AN ANNOTATED SECONDARY BIBLIOGRAPHY SERIES ON ENGLISH LITERATURE IN TRANSITION

1880–1920

W. EUGENE DAVIS

GENERAL EDITOR

JOSEPH CONRAD

THOMAS HARDY

E. M. FORSTER

JOHN GALSWORTHY

GEORGE GISSING

D. H. LAWRENCE

H. G. WELLS

WALTER PATER

G. B. SHAW

Dennis Jackson, *Associate Editor and Contributor*

The Contributors, Volume One

James Cox
Bethany K. Dumas
Duane Edwards
Langdon Elsbree
David Farmer
Giles Mitchell

Charles R. Rossman
Bob L. Smith
Alvin Sullivan
Jim E. Tanner
George Y. Trail

Foreign Language Contributors

Bengt Altenberg
Simonetta de Filippis
Jacqueline Gouirand
Konrad Gross
Sadanobu Kai

Arnold Odio
Yasuichirô Ôhashi
Taiji Okada
Tohru Okumura

The Contributors, Volume Two

Margaret Bolsterli
Carol Cloos
Patricia Elliott
Christopher Gould
Donald Gutierrez

Anne Kiley
Hebe Riddick Mace
Charles L. Ross
T. A. Smailes
Sharon Wevill

D. H. Lawrence

AN ANNOTATED BIBLIOGRAPHY OF WRITINGS ABOUT HIM

VOLUME II

COMPILED AND EDITED BY

JAMES C. COWAN

NORTHERN ILLINOIS UNIVERSITY PRESS

DE KALB, ILLINOIS

James C. Cowan is Founder and former Editor (1968-1983) of *The D. H. Lawrence Review*. He is the author of *D. H. Lawrence's American Journey: A Study in Literature and Myth* (1970) and compiler and editor of *D. H. Lawrence: An Annotated Bibliography of Writings about Him,* Vol. I (1982).

Library of Congress Cataloging in Publication Data
(Revised for vol. 2)

Cowan, James C.
    D. H. Lawrence, an annotated bibliography of writings about him.

    An Annotated secondary bibliography series on English literature in transition, 1880-1920.
    Includes indexes.
    1. Lawrence, D. H. (David Herbert), 1885-1930--Criticism and interpretation--Bibliography. I. Title.
Z8490.5.C68 1982 [PR6023.A93] 016.823'912 80-8664
ISBN 0-87580-077-7 (v. 1)
ISBN 0-87580-105-6 (v. 2)

Copyright © 1985 by Northern Illinois University Press
Published by the Northern Illinois University Press, DeKalb, Illinois 60115
Manufactured in the United States of America
All Rights Reserved

Preface

D. H. Lawrence: An Annotated Bibliography of Writings about Him follows principles established in preceding volumes in the Annotated Secondary Bibliography series. The 2,566 entries, dated between 1961 and 1975, in Volume II include entries and abstracts of published writings on Lawrence in fifteen languages, with foreign language titles listed bibliographically in the original language followed by an English translation and annotation in English. Broadly representative of secondary materials on Lawrence, the bibliography includes various kinds of publications: historical scholarship, biography, comparative and influence studies, introductions to primary and secondary works, criticism, bibliography, reviews, adaptations of Lawrence's works to other media, news items, letters to the editor, imaginative writing, and doctoral dissertations. The length of abstracts varies from brief annotations to fairly long abstracts of major sources and materials not readily accessible.

While response to the extensive bibliographical coverage of Volume I was gratifying, such a large-scale compilation as the two volumes on Lawrence inevitably falls short of the goal of being definitive. Short reviews and notices, letters, news reports, and comments in periodicals of limited circulation are included in representative examples throughout the bibliography; but items not directly accessible to our contributors are not included. The reason is that inaccuracies in indexes, catalogues, and bibliographies used as sources for the present compilation and inadequate resources in foreign language areas and ephemeral publications have made verification and annotation essential to accuracy. I hope that users of this bibliography will call to my attention items which have been omitted so that they can be added to a supplementary listing.

The principles I have followed in the matter of inclusions and exclusions are those established in preceding volumes in this series. Since secondary works are themselves abstracted, reviews of these works are not generally included unless they comment directly on Lawrence or his work. Secondary comments on Frieda Lawrence and reviews of her memoirs or of writings about her are sometimes included for their illumination of Lawrence. Doctoral dissertations, catalogued under the years of acceptance for the doctorate, are listed without abstract but with reference to **DISSERTATION ABSTRACTS INTERNATIONAL** or similar series, whenever applicable. Dissertation titles are verified in such sources as DAI, Lawrence F. McNamee's DISSERTATIONS IN ENGLISH AND AMERICAN LITERATURE (1968) and its SUPPLEMENT I (1969) and SUPPLEMENT II (1974), in INDEX TO THESES, edited by Geoffrey M. Paterson and Joan E. Hardy, and at times in separate university or national listings. Whenever possible, I have provided abstracts of foreign language dissertations, since these were often printed, although some foreign language dissertations may have been omitted inadvertently because they were not listed in standard bibliographical sources or were inaccessible for verification. Even so, the two volumes of this bibliography include more dissertations than has been usual in the A.S.B. Series or in previous secondary bibliographies of Lawrence.

As in Volume I, I have tried, insofar as possible, to list entries under the date of first publication and to provide cross references to later reprintings, revisions, or translations. I have avoided listing essentially the same material under different dates except when, as noted, the material is incorporated or absorbed in a subsequent larger work which is listed and abstracted under its date of publication. In point of view, the abstracts maintain the original author's voice as accurately as possible by means of paraphrases and selected quotations, with all editorial comments, cross references to related materials, and some indicative abstracts enclosed in square brackets. For each volume of this bibliography, five separate indexes are provided to index the bibliography by authors, titles of secondary works, periodicals and newspapers, foreign languages, and primary titles.

As in Volume I, I must add that this bibliography of D. H. Lawrence, although more than a decade in the making, has to be seen as a beginning on a project that will require further updating and supplementation.

ACKNOWLEDGMENTS

The two volumes of the D. H. Lawrence bibliography, like other volumes in the A.S.B. Series, have been cooperative ventures. Again as in Volume I, my greatest debt is to Dennis Jackson, for his work as associate editor. His thorough knowledge of Lawrence and what has been written about him; his resourcefulness in searching out fugitive items in the Library of Congress, the New York Public Library, and elsewhere; and his faithfulness to the project for a number of years have made his contribution indispensable. I am grateful to the late Helmut E. Gerber, general editor of the Annotated Secondary Bibliography Series, for his unfailing support and encouragement as well as practical assistance during the years in which we pursued this project. I am also indebted to the contributors (listed opposite the title page) for their patience and hard work. The original group of contributors, those listed for Volume I, continued their work throughout the bibliography; they were joined, for the later years, by an additional group of contributors, those listed for Volume II, to help in verifying and abstracting the increased amount of material for those years. Foreign language contributors made especially valuable contributions that will make this bibliography a useful research tool in fourteen languages besides English. While I wrote a substantial number of the abstracts and am responsible for the final form of all abstracts, I cannot claim anything like single authorship of a work that could not have been nearly so definitive in form without the contributions of these scholars.

I am also indebted to several scholars for direct and indirect contributions to this bibliographical work. C. J. Burkhart, an early contributor to the A.S.B. Series, and Fleda Brown Jackson each wrote several abstracts. Sonja Miletić and Miroslav Beker in Serbo-Croatian and Margarida Losa and John Remsbury in Portuguese provided valuable listings and verifications of secondary materials on Lawrence. Earlier secondary bibliographies, especially those of William White, Maurice Beebe and Anthony Tommasi, Richard Beards, and I. R. Willison, provided useful checklists of writings on Lawrence. And the definitive primary bibliography by Warren Roberts proved to be an invaluable resource to which I turned repeatedly for authoritative information about Lawrence's works, their publication, variants, translations, and reviews.

Several of the contributors wish to acknowledge the support of research grants or other assistance. Dennis Jackson's work on this project was carried out with the support of the University of Delaware Research Fund. David Farmer had the help of Linda Secord as a graduate assistant at the University of Texas at Austin. Charles L. Ross had the help of C. Stephen Finley as a graduate assistant at the University of Virginia. I am indebted to my wife, Judith R. Cowan, M.D., for her unfailing support throughout this project. The associate editor, the contributors and I gratefully acknowledge the many libraries in which this bibliographical research was done, in particular the interlibrary loan staffs through whose services the resources of more than a hundred libraries were made available. Among those libraries providing especially helpful or extensive service are the University of Arkansas Library, British Museum, Library of Congress, University of Delaware Library, Duke University Library, New York Public Library, University of North Carolina Library, University of Oklahoma Library, and the Humanities Research Center and the Library of the University of Texas. Finally, I want to thank Leslie Wildrick and Philip Rider for their valuable assistance with the manuscript of this book as editors at Northern Illinois University Press.

James C. Cowan

Contents

PREFACE	v
A CHECKLIST OF THE WORKS OF D. H. LAWRENCE	xi
INTRODUCTION	xxi
THE BIBLIOGRAPHY	1
INDEX OF AUTHORS	659
INDEX OF TITLES OF SECONDARY WORKS	679
INDEX OF PERIODICALS AND NEWSPAPERS	743
INDEX OF FOREIGN LANGUAGES	755
INDEX OF PRIMARY TITLES	757

NOTE ON ENTRY STYLE

Titles of Lawrence's books appear in italic type; titles of his stories, in roman capitals and lower case with quotation marks. Titles of books by other authors, collections of stories and letters edited by other writers, and names of periodicals and newspapers appear in capitals. The translations appearing in parentheses are confined to meanings of the phrases; however, it should be noted that the titles of translations are seldom literal ones.

A Checklist

OF THE WORKS OF D. H. LAWRENCE
CITED IN THIS BIBLIOGRAPHY

I. FICTION

A. SEPARATE WORKS

The White Peacock. Lond, 1911; NY, 1911; reissued, Lond, 1915, 1921, 1927, 1935, 1951; Leipzig, 1932; Harmondsworth, Middlesex, England, 1950; reissued with textual emendations and restorations, ed Matthew J. Bruccoli, Carbondale and Edwardsville, IL, 1966; textual ed, ed Andrew Robertson, Cambridge, 1983.

The Trespasser. Lond, 1912; NY, 1912; textual ed, ed Elizabeth Mansfield, Cambridge, 1982.

Sons and Lovers. Lond, 1913; NY, 1913; reissued, Lond, 1927, 1935; NY, 1922, 1923, 1931, 1951; Leipzig, 1929, 1936; facsimile of manuscript, ed Mark Schorer, Berkeley, 1978; reissued, ed Keith Sagar, Harmondsworth, Middlesex, England, 1981.

The Prussian Officer and Other Stories. Lond, 1914; NY, 1916; reissued, Lond, 1924, 1927; Harmondsworth, Middlesex, England, 1945; textual ed, ed John Worthen, Cambridge, 1983. Contents: "The Prussian Officer," "The Thorn in the Flesh," "Daughters of the Vicar," "A Fragment of Stained Glass," "The Shades of Spring," "Second Best," "The Shadow in the Rose Garden," "Goose Fair," "The White Stocking," "A Sick Collier," "The Christening," "Odour of Chrysanthemums."

The Rainbow. Lond, 1915; NY, 1915; reissued, Lond, 1929, 1935; NY, 1916, 1924, 1931; reissued, ed John Worthen, Harmondsworth, Middlesex, England, 1981.

Women in Love. NY, 1920; Lond, 1921; reissued, NY, 1922, 1931, 1933, 1937; Lond, 1925, 1936, 1946, 1950; reissued, ed Charles L. Ross, Harmondsworth, Middlesex, England, 1982.

The Lost Girl. Lond, 1920; NY, 1921; reissued, Lond, 1925; textual ed, ed John Worthen, Cambridge, 1981.

Aaron's Rod. NY, 1922; Lond, 1922; reissued, NY, 1930, 1933; Lond, 1927, 1935, 1948.

England, My England and Other Stories. NY, 1922; Lond, 1924. Contents:

"England, My England," "Tickets, Please," "The Blind Man," "Monkey Nuts," "Wintry Peacock," "You Touched Me," "Samson and Delilah," "The Primrose Path," "The Horse Dealer's Daughter," "Fanny and Annie."

The Ladybird. Lond, 1923; pub as *The Captain's Doll: Three Novelettes.* NY, 1923; reissued, Lond, 1928; NY, 1930, 1931. Contents: *The Ladybird, The Fox, The Captain's Doll.*

Kangaroo. Lond, 1923; NY, 1923; reissued, Lond, 1950.

The Boy in the Bush (with M. L. Skinner). Lond, 1924; NY, 1924; reissued, NY, 1931; reissued from 1st ed, Carbondale and Edwardsville, IL, 1971.

St. Mawr Together with The Princess. Lond, 1925; reissued, Lond, 1928. Pub as *St. Mawr* [without "The Princess"]. NY, 1925. Textual ed, *St. Mawr and Other Stories*, ed Brian H. Finney. Cambridge, 1983. Contents: "The Overtone," *St. Mawr*, "The Princess"; Appendixes: "The Wilful Woman," "The Flying-Fish."

The Plumed Serpent. Lond, 1926; NY, 1926; reissued, Lond, 1927, 1950; NY, 1950.

Sun. Lond, 1926; unexpurgated ed, Paris, 1928; pirated ed, U.S., 1929. Expurgated ed collected in *The Woman Who Rode Away and Other Stories.* Lond, 1928; NY, 1928. Unexpurgated ed collected in *The Princess and Other Stories*, ed Keith Sagar. Harmondsworth, Middlesex, England, 1971.

Glad Ghosts. Lond, 1926; collected in *The Woman Who Rode Away and Other Stories.* Lond, 1928; NY, 1928.

Rawdon's Roof. Lond, 1928; collected in *The Lovely Lady.* Lond, 1933; NY, 1933.

The Woman Who Rode Away and Other Stories. Lond, 1928; NY, 1928. Contents: "Two Blue Birds," "Sun," "The Woman Who Rode Away," "Smile," "The Border Line," "Jimmy and the Desperate Woman," "The Last Laugh," "In Love," "Glad Ghosts," "None of That," and [in American ed only] "The Man Who Loved Islands."

Lady Chatterley's Lover. Florence, 1928; Paris, 1929; authorized expurgated ed, Lond, 1932; NY, 1932; Paris, 1933; authorized unexpurgated ed, NY, 1959; Harmondsworth, Middlesex, England, 1960. [See Warren Roberts, A BIBLIOGRAPHY OF D. H. LAWRENCE, 2nd ed (Cambridge: Cambridge UP, 1982), Appendix I, pp. 561-65, for a list of parodies and a list of piracies and forgeries of *Lady Chatterley's Lover.*]

The Escaped Cock. Paris, 1929; pub as *The Man Who Died.* Lond, 1931; NY, 1931; illustrated ed, Lond, 1935; critical textual ed, ed Gerald M. Lacy, pub as *The Escaped Cock.* Los Angeles, 1973.

The Virgin and the Gipsy. Florence, 1930; Lond, 1930; NY, 1930; reissued, Lond, 1931; NY, 1934, 1944.

Love among the Haystacks and Other Pieces. Lond, 1930; NY, 1933; reissued, Lond, 1933; Berne, 1943. Contents: *Love among the Haystacks*, "A Chapel among the Mountains," "A Hay Hut among the Mountains," "Once," and [in American ed only] "Christs in the Tirol."

The Lovely Lady. Lond, 1933; NY, 1933; reissued, Lond, 1934. Contents: "The Lovely Lady," "Rawdon's Roof," "The Rocking-Horse Winner," "Mother and Daughter," "The Blue Moccasins," "Things," "The Overtone," "The Man Who Loved Islands."

A Modern Lover. Lond, 1934; NY, 1934; reissued, Lond, 1936; NY, 1948, 1969. Contents: "A Modern Lover," "The Old Adam," "Her Turn," "Strike-Pay," "The Witch a la Mode," "New Eve and Old Adam," "Mr. Noon."
The First Lady Chatterley (1st manuscript version of *Lady Chatterley's Lover*). NY, 1944; Lond, 1972.
A Prelude [rptd from the NOTTINGHAMSHIRE GUARDIAN, 7 Dec 1907]. Thames Ditton, Surrey, England, 1949.
John Thomas and Lady Jane (2nd manuscript version of *Lady Chatterley's Lover*). Lond, 1972; NY, 1972. [1st ed of this version pub in Italian as *La Seconda Lady Chatterley*, trans by Carlo Izzo, in *Le Tre "Lady Chatterley."* Milan and Verona, 1954.]
Mr. Noon. Textual ed, ed Lindeth Vasey, Cambridge, 1984.

B. COLLECTED EDITIONS

Uniform Pocket Edition of the Novels, 20 vols. Lond, 1927-1934.
The Phoenix Edition of D. H. Lawrence, 21 vols. Lond, 1955-1958.
The Cambridge Edition of the Works of D. H. Lawrence. Cambridge, 1979- .
The Tales of D. H. Lawrence. Lond, 1934; rptd, Lond, 1948, 1949. Contents: Reprints all stories from *The Prussian Officer and Other Stories, England, My England and Other Stories, The Ladybird, The Fox, The Captain's Doll, St. Mawr Together with The Princess, The Woman Who Rode Away and Other Stories, The Lovely Lady, The Virgin and the Gipsy, The Man Who Died.*
Stories, Essays, and Poems. Lond, 1939.
Full Score: Twenty Tales. Lond, 1943. Contents: "The Prussian Officer," "Second Best," "The White Stocking," "Samson and Delilah," "The Horse Dealer's Daughter," "Fanny and Annie," *The Ladybird, The Fox,* "Two Blue Birds," *The Captain's Doll,* "The Princess," "The Woman Who Rode Away," "Jimmy and the Desperate Woman," "None of That," "The Man Who Loved Islands," "Rawdon's Roof," "The Rocking-Horse Winner," "The Blue Moccasins," "Adolf," "Things."
The Portable D. H. Lawrence, ed Diana Trilling. NY, 1947.
The Later D. H. Lawrence, ed William York Tindall. NY, 1952.
The Complete Stories of D. H. Lawrence, 3 vols. Lond, 1955.
D. H. Lawrence: The Short Novels, 2 vols. Lond, 1956.
Selected Tales, with Introduction by Ian Serraillier. Lond, 1963; reissued, Lond, 1972. Contents: "The Rocking-Horse Winner," "Odour of Chrysanthemums," "Strike-Pay," "The Christening," "Tickets, Please," "Monkey Nuts," "Fanny and Annie," "You Touched Me," "The Man Who Loved Islands," "Things," "Daughters of the Vicar."
D. H. Lawrence: Four Short Novels. NY, 1965. Contents: *Love among the Haystacks, The Ladybird, The Fox, The Captain's Doll.*
D. H. Lawrence, ed Mark Schorer. NY, 1968.
D. H. Lawrence: A Selection, eds R. H. Poole and P. J. Shepherd. Lond, 1970.
The Mortal Coil and Other Stories, ed with Introduction by Keith Sagar. Harmondsworth, Middlesex, England, 1971; rptd 1972. Contents: "Adolf," "Rex," "A Prelude," "Lessford's Rabbits," "A Lesson on a Tortoise," "A Fly

in the Ointment," "The Old Adam," "The Witch a la Mode," "The Miner at Home," "Her Turn," "Delilah and Mr. Bircumshaw," "A Chapel and a Hay Hut among the Mountains," "Once," "New Eve and Old Adam," "The Thimble," "The Mortal Coil."

The Princess and Other Stories, ed with Introduction by Keith Sagar. Harmondsworth, Middlesex, England, 1971; rptd, 1972, 1974, 1976, 1978. Contents: "The Wilful Woman," "The Princess," "The Overtone," "The Flying Fish," "Sun," "Mercury," "The Man Who Was Through with the World," "A Dream of Life," "The Undying Man," "The Blue Moccasins," "Things," "Mother and Daughter."

II. POEMS

A. SEPARATE VOLUMES

Love Poems and Others. Lond, 1913; NY, 1913; reissued, Lond, 1914, 1923, 1934.

Amores. Lond, 1916; NY, 1916.

Look! We Have Come Through! Lond, 1917; NY, 1918; illustrated ed, as *Look! We Have Come Through! A Cycle of Love Poems.* Marazion, Cornwall, England, 1958; Austin, TX, 1959.

New Poems. Lond, 1918; NY, 1920.

Bay. Westminster, England, 1919.

Tortoises. NY, 1921; collected in *Birds, Beasts and Flowers.* NY, 1923; Lond, 1923.

Birds, Beasts and Flowers. NY, 1923; Lond, 1923; illustrated ed, Lond, 1930.

Pansies. Lond, 1929; NY, 1929; reissued, Lond, 1930; definitive ed, Lond, 1929; limited ed, Brooklyn, NY, 1954.

Nettles. Lond, 1930; rptd in *Pornography and So On.* Lond, 1936.

Triumph of the Machine. Lond, 1930; collected in *Last Poems.* Florence, 1932; NY, 1933; Lond, 1933.

Last Poems, ed Richard Aldington. Florence, 1932; NY, 1933; Lond, 1933; reissued, Lond, 1935.

An Original Poem ["The wind, the Rascal," rptd from POETRY, III (Jan 1914)]. Lond, 1934.

B. COLLECTED EDITIONS

D. H. Lawrence [Selected Poems]. Lond, 1928.

The Collected Poems of D. H. Lawrence, 2 vols. Lond, 1928; NY, 1929; rptd, Lond, 1929, 1932.

The Ship of Death and Other Poems. Lond, 1933.

D. H. Lawrence: Selected Poems. Lond, 1934.

Poems, 2 vols. Lond, 1939.

Fire and Other Poems. San Francisco, 1940.

D. H. Lawrence: Selected Poems, with Introduction by Kenneth Rexroth. NY, 1947.
Selected Poems, ed W. E. Williams. Harmondsworth, Middlesex, England, 1950.
Selected Poems, ed James Reeves. Lond, 1951.
D. H. Lawrence: The Complete Poems, 3 vols. Lond, 1957.
D. H. Lawrence, 20 Poems. Lond, 1959.
D. H. Lawrence: Tutte le Poesie, trans into Italian and with Introduction and notes by Piero Nardi, 2 vols. Milan and Verona, 1959.
Four D. H. Lawrence Songs, with music by Vittorio Rieti. Lond, 1964; NY, 1964. Contents: "Aware," "Thomas Earp," "December Night," "Quite Forsaken."
The Complete Poems of D. H. Lawrence, ed Vivian de Sola Pinto and F. Warren Roberts. Lond, 1964; NY, 1964; reissued with emendations and additions, Lond, 1967; reissued with further emendations and additions, NY, 1971; reissued with further emendations and additions, Lond, 1972.
D. H. Lawrence: Poems Selected for Young People, ed by William Cole. NY, 1967.
The Body of God: A Sequence of Poems, selected and arranged by Michael Adam. Penzance, Cornwall, England, 1970.
D. H. Lawrence: Selected Poems, ed by Keith Sagar. Harmondsworth, Middlesex, England, 1972.
Consciousness. N.p.: Privately Printed, 1974. Contents: "For God's Sake," "O! Start a Revolution," "It's Either You Fight or You Die."
Birds, Beasts and the Third Thing, selected and illustrated by Alice and Martin Provensen, with Introduction by Donald Hall. NY, 1982.

III. PLAYS

A. SEPARATE WORKS

The Widowing of Mrs. Holroyd. NY, 1914; Lond, 1914.
Touch and Go. Lond, 1920; NY, 1920.
David. Lond, 1926; NY, 1926; rptd, Lond, 1927, 1930.
A Collier's Friday Night. Lond, 1934.

B. COLLECTED EDITIONS

The Plays of D. H. Lawrence. Lond, 1933; reissued, Lond, 1938. Contents: *The Widowing of Mrs. Holroyd, Touch and Go, David.*
The Complete Plays of D. H. Lawrence. Lond, 1965; NY, 1966. Contents: *The Widowing of Mrs. Holroyd, David, The Married Man, The Daughter-in-Law, The Fight for Barbara, Touch and Go, The Merry-Go-Round, A Collier's Friday Night, Altitude, Noah's Flood.*
Three Plays by D. H. Lawrence, with an Introduction by Raymond Williams. Harmondsworth, Middlesex, England, 1969. Contents: *A Collier's Friday Night, The Daughter-in-Law, The Widowing of Mrs. Holroyd.*

IV. NON-FICTION PROSE: ESSAYS, TRAVEL BOOKS, LETTERS

A. SEPARATE WORKS

Twilight in Italy. Lond, 1916; NY, 1916; reissued, Lond, 1924, 1926, 1934.

Movements in European History. Lond, 1921; illustrated ed, Oxford, 1925; rvd ed for Irish schools, Dublin and Cork, 1927; new ed, with Introduction by James T. Boulton, Oxford, 1971.

Psychoanalysis and the Unconscious. NY, 1921; Lond, 1923; reissued, Lond, 1931.

Sea and Sardinia, with eight pictures in color by Jan Juta. NY, 1921; Lond, 1923; reissued, Lond, 1927, 1950; NY, 1931; Harmondsworth, Middlesex, England, 1944.

Fantasia of the Unconscious. NY, 1922; Lond, 1923; reissued, NY, 1931; Lond, 1931.

Studies in Classic American Literature. NY, 1923; Lond, 1924; reissued, NY, 1931, 1964; Lond, 1933; Harmondsworth, Middlesex, England, 1971. Contents: "Foreword" [in American ed only], "The Spirit of Place," "Benjamin Franklin," "Hector St. John Crèvecoeur," "Fenimore Cooper's White Novels," "Fenimore Cooper's Leatherstocking Novels," "Edgar Allan Poe," "Nathaniel Hawthorne and *The Scarlet Letter*," "Hawthorne's *Blithedale Romance*," "Dana's *Two Years before the Mast*," "Herman Melville's *Typee* and *Omoo*," "Herman Melville's *Moby Dick*," "Whitman."

Reflections on the Death of a Porcupine and Other Essays. Phila, 1925; Lond, 1934; reissued, Bloomington, IN, 1963. Contents: "The Crown," "The Novel," "Him with His Tail in His Mouth," "Blessed Are the Powerful," "Love Was Once a Little Boy," "Reflections on the Death of a Porcupine," "Aristocracy."

Mornings in Mexico. Lond, 1927; NY, 1927; reissued, Lond, 1930, 1950; reissued, with Introduction by Ross Parmenter, Salt Lake City, 1982. Contents: "Corasmin and the Parrots," "Walk to Huayapa," "The Mozo," "Market Day," "Indians and Entertainment," "The Dance of the Sprouting Corn," "The Hopi Snake Dance," "A Little Moonshine with Lemon."

Sex Locked Out [rptd from the SUNDAY DISPATCH (Lond), 25 Nov 1928]. Lond, 1929; collected as "Sex versus Loveliness," in *Assorted Articles.* Lond, 1930; NY, 1930.

My Skirmish with Jolly Roger [1st pub as Introduction to *Lady Chatterley's Lover.* Paris, 1929]. NY, 1929; rvd and pub as *A Propos of "Lady Chatterley's Lover."* Lond, 1930.

Pornography and Obscenity. Lond, 1929; NY, 1930; collected in *Pornography and So On.* Lond, 1936; collected in *Sex, Literature and Censorship.* NY, 1953; Lond, 1955.

Assorted Articles. Lond, 1930; NY, 1930; reissued, Lond, 1932, 1936. Contents: "The 'Jeune Fille' Wants to Know," "Laura Philippine," "Sex versus Loveliness," "Give Her a Pattern," "Do Women Change?," "Master in His Own House," "Matriarchy," "Cocksure Women and Hensure Men," "Is England

Still a Man's Country?," "Dull London," "Red Trousers," "The State of Funk," "The Risen Lord," "Enslaved by Civilization," "Men Must Work and Women as Well," "Autobiographical Sketch," "Hymns in a Man's Life," "Making Pictures," "Pictures on the Walls," "On Being a Man," "On Human Destiny."

Apocalypse. Florence, 1931; NY, 1931; Lond, 1932; reissued, NY, 1966. Textual ed, *Apocalypse and the Writings on Revelation*, ed Mara Kalnins. Cambridge, 1980. Contents: "A Review of *The Book of Revelation* by Dr. John Oman," "Introduction to *The Dragon of the Apocalypse* by Frederick Carter," *Apocalypse*; Appendixes: *Apocalypse*, Fragment 1; *Apocalypse*, Fragment 2; *Apocalypsis II.*

A Letter from Cornwall. Yerba Buena P, 1931. [Letter to J. D. Beresford, 5 Jan 1916.] Collected in *The Letters of D. H. Lawrence*, ed Aldous Huxley. Lond, 1932; NY, 1932.

Etruscan Places. Lond, 1932; NY, 1932; reissued, Lond, 1933, 1938.

The Letters of D. H. Lawrence, ed with an Introduction by Aldous Huxley. Lond, 1932; NY, 1932, reissued, Lond, 1934; NY, 1936; reissued, 3 vols, Leipzig, 1938 and 1939.

We Need One Another. NY, 1933; collected in *Phoenix: The Posthumous Papers of D. H. Lawrence*, ed Edward D. McDonald. NY, 1936. Contents: "We Need One Another," "The Real Thing."

Foreword to "Women in Love." San Francisco, 1936; pub as Foreword in *Women in Love.* NY, 1937; collected in *Phoenix II: Uncollected, Unpublished and Other Prose Works by D. H. Lawrence*, ed Warren Roberts and Harry T. Moore. NY, 1968; Lond, 1968.

Phoenix: The Posthumous Papers of D. H. Lawrence, ed with an Introduction by Edward D. McDonald. NY, 1936; Lond, 1936; reissued, Lond, 1938, 1961, 1968; NY, 1968.

D. H. Lawrence's Letters to Bertrand Russell, ed Harry T. Moore. NY, 1948.

Eight Letters by D. H. Lawrence to Rachel Annand Taylor. Pasadena, CA, 1956.

The Collected Letters of D. H. Lawrence, ed with an Introduction by Harry T. Moore, 2 vols. NY, 1962; Lond, 1962.

The Symbolic Meaning: The Uncollected Versions of "Studies in Classic American Literature," ed with an Introduction by Armin Arnold. Lond, 1962; NY, 1964. Contents: Early versions of the essays "The Spirit of Place," "Benjamin Franklin," "Hector St. John de Crèvecoeur," "Fenimore Cooper's Anglo-American Novels," "Fenimore Cooper's Leatherstocking Novels," "Edgar Allan Poe," "Nathaniel Hawthorne I," "Nathaniel Hawthorne II," "The Two Principles," "Dana's *Two Years before the Mast*," "Herman Melville's *Typee* and *Omoo*," "Herman Melville's *Moby Dick*," "Whitman."

D. H. Lawrence and German Literature with Two Hitherto Unknown Essays by D. H. Lawrence, by Armin Arnold. Montreal, 1963. Contents: "Review of H. G. Fiedler's *Oxford Book of German Verse*," "Review of Jethro Bithell's *The Minnesingers.*" These two essays collected in *Phoenix II: Uncollected, Unpublished, and Other Prose Works by D. H. Lawrence*, ed Warren Roberts and Harry T. Moore. NY, 1968; Lond, 1968.

Lawrence in Love: Letters to Louie Burrows, ed with an Introduction by James T. Boulton. Nottingham, 1968; rptd, 1969.

The Quest for Rananim: D. H. Lawrence's Letters to S. S. Koteliansky, 1914 to

1930, ed with an Introduction by George J. Zytaruk. Montreal and Lond, 1970.
Letters from D. H. Lawrence to Martin Secker, 1911-1930, ed by M[artin] S[ecker]. Bridgefoot Iver, Bucks., England, 1970.
The Centaur Letters, with an Introduction by Edward D. McDonald. Austin, TX, 1970.
D. H. Lawrence: Letters to Thomas and Adele Seltzer, ed Gerald M. Lacy. Santa Barbara, CA, 1976.
The Letters of D. H. Lawrence, Vol. I: *September 1901-May 1913*, ed James T. Boulton. Cambridge, 1979.
The Letters of D. H. Lawrence, Vol. II: *June 1913-October 1916*, ed George J. Zytaruk and James T. Boulton. Cambridge, 1981.
The Letters of D. H. Lawrence, Vol. III: *1916-1921*, ed James T. Boulton and Andrew Robertson. Cambridge, 1984.

B. COLLECTED EDITIONS

Pornography and So On. Lond, 1936. Contents: "Pornography and Obscenity," "Introduction to Painting," *Nettles.*
Selected Essays. Harmondsworth, Middlesex, England, 1950. Contents: Reprints selections from *Assorted Articles*, *Phoenix*, *Reflections on the Death of a Porcupine*, *Twilight in Italy*, *The Letters of D. H. Lawrence*, *Mornings in Mexico*, *Studies in Classic American Literature.*
Letters, selected by Richard Aldington. Harmondsworth, Middlesex, England, 1950.
Art and Painting. Lond, 1951. Contents: "Making Pictures," "Art and Morality," "Introduction to These Paintings" (excerpts), "Pictures on the Walls."
Sex, Literature and Censorship, ed with Introduction by Harry T. Moore. NY, 1953; Lond, 1955. Contents: "Love," "Making Love to Music," "Cocksure Women and Hensure Men," "Sex versus Loveliness," "Introduction to Pansies," "The State of Funk," "Pornography and Obscenity," "A Propos of *Lady Chatterley's Lover*"; and [in English ed only] "The Novel," "Love Was Once a Little Boy," "Introduction to His Paintings," and reproductions of the paintings *The Finding of Moses* (in color), *Resurrection*, *Fauns and Nymphs*, and *Under-the-Haystack.*
Selected Literary Criticism, ed Anthony Beal. Lond, 1955; NY, 1966. Contents: Reprints selections from *Assorted Articles*, *The Letters of D. H. Lawrence*, *Phoenix*, *Studies in Classic American Literature.*
The Selected Letters of D. H. Lawrence, ed with an Introduction by Diana Trilling. NY, 1958.
Phoenix II: Uncollected, Unpublished, and Other Prose Works by D. H. Lawrence, ed with Introduction by Warren Roberts and Harry T. Moore. Lond, 1968; NY, 1968.
D. H. Lawrence and Italy, with an Introduction by Anthony Burgess. NY, 1972. Contents: *Twilight in Italy*, *Sea and Sardinia*, *Etruscan Places.*
Lawrence on Hardy and Painting: "Study of Thomas Hardy" and "Introduction to These Paintings," ed J. V. Davies. Lond, 1973.

D. H. Lawrence on Education, eds Joy and Raymond Williams. Harmondsworth, Middlesex, England, 1973. Contents: "Autobiographical Sketch," "The Proper Study," "The Novel and the Feelings," "Why the Novel Matters," "Schoolgirl" and "Assistant Teacher" (excerpts from *The Rainbow*), "Classroom" (excerpt from *Women in Love*), "Lessford's Rabbits," "A Lesson on the Tortoise," "Last Lesson of the Afternoon," "Men Must Work and Women as Well," "Education of the People," "Education and Sex in Man, Woman and Child" (excerpt from *Fantasia of the Unconscious*), "Letter to Lady Cynthia Asquith," "Benjamin Franklin," "On Human Destiny," "Hymns in a Man's Life," "Nottingham and the Mining Countryside," "Return to Bestwood."

D. H. Lawrence and New Mexico, ed with an Introduction by Keith Sagar. Salt Lake City, 1982. Contents: Reprints selections and excerpts from *Birds, Beasts and Flowers, Phoenix II, Mornings in Mexico, The Letters of D. H. Lawrence, Phoenix, Fire and Other Poems*, "The Princess," *St. Mawr*, "The Wilful Woman," "The Woman Who Rode Away."

V. TRANSLATIONS

All Things Are Possible, by Leo Shestov, trans by S. S. Koteliansky, with Foreword [and collaboration] by D. H. Lawrence. Lond, 1920.

The Gentleman from San Francisco and Other Stories, by I. A. Bunin, trans by S. S. Koteliansky and Leonard Woolf. Richmond, England, 1922; NY, 1923. [D. H. Lawrence collaborated with S. S. Koteliansky in the translation of "The Gentleman from San Francisco."]

Mastro-Don Gesualdo, by Giovanni Verga, trans by D. H. Lawrence. NY, 1923; Lond, 1925; reissued, Lond, 1928.

Little Novels of Sicily, by Giovanni Verga, trans by D. H. Lawrence. NY, 1925; Lond, 1925; reissued, Lond, 1928, 1929, 1937; NY, 1953; reissued, with Introduction and Glossary by Andrew Wilkin, Harmondsworth, Middlesex, England, 1973. Contents: "Notes on Giovanni Verga," "His Reverence," "So Much for the King," "Don Licciu Papa," "The Mystery Play," "Malaria," "The Orphans," "Property," "Story of the Saint Joseph's Ass," "Black Bread," "The Gentry," "Liberty," "Across the Sea."

Cavalleria Rusticana and Other Stories, by Giovanni Verga, trans by D. H. Lawrence. Lond, 1928; NY, 1928; reissued, Lond, 1931, 1932. Contents: "Translator's Preface," "Cavalleria Rusticana," "La Lupa," "Caprice," "Jeli the Herdsman," "Rosso Malpelo, or the Red-Headed Brat," "Gramigna's Lover," "War of Saints," "Brothpot," "The How, When, and Wherefore."

The Story of Doctor Manente, Being the Tenth and Last Story from the Suppers of A. F. Grazzini, called Il Lasca, trans by D. H. Lawrence. Florence, 1929.

VI. PAINTINGS

The Paintings of D. H. Lawrence. Lond, 1929. Contents: Oil Paintings: *Resurrection, A Holy Family, Red Willow Trees, Finding of Moses, Contadini, Rape of the Sabine Women, Flight Back into Paradise, Boccaccio Story, Accident* in a Mine, North Sea, Fight with an Amazon, Fauns and Nymphs, Family on a Verandah, Close-Up (Kiss), Dance-Sketch; Water Colours: *Spring, Summer Dawn* (actually in oils), *Fire-Dance, Under the Hay-Stack, Yawning, Leda, Renascence of Men, The Mango Tree, Throwing Back the Apple, The Lizard, Singing of Swans.*

Paintings of D. H. Lawrence, ed Mervyn Levy, with essays by Harry T. Moore, Jack Lindsay, and Herbert Read. NY, 1964; Lond, 1964. Contents: Plates in Colour: *Coastal Scene with Figures, Landscape with Figure, Copy from a Print of Giotto's "Joachim and the Shepherds," The Kiowa Ranch, New Mexico, The Feast of the Radishes, Resurrection, Red Willow Trees, Villa Mirenda, Flight Back into Paradise, Family on a Verandah, Fauns and Nymphs, Dance Sketch, Rape of the Sabine Women, Italian Landscape, Jaguar Leaping at a Man, Leda;* and thirty-one black and white reproductions.

Etruscan Places [not the travel book but a separate issue of the needlepoint design *Etruscan Figure*], with commentary by David Farmer. Tulsa, 1981.

Ten Paintings. Redding Ridge, CT, 1982. Contents: Frontispiece: Photograph of D. H. Lawrence, by Edward Weston; "Making Pictures," by D. H. Lawrence; Paintings (color plates): *A Holy Family, Boccaccio Story, Fight with an Amazon, Flight Back into Paradise, Resurrection, Red Willow Trees, Behind the Villa Mirenda, Fauns and Nymphs, Dance Sketch, Finding of Moses;* "Excerpts from Letters," "Afterword."

Introduction

The first "key points" in the development of Lawrence's critical reputation, as J. C. F. Littlewood comments in "Lawrence Old and New," ESSAYS IN CRITICISM (1971) [3744], came in the early 1930s when some of his "most influential contemporaries" gave "their considered accounts of his work as a whole." Littlewood has in mind such studies as F. R. Leavis's Minority Pamphlet, D. H. LAWRENCE (1930) [551], and Aldous Huxley's "Introduction" to *The Letters of D. H. Lawrence* (1932) [723]. Following the decline of critical interest in Lawrence in the early 1940s, as I suggested in my "Introduction" to Volume I of this bibliography, serious criticism of Lawrence reemerged in the late 1940s and early 1950s in such key essays as Mark Schorer's "Technique as Discovery," HUDSON REVIEW (1948) [1243] and Leavis's essays on "The Novel as Dramatic Poem," SCRUTINY (1950) [1296, 1297], (1951) [1334, 1335, 1336], and (1952) [1373, 1374]. The turning point in the establishment of Lawrence's critical reputation was marked by the publication in the mid-1950s of Harry T. Moore's biography THE INTELLIGENT HEART: THE STORY OF D. H. LAWRENCE (1954) [1460] and F. R. Leavis's critical study D. H. LAWRENCE: NOVELIST (1955) [1494]. By the 1960s the Lawrence revival was in full swing.

The increased interest in D. H. Lawrence in the fifteen-year period from 1961 to 1975 is indicated by the fact that Volume II of this bibliography is of comparable length to Volume I, which included some 2,061 annotated entries for the years 1909 to 1960. Some have deprecated this productivity as "industrial literary scholarship," as F. R. Leavis did in "Lawrence 'Scholarship' and Lawrence," his review in the SEWANEE REVIEW (1963) [2408] of Harry T. Moore's edition of *The Collected Letters of D. H. Lawrence* (1962) [2294]. The term surfaced again in "The Lawrence Industry," an omnibus review in the TIMES LITERARY SUPPLEMENT (London) (1970) [3547], and in several other reviews. While it would be idle to pretend that the exigencies of the academic marketplace in the third quarter of the twentieth century did not contribute to the growth of research and publication in Lawrence scholarship as in other areas, I cannot agree that the major Lawrence studies between 1961 and 1975 should be characterized as merely industrial products, mass produced with minimal quality control. A number of examples from among the many items abstracted for the years covered in this bibliography attest to both the breadth and depth of scholarly interest in Lawrence. Some of them are distinguished.

These years saw a continuation, with modifications, of the four areas of published responses to Lawrence discussed in the Introduction to Volume I: first, the view of Lawrence as an ignorant genius; second, the psychoanalytic criticism that examines Lawrence and his work from a Freudian perspective or that studies his own psychological theories; third, the memoirs and letters written by people who knew Lawrence; and fourth, the canon of serious academic scholarship and criticism. Within these broad categories, I should like to survey the further developments in Lawrence's critical reputation in this period.

By the 1960s and 1970s, Lawrence is scarcely spoken of as an "ignorant genius." For one thing, there is altogether too much scholarship on Lawrence's art and ideas for a view of him as ignorant to remain credible. For another, Leavis had been quite effective in his answers, in "Mr. Eliot and Lawrence," SCRUTINY (1951) [1333] and elsewhere, to T. S. Eliot's repeated charge against Lawrence of "ignorance," in Eliot's review "Son of Woman," CRITERION (1931) [646], in AFTER STRANGE GODS: A PRIMER OF MODERN HERESY (1933) [810], and in his Foreword to D. H. LAWRENCE AND HUMAN EXISTENCE, by Father William Tiverton (Martin Jarrett-Kerr) (1951) [1326], although to Eliot's mind what Lawrence lacked was not education but "a wise and large capacity for orthodoxy." Whatever one's view of that deficiency, after the publication of Rose Marie Burwell's "A Catalogue of D. H. Lawrence's Reading from Early Childhood," D. H. LAWRENCE REVIEW (1970) [3448], few could doubt the extent of his knowledge.

The psychoanalytic critical technique of examining the text for the unconscious motives it conceals led to the discovery by academic critics of a neurotic latent content and even an unsuspected sexual subtext in Lawrence's fiction. Daniel A. Weiss, in OEDIPUS IN NOTTINGHAM: D. H. LAWRENCE (1962) [2348] finds the Oedipal conflict in *Sons and Lovers* projected as the basic opposition in Lawrence's fiction between "The Mother in the Mind" and "The Father in the Blood." David Cavitch, in D. H. LAWRENCE AND THE NEW WORLD (1969) [3272], sees in Lawrence's fiction the writer's unsuccessful attempt to liberate himself psychologically through artistic creation from conflicts growing out of his suppressed homosexual yearnings. Both R. E. Pritchard, in D. H. LAWRENCE: BODY OF DARKNESS (1971) [3782], and John E. Stoll, in THE NOVELS OF D. H. LAWRENCE: A SEARCH FOR INTEGRATION (1971) [3806], examine Lawrence's recurrent images and principal fictional characters to discover his attempt to liberate through his fiction the buried primary self suppressed by self-conscious existence (Pritchard) and a consequent search for integration of this vital being by overcoming duality through art (Stoll). At least one medical writer, William B. Ober, M.D., in "Lady Chatterley's *What*?" ACADEMY OF MEDICINE OF NEW JERSEY BULLETIN (1969) [3369], views the emphasis on Mellors's potency as compensating for Lawrence's impotence at the time and the concealed suggestion of anal intercourse as deriving from repressed homosexual strivings.

Several commentaries examine Lawrence's own psychological theories of the unconscious. One of the most useful of these is Philip Rieff's "The Therapeutic as Mythmaker: Lawrence's True Christian Philosophy," in THE TRIUMPH OF THE THERAPEUTIC: USES OF FAITH AFTER FREUD (1966) [2864], which finds in *Psychoanalysis and the Unconscious* and *Fantasia of the Unconscious* Lawrence's rejection of the philosophy of both Christianity and rational science and his trust in man's irrational faculty as a means of achieving harmony with the universe. Claudia C. Morrison, in FREUD AND THE CRITIC: THE EARLY USE OF DEPTH PSYCHOLOGY IN LITERARY CRITICISM (1968) [3156], sees Lawrence himself, in *Studies in Classic American Literature*, as making "a highly idiosyncratic application of the principles of depth psychology to literature" by way of the "essentially religious" system of *Psychoanalysis* and *Fantasia*. And Howard M. Harper, Jr., in "*Fantasia* and the Psychodynamics of *Women in Love*," in THE CLASSIC BRITISH NOVEL (1972) [3923], examines characters and relationships in that novel in light of a detailed explanation of Lawrence's psychological theory.

Reminiscences by people who had known Lawrence were once the most prevalent form of published commentary on him. An article by Jeffrey Meyers, aptly titled "Memoirs of D. H. Lawrence: A Genre of the Thirties," D. H. LAWRENCE REVIEW, XIV (Spring 1981), 1-32, defines the distinct literary type to which they belong. But after the publication of Edward Nehls's D. H. LAWRENCE: A COMPOSITE BIOGRAPHY, 3 vols. (1957, 1958, 1959) [1634, 1708, 1840], what remained to be remembered? As it turns out, a number of things. I should like to consider this question briefly in a survey of the memoirs of Lawrence, comments on Lawrence in other memoirs, and collections of Lawrence's letters published in this period and to indicate the use to which Lawrence biographers have put the information derived from these sources.

FRIEDA LAWRENCE: THE MEMOIRS AND CORRESPONDENCE, edited by E. W. Tedlock, Jr. (1961) [2112], presents Frieda's only slightly fictionalized account of the life of "Paula" (Frieda) with "Edna" (her sister Else), "Octavio" (Otto Gross), "Charles Widmer" (Ernest Weekley), "Andrew" (D. H. Lawrence), and "Dario" (Angelo Ravagli), together with several short essays and a collection of her letters, most notably those to John Middleton Murry. Helen Corke's D. H. LAWRENCE: THE CROYDON YEARS (1965) [2620] collects several of her earlier memoirs of Lawrence in Croydon in 1909-1910 [2223], of Jessie Chambers [1323], of the background and writing of *The White Peacock* [1760], and her critique of Lawrence's reading of the Book of Revelation [799]. Joseph Foster's D. H. LAWRENCE IN TAOS (1972) [3902] recounts, in questionable detail, Lawrence and Frieda's initial journey to Taos, to Mexico, and back to Taos; their conversations; and their relationships with people there, mainly with Mabel Dodge Luhan. A CONVERSATION ON D. H. LAWRENCE, edited by Haruhide Mori (1974) [4370], transcribes a 1952 tape recording of a discussion in the UCLA library among Aldous Huxley, Lawrence Clark Powell, Frieda Lawrence, Dorothy G. Mitchell, and Majl Ewing. Martha Gordon Crotch's MEMORIES OF FRIEDA LAWRENCE (1975) [4469] gives a clear picture of Frieda in the months immediately following Lawrence's death.

Several personal memoirs include material that casts new light on Lawrence and his life. Lina Waterfield, in "The Fortress of Aulla and D. H. Lawrence," in CASTLE IN ITALY: AN AUTOBIOGRAPHY (1961) [2180], gives a picture of

Lawrence in Italy in 1913 and is the source of the information that Lawrence claimed to have actually given his mother an overdose of morphia, as Paul does in *Sons and Lovers*. Sir Compton Mackenzie, in "Memories of D. H. Lawrence," ON MORAL COURAGE (1962) [2282], as well as in several volumes of his ten-volume autobiography, MY LIFE AND TIMES (1966, 1967, 1968, 1969) [2833, 2967, 3141, 3352], gives information on Lawrence's concerns about his sexuality and provides insights on his relationship with the man he satirized in "The Man Who Loved Islands." THE EARLY MEMOIRS (1873-1915) OF LADY OTTOLINE MORRELL (1963) [2421] and OTTOLINE AT GARSINGTON: MEMOIRS OF LADY OTTOLINE MORRELL, 1915-1918 (1974) [4374], both edited by Robert Gathorne-Hardy, recount Lawrence's visits to Garsington, offering valuable accounts of social life at the manor, Lawrence's short friendship with Bertrand Russell, and his hostess's pain on being caricatured as Hermione in *Women in Love*. Lady Beatrice Glenavy, in TODAY WE WILL ONLY GOSSIP (1964) [2501], remembers Lawrence's friendship in the war years with her husband, Gordon Campbell, and herself, John Middleton Murry and Katherine Mansfield, and others of their circle. Lady Cynthia Asquith's DIARIES, 1915-1918, edited by E. M. Horsley (1968) [3033], includes valuable information about her friendship with Lawrence, his reaction to the war, the suppression of *The Rainbow*, the expulsion from Cornwall, and her reading of *Women in Love*. Helen Corke's IN OUR INFANCY: AN AUTOBIOGRAPHY, Part I: 1882-1919 (1975) [4465] provides an account of her tragic love affair with a married violinist, "H. B. M." (Herbert Baldwin Macartney), and of her friendship with Lawrence, who adapted the tragedy in the "saga" that became *The Trespasser*.

This period also saw the publication of several collections of Lawrence's correspondence. *The Collected Letters of D. H. Lawrence*, 2 vols., edited by Harry T. Moore (1962) [2294], is not "the definitive edition" its publisher claimed, as several reviewers pointed out, albeit a somewhat more inclusive collection than Aldous Huxley's edition of *The Letters of D. H. Lawrence* (1932) [723]. For a representative sampling of opinion, see the negative reviews by H. Coombes [2376], Andor Gomme [2248], and F. R. Leavis [2408] and the defense by Mark Schorer [2336]. Despite the limitations, which were primarily those imposed by publisher's restrictions, *Collected Letters* remained for a generation the best available collection of Lawrence's correspondence. But the scholarly deficiencies noted by some reviewers could be corrected only by a definitive scholarly edition such as the Cambridge Edition of *The Letters of D. H. Lawrence*, 7 vols., published beginning in 1979 under the general editorship of James T. Boulton.

Meanwhile, in the late 1960s and 1970s, various individual collections of Lawrence letters were issued in book form, in addition to other collections appearing in periodicals. *Lawrence in Love: Letters to Louie Burrows*, edited by James T. Boulton (1968) [3044], in a form carefully edited and introduced with scholarly annotations, makes available for the first time a major collection of 165 letters Lawrence wrote to the young lady to whom he was engaged for a short time and whose background he used in *The Rainbow*. *The Quest for Rananim: D. H. Lawrence's Letters to S. S. Koteliansky, 1914 to 1930*, edited by George J. Zytaruk (1970) [3653], also with complete editorial apparatus and a scholarly introduction, prints 343 letters, 239 of which were not included in the Moore and Huxley collections, and illuminates Lawrence's search for community and his relationship with the Russian emigre who became his most reliable friend. Three further collections, these without scholarly apparatus, are *The Centaur Letters*, with a Foreword by Edward D. McDonald (1970) [3553], which includes thirty Lawrence letters to Harold T. Mason and others at The Centaur Book Shop, Philadelphia; the privately published *Letters from D. H. Lawrence to Martin Secker, 1911-1930* (1970) [3608], which includes 196 letters to Lawrence's longtime English publisher; and LETTERS FROM A PUBLISHER: MARTIN SECKER TO D. H. LAWRENCE AND OTHERS, 1911-1929 (1970) [3607].

New biographical studies of Lawrence, like earlier ones, rely extensively on the evidence provided by these and other memoirs and letters. Émile Delavenay's D. H. LAWRENCE: L'HOMME ET LA GENÈSE DE SON OEUVRE. LES ANNÉES DE FORMATION (1885-1919) (1969) [3292], the most controversial and influential critical biography of the period, is a "genetic" study which depends on the published memoirs and personal communications of Jessie Chambers, Ada Lawrence Clarke, and others to show that Lawrence's work was shaped by conflicts and contradictions in his psyche, and on a close analysis of internal evidence to trace Lawrence's ideas to those of German theorists of mystical racial ideology such as Houston S. Chamberlain and Otto Weininger. Harry T. Moore's THE PRIEST OF LOVE: A LIFE OF D. H. LAWRENCE (1974) [4369] is a new version of his THE INTELLIGENT HEART (1954) [1460], revised and expanded to include information made available by the publication of new materials. Martin Green's THE VON RICHTHOFEN SISTERS: THE TRIUMPHANT AND THE TRAGIC MODES OF LOVE: ELSE AND FRIEDA VON RICHTHOFEN, OTTO GROSS, MAX WEBER, AND D. H. LAWRENCE IN THE YEARS 1870-1970 (1974) [4320] studies the German intellectual background of Frieda and Else, Gross, Weber, and Edgar Jaffe, and Lawrence's indirect contact, through them, with the sexual ideas of Schwabing and the *kosmische Runde*. Robert Lucas's FRIEDA VON RICHTHOFEN. IHR LEBEN MIT D. H. LAWRENCE (1972) [3948], Geoffrey Trease's THE PHOENIX AND THE FLAME: D. H. LAWRENCE (1973) [4227], Philip Callow's SON AND LOVER: THE YOUNG LAWRENCE (1975) [4457], and Emily Hahn's LORENZO: D. H. LAWRENCE AND THE WOMEN WHO LOVED HIM (1975) [4498] are popular biographies based largely on previously published memoirs and biographies.

Almost every year catalogued in the second volume of this bibliography enters and abstracts serious books of academic scholarship and criticism on Lawrence not included in any of the foregoing categories. There is now such variety of approach and topics in Lawrence studies that they are hard to categorize. Although they vary in purpose and quality from the introductory survey to the full-scale authoritative critical analysis, these academic studies, taken together, demonstrate the lasting literary significance of Lawrence's work.

Some critics see Lawrence in terms of earlier traditions in English literature, as F. R. Leavis did in naming him as the modern successor to the nineteenth-century English novelists, in THE GREAT TRADITION: GEORGE ELIOT, HENRY JAMES, JOSEPH CONRAD (1948) [1234]. Julian Moynahan's THE DEED OF LIFE: THE NOVELS AND TALES OF D. H. LAWRENCE (1963) [2423] also sees Lawrence as continuing the tradition of English realistic fiction with the addition of attributing "paramount importance" to feeling. Keith Sagar's

THE ART OF D. H. LAWRENCE (1966) [2869], which correlates the four phases of Lawrence's career with the appropriate form of his art in each period, places him in a much older tradition, "with Sophocles, Shakespeare, Tolstoy and Hardy, ... of 'setting behind the small action of the protagonists the terrific action of unfathomed nature.'" Colin Clarke's RIVER OF DISSOLUTION: D. H. LAWRENCE AND ENGLISH ROMANTICISM (1969) [3279] approaches Lawrence's work, particularly *Women in Love*, in terms of the romantic theme of dissolution and disintegration.

Other critics, emphasizing Lawrence's role as a visionary or prophet, read his work in terms of his own radical "metaphysic." Eugene Goodheart's THE UTOPIAN VISION OF D. H. LAWRENCE (1963) [2394] sees Lawrence as a Nietzschean "tablet-breaker," diverting "the current of tradition" away from the Victorian view of society as a system of obligations to a Utopian view of society as the outgrowth of an impulse toward community in the dialectic between impulse and resistance within which the individual develops. D. H. LAWRENCE, ARTIST AND REBEL: A STUDY OF LAWRENCE'S FICTION (1963) [2456], a study by E. W. Tedlock, Jr., of Lawrence's vitalist ethic, focuses on the inseparability of his fictional art as it develops in the four phases of his career from his rebellion against conventions or institutions that inhibit the natural life. H. M. Daleski's THE FORKED FLAME: A STUDY OF D. H. LAWRENCE (1965) [2624] delineates the opposing terms of Lawrence's dualism, at the core of which is the tension between the male principle and the female principle, especially as developed in the *Study of Thomas Hardy*, as the all-pervading principle in his work. George H. Ford's DOUBLE MEASURE: A STUDY OF THE NOVELS AND STORIES OF D. H. LAWRENCE (1965) [2639] sees in Lawrence's fiction a "double rhythm" of "creating and destroying": the cycle of rural life associated with the men and the impulse of the women toward the civilized world of the town in *The Rainbow*, and the assertion of the need for relationship between man and woman and the evocation of societal corruption and doom in *Women in Love*. Baruch Hochman's ANOTHER EGO: THE CHANGING VIEW OF SELF AND SOCIETY IN THE WORK OF D. H. LAWRENCE (1970) [3514], characterizing Lawrence as "the radical individualist," explores the pervasive tension in his work between the "social and moral ego of character" and "another ego" or self. Frank Kermode's LAWRENCE (1973) [4132] critically examines the way that Lawrence's "metaphysic" is encompassed by his fiction in the four phases of his career.

Another kind of study sees Lawrence's work in terms of the positive alternative religious values it evokes. George A. Panichas's ADVENTURE IN CONSCIOUSNESS: THE MEANING OF D. H. LAWRENCE'S RELIGIOUS QUEST (1964) [2563] sees Lawrence's art as inseparable from his religious quest as a thought-adventurer on a "voyage of discovery." LITERATURE AND RELIGION: VIEWS ON D. H. LAWRENCE, edited by Charles A. Huttar (1968) [3110], collects a group of papers written primarily from a traditional Christian perspective. Chaman L. Nahal's D. H. LAWRENCE: AN EASTERN VIEW (1970) [3570] examines the wider religious affinities between Lawrence's ideas and the approach to life in the Vedas and other Hindu Scriptures.

If myth, as Joseph Campbell has suggested, is what we call other people's religion, then studies of Lawrence's evocation of mythic images and principles are a means of arriving at his religious positives. Evelyn J. Hinz's series of studies elucidating Lawrence's archetypal imagination began with a trilogy of articles in the D. H. LAWRENCE REVIEW on the novels of Lawrence's apprenticeship period: "Juno and *The White Peacock*: Lawrence's English Epic" (1970) [3512]; "*The Trespasser*: Lawrence's Wagnerian Tragedy and Divine Comedy" (1971) [3722]; "*Sons and Lovers*: The Archetypal Dimensions of Lawrence's Oedipal Tragedy" (1972) [3927]. My book D. H. LAWRENCE'S AMERICAN JOURNEY: A STUDY IN LITERATURE AND MYTH (1970) [3462] discusses the fiction of Lawrence's American period together with his psychological treatises and his criticism of American literature in terms of his romantic quest for regenerative myths and symbols. John B. Vickery's THE LITERARY IMPACT OF "THE GOLDEN BOUGH" (1973) [4230] includes two chapters on Lawrence's use of Frazer. Materials from Vickery's articles "Myth and Ritual in the Shorter Fiction of D. H. Lawrence," MODERN FICTION STUDIES (1959) [1869]; "*The Plumed Serpent* and the Eternal Paradox," CRITICISM (1963) [2462]; "*The Plumed Serpent* and the Reviving God," JOURNAL OF MODERN LITERATURE (1972) [4013]; and "D. H. Lawrence's Poetry: Myth and Matter," D. H. LAWRENCE REVIEW (1974) [4426], are incorporated in his book MYTHS AND TEXTS: STRATEGIES OF INCORPORATION AND DISPLACEMENT (1983). Samuel A. Eisenstein's BOARDING THE SHIP OF DEATH: D. H. LAWRENCE'S QUESTER HEROES (1974) [4305] compares Lawrence's heroes with the questing heroes in religious literature and myth to demonstrate the process of growth by which his protagonists emerge from the mass to become individuals.

Various critical approaches, from the traditional to the specialized, are represented by full-length studies of Lawrence. Claude M. Sinzelle's THE GEOGRAPHICAL BACKGROUND OF THE EARLY WORKS OF D. H. LAWRENCE (1964) [2587] examines the matrix of place out of which the fiction of Lawrence's first period arose. Yudhishtar's CONFLICT IN THE NOVELS OF D. H. LAWRENCE (1969) [3419] defends Lawrence as an exception to whom the rules of aesthetic criticism do not apply, making almost all previous criticism inadequate or misleading. Claude Negriolli's LA SYMBOLIQUE DE D. H. LAWRENCE (1970) [3574] analyzes Lawrence's symbolism by a structuralist method. Keith Alldritt's THE VISUAL IMAGINATION OF D. H. LAWRENCE (1971) [3658] examines the visual element in Lawrence's fiction. Kenneth Inniss's D. H. LAWRENCE'S BESTIARY: A STUDY OF HIS USE OF ANIMAL TROPE AND SYMBOL (1971) [3727] analyzes the function of animal imagery in Lawrence's fiction and poetry as well as nonfiction prose. Stephen J. Miko's TOWARD "WOMEN IN LOVE": THE EMERGENCE OF A LAWRENTIAN AESTHETIC (1971) [3756] studies the development of Lawrence's aesthetic in the ideas and fiction culminating in *Women in Love*. Scott Sanders's D. H. LAWRENCE: THE WORLD OF THE MAJOR NOVELS (1973) [4199] sees the five major novels in terms of Lawrence's response to specific historical circumstances of class division, personal alienation, increased mobility, the decline of religion, the rise of industry, widespread education, and the First World War. Biyot K. Tripathy's THE MAJOR NOVELS OF D. H. LAWRENCE (1973) [4229] explicates structure and characterization in the novels, which he finds to be organized on two distinct time schemes, objective and subjective, with characters considered individually rather than as types.

Several critical books are influence studies or explorations of Lawrence's relation to other literary figures. Mary Corsani's D. H. LAWRENCE E L'ITALIA (1965) [2621] is the first major study of the influence of Italy and its culture on Lawrence's work. Norman J. Fedder's THE INFLUENCE OF D. H. LAWRENCE ON TENNESSEE WILLIAMS (1966) [2794] demonstrates Lawrence's importance for the work of the American dramatist. Émile Delavenay's D. H. LAWRENCE AND EDWARD CARPENTER (1971) [3695] explores the unacknowledged influence of Carpenter on Lawrence. George J. Zytaruk's D. H. LAWRENCE'S RESPONSE TO RUSSIAN LITERATURE (1971) [3834] discusses Lawrence's relation to Russian writers such as Tolstoy, Dostoevsky, and Rozanov. Richard Swigg's LAWRENCE, HARDY, AND AMERICAN LITERATURE (1972) [4001] relates Lawrence's view of tragedy in his work through *Women in Love* to the art and ideas of Thomas Hardy and of the classic American writers.

A number of other books are studies of individual novels or of Lawrence's work in genres other than the novel. The former include brief introductions intended primarily for students, casebooks, and study guides to several of Lawrence's major novels as well as works of academic scholarship such as L. D. Clark's DARK NIGHT OF THE BODY: D. H. LAWRENCE'S "THE PLUMED SERPENT" (1964) [2480], which presents a critical defense supported by scholarship on the manuscripts, the sources, and the influences of travel and place; and Peter Balbert's D. H. LAWRENCE AND THE PSYCHOLOGY OF RHYTHM: THE MEANING OF FORM IN "THE RAINBOW" (1974) [4264], which shows how meaning emerges from form in Lawrence's use of the womb symbol and the rhythmic arrangement of language in a coherent whole. Studies of the short fiction include Kingsley Widmer's THE ART OF PERVERSITY: D. H. LAWRENCE'S SHORTER FICTIONS (1962) [2351], which explicates the short fiction in terms of the demonic elements; Adrian Hsia's D. H. LAWRENCE: DIE CHARAKTERE IN DER HANDLUNG UND SPANNUNG SEINER KURZGESCHICHTEN (1968) [3109], which examines the stories chronologically with reference to character development and major themes such as the polarity of mind consciousness and "blood consciousness"; M. G. Krishnamurthi's D. H. LAWRENCE: TALE AS MEDIUM (1970) [3536], which surveys Lawrence's stories, grouped according to theme; and Reloy Garcia and James Karabatsos's A CONCORDANCE TO THE SHORT FICTION OF D. H. LAWRENCE (1972) [3910], a computer-generated word index to the short novels and stories that employs current paperback reprints rather than authoritative texts. D. H. Lawrence's criticism has been discussed in David J. Gordon's D. H. LAWRENCE AS A LITERARY CRITIC (1966) [2799], the first full-length study of Lawrence's critical ideas; Ileana Čura-Sazdanič's D. H. LAWRENCE AS CRITIC (1969) [3285], which places Lawrence's criticism, with its condemnation of a machine civilization, in the moral tradition of Arnold, Carlyle, and Leavis; and Aruna Sitesh's D. H. LAWRENCE: THE CRUSADER AS CRITIC (1975) [4586], which views Lawrence, both as artist and critic, as a moralist whose judgments are centered in his vision of life. Lawrence's poetry has been considered in Tom Marshall's THE PSYCHIC MARINER: A READING OF THE POEMS OF D. H. LAWRENCE (1970) [3559], which correlates his analysis of the forms, rhythms, and language of the poems with the growth of Lawrence's ideas on death and rebirth, modern mechanized society and man's primitive nature, and the need to reconcile flesh and spirit; T. A. Smailes's SOME COMMENTS ON THE VERSE OF D. H. LAWRENCE (1970) [3620], which discusses the evolution of some poems and provides unpublished variants and corrections to published versions of others; Sandra M. Gilbert's ACTS OF ATTENTION: THE POEMS OF D. H. LAWRENCE (1972) [3913], which focuses on the "effort of attention" in Lawrence's poetry from the tentative early verse, through the mature style of *Birds, Beasts and Flowers*, to the visionary journey of *Last Poems*; and Reloy Garcia and James Karabatsos's A CONCORDANCE TO THE POETRY OF D. H. LAWRENCE (1970) [3497], a computer-generated word index to the unrevised edition of *The Complete Poems of D. H. Lawrence* (1964). The first full-length study of the drama is Sylvia Sklar's THE PLAYS OF D. H. LAWRENCE (1975) [4587], which includes detailed critical responses to the eight plays and two fragments.

The indispensable standard primary bibliography, Warren Roberts's A BIBLIOGRAPHY OF D. H. LAWRENCE (1963) [2438], has been updated in a second edition (1982). Secondary bibliography in this period, subsumed in the present volume, includes "D. H. Lawrence: Ten Years of Criticism, 1959-1968, a Checklist," by Richard D. Beards, assisted by G. B. Crump, D. H. LAWRENCE REVIEW (1968) [3040], with annual supplementary checklists by Beards through 1979; and the D. H. LAWRENCE REVIEW foreign-language bibliographies for French, German, Italian, Japanese, Portuguese, Scandinavian, and Yugoslavian publications on Lawrence. Lawrence's contemporary critical reception is well represented in R. P. Draper's D. H. LAWRENCE: THE CRITICAL HERITAGE (1970) [3472], a collection of early reviews of Lawrence's works on their original publication. Lawrence's relation to little magazines is suggested by Nicholas Joost and Alvin Sullivan's D. H. LAWRENCE AND "THE DIAL" (1970) [3525], a study of Lawrence's primary publications and reviews of his work in the American periodical. Reliable introductions to Lawrence's work include Anthony Beal's D. H. LAWRENCE (1961) [2068]; R. P. Draper's D. H. LAWRENCE (1964) [2490]; R. P. Draper's D. H. LAWRENCE ("Profiles in Literature") (1969) [3302]; Tony Slade's D. H. LAWRENCE (1970) [3396], and Armin Arnold's D. H. LAWRENCE (1972) [3841]. Two periodicals devoted to Lawrence in this period are the D. H. LAWRENCE REVIEW, founded under my editorship (1968) [3064, 3065, 3066] and continuing publication with three issues for each annual volume as a forum for criticism, scholarship, reviews, and bibliography; and the D. H. LAWRENCE STUDIES (Kyoto), founded under the leadership of Sadanobu Kai (1973) [4071] and continuing publication in single annual numbers devoted to individual major works by Lawrence. Special issues include Lawrence numbers of PAUNCH, under the guest editorship of E. W. Dawson, No. 26 (1966) [2853]; and LITERATURE/FILM QUARTERLY, edited by Thomas L. Erskine, Vol. I, No. 1 (1973) [4145].

Finally, I should like to call attention to seven additional issues or events that are important for the development of Lawrence's literary reputation in this period.

First, the English censorship trial of *Lady Chatterley's Lover* (1960) generated a heated debate among scholars, clergymen, literati, and the reading public. THE TRIAL OF LADY CHATTERLEY: REGINA V. PENGUIN BOOKS LIMITED, by C. H. Rolph (C. R. Hewitt) (1961) [2154], is a narrative account and edited transcript of the trial. A substantial number of discussions in books, news reports, accounts and commentaries in periodicals, and letters to the editor concerning the trial are included in this bibliography and identified in a sublisting under *Lady Chatterley's Lover* in the index to primary titles.

Second, the question of whether Lawrence's treatment of sex in *Lady Chatterley's Lover* involved anal intercourse in the "night of sensual passion" scene developed into a major critical controversy. First raised by G. Wilson Knight, in "Lawrence, Joyce and Powys," ESSAYS IN CRITICISM (1961) [2107], and John Sparrow, in "Regina v. Penguin Books Ltd.: An Undisclosed Element in the Case," ENCOUNTER (1962) [2340], the issue of buggery was argued pro and con largely in these two periodicals (see cross-references in abstracts for these two articles) and echoed in criticism throughout the period.

Third, the commercially successful filming of four Lawrence works—*Sons and Lovers* (1960), *The Fox* (1967), *Women in Love* (1969), and *The Virgin and the Gypsy* (1970)—generated wide discussion of the adaptations. Both current reviews and publicity on the films and academic critiques are included in this bibliography and sublisted under the titles in the index to primary titles.

Fourth, Lawrence came into his own as a playwright in the acclaimed naturalistic productions of *A Collier's Friday Night*, *The Daughter-in-Law*, and *The Widowing of Mrs. Holroyd* in the "Season of Plays" (1968) directed by Peter Gill at the Royal Court Theatre in London with meticulous attention to details of setting and the daily rituals of a Midlands collier's home, as most reviews emphasized. The productions won for Lawrence the audience that his plays had never had during his lifetime and established him as a significant dramatist whose plays are worthy of serious critical consideration, as subsequent books and articles on Lawrence's dramatic oeuvre have borne out.

Fifth, the feminist critique of Lawrence's work seemed at the time to have been launched almost singlehandedly by Kate Millett's chapter on Lawrence in SEXUAL POLITICS (1970) [3563], which provoked Norman Mailer's response in THE PRISONER OF SEX (1971) [3749] and other refutations (see cross-references in the abstract for the book). In retrospect, reservations about Lawrence from the feminist perspective are to be found in some earlier responses by women, such as the novelist Ruth Suckow's "Modern Figures of Destiny: D. H. Lawrence and Frieda Lawrence," in the D. H. LAWRENCE REVIEW (1970) [3629] and the comments of Dorothy G. Mitchell in A CONVERSATION ON D. H. LAWRENCE, edited by Haruhide Mori (1974) [4370]. Whatever the merits of any particular reading of Lawrence from this approach, the questions brought to the forefront of critical debate by Millett in 1970 have reverberated in Lawrence criticism from then on.

Sixth, the D. H. Lawrence Festival in Taos (1970), which commemorated the fortieth anniversary of Lawrence's death, was a forum for panel discussions among Lawrence scholars, creative writers, and people who had known Lawrence in his lifetime. Often marked by free-wheeling questions and comments from the floor, the five-day conference generated little new scholarship but established many important relationships among Laurentians that have contributed indirectly to the direction and growth of Lawrence's critical reputation since then. The Festival was itself the occasion of many newspaper items and reviews, a representative selection of which are included in this bibliography. For a varied sampling of opinion, see L. D. Clark, "The D. H. Lawrence Festival: Kiowa Ranch, New

Mexico, September 30-October 4, 1970," D. H. LAWRENCE REVIEW (1971) [3682]; Émile Delavenay, "David Herbert Lawrence et la crise de conscience américaine," LE MONDE (1971) [3692]; and Martin Green,"Old Flames at the Ranch," LONDON MAGAZINE (1971) [3714].

Seventh, YOUNG BERT: AN EXHIBITION OF THE EARLY YEARS OF D. H. LAWRENCE, compiled by Lucy I. Edwards, David Phillips, Arnold Rattenbury, and Jo Barnes (1972) [3888], assembled some 293 works of art, artifacts, photographs, and memorabilia associated with the young Lawrence for a widely discussed exhibition at the Castle Museum, Nottingham. This important exhibition signaled a renewed interest in Lawrence's relation to the art and culture of his home county, an interest evidenced also by the publication in that same year of two local guidebooks—Michael Bennett's A VISITORS GUIDE TO EASTWOOD AND THE COUNTRYSIDE OF D. H. LAWRENCE (1972) [3853] and Bridget Pugh's THE COUNTRY OF MY HEART: A LOCAL GUIDE TO D. H. LAWRENCE (1972) [3978]. Despite a small anti-Lawrence faction in Eastwood, as reported by Arthur Osman in the TIMES (London) (1972) [3972], efforts to restore Lawrence's boyhood home and to develop the tourist potential of Erewash Valley continued.

James C. Cowan

D. H. Lawrence

AN ANNOTATED BIBLIOGRAPHY
OF WRITINGS ABOUT HIM

The Bibliography

1961

2062 Armytage, W. H. G. "From Rananim to Thelnetham," HEAVENS BELOW: UTOPIAN EXPERIMENTS IN ENGLAND, 1560-1960 (Toronto: University of Toronto P; Lond: Routledge & Kegan Paul, 1961), pp. 385-399; additional references, pp. 303, 417.

DHL discussed plans for "his Utopia of revolt--Rananim" with S. S. Koteliansky (August 1914) and asked Lady Ottoline Morrell (February 1915), " 'to form the nucleus of a new community' " which would " 'bring church and house and shop together.' " Later DHL recruited Aldous Huxley, Bertrand Russell, and Lady Cynthia Asquith. DHL started THE SIGNATURE as a means of furthering his ideas, but, like his friendship with Russell, this too failed. Concluding that in England "decomposition" had set in, DHL "began to concentrate on America." He moved to Cornwall near the John Middleton Murrys, but after various difficulties, the Murrys left. Catherine Carswell and Esther Andrews, as new disciples, helped DHL sustain the dream. By fall 1917, the group was to include Dr. and Mrs. David Eder, William Henry, Cecil Gray, several others, and the venue was changed to the Andes. After the war, DHL and Frieda's travels brought them to Taos, New Mexico, where Mabel Dodge Luhan gave DHL a ranch at which he planned to establish Rananim. At a Cafe Royal dinner, DHL asked a group of friends to join him there, but "only the deaf Dorothy Brett really heard the appeal." Rananim was dead, but DHL made his final statement on it in *The Plumed Serpent*, "his Utopia made literate, the idea allegorized." The idea was later paralleled in plans by J. P. Cooney, John Middleton Murry, and Max Plowman for various agrarian communities.

2063 Arnold, Armin. "D. H. Lawrence and Thomas Mann," COMPARATIVE LITERATURE, XIII (Winter 1961), 33-38; rptd in D. H. LAWRENCE AND GERMAN LITERATURE WITH TWO HITHERTO UNKNOWN ESSAYS BY D. H. LAWRENCE, by Armin Arnold (Montreal: Mansfield Book Mart, H. Heinemann, 1963), pp. 49-58.
With the exception of two articles written by Germans, DHL wrote the first article on Thomas Mann in English (in the BLUE REVIEW, July 1913), though he seems to have read only DEATH IN VENICE, TONIO KRÖGER, and TRISTAN. Identifying Mann with Tonio and Aschenbach, DHL dismissed Mann as " 'the last sick sufferer from the complaint of Flaubert.' "

2064 Arnold, Armin. "In the Footsteps of D. H. Lawrence in Switzerland: Some New Biographical Material," TEXAS STUDIES IN LITERATURE AND LANGUAGE, III (Summer 1961), 184-88.
Harry T. Moore's account of DHL's walking tour through Switzerland, 19-26 Sept 1913, based on DHL's essays "Italians in Exile" and "The Return Journey," is not wholly accurate because by the time he wrote the essays, DHL had forgotten the names of places, inns, people. From DHL's "very accurate descriptions, however, it is possible to identify almost all localities he mentions." [By following the same streets on foot and even sleeping in the same places, the author offers his own corrections and identifications.]

2065 Asakawa, Jun. "Oboegaki Lawrence (II)" (A Note on Lawrence [II], ENGLISH LANGUAGE AND ENGLISH AND AMERICAN LITERATURES (Chūo University), No. 2 (Nov 1961), 21-28.
[On *The Rainbow*.] [In Japanese.]

2066 Baldanza, Frank. "D. H. Lawrence's Song of Songs," MODERN FICTION STUDIES, VII (Summer 1961), 106-14.
DHL's rejection of the Bible was a rejection of Jewish morality, not of Jewish poetry. In fact, Biblical imagery and allusion are embedded in most of DHL's works, and Biblical prosodic method contributed to his style throughout his career. In his earlier and middle years, the Biblical influence on DHL was apparently a subconscious one; however, the conscious Biblical influence in later works reflects DHL's intellectual respect for the Bible, derived from his reading of the Moffat translation and Frederick Carter's DRAGON OF THE APOCALYPSE. The most convenient index of the Biblical influence upon DHL's style is a close analysis of *The Rainbow* and *Women in Love*.

2067 Bayley, John. "The Novel and the Life Standard," LONDON MAGAZINE, VIII (Feb 1961), 60-66, espec pp. 62-63.
Believing that the novel can help one " 'to be whole man alive,' " DHL, in his novels, forces "a symbolic choice . . . upon us." But DHL's " 'death' figures, like Skrebensky, Loerke, Chatterley, show his refusal to admit that any life worthy of the name could exist outside his own vision of it."

2068 Beal, Anthony. D. H. LAWRENCE (Edinburgh: Oliver and Boyd; NY: Grove P, 1961; rptd, NY: Capricorn Books, 1972).

DHL's early novels, *The White Peacock, The Trespasser,* and *Sons and Lovers,* depict the world as he knew it, the protagonists in *The White Peacock* being just above his own family on the social scale. Basic to these novels, as well as to his later works, is the conflict between abstract ideas and warm life. DHL's subject matter, if not his technique, differs from that of his predecessors. *The Rainbow* is unique and original, unlike any novel before it and unlike any of DHL's novels that follow it: Ursula Brangwen, the product of three generations, develops to the same point reached by Paul Morel in *Sons and Lovers.* DHL increasingly condemns the world of his own youth, the physical as well as the social world. In *Women in Love,* Gerald Crich, who perfects the industrial system and becomes a kind of god to his employees, is as possessive, selfish, ruthless, and efficient in love as he is in business--and finds happiness in neither. The contrasts between the various couples and the worlds they inhabit structure the novel, and the symbolism is conscious. DHL's antipathy toward the war and toward England are part of the novel, as is his fulfilling relationship with Frieda. *The Lost Girl* stands alone, the only novel in which DHL is not working out his own problems. *Aaron's Rod* is a disappointment: Aaron discovers Italy, has his flute destroyed, attempts to establish a meaningful relationship with Lilly; but, for all that, there is no real conflict in the novel. *Kangaroo* is interrupted by fifty pages of autobiography; despite this, there is coherent development of the artist as activist theme and a recognition that political activity is useless since it cannot change men. DHL's dark gods and Australia as setting are equally significant, and this novel includes some of DHL's most beautiful natural description. In *The Plumed Serpent,* which must be considered a major work, setting is inseparable from spiritual action, and sex between man and woman is basic to the religious theme. This treatment of sexual love anticipates DHL's directly phallic book, *Lady Chatterley's Lover,* which was legally banned in England for thirty-two years. As DHL's attempt to restore innocence and vitality to forbidden Anglo-Saxon words, *Lady Chatterley's Lover* fails, though it does present an effective statement of tenderness and phallic consciousness. It is DHL's most carefully wrought novel after *Women in Love.* Though the ten novels, seven novellas, and fifty plus short stories are among his best works, DHL's canon is not restricted to fiction. His travel books, literary criticism, philosophy texts, and letters are also significant. Though his work was not understood during his lifetime, the post-World War II generation saw DHL as a positive creative force, not as an iconoclast prophesying sexual liberty, as the generation of the twenties apparently saw him. Now DHL is being read widely, and not just by academicians. He is taken seriously as artist and critic, and readers are coming to recognize that DHL did not create a vast monolithic system embodying a progressive, coherent doctrine.

2069 Bedford, Sybille. "The Last Trial of Lady Chatterley," ES-QUIRE, LV (April 1961), 132-36, 138, 141-55.

The 1960 British trial of *Lady Chatterley's Lover* (Regina v. Penguin Books, Ltd.), unlike the one in America, was a criminal trial under the 1959 Obscene Publications Act, which allowed the defense to present evidence justifying the book on the basis of its literary merit judged as a whole. As a criminal proceeding, the case was automatically tried by a jury. In his opening speech, the prosecutor said that there were two questions to decide: whether the book was obscene and, if so, whether its publication would be for the public good. In stating the case for the Crown, the prosecutor said that the novel was about a sex-starved woman who satisfied her lust with a man other than her husband and that there were "thirteen passages of sexual intercourse" which were unvaried except in location. The prosecutor then read aloud passages containing the four-letter words. Defense strategy was to call expert witnesses [excerpts of testimonies given], most of whom said that the book was artistically successful, in the main, and that it was not obscene. The prosecutor concluded his case by reminding the jury that their opinions were the only ones that mattered. The presiding judge summed up by seconding this view, saying that the jury need not take evidence into account, and pointing out the absurdity of "reverencing a man's balls." Three hours later, the jury returned a "Not Guilty" verdict.

2070 Bedford, Sybille. "The Wife's Tale," SPECTATOR, CCVII (8 Dec 1961), 863-64.
[Review of FRIEDA LAWRENCE: THE MEMOIRS AND CORRESPONDENCE, ed by E. W. Tedlock (1961). Discusses DHL's relationship with Frieda and with her aristocratic family.]

2071 Berg, Robert von. "T. S. Eliot über D. H. Lawrence" (T. S. Eliot on D. H. Lawrence), SÜDDEUTSCHE ZEITUNG, 12 Dec 1961.
[Report of T. S. Eliot's speech to the Young Men's Hebrew Association in New York on the role of the literary critic, in which Eliot considered DHL as an opponent whose work has been overestimated.] [In German.]

2072 Booth, Wayne C. THE RHETORIC OF FICTION (Chicago: University of Chicago P, 1961), pp. 53n, 79-81, 138-39, 154, 293.
Most critics respond to *Lady Chatterley's Lover* in terms of its thesis. What mars the novel is Mellors's preachments as they appear in dramatized form. DHL dishonestly tips the scales in favor of Mellors's ideas. DHL as "implied narrator" thus becomes part of the drama and as such is aesthetically objectionable.

2073 Bugarski, Ranko. "Kraj jedne knijiževne i legalnosti" (End of Literary Illegality), ŽIVOT, Nos. 1-2 (1961), 109-10.
[On the publication of the unexpurgated text of *Lady Chatterley's Lover* in England.] [In Serbo-Croatian.]

2074 "Canadian Customs Seize Books," TIMES (Lond), 11 May 1961, p. 13.
[Brief news story.] Customs officials in Vancouver have held up distribution of three books, including THE TRIAL OF LADY CHATTERLEY: REGINA V. PENGUIN BOOKS LIMITED, by C. H. Rolph. Earlier *Lady Chatterley's Lover* was seized by Montreal police, an action upheld by the Quebec appeals court and now being appealed to the Supreme Court of Canada.

2075 Casey, Paul C. "The Casey Judgement," TAMARACK REVIEW, XXI (Autumn 1961), 58-70.
[Reprint of Mr. Justice Casey's adverse opinion on *Lady Chatterley's Lover*,

which he wrote on the unanimous judgment of the Court of Queen's Bench, Quebec, on the appeal instituted at the direction of the publisher, New American Library, of the 1960 conviction, under Section 150 (8) of the Criminal Code, of three Montreal newsdealers for selling the book. Under the definition given by Parliament in the 1959 statute under which the 1960 proceedings were taken--
" '*any publication a dominant characteristic of which is the undue exploitation of sex . . . shall be deemed to be obscene*' "--the appeal was dismissed. See also "Lady Chatterley in Ottawa," CANADIAN FORUM, XLII (April 1962), 11-13, for an account of the reversal of this decision on the subsequent appeal of this case to the Supreme Court of Canada.]

2076 Cox, C. B. "Symposium: Pornography and Obscenity. Editorial Comment: The Teaching of Literature," CRITICAL QUARTERLY, III (Summer 1961), 99-103.

Our muddled thinking about "the relationship between art and morality"--revealed by the censorship trial of *Lady Chatterley's Lover*--issues out of the conflict between the old upper-class view of literature as *belles lettres* and the "new lower class, non-conformist, puritan view of literature as the expression of the whole man." Proponents of the latter view often adopt an all-or-nothing stance, as did DHL in *Lady Chatterley's Lover* and *The Man Who Died*: having become "dissatisfied with the human condition itself," he lost himself in "an Arcadian dream . . . out of touch with the actual problems of marriage." [See also, in the same "Symposium: Pornography and Obscenity," CRITICAL QUARTERLY, III (Summer 1961), the following comments: Donald Davie, "Literature and Morality," pp. 109-13; Martin Jarrett-Kerr, "A Christian View," pp. 113-18 (not abstracted as not specifically on DHL); C. S. Lewis, "Four-Letter Words," pp. 118-22; and Norman St. John-Stevas, "The English Censorship Laws," pp. 103-9.]

2077 Davie, Donald. THE HEYDAY OF SIR WALTER SCOTT (Lond: Routledge & Kegan Paul; NY: Barnes & Noble, 1961), pp. 105, 129-33, 145, 146, 157.

DHL was "right to insist that the five Leatherstocking novels should be read in the order in which they were composed." DHL's revisions of the essay "Fenimore Cooper's Leatherstocking Novels" make the tone "less attractive," "more derisive." But "we look in vain among later commentators for the enthusiasm which Lawrence expresses" for THE PIONEERS.

2078 Davie, Donald. "Symposium: Pornography and Obscenity. Literature and Morality," CRITICAL QUARTERLY, III (Summer 1961), 109-13.

Dr. Leavis's point that "the more artful and sophisticated" a work is, the more moral it is "is a lesson seldom learned." One of the dispiriting things about the *Lady Chatterley's Lover* case (Regina v. Penguin Books, Ltd.) was the assumption "that once Lawrence could be proved to have approached the matter of sexual relations with awful solemnity, the novel would thereby be shown to be a moral work." [See also, in the same "Symposium: Pornography and Obscenity," CRITICAL QUARTERLY, III (Summer 1961), the following comments:

C. B. Cox, "Editorial Comment: The Teaching of Literature," pp. 99-103; Martin Jarrett-Kerr, "A Christian View," pp. 113-18 (not abstracted as not specifically on DHL); C. S. Lewis, "Four-Letter Words," pp. 118-22; and Norman St. John-Stevas, "The English Censorship Laws," pp. 103-9.]

2079 Dehring, Erna. "Das Tier bei D. H. Lawrence" (The Animal in the Work of D. H. Lawrence). Unpublished dissertation, University of Göttingen, 1961. [Listed in Lawrence F. McNamee, DISSERTATIONS IN ENGLISH AND AMERICAN LITERATURE (NY & Lond: Bowker, 1968), p. 613.]

The description of animals in DHL's works often serves as a contrasting background to human life. Animals embody his creed that only "sense-awareness" can bring about the recreation of man, whose mechanized life has destroyed the links to nature. DHL does not preach man's return to animalism, but attempts to comprehend the otherness of animals. Since the mystery of animal life cannot be revealed by the language of science, DHL frequently uses metaphors and emphasizes the natural environments of the animals. Animal imagery appears very rarely in his early works but assumes an important place later on. DHL often seizes on traditional images whose underlying meaning he converts to suit his own message. His animal imagery is strongly didactic and often hints at traits man and animals have in common. Animals turn up as symbols, metaphors, in comparisons, and only occasionally in allegories. [In German.]

2080 de Michelis, Eurialo. "Ancora su Lady Chatterley" (On Lady Chatterley Again), IL GIORNALE D'ITALIA (Rome), 2 March 1961, p. 3.

The trial of *Lady Chatterley's Lover* (Regina v. Penguin Books, Ltd.) shows that a book is often more a platform for controversial discussion than an artistic event. This novel can be defended against the accusation of obscenity in that the relationship between Constance and Mellors is not only physical but spiritual as well. The weakness of the book lies in DHL's prophetic attitude; in the end *Lady Chatterley's Lover* becomes more a manifesto of DHL's ideas than a fictional work. [In Italian.]

2081 de Michelis, Eurialo. "Lawrence in versi" (Lawrence in Verse), LETTERATURE MODERNE (Bologna), March-April 1961, pp. 232-44.

[Review of *Tutte le poesie di D. H. Lawrence* (*The Complete Poems of D. H. Lawrence*), 2 vols., trans and ed and with an Introduction by Piero Nardi (1959).] DHL's poetic works do not constitute real poetry because their artistic aspects are often subordinated to the demands of theories. Poetry and conceptual structures are strictly linked in DHL's poems. They can be grouped in relation to biographical elements. The most relevant concern the various female figures (DHL's mother, Jessie Chambers, Frieda) who had an important role in his life. From a reading of the poems written under the influence of Frieda's love, one can see how important she was in determining his theories of sex and his approach to Freudianism. [In Italian.]

2082 Fiedler, Leslie A. "The Literati of the Four-letter Word," PLAYBOY, VIII (June 1961), 85, 125-28.

DHL is one of several writers like "small boys writing dirty words on sidewalks and fences." He seems shocking and rebellious when he wishes to "be tender or merely matter of fact." While DHL makes "all the typical modern errors," he contrived "*for the first time* a pseudo-poetry and sentimentality proper to sexual frankness." It is not "mere masculine narcissism which demands the fantasies of erotic fiction" but "the deep need of the male to know what he is to someone utterly other."

2083 Foster, D. W. "Lawrence, Sex and Religion," THEOLOGY, LXIV (Jan 1961), 8-13.

As the Christian pastorate struggles to find an inspired method for sex education, the advice to use English literature is welcome. The case against DHL, who comes to mind in this connection, was best countered by his own *Pornography and Obscenity*. *Lady Chatterley's Lover* can be read by a mature public for the vision it gives of the "sacred mystery" of human love. DHL's sexual polarity, unlike that of Freud, Zola, or Maupassant, is not reductive. To the charge of pantheism, one can answer that DHL wants both "Word and Flesh," and his range of possibilities leaves us with a sense of necessary worldly tension. DHL's social criticism shows an ethical sense, and his view of the difficult but satisfying rebirth through marriage is meaningful.

2084 Fraiberg, Selma. "Two Modern Incest Heroes," PARTISAN REVIEW, XXVIII, Nos. 5-6 (1961), 646-61, espec pp. 647-51.

Sigmund Freud's work on incest has changed the impact of that subject as a tragic literary theme. DHL in *Sons and Lovers* confronts this problem, though he is unable to make it dynamic for the modern reader. In "The Rocking-Horse Winner" the incest theme is much more compelling because of DHL's use of symbolism which avoids a standard Oedipal story line. [The essay continues with a treatment of incest in Ralph Ellison's INVISIBLE MAN and Thomas Mann's THE HOLY SINNER.]

2085 Gifford, Henry. "The Defect in Lawrence's Poetry," CRITICAL QUARTERLY, III (Summer 1961), 164-66.

[Reply to Vivian de Sola Pinto, "Poet Without a Mask," CRITICAL QUARTERLY, III (Spring 1961), 5-18.] Because DHL had no ear for rhythms his poems remain notebook jottings. Looseness and lack of respect for the past inevitably mean decay. DHL's random successes do not make him a poet. [See also rejoinders by Vivian de Sola Pinto, "Mr. Gifford and D. H. Lawrence," CRITICAL QUARTERLY, III (Autumn 1961), 267-68; and Gāmini Salgādo, "Mr. Gifford and D. H. Lawrence," CRITICAL QUARTERLY, III (Autumn 1961), 268-70; and further comment by Vivian de Sola Pinto, "Lawrence's Poetry," CRITICAL QUARTERLY, IV (Spring 1962), 81.]

2086 Goldberg, S. L. "*The Rainbow*: Fiddle-Bow and Sand," ESSAYS IN CRITICISM (Oxford), XI (Oct 1961), 418-34; rptd in D. H. LAWRENCE: "THE RAINBOW" AND "WOMEN IN LOVE": A CASEBOOK, ed by Colin Clarke (Lond: Macmillan, 1969; Nash-

ville: Aurora Publishers, 1970), pp. 117-34.
Each chapter in *The Rainbow* "crystallizes" a different basic Lawrentian intuition about life, and the intuitions fall into a pattern. [Examples are given.] The chief flaw in *The Rainbow* is DHL's "*over*-certainty," especially in the second half of the novel. Far too often we are asked to accept a position simply because it is Ursula's or to reject a person or an institution for the same reason. Only Ursula's feelings, not the bases of her arguments, are shown.

2087 Goodheart, Eugene. "The Utopian Vision of D. H. Lawrence," DISSERTATION ABSTRACTS, XXII (1962), 4015A. Unpublished dissertation, Columbia University, 1961, rvd and pub as THE UTOPIAN VISION OF D. H. LAWRENCE (Chicago and Lond: University of Chicago P; Toronto: University of Toronto P, 1963).

2088 Gordon, David J. "D. H. Lawrence as Literary Critic." Unpublished dissertation, Yale University, 1961. [Listed in INDEX TO AMERICAN DOCTORAL DISSERTATIONS, 1960-61 (Ann Arbor, Mich.: University Microfilms, 1961), p. 124], rvd and pub as D. H. LAWRENCE AS A LITERARY CRITIC (New Haven and Lond: Yale UP [Yale Studies in English, Vol. 161], 1966).

2089 Green, Martin. A MIRROR FOR ANGLO-SAXONS (Lond: Longmans, 1961), pp. 51-52, 107-108, 176-77, and *passim.*
DHL is the only English writer of this century who is not "British"; i.e., he takes seriously those who don't speak BBC English. Alien to his native country, DHL is a failure in England for precisely the same reasons that T. S. Eliot is successful there. In *Lady Chatterley's Lover*, he presents the essential conflict for Englishmen today. The most important dichotomy for us is that between Oliver Mellors, the essential Englishman, and Sir Clifford Chatterley, the "British" gentleman.

2090 Hashimoto, Hiroshi. "D. H. Lawrence ni Okeru Ai" (Love Ethic of D. H. Lawrence), SCIENTIFIC RESEARCHES (Waseda University), No. 10 (Dec 1961), 43-52.
[In Japanese.]

2091 Heilbrun, Carolyn G. THE GARNETT FAMILY (NY: Macmillan, 1961), pp. 77, 90-92, 95, 101, 106, 134, 139, 142-62, 164, 188-89, 197.
DHL's relationship with Edward Garnett, a confidant and friend, is misrepresented in Harry T. Moore's biography, THE INTELLIGENT HEART: THE STORY OF D. H. LAWRENCE (1954). Garnett was not, as Moore suggests, responsible for the bowdlerization of *Sons and Lovers* but merely responded to pressure from the publisher, Gerald Duckworth, and the puritanical reading public; nor was Garnett a proponent, as charged, of literary traditionalism but actively encouraged innovation. In general, DHL eventually accepted each of Garnett's criticisms of his writing, although he typically fought them initially. The incident which has been assumed to be the cause of the final rupture between Garnett and DHL was the former's remarks concerning the manuscript *The Sisters* in

a letter in which Garnett suggested that DHL go to another publisher. In discussing this incident, Moore neglects to point out that DHL distinguished his anger with the reading public from his feelings for Garnett.

2092 Heppenstall, Rayner. THE FOURFOLD TRADITION: NOTES ON THE FRENCH AND ENGLISH LITERATURES, WITH SOME ETHNOLOGICAL AND HISTORICAL ASIDES (Lond: Barrie & Rockliff, 1961), pp. 12, 75, 93, 95, 100, 103-4, 114, 130-39, 157, 181, 190, 202, 244.

[Taking his departure from F. R. Leavis's seeing one's opposing responses to DHL and James Joyce as the crucial test of how one judges greatness in a creative writer, the author makes an extended contrast between the two in terms of their personal backgrounds and literary practices, their lack of sympathy with each other's work, the differing allegiances they inspired in critics such as Leavis and T. S. Eliot, and the opposing enclaves that formed around the two writers. Later Albert Camus's NOCES and some of his later stories are "strongly reminiscent" of DHL.]

2093 Hirashima, Junko. "Ishikika no Sekai (D. H. Lawrence: *The Fox* no Buntai)" (D. H. Lawrence: The Style of *The Fox*), BAIKA TANKIDAIGAKU KENKYUKIYO (Baika Tankidaigaku), No. 10 (Dec 1961), 30-48.

[In Japanese.]

2094 Hoggart, Richard. "*Chatterley*, the Witnesses, and the Law: Black Magic? White Lies?" ENCOUNTER, XVI (March 1961), 54-55.

[Letter in reply to Colin Welch, "Black Magic, White Lies," ENCOUNTER, XVI (Feb 1961), 75-79.] If Welch is going to support his case with quotation out of context and from sources other than *Lady Chatterley's Lover*, then he ought to consider those that directly refute his case. [Examples cited.] [See also additional letters in reply to Welch by Rebecca West, William Emrys Williams, and Martin Jarrett-Kerr, in "*Chatterley*, the Witnesses, and the Law: Black Magic? White Lies?" ENCOUNTER, XVI (March 1961), 52-53, 54, 55-56, respectively.]

2095 Hoggart, Richard. "Introduction," *Lady Chatterley's Lover*, by D. H. Lawrence, 2nd ed (Harmondsworth, Middlesex, England: Penguin Books, in association with William Heinemann, 1961; rptd, 1961, 1965, 1966, 1967, 1969 [twice], 1970, 1971, 1972, 1973), pp. v-[xv].

"*Lady Chatterley's Lover* is *not* a dirty book. It is clean and serious and beautiful." It challenges the reader "to shake off the habits of a society which manages to be smutty and ashamed at the same time about sexual questions." Even the thirty pages concerned directly with sex are very different from pornographic writing. The baby chicks scene in *Lady Chatterley's Lover* is marked by "respect--reverence" for both the other person and oneself. "Body without mind is brutish; mind without body . . . is a running-away from our double being." Because our very language for sex shows us to be "knotted and ashamed," DHL sought to cleanse the "four-letter words" of their dirt. DHL points the moral by depicting Connie's early affairs in Germany and later with Michaelis as joyless. Hammond relegates sex to a slightly degrading, pointless, physical coupling; similarly, Clifford's suggestion that a suitable man be found to father the baby he has decided Connie "needs" is made without regard for the moral or emotional implications. Connie and Mellors, on the other hand, are "lovers" in the fullest sense, and their sexual encounters are neither "bouts" (as the prosecutor in Regina v. Penguin Books, Ltd., 1960, called them) nor an attack on the institution of marriage. In accomplishing his stated purpose, to encourage " 'men and women to be able to think sex, fully, completely, honestly, and cleanly' " DHL explores "the theme of industrialism and its effects on man" and speaks for " 'the holiness of the heart's affections'; and for sex as part of that holiness." [The 1960 Penguin Books unexpurgated ed of *Lady Chatterley's Lover* was the occasion for the English censorship trial, Regina v. Penguin Books (1960) under the Obscene Publications Act of 1959. After the acquittal of Penguin Books, the second edition, with this introduction by Richard Hoggart, one of the expert witnesses for the defense, was published in 1961.]

2096 Idema, James M. "The Hawk and the Plover: 'The Polarity of Life' in the 'Jungle Aviary' of D. H. Lawrence's Mind in *Sons and Lovers* and *The Rainbow*," FORUM (Houston), III (Summer 1961), 11-14.

In *Sons and Lovers,* Paul Morel absorbs, and even becomes, the polarity between his mother and father. In *The Rainbow,* Anna and Will Brangwen show similar polarities, but Ursula is a product, not an element, of the marriage. Nature in the novels serves to intensify the ugliness of social life as well as to reflect happy human intercourse at moments of intense alienation. DHL finds polarities even within nature, between its "crust" and the "shimmer inside." DHL's greatest skill is in his ability to assimilate opposing points of view, to be both Paul and Miriam, Ursula and Skrebensky. Although his characters lack roundness, DHL plumbs "their very souls and realizes complete identification" with each character and his opposite.

2097 Irwin, W. R. "The Survival of Pan," PUBLICATIONS OF THE MODERN LANGUAGE ASSOCIATION, LXXVI (June 1961), 159-67.

Despite his marked disapproval of romance in *Studies in Classic American Literature,* DHL nowhere shows more dedication to the romantic values of wonder and veneration for the "old" than in frequent references to Pan. In "Pan in America," what DHL calls "Pan power" is a primitive emanation of the "Old Allness" which survives even in our mechanistic age. DHL incorporated the Pan myth into works from *The White Peacock* to *Lady Chatterley's Lover.* Aaron Sisson's flute in *Aaron's Rod* is an intimation of Pan, and the stallion in *St. Mawr* is linked with Pan power. Not surprisingly, Mellors in *Lady Chatterley's Lover* shares this power and urges the masses to forget their money-greed and recognize the great god. One can also find forms of Pan in *The Ladybird* and *The Plumed Serpent.* DHL distinguished between a genuine and pure, if dangerous, Pan spirit and a fallen, civilized, and deteriorated one which the world both overtly condemns and covertly lusts after. DHL's Pan represents an affirmative constituent in his unstable image of the "dark god."

2098 Ishihara, Fumio. "Lawrence Bungaku no Jigen (III)" (The Dimensions of Lawrencean Literature, III), BULLETIN OF THE FACULTY OF FOREIGN LANGUAGES (Kitakyûshû University), Special Number (1961), pp. 1-33.
[On "Odour of Chrysanthemums."] [In Japanese.]

2099 Iwata, Noboru. "*The Fox* ni Tsuite" (On *The Fox*), LITERARY SYMPOSIUM (Aichi University), No. 21 (Feb 1961), 183-202. [In Japanese.]

2100 Jacobson, Dan. "Surer Than Sure," NEW STATESMAN, ns LXII (8 Dec 1961), 886-87.
Although FRIEDA LAWRENCE: THE MEMOIRS AND CORRESPONDENCE, ed by E. W. Tedlock, Jr., does not compare with her earlier "NOT I, BUT THE WIND...," it has the value, in the letters it includes from other people (such as Alice Dax and Ernest Weekley), of making us realize the importance of DHL's life in relation to his art and the sort of impact (in some cases, one of large suffering) his marriage created for other people, especially if we see DHL's life as in some way an exemplary one.

2101 Jarrett-Kerr, Martin. "*Chatterley*, the Witnesses, and the Law: Black Magic? White Lies?" ENCOUNTER, XVI (March 1961), 55-56.
[Letter in reply to Colin Welch, "Black Magic, White Lies," ENCOUNTER, XVI (Feb 1961), 75-79.] DHL is not a black magic magus. There is much of the Book, especially the Old Testament, in DHL. [See also additional letters in reply to Welch by Rebecca West, William Emrys Williams, and Richard Hoggart, in "*Chatterley*, the Witnesses, and the Law: Black Magic? White Lies?" ENCOUNTER, XVI (March 1961), 52-53, 54, 54-55, respectively.]

2102 Jarrett-Kerr, Martin. "Manalive," NEW STATESMAN, LXI (24 March 1961), 480-81.
"Open Lawrence's literary criticism at almost any point in either" *Phoenix: The Posthumous Papers of D. H. Lawrence,* ed and with an Introduction by Edward D. McDonald (republished 1961), or *Selected Literary Criticism,* by DHL, ed by Anthony Beal, "and you will realise again what a fine technician the man was." [Also reviews A D. H. LAWRENCE MISCELLANY, ed by Harry T. Moore (1959).]

2103 Järv, Harry. "D. H. Lawrence--'vår tids skapande geni'" (D. H. Lawrence: 'The Creative Genius of Our Time'), HORISONT (Vasa, Finland), VIII (1961), 16-19.
The reason for the late appreciation of DHL's works was partly his original technique, partly T. S. Eliot's unjustified accusation that DHL was ignorant and incapable of intellectual thinking. Although uneven and inconsistent as artist and

critic, DHL was also frequently misunderstood. [Includes a short account of DHL criticism since the 1940s and of the reception of his *Studies in Classic American Literature.*] [In Swedish.]

2104 Kael, Pauline. "Commitment and the Straitjacket," FILM QUARTERLY, XV (Fall 1961), 4-13, espec pp. 9-11; rptd in I LOST IT AT THE MOVIES, by Pauline Kael (Bost: Little, Brown, 1965), pp. 62-78, espec pp. 72-74; rptd. (NY: Bantam Books, 1966), pp. 55-69, espec pp. 63-65.

The film of *Sons and Lovers,* "a rather tepid series of scenes illustrating Lawrence themes," "fulfills a genuine function if it directs people to the book." Two "post coital discussions" in the movie are "embarrassing, even grotesque." "Lawrence does have scenes like this, but they're the culminations of relationships that have been developed over hundreds of pages; they're not really adaptable to the theatrical convention that speeds them up."

2105 Kai, Sadanobu. "D. H. Lawrence ni Okeru Shi to Fukkatsu *Shinda Otoko* no Daimei o Megutte" (Death and Resurrection in D. H. Lawrence, with Special Reference to *The Man Who Died*), STUDIES IN FOREIGN LITERATURES (Ritsumeikan University), No. 4 (Dec 1961), 13-24.

[In Japanese.]

2106 Katô, Muneyuki. "*Musuko to Koibitotachi* o Chûshin to Shite Mita Lawrence no Ai to Jitsuzon to Sogai to Jyûtai" (Lawrence's Love, Real Existence, Alienation, and Bond Themes Seen Mainly Through *Sons and Lovers*), TREATISES IN COMMEMORATION OF THE 15TH ANNIVERSARY OF THE FOUNDATION OF KITAKYÛSHÛ UNIVERSITY (Dec 1961), 97-155.

[In Japanese.]

2107 Knight, G. Wilson. "Lawrence, Joyce and Powys," ESSAYS IN CRITICISM, XI (Oct 1961), 403-17; rptd in NEGLECTED POWERS: ESSAYS ON NINETEENTH AND TWENTIETH CENTURY LITERATURE, by G. Wilson Knight (Lond: Routledge & Kegan Paul; NY: Barnes & Noble, 1971), pp. 142-55; excerpt rptd as " 'Through . . . degradation to a new health'--A Comment on *Women in Love*," in D. H. LAWRENCE: "THE RAINBOW" AND "WOMEN IN LOVE," A CASEBOOK, ed by Colin Clarke (Lond: Macmillan, 1969; Nashville: Aurora Publishers, 1970), pp. 135-41.

Lady Chatterley's Lover represents DHL's "final and comprehensive sexual statement." However, the book should not be taken merely as an endorsement of revitalized normality but rather as an appeal to eradicate the stigma attached to anal sex. The anal intercourse scene in the book is prepared for carefully by image patterns which show that DHL was questing for a largeness of being beyond the normal. Numerous passages in the novel and in "A Propos of *Lady Chatterley's Lover*" show that sodomy did occur in the disputed scene. Similar passages in *Women in Love* show that either partner may be the active one. In such poems as

"New Heaven and Earth," "Elysium," and "Manifesto," the "deathly is found to be the source of some higher order of being." Believing that "contact with a basic materiality liberates a person," DHL urges modern man to break through this degradation "to a new health." [See also reply by John Peter, "The Bottom of the Well," ESSAYS IN CRITICISM, XII (April 1962), 226-27; and additional discussions in the controversy as follows: John Sparrow, "Regina v. Penguin Books Ltd.: An Undisclosed Element in the Case," ENCOUNTER, XVIII (Feb 1962), 35-43; John Sparrow, "Afterthoughts on Regina v. Penguin Books Ltd.," ENCOUNTER, XVIII (June 1962), 83-88; John Peter, "Lady Chatterley Again," ESSAYS IN CRITICISM, XII (Oct 1962), 445-47; William Empson, "Lady Chatterley Again," ESSAYS IN CRITICISM, XIII (Jan 1963), 101-4; John Sparrow, "Lady Chatterley Again," ESSAYS IN CRITICISM, XIII (April 1963), 202-5; John Peter, "Lady Chatterley for the Last Time I," ESSAYS IN CRITICISM, XIII (July 1963), 301-2; and John Sparrow, "Lady Chatterley for the Last Time II," ESSAYS IN CRITICISM, XIII (July 1963), 303.]

2108 Kuo, Carol Haseley. "Lawrence's *The Rainbow*," EXPLICATOR, XIX (June 1961), Item 70; rptd in THE EXPLICATOR CYCLOPEDIA, ed by Charles Child Walcutt and J. Edwin Whitesell, Vol. III: PROSE (Chicago: Quadrangle Books, 1968), pp. 121-22.

Ursula Brangwen in *The Rainbow* and St. Ursula are parallel. Both are teachers. After three years of freedom, St. Ursula returns home to marry; after teaching Ursula rejects freedom for a time. St. Ursula is killed by Attila's hordes; Ursula is set upon, symbolically, by horses representing "the man's world." St. Ursula is beatified; Ursula is given the beatific vision of the rainbow.

2109 Kuramochi, Saburô. "*Niji* no Ursula" (Ursula in *The Rainbow*), RONSHÛ (Senshû University), No. 14 (Sept 1961), 19-50. [In Japanese.]

2110 Lacher, Walter. "D. H. Lawrence," in L'AMOUR ET LE DIVIN (Love and the Divine), (Geneva: Perret-Gentil, 1961), pp. 63-102.

While some similarities between DHL and Henri Bergson can be found, the novelist's language is completely different from the French philosopher's. DHL has his own cosmogony, composed of the elements of his *Psychoanalysis and the Unconscious* and *Fantasia of the Unconscious*. [After analyzing DHL's ideas as developed in these works, the author examines the novelist's credo in detail and explains the myth of *The Plumed Serpent*, concluding that DHL's philosophic terrain is as uneven as the volcanic terrain of Mexico. After studying the writer's conception of politics and his choice for dictatorship, the author deals with DHL's novels, first and at greatest length with *The Plumed Serpent*, the first of DHL's novels translated into French, then alludes briefly to *The Boy in the Bush, St. Mawr,* and "The Man Who Loved Islands."] The novels of liberation constitute an important group; *Sons and Lovers* remains their unforgettable prototype. DHL's tenderness and love for his mother are revealed as well in many of his poems. DHL loved his mother too much to describe her as a genitrix, the role assigned to the heroines of some works that are the reverse of *Sons and Lovers*;

e.g., *The Virgin and the Gipsy* and "The Lovely Lady." [After dealing briefly with *Aaron's Rod* and *Kangaroo,* the author considers DHL's contradictions, one of them being his rejecting introspection and at the same time thinking the awareness of self and self-limits necessary. He examines the Laurentian theme of the failure of love in the modern world in such novels as *The White Peacock, The Trespasser, The Rainbow, Women in Love,* and *Lady Chatterley's Lover.*] [In French.]

2111 Laski, Marghanita. ECSTASY: A STUDY OF SOME SECULAR AND RELIGIOUS EXPERIENCES (Lond: Cresset P, 1961; rptd NY: Greenwood P, 1968), pp. 73-76, 84n, 116, 145n, 148-53, 185n, 211-12.
[DHL's "ecstatic veracity" is impugned in an examination of two passages from his fiction: the first, labelled L17a in the appendix where it is fully quoted, is a five-paragraph extract from Chap. VII, "The Cathedral" in *The Rainbow,* a narration of Will Brangwen's ecstasy in Lincoln Cathedral; the second, L17b, is a paragraph extract from Chap. XIII, "Baxter Dawes" in *Sons and Lovers,* a description of Paul's ecstatic sex with Clara.] DHL's descriptions of ecstatic experience are idiosyncratic. For example, when an image in ecstatic descriptions is a sexual one, the ecstatic, or his soul, normally plays the part of the female. But in text L17a, the writer sets his hero Will's soul in the part of the male, "every jet of him" straining and leaping to the "fecundity" in the close embrace of Lincoln Cathedral. DHL's apparent *frequency* of ecstasy is also peculiar. In the Cathedral, Will experiences two immediately successive ecstasies. In text L17b, it is suggested that Paul "as a rule" feels ecstasy when he starts love-making. If DHL did indeed believe that ecstasy should be the "rule," instead of a rare exception, during love-making, then one must wonder whether he had ever himself known satisfactory love-making by the time he came to write *Sons and Lovers.*

2112 Lawrence, Frieda [Frieda Lawrence Ravagli]. FRIEDA LAWRENCE: THE MEMOIRS AND CORRESPONDENCE, ed by E[rnest] W. Tedlock, Jr. (Lond: William Heinemann, 1961; 1st American ed, NY: Knopf, 1964),
[The expanded 1964 collection includes a manuscript version of the memoirs, with fragments printed in an appendix, 257 letters, and twelve essays. After the publication of her "NOT I, BUT THE WIND..." (1934), Frieda Lawrence made occasional attempts from 1935 until her death to write a slightly fictionalized account of her life. These manuscripts, none complete or in finished form, were found scattered among her papers after her death in 1956; the editor has arranged the manuscripts according to the plan Frieda had discussed in several letters (in particular one to Angelo Ravagli dated 21 Dec 1937). Entitled "AND THE FULLNESS THEREOF...," the memoirs are presented within the frame narrative of a trip Frieda made with Ravagli from Taos to Buenos Aires; at points during the journey, the Frieda character, "Paula," remembers scenes from her childhood, adolescence, first marriage and uneasy attempts at English housewifery, the meeting and elopement with "Andrew" (DHL), Andrew's death, and her life in New Mexico with "Dario" (Ravagli). The selection of letters dates from February 1890 to August 1956. Frieda's letters are addressed to members

of her family, notably her elder sister Elsa Jaffe and her son Montague Weekley, to various people, literary and otherwise, with whom she had become acquainted as DHL's wife or who were engaged, with or without her blessings, in studying his work after his death, and to Angelo Ravagli. Also included is a letter to Frieda from Ernest Weekley, dated 10 May 1912, about her elopement with DHL, three letters from Weekley to Frieda's parents, discussing impending divorce arrangements, a letter to Frieda from Alice Dax, dated 23 Jan 1935, in which Mrs. Dax tries to explain the nature of her relationship with DHL, and a ten-year correspondence (1946-1956) between Frieda and John Middleton Murry, in which they discuss their brief love affair in September 1923, Murry's relationship with DHL, and DHL's treatment of Murry in several short stories. The essays include both published and previously unpublished work. Among the unpublished material is a sketch of Katherine Mansfield, a tribute to A. R. Orage, and a description of lunch with George Bernard Shaw. Published work reprinted here includes a trenchant criticism of William York Tindall's D. H. LAWRENCE AND SUSAN HIS COW (1939), a letter replying to Bertrand Russell's "Portrait from Memory," which had appeared in HARPER'S (Feb 1953), and Frieda's Foreword to *The First Lady Chatterley* (1944) and to D. H. LAWRENCE: A COMPOSITE BIOGRAPHY, ed by Edward Nehls, Vol. I: 1885-1919 (Madison: University of Wisconsin P, 1957).]

2113 "Lawrence Play Skilfully Adapted to Television," TIMES (Lond), 24 March 1961, p. 18.
[Review of *The Widowing of Mrs. Holroyd*, as adapted by Ken Taylor and directed by Claude Whatham for presentation in the Television Playhouse series, Granada TV Network, 23 March 1961.] The smoothness of the adaptation, despite its reduction of the play to "an hour minus commercials," raises the question of how far the adaptor has gone in smoothing over DHL's "rough passages" and untangling "knots in the construction." The dialogue is "convincingly Lawrentian": "crisp, spare and genuinely dramatic."

2114 Leavis, F[rank] R[aymond]. "Genius as Critic," SPECTATOR, CCVI (24 March 1961), 412, 414; rptd in D. H. LAWRENCE: A CRITICAL ANTHOLOGY, ed by H. Coombes (Harmondsworth, Middlesex, England: Penguin Books, 1973), pp. 419-23.
Phoenix: The Posthumous Papers of D. H. Lawrence reveals that DHL was a sure critic of poetry, a versatile critic, and a powerful, original thinker whose "response to art is a response to life." Its "un-Eliotic freedom of utterance" makes it the "finest body of criticism in existence." [*Phoenix*, ed by Edward D. McDonald, reissued 1961.]

2115 Leavis, F[rank] R[aymond]. "The New Orthodoxy," SPECTATOR, CCVI (17 Feb 1961), 229-30; rptd as "The Orthodoxy of Enlightenment," in ANNA KARENINA AND OTHER ESSAYS, by F. R. Leavis (Lond: Chatto & Windus; NY: Pantheon Books, 1967), pp. 235-41; and rptd as "The New Orthodoxy," in D. H. LAWRENCE: A CRITICAL ANTHOLOGY, ed by H. Coombes

(Harmondsworth, Middlesex, England: Penguin Books, 1973), pp. 413-19.

[Comment on "the court proceedings over *Lady Chatterley's Lover*" (Regina v. Penguin Books, Ltd., 1960).] Although it was "essential to the case for the Defence" that "the book should be current as an unquestioned literary classic," *Lady Chatterley's Lover* "is a bad novel" in that it reveals "a disrupted disintegration of the artist" and handles Sir Clifford ineffectively. Ultimately, DHL himself was not satisfied with the book.

2116 Lewis, C[live] S[taples]. AN EXPERIMENT IN CRITICISM (Lond: Cambridge UP, 1961), pp. 124-26.

For the vigilant school of critics, criticism is a form of ethical and social hygiene, and their goal is to stamp out evil. An objective or disinterested reader can enjoy the copulation scene in *Sons and Lovers* in which the young couple are grains in a great heave of life, and--at the same time--see the practical conclusions drawn as muddled and pernicious. The vigilants do not permit such liberty.

2117 Lewis, C[live] S[taples]. "Symposium: Pornography and Obscenity. Four-Letter Words," CRITICAL QUARTERLY, III (Summer 1961), 118-22.

Four-letter words have never been used to " 'move desire' ": "They are the vocabulary either of farce or vituperation." Hence, DHL's "usage is not to be reckoned a return to nature from some local or recent inhibition. It is ... artificial ... a rebellion against language." [See also, in the same "Symposium: Pornography and Obscenity," CRITICAL QUARTERLY, III (Summer 1961), the following comments: C. B. Cox, "Editorial Comment: The Teaching of Literature," pp. 99-103; Donald Davie, "Literature and Morality," pp. 109-13; Martin Jarrett-Kerr, "A Christian View," pp. 113-18 (not abstracted as not specifically on DHL); and Norman St. John-Stevas, "The English Censorship Laws," pp. 103-9.]

2118 Loth, David. THE EROTIC IN LITERATURE (NY: Julian Messner, 1961; Lond: Secker & Warburg, 1962), pp. 10, 21, 23, 39, 40, 149-50, 162, 187, 209, 222, 223, 230.

DHL, "persecuted almost all his working life" as a "purveyor of smut," would have banned both Charlotte Bronte's JANE EYRE and James Joyce's ULYSSES for using "sex excitement with a desire to spite the sex feeling, to humiliate and degrade it." As early as 1911, DHL was forced to substitute new wording for the "dangerous" phraseology of a single paragraph in *The White Peacock*; in 1915, the publisher agreed to a "destruction order" for *The Rainbow* "without giving Lawrence a chance to defend it." In 1951, the Customs refused to allow a biographer to import a copy of *The Paintings of D. H. Lawrence*; but in 1959, after the Postmaster General had barred *Lady Chatterley's Lover* from the mails, Judge Frederick vanPelt Bryan held (in Grove Press vs. Christenberry) that the novel was not obscene in the meaning of the statute. Nevertheless, the mayor of Taunton, Massachusetts, in 1960 was able to get booksellers to abide by his unilateral decision to ban certain books, including *Lady Chatterley's Lover*.

2119 Lucas, Barbara. "A propos of 'England, My England,'" TWENTIETH CENTURY, CLXIX (March 1961), 288-93; rptd in D. H. LAWRENCE: A CRITICAL ANTHOLOGY, ed by H. Coombes (Harmondsworth, Middlesex, England: Penguin Books, 1973), pp. 424-30.

[The author sets out to correct minor errors in Harry T. Moore's account in THE INTELLIGENT HEART: THE STORY OF D. H. LAWRENCE (1954) of the "real-life sources" for "England, My England" and to refute Moore's opinion that her father, Percy Lucas, was the model for Egbert.] DHL did "not know Percy . . . nor did he need to for the creation of Egbert. What he needed was simply the *pattern* of Percy, and his wife, and his children, and his in-laws, and his cottage, *and the accident* [the author's sister Sylvia was lamed by falling on a sickle]." "England, My England" incorporates this pattern imaginatively in a story so typically Laurentian that "readers are amazed to think that real-life sources could possibly be needed."

2120 MacDonald, Dwight. "London Letter," PARTISAN REVIEW, XXVII (March-April 1961), 248-59.

The Regina v. Penguin Books, Ltd., trial over *Lady Chatterley's Lover* was an event of dramatic and social interest. Under the provisions of the 1959 Obscene Publications Act, the defense called thirty-five expert witnesses to attest to the merits of the novel, opposing a recent TIMES editorial to the contrary. The various testimonies and legal approaches of the defense and prosecution considered whether the book as a whole would be "for the public good." [See also the editorial, "A Decent Reticence," TIMES (Lond), 3 Nov 1960, p. 13, three selections of letters to the TIMES in response to it (1960), and news accounts of the trial.]

2121 McWilliam, G. H. "Verga and 'Verismo,'" HERMATHENA (Dublin), XCV (July 1961), 3-20.

Giovanni Verga and DHL probably never met, sincer Verga was 81 and near death in 1921 when his work first attracted the attention of DHL, then living in Sicily. Drawn by the dynamism of Verga's prose, especially his use of Sicilian vernacular, and his modern sense of realism ("verismo") in the later works *I Malavoglia* and *Mastro-Don Gesualdo*, DHL set out to translate Verga, publishing the *Mastro-Don* in 1923 followed by *Little Novels of Sicily* (1925) and *Cavalleria Rusticana and Other Stories* (1928). Far excelling the English versions of 1891 and 1893 by Mary A. Craig, these remain the best translations of Verga available, though a recent Verga revival is producing new translations in America. [There is no further mention of DHL, and the remaining three fourths of the essay is a critique of Verga's style and content.]

2122 Magalaner, Marvin, and Edmond L. Volpe. "D. H. Lawrence," TWELVE SHORT STORIES (NY: Macmillan, 1961; rptd in 12th printing, 1970), pp. 103-7; rvd and rptd in TWELVE SHORT STORIES, SECOND SERIES, ed by Marvin Magalaner and Edmond L. Volpe (NY: Macmillan, 1969), pp. 111-16.

Nothing in DHL's early life suggests his later "literary fame." *Sons and Lovers*, a "classic study of an Oedipus complex," "shocked middle class readers" and established the pattern of "antagonism between author and uninformed public" that has typified DHL's relationship with his "potential audience," a conflict deriving from his "ideas, rather than his actions." Finding "the civilization of cities . . . evil, decadent, and unwholesome, he sought constantly to discover the ideal Lawrentian community" in which machines would be rejected in favor of his "principles of life, love, religion, ethics, and emotional relationships." [Introduces "The Blind Man," which is reprinted in the anthology, pp. 108-26. The revised version (1969) introduces "Odour of Chrysanthemums," which is reprinted in TWELVE SHORT STORIES, SECOND SERIES, pp. 111-16, pointing out both its "realistic depiction" of life and the "literary shorthand" of its symbolism.]

2123 Masugi, Tadashi. "*The White Peacock*--Tsuki to Kujaku" (*The White Peacock*: The Moon and the Peacock), SHIRON (Tôhoku University), No. 3 (May 1961), 41-59.
[In Japanese.]

2124 Mauriac, Francois. "D. H. Lawrence," SECOND THOUGHTS: REFLECTIONS ON LITERATURE AND ON LIFE, trans from the French by Adrienne Foulke (Lond: Darwen Finlayson, 1961), pp. 113-16.
Never a social climber, DHL tried instead "to swim back upstream . . . recovering his lost dignity as a son of light." Despite his pagan sentiments, however, DHL rejected the idea of the "noble savage," believing that both civilized and primitive cultures were waiting for a revelation from him. Basically envious of Christ, DHL did not wish to be an Antichrist; he wanted rather to be another Christ. DHL believed that mankind could not fully realize its potential so long as it neglected "the strength, the elemental potency of blood and flesh."

2125 Maxwell, J. C. "*Lady Chatterley's Lover*: A Correction," NOTES AND QUERIES, VIII (March 1961), 110.
[Suggested emendation of "his eyes, immediate knowledge" to "his eyes' immediate knowledge" in a sentence in Chapter XVI of *Lady Chatterley's Lover*, p. 294, in the 1933 Odyssey P edition and p. 259 in the 1960 Penguin Books edition. See reply by M. T. Tudsbery, C. B. E., "*Lady Chatterley's Lover*," NOTES AND QUERIES, VIII (April 1961), 149.]

2126 Michot, P[aulette]. "D. H. Lawrence: A Belated Apology," REVUE DES LANGUES VIVANTES, XXVII, No. 4 (1961), 290-305.
[A detailed discussion of the English censorship proceedings against *Lady Chatterley's Lover* (Regina v. Penguin Books, Ltd., 1960) under the Obscene Publications Act of 1959, including the rationale and provisions of the statute, the decision to make a test case of the Penguin edition of DHL's novel, the four-

day progress of the trial, with arguments by Mr. Griffith-Jones for the Prosecution and Mr. Gardiner for the Defence and a complete list with identification of the thirty-six expert witnesses for the Defence, the surprise verdict, results of the acquittal, public and press opinion, DHL's *A Propos of "Lady Chatterley's Lover,"* and the author's concluding comments *a propos* of the trial.]

2127 Montale, Eugenio. "Tutte le poesie di D. H. Lawrence" (*The Complete Poems of D. H. Lawrence*), CORRIERE DELLA SERA (Milan), 27 May 1961, p. 3.

[Review of *Tutte le poesie di D. H. Lawrence* (*The Complete Poems of D. H. Lawrence*), 2 vols., trans and ed and with an Introduction by Piero Nardi (1959).] In DHL's poems all the themes that can be found in his work are treated: women, Freudianism, the attack on industrialism, the exaltation of nature. The best verses are those in which state of mind and ideas appear free from the typical didactic attitude of Puritan writers. [In Italian.]

2128 Moore, Harry T. "The Prose Style of D. H. Lawrence," in LANGUE ET LITTÉRATURE: ACTES DU VIIIe CONGRÈS DE LA FÉDÉRATION INTERNATIONALE DES LANGUES ET LITTÉRATURES MODERNES (Language and Literature: Acts of the Eighth Congress of the International Federation of the Modern Languages and Literatures) (Paris: Societe d'Edition "Les Belles Lettres," 1961), pp. 317-18.

"As a spontaneous rather than a deliberate writer, D. H. Lawrence had no separate 'style' for his imaginative work; he wrote his essays and letters in the same heightened and incantatory language that is found in his novels and stories." DHL's career is divided into four periods: in the first period, 1909-1912, he assimilates Biblical images and rhythms with the "sturdy colloquialisms" of his native idiom; in the second period, 1913-1919, he writes his finest novels in a "prose of ecstasy"; in the third period, 1920-1925, he writes a more flexible prose, though in less successful fiction; and in the fourth period, 1926-1930, "the prose of the dying Lawrence is usually characterized by fading colors and slackening rhythms." [A passage from "Smile" is analyzed.] [See also Harry T. Moore, "The Prose of D. H. Lawrence," in D. H. LAWRENCE: THE MAN WHO LIVED, ed by Robert B. Partlow, Jr., and Harry T. Moore (Carbondale and Edwardsville: Southern Illinois UP, 1980).]

2129 Mothersill, Mary. "Vivas on D. H. Lawrence," CHICAGO REVIEW, XIV (Spring 1961), 113-24.

DHL tended to regard all individuals with whom he came in contact as either friends or enemies; tastes and manners which DHL found unappealing he could not tolerate in his friends. Acquaintances therefore found DHL difficult to ignore but discovered that "to engage with him was to adopt his level of argument, one which by ordinary intellectual standards was extremely low." Even critics have found it nearly imposible to deal with DHL's work "without going off one deep end or another" in response to the author's personality.

The publication of Eliseo Vivas's book D. H. LAWRENCE: THE FAILURE AND THE TRIUMPH OF ART (1960), is the beginning of a dispassionate critical approach to DHL.

2130 Muir, Kenneth. "The Three Lady Chatterleys," LITERARY HALF-YEARLY, XI (Jan 1961), 18-25.

The three versions of *Lady Chatterley's Lover* differ greatly in plot, theme, and characterization. The first version is notably the only one to deal with politics. The second has not been published in English, and the third describes what DHL wanted of marriage.

2131 Muir, P. H. "Further Reminiscences XV," BOOK COLLECTOR, X (Winter 1961), 435-39.

[Memoir of S. S. Koteliansky.] "Kot retained his affection for Katherine [Mansfield] and his adoration of Lawrence all his life; but for [John Middleton] Murry he had nothing but loathing." He recalled the activities of "this small band of intellectuals" in rafia- and batik-work and pottery decoration as well as laundry and gardening. "Kot cannot have been much of a business manager for the Lawrence-Murry periodical," THE SIGNATURE.

2132 Murray, W. "Why Did the S. A. Censors Ban *Lady Chatterley's Lover?*" FORUM (South Africa), IX (Jan 1961), 29.

The Bible was once a banned book. The South African censors banned *Lady Chatterley's Lover* hard upon a British court's finding (Regina v. Penguin Books, Ltd.) that the book was not obscene. Was it banned simply because it contains words that might offend in library, lounge, or bedroom, or because it is a social document of radical intent, or for both reasons? [The author has no answer, but he regrets the frivolous abuse of censorship which denies access to "the precious life-blood of a master spirit."]

2133 Nahal, Chaman Lal. "D. H. Lawrence: An Eastern Interpretation." Unpublished dissertation, University of Nottingham, 1961. [Listed in Sheila M. Cooke (compiler), D. H. LAWRENCE: A FINDING LIST: A CATALOGUE OF THE PRINTED MATERIAL IN THE COUNTY AND UNIVERSITY LIBRARIES OF NOTTINGHAM, 2nd ed (Nottingham: Nottinghamshire County Council, 1980), p. 107.] Rvd, enlgd, and pub as D. H. LAWRENCE: AN EASTERN VIEW (Lond: Thomas Yoseloff; South Brunswick and NY: A. S. Barnes, 1970; Delhi: Atma Ram, 1971).

2134 Nakamura, Yoshio. "*The Rainbow* ni Tsuite" (On *The Rainbow*), LITERARY SYMPOSIUM (Aichi University), No. 21 (Feb 1961), 157-81.

[In Japanese.]

2135 Nardi, Piero. "Introduzione" (Introduction), *Libri di viaggio e pagine di paese* (*Complete Collection of Travel Books*), by D. H. Lawrence (Milan: A. Mondadori, 1961), pp. xv-xl.

Twilight in Italy deals above all with the religious problem: DHL rejects the Christian ideal for a pagan one. This is the period in which he had begun a new life with Frieda and was led to identify the sensual with sexual experience. The Italians seemed to DHL a people who lived a life very close to the principles of his religion of sex. DHL's "Introduction" to MEMOIRS OF THE FOREIGN LEGION by Maurice Magnus is one of his most vivid autobiographical writings. In *Sea and Sardinia*, DHL's aspiration to a return to primitive values is encouraged by the faith in primitive sexuality that he finds still alive in the Sardinian people. In the essays collected in the "Peoples, Countries, Races" section of *Phoenix: The Posthumous Papers of D. H. Lawrence,* ed by Edward D. McDonald (1936), DHL seems torn between the world of progress and the primitive countries, but in *Mornings in Mexico* he turns to the latter. *Etruscan Places*, even though it reveals DHL's lack of any scientific knowledge, constitutes his example of an ideal life for humanity. [In Italian.]

2136 Nishikawa, Masaharu. "Annable no Sôwa" (On the Episode of Annable), ENGLISH LITERATURE (Waseda University), No. 19 (Jan 1961), 210-23.

[On Annable in *The White Peacock.*] [In Japanese.]

2137 O'Faolain, Sean (ed). SHORT STORIES: A STUDY IN PLEASURE (Bost and Toronto: Little, Brown, 1961), pp. 461-64.

"The Horse-Dealer's Daughter" takes us away from reality beyond reason to lead us to "moral shock." [The story is included in the anthology.]

2138 Ôhashi, Yasuichirô. "Lawrence no Shi ni Arawareta Ganseki to Kôbutsu ni Tsuite" (Rocks and Minerals in D. H. Lawrence's Poetry), STUDIES IN FOREIGN LITERATURES (Ritsumeikan University), No. 4 (Dec 1961), 52-68.

[In Japanese.]

2139 Okumura, Osamu. "D. H. Lawrence the Preacher," AOYAMA JOURNAL OF GENERAL EDUCATION (Aoyama Gakuen University), No. 2 (Nov 1961), 63-84.

2140 Okumura, Tôru. "Ai to Kunô no Henreki *Miyo Warera Wa Yatte Kita!*" (Lawrence's Pilgrimage of Love and Agony--*Look! We Have Come Through!*), ENGLISH LITERATURE REVIEW (Kyôto Women's University), No. 5 (March 1961), 12-38.

[In Japanese.]

2141 Panichas, George A. "F. M. Dostoevsky and D. H. Lawrence: Their Visions of Evil," RENAISSANCE AND MODERN STUDIES, V (1961), 49-75; rptd in ADVENTURE IN CONSCIOUSNESS: THE MEANING OF D. H. LAWRENCE'S RELIGIOUS QUEST, by George A. Panichas (The Hague: Mouton, 1964), pp. 151-79; and rptd in THE REVERENT DISCIPLINE: ESSAYS IN LITERARY CRITICISM AND CULTURE, by George A. Panichas (Knoxville: University of Tennessee P, 1974), pp. 205-28.

Always disturbed and fascinated by Dostoevsky, DHL detested the Russian's "moral scheme" and dismissed his art, but was nonetheless held by his view of certain aspects of human nature. Loerke in *Women in Love* has affinities with the voluptuary Svidrigaylov in CRIME AND PUNISHMENT. Both are sinister, demonic characters, holding insidious power over others and representing moral depravity and evil. Loerke's excess is more cerebral than carnal, a revealing distinction between him and Svidrigaylov. Like Dostoevsky, DHL describes his evil character by likening him to an insect. Although both Raskolnikov and Gerald Crich detest their debased and immoral acquaintances, both have something in common with these evil characters, and both must be viewed as supermen who failed. Both Dostoevsky and DHL refused to submit to the relentless reality of their visions of evil.

2142 Peerman, Dean. "D. H. Lawrence: Devout Heretic," CHRISTIAN CENTURY, LXXVIII (22 Feb 1961), 237-41.

DHL was an animist or pantheist, *not* a Christian. Nevertheless, his penetrating criticisms of Christianity and the Church--especially of the "Christian view" of sex--have much to teach the Christian.

2143 Perosa, Sergio. "D. H. Lawrence: *Tutte le poesie*" (*The Complete Poems of D. H. Lawrence*), IL VERRI (Milan), 1 Feb 1961, pp. 97-103.

[Review of *Tutte le poesie di D. H. Lawrence* (*The Complete Poems of D. H. Lawrence*), 2 vols., trans and ed and with an Introduction by Piero Nardi (1959).] DHL's poetry is at times a real literary offense, but it reveals a great vitality and will. DHL's poems are strictly connected to his life, as can be seen in *Rhyming Poems*. The poems of *Look! We Have Come Through!*, written in free verse, constitute a real narrative. In *Birds, Beasts and Flowers*, DHL succeeds in expressing his emotions in poetic images, while in *Pansies* his Messianic tone prevails, and his "poetic" thoughts are devoted to mass man, the dullness of the bourgeoisie, mechanization, and rationality. [In Italian.]

2144 Pinto, Vivian de Sola. "Mr. Gifford and D. H. Lawrence," CRITICAL QUARTERLY, III (Autumn 1961), 267-68.

[Rejoinder to Henry Gifford, "The Defect In Lawrence's Poetry," CRITICAL QUARTERLY, III (Summer 1961), 164-66.] Shakespeare's "loosening" does not show decay. DHL's concern for rhythm is clear in his revisions. DHL does respect the past and builds on other poetry. Gifford, like his nineteenth-century namesake, is "altogether petty, captious and literal." [See also Vivian de Sola Pinto, "Poet without a Mask," CRITICAL QUARTERLY, III (Spring 1961), 5-18, to which Gifford's note was a reply; Gāmini Salgādo, "Mr. Gifford and D. H. Lawrence," CRITICAL QUARTERLY, III (Autumn 1961), 268-70; and Vivian de Sola Pinto, "Lawrence's Poetry," CRITICAL QUARTERLY, IV (Spring 1962), 81.]

2145 Pinto, Vivian de Sola. "The Poems of D. H. Lawrence," TIMES LITERARY SUPPLEMENT (Lond), 31 March 1961, p. 201. [Letter to the Editor replying to Geoffrey Strickland, "The Poems of D. H. Lawrence," TIMES LITERARY SUPPLEMENT (Lond), 24 March 1961, p. 185.] As Strickland comments, there should be wider publication of foreign editions of DHL. Work on an edition of the complete poems of DHL (ed by Vivian de Sola Pinto and F. Warren Roberts) is in progress. Indebtedness to Piero Nardi's edition [*D. H. Lawrence: Tutte le Poesie,* 2 vols. (1959)] will be acknowledged in the preface.

2146 Pinto, Vivian de Sola. "Poet without a Mask," CRITICAL QUARTERLY, III (Spring 1961), 5-18; rptd in D. H. LAWRENCE: A COLLECTION OF CRITICAL ESSAYS, ed by Mark Spilka (Englewood Cliffs, N. J.: Prentice-Hall, 1963), pp. 127-41; and rvd and enlgd as the Introduction, "D. H. Lawrence: Poet without a Mask," *The Complete Poems of D. H. Lawrence,* 2 vols., ed by Vivian de Sola Pinto and F. Warren Roberts (NY: Viking P, 1964), pp. 1-21.
While DHL recognized the value of traditional form, his poetic form was "expressive," as Blackmur calls it, or, from Coleridge, "organic." The mask of "living" traditional form no longer fits because of increasing isolation of the poet and loosening rhythms. Major prophetic poets like Blake and DHL abandon the mask. The Imagists and the Futurists helped DHL escape from literary diction, vague romanticism, and saccharine rhythms. Whitman was the greatest liberating influence. *Birds, Beasts and Flowers* leads DHL into the celebration of "divine otherness," allowing him to escape from the autobiographical. *Last Poems* shows DHL developing into a mythological poet. DHL, like Wordsworth, wrote much bad poetry, but his poems, like Wordsworth's, are the important experiments of a major poet. [See also reply by Henry Gifford, "The Defect in Lawrence's Poetry," CRITICAL QUARTERLY, III (Summer 1961), 164-66; rejoinders by Vivian de Sola Pinto, "Mr. Gifford and D. H. Lawrence," CRITICAL QUARTERLY, III (Autumn 1961), 267-68, and Gāmini Salgādo, "Mr. Gifford and D. H. Lawrence," CRITICAL QUARTERLY, III (Autumn 1961), 268-70; and further comment by Vivian de Sola Pinto, "Lawrence's Poetry," CRITICAL QUARTERLY, IV (Spring 1962), 81.]

2147 Praz, Mario. "D. H. Lawrence trent'anni dopo" (D. H. Lawrence Thirty Years After), IL TEMPO (Milan), 16 July 1961, p. 3.
Until 1950, critical studies on DHL pointed out above all the diabolic character of his work. After 1950, critics like Harry T. Moore and Edward Nehls

gave readers a less mythical image of DHL. His treatment of sex is not to be taken as an obsession but as a glorification of the natural instincts in man as opposed to the general mechanization of society. His ideal world was to be based not on the leadership of a superior man but on tenderness. Today DHL should be studied exclusively from an artistic point of view. [In Italian.]

2148 Pritchett, V[ictor] S. "In Writing Nothing Fails Like Success," NEW YORK TIMES BOOK REVIEW, 22 Jan 1961, pp. 1, 38.

Although Cyril Connolly maintains that literary success "liberates the tensions of a hostile environment and so prepares the way for literary failure," DHL's "earliest and best work" did not help him to escape from later hostile environments nor did it result in later literary failures. [Only a brief portion of the essay deals with DHL.]

2149 Radcliffe, [Cyril John], Baron. CENSORS: THE REDE LECTURE, 1961 (Lond: Cambridge UP, 1961).

[The Rede Lecture delivered at the University of Cambridge, 4 May 1961. In bringing "under review the subject of censorship," Lord Radcliffe here discusses changing British attitudes toward "freedom" of the printed word since the time of Milton's AREOPAGITICA, and he comments on the recent unsuccessful prosecution of the publishers of *Lady Chatterley's Lover* in England (Regina v. Penguin Books, Ltd., 1960) .] In a way, the *Lady Chatterley's Lover* case was a "posthumous trial" and subsequent "vindication" of the "literary reputation and artistic integrity" of DHL. He "got his verdict," one he never got during his life, "though it must have been very hard at any time since his . . . 'Apropos of *Lady Chatterley's Lover*' for even an unenthusiastic reader to doubt his patent sincerity of purpose." This trail "marked dramatically a final turning away from the older idea that written words can be things dangerous enough in themselves to merit punishment for the man who has let them loose on society." Among the "least satisfactory" results of the trial would be "that it should set off one more cannibal dance round the idea of authority," for "it is high time that the literate section of the English public grew up and reached adulthood in its image of authority and abandoned this endless projection of a force styled 'They.' "

2150 Rees, Richard. "The Listener's Book Chronicle," LISTENER AND BBC TELEVISION REVIEW, LXVI (7 Dec 1961), 993.

Frieda Weekley's meeting DHL in 1912 "was tragedy for her admirable first husband," and some have suggested "that she was spoiling Lawrence's life as well," a charge that "cannot be maintained." [Review of FRIEDA LAWRENCE: THE MEMOIRS AND CORRESPONDENCE, ed by E. W. Tedlock (1961).]

2151 Requardt, Egon. "David Herbert Lawrence: *Sons and Lovers*," DIE NEUEREN SPRACHEN, (Frankfurt) ns X (1961), 230-35.

Sons and Lovers, an autobiographical novel, contains the germs of DHL's future ideas: his protest against spiritual love and the cosmic dimension of the man-woman relation. Although DHL portrays family life naturalistically, he is not a social critic but analyzes psychological problems. Some of the questions raised in *Sons and Lovers* are also treated and answered in DHL's short story "The Lovely Lady." [In German.]

2152 Robbins, Patricia. LADY CHATTERLEY'S DAUGHTER (NY: Ace Books, 1961).
[This novel, a "sequel" to *Lady Chatterley's Lover,* centers on the inhibited loves of Clare Mellors, presented as the daughter of Connie and Mellors, who "sought from each of her lovers release from the pent-up desires that brought her to the brink of passion but never beyond." A V.A.D. nurse during World War II, Clare lives in London with her Aunt Hilda. Distressed to learn that her birth was illegitimate, Clare upbraids her parents for not waiting until marriage to express their passion. She also visits Wragby Hall and becomes friends with Sir Clifford Chatterley and finds the lack of passion in his world congenial. At his death, Clifford leaves "Wragby Hall and everything that goes with it" to her.]

2153 Robson, W[illiam] W[allace]. "D. H. Lawrence and *Women in Love,*" THE MODERN AGE, ed by Boris Ford (Harmondsworth, Middlesex, England, and Baltimore: Penguin Books, 1961; 2nd ed. 1963; rvd and rptd, 1964; rptd, 1966, 1967, 1969), pp. 280-300; rptd in CRITICAL ESSAYS, by W. W. Robson (Lond: Routledge & Kegan Paul, 1966), pp. 264-84.
DHL's life is difficult to separate from his writing, which often represents "the writer's living-through of his personal problems and conflicts, as well as his more general pre-occupations." Though he sometimes repels the reader by the "preaching" and "pleading" with which he presents his moral, social, and political beliefs, he is also able to make "us *see* the complexity of many of the concrete human situations to which moral judgments are undoubtedly relevant, but which do not lend themselves to description and analysis." This ability is best realized in *Women in Love,* DHL's most "complex, difficult and 'modern'" novel. Here, although DHL is "personally involved" in the characterizations of both Rupert Birkin and Gerald Crich, they remain convincing dramatic characters open to both the objections and sympathies of others and, as a result, in touch with "ordinary reality."

2154 Rolph, C. H. [pseud of C. R. Hewitt]. THE TRIAL OF LADY CHATTERLEY: REGINA V. PENGUIN BOOKS LIMITED (Harmondsworth, Middlesex, England: Penguin Books, 1961).
[A narrative and edited transcript of the trial of 1960, prosecuting Penguin Books, Ltd., under the Obscene Publications Act of 1959, for its publication of the unexpurgated *Lady Chatterley's Lover,* the first novel to be tried under the new law. Rather than a trial of the publisher, it was, as conducted, "a fifteenth-century trial for adultery, Constance Chatterley was there in the Court." Mr. Justice Byrne presided, the prosecutor was Mr. Griffith-Jones, and the defense was represented by Messrs. Gerald Gardiner, Jeremy Hutchinson,

and Richard du Cann. The testimony of the thirty-five distinguished witnesses for the defense gave evidence, often under precise cross-examination, of the literary merits and social and moral importance of the novel. These witnesses, including critics, authors, educators, clergymen, and a Member of Parliament, were as follows: Graham Hough, Helen Gardner, Joan Bennett, Dame Rebecca West, Dr. John Robinson, the Bishop of Woolwich, Dr. Vivian de Sola Pinto, Sir William Emrys Williams, Prebendary A. Stephan Hopkinson, Richard Hoggart, Francis Cammaerts, Sarah Beryl Jones, Dr. C. V. Wedgewood, Francis Williams, E. M. Forster, Ray Jenkins, M. P., Walter Allen, Anne Scott-James, Dr. James Hemming, Raymond Williams, Norman St. John-Stevas, J. W. Lambert, Sir Allen Lane, Canon T. R. Milford, Professor Kenneth Muir, Sir Stanley Unwin, Dilys Powell, C. D. Lewis, Stephen Potter, Janet Adam Smith, Noel Annan, the Reverend Donald Tytler, John Connell, C. K. Young, Hector Hetherington, Bernardine Wall. The acquittal of Penguin Books, Ltd., marked a turning point in the history of English literary censorship. See also "Canadian Customs Seize Books," TIMES (Lond), 11 May 1961, p. 13, which reveals that THE TRIAL OF LADY CHATTERLEY was among books held up by Canadian Customs in Vancouver.]

2155 St. John-Stevas, Norman. "Symposium: Pornography and Obscenity. The English Censorship Laws," CRITICAL QUARTERLY, III (Summer 1961), 103-9.

"The prosecution of *Penguin Books* for publishing *Lady Chatterley's Lover* last year [Regina v. Penguin Books, Ltd.] provided an admirable test case" for the Obscene Publications Act of 1959. "The Act works. It effectively protects works of literature." [See also, in the same "Symposium: Pornography and Obscenity," CRITICAL QUARTERLY, III (Summer 1961), the following comments: C. B. Cox, "Editorial Comment: The Teaching of Literature," pp. 99-103; Donald Davie, "Literature and Morality," pp. 109-13; Martin Jarrett-Kerr, "A Christian View," pp. 113-18 (not abstracted as not specifically on DHL); and C. S. Lewis, "Four-Letter Words," pp. 118-22.]

2156 Salgādo, Gāmini. "Mr. Gifford and D. H. Lawrence," CRITICAL QUARTERLY, III (Autumn 1961), 268-70.

[Reply to Henry Gifford, "The Defect in Lawrence's Poetry," CRITICAL QUARTERLY, III (Summer 1961), 164-66.] Gifford's case against DHL's poetry is like R. P. Blackmur's [in "D. H. Lawrence and Expressive Form," THE DOUBLE AGENT (NY: Arrow Editions, 1935), pp.103-20], but is more compact and without "numbing jargon." Trying to finish one of DHL's "unfinished" poems shows that the charge is not just. While DHL sometimes failed as a poet, greater attention to form would not have helped him. DHL's prose makes it evident that he was concerned with rhythm, as do his revisions. DHL's "formal norm" is not standard English metrical patterns, but the rhythms of the Authorized Version and the parallelisms of Hebrew poetry. [See also Vivian de Sola Pinto, "Poet without a Mask," CRITICAL QUARTERLY, III (Spring 1961), 5-18, to which Gifford's note was a reply; and two rejoinders by Vivian de Sola Pinto, "Mr. Gifford and D. H. Lawrence," CRITICAL QUARTERLY, III (Autumn 1961), 267-68; and "Lawrence's Poetry,"

CRITICAL QUARTERLY, IV (Spring 1962), 81.]

2157 Sargent, Robert. "For D. H. Lawrence," SHENANDOAH, XII (Winter 1961), 11.
[A poem addressed to DHL in which the speaker, having received DHL's "communication" and turned his "head Upward, heavenward," concludes that "Somehow, it didn't seem right./ Either for heaven or you."]

2158 Sawyer, Paul W. "The Religious Vision of D. H. Lawrence," CRANE REVIEW (Tufts University), III (Spring 1961), 105-12.
The obscenity question surrounding *Lady Chatterley's Lover* obscures DHL's artistry. In this novel, Connie is spiritually revived through a tender sexual relationship with the gamekeeper that is like a "sacred communion ritual," allowing her to become aware of many sources of life. Repeating this theme is *The Man Who Died,* a more allegorical work that tries to revitalize Christian doctrine. The rebirth here is through a similar love communion in which man is mystically at one with the universe, reminiscent of ancient religious rites that Christianity would do well to recover.

2159 Saxena, H. S. "The Critical Writings of D. H. Lawrence," INDIAN JOURNAL OF ENGLISH STUDIES, II (1961), 130-37.
DHL's critical remarks in essays, reviews, and letters should be related to his concept of a well-written novel. His attacks on his contemporaries also demonstrate his ideas about technique and content.

2160 Schönfeld, Herbert M. "*Lady Chatterley:* Eine Darstellung und Würdigung des vielumstrittenen Romans" (*Lady Chatterley:* An Evaluated Account of the Much-Debated Novel), NEUE ZEITSCHRIFT FÜR ÄRZTLICHE FORTBILDUNG, L (Stuttgart, 1961), 243.
Lady Chatterley's Lover, partly a social problem novel, is mainly concerned with DHL's attacks on sham marriages. The lapse into "obscene" scenes results from the author's overemphasis on man's physcial life. [In German.]

2161 Schroeter, James. "A Misreading of Poe's 'Ligeia,'" PUBLICATIONS OF THE MODERN LANGUAGE ASSOCIATION, LXXVI (Sept 1961), 397-406.
[Refutation of Roy Basler, "The Interpretation of 'Ligeia,'" COLLEGE ENGLISH, V (April 1944), 363-72.] DHL's was "the earliest and probably the most influential reading" of "Ligeia." Basler "borrowed from Lawrence" the image of Ligeia as a vampire. "Indeed, most of the ideas Basler represents as his own are freely translated from Lawrence," who is "the only outstanding critic of 'Ligeia' that Basler never refers to." [See also reply by Roy Basler and rejoinder by James Schroeter, "Poe's 'Ligeia,'" PUBLICATIONS OF THE MODERN LANGUAGE ASSOCIATION, LXXVII (Dec 1962), 675.]

2162 "Searcher for Atlantis," TIMES LITERARY SUPPLEMENT (Lond), 12 May 1961, p. 292.

DHL's power to make the known world 'strange again'" is part of the romantic inheritance which makes DHL the latest and most compelling writer in the English Romantic tradition; indeed, Coleridge's definition of the secondary imagination is virtually an "exact description of Lawrence's art." The philosophy expressed in *Phoenix: The Posthumous Papers of D. H. Lawrence,* ed by Edward D. McDonald (reissued, 1961), is "an invaluable, if cabalistic, interpretation of [DHL's] own artistic process." The concomitant sympathy and detachment with which DHL regards the past is expressed in language "which exactly fits Cassirer's notion of the artist as one who preserves, but does not reinstate, the original power of the word." [A D. H. LAWRENCE MISCELLANY, ed by Harry T. Moore (1959) is also reviewed.]

2163 Sharpe, Michael C. "The Genesis of D. H. Lawrence's *The Trespasser,*" ESSAYS IN CRITICISM, XI (Oct 1961), 34-39.

Unjustly neglected as the least characteristic of DHL's works, *The Trespasser* actually involved DHL deeply and personally. DHL came to know Helen Corke through his attempts to revive her, as Siegmund tries to awaken Helena in *The Trespasser* and as Derrick Hamilton (DHL) tries to awaken Ellis in NEUTRAL GROUND (1933), Miss Corke's novel based largely on the same five-day diary as *The Trespasser.*

2164 Sheed, Wilfrid. "The Trial of Lady Chatterley," JUBILEE, IX (Aug 1961), 33-35.

In their eagerness to prevent the censorship of *Lady Chatterley's Lover*, the thirty-five literary experts who testified for the defense in the British censorship trial (Regina v. Penguin Books, Ltd.) made unconsidered and even foolish remarks about the literary merit of the book. Katherine Anne Porter's criticism of the novel, essentially, is that, given the resemblance between Mellors and DHL, readers are told how wonderful it feels to have sex with the author. The expert witnesses not only did not consider Porter's written comments but also failed to analyze the crucial difference between DHL's art and his ability through that art to make the adolescent fantasy of impersonal sex appear actually to be an advance over adult courtship. By means of his own intensity and the stream of his dark poetry, DHL can exalt a sub-human love story and make it seem important. The book can have a negative influence because young people reading it may be wildly misled as to the psychology of sex.

2165 Shimpachirō, Miyata. "The Marquis on Trial," JAPAN QUARTERLY, VIII (Oct-Dec 1961), 494-96.

[A reportorial account of the last three Japanese censorship trials of *Lady Chatterley's Lover* in the 1950s, as background to another narrative account of a newly begun trial in a Tokyo court concerning the publication of a Japanese translation of the Marquis de Sade's JULIETTE.] Between 1950 and 1957, three trials were held in the Japanese Supreme Court to decide whether the Japanese translation of *Lady Chatterley's Lover* was "a work of art or of pornography." In the end, the Court declared that "art and obscenity can coexist in the same work" and that "art does not have the privilege of being obscene." The Court branded DHL's novel a pornographic work and placed a ban on its sale. Now, four years later, a similar trial has opened in the Tokyo District Court to decide whether a Japanese translation of the Marquis de Sade's JULIETTE is "pornographic." The prosecution claimed that the work *was* pornographic in the same way as *Lady Chatterley's Lover*; the defense counsel countered that in London the publishers of *Lady Chatterley's Lover* had been exonerated and "stressed that the time had come for a revision of the Chatterley" decision in Japan too. Whatever the outcome of this new struggle in the Japanese courts, it is hoped that this trial will "do more than the Chatterley trial to clarify the nature of 'obscenity,' 'thought,' and 'art,' and the relationship between the part and the whole in a work of art."

2166 Shirai, Toshitaka. "D. H. Lawrence: *Women in Love* no Kosei" (D. H. Lawrence: The Structure of *Women in Love*), BULLETIN OF YAMAGATA UNIVERSITY, IV (Feb 1961), 57-80.
[In Japanese.]

2167 Shonfield, Andrew. "Lawrence's Other Censor," ENCOUNTER, XVII (Sept 1961), 63-64.
In *Lady Chatterley's Lover*, DHL disguises perversions in rhetoric. If whatever Mellors did with Connie on the night before her departure was as important as DHL says, then DHL ought to say plainly what it was, if we are to profit by it. The truth is that DHL was ashamed to be plain about it. In any case, "copulation" is ridiculed by Connie at one point.

2168 Sillitoe, Alan. "Lawrence's Republic," TIME AND TIDE, XLII (19 Oct 1961), 1756.
Fantasia of the Unconscious, a "brilliant, erratic and fascinating book" and the key to DHL's "whole character and philosophy," deals with "those shadowy zones of human reaction that precede a state of complex social awareness." But the "return to that shadowy womb state of the pre-Fall Eden" which DHL, "for whatever reason, wanted to inhabit" is an "impossible" solution: mankind cannot "sacrifice" the "many worthwhile things in civilization" and must continue to "lurch forward." [Briefly discusses DHL's views on leadership, education, and the family.]

2169 Sparrow, John. "The Censor as Aedile," TIMES LITERARY SUPPLEMENT (Lond), 4 Aug 1961, pp. 473-75; rptd in INDEPENDENT ESSAYS, by John Sparrow (Lond: Faber & Faber; Westport, CT: Greenwood P, 1963), pp. 193-209.
[Review essay on Lord Radcliffe's CENSORS: THE REDE LECTURE and C. H. Rolph (ed), THE TRIAL OF LADY CHATTERLEY: REGINA V. PENGUIN BOOKS LIMITED (1961).] In Regina v. Penguin Books, Ltd. (1960), *Lady Chatterley's Lover* was prosecuted under the Jenkins Act, which makes "corruption" the essential element in obscenity. But if proceedings had been under Common Law, questions of the work's tendency "as a whole" and of its literary merit would not have applied, and attention could have been focused upon "the sheer indecency of the book": its " 'unmentionable' words," "profuse

descriptions of male and female *pudenda*," "allusions to the two 'entrances,' " betraying the author's "anal obsession," and its varied depictions of "natural and unnatural sex acts." Whereas Yeats and Dryden, in his translation of Lucretius, succeeded in rendering frank sexuality in artistically valid terms, DHL did not. The real issues of the trial were missed, the issues actually debated were clouded, and the testimony of the witnesses offered mere opinions instead of evidence. It is doubtful that the twenty-one-year-old girl who testified understood the point of the "night of sensual passion."

2170 Stolpe, Herman. "*Lady Chatterley* vann processen" (*Lady Chatterley* Won the Case), BOKVANNEN (Stockholm), XVI (1961), 168-69.
[Brief report of the 1960 British censorship trial of *Lady Chatterley's Lover* (Regina v. Penguin Books, Ltd.).] [In Swedish.]

2171 Strickland, Geoffrey. "The Poems of D. H. Lawrence," TIMES LITERARY SUPPLEMENT (Lond), 24 March 1961, p. 185.
[Letter to the Editor.] The best available English text of DHL's poems is Piero Nardi's edition [*D. H. Lawrence: Tutte le Poesie*, 2 vols. (1959)], which contains not only both the English text and Professor Nardi's Italian translation but also forty-five heretofore uncollected poems and all four of DHL's prefaces. [See also reply by Vivian de Sola Pinto, "The Poems of D. H. Lawrence," TIMES LITERARY SUPPLEMENT (Lond), 31 March 1961, p. 201.]

2172 Tanner, Tony. "A Hungry Woman," TIME AND TIDE, XLII (14 Dec 1961), 2121.
FRIEDA LAWRENCE: THE MEMOIRS AND CORRESPONDENCE, ed by E. W. Tedlock, Jr., answers the questions: "What was it like being the focus of all Lawrence's moods, needs and antagonisms; what was it like to walk with him, nurse him, sometimes beg for him, leave children for him: what was it like to watch him die: more, what was it like to outlive him for twenty-six years, to see the penurious exile transformed into an industry for critics, to watch the man give way to the monument?"

2173 Thody, Philip. "*Lady Chatterley's Lover*: A Pyrrhic Victory," THRESHOLD, V (Autumn-Winter 1961-1962), 36-49.
In reading THE TRIAL OF LADY CHATTERLEY: REGINA V. PENGUIN BOOKS LIMITED, ed by C. H. Rolph, one is reminded of the trial one hundred years earlier (1857) of Flaubert's MADAME BOVARY. Whereas Flaubert's novel was acquitted on aesthetic grounds, DHL's was successfully defended as being moral in a Christian tradition. But surely the message of the novel is far more pagan than Christian; hence, the tactics of the defense won a Pyrrhic victory.

2174 Tillyard, E. M. W. SOME MYTHICAL ELEMENTS IN ENGLISH LITERATURE (Lond: Chatto & Windus, 1961), pp. 73-74.

[The Clark Lectures, Trinity College, Cambridge, 1959-1960.] DHL exemplifies the process of withdrawing from civilization to make "a series of unsuccessful attempts to find the right place to retire to for the exercise of the particular forms of religion he came to express." *The Plumed Serpent,* "his most ambitious book," concerns such an attempt but fails to convince. "The very struggles of Kate to get clear of her Mexican retreat can be matched by eighteenth-century accounts of the temptations suffered by the retired man in his country retreat to return to the bustle of the town."

2175 Tomlinson, T. B. "Literature and History--The Novel," CRITICAL REVIEW (Melbourne), IV (1961), 93-101.
[This essay examines the basic differences between "art and history" and discusses some of the problems of "literary fiction," briefly quoting such critics as Collingwood, Kingsley, Trollope, and Leavis, and commenting on George Eliot, Dickens, and finally DHL's *Sons and Lovers, The Rainbow, Women in Love,* and *Lady Chatterley's Lover.*] DHL is "best when not attempting completeness and truth-to-the-facts in the historian's or sociologist's sense." The completely "sociological novel" will probably never be written.

2176 Tudsbery, M. T., C.B.E. "*Lady Chatterley's Lover,*" NOTES AND QUERIES, VIII (April 1961), 149.
[Reply to J. C. Maxwell, "*Lady Chatterley's Lover*: A Correction," NOTES AND QUERIES, VIII (March 1961), 110.] In the sentence in question in Chap. XVII of *Lady Chatterley's Lover,* the original text prints a comma after the word *eyes.*

2177 Turnell, Martin. MODERN LITERATURE AND CHRISTIAN FAITH (Westminster, MD: Newman P, 1961), pp. 30-34.
Although his achievements in other genres were considerable, DHL was a great master of prose fiction. He was also a moralist, but his novels are not "*romans à thèse*" but attempts "to discover a new mode of consciousness." His genius in describing "strange states of consciousness" is evident not only in stories like "The Woman Who Rode Away" but also in such passages in his novels as the description of Ursula's feelings in "Excurse" in *Women in Love.* The rhythm of his greatest novels -- . . . *The Rainbow* and *Women in Love*--is essentially dual." In both DHL presents marriage as a "love-hate relationship," a "contradiction" he discusses in *Fantasia of the Unconscious.*

2178 Waldron, P[hilip]. "Book Reviews," JOURNAL OF THE AUSTRALASIAN UNIVERSITIES LANGUAGE AND LITERATURE ASSOCIATION, No. 16 (Nov 1961), 223-24.
Love Among the Haystacks and Other Pieces is a collection of stories which "show Lawrence's style and thought at their most mature." *Mornings in Mexico* and *Etruscan Places* (reissued together) are "chiefly interesting" for the account in the latter of DHL's "trip through the sites of several Etruscan cities." "But Lawrence idealized the Etruscans into symbols of his own thought. *Etruscan Places* is a *Utopia.*" [THE INTELLIGENT HEART: THE STORY OF D. H. LAWRENCE, by Harry T. Moore, is also reviewed.]

2179 Walker, Warren S. "D. H. Lawrence," TWENTIETH- CENTURY SHORT STORY EXPLICATION: INTERPRETATIONS, 1900-1961, OF SHORT FICTION SINCE 1800 (Hamden, CT: Shoe String P, 1961); enlgd and rptd as TWENTIETH-CENTURY SHORT STORY EXPLICATION: INTERPRETATION, 1900-1966, OF SHORT FICTION SINCE 1800, 2nd ed (Hamden, CT: Shoe String P, 1967), pp. 414-36; two supplements pub as TWENTIETH-CENTURY SHORT STORY EXPLICATION, 1967-1969: SUPPLEMENT I TO SECOND EDITION (Hamden, CT: Shoe String P, 1970), pp. 153-56, and TWENTIETH-CENTURY SHORT STORY EXPLICATION, 1970-1972: SUPPLEMENT II TO SECOND EDITION (Hamden, CT: Shoe String P, 1973), pp. 86-88; further enlgd and rptd as TWENTIETH-CENTURY SHORT STORY EXPLICATION: INTERPRETATIONS, 1900-1975, OF SHORT FICTION SINCE 1800, 3rd ed (Hamden, CT: Shoe String P, 1977), pp. 450-64.

[Secondary bibliography of critical commentaries on fifty-eight DHL short stories, listing both articles and sections of books devoted to particular stories.]

2180 Waterfield, Lina. "The Fortress of Aulla and D. H. Lawrence," CASTLE IN ITALY: AN AUTOBIOGRAPHY (Lond: Murray; NY: Thomas Y. Crowell, 1961), pp. 119-43, espec pp. 134-43.

[After the author and her husband, the painter Aubrey Waterfield, called on DHL and Frieda at Fiascherino, Italy, in November 1913, a friendly relationship developed between the two couples. DHL proved a charming companion: "His passionate love of nature . . . made every walk seem to be an adventure." In response to the author's view that in *Sons and Lovers* Paul hastens his mother's death selfishly "because he cannot bear to see her suffer," DHL replied emphatically, " 'You are quite wrong. You see *I* did it--I gave the over-dose of morphia and set her free.' " DHL and Frieda visited the Waterfields at their castle at Aulla for three days in December 1913, and the Waterfields saw them for the last time in May 1914. Includes letters from DHL to the Waterfields and letters from Aubrey Waterfield to others about DHL.]

2181 Weales, Gerald. RELIGION IN MODERN ENGLISH DRAMA (Phila: University of Pennsylvania P, 1961), pp. 34-35.

In DHL's play *David* the visionary Saul is challenged and defeated by the practical David, who presents a concept of a God made in man's image rather than the faceless flame that transfigured men. Through the figures of Samuel and Jonathan, however, DHL's deeply religious work holds out a promise of a rebirth of Saul's deity.

2182 Weaver, Robert. "Lady Chatterley and All That," TAMARACK REVIEW, XXI (Autumn 1961), 49-57.

[An article on censorship in Canada. *Lady Chatterley's Lover* is mentioned along with Henry Miller's TROPIC OF CANCER, James Joyce's ULYSSES, and others.]

2183 Weisburg, Edzia. "The Triumph and Failure of D. H. Lawrence," PARTISAN REVIEW, XXVIII (March-April 1961), 309-14.

Eliseo Vivas's study, D. H. LAWRENCE: THE FAILURE AND THE TRIUMPH OF ART (1960), which marks the initiation of detached, dispassionate critical attention to DHL's fiction, points to the need for fresh approaches to the problems posed by DHL's unsuccessful works. Themes such as homosexuality, which have been practically undiscussed, need more thorough examination. Two tendencies in DHL's writing that are problematic are his dogmatic attitudes toward sex and the monotonous repetition of a single theme that was exhausted in *Women in Love*. On the positive side, "it is the ability to 'render' rather than to 'state' which makes Lawrence a great writer."

2184 Welch, Colin. "Black Magic, White Lies," ENCOUNTER, XVI (Feb 1961), 75-79.

Although clergy defended *Lady Chatterley's Lover* at the censorship trial (Regina v. Penguin Books, Ltd.) as a guide to Christian love and marriage, the truth is that the book seeks to destroy the Christian idea of love and marriage. Connie and Mellors copulate before they fall in love, and their love does not increase their reverence for life. *Lady Chatterley's Lover* is, in the tradition of witchcraft, a celebration of a Black Mass. "What it preaches is this: that mankind can only be regenerated by freeing itself from the tyranny of the intellect and the soul, from the tyranny of Jesus Christ, and by prostrating itself before its own phallus." [See also three letters in reply to Welch by Rebecca West, Richard Hoggart, and Martin Jarrett-Kerr, and one letter of support by William Emrys Williams, in "*Chatterley*, the Witnesses, and the Law: Black Magic? White Lies?" ENCOUNTER, XVI (March 1961), 52-53, 54-55, 55-56, and 54, respectively; and rejoinders by Colin Welch and E. L. Mascall, "Chatterley and the Law," ENCOUNTER, XVI (April 1961), 85.]

2185 Welker, Robert H. "Advocate for Eros: Notes on D. H. Lawrence," AMERICAN SCHOLAR, XXX (Spring 1961), 191-202.

The unabridged *Lady Chatterley's Lover* (NY: Grove P, 1959) brings to American culture, for the first time, a hero whose maleness is defined by his tenderness and eroticism, a hero alive to the "natural riches of desire." Typical male figures of American art [examples discussed] are "the sexually crippled or confused, the compulsive, the cynical, the violent, the romantically doomed." [Includes a brief discussion of how Connie Chatterley is psychologically more healthy than the typical American heroine.]

2186 Werner, Alfred. "Lawrence and Pascin," KENYON REVIEW, XXIII (Spring 1961), 217-28.

Although they never met, DHL and Jules Pascin, a Bulgarian-born painter (1885-1930), had much in common, both in their lives and in their art. Both DHL and Pascin tried to break through the conventional restraints of art and society while expressing their instincts in a highly individualistic manner. Although both viewed flesh and blood as wiser than intellect, "the sexual theme so boldly stated in the work of both . . . always falls short of the complete fulfillment and happiness they claimed for it." DHL "seems to have had 'a secret dread of Absolute Beauty,' considering it to be 'immoral and against mankind,' " whereas Pascin, who was devoid of DHL's missionary zeal, sought after Absolute Beauty in both life and art.

2187 West, Rebecca [pseud of Cicily Isabel Fairfield Andrews]. "*Chatterley,* the Witnesses, and the Law: Black Magic? White Lies?" ENCOUNTER, XVI (March 1961), 52-53.

[Letter to the Editor in reply to Colin Welch, "Black Magic, White Lies," ENCOUNTER, XVI (Feb 1961), 75-79.] *Lady Chatterley's Lover* is not intended to "undermine the Christian attitude to sex, love and marriage." DHL is dealing with a "coldness of the flesh" which could signal the death of the species. This is why in the sexual awakening of Connie and Mellors, DHL shows them feeling reciprocal tenderness and respect. [See also letter of support from William Emrys Williams and additional replies to Welch by Richard Hoggart and Martin Jarrett-Kerr, in "*Chatterley,* the Witnesses, and the Law: Black Magic? White Lies?" ENCOUNTER, XVI (March 1961), 54, 54-55, 55-56, respectively; and rejoinder by Colin Welch and a supportive response by E. L. Mascall, "Chatterley and the Law," ENCOUNTER, XVI (April 1961), 85.]

2188 Whitaker, Thomas R. "Lawrence's Western Path: *Mornings in Mexico,*" CRITICISM, III (Summer 1961), 219-36.

Using a novelistic, dramatic method, DHL "selected and arranged" the essays in *Mornings in Mexico* "so that the book 'places' his various points of view as stages on a literary and quite unchronological journey." The implicit theme of the book is "the limits and the uniqueness of each being." The paradox is "that one who accepts his limits . . . opens himself to the tide of a continual creation, which may then carry him onward." The action of the book "appears in the gradually deepening insight" of DHL's " 'tourist' *persona*": if the ego descends to "accept what seems darkly inferior and destructive . . . a new self may step free." "There is a clear symbolic continuity" from Boehme to Blake to DHL.

2189 Widmer, Kingsley, and Eleanor Widmer (eds). LITERARY CENSORSHIP: PRINCIPLES, CASES, PROBLEMS (Belmont, CA: Wadsworth Publishing, 1961).

Casebook on censorship, with excerpts organized in five parts, only the fourth of which is concerned with DHL. Contents of Part Four: "Sex and the Novel: American Censorship of *Lady Chatterley's Lover,*" excerpts from items abstracted under year of first publication: Malcolm Cowley and Alfred Kazin, pp. 94-101, from Hearing Before the Judicial Officer of the Post Office Department, "Transcript of Proceedings, May 14, 1959," APPENDIX TO THE BRIEF ON BEHALF OF PLAINTIFF-APPELLEE, U. S. Court of Appeals for Second Circuit, GROVE PRESS v. CHRISTENBERRY (1959); Post Office Department, pp. 102-4, from PROPOSED FINDINGS (Washington, D. C.: Post Office Department, May 21, 1959); Judge Frederick vanPelt Bryan, pp. 105-9, from U. S. District Court opinion in GROVE PRESS v. CHRISTENBERRY, U. S. D. C. S. D. N. Y. 175 F. Supp. 488 (1959); Judge Charles E. Clark, pp. 110-11, from U. S. Court of Appeals majority opinion in GROVE PRESS v.

CHRISTENBERRY, 182 F. (2d Cir. 1960); Judge Leonard P. Moore, pp. 111-13, from U. S. Court of Appeals opinion in GROVE PRESS v. CHRISTENBERRY, 182 F. (2d Cir. 1960); Harry T. Moore, "*Lady Chatterley's Lover* as Romance," pp. 114-16, from THE NEW YORK TIMES BOOK REVIEW, 2 May 1959, Sect. 7, p. 5; Bergen Evans, from "The Storm over *Lady Chatterley's Lover*," pp. 116-19, from CORONET, XLVII (Dec 1959), 144-50; John Benedict, from "The *Lady Chatterley's Lover* Case: A Legal Left-Wing Softening of Public Morality," pp. 119-21, from THE AMERICAN MERCURY, XC (Jan 1960), 3-15; Eliseo Vivas, pp. 121-24, from Chap. V, "*Lady Chatterley's Lover*," D. H. LAWRENCE: THE FAILURE AND THE TRIUMPH OF ART (Evanston, IL: Northwestern UP, 1960), pp. 138-47; Stanley Kauffmann, pp. 124-28, from "*Lady Chatterley* at Last," THE NEW REPUBLIC, CXL (25 May 1959), 13-16; DHL, pp. 129-34, from "Pornography and Obscenity" [not abstracted], DHL, pp. 134-38, from *A Propos of Lady Chatterley's Lover* [not abstracted]; Part Five: "The Cultural Context of American Censorship" [not abstracted]; Kingsley Widmer and Eleanor Widmer, "Questions and Suggestions," pp. 175-82 [not abstracted].

2190 [*The Widowing of Mrs. Holroyd*], TV TIMES (Lond), 18-25 March 1961, pp. 13 and 33.

[Review of the adaptation by Ken Taylor, directed by Claude Whatham for presentation in the Television Playhouse series, Granada TV Network, 23 March 1961.] This "powerful play" centers on a woman's choosing between her "handsome husband" and "the young man in whom she sees a chance to escape from married strife."

2191 Wiehe, R. E. "Lawrence's 'Tickets, Please,'" EXPLICATOR, XX (Oct 1961), Item 12.

In "Tickets, Please," Coddy (John Thomas Raynor), unlike his Orphic counterpart, counterattacks when set upon by the women. The form his counterattack takes is to choose Annie, who, as his strongest assailant, wants him less than any of the others do.

2192 Williams, Raymond. "The Law and Literary Merit," ENCOUNTER, XVII (Sept 1961), 66-69.

A question not yet dealt with by those concerned in the *Lady Chatterley's Lover* case (Regina v. Penguin Books, Ltd.) is how far literary merit can be established within the legal process and the reference a literary judgment has to moral and social judgments. In the *Lady Chatterley's Lover* case, literary critics had to deal with terms not of their own choice: evidence of literary merit was tied to questions of obscenity, whereas in point of law the questions are separable. Had they been regarded as separable in the trial, many witnesses could have honestly said that they regarded the book as mediocre without risking loss of the case.

2193 Williams, Raymond. "The Variety of D. H. Lawrence," TIME AND TIDE, XLII (17 Feb 1961), 251-52.

Although the typical "man in the pub" thinks DHL had a " 'one-track mind,' " "his real importance . . . is as . . . a many-sided writer, of unusual range and variety: novelist, poet, translator, essayist, travel-writer, literary critic, social critic." No book shows his range better than *Phoenix: The Posthumous Papers of D. H. Lawrence,* ed by Edward D. McDonald (1936, rptd 1961). More than any writer in English since Dickens, DHL had a "quickness" in "getting a feeling, a person, a place alive in a few words." As *Study of Thomas Hardy* (written 1914) reveals, DHL in that year "died as the writer he was evidently shaping to be; remade himself, and was in part re-made, as a different and more disturbing voice." "From *The Rainbow* on-- . . . the centre of interest is in general living processes rather than in one particular living process." Most of the things that made the change are described in *Phoenix,* the importance of which is "as writing, not as prophecy; as communication, not as mystique."

2194 Williams, William Emrys. "*Chatterley,* the Witnesses, and the Law: Black Magic? White Lies?" ENCOUNTER, XVI (March 1961), 54.
[Letter to the Editor in response to Colin Welch, "Black Magic, White Lies," ENCOUNTER, XVI (Feb 1961), 75-79, basically in support of Welch's position. See also replies to Welch by Rebecca West, Richard Hoggart, and Martin Jarrett-Kerr, in "*Chatterley,* the Witnesses, and the Law: Black Magic? White Lies?" ENCOUNTER, XVI (March 1961), 52-53, 54-55, 55-56, respectively; and rejoinder by Colin Welch and a supportive response by E. L. Mascall, "Chatterley and the Law," ENCOUNTER, XVI (April 1961), 85.]

2195 Wright, Raymond. "Lawrence's Non-Human Analogues," MODERN LANGUAGE NOTES, LXXVI (May 1961), 426-32.
Descriptions of animals, and occasionally plants, in DHL's fiction can be classified into two general types--those that are so clearly inconspicuous as to be seen merely as a part of the author's description of natural setting and those that are so pointed that DHL must have intended an analogous relationship between them and his human characters. The scene in Chapter VI of *The Rainbow* typifies the second type of description, in that the squabbling of two blue-caps corresponds to the marital state of the principal characters. When such descriptions are so obviously analogous to events in the main narrative, they "anticipate, modify, or replace discursive analysis." They can be expected in DHL's novels particularly at moments of tension or revelation, although they are relatively trivial in significance as compared to DHL's symbolic episodes.

2196 Yamaji, Katsuyuki. "On the Sun (II)--Three Types of Love in D. H. Lawrence's Literature," CULTURAL SCIENCE REPORTS (Kagoshima University), No. 10 (July 1961), 47-64.

1962

2197 Adelman, Gary Stephen. "Lawrence's *Rainbow*," DISSER-

TATION ABSTRACTS, XXIV (1964), 5402. Unpublished dissertation, Columbia University, 1962.

2198 Agee, James. LETTERS OF JAMES AGEE TO FATHER FLYE (NY: George Braziller, 1962), p. 73.
"[D. H. Lawrence] seems to me somewhat crazy all right, and certainly a man of genius, and I am at present convinced one of the greater and more nearly saint-like people. No one certainly was ever more honest." [In context (letter of 26 Nov 1934), the reference is to *The Letters of D. H. Lawrence,* ed by Aldous Huxley (1932). Brief but telling comment.]

2199 Alcibiade [pseud of Mario Praz]. "Incanto pagano di D. H. Lawrence" (Pagan Enchantment in D. H. Lawrence), PAESE SERA (Rome), 23 March 1962, p. 3.
[Review of *Libri di viaggio e pagine di paese (Complete Collection of Travel Books),* by D. H. Lawrence, with an Introduction by Piero Nardi (1961).] DHL's travel books are among his best works because, in them, he shows a peculiar taste for proselytism and an extraordinary capacity for capturing the vital essence of things. These aspects of his artistic temperament call to mind, in a way, Rousseau and Van Gogh. [In Italian.]

2200 Aldington, Richard. "Sutures in the Saga of Lorenzo," SATURDAY REVIEW (NY), XLV (17 March 1962), 26.
The Collected Letters of D. H. Lawrence, ed by Harry T. Moore (1962), an excellent collection designed for the specialist, can also be read understandably by the casual reader, thanks to Moore's skillful guidance. [Includes portrait.]

2201 Amado Lévy-Valensi, Eliane. "L'en-deçà de la connaissance. Le péché et les voies du salut dans l'ontologie Lawrencienne" (On This Side of Knowledge: Sin and the Roads to Salvation in the Lawrentian Ontology), LES NIVEAUX DE L'ÊTRE ET LA CONNAISSANCE DANS LEUR RELATION AU PROBLÈME DU MAL (The Levels of Being and Knowledge and Their Relationship to the Problem of Evil) (Paris: Presses Universitaires de France, 1962), pp. 280-333.
In spite of several theoretical essays, DHL is more an artist than a philosopher. His thought has its roots in his own life; it is transposed human experience. Apprehended intuitively, his world is that of Schopenhauer, with an important difference: whereas Schopenhauer condemns physical desire, DHL wants to reveal its metaphysical dimension. Sexuality is the consequence of sin, but at the same time it is the means to redemption and union. Behind the discontinuity of appearances, DHL looks for the secret connection: he dreams of the polarity of a vital circuit linking the sun, the moon, and living beings. The secret heart of the world is sometimes revealed in the fascinating Lawrentian landscapes. His world is both nocturnal and bright. DHL's essential intuition is a negation of evil, an intuition of the primitive reality of the world before sin. *St. Mawr* is a significant text on this subject. The world of knowledge, for DHL, is actually the negative world of illusion and sin, and his characters manifest his disgust of mental power.

Rather than a poet of eroticism, DHL is the philosopher of one of the ways of restoring lost unity. Yet the sexuality of sin is also present in DHL's work; it is characterized by the strengthening of the will and the ego and the possession of the other. The major theme of *The White Peacock* is the destructive power of women. In *Sons and Lovers,* DHL attributes to the mother man's inhibition in the face of life and love. But woman can also be man's victim. Alienated sexuality that is only the result of avid individuality is solved by destruction. The individual can reach redeeming knowledge when the communion of sexuality is revealed to him, but this revelation can exist only when man or woman surrenders his or her will. Although the assertion of life in DHL's vision is never free of a fascination for death, DHL's philosophy goes deeper into actual experience than that of Schopenhauer. [The author gives specific examples illustrating her thesis and comments on DHL's contradictions and on his attitude towards the Jews.] [In French.]

2202 André, Robert. "Lettres Étrangères" (Foreign Letters), LA NOUVELLE REVUE FRANÇAISE, ns X (April 1962), 728-30.

There is no growth in DHL's work--he only repeats himself. It is impossible to enter the Lawrentian universe by means of our intelligence. [Commentary on *The Virgin and the Gipsy* and "Daughters of the Vicar."] [In French.]

2203 Arnold, Armin (ed). *The Symbolic Meaning: The Uncollected Versions of "Studies in Classic American Literature,"* by D. H. Lawrence, ed by Armin Arnold, with a Preface by Harry T. Moore (Lond: Centaur P, 1962; NY: Viking P, 1964).

Editorial commentary in this edition of the earliest versions of DHL's critical essays on "classic American literature" is presented in the editor's Introduction and textual headnotes to the individual essays, recording any earlier publications and noting variations between the earlier versions published here and the versions (usually the third) published in *Studies in Classic American Literature.* Contents, abstracted under 1962: Harry T. Moore, "Preface," pp. ix-xi; Armin Arnold, "Introduction," pp. 1-11, rvd and enlgd from "The Transcendental Element in American Literature: A Study of Some Unpublished D. H. Lawrence Manuscripts," MODERN PHILOLOGY, LX (Aug 1962), 41-46; and individual headnotes [not otherwise abstracted] as follows: 1. "The Spirit of Place," p. 15; 2. "Benjamin Franklin," p. 33; 3. "Hector St. John de Crèvecoeur," p. 49; 4. "Fenimore Cooper's Anglo-American Novels," pp. 67-68; 5. "Fenimore Cooper's Leatherstocking Novels," pp. 83-85; 6. "Edgar Allan Poe," pp. 105-6; 7. "Nathaniel Hawthorne I," pp. 121-22; 8. "Nathaniel Hawthorne II," pp. 147-48; 9. "The Two Principles," p. 159; 10. "Dana's *Two Years Before the Mast,*" p. 175; 11. "Herman Melville's *Typee* and *Omoo,*" pp. 197-98; 12. "Herman Melville's *Moby Dick,*" pp. 211-13; 13. "Whitman," pp. 229-30.

2204 Arnold, Armin. "The Transcendental Element in American Literature: A Study of Some Unpublished D. H. Lawrence Manuscripts," MODERN PHILOLOGY, LX (Aug 1962), 41-46; also pub as "The Transcendental Element," MIDWAY, No. 12 (Oct 1962), 28-33; and enlgd as "Introduction," *The Symbolic Meaning: The Uncol-*

lected Versions of "Studies in Classic American Literature," by D. H. Lawrence, ed by Armin Arnold (Lond: Centaur P, 1962; NY: Viking P, 1964), pp. 1-11.

Three versions of DHL's essays on American literature, originally entitled *The Transcendental Element in American Literature,* can be distinguished: (1) the twelve essays written in Cornwall (1917-1918), eight of which were published in ENGLISH REVIEW; (2) the second version written in Sicily (1920), of which only the Whitman essay was published, though typescripts of the two Melville essays and the second Hawthorne essay are extant; and (3) the twelve essays "radically" rewritten in America and published as *Studies in Classic American Literature* (1923). The first two versions reveal a philosophical, rather than a purely literary, dynamic; the second version lacks vitality; and the third version, "spoilt" by a "hysterical tone," presents DHL at his worst, noisily "grinding his ax." [Surveys English and American reviews of *Studies in Classic American Literature*.]

2205 "At the Drop of a Stamp," TIME, LXXIX (27 April 1962), 88, 91.

The Collected Letters of D. H. Lawrence, ed by Harry T. Moore, "comprises a remarkably complete autobiography of the contentious, witty, prickly and tender novelist, who corresponded voluminously because he was so often away from home--driven first by a consuming desire for utopia, then by a consumptive body that forced him to seek out hot, dry climates." [Quotes various comments by DHL on society, writing, modern painting, Christianity, democracy, and life.]

2206 Balakian, Nona. "The Prophetic Vogue of the Anti-Heroine," SOUTHWEST REVIEW, XLVII (Spring 1962), 134-41.

[Essay on the "denigration or deflation of women in present-day literature," including Mailer, Nabokov, and others; DHL and Shaw are held up as "the two male writers" who have done most to "liberate" women in fiction by "de-romanticization."] Connie in *Lady Chatterley's Lover* is "a genuine woman, warm ... spontaneous," "universal," but still "'modern.'" "Released from bondage," DHL's "exceptional woman" "demands a more equal footing with her partner" and is "wary of surrendering her deeper self." The heroines of DHL and Shaw "remained models of possibility still to be achieved in fact."

2207 Basler, Roy, and James Schroeter. "Poe's 'Ligeia,'" PUBLICATIONS OF THE MODERN LANGUAGE ASSOCIATION, LXXVII (Dec 1962), 675.

[Reply by Roy Basler and rejoinder by James Schroeter on Schroeter's "A Misreading of Poe's 'Ligeia,'" PUBLICATIONS OF THE MODERN LANGUAGE ASSOCIATION, LXXVI (Sept 1961), 397-406. The relevance of DHL in this critical exchange between two Poe scholars is whether James Schroeter's charge that Basler, in his interpretation of "Ligeia," plagiarized DHL's reading of the story is true. While he had read DHL's "Edgar Allan Poe" essay twenty years previously, Basler says that any borrowing from it was unconscious on his part.]

2208 Beck, Warren. "Lawrence Letters--The Heart of the Man,"

CHICAGO SUNDAY TRIBUNE MAGAZINE OF BOOKS, 8 April 1962, p. 4.
The Collected Letters of D. H. Lawrence, ed by Harry T. Moore (1962) "gives everything of first importance and much of interest besides." Moore has provided a useful introduction and index as well as helpful commentaries here and there.

2209 Beer, J. B. THE ACHIEVEMENT OF E. M. FORSTER (Lond: Chatto & Windus, 1962), pp. 112, 172, 184, 195-98, 206-7.
E. M. Forster's novels have greater breadth than DHL's--more "total consistency and truth to the whole"--but they lack DHL's "singleness of vision." DHL's novels (*The Rainbow,* in particular) develop some of Forster's themes, but this is perhaps less a case of conscious borrowing than of two authors' responding to current ideas.

2210 Bergonzi, Bernard. "Private Eye," TABLET (Lond), CCXVI (30 June 1962), 617-18.
The Symbolic Meaning: The Uncollected Versions of "Studies in Classic American Literature," ed by Armin Arnold, reprints the original versions of the "slangy, informal, intuitive work" on American literature which, in the 1923 version, showed DHL to be a "fine," if sometimes "barely coherent," critic. With his "intensely personal" interest in American literature, DHL "helped to set in motion" the now widely accepted study of American literature as a subject distinct from English literature. However, "Lawrence had too many axes to grind and too little detachment to be a great critic."

2211 "Biography," BOOKLIST AND SUBSCRIPTION BOOKS BULLETIN: A GUIDE TO CURRENT BOOKS, LVIII (1 May 1962), 604.
"Aside from its intrinsic literary value," *The Collected Letters of D. H. Lawrence* (2 vols., ed and with an Introduction by Harry T. Moore) "will serve as a frame of reference for Lawrence's previously published books and for the bulk of criticism and memoirs which his works and life have inspired."

2212 Bo, Carlo. "La rivolta di Lawrence e la fuga dalla civiltà" (Lawrence's Revolt and His Flight from Civilization), LA STAMPA (Turin), 6 April 1962, p. 3.
DHL tried to escape civilization and spent his life traveling around the world looking for possible alternatives. He was never fully satisfied because his ideal world was artificial and illusory. [In Italian.]

2213 Bogdanovich, Peter. "Talkies: A Conversation Piece in Short Takes, Starring the Last Tycoons," ESQUIRE, LVIII (Aug 1962), 33-40, espec p. 39; rptd as "Talkies," in PIECES OF TIME: PETER BOGDANOVICH ON THE MOVIES (NY: Arbour House and Dell Publishers [Delta Books], 1973), pp. 25-45, espec pp. 38-40.
[In an interview with the author, the film producer Jerry Wald gives an account of his numerous attempts, since his introduction to *Sons and Lovers* in a class taught by Thomas Wolfe, to make a film version of the novel. Among the actors

proposed, at various times, for the leading role (Paul Morel) were Leslie Howard, Marlon Brando, James Dean, and Montgomery Cliff, while Alec Guinness was once considered for the role of the father and Joan Collins for the part ultimately played by Mary Ure (Clara Dawes). The producer declares that Gavin Lambert, who wrote the initial screenplay, and Jack Cardiff, who directed the film, were wholly inexperienced but were "enthusiastic." The author adds a footnote to the article as reprinted in PIECES OF TIME to demonstrate that Wald's account was for the most part unreliable: Wald would have been only seventeen at the time of Wolfe's class in 1929, Dean was unknown in 1948, Lambert had written a feature film, and Cardiff had been both director of photography and director on previous films.]

2214 Bradbrook, Frank. "Camus and Lawrence," TIMES LITERARY SUPPLEMENT (Lond), 20 July 1962, p. 525.
[Letter to the Editor.] *The Letters of D. H. Lawrence,* ed by Aldous Huxley (1932) is the source of a quotation in Albert Camus's CAHIERS.

2215 Brady, Emily Kuempel. "The Literary Faulkner: His Indebtedness to Conrad, Lawrence, Hemingway, and Other Modern Novelists," DISSERTATION ABSTRACTS, XXIII (1962), 2131A. Unpublished dissertation, Brown University, 1962.

2216 Busch, Günther. "Kritische These über D. H. Lawrence" (A Critical Approach to D. H. Lawrence), WORT IN DER ZEIT (Vienna), VIII, No. 4 (1962), 44-48.
DHL gives a modern version of the Rousseauesque ideal. He attacks the one-sided view of nature as the object of exploitation and sentimental reveries. At the same time he sees nature in a pseudoreligious way, as a kind of retreat from the insufferable monotony of modern life. [In German.]

2217 Callaghan, Morley. "Would You Give This Book to a Fifteen-Year Old?" TORONTO STAR WEEKLY, 23 July 1960 [not seen in this form]; long excerpts rptd in D. H. LAWRENCE NEWS AND NOTES, II, No. 2 (1962), 2-6.
[Account of the author's testimony as witness for the defense in the Montreal obscenity trial of *Lady Chatterley's Lover.* Suggesting " 'dirt for dirt's sake' " as a definition of obscenity, the author defends DHL's direct treatment of sex and his use of four-letter words and calls DHL "fiercely honest."]

2218 Ceserani, Remo. "D. H. Lawrence in viaggio: Frati anarchici, Etruschi e Messicani" (D. H. Lawrence's Travels: Anarchist Monks, Etruscans and Mexicans), IL MONDO (Rome), 9 June 1962, pp. 10-11.
[Review of *Libri di viaggio e pagine di paese* (*Complete Collection of Travel Books*), by D. H. Lawrence, with an Introduction by Piero Nardi (1961).] All of DHL's works reveal his profound knowledge of places, peoples, and customs, but this knowledge emerges most clearly in his travel books. These writings often appear weighted down with theoretical discussions, but they also reveal DHL's

extraordinary sincerity and intelligence. This is particularly evident in *Twilight in Italy*. The leit-motif of the travel books is DHL's escape from England in search of an ideal place and a perfect community. DHL's main merit lies in his having expressed solidarity among men and between man and nature. [In Italian.]

2219 "A Child's Guide to Modern Culture: N Is for New Establishment," SPECTATOR, CCIX (23 Nov 1962), 810-11.

[Satire. Two-page genealogy showing DHL's literary descendants as Leavis, Orwell, J. B. Priestley, and H. Miller; and as further descendants, through Leavis: Hoggart, Williams, Wesker, Olivier, the Redgrave family, A. Finney, and T. Courtney; through Priestley: Waterhouse, Amis, Wain, Clayton, Braine, Stan Barstow, Osborne, George Divine, J. Littlewood, Schlesinger, L. Anderson, Brecht, P. Gilliatt, S. Delaney, B. Behan, L. Bart, and Colin MacInnes; and through Miller: L. Durrell. A cartoon caricature of DHL asks: "F Dash Me! Am I really responsible for all that?"]

2220 Clark, L. D. "The Habitat of *The Plumed Serpent*," with photographs by LaVerne H. Clark, TEXAS QUARTERLY, V (Spring 1962), 162-67.

[A series of twenty black-and-white photographs and two line drawings on Aztec motifs, accompanied by a running commentary and brief quotations from *The Plumed Serpent*, of hotels and homes, monuments and pyramids, churches, people, and natural settings referred to or used in the novel. Taken in 1960 and 1961, the photographs give some indication of DHL's exposure to Mexico: more than two years from his first visit to his final leaving, living there for more than ten months, visiting "at least twenty of its states," and staying "for periods of one to four months in Mexico City, Chapala, Guadalajara, and Oaxaca."]

2221 Clements, A. L. "The Quest for the Self: D. H. Lawrence's *The Rainbow*," THOTH, III (Spring 1962), 90-100.

In *The Rainbow*, the relationship between man and woman and the concern for sexual fulfillment are essential elements in the larger quest for self. Ursula seeks in successive acts of rejection--of Skrebensky, Winifred Inger, her parents' way of life, the church, school-teaching, and college--the answer to the question: "Whither to go, how to become oneself?" The final rejection of Skrebensky comes out of her hard-won awareness that she cannot create the man she is to love, that he must come to her out of the Infinite. This structure of rejection and quest, death and rebirth, leads up to Ursula's vision of the rainbow at the end of the novel.

2222 Connolly, Cyril. "The Fire That Consumes," SUNDAY TIMES (Lond), "Magazine Section," 18 March 1962, p. 31; rptd as "The Letters of D. H. Lawrence," in PREVIOUS CONVICTIONS, by Cyril Connolly (Lond: Hamish Hamilton, 1963), pp. 265-68.

The Collected Letters of D. H. Lawrence, ed by Harry T. Moore, includes most of the letters in the Aldous Huxley edition (1932) and adds many previously undiscovered or unpublished letters. [The author speculates on what DHL would have thought of the trial of *Lady Chatterley's Lover* (Regina v. Penguin Books, Ltd., 1960), mentions several of his correspondents, and hopes that "some of those who confiscated his paintings, burnt his books, impounded his manuscripts, pilfered his mail, badgered him out of the country and campaigned against *The Rainbow, Pansies* and *Lady Chatterley's Lover* are alive to read these letters and are in sufficient possession of their faculties to understand something of the damage they caused." In PREVIOUS CONVICTIONS, the review is preceded, pp. 262-64, by "D. H. Lawrence and a Disciple," a review of Witter Bynner, JOURNEY WITH GENIUS: RECOLLECTIONS AND REFLECTIONS CONCERNING THE D. H. LAWRENCES (1951) (not abstracted).]

2223 Corke, Helen. "Portrait of D. H. Lawrence, 1909-1910," TEXAS QUARTERLY, V (Spring 1962), 169-77; rptd in D. H. LAWRENCE: THE CROYDON YEARS, by Helen Corke (Austin: University of Texas P, 1965), pp. 1-16.

[Drawn from the period when DHL was working on *The Trespasser,* using Helen Corke's diary, notes, and experiences as sources for the novel, this memoir stresses her gratitude for DHL's taking "upon himself the responsibility of recharging my depleted energy" after her "personal tragedy" by his visits and poetry reading; her gradual involvement in his relationship with "Muriel" (Jessie Chambers); and her realization that DHL, "cynical and impatient" with uncertainty, and she were gradually drawing apart.] [The memoir is introduced by Warren Roberts, "Helen Corke's 'Portrait of D. H. Lawrence, 1909-1910': An Introductory Note," TEXAS QUARTERLY, V (Spring 1962), 168 (not abstracted).]

2224 Cornwell, Ethel F. "The Sex Mysticism of D. H. Lawrence," THE "STILL POINT": THEME AND VARIATIONS IN THE WRITINGS OF T. S. ELIOT, COLERIDGE, YEATS, HENRY JAMES, VIRGINIA WOOLF, AND D. H. LAWRENCE (New Brunswick, NJ: Rutgers UP, 1962), pp. 12-14, 208-41.

In response to traditional religion and a conventional god, which DHL thought of as dead forms that had outlived their viability, and to modern industrial civilization, which he felt fostered the pursuit of a false individualism, DHL evolved a personal "religion" which would lead to personal integration and renewed connections with other men and the cosmos. Examination of DHL's total canon reveals that this religion begins with his early belief " 'in the blood, the flesh, as being wiser than the intellect.' " DHL's early novels offer three basic ideas that remain the core of his thought: "that the 'law of polarity' is the basic law of the universe," that personal integration requires the reconciliation of opposites, and that the means to both personal integration and relationship with the creative principle of the universe is physical union with the opposite sex. DHL explored facets of these ideas throughout his life, evolving his concepts and examining the social circumstances that might allow their implementation. Regardless of which tack his explorations might take, one characteristic always marked DHL's thought-- his sense of wonder at the mystery of creation.

2225 Craig, Alec. THE BANNED BOOKS OF ENGLAND AND OTHER COUNTRIES (Lond: George Allen & Unwin, 1962); rvd version of 1st ed pub in America as SUPPRESSED BOOKS: A HISTORY OF THE CONCEPTION OF LITERARY OBSCENITY

(Cleveland and NY: World Publishing Co., 1963), pp. 33, 42, 75-77, 84, 95, 97, 107, 114, 115, 118, 132, 145, 146-63, 164, 166, 167, 173, 175, 187, 188, 191, 192, 193-94, 196, 200, 207, 209, 231-48.

DHL's "calculated challenge to convention" in the sexual scenes and vocabulary of *Lady Chatterley's Lover* prevented his publishing the original edition in English-speaking countries. [The author recounts the grudging decision by Magistrate W. E. Batt in London in 1953 not to order destruction of the expurgated edition; surveys the proceedings and the decision by Judge Frederick vanPelt Bryan in a court action brought by the publishers of the first unexpurgated American edition in 1959 (Grove Press v. Christenberry), which lifted the ban imposed on the book by postal authorities; and discusses briefly the proceedings against the book in London 1960 (Regina v. Penguin Books, Ltd.), which resulted in acquittal of the British publishers of the unexpurgated edition. The author also devotes a chapter to the Obscene Publications Act of 1959, under which the proceedings against *Lady Chatterley's Lover* were taken in 1960, and distinguishes the differences between this legal statute and the statute which it superseded, Lord Campbell's original Obscene Publications Act of 1857 (under which proceedings against *The Rainbow* had been taken in 1915, although that case is not discussed here). See also Frederick vanPelt Bryan, U.S.D.J. UNITED STATES DISTRICT COURT, SOUTHERN DISTRICT OF NEW YORK, CIVIL 147-87: GROVE PRESS, INC. AND READERS' SUBSCRIPTION, INC., PLAINTIFFS, AGAINST ROBERT K. CHRISTENBERRY, INDIVIDUALLY AND AS POSTMASTER OF THE CITY OF NEW YORK, DEFENDANT: OPINION: 175 F. Supp. 488 (21 July 1959), which is reprinted here in the Appendix, pp. 231-48.]

2226 Craig, David. "Love and Society: MEASURE FOR MEASURE and Our Own Time," SHAKESPEARE IN A CHANGING WORLD, ed by Arnold Kettle (NY: International Publishers, 1962), pp. 195-216; rptd as Chap. I: "Shakespeare, Lawrence and Sexual Freedom," in THE REAL FOUNDATIONS: LITERATURE AND SOCIAL CHANGE, by David Craig (NY: Oxford UP, 1974), pp. 17-38.

Four tales by DHL ("Daughters of the Vicar," *The Captain's Doll, St. Mawr,* and *The Virgin and the Gipsy*) are the modern works of English literature most akin to Shakespeare's MEASURE FOR MEASURE. They resemble Shakespeare's play in that they treat the themes of fulfillment through love and personal freedom by means of a contrast between what is life affirming and what is life denying. Just as Shakespeare presents Claudio as the antithesis of Angelo, "with his deathly wish to ignore and repress real feelings," DHL defines fullness of experience "by contrasting pairs of people through the imagery that establishes the contrasting types." DHL depicts characters who, like Shakespeare's Angelo, do not know themselves because of the repression which is inherent to their dignified public roles. It is this aspect of characterization that enables both writers to treat public values such as justice, authority, and discipline. However, there is no simplistic contrast between the artificiality of social roles and the reality of personal feelings, and neither Shakespeare nor DHL presents a "primitivist or anarchic opposition . . . between control and freedom." Rather, both authors are concerned with social responsibility. In this respect, however, the comparison between Shakespeare and DHL proves imperfect, since despite the fact that DHL valued the societal impulse, he often spoke contemptuously of it and "regarded social organization as something only minimally relevant to our deeper experience."

2227 Cunningham, J. S. "Lady Chatterley's Husband," LITERARY HALF-YEARLY, III (July 1962), 20-27.

Critics asserting that Clifford's physical condition is a flaw in *Lady Chatterley's Lover* tend to overlook other ways in which he is isolated from Connie. A thorough study of Clifford reveals DHL's subtlety and penetration in this characterization.

2228 "Current Books," NINETEENTH CENTURY FICTION, XVII (Sept 1962), 196.

The Collected Letters of D. H. Lawrence, ed by Harry T. Moore, is actually a selection which skims the cream of available letters, not the definitive edition which the publisher claims. [Brief notice.]

2229 Dalton, Robert O. " 'Snake': A Moment of Consciousness," BRIGHAM YOUNG UNIVERSITY STUDIES, IV, Nos. 2-3, (1962), 243-53.

DHL's profound earnestness in conveying an insight justifies his poetry. DHL's belief that man should follow his instincts and forget his "mental indoctrination" explains why he writes "naturally" in "Snake." DHL recognized that man, in living less in contact with the living world, is becoming an automaton. The encounter with the snake shows DHL's recognition of the life existing beneath the vicissitudes of everyday concerns.

2230 Davis, Edward. FESTIVAL OF ENGLISH POETRY (South African Broadcasting Corp., 1962), pp. 88-93.

DHL's verse is better than his prose. He is a far greater poet than is generally recognized. "The Hands of God," "Abysmal Immortality," "The Ship of Death," "Intimates," "The Triumph of the Machine," and "The English Are So Nice" [all quoted in full] demonstrate his versatility. DHL, Eliot, and Yeats may make their century seem brave to those born in the next.

2231 dell'Arco, Mario. "Lawrence etrusco" (Lawrence Student of Etruscan Civilization), LA SICILIA (Catania), 13 March 1962, p. 3.

Etruscan Places is one of DHL's best works because of its style and the concreteness and rationality of the subject matter. DHL shows himself to be a sharp observer of modern man. He hated Roman civilization as much as he hated fascism. He can be considered a humanitarian socialist who disliked the concept of leadership under any political label. [In Italian.]

2232 DeWinter, Oswald. "*Lady Chatterley's Lover* and the Aubade," D. H. LAWRENCE NEWS AND NOTES (California, PA), II, No. 3 (1962), 4-5.

Lady Chatterley's Lover depicts the same situation found in the Provencal *aubade,* "the intrusion of the world upon the perfect (and incidentally, extra-societal) union of two lovers."

2233 D. H. LAWRENCE NEWS AND NOTES (California, PA), II (Spring 1962), 1-8.
[Mimeographed newsletter, ed by Dexter Martin.] "To spread interest in Lawrence without idealizing or devitalizing him." Contents, abstracted under year of first publication: Introductory note, p. 1, "Some Future Issues," p. 1, and bibliography, interalia commentary, and notes by Dexter Martin [not abstracted]; [Dexter Martin], "An Informal Bibliography (from June 1960 to April 1962)," pp. 1-5; comments on DHL MSS, on Harry T. Moore, and on Jerry Wald, pp. 6, 7 [not abstracted]; [Dexter Martin], "A Note about Frieda," pp. 7-8; [Dexter Martin], "Vs. Diana Trilling's Preface to Her Portable Lawrence," p. 8; [Andor Gomme], "High-Handed Publishers?" pp. 6-7, rptd from "Friends and Enemies," TIMES LITERARY SUPPLEMENT (Lond), 27 April 1962, pp. 273-75; untitled news quotation, p. 7, rptd from PITTSBURGH POST-GAZETTE, 28 June 1962 [not abstracted].

2234 D. H. LAWRENCE NEWS AND NOTES (California, PA), II, No. 2 (1962), 1-6.
[Offset newsletter, ed by Dexter Martin.] Contents, abstracted under year of first publication: Interalia commentary and notes by Dexter Martin: "Degradation" (commentary on presentation in PLAYBOY of selected DHL letters with captions), pp. 1-2 [not abstracted]; Ed Zern, [Review of *Lady Chatterley's Lover*], p. 2, rptd from FIELD AND STREAM, Nov 1959, p. 142; Morley Callaghan, "Would You Give This Book to a Fifteen-Year Old?" pp. 2-6, rptd from TORONTO STAR WEEKLY, 23 July 1960; Bergen Evans, "Bergen Evans on LC'sL," p. 6, excerpt rptd with commentary from "The Storm over *Lady Chatterley's Lover*," CORONET, XLVII (Dec 1959), 144-50.

2235 D. H. LAWRENCE NEWS AND NOTES (California, PA), II, No. 3 (1962), 1-8.
[Offset newsletter, ed by Dexter Martin.] Contents, abstracted under year of first publication: William White, "Lawrence and Marquand," p. 1; Bernard S. Oldsey, "Lawrence's 'Error' about Hawthorne's Pearl," pp. 2-4; Oswald DeWinter, "*Lady Chatterley's Lover* and the Aubade," pp. 4-5; Dean H. Keller, "An Uncollected Poem by Lawrence," p. 6; D[exter] M[artin], "Note by D. M.," pp. 6-7; Dexter Martin, "Three Types of Vitalism in *The Rainbow*," p. 8.

2236 Drain, Richard Leslie. "Formative Influences on the Work of D. H. Lawrence." Unpublished dissertation, Cambridge University, 1962. [Listed in Lawrence F. McNamee, DISSERTATIONS IN ENGLISH AND AMERICAN LITERATURE (NY and Lond: Bowker, 1969), p. 613.]

2237 Drain, Richard L. "Reviews," ENGLISH STUDIES (Amsterdam), XLIII (Feb 1962), 69-72.
Phoenix: The Posthumous Papers of D. H. Lawrence, ed by Edward D. McDonald

(reissued 1961), "remains an indispensable volume." [Also reviews A D. H. LAWRENCE MISCELLANY, ed by Harry T. Moore, noting its inclusion of the first version of *The Fox* with a facsimile of the manuscript and commenting on "this American advocacy of the man rather than the books, 'Life' rather than art."]

2238 Eichrodt, John Morris. "D. H. Lawrence and the Protestant Crisis," DISSERTATION ABSTRACTS, XXV (1965), 4144A. Unpublished dissertation, Columbia University, 1962.

2239 Enright, D[ennis] J. "Never Trust the Editor," NEW STATESMAN, LXIV (10 Aug 1962), 178.
[Review of *The Symbolic Meaning: The Uncollected Versions of "Studies in Classic American Literature,"* ed by Armin Arnold.] "To make these early versions available is one thing. To assert again and again that they are superior to the *Studies,* as Dr. Arnold does, is another thing altogether: a great big untruth." [Compares sample passages on "art-speech."] "The early versions throughout are composed largely in a conventional lecture style."

2240 Fabiani, Enzo. "Pagine di viaggio del romanziere dell'amore" (Travel Books of the Novelist of Love), GENTE (Milan), 16 Feb 1962.
[Review of *Libri di viaggio e pagine di paese (Complete Collection of Travel Books)* by D. H. Lawrence, with an Introduction by Piero Nardi (1961).] DHL wandered all his life and tried to approach people and study their way of life. But his obsession with the idea of his "new religion" led him to see a mythical divinity in any person in whom some elements of primitivism could be found. All this emerges very clearly from his travel books, where, when the writer prevails over the thinker, there are many wonderful pages of description. [In Italian.]

2241 Fairchild, Hoxie Neale. RELIGIOUS TRENDS IN ENGLISH POETRY, Vol. V: 1880-1920: GODS OF A CHANGING POETRY (NY and Lond: Columbia UP, 1962), pp. 261, 276-84, 323.
DHL, whose pre-1920 poems embody ideas which, in later guises, become "the central core of his prophecy," reflects "the shift from Evangelical Protestantism through latitudinarianism to romanticism." "His heresies may be thought of as protests against the incomplete orthodoxy of Christians." For him, "the seat of authority is not the cerebrum but the solar plexus." "In completely satisfying union with a woman," as in the victorious struggle in *Look! We Have Come Through!,* "we achieve union with the godhead of nature." The later DHL's "genuine wisdom was lost in . . . hysterical exaggeration, incoherence, embittered outrage, and mystagogic posturing." [See also Hoxie Neale Fairchild, RELIGIOUS TRENDS IN ENGLISH POETRY, Vol. VI: 1920-1965: VALLEY OF THE DRY BONES (NY and Lond: Columbia UP, 1968), pp. 22, 35, 100, 117-18, 129, 182-83, 193, 200-1, 218, 219-20, 221-22, 225, 226-27, 227-28, 254, 263, 271, 277, 279-81, 288, 290, 292-93, 299, 313-14, 355, 364, 366-70, 387-88, 394, 411, 435.]

2242 Fedder, Norman Joseph. "The Influence of D. H. Lawrence on Tennessee Williams," DISSERTATION ABSTRACTS, XXIV (1963), 742. Unpublished dissertation, New York University, 1962; rvd and pub as THE INFLUENCE OF D. H. LAWRENCE ON TENNESSEE WILLIAMS (The Hague, Lond, Paris: Mouton, 1966).

2243 Ford, George H. "Shelley or Schiller? A Note on D. H. Lawrence at Work," TEXAS STUDIES IN LITERATURE AND LANGUAGE, IV (Summer 1962), 154-56.
[A note to explain how, in describing the tastes Gudrun and Loerke share, DHL could overlook the error: " 'Particularly they liked the late eighteenth century, the period of Goethe, and of Shelley, and Mozart.' " T. S. Eliot's charge that DHL was inadequately educated notwithstanding, DHL's failure to delete "Shelley" was the result of his revising for "unity" and, in his haste, failing to note the error.]

2244 Gardner, John, and Lennis Dunlap. THE FORMS OF FICTION (NY: Random House, 1962), pp. 521-24.
"In form, 'The Fox' is a short novel. All three important characters change, and action is episodic. One way of seeing the structure of the short novel is to separate the episodes and to examine the part each episode plays in the total scheme."

2245 Garnett, David. THE FAMILIAR FACES (Lond: Chatto & Windus; NY: Harcourt, Brace & World, 1962), pp. xiii, 26, 79, 81, 105.
Although writers who "preach a gospel" inspire "enthusiasm and hero-worship," "sooner or later the message becomes boring and their reputations fade," a process which will overtake DHL, making *Women in Love* "unreadable," while non-message novels will survive. T. E. Lawrence once referred obliquely to the exhibition of DHL's pictures at the Warren Gallery (July 1929) as "Maddox Street prostitution," but on returning a copy of *Lady Chatterley's Lover,* which he had borrowed from David Garnett, he called DHL an artist.

2246 Gentry, Curt. "A New Collection of D. H. Lawrence Letters," in "A Bookman's Notebook," SAN FRANCISCO CHRONICLE, 21 March 1962, p. 41.
The Collected Letters of D. H. Lawrence, ed by Harry T. Moore, includes some 600 previously unpublished letters and reprints many others from *The Letters of D. H. Lawrence,* ed by Aldous Huxley (1932) and other volumes, restoring passages and names which were deleted on original publication. [Includes drawing of DHL.]

2247 Germer, Rudolph, and T. A. Burkill. "Modern Writers: D. H. Lawrence," PRAXIS DES NEUSPRACHLICHEN UNTERRICHTS (Practice of Modern Languages Instruction) (Dortmund, 1962), pp. 89-93.
There is some truth in T. S. Eliot's censure of DHL: The prophet DHL lacks a sense of humor and is too conscious of class distinctions and of his own low

birth; he is certainly not at his best in discursive thinking, and there is a certain morbidity in his emphasis on sex. However, the difficulties of the task envisaged by DHL must be taken into account. He broke into new intellectual territory outside orthodoxy and tradition. His "essential philosophy resolved itself into a form of sacramental or physicalistic mysticism." ...DHL's major ideas, many of them already present in *The White Peacock,* are developed and elaborated--sometimes *ad nauseam*--in later novels. [DHL's life, his literary activity and school editions are described briefly, and "Odour of Chrysanthemums" is highly recommended for German class discussion.]

2248 [Gomme, Andor]. "Friends and Enemies," TIMES LITERARY SUPPLEMENT (Lond), 27 April 1962, pp. 273-75; excerpt rptd as "High-Handed Publishers?" D. H. LAWRENCE NEWS AND NOTES, II (Spring 1962), 6-7; rptd in D. H. LAWRENCE: A CRITICAL ANTHOLOGY, ed by H. Coombes (Harmondsworth, Middlesex, England: Penguin Books, 1973), pp. 430-35.

The Collected Letters of D. H. Lawrence, ed by Harry T. Moore (1962), is not the definitive edition of DHL's letters. Many letters published in the Huxley edition (1932) and subsequent collections are duplicated here, but there is no record of letters not reprinted nor a list of unpublished letters. DHL's incredible energy, his courage and integrity, and the sensitivity and thoughtfulness he displayed in his personal relations are all found, direct and unrehearsed, in his letters. The letters constitute an autobiography and testify to the "wholeness of Lawrence's genius." Reading his letters is "an extraordinary experience, affording as no other can a real opening into the quality of Lawrence as a man and the intimate union between his life and his art."

2249 Gransden, K[arl] W[atts]. E. M. FORSTER (Edinburgh: Oliver & Boyd; NY: Grove P, 1962), pp. 108-18.

Although E. M. Forster was in some ways influenced by DHL, most noticeably in terms of didacticism, Forster became "ever more tentative" while DHL "became ever more emphatic."

2250 Greenwood, E. B. "Reflections on Professor Wellek's Concept of Realism," NEOPHILOLOGUS, XLVI (April 1962), 89-97, espec 90, 94.

The "fiction of art" is truer than the "universal fiction of ordinary perception." Symbolic art, as in the "Moony" chapter in *Women in Love,* is realistic art in that the actions do convincingly convey something other than themselves.

2251 Gregor, Ian, and Brian Nicholas. "The Novel as Prophecy: *Lady Chatterley's Lover* (1928)," THE MORAL AND THE STORY (Lond: Faber and Faber, 1962), pp. 217-48.

Two dominant ideas in *Lady Chatterley's Lover* are important for understanding the centrality of sex for DHL. The fulfillment of an individual's life depends on his capacity for an intimate sensual relationship with another, found most completely in sex. The achievement of that relationship brings the individual into union with the very source of life itself. DHL's interest in *Lady Chatterley's*

Lover is in the creation not of a realistic human situation but of a fable of life and death, with Mellors representing life and Clifford death. In Connie's rejection of Clifford and her acceptance of Mellors, she learns to live her own life. Disputes regarding DHL's attitude derive from a fundamental ambiguity in the pattern of the novel itself. The characters do not, as *characters,* convey the basic antithesis that DHL intends in the novel. His problem lies in trying to say something that cannot be dramatized in terms of the novel. *Lady Chatterley's Lover* is a religious novel, like THE END OF THE AFFAIR and THÉRÈSE DESQUEVRAUX. Sex, rather than characters, is the touchstone of DHL's concept of consciousness. Hence, DHL's dilemma: he wanted to restore a sacred character to sex but, because he was equally concerned to restore the shameless character of sex, he was unwilling to admit the corollary--sex is also taboo. With all this uncertainty, there is an over-simplification in *Lady Chatterley's Lover* not to be found in earlier novels. Unequivocal assertion has replaced complexity, and the novel clearly rejects interest in character, symbol, a public theory of "right and wrong." An interest in the personal and moral gradations of human beings may be a minimum requirement for the novelist.

2252 Gribble, Jennifer, and Alexander Porteous. "Leavis, Lawrence and Porteus [sic]," QUADRANT, VI, No. 2 (1962), 67-71.
[Jennifer Gribble's reply to Alexander Porteous, "The Strange Case of Dr Leavis and Mr Lawrence," QUADRANT, VI, No. 1 (1962), 11-22; and Porteous's rejoinder to her.] **Gribble**: Leavis's essay on *The Rainbow* demonstrates that a work's function beyond its validity as an "imaginative-moral" structure "arises from the achievement of the work as a whole, and can only be apprehended *through* a complete critical response to the work itself." "Lawrence's departure from 'tradition' lay in his opening up of areas of exploration quite new in the English novel." His style is indicative of his concern "with a more basic and intensive study of human relationships" than his predecessors. For a statement of DHL's idea of "fulfilment," one may turn to *Psychoanalysis and the Unconscious,* although "the notion is rendered satisfactorily by *The Rainbow* itself." DHL rejects the Christian concern with "love" because it involves the ego. **Porteous**: "Miss Gribble's . . . admirable exposition of a view of Lawrence's achievement in *The Rainbow*" arises "from a generous warmth in the reader's reception of some leading ideas derived from the work rather than from anything realized by the work itself." "The episode of the animal-child" exemplifies DHL's "central weaknesses as a novelist." "This imaginative and moral restriction" goes "hand in hand with the limitations and deficiencies of Lawrence's use of language." While Miss Gribble forcefully sets forth the "love ethic implicit in the novel," she does not show explicitly "its realization in the work itself."

2253 Gullason, Thomas A., and Leonard Gaspar (eds). THE WORLD OF SHORT FICTION: AN INTERNATIONAL COLLECTION (NY: Harper & Brothers, 1962), pp. 126-28, 535-36.
[Brief interpretive biography stresses that DHL was "a priest of love" whose primary interest was humanity. Cites Aldous Huxley's statements that DHL was concerned with "the otherness that lies beyond the boundaries of man's conscious

mind" and that DHL would force a work of art "into a semblance of more than human perfection."]

2254 Gurko, Leo. "*The Trespasser*: D. H. Lawrence's Neglected Novel," COLLEGE ENGLISH, XXIV (Oct 1962), 29-35.
The Trespasser "is more than a swatch of early Lawrence. . . .Though it is certainly a compendium of all his faults, it is also a coherent assemblage of nearly all his virtues." Chap. XXII, for example, "is one of the memorable sequences in Lawrence."

2255 Hall, Roland. "D. H. Lawrence and A. N. Whitehead," NOTES AND QUERIES, IX (May 1962), 188.
"The passages Sir Clifford reads out" in Chap. XVI of *Lady Chatterley's Lover* are "the last 2 1/3 paragraphs of A. N. Whitehead's RELIGION IN THE MAKING" (Cambridge UP, 1926), although the "quotations are not entirely accurate."

2256 Hasegawa, Toshimitsu. "D. H. Lawrence no *Women in Love* ni Tsuite" (On D. H. Lawrence's *Women in Love*), THE RITSUMEIKAN BUNGAKU (Ritsumeikan University), No. 208 (Oct 1962), 23-44.
[In Japanese.]

2257 Hassall, Christopher. "D. H. Lawrence and the Etruscans," ESSAYS BY DIVERS HANDS, ns XXXI (1962), 61-78.
[Begins with a brief history of our knowledge of the Etruscans.] DHL's Etruscan experience brought him to maturity as a poet and gave him insight into his relationship to traditional English poetry. Increasingly unable to accept the view of life embodied in an industrial civilization, DHL sought and found in Etruria a justification of the principles underlying his own conception of poetry. He saw the traditional poet sitting in contemplation, looking into the past or the future, but DHL concerned himself with the now, the present. Hence, he presented images that cannot last, cannot become static. His dominant theme in his Etruscan essays is that the beauty of Etruscan things lies in their evanescence. From the Etruscans DHL also learned an acceptance of death as part of the process of life. Etruscan art, like DHL's own writing, is suggestive rather than finished. Both in his poems and in his novels, DHL prefers a natural discipline of sincerity to a craftsman's discipline of form.

2258 Höltgen, K. J. "D. H. Lawrence's Poem 'Masses and Classes,' " NOTES AND QUERIES, IX (Nov 1962), 428.
DHL's "God cannot do without me" more likely comes from Angelus Silesius (Johann Scheffler) than from an "old Frenchman."

2259 Hough, Graham. "The Listener's Book Chronicle," LISTENER AND BBC TELEVISION REVIEW, LXVII (19 April 1962), 697.
"From the start, Lawrence had the gift of making letter-writing as lively and natural as talking." In *The Collected Letters of D. H. Lawrence*, both the writer and the recipients are "clearly present" in a relationship. DHL writes about both ideas and the "immediate scene."

2260 Hough, Graham. "The Listener's Book Chronicle," LISTENER AND BBC REVIEW, LXVII (21 June 1962), 1085, 1087.

The essays in *Studies in Classic American Literature* "were written in a very different frame of mind from . . . the far quieter and more considered original version[s]," now collected in *The Symbolic Meaning: The Uncollected Versions of "Studies in Classic American Literature,"* ed by Armin Arnold, which is arguably a better book. "It is certainly good to see Lawrence speaking of the American writers whom he loved in this temperate and sympathetic tone."

2261 Kai, Sadanobu. "D. H. Lawrence ni Okeru Shi to Fukkatsu--Shocho to Shiteno Fushicho ni Tsuite" (The Death and Resurrection in D. H. Lawrence, II: Phoenix as His Personal Symbol), STUDIES IN FOREIGN LITERATURES (Ritsumeikan University), No. 5 (Dec 1962), 50-72.

DHL's design of " 'a phoenix rising from the nest in flames' " for the cover of *Lady Chatterley's Lover* is described in *A Propos of "Lady Chatterley's Lover"* as " 'rising from the nest *of* flames' " (italics added), i.e., from the experience of death. The image of the phoenix appears repeatedly in DHL's earlier works: Will's buttermold in *The Rainbow*; husband and wife, soul and body in *Kangaroo*; the pattern of rebirth in the essay "Life"; and the poem "Phoenix" in *Last Poems*, a self-portrait in which the phoenix as "she" is related to the mother and the "bub" to the son or brother. [Examples are discussed in detail.] [In Japanese.]

2262 Karl, Frederick R. THE CONTEMPORARY ENGLISH NOVEL (NY: Farrar, Straus, & Girous; Toronto: Ambassador Books, 1962), pp. 3-8, 11, 18, 20, 40, 45, 48, 58, 59, 60, 63, 86, 96, 111, 126, 142-45, 152, 153, 164, 176, 189, 193, 195, 237, 249, 252, 263.

[DHL and other major modern novelists are used as touchstones for measuring the achievement of later contemporary novelists.] Of three modern English novelists, Conrad, Joyce, and DHL, who "pumped new life into a genre that had been declared dead," only DHL was native born. After DHL, no novelist fully believed "that man, like the phoenix, will rise from his own ashes." Lawrence Durrell "points toward but hardly reaches Lawrence's examination of love" and, like DHL, tries to replace traditional religious views with secular philosophy. Joyce Cary's characters, unlike DHL's, do not incorporate both mental and physical faculties in striving after balance but emphasize the lower plane at the expense of the higher. [Other novelists seen in brief parallels to DHL include Samuel Beckett, C. P. Snow, Elizabeth Bowen, George Orwell, Henry Green, John Osborne, Colin Wilson, and Nigel Dennis.]

2263 Kazin, Alfred. "Sons, Lovers, and Mothers," PARTISAN REVIEW, XXIX (Summer 1962), 373-85; also pub as "Introduction," *Sons and Lovers,* by D. H. Lawrence (NY: Random House, Modern Library, 1962), pp. vii-xix; rptd in D. H. LAWRENCE AND "SONS AND LOVERS": SOURCES AND CRITICISM, ed by E[rnest] W. Tedlock, Jr. (NY: New York UP, 1965), pp. 238-50; rptd in D. H.

LAWRENCE, "SONS AND LOVERS": TEXT, BACKGROUND, AND CRITICISM, ed by Julian Moynahan (NY: Viking P [Viking Critical Library Edition], 1968), pp. 597-610; rptd in TWENTIETH CENTURY INTERPRETATIONS OF "SONS AND LOVERS": A COLLECTION OF CRITICAL ESSAYS, ed by Judith Farr (Englewood Cliffs, NJ: Prentice-Hall, 1970), pp. 74-84; rptd in D. H. LAWRENCE: A COLLECTION OF CRITICISM, ed by Leo Hamalian (NY: McGraw-Hill, 1973), pp. 22-32.

"The striking thing about Lawrence . . . is his sense of his own authority." This sense of authority, on which rests all his power, grows out of the sacred, intense relationship with his mother. "The struggle in *Sons and Lovers* is not between love of the mother and love of a young woman; it is the hero's struggle to *keep* the mother as his special strength, never to lose her."

2264 Keller, Dean H. "An Uncollected Poem by Lawrence," D. H. LAWRENCE NEWS AND NOTES (California, PA), II, No. 3 (1962), 6.

DHL's poem "Creative Evolution" was published in TWO WORLDS (March 1926) but not included in either *The Collected Poems of D. H. Lawrence* (1928) or *The Complete Poems of D. H. Lawrence* (1957). [The poem is reproduced in full.] [See also D[exter] M[artin], "Note by D. M.," D. H. LAWRENCE NEWS AND NOTES, 11, No. 3 (1962), 6-7.]

2265 Kermode, Frank. "Lawrence in His Letters," NEW STATESMAN, ns LXIII (23 March 1962), 422-23.

The Collected Letters of D. H. Lawrence, ed by Harry T. Moore (1962), neither sufficiently conclusive nor adequately annotated, is not a significant addition to *The Letters of D. H. Lawrence,* ed by Aldous Huxley (1932). Although some of the letters could have been written only by a great man, others show how violent, vindictive, or egocentric a great man can be. *Collected Letters* covers DHL's theorizing on such concerns as the unhealthiness of modern English life, body vs. mind, darkness and light, and instinct. Equally prominent is his obsession with apocalypse and messianism. DHL is at his best in his sense of the quick as a form of creative reality, and our criticism of DHL's penchant to posit universals is based on criteria derived from his own great work.

2266 Kermode, J[ohn] Frank. "Spenser and the Allegorists," PROCEEDINGS OF THE BRITISH ACADEMY, XLVIII (1962), 261-79; rptd in SHAKESPEARE, SPENSER, DONNE, by Frank Kermode (NY: Viking P, 1971), pp. 12-32.

Although poetic allegorists have declined in esteem since Spenser, such modern writers as T. S. Eliot, Ezra Pound, and DHL are covertly allegorical. Whereas Spenser in THE FAERIE QUEENE converts myth into event by providing contemporary historical contexts for the biblical archetypes, DHL converts events into myths, fleeing from history into archetypes and "buried" apocalyptic meanings. For example, the sexual initiation of Connie and Mellors in *Lady Chatterley's Lover* is an allegory of personal rebirth (see the Opening of the Seals in Revelation) and also of national rebirth: Connie is England and Mellors is DHL's Arthur, emperor of the Last Days. Unlike Spenser, DHL pursues apocalyptic researches that are secret and remote from the modern world and sacrifices presence to type, making history part of a private myth.

2267 King, Willard L., and Kenneth B. Hawkins. "Lady Chatterley," AMERICAN BAR ASSOCIATION JOURNAL, XLVIII (Jan 1962), 43-47.
[Review of THE TRIAL OF LADY CHATTERLEY: REGINA v. PENGUIN BOOKS LIMITED, ed by C. H. Rolph (1961). Discusses the 1960 British trial in relation to English and American obscenity laws and compares the trial to other important American obscenity trials.]

2268 Koljevič, Svetozar. "Putevi suvremenog engleskog romana" (The Contemporary English Novel), DELO (Belgrade), No. 7 (1962), 870-89.
[DHL is one of the novelists considered.] [In Serbo-Croatian.]

2269 Kuramochi, Saburô. "D. H. Lawrence no Sekai" (The World of D. H. Lawrence), RONSHÛ (Senshû University), No. 31 (Dec 1962), 33-41.
[In Japanese.]

2270 "Lady Chatterley in Ottawa," CANADIAN FORUM, XLII (April 1962), 11-13.
[An account of the opinion of the Supreme Court of Canada on the appeal by the publishers, New American Library, of the 1960 conviction, under Section 150 (8) of the Criminal Code, of three Montreal newsdealers for selling copies of *Lady Chatterley's Lover*. The five to four decision reversed the judgment of the lower Court of Queen's Bench, Quebec, which had rejected the appeal, and returned confiscated copies of the novel to the Montreal newsdealers. Substantial passages from three of the seven written opinions by justices of the Supreme Court of Canada (one from a justice who voted with the majority and two from dissenting justices) are included. See also Paul C. Casey, "The Casey Judgement," TAMARACK REVIEW, XXI (Autumn 1961), 58-70, for a reprint of the Court of Queen's Bench opinion which had dismissed the appeal.]

2271 Lesser, M. X., and John N. Morris. THE FICTION OF EXPERIENCE: MODERN SHORT STORIES (NY: McGraw Hill, 1962), p. 58.
[Brief biographical headnote to "The Rocking-Horse Winner," which is reprinted in the anthology, pp. 59-73, mentioning DHL's Eastwood background, his early fiction, his elopement with Frieda Weekley, his censorship problems, and his " 'essentially poetic' " ideas.]

2272 Levy, Mervyn, Colin Wilson, and John Cohen. "The Paintings of D. H. Lawrence," THE STUDIO, CLXIV (Oct 1962), 130-35.
[Levy: Surveys the history of DHL's paintings and quotes from DHL's July 1929 article in THE STUDIO describing how he feels while painting.]

[Wilson] : DHL used sex as "the symbol of all that was opposed to what he hated," delighted in nakedness, and dealt with the sadistic, though not the homosexual, element of sex in his paintings.

[Cohen] : DHL's paintings emphasize the oral, anal, and genital centers of the body, illustrate "priapic themes," have allusive significance, present, allegorically, the man-woman relationship, and convey "some ineffably orgiastic and yet mystical message." [Five DHL paintings are reproduced.]

2273 Lindsay, Jack. "D. H. Lawrence," FANFROLICO AND AFTER (Lond: Bodley Head, 1962), pp. 149-52.

[Refutes the account of DHL's association with the Fanfrolico Press given by P(ercival) R(eginald) Stephensen, the author's partner in the firm.] Far from rejecting, DHL accepted the plan for Fanfrolico Press to publish a volume of reproductions of his paintings. After the Fanfrolico partnership was dissolved, Stephensen joined with the bookseller Edward Goldston to form the Mandrake Press, which brought out the book. Earp's criticism, " 'Alternately muddy and garish' as a description of Lawrence's colours will not do," but it accurately describes the "colour-work" of the Mandrake Press reproductions. DHL asked the author to check the statement about Henry VIII's syphilis in his "Introduction to These Paintings." The exhibition of DHL's paintings at the Dorothy Warren galleries opened on 15 June and was raided by the police on 5 July 1929. [See also Jack Lindsay, "Expatriate Publishing II," MEANJIN QUARTERLY, XXXIII (June 1974), 176-79.]

2274 Lo Curzio, Guglielmo. "Poesia di Lawrence" (Lawrence's Poetry), GAZZETTA DEL SUD (Messina), 24 Feb 1962, p. 3.

Tutte le poesie di D. H. Lawrence (*The Complete Poems of D. H. Lawrence*), trans and ed and with an Introduction by Piero Nardi (1959) has been considered by many critics the best in the world. DHL's poems are very useful for a deeper knowledge of his life and novels, even though in many poems DHL was not able to reach real poetic expression. The best poems are those about nature and instinct. [In Italian.]

2275 Lo Curzio, Guglielmo. "Tre romanzi di Lawrence" (Three Novels by Lawrence), GAZZETTA DEL SUD (Messina), 8 Dec 1962, p. 3.

Canguro, Il ragazzo nella boscaglia, Il serpente piumato (*Kangaroo, The Boy in the Bush, The Plumed Serpent*) published together in the Italian translation (1962), are among DHL's best novels. Australia provides the setting for the first two novels; in that country, DHL found an answer to his need for a natural life as opposed to progress and civilization. *The Boy in the Bush* is particularly well written because it is supported by a very solid narrative structure and is not weighted down with digressions. [In Italian.]

2276 Lohf, Kenneth A. (comp). THE COLLECTION OF BOOKS, MANUSCRIPTS, AND AUTOGRAPH LETTERS IN THE LIBRARY OF JEAN AND DONALD STRALEM (NY: Athoensen P, 1962), pp. 31-32.

[The Stralem library contains first editions of *The Prussian Officer and Other Stories* (Lond: Duckworth, 1914), *The Rainbow* (Lond: Methuen, 1915), *Women in Love* (NY: Privately Printed for Subscribers Only, 1920), and "nineteen additional titles in first edition."]

2277 Longville, Timothy. "The Longest Journey: D. H. Lawrence's *Phoenix*," CRITICAL QUARTERLY, IV (Spring 1962), 82-87.

All of DHL's work is unified by his vision--deriving "from the evangelical Christianity of his youth"--of the perpetual re-creation of the agony of Christ, which ought to issue in a re-creation of Eden. But the imagery DHL associates with "the moment of conversion from the New to the Old Testament attitudes, the central event in [his] work," "lays bare some of [his] deepest indecisions." As the pieces in *Phoenix: The Posthumous Papers of D. H. Lawrence* reveal, his analyses of the darkness "are far more alive and convincing than his visions of a recreated paradise."

2278 Lowe, Victor. UNDERSTANDING WHITEHEAD (Baltimore: The John Hopkins P, 1962), pp. 24, 106, 287.

Alfred North Whitehead has made it possible for "thinking man" to respond to DHL's feeling for nature "without having to swallow Lawrence's antiscientific extravagances." In Chap. XVI of *Lady Chatterley's Lover,* Clifford reads to Connie four sentences, without identification, from the conclusion to Whitehead's RELIGION IN THE MAKING, but DHL misinterprets the passage "as predicting a nonphysical order of nature" and mistakenly sees in Whitehead only another "despiser of the body."

2279 McCann, Charles. "Portraits of the Artists as Young Men: Fact versus Fiction," ENGLISH FICTION IN TRANSITION, V (1962), 27-29.

The ending of the artist-novel is defective because the artist-hero's success depends upon his "escape" from the fictional laws to which all the other characters of the novel are subject. In Joyce, Stephen Dedalus is exempted from these laws, while DHL's Paul Morel rises like a phoenix from the ruins about him. DHL intended a tragic view of life in *Sons and Lovers* (as he wrote to Edward Garnett). But he loaded the deck against the world for Paul Morel, making "escape" the right and inevitable thing. DHL tries to forestall the reader's reaction to this escape by emphasizing Morel's loneliness in the last paragraphs.

2280 MacInnes, Colin. "Experts on Trial: A Comment on Mr. Sparrow," ENCOUNTER, XVIII (March 1962), 63-65.

[Reply to John Sparrow, "Regina v. Penguin Books Ltd.: An Undisclosed Element in the Case," ENCOUNTER, XVIII (Feb 1962), 35-43.] The worst thing about the trial of *Lady Chatterley's Lover* is not that it failed to deal honestly with the book, e. g., with the passage to which Mr. Sparrow objected, but that people would betray DHL's greatness by agreeing to witness in defense of that which is superior to legal opinion. Mr. Sparrow's tone is that of a coroner's inquest, "but who cares if dopes, barristers, and idiots make idiots of themselves?" [See also rejoinder by John Sparrow, "Afterthoughts on Regina v. Penguin Books

Ltd.," ENCOUNTER, XVIII (June 1962), 83-88.]

2281 Mackenzie, Compton. "The Case of *Lady Chatterley's Lover*," ON MORAL COURAGE (Lond: Collins, 1962), pub in America as CERTAIN ASPECTS OF MORAL COURAGE (Garden City, NY: Doubleday, 1962), pp. 120-38.

The acquittal of the publisher in the prosecution of *Lady Chatterley's Lover* (Regina v. Penguin Books Ltd., 1960) was a signal victory for freedom of the press. [The account of the trial includes summaries and running commentary on the testimony given by the expert witnesses for the defense, including critics, writers, educators, and clergy.] Two motives for the novel were to project through Mellors what DHL would have liked to be physically and "to snatch from the head of James Joyce" the laurel wreath bestowed by Bloomsbury. The witnesses, in defense of a good cause, made themselves ridiculous by maintaining that in *Lady Chatterley's Lover* DHL really had offered to this " 'tragic age' " a means of salvation.

2282 Mackenzie, Compton. "Memories of D. H. Lawrence," ON MORAL COURAGE (Lond: Collins, 1962), pub in America as CERTAIN ASPECTS OF MORAL COURAGE (Garden City, NY: Doubleday, 1962), pp. 104-19.

[Taken by Gilbert Cannan to meet DHL and Frieda in August 1914, the author discovered DHL scrubbing the floor and found Frieda a genial hostess. When DHL and Frieda left England in 1919, they lived near Mackenzie in a small place above the Bay of Naples.] The beard which DHL had grown undoubtedly helped "in developing the messianic belief in himself . . . encouraged by his female disciples," who, he thought, represented, albeit somewhat subserviently, " 'the threshold of a new underworld of knowledge and being.' " Once DHL insisted that we must give up thinking with our minds and, pointing to his fly-buttons, " 'learn to think here.' " [The MS of *Fantasia of the Unconscious* was typed on Mackenzie's typewriter "of which only the red half of the ribbon was still usable."] Reading ULYSSES, as serialized in THE LITTLE REVIEW, DHL was "horrified" at Joyce's "old fags" and quotations stewed in "journalistic dirty-mindedness." Concerned about his inability to attain simultaneous sexual climax with his wife, DHL said that the nearest he had come to perfect love was with a young coalminer. Expounding on his theories of sex, DHL insisted that the Etruscans had thought with their genitals. DHL's treatment during the war years probably helped to unbalance him. The attack on *The Rainbow* resulting in its prosecution was led by James Douglas, and shamefully, no prominent author came to DHL's defense. DHL's "anti-Christian obsession was based on a personal jealousy of Jesus Christ." "His mind was as much hag-ridden by sex as that of John Knox." [This memoir formed the basis for reminiscences and comments on DHL scattered throughout Compton Mackenzie's ten-volume autobiography. See especially his MY LIFE AND TIMES, OCTAVE FIVE: 1915-1923 (Lond: Chatto & Windus, 1966), pp. 164-73, 176-79, 183-85, 189, 190-93, 235; MY LIFE AND TIMES, OCTAVE SIX: 1923-1930 (Lond: Chatto & Windus, 1967), pp. 84-85, 131-32, 170; MY LIFE AND TIMES, OCTAVE SEVEN: 1931-1938 (Lond: Chatto & Windus, 1968), pp. 35-36, 282; and MY LIFE AND TIMES, OCTAVE EIGHT:

1939-1946 (Lond: Chatto & Windus, 1969), p. 265.]

2283 Maldonado Denis, Manuel. "Sobre la lectura de *Lady Chatterley's Lover*" (Notes on *Lady Chatterley's Lover*), LA TORRE (University of Puerto Rico, San Juan), X (Jan-March 1962), 159-71.
Lady Chatterley's Lover shows DHL's desire to moralize, to make a value of eroticism. [See André Malraux, "D. H. Lawrence et l'érotisme. À propos de *l'Amant de Lady Chatterley*" (D. H. Lawrence and Eroticism: A propos of *Lady Chatterley's Lover*), LA NOUVELLE REVUE FRANÇAISE, XXXVIII (Jan-June 1932), 136-40, widely reprinted in Spanish translation in Latin America as a Preface to the novel.] DHL's preoccupation with the consequences of industrialism for modern man, and his rejection of money, give his work prophetic characteristics. The story of Constance and Mellors must be examined in the context of this sociological content of the novel. If there is any paganism in the work, it is in DHL's desire to elevate the rediscovery of the body to an aesthetic principle. Love for DHL is the fusion of two bodies into one, a fusion in which the lost communion between man and Cosmos is restored. DHL wanted to go beyond tragedy with its association of passion with suffering and death. Rather, his Romantic purpose was to return to man his lost innocence in relation to nature. Although *The Plumed Serpent* is a better novel in content and structure, *Lady Chatterley's Lover* has passages of great poetic beauty, and few writers have described the relationship between a man and a woman with greater artistic power. [In Spanish.]

2284 Marcuse, Ludwig. "London 1960: D. H. Lawrence oder purissimus penis (Kaiser Augustus über Horaz)" (London 1960: D. H. Lawrence or purissimus penis--Emperor Augustus on Horace), OBSZÖN: GESCHICHTE EINER ENTRÜSTUNG (Munich: Paul List Verlag, 1962), pp. 265-311; additional references, pp. 29, 39n, 41, 45, 143, 161, 263, 315, 316, 371, 391; pub in England as OBSCENE: THE HISTORY OF AN INDIGNATION, trans by Karen Gershon (Lond: MacGibbon & Kee, 1965), pp. 215-54; additional references, pp. 20, 22, 23, 24, 26, 27, 31, 44, 77, 79, 93, 96, 99, 107, 209, 214, 257, 283, 285, 286, 288, 304, 306, 321.
In the obscenity trial of *Lady Chatterley's Lover* in 1960 (Regina v. Penguin Books, Ltd.), the public prosecutor attempted to conjure up almost Victorian standards and outdated psychological views, contending that the novel does not condemn adultery. Even the defense counsel and thirty-five literary expert witnesses avoided a discussion of the artistic values and defended DHL with arguments which turned the contested scenes into pseudoreligious episodes. The "artistic power of the story-teller" was not made plausible. *Lady Chatterley's Lover* is a utopian book in which DHL sees sexuality as the deliverance from misery. [In German.]

2285 Marshall, Percy. MASTERS OF THE ENGLISH NOVEL (Lond: Dennis Dobson, 1962), pp. 11, 19, 23, 200-13.
[Literary history. Biographical sketch mentions the decimation by coal-mining interests of the once pastoral country of DHL's origin, the tensions between his parents, his high school scholarship, his serious illnesses, his friendship with

Jessie Chambers, his early publication in the ENGLISH REVIEW, his schoolteaching, his elopement with Frieda Weekley. Historical survey of his major fiction emphasizes the quality of "autobiography, lifted to the region of poetry," in *The White Peacock, The Trespasser,* and *Sons and Lovers;* the cycle of life and human relationships in *The Rainbow;* Philip Heseltine's threatened legal action against *Women in Love;* the autobiographical content, Australian scenery, and rejection of politics in *Kangaroo;* the conjunction between *The Plumed Serpent* and *Mornings in Mexico;* and the censorship of *Lady Chatterley's Lover.*]

2286 [Martin, Dexter]. "An Informal Bibliography (from June 1960 to April 1962)," D. H. LAWRENCE NEWS AND NOTES (California, PA), II (Spring 1962), 1-5.
[A bibliography of DHL, divided into eight sections as follows: "Articles," "Recent Hardbound Books about Lawrence," "Recent Paperbound Books about L(awrence) (American editions)," "Recent Paperbound Books about L(awrence) (English editions)," "Hardbound American Editions of L(awrence)," "Hardbound English Editions of L(awrence)," "Paperbound American editions of L(awrence)," and "Miscellaneous."]

2287 [Martin, Dexter]. "A Note about Frieda," D. H. LAWRENCE NEWS AND NOTES (California, PA), II (Spring 1962), 7-8.
Although DHL said of Frieda in 1930, " 'She's killing me, she's killing me,' " nothing has appeared in print about her "flaunting a love affair in his face while he was visibly dying." After his death she had an affair in London "with one of L's worst enemies, Murry." In SON OF WOMAN, "Murry includes certain sexual information--*or misinformation*--about L which could only have come from her."

2288 M[artin], D[exter]. "Note by D. M.," D. H. LAWRENCE NEWS AND NOTES (California, PA), II, No. 3 (1962), 6-7.
[This response to Dean H. Keller, "An Uncollected Poem by Lawrence," D. H. LAWRENCE NEWS AND NOTES, II, No. 3 (1962), 6, uses DHL's poem "The Work of Creation" as a gloss on his "Creative Evolution."]

2289 Martin, Dexter. "Three Types of Vitalism in *The Rainbow*," D. H. LAWRENCE NEWS AND NOTES (California, PA), II, No. 3 (1962), 8.
The microscope scene in "The Bitterness of Ecstasy" chapter in *The Rainbow* reveals DHL as "a mystical, non-Christian vitalist," but not yet a pantheist.

2290 [Martin, Dexter]. "Vs. Diana Trilling's Preface to her Portable Lawrence," D. H. LAWRENCE NEWS AND NOTES (California, PA), II (Spring 1962), 8.
[Refutes Diana Trilling's "Editor's Introduction" to *The Portable D. H. Lawrence* (1947), specifically with respect to her claims that DHL's " 'only god is the god of the sexual mystery,' " that DHL believed that man " 'achieved godhead' " in fulfilling " 'his sexual nature,' " that *The White Peacock* contains DHL's " 'loveliest descriptions' " of nature, and that Ramón in *The Plumed Serpent* " 'is the archetype of the fascist dictator.' "]

2291 Martin, W. R. "Fancy or Imagination? 'The Rocking-Horse Winner,' " COLLEGE ENGLISH, XXIV (Oct 1962), 64-65; rptd in D. H. LAWRENCE: "THE ROCKING-HORSE WINNER," ed by Dominick P. Consolo (Columbus, OH: Merrill [The Merrill Literary Casebook Series], 1969), pp. 52-54.

In "The Rocking-Horse Winner," the rocking horse, in ironic contrast with real race horses, which symbolize a fully lived life, symbolizes "the unlived, merely mimetic, life of Paul's parents." [See also replies by William D. Burroughs, "No Defense for 'The Rocking-Horse Winner,' " COLLEGE ENGLISH, XXIV (Jan 1963), 323; and Robert G. Lawrence, "Further Notes on D. H. Lawrence's 'Rocking-Horse,' " COLLEGE ENGLISH, XXIV (Jan 1963), 324.]

2292 Mibu, Ikuo. "Lawrence no Buntai" (Lawrence's Style), ENGLISH STUDIES (Nihon University), No. 12 (March 1962), 21-40.

[The style of *The Man Who Died.*] [In Japanese.]

2293 Miller, Nolan. "The 'Success' and 'Failure' of D. H. Lawrence," ANTIOCH REVIEW, XXII (Fall 1962), 380-92.

[Review article on DHL considering principally D. H. LAWRENCE: A COMPOSITE BIOGRAPHY, 3 vols., ed by Edward Nehls (1957, 1958, 1959), and *The Collected Letters of D. H. Lawrence,* ed by Harry T. Moore (1962).] The literary biographer's knowledge that typically he will be dealing with a man of many personal weaknesses gives him license to assume the "heroic authority of a point of view" to the detriment of the truth of his subject. In the more than eighty "memoirs" about DHL in Nehls's 1,800-page "composite biography" even the physical description of DHL is so inconsistent that he emerges as a faint blur. It is, therefore, still necessary to read the primary sources--the letters--to get an unblurred picture of him. These letters reveal that DHL from the beginning of his career suffered little from the problems that typically beset writers. Publishers were cooperative, and DHL had serene confidence in his spontaneity and judgment as an artist. The trouble with DHL was that this self-belief gradually became "belief," and his work became increasingly formulaic and unspontaneous. DHL diminished in point of "wholeness," partially because of Frieda, who saved him as a man, originally, but who ultimately destroyed him as a writer by not believing in his art.

2294 Moore, Harry T. "Introduction" and "Who's Who in the Lawrence Letters," *The Collected Letters of D. H. Lawrence,* 2 vols., ed by Harry T. Moore (NY: Viking P; Lond: Heinemann, 1962), pp. ix-xxvii, xxix-lvi.

DHL's letters are a "useful basis for biography" and tell "the full story of his life as no other medium can." They reveal the development of his works and ideas--especially in the large groups of letters to Blanche Jennings, Helen Corke, Edward Garnett, J. M. Murry, and S. S. Koteliansky--and serve as "comments on modern civilization." The "full texts of as many letters as possible" are reproduced; annotation is sparse because of space restrictions and because "after a while the letters explain one another." [The editor provides an alphabetical guide to correspondents and persons mentioned significantly in DHL's letters.]

2295 Moore, Harry T. "*Lady Chatterley's Lover*: The Novel as Ritual," pub as "Afterword" to *Lady Chatterley's Lover,* by D. H. Lawrence, "Complete, Unexpurgated Authorized Edition" (NY: New American Library, Signet Books, 1962), pp. 285-99.

Beginning *Lady Chatterley's Lover* in Oct 1926 at age forty-one, DHL completed the final version in Jan 1928, "barely two years before his death." Knowing that it could not be published in England and America and unable to cut it, DHL brought out the first edition in unexpurgated form in Florence; later, because of piracies, he authorized a cheap Paris edition. Although the first unexpurgated American edition, which was banned from the mails in 1959, was judged by Judge Frederick vanPelt Bryan not to be legally obscene (Grove Press v. Christenberry), in the Canadian trial the book was ruled obscene by Judge T. A. Fontaine in a decision later reversed by the Supreme Court of Canada. In *Lady Chatterley's Lover,* DHL attempted "to create a harmony" between "mind knowledge" and "blood knowledge," and used "the shock words as weapons on his side of the war" between the two. In the background of the novel's composition are DHL's visit to the Midlands in 1926, which inspired the "industrialized setting," and his tour of the Etruscan tombs in 1927. DHL thought that the "way to salvation was through love, . . . a tender, even sacred, complete union of a man and a woman who . . . retain their separate identities." DHL recognized, after the fact, that Clifford was symbolic of a " 'deeper emotional or passional paralysis' "; yet the character would have served him better had he been, like Gerald Crich, "crippled only within." But DHL sympathized with Clifford even in satiric scenes, and he could "now be a Mellors only in theory." Wragby, based on Lambclose, near Eastwood, has symbolic dimensions in the novel. DHL drew on the Sleeping Beauty motif for the love story and continued the Medieval romance tradition of Tristan and Iseult.

2296 Moore, Harry T. "Preface," *The Symbolic Meaning: The Uncollected Versions of "Studies in Classic American Literature,"* by D. H. Lawrence, ed by Armin Arnold (Lond: Centaur P, 1962; NY: Viking P, 1964), pp. ix-xi.

The original versions of the essays collected in *Studies in Classic American Literature* resulted not only from DHL's "wartime dissatisfaction with England and his desire to go to America" but also from his long admiration of Cooper, his profound influence by Whitman, and his discovery during the war years of Melville's moving fiction about the Pacific. Today DHL's critical insights are recognized along with his "creative powers."

2297 Mori, Haruhide. "Mujun to Shôsô no Hyôgen: *Women in Love,* Jinbutsu to Imêji" (Expression of Irritation and Contradiction: Characterization and Imagery in *Women in Love*), PRELUDE (Osaka University), No. 6 (Sept 1962), 26-35.

[In Japanese.]

2298 Mori, Haruhide. "*The Rainbow* no Kôzô Imeiji no Hassô Oyobi Sakusô to Tenkai" (The Structure of *The Rainbow* and a Study of Its Imagery), ÔSAKA LITERARY REVIEW (Ôsaka University), No. 1 (April 1962), 57-69.

[In Japanese.]

2299 Morrill, Claire. "Taos Echoes of D. H. Lawrence," SOUTH-WEST REVIEW, XLVII (Spring 1962), 150-56.
[Anecdotes, impressions, snatches of DHL's poetry, assembled by a writer who arrived in Taos, New Mexico, twenty-two years after DHL left.] In Taos DHL made a "personal impact" on "the Lawrence circle," but, although he was "happier here" than anywhere else, he "had almost no connection" with the village itself. [See also Claire Morrill, A TAOS MOSAIC: PORTRAIT OF A NEW MEXICO VILLAGE (Albuquerque: University of New Mexico P, 1973), pp. 106-28.]

2300 Moseley, Edwin M. "Christ as Artist and Lover: D. H. Lawrence's *Sons and Lovers,*" PSEUDONYMS OF CHRIST IN THE MODERN NOVEL (Pittsburgh, PA: University of Pittsburgh P, 1962), pp. 69-87, additional references pp. 89-91, 102.
Examination of *Sons and Lovers,* with the Freudian Oedipus complex in mind, sharply outlines one aspect of the novel, the antagonism of mother and son against the father, who figuratively imprisons the spiritual and intellectual Gertrude in a hellish life as a collier's wife. But the oedipal pattern is modified by the fact that Gertrude can fight her own battles, whereas Walter Morel is quickly and decisively defeated. Consequently, the book focuses on the problem of possessive and jealous mother love. In a sense the father's defeat is so complete that Gertrude Morel is a virgin-Madonna who conceived Paul "immaculately." Similarly, Miriam expects Paul to be Christ-like in abnegating the flesh. Paul's growth beyond--and survival of--both these women suggests that, for DHL, the traditional soul-body dualism expressed man's basic quest, with the significant qualification that DHL reversed the emphasis to stress the physical-emotional self rather than the spiritual one. In *The Man Who Died,* DHL confirms this reversal by depicting Christ's "rebirth" as a reversal of attitudes, an abandonment of his youthful sense of mission, and a quest for life in the flesh.

2301 Myers, Neil. "Lawrence and the War," CRITICISM, IV (Winter 1962), 44-58.
The compelling force of DHL's post-war work "rises directly from horrified experience of the universe" described in " 'The Nightmare,' *England My England,* and *Aaron's Rod* . . . , from a vision of nothing less than what was to emerge in the corruption of slayer and slain at Auschwitz and Hiroshima."

2302 Nardi, Piero. "Introduzione" (Introduction), *Canguro, Il ragazzo nella bescaglia, Il serpente piumato* (*Kangaroo, The Boy in the Bush, The Plumed Serpent*) (Milan: A. Mondadori, 1962), pp. xv-xl.
Kangaroo is based on DHL's own experience and reveals how much he was impressed by Australia as an untouched country. The central idea of this novel is the proposal of a new political order based on the authority principle. *The Boy in the Bush* is centered on DHL's idea of the need to replace the spiritual concept of life with a sensual one. The contribution of Mollie Skinner to the writing of this novel was decisive in giving it a solid narrative structure. *The Plumed Serpent* reflects DHL's experience in New Mexico, above all his knowledge of the "pueblo" of Taos and his subsequent recognition of the Indians' way of life

as more meaningful than that of civilized peoples. [In Italian.]

2303 Nardi, Piero. "Introduzione" (Introduction), *Racconti (Complete Short Stories)* by D. H. Lawrence (Milan: A. Mondadori, 1962), pp. xvii-xxx.

"A Prelude to a Happy Christmas," the first short story written by DHL, is free of any Messianic ambition and reflects only real life. This is true also for his other early short stories. Among these, "Odour of Chrysanthemums," which can be considered an excellent example of realism, is particularly important from an artistic point of view. "A Fragment of Stained Glass," "A Modern Lover," and "The Shades of Spring" reveal a tendency to aestheticism but always as an aspect of reality. "Adolf" and "Rex" are about DHL's childhood as seen by the mature DHL. This is the source of some contradictions: because DHL is mainly interested in communicating his ideas on instinct and the importance of the primitive way of life, he is sometimes led to distort the meaning of what really happened in his childhood. The change determined in his life and ideas by Frieda appears very clearly in "A Chapel Among the Mountains," "A Hay Hut Among the Mountains," and "Once," while "The Prussian Officer" and "The Thorn in the Flesh" reveal Frieda's contribution to DHL's understanding of Freudianism and to the accentuation of his Messianism. [In Italian.]

2304 Nardi, Piero. "I viaggi di Lawrence" (Lawrence's Travels), IL RESTO DEL CARLINO (Bologna), 7 April 1962, p. 3.

DHL's restless nature drove him to seek relief in voyages and the new experiences afforded by far away countries and alien cultures, which find reflection also in many of his writings. Two typical examples are *Kangaroo* and *The Boy in the Bush,* now for the first time translated into Italian. [In Italian.]

2305 Nardi, Piero. "Lawrence amava l'Italia come si ama una bella donna" (Lawrence Loved Italy as One Loves a Beautiful Woman), IL TEMPO (Rome), 3 March 1962, p. 3.

[Comment on *Libri di viaggio e pagine di paese (Complete Collection of Travel Books)* by D. H. Lawrence, with an Introduction by Piero Nardi (1961).] In his travel books DHL is concerned with the search for proofs to sustain his belief in instinct as opposed to intellect. But this proves to be a weakness, because it leads him to interpret everything in terms of this idea. For instance, he states that the Italians considered sex as a manifestation of divinity. In any case DHL's travel books contain many wonderful descriptions of places and people, above all in relation to Italy. [In Italian.]

2306 Nardi, Piero. "Lawrence scoperse l'Australia come un mondo ancora vergine" (Lawrence's Discovery of Australia as an Untouched World), IL TEMPO (Rome), 22 April 1962, p. 3.

Kangaroo and *The Boy in the Bush* (trans into Italian, with an Introduction by Piero Nardi) can be considered travel books. The latter is more effective because it has a very tightly knit structure, while *Kangaroo,* like other DHL novels, is often interrupted by pointless digressions. [In Italian.]

2307 Nazareth, Peter. "D. H. Lawrence and Sex," TRANSITION, II (Oct 1962), 54-57.

[First part of a two-part article, the second part of which is pub in TRANSITION, III (March 1963), 39-43.] In order to see beyond DHL's popular reputation as a writer on sex, one must examine his style and convictions, which show sexuality as part of the fundamental rhythm and pattern of physical life and of the expression of the constant amid discontinuity. Denouncing those who love mechanically, only with the body or only through the mind, DHL advocates experiencing love with one's whole being in a sensual, yet tender, passion. [These ideas are examined in the lives of the characters in *Lady Chatterley's Lover* and *The Rainbow,* as are DHL's concepts of the unconscious self and the mind (akin to Freud's "ego" and "id"), and of separateness and otherness.]

2308 Newman, Paul B. "D. H. Lawrence and THE GOLDEN BOUGH," KANSAS MAGAZINE, 1962, pp. 79-86.

The essential organizing myths of *Women in Love* are taken directly from Frazer's THE GOLDEN BOUGH. Birkin and Gerald are incarnations of vegetative dying gods, with Birkin twice born but Gerald refusing rebirth. The two Brangwen sisters are embodiments of the moon goddess, with Ursula, initially destructive, ultimately foregoing conscious will and assuming the beneficent features of the fertility goddess, while Gudrun remains a sinister incarnation of Cybele, mating with her lover on a mountain top, destroying him, and taking the artist Loerke as her sodomitic priest.

2309 Nogara, Gino. "Il lungo viaggio italiano dell'autore di *Lady Chatterley*" (The Long Italian Journey of the Author of *Lady Chatterley*), LA PROVINCIA (Cremona), 4 July 1962, p. 7.

[Review of *Libri di viaggio e pagine di paese* (*Complete Collection of Travel Books*) by D. H. Lawrence, with an Introduction by Piero Nardi (1961).] DHL is among the most authentic and honest writers of the twentieth century; therefore, even though many of the ideas he expresses in his travel books are highly debatable, they must be respected. On the whole, DHL's travel books are very useful for a deeper knowledge of his work. [In Italian.]

2310 Noon, William T. "God and Man in Twentieth-Century Fiction," THOUGHT (NY), XXXVII (Spring 1962), 35-56, espec 43-49.

The art of Kafka, DHL, and Joyce presents three theological perspectives. Kafka's distorted inner world contains in itself no clue to an incarnation; transcendence lies beyond. DHL looks inward to the underlying immanence. As an "apostate Protestant," DHL must fashion his own vision based not on impotence, as in Kafka, but on physical-mystical sexual powers. Exaggeration often mars his message, as in *Lady Chatterley's Lover,* where the characterization defies realism, but seen as parables, his works are effective. The Holy Ghost, who brings light and order out of chaos, is missing in DHL's phallic religion. Human love finds it difficult to survive, and DHL chronicles mostly failures. Yet his intensity, if we can avoid its desperation, is illuminating. Joyce's artistic tactic was to set himself up in deliberate opposition to the word of the Church and to place his faith only in art.

2311 Nordell, Rod. "A Writer in His Letters," in "From the Book-Shelf" column, CHRISTIAN SCIENCE MONITOR, 21 March 1962, p. 9.

Although DHL's letters reveal his "vivid personality," they have "the shortcomings of that personality," as when, preoccupied with *Lady Chatterley's Lover,* DHL "talks less about art and more about his sexual theories," thus revealing "the fundamental narrowness of his superficially expansive view of life." [Review of *The Collected Letters of D. H. Lawrence,* ed by Harry T. Moore.]

2312 Nott, Kathleen. "Whose Culture?" LISTENER AND BBC TELEVISION REVIEW, LXVII (12 April 1962), 631-32, and (19 April 1962), 677-78; rvd and expanded in "Lawrence by Leavis," in A SOUL IN THE QUAD, by Kathleen Nott (Lond: Routledge & Kegan Paul, 1969), pp. 283-96.

F. R. Leavis, by placing DHL in the line of "The Great Tradition," has forced him into a fabricated moral and aesthetic tradition in which he does not belong. DHL does not exhibit a great artist's "maturing awareness," which brings about "a greater depth in characterization, a more persuasive illusion of reality, a more closely bound and complex logic of action, and a more subtly contrapuntal kind of dialogue." Dr. Leavis "believes that the germ of culture is in the creative responses of individuals. . . . But in Lawrence he seems to have chosen the wrong cultural hero." [Polemic aimed chiefly at Leavis.]

2313 Ôhashi, Yasuichirô. "Shijin Lawrence to Girisha Shinwa" (Greek Mythology in D. H. Lawrence's Poetry), MEMOIRS OF HUMANISTIC AND SOCIAL SCIENCES (Kyôto Technical University), No. 11 (Dec 1962), 63-95.

[In Japanese.]

2314 Okada, Taiji. "D. H. Lawrence to Indo" (D. H. Lawrence and India), REVIEW OF KÔBE UNIVERSITY OF MERCANTILE MARINE: PART I: STUDIES IN HUMANITIES AND SOCIAL SCIENCE, No. 10 (March 1962), 177-207.

[In Japanese.]

2315 Okumura, Tôru. "Lawrence to Daiichiji Taisen" (Lawrence and the First World War), ENGLISH LITERATURE REVIEW (Kyôto Women's University), No. 6 (March 1962), 1-21.

[In Japanese.]

2316 Oldsey, Bernard S. "Lawrence's 'Error' about Hawthorne's Pearl," D. H. LAWRENCE NEWS AND NOTES (California, PA), II, No. 3 (1962), 2-4.

DHL's error, in "Nathaniel Hawthorne and THE SCARLET LETTER," in saying that Pearl "married an Italian Count" is explained by his attitude in the following essay, "Hawthorne's BLITHEDALE ROMANCE," toward Zenobia, a character based on Margaret Fuller, who "apparently" married Giovanni Angello, Marquis Ossoli.

2317 Panichas, George A. "D. H. Lawrence, Religious Seeker." Unpublished dissertation, University of Nottingham, 1962. [Listed in Lawrence F. McNamee, DISSERTATIONS IN ENGLISH AND AMERICAN LITERATURE (NY and Lond: Bowker, 1968), p. 613]. Rvd and pub as ADVENTURE IN CONSCIOUSNESS: THE MEANING OF D. H. LAWRENCE'S RELIGIOUS QUEST (The Hague, Lond, Paris: Mouton, 1964).

2318 Panichas, George A. "Voyage of Oblivion: The Meaning of D. H. Lawrence's Death Poems," ENGLISH MISCELLANY (Rome), XIII (1962), 135-64; rptd as Chap. VIII: "Voyage of Oblivion," in ADVENTURE IN CONSCIOUSNESS: THE MEANING OF D. H. LAWRENCE'S RELIGIOUS QUEST, by George A. Panichas (The Hague: Mouton, 1964), pp. 180-207.

DHL's "preoccupation with the meaning of death" is powerfully revealed in *Last Poems,* a profound part of a "spiritual autobiography," written during his final illness. As death drew nearer, DHL "gained a greater tranquility" and "turned his thoughts to the ancient Greeks, to God, and to death itself." DHL's interest was not in classic Hellenism but in the pre-Socratic world. In "The Greeks Are Coming!" he describes "the voyagers from Cnossos," and in "For the Heroes Are Dipped in Scarlet," he celebrates "men who bravely adventure into life." "The full religious significance of his vision of life and of death" emerges in "the interrelationship of Lawrence's death poems with those on his concept of God and the pagan Greeks." "Bavarian Gentians," with its "mythological framework" and its freedom from "intellectual deliberateness," presents the "religious seeker" in a "synthesis of Christian and pagan symbols" and "sets the theme of all his death poetry." The image of death as a journey is reiterated in "Difficult Death" and "All Soul's Day." The poems "Death," "Two Ways of Living and Dying," "The Houseless Dead," and "Beware the Unhappy Dead" concern the "unhappy dead," those who, having been life-deniers, are unprepared for the final voyage. "The End, the Beginning," "Sleep," "Sleep and Waking," and "Tabernacle" suggest that death, like life, is a mystery indefinable in absolute terms. The concept of death as "decay and corruption, followed by rebirth and renewal," as seen in "Shadows," is "endemic to most" of the death poetry. The most remarkable of these poems is "The Ship of Death," with its effect of "a deep religious intensity arising from the poet's integrity of affirmation." "It should be read in conjunction with" *The Man Who Died, Apocalypse,* and *Etruscan Places* for its presentation of DHL's "belief that the resurrection of life is not a matter of sin and salvation," his "distrust of doctrinal promises of after-life," and his approval of the Etruscan concept of "death as a further sojourn in the 'living continuum.' " [The ten sections of "The Ship of Death" are discussed in detail.] "Not only in its dignity and hope, but also in its piety and humility, his vision echoes an unqualified message of rebirth and renewal."

2319 Peter, John. "The Bottom of the Well," ESSAYS IN CRITICISM, XII (April 1962), 226-27.

[Reply to G. Wilson Knight, "Lawrence, Joyce and Powys," ESSAYS IN CRITICISM, XI (Oct 1961), 403-417. Refutes Knight's theory that *Lady Chatterley's*

Lover celebrates sodomy, suggesting that Knight has based his argument on quotations taken out of context and a confusion of the literal and figurative. See also further discussions in the controversy as follows: John Sparrow, "Regina v. Penguin Books Ltd.: An Undisclosed Element in the Case," ENCOUNTER, XVIII (Feb 1962), 35-43; "Afterthoughts on Regina v. Penguin Books Ltd.," ENCOUNTER, XVIII (June 1962), 83-88; John Peter, "Lady Chatterley Again," ESSAYS IN CRITICISM, XII (Oct 1962), 445-47; William Empson, "Lady Chatterley Again," ESSAYS IN CRITICISM, XIII (Jan 1963), 101-4; John Sparrow, "Lady Chatterley Again," ESSAYS IN CRITICISM, XIII (April 1963), 202-5; John Peter, "Lady Chatterley for the Last Time I," ESSAYS IN CRITICISM, XIII (July 1963), 301-2; and John Sparrow, "Lady Chatterley for the Last Time II," ESSAYS IN CRITICISM, XIII (July 1963), 303.]

2320 Peter, John. "Lady Chatterley Again," ESSAYS IN CRITICISM, XII (Oct 1962), 445-47.
[Rejoinder to John Sparrow, "Regina v. Penguin Books Ltd.: An Undisclosed Element in the Case," ENCOUNTER, XVIII (Feb 1962), 35-43. Refutes Sparrow's support of G. Wilson Knight's reading of *Lady Chatterley's Lover* as in part a celebration of sodomy; cites quotations from Chap. XIV of the novel as evidence that DHL rejected unconventional sexual practices. See also further discussions in the controversy as follows: G. Wilson Knight, "Lawrence, Joyce and Powys," ESSAYS IN CRITICISM, XI (Oct 1961), 403-17; John Peter, "The Bottom of the Well," ESSAYS IN CRITICISM, XII (April 1962), 226-27; John Sparrow, "Afterthoughts on Regina v. Penguin Books Ltd.," ENCOUNTER, XVIII (June 1962), 83-88; William Empson, "Lady Chatterley Again," ESSAYS IN CRITICISM, XIII (Jan 1963), 101-4; John Sparrow, "Lady Chatterley Again," ESSAYS IN CRITICISM, XIII (April 1963), 202-5; John Peter, "Lady Chatterley for the Last Time I," ESSAYS IN CRITICISM, XIII (July 1963), 301-2; and John Sparrow, "Lady Chatterley for the Last Time II," ESSAYS IN CRITICISM, XIII (July 1963), 303.]

2321 Pinto, Vivian de Sola. "Lawrence's Poetry," CRITICAL QUARTERLY, IV (Spring 1962), 81.
[Further comment on Henry Gifford, "The Defect in Lawrence's Poetry," CRITICAL QUARTERLY, III (Summer 1961), 164-66.] Dislike as intense as that directed at DHL's poetry has been incurred by Wordsworth and Byron, both of whom, like DHL, wrote a lot of inferior verse. But hell and DHL are preferable to heaven and Pound and his adulators! [See also Vivian de Sola Pinto, "Poet Without a Mask," CRITICAL QUARTERLY, III (Spring 1961), 5-18, to which Gifford's note was a reply; and rejoinders by Vivian de Sola Pinto, "Mr. Gifford and D. H. Lawrence," CRITICAL QUARTERLY, III (Autumn 1961), 267-68; and Gāmini Salgādo, "Mr. Gifford and D. H. Lawrence," CRITICAL QUARTERLY, III (Autumn 1961), 268-70.]

2322 Porteous, Alexander. "The Strange Case of Dr Leavis and Mr Lawrence," QUADRANT, VI, No. 1 (1962), 11-22.
"Rival twin-hegemonies" have reared "two stern citadels," each proclaiming "a body of inoppugnable doctrine: the votaries of Pound and his prophet Eliot; and

those of Lawrence and his prophet Leavis," although in recent years Pound's reputation has declined while DHL's has risen. Leavis was wrong about both "the importance of Lawrence's achievement . . . and its nature." *The Rainbow* has "two main strengths": a "robust rendering of . . . vernacular rural life" and a "delicate reporting of certain occasions . . . where the human and the natural situation" are serenely harmonized. But DHL's "function as 'a social historian,' " which Leavis emphasizes, is "peripheral to the achievement of his novel as a structure of imagination." Leavis deals inadequately with the critical charges that *The Rainbow* lacks formal artistic structure, that it fails to transmute into art the "great gobbets of Lawrence's own experience which it incorporates," and with its "gravest weakness," its "very damaging inelegance of language." [Instances in the novel of each of these "weaknesses" are discussed.] Leavis's comments serve only "to isolate and render inescapable the problem of the second-rate Romanticism of Lawrence's basic attitudes," as "a prophet of Romantic self-fulfilment, including sexual fulfilment, spiced with Nonconformist righteousness." Both DHL and Leavis emphasize the abstraction "sex" and avoid the word "love." [See also reply to Jennifer Gribble and rejoinder by Alexander Porteous, "Leavis, Lawrence and Porteus [sic]," QUADRANT, VI, No. 2 (1962), 67-71.]

2323 Prisco, Michele. "Lawrence in Italia" (Lawrence in Italy), IL MATTINO (Naples), 21 April 1962, p. 3.

[Review of *Libri di viaggio e pagine di paese* (*Complete Collection of Travel Books*) by D. H. Lawrence, with an Introduction by Piero Nardi (1961).] The Italian experience was very important in DHL's life, as can be seen from his books on Italy. Particularly interesting is his description of Southern Italy, which is always unconventional even when he dwells on the commonplace. [In Italian.]

2324 Raymond, John. "The Georgian Literary Scene: Secker's World," SUNDAY TIMES (Lond), "Magazine Section," 18 March 1962, pp. 32-33.

[Feature article based on interviews with Martin Secker at age eighty, including discussion of Secker's publication of DHL's books from 1920 on, his friendship with DHL, and his preference for the expurgated text of *Lady Chatterley's Lover* as published in 1932. Illustrated with photographs of Secker.]

2325 "Regina v. Penguin," ENCOUNTER, XVIII (March 1962), 94-96.

[Four Letters to the Editor in reply to John Sparrow, "Regina v. Penguin Books Ltd.: An Undisclosed Element in the Case," ENCOUNTER, XVIII (Feb 1962), 35-43. Views expressed by the correspondents are as follows: **David Sylvester**: Sparrow's objection to DHL's " 'covert and oblique' " language in the scene in question in *Lady Chatterley's Lover* "evaporates" when one realizes that, unlike such erotic writers as Cleland, Sade, Apollinaire, and Miller, DHL nowhere speaks "of the physiology and technology of sex" in " 'plain and forthright' " language and gives " 'detailed descriptions' " only of "emotions and feelings"; **Stephen Potter**: Although Sparrow charges both "Crown and Defence" with "bungling" and the witnesses with "humbug," his own account is riddled with inconsistencies and inaccuracies, falsely generalizes from the particular instance, and never mentions "that in the poems and the novels as a whole, sex is certainly not the predominating theme"; **Francis Bondy**: cites a Goethe parallel to DHL's reference to Cellini; and **R. T.**: asks (in verse), *"But can a soul-sick Sparrow tell / The orifice that leads to Hell?"* See also two additional selections of letters: "Regina v. Penguin," ENCOUNTER, XVIII (April 1962), 93-95; and "Regina v. Penguin," ENCOUNTER, XVIII (May 1962), 91-94; and rejoinder by John Sparrow, "Afterthoughts on Regina v. Penguin Books Ltd.," ENCOUNTER, XVIII (June 1962), 83-88.]

2326 "Regina v. Penguin," ENCOUNTER, XVIII (April 1962), 93-95. [Five Letters to the Editor in reply to John Sparrow, "Regina v. Penguin Books Ltd.: An Undisclosed Element in the Case," ENCOUNTER, XVIII (Feb 1962), 35-43. Views expressed by the correspondents are as follows: **Frederick May**: "It is not . . . a failure in honest writing if Lawrence expresses himself in a formal pattern of symbols and classical references" rather than a prose statement such as " 'He then effected anal connection' "; **Jayanta Padmanabha**: citing DHL's allusion to Abelard's statement on passing " 'through all the stages and refinements of passion,' " quotes two Latin extracts from Abelard and supports Sparrow's reading by pointing out Mellors's reference to intercourse " 'in the Italian manner' " and his use of a "more forceful" term in conversation with Sir Clifford; **Alec Craig**: DHL's advocacy of anal intercouse, a "not uncommon" practice which the British working class call " 'to soldier,' " "is an integral part of Lawrence's general gospel of primitive sexuality, phallic worship,'dark gods,' and the like"; **R. A. Raphael**: comments on Sparrow (in verse): *"Let us revere this interchange of roles / As Warden of All Bodies, not All Souls"*; **David Tudor-Pole**: History will show that the trial was not "the apogee of humbug" but "a significant breakthrough in releasing hitherto 'undiscussable' problems into a wider area of enquiry and debate." See also two additional selections of letters: "Regina v. Penguin," ENCOUNTER, XVIII (March 1962), 94-96; and "Regina v. Penguin," ENCOUNTER, XVIII (May 1962), 91-94; and rejoinder by John Sparrow, "Afterthoughts on Regina v. Penguin Books Ltd.," ENCOUNTER, XVIII (June 1962), 83-88.]

2327 "Regina v. Penguin," ENCOUNTER, XVIII (May 1962), 91-94. [Fourteen Letters to the Editor in reply to John Sparrow, "Regina v. Penguin Books Ltd.: An Undisclosed Element in the Case," ENCOUNTER, XVIII (Feb 1962), 35-43. Views expressed by the correspondents are as follows: **Isabella Halstead, Jacqueline Ross**, and **James Ross**(satirically): "We demand, in accordance with English Law, that the case of D. H. Lawrence be reconsidered" for such crimes as "committing underhanded literary indirection when we all expect and prefer the horrid details"; **Hector Hawton**: "I don't believe the novel will entice anyone to practice the vice [of buggery]," but DHL's "whole attitude to women was distorted and pernicious"; **Francois Bondy**: corrects errors in his "erratically printed" earlier letter (March 1962); **Nicolas Walter**: The witnesses "were forced into the position of having to defend the bad against the worse," but the trial was a necessary step toward "the freedom to read"; **Osbert Lancaster** (on Mellors, in verse): *"But now the Oxford Commissars insist / He was a backwing deviationist"*; **Pandora**: The critics "claim for Lawrence's sexual philosophy a respect for *nature,*" but "Lawrence resents the natural female orgasm" and hammers "at the notion that the woman must be a 'thing' "; **Henry Adler:** *Pornography and Obscenity* shows that DHL hated diversions from sexual fulfillment, such as masturbation, and attacked "the vulgar confusions between the 'sex functions and the excrementory functions' "; **Nathaniel Tarn:** "It would have been cleaner and saner in the long run for *Lady Chatterley* to have been damned for what it is than to have had it saved for only a part of what it could be"; **Alan M. Cohn:** Sparrow and G. Wilson Knight ["Lawrence, Joyce and Powys," ESSAYS IN CRITICISM, XI (Oct 1961), 403-17] "have independently made the same discovery at almost the same time"; **M. B. Simms:** "The *real* point at issue in the trial was, not whether this particular book was obscene, but whether serious works may be freely published in a civilised community, *irrespective of subject*"; **H. L.:** "In real life, Lady C. and Mellors would surely have had to think about the possibility of pregnancy--and wouldn't this have made a world of difference in terms of the uninhibited enjoyment and spontaneity of their get-togethers?"; **M. M.** (in verse): Sparrow is "more specious" than "Lucretius," a Latin extract from whom is quoted in support; **Michael Boston:** Sparrow's case is entirely convincing but ridiculously solemn and lacks the insight of Mann or Shakespeare; **Wensley Pithet:** "It was up to the prosecution to have pursued the implications of the 'night of sensual passion' . . . rather than for the defence to have prejudiced the winning of so important a victory on a point of pedantic accuracy." See also two additional selections of letters: "Regina v. Penguin," ENCOUNTER, XVIII (March 1962), 94-96; and "Regina v. Penguin," ENCOUNTER, XVIII (April 1962), 93-95; and rejoinder by John Sparrow, "Afterthoughts on Regina v. Penguin Books Ltd.," ENCOUNTER, XVIII (June 1962), 83-88.]

2328 Roberts, Walter. "After the Prophet: The Reputation of D. H. Lawrence," MONTH, ns XXVII (April 1962), 237-40.
[Review of FRIEDA LAWRENCE: THE MEMOIRS AND CORRESPONDENCE, ed by E. W. Tedlock, Jr. (1961), characterized chiefly by a derisive, sharp-tongued, mocking tone: Frieda's book is the "final supplement to the Koran" and might well be subtitled "Documents of the Primitive Lawrentian Church." DHL is "the Prophet," "the holy one," the "latter-day Messiah," and Frieda is "the Fatima of the Lawrentian sect," the "spiritual daughter of the holy one, gathering round her the authenticated heirs and heiresses of the mysteries." Other DHL followers and memoirists are "the faithful," "surviving apostles" of the "Lawrentian Church Militant."] Some of Frieda's "extraordinary claims go unchallenged" by the editor; for example, DHL can hardly be called a philosopher. Artists should be trained in the humanities; "Frieda did a remarkable job as a one-woman university in the wilderness," but "intending world figures should try to make sure that they are less exposed to the random pulsations of *fin de siècle* barbarism."

2329 Rosenthal, T. G. "The Writer as Painter," LISTENER AND BBC TELEVISION REVIEW, LXVIII (6 Sept 1962), 349-50.
DHL was "the most literary of all the writer-painters": "he would not have painted as he did had he not written as he did." The writer is basically "an artist who creates and re-creates from what is within himself while the painter is one who creates, as it were, from scratch." Since DHL could not do this, he was a "bad

painter" whose paintings are a "visual extension of his writings." [Compares DHL as an unsuccessful writer-painter with Henry Miller, Lorca, and Strindberg, who were successful writer-painters.]

2330 Rowse, A[lfred] L[eslie]. "The Miner's Son, Who Was 'No Gentleman,'" NEW YORK HERALD TRIBUNE BOOKS, 1 July 1962, p. 8.

The letters in *The Collected Letters of D. H. Lawrence,* ed by Harry T. Moore, are, except with regard to sex, "coterminous with his work and representative of all its facets and qualities." Two new groups of letters are those to Blanche Jennings, which give "a better picture of Jessie [Chambers] and her frustrated love," and "the rude correspondence with Bertrand Russell." These "immensely readable" "letters afford a remarkable picture of the literary side of Lawrence's time."

2331 Ryals, Clyde de L. "D. H. Lawrence's 'The Horse Dealer's Daughter': An Interpretation," LITERATURE AND PSYCHOLOGY, XII (Spring 1962), 39-43.

The symbolism in "The Horse Dealer's Daughter" vividly reveals a Jungian "rebirth archetype." Mabel's attempted suicide and her rescue by Ferguson are symbolically related to the rebirth archetype in three basic areas: the rite of baptism, the desire to return to the maternal depths, and the birth of a child--especially in that the rescue is effected by a doctor. When Mabel and Ferguson return to the real world at the end of the story, they are so changed by the transcendent experience that Ferguson's rescue of Mabel from death by water becomes "a psychic rebirth for both of them."

2332 Sagar, K[eith] M. "Lawrence and the Wilkinsons," REVIEW OF ENGLISH LITERATURE, III (Oct 1962), 62-75.

Gair Wilkinson and his brother Walter, English puppet artists, were neighbors of DHL and Frieda at Villa Mirenda, Italy, 1927-1928. "A number of extracts from the Wilkinson diaries and from Lawrence's letters, all previously unpublished, [are printed] with a minimum of explanatory comments."

2333 Sagar, Keith M. "Vision and Form in the Works of D. H. Lawrence." Unpublished dissertation, University of Leeds, 1962. [Listed in Lawrence F. McNamee, DISSERTATIONS IN ENGLISH AND AMERICAN LITERATURE (NY & Lond: Bowker, 1969), p. 613.]. Rvd and pub as THE ART OF D. H. LAWRENCE (Cambridge: Cambridge UP, 1966).

2334 Saxena, H. S. "D. H. Lawrence and the Impressionistic Technique," INDIAN JOURNAL OF ENGLISH STUDIES, III, No. 1 (1962), 145-52.

DHL extended the "technique of the impressionist painters to the novel in his attempt to describe the subjective experience of his characters and their sensations in the presence of one another." As a painter himself from age fifteen, DHL "treated painting as a serious art medium." "Morality and the Novel" begins with an example from Van Gogh, and Paul Morel's discussion of his art is related to impressionist technique. DHL's landscape descriptions in his novels and stories, "like impressionist pictures, are not visually clear but are peculiarly radiant and full." The impressionistic techniques of "rapid and rough sketching, and loose and abrupt" brush strokes, which make the painting appear instinctive, are paralleled in DHL's prose by rapidly flowing words and scenes, which render the sensation "whole and pure." Although a close observer of life, like Hardy or Dickens, DHL was not content merely to observe but sought "to render [the] 'endless flow of vitalistic communication' by translating into language, the drama of instincts."

2335 Schmoller, Hans. "D. H. Lawrence," TIMES LITERARY SUPPLEMENT (Lond), 4 May 1962, p. 309.
[Letter to the Editor in response to (Andor Gomme), "Friends and Enemies," TIMES LITERARY SUPPLEMENT (Lond), 27 April 1962, 273-75. While admitting that he has not seen the original, the author offers his own reading of Frieda Lawrence's phrasing in her German postscript to DHL's letter of 21 May 1926 to Carl Seelig as a correction of the readings suggested by Harry T. Moore, in *The Collected Letters of D. H. Lawrence* (1962), p. 916, and by the reviewer. In a brief reply, the reviewer accepts Schmoller's reading as correct.]

2336 Schorer, Mark. "The Line of a Life Made Clear," NEW YORK TIMES BOOK REVIEW, 18 March 1962, pp. 6, 18.
The Collected Letters of D. H. Lawrence, ed by Harry T. Moore, identifies names and includes many letters unavailable for *The Letters of D. H. Lawrence,* ed by Aldous Huxley (1932). But limitations in space have led to the exclusion of many other letters now available and have imposed editorial restrictions on the present edition. Nevertheless, with its publication, "suddenly, the whole line of life is clear in a way that it has never been. This is one of the greatest autobiographical revelations in literary history." The life falls into four stages: the young DHL up to age twenty-seven, when he elopes with Frieda Weekley; his response of intensely personal rage and an elegiac sense of loss for England during the war years; the dream of Rananim; and, finally, "withdrawal": "There was at last only the self alone, and the imagery of resurrection."

2337 Shirai, Toshitaka. "D. H. Lawrence no Working Method" (D. H. Lawrence's Working Method), SHIRON (Tôhoku University), No. 4 (Feb 1962), 19-36.
[In Japanese.]

2338 Singleton, Ralph Herbert (ed). TWO AND TWENTY: A COLLECTION OF SHORT STORIES (NY: St. Martin's P, 1962).
[This anthology includes "The Rocking-Horse Winner," pp. 215-35, and biographical information on DHL, emphasizing the influence of Jessie Chambers and Ford Madox Hueffer on his literary career, his problems with censors, and his stormy life with Frieda.]

2339 Sparrow, John. "Afterthoughts on Regina v. Penguin Books Ltd.," ENCOUNTER, XVIII (June 1962), 83-88; rptd in CONTRO-

VERSIAL ESSAYS, by John Sparrow (Lond: Faber & Faber; NY: Chilmark, 1966), pp. 59-70.
[Rejoinder to Colin MacInnes, "Experts on Trial: A Comment on Mr. Sparrow," ENCOUNTER, XVIII (March 1962), 63-65; and to Letters to the Editor by David Sylvester, Stephen Potter, Francois Bondy, and R. T., "Regina v. Penguin," ENCOUNTER, XVIII (March 1962), 94-96; and to Letters to the Editor by Frederick May, Jayanta Padmanabha, Alec Craig, David Tudor-Pole, and R. A. Raphael, "Regina v. Penguin," ENCOUNTER, XVIII (April 1962), 93-95.] Reluctant critics, finding the evidence irrefutable that DHL depicted anal penetration with approval in *Lady Chatterley's Lover,* tried to minimize its importance in the novel as a whole. The episode has major significance, however, in that DHL advocates anal sex as an important element in a mature heterosexual relationship; specifically, the scene demonstrates the need for "complete submission" on the part of the woman and "an entire absence of shame." Because the defense omitted reference to this passage in the trial (Regina v. Penguin Books Ltd., 1960), *Lady Chatterley's Lover* was not judged for what it was; the verdict might have been different if this issue had been clarified rather than concealed. [See also John Sparrow, "Regina v. Penguin Books Ltd.: An Undisclosed Element in the Case," ENCOUNTER, XVIII (Feb 1962), 35-43; and further discussions in ESSAYS IN CRITICISM as follows: G. Wilson Knight, "Lawrence, Joyce and Powys," XI (Oct 1961), 403-17; John Peter, "The Bottom of the Well," XII (April 1962), 226-27; John Peter, "Lady Chatterley Again," XII (Oct 1962), 445-47; William Empson, "Lady Chatterley Again," XIII (Jan 1963), 101-4; John Sparrow, "Lady Chatterley Again," XIII (April 1963), 202-5; John Peter, "Lady Chatterley for the Last Time I," XIII (July 1963), 301-2; and John Sparrow, "Lady Chatterley for the Last Time II," XIII (July 1963), 303.]

2340 Sparrow, John. "Regina v. Penguin Books Ltd.: An Undisclosed Element in the Case," ENCOUNTER, XVIII (Feb 1962), 35-43; rptd in CONTROVERSIAL ESSAYS, by John Sparrow (Lond: Faber & Faber; NY: Chilmark, 1966), pp. 40-58.
Although unremarked at the English censorship trial (Regina v. Penguin Books Ltd., 1960) and unacknowledged by DHL's admirers, the text of *Lady Chatterley's Lover* makes clear that the " 'night of sensual passion' " between Connie and Mellors involved anal penetration as the means to "burn out shame" in Connie. DHL explicitly approves the act, but he compromises his declared artistic intentions of dealing candidly with sexuality by veiling the true meaning of this scene. Had the jury understood the scene and thus the novel's sexual creed, the verdict might have been different. [See also John Sparrow, "Afterthoughts on Regina v. Penguin Books Ltd.," ENCOUNTER, XVIII (June 1962), 83-88; and Colin MacInnes, "Experts on Trial: A Comment on Mr. Sparrow," ENCOUNTER, XVIII (March 1962), 63-65; as well as further discussions in ESSAYS IN CRITICISM as follows: G. Wilson Knight, "Lawrence, Joyce and Powys," XI (Oct 1961), 403-17; John Peter, "The Bottom of the Well," XII (April 1962), 226-27; John Peter, "Lady Chatterley Again," XII (Oct 1962), 445-47; William Empson, "Lady Chatterley Again," XIII (Jan 1963), 101-4; John Sparrow, "Lady Chatterley Again," XIII (April 1963), 202-5; John Peter, "Lady Chatterley for the Last Time I," XIII

(July 1963), 301-2; and John Sparrow, "Lady Chatterley for the Last Time II," XIII (July 1963), 303.]

2341 Stavrou, C[onstantine] N. "Hawthorne on Don Juan," GEORGIAN REVIEW, XVI (Summer 1962), 210-21.

DHL's "inverted" Puritanism led him to misunderstand Hawthorne's intent in THE SCARLET LETTER. Actually, Hawthorne was firmly against DHL's Miltonic duality in which man was expected to give himself to woman in "blood-consciousness" while remaining in control.

2342 Steiner, George. "F. R. Leavis," ENCOUNTER, XVIII (May 1962), 37-45, espec p. 43.

F. R. Leavis's "obsessive" relation to DHL ignores the fact "that there is much in Lawrence which is monotonous and hysterical, that very few of his works are unflawed by hectoring idiosyncrasies, that there was little in his genius either of laughter or tolerance." To Leavis, for C. P. Snow to propose "that there are crises of spirit and political fact more actual or different than those dreamt of in *Women in Love,* is to query 'life.' "

2343 Tanner, Tony. "The Man Who Lived," SPECTATOR, CCVIII (23 March 1962), 373-74.

The Collected Letters of D. H. Lawrence, ed by Harry T. Moore (1962) reveal that he was a sensitive, disillusioned man who felt hemmed in by the world; that he searched for a new world; that he opposed anything formalized in art or society; that he advocated "a tender, wondering reverence for life." Each letter offers "a momentary glimpse of the man" while the collection provides more comprehensive coverage than *The Letters of D. H. Lawrence,* ed by Aldous Huxley (1932).

2344 Temple, Frédéric. "Au Nouveau-Mexique sur les pas de D. H. Lawrence" (To New Mexico in the Steps of D. H. Lawrence), LA NOUVELLE REVUE FRANÇAISE, ns X (March 1962), 562-67.

[An account of the author's journey to New Mexico, his conversations with acquaintances of DHL, and his visit to the Lawrence ranch.] [In French.]

2345 Toraiwa, Masazumi. "Nikutai to Sono Kage: D. H. Lawrence Oboegaki" (Body and Illusion: A Note on D. H. Lawrence), ENGLISH LITERATURE (Waseda University), No. 22 (Nov 1962), 45-56.

[In Japanese.]

2346 Vigorelli, Giancarlo. "Lawrence in Italia" (Lawrence in Italy), IL TEMPO (Milan), 24 Feb 1962, p. 66.

DHL spent his life in search of places untouched by civilization. He saw in Italians the followers of his idea of a religion of sex. DHL was not a good prophet, but he was an ingenious writer when he expressed his "vitalism." [In Italian.]

2347 Watson, George. THE LITERARY CRITICS: A STUDY OF ENGLISH DESCRIPTIVE CRITICISM (Harmondsworth, Middlesex, England: Penguin Books, 1962), pp. 21-22, 194, 212, 215, 217-19.

DHL is a fair representative of the modern moralist, who tends to shout. In particular, he indicts the sanctions of White Protestant Societies, whether British or American. Like others, he is self-righteously nonprofessional, despises scholarship, is prone to conspiratorial theories of "Establishments," and insists on being regarded as an outcast. [Brief and superficial.]

2348 Weiss, Daniel A. OEDIPUS IN NOTTINGHAM: D. H. LAWRENCE (Seattle: University of Washington P, 1962); excerpts from Chap. III: "The Mother in the Mind," pp. 39-68, rptd in E[rnest] W. Tedlock, Jr. (ed), D. H. LAWRENCE AND "SONS AND LOVERS": SOURCES AND CRITICISM (NY: New York UP, 1965), pp. 112-36, and in Judith Farr (ed), TWENTIETH CENTURY INTERPRETATIONS OF "SONS AND LOVERS" (Englewood Cliffs, N. J.: Prentice-Hall, 1970), pp. 28-41; excerpts from Chap. VI: "The Great Circle," pp. 69-111, rptd in Stephen J. Miko (ed), TWENTIETH CENTURY INTERPRETATIONS OF "WOMEN IN LOVE" (Englewood Cliffs, N. J.: Prentice-Hall, 1969), pp. 111-13; a rvd version of Chap. IV also pub as "D. H. Lawrence's Great Circle: From *Sons and Lovers* to *Lady Chatterley*," PSYCHOANALYTIC REVIEW, L (Fall 1963), 112-38. In *Sons and Lovers,* the "Oedipal situation" is not only evident in the Paul-Gertrude-Walter Morel relationships but also "prevails *against* Lawrence's attempt to direct it" by its symbolic representation in Paul's relationships with Miriam and Clara, both of whom are surrogate mothers, and with Baxter Dawes, a surrogate father. Paul's rejection of death at the conclusion is a symbolic rejection of "his acceptance of the mother," and his turning toward the town is an implicit acceptance of his father's values. In the *Prussian Officer* stories, DHL "recapitulates, reconsiders, and reorders the events, characters and moral judgments" of *Sons and Lovers.* The incomplete resolution of the father-son relationship in *Sons and Lovers* produces in DHL's stories a succession of protagonists who tend steadily and progressively toward a "fusion of these filial and paternal strains." The process of identification with the father can be seen in the orderly's ambivalence in "The Prussian Officer," the old collier's confession in "The Christening," the sympathy with the dead father in "Odour of Chrysanthemums," the indictment of the "mother" (Hilda) in the "attempt to resolve the conflict between father and son" (Pilbeam and Syson) in "The Shades of Spring," the "family romance" incorporating DHL's initial response to Ernest and Frieda Weekley in "The Old Adam," and Alfred Durant's ultimate identification with his father in "The Daughters of the Vicar." Descriptions of sexual relations in DHL's novels always contain recognizable imagery of "coitus anxiety" (fear of orgasm in the male), which, becoming more pronounced in the later work, "can only be interpreted as an unconscious equation" between orgasm and annihilation or castration, implying a neurotic regression to the oral stage. The latent, unresolved Oedipal complex, thus, not only determines the central situation of *Sons and Lovers* but also is found in virtually all of DHL's work, determining the structure of his fiction, including *Lady Chatterley's Lover* and *The Man Who Died.* [Illustrated with seven black and white reproductions of pictures by Edvard Munch.]

2349 White, William. "Lawrence and Marquand," D. H. LAWRENCE

NEWS AND NOTES (California, PA), II, No. 2 (1962), 1.
John P. Marquand met DHL in Taormina, Sicily, in the early twenties.

2350 Wickes, George. "The Art of Fiction: XXVIII," PARIS REVIEW, VII (Summer-Fall 1962), 129-59; rptd in WRITERS AT WORK: THE "PARIS REVIEW" INTERVIEWS, Second Series (NY: Viking P, 1963; Viking P, Compass Books, 1965), pp. 165-91, espec pp. 167, 171, 181, 182.
[An interview with Henry Miller, who speaks of his often writing as if possessed, as was the case with his unfinished work on DHL, which required so much thought and attention to form that he wrestled with it for two obsessive years of sleepless nights and feverish days. This struggle produced some "cadenza" passages in which, as in TROPIC OF CAPRICORN, the words tumble out one after the other. Yet Miller found that he could not finish the book, becoming entangled in DHL's contradictions while admiring his quest. No longer distracted by DHL, Miller is now able to see his flaws. See also the "unfinished" book in question, THE WORLD OF LAWRENCE: A PASSIONATE APPRECIATION, by Henry Miller, ed and with an Introduction and Notes by Evelyn J. Hinz and John J. Teunissen (Santa Barbara: Capra P, 1980).]

2351 Widmer, Kingsley. THE ART OF PERVERSITY: D. H. LAWRENCE'S SHORTER FICTIONS (Seattle: University of Washington P, 1962); excerpt, pp. 92-95, rptd as "The Triumph of the Middleclass Matriarch," in D. H. LAWRENCE: "THE ROCKING-HORSE WINNER," ed by Dominick P. Consolo (Columbus, OH: Merrill [The Merrill Literary Casebook Series], 1969), pp. 43-46; excerpt, pp. 225-26, rptd in TWENTIETH CENTURY INTERPRETATIONS OF "SONS AND LOVERS": A COLLECTION OF CRITICAL ESSAYS, ed by Judith Farr (Englewood Cliffs, NJ: Prentice-Hall, 1970), p. 105.
"Perversity" in DHL's short fictions takes three forms: (1) refusing to idealize love and marriage, (2) seeing morality as inapplicable to meaningful areas of human experience, and (3) asserting death and destruction as the foundations of consciousness and meaning. DHL focuses on desire for annihilation, the demonic, social denial of modern woman, egoistic conflict in love, and religious renewal.

Self-destructive yearnings may be both the characters' destiny and a process that frees as well as destroys them. The youth in "The Prussian Officer" is transformed in the extremity of his relation with the officer. The satire of a rationalistic idealist in "The Man Who Loved Islands" ends with the destruction of a mind that isolated itself. Self-annihilation in "England, My England" lies in nostalgic disengagement from modern society. "Odour of Chrysanthemums" realistically relates passion and death in a mining family, and the primitivism of "The Woman Who Rode Away" is counterpoised with DHL's insistence that "we cannot go back to the savages." The demonic in DHL becomes a negative way to wisdom. In "A Fragment of Stained Glass" and "The Border Line," it is opposed to conventional social order. Demon lovers, like Henry in "The Fox," who destroys a fraudulent female farm "community," are alien to the established order and depend on magical knowledge related to death. In *St. Mawr,* Lou responds deeply to the demonic traits of the rebellious stallion but ultimately transcends what he represents to confront a future between civilized life and primitive sordidness.

DHL misogynistically uses the Anglo-American woman, in her quest for emancipation, comfort, and happiness, to represent destructiveness. "None of That" and "The Princess" culminate in rape of willful female protagonists. "The Rocking-Horse Winner," "The Lovely Lady," and "Mother and Daughter" show modern women transforming their children into objects in service of their worship of things. "New Eve and Old Adam," "The Witch a la Mode," and "Blue Mocassins" show women more involved in rebellion, adultery, erotic torment, and self-destruction than in courtship or marital domesticity. Since it violates the innate isolation of the organism, love is potentially self-annihilation. DHL's love stories, ranging from pastoral life in "Love Among the Haystacks," to realism and anticlericalism in "Daughters of the Vicar," to satiric comedy in "Tickets, Please" and "Jimmy and the Desperate Woman," combine strong passions and ordinary provincial life. Love is charged with hatred in "The White Stocking," and the being of the lovers in "The Shadow in the Rose Garden" is defined by the quality of their passion. Love remains troubled even in positive stories like *The Captain's Doll*, which turns on surmounting false notions of love.

DHL's work assumes Christianity's collapse and the need for a new effort to reach deity through demonic perversity. The rebirth motif permeates "The Horse-Dealer's Daughter," *The Virgin and the Gipsy,* and "Sun." In *The Man Who Died* the "risen Christ," a phallic combination of ancient fertility gods, is DHL's negation of Christian humanist universality. DHL's nihilism is a search by the path of destruction for the affirmation of a "higher unconsciousness" beyond it.

2352 Williams, Raymond. "Letters from Lawrence," MANCHESTER GUARDIAN WEEKLY, 29 March 1962, p. 11; rptd in "D. H. Lawrence," A LIBRARY OF LITERARY CRITICISM (MODERN BRITISH LITERATURE), ed by Ruth Z. Temple and Martin Tucker (NY: Ungar Publishing, 1966), II, 162-64.

The "personal quickness" of DHL's letters is ultimately "a public literary style" by which he could "dramatise himself, without the deep responsibilities and disciplines of real creation." [Reviews *The Collected Letters of D. H. Lawrence.*]

2353 Williams, Raymond. "Strindberg and the New Drama in Britain"; "La Nouvelle Vague Anglaise et Strindberg," WORLD THEATRE, XI (Spring 1962), 61-66.

It is difficult to tell whether contemporary British dramatists like John Osborne, Arnold Wesker, and Shelagh Delaney have been influenced by the meager sources of Strindberg available to them (FRÖKEN JULIE and FADREN) or by DHL, whose *Women in Love, Sons and Lovers,* and many of the later short stories treat the same themes as Strindberg, i.e., "intense sexual conflict, in a mainly naturalist mode." [Printed in English and French versions in parallel columns on each page.]

2354 Willingham, John R. "Literature," LIBRARY JOURNAL,

LXXXVII (15 April 1962), 1611.
The Collected Letters of D. H. Lawrence, ed by Harry T. Moore, is "one of the major publications of the year" for both students and laymen.

2355 Wilson, Colin. "D. H. Lawrence," in THE STRENGTH TO DREAM: LITERATURE AND THE IMAGINATION (Lond: Gollancz, 1962), pp. 157-62; additional references, pp. 14, 115, 142, 143, 154, 163, 180, 189, 190, 197, 200; (Bost: Houghton Mifflin, 1962), pp. 180-86; additional references, pp. xv, 124, 161, 162, 176, 209, 220, 221, 227, 231.

In DHL's very personal "sexual mysticism," sex cannot be separated from human personality. Rather than functioning as a "detached artist," DHL is down among his characters, reacting to them on a human level, with a personal involvement that often wrecks his "artistic intentions." Thus, in works like *The Fox,* "when the sexual relationships that bring freedom are at last achieved, there is always a further state of conflict." DHL similarly "shirks the issue" of "What now?" at the end of "The Prussian Officer," "The Man Who Loved Islands," and *Lady Chatterley's Lover.* The latter novel "is only an ugly parody of his early vision of sex," in such works as *Love Among the Haystacks* and *The White Peacock,* which "seem free from the disgust and malice that disfigures so much of his later work."

2356 Winterich, John T. "*The Collected Letters of D. H. Lawrence,*" BOOK-OF-THE-MONTH CLUB NEWS (NY), June 1962, p. 11.

There is a "remarkable absence of trivia" in *The Collected Letters of D. H. Lawrence,* ed by Harry T. Moore. DHL did not exactly treat letters as an art form, but he did approach their composition "as seriously as he did the fashioning of his imaginative productions."

2357 Woerner, Robert Frederick. "D. H. Lawrence and Hermann Hesse: A Comparative Study of Two Critics of Modern Culture," DISSERTATION ABSTRACTS, XXIV (1963), 306. Unpublished dissertation, Indiana University, 1962.

2358 Yamaguchi, Keizabrô. "D. H. Lawrence no Ikyôsei" (Paganism in D. H. Lawrence's Literature), STUDIES IN ENGLISH LITERATURE (Hôsei University), No. 5 (Dec 1962), 40-64.

[In Japanese.]

2359 Young, Jessica [Hankinson] Brett. FRANCIS BRETT YOUNG: A BIOGRAPHY (Lond: William Heinemann, 1962), pp. 95-117 and passim.

Francis Brett Young, acquainted with DHL personally during his residence in Capri and familiar with his fiction, could not easily assess DHL's achievement as a writer. On the other hand, Young regarded DHL as "the only authentic genius ... of the generation" to which they belonged. However, he believed that DHL's genius was "not constant or infallible ... for genius, by its very nature, is a little superhuman, and its vision, for this reason, incurs the charge of inhumanity." Although DHL at times manifested a "pathological soul," Young never questioned his sincerity--an "almost puritanical . . . earnestness and austerity."

2360 Zampa, Giorgio. "Lawrence cercava in Italia le tracce di una razza selvaggia" (Lawrence Searched in Italy for the Traces of a Savage Race), CORRIERE DELLA SERA (Milan), 21 April 1962, p. 3.
[Review of *Libri di viaggio e pagine di paese* (*Complete Collection of Travel Books*) by D. H. Lawrence, with an Introduction by Piero Nardi (1961).] In *Twilight in Italy*, DHL's intelligence, intuition, and spontaneity appear quite clearly, though many of the ideas expressed in this work are highly debatable. *Sea and Sardinia* is more fictional and contains wonderful descriptions. *Etruscan Places* is the best of DHL's travel books, even though its interpretations of Etruscan civilization are questionable, while its descriptive elements confirm DHL's art. [In Italian.]

1963

2361 Adelman, Gary. "Beyond the Pleasure Principle: An Analysis of D. H. Lawrence's 'The Prussian Officer,'" STUDIES IN SHORT FICTION, I (Fall 1963), 8-15.
In "The Prussian Officer," "a dramatization of the consequences of twenty-five centuries of evasion and denial of life," the Captain is "an exaggerated picture of modern man," the result of "mechanical insistence on an ideal of impersonal service." Schöner, his orderly, living instinctively and innocently, makes the Captain realize that he is "only the simulacrum of a man." The love and hate the Captain feels are symbolized by the horse, an archetype of the unconscious and DHL's symbol for the spontaneous self. In losing his innocence, Schöner is "initiated into personal consciousness by a society which has produced the Captain," and he "begins to play an active role in the perverse love affair." The sexually described murder and its aftermath suggest DHL's view of modern man destroying naturalness and committing himself to "perversity and death."

2362 Arnold, Aerol. "D. H. Lawrence," TIMES LITERARY SUPPLEMENT (Lond) 21 Nov 1963, p. 956.
[Letter to the Editor in reply to a review of Warren Roberts, A BIBLIOGRAPHY OF D. H. LAWRENCE (1963). Cites DHL's letter from Del Monte Ranch to Catherine Carswell (8 Oct 1924) as evidence in support of Roberts's placing the setting of "The Woman Who Rode Away" in New Mexico. In a rejoinder, the anonymous reviewer says that while Arnold is right and while the cave resembles the one near Arroyo Seco described by Mabel Dodge Luhan, "the action itself could scarcely be conceived in New Mexico." See also further comment by Harry T. Moore, "D. H. Lawrence," TIMES LITERARY SUPPLEMENT (Lond), 19 Dec 1963, p. 1038.]

2363 Arnold, Armin. D. H. LAWRENCE AND GERMAN LITERATURE WITH TWO HITHERTO UNKNOWN ESSAYS BY D. H.

LAWRENCE (Montreal: Mansfield Book Mart, H. Heinemann, 1963); material in the "Introduction" and "Postscript" and D. H. Lawrence's "Review of H. G. Fiedler's OXFORD BOOK OF GERMAN VERSE" and "Review of Jethro Bithell's THE MINNESINGERS" also pub in Armin Arnold, "D. H. Lawrence's First Critical Essays: Two Anonymous Reviews Identified," PUBLICATIONS OF THE MODERN LANGUAGE ASSOCIATION, LXXIX (March 1964), 185-88.

As shown by DHL's letters to May Chambers Holbrook (6 Dec 1911) and to Else Jaffe (10 Feb 1913), two anonymous reviews, one on H. G. Fiedler's OXFORD BOOK OF GERMAN VERSE [review rptd in full, pp. 21-25], the other on Jethro Bithell's THE MINNESINGERS [review rptd in full, pp. 29-32], published in the ENGLISH REVIEW (Jan 1912), were written by DHL. DHL's works were regularly translated into German, most of them being available by 1938, thanks in part to Douglas Goldring. German women critics were more drawn to DHL than their male counterparts, but despite increasing interest, DHL's work was eclipsed by World War II and was out of favor until a post-war revival which began in Switzerland. DHL wrote probably the first article on Thomas Mann by an Englishman, a negative review in BLUE REVIEW (July 1913). Mann's intellectual control and his artistic speculations provide strong contrast to DHL, who saw commitment to art as an ailment of the soul. DHL's German letters to the Baroness von Richthofen, published in NEUE RUNDSCHAU (Dec 1934) and superficially translated, with omissions, in Frieda Lawrence's "NOT I, BUT THE WIND . . ." (1934), are valuable for their outspoken revelation of DHL's attitude toward friends and toward Frieda's first marriage and her children.

2364 Arnold, Armin. "Die deutschen Briefe von D. H. Lawrence" (The German Letters of D. H. Lawrence), NEUE ZÜRCHER ZEITUNG, 24 Aug 1963, pp. 12-13; rvd and trans by the author with notes as "D. H. Lawrence's German Letters," in D. H. LAWRENCE AND GERMAN LITERATURE, WITH TWO HITHERTO UNKNOWN ESSAYS BY D. H. LAWRENCE, by Armin Arnold (Montreal: Mansfield Book Mart, H. Heinemann, 1963), pp. 59-64; original article trans with minor revisions as "The German Letters of D. H. Lawrence," COMPARATIVE LITERATURE, III, No. 3 (1966), 285-98.

NUR DIE WIND (1936), the German edition of Frieda Lawrence's memoir prepared by her sister, Else Jaffe, includes some fifteen letters and passages from letters by DHL which do not appear in "NOT I, BUT THE WIND . . ." (1934). Apparently Else had not sent Frieda all of DHL's letters to their mother and others; and Frieda, for both personal and political reasons, had "radically censored and shortened in the process of translation" some of the letters in her possession. These inconsistencies and the fact that a selection of DHL's letters to the Baroness von Richthofen (published in NEUE RUNDSCHAU [Dec 1934]) seems to contain the originals, have not been considered in *The Collected Letters of D. H. Lawrence,* ed by Harry T. Moore (1962). [The letters appear in English for the first time in the English version of this article, which also reprints the original German letters, pp. 294-98.] [In German.]

2365 Asakawa, Jun. "Oboegaki Lawrence (III)" (A Note on

Lawrence [III], ENGLISH LANGUAGE AND ENGLISH AND AMERICAN LITERATURES (Chūo University), No. 3 (Dec 1963), 84-94. [On symbol in DHL.] [In Japanese.]

2366 Asakawa, Jun. "Oboegaki Lawrence (IV)" (A Note on D. H. Lawrence [IV], ENGLISH LANGUAGE AND ENGLISH AND AMERICAN LITERATURES (Chūo University), No. 4 (Dec 1963), 33-40. [On *The Ladybird*.] [In Japanese.]

2367 Bantock, G[eoffrey] H[erman]. EDUCATION IN AN INDUSTRIAL SOCIETY (Lond: Faber & Faber, 1963), pp. 59, 78, 81n, 98, 116, 151-52, 163-65, 184, 211n, 214-15, 217-18.
Suggesting that " 'radical unlearnedness' " may be as valid a form of self-expression for some natures as learnedness, DHL "pointed to the extent to which elementary education as it existed in his day contributed to the drying up of the affective centres, through the imposition of an alien and 'genteel' culture upon the native resources of the people or 'folk.' " DHL "indicts industrialization and mechanization for its 'inhumanity' " and seeks "to reawaken the old spontaneous intuitive faculties" for "direct sensuous awareness of the external world," unclouded by rationalist abstraction. In "Education of the People," he suggests that working men need to be educated to proficiency in the minor domestic trades.

2368 Beebe, Maurice. "Lawrence's Sacred Fount: The Artist Theme of *Sons and Lovers*," TEXAS STUDIES IN LITERATURE AND LANGUAGE, IV (Winter 1963), 539-52; rptd in IVORY TOWERS AND SACRED FOUNTS: THE ARTIST AS HERO IN FICTION FROM GOETHE TO JOYCE, by Maurice Beebe (NY: New York UP, 1964), pp. 101-13; rptd as "The Artist Theme," in D. H. LAWRENCE: "SONS AND LOVERS," A CASEBOOK, ed by Gāmini Salgādo (Lond: Macmillan, 1969; Nashville: Aurora Publishers, 1970), pp. 177-90.
Sons and Lovers is about art as well as love: DHL "sees the sexual act as similar to the creative process"--each success in sex and art alike representing "a creative renewal." DHL follows the "Sacred Fount theme": life is a resource that may be used up--either life may be destroyed when turned into art or the artist may be destroyed when submitting to life. The artist theme, though not the central focus of the novel, is a "buried theme" that enabled DHL "subconsciously to solve conflicts which are unsolvable on a conscious level." Paul Morel, with his artistic talent and temperament, is the object in "the jealous struggle of two patronesses," Gertrude and Miriam, for his homage. But only Clara's passion can help begin his liberation. One side of Paul, his work as an artist, remains untouched. He begins to free himself from his mother "when he assumes the role of father" in relation to Clara and Baxter Dawes, and he destroys "his dead self" when he kills his mother. His despair after her death represents his own "symbolic death" before rebirth. Miriam's visit makes him realize that the past is dead, and he is free, like Stephen Dedalus, both to experience "a moment of consecration" and to follow "an exile which is to lead . . . to creative renewal." DHL, too, killed his experience as a son by "transforming it into art" and going on to *The Rainbow*.

2369 Bertaccini, Renato. "Lawrence e Vittorini" (Lawrence and Vittorini), PERSONA (Rome), 1 March 1963, pp. 23-24.

In *Canguro, Il ragazzo nella boscaglia, Il serpente piumato* (*Kangaroo, The Boy in the Bush, The Plumed Serpent*) (1962), Australia and Mexico represent an alternative to the European-American civilization. *The Plumed Serpent,* in particular, proposes a return to the Aztec cult. The Italian edition of this novel avails itself of a very good translation by Elio Vittorini. [In Italian.]

2370 Blöcker, Gunter. "Einübung in D. H. Lawrence" (Introduction to D. H. Lawrence), SÜDDEUTSCHE ZEITUNG, 6 April 1963.

[Review of *Mexikanischer Morgen und Italienische Dämmerung* (1963), which includes *Twilight in Italy, Sea and Sardinia,* and *Mornings in Mexico,* translated by Georg Goyert, Alfred Kuoni, and Oswalt von Nostitz.] In his travel impressions, DHL, rather than functioning as a tourist guide, tries to portray spontaneous life, though at times he dwells, for didactic reasons, too long on the effects of civilization or sham philosophies. [In German.]

2371 Brophy, Brigid. "The British Museum and Solitary Vice," LONDON MAGAZINE, II (March 1963), 55-58.

In *Lady Chatterley's Lover,* DHL challenges "the definition not of pornography but of obscenity." He was right to challenge the taboo of language, for both sexual and excretory functions, "if only to disprove the primitive superstition" concerning these words. But DHL's strictures against masturbation on the ground that "it leaves the masturbator ashamed" and is practiced in secret are unjustified. Shame is a response learned from puritans and scoutmasters, and masturbation shares with reading the characteristic of being an anti-social, solitary activity.

2372 Burroughs, William D. "No Defense for 'The Rocking-Horse Winner,'" COLLEGE ENGLISH, XXIV (Jan 1963), 323; rptd in D. H. LAWRENCE: "THE ROCKING-HORSE WINNER," ed by Dominick P. Consolo (Columbus, OH: Merrill [The Merrill Literary Casebook Series], 1969), pp. 55-56.

[Reply to W. R. Martin, "Fancy or Imagination? 'The Rocking-Horse Winner,'" COLLEGE ENGLISH, XXIV (Oct 1962), 64-65.] Martin fails in his attempt to defend "The Rocking-Horse Winner" against the strictures of Hough and Leavis (and Gordon and Tate). Technically perfect, the story is finally both pathetic and didactic, failing to present life. [See also another reply to Martin by Robert G. Lawrence, "Further Notes on D. H. Lawrence's 'Rocking-Horse,'" COLLEGE ENGLISH, XXIV (Jan 1963), 324.]

2373 Chamberlain, Robert L. "Pussum, Minette, and the Africo-Nordic Symbol in Lawrence's *Women in Love*," PUBLICATIONS OF THE MODERN LANGUAGE ASSOCIATION, LXXVIII (Sept 1963), 407-16.

The major symbol of *Women in Love* is a metaphor of destruction, either by heat or by cold. Differences between the two principal current editions of the novel (Viking Press and Random House), which derive from different plates, concern the conversion of Pussum into Minette. In the first trade edition (Martin Secker),

Pussum is so dark in hair, eyes, and mood that her association with the dark African motif is obvious. Almost as important in the complex Africo-Nordic color symbolism is yellow as a Nordic image: Gerald, Hermione, and the Brangwen sisters have yellow hair, and Minette's association with yellow, in hair and dress, signals her triumph over Halliday and prefigures the mortal conflict between the two Nordics Gerald and Gudrun. The impossibility of change in Minette and Halliday is a foil for the progress of Ursula and Birkin until "Excurse," when they have "come through" the limits of sensational experience and the imposition of will by one over the other. Gerald takes the path of suicide. Birkin's attraction to him suggests that Gerald's fate might have been his, though he is in greater danger of undergoing a slow dissolution, as Loerke does. Minette is the key to the dualistic symbolism of *Women in Love* precisely because her blondeness combined with symbolic darkness incorporates both Northern and African, Apollonian and Dionysian, mind and feeling. Finally, one comes to see, through the Pussum-to-Minette transformation, that the Nordic and African modes of destruction--industrialization and mindless dissolution, will and sensuality, snow and mud--are one and the same.

2374 Clark, L. D. "D. H. Lawrence's *The Plumed Serpent*," DISSERTATION ABSTRACTS, XXIV (1963), 5405A. Unpublished dissertation, Columbia University, 1963: rvd and pub as DARK NIGHT OF THE BODY: D. H. LAWRENCE'S "THE PLUMED SERPENT" (Austin: University of Texas P, 1964).

2375 Coffey, Warren. "Wyndham Lewis: Enemy of the Rose," RAMPARTS, II (May 1963), 70-76.
Wyndham Lewis was the best and "the most neglected major writer of our time and its most resolute enemy." Antilyrical and antipastoral, Lewis thought that DHL was the best of the primitivist, pastoral writers, but he himself "never trafficked in primitivist solutions."

2376 Coombes, H. "The Uncollected Letters of D. H. Lawrence," ESSAYS IN CRITICISM, XIII (Jan 1963), 81-85.
[This review of *The Collected Letters of D. H. Lawrence*, ed by Harry T. Moore, begins with an attack on the editor's lack of inclusiveness, selection, and introduction.] "One impression we receive from the letters as a whole, despite moments and periods of stress, anger, misery, is the unparalleled, strictly unparalleled, spontaneity with perspective. With all his intensity of feeling, he was always alive to the outer world and to the condition and feelings of the person he was writing to."

2377 Cox, C. B., and A. E. Dyson. " 'Bavarian Gentians' by D. H. Lawrence," MODERN POETRY: STUDIES IN PRACTICAL CRITICISM (Lond: Edward Arnold, 1963), pp. 66-71.
"Bavarian Gentians," "certainly a great poem," fully justifies DHL's "principles of composition." "Diffuse and sentimental" in his early verse, DHL, under the influence of Ezra Pound, the Imagists, Walt Whitman, and the Authorized Version of the Bible, developed "a highly original type of formal composition," moving

toward "the intensely evocative images and rhythms" of *Birds, Beasts and Flowers* and *Last Poems*. "The organic form of 'Bavarian Gentians', based on repetitions and incantatory rhythms," uses "rhetorical phrases without principal verbs" and irregular lines. The dark and light imagery of the Pluto-Persephone pattern in the poem create the "double effect" of conflicting emotions.

2378 "Current Books," NINETEENTH CENTURY FICTION, XVII (Sept 1963), 195-96.
The Collected Letters of D. H. Lawrence, edited by Harry T. Moore, is "carefully transcribed and fully annotated." It is not, however, a "definitive" edition, as the publisher describes it, but only a selection that skims the cream of available letters.

2379 Daiches, David. D. H. LAWRENCE (Brighton: Privately Printed at the Dolphin P, 1963).
[This 24-page pamphlet, printed from an original recording for the Canadian Broadcasting Company, was published in an edition of seventy copies only for private distribution.] DHL's two masterpieces, *The Rainbow* and *Women in Love,* should be "read as symbolic and dramatic poems in prose." In them DHL explores the potentialities and distortions of human nature. In the first of these works, DHL develops his doctrine about marriage "as a fight and at the same time, if properly realized, a means of mystic knowledge through the awareness by one partner ... of the essential *otherness* of the other." In *Women in Love,* DHL carries this basic doctrine further while exploring also the ills of modern industrial society. Following a series of works concerned with the issue of political leadership, DHL returned to his earlier theme in *Lady Chatterley's Lover*; in this novel he was less successful in carrying out his aims because of "simplifications and contradictions that at times make the novel read almost like a parody of itself." Because DHL challenges his reader with disturbing insights, his works have naturally been controversial.

2380 Dawson, Eugene. "D. H. Lawrence and Trigant Burrow: Pollyanalytics and Phylobiology, An Interpretive Analysis," DISSERTATION ABSTRACTS, XXIV (1964), 2906A. Unpublished dissertation, University of Washington, 1963.

2381 Delbaere-Garant, Jane. "The Call of the South," REVUE DES LANGUES VIVANTES (Brussels), XXIX, No. 4 (1963), 336-57.
When we compare E. M. Forster's WHERE ANGELS FEAR TO TREAD and DHL's *The Lost Girl,* we are first struck by the resemblance of the two Italian heroes, but the two heroines, Lilia and Alvina, have little in common. [The author summarizes the plot of *The Lost Girl* and comments on DHL's ideas: the opposition of instinct and education, past beauty and modern vulgarism, which leads to DHL's condemnation of modern civilization.] Both Forster and DHL turned to the still vivid and imaginative South because they feared that man would become a mere machine in our modern, mechanized world. DHL turned to Italy because he was in search of a great past in which the relation between the mind and the senses had not yet been broken. Neither Forster nor DHL was satisfied with what he

found in Italy. What they present in their novels is not so much Italy as such as a general idea of the "South" as the embodiment of what is lacking in England. DHL's desperate search was for a country that had not received the stamp of modern civilization.

2382 Draper, Ronald. "Great Writers--4: D. H. Lawrence," TIME AND TIDE, XLIV (24-30 Jan 1963), 23-24.

[Popularized overview of DHL's life and work, stressing autobiographical elements of *Sons and Lovers,* DHL's hatred of industrialism and his passion for "natural life" and roots, and his treatment of sex as "simply part of the rich communion between man and Nature."] DHL's major theme is neither sex nor love but, as seen in his two greatest novels, *The Rainbow* and *Women in Love,* "the theme that his own childhood thrust upon him, of marriage."

2383 Drew, Elizabeth. "D. H. Lawrence, 1885-1930: *Women in Love,*" in THE NOVEL: A MODERN GUIDE TO FIFTEEN ENGLISH MASTERPIECES, by Elizabeth Drew (NY: W. W. Norton, 1963), pp. 208-23.

At the beginning of *Women in Love,* the Crich wedding scene establishes the attraction between Gudrun and Gerald and Ursula and Birkin, introduces the macabre figure of Hermione Roddice, conveys "the strange undercurrents in the Crich family," and suggests the theme of "suppressed homosexuality." Despite Birkin's concern for "societal instincts," it is hard to believe "that Lawrence saw any hope for his society." "Gerald's egocentric will expresses itself in the mechanization of both the work and lives of the miners." The Arab mare and rabbit scenes show his subjugation of these symbols of "pure living organism" to will, and the latter culminates in a " 'hellish recognition' " between him and Gudrun. Their union "dwindles into a battle of wills in which she finally worsts him" before turning to the "repellent" Loerke. "Lawrence senses mystical depths of evil below sexuality which match the mystical heights above it." Against such death-oriented relations "Birkin and Ursula work out their final creative affirmation" in "star-equilibrium." "Critics differ as much about Lawrence's success in formal quality as about his ultimate place in literary history." But although we are often "*told*" in "incantatory prose" of feelings and experiences that are not presented dramatically, there are some "episodes where the external scene and the psychic content are perfectly fused into a complete harmony."

2384 Dudek, Louis. "Art, Entertainment and Religion," QUEEN'S QUARTERLY, LXX (Autumn 1963), 413-30.

In modern culture, the religious tradition has forced a rift between art and entertainment, and driven art to the periphery of society. DHL is an iconoclast in search of "new affirmations and new bearings" and belongs with Blake, Whitman, Nietzsche, Shaw, Ibsen, Pound, Jeffers, Gide, and Camus as an advocate of an individual, "secular approach to life." The objection to *Lady Chatterley's Lover* was not really to its alleged obscenity but to "its elevation of sexuality to the dignity of a new religion." DHL comes "very close to bridging the gap between art and entertainment." [Focus of the article is not on DHL but on the cultural thesis.]

2385 Durrell, Lawrence, and Henry Miller. LAWRENCE DURRELL / HENRY MILLER: A PRIVATE CORRESPONDENCE, ed by George Wickes (NY: Dutton, 1963), pp. 3, 6, 8, 9, 12, 17-18, 22, 27, 34, 46-47, 52, 56, 57, 64, 72, 78-79, 108, 217, 228, 237, 312, 361.
[Although neither Miller nor Durrell ever met DHL, their correspondence shows clearly the impact that his work had on both writers. Miller struggled with an uncompleted manuscript, THE WORLD OF LAWRENCE, fragments of which he published in other books. Durrell (Spring 1936) resents "a filthy attack" on DHL. In an exchange of letters on art and the artist, Miller (Summer 1936) sees art as "a lifelong struggle to find yourself" and compares DHL in this respect to Cézanne, Van Gogh, and Gauguin. Durrell (Fall 1936) sees the driving force behind these and other artists as "self-isolation, the dislocation of the societal instinct." Miller (3 Jan 1937) continues: "When man becomes fully conscious of his powers, his role, his destiny, he is an artist and ceases to struggle with reality" --a point he makes in his DHL book. Both writers are delighted to meet DHL's associates. Miller (22 Jan 1946) confides that Frieda Lawrence, visiting him at Big Sur, had said, " 'If only Lawrence had known you when alive. You would have been the very friend he was looking for,' " but Miller adds, "(I wonder.)" Durrell (June 1957) finds himself childishly thrilled, on meeting Richard Aldington, "to talk to a writer who knew Lawrence for years and years."]

2386 Dutton, Geoffrey. "The Novels of Patrick White," CRITIQUE: STUDIES IN MODERN FICTION, VI (Winter 1963-1964), 7-28, espec p. 15.
[Briefly compares White and DHL. Notes the relevance to White of DHL's division of people, in his essay "John Galsworthy," into human beings and social beings.]

2387 Elsbree, Langdon. "The Breaking Chain: A Study of the Dance in the Novels of Jane Austen, George Eliot, Thomas Hardy, and D. H. Lawrence," DISSERTATION ABSTRACTS, XXIV (1963), 2476A. Unpublished dissertation, Claremont Graduate School, 1963.

2388 Empson, William. "Lady Chatterley Again," ESSAYS IN CRITICISM, XIII (Jan 1963), 101-4.
[Reply to John Peter, "The Bottom of the Well," ESSAYS IN CRITICISM, XII (April 1962), 226-27. Refutes Peter's objections to G. Wilson Knight's reading of *Lady Chatterley's Lover* as a celebration of anal sex. See also further discussions in the controversy as follows: G. Wilson Knight, "Lawrence, Joyce and Powys," ESSAYS IN CRITICISM, XI (Oct 1961), 403-17; John Sparrow, "Regina v. Penguin Books Ltd.: An Undisclosed Element in the Case," ENCOUNTER, XVIII (Feb 1962), 35-43; John Sparrow, "Afterthoughts on Regina v. Penguin Books Ltd.," ENCOUNTER, XVIII (June 1962), 83-88; John Peter, "Lady Chatterley Again," ESSAYS IN CRITICISM, XII (Oct 1962), 445-47; John Sparrow, "Lady Chatterley Again," ESSAYS IN CRITICISM, XIII (April 1963), 202-5; John Peter, "Lady Chatterley for the Last Time I," ESSAYS IN CRITICISM, XIII (July 1963), 301-2; and John Sparrow, "Lady Chatterley for the Last Time II," ESSAYS IN CRITICISM, XIII (July 1963), 303.]

2389 Engelberg, Edward. "Escape from the Circles of Experience: D. H. Lawrence's *The Rainbow* as a Modern *Bildungsroman*," PUBLICATIONS OF THE MODERN LANGUAGE ASSOCIATION, LXXVIII (March 1963), 103-13; rptd in CRITICS ON D. H. LAWRENCE, ed by W. T. Andrews (Lond: Allen & Unwin; Coral Gables, FL: University of Miami P, 1971), pp. 67-80.

DHL's problem as a novelist was the meaning of experience. In *The Rainbow* he achieves a balance between tradition and innovation. Ursula's value--DHL's theory of "another ego" notwithstanding--is precisely her humanness, her consistency as a character in the *Bildungsroman* convention. Rejecting Proust's and Joyce's method of exploring the inner lives of their characters, DHL substitutes a persona whose deeper being functions as a kind of antipodal self. This gives the novel a modernist subtlety without sacrificing realism. "The Wedding Ring" was an inappropriate title because Ursula's triumphant growth beyond the encirclements of experience is basic to the meaning. Though Lydia and Anna also have a prodigious appetite for experience, their inadequate accommodations stress by contrast the purposive nature of Ursula's commitment to experience. Ursula's manner of stripping away everything that hides the truth about herself leads to a higher consciousness but fills the novel with a negativity from which DHL must remove her in the final vision. In the scene with the horses, Ursula finally surmounts the circles which they symbolize by entering a consciousness of separateness from time and space. The originality of *The Rainbow* is that at the end of experience the protagonist is granted release from it.

2390 Englander, Ann. " 'The Prussian Officer': The Self Divided," SEWANEE REVIEW, LXXI (Oct-Dec 1963), 605-19.

The inability of critics to agree on the meaning of "The Prussian Officer" results from "a radical incoherence in the relationship of the characters that can be traced to the fact that the story is controlled by a theory itself poorly thought through." To satisfy his theory, DHL schematizes "the psyche of each character into two opposed forces, Consciouness and the Unconscious, and . . . project[s] that schema symbolically into two opposed characters." DHL wants the reader to "view each character in three ways: 1) as a symbol of one half of the psyche; 2) as a complete psyche divided into the warring opposites of Consciousness and the Unconscious; 3) as a human being." The result of the story's failure to "operate harmoniously on all levels" is "frustrated expectation."

2391 Feltes, N. N. "Correspondence," SEWANEE REVIEW, LXXI (Oct-Dec 1963), 696-97.

[Letter to the Editor in reply to Harry T. Moore, "Correspondence," SEWANEE REVIEW, LXXI (April-June 1963), 347-48, refuting Moore's rebuttal to F. R. Leavis's criticism of Moore's editing of *The Collected Letters of D. H. Lawrence* (1962). See also F. R. Leavis, " 'Lawrence Scholarship' and Lawrence," SEWANEE REVIEW, LXXI (Jan-March 1963), [25]-35.]

2392 Fitzgerald, F[rancis] Scott. THE LETTERS OF F. SCOTT FITZGERALD, ed and with an Introduction by Andrew Turnbull (NY: Scribner's, 1963), pp. 73, 97, 179, 433, 527, 581.

[Fitzgerald frequently compares other modern writers unfavorably to DHL. The "original D. H. Lawrence is infinitely greater than" John Steinbeck, "a cheap, blatant imitation" of him. Thomas Wolfe is "too 'smart' " to risk comparison with "a solid gold bar" like Hemingway's "courage" or DHL's "intense cohabitation." Glenway Westcott's work is "old stuff" that DHL and others did long before him. Concerning "the world into which willy-nilly one's children will grow up the most accurate data can be found in the European leaders such as Lawrence, Jung and Spengler."]

2393 Ford, George H. "An Introductory Note to D. H. Lawrence's Prologue to *Women in Love*," TEXAS QUARTERLY, VI (Spring 1963), 92-97.

This newly published manuscript of the cancelled "Prologue" to *Women in Love* provides a key both to the novel and to a basic conflict in DHL's own character. It reveals that DHL's objective in the novel was to explore love between man and man, as well as love between man and woman. Friendship between men was a preoccupation of DHL's in much of his fiction and in his personal life, where he conceived of it as a "possible cure for man's loneliness." Evidence suggests that this "Prologue" was written in 1916 when DHL undertook a complete rewriting of the novel. Perhaps DHL abandoned this chapter because he feared trouble with censors, but several technical, artistic advantages also justify exclusion of the "Prologue."

2394 Goodheart, Eugene. THE UTOPIAN VISION OF D. H. LAWRENCE (Chicago: University of Chicago P, 1963); excerpt from Chap. V, pp, 149-59, rptd as "*The Man Who Died*," in CRITICS ON D. H. LAWRENCE, ed by W. T. Andrews (Lond: Allen & Unwin; Coral Gables, FL: University of Miami P [Readings in Literary Criticism 9], 1971), pp. 109-16.

DHL was a Nietzschean "tablet-breaker," a figure possessed of a prophetic vision "whose characteristic impulse is to divert the current of tradition into new and hitherto unknown channels." Turning away from the Victorian conception of society as a system of obligations, DHL emphasized his Utopian conception of society as the outgrowth of the fulfillment of the "profound spontaneous soul of men." The human impulse toward community, not obligation or duty, makes the spontaneous creative act both "purposive and selfless." Within the spontaneous mode, the individual develops through the dialectic between impulse and resistance toward the free surrender of the self to the human community. Like his vision of society, DHL's artistic practice was new. His art, as in *The Rainbow,* is not an imitation of "already enacted life" but "an imaginative adventure in which the imagination seeks to transcend the old life." Beginning with the individual and imagining his fulfillment in a Utopian society which offers such opportunities, DHL sometimes loses track of the concrete facts of the world--which would have helped to define his characters--and lapses into abstraction. Too often his characters are not really dramatically there, partially because DHL dissolves before them the hard, resistent obstacles to their fulfillment. What DHL attempted, as a prophetic artist trying through his art to effect change in the world, was to reawaken in modern man a mythical consciousness of the archetypal patterns that recur in the lives of man. He worked, therefore, as in *The Fox* and *St. Mawr,* with dynamic symbolism of the attempt to redirect modern man to the "idea of the fulfilment of the individual in the cosmic order." If *The Fox* is successful, the reader experiences an apprehension of "nature as a field charged with divinity." This effect is much more difficult to achieve in a novel, where length and the necessary repetition of symbols may produce fatigue as well as incantation.

Like all Utopians, DHL saw life as "a fabrication or falsification of natural life," and so, having rejected the actual, he imitated nature. "Like those of the romantics and Whitehead, Lawrence's appeal to nature is part of an imaginative effort to overcome the *bifurcations* of the modern world." Like the young Wordsworth, he particularly valued nature's defiant otherness, its aspect of fierceness and terror. Like Nietzsche he wanted to say yes to life in the Dionysian mode, to experience the extreme moments of being alive. Though, like Hardy, DHL was aware that the natural life could lead to the annihilation or disintegration of identity, his emphasis was on the natural life as opportunity. Indeed his "imaginative career can be understood as a sustained effort to bind nature once again to the civilized life of man." DHL was also a religious artist, though not a Christian. Despite his interest in the figure of Christ, DHL emphasized the body, not the soul. He saw the physical, passional relationship between man and woman as the source of the religious life, indeed, of all life, of all man's creative expressions. In contrast to Freud, DHL saw the unconscious as the seat of man's impulse toward vital, spontaneous self-realization, not as the seat of sexual repression and incest craving. As DHL stresses in *The Rainbow* and *Women in Love,* man truly realizes himself only in a transcendent experience of oneness with the cosmos. The goal is not the woman, who is for DHL ideally a submissive lover and a domestic, nor the world of men beyond, but "the right connection with the cosmos," alone "on the frontier of the unknown."

In such works as *Aaron's Rod* and *Kangaroo,* therefore, DHL moves beyond the love mode to concentrate on the power urge. Though the principal theme of these works is power as "the capacity to be single and self-sufficient," the corollary of the self's making "*voluntary* connections with other vital beings" leads DHL into the most obvious failures of his career. His political imagination reveals itself to be "either feeble or 'hysterical' " as his protagonists' desperate searches for leaders lay him open to the charge of fascism. These works, nevertheless, allowed DHL to develop his understanding of power as that which protects him from "every enticement, every coercion, every narcotic that might cheat" him of his true being. This conception is important in the works of his final period, the period of the reciprocity of tenderness, of which *The Man Who Died* is the masterpiece and "a kind of grand summation of Lawrence's principal themes, a revelation of the strengths and weaknesses of his Utopian ambitions." "Lawrence is essentially like Blake and Nietzsche in his address to the untapped powers of man and his hatred of the rules and forms that curb those powers." Like them, too, he is a visionary "artist beyond good and evil who compels our admiration and mistrust."

2395 Gordyshevskaya, M. "The Circle Completes Itself: Notes on the Contemporary Colonial Novel," INOSTRANNAIA LITERATURA

(Foreign Literature), IX, No. 6 (April 1963), 190-99.
[DHL is among the modern "colonial" novelists considered.] [In Russian.]

2396 Grant, Douglas. "Hands Up, America!" REVIEW OF ENGLISH LITERATURE, IV (Oct 1963), 11-17.

While DHL's "unambiguously personal" *Studies in Classic American Literature* has coherence and an occasional brilliant illumination, it also reveals that DHL "read for the purpose of seeing reflected a revelation which he had already had."

2397 Green, Martin. RE-APPRAISALS: SOME COMMONSENSE READINGS IN AMERICAN LITERATURE (Lond: Hugh Evelyn, 1963), pp. 14, 27, 47-48, 89-90, 109, 181-82, 231-32, 233, 239.

Studies in Classic American Literature helped to initiate American literature as a subject, yet treats literature radically and prophetically, reducing it to psychic or symbolic significance, rather than engaging the totality of meaning in the text. DHL's arbitrary method, characterized by excessive dependence on intuition to interpret a whole national culture, is not criticism, but it has influenced recent American critics like Marius Bewley, Richard Chase, and Leslie Fiedler. In comparison to modern American novelists, both DHL and J. D. Salinger have been called writers for adolescents. In contrast to William Faulkner, DHL always presents his mind in his work and involves our intelligence as Faulkner never does.

2398 Gurko, Leo. "*The Lost Girl*: D. H. Lawrence as a 'Dickens of the Midlands,'" PUBLICATIONS OF THE MODERN LANGUAGE ASSOCIATION, LXXVIII (Dec 1963), 601-5.

DHL's gift of mimicry as a potential "'Dickens of the Midlands'" is evident in his critically unpopular novel, *The Lost Girl*, the ragged shape of which is the result of its split composition, started in 1912 and finished in 1920. The heroine, Alvina, survives in the unattractive Midlands through her double nature, making the typical Laurentian progression from conventional surface to deeper being. In DHL's sexual comedy, Alvina grows up in the middle class only half alive and thus is driven to sexual actions which never help her to realize herself. Rescued from this Philistine world by a European troupe of actors masquerading as American Indians, she finds in this group her lost self and gets a new name which allows her to transcend her old life. The troupe's Wild West show, rather than implying that one must literally go primitive to rise above civilized death, dramatizes the rejuvenating effect of the imaginative gesture in reaching as far as possible towards an antithetical persona. Although the novel is banal in its treatment of Cicio and the troupe and in its use as a medium for DHL's opinions, nowhere else do DHL's Dickensian qualities of caricature and great narrative energy appear in so pure a form.

2399 Hartt, Julian N. "The Travail of Erotic Man," THE LOST IMAGE OF MAN (Baton Rouge: Louisiana State UP, 1963), pp. 55-60.

Lady Chatterley's Lover exemplifies the first of two phases in the modification of romantic ideals of love and sex in the twentieth century. DHL presents the "image of a person who discovers in fulfilled sexual love the key to fulfilled human life." DHL's concepts were subsequently displaced by a second phase "by which sexual love is stripped of the last shred of traditional *and* Lawrentian sentimentality."

    2400 Hirashima, Junko. "Jiyû to Sokubaku (D. H. Lawrence: 'The Thorn in the Flesh' no Sekai)" (D. H. Lawrence: "The Thorn in the Flesh"), BAIKA TANKIDAIGAKU KENKYUKIYO (Baika Tankidaigaku), No. 12 (Oct 1963), 44-58.

[In Japanese.]

    2401 Iida, Kôsaku. "D. H. Lawrence Sonzai to Ai" (D. H. Lawrence-- Existence and Love), COLLECTED TREATISES FOR THE 35TH ANNIVERSARY OF KANAGAWA UNIVERSITY, Autumn 1963, pp. 663-77.

[In Japanese.]

    2402 Ingamells, John. "Cézanne in England 1910-1930," BRITISH JOURNAL OF AESTHETICS, V (Oct 1965), 341-50, espec 346-47.
The fallacy of "the absolute and plastic approach" to Cézanne's painting was exposed by DHL in 1929. Whereas Bloomsbury saw in Cézanne's work "the full realization of their aesthetic emotion," DHL recognized an expression of his "life force." The important contribution of DHL to the appreciation of Cézanne is that he "made significant form seem an extremely trivial aspect of Cézanne's work."

    2403 Iwata, Noboru. "*St. Mawr* no Hyôka" (The Evaluation of *St. Mawr*), LITERARY SYMPOSIUM (Aichi University), No. 24 (Feb 1963), 105-29.

[In Japanese.]

    2404 Kitazawa, Yoshihiro. "D. H. Lawrence no Kaikyûkan (Dai Ikki no Baai)" (Class Consciousness of D. H. Lawrence), PRELIMINARY ESSAY (Tôhoku University), No. 5 (March 1963), 31-36.

[In Japanese.]

    2405 Koljević, Svetozar. "Lorensovo traganje za izgubljenim rajem" (Lawrence's Search for Paradise Lost), in TRIJUMF INTELIGENCIJE (Belgrade, 1963), pp. 43-61.

[DHL's quest for recovery of paradise.] [In Serbo-Croatian.]

    2406 Land, Myrick. "As a Would-be Messiah, Mr. D. H. Lawrence Endures his Sad Lot Among a Host of Friends," THE FINE ART OF LITERARY MAYHEM: A LIVELY ACCOUNT OF FAMOUS WRITERS AND THEIR FEUDS (NY: Holt, Rinehart & Winston; Lond: Hamilton, 1963), pp. 136-60.
The elopement of DHL and Frieda von Richthofen Weekley in the spring of 1912 coincided with the first months of the relationship between Katherine Mansfield and John Middleton Murry. Shortly after Murry's little magazine, RHYTHM,

accepted a story by DHL, the two couples met and became friends. DHL undertook to advise Murry, with insufferable pomposity, about the course his financial and romantic affairs should take. When the two couples lived as neighbors in Cornwall, Katherine's reservations about DHL's wish to make a Utopian experiment of living together were reinforced by the Lawrences' frequent battles with thrown crockery and physical blows. After the Murrys left, the relationship was not renewed until 1919, when Murry, as editor of ATHENAEUM, accepted one of DHL's articles but rejected another, particularly bitter one. DHL responded with a hate-filled letter to Katherine. Murry expressed his hostility in two scathing reviews of *The Lost Girl* and *Women in Love*. Then suddenly he wrote contritely to DHL, begging for a reconciliation. When DHL returned to England from America briefly in 1923-1924, he gave a dinner at the Cafe Royal for a group of friends, including Murry, S. S. Koteliansky, Donald and Catherine Carswell, Mark Gertler, Mary Cannan, and Dorothy Brett, in what Mrs. Carswell saw as a gathering of disciples at the Last Supper. This impression was furthered, after DHL asked each in turn to leave dying England and to follow him to the New World, when Murry kissed him effusively and declared, " 'In the past I *have* betrayed you. But never again.' " Despite his promise to come to New Mexico, Murry showed no interest in doing so. On his return to America, DHL wrote to Murry, with reference to the Cafe Royal dinner, " 'Let's wipe off all that Judas-Jesus slime.' " In 1929 Murry wrote suggesting that they meet again, but DHL declined: ' 'We are a dissonance.' " The following year DHL died, but Murry spent the rest of his life rehashing "the troubled friendship he could neither sustain nor surrender." [An informal, entertaining survey that is journalistic rather than scholarly in tone.]

2407 Lawrence, Robert G. "Further Notes on D. H. Lawrence's 'Rocking-Horse,' " COLLEGE ENGLISH, XXIV (Jan 1963), 324; rptd in D. H. LAWRENCE: "THE ROCKING-HORSE WINNER," ed by Dominick P. Consolo (Columbus, OH: Merrill [The Merrill Literary Casebook Series], 1969), p. 57.
[Comment on W. R. Martin, "Fancy or Imagination? 'The Rocking-Horse Winner,' " COLLEGE ENGLISH, XXIV (Oct 1962), 64-65.] In "The Rocking-Horse Winner,' " the rocking horse is also an allusion to the Trojan horse, "a familiar symbol of deception." [See also another reply to Martin by William D. Burroughs, "No Defense for 'The Rocking-Horse Winner,' " COLLEGE ENGLISH, XXIV (Jan 1963), 323.]

2408 Leavis, F[rank] R[aymond]. " 'Lawrence Scholarship' and Lawrence," SEWANEE REVIEW, LXXI (March 1963), 25-35; rptd in ANNA KARENINA AND OTHER ESSAYS, by F. R. Leavis (Lond: Chatto & Windus; NY: Random House, Pantheon Books, 1967), pp. 167-76.
[Primarily an attack on Harry T. Moore's edition of *The Collected Letters of D. H. Lawrence* as a "signal and peculiarly offensive instance" of the "growth of industrial literary scholarship" and of " 'authorities.' "] DHL's correspondence reveals his "marvellous sympathetic responsiveness," his varying of "tone and manner" with the correspondent. His letters to "ladies of the *beau monde*," such as Lady Cynthia Asquith and Lady Ottoline Morrell, are among his "most intensely ear-

nest letters to women" and are worth an essay in themselves. Part of DHL's genius is seen in his "comedy, alive with amused and placing observation, but wholly free from malice or complacency." [A letter to Ottoline Morrell is discussed in detail to illustrate the point. See also response by Harry T. Moore, "Correspondence," SEWANEE REVIEW, LXXI (Spring 1963), 347-48; and N. N. Feltes's rejoinder in defense of Leavis, "Correspondence," SEWANEE REVIEW, LXXI (Oct-Dec 1963), 696-97.]

2409 Lerner, Laurence. "How Beastly the Bourgeois Is," CRITICAL SURVEY, I (Spring 1963), 87-89; rptd as " 'How beastly the bourgeois is': Lawrence's Poetry," in THE TRUTHTELLERS: JANE AUSTEN, GEORGE ELIOT, D. H. LAWRENCE, by Laurence Lerner (NY: Schocken Books, 1967), pp. 220-24.

In "How Beastly the Bourgeois Is," DHL perfectly captures the tone of a witty female speaker, but the effect breaks down when we realize that the poem is serious. Lacking the formality of good satire, the poem becomes merely unpleasant grumbling. DHL's poetry does not express emotion; it betrays it by relying on luck rather than work.

2410 Levin, Richard. "The Lady and Her Horsekeeper: Middleton or Rowley?" NOTES AND QUERIES, X (Aug 1963), 303-6.

In attributing a special virility to keepers of animals (*St. Mawr, Lady Chatterley's Lover*), DHL is drawing on a very old conception that appears in folk tales, legends, myths--and particularly in the plays of Thomas Middleton.

2411 Lo Curzio, Guglielmo. "Il viaggiatore Lawrence" (Lawrence's Travels), LA SICILIA (Catania), 8 Jan 1963, p. 3.

[Review of *Libri di viaggio e pagine di paese* (*Complete Collection of Travel Books*) by D. H. Lawrence, with an Introduction by Piero Nardi (1961).] In his travel books, DHL shows his great incisiveness when he discusses the main themes of his thought--sex, in particular. In Italian people he saw the fulfillment of a primordial way of life, and in the Etruscans he found an erotic message. Sex was for DHL a means of revolt against the establishment, civilization, progress. [In Italian.]

2412 Maetzke, Ernst-Otto. "Männer mit roten Hosen" (Men in Red Trousers), FRANKFURTER ALLGEMEINE ZEITUNG, 8 Oct 1963.

DHL's *Mornings in Mexico,* mainly concerned with the author's search for unsophisticated life, revives the stereotype of the indomitable male. [In German.]

2413 Marković, Vida E. "David Herbert Lorens" (David Herbert Lawrence), in ENGLESKI ROMAN XX VEKA (The English Novel of the Twentieth Century), I (Belgrade: Naučna, 1963), pp. 78-99, 170-73.

[Introduction to DHL's life and work, pp. 78-99, and a bibliographical note, pp. 170-73.] [In Serbo-Croatian.]

2414 Masugi, Tadashi. "D. H. Lawrence no Kaikyûkan--Dai Sanki no Baai" (D. H. Lawrence's View of Social Class, Especially in His

Third Period), SHIRON (Tôhoku University), No. 5 (March 1963), 44-52. [In Japanese.]

2415 Moore, Harry T. "Correspondence," SEWANEE REVIEW, LXXI (Spring 1963), 347-48; rptd as "Comment on Leavis," in AGE OF THE MODERN AND OTHER LITERARY ESSAYS, by Harry T. Moore (Carbondale and Edwardsville: Southern Illinois UP; Lond and Amsterdam: Feffer & Simons, 1971), pp. 70-72.
[Reply to F. R. Leavis, " 'Lawrence Scholarship' and Lawrence," SEWANEE REVIEW, LXXI (Jan-March 1963), 25-35, citing Moore's scholarly credentials and editorial problems, comparing Leavis's and his followers' use of literary criticism to the Storm Troopers' bludgeoning of those who disagreed, and suggesting that Leavis's concern with side issues diverts "attention from those twelve hundred Lawrence letters." See also N. N. Feltes's rejoinder in defense of Leavis in "Correspondence," SEWANEE REVIEW, LXXI (Oct-Dec 1963), 696-97.]

2416 Moore, Harry T. "D. H. Lawrence," TIMES LITERARY SUPPLEMENT (Lond), 19 Dec 1963, p. 1038.
[Letter to the Editor in further comment on issues raised in the letter by Aerol Arnold, "D. H. Lawrence," TIMES LITERARY SUPPLEMENT (Lond), 21 Nov 1963, p. 956.] While DHL in "The Woman Who Rode Away" "made use of that sacrificial cave above Arroyo Seco" near Taos, "he really intended the setting of the story to be Mexico." The woman in the story is partly based on Mabel Dodge Luhan. "The landscape is a blending of Sangre de Cristo and Sierra Madre, but mostly the latter."

2417 Moore, Harry T. "*The Plumed Serpent*: Vision and Language," in D. H. LAWRENCE: A COLLECTION OF CRITICAL ESSAYS, ed by Mark Spilka (Englewood Cliffs, NJ: Prentice-Hall, 1963), pp. 61-71.
The Plumed Serpent is both DHL's most ambitious undertaking and his greatest failure. The basic vision embodied in the work derives from DHL's fascination with the Nietzschean *Übermensch* who will lead mankind to a better future and from his readings of American literature, which led him to an exploration of the American spirit and a perception of the latent primitivism of the New World. Although DHL harshly criticized civilization in other works, "he attempted melioration only in terms of a seemingly plausible social order." But in *The Plumed Serpent,* DHL's criticism is more destructive, since he endorses the replacement of the established order with a new one, "really an ancient and entirely outmoded one," which he envisions as the basis for future human progress. Predictably, critics have cited *The Plumed Serpent* as evidence for the erroneous conclusion that DHL was a Fascist.

2418 Moore, Harry T. "Richard Aldington in His Last Years," TEXAS QUARTERLY, VI (Autumn 1963), 60-74; rptd in RICHARD ALDINGTON: AN INTIMATE PORTRAIT, ed by Alister Kershaw and F.-J. Temple (Carbondale and Edwardsville: Southern Illinois

UP, 1965), pp. 80-105, espec pp. 80-91, 98-101.
[Recalling Richard Aldington's stories and letters about DHL, the author discusses DHL's reactions to Aldington's DEATH OF A HERO, Aldous Huxley's POINT COUNTER POINT, and the reviews of *Lady Chatterley's Lover,* and recounts Aldington's treatments of DHL in several books.]

2419 Mori, Haruhide. "Geijutsu no Hôkai--*Aaron's Rod* to *Kangaroo* no Shisô to Hyôgen" (Failure of Art: Ideas and Expression in *Aaron's Rod* and *Kangaroo*), ÔSAKA LITERARY REVIEW (Ôsaka University), No. 2 (July 1963), 51-61.
[In Japanese.]

2420 Mori, Haruhide. "Lawrence no Gikyoku ni Kansuru Oboegaki: *Mrs. Holroyd, Touch and Go, David*" (Notes on Lawrence's Plays: *Mrs. Holroyd, Touch and Go, David*), PRELUDE (Ôsaka University), No. 7 (Nov 1963), 26-36.
[In Japanese.]

2421 Morrell, Lady Ottoline. THE EARLY MEMOIRS (1873-1915) OF LADY OTTOLINE MORRELL, ed by Robert Gathorne-Hardy (Lond: Faber & Faber, 1963), pp. 177, 219, 270-74, 279-80, 283; pub in America as MEMOIRS OF LADY OTTOLINE MORRELL: A STUDY IN FRIENDSHIP, 1873-1915, ed by Robert Gathorne-Hardy (NY: Knopf, 1964), pp. 147, 204, 273-78, 283-84, 289.
[Account of Lady Ottoline Morrell's meeting DHL in Feb 1915, of her visits to the Lawrences at Greatham, and of acquaintances' brief remarks about DHL.] Raymond Asquith did not believe peasants talked as DHL represented in *The White Peacock.* Bertrand Russell thought DHL a prophet who was always right. ["Lawrence is the spirit of flame," Lady Ottoline wrote in her journal.] Raised by a mother who was "a very remarkable woman," DHL, like Burns, sprang from a working-class home but, "unlike Burns, was never at one with his old companions." Although *The Rainbow* seemed written in a "slapdash amateurish style," it also contained passages of intensity and passion that must have grown out of DHL's "own life and struggles with his wife, Frieda."

2422 Morse, J. Mitchell. "Notes and Questions on D. H. Lawrence's *Sons and Lovers,*" EXERCISE EXCHANGE, X (March 1963), 16-19.
[A list of study questions and a brief discussion of symbol and vocabulary.]

2423 Moynahan, Julian. THE DEED OF LIFE: THE NOVELS AND TALES OF D. H. LAWRENCE (Princeton, NJ: Princeton UP, 1963, rptd 1966; Lond: Oxford UP, 1966); excerpt, pp. 13-31, rptd as "*Sons and Lovers*: The Search for Form," in D. H. LAWRENCE, "SONS AND LOVERS": TEXT, BACKGROUND, AND CRITICISM, ed by Julian Moynahan (NY: Viking P [Viking Critical Library Edition], 1968), pp. 560-76; excerpt, pp. 72-89, rptd as "The Discovery of Form," in TWENTIETH CENTURY INTERPRETATIONS OF "WOMEN IN LOVE": A COLLECTION OF CRITICAL ESSAYS, ed by Stephen J. Miko (Englewood Cliffs, NJ: Prentice-Hall, 1969), pp. 61-72; excerpt, pp. 63-72, rptd as "Ritual Scenes in *The Rainbow*," in D. H. LAWRENCE: "THE RAINBOW" AND "WOMEN IN LOVE," A CASEBOOK, ed by Colin Clarke (Lond: Macmillan, 1969); Nashville: Aurora Publishers, 1970), pp. 142-50.

The "most important and interesting work" of DHL, a great, though "uneven," novelist, includes *Sons and Lovers, The Rainbow, Women in Love, The Lost Girl, Lady Chatterley's Lover,* and selected shorter tales. "A writer of tales first and last," DHL continues the "richest traditions of English fiction beginning with Richardson" and "modifies tradition by adding something new." For DHL, "values are discovered or created outright in the act of living," and his "paramount importance" is that he "looked more closely than any other modern writer in English at the knotty fibers of human feeling and instinct which tie ordinary men to one another." *The White Peacock* and *The Trespasser* are "improvisations," the beginnings of DHL's "search for form," the *donne* of both novels being "women undermine men's hold on life." *Sons and Lovers* is DHL's breakthrough: "the insight it bred is released to become the driving power in subsequent books of a new, major exploration of human relationships." Full of "richly detailed specifications of place and person," *Sons and Lovers* is organized by three interrelated "orders of matrices"--autobiographical narrative, psychoanalytic theory, and " 'passional' " or " 'vital' " logic. This last matrix, in which "short of death there is no occasion in experience when the individual cannot make the correct, life-enhancing choice," accounts for Paul's heroism and the ending of the novel: he "holds and uses this freedom." *The Rainbow* and *Women in Love* are DHL's "discovery of form." *The Rainbow* is DHL's "sacred book"--its theme "salvation"--for which he draws on materials from religious tradition for "his secular but visionary ends." Salvation is "a wholesome state of being attainable here and now," and the "crucial relationship" is "between a man and woman." The "expanding symbols" (arch, rainbow, cathedral), "symbolic characters," and "ritual scenes" help to deepen "one's sense of vital human realities as they exist within society and history, and of vital forces of nature underlying civilization." Throughout *Women in Love,* DHL's "most difficult" and "fully achieved" novel, the "process of dissolution is universal," determining both the "form of the society represented and ... the nature of human experience ... within society." Bleaker than *The Rainbow,* the novel completes a cycle in DHL's development as a novelist: having achieved a "dazzlingly original narrative form" by which to confront "systems of custom and convention" with " 'profound intuitions of life,' " DHL found there was no longer "any common ground where life and history could meet, mingle, and enhance each other." *Aaron's Rod, Kangaroo,* and *The Plumed Serpent,* DHL's "breaking of form" and among his worst works, represent his "hapless infatuation with notions of anti-democratic leadership." The main characters are self-exiles from the European bourgeoisie who despair of hope and fall into "political and social extremism"--a formula which also covers DHL "during some of these years." *The Lost Girl* and *Lady Chatterley's Lover* "dramatize a recoil from dead things" and are "pastoral" novels in which "courage, cunning, endurance and an unimpaired will" are demanded of the lovers as they "create or recreate their own freedom." DHL's "deed of life," the "most valuable and moving" thing in them is his "absolute insistence that the experience which is wholly private and personal shall not be submerged and lost in the tumult of public catastrophe or sacrificed to any set of merely general standards." DHL's tales like "Odour of Chrysanthemums," *The Fox,* "The Man Who Loved Islands," and *The Virgin and the Gipsy* contain "less strained argument" and a "more direct release of his peculiarly rich sense of life" than the novels often do.

2424 Murphy, Terrence J. CENSORSHIP: GOVERNMENT AND OBSCENITY (Baltimore and Dublin: Helicon P, 1963), pp. 3, 100, 127, 181-86, 199, 200, 209, 218.

Only two books have been challenged in twenty-five years under federal law in the United States--Joyce's ULYSSES and DHL's *Lady Chatterley's Lover*--and both were then allowed to circulate. "When *Lady Chatterley's Lover* became a topic of public conversation twenty-five members of Congress made . . . speeches or insertions in the [CONGRESSIONAL] RECORD." In 1959 the New York Court of Appeals upheld the statute under which the film of *Lady Chatterley's Lover* was banned for presenting adultery as "a proper pattern of behavior," but this decision was later reversed by the U. S. Supreme Court in an opinion (Kingsley International Pictures v. Board of Regents), which "never met the argument that the state must protect 'order and morality.' " The "popular image of the anti-obscenity program of the Post Office Department" was "distorted" by the front-page publicity given the *Lady Chatterley's Lover* censorship case (Grove Press v. Christenberry), which created a demand for the novel disproportionate to its literary merits.

2425 Nakamura, Yoshio. "*The Lost Girl* Oboegaki" (Notes on *The Lost Girl*), LITERARY SYMPOSIUM (Aichi University), No. 24 (Feb 1963), 81-103.

[In Japanese.]

2426 Nazareth, Peter. "D. H. Lawrence and Sex," TRANSITION, III (March 1963), 38-43.

[Second part of a two-part article, the first part of which is pub in TRANSITION, II (Oct 1962), 54-57.] To offset historically destructive attitudes, DHL tries to strike a balance between the consciousness of sex and the experience of sex. His use of four-letter words in *Lady Chatterley's Lover* (of which Aldous Huxley approved) is an attempt to promote healthy realism. Upholding the traditional Christian beliefs on marriage, DHL strives to show how the vitality of this union is preserved by a sacred regard for sexuality in all its complexity. He also has pointed out the perverse or false loves with which man can be preoccupied and deluded. Examining Birkin's stoning of the moon's reflection in *Women in Love,* we can see, contrary to Forster's opinion, the wholeness of DHL idealized. The primitivism often charged to DHL could not have fostered this wholeness.

2427 Ninomiya, Takamichi. "Futatsu no 'Hi-Gakkyuteki' Lawrence Ron (Anais Nin to Henry Miller)" (Two Unprofessional Studies of Lawrence--Anaïs Nin's and Henry Miller's), KÔBE MISCELLANY (Kôbe University), No. 2 (June 1963), 43-69.

[On the treatment of DHL in Anaïs Nin, D. H. LAWRENCE: AN UNPROFES-

SIONAL STUDY and Henry Miller's uncompleted THE WORLD OF LAWRENCE.] [In Japanese.]

2428 Nishikawa, Masaharu. "D. H. Lawrence ni Okeru Shi no Ishiki" (On the Consciousness of Death in D. H. Lawrence's Works), YAMATO BUNKA (Tenri University), No. 41 (March 1963), 28-40. [In Japanese.]

2429 "Notes on Current Books," VIRGINIA QUARTERLY REVIEW, XXXIX (Winter 1963), xxiii.

The "extraordinarily vivid" letters in *The Collected Letters of D. H. Lawrence,* ed by Harry T. Moore, "supply information" needed by the scholar and teacher of DHL's poetry and prose.

2430 O'Connor, Frank [pseud of Michael O'Donovan]. THE LONELY VOICE: A STUDY OF THE SHORT STORY (Lond: Macmillan; Cleveland and NY: World, 1963), pp. 143-55; excerpt, pp. 153-55, rptd as "Poe and 'The Rocking-Horse Winner,'" in D. H. LAWRENCE: "THE ROCKING-HORSE WINNER," ed by Dominick P. Consolo (Columbus, OH: Merrill [The Merrill Literary Casebook Series], 1969), pp. 58-59.

Although DHL's novels after *Sons and Lovers* are unreadable, his stories are very good, especially in the treatment of nature at which DHL excelled. [Includes speculation on the implication of the homosexual subject matter.]

2431 Panichas, George A. "D. H. Lawrence's Biblical Play *David,*" MODERN DRAMA, VI (Sept 1963), 164-76; rptd as Chap. VI, "The Biblical Play *David,*" ADVENTURE IN CONSCIOUSNESS: THE MEANING OF D. H. LAWRENCE'S RELIGIOUS QUEST (The Hague: Mouton, 1964), pp. 136-50.

DHL's play *David,* written in 1925 shortly after diagnosis of his advanced tuberculosis, shows DHL's reliance on the power of endurance to save him from despair. Although DHL disliked his own name David, he identified himself with the Biblical David, whose endurance DHL thought one of his most attractive qualities. The Biblical David, as well as Michaelangelo's Florentine sculpture *David,* represented for him the spirit of life, light, love, whereas Saul represented violent negation. [Includes analysis of the ideas in *David.*]

2432 Panichas, George A. "D. H. Lawrence's War Letters," TEXAS STUDIES IN LITERATURE AND LANGUAGE, V (Autumn 1963), 398-409; absorbed into Chap. III, "The Great War of 1914-1918," ADVENTURE IN CONSCIOUSNESS: THE MEANING OF D. H. LAWRENCE'S RELIGIOUS QUEST (The Hague: Mouton, 1964), pp. 62-94.

DHL's correspondence of the 1914-1918 period reveals "with astonishing intensity," a "response to World War I . . . so direct and unequivocal, so real and unvarnished, that to dismiss or misinterpret it as being exaggerated, selfish, egotistical, and hysterical . . . is to deprecate an integrity and seriousness inhering in a consciousness that is in profound travail." DHL's despair, rage, and intransigence and his "portrayals of the soldier type" were centered in his belief that the war was a "blasphemy against life." [Frequent quotations support the discussion.]

2433 Peter, John. "Lady Chatterley for the Last Time I," ESSAYS IN CRITICISM, XIII (July 1963), 301-2.
[Rejoinder to William Empson, "Lady Chatterley Again," ESSAYS IN CRITICISM, XIII (Jan 1963), 101-4; and John Sparrow, "Lady Chatterley Again," ESSAYS IN CRITICISM, XIII (April 1963), 202-5. Refutes arguments put forth by Empson and Sparrow as rejoinders to Peter's attack on G. Wilson Knight's and Sparrow's reading of *Lady Chatterley's Lover* as a celebration of sodomy. Followed by a further rejoinder from John Sparrow, "Lady Chatterley for the Last Time II," ESSAYS IN CRITICISM, XIII (July 1963), 303. See also further discussions in the controversy as follows: G. Wilson Knight, "Lawrence, Joyce and Powys," ESSAYS IN CRITICISM, XI (Oct 1961), 403-17; John Peter, "The Bottom of the Well," ESSAYS IN CRITICISM, XII (April 1962), 226-27; John Sparrow, "Regina v. Penguin Books Ltd.: An Undisclosed Element in the Case," ENCOUNTER, XVIII (Feb 1962), 35-43; John Sparrow, "Afterthoughts on Regina v. Penguin Books Ltd.," ENCOUNTER, XVIII (June 1962), 83-88; and John Peter, "Lady Chatterley Again," ESSAYS IN CRITICISM, XII (Oct 1962), 445-47.]

2434 Pinto, Vivian de Sola. "Lawrence and Frieda," ENGLISH, XIV (Spring 1963), 135-39.
DHL lies somewhere between Keats and Byron as one of the three great poet letter-writers in English. *The Collected Letters of D. H. Lawrence,* ed by Harry T. Moore (1962), however, is deficient in its incompleteness, its lack of source identification, and its failure to correct "slips." FRIEDA LAWRENCE: THE MEMOIRS AND CORRESPONDENCE ed by E. W. Tedlock, Jr. (1961) preserves the essence of a great-hearted woman who shares with us her vision of "the great English writer to whom she was at once wife, mother, and devoted comrade."

2435 Powell, Lawrence Clark. SOUTHWESTERN BOOK TRAILS: A READER'S GUIDE TO THE HEARTLAND OF NEW MEXICO AND ARIZONA (Albuquerque: Horn & Wallace, 1963), pp. 25, 42, 43-44, 45.
"D. H. Lawrence *was* a mystic. Indians and landscape moved him to brood on the cosmos and to write *The Plumed Serpent,* a religious-philosophical-political novel about Mexico." DHL was lured to New Mexico by Mabel Dodge Luhan, who gave him Kiowa Ranch, from which the view was "one of the most fabulous of New Mexico's panoramas."

2436 Rehder, Jessie (ed). THE STORY AT WORK: AN ANTHOLOGY (NY: Odyssey P, 1963), pp. 240-41.
[Brief commentary on the symbolism in "The Horse-Dealer's Daughter," which is reprinted in the anthology, pp. 223-40.]

2437 Requardt, Egon. "D. H. Lawrence: Solipsist oder Prophet einer neuen Gemeinschaft?" (D. H. Lawrence: Solipsist or Prophet of a New Community?), DIE NEUEREN SPRACHEN, ns XII (Frankfurt, 1963), 506-15.

DHL's portrayal of a new community in *The Plumed Serpent* is, despite its fascination, naive and unconvincing. His cult of natural leadership and the glorification of the unconscious result in cruelty and barbarity. Although DHL rejects nationalism and faith in political creeds, the members of the new community are linked together by their hatred of the "gringos" and the party-like discipline of Ramón's and Cipriano's troops. DHL's wavering between the extremes of a new community and solipsism may be explained by disappointment in his personal life. [In German.]

2438 Roberts, Warren. A BIBLIOGRAPHY OF D. H. LAWRENCE (Lond: Rupert Hart-Davis, 1963); 2nd ed rvd: (Cambridge: Cambridge UP, 1982).

[Containing sections devoted to books and pamphlets, contributions to books, contributions to periodicals, translations, manuscripts, and books and pamphlets about DHL, this is the definitive bibliography of DHL. Entries for books by DHL provide quasi-facsimile title-page transcription, physical description of binding and contents, information on publishing dates, price, and number of copies printed, and a list of variant copies when known.] "An attempt has been made to identify all first appearances in print of the works of D. H. Lawrence, both in periodical and book form, with sufficient cross references to permit the student to follow each work through its significant publications."

2439 Rovit, Earl. "Books in English," BOOKS ABROAD, XXXVII (Autumn 1963), 458.

The Collected Letters of D. H. Lawrence, ed by Harry T. Moore, reveals a "radical change in Lawrence's style and personality . . . at about the time of World War I." Whereas the pre-war letters are engagingly eloquent, "Lawrence's voice becomes increasingly arrogant, gossipy, and pretentiously shrewish from 1916 on."

2440 Saibara, Susumu. "D. H. Lawrence no Doku Shin Jidai (I)" (The Early Life of D. H. Lawrence--His Life and World [I]), STUDIES OF SOCIAL SCIENCE (Kôchi Junior College), No. 14 (Feb 1963), 1-20.

[In Japanese.]

2441 Saxena, H. S. "Lawrence's Views on Character," INDIAN JOURNAL OF ENGLISH STUDIES, IV, No. 1 (1963), 175-82.

DHL mainly portrays his characters not through objective descriptions of behavior but through "the expression of feelings that surge beneath and border with the unconscious." His "most distinctive gift was his insight into the obscure origins of human relationships." Yet he "could draw unforgettable characters with almost Dickensian facility," and he thought " 'there ought to be a bit of both' " external and internal action. Whereas Thomas Hardy presents Egdon Heath as a dominant force in the action of human characters, DHL's characters are not dominated by physical setting but rather enter into a " 'quick relatedness to all the other things in the novel.' " Thus, "instead of merely creating social and mental personalities," as he accused John Galsworthy, E. M. Forster, and Jane Austen of doing, DHL sought "to change the quality of human relationship" by restoring " 'the natural warm flow of common sympathy between man and man, man and woman.' "

2442 Serraillier, Ian. "Introduction," *D. H. Lawrence: Selected Tales* (Lond: Heinemann Educational Books, 1963; rptd [New Windmill Series], 1972), pp. vii-xi.

[Brief biographical sketch mentioning DHL's contrasting parents, his youthful illnesses, his friendship with Jessie Chambers, his elopement with Frieda, the hostility against him during the war, his wanderings throughout the world.] Of the stories included in this collection, "Odour of Chrysanthemums" and "The Christening" portray life in the miner's home as DHL knew it in youth, "Monkey Nuts" and "Tickets, Please" "re-create war-time experiences on the home front," "Things" and "The Man Who Loved Islands" cruelly satirize friends of DHL's, and "Daughters of the Vicar" presents the repressive "life of the vicarage . . . as a destructive force."

2443 Shirai, Toshitaka. "D. H. Lawrence no Kaikyû Kan" (D. H. Lawrence and Class), SHIRON (Tôhoku University), No. 5 (March 1963), 37-43.

[In Japanese.]

2444 Smith, L. E. W. "Snake," CRITICAL SURVEY, I (Spring 1963), 81-86; rptd in TWELVE POEMS CONSIDERED, by L. E. W. Smith (Lond: Methuen, 1964), pp. 131-43.

"Snake" is a perfect example of the union of form and content. [Line by line analysis of rhythm, grammar, and syntax supports the point.]

2445 Sparrow, John. "Lady Chatterley Again," ESSAYS IN CRITICISM, XIII (April 1963), 202-5.

[Rejoinder to John Peter, "Lady Chatterley Again," ESSAYS IN CRITICISM, XII (Oct 1962), 445-47. Refutes Peter's objections to G. Wilson Knight's and Sparrow's reading of *Lady Chatterley's Lover* as a celebration of anal sex. See also further discussions in the controversy as follows: G. Wilson Knight, "Lawrence, Joyce and Powys," ESSAYS IN CRITICISM, XI (Oct 1961), 403-17; John Peter, "The Bottom of the Well," ESSAYS IN CRITICISM, XII (April 1962), 226-27; John Sparrow, "Regina v. Penguin Books Ltd.: An Undisclosed Element in the Case," ENCOUNTER, XVIII (Feb 1962), 35-43; John Sparrow, "Afterthoughts on Regina v. Penguin Books Ltd.," ENCOUNTER, XVIII (June 1962), 83-88; William Empson, "Lady Chatterley Again," ESSAYS IN CRITICISM, XIII (Jan 1963), 101-4; John Peter, "Lady Chatterley for the Last Time I," ESSAYS IN CRITICISM, XIII (July 1963), 301-2; and John Sparrow, "Lady Chatterley for the Last Time II," ESSAYS IN CRITICISM, XIII (July 1963), 303.]

2446 Sparrow, John. "Lady Chatterley for the Last Time II," ESSAYS IN CRITICISM, XIII (July 1963), 303.

[Further rejoinder to John Peter, "Lady Chatterley for the Last Time I," ESSAYS

IN CRITICISM, XIII (July 1963), 301-2. Refutes Peter's objections to arguments advanced by William Empson and Sparrow as rejoinders to Peter's attack on G. Wilson Knight's and Sparrow's reading of *Lady Chatterley's Lover* as a celebration of sodomy. See also further discussions in the controversy as follows: G. Wilson Knight, "Lawrence, Joyce and Powys," ESSAYS IN CRITICISM, XI (Oct 1961), 403-17; John Peter, "The Bottom of the Well," ESSAYS IN CRITICISM, XII (April 1962), 226-27; John Sparrow, "Regina v. Penguin Books Ltd.: An Undisclosed Element in the Case," ENCOUNTER, XVIII (Feb 1962), 35-43; John Sparrow, "Afterthoughts on Regina v. Penguin Books Ltd.," ENCOUNTER, XVIII (June 1962), 83-88; John Peter, "Lady Chatterley Again," ESSAYS IN CRITICISM, XII (Oct 1962), 445-47; William Empson, "Lady Chatterley Again," ESSAYS IN CRITICISM, XIII (Jan 1963), 101-4; and John Sparrow, "Lady Chatterley Again," ESSAYS IN CRITICISM, XIII (April 1963), 202-5.]

2447 Spender, Stephen. "Lawrence," THE CONCISE ENCYCLOPEDIA OF ENGLISH AND AMERICAN POETS AND POETRY, ed by Stephen Spender and Donald Hall (NY: Hawthorne, 1963), pp. 188-89.

DHL's poetic powers are more evident in his novels and short stories than in his poetry. DHL is most at home in free verse and his greatest strength lies in his images. The death poems in *Last Poems* show the beginning of a new development in his poetry.

2448 Spender, Stephen. "The Modern Necessity," THE STRUGGLE OF THE MODERN (Berkeley: University of California P, 1963), pp. 98-109.

Gerard Manley Hopkins and DHL were both forced by the pressures of modern life into a modern idiom. Whereas Hopkins was overly concerned with poetic form, DHL had little knowledge of it. In contrast to the aesthetic moderns, DHL held that art was an imitation of life as it is, but he had more feelings than ideas about artistic procedure. His poetry is marred by formlessness and a search for remembered Biblical forms. Although DHL did not consider himself a poet, he gave us more poetry to be grateful for than most professionals.

2449 Spilka, Mark (ed). D. H. LAWRENCE: A COLLECTION OF CRITICAL ESSAYS (Englewood Cliffs, NJ: Prentice-Hall [Twentieth Century Views], 1963).

Essays are organized under the categories "The Major Novels," "The Tales," and "Other Genres," followed by a chronology, notes on contributors, and bibliography. Contents, abstracted under year of first publication: Mark Spilka, "Introduction," pp. 1-14; Dorothy Van Ghent, "On *Sons and Lovers*," pp. 15-28, from THE ENGLISH NOVEL: FORM AND FUNCTION (NY: Holt, Rinehart, and Winston, 1953), pp. 245-61; Marvin Mudrick, "The Originality of *The Rainbow*," pp. 29-49, from SPECTRUM, III (Winter 1959), 3-28; Mark Schorer, "*Women in Love* and Death," pp. 50-60, from HUDSON REVIEW, VI (Spring 1953), 34-47; Harry T. Moore, "*The Plumed Serpent*: Vision and Language," pp. 61-71 (original publication, 1963); Julian Moynahan, "*Lady Chatterley's Lover*: The Deed of Life," pp. 72-92, from ELH, XXVI (March 1959), 66-90; Monroe Engel, "The

Continuity of Lawrence's Short Novels," pp. 93-100, from HUDSON REVIEW, XI (Summer 1958), 201-10; Graham Hough, "Lawrence's Quarrel with Christianity: *The Man Who Died*," pp. 101-11, from THE DARK SUN: A STUDY OF D. H. LAWRENCE (Lond: Duckworth, 1956; NY: Macmillan, 1957), pp. 241-54; Mark Spilka, "Ritual Form in 'The Blind Man,' " pp. 112-16, from THE LOVE ETHIC OF D. H. LAWRENCE (Bloomington: Indiana UP, 1955), pp. 22-31; W. D. Snodgrass, "A Rocking-Horse: The Symbol, the Pattern, the Way to Live," pp. 117-26, from HUDSON REVIEW, XI (Summer 1958), 191-200; V[ivian] de S[ola] Pinto, "Poet Without a Mask," pp. 127-41, from CRITICAL QUARTERLY, III (Spring 1961), 5-18; Arthur E. Waterman, "The Plays of D. H. Lawrence," pp. 142-50, from MODERN DRAMA, II (Feb 1960), 349-57; Richard Foster, "Criticism as Rage: D. H. Lawrence," pp. 151-61, from A D. H. LAWRENCE MISCELLANY, ed by Harry T. Moore (Carbondale: Southern Illinois UP, 1959), pp. 312-25; Raymond Williams, "Lawrence's Social Writings," pp. 162-74 (originally entitled "D. H. Lawrence"), from CULTURE AND SOCIETY, 1780-1950 (Lond: Chatto & Windus; NY: Columbia UP, 1958), pp. 199-215; "Chronology of Important Dates," pp. 175-76 [not abstracted]; "Notes on the Editor and Authors," pp. 177-78 [not abstracted]; "Selected Bibliography," pp. 179-82 [not abstracted].

2450 Stanley, F. R. "The Artist as Pornographer: The Evaluation of D. H. Lawrence's Genius," LITERARY HALF-YEARLY, IV (Jan 1963), 14-27.

The obscenity trial of *Lady Chatterley's Lover* proved one thing: it revealed the meanness of men when confronted by genius.

2451 Steiner, George. "Life of Letters," KENYON REVIEW, XXV (Winter 1963), [174]-77.

Although DHL's moral outrage at times descends to "sheer derision," his letters are equaled only by those of Van Gogh in conveying a "power of presence." DHL's mind was a totalitarian one in the sense that "all facets of private life, of fiction, of doctrine cohere"; in his attitudes about any topic, "the central demon of the novels and paintings leaps at you." Therefore, nothing in DHL's experience can be considered irrelevant to his art; the unpleasantness, the egotism, and the bullying all "relate to the strong center of creation." [Includes a review of *The Collected Letters of D. H. Lawrence*, ed by Harry T. Moore (1962).]

2452 Steinhoff, Anneliese. "Drei alte Frauen im Hochtal von Taos" (Three Old Women in Taos), NEUE DEUTSCHE HEFTE, No. 93 (Gütersloh, 1963), 5-22.

[Report on a visit to Dorothy Brett, Mabel Dodge Luhan, and Frieda Lawrence, mentioning a few reminiscences of their lives with DHL.] [In German.]

2453 Stewart, J. I. M. "Lawrence," EIGHT MODERN WRITERS (Oxford: Oxford UP [Oxford History of English Literature, Vol. XII], 1963), pp. 484-593.

"Like most oracles Lawrence can be readily misinterpreted and like most prophets he can be easily mocked." *The White Peacock*, although flawed in point of view and "flowery" prose, has a "strongly realized" story which introduces major Laurentian themes such as "sacramental" friendship and characters such as the gamekeeper, Annable. *The Trespasser* is "vitiated by an adherence" to the fashionable Russian manner, but *Sons and Lovers,* which "alone would establish him as the foremost English writer of his generation," "gives the effect of one whole and completed action" through its "vivid evocation of one English working class home" as a representative one. In *The Rainbow,* through the theme of marriage, considered in terms less of social relations than of DHL's developing "gospel of the flesh," he "most consistently achieves a purely dramatic projection of his problems." *Women in Love,* for all its simplicity of structure, which sets the "life-theme" in Ursula and Birkin over against the "death-theme in Gudrun and Gerald," is perhaps "the radically original English novel of its age," one which presents complex people who "live at the end of abnormally open channels of communication with infra-personal worlds." [Detailed discussion of the development of the relationships of the two principal couples and of such key scenes and symbols as the African statuette, the Arab mare, the "gladiatorial" scene, and Gerald's death in the snow.] *The Lost Girl,* written in imitation of Arnold Bennett, "is commonly regarded as the least interesting of Lawrence's novels"; "yet its heroine, Alvina Houghton, is the most humanly appealing of his women." DHL's authorial intrusions in *Aaron's Rod* and *Kangaroo* may make us feel that as a novelist he "does not consistently respect his medium." *Aaron's Rod* demonstrates DHL's "high command of the spirit of place" in "sketches of Bohemian society" and expatriate life and "striking evocations of Italian cities and the Italian countryside." Its autobiographical characters, under different names, and its dominant theme of power are carried over into *Kangaroo,* in which DHL's descriptions of bush, beach, ocean, and bungalow have the "rapt quality" of Coleridge's notebooks, and only "Somers's finding himself, hard upon arrival in Australia, in demand as a potential leader of contending political movements" is "fantasy." *The Plumed Serpent,* DHL's contribution to Atlantean myth, asserts "the existence of a long-buried wisdom the recovering of which must marvelously mend the world." Kate Leslie's fascination with Ramón's bizarre Quetzalcoatl movement is credible, but not her involvement in it "believingly," eventually as Cipriano's wife in a marriage consummated only after the ritual killing of the prisoners and some time before the even more brutal death of Carlota, Ramón's Christian wife. *Lady Chatterley's Lover* returns to the industrial English midlands setting and central theme of *The Rainbow* and *Women in Love*: "sexual fulfilment as an absolute, and its near desuetude among us as the effective cause of the ills of modern society." Despite Mellors's "melancholy," which prevents his projecting "out upon the world...the warmth and joy he experiences on the phallic level," the action of the novel "is felt as issuing from, and steadily conditioned by, a complex society which is masterfully grasped, examined, and judged" in an artistically coherent whole. [The author also examines briefly "Daughters of the Vicar," *St Mawr, The Captain's Doll,* "The Woman Who Rode Away," and *The Man Who Died* (the last of which betrays DHL's "intuition that Christianity isn't quite so dead, after all")and examines selections from DHL's poetry in light of his conception of the distinguishing qualities of Etruscan art as " 'naturalness verging on the commonplace' " and disregard of "convention."]

2454 Sumimoto, Akiko. "*Women in Love* Ron: Shi to Sei" (A Study of *Women in Love*), MULBERRY (Aichi Women's College), No. 12 (Feb 1963), 19-25.
[In Japanese.]

2455 Swinnerton, Frank. FIGURES IN THE FOREGROUND: LITERARY REMINISCENCES, 1917-40 (Lond: Hutchinson, 1963), pp. 27, 29, 35, 42, 43, 46, 59, 61, 64, 68, 72, 73, 75, 87, 97, 107, 115, 126, 127, 128, 141, 147, 162, 165, 187, 189, 194, 195, 207, 224, 236, 264.

["One long-lived man's impressions, gathered at first hand . . . , of literary fashion in the first half of the twentieth century."] Virginia Woolf in 1925 listed DHL among the only five "significant novelists" of the time, but she "resented Lawrence's 'schoolboy tweaking and smacking of anyone opposed to him.'" Although in 1919 he did not list DHL, Joyce, or Woolf among the leading novelists, Hugh Walpole found DHL "very strong" in personality, but later wrote, "'Lawrence of course beats us with the eccentrics but we are more steadily and generally popular.'" John Middleton Murry and Katherine Mansfield at one time consorted intimately with DHL, but DHL later referred to Murry as a "mud-worm." H. M. Tomlinson "had no sympathy with Lawrence's immoderate angers." Aldous Huxley was "equally at home with Bennett and D. H. Lawrence." George Moore thought DHL "a man of plenty of talent," though in his one undoubted success, *Sons and Lovers,* he had trouble with ending the novel. "Mrs. F. R. [Q. D.] Leavis" despised popular novels and admired only Woolf, Forster, DHL, and T. F. Powys. "On Lawrence [F. R. Leavis] is not only superlatively enthusiastic but illuminating."

2456 Tedlock, E[rnest] W., Jr. D. H. LAWRENCE, ARTIST AND REBEL: A STUDY OF LAWRENCE'S FICTION (Albuquerque: University of New Mexico P, 1963; Cambridge: Cambridge UP, 1965); excerpt, pp. 209-10, rptd as "Values and 'The Rocking-Horse Winner,'" in D. H. LAWRENCE: "THE ROCKING-HORSE WINNER," ed by Dominick P. Consolo (Columbus, OH; Charles E. Merrill [The Merrill Literary Casebook Series], 1969), pp. 69-70.

[This study of DHL's vitalist ethic focuses on the inseparability of his art from his rebellion against conventions and institutions that damage or deny the natural life. The study is organized chronologically into four main periods: "Early Patterns of Revolt," "Alienation and Exile," "Search for a New World," and "Mediterranean and English Salvations." Each section is introduced with a biographical note, followed by detailed synopses of the short fiction, novels, and major non-fiction of the period. Critical exegesis incorporates life, work, and the development of DHL's vitalist philosophy.] After his meeting and elopement with Frieda Weekley confirmed his vitalist theories and marked the beginning of his mature art, DHL's fictional prototypes, narrative situations of conflict, protests against the mechanistic blighting of human life, and discovery in nature of a saving vision of wholeness were already firmly established. The early short fiction and novels delineate DHL's characteristic fictional worlds ("the miner's home and life; the town of trade and manufacture, fairs, churches and vicars; the countryside of wood, lake, farm and field"), his major protagonist types (the darkly intuitive farmer/miner/keeper and the "young intellectual"), and his central themes (the conflict between these instinctively alive beings and their "conscience keepers"--wives, mothers, lovers--and the difficulties of love-sex relationships). The early work is thus concerned with those barriers, rooted in cultural and class attitudes, which frustrate true relationships between people. This "split" is a dominant feature in female characters; in men, it springs from an excessive attachment to the mother. Since the barriers to relationships originate in the woman, "her plight is . . . central to all of Lawrence's work," and she gains salvation only "by the mastery of a vital man from the lower class, or of an alien culture, who is opposed to the values of her culture." In this "contrapuntal handling of character and incident," characters are paired in conflict. "Among his women, Lawrence's favorite pairing is of two sisters; among men, two friends, usually of different classes." Plot incidents are structured in "thesis-antithesis cycles of crisis moving to an ending that is often a last anti-social choice." DHL's diction also tends to fall on either side of a division between concrete, vitalist words, such as *blood* and *touch*, and an abstract vocabulary for anti-life experience and event.

In *Sons and Lovers,* DHL turns to a more direct confrontation of his own life, after attempting to mask his subjective involvement in *The White Peacock* and *The Trespasser.* Although *Sons and Lovers* is occasionally disrupted by long expository passages, its "power lies in the intensely felt objectification of experience." After *Sons and Lovers,* DHL concentrates more on the "cultural-psychological forces" which deny life, a thematic focus leading him toward his later obsessions with leadership. These developing themes express DHL's desire "for an existence untroubled by time and consciousness, governed only by the laws of being, or the life force revealing itself in nature." This "lovely but terrible vision" informs *The Rainbow*; it becomes Birkin's preachment in *Women in Love,* Lilly's in *Aaron's Rod,* and Somers's predicament in *Kangaroo,* and evolves into "a program for gods and supermen" in *The Plumed Serpent,* a flawed mixture of mythic prophecy and dogmatic argument. At the end of the periods of alienation, exile, and the search for a new life, DHL articulated in *Psychoanalysis and the Unconscious* and *Fantasia of the Unconscious* the psychology of character which "he had already explored intuitively in his fiction" in plots that analyze "the psychological, ethical consequences of succumbing to, or breaking with, a culturally distorted view of relationship." His characters, in the fiction, move through "psychic stages" seeking "the absolute in a world of disastrous relativity and irreligiousness." DHL's work in his last years continues to express his alienation from northern civilizations, but he turns back to "a softer, strongly sexual Mediterranean sun pride and power," replacing the leadership themes with "a more humanly limited quality of vitalistic relationship." His "perception of nature . . . is revivified, diversified and softened"; he returns to the more traditional myths of Pan, Dionysus, Isis, and Osiris. "Ultimately his imagination turns again to England, the original and deepest cause of his *saevo indignatio,* in an attempt to establish new roots in native ground." In *Lady Chatterley's Lover,* DHL accepts "both the sexual and social condition of man without excessive bitterness, and without wishing to transcend it in the nonhuman vitalistic mystery, or to make men into gods with a revolutionary program." His best work, in *The Rainbow, Women in Love,* and *Lady*

Chatterley's Lover, centers "on the human struggle for fulfillment, in the contemporary condition."

2457 Tetsumura, Haruo. "D. H. Lawrence Kenkyû (II) (Sono Shinpi Shugi o Sasaeru Mono)" (A Study of D. H. Lawrence, II: An Aspect of His Mysticism), SHIMONOSEKI ECONOMIC REVIEW (Shimonoseki Ichiritsu College), VII (July 1963), 61-90.
[In Japanese.]

2458 Tetsumura, Haruo. "D. H. Lawrence no Shinpishugi (Tsuki no Imisuru Mono)" (D. H. Lawrence's Mysticism: What the Moon Signifies), HIROSHIMA STUDIES IN ENGLISH LANGUAGE AND LITERATURE (Hiroshima University), IX (June 1963), 51-65.
[In Japanese.]

2459 Uchiki, Jôtarô. "Lawrence no *Niji* no Kôsei ni Kansuru Ichi Kenkyû" (A Study on the Composition of Lawrence's *The Rainbow*), SYLVAN (Tohoku University), No. 8, (May 1963), 14-24.
[In Japanese.]

2460 Usui, Yoshitaka. "Lawrence to Hihyôka-Tachi" (Lawrence and His Critics), ENGLISH LITERATURE (Waseda University), No. 28 (March 1963), 135-45.
[In Japanese.]

2461 Vickery, John B. "THE GOLDEN BOUGH: Impact and Archetype," VIRGINIA QUARTERLY REVIEW, XXXIX (Winter 1963), 37-57; rvd and enlgd as Chap. IV in THE LITERARY IMPACT OF "THE GOLDEN BOUGH," by John B. Vickery (Princeton: Princeton UP, 1973), pp. 106-38.
Frazer's THE GOLDEN BOUGH "was grounded in the essential realism of anthropological research, informed with the romance quest of an ideal, and controlled by the irony in divine myth and human custom." For these reasons it is "responsible for the form and shape of modern literature," including the work of DHL.

2462 Vickery, John B. "*The Plumed Serpent* and the Eternal Paradox," CRITICISM, V (Spring 1963), 119-34.
The Plumed Serpent is not a program novel but a novel focused on DHL's recognition of a cultural crisis which demands that man change his consciousness. The "dances, hymns, rituals, and myths .... delineate the form, not the content, of the human quest" for an integrated personality, for "the recovery of meaning and wholeness for the individual and his fragmented society." The structural pattern is a quest motif recalling that of Eliot's THE WASTE LAND, with Ramón representing the achieved goal and Kate the person struggling, through stages presented in sexual terms, to move out of a cynical, rational consciousness and into an intuitive, integrated one.

2463 Wada, Shizuo. "D. H. Lawrence Oboegaki (I)" (A Note on D.H.

Lawrence [I]), KYÛSHÛ SHÔKA DAIGAKU SHÔKEI RONSÔ (Kyûshû Shôka University), III (April 1963), 111-35. [In Japanese.]

2464 Warschausky, Sidney. "D. H. Lawrence," INSIGHT II: ANALYSES OF MODERN BRITISH LITERATURE, ed by John V. Hagopian and Martin Dolch (Frankfurt: Hirschgraben, 1963; rptd, 1975), pp. 220-33.
[This handbook for German high-school teachers contains brief analyses of "The Blind Man" and "The Rocking-Horse Winner," explaining structure, development of action, characterization, use of symbols, and referring to various readings by other critics. Offers sample questions and answers for treatment in class.]

2465 Weintraub, Stanley. "Books in English," BOOKS ABROAD, XXXVII (Winter 1963), 76.
The Symbolic Meaning: The Uncollected Versions of "Studies in Classic American Literature," ed by Armin Arnold, is DHL's much less poetic, less emotional consideration of his material." In the three versions of the essays in "his greatest work of criticism," DHL's "attitude toward American literature changed from sympathetic respect to grudging admiration."

2466 Weiss, Daniel. "D. H. Lawrence's Great Circle: From *Sons and Lovers* to *Lady Chatterley*," PSYCHOANALYTIC REVIEW, L (Fall 1963), 112-38; also pub in different form as Chap. IV, "The Great Circle," in OEDIPUS IN NOTTINGHAM: D. H. LAWRENCE, by Daniel Weiss (Seattle: University of Washington P, 1962), pp. 69-109.
In "The Prussian Officer," characterized by both artistic and psychological inevitability, DHL's depiction of homoerotic and sadomasochistic elements demonstrates keen observation and suggests autobiographical analogues. In *Sons and Lovers,* Paul's loves are determined by his original family situation: Miriam and Clara divide the mother's role, and Baxter Dawes is an extension of the father. Ambivalent about both, Paul "makes the patricidal gesture" against Dawes, rejects it, and gives up Clara to return to a child's dependency on his mother. Similar Oedipal motifs occur in "The Old Adam" and "Daughters of the Vicar." In all these works, the son "submits to the sadomasochistic desire to be beaten by the father," but only "The Prussian Officer" explicitly completes the homoerotic pattern. In later works, the elemental situation of *Sons and Lovers* is transformed into its opposite. DHL assigns his sensitive, intellectual side to spokesmen for a cult: the vital artisans and gamekeepers modeled on the "father-ideal." His rejection of mental consciousness is a rejection of his mother fixation. Sexual description in DHL's novels show both regression to the oral stage and coitus anxiety which equates orgasm with loss. It is Gerald, with his "fear of intrauterine absorption," not Birkin, who most resembles DHL himself, and DHL's women draw men to them in order to destroy them. Cipriano, the ultimate father figure, is safe from women because he never permits Kate to attain orgasm. The seeming shift in *Lady Chatterley's Lover* is possible only because the cycle was completed and DHL was dying.

2467 Williams, Raymond. "Tolstoy, Lawrence, and Tragedy," KENYON REVIEW, XXV (Autumn 1963), 633-50; rvd and rptd as "Social and Personal Tragedy: Tolstoy and Lawrence," in MODERN TRAGEDY, by Raymond Williams (Lond: Chatto & Windus; Stanford: Stanford UP, 1966), pp. 121-38.

The division of experience into social and personal categories has shaped modern tragedy and divided it into social tragedy ("a civilization destroyed or destroying itself") and personal tragedy ("men and women suffering and destroyed in their closest relationships"). The process of this division is seen most clearly in ANNA KARENINA and *Women in Love,* each of which contains an important relationship that ends in tragedy and is set in a social context formed by other relationships. Although ANNA KARENINA and *Women in Love* are similar in movement, they are different in several important respects. Tolstoy set the personal tragedy within a tragic context of a real society; DHL abstracted the personal tragedy from any social setting, real or fabricated. Whereas ANNA KARENINA is a tragedy resting on contrasts (Karenin and Vronsky, Vronsky and Levin, Levin-Kitty and Vronsky-Anna), *Women in Love* is a "tragedy of a single action, in varying forms" (the Birkin-Ursula relationship is a variation of and not a contrast to the Gerald-Gudrun relationship).

2468 Wood, Frederick T. "Prose, Poetry, and Drama," in "Current Literature 1962," ENGLISH STUDIES (Amsterdam), XLIV (June 1963), 222-33, espec p. 226.

The Collected Letters of D. H. Lawrence, ed by Harry T. Moore, "does not represent all the Lawrence correspondence that is available." It should have indicated "what is omitted, where each item fits in the chronological sequence, and where we may look for it if we wish."

2469 Zinnes, Harriet. "Anais Nin's Works Reissued," BOOKS ABROAD, XXXVII (Summer 1963), 283-86.

Anais Nin, whose D. H. LAWRENCE: AN UNPROFESSIONAL STUDY (1932) helps one "to understand the real Lawrence," like DHL approached fiction as a poet. "Like Lawrence, too, Anais Nin is one of the few writers to understand modern woman's striving," and again like him, "is particularly interested in today's neurotic woman." In SEDUCTION OF THE MINOTAUR, Lillian, the jazz pianist, comes "to Mexico seeking like a true Laurentian a passional renewal after an unhappy marriage."

1964

2470 Allen, Walter. TRADITION AND DREAM: THE ENGLISH AND AMERICAN NOVEL FROM THE TWENTIES TO OUR TIME (Lond: Phoenix House, 1964); also pub as THE MODERN NOVEL IN BRITAIN AND THE UNITED STATES (NY: Dutton, 1964), pp. 2, 21-29, 36, 43, 54, 56, 77, 153, 154, 196, 238, 247, 250, 266, 276, 287.

"Closer in spirit and in his view of the novel to George Eliot than to Flaubert," DHL is "the novelist as moralist" or "the moralist as novelist." Though "a traditional autobiographical novel in form," *Sons and Lovers* is far beyond such works as Bennett's CLAYHANGER in impact. Caught in the clash between his miner father and his refined mother, DHL is on his mother's side, though he was later to change sides. "In *The White Peacock* Annable is defeated by the high-born lady: almost twenty years later, as Mellors, the gamekeeper of *Lady Chatterley's Lover*, he gets his own back on her. But until *The Plumed Serpent* the situation--the destruction of instinctive man by the spiritual woman--is fundamental to Lawrence." Expressing his anti-intellectual vision in the "Edgar Allan Poe" essay, DHL had to an "extraordinary degree the faculty Jung calls primitive thinking and feeling," which enabled him to convey "felt experience" through what Eliseo Vivas calls "the constitutive symbol," a concept related to Jung's definition of the symbol as the living " 'expression of a thing not to be characterized in any other or better way.' " *Women in Love,* in many ways a modern PILGRIM'S PROGRESS, is more difficult than *The Rainbow* because of Birkin's presence as a persona for DHL. The "indictment of industrialism as the final blasphemy against life Lawrence took up again, with much less art, in *Lady Chatterley's Lover*." [In this literary history, comparisons are drawn between DHL and such writers as Aldous Huxley, Stephen Hudson, Sherwood Anderson, Edward Dahlberg, Rosamond Lehmann, Joyce Cary, P. H. Newby, Doris Lessing, and Lawrence Durrell.]

2471 "Among the New Books--The Time of Dickens," SAN FRANCISCO CHRONICLE, THIS WORLD, 22 March 1964, p. 29.
The Symbolic Meaning: The Uncollected Versions of "Studies in Classic American Literature," ed by Armin Arnold, is not " 'in effect a new work' " by DHL as claimed but a collection of the original articles which he revised and rewrote as *Studies in Classic American Literature.* Less "imaginative and daring" than that book, "it is important largely for purposes of comparison."

2472 Arnold, Armin. "D. H. Lawrence's First Critical Essays: Two Anonymous Reviews Identified," PUBLICATIONS OF THE MODERN LANGUAGE ASSOCIATION, LXXIX (March 1964), 185-88; also pub in expanded form in D. H. LAWRENCE AND GERMAN LITERATURE WITH TWO HITHERTO UNKNOWN ESSAYS BY D. H. LAWRENCE, by Armin Arnold (Montreal: Mansfield Book Mart, H. Heinemann, 1963), pp. 13-36.
Two passages in DHL's correspondence give evidence of his authorship of two anonymous reviews published in the ENGLISH REVIEW in 1912. These essays, the first favorably reviewing H. G. Fiedler's anthology, the OXFORD BOOK OF GERMAN VERSE, and the second favorably reviewing Jethro Bithell's anthology of translations of German poetry, THE MINNESINGERS, "tell us a great deal about his taste in poetry at that time." [The two reviews are quoted in full. See also correction by Carl E. Baron, "Two Hitherto Unknown Pieces by D. H. Lawrence," ENCOUNTER, XXXIII (Aug 1969), 3-5.]

2473 Austin, Allan Edward. "D. H. Lawrence's Shorter Fiction: The Question of Chronology," DISSERTATION ABSTRACTS,

XXV (1964), 2976A. Unpublished dissertation, University of Rochester, 1964.

2474 Bartlett, Norman. "Aldous Huxley and D. H. Lawrence," AUSTRALIAN QUARTERLY, XXXVI (March 1964), 76-84.
Huxley tries intellectually to justify DHL's "instinctive religion of sensuality" and to resolve the contradiction of flesh and spirit in synthesis. DHL sought "mindlessness," while Huxley derived from the tantrism of Mahāyāna Buddhism the principle that "all the senses are means . . . of liberation from the prison of the self." Huxley's move from satire to mysticism amounts to "spiritual onanism," and his isolation from everyday experience made him "susceptible to the archheretic of western civilization, D. H. Lawrence," whose influence is apparent in POINT COUNTER POINT, DO WHAT YOU WILL, BRAVE NEW WORLD, and BRAVE NEW WORLD REVISITED. Both Huxley and DHL repudiated the human tradition, strove to be faithful to their internal perceptions, expressed a common belief that the atrophy of modern society leads to "individual madness and social revolution," exposed the moral void created by industrialism, and sought compensation in exoticism and eccentricity.

2475 Bedient, Calvin Bernard. "The Fate of the Self: Self and Society in the Novels of George Eliot, D. H. Lawrence, and E. M. Forster," DISSERTATION ABSTRACTS, XXV (1964), 1187A. Unpublished dissertation, University of Washington, 1964. Rvd and pub as ARCHITECTS OF THE SELF: GEORGE ELIOT, D. H. LAWRENCE, AND E. M. FORSTER (Berkeley, Los Angeles, and Lond: University of California P, 1972).

2476 Branda, Eldon S. "Textual Changes in *Women in Love*," TEXAS STUDIES IN LITERATURE AND LANGUAGE, VI (Autumn 1964), 306-21.
The two current American editions of *Women in Love*, the Random House Modern Library and the Viking Compass Book editions, "contain important textual differences." The textual history of these differences begins with minor changes made from the final typescript of the first printing, a private printing by Thomas Seltzer in New York, and continues in Seltzer's clumsy corrections for the first American trade edition, and in a variety of errors as well as DHL's addition of chapter titles for this edition, which is the basis of the current Modern Library version. Textual differences in the Viking Compass Book edition begin with changes in the first British edition on which it is based and in which DHL made revisions to be less explicit about Birkin's and Gerald's relationship and, for the next two printings, substantially modified the Halliday sections, when threatened by Philip Heseltine's libel suit. The edition probably most closely reflecting DHL's intentions is the first privately printed American one.

2477 Burbank, Rex. SHERWOOD ANDERSON (NY: Twayne [Twayne United States Authors Series T-65], 1964), pp. 20, 110, 113-16.
For Sherwood Anderson, DHL was "a greatly admired fellow novelist who shared

his general views on the importance of sex" and his "repugnance for bloodless spirituality and intellectualism." Fred and Aline Grey and Dudley in Anderson's DARK LAUGHTER prefigure Clifford and Connie Chatterley and Mellors. But DHL, unlike Anderson, was able to study Freud, accepting some of his principles and rejecting others, and with "self-assurance, he could affirm the vitalism of the unconscious and the centrality of sex as a life-generating force."

2478 Cecchi, Emilio. SCRITTORI INGLESI E AMERICANI: SAGGI, NOTE E VERSIONI (English and American Writers: Comments, Notes, and Versions), Vol. II (Milan: Alberto Mondadori, 1964; 2nd ed 1968), pp. 70-86; additional references, pp. 23, 102, 119, 123, 155-57, 168-69, 175, 179-80, 203, 215, 219, 221, 227, 239, 241, 249-50, 269, 273, 301, 304, 332, 334.

Contents on DHL, reprinted from earlier publication but not abstracted except as noted: "Il 'Messaggio' di D. H. Lawrence" (D. H. Lawrence's "Message"), pp. 70-73, from "D. H. Lawrence," L'ITALIA LETTERARIA (Rome), II (25 May 1930), 1-2; "*L'amante di Lady Chatterley*" (*Lady Chatterley's Lover*) (1945), pp. 74-78; "L'amica di D. H. Lawrence" (D. H. Lawrence's Friend) (1948), pp. 78-81; " 'Classici americani' di D. H. Lawrence" (D. H. Lawrence's "Classic Americans") (1948), pp. 81-84; "Versioni da D. H. Lawrence" (Versions of D. H. Lawrence) [Italian translations of DHL's poems "Cry of the Masses," "The People," and "What Have They Done to You--?"] (1930), pp. 84-86. [In Italian.]

2479 Chambers, Maria Cristina. "Afternoons in Italy with D. H. Lawrence," TEXAS QUARTERLY, VII (Winter 1964), 114-20; rptd as a pamphlet, AFTERNOONS IN ITALY WITH D. H. LAWRENCE (a private edition of 100 copies signed by Maria Cristina Chambers).

[Reminiscences of a visit with DHL in 1929, at his invitation, when the author was in her twenties and in youthful awe of DHL, who was well mannered and thoughtful, despite his illness. Contains his last letter to her, published for the first time. The private edition is issued "Together with a photograph of Lawrence, his sister-in-law, and Frieda."]

2480 Clark, L. D. DARK NIGHT OF THE BODY: D. H. LAWRENCE'S "THE PLUMED SERPENT" (Austin: University of Texas P, 1964).

Despite its excesses of language and prophecy, *The Plumed Serpent* is saved by DHL's deep sympathy with Mexico and his skill in synthesizing form, setting, and symbol. His choice of a woman as the protagonist of his American works invokes old religious and mystical traditions of the soul in search of its lover, God. *The Plumed Serpent* is unified by Kate's perspective, which reflects DHL's real purpose to treat the conflicts within the European soul in quest of the oldest manifestation of deity. The meaning emerges out of Kate's ambivalence to the spirit and land of Mexico. In early chapters her disillusionment with the moribund society of modern Mexico, as seen in her response to motifs of death in art, ritual, and politics, leaves her vulnerable to the implications of a proclamation of the rebirth of Quetzalcoatl. Kate's journey to the lake of Sayula, presented in organic description," involves both body and soul of the character and a religious quality in the landscape. Kate distinguishes between primitive modes, seeing the banditry and murder as "hopeless, panic reversal," while regarding the ritual dancing in the plaza as an attempt to get into touch with "the mystery of the cosmos." Her acceptance of godhead as Malintzi, bride of Huitzilopochtli-Cipriano, returns her to a virginal state in a "dark night of the body" in which she moves beyond polarities of wish and will to engagement with eternal life-forces. Faced with the alternative between Europe, independence, and London drawing rooms, and submissive revitalization with Ramón and Cipriano, Kate chooses the latter. *The Plumed Serpent* thus reverses the historical conquest of Mexico as dark mother forced by white father and offers a new blending of white European and dark American spirits, obviating conquest through mutual submission to the gods. Kate's story follows traditional novel form, but the religious movement reveals elements peculiarly Laurentian. Bell and drum, representing Christian church vs. the Quetzalcoatl religion, embody the opposites of the book. Finding DHL's pantheon implausible reflects a cultural blindness. DHL's Mexico and its religion are not realistic but prophetic. The seeming fascism of some aspects of the movement is countered by Kate's own reservations. Ramón wants to make men into "lords of life," but Cipriano, it is implied, might become a master of death in his propensity toward human sacrifice. DHL, who had read widely in archaeology and anthropology, set his Indian revival in Mexico rather than New Mexico because the kind of revolution he projected seemed more plausible there. As an ancient symbol, the circle attracted DHL, as it did other great modern writers. The need for a new circle with a new center presupposes the deterioration of the old circle. A Gnostic conception, shared by Indians, Theosophists, and *The Plumed Serpent*, is that the giant bird or the serpent or a combination of the two, symbolized by cross and circle, incarnates the deepest power of the universe. Sun, stars, and lake become symbols whose centers are everywhere and whose circumferences are nowhere. Ultimately, *The Plumed Serpent* describes a symbolic descent of the body to a center of renewal and return that, corresponding to the ascent of the soul in the poems of St. John of the Cross and suggesting a cyclical universe that includes rejection as well as acceptance, reconciles contradictions in a way akin to the affirmation of Heraclitus that the way up and the way down are one and the same.

2481 Cowan, James Costello. "Lawrence in Old and New Mexico: The Quest and the Art," DISSERTATION ABSTRACTS, XXV (1964), 3567A. Unpublished dissertation, University of Oklahoma, 1964. Extensively rvd and pub as D. H. LAWRENCE'S AMERICAN JOURNEY: A STUDY IN LITERATURE AND MYTH (Cleveland and Lond: P of Case Western Reserve University, 1970).

2482 Craig, David. "Love and Society: MEASURE FOR MEASURE and Our Own Time," in SHAKESPEARE IN A CHANGING WORLD, ed by Arnold Kettle (Lond: Lawrence and Wishart; NY: International Publishers, 1964), pp. 195-216; rptd as Chap. I: "Shakespeare, Lawrence and Sexual Freedom," in THE REAL FOUNDATIONS: LITERATURE AND SOCIAL CHANGE, by David Craig (Lond: Chatto & Windus, 1973; NY: Oxford UP, 1974), pp. 17-38.

Four tales by DHL ("Daughters of the Vicar," *The Captain's Doll, St. Mawr,* and *The Virgin and the Gipsy*) are the modern works of English literature most akin to Shakespeare's MEASURE FOR MEASURE in that they treat the themes of fulfillment through love and personal freedom by means of a contrast between what is life-affirming and what is life-denying. Just as Shakespeare presents Claudio as the antithesis of Angelo, "with his deathly wish to ignore and repress real feelings," DHL likewise defines fullness of experience "by contrasting pairs of people through the imagery that establishes the contrasting types." DHL depicts characters who, like Shakespeare's Angelo, do not know themselves because of the repression inherent to their dignified public roles. It is this aspect of characterization which enables both writers to treat public values such as justice, authority, and discipline. However, there is no simplistic contrast between the artificiality of social roles and the reality of personal feelings, and neither Shakespeare nor DHL presents a "primitivist or anarchic opposition . . . between control and freedom." Rather, both authors are concerned with social responsibility. In this respect, however, the comparison between Shakespeare and DHL proves imperfect, since despite the fact that DHL valued the societal impulse, he often spoke contemptuously of it and "regarded social organization as something only minimally relevant to our deeper experience."

2483 Cross, Amanda [pseud of Carolyn G. Heilbrun]. IN THE LAST ANALYSIS (NY: Macmillan [Cock Robin Mystery], 1964), pp. 138-39, 158, 168-69.

[In this mystery novel, identification of the murderer turns on the fact that he cannot identify a passage from DHL--Anna Lensky and her step-father in the barn in *The Rainbow*.]

2484 Cross, Gustov. "Little Magazines in Australia," REVIEW OF ENGLISH LITERATURE, V (Oct 1964), 20-28.

While in Australia in 1922, DHL found "material for nearly half a chapter of *Kangaroo*" in the pages of the SYDNEY BULLETIN, the only Australian journal serving the function of a little magazine, though the number has grown since then.

2485 Crossman, R. H. S. "Carlyle and Froude," NEW STATESMAN, ns, LXVII (17 Jan 1964), 81-82.

The works of Thomas Carlyle, particularly LATTER-DAY SAINTS, and the worst of DHL's didactic writings are similar in philosophy. Both writers have been discredited as prophets, but DHL, unlike Carlyle, will continue to command interest as "a poet and a novelist of genius," though he "spoiled much of what he wrote with hysterical rant."

2486 Davis, Edward. READINGS IN MODERN FICTION (Cape Town, South Africa: Simondium, 1964), pp. 258-81.

DHL's best writing on sex is sane. He does not magnify it but regards it as a normal function. His revolt against prudery merely underlines the necessity of "stable and loyal marriages." He respects the integrity of his characters, each of whom is credible and important in his own right. DHL sees further than most and evaluates what he sees in diction that is neither inflated nor dull. [Includes a synopsis of *The Rainbow* and a study of characters in both *The Rainbow* and *Women in Love*.]

2487 Dekker, George. "Lilies That Fester: THE LAST OF THE MOHICANS and 'The Woman Who Rode Away,' " NEW LEFT REVIEW, No. 28 (Nov-Dec 1964), 75-84.

Leslie Fiedler, somewhat misled by *Studies in Classic American Literature,* misrepresents the vital personal relationships developed in James Fenimore Cooper's THE LAST OF THE MOHICANS. DHL's valuable essay "Fenimore Cooper's Leatherstocking Novels" is pointed in its analysis of Cooper's female characters and consistent with a miscegenation theme illustrated in *St. Mawr* and "The Woman Who Rode Away." Neither Cooper nor DHL can successfully resolve the social dilemma of white supremacy.

2488 "D. H. L.'s American Digest," TIMES LITERARY SUPPLEMENT (Lond), 28 May 1964, p. 448.

Studies in Classic American Literature (reissued 1964) is "among the finest criticism of the century and essential reading for anyone seriously interested in American literature." Even when DHL "misses the mark," as in his overvaluation of Cooper, his criticism shows a "great mind at work on things that interested him."

2489 Donald, D. R. "The First and Final Versions of *Lady Chatterley's Lover*," THEORIA, XXII (June 1964), 85-97.

The final version of *Lady Chatterley's Lover* is one of DHL's failures; *The First Lady Chatterley* is "comparable with his best." In the first version, DHL's convictions are woven skillfully into the complex web of human relations among characters who are more convincing, spontaneous, and complex than the wooden effigies in the final version. Parkin [in the first version] loves Constance, but he makes her feel the "ferocity of his resentment" at their social incompatibility and, out of manliness, refuses marriage because it would imperil his integrity and lower Constance in her own and others' estimation. Mellors, on the contrary, tailored for matrimony, is an unconvincing social compromise whose lengthy discourses proclaim him another Laurentian mouthpiece. DHL's recognition of social barriers gives the first version a tragic inevitability that was lost when he altered character to circumvent those barriers. Because the first Constance is chaste, her eventual spring awakening by Parkin has greater significance for us than the Mellors relationship, which merely culminates a series of other indiscretions.

2490 Draper, R[onald] P. D. H. LAWRENCE (NY: Twayne [TEAS 7], 1964).

The two principal aims of DHL's writings are "to communicate the whole man" and to reveal "the changing rainbow of our living relationships." DHL's early novels, which, except for *The Trespasser,* are about his native area, form a prelude to *The Rainbow* and *Women in Love*. They are also of great interest in themselves: *Sons and Lovers* especially shows the development of DHL's romanticism and his fidelity to actual life. DHL's next novel, *The Rainbow,* parallels the life struggle of one generation with that of another, with sex, courtship, and marriage emerging as prominent themes throughout the novel. Its sequel, *Women in Love,* combines structural simplicity and toughness, psychological penetration, the presentation of men and women in relation to industrialism, and scenes of symbolic power. The novels that follow, *The Lost Girl, Aaron's Rod,* and *Kangaroo,* marred by casualness and diffuseness, lack artistic wholeness and the independent reality of the preceding novels. In the late novels, *The Plumed Serpent* and *Lady Chatterley's Lover,* DHL confronts and comes to terms with the basic sexual problem of *Women in Love.* DHL's tales are an important part of his total work: some are mere sketches, some realistic vignettes, and some virtually prose poems. Finally, DHL's poems, unconventionally yet carefully written, are either autobiographical or satirical.

2491 Enright, D[ennis] J[oseph]. "A Haste for Wisdom: The Poetry of D. H. Lawrence," NEW STATESMAN, ns LXVIII (30 Oct 1964), 653-54; rptd in CONSPIRATORS AND POETS, by D. J. Enright (Lond: Chatto & Windus, 1966), pp. 95-101; and rptd in D. H. LAWRENCE: A CRITICAL ANTHOLOGY, ed by H. Coombes (Harmondsworth, Middlesex, England: Penguin Books, 1973), pp. 442-48.

[Review of *The Complete Poems of D. H. Lawrence,* ed by Vivian de Sola Pinto and F. Warren Roberts (1964).] Critics have seen DHL's poetry either as "vitiated by formlessness" or as "organic" or "expressive" in form. DHL suffers most, however, from the lack of a critical "selected poems." While sometimes "uniquely sensitive and refreshing," DHL is sometimes bumbling, but occasional exasperation "is a small enough price ... for a sizeable body of major poetry."

2492 Ernst, Morris L., and Alan U. Schwartz. CENSORSHIP: THE SEARCH FOR THE OBSCENE (NY: Macmillan; Lond: Collier-Macmillan [Milestones of Law series], 1964), pp. 117, 127-32, 247-48, 271n.

The case of *Lady Chatterley's Lover* (Grove Press v. Christenberry), "although it introduced no new theories or standards of the Law of Obscenity, did serve as a platform upon which Judge Frederick vanPelt Bryan could present an admirably clear and graciously written opinion of the state of Federal obscenity law circa 1959." Judge Leonard Moore of the Circuit Court of Appeals, while agreeing with the result, raised some unanswered questions about the complex problems of establishing "contemporary community standards," whether "natural man" ought in some cases to be inhibited and whether "literary merit" gives an author "carte blanche." [Quotations from Judge Bryan's and Judge Moore's opinions.] In the English censorship trial (Regina v. Penguin Books, Ltd., 1960), in which the defense put thirty-five expert witnesses on the stand, the last word belonged to Viscount Gage, who quoted a fellow peer as saying that he had no objections to his daughter's reading *Lady Chatterley's Lover* but objected strongly to its being read by his gamekeeper.

2493 Fahey, William Arthur. "The Travel Books of D. H. Lawrence: Records of a Spiritual Pilgrimage," DISSERTATION ABSTRACTS, XXV (1965), 5927A. Unpublished dissertation, New York University, 1964.

2494 Fiedler, Leslie A. "The Stockings Are Rough but They Haven't Run," SUNDAY HERALD TRIBUNE BOOK WEEK (NY), 12 April 1964, pp. 5, 19.

[Review of *The Symbolic Meaning: The Uncollected Versions of "Studies in Classic American Literature,"* ed by Armin Arnold.] "Lawrence's was the first critical study to reveal how interesting and how subversive our literary tradition in fact is." DHL saw "first, that our literature is in some sense encoded, has to be deciphered rather than simply read; and, second, that its essential sentimentality is based not on the love of men for women but on an exclusive love of males, joined together in a homoerotic anti-marriage." Drawn to America by the " 'clues to a real solution' " offered by Whitman's Calamus poems, DHL experienced the actual confrontation of the Indians as a "traumatic betrayal," from which the final version of the *Studies* emerged. The book, which scarcely registers the existence of Negroes, shows "that the myth of the Indian rather than that of the Negro lives at the deepest levels of our national psyche."

2495 "The Fleshly Muse," TIME, LXXXIV (18 Dec 1964), 92.

"For 26 years, . . . Frieda loyally supported the image of Lawrence as the ultimate male"; but the extensive memoir she was writing, published as FRIEDA LAWRENCE: THE MEMOIRS AND CORRESPONDENCE, ed by E. W. Tedlock, Jr. (1961, 1964), illuminates the couple's "stormy relationship." DHL's "Sunday paintings," now collected in *Paintings of D. H. Lawrence,* ed by Mervyn Levy, present "a sampling of candid nudes, but the approach is less pornographic or primitive than merely earnest."

2496 Foltinek, Herbert. "Über die Methode des Motivvergleichs--Dargestellt an englishen Literaturwerken" (On the Method of Motif Comparison--Presented in English Literary Works), ENGLISH MISCELLANY (Rome), XV (1964), 103-33, espec 126-30.

Edmund Spenser's THE FAERIE QUEENE, Book VI, canto viii, ll. 31-51, and DHL's "The Woman Who Rode Away" share the motif of a civilized woman captured by barbarians who seek to sacrifice her to their primitive god. Comparison of such parallels in literature can serve to illuminate the sources of literary texts, to render the uniqueness of a writer's personality, or to establish the basis for a broad analysis of the literary representation of culture. DHL's woman feels the emptiness of her life, and beside the powerful certainty, emotion, and visionary raptures of the Indians, the civilization she abandoned seems spiritless, rotten, and deadly. DHL's theme of death and rebirth is bound in this story to a cultural prognosis that exemplifies much twentieth-century literature: the seeking after the values of primitive cultures with which to renounce the diseased achievements of our modern civilization. Spenser's Serena, in contrast to the events in "The Woman Who Rode Away," is saved from the cannibals by her knight. The primitive in Spenser stands in total opposition to a Christian, knightly society, and the conflict is between a strange, barbaric force and ideal virtue. Spenser uses his motif to stress the values of his civilization, of law against lawlessness, order over chaos, and humanity against inhumanity. [Contains extensive theorizing on the method of *Motivvergleiche* and further examples from the work of Jonson, Shakespeare, Smollett, and Dickens.] [In German.]

2497 Ford, George H. " 'The Wedding' Chapter of D. H. Lawrence's *Women in Love*," TEXAS STUDIES IN LITERATURE AND LANGUAGE, VI (Summer 1964), 134-47.

Two chapters of earlier versions of *Women in Love* survive: the "Prologue," concerning Birkin and Gerald, and "The Wedding," portraying Gudrun and Ursula, now published for the first time. The "Wedding" chapter, "essentially another version" of the opening chapter, "Sisters," in the published version of the novel, provides an interesting example of DHL's methods of revising. Contrary to the notion that he never revised, DHL sometimes made extensive deletions and changes, sometimes became dissatisfied with a draft and wrote a whole new one, and sometimes "copied large parts of one draft into another." A comparison of the rejected and published versions of the "Wedding" chapter suggests that the rewriting was "a fresh one," though the basic conception of Ursula and Gudrun and the convention of two sisters' talking did not change. [Text of the original version included.]

2498 Friedman, Alan Howard. "The Turn of the Novel: Changes in the Pattern of English Fiction Since 1890, Conrad, Forster, and Lawrence," DISSERTATION ABSTRACTS, XXV (1965), 6622A. Unpublished dissertation, University of California at Berkeley, 1964. Rvd and pub as THE TURN OF THE NOVEL (NY: Oxford UP, 1966).

2499 Gillès, Daniel. "D. H. Lawrence ou la Poésie Immédiate" (D. H. Lawrence or Immediate Poetry), REVUE GÉNÉRALE BELGE (Brussels), C (Jan 1964), 43-59.

DHL's early poetry, as he himself recognized, was impressionist poetry, written out of direct emotional experience. His poetry is of an extraordinary intensity and an overwhelming sincerity and immediacy. The poems of the young DHL, cries of revolt and of refusal to obey, are true poems of youth. But in this period, DHL, whose life is still sentimental and totally dominated by his mother, is not entirely free to love, as the portrait of his mother in "The Bride" shows. After he elopes to Germany with Frieda von Richthofen, his poetry reflects the romantic setting of the Bavarian Alps and the Italian lakes and the discovery of total love, in poems such as "Bei Hennef" and "Epithalamion." A poet of instinct, DHL is not a man who reflects on his art and its rules. Although he collaborates briefly with the Imagists, DHL avoids identification with all aesthetic theories and schools. After spending the war years in England with Frieda, who has become his wife, DHL and she travel for six years. With *Birds, Beasts and Flowers,* he discovers a new field of poetic exploration, as shown in "Fish." After his return to Europe in 1925, he writes *Pansies,* a collection of didactic verse, in the form of fugitive, intuitive thoughts in the tradition of Pascal and La Rochefoucauld, as in "The Mosquito Knows." His last poetry considers the theme of death in such works as "The Ship of Death." [Cited poems are quoted in translations by the author.] [In French.]

2500 Gillès, Daniel. D. H. LAWRENCE OU LE PURITAIN SCANDALEUX (D. H. Lawrence or the Scandalous Puritan) (Paris: Rene

Julliard, 1964).

[After a biographical survey of DHL's early life in the first part of this work, the author, in the second part entitled "Changer la vie," analyzes DHL's dreams of a promised land. Then he traces DHL and Frieda's travels in Italy and New Mexico. The last two chapters are symbolically entitled "La barque de la mort" (The Ship of Death) and "Le Phénix" (The Phoenix). Popular biographical study of DHL and his work, relying principally on DHL's letters and earlier biographies of the novelist.] [In French.]

2501 Glenavy, Lady Beatrice [Beatrice Elvery Campbell]. TODAY WE WILL ONLY GOSSIP (Lond: Constable, 1964), pp. 63-68, 98, 99, 139-40, 141.

[Personal reminiscence of the friendship during the war years of the author and her husband, Gordon Campbell, who succeeded his father as second Baron Glenavy of Milltown in 1931, with DHL and Frieda, John Middleton Murry and Katherine Mansfield, and others of their circle. The author recounts with tolerance and tact such incidents as S. S. Koteliansky's and Mark Gertler's wrecking a party, discusses Campbell's withdrawal from the intense, intimate friendship with Murry, and describes Lady Ottoline Morrell as "a great and gracious lady" who "was a generous and good friend to all those young people." See also Peter L. Irvine and Anne Kiley, "D. H. Lawrence: Letters to Gordon and Beatrice Campbell," D. H. LAWRENCE REVIEW, VI (Spring 1973), 1-20.]

2502 G[ohdes], C[larence]. "Brief Mention," AMERICAN LITERATURE, XXXVI (Nov 1964), 403.

[Brief notice of *The Symbolic Meaning: The Uncollected Versions of "Studies in Classic American Literature,"* ed by Armin Arnold.] "These *Ur-studien* are less vitriolic in tone, but, like the final versions, they betray more of the disordered mentality of their author than they clarify the subject about which he knew so very little."

2503 Goodheart, Eugene. "Lawrence and Christ," PARTISAN REVIEW, XXXI (Winter 1964), 42-59; rvd and rptd in THE CULT OF THE EGO: THE SELF IN MODERN LITERATURE, by Eugene Goodheart (Chicago and Lond: University of Chicago P, 1968), pp. 161-82.

DHL has recently been "remade" in an attempt to stress his connection with various causes, particularly Christianity. This is directly counter to DHL's own insistence on his aversion to any commitment to a conventional view of Christ or the myths of Christianity. In *The Man Who Died,* misanthropy links DHL with Nietzsche. DHL both courts and fears Nietzsche's concept of Dionysian energy and Blake's distrust of institutions and his transcendence through single life. DHL's treatment of Christ is often a symbol of this single life and its aristocracy. Seeing no opposition between the visionary and the ethical leads to critical misunderstanding of DHL's meaning.

2504 Gordon, David J. "D. H. Lawrence's Quarrel with Tragedy," PERSPECTIVE, XIII (Winter 1964), 135-50; rvd and rptd in D. H.

LAWRENCE AS A LITERARY CRITIC, by David J. Gordon (New Haven and Lond: Yale UP [Yale Studies in English, Vol. 161], 1966), pp. 75-95.

DHL's belief in man's radical innocence forced him to question the concept of determinism in tragic works of other artists. Refusing to recognize inherent evil in existence, DHL instead uses his principles of blood and mind to show that self-consciousness, a "fall" from instinct, causes evil. This theory informs his creation of characters who are not heroes in the sense of Flaubert, Dostoevsky, or Shakespeare, writers who are either too pitying or too conscious. Hardy's characters avoid that fate but fail to achieve wholeness. After *The Rainbow* DHL's vision of the tragic becomes more skeptical, and he sees the vital destruction of the old as necessary for rebirth. Still rejecting the negating destruction of mechanism, of denial, DHL's tragic sense, when fully realized, is highly individual.

2505 Gottwald, Johannes. "Die Erzählformen der Romane von Aldous Huxley und David Herbert Lawrence" (Narrative Techniques in the Novels of Aldous Huxley and David Herbert Lawrence). Published dissertation, University of Munich, 1964. [Listed in Lawrence F. McNamee, DISSERTATIONS IN ENGLISH AND AMERICAN LITERATURE, SUPP I (NY and Lond: Bowker, 1969), p. 249.]

Aldous Huxley and DHL are the exponents of extreme, formal concepts in modern fiction writing. Both write for didactic reasons and abandon the realistic tradition of nineteenth-century fiction. DHL's novels are not so neatly constructed as Huxley's. His sole subject is the basic antagonism between life-affirming and life-denying values. Accordingly, he portrays the individual development of only few characters and rejects a plot that is elaborated on the principle of cause and effect. Despite the episodic structure of his novels there are no abrupt transitions between the single parts, and the action does not lack coherence. It is held together by recurring symbols, images, *leit-motifs,* and the description of the unconscious processes within his protagonists. Contrary to Huxley, DHL does not appeal to the readers' intellects but to their emotions. [In German.]

2506 Greet, T. Y., Charles E. Edge, and John M. Munro (eds). THE WORLDS OF FICTION: STORIES IN CONTEXT (Bost: Houghton Mifflin, 1964), pp. 230-34.

[Detailed notes on "Odour of Chrysanthemums" quote extensively from "Nottingham and the Mining Countryside," *The Collected Letters of D. H. Lawrence,* "Edgar Allan Poe," "We Need One Another," "The Real Thing," and "Morality and the Novel" as glosses on the story, which is reprinted in the anthology, pp. 213-30.]

2507 Gregory, Horace. "A Young Man Speaking for His Own Generation," NEW YORK TIMES BOOK REVIEW, 15 Nov 1964, pp. 4, 64.

The younger generation today reads DHL not only as a "once banned and censored writer" but also, more importantly, as one who "wrote directly in the language of the senses" and whose "volatile, kinetic thinking makes its strongest appeal to freshly awakened youthful intelligence." *The Complete Poems of D. H.*

Lawrence, ed by Vivian de Sola Pinto and F. Warren Roberts, shows "the enduring freshness of some of the poems," though many are more like "notes for poems." [The author also comments briefly on *Paintings of D. H. Lawrence,* ed by Mervyn Levy, and FRIEDA LAWRENCE: THE MEMOIRS AND CORRESPONDENCE, ed by E. W. Tedlock, Jr.]

2508 Gurko, Leo. "*Kangaroo*: D. H. Lawrence in Transit," MODERN FICTION STUDIES, X (Winter 1964-1965), 349-58.

Until 1922, the main theme of DHL's art was personal relationships. Beginning with *Kangaroo,* his protagonists search for something larger than themselves in landscape, religion, and mythology, seeking to meld with the spirits and gods of place. The central principle of *Kangaroo* is an anthropomorphism in reverse: DHL breathed the qualities of the land into the people. On the surface, both land and people appear flat, undifferentiated, empty. But near the end of the novel, Somers experiences a powerful intuition of the "emanation of place ... a lurking liveness," in which he discovers his desire for the impersonal god.

2509 Guttmann, Allen. "D. H. Lawrence: The Politics of Irrationality," WISCONSIN STUDIES IN CONTEMPORARY LITERATURE, V (Summer 1964), 151-63.

When DHL turned from the "private concerns of *Women in Love*" to the "public themes of *Kangaroo* and *The Plumed Serpent,* he became the prophet of an authoritarian irrationality *similar to* (not *identical with*) ... Fascism." Making available "the vision of an ideology otherwise misunderstood wrongly as diabolism," DHL "forces the limits of our vicarious experience until the politically abominable becomes uncomfortably imaginable." Read as a realistic novel, *The Plumed Serpent* is "absurd"; read "as a series of shimmering tableaux, as a mysterious movement from novel to fantasy," it is "an authentic masterpiece." The book shows that the poor have benefited little from the Mexican Revolution, that "equality of opportunity" has never stopped "charismatic leaders" from taking over, and that "the nineteenth century faith in rationality was based unstably on an inadequate conception of human behavior."

2510 Hardy, Barbara. "Truthfulness and Schematism: D. H. Lawrence," THE APPROPRIATE FORM: AN ESSAY ON THE NOVEL (Lond: Athlone P, 1964), pp. 132-73.

The novel is seen in its freer forms in the work of DHL, whose aims are directly opposite to those of Henry James or James Joyce. DHL's respect for the novel is not that of an artist but that of a human being. Regarding both conspicuous artistry and "the old stable ego" as static forms imposed on the fluidity of human nature, DHL preferred the ambivalence of psychological distinctions to ideological schemes and moral categories. In *Sons and Lovers,* by having Paul's relationships with both Clara and Miriam fail, DHL shows that the impasse with Miriam derives in part from Paul's relationship with his parents. The ambivalence of Paul's feelings toward his mother accounts for his decision at the end to turn away from her and death. This is a story of an artist who owes his mother "both his wound and his bow." The debates in *Women in Love* have a life and individuality that transcend schemes. Love in this novel ranges from "bestial passion" and "perversion" to tenderness. *Lady Chatterley's Lover* shows the element of "bestiality" in tender passion. The lovers' private, "obscene" language is true, whereas Sir Clifford's language is artificially literary, though in characterizing the latter, DHL " 'puts his thumb in the [scale].' "

2511 Hardy, John Edward. THE MODERN TALENT: AN ANTHOLOGY OF SHORT STORIES (NY: Holt, Rinehart & Winston, 1964), pp. 496-97.

[Brief biographical note, citing DHL's championing of "sexual freedom," his artistic integrity, his "considerable talent" as a painter. "The Christening" is reprinted in the anthology, pp. 36-45.]

2512 Hardy, John Edward. "*Sons and Lovers*: The Artist as Savior," MAN IN THE MODERN NOVEL (Seattle: University of Washington P, 1964), pp. 52-66.

Sons and Lovers exhibits a "half-emergent" form. DHL remained too close to the vital, undifferentiated mass of experience and feeling, and his novel records the struggle of the artist-hero to "think his way out" of immersion in experience in order to recreate it from the perspective of the isolated artist. Paul's struggle as an artist, like DHL's, is to separate himself from his family--specifically his mother-- to achieve himself as isolate being. Paul, like Christ, "is wasted by compassion," sacrificing himself for the benefit of the women with whom he comes into contact, either beautifying them, helping them to perceive and understand more fully, or leading them to fuller vitality. But his sacrifices do not redeem his world, and he is unable, himself, to triumph over suffering or even, despite DHL's attempt at an affirmative ending, to complete his own separation from his mother and achieve self-responsibility. The ending, consequently, seems forced, tacked on, a *non sequitur.* One wonders if DHL himself "ever achieved the final detachment" to which Paul aspires.

2513 Harris, Marguerite (ed). MAXIMS & APHORISMS FROM THE LETTERS OF D. H. LAWRENCE, compiled, and with appended poems by Marguerite Harris (NY: "Printed, designed, & zapped in an edition of 250 copies by Ed Sanders," 1964).

[This mimeographed pamphlet is a collection of statements from DHL's letters, organized in four parts. The two appended poems by Marguerite Harris, "The Race" and "The Thread of Love," are Laurentian in tone and take statements by DHL as their points of departure.]

2514 Heagarty, Mary Alice. "Aesthetic Distance in the Techniques of the Novel," DISSERTATION ABSTRACTS, XXV (1965), 4687-88. Unpublished dissertation, University of Illinois, 1964.

[Studies works by Austen, George Eliot, Lawrence, Henry James, Dreiser. The moon symbol is traced from *Sons and Lovers* through *The Rainbow* and *Women in in Love.*]

2515 Hicks, Granville. "D. H. L. the Second Time Around," SATURDAY REVIEW, XLVII (7 March 1964), 31-32.

The Symbolic Meaning: The Uncollected Versions of "Studies in Classic American Literature," ed by Armin Arnold, "is not only a different book" from the 1923 version "but in some ways a superior one." As a vehicle for expressing the philosophy and psychology that DHL was evolving at the time, however, "the revised version is an improvement." "Both versions show an extraordinary insight into American literature," as evidenced in DHL's trusting the tale in Cooper and his early "recognition of the importance of MOBY DICK." Only about Whitman did DHL "drastically alter his opinion" in the revised version. "A comparison of the two volumes helps us to see Lawrence more clearly."

2516 Hirashima, Junko. "Gûwa (D. H. Lawrence--'The Man Who Loved Islands' no Sekai)" (D. H. Lawrence: "The Man Who Loved Islands"), BAIKA JOSHIDAIGAKU BUNGAKUBU KIYÔ (Baika Joshidaigaku), No. 1 (Dec 1964), 49-72.
[In Japanese.]

2517 Hochman, Baruch. "'Another Ego': The Changing View of Self and Society in the Work of D. H. Lawrence," DISSERTATION ABSTRACTS, XXV (1964), 7269A. Unpublished dissertation, Columbia University, 1964. Rvd and pub as ANOTHER EGO: THE CHANGING VIEW OF SELF AND SOCIETY IN THE WORK OF D. H. LAWRENCE (Columbia, SC: University of South Carolina P, 1970).

2518 Hoffman, Frederick J. THE MORTAL NO: DEATH AND THE MODERN IMAGINATION (Princeton: Princeton UP, 1964), pp. 395, 406-23, 491-93.
DHL attempted to reshape the entire range of religious thought along the lines of individual definition. Basically, DHL viewed experience as a struggle for balance, "polarity," or a state of "still tension"; sexual union is an important means by which man approaches such a state. However, a balance between sensuality and spirituality (either extreme being destructive in itself) is made difficult by the pervasive influence of Christianity, and indeed, DHL's early fiction records the failures of individuals to achieve such balance. These contradictions are tentatively reconciled in the character of Rupert Birkin, and *Women in Love,* therefore, can be seen as a turning point in DHL's career. After this, DHL "cast about for a proper definition of 'political activity,' of some literary extension of the male power . . . contained in Birkin's balanced view." His search led to "excesses of banality and querulousness." Believing that Christianity was dead but that man was continuous, DHL rejected the Christian ideal of grace but wished to assert the "analogical responsibility" of Christianity "to the actual circumstances of human relationship." In short, therefore, he attempted to revise along secular lines "the religious metaphors used to support man's reaction to mortality."

2519 Hoggart, Richard. "Lawrence's Voices," LISTENER AND BBC TELEVISION REVIEW, LXXII (29 Oct 1964), 673-74; rptd in SPEAKING TO EACH OTHER: ESSAYS, by Richard Hoggart, Vol. II: ABOUT LITERATURE (NY: Oxford UP, 1970), pp. 103-6.
In reading *The Complete Poems of D. H. Lawrence,* ed by Vivian de Sola Pinto

and F. Warren Roberts, it would be more useful now to pay attention to DHL's tone than to the old free or formal arguments. DHL's voices range from the quick, irreverent, and quirky working class accents of "Red Geranium and Godly Mignonette" to the prophetic and mystical tones of "Bavarian Gentians." Like Orwell and other writers whose lives and art are interdependent, DHL had to reject most social and literary tones to have his say.

2520 Hoyt, C. A. "D. H. Lawrence: The Courage of Human Contact," ENGLISH RECORD, XIV (April 1964), 8-15.

Lady Chatterley's Lover is DHL's best statement in fiction of his beliefs. The novel has an important relationship with the apocalyptic elements in the Romantic poets, particularly Blake and Shelley.

2521 Iwata, Noboru. "*St. Mawr* Sairon (I)" (On *St. Mawr* Again [I]), LITERARY SYMPOSIUM (Aichi University), No. 26 (Feb 1964), 185-214.

[In Japanese.]

2522 Johnson, Spud [pseud of Willard Johnson]. "The Santa Fe Gadfly," SANTA FE NEW MEXICAN, PASATIEMPO (Sunday Magazine Section), 22 March 1964, pp. 7, 12.

[Column.] A search for brief newspaper items appearing in the NEW MEXICO SENTINEL uncovers a report by Knud Merrild of DHL's alleged abusive treatment of a bull terrier bitch, Pipsy, given to him by Mabel Dodge Luhan. [See also Knud Merrild, "D. H. Lawrence and Bibsy Bubastis," NEW MEXICO SENTINEL ("New Mexico Writers" page, ed by Hanniel Long), 24 Aug 1937 and 31 Aug 1937; and five Letters to the Editor in reply by Mabel Dodge Luhan, Spud Johnson, Dorothy Brett, Witter Bynner, and Frieda Lawrence, in NEW MEXICO SENTINEL ("New Mexico Writers" page, ed by Hanniel Long), 21 Sept 1937, rptd and discussed in Spud Johnson, "The Santa Fe Gadfly," SANTA FE NEW MEXICAN, PASATIEMPO (Sunday Magazine Section), 29 March 1964, pp. 5, 12.]

2523 Johnson, Spud [pseud of Willard Johnson]. "The Santa Fe Gadfly," SANTA FE NEW MEXICAN, PASATIEMPO (Sunday Magazine Section), 29 March 1964, pp. 5, 12.

[Column. Quotes Letters to the Editor by Mabel Dodge Luhan, Spud Johnson, and Dorothy Brett, defending DHL against the charge that he mistreated his terrier bitch, Pipsy; from Witter Bynner, supporting the veracity of Knud Merrild, who had made the charge; and from Frieda Lawrence, recounting how DHL had nursed the dog when she was sick. See also Knud Merrild, "D. H. Lawrence and Bibsy Bubastis," NEW MEXICO SENTINEL ("New Mexico Writers" page, ed by Hanniel Long), 24 Aug 1937 and 31 Aug 1937; and the five Letters to the Editor in reply by Mabel Dodge Luhan, Spud Johnson, Dorothy Brett, Witter Bynner, and Frieda Lawrence, in NEW MEXICO SENTINEL ("New Mexico Writers" page, ed by Hanniel Long), 21 Sept 1937. The question is also discussed in Spud Johnson, "The Santa Fe Gadfly," SANTA FE NEW MEXICAN, PASATIEMPO (Sunday Magazine Section), 22 March 1964, pp. 7, 12.]

2524 Junkins, Donald. " 'The Rocking-Horse Winner': A Modern Myth," STUDIES IN SHORT FICTION, II (Fall 1964), 87-89.
In overlooking its mythic qualities, critics have failed to recognize "The Rocking-Horse Winner" as a story "of meaning, not morality," which dramatizes "modern man's unsuccessful attempt to act out and emerge from his oedipal conflict with the woman-mother." Paul takes on the impossible task of trying to solve the mother's " 'problems' ": an "unrealized man-boy," unable to "overcome his oedipal confrontation," he dies, killed by the "man-devouring woman . . . re-created in modern terms."

2525 Kawabata, Takashi. "D. H. Lawrence (Atara Shii Sekai no Kokai)" (D. H. Lawrence: His Voyage of Discovery to the New World), ENGLISH LITERATURE IN HOKKAIDÔ (Hokkaidô University), No. 9 (Jan 1964), 50-57.
[In Japanese.]

2526 Kendle, Burton S. "D. H. Lawrence: The Man Who Misunderstood Gulliver," ENGLISH LANGUAGE NOTES, II (Sept 1964), 42-46.
DHL misreads Swift's "The Lady's Dressing Room" in missing the comic tone, which invites acceptance of the whole human being instead of underlining the "deranged" rejection of Celia because of her bodily functions. DHL's humorlessness makes him unable to see Swift's wit. His misreading includes several literal errors as well. DHL also misreads GULLIVER'S TRAVELS because he identifies Gulliver with Swift, whereas Gulliver is most like DHL's character Cathcart in "The Man Who Loved Islands."

2527 Kessler, Jascha. "D. H. Lawrence's Primitivism," TEXAS STUDIES IN LITERATURE AND LANGUAGE, V (Winter 1964), 467-88.
DHL's primitivism is really a "modern primitivism," which represents destructive impulses that are socially ahistorical and psychologically regressive. DHL chose to tell "the story of a person's life by dramatizing his instinctual imperatives." His "inverted Manicheanism" characterizes "civilization as the effect of conscious thought, claims that the pursuit of its 'ideal' goals was ruining man, promotes the unconscious as the source of love, and calls the release of instinctual drives good." DHL was "a familiar sort of modern mechanist," whose stories "represent . . . unindividualized and unindividualizing process" and are as "impersonal . . . as a physics without history." [Draws on *Psychoanalysis and the Unconscious* and *Fantasia of the Unconscious* and compares DHL with Freud.]

2528 Kuramochi, Saburô. "Personification and De-Personification in D. H. Lawrence's Poetry," ÔTSUKA REVIEW (Tôkyô University of Education), No. 1 (June 1964), 49-58.

2529 "Language and Literature," CHOICE, 1 (May 1964), 98.
The Symbolic Meaning: The Uncollected Versions of "Studies in Classic American Literature," ed by Armin Arnold, "is significant because his style of writing is less

eccentric here" than in the *Studies.* Comparison between the two versions reveals "the ever-changing, non-fixed character of Lawrence's ideas."

2530 Levy, Mervyn. "Foreword," *Paintings of D. H. Lawrence,* ed by Mervyn Levy (NY: Viking P; Lond: Cory, Adams & Mackay, 1964), pp. 10-14.

Although incidental to his writing, DHL's interest in painting is basic to understanding "his evolution as man, and writer." Though "versed in the basic principles of perspective and composition," DHL shows "little academic knowledge of human anatomy," and his nudes, "weak in construction," suggest that he made no "positive, first-hand study of anatomy" by drawing "from the life." DHL's puritanism and his belief that the body is sacramental may explain his "unwillingness to study the human form in any coldly detached or purely scientific context." His nudes are "always a struggle, and in this respect they are profoundly revealing."

2531 Levy, Mervyn (ed). *Paintings of D. H. Lawrence* (NY: Viking P; Lond: Cory, Adams & Mackay, 1964).

Contents, abstracted under year of first publication: DHL, "Making Pictures," front endpaper [not abstracted]; Mervyn Levy, "Foreword," pp. 10-14; Harry T. Moore, "D. H. Lawrence and His Paintings," pp. 17-34; Jack Lindsay, "The Impact of Modernism on Lawrence," pp. 35-53; Herbert Read, "Lawrence as a Painter," pp. 55-64; and "Notes on the Pictures," pp. 67-79 [not abstracted]. [Includes 16 full-page color plates and 24 pages of monochrome plates.]

2532 Levy, Raphael. "Lawrence's 'Song of a Man Who Has Come Through,'" EXPLICATOR, XXII (Feb 1964), Item 44.

The "three strange angels" derive from the angels in Genesis who appeared to Abraham to foretell the birth of Isaac and the destruction of Sodom.

2533 Lindsay, Jack. "The Impact of Modernism on Lawrence," *Paintings of D. H. Lawrence,* ed by Mervyn Levy (NY: Viking P; Lond: Cory, Adams & Mackay, 1964), pp. 35-54.

DHL's sympathy with impressionism--its " 'shimmer of lights and colours' "-- did not prevent him from seeing the need to go beyond it. Like Cézanne, whom he admired, DHL wished " 'to touch the world of substance' " with " 'the intuitive touch.' " In analyzing Cézanne's art-crisis, DHL was also "analyzing his own deep creative conflicts, which were powerfully resolved in *The Sisters*" by "something quite new in prose." DHL's letter to Edward Garnett of 5 June 1914 shows that, while he did not accept the position of the Futurists, he was "finding his place in the tumultuous social and artistic conflicts which Futurism ushered in." DHL's interest in primitive art, as seen in *Women in Love,* is not one of simple acceptance but a part of his own self-clarification. Opposed to the mechanical and theoretical in modern art, DHL uses modernism to gain his own perspective and aims.

2534 "Literature," BOOKLIST AND SUBSCRIPTION BOOKS BULLETIN: A GUIDE TO CURRENT BOOKS, LXI (15 Dec 1964), 372.

The Complete Poems of D. H. Lawrence, ed with notes by Vivian de Sola Pinto and F. Warren Roberts and with an Introduction by Pinto, is "a welcome definitive edition for browsing or study," containing "hitherto uncollected poems, . . . juvenilia, . . . variants and early drafts of published poems."

2535 Lochhead, Marion. THE VICTORIAN HOUSEHOLD (Lond: John Murray, 1964), pp. 145-46.

DHL grew up in the "English Black Country" in harsh circumstances of poverty. His mother, the "dominant influence" in his boyhood, was once a school mistress and could not forgive "the conditions to which her marriage had reduced her." The "spiritual background" of DHL's childhood was "the evangelical missions or 'revivals' " of the local Congregational chapel. [The first four stanzas of DHL's poem "Red-Herring" are quoted as evidence of his childhood milieu.]

2536 "Lost Paradise," NEWSWEEK, LXIV (23 Nov 1964), 118, 120.

"Almost every word of" FRIEDA LAWRENCE: THE MEMOIRS AND CORRESPONDENCE, ed by E. W. Tedlock, Jr., diminishes Frieda's stature from mythic personage to *hausfrau*. *The Complete Poems of D. H. Lawrence*, ed by Vivian de Sola Pinto and F. Warren Roberts, reveals DHL's "profound sense of life as an ordeal, 'coming through' to glory and degradation, inevitably and simultaneously." "No modern poet has brought word and object closer together than Lawrence. His ability not simply to sympathize with, but to identify himself with any living thing is fantastic." *Paintings of D. H. Lawrence*, ed by Mervyn Levy, "shows Lawrence as a half-primitive image maker." "The sense of a lost paradise is the human condition," and as DHL expressed it, the " 'ache for being is the ultimate hunger.' "

2537 Macauley, Robie, and George Lanning. TECHNIQUE IN FICTION (NY, Evanston, and Lond: Harper & Row, 1964), pp. 59, 70, 187, 191-93.

In *Lady Chatterley's Lover,* Mellors's habit of speaking sometimes like an educated man and sometimes like a collier is a "mannerism which very quickly wears out the reader's patience." In the organic design of *The Rainbow* and *Women in Love,* "there are five major examples of a love relationship, the first three (in *The Rainbow*) being progressively deeper and more complex explorations" in a threefold plan which proves unsuccessful "because the Ursula-Skrebensky affair, which is intended to be the most searching and profound development of the theme, falls somewhat short." In *Women in Love* the same theme is, therefore, divided "into two different treatments in the concurrent stories" of the relationships of Gudrun and Gerald Crich, which "ends in catastrophe," and Ursula and Rupert Birkin, which "ends in concord."

2538 Mandrillo, P. "D. H. Lawrence as a Critic and Translator of Verga," PROCEEDINGS OF THE NINTH CONGRESS OF THE AUSTRALASIAN UNIVERSITIES' LANGUAGE AND LITERATURE ASSOCIATION, ed by Marion Adams (Melbourne: University of Melbourne, 1964), p. 87.

Although there are limitations to DHL's ability as a critic and translator of Giovanni Verga, his affinity for Verga's language and feelings resulted in DHL's spiritual development and growth in studies of the Italian writer. *Kangaroo* and *The Plumed Serpent* display feelings similar to Verga's in the search for the primitive life.

2539 Marks, William Sowell, III. "The Novel as Puritan Romance: A Comparative Study of Samuel Richardson, The Brontës, Thomas Hardy, and D. H. Lawrence," DISSERTATION ABSTRACTS, XXV (1964), 1214A. Unpublished dissertation, Stanford University, 1964.

2540 Merivale, Patricia. "D. H. Lawrence and the Modern Pan Myth," TEXAS STUDIES IN LITERATURE AND LANGUAGE, VI (Autumn 1964), 297-305; rptd as Chap. VI, "Culminations: D. H. Lawrence," PAN THE GOAT-GOD: HIS MYTH IN MODERN TIMES, by Patricia Merivale (Cambridge, MA: Harvard UP, 1969), pp. 194-219.
As both "critic and exponent" of the Pan-tradition, DHL has "no serious competitors" in a modern literary context, which includes treatments of this tradition by Arthur Machen, E. M. Forster, and others. Seldom falling below his own "standard of vividness and concreteness" in employing "the neo-Romantic symbol of ineffable visionary experience," DHL "respected the paradox . . . in the mysterious synthesis of goat and god and took it to one possible logical conclusion: he sees the goat in man--the demonically and often sinisterly sexual--as synonymous with the divine in man." [Discusses DHL's handling of the tradition in detail in "Pan in America," *St. Mawr, The Plumed Serpent,* and "The Last Laugh."]

2541 Mibu, Ikuo. "Birkin ni Tsuite" (On Birkin) ENGLISH STUDIES (Nihon University), No. 12 (March 1964), 79-91.
[A study of Birkin in *Women in Love.*] [In Japanese.]

2542 Mibu, Ikuo. "Zenki Sakuhin no Josei" (Women in Early Works), ENGLISH STUDIES (Nihon University), No. 15 (Nov 1964), 199-224.
[Women in DHL's early works.] [In Japanese.]

2543 Miller, James E., and Bernice Slote (eds). THE DIMENSIONS OF THE SHORT STORY: A CRITICAL ANTHOLOGY (NY: Dodd, Mead, 1964), p. 561.
[This anthology includes "Two Blue Birds," pp. 363-76, and biographical note mentioning DHL's coal miner father and his domineering mother, his teaching experience, his connections with Hueffer, his major novels, his marriage and travels with Frieda, and his problems with censors.]

2544 Millett, Fred B. "D. H. Lawrence," in A HISTORY OF ENGLISH LITERATURE, by William Vaughn Moody and Robert Morss Lovett, 8th ed (NY: Charles Scribner's Sons, 1964), pp. 429-31, 475-76, 497, 502.
DHL's career as a novelist was dedicated to "an assault on the psychological and aesthetic limitations of realism." DHL believed that realism had lent support to unsavory social forces in the modern world: materialism, commercialism, and

nationalism; he felt that a more creative, enriching kind of life could be realized by coming to terms with deeper instincts. Two of DHL's main concerns as a writer of fiction were an attack on prudishness and a preoccupation with the doctrine of psychoanalysis. In his hostility to the prevailing social-political order of the twentieth century, DHL became anti-intellectual. As a poet, DHL was temporarily connected with the Imagists, sharing their conviction that poetry should be implicit rather than explicit and that verse should be freed from the restrictions of conventional form. DHL viewed poetry as a medium in which to present sudden intuitions; his verse, therefore, typically lacks a "completely satisfactory form."

2545 Moore, Harry T. "D. H. Lawrence and His Paintings," *Paintings of D. H. Lawrence,* ed by Mervyn Levy (NY: Viking P; Lond: Cory, Adams & Mackay, 1964), pp. 17-34.

The paintings have recognizably Lawrencean features: 'the eye that was responsible for refracting landscapes" in the fiction and nonfiction depends on "vitality" to carry the works beyond "considerations of careless haste." This vitality comes from "one of the constituents of his vision"--what he called "quickness," an " 'odd sort of fluid, changing, grotesque or beautiful relatedness.' " DHL, who learned to paint by copying other works, cultivated a thorough acquaintance with European art--particularly the Italian Renaissance, "the modern French School," African and Melanesian statuary, and Futurism. Though he was basically "a Sunday painter," DHL's Warren Gallery-Mandrake Press pictures were his most ambitious. [Detailed discussion of the pictures shown at the 1929 Warren Gallery exhibit, the paintings reproduced here in color or monochrome.]

2546 Mori, Haruhide. "Lawrence's Imagistic Development in *The Rainbow* and *Women in Love,*" ELH, XXXI (Dec 1964), 460-81.

In *The Rainbow,* the meaning of an image grows in the reader's unconscious or memory, and the meaning of the novel emerges organically out of images of birds, flood, darkness, acorn, horses, and rainbow as they develop. The meaning of *Women in Love* grows not out of its poetry but out of Birkin's philosophy so that many important verbal statements, especially those regarding death and love, are unmotivated except in relation to Birkin's ideas, even when they are uttered by another character. Images carried over from *The Rainbow* to *Women in Love* are used in static patterns to support Birkin's philosophy, which is not coherent because Birkin is not a fully credible character.

2547 Nakamura, Yoshio. "Chatterley Fujin no Ichiya" (A Night Spent by Lady Chatterley), FOCUS (Aichi University), No. 1 (Dec 1964), 43-51.

[In Japanese.]

2548 Nakano, Kimiko. "*The Rainbow* ni Okeru D. H. Lawrence no Shisô" (D. H. Lawrence's Attitude to Love and Religion as Found in *The Rainbow*), KÔNAN WOMEN'S COLLEGE STUDIES IN ENGLISH LITERATURE, No. 1 (Dec 1964), 118-35.

[In Japanese.]

2549 Nardi, Piero. "Le donne di Lawrence" (Lawrence's Women), IL RESTO DEL CARLINO (Bologna), 16 June 1964, p. 3.

In one of his letters to Edward Garnett, DHL states that the fundamental problem of modern times is the establishment of a new man-woman relationship. This problem, incidental to *Aaron's Rod,* in which DHL portrays the character of the "real man," becomes paramount in *Women in Love.* [In Italian.]

2550 Nardi, Piero. "Introduzione" (Introduction), *L'arcobaleno--Donne innamorate (The Rainbow--Women in Love)* (Milan: A. Mondadori, 1964), pp. xiii-xxxix.

The major themes of *The Rainbow* are woman's achievement of her own individuality and her sexual fulfillment in marriage as an approach to divinity. The relationship between two men and DHL's attack on intellectualism fade into the background in *Women in Love.* In this novel DHL's social aim is apparent. [In Italian.]

2551 Nardi, Piero. "Il problema dell'amore nei romanzi di Lawrence" (The Problem of Love in Lawrence's Novels), IL TEMPO (Rome), 7 July 1964, p. 3.

The Rainbow and *Women in Love* have been published in Italy in a single volume because they are both derived from a projected novel whose title was to be "The Sisters." These novels, in which DHL thoroughly analyzes the man-woman relationship, are perhaps among his best works. [In Italian.]

2552 Nardi, Piero. "Il puritano Lawrence" (Lawrence the Puritan), IL RESTO DEL CARLINO (Bologna), 24 April 1964, p. 3.

Venice has often inspired the sensual immoralist; it was not so in the case of DHL. In fact DHL's fundamental attitude is typical of the stern moralist, though his moralism is based on heterodox principles, as D. Gillĕs rightly points out in his D. H. LAWRENCE OU LE PURITAIN SCANDALEUX (Paris, 1964). [In Italian.]

2553 Newman, Paul B. "The Natural Aristocrat in Letters," UNIVERSITY REVIEW (Kansas City), XXXI (Oct 1964), 23-31.

Like Yeats and Conrad, DHL tried to recover a heroic "mythical insight" that could inform personality with the power to struggle against materialism. Such a personality, like the heroic figures of Greek literature, would present to society an aristocracy of moral ideals. The natural aristocrat is both anti-self and anti-democratic, respecting not the equality but the polarity of every man. DHL used the concept of the Holy Ghost as an image of individual divinity and saw a moral breakdown, much as Paul Tillich did, in the refusal to recognize the moral in the ontological. Other religious comparisons can be made with Richard Wagner's *Ring* cycle. Love has the power of salvation, if it is used for regeneration, for unity through sublimation rather than for destruction through egoistic will. All the characters in *Women in Love* search for an anti-self, but Gerald suffers a tragic failure to find a moral model and, thus, regeneration.

2554 Ninomiya, Takamichi. "Lawrence no Tolstoi Kan (I)" (Law-

rence's View of Tolstoy [I]), TAUROS (Kôbe University), No. 4 (Jan 1964), 47-55.
[In Japanese.]

2555 Ninomiya, Takamichi. "Lawrence no Tolstoi Kan (II)" (Lawrence's View of Tolstoy [II]), TAUROS (Kôbe University, No. 5 (June 1964), 33-44.
[In Japanese.]

2556 Nogara, Gino. "Intelletto e sesso" (Intellect and Sex), LA PROVINCIA (Cremona), 9 Oct 1964, p. 3
The central point in *The Rainbow* and *Women in Love* is woman's search for her own individuality, for her fulfillment in a complete sexual life. [In Italian.]

2557 Nosaka, Tôsaku. "*Sons and Lovers* ni Okeru Buntai" (The Style in *Sons and Lovers*), KENKYÛ RONBUN-SHÛ (Miyagi Women's College), No. 24 (July 1964), 18-38.
[In Japanese.]

2558 Ôhashi, Yasuichirô. "Shijin Lawrence to Tsuki" (The Moon in D. H. Lawrence's Poetry), MEMOIRS OF HUMANISTIC AND SOCIAL SCIENCES (Kyôto Technical University), No. 12 (March 1964), 59-84.
[In Japanese.]

2559 Ohmann, Richard. "Generative Grammars and the Concept of Literary Style," WORD, XX (1964), 422-39, espec pp. 437-38; rptd in LINGUISTICS AND LITERARY STYLE, ed by Donald C. Freeman (NY: Holt, Rinehart & Winston, 1970), espec pp. 275-76.
Literary styles may be contrasted on the basis of which of four possible "transformational operations" they are built on: "addition, deletion, reordering, and combination." DHL's "especially brusque, emphatic style" in *Studies in Classic American Literature* is idiosyncratic in "the use of truncated sentences, which have gone through a variety of deletion transformations." [Stylistic analysis of a passage from "Herman Melville's TYPEE and OMOO" quotes the passage first as written, then with DHL's stylistic deletions restored.]

2560 Okada, Taiji. "D. H. Lawrence no Mashin to Seirei" (D. H. Lawrence's Demon and Holy Ghost), REVIEW OF KÔBE UNIVERSITY OF MERCANTILE MARINE, PART I: STUDIES IN HUMANITIES AND SOCIAL SCIENCE, No. 12 (March 1964), 157-80.
[In Japanese.]

2561 Okumura, Tôru. "Paul no Higeki--*Musuko to Koibito*" (The Tragedy of Paul--*Sons and Lovers*), REVIEW OF ENGLISH LITERATURE (College of Liberal Arts, Kyôto University), No. 16 (Oct 1964), 106-40.
[In Japanese.]

2562 "The Painter of the Rainbow," TIMES LITERARY SUPPLEMENT (Lond), 19 Nov 1964, p. 1034.

"The conventional terms of conventional art-criticism seem curiously irrelevant when applied to Lawrence's paintings," which are reproduced in *Paintings of D. H. Lawrence*, ed by Mervyn Levy. One is inclined "to suggest that Lawrence could not draw very well, that . . . he did not know enough about anatomy to produce convincing nudes." Because DHL "did not approach painting as a painter," although he "was perfectly well aware of a deliberate purpose behind his painting," he failed to communicate his vision in this medium as he did in his prose. [Discussion of the effect of *Boccaccio Story, Resurrection, Close-Up, Yawning, The Mango Tree,* and *Fight with an Amazon.*] Thus the view that one cannot understand DHL as a writer without taking his painting into account remains unproven. [Comments on the critical essays by Harry T. Moore, Jack Lindsay, and Herbert Read in the volume.]

2563 Panichas, George A. ADVENTURE IN CONSCIOUSNESS: THE MEANING OF D. H. LAWRENCE'S RELIGIOUS QUEST (The Hague: Mouton, 1964).

[Revealing DHL as a religious seeker, a thought-adventurer on a "voyage of discovery," this book sees DHL's art as inseparable from religion understood as a creative act. A number of essays, abstracted under year of first publication, are revised and reprinted here as chapters: "The Third Ground, the Holy Ground," GONG, XI (Summer 1961), 8-11, enlgd as Chap. 1, pp. 15-30; "F. M. Dostoevsky and D. H. Lawrence: Their Visions of Evil," RENAISSANCE AND MODERN STUDIES, V (1961), 49-75, rptd as Chap. VII, pp. 151-79; "Voyage of Oblivion: D. H. Lawrence's Death Poems," ENGLISH MISCELLANY, XII (1962), 131-64, rptd as Chap. VIII, pp. 180-207; "D. H. Lawrence's War Letters," TEXAS STUDIES IN LITERATURE AND LANGUAGE, V (Autumn 1963), 398-409, absorbed into Chap. III, pp. 62-94; "D. H. Lawrence's Biblical Play *David*," MODERN DRAMA, VI (Sept 1963), 164-76, rptd as Chap. VI, pp. 136-50; "D. H. Lawrence's Concept of the Risen Lord," CHRISTIAN SCHOLAR, XLVII (Spring 1964), 56-65, rptd as Chap. V, pp. 124-35.]

2564 Panichas, George A. "D. H. Lawrence's Concept of the Risen Lord," CHRISTIAN SCHOLAR, XLVII (Spring 1964), 56-65; rvd and rptd as Chap. V, "Christ Risen," in ADVENTURE IN CONSCIOUSNESS: THE MEANING OF D. H. LAWRENCE'S RELIGIOUS QUEST, by George A. Panichas (The Hague: Mouton, 1964), pp. 124-35.

DHL's insistence on the risen Christ as a symbol of the affirmation of life, as opposed to the Church's stress on the crucified Christ, was a valid emphasis. However, his depiction in *The Man Who Died* of Christ's resurrection *into* the flesh, particularly in Part II of Christ's phallic fulfillment, becomes dogmatically tendentious and reveals "a distinct if not crippling limitation both to his vision and understanding of life."

2565 Pearsall, Robert Brainard. "The Second Art of D. H. Lawrence," SOUTH ATLANTIC QUARTERLY, LXIII (Autumn 1964), 457-67.

Though a writer, DHL took up a second art during three periods of great stress in his life to comfort and rebuild himself--"once during his troubled adolescent years, once in the wartime years that paralyzed him, and once, finally, when he was dying a long hard death from tuberculosis." The "imitative, bourgeois, and mother-ridden" drawing and painting of his adolescence, the "practical and useful" "little boxes and embroidered objects" of the war years, and the "phallic painting" of his last years show how "he resisted separation from his mother, resisted the inutile status assigned to him in wartime, and resisted the approach of his own death."

2566 P[eterson], L. "D. H. Lawrences 'The Rocking-Horse Winner,'" HORISONT (Vasa, Finland), XI (1964), 32-33.

"The Rocking-Horse Winner" shows man's inability to master "the unknown" in life. Greed was to DHL a stifling human disease, but Paul's desperate efforts to help and to "know" by making his will dominate the vital instincts are disastrous. Paul's control of the rocking-horse and his futile "mechanical gallop" are DHL's judgment of our materialistic and mechanical society. [In Swedish.]

2567 Pickrel, Paul. "They Know They're Monsters: Some Recent Books on Art," HARPER'S MAGAZINE, CCXXIX (Dec 1964), 124-30, espec p. 130.

Paintings of D. H. Lawrence, ed by Mervyn Levy, "makes available work that has been extremely hard to come by. The reproductions are inferior to those in the Mandrake edition." "Once they [the paintings] were enough to bring out the police, but now they hardly figure as anything more than documentation of a career whose genius lay elsewhere." They might be collectively titled " 'a dream of hedonism by a Puritan who never learned to draw.' "

2568 Pieraccini, Leonetta. "Lawrence e Casanova" (Lawrence and Casanova), IL MONDO (Rome), 2 June 1964, p. 12.

Aldo Palazzeschi, in whose villa near Scandicci the Lawrences lived for some time, recalls a few small episodes of their married life to demonstrate how they loved each other. He remembers also how offended DHL was by reading Casanova's MEMOIRS, in spite of the fact that in the same period he was writing *Lady Chatterley's Lover.* DHL's reaction can be explained by the fact that he was convinced that his novel had intrinsic poetic and moral values, while Casanova's writings were merely examples of libertinism. [In Italian.]

2569 Pinto, Vivian de Sola, and F. Warren Roberts. "Editors' Note on the Text," *The Complete Poems of D. H. Lawrence* (NY: Viking P; Lond: Heinemann, 1964), pp. 23-26.

[Identifies the sources for the compilation of the *Complete Poems.*]

2570 "Places, Races and Faces," SUNDAY HERALD TRIBUNE BOOK WEEK (NY), 13 Dec 1964, p. 10.

Paintings of D. H. Lawrence, ed by Mervyn Levy, is "the first representative collection of paintings by Lawrence, a self-taught painter." [Brief notice.]

2571 Potter, Stephen. "Towards the Great Secret," SPECTATOR,

CCXIII (23 Oct 1964), 545.

The order of poems in *The Complete Poems of D. H. Lawrence,* ed by Vivian de Sola Pinto and F. Warren Roberts, shows DHL's evolution to a more complete and perfect power: the thought of his prose is improved by compression in the poems.

2572 Powell, Lawrence Clark. THE LITTLE PACKAGE: PAGES ON LITERATURE AND LANDSCAPE FROM A TRAVELING BOOKMAN'S LIFE (Cleveland and NY: World, 1964), pp. 109, 136-37, 150, 180, 243.

A writer's "sensitivity," "absorptive capacity," and "creative stamina" allow him to "soak up" a locale and render it quickly. *Sea and Sardinia* is "a two-week walking trip through the mountainous island." Although DHL "spent only four months in Australia," *Kangaroo* "is a classic expression of the little continent." In "The Princess," DHL successfully renders the Sangre de Cristo Mountains. DHL has kept the author occupied for twenty years as a book collector, "starting with the Modern Library edition of *The Rainbow* and culminating with the rarissime second edition of *Lady Chatterley's Lover.*"

2573 Praz, Mario. "D. H. Lawrence," STORIA DELLA LETTERATURA INGLESE (History of English Literature) (Florence: Sansoni, 1964), pp. 700-703.

DHL's work reflects the psychoanalytic interests of the first post-war novelists. He is an intellectual, but in his opinion, intellectualism and progress destroy real life. To avoid the deadly influence of modern society he proposes a new religion based on nature and sexual experience as means of immediate knowledge. DHL is one of the most original modern writers. [In Italian.]

2574 Prisco, Michele. "Due romanzi di Lawrence" (Two Novels of Lawrence), IL MATTINO (Naples), 6 Aug 1964, p. 3.

DHL's aspiration to establish a sort of Eden, free from any social restraints, led him to search for an ideal area to suit his needs. Many writings register DHL's experience in Italy, where *The Rainbow* and *Women in Love* have recently come out in a single volume (with an Introduction by Piero Nardi). The latter novel is a protest against women's emancipation. [In Italian.]

2575 Read, Herbert. "Lawrence as a Painter," *Paintings of D. H. Lawrence,* ed by Mervyn Levy (NY: Viking P; Lond: Cory, Adams & Mackay, 1964), pp. 55-66.

Knud Merrild's A POET AND TWO PAINTERS (1938) is "the most professional and understanding treatment of Lawrence as a painter." The main reasons that DHL did most of his painting in the last few years of his life were the inspiration of watching Merrild paint and the fact that DHL was "an expressionist, an extreme example" of the artist "who seeks a direct correspondence between feeling and representation, to the neglect of the more sophisticated values of proportion and harmony." DHL's paintings achieve what he sought--"vitality." Their value, in fact, may not be artistic or biographical but moral: "They challenge us to cast off our own inhibitions and experience a similar delight."

2576 Rees, Marjorie. "Mollie Skinner and D. H. Lawrence," WESTERLY, I (March 1964), 41-49.
[Quoted passages from Mollie Skinner's unpublished autobiography, THE FIFTH SPARROW, concern her first meeting with DHL, his encouraging her to write, and their joint work on *The Boy in the Bush.* She states that one of her reasons for writing an autobiography was to vindicate DHL, for whom she had the greatest admiration. Several letters from DHL to Miss Skinner are included.] [See also M. L. Skinner, THE FIFTH SPARROW (Sydney, Australia: Sydney UP, 1972), pp. 109-33, 138-59.]

2577 Rexroth, Kenneth. "Poet in a Fugitive Cause," NATION (NY), CXCIX (23 Nov 1964), 382-83.
[Review article on *The Complete Poems of D. H. Lawrence,* ed by Vivian de Sola Pinto and F. Warren Roberts, and *Paintings of D. H. Lawrence,* ed by Mervyn Levy.] DHL, allowing himself to become the prophet of an outmoded religion of sexual revolution, attacked Victorian morality after it was a dead issue. Although the incongruity of his puritanism corrupted him as man and stylist, DHL fulfilled countless programs from the LYRICAL BALLADS to the Imagist manifesto. Only DHL's illness distracted his poise and injures his later poems. Like most major poets of the twentieth century, DHL was anti-humane, anti-humanist, and anti-humanitarian and needs, with others, to be re-evaluated in this light.

2578 Ricks, Christopher. "A Genius But ... ," NEW YORK REVIEW OF BOOKS, III, 19 Nov 1964, 6-7.
[Review article on *Paintings of D. H. Lawrence,* ed by Mervyn Levy, and *The Complete Poems of D. H. Lawrence,* ed by Vivian de Sola Pinto and F. Warren Roberts.] While DHL's paintings show a brutal mindlessness, they are redeemed by his poems, astonishing in their "mercurial versatility." The early poems are more artistically satisfying, but the later poems show more of DHL. DHL's hatreds are inexcusable, and he could not recognize the difference between passion and affection. [Also reviews FRIEDA LAWRENCE: THE MEMOIRS AND CORRESPONDENCE, ed by E. W. Tedlock, Jr. (1961, 1964).]

2579 Satin, Joseph. READING PROSE FICTION (Bost: Houghton, Mifflin, 1964), p. 479.
[Brief headnote to "The Shadow in the Rose Garden," which is reprinted in the anthology, pp. 479-90.] "Ever since Eden, apples and gardens have had special significance."

2580 Saunders, J. W. THE PROFESSION OF ENGLISH LETTERS (Lond: Routledge and Kegan Paul; Toronto: University of Toronto P, 1964), pp. 204, 214, 216-20, 221, 222, 224, 242, 243, 247.
Appalled by the prevailing ugliness wrought by the Industrial Revolution, DHL, like Hardy and Joyce, lived out his career in the context of a conflict engendered by the demands of a mass market. Though courageous in trying " 'to break a way through,' " DHL, even as a struggling young author, "had to contend with public hostility." Though *The White Peacock* was "a fair success," *The Trespasser* and *Sons and Lovers* both initially lost money. *The Rainbow* was seized and sup-

pressed as obscene, but DHL won a victory in the 1920 American vice case brought against *Women in Love,* making a turning-point in his recognition. *The Lost Girl* was successful, and *The Plumed Serpent* ran through five editions in as many years. Yet DHL's view of life, "associated too easily in the public mind either with a 'highbrow' image" or with "sexual licence and anarchy," was not easily commendable to a mass market. Like the eighteenth-century novelists, "Lawrence saw the novel as a medium of social reform." Working "in almost continuous uproar," DHL, besides his twelve novels, produced in profusion his volumes of poems, short stories, plays, travel books, translations, history, criticism, and paintings in "a professional career as earnest as Pope's or Carlyle's." Increasingly successful financially, DHL made a profit of £1,024 on *Lady Chatterley's Lover* in 1928 and £500 on *Pansies* in 1929, leaving at his death in 1930 an estate of £4,000, "exclusive of the value of his books, paintings, and manuscripts." The subsequent good sales record of DHL's books demonstrates "the victory of a dedicated man of letters within the mass market."

2581 Schmidt, Sandra. "Indians and Palefaces," CHRISTIAN SCIENCE MONITOR, 2 July 1964, p. 7.

In *The Symbolic Meaning: The Uncollected Versions of "Studies in Classic American Literature,"* ed by Armin Arnold, "Lawrence's mythical America is a battleground between the evil forces of intellectual knowledge and the good forces of 'blood knowledge' in which the baddies have the clear advantage." While his attitude toward the writers examined is "somewhat ambiguous," he "reveals odd twists of 19th century thinking" and illuminates the subject with "quick flashes of insight." But "the book is lumpy with crochets, prejudices, and obsessions."

2582 Scholes, Robert. "Return to Alexandria: Lawrence Durrell and Western Narrative Tradition," VIRGINIA QUARTERLY REVIEW, XL (Summer 1964), 411-20.

The lack of emphasis on form in Lawrence Durrell's early novel, THE BLACK BOOK, is an indication of the influence that DHL once exerted on him. Although in Durrell's mature work "form . . . is nearly everything," traces remain of DHL and Henry Miller, authors who were disdainful of form.

2583 Shimizu, Kazuyoshi. "Lawrence no Bungaku Hihyô" (Literary Criticism of Lawrence), SHIRON (Tôhoku University), No. 6 (June 1964), 57-74.

[In Japanese.]

2584 Shirai, Toshitaka, and Takashi Fujita. "Word-List of *The Rainbow*--A Study of D. H. Lawrence's Vocabulary," BULLETIN OF YAMAGATA UNIVERSITY, V (Feb 1964), 31-156.

2585 Simpson, Louis. "Demons All Along," SUNDAY HERALD TRIBUNE BOOK WEEK (NY), 1 Dec 1964, pp. 1, 18.

The Complete Poems of D. H. Lawrence, ed by Vivian de Sola Pinto and F. Warren Roberts, brings together "all the poems Lawrence wrote, including poems that until now have been available only in manuscript or in obscure publications," and including variant drafts and juvenilia. After he left England, "the new demon expressed himself in free verse." R. P. Blackmur's attack on Lawrence's principles [in "D. H. Lawrence and Expressive Form," THE DOUBLE AGENT (1935)] does not do justice to DHL's craftsmanship, which, in his best poems, cannot be faulted. If in his best work DHL "could slip into the skin of an animal, or bird, or reptile," much of his poetry is "peevish" and *Nettles* is "doggerel." "At the worst he was a poet and could do no harm; at his best, he wrote the strongest English in this century."

2586 Singh, T. N. "D. H. Lawrence: The Evolution of a Genius," CRITICISM AND RESEARCH (Banaras Hindu University), 1964, pp. 69-83.

The works of DHL were affected not only by his own personal experiences but also by social conditions based on a denial of life values. His primary concern is to safeguard the integrity of the individual personality against collectivism in recent times.

2587 Sinzelle, Claude M. THE GEOGRAPHICAL BACKGROUND IN THE EARLY WORKS OF D. H. LAWRENCE (Paris: Librairie Marcel Didier [Études Anglaises, Cahiers et Documents 1], 1964).

A survey of the Eastwood area, an itinerary of the houses in which DHL lived, in the Bottoms, in Walker Street, in Lynncroft Road, as well as the coal pits at Cossal, the Eastwood Colliery, the Nottingham Canal, Sherwood Forest, the Congregational Chapel, the Three Tuns Inn, Haggs Farm, and the Moorgreen Reservoir traces the topography of DHL's childhood, which became that of *The White Peacock*. From DHL's first visit to Haggs Farm in 1901, "he established a more permanent contact with nature, and especially farm-life." Far from being cut off from nature, he responded to it from early childhood and spent many holidays and weekends between the ages of sixteen and twenty-three at Haggs Farm. *The White Peacock* draws on this experience for a poetical response to nature. The novel shows DHL's "sense of discernment in social matters," but its snobbery is educational, not social. "Although the talk about Daphnis, Amaryllis, Nais . . . seems improbable in a hayfield," DHL was reading Virgil's GEORGICS, translating from the Latin, while he was writing the novel. Both romanticism and naturalism are "facets of Lawrence's treatment of the background." DHL's "scientific investigation into Nature," as seen in his teaching botany, was "an essential part of a search for a philosophy of life." His botanical descriptions reveal a "close observation of Nature, but at a deeper level, the author derives a symbol from this almost scientific description." Tactile impressions, which define physical contacts with nature and relations with others, lead to the pulse of the seasons in *The Rainbow*. "*The White Peacock* can be read on three levels": as "a romantic idyll clothed in a network of symbols," as "a naturalistic novel of manners," and as "a poem of Nature." "The constant assimilation of human characters to plants or animals and the animism of Nature makes it difficult to draw a line between the human and the non-human." The poetic qualities of the prose--inverted modification, rhythm, onomatopoeia--make the novel a hymn to life. *Sons and Lovers* "is not written as a novel of manners from the outside" but, in the first part at least, "is entirely written from the inside." Contrary to the popular conception that young DHL "suffered from the spoiling of the countryside by the collieries, ... they were for him at the time an integral part of the landscape." The first part of the novel, dealing almost exclusively with the home of the Morels, evokes the small town only through description of the Bottoms. The life of the miners is not revealed through sociological surveys but dramatized from within through characters of flesh and blood. Although it seems ample enough from the outside, the house in the Bottoms, from the inside, was a small setting for such a large family. Though both parents seem at fault in different ways, there are no villains in the novel--only characters shown as living people caught in a vicious circle. "The absolute need for a living wage, the impossibility to get it through a strike ... , and the impossiblity to get it otherwise make the situation hopeless and cause a tragic dissension between the husband and the wife." The importance of the butty system, whereby a butty subcontracted the labor of several day-men to whom he paid a fixed salary, or of the Nonconformist Church, as an educational center for the poor rivaling the Anglican Church, cannot be overestimated. Nonconformism led to a rich culture but also to a middle-class establishment against which DHL rebelled. "As Lawrence was growing up, he witnessed the supercession of the old patriarchal relationship between the coal-owners and their men, by the modern system of impersonal rule," a theme developed in *Women in Love*. [Contains two appendices and eight photographic plates with notes.]

2588 Sklar, Robert. "Our Literary Tocqueville," REPORTER, XXXI (5 Nov 1964), 50.

[Review of *The Symbolic Meaning: The Uncollected Versions of "Studies in Classic American Literature,"* ed by Armin Arnold; and *Paintings of D. H. Lawrence,* ed by Mervyn Levy.] "Five critical years, years beginning in defeat and ending in international fame and success, separate *The Symbolic Meaning* from the later *Studies.*" When DHL revised the essays in Taos, "he dropped the slow, reasoned perceptions of his desperate years. Instead he wrote in a clipped, forceful style and ironic humor that reflect his success, his certainty, his confidence." In Italy, DHL painted twenty-six oils and water colors which were in the 1929 London exhibition that was "closed by the police." These pictures, together with his "youthful landscapes," are brought together in *Paintings of D. H. Lawrence.*

2589 Storey, David. "Slabs of Slate," NEW STATESMAN, ns LXVIII (30 Oct 1964), 654-55.

[Review of *Paintings of D. H. Lawrence,* ed by Mervyn Levy.] DHL immersed himself in the center of his experience as a way of establishing the truth of his insights; Cézanne, conversely, withdrew to a point where he could see a totality of design. The conflict of values represented in these two postures toward art and experience suggests a need to transcend revelation and circumspection by combining them. DHL's reliance on intuition to achieve its own rationale made him incapable of managing a realized artistic end, as his pictures of "heavy limbs and sinuous thrashing branches" suggest in their unresolved energy.

2590 Tanselle, G. Thomas. "The Thomas Seltzer Imprint," PAPERS OF THE BIBLIOGRAPHICAL SOCIETY OF AMERICA, LVIII (Fourth Quarter 1964), 380-448.

Thomas Seltzer's publishing house existed for only six and a half years. In that time he provided a valuable service as a small and personal publisher. This courage brought the question of censorship before the reading public, and he presented to America the "People's Theatre" drama series, mysteries and popular novels (both British and American), poetry, and more than twenty items by DHL. [The chronological checklist that is included is not intended as a descriptive bibliography.]

2591 Tetsumura, Haruo. "Ai no Shigan *The Rainbow*" (On *The Rainbow*: Love as It Is to Be Transcended), SHIMONOSEKI ECONOMIC REVIEW (Shimonoseki Ichiritsu College), VII (March 1964), 53-74. [In Japanese.]

2592 Uehata, Yoshikazu. "D. H. Lawrence to Dentô" (D. H. Lawrence and Tradition), KANSAI-DAIGAKU BUNGAKU RONSHŪ (Kansai University), No. 12 (Jan 1964), 58-71. [In Japanese.]

2593 Wada, Shizuo. "D. H. Lawrence Oboegaki (II) (*Shirokujaku* ni Tsuite)" (A Note on D. H. Lawrence [II] --A Study of *The White Peacock*), KYÛSHÛ SANGYÔ DAIGAKU KYÔYÔBU KIYÔ (Kyûshû Sangyô University), I (Nov 1964), 27-62. [In Japanese.]

2594 Walsh, William. "Ursula in *The Rainbow*" and "The Writer as Teacher: The Educational Ideas of D. H. Lawrence," THE USE OF IMAGINATION: EDUCATIONAL THOUGHT AND THE LITERARY MIND (Lond: Chatto & Windus, 1964), pp. 137-38, 163-74, 199-228; excerpt, pp. 163-74, rptd as "The Childhood of Ursula," in TWENTIETH CENTURY INTERPRETATIONS OF "THE RAINBOW": A COLLECTION OF CRITICAL ESSAYS, ed by Mark Kinkead-Weekes (Englewood Cliffs, NJ: Prentice-Hall, 1971), pp. 82-91.
In *The Rainbow*, DHL depicts in Ursula "the too intensely loved, the over-possessed child." The partially subconscious conflict between her parents is the cause of Ursula's troubled relationship with Will. Will's possessiveness puts "an intolerable strain on the child" which shatters the "relaxed rhythm of childhood," pulls Ursula "too early into a too sharpened awareness," and ultimately stunts her emotional growth. While Will's distorted affection leads Ursula to perceive "a disturbed and malicious world" from which she must flee into herself, three influences of her childhood serve to mitigate the destructive effects of this relationship: her grandmother, the Grammar School, and religion. Conceiving the purpose of the novel as revealing " 'the relation between man and his circumambient universe,' " DHL held that "the novel has to help us develop 'an instinct for life,' not 'a theory of right and wrong.' " Although he opposed the cerebral ideal, DHL was never "an opponent of consciousness" but an advocate of extending and opening it to include the "neglected springs of life which are the origins of full consciousness." Education could assist in "reforming . . . the broken connection with the root of being" by helping man "to achieve a true relatedness to the living

universe about him." Since our injured modern psyche is able to understand only "in a restricted and mechanical way," education involved educating our feelings, the voice of our real identity. In *Education of the People,* DHL sets forth the application of his beliefs to education and describes how the system he proposes would work. As a professional teacher, he understood that education depends on a metaphysic. Although for him, "equality" was a worn ideal, he did not advocate inequality but a system in which such categories, based on mechanistically quantified comparisons, are irrelevant because the emphasis is on individual, organic development in quality of life. The present system "in which we stand for idealism but live by materialism" breeds vulgarity and produces cynicism. DHL wants both home and school to foster the virtues of courage and independence. DHL's final educational principle is "the exclusion of irrelevant modes of consciousness." The lasting impression of DHL's educational writings is "that he was an artist with an extraordinarily undeceived and exact sense for 'truth in being,' a man with a superlative sense of reality."

2595 Warner, Oliver. "D. H. Lawrence, 1885-1930," ENGLISH LITERATURE: A PORTRAIT GALLERY (Lond: Chatto & Windus, 1964), pp. 98-99.

[Brief biographical sketch, mentioning DHL's Nottinghamshire mining background, his teaching, his rebellious nature and notoriety, and referring only in passing to three of his novels. Includes photographic portrait.]

2596 Way, Brian. "Sex and Language: Obscene Words in D. H. Lawrence and Henry Miller," NEW LEFT REVIEW, No. 27 (Sept-Oct 1964) 66-80.

The works of DHL and Henry Miller are comparable in the use of "obscene" words because they, unlike James Joyce, have many readers and because they use the words with self-conscious drama. There are affinities between the two in their portrayal of sex with directness, though judged by DHL's puritanical standards, Miller is often more crude. DHL wishes to purify words associated with sex; Miller wishes to vitalize them. This difference often restricts DHL's expressive power, while unleashing Miller's originality. Geoffrey Gorer, in his review of *Lady Chatterley's Lover,* would like to defuse the obscenities.

2597 "The We's," TIME, XXXIII (20 March 1964), 104.

DHL's "famed *Studies in Classic American Literature* was shrill, derisive, but continuously provocative. *The Symbolic Meaning,* a collection of earlier versions of the same essays, is considerably calmer in tone, but both versions bear the unmistakable stamp of Lawrence's chaotic, irascible mind. He saw the underlying theme of U. S. literature as the 'disintegration of the primal self.' "

2598 Wilde, Alan. "The Illusion of *St. Mawr*: Technique and Vision in D. H. Lawrence's Novel," PUBLICATIONS OF THE MODERN LANGUAGE ASSOCIATION, LXXIX (March 1964), 164-70.

Adverse critics of *St. Mawr* object to the structurally uneven use of the horse, an interpretive error that confuses narrative structure with total organization. Lou Witt's transcendence of Rico's world moves the novella toward a change in tone and purpose that makes St. Mawr superfluous. Lou's receptivity to profound experience in the "presentational symbol" of the New Mexican ranch implies a need to control the presence in herself of the rejected civilization in order to mold the wilderness while not being overwhelmed by the sordid in nature.

2599 Willingham, John R. "Fine Arts," LIBRARY JOURNAL, LXXXIX (15 Dec 1964), 4899-4900.
Paintings of D. H. Lawrence, ed by Mervyn Levy, collects "every extant piece" of DHL's "prodigious flights on canvas" in "a triumph of beautiful bookmaking."

2600 Willingham, John R. "Literature," LIBRARY JOURNAL, LXXXIX (15 April 1964), 1748.
The Symbolic Meaning: The Uncollected Versions of "Studies in Classic American Literature," ed by Armin Arnold, collects the forgotten early versions of DHL's "12 exploratory essays on the strange phenomenon of American literature."

2601 Willingham, John R. "Poetry," LIBRARY JOURNAL, LXXXIX (15 March 1964), 1251.
The Complete Poems of D. H. Lawrence, ed by Vivian de Sola Pinto and F. Warren Roberts, redresses the imbalance whereby "Lawrence the poet has never been so satisfactorily on record as Lawrence the writer of fiction."

2602 Zuckerman, Elliott. THE FIRST HUNDRED YEARS OF WAGNER'S TRISTAN (NY and Lond: Columbia UP, 1964), pp. 124-27, and *passim.*
DHL's *The Trespasser* is like a Wagnerian opera set on the Isle of Wight. The characters "display a remarkable aptitude for performing excerpts from the music-dramas that are presumably recognizable without accompaniment." This early novel, of which DHL himself held a low opinion, "is neatly representative of the absurdities of an amateur Wagnerism that was prevalent in England at the turn of the century." An example of DHL's more successful adaptations of Wagner (in a novel that is more representative of DHL's talents) is the images of Valhalla in the closing chapters of *Women in Love.*

1965

2603 Alexander, John. "D. H. Lawrence's *Kangaroo*: Fantasy, Fact or Fiction?" MEANJIN QUARTERLY, XXIV (June 1965), 179-95.
Adverse criticism of the content of *Kangaroo* assumes that DHL had little factual knowledge of Australian people or politics. Actually, DHL knew much about Australian politics and arranges the political content of *Kangaroo* so that it develops in five stages. [The point is supported with evidence and developed in detail.] Basically, *Kangaroo* is an analysis of Whitman's "The Law of the Average and The Principle of Identity," as DHL calls them in his essay on democracy. Cooley is not a Fascist but an example of Whitman's "nauseating benevolence." [See also

reply by Curtis Atkinson, "Was There Fact in D. H. Lawrence's *Kangaroo*?" MEANJIN QUARTERLY, XXIV (1965), 358-59.]

2604 Altick, Richard D. LIVES AND LETTERS: A HISTORY OF LITERARY BIOGRAPHY IN ENGLAND AND AMERICA (NY: Knopf, 1965), pp. 335, 375-76, 377, 391.
[Briefly comments on memoirs of DHL, Richard Aldington's PORTRAIT OF A GENIUS, BUT . . . (1950), and D. H. LAWRENCE: A COMPOSITE BIOGRAPHY (3 vols.), ed by Edward Nehls (1957, 1958, 1959).] "Although D. H. Lawrence's adolescent experience was as various as that of any youth, more than one of his biographers discussed those years almost wholly in terms of 'the son and the lover,' a young man torn by a protracted conflict of loyalties between his possessive mother and Jessie Chambers."

2605 Aoyama, Seiko. "*The Virgin and the Gipsy* ni Tsuite (Lawrence no Tanpen-Shôse-Tsu ni Okeru Seimeishugi no Keifu)" (Lawrence's Idea of Life in *The Virgin and the Gipsy*), COLLECTED ESSAYS (Kyôritsu Women's Junior College), No. 9 (Dec 1965), 83-101.
[In Japanese.]

2606 Arnold, Armin. "D. H. Lawrence, the Russians, and Giovanni Verga," COMPARATIVE LITERATURE STUDIES, II (1965), 249-57.
DHL discovered in Verga a writer unknown in English whom he could offer as the "blank opposite" of the French (Flaubert, Maupassant, Zola) and Russian (Chekhov, Dostoevsky, Tolstoy, Turgenev) writers championed and translated by the Garnetts, Katherine Mansfield and John Middleton Murry, with whom DHL had fallen out.

2607 Atkinson, Curtis. "Was There Fact in D. H. Lawrence's *Kangaroo*?" MEANJIN QUARTERLY, XXIV (Sept 1965), 358-59; rptd in CRITICS ON D. H. LAWRENCE, ed by W. T. Andrews (Lond: Allen & Unwin; Coral Gables, FL: University of Miami P, 1971), pp. 87-88.
[Reply to John Alexander, "D. H. Lawrence's *Kangaroo*: Fantasy, Fact or Fiction?" MEANJIN, XXIV (June 1965), 179-95.] A series of incidents which "took place in Sydney a year before Lawrence wrote *Kangaroo* at Thirroul, about thirty miles south of Sydney," "may throw light on the politics of the novel." These incidents included a Labour meeting (Sunday, 1 May 1921) at which "some speakers introduced irrelevant abuse of returned soldiers," and a counter-demonstration the following week (Sunday, 8 May 1921) by veterans, about half of them in uniform and the rest wearing badges of the Returned Soldiers' League. The author [Curtis Atkinson] spoke from the League's platform, denouncing "anti-British and anti-Australian sentiments." C. H. Murphy, Labour M. L. A., was heckled by the rioting crowd estimated at about 100,000, which was kept from violence by the police. "Elsewhere in the Domain a socialist and a communist meeting were broken up and portable platforms smashed." DHL, "a tireless questioner on any subject which interested him," had probably heard and read about these incidents that "left their mark on the politics of the period."

2608 Bantock, G[eoffrey] H[erman]. EDUCATION AND VALUES: ESSAYS IN THE THEORY OF EDUCATION (Lond: Faber & Faber, 1965), pp. 31-32, 41-42, 44, 56-57, 65n, 66, 117, 163.

"The two writers on education in English in the twentieth century of major importance are D. H. Lawrence and T. S. Eliot ... because they, alone, ask the fundamental questions; in the one case, about the psychic nature and development of the individual, and, in the other, about the nature of our social order." Exploring the realities that lie beneath appearances, *Fantasia of the Unconscious* is at once a "penetrating" analysis of modern life and "the major educational textbook of our day; it persuades that our precarious complacencies form but a thin surface over the abyss." [See also G. H. Bantock, "D. H. Lawrence and the Nature of Freedom," FREEDOM AND AUTHORITY IN EDUCATION (Lond: Faber & Faber, 1952), pp. 133-81.]

2609 Barbati, Claudio. [*The Prussian Officer and Other Stories*], LA FIERA LETTERARIA (Rome), 20 June 1965, p. 4.

When DHL was writing his short stories, his interest in the primordial instinctive nature of man was becoming manifest. For this reason, the short stories in *The Prussian Officer and Other Stories* reflect a phase of DHL's literary research which was to lead to his Messianism and to the main themes and characters that were to be developed in his later novels. [In Italian.]

2610 Barfield, Owen. UNANCESTRAL VOICE (Middletown, CT: Wesleyan UP, 1965), pp. 11-17, 22, 28-33.

[Philosophical discourse. Three men, Burgeon, Middleton, and Rodney, discuss "the recent prosecution and acquittal" of DHL's *Lady Chatterley's Lover* (Regina v. Penguin Books, Ltd., 1960), as a point of departure for wider philosophical speculations. First, they consider the questions of "obscenity" versus "pornography," DHL's ideas of "the body" and the death of the "cosmos" in *Apocalypse,* and the "great change" in our time "in the very constitution of Western man." Then Burgeon's discovery of R. J. Z. Werblowski's book JOSEPH KARO: LAWYER AND MYSTIC, leads him, in the light of the sixteenth-century kabbalistic Rabbi Karo's visitant angel, the "Maggid" or "Meggid," whom Burgeon identifies as an archetype of "the inner depths of his being," to a consideration of "the enigma of Lawrence's reputation as a prophet" and the changes in Western conceptions of sex: "Sex in the heart, sex in the head, sex in the loins--and what next?" In the subsequent discourse, the question, "If the evolution of the earth and of humanity is in any sense guided by spiritual beings more powerful than man, why does it not proceed smoothly to an appointed end?," is considered in relation to Marxism (which is compared to the calculating spirit Ahriman), and the thought of evolutionary biologists like Julian Huxley, philosophers like Herbert Spencer and Teilhard de Chardin, historiographers like Arnold Toynbee and Nicolas Berdyaev, oriental religious philosophy, the thoroughly "Roman" character of Western Christianity (which dismisses the concept of "spirit" while keeping the word), and other speculations.]

2611 Beards, Richard Douglas. "The Novels of Thomas Hardy and D. H. Lawrence: A Comparative Study," DISSERTATION AB-

STRACTS, XXVI (1965), 2743A. Unpublished dissertation, University of Washington, 1965.

2612 Bergonzi, Bernard. HEROES' TWILIGHT: A STUDY OF THE LITERATURE OF THE GREAT WAR (Lond: Constable, 1965), pp. 51, 141-44, 160, 179.

DHL's hatred of the war may be traced in his letters written during the First World War and in the chapter "The Nightmare" in *Kangaroo,* in which his "account of the tribulations he endured during the war frequently rises to the level of hysteria." Both DHL and Ford Madox Ford were "conscious of living in a doomed society."

2613 Boren, James L. "Commitment and Futility in *The Fox,*" UNIVERSITY REVIEW (Kansas City), XXXI (June 1965), 301-4.

In *The Fox,* "estrangement of nature" denies sexual identification. Henry intrudes, as does the fox, upon March's life of balanced futility, demanding that she accept a rending fulfillment. The etymology of DHL's fictional names reveals the conflict in its complexity; e. g., Henry is "the ruler" who intrudes into the "borderland" of March's identity. Recalling the demonic tradition, Henry's role as fox is purposefully ambiguous. Within the Laurencean framework, there can be no satisfaction at the end, no moral affirmation.

2614 Bramley, J. A. "D. H. Lawrence's Sternest Critic," HIBBERT JOURNAL, LXIII (Spring 1965), 109-11.

DHL was at once an inspired poet, "acutely sensitive to the beauty of the natural world," and an "almost insane egotist, reacting violently from a robot civilization which he detested, and fulminating against whole societies and people. This attitude led him to propose preposterous theories, mostly of a sexual nature, for the betterment of mankind." Though "one can sympathise" with DHL's reactions against materialistic and mechanical civilization, "it is not so easy to accept the primitive life of the sexual urges and the jungle which he offers instead."

2615 Brennan, Neil F. "Sweet Georgian Brown," ENGLISH LITERATURE IN TRANSITION, VIII (May 1965), 269-71.

In "Snap-Dragon," emotion exceeds the "form devised for it," and in "Snake," DHL laments what he should regard as a public service. [Review of Robert H. Ross, THE GEORGIAN REVOLT (1965). See also reply by Leslie B. Mittleman, "Lawrence's 'Snake' Not 'Sweet Georgian Brown,' " ENGLISH LITERATURE IN TRANSITION, IX (1966), 45-46.]

2616 Buckley, Brian. "Lawrence the Poet," TIMES LITERARY SUPPLEMENT (Lond), 16 Sept 1965, p. 809.

[Letter to the Editor in reply to Andor Gomme, "Lawrence the Poet: Achievement and Irrelevance," TIMES LITERARY SUPPLEMENT (Lond), 26 Aug 1965, pp. 725-27.] In their otherwise fine edition of *The Complete Poems of D. H. Lawrence,* Vivian de Sola Pinto and F. Warren Roberts err concerning three poems first printed in the ENGLISH REVIEW. The *TLS* reviewer's selection of poems does not show the quality of DHL's early verse. DHL's pre-1920 poems are not great, but some of them "throw up sparks of promise of the great novelist," and their "steady, independent emancipation from Victorian verse conventions is in itself a manifestation of his genius."

2617 Chambers, J[onathan] D[avid]. "Introduction to the Second Edition," D. H. LAWRENCE: A PERSONAL RECORD, by E. T. [pseud of Jessie Chambers], 2nd ed, ed by J. D. Chambers (Lond: Frank Cass; NY: Barnes & Noble, 1965), pp. xi-xvii.

DHL's friendship with Jessie Chambers, which ended abruptly in 1913, is the basis of her memoir. The book is an invaluable source for the study of the early development of DHL's mind. It depicts the manner in which DHL's relationship with his mother undermined the rapport he might have had with his father.

2618 Charlesworth, Barbara. DARK PASSAGES (Madison: University of Wisconsin P, 1965), pp. 17-25.

[This work, devoted to the decadents, contains a comparison of Swinburne's LESBIA BRANDON and DHL's *Lady Chatterley's Lover*.]

2619 Clark, L. D. "Lawrence / *Women in Love*: The Contravened Knot," in APPROACHES TO THE TWENTIETH-CENTURY NOVEL, ed and with an Introduction by John Unterecker (NY: Crowell, 1965), pp. 51-78.

Women in Love marks DHL's emergence as a mature artist. Owing its major debt to the Bible, "with a contest between the powers of good and evil enveloping the action and destruction hanging imminent," the novel's world is one of free will in which each character must choose salvation or damnation. Within this context, "the transcendent vision supersedes all others" to produce a novel uniquely Lawrentian in a form representing a complex interweaving of thematic strands, a "contravened knot," in which the characters stand in relation to those larger realities--"the world of myth, of epic, and of the Bible"--which reveal the innermost springs of being beneath " 'the old stable ego.' " Each character, therefore, becomes a voice for universal themes, with Birkin as the "keystone" of their interrelationships. Because he is a fully humanized savior, laboring under his own doubts, the novel escapes becoming a fable, like *The Man Who Died,* but succeeds in exploring human nature beneath the narrow limits of existing social, political, and moral systems. In this effort to express a stratum of existence normally considered inexpressible, DHL relies extensively on symbolism. A careful analysis of "Water-Party" reveals a complex patterning of water, dance, light, and dark images which flow together to express both the tangible and the intangible, yet which never lose sight of DHL's central theme, "the mystery of interdependence between unity and duality." Similarly, the entire structure of the novel, "a rhythm magnified by the lens of symbolism, is one of ebb and flow, of climax and subsidence," in which "experience oscillates between the consummation of attraction and the consummation of repulsion." Four chapters--"Rabbit," "Moony," "Excurse," and "Death and Love"--constitute the novel's narrative center, celebrating "the rites of matrimony according to the opposing mystiques of good and evil." While the conjunction of Gerald and Gudrun is an evil parody of true union, that of Birkin and Ursula represents a creative union "attained through the continuous reconciliation of opposites." Birkin's vision of *Blutbrüderschaft* remains a hope, albeit a faint one, but the gradual separation of the sisters reaches the finality of total rupture. Although Birkin's dream of Utopia thus fails, his victorious union with Ursula makes *Women in Love* "a document of love and affirmation in spite of the large shares of misanthropy and negation that darken its pages." DHL speaks with the double voice of the New Testament prophet: the apocalyptist who wishes "to be rid of a troubled and troublesome society," and the evangelist who "proposes a new heaven and earth founded on love."

2620 Corke, Helen. D. H. LAWRENCE: THE CROYDON YEARS. With an Introduction by Warren Roberts (Austin: University of Texas P, 1965).

Contents, abstracted under year of first publication: Warren Roberts, "Introduction," pp. ix-xi; Helen Corke, "Preface," pp. xiii-xiv, and acknowledgements [not abstracted]; and Helen Corke, "Portrait of D. H. Lawrence, 1909-1910," TEXAS QUARTERLY, V (Spring 1962), 168-77; "D. H. LAWRENCE'S 'PRINCESS': A MEMORY OF JESSIE CHAMBERS" (Thames Ditton, Surrey, England: Merle Press, 1951); "Concerning *The White Peacock*," TEXAS QUARTERLY, II (Winter 1959), 186-90; "LAWRENCE & APOCALYPSE" (Lond: William Heinemann, 1933).

2621 Corsani, Mary. D. H. LAWRENCE E L'ITALIA (D. H. Lawrence and Italy) (Milan: Mursia, 1965).

The aim of this book is to study the influence of Italy and its culture in DHL's works. The first phase is *Twilight in Italy,* in which the basis of DHL's religious belief and his vision of humanity are to be found: man has to find his fulfilment in spirit as well as in flesh, keeping these two spheres separated; the Italian people reach their individual immortality through procreation, while the English people exhaust their vital impulses through physical strength and science. In this first book on Italy, DHL was able to catch the beauty of the natural landscape and the capacity of the Italians to experience all aspects of life through the senses. In the second phase, the two main novels, *The Rainbow* and *Women in Love,* bear traces of the Italian experience as well. In *Women in Love,* the contrast between the humanitarian Thomas Crich and his efficient son Gerald in relation to industrial management reflects the comparison DHL had drawn between Italy, where industrial development was still at its initial stages, and England, where advanced industrialism was now making new and different demands. In *The Rainbow,* DHL attacks the sort of democracy based on money which he had already criticized in *Twilight in Italy.* In *Twilight in Italy,* in fact, DHL goes back to the old social order of the Italian peasant world in which the principle of inequality among men was accepted. In the third phase, with *The Lost Girl* and *Aaron's Rod,* DHL again underlines the difference between Italian and English social classes. The last part of *The Lost Girl* is set in Italy in an area known for the wild beauty of its landscape and the primitive way of life which derives, according to DHL, from a far-away pagan past. In *Aaron's Rod,* in particular, many of DHL's personal experiences in Italy are recorded, and he rebels against the sentimentalism and humanitarianism of the English conception of domestic life. In *Sea and Sardinia,* DHL also deals with the enormous differences between the English people and the old peasant society he found in Sardinia. He is attracted above all by the sense of detachment and solitude of the Sardinians and by the sharp separation of the sexes and the subsequent antagonism between them. His search through the past for the remote sources of life sharpens his capacity to penetrate the essence of things, as is apparent in the poems of *Birds, Beasts and Flowers.*

To understand Italian reality in a more concrete way, DHL began a critical study of Italian literary movements and undertook some translations from the Italian. The first of these translations, Verga's *Mastro-Don Gesualdo,* in spite of some imperfections, reveals DHL's capacity to recreate atmosphere, reproduce dialogue, and depict characters. The translation of Verga's *Little Novels of Sicily* is less well done because their fragmentary nature prevents the translator from expressing convincingly the essence of a peasant world so different from the English one. The best translation from the standpoint of style is Verga's *Cavalleria Rusticana and Other Stories.* DHL also wrote some essays on Verga, Lasca, and Grazia Deledda and underlined how these authors dealt above all with a regional society. In his works as a critic and translator DHL shows a profound sense of language as a means of expression and communication of the passions. In the writings of the last phase--*Etruscan Places, Lady Chatterley's Lover, The Man Who Died,* and "The Ship of Death"--DHL considered the man-woman relationship as the only means of understanding reality. Studying Etruscan civilization he found the spontaneity between men and women, masters and slaves, men and beasts that was lacking in industrial society. In the writings of this period, DHL criticizes English society as lacking that "sheer physical flow" which establishes harmonious communion among human beings. In the end it can be said that Italy and its culture sharpened DHL's awareness as a man of the twentieth century who tried to give a sense of unity to the plurality of the universe. [In Italian.]

2622 Cowan, James C. "The Symbolic Structure of *The Plumed Serpent,*" TULANE STUDIES IN ENGLISH, XIV (1965), 75-96; enlgd and rptd as Chap. VII in D. H. LAWRENCE'S AMERICAN JOURNEY: A STUDY IN LITERATURE AND MYTH, by James C. Cowan (Cleveland and Lond: P of Case Western Reserve University, 1970), pp. 99-123.

In *The Plumed Serpent,* which is structured on dualities of theme, motive, narrative movement, mythic patterns, and consciousness, DHL attempts "the reconciliation of a series of paired opposites, presented on ascending levels of abstraction from the personal to the cosmic." Subordinating character to "symbolic structure," DHL presents the values of the novel mainly through "image, incident, and ritual." "The disparity between white consciousness and dark consciousness," first signaled in color imagery, is further established in contrasting attitudes "toward the counters of violence and nakedness" in a distinction "between sensation and being," "blood lust and blood consciousness." DHL's consistent reversal of the Christian pattern, in "mythico-conceptions" of creation, birth, and rebirth, prayer and liturgy, and biblical allusions, recalls the "inversions of Christian forms in the Witches' Sabbath or Black Mass." "If the dark sun, the circle dance, the plumed serpent, and some of the hymns are artistically effective, the ersatz rituals often seem" bombastic political propaganda. Although Ramón proclaims himself " 'Lord of the Two Ways' " and symbols of reconciliation in circle imagery offer a "centrality" intended to unify the opposites of white and dark consciousness, there is "a failure in coherence between the realistic and metaphorical modes of the novel." Although at its completion DHL considered *The Plumed Serpent* his " 'most important novel, so far,' " three years later he rejected its militant and political side in favor of tenderness in human relationships.

 2623 Čura-Sazdanić, Ileana. "D. H. Lawrence as Critic." Unpublished dissertation, University of Exeter, 1965. [Listed in Lawrence F. McNamee, DISSERTATIONS IN ENGLISH AND AMERICAN LITERATURE, SUPP I (NY & Lond: Bowker, 1969), p. 246]. Rvd and pub as D. H. LAWRENCE AS CRITIC (Delhi: Munshiram Manoharlal, 1969).

 2624 Daleski, H[erman] M. THE FORKED FLAME: A STUDY OF D. H. LAWRENCE (Evanston, IL: Northwestern UP; Lond: Faber & Faber, 1965); excerpt from Chap. II: "The Release: The First Period," pp. 49-63, rptd in D. H. LAWRENCE: "SONS AND LOVERS," A CASEBOOK, ed by Gāmini Salgādo (Lond: Macmillan, 1969; Nashville: Aurora Publishers, 1970), pp. 191-207; excerpt from Chap. II, pp. 174-87, rptd as "*Women in Love*: 'Firm Singleness and Melting Union,' " in D. H. LAWRENCE: "THE RAINBOW" AND "WOMEN IN LOVE": A CASEBOOK, ed by Colin Clarke (Lond: Macmillan, 1969; Nashville: Aurora Publishers, 1970), pp. 151-66; excerpt from Chap. I: "The Tiger and the Lamb: The Duality of Lawrence," pp. 20-31, rptd in CRITICS ON D. H. LAWRENCE, ed by W. T. Andrews (Lond: Allen & Unwin; Coral Gables, FL: University of Miami P, 1971), pp. 105-8; excerpt from Chap. III, pp. 79-106, rptd as "The First and Second Generations," in TWENTIETH CENTURY INTERPRETATIONS OF "THE RAINBOW": A COLLECTION OF CRITICAL ESSAYS, ed by Mark Kinkead-Weekes (Englewood Cliffs, NJ: Prentice-Hall, 1971), pp. 33-57.

DHL's dualism is both an all-pervading principle of the universe and a necessary tension of opposites in which all things have their being. At its core is the duality between male and female, especially as developed in the *Study of Thomas Hardy*. The female principle is of infinite oneness and stability, an emphasis on feeling and the law of the body. The male principle is of ceaseless change and will to motion, an emphasis on knowledge and the law of the spirit. Paradoxically, the female principle is almost identical with the "phallic consciousness" that DHL espoused, while the male principle represents the abstracting, idealizing "mental consciousness" that he warred against. DHL believed in himself strongly as a male, yet was fundamentally identified with the female principle. DHL's creative work is a lifelong effort to heal this breach in his nature, to reconcile the opposite elements of male and female within himself.

DHL's internal division is manifested in *Sons and Lovers* in his treatment of the Morels, who are a projection of the violent clash within the author. DHL unconsciously sympathized with Mr. Morel, who paradoxically represents the female principle, although he consciously sympathized with Mrs. Morel, who represents the male principle. None of the distortions that enter into DHL's portrayal of the Morels impinge on Paul's relations with Mrs. Morel, Miriam, and Clara. These three relationships are without the internal inconsistencies, and without the unfairness to Miriam and Clara, that critics often perceive. *Sons and Lovers* liberated DHL from the problems of young manhood but left him with an abiding sense of male-female duality.

In his finest novel, *The Rainbow*, DHL "made his most strenuous effort to show how the male and female principles could be reconciled both within the individual psyche and within marriage." The first two generations of Brangwens fail to achieve this harmony because one partner in the marriages has a reductive effect on the other. Both marriages are predominantly on "female" terms. In Ursula, however, DHL depicts the only character in all his works who fully reconciles the male and female principles, but no man is found to match her achievement. *Women in Love* ostensibly presents two psychically balanced persons, Ursula and Birkin, who achieve a marriage that fulfills their separate identities without usurping them. Close examination of Birkin's character and marriage, however, reveals that he leads Ursula into withdrawal from the "man's world" and into a marriage which, once again, is on essentially "female" terms. The fact that female characteristics gain the upper hand in *Women in Love,* under the guise of harmony, compels DHL "to redefine the meaning of 'man-being' and to explore alternative ways of effecting a return to the world of men."

This effort leads DHL to the compensatory male assertion found in *Aaron's Rod* and *Kangaroo* and the cul-de-sac of *The Plumed Serpent*, clearly the worst of his mature novels. The goal of reconciliation and harmony gives way in *The Plumed Serpent* to a repugnant insistence on mastery and domination, not only of the female by the male but of one male by another as well. During this period, DHL wrote against his own deepest values. *Lady Chatterley's Lover* effects a return to those values. DHL abandons his emphasis on power and leadership and renews his search for reconciliation between the male and female principles, with an emphasis on tenderness in relationships. Connie Chatterley's experiences repudiate those of Kate in *The Plumed Serpent*. Whereas Kate had merely surrendered herself to Cipriano's control, Connie finds her true full self through a deep act of giving in love, as Mellors himself does. Nevertheless, the "night of sensual passion," during which Mellors vents his anger with Hilda by "burning out the shames" in Connie's "most secret places," indicates that neither Mellors nor DHL has succeeded in reconciling within himself the two principles, male and female. DHL, through Mellors, continues to assert a covert masculine significance which is a major blemish in the novel. [See also reply to Daleski, pp. 107-25, by Joseph Spano, "A Study of Ursula (of *The Rainbow*) and H. M. Daleski's Commentary," PAUNCH, No. 33 (Dec 1968), 21-33.]

2625 De Villeneuve-Trans, Roméo. CHRONIQUES ET ROMANS SOCIAUX (Chronicles and Social Novels) (Avignon: Aubanel père, 1965), pp. 243-63.
[A biography of DHL with brief evocations of his principal novels.] [In French.]

2626 Díaz de León, Martha. "El México visto por D. H. Lawrence" (Mexico as Seen by D. H. Lawrence), CUADERNOS AMERICANOS, XXIV (March-April 1965), 262-83.

Although *The Plumed Serpent* has brilliant descriptions of Mexico, the nationalistic tone is quite exaggerated. Some of DHL's observations seem to anticipate recent sociological studies of family life in Mexico by Oscar Lewis in his book LOS HIJOS DE SANCHEZ; thus, DHL offers insight into what could be sociohistorical reality. But DHL was able to see beyond Mexico's immediate reality; by searching within the past, he foresaw its future. Were it not for the exaggerated symbolic-mythological solution, *The Plumed Serpent* would have been a great novel. Furthermore, DHL's impressions of Mexico and its people were probably conceived near the bullfighting ring: "the mongrel men of a mongrel city." As a result, when he finally began to write *The Plumed Serpent* he identified himself with Quetzalcoatl, the redeeming god that the old inhabitants of Mexico were left expecting and who, in DHL's mind, assumes the form of a modern Messiah who will save Mexico. Certainly, the most important part of the country which must be redeemed by Quetzalcoatl-Lawrence is the native portion. His hope is to change the country into something distinctly different: "a new being 'where the basic matter--the blood--is found in the land proper and the new, the anemic, in the white imported element.'" DHL feels in the Mexican Indians the presence of a strong and remote power which is dormant and needs to be reawakened. [In Spanish.]

2627 Donoghue, Denis. "Action is Eloquence," LUGANO REVIEW, I, Nos. 3-4 (1965), 147-54; rptd in THE ORDINARY UNIVERSE: SOUNDINGS IN MODERN LITERATURE, by Denis Donoghue (Lond: Faber & Faber; NY: Macmillan, 1968), pp. 169-79.

In "Odour of Chrysanthemums," the chrysanthemums are emblems of life itself, their odor the smell of life. DHL's wish for his work to redeem consciousness partly explains his forcing on the reader a terminology of redemption, expiation, and victimage. This story is life enhancing, for Walter, like Christ, is an appropriate sacrificial victim, and Elizabeth's conversion, upon seeing the body of her dead husband, becomes a seeking-for-life.

2628 Donoghue, Denis. "Melville," LUGANO REVIEW, I (1965), 67-82.

DHL's poems, unlike Melville's, rarely go wrong, for they have a fine, modest adequacy, existing for the sake of the fiction as footnotes to the great text. [DHL mentioned only in the introduction, by comparison.]

2629 Drain, Richard L. "Reviews," ENGLISH LANGUAGE NOTES, III (Dec 1965), 158-61.

The Complete Poems of D. H. Lawrence, ed by Vivian de Sola Pinto and F. Warren Roberts, shows that DHL's poetry "is worth reconsidering in its own right." Although "much of Lawrence's poetry fails--fails even when the old conventions have been sloughed off," "writing of this sort involves a free range of diverse attitudes as well as of descriptive notations."

2630 Duncan, Iris June Autry. "The Theme of the Artist's Isolation

in Works by Three Modern British Novelists," DISSERTATION ABSTRACTS, XXVI (1965), 3332. Unpublished dissertation, University of Oklahoma, 1965.
[Examines novels by James Joyce, DHL, and George Orwell.]

2631 Dyson, A. E. THE CRAZY FABRIC: ESSAYS IN IRONY (Lond: Macmillan; NY: St. Martin's P, 1965), pp. 27, 149-50, 168, 171, 173-75, 176-78, 185, 202-3.
[DHL is compared briefly with several other modern writers.] Oscar Wilde's "The Soul of Man Under Socialism" and DHL's essay "Democracy" have "strikingly similar" "underlying ideas," such as belief in "individualism." The difference between Aldous Huxley and DHL may be seen "in terms of temperament rather than of integrity." George Orwell "accepts sex with almost Lawrentian completeness," but differs from DHL in the extent of hope for humanity he found in it.

2632 "The Economics of Affection," TIMES (Lond), 9 Aug 1965, p. 5.
"Whether or not [DHL] knew Chekhov when he wrote it, the same temperamental affinity runs through *A Collier's Friday Night,* his first play." "Ernest, the young student, is not even the main character: it is the *collier's* night, and the shape of the play is dominated by his movements." "Ernest hates the sight of him, but the play treats him tenderly," a "fair-mindedness" that extends to the other parts. [Review of the Royal Court Theatre one-performance production, directed by Peter Gill.]

2633 Ehrstine, John W. "The Dialectic in D. H. Lawrence," RESEARCH STUDIES (Washington State University), XXXIII (March 1965), 11-26.
[Concentrates on *Sons and Lovers, The Rainbow, Women in Love,* and *Lady Chatterley's Lover* in an effort to answer two questions: what use does DHL make of the "sexual theme," and how effective is it?] DHL organically developed the symbols that embody his philosophical attitudes. Starting with the novels themselves, one can interpret the Laurentian world dialectically, seeing man's fullest existence not as fusion but as "constant synthesis between the spiritual and physical aspects of life." These two aspects are brought together in sexual union; the act "serves as a gateway to higher experience and awareness for both partners." In *Sons and Lovers,* there is no complete synthesis. Paul Morel can "never bring the duality of life into harmony." He meets Miriam only spiritually and Clara only physically. In *The Rainbow* and *Women in Love,* sexual synthesis between man and woman overcomes death. The image of the rainbow itself is a "perfect symbol for such a dialectic," with both sides rooted to the ground and a high arch over the earth in the middle. Tom and Lydia reach a synthesis through the "physical world of the senses," but it is Anna's birth that evokes the symbol of the rainbow "in its full significance." However, the question remains, "Is this all life offers?" The perfectly synthesized individual appears in *Women in Love* and *Lady Chatterley's Lover.* Rupert Birkin's rejection in *Women in Love* of "pure sensualism" completes the relationship between sex and the spiritual world. When Ursula is eventually able to accept the higher spiritual love that Rupert offers her, a new world

unfolds. Rupert and Ursula "affirm to each other that, unlike Gerald, they will never have any fear of death." Since death has meaning only in the physical realm, they have "totally overcome the physical world." In *Lady Chatterley's Lover,* the statement of synthesis is clearer still. The flame between Connie and Mellors, as a symbol of synthesis, includes "peace" and "chastity" and contains "all contraries." DHL follows certain patterns throughout all four novels--the "clashes of opposites within the individual" which are like the opposition between men and women. All these contraries are further associated with "the relationship between the individual and society." The social theme in *Lady Chatterley's Lover* is more intricately woven into the work than in the other novels because "the two themes-- rebirth through sexual union, and salvation from social conditions--demand each other."

  2634 Eisenstein, Samuel Abraham. "The Quester Hero: A Study of Creative Evolution in the Fiction of D. H. Lawrence," DISSERTATION ABSTRACTS, XXVI (1966), 3950A. Unpublished dissertation, University of California at Los Angeles, 1965. Rvd and pub as BOARDING THE SHIP OF DEATH: D. H. LAWRENCE'S QUESTER HEROES (The Hague and Paris: Mouton, 1974).

  2635 Eisenstein, Samuel A. " 'The Woman Who Rode Away,' " KYUSHU AMERICAN LITERATURE (Fukuoka, Japan), No. 9 (1965), 1-18; rptd in BOARDING THE SHIP OF DEATH: D. H. LAWRENCE'S QUESTER HEROES, by Samuel A. Eisenstein (The Hague and Paris: Mouton, 1974), pp. 114-25.

In "The Woman Who Rode Away," the Woman moves "inexorably to an epiphany of self-immolation that assures her of a place in the pantheon of gods and goddesses." Dying "for a cause that is not personal but cosmic," she is, "in the mode of Leda," the hero as victim. Leaving "her old existence" in which "the fountains of life" have dried up at the source, she gives up her useless independence "so that the Indians can regain their lost power." "The number three is a *leitmotif* in the story--three Indians, three days," and other triadic configurations--and refers to " 'the number and nature of God.' " Other important symbols are her roan horse [which the author relates to various horses in world mythology and in DHL's writings] ; rituals of question and answer, magic formula, narcotic drink and dance; and color imagery. One should not interpret DHL's "parable" as a "simple-minded approval" of the blood-thirsty sacrifice: "The author only tells the story." "The vegetative Jesus-Osiris begins where" "The Woman Who Rode Away" ends--with the knowledge that "an entire race cannot be redeemed by one man or woman," but that "the hero must redeem himself by conscious sacrifice of the dead stuff within his own psyche." [Myth criticism.]

  2636 Ellmann, Richard, and Charles Feidelson, Jr. (eds). THE MODERN TRADITION: BACKGROUNDS OF MODERN LITERATURE (NY: Oxford UP, 1965), pp. 383, 541, 686.

[Introductions to separate sections of this anthology incorporating excerpts from "Pan in America," retitled "The Death of Pan," pp. 416-23; from DHL's letter to Edward Garnett, 5 June 1914, here entitled "The Physics of Human Character," pp. 435-36; from *Psychoanalysis and the Unconscious,* here entitled "A Non-Freudian Unconscious," pp. 591-95; and from "Why the Novel Matters," here entitled "The Living Self," pp. 703-7.] Although "usually opposed to mechanics," DHL at times treats "people as inorganic solids and energies" rather than as "personal 'minds.' " Finding the Freudian unconscious "a grotesque figment of the conscious mind," DHL gave an "unscientific, intuitive account of the deeper psyche" as having "a complex balance" and "creative function." Against the "depression of natural energy and impulse" that was "the great peril of our time," DHL offers "the living ambiguity of a successful fictional character as an exemplar of vital freedom in human beings."

2637 Engelberg, Edward. "Books," WESTERN HUMANITIES REVIEW, XIX (1965), 275-77.

Although DHL misled the reader by rewriting and rearranging the order of his poems, *The Complete Poems of D. H. Lawrence,* ed by Vivian de Sola Pinto and F. Warren Roberts (1964), comes "as close to a reliable text as we are likely to have in the foreseeable future." Although "there are many bad poems here--many good ones, too; and a very few that stand with the best," "that he was a poet . . . --and not merely a 'potential'--is amply evidenced in this two-volume edition." [The reliability of the text was questioned by T(homas) A. Smailes, in *"More Pansies* and *Last Poems*: Variant Readings Derived from MS Roberts E192," D. H. LAWRENCE REVIEW, I (Fall 1968), 201-13; and "Lawrence's Verse: More Editorial Lapses," NOTES AND QUERIES, ns XVII (Dec 1970), 465-66; and defended by Vivian de Sola Pinto and F. Warren Roberts, "A Note on Editing *The Complete Poems,*" D. H. LAWRENCE REVIEW, I (Fall 1968), 213-14. Hebe Bair, in "Lawrence as Poet," D. H. LAWRENCE REVIEW, VI (Fall 1973), 313-25, counted "a total of 414 revisions involving some 243 poems" in the text of *The Complete Poems of D. H. Lawrence* as reissued in 1971.]

2638 Ford, Ford Madox [formerly Ford Madox Hueffer]. LETTERS OF FORD MADOX FORD, ed by Richard M. Ludwig (Princeton: Princeton UP, 1965), pp. 137, 140, 237, 247, 248, 269.

[Ford wrote about DHL briefly in an essay on the "second flight of English Novelists" (1922), and more fully in a reminiscence of DHL (1936), to which Frieda Lawrence took exception. Neither her Letter to the Editor of AMERICAN MERCURY nor Ford's response was published in the "Letters to the Editor" column, though Ford's is printed here. See also Ford Madox Ford, "A Haughty and Proud Generation," YALE REVIEW, XI (July 1922), 703-717; and "D. H. Lawrence," AMERICAN MERCURY, XXXVIII (June 1936), 167-79.]

2639 Ford, George. DOUBLE MEASURE: A STUDY OF THE NOVELS AND STORIES OF D. H. LAWRENCE (NY: Holt, Rinehart and Winston, 1965); excerpt from Chap. III, pp. 28-47, rptd as "The 'S' Curve: Persephone to Pluto," in D. H. LAWRENCE, "SONS AND LOVERS": TEXT, BACKGROUND, AND CRITICISM, ed by Julian Moynahan (NY: Viking P [Viking Critical Library Edition], 1968), pp. 577-96; excerpt from Chap. VIII, pp. 187-207, rptd as "Dies Irae," in TWENTIETH CENTURY INTERPRETATIONS OF "WOMEN

IN LOVE": A COLLECTION OF CRITICAL ESSAYS, ed by Stephen J. Miko (Englewood Cliffs, NJ: Prentice-Hall, 1969), pp. 20-39; excerpt from Chap. VIII, pp. 189-207, rptd as "*Women in Love*: The Degeneration of Western Man," In D. H. LAWRENCE: "THE RAINBOW" AND "WOMEN IN LOVE," A CASEBOOK, ed by Colin Clarke (Lond: Macmillan, 1969; Nashville: Aurora Publishers, 1970), pp. 167-87; excerpt from Chap. III, pp. 28-44, rptd as "The 'S' Curve: Persephone to Pluto," in TWENTIETH CENTURY INTERPRETATIONS OF "SONS AND LOVERS": A COLLECTION OF CRITICAL ESSAYS, ed by Judith Farr (Englewood Cliffs, NJ: Prentice-Hall, 1970), pp. 64-73; excerpt from Chap. VI, pp. 126-37, rptd as "*The Rainbow* and the Bible," in TWENTIETH CENTURY INTERPRETATIONS OF "THE RAINBOW": A COLLECTION OF CRITICAL ESSAYS, ed by Mark Kinkead-Weekes (Englewood Cliffs, NJ: Prentice-Hall, 1971), pp. 73-82.

DHL employs in his fiction an antipodal "double rhythm" of "creating and destroying" expressed variously as thesis and antithesis, darkness and light, unconscious and conscious, dynamic and static, and the contrary drives toward isolation and toward union. DHL's development after *Sons and Lovers* follows an " 'S' curve," a shifting of parental preference, in which DHL makes up, in later novels, for injustices to his father in *Sons and Lovers*. Something in DHL that impelled him to isolation is incorporated into his fiction. In "The Prussian Officer," the officer's violence toward the soldier and the soldier's resulting increased consciousness lead to a sense of separateness in both. In "The Man Who Loved Islands," the protagonist is deprived of layer after layer until he is absolutely alone. Isolation is ended, if at all, only in "a connection between the vigorous flow of two lives."

The two contrasting rhythms in *The Rainbow* are the cycle of rural life associated with men and the impulse of the women toward the civilized world. As in the Bible, *The Rainbow* is the story of the ancestry, birth, development, trials, and triumphs of a prophetess, Ursula Brangwen, whose purpose is to show the way out of a wilderness toward a "Promised Land." DHL conveys a sense of timelessness by minimizing topicality and using biblical analogues. In human relationships, however, *The Rainbow* remains novelistic. In the triadic, symphonic structure, the first movement, pastoral and Edenic, appropriately has the most harmonious resolution. In the second movement, the marriage of Will and Anna, with its pattern of conjugal affections and revulsions, is an arena for conflict and tension rather than for resolution. In the third movement, Ursula's quest for "unknown realities" gathers all the strands of the narrative. The biblical passage about the Sons of God choosing the daughters of men, invoked as a measure of men, places high expectations on Skrebensky, whose destruction results from the idea that preoccupation with civilized consciousness leaves out the area of darkness.

"Dies Irae" would have been a more appropriate title for *Women in Love,* for during World War I, DHL had the sense that the world might simply be wiped out, an idea reflected in cataclysmic images of flood, fire, ice, and bomb. DHL's study of collapsing past civilizations is evident in his references to societal doom as slow extinction. The novel encapsulates DHL's realization of the societal hatred in modern man. DHL's deliberate vagueness about the time period of *Women in Love* extends its contemporaneity throughout the twentieth century. Birkin's pondering the African statuette and his meditations on "dreadful mysteries" beyond the phallic suggest some form of sexual perversion, and several key characters are related obliquely to anal intercourse, leaving the artistic problem of distinguishing between the death-oriented and the life-oriented couples. The complexity of Birkin's character derives from the fact that he is partly death-oriented himself.

DHL employs an analogical method which, by parallels with the Bible, myth, history, and legend, encircles his characters with clusters of associations that imbue their individual experience with historical significance. Birkin's assertion that only the perfect relation with a woman is available to us in a time of societal disintegration is placed in the frame of DHL's impressive artistic evocations of hate, corruption, and transience.

2640 Frierson, William C. THE ENGLISH NOVEL IN TRANSITION, 1885-1940 (NY: Cooper Square Publishers, 1965), pp. x, 134, 165, 169, 193, 201, 210, 213, 224-28, 229-34, 235, 243, 244, 246, 250, 251, 263, 264, 282-84, 297, 306, 314, 320, 321.

DHL's letter to Edward Garnett (5 June 1914) about "another ego" is his clearest expression of "his special view of fiction." DHL did not pursue his life-long search for harmony unaided: "The central ideas of Whitman dominated his consciousness." Though "convinced that his own fulfillment would come through sex," DHL showed, through the experiences recorded in *Sons and Lovers,* that "relationships must be perfected . . . to be significant, and that even then sex is a part of something else, something greater": "Sex is not an end in itself but a spur to activity, not instrumental but inspirational." "So a rebirth, a renewal, a surrender to the forces of life is the end." [Brief discussion of *The Rainbow, Women in Love, The Lost Girl, Aaron's Rod, Kangaroo, The Plumed Serpent, St. Mawr,* and *Lady Chatterley's Lover* in light of these principles.] "With Lawrence the range of the novelist's perception extended beyond the tangible and the finite" to a drama between "symbolic presences." Like other novelists of the twenties, he "created a private world of his own." Though Huxley was attracted to him, DHL "provided no essential stimulus." H. E. Bates resembles DHL in "responding to the elements and to the spirit of forest and river." [In surveying criticism of the English novel since the 1880s, critical references to DHL are frequently cited.]

2641 Gertler, Mark. SELECTED LETTERS, ed by Noel Carrington, with an Introduction on His Work as an Artist by Quentin Bell (Lond: Rupert Hart-Davis, 1965), pp. 13-14, 76-77, 79-82, 96n, 101-2, 109n, 127, 128-33, 157n, 160-62, 171n, 175, 185, 210, 218-19, 222, 223n, 228, 232, 236, 253-54.

[In letters to Gertler, DHL (9 Oct 1916) calls his painting *The Merry-Go-Round* "the best *modern* picture I have seen," and (1918) asks Gertler to help bring him back into Lady Ottoline Morrell's circle. S. S. Koteliansky writes Gertler (26 Aug [1918]) that Frieda was "devouring [DHL] bit by bit, gradually, permanently."

Gertler writes to Kotelianksy (7 Aug 1923) that DHL should see a doctor for his health, but two years later (8 Oct 1925) expresses "no desire to see" DHL on his planned trip to London since "the kind of disturbance he creates . . . does only harm." In the last year of DHL's life, Gertler writes to Koteliansky, blaming Frieda for DHL's not getting adequate medical treatment. After DHL's death in March 1930, Gertler reports having talked to Huxley about Koteliansky's taking part in editing DHL's letters: "The only trouble is Frieda."]

2642 Gilbert, Sandra. D. H. LAWRENCE'S "SONS AND LOVERS" AND "THE RAINBOW," "WOMEN IN LOVE," "THE PLUMED SERPENT" (NY: Simon & Schuster, Monarch P, 1965).
[Study guide to *Sons and Lovers*. The "Introduction" surveys DHL's early career, his relationship with Jessie Chambers and elopement with Frieda Weekley, the plan of *Sons and Lovers*, its relation to Freud, DHL's later novels and other work, and his last illness and death. This survey is followed by a detailed, chapter-by-chapter summary of the novel with analytic commentary, a description and analysis of the characters, a survey of criticism on DHL and his works, and brief summaries and analyses of *The Rainbow, Women in Love*, and *The Plumed Serpent*. Sample essay test questions and detailed answers, and a short primary and secondary bibliography and guide to research papers are provided.]

2643 Gillie, Christopher. "Human Subject and Human Substance: Stephen Dedalus of A PORTRAIT OF THE ARTIST and Rupert Birkin of *Women in Love*," CHARACTER IN ENGLISH LITERATURE (Lond: Chatto & Windus; NY: Barnes & Noble, 1965), pp. 177-202, espec pp. 187-202.
DHL opens *Women in Love* with a scene in which Ursula and Gudrun contemplate marriage with skepticism. Because such skepticism leads to fear, DHL calls into question the validity of the central institution of society and thus the validity of society itself. The focal issue of DHL's novel is "what constitutes the meaningfulness of human relationships, and what frustrates them." DHL's characters, like those of his predecessors in the tradition of the novel, are engaged in self-discovery, but they differ in that the reader does not commit "himself to the writer as to God, secure that, if he does so alertly and not blindly, the character will unfold so that what is hidden in his destiny shall be made manifest." On the other hand, DHL's "ruthless skepticism takes nothing for granted, so that we are not offered characters who unfold, but characters who are seeking what exists in them to be unfolded." The opposition between the individual and society in *Women in Love* involves the resolution of our relationships: the marriage of Ursula and Rupert Birkin, the antagonism of Gudrun and Gerald Crich, the alienation of the two sisters, and the failed friendship between Rupert and Gerald. The success of the one and the failure of the other three reveals "a success in relationship and a failure in society." For this reason, DHL "takes us far within the personality, into the pre-social, pre-conscious regions, out of which both personality and community must arise, if at all."

2644 Gomme, A[ndor] H. "D. H. Lawrence," in CRITICS WHO HAVE INFLUENCED TASTE, ed by A. P. Ryan (Lond: Geoffrey

Bles, 1965), pp. 95-97.
DHL's "vigour, insight and sanity" as a literary critic were unappreciated in his time. Objections to *Studies in Classic American Literature* centered on the "metaphorical, abrupt, repetitive" style, through which DHL focused on essential questions about the life behind the American classics rather than on the rules of fiction, which he thought applicable " 'only for novels which are copies of other novels. ' " DHL's critical principles are set forth in the letter to Edward Garnett about *The Rainbow* (5 June 1914) and in the "John Galsworthy" essay, but Garnett, "a representative intellectual of his day," failed to grasp them.

2645 Gomme, Andor. "Lawrence the Poet: Achievement and Irrelevance," TIMES LITERARY SUPPLEMENT (Lond), 26 Aug 1965, pp. 725-27.

[Review of *The Complete Poems of D. H. Lawrence,* ed by Vivian de Sola Pinto and F. Warren Roberts.] As a novelist, DHL belongs to the "central tradition," but as a poet, he does not fit the literary map, and his poetry only rarely escapes into the nonhuman. DHL often slips into jargon to prevent himself from discovering what he means. Injecting meaning into all that he saw, DHL substitutes repetition and assertion for argument and demonstration. *Pansies* gives no experience that would allow the reader to share the "thought," although the collection as a whole is lively if too thickly planted. The death poems in *Last Poems* give the "superb courage of Lawrence's steady contemplation." It would be a work of piety to publish a well-chosen selection of the poems less likely to put readers off. [See also comment by Malcolm Pittock, "Lawrence the Poet," TIMES LITERARY SUPPLEMENT (Lond), 2 Sept 1965, p. 755; and replies to Gomme by Brian Buckley, "Lawrence the Poet," TIMES LITERARY SUPPLEMENT (Lond), 16 Sept 1965, p. 809, and by Vivian de Sola Pinto, "Lawrence the Poet," TIMES LITERARY SUPPLEMENT (Lond), 24 Oct 1965, p. 946.]

2646 Gordan, John D. "Novels in Manuscript: An Exhibition from the Berg Collection, Part II (Conclusion)," BULLETIN OF THE NEW YORK PUBLIC LIBRARY, LXIX (June 1965), 396-413, espec 407-8.

The public has been hostile to DHL because he tried "tempestuously" to restore primitive vigor and balance to human relations and to combat what he felt were unhealthy conventions in regard to sex." [Describes the manuscript on display, a 569-page corrected typescript of *Kangaroo* with slight and sparse corrections.]

2647 Gray, Ronald. THE GERMAN TRADITION IN LITERATURE, 1871-1945 (Cambridge: Cambridge UP, 1965), pp. 6, 101, 159, 327-28, 340-54; excerpt, pp. 340-54, rptd as "*Women in Love* and the German Tradition in Literature," in D. H. LAWRENCE: "THE RAINBOW" AND "WOMEN IN LOVE," A CASEBOOK, ed by Colin Clarke (Lond: Macmillan, 1969; Nashville: Aurora Publishers, 1970), pp. 188-202.

Although DHL recoiled from German culture and did not admire German writers, *Women in Love* is deeply indebted to German ideas. Remaining essentially an English novel, the book "marries something from the English world, especially an insistence on individuality and morality, with something from the German world that had better just be called mysticism." By avoiding a "message" and refusing to endorse a "*Weltanschauung*," DHL provides "insights we might well not have, if the novel had remained entirely within the 'German' tradition." The influence of three German writers can be recognized in *Women in Love*. Structurally, DHL's novel closely resembles Goethe's ELECTIVE AFFINITIES, in that DHL's plot concerns "polarity," or "attraction and repulsion within pairs and between them." In terms of theme, DHL "ranges up and down Nietzsche's ideas, the Dionysian and the Apolline." Yet, whereas in Nietzsche's work "there is no comprehensive pattern, no exposition, development, climax, catastrophe, and taking stock, as there is in the novel," DHL traces the inhumane consequence of Nietzschean idealism. Finally, DHL's way of feeling about love resembles that of Rilke, the latter's "ideal of love without reciprocity" being very similar to DHL's "twin stars, 'asked for nothing, giving nothing.'"

2648 Green, Martin. SCIENCE AND THE SHABBY CURATE OF POETRY: ESSAYS ABOUT THE TWO CULTURES (NY: W. W. Norton, 1965), pp. 10, 26, 30, 44-45, 48, 50-51, 66-68, 70, 72, 82, 85, 87, 91, 94, 96, 125, 129-30, 148, 158.

[A consideration of the pros and cons of C. P. Snow's essay THE TWO CULTURES (Rede Lecture, 1959) in light of F. R. Leavis's rebuttal, TWO CULTURES: THE SIGNIFICANCE OF C. P. SNOW (Richmond Lecture, 1962), with passing references to DHL throughout.] For DHL, who relied on the literary mind to interpret events, what the mind failed to grasp lost all dignity and interest. In *Kangaroo*, DHL's presentation of the political party is unconvincing because, considering political events out of context, "his intuition has no authority on this subject." But DHL's description of nature, e.g., of the Alpine scenery in *Women in Love*, is convincing because, knowing about natural beauty of all kinds, he has established his authority in this matter.

2649 Gregor, Ian. "Towards a Christian Literary Criticism," MONTH, ns XXXIII (1965), 239-49.

The bringing together of four relationships in *Women in Love* is DHL's attempt to purify the dialectic of love. Gerald's love is entirely egocentric; a tormented consciousness drives him to impose himself on the world in which he lives. Birkin's impetus, on the other hand, is to see what is beyond love. Ursula pits herself against Birkin's drive for impersonality. Through her as a genuinely imagined creation, DHL is able to subject his own views to constant scrutiny. Because the work is a fiction and not a treatise, the imaginative pressures of the novel remorselessly expose the author's own conceptualizations. In the end result, it is Ursula who wins the day because Birkin ceases to focus the reader's imagination as he stiffens into an idea.

2650 Grubb, Frederick. A VISION OF REALITY: A STUDY OF LIBERALISM IN TWENTIETH-CENTURY VERSE (Lond: Chatto & Windus, 1965), pp. 14, 58, 95, 123, 164-67, 169, 214, 218, 220.

DHL charged Bloomsbury with "shallow rationalism": "overblown, inbred liberalism talking out the power of action." As his comments to Bertrand Russell and E. M. Forster show, he "hated Bloomsbury because it put mental idealism before practical being." "He reiterates the need for differences, and he can see how power is perverted by envy and ambition--knowledge which might save liberals much fretful bewilderment." [Brief references to echoes of DHL in poems by Robert Graves and Ted Hughes.]

2651 Gurtoff, Stanley Arthur. "The Impact of D. H. Lawrence on His Contemporaries," DISSERTATION ABSTRACTS, XXVI (1966), 5412A. Unpublished dissertation, University of Minnesota, 1965.

2652 Hall, James B. (ed). THE REALM OF FICTION: SIXTY-ONE SHORT STORIES (NY: McGraw-Hill, 1965).
[This anthology includes "The Blind Man" and a brief headnote mentioning DHL's collier background, his education, his fight with the censors, and a few of his better-known works.]

2653 Harding, D. W. "Courting," NEW STATESMAN, LXIX (23 April 1965), 650; rptd in D. H. LAWRENCE: A CRITICAL ANTHOLOGY, ed by H. Coombes (Harmondsworth, Middlesex, England: Penguin Books, 1973), pp. 448-50.
[Review of Jessie Chambers ("E. T."), D. H. LAWRENCE: A PERSONAL RECORD, 2nd ed (1965).] In "The Test on Miriam," DHL "gropes for the truth when he classes himself with the men who are bound in by their own virginity because they are 'the sons of mothers whose husbands had blundered rather brutally through their feminine sanctities.'" But he abandons this insight for the fantasy that his sexual encounter with "Miriam" was a failure on account of her having merely endured it. "A girl who commanded his respect and was 'good' fell into the prohibited class; and eventually he found his compromise in marrying an adultress whom he could respect."

2654 Harding, D. W. "Womenfolk," NEW STATESMAN, LXX (24 Sept 1965), 441-42; rptd in D. H. LAWRENCE: A CRITICAL ANTHOLOGY, ed by H. Coombes (Harmondsworth, Middlesex, England: Penguin Books, 1973), pp. 450-52.
DHL and Helen Corke, "one of the many young women who attracted" him during his Croydon period, shared emotional experiences and poetry and, in their twenties, explored "the possibilities of personal relationship between the sexes in a way that would now be attempted at an earlier age." [Review of Helen Corke, D. H. LAWRENCE: THE CROYDON YEARS (1965).]

2655 Harvey, J. R. "*The Paintings of D. H. Lawrence,*" DELTA (Cambridge University), No. 36 (Summer 1965), 10-12.
The Paintings of D. H. Lawrence, ed by Mervyn Levy (1964) is not "the definitive collection ... but a fairly loose gathering with some fairly loose prose" and some color plates of questionable reliability. "In the short time he devoted to painting, Lawrence just did not find a satisfactory way of communicating his understanding of the body in paint." Despite the editor's claims, DHL's painting is not the by-product of his novelistic art but of his insight in art criticism, through which he

made a creative contribution. [DHL's training and technique as a painter are compared to William Blake's.]

2656 Häusermann, H. W. "Vorwort" (Preface), *Zwei Blaue Vogel und Andere Erzählungen* (*Two Blue Birds and Other Stories*), by D. H. Lawrence, ed by Elisabeth Schnack (Zurich, 1965), pp. 7-29.
DHL's narrative technique owes much to tradition, since he had to submit to the taste of a reading public that expected entertainment and illusion, not the presentation of shocking ideas. Departing from unity of form and the demand for objectivity, DHL conveys his message by means of symbols, the change from personal to impersonal style, and unrealistic events. [In German.]

2657 Helwig, Werner. "Meisternovellen" (Master Tales), SÜDDEUTSCHE ZEITUNG (24 Nov 1965).
DHL's tales and novellas are more perfect in form than his novels. [In German.]

2658 Hepburn, James G. "D. H. Lawrence's Plays: An Annotated Bibliography," BOOK COLLECTOR, XIV (Spring 1965), pp. 78-81.
[Bibliography.] Earlier bibliographies are incomplete or inaccurate, and evidence suggests that "there may be one or two lost plays."

2659 Hildick, Wallace. "D. H. Lawrence," WORD FOR WORD: A STUDY OF AUTHORS' ALTERATIONS (Lond: Faber & Faber, 1965), pp. 58-69; rptd in abridged form as WORD FOR WORD: THE REWRITING OF FICTION (NY: W. W. Norton, 1965), pp. 52-63.
[Excerpts from the mss and published texts of *The White Peacock* and "Odour of Chrysanthemums," and from the draft before alteration, the ms with alterations, and the published text of *The Rainbow* are reproduced side-by-side to show DHL's revisions in progress.] "The first shows the sort of general tightening and tidying that must be undertaken by the intelligent, sensitive but raw young writer. The second shows the sort of recasting that must often be done by the more experienced but still not fully technically competent writer. And the third gives a glimpse of the sort of improvement--the increase in penetrative power--that can be made by an inspired, experienced and technically accomplished author."

2660 Hirashima, Junko. "D. H. Lawrence: *The Man Who Died* no Buntai" (D. H. Lawrence: The Style of *The Man Who Died*), BAIKA JOSHIDAIGAKU BUNGAKUBU KIYÔ (Baika Joshidaigaku), No. 2 (Dec 1965), 105-30.
[In Japanese.]

2661 Hoggart, Richard. "A Question of Tone: Some Problems in Autobiographical Writing," ESSAYS BY DIVERS HANDS, XXXIII (1965), 18-38.
The audience for autobiography today is undiscriminating. As a result, writers of autobiography tend, out of convenience, to use tones that are essentially false, often relying on either rampant sensibility or its obverse, laying bare one's soul.

Because autobiography has few formal rules, it needs some controls. The writer of autobiography should seek to divest his tone of imitations of established literary voices and employ available social tones, which make a stronger and more ironic texture possible. Honesty and patience should be the first objectives. It is most difficult for a working-class writer to find his style. The opening of *Sons and Lovers* is successful. Its tone is that of a working-class man who has become articulate but has also kept the rhetoric of his kind. [Quotations illustrate the point.]

2662 Holbrook, David. THE QUEST FOR LOVE (Lond: Methuen, 1964; University, AL: University of Alabama P, 1965), pp. 19, 20, 21, 24, 26, 38, 45, 51, 54, 62, 79, 87, 89, 92, 101, 112, 140, 192-366. [DHL and *Lady Chatterley's Lover* analyzed in the context of recent psychoanalytic theories of the origins of consciousness.] *Lady Chatterley's Lover,* at once DHL's bravest book and his greatest falsification, depicts "neurotic genitality, conditioned by infantile oral aggressiveness," rather than adult relationships. Sex between Mellors and Connie satisfies DHL's unconscious, narcissistic need for "coition [with] himself in place of his father and mother." In concentrating on "verbal-oral *accounts* of the erotic," DHL forgets the complexities of love in real life and thus moves the novel away from realism toward "the pastoral idyll." In making the baby "a side issue," DHL refuses to acknowledge the adult reality that the act of love culminates not in orgasm but in the birth and nurturing of a child in the next generation. The "sexual unreality" of the novel is seen in Mellors's never submitting "to the rhythm of the awakening woman" but treating her inert passivity in a "masterly over-bearing" manner. Finally, DHL's argument that "loyalty to the 'industrial system' " prevents one's "achieving orgasm adequately" denies "the life-seeking impulse in human nature and its creativity." "We shall not improve human life merely by episodes of 'warm-hearted fucking' in huts in the woods, irresponsible to the procreation between our loins, and to the realities of our social context." [The long essay on *Lady Chatterley's Lover* is supplemented by brief appendices on *Aaron's Rod* and *Women in Love.*]

2663 Hortmann, Wilhelm. "D. H. Lawrence," ENGLISCHE LITERATUR IM 20. JAHRHUNDERT (English Literature in the Twentieth Century) (Bern: Dalp Taschenbücher, 1965), pp. 52-57.
In *Psychoanalysis and the Unconscious* and *Fantasia of the Unconscious,* DHL attaches great importance to instinct as the decisive form for human self-fulfillment. The underlying theme in most of his novels is man's response to his natural impulses and the dualism of body and mind. Instinct-oriented love relations show that this dualism must be overcome to effect the balance of the conscious and the unconscious forces in man. DHL's style lapses occasionally in his later novels and stories (*The Plumed Serpent,* "Sun," "None of That") into erotic verbosity which, at times, leaves the laws of psychology out of consideration. [In German.]

2664 Hsia, Adrian Rue Chun. "Die Kurzgeschichten von D. H. Lawrence" (The Short Stories of D. H. Lawrence). Unpublished dissertation, University of Berlin, 1965. [Listed in Lawrence F. McNamee, DISSERTATIONS IN ENGLISH AND AMERICAN LITERATURE,

SUPP I: 1964-1968 (NY and Lond: Bowker, 1969), p. 246.] Pub as D. H. LAWRENCE: DIE CHARAKTERE IN DER HANDLUNG UND SPANNUNG SEINER KURZGESCHICHTEN (D. H. Lawrence: The Characters of His Short Stories in Action and Tension) (Bonn: H. Bouvier [Abhandlungen zur Kunst-, Musik- und Literaturwissenschaft, Vol. 56], 1968).
[In German.]

2665 Hyman, Stanley Edgar. "The Lawrence Mob," NEW LETTERS, 18 Jan 1965, pp. 19-20; rptd in THE CRITIC'S CREDENTIALS: ESSAYS AND REVIEWS, by Stanley Edgar Hyman, ed by Phoebe Pettingell (NY: Atheneum, 1978), pp. 130-34.

The Complete Poems of D. H. Lawrence, ed by Vivian de Sola Pinto and F. Warren Roberts, reveals DHL's seven poetic voices, "six of them in various degrees objectionable."

2666 Ingamells, John. "Cézanne in England 1910-1930," BRITISH JOURNAL OF AESTHETICS, V (Oct 1965), 341-50.

[Portion of article, pp. 346-47, discusses DHL as a critic of Cézanne.] The fallacy of "the absolute and plastic approach" to Cézanne's painting was exposed by DHL in 1929. Whereas Bloomsbury saw in Cézanne's work "the full realization of their aesthetic emotion," DHL recognized an expression of the "life force." The important contribution of DHL to the appreciation of Cézanne is that he "made significant form seem an extremely trivial aspect of Cézanne's work."

2667 Inniss, Kenneth B. "D. H. Lawrence's Bestiary: A Study of His Use of Animal Trope and Symbol," DISSERTATION ABSTRACTS, XXVI (1965), 3340A. Unpublished dissertation, University of Kansas, 1965. Rvd and pub as D. H. LAWRENCE'S BESTIARY: A STUDY OF HIS USE OF ANIMAL TROPE AND SYMBOL (The Hague and Paris: Mouton, 1971).

2668 Irie, Takanori. "D. H. Lawrence no Shisôteki Igi" (D. H. Lawrence as a Thinker), METROPOLITAN (Tôkyô Metropolitan University), X (1965), 1-17.
[In Japanese.]

2669 Isaacs, Neil D. "The Autoerotic Metaphor in Joyce, Sterne, Lawrence, Stevens, and Whitman," LITERATURE AND PSYCHOLOGY, XV (Spring 1965), 92-106.

In "The Rocking-Horse Winner," DHL sets up an equation in which money equals luck, which in turn equals love. Paul's riding the rocking horse is a complex metaphor for achieving, through autoeroticism, an orgasmic exaltation accompanied by a visionary state, in which Paul foresees the winner's name, finds a means of fulfilling his love, and tries to project all three--money, luck, love--to his mother. But the overtly Oedipal gestures of his autoerotic act result in an accompanying guilt. Paul, unable to bear the "monstrous burden of guilt" for implicating his mother in his autoerotic act of love, dies.

2670 Ishihara, Fumio. "Lawrence Bungaku no Jigen (IV)" (The Dimensions of Lawrencean Literature [IV]), BULLETIN OF THE FACULTY OF FOREIGN LANGUAGES (Kitakyûshû University), No. 11 (Nov 1965), 1-16.
[An approach to Lawrence's view of life: resistance and human alienation.] [In Japanese.]

2671 Iwata, Noboru. "Hana to Dôbutsu (*Sons and Lovers* no Baai)" (Flowers and Animals in *Sons and Lovers*), LITERARY SYMPOSIUM (Aichi University), No. 29 (Feb 1965), 99-126.
[In Japanese.]

2672 Jarvis, F. P. "A Textual Comparison of the First British and American Editions of D. H. Lawrence's *Kangaroo*," PAPERS OF THE BIBLIOGRAPHICAL SOCIETY OF AMERICA, LIX (Fourth Quarter 1965), 400-24.
Collation of the first British edition (Secker's) and first American edition (Seltzer's) of *Kangaroo* shows a four to one "ratio of accidental to substantive and semisubstantive variants." Whereas "accidental discrepancies" seldom alter the meaning but affect "the texture of the work as a whole," "the substantive discrepancies appear to be of such magnitude in some places that the two editions seem almost to be at cross-purposes in very critical passages of the book." Textual comparison of the two editions reveals the differences and establishes "the Seltzer edition as the one containing more scrupulous and judicious revisions, and consequently as the edition whose text is 'cleaner' and more authoritative."

2673 Jorgensen, Paul A., and Frederick B. Shruyer. "D. H. Lawrence," THE ART OF PROSE (NY: Charles Scribner's Sons, 1965), p. 358.
[Brief biographical headnote to "The Hopi Snake Dance," which is reprinted in the anthology, pp. 359-76, mentions DHL's early publication in ENGLISH REVIEW, his early novels, his elopement with "a married woman, a German," and his interest in primitivism.]

2674 Kamimura, Tatsuhiko. "*Yamaarashi no Shi ni Omou* Kara" (On *Reflections on the Death of a Porcupine*), ENGLISH LITERATURE REVIEW (Kyôto Women's University), No. 8 (March 1965), 55-70.
[In Japanese.]

2675 Kay, Wallace Grant. "The Cortege of Dionysus: A Study of the Fiction of D. H. Lawrence and Jean Giono," DISSERTATION ABSTRACTS, XXVII (1966), 208A. Unpublished dissertation, Emory University, 1965.

2676 Kenner, Hugh (ed). STUDIES IN CHANGE: A BOOK OF THE SHORT STORY (Englewood Cliffs, NJ: Prentice-Hall, 1965), p. 89.
[Brief critical headnote to "The Shadow in the Rose Garden," which is reprinted in the anthology, pp. 89-99.] "As usual, Lawrence spurns narrators and works

with unsettling closeness to his characters. This study in reciprocal cruelty springing from an intimacy neither protagonist can govern is itself intimate, as though the reader were present, invisible, at confrontations not meant for anyone's eyes."

2677 Kermode, Frank. "Rammel," NEW STATESMAN, LXIX (14 May 1965), 765-66.

The prose in Alan Sillitoe's novels is "dangerously stretched" in ways reminiscent of *Lady Chatterley's Lover,* at one point in THE DEATH OF WILLIAM POSTERS seeming almost to parody talks between Connie and Mellors in their combination of blunt conversation and coitional therapy.

2678 Kershaw, Alister, and Frédéric-Jacques Temple (eds). RICHARD ALDINGTON: AN INTIMATE PORTRAIT (Carbondale and Edwardsville: Southern Illinois UP, 1965), pp. 14, 19, 42, 65-70, 77, 80-91, 98-101, 141-42.

[Brief memoirs of Richard Aldington by various contributors. Those discussing his connections with DHL are as follows: **Richard Church**: Aldington's contacts with DHL near the end of DHL's life. **Lawrence Durrell**: Aldington's "brilliant" defense of *The Rainbow* and *Sons and Lovers.* **Sir William Haley**: Aldington's objectivity "about what was good and what was poor" in DHL's works. **Morikimi Megata**: Aldington's correspondence with the author about *The Man Who Died* and the origins of "The Border Line" and "Glad Ghosts." **Harry T. Moore**: Aldington's stories, letters, and several books about DHL. **Sir Alec Randall**: DHL as one of the Mecklenburg Square group. **F. -J. Temple**: The author's "passion for D. H. Lawrence" led to his meeting Aldington. **Paul Schlueter** (in "A Chronological Check List of the Books by Richard Aldington" [pp. 175-86]): Lists books on DHL written, edited, or introduced by Aldington.]

2679 KINDLERS LITERATUR LEXIKON (Kindler's Handbook of Literature) [adapted from DIZIONARIO DELLE OPERE DI TUTTI I TEMPI E DI TUTTE LE LETTERATURE, ed by Valentino Bompiani], 7 vols. (Zürich: Kindler Verlag, 1965-1974), I, 2-3, 774, 2138-39; III, 191; IV, 303, 913-18, 2014; V, 2161-63, 2342, 2995-98; VI, 1731-34, 1954; VII, 1214-17; Supp., 1074-75; rptd, 12 vols. (Zürich: Kindler Verlag, 1970), ed by Gert Woerner (Vols. for entries A-G) and Rolf Geisler and Rudolf Radler (Vols. for entries H-Z), with contributions by Jerome V. Gebsattel, Johann N. Schmidt, and Horst Strittmatter in individual entries on D. H. Lawrence as follows: I, [D. H. Lawrence], 311; *"Aaron's Rod,"* 705-6; II, *"Apocalypse,"* 1091; *"The Captain's Doll,"* 1773-74; IV, *"The Fox,"* 3642; VI, *"Kangaroo,"* 5147-48; *"Lady Chatterley's Lover,"* 5452-54; VII, *"The Man Who Died,"* 6002; IX, *"The Plumed Serpent,"* 7572-73; *"Pornography and Obscenity,"* 7662-63; *"The Rainbow,"* 7989-90; X, *"Sons and Lovers,"* 8903-4; *"St. Mawr,"* 9014; XI, *"Women in Love,"* 10267-69; XII, *"Studies in Classic American Literature,"* 10963-64: excerpts rptd in HAUPTWERKE DER ENGLISCHEN LITERATUR DARSTELLUNGEN UND INTERPRETATIONEN (Main Works of English Literature, Concise Commentaries and Interpretations), ed by Manfred Pfister (Munich: 1975), pp. 443-44, 448-49, 451-52, 456, 459-60, 462-63.

Aaron's Rod, one of DHL's weaker works, connects the central theme, the man-to-man relationship, to that of man in society. In *Apocalypse,* DHL idealizes a heathenish union of man and cosmos. His approach to questions of religion, philosophy, and history is unscholarly. The book is full of reactionary sentiment. *The Captain's Doll* and *The Fox* rank among DHL's best stories because they are free from dogmatism. The style of *Kangaroo* shows DHL at his best and his worst. Here he relates man's lust for power with the theme of love. *Lady Chatterley's Lover* is an indictment of English society in the twenties. Mellors is realistically convincing, whereas Clifford's flatness serves to indicate man's loss of contact with nature. DHL's essay "Resurrection" provides the key for all his following works. In *The Man Who Died* the theme of resurrection is deprived of its Christian meaning and points to man's sensual emancipation. Sexual, political, and religious subjects are linked together in *The Plumed Serpent,* a novel marred by long-winded discussions, sensational events, and the vagueness of central terms such as "life" and "blood." *Pornography and Obscenity* traces the origin of pornography to an unnatural attitude toward sex in modern society without considering social, historical, and other reasons. In *The Rainbow,* DHL moves away from traditional plot-cum-character technique and uses an episodic structure in which the flow of action is determined by the rhythm of biological life. The main theme of *Sons and Lovers* is man's alienation as caused by the domination of either reason or passion. DHL's criticism of industrial society in *St. Mawr* is very didactic. His *Studies in Classic American Literature,* one of the most original contributions to an understanding of American literature, views America as a possible source for a mythic rebirth of Europe. DHL's most complex novel, with intricate psychological relationships, *Women in Love,* is concerned with the disintegrating world of a generation that wavers helplessly between the most contradictory views of life. [Information in digest form on the origin, content, and meaning of DHL's works.] [In German.]

2680 Kitazawa, Yoshihiro. "D. H. Lawrence no Saku Hin ni Arawareta Shokubutsu to Sono Gihô ni Tsuite" (Plants in D. H. Lawrence's Works and His Treatment of Them), SYLVAN (Tôhoku University), No. 6 (May 1965), 23-35.

[In Japanese.]

2681 Kitchin, Laurence. "The Zombie's Lair," LISTENER AND BBC TELEVISION REVIEW, LXXIV (4 Nov 1965), 701-2, 704.

"The first literary collision" between the world of the working-class industrial culture and the world of the Edwardian intellectuals took place in *Women in Love* when DHL represented Breadalby, Shortlands, and their inhabitants as relics of an irrecoverable past. Although his balanced view of class conflict in *Women in Love* gave way to emphasis on "the analysis of sexual interplay" in *Lady Chatterley's Lover,* DHL's "critique of the country-house intelligentsia" was "a foretaste of the resentful subversiveness which Lawrence bequeathed to the novelist of our day," an influence that can be seen in Braine's ROOM AT THE TOP, Amis's LUCKY JIM and TAKE A GIRL LIKE YOU, Wain's HURRY ON DOWN,

Murdoch's THE BELL, Hartley's THE GO-BETWEEN, and Cary's TO BE A PILGRIM. [Informal literary history and influence study.]

2682 Kreuzer, James R., and Lee Cogan (eds). "Techniques of Description: Adjectives, Figures of Speech, Imagery," LITERATURE FOR COMPOSITION (NY: Holt, Rinehart & Winston, 1965), pp. 289-91.

[Analysis of DHL's descriptive technique in the use of adjectives, figures of speech, and imagery in selected sentences or sentence elements in "Market Day," from *Mornings in Mexico,* which is reprinted in the anthology, pp. 285-89.]

2683 "Language and Literature," CHOICE, I (Jan 1965), 479.

The Complete Poems of D. H. Lawrence, ed by Vivian de Sola Pinto and F. Warren Roberts, is "almost a definitive edition," although the editors throughout "break lines because of printing format and do not follow Lawrence's exact placement as given in the *Collected Poems.*"

2684 Lasch, Christopher. "Mabel Dodge Luhan: Sex as Politics," THE NEW RADICALISM IN AMERICA (1889-1963): THE INTELLECTUAL AS A SOCIAL TYPE (NY: Knopf, 1965), pp. 104-40.

After the collapse of their friendship in 1924, Mabel Dodge Luhan sought DHL's advice, through correspondence, concerning the writing of her autobiography. Although critical of her lack of "restraint," DHL was impressed by her manuscript, calling it "the most serious 'confession' that ever came out of America." The theme of "sexual rivalry and hostility" in Luhan's work was a favorite subject of DHL's as well. The difference in the authors' treatments of it, however, is that whereas DHL "ruthlessly dragged what he knew ... to consciousness and managed ... to write about himself with a rare honesty," Luhan "allowed most of her understanding of sexual conflict to remain only half articulated, buried under layers of ideology." Like many American radicals of her day, Luhan misunderstood DHL, seeing him merely as "a propagandist who wanted white men to live like Indians" and failing to recognize the function of art in DHL's primitivism.

2685 Latta, William. "More Books," COLLEGE ENGLISH, XXVI (April 1965), 580.

The Complete Poems of D. H. Lawrence, ed by Vivian de Sola Pinto and F. Warren Roberts (1964) includes juvenilia as well as numerous variants and drafts of published poems. Although not a "Variorum Edition," the collection also includes textual and explanatory notes, a glossary of dialect and other unfamiliar terms, and an index. [Brief review.]

2686 Latta, William Charlton, Jr. "The Theme of Spiritual Death and Rebirth in the Novels of D. H. Lawrence," DISSERTATION ABSTRACTS, XXVI (1966), 5439A. Unpublished dissertation, University of Nebraska, 1965.

2687 Leavis, F[rank] R[aymond]. "ANNA KARENINA," CAMBRIDGE QUARTERLY, I (Winter 1965-1966), 5-27; rptd as "ANNA

KARENINA: Thought and Significance in a Great Creative Work," in ANNA KARENINA AND OTHER ESSAYS, by F. R. Leavis (Lond: Chatto & Windus; NY: Pantheon, 1967), pp. 9-32.

DHL's statement that " 'the novel is the highest form of subtle inter-relatedness that man has discovered' " is applicable to Tolstoy's ANNA KARENINA, although DHL says that in that book " 'all the tragedy comes from Vronsky's and Anna's fear of society.' " Although usually "so marvellously perceptive" as a critic, DHL, in "referring . . . to Anna's finally going off undivorced with Vronsky, and to the absence of any cheering example of happiness so won," is surprisingly simplistic and distorting in effect. But there are differences between this novelistic situation and DHL's: "Anna was not an amoral German aristocrat," and Vronsky, "altogether unlike Lawrence," has "nothing of the artist in him." While the conditions of DHL's life with Frieda had certain advantages, "it is impossible . . . not to feel that his work reveals a loss, a certain disablement entailed by those conditions: the life of nomadic, childless, improvised, and essentially impermanent domesticities." DHL could not have written *Lady Chatterley's Lover* from such "a profound *corrective* impulse" "if he hadn't lost his sense of what a normal human life was like."

2688 Levin, Harry. "Reflections on the Final Volume of THE OXFORD HISTORY OF ENGLISH LITERATURE," FORUM FOR THE MODERN LANGUAGE STUDIES (St. Andrews University), I (Jan 1965), 4-16, espec 5-6, 7; rptd in REFRACTIONS: ESSAYS IN COMPARATIVE LITERATURE, by Harry Levin (NY: Oxford UP, 1966), pp. 151-70, espec pp. 153-55, 158, 165.

In retrospect, DHL seems "the most prophetic of the figures" discussed in J. I. M. Stewart's EIGHT MODERN WRITERS (1965): "his sexual candor, his class-consciousness, and his other quarrels with his time and place make him the progenitor of today's angry young men."

2689 Lodge, David. THE BRITISH MUSEUM IS FALLING DOWN (Lond: MacGibbon & Kee, 1965; NY: Holt, Rinehart, 1967).

[The hero of this comic novel is a young English graduate student who is researching his thesis on "long sentences" in British novels. At the British Museum, he orders DHL's books, but spends most of his day fighting off fears that his wife-- a Catholic with whom he has already had three children--is pregnant again, and fighting off the advances of a lecherous young virgin (to him, "sex" means "babies"). He shows little inclination toward the "Dionysiac abandon" symbolized in a comic way by the "huge, tottering pile of unread Lawrentiana" that awaits him, through most of the story, on his Reading Room desk.]

2690 Lowry, Malcolm. SELECTED LETTERS OF MALCOLM LOWRY, ed by Harvey Breit and Marjorie Bonner Lowry (Phila & NY: J. B. Lippincott, 1965), pp. 115, 116, 146, 178.

[In a letter to Albert Erskine (30 June 1946), the author discusses a statement in DHL's *Letters* that the " 'personal battle' . . . should be carried into the soul of every man in England." Lowry also asks Erskine to check a reference in another DHL letter to "their secret mines of silver." In another letter, he mentions

DHL's praise of Anna Wickham's poetry and his having lived in the house Wyewurk in Australia.]

2691 Mackenzie, Compton. MY LIFE AND TIMES, OCTAVE FOUR: 1907-1915 (Lond: Chatto & Windus, 1965), pp. 199, 216, 224-25.
[In 1913, Ford Madox Hueffer's "Literary Portrait" pinned great hopes for literature upon DHL and Ezra Pound, also mentioning Mackenzie's SINISTER STREET. The following year Henry James, in the second of two articles about the younger generation of novelists, included both DHL and Mackenzie. In August 1914, Mackenzie went with Gilbert Cannan to visit DHL, finding him scrubbing the floor and shouting at Frieda. Mackenzie, who was anxious "to get into the war," offered DHL his cottage in Italy for the winter, on the assumption that the war would be over by then. See also Compton Mackenzie, THE SOUTH WIND OF LOVE (Vol. II of THE FOUR WINDS OF LOVE) (Lond: Rich & Cowan; NY: Dodd, 1937), pp. 243-53, for a fictional rendering of the author's first meeting with DHL and Frieda.]

2692 MacShane, Frank. THE LIFE AND WORK OF FORD MADOX FORD (NY: Horizon P, 1965), pp. 78-79, 80, 81, 87, 96, 101, 124, 128, 136, 157, 163, 196, 248, 254.
DHL acknowledged his debt to Ford Madox Ford for publishing his work, the most important by any unknown writer, in the ENGLISH REVIEW, which "became the centre of a revival in English letters." Though others complained about Ford's arrogance, DHL, who had visited him at South Lodge, thought him " 'a lot better fellow than he thinks he ought to be.' " When Ezra Pound left the Imagist group, DHL joined in signing the Imagist manifesto. Ford, who once visited Nottingham with DHL "to discover at first hand the atmosphere of *Sons and Lovers*," later wrote an article on DHL. [See also Ford Madox Ford, "D. H. Lawrence," AMERICAN MERCURY, XXXVIII (June 1936), 167-79.]

2693 Mahnken, Harry E. "The Plays of D. H. Lawrence: Addenda," MODERN DRAMA, VII (Feb 1965), 431-32.
[Note offering two corrections to Arthur E. Waterman, "The Plays of D. H. Lawrence," MODERN DRAMA, II (Feb 1960), 349-57.] Internal evidence and biographical data show that DHL's play *Altitude* could not have been written earlier than the period of DHL's "sojourn" in New Mexico. *Keeping Barbara* or *The Fight for Barbara*, written in 1912 but not published until 1933, should be added to the list of DHL's plays.

2694 Marks, William S., III. "The Psychology of the Uncanny in Lawrence's 'The Rocking-Horse Winner,' " MODERN FICTION STUDIES, XI (Winter 1965-1966), 381-82; rptd in D. H. LAWRENCE: "THE ROCKING-HORSE WINNER," ed by Dominick P. Consolo (Columbus, OH: Merrill, 1969), pp. 71-83.
Freud shows that the horse, when it becomes a totemic animal for the neurotic, represents surrogate parents and indicates libido fixation at a narcissistic and Oedipal stage of development. DHL shows that for Paul, the child, there is a causal and magical equation of money, riding, and narcissistic sexuality (disguised

masturbation). The repetition compulsion shown in Paul's obsessional riding is a form of ritual magic by which the narcissistic, power-obsessed child establishes contact with the demonic (uncanny) world which in turn demands the sacrifice of his life. [Contains copious references to Freud's theories and case histories and relates Paul's mother, as a form of the witch who sacrifices children, to Hawthorne's "vengeance-seeking" Hester Prynne.]

2695 Martin, W. R. " 'Freedom Together' in Lawrence's *Women in Love*," ENGLISH STUDIES IN AFRICA, VIII (Sept 1965), 111-20.
In *Women in Love,* Gerald on his mare and Loerke's picture of the girl on the stallion are obverse representations of what marriage should not be. Birkin's "star equilibrium" involves a new harmony within the individual and a new relationship between individuals. Gerald, a stickler for convention, is as amoral as Loerke, whereas Birkin, the advocate of spontaneity, behaves with conventional decorum, speaking to the father before proposing to Ursula, "walking out" during courtship, resigning from his inspectorship, taking out a marriage license, and going on a honeymoon. Birkin and Ursula, rather than being trapped by convention, have reached an internal harmony with tradition that gives it fresh meaning for them. Marriage has not been imposed upon them; it is what they both deeply need, an eternal conjunction of free agents.

2696 Massey, Irving. "An End to Innocence," QUEEN'S QUARTERLY, LXXII (Spring 1965), 178-94.
DHL stands in a long tradition of writers who equate consciousness and developed culture with the loss of innocence, with the end of inner harmony and the ability of man to express himself in unity. This tradition asserts the eventual return of innocence, which can be attained, as Blake saw it, "through the improvement of sensual delight, until the whole body becomes an erogenous zone."

2697 Mayhall, Jane. "D. H. Lawrence: The Triumph of Texture," WESTERN HUMANITIES REVIEW, XIX (Spring 1965), 161-74.
A "list of contrarieties," both in the ways DHL has been evaluated and in his life and art, establishes the principle of paradox in DHL. Committed to "the immediate," yet an "indefatigable disciplinarian," DHL did not want to " 'build' a plot" but to give "the feeling of the plot's flowing"--to "project the way our lives are lived." The drama of his work is "gleaned form *organic surprise,* and based on the indeterminateness of life itself." DHL excels where "passions are not spared," especially in his short stories and novelettes, where "he shows a particular aptitude for the dramatic." At the heart of this drama is his style--from the movement of the paragraphs to the energies and fluidity of individual sentences and words-- stemming from DHL's "being his old divided self" and "presenting the immediate, divided situation." [Includes discussion of the sheaf-gathering scene in *The Rainbow* for its "fluidity," of *Lady Chatterley's Lover* as a dull sermon, of "The Fox" for the superb mimetic "energy of the writer," and of "The Rocking-Horse Winner" as the "allegory" of DHL the writer.]

2698 Mayhead, Robin. UNDERSTANDING LITERATURE (Cambridge: Cambridge UP, 1965), pp. 30-34.

The passage in *Aaron's Rod* in which the child Millicent first questions her father about the blue ball Christmas ornament, then carelessly breaks it, illustrates, whether it calls to mind particular experiences or not, the "universal significance" of "what family tensions are like."

    2699 Millet, Robert Walker. "The Question of the Relationships between the Painting and Written Works of D. H. Lawrence." Unpublished dissertation, University of Ottawa, 1965. [Listed in D. H. LAWRENCE REVIEW, III (Spring 1970), 84.]

    2700 Mitchell, Peter Todd. "Lawrence's *Sea and Sardinia* Revisited," TEXAS QUARTERLY, VIII (Spring 1965), 67-72.
[The author, a painter, retraced the steps of the Lawrences' tour of Sardinia in 1921, visiting the towns, the kinds of inns, and parts of the island they had visited. The essay, a pleasant travelogue with quotations from *Sea and Sardinia,* is followed by several pages of black-and-white photographs of the author's paintings, based on excerpts from DHL's book.]

    2701 Moore, Harry T. "A Postscript," D. H. LAWRENCE AND "SONS AND LOVERS": SOURCES AND CRITICISM, ed by E. W. Tedlock, Jr. (NY: New York UP, 1965; Lond: University of London P, 1966), pp. 63-65.
A sentence near the end of *Sons and Lovers* in the final manuscript version reads, " 'Mother!' he whimpered--'mother!' " "In several current editions, the word *whispered* appears instead of *whimpered*." The two manuscript fragments of *Paul Morel* show this earlier version of *Sons and Lovers* to be much inferior to the final published version. [Textual commentary.]

    2702 Mori, Haruhide. "D. H. Lawrence no Hyôgen Keishiki" (Pattern in the Style of D. H. Lawrence), KÔBE MISCELLANY (Kôbe University), No. 3 (Feb 1965), 27-40.
[In Japanese.]

    2703 Mori, Haruhide. "D. H. Lawrence: *The Plumed Serpent,*" STUDIES IN STYLISTICS (Ôsaka Women's University), No. 6 (Jan 1965), 66-67.
[In Japanese.]

    2704 Morrill, Claire. "Three Women of Taos: Frieda Lawrence, Mabel Luhan, and Dorothy Brett," SOUTH DAKOTA REVIEW, II (Spring 1965), 3-22; rptd as "Three Women of Taos," in A TAOS MOSAIC: PORTRAIT OF A NEW MEXICO VILLAGE, by Claire Morrill (Albuquerque: University of New Mexico P, 1973), pp. 106-21.
In Taos lived three women who had been "brought into confrontation here by D. H. Lawrence": Mabel Dodge Luhan, the wealthy socialite and arts patron who found in Taos and her Indian husband something that held her for more than forty years; Dorothy Brett, who found independence and freedom in Taos after

an English youth of meekness and submission; and Frieda Lawrence, who "ripened" at the ranch where DHL did much of his writing and was happiest. [Memoir.]

2705 Morse, Donald E. "Love and Three Generals: A Fable," CEA CRITIC, XXVIII (Nov 1965), 1-2.

The recent Massachusetts judicial decision prohibiting sale of John Cleland's FANNY HILL is similar to the 1959-1960 case of *Lady Chatterley's Lover*, which can be likened to a fable concerning the good General Eisenhower, the Postmaster General Summerfield, and the Attorney General, all three of whom were shocked by the four-letter words in the novel, though the Supreme Court refused to ban the book.

2706 Nakano, Kimiko. "*Sons and Lovers* ni Tsuite" (On *Sons and Lovers*), KÔNAN WOMEN'S COLLEGE STUDIES IN ENGLISH LITERATURE, No. 2 (Dec 1965), 75-90.

[In Japanese.]

2707 Nakano, Kimiko. "*Women in Love* ni Okeru Gerald Crich" (Gerald Crich in *Women in Love*), KÔNAN WOMEN'S COLLEGE RESEARCHES, No. 1 (March 1965), 179-94.

[In Japanese.]

2708 Nardi, Piero. "Taccuino veneziano: la laguna di Lawrence" (Venetian Notebook: Lawrence's Lagoon), IL RESTO DEL CARLINO (Bologna), 8 May 1965, p. 3.

In the poem "St. Mark," in "The Evangelistic Beasts" section of *Birds, Beasts and Flowers,* Daniele Manin [a figure of the Italian Risorgiment in Venice] is mentioned. This allusion probably results from DHL's topographical knowledge of Venice, where one of the best-known squares is named after Manin. DHL had visited Venice for the first time in 1920 and had settled there for a longer period in 1921. As a result he had planned a book on Venice and later used Venice as the setting of Chapter XVII of *Lady Chatterley's Lover*. [In Italian.]

2709 Nichols, Ann Eljenholm. "Syntax and Style: Ambiguities in Lawrence's *Twilight in Italy*," COLLEGE COMPOSITION AND COMMUNICATION, XVI (Dec 1965), 261-66.

[Linguistic analysis of style.] The syntax and style of *Twilight in Italy* are epic in quality; DHL's epic journey demanded a high style.

2710 Ninomiya, Takamichi. "Higeki no Keishô (Lawrence no Thomas Hardy Ron)" (Tragedy Bequeathed: Lawrence on Thomas Hardy), TAUROS (Kôbe University), No. 7 (Feb 1965), 2-12.

[In Japanese.]

2711 Nolte, William H. "The Sex Uproar," MENCKENIANA, XVI (Winter 1965), 3-7.

Although Mencken believed in complete freedom of the press, including freedom to use sexual language, he found DHL's novels badly flawed by their sole concern with sex. Mencken hated DHL's irrationalism and did not think his characters credible.

2712 "Notes on Current Books," VIRGINIA QUARTERLY REVIEW, XLI (Winter 1965), xxviii.

Now that DHL's pictures may be seen in *Paintings of D. H. Lawrence*, ed by Mervyn Levy, "One wonders at the shock of the whispered descriptions or at the serious consideration which had been given them in earlier years."

2713 Oda, Motoi. "*Lady Chatterley's Lover*--Sono Shippai to Shôri" (*Lady Chatterley's Lover*--Its Failure and Triumph), ENGLISH LITERATURE IN HOKKAIDÔ (Hokkaidô University), No. 10 (July 1965), 53-62.

[In Japanese.]

2714 Okada, Taiji. "Chichi no Ko Lawrence" (Lawrence: Son of Father), REVIEW OF KÔBE UNIVERSITY OF MERCANTILE MARINE: PART I, STUDIES IN HUMANITIES AND SOCIAL SCIENCE, No. 13 (March 1965), 108-30.

[In Japanese.]

2715 Okumura, Tôru. "Michinaru Sekai o Motomete--*Niji*" (In Search of the Unknown World--*The Rainbow*), REVIEW OF ENGLISH LITERATURE (College of Liberal Arts, Kyôto University), No. 17 (March 1965), 74-108.

[In Japanese.]

2716 Oppel, Horst. "D. H. Lawrence: *St. Mawr*," in DER MODERNE ENGLISCHE ROMAN: INTERPRETATIONEN (The Modern English Novel: Interpretations), ed by Horst Oppel (Berlin: E. Schmidt, 1965), pp. 115-34.

Several faults in *St. Mawr* have, on occasion, prevented the critics from making an adequate assessment: obviously incompatible levels of style, incomplete characterization of Rico, exaggerated use of symbols, and interruption of the narrative by theoretical reflections. Only Lou Carrington and Mrs. Witt are fully characterized. Both are weary of modern life, but they respond differently to the frictions of civilization. Lou's escape to the desolate ranch does not mean a retreat into an earthly paradise, since natural life involves both the lovely and the terrible. The stallion, the central image of the tale, is both a symbol of instinctive life and a means to analyze the characters. Rico's fall from the horse, the turning point of the narrative, exemplifies nature's revenge for man's enslavement of animals. St. Mawr's disappearance is not a structural fault but symbolizes the return to nature. Its function, the portrayal of unperverted life, is taken up in the unbroken magic of the wilderness. [In German.]

2717 Ôta, Saburô. "D. H. Lawrence: *Shojo to Jipshi* Hihyô" (On D. H. Lawrence: *The Virgin and the Gipsy*), GAKUEN (Shôwa Women's University), No. 308 (Aug 1965), 2-13.

[In Japanese.]

2718 Panichas, George A. "D. H. Lawrence and the Ancient Greeks," ENGLISH MISCELLANY (Rome), XVI (1965), 195-214; rptd in THE REVERENT DISCIPLINE: ESSAYS IN LITERARY CRITICISM AND CULTURE, by George A. Panichas (Knoxville: University of Tennessee P, 1974), pp. 335-50.

DHL appreciated the Greeks for their vitality, sensuousness, and direct contact with "the everlasting *wonder* in things." DHL read Homer's epics as "the supreme old novels," still filled with a sense of immediacy. DHL disliked Plato, however, whose vision of balance and equilibrium seemed to him static and enervating, and he preferred the pre-Socratic philsophers because they seemed to have a more "living understanding." Heracleitus, with whom he agreed on the evils of education, the necessity of strife, perpetual flux, and the need for a "sensitive soul," is closest in spirit to DHL. DHL's response to myth was derived from the Greeks. DHL's debt to the Greeks, however, must be seen as qualified. Wanting "tragedy purged of the metaphysics of fatalism," DHL is a tragic poet in *Sons and Lovers, The Rainbow,* and *Women in Love,* but ultimately rejects the Hellenic concept of tragedy in favor of *phallus* in *The Plumed Serpent, Lady Chatterley's Lover,* and *The Man Who Died.* Although his art never comes to terms with the tragic, something of the tragic spirit reappears in *Last Poems.*

2719 Pinto, Vivian de Sola. "Lawrence the Poet," TIMES LITERARY SUPPLEMENT (Lond), 24 Oct 1965, p. 946.

[Letter to the Editor in reply to Andor Gomme, "Lawrence the Poet: Achievement and Irrelevance," TIMES LITERARY SUPPLEMENT (Lond), 26 Aug 1965, pp. 725-27, which had reviewed *The Complete Poems of D. H. Lawrence,* ed by Vivian de Sola Pinto and Warren Roberts. Pinto defends that edition, saying that it was never intended as a "Variorum Edition" recording all extant variants of DHL's poems.]

2720 Pittock, Malcolm. "Lawrence the Poet," TIMES LITERARY SUPPLEMENT (Lond), 2 Sept 1965, p. 755.

[Letter to the Editor in reply to Andor Gomme, "Lawrence the Poet: Achievement and Irrelevance," TIMES LITERARY SUPPLEMENT (Lond), 26 Aug 1965, pp. 725-27. *The Complete Poems of D. H. Lawrence,* ed by Vivian de Sola Pinto and Warren Roberts, does not contain the earlier version of "The Bride" entitled "The Dead Mother," which is printed only in Ada Lawrence and G. Stuart Gelder, EARLY LIFE OF D. H. LAWRENCE (1932).["The Dead Mother" is reprinted with Pittock's letter, and a brief comparison shows DHL's improvements. See also Vivian de Sola Pinto, "Lawrence the Poet," TIMES LITERARY SUPPLEMENT (Lond), 24 Oct 1965, p. 946.]

2721 Raes, Hugo. "Struisvogeltje Spelen: De Evolutie van de Erotische Literatuur" (Ostrich Play: The Evolution of Erotic Literature), VLAAMSE GIDS, XLIX (Nov 1965), 698-706.

The publication of the unexpurgated *Lady Chatterley's Lover* in 1959 is a step toward making the erotic in literature acceptable. [In Dutch.]

D. H. LAWRENCE

2722 Raina, M. L. "The Use of the Symbol by English Novelists 1900-1930, with Particular Reference to E. M. Forster, D. H. Lawrence, and Virginia Woolf." Unpublished dissertation, University of Manchester, 1965. [Listed in Lawrence F. McNamee, DISSERTATIONS IN ENGLISH AND AMERICAN LITERATURE, SUPP I (NY and Lond: Bowker, 1969), p. 245.]

2723 Rich, Adrienne. "Reflections on Lawrence," POETRY, CVI (June 1965), 218-25.
[Review of *The Complete Poems of D. H. Lawrence*, ed by Vivian de Sola Pinto and F. Warren Roberts.] "Poetry of the Present" is a poet's essay, important to the historian and to all readers of poetry. *The Complete Poems of D. H. Lawrence* reveals DHL as a major poet. *Look! We Have Come Through!* is rooted not only in biography but also in the development of a mind. A large number of poems in *Pansies* are part of DHL's central achievement. His language, related to the King James version of the Bible, shows a "passionate grasp of the physical world."

2724 Roberts, Warren. "Introduction," D. H. LAWRENCE: THE CROYDON YEARS, by Helen Corke (Austin: University of Texas P, 1965), pp. ix-xi.
Publication of *Sons and Lovers* "marked the turning point in [the] relationship" between DHL and Helen Corke because Jessie Chambers, with whom she had developed a "vivid friendship" and whose portrait as Miriam both women considered unjustifiable, turned away from all reminders of DHL, including Helen. No one who knew DHL has written about him "with more perception or less ostentation than Helen Corke."

2725 Roland, Christoph. "David Herbert Lawrence. Berühmt-berüchtigt seine Lady Chatterly [sic] --Eine Genie--von düsterer Krankheit gezeichnet" (David Herbert Lawrence: Notorious for His Lady Chatterley--A Genius--Stricken by an Incurable Disease), INTERPRESS (KULTUR). INTERNATIONALER BIOGRAPHISCHER PRESSEDIENST, No. 121 (25 Aug 1965).
[Short biographical-bibliographical account of DHL's career.] [In German.]

2726 Ross, Robert H. THE GEORGIAN REVOLT: RISE AND FALL OF A POETIC IDEAL, 1910-1922 (Carbondale and Edwardsville: Southern Illinois UP, 1965; Lond: Faber & Faber, 1967), pp. 15, 51, 89-91, 100, 101, 108, 115, 116, 119, 129-30, 138, 168, 212, 237, 239-41.
A spokesman for the "spiritual vigor" by which modern poets were "casting off the ennui of the fin de siecle," DHL contributed an "eloquent paean to the 'Georgian Renaissance,' " to Murry's RHYTHM, exulting in " 'the vast freedom, the illimitable wealth that we have suddenly got.' " When Edward Marsh, who included "Snap-dragon" in his GEORGIAN POETRY, 1911-1912, returned some DHL poems because they were "cast in vers libre," he provoked a controversy in which DHL attacked Marsh's "Prosodic canons as not only outmoded but insensitive as well." DHL objected angrily to Lascelles Abercrombie's "End of the World" as " 'mean and rather sordid, and full of rancid hate.' "

2727 Sagar, Keith. "Three Separate Ways: Unpublished D. H. Lawrence Letters to Francis Brett Young," REVIEW OF ENGLISH LITERATURE (Leeds), VI (July 1965), 93-105.

Seven previously unpublished DHL letters to Mr. and Mrs. Francis Brett Young are a record of the Lawrences' relationship with the Brett Youngs and Compton Mackenzie in 1920-1921.

2728 Sale, Roger. "D. H. Lawrence, 1912-1916," MASSACHUSETTS REVIEW, VI (Spring-Summer 1965), 467-80; enlgd and rptd as "D. H. Lawrence, 1910-1916," in MODERN HEROISM: ESSAYS ON D. H. LAWRENCE, WILLIAM EMPSON, & J. R. R. TOLKIEN, by Roger Sale (Berkeley, Los Angeles, Lond: University of California P, 1973), pp. 16-106.

The last four chapters of *Sons and Lovers*, in which DHL fits his characters into symbolic roles and discovers a "new relation" between men and women as his subject, foreshadow the kind of novelist he was to become. The success of Tom and Lydia's marriage in *The Rainbow* lies in their ability to accept each other's "otherness," as the Morels could not, and thereby to make of their marriage a cosmic family. Anna and Will reject the "otherness" in each other; hence, Ursula is more conscious, more vulnerable to the destructiveness of mechanized history, and closer at times to death. Birkin in *Women in Love,* until the "Excurse" chapter, is a violent character who attempts to escape the destructiveness of phallic sexuality by means of dominating either Ursula or Gerald. DHL must murder life that is "industrial and dominating, but the price is high; no man and no society for Birkin, and so no further imaginative exploration for Lawrence."

2729 Salgādo, Gāmini. "Reviews and Comment," CRITICAL QUARTERLY, VII (Winter 1965), 389-92.

[Review of *The Complete Poems of D. H. Lawrence,* ed by Vivian de Sola Pinto and F. Warren Roberts (1964).] DHL has survived his critics, who have finally only one complaint about him--that he lacked discipline. But if DHL's method led sometimes to bad writing, it is also the inescapable condition of his successes. DHL's view of poetry is directly linked to his view of experience; objecting to the one may be objecting to the other. DHL wrote poetry that recalls the best of Hardy, Pound, even Yeats, but finally he will stand or fall by having qualities of awareness uniquely his own.

2730 Sepčić, Višnja. "Romansijerska tehnika D. H. Lawrencea" (D. H. Lawrence's Art of the Novel). Unpublished dissertation, University of Zagreb, 1965. [Listed in "Criticism of D. H. Lawrence in Yugoslavia: 1916-1976: A Bibliography," by Sonja Miletić and Miroslav Beker, D. H. LAWRENCE REVIEW, XI (Spring 1978), 75.]
[In Serbo-Croatian.]

2731 Shaw, Rita Granger. "SONS AND LOVERS": NOTES (Lincoln, NE: Cliff's Notes, 1965).

[Contains an "Introduction," "Background of the Novel," brief "Plot Summary," a short summary and commentary on each chap., discussions of "Lawrence's

Style," "Major Characters," and "Minor Characters," "Selected Bibliography," "Chronological Chart" of DHL's life and literary career, and "Examination Questions." "This outline is designed not as a substitute for the text of *Sons and Lovers* but as an instructive and motivating guide."]

2732 Shimizu, Kazuyoshi. "Lawrence no Rakuen (Risô Shakai 'Rananim' no Kôsatsu)" (Utopian World of D. H. Lawrence--A Consideration of "Rananim") LITERARY SYMPOSIUM (Aichi University), No. 29 (Feb 1965), 75-97.
[In Japanese.]

2733 Singh, G. S. "Better History and Better Criticism: The Significance of F. R. Leavis," ENGLISH MISCELLANY, XVI (1965), 215-79.
DHL is accorded the pride of place in Leavis's critical scale not only as the greatest English novelist but also as the greatest Englishman of this century. Leavis thought the maturest accomplishments of DHL's creative genius to be *The Rainbow* and *Women in Love,* novels that enact the problems of our civilization in a compelling moral and artistically impressive way. Unlike Eliot, DHL had a positive attitude toward life and an essential reverence for its multiplicity of forms. Leavis thought the burden of DHL's art to be the fulfillment of individual life through a true marital relationship. [Extended analysis of Leavis's major critical positions.]

2734 Sitwell, Edith. "A Man with Red Hair," TAKEN CARE OF: AN AUTOBIOGRAPHY (Lond: Hutchinson, 1965), pp. 107-11; pub in America as TAKEN CARE OF: THE AUTOBIOGRAPHY OF EDITH SITWELL (NY: Atheneum, 1965), pp. 122-27.
[A sardonic, hostile account of a visit Edith Sitwell and her brother Osbert paid the Lawrences in Tuscany, during which DHL looked like "a plaster gnome on a stone toadstool" and, "though courteous and amiable," was "determined to impress upon us that he was a son of toil." Includes fragmentary criticism of *Lady Chatterley's Lover,* which shows, in DHL's loathing of Sir Clifford Chatterley, his hatred of all "gentlemen," and in the "adulterous gamekeeper," lapses of taste, though his four-letter words are not "as harmful as the descriptions of sexual intercourse, which in my opinion would freeze any impulse to love between boy and girl." This account should be compared with Osbert Sitwell's friendly version of the same visit in his PENNY FOOLISH: A BOOK OF TIRADES AND PANEGYRICS (Lond: Macmillan, 1935), pp. 293-97; and with Edith Sitwell's assessment of DHL in her SELECTED LETTERS, ed by John Lehmann and Derek Parker (Lond: Macmillan, 1970), p. 200.]

2735 Spilka, Mark. "The Affective Fallacy Revisited," SOUTHERN REVIEW (Adelaide), I (1965), 57-70.
Eliseo Vivas, relying on the New Critical doctrine of the Affective Fallacy, argues that DHL, by forcing his readers to respond emotionally, causes them to lose aesthetic distance. But conscious distance from the work of art is not the same as unconscious distance. While reading, the reader has an unconscious response that determines much of his subsequent conscious response.

2736 Suehiro, Yoshitaka. "D. H. Lawrence no Ai to Seimei no Rinri" (The Love and Life Ethics of D. H. Lawrence), JOURNAL OF THE SECOND COLLEGE OF ENGINEERING, NIHON UNIVERSITY, VI (March 1965), 21-26.
[In Japanese.]

2737 Talon, Henri. D. H. LAWRENCE: "SONS AND LOVERS": LES ASPECTS SOCIAUX, ÉCONOMIQUES, LA VISION DE L'ARTISTE (D. H. Lawrence: *Sons and Lovers*: The Social and Economic Aspects and the Artist's Vision) (Paris: Archives des Lettres Modernes, 1965).
[This pamphlet of 63 pages is an academic study analyzing the social and economic aspects of *Sons and Lovers* and using precise factual details to examine systematically the text of the novel.] [In French.]

2738 Tedlock, E[rnest] W., Jr. (ed). D. H. LAWRENCE AND "SONS AND LOVERS": SOURCES AND CRITICISM (NY: New York UP, 1965; Lond: University of London P, 1966).
Contents, abstracted under date of first publication: E[rnest] W. Tedlock, Jr., "Introduction," pp. 3-4 (1965); I. **Origins:** 1. "From Lawrence's Letters," pp. 12-32 [excerpts from DHL letters to Blanche Jennings, Sydney S. Pawling, Rachel Annand Taylor, Helen Corke, Ada Lawrence Clarke, Edward Garnett, A. W. McLeod, and Barbara Low, including "Foreword to *Sons and Lovers*"--not abstracted]; 2. Alice Dax, "From a Letter by Alice Dax ("Clara") to Frieda Lawrence," pp. 33-35, excerpt of letter pub in FRIEDA LAWRENCE: THE MEMOIRS AND CORRESPONDENCE, ed by E. W. Tedlock, Jr. (Lond: William Heinemann, 1961; NY: Knopf, 1964), pp. 246-49 [letter not abstracted separately]; 3. Frieda Lawrence, "From Letters by Frieda Lawrence," pp. 36-38, excerpts from Frieda's letters to Edward Garnett, Harry T. Moore, and Edward Gilbert pub in FRIEDA LAWRENCE: THE MEMOIRS AND CORRESPONDENCE, ed by E. W. Tedlock, Jr. (Lond: William Heinemann, 1961; NY: Knopf, 1964), pp. 171-72, 182-83, 328-29, 333 [letters not abstracted separately]; 4. Jessie Chambers, "From D. H. LAWRENCE: A PERSONAL RECORD," pp. 39-42, from D. H. LAWRENCE: A PERSONAL RECORD by E. T. (Lond: Jonathan Cape, 1936), pp. 156-61; 5. Harry T. Moore, "The Genesis as Revealed in the Miriam Papers," pp. 43-62, from Appendix B: "The Genesis of *Sons and Lovers*," D. H. LAWRENCE: HIS LIFE AND WORKS, 2nd rvd ed (NY: Twayne, 1964), pp. 285-305; 6. Harry T. Moore, "A Postscript," pp. 63-65 (1965); 7. E. W. Tedlock, Jr., "A Report on the Final Manuscript," pp. 66-69 (1965); II. **Freudian Connections and Approaches:** 8. Alfred Booth Kuttner, "A Freudian Appreciation," pp. 76-100, rptd from "*Sons and Lovers*: A Freudian Appreciation," PSYCHOANALYTIC REVIEW, III (July 1916), 295-317; 9. Frederick J. Hoffman, "Lawrence's Quarrel with Freud," pp. 101-11, excerpted from FREUDIANISM AND THE LITERARY MIND (Baton Rouge: Louisiana State UP, 1945; 2nd ed, 1957), pp. 151-76; 10. Daniel A. Weiss, "The Mother in the Mind," pp. 112-36, from OEDIPUS IN NOTTINGHAM: D. H. LAWRENCE (Seattle: University of Washington P, 1962), pp. 39-67; Frank O'Connor [pseud of Michael O'Donovan], "D. H. Lawrence: *Sons and Lovers*," pp. 137-44, from THE MIRROR IN THE

ROADWAY (NY: Knopf, 1955), pp. 270-79; III. **Techniques and Values:** 12. John Middleton Murry, "Son and Lover," from SON OF WOMAN: THE STORY OF D. H. LAWRENCE (Lond: Jonathan Cape, 1931), pp. 19-38; 13. Mark Schorer, "Technique as Discovery," pp. 164-69, from "Technique as Discovery," HUDSON REVIEW, I (Spring 1948), 67-87; 14. Dorothy Van Ghent, "On *Sons and Lovers,*" pp. 170-87, from THE ENGLISH NOVEL: FORM AND FUNCTION (NY: Holt, Rinehart and Winston, 1953), pp. 245-61; 15. Mark Spilka, "How to Pick Flowers," pp. 188-99, from THE LOVE ETHIC OF D. H. LAWRENCE (Bloomington: Indiana UP, 1955), pp. 39-59; 16. Mark Spilka, "Counterfeit Loves," pp. 200-216, from THE LOVE ETHIC OF D. H. LAWRENCE (Bloomington: Indiana UP, 1955), pp. 60-89; 17. Louis Fraiberg, "The Unattainable Self," pp. 217-37, from "The Unattainable Self: D. H. Lawrence's *Sons and Lovers,*" TWELVE ORIGINAL ESSAYS ON GREAT ENGLISH NOVELS, ed by Charles Shapiro (Detroit: Wayne State UP, 1960), pp. 175-201; 18. Alfred Kazin, "Sons, Lovers and Mothers," pp. 238-50, from "Sons, Lovers and Mothers," PARTISAN REVIEW, XXIX (Spring 1962), 373-85.

2739 Tedlock, E[rnest] W., Jr. "Introduction," D. H. LAWRENCE AND "SONS AND LOVERS": SOURCES AND CRITICISM, ed by E. W. Tedlock, Jr. (NY: New York UP, 1965; Lond: University of London P, 1966), pp. 3-4, 7-11, 73-75, 147-50.

[Introductions to the anthology and to individual sections entitled "Origins," "Freudian Connections and Approaches," and "Techniques and Values."] This collection of letters and essays is designed "to give the reader of *Sons and Lovers* an opportunity to range through the problems of meaning and technique that have been connected with it, and the solutions that have been offered." The letters illuminate many of the personal problems contained in the novel. DHL's unpublished foreword "expounds the novel's theme in parabolic language" and reveals "a Lawrence who through a tremendous effort of consciousness, understanding, and activity has at least partially transcended his fictional counterpart." Early psychoanalytical critics hailed *Sons and Lovers* as a "vindication by art of [Freud's] scientific analysis"; recent psychoanalytically oriented critics "tend to reduce the artist to the role . . . of psychological medium . . . of predestinated case history." The essays that discuss *Sons and Lovers* "in terms of techniques and values" represent the stages of critical concern with the novel's unity and the increasing critical attention to DHL's symbolism as his particular technical innovation and as a reliable clue to the characters, relationships, and values of the novel.

2740 Tedlock, E[rnest] W., Jr. "A Report on the Final Manuscript," D. H. LAWRENCE AND "SONS AND LOVERS": SOURCES AND CRITICISM, ed by E. W. Tedlock, Jr. (NY: New York UP, 1965; Lond: University of London P, 1966), pp. 66-69.

The final manuscript of *Sons and Lovers* [at the University of California at Berkeley] contains extensive revisions "between the lines" by DHL and also shows that Edward Garnett "had an exceptionally, significantly free hand in cutting and otherwise preparing the manuscript for the printers." Cut from the final manuscript version were eighty-eight passages varying in length from three to eighty-nine lines. Most of the cuts were made by Garnett "to bring the novel to a length the publishers of the day found economically feasible." [Textual analysis.]

2741 Tetsumura, Haruo. "*Aaron's Rod* Danshô (Sakuhin to Ningen Lawrence)" (On *Aaron's Rod* by Lawrence), HIROSHIMA STUDIES IN ENGLISH LANGUAGE AND LITERATURE (Hiroshima University), XII (Nov 1965), 33-43.
[In Japanese.]

2742 Tetsumura, Haruo. "*Sons and Lovers* kara *Women in Love* e (Shi no Gutaitekina Kankaku ni Mukatte)" (From *Sons and Lovers* to *Women in Love*: Toward a More Concrete Sense of Death), SHIMONOSEKI ECONOMIC REVIEW (Shimonoseki Ichiritsu College), VIII (March 1965), 81-104.
[In Japanese.]

2743 Titta Rosa, Giovanni. "La moglie di Lawrence" (Lawrence's Wife), IL GAZZETTINO (Venice), 24 Oct 1965, p. 3.
At a conference on DHL, Frieda Lawrence Ravagli spoke of her recollections of her life with DHL and told some anecdotes to illustrate it. She did not say anything about DHL's ideas but spoke only of their love and her escape from her family environment and social conventions in order to follow him. [In Italian.]

2744 Tomlinson, T. B. "Lawrence and Modern Life: *Sons and Lovers, Women in Love*," CRITICAL REVIEW (Melbourne), No. 8 (1965), 3-18; excerpt rptd in CRITICS ON D. H. LAWRENCE, ed by W. T. Andrews (Coral Gables, FL: University of Miami P, 1971), pp. 58-66; rptd as "D. H. Lawrence: *Sons and Lovers, Women in Love*," in THE ENGLISH MIDDLE-CLASS NOVEL, by T. B. Tomlinson (NY: Harper and Row, 1976), pp. 185-98.
The crucial works in any evaluation of DHL are *Women in Love* and, secondarily, *Sons and Lovers*. DHL's disgust with modern "mechanistic" society and his distrust for "humanity itself" come to a climax in *Women in Love*. Birkin's attitude is marked by "solipsistic contemptus mundi," though DHL pretends sensual vitality over despair and sees humanity in mass as "a huge aggregate lie." When DHL's prose "disintegrates," it unveils a "fiercely destructive urge" seldom "absent from his work." Paul's treatment of Miriam in *Sons and Lovers* is far "less humane" than his father Walter's treatment of his mother. Gerald Crich and Walter Morel, though often misread, have a "baffled strength" greater than Birkin's philosophizing. Gerald is not essentially negative but possibly "in touch with deeper sources of life," though his "impotent will" finally kills him. Much of the "extraordinary range and density" of *Women in Love* is established on "Gerald's life and death," though Birkin's exploratory spirit is also essential.

2745 Uchiki, Jôtarô. "*Koisuru Onnatachi* ni Okeru Kôseijô no Tokuchô ni Tsuite" (On the Characteristics in the Composition of *Women in Love*), SYLVAN (Tôhoku University), No. 10 (May 1965), 10-22.
[In Japanese.]

D. H. LAWRENCE

2746 Uchiki, Jôtarô. "*Sons and Lovers* ni Tsuite" (On *Sons and Lovers*), REPORT OF THE CHIBA INSTITUTE OF TECHNOLOGY (HUMANE STUDIES), No. 7 (Dec 1965), 17-40.
[In Japanese.]

2747 Uehata, Yoshikazu. "D. H. Lawrence to Shakai" (D. H. Lawrence and Society), STUDIES IN ENGLISH LANGUAGE AND LITERATURE (Kansai University), No. 9 (Feb 1965), 1-15.
[In Japanese.]

2748 "Verse," in "Briefly Noted," NEW YORKER, XLI (13 March 1965), 204.
The Complete Poems of D. H. Lawrence, ed by Vivian de Sola Pinto and F. Warren Roberts (1964) shows that DHL's "collected poems stand as one of the most invigorating contributions to the verse of the early twentieth century." "He was-- at his best--original, fearless, and emotionally open."

2749 Wada, Shizuo. "D. H. Lawrence Oboegaki (III) (*Musuko to Koibito* ni Tsuite)" (A Note on D. H. Lawrence [Part III] : On *Sons and Lovers*), KYÛSHÛ SANGYÔ DAIGAKU KYÔYÔBU KIYÔ (Kyûshû Sangyô University), II (Dec 1965), 21-60.
[On the Oedipus complex in *Sons and Lovers.*] [In Japanese.]

2750 Waldron, Philip. "The Education of D. H. Lawrence," JOURNAL OF THE AUSTRALASIAN UNIVERSITIES LANGUAGES AND LITERATURE ASSOCIATION, No. 24 (1965), 239-52.
A study of DHL's formal and informal education shows that his attempt to shake off inhibiting forces of tradition was not caused by ignorance, as some have claimed, but by his desire to be fully alive.

2751 Wardle, Irving. "Lawrence on Stage," OBSERVER (Lond), 12 Dec 1965, p. 26.
Although "Lawrence the dramatist . . . has so far escaped the attentions of the Lawrence industry," *The Complete Plays of D. H. Lawrence* reveals a substantial output of eight full-length plays and two fragments. Although *Touch and Go* is "substandard" in construction and in *David* "the shade of Barrie speaks in the accents of a Hollywood Biblical," the early plays "--all concerned with hypergamous relationships, working-class values, and the figure of the dominant mother-- vitally enlarge our understanding of Lawrence's imagination."

2752 Wasserstrom, William (ed). THE MODERN SHORT NOVEL (NY: Holt, Rinehart & Winston), 1965), pp. 157-58.
[This anthology includes "The Woman Who Rode Away," pp. 157-92.] In all his writings, DHL seeks a new moral system that would incorporate his concept of blood-consciousness. In "The Woman Who Rode Away," he uses the Chilchui myth from ancient Aztec civilization to reinforce his prophecy that a new religion based on myths and rooted in passion is necessary to save man from the modern world of mind and machine. The vibrant woman abandons her static mate

and achieves a new release of her passions among primitive men.

2753 Weales, Gerald. "Tennessee Williams Borrows a Little Shaw," SHAW REVIEW, VIII (May 1965), 63-64.
Converting a Freudian tale into a romantic comedy, Tennessee Williams and Donald Windham based their play YOU TOUCHED ME! (1945) on DHL's short story by that title.

2754 Weintraub, Stanley. REGGIE: A PORTRAIT OF REGINALD TURNER (NY: George Braziller, 1965), pp. 136, 191, 193-205.
Introduced to Reginald Turner by Norman Douglas in Florence in Nov 1919, DHL spent "many evenings in Reggie's company," both in his flat and in cafés. *Aaron's Rod* includes "wickedly accurate" caricatures of Douglas as Argyle, Maurice Magnus as Mee, and Turner as Algy Constable. In the give-and-take between Algy and the Marchesa [Chap. XVI], "we have a travesty on Reggie's own small-talk," captured with fidelity. Later, DHL may have used the half-Jewish Turner in part for his description of Ben Cooley, the Jewish leader of the Diggers in *Kangaroo,* for whom General Sir John Monash, a Jewish military leader whom DHL did not know, served as the chief prototype.

2755 West, Paul. "D. H. Lawrence: Mystical Critic," SOUTHERN REVIEW (Baton Rouge), ns I (Jan 1965), 210-28; rvd and rptd as "D. H. Lawrence," in THE WINE OF ABSURDITY: ESSAYS ON LITERATURE AND CONSOLATION, by Paul West (University Park, PA, and Lond: Pennsylvania State UP, 1966), pp. 19-38; additional references, pp. 3-4, 244-45, 247.
Although DHL deserves the critical attention he is receiving, his main theme cannot be engaged at the "conceptual, disciplined level," and the critic must avoid manipulating DHL's utterances "into a symmetry" DHL himself never achieved. Because DHL's "emotional core . . . is inscrutable," each reader must respond to DHL's work personally and individually. The original versions of *Studies in Classic American Literature* best illustrate how DHL should be approached critically. *The Symbolic Meaning* reveals DHL "the mystic and mystical critic" and shows that the intuitional critic who lacks most of the orthodox critical values can sometimes do more for book, author, or whole literature than the institutional critic. Among earlier studies of DHL, only Anais Nin's "unprofessional study" approaches DHL as he himself approached Cooper, Melville, and Whitman, authors in whom DHL found the blood-consciousness and reverence for life that were the basis of his own work. [Chiefly a review essay on *The Symbolic Meaning: The Uncollected Versions of "Studies in Classic American Literature,"* ed by Armin Arnold (1964), framed in a brief critical overview of the state of DHL criticism since 1930.]

2756 White, Victor. "Frieda and the Lawrence Legend," SOUTHWEST REVIEW, L (Autumn 1965), 388-97.
[Mainly an attack on Frieda as "less a fascinating woman than a fascinating example of a promoter of the first order, one who was chiefly responsible for the creation of a literary legend which secured Lawrence a rather larger place in the his-

tory of literature than he would otherwise have had." Her "engaging qualities" were, apparently, her "booming-voiced vitality" and her "sincerity" of belief in DHL's greatness. Though the writer has a caustic familiarity with Frieda's and DHL's past and with their domestic life, he remains untouched by DHL's work. An exercise in resentment, deftly argued and observed.]

2757 Widmer, Kingsley. THE LITERARY REBEL (Carbondale and Edwardsville: Southern Illinois UP, 1965), pp. 32, 39, 78, 132, 165.

DHL wrote "strident 'pollyanalytics' " to "justify his insights," and much of his travel writing really concerns his flight to deeper awareness.

2758 Wolf, Harold R. "British Fathers and Sons, 1773-1913: From Filial Submissiveness to Creativity," PSYCHOANALYTIC REVIEW, LII (Summer 1965), 53-70.

Submission to paternal authority was characteristic of eighteenth-century fiction, but Victorian literature, as evidenced by Matthew Arnold's SOHRAB AND RUSTUM and the autobiographies of John Stuart Mill and Edmund Gosse, shows the growing awareness in the son of his role in liberating himself from the father and the growing importance of the mother. In *Sons and Lovers* there is no submission to the father except insofar as the son must accept the fact that he cannot have the mother as wife. Fear of losing the integrity of the self and communion with the natural order are dominant themes in the novel. The struggle between the desire to merge with woman and the desire to be individual is the struggle between death and life, but it is his feminine identification that makes Paul a creative artist.

2759 Yamaguchi, Keizabrô. "Chijô no Shinwa" (D. H. Lawrence's *The Plumed Serpent*), BULLETIN OF THE FACULTY OF LIBERAL ARTS (Hôsei University), No. 9 (April 1965), 85-104.

[In Japanese.]

2760 Yamaguchi, Keizabrô. "D. H. Lawrence no Tanpen Shôsetsu no Gihô to Stairu" (Technique and Style of D. H. Lawrence's Short Stories), STUDIES IN ENGLISH LITERATURE (Hôsei University), No. 8 (Dec 1965), 69-83.

[In Japanese.]

2761 Zanger, Jules. "D. H. Lawrence's Three Strange Angels," PAPERS ON LANGUAGE AND LITERATURE, I (Spring 1965), 184-87.

That the "three strange angels" in "Song of a Man Who Has Come Through" allude to the three angels of Genesis 18:2 is reinforced by the poem "Lady Wife." Tentative dating indicates that the triumphant event celebrated is the marriage of DHL and Frieda. The three "song" poems of *Look! We Have Come Through!* show DHL fearing the "space of the world," shutting it out, and finally rejecting the fear.

2762 Zytaruk, George John. "D. H. Lawrence's Response to Russian Literature," DISSERTATION ABSTRACTS, XXVI (1966), 4678A. Unpublished dissertation, University of Washington, 1965. Rvd and pub as D. H. LAWRENCE'S RESPONSE TO RUSSIAN LITERATURE (The Hague and Paris: Mouton, 1971).

1966

2763 Alcorn, John Marshall. "Hardy to Lawrence: A Study in Naturism," DISSERTATION ABSTRACTS, XXIX (1968), 251A. Unpublished dissertation, New York University, 1966. Rvd and pub as THE NATURE NOVEL FROM HARDY TO LAWRENCE (NY: Columbia UP, 1977).

2764 Alexander, John C. "Teilhard de Chardin and D. H. Lawrence: A Study in Agreements," ORMOND PAPERS (Parkville, Victoria, Australia), I (1966), 5-13; rvd and rptd as "D. H. Lawrence and Teilhard de Chardin: A Study in Agreements," D. H. LAWRENCE REVIEW, II (Summer 1969), 138-56.

Although there seems to be little compatibility between the aristocratic French Jesuit scientist-priest and the "plebian free-thinking intuitive English poet-novelist," there are a number of biographical and ideological points of comparison between Teilhard de Chardin and DHL. Both were "perceptive phenomenologists"; "for each, experience preceded rationalisation." Both sought a synthesis of experience which "gathers man, nature, and God into a personal, universalist, dynamic unity." In DHL's thought, "the feminine 'earth' element is prominent," while in Teilhard's "the masculine universal" predominates. Since Love was a "supreme dynamic" for both, "any misuse of this energy in its sexual form" was a " 'shocking waste' of a prime resource." In works such as Teilhard's ESQUISSE D'UN UNIVERS PERSONNEL, LE MILIEU DIVIN, and THE PHENOMENON OF MAN, and DHL's *Apocalypse,* both writers sought the cosmic sense, that " 'conscious affinity which binds us psychologically to the whole in which we are enveloped.' " "Both see the need for a personalized universal centre that will draw men upwards . . . towards itself and so towards their true selves. Teilhard places Christ at this centre," while DHL prefers the darker God of life, rather than the God of light. "As both were convinced of the need for a spiritual and cultural elite in society, a hierarchical structure" emerges in their writings: both "visions have in common--the vivifying centre, the surge of new vitality, the fusion of many men into a single, coordinated enterprise, the drawing of the concentric spheres upwards by the 'centre' into a cone with the maximum intensity at the apex," like DHL's "spiral flame." DHL, while acknowledging the collective, came back to an emphasis on the individual. Teilhard postulates an etherealized "telos," an "ecstasy" of man into God.

2765 Allott, Miriam. "Reviews," MODERN LANGUAGE REVIEW, LXI (Jan 1966), 120-22.

The Complete Poems of D. H. Lawrence, ed by Vivian de Sola Pinto and F. Warren Roberts, "may possibly satisfy the general reader but it will frustrate the serious student." Although it contains such new material as "over thirty pieces assigned to 1904-12" and a similar number of "Additional Pansies," this two-volume edition "is essentially an expansion of the existing three-volume Phoenix edition," fails to make use of some new manuscript material, and in the editorial commentary is often inconsistent or perfunctory.

2766 Amorós, Andrés. "Vitalismo Sexual" (Sexual Vitalism), INTRODUCCIÓN A LA NOVELA CONTEMPORÁNEA (Introduction to the Contemporary Novel) [1st ed., 1966 (not seen)], 2nd ed. (Salamanca, Spain: Ediciones Anaya, 1971), pp. 201-6.

DHL in *Lady Chatterley's Lover* and Henry Miller in TROPIC OF CANCER and TROPIC OF CAPRICORN sought to give a comprehensive treatment of sexuality. [In Spanish.]

2767 Andrews, W. T. "D. H. Lawrence's Favourite Jargon," NOTES AND QUERIES, ns XIII (March 1966), 97-98.

A study of DHL's "set vocabulary"--words suggesting irritation, anger, mockery, and cruelty, and then weariness and loneliness--reveals the "set pattern" for his characters: a "cycle of nervous excitement followed by frustration and apathy."

2768 Andrews, W. T. "D. H. Lawrence's Novels as Irritants," NOTES AND QUERIES, ns XIII (Nov 1966), 418-19.

Angry scenes in DHL's work, in which "characteristically irritable characters irritate one another," give his "work as a whole its strongly marked unity of tone and feeling." DHL uses these scenes to irritate his reader "into full participation" and ultimately into recognition of "the inevitable frictions" in the attempts of human beings to get into "touch."

2769 Barry, Sandra. "Singularity of Two; The Plurality of One," PAUNCH, No. 26 (April 1966), 34-39.

In *Aaron's Rod,* DHL demonstrates the equilibrium between the principles of Law (man acting according to his own nature) and Love (the spiritual which is abstract and beyond man).

2770 Battye, Louis. "The Chatterley Syndrome," STIGMA: THE EXPERIENCE OF DISABILITY (Lond, Dublin, Melbourne: Geoffrey Chapman, 1966), pp. 1-16.

[The author, himself "permanently disabled by a congenital neuro-muscular condition," uses the word "cripple" throughout to describe Sir Clifford Chatterley.] Although he at first tries to be "fair" in his characterization of Clifford in *Lady Chatterley's Lover,* "Lawrence's irrational 'philosophy' of the physical, the sensual and the intuitive deeply prejudiced him against the abnormal," a bias evident in the shift of sympathy from Clifford to Connie. "Even Sir Clifford's attempt to fulfil himself by becoming a writer is neatly turned against him." The "process of denigration" continues, at first with "subtlety, then with increasing crudeness and brutality," culminating in "Mellors's elegant statement that his employer has 'no balls.' " This love triangle is a perfectly allowable theme in fiction, calling for compassion toward all three characters. But in DHL's "pagan hymn to physical love . . . a feeble broken body [is] an insult to the dark gods," "the primitive belief that a weak, malformed and ugly body probably enshrines a weak, malformed and ugly soul." [Detailed discussion of the real situation of the "cripple," who "wants to resume his former social, sexual and emotional life," but who finds others' love for him "inevitably . . . adulterated with pity."] DHL saw clearly "our essential irrelevance to the real business of living, and brutally though he expressed that terrible vision, we should be grateful to him."

2771 Bedient, Calvin. "The Radicalism of *Lady Chatterley's Lover*," HUDSON REVIEW, XIX (Autumn 1966), 407-16; extensively rvd and rptd as Chap. VII: "Oliver & Constance / John Thomas & Lady Jane," in ARCHITECTS OF THE SELF: GEORGE ELIOT, D. H. LAWRENCE, AND E. M. FORSTER, by Calvin Bedient (Berkeley, Los Angeles, and Lond: University of California P, 1972), pp. 172-82.

Lady Chatterley's Lover was brought to trial in Britain on the "wrong charge," for though "not pornographic, it is subversive" in its intention not to corrupt but "to eradicate the sense of morality altogether--to exclude from experience the conceptualization and codification of good and evil." DHL's radicalism may be seen in his "wish to de-create the ego."

2772 Blissett, William. "D. H. Lawrence, D'Annunzio, Wagner," WISCONSIN STUDIES IN CONTEMPORARY LITERATURE, VII (Winter-Spring 1966), 21-46.

The "important influence and analogue" for *The Trespasser* is "not Helen Corke but Gabriele D'Annunzio," whose emphasis on "blood, the mindless, flow" drew DHL's "troubled admiration." "Apart from D'Annunzio," DHL is "almost untouched by the many attempts to use Wagnerian themes, myths, or techniques in literature." Though he was aware of "the depth of German irrationalism" and shared the "visionary and inward" in German culture, DHL differed from Wagner in aspiring neither to the " 'condition of music' " nor to " 'total art' " in his writing. [Isolates Wagnerian elements in *The Trespasser* and in other fiction and several poems.]

2773 Burns, Wayne. "*Lady Chatterley's Lover*: A PILGRIM'S PROGRESS for Our Time," PAUNCH, No. 26 (April 1966), 16-33.

Although DHL had expressed his philosophy in *Fantasia of the Unconscious*, it was not until *Lady Chatterley's Lover* that he gave full and direct expression to the concept of the good life. [Quotes extensive extracts from *Fantasia, Lady Chatterley,* and DHL's letters.]

2774 Cameron, Mary Carolyn Davis. "The Reputation of D. H. Lawrence: 1912-1960," DISSERTATION ABSTRACTS, XXVII (1966), 176A. Unpublished dissertation, Yale University, 1966.

2775 Cavitch, David Berl. "D. H. Lawrence and the New World," DISSERTATION ABSTRACTS, XXVII (1966), 1052A. Unpublished dissertation, University of California at Berkeley, 1966. Rvd and pub as D. H. LAWRENCE AND THE NEW WORLD (NY: Oxford UP, 1969).

2776 Cavitch, David Berl. "Solipsism and Death in D. H. Lawrence's Late Works," MASSACHUSETTS REVIEW, VII (Spring 1966), 495-508; rvd and rptd as Chap. VIII: "An Exit from the Fallen Self," in D. H. LAWRENCE AND THE NEW WORLD, by David Cavitch (NY: Oxford U P, 1969), pp. 194-218.

Lady Chatterley's Lover marks a retreat from mimetic representation of life and the end of DHL's search for a world of communal experience. Mellors's situation at the end "implies the stability of maternal rather than conjugal relations." *The Man Who Died* shows a similar rejection of direct, personal relationships: the Man's fatherhood "points to his prenatal identification." The later DHL shows little interest in actual examination of the world. The inward turning is evident in *Pansies* in DHL's impatience with objective reality. *Last Poems* and *Etruscan Places* draw on immediate knowledge of the preparations for dying. In "Bavarian Gentians" words express facts of consciousness without being outwardly referential symbols. Only death "could finally promise Lawrence to remove the basic human sense of self-division and alienation from the life of the body" after hope is abandoned for improved sexual and social human relationships.

2777 Cohn, Dorrit. "Narrated Monologue: Definition of a Fictional Style," COMPARATIVE LITERATURE, XVIII (Spring 1966), 97-112.

DHL's rendering of Kate Leslie's consciousness in *The Plumed Serpent* is one example of *erlebte Rede*, "the rendering of a character's thoughts in his own idiom, while maintaining the third-person form of narration."

2778 Corsani, Mary. "D. H. Lawrence traduttore dall'italiano" (D. H. Lawrence as Translator from the Italian), ENGLISH MISCELLANY (Rome), XVII (1966), 249-78.

DHL's translation of Giovanni Verga's *Mastro-Don Gesualdo* shows some imperfections but many positive aspects, such as quick and captivating narration and a characteristic rendering of dialogue. The *Little Novels of Sicily*, on the contrary, though less flawed is more confused and fails to give a realistic picture of the environment. *The Story of Doctor Manente* by Lasca shows how well DHL has learned the art of translation. He succeeds in reproducing the short story style, the liveliness of Tuscan speech, and the atmosphere of sixteenth-century Florence. [In Italian.]

2779 Cox, C. B. "Lawrence's Vicious Art," SPECTATOR, CCXVI (24 June 1966), 797.

Post-Leavis criticism tends to minimize the vicious, destructive impulses in DHL's art. The defence witnesses at the censorship trial of *Lady Chatterley's Lover* (Regina v. Penguin Books, Ltd., 1960) had to make DHL acceptable to society at the expense of diluting the full force of his genius. Although at his best DHL "presents an extraordinary interplay of realism and myth, combining reverence for what things are with a mystical vision of what they might be, . . . the impossibility of actualising his vision . . . drove him to despair." [Review of Keith Sagar, THE ART OF D. H. LAWRENCE (1966); Anthony West, D. H. LAWRENCE (1950, rptd 1966); and David J. Gordon, D. H. LAWRENCE AS A LITERARY CRITIC (1966).]

2780 Cummins, P. D. "*Sons and Lovers*/D. H. Lawrence," 100 GREAT BOOKS: MASTERPIECES OF ALL TIME (Lond: Odhams Books, 1966; rptd, 1967), pp. 464-69.
[Brief account of DHL's early life as it is related in *Sons and Lovers*, emphasizing his mother's "indomitable will" and "stubborn self-sacrifice" in seeing that her sons did not go to the pits, DHL's early delicacy and later illness, his adolescent friendship with Jessie Chambers, who encouraged his writing and on whom the character of Miriam is based, the deaths of his brother Ernest and his mother.] "The first half of *Sons and Lovers* is entirely autobiographical." "The first, and by far the finest, of the novels whose theme is the Oedipus complex," it handles "the tragic relationship between mother and son . . . with great restraint, without sentimentality or self-pity." DHL's later belief "that he had treated his father too harshly in *Sons and Lovers* . . . is unjustified."

2781 Davie, Donald. "Sincerity and Poetry," MICHIGAN QUARTERLY REVIEW, V (Winter 1966), 3-8; rptd with minor changes as "On Sincerity: From Wordsworth to Ginsberg," ENCOUNTER, XXXI (Oct 1968), 61-66; largely incorporated in "A Doggy Demos: Hardy and Lawrence," THOMAS HARDY AND BRITISH POETRY, by Donald Davie (NY: Oxford UP, 1972; Lond: Routledge & Kegan Paul, 1973), pp. 130-51.
Kenneth Rexroth's Introduction to *D. H. Lawrence: Selected Poems* implies that DHL is always sincere, while Hardy is not, in that DHL's "I" is always himself. While Pound's "persona," Yeats's "mask," and Eliot's notion of the "dramatic" in poetry combine to put the confessional out of bounds and make the question of sincerity impertinent and illegitimate, sincerity is clearly important in Lowell, Ginsberg, and DHL. Although acceptance of the poetic life as more important than the poems it produces is filled with dangers, it must be welcomed. The biographer must be reinstated, and confessional poetry must be read as autobiography, with more attention to tone and less to irony and paradox.

2782 Dawson, E[ugene] W. "Lawrence's Pollyanalytic Esthetic for the Novel," PAUNCH, No. 26 (April 1966), 60-68.
The basis for DHL's esthetic for the novel is expressed in "The Novel": he insists that it be (1) quick, (2) interrelated in all parts, vitally and organically, and (3) honorable.

2783 Decker, Randall E. (ed). "D. H. Lawrence," PATTERNS OF EXPOSITION (Bost: Little, Brown, 1966), p. 223.
In "New Mexico" [which is reprinted in the anthology, pp. 223-30], "the vividness and natural spontaneity of style which is characteristic of Lawrence's writing" is exemplified. [Brief headnote.]

2784 DeNitto, Dennis. "Modern Literary Primitivism in the Writings of D. H. Lawrence and Other British Novelists," DISSERTATION ABSTRACTS, XXVII (1967), 3867A. Unpublished dissertation, Columbia University, 1966.

2785 Doheny, John. "The Novel Is the Book of Life: D. H. Lawrence and a Revised Version of Polymorphous Perversity," PAUNCH, No. 26 (April 1966), 40-59.

Sons and Lovers clarifies some confusion created in Norman O. Brown's LIFE AGAINST DEATH by Brown's exclusive reference to poetry for his theory of literature. Had he discussed the novel, Brown's conclusion would have been significantly different.

2786 Draper, R[onald] P. "The Defeat of Feminism: D. H. Lawrence's *The Fox* and 'The Woman Who Rode Away,'" STUDIES IN SHORT FICTION, III (1966), 186-98.

The Fox and "The Woman Who Rode Away," though cruder in their "anti-feminist attitude" than *The Rainbow* and *Women in Love,* have two "important compensating qualities." First, from the woman's defeat comes the recovery of "her lost self," a theme which, though it distorts masculine and feminine roles, releases DHL's "own feminine awareness in passages of great visionary power." Second, DHL pushes "to an extreme the more reactionary view of woman" and exposes "the extravagances and vindictive motivation of this view." In *The Fox,* some of Banford's criticisms of Henry's bullying do apply, and despite Henry's efforts to dominate, neither March nor DHL can " 'tell what it will be like over there.' " March's final reluctance to submit to her husband is "a sign of health." More extreme in its anti-feminism, "The Woman Who Rode Away" repeats "on a larger mythical scale" the "contradictions" of *The Fox*: again the woman is "the object of compassionate rescue and of vindictive outrage." [Detailed analyses of both stories reveal DHL's ambivalent views.]

2787 Draper, R[onald] P. "Satire as a Form of Sympathy: D. H. Lawrence as a Satirist," RENAISSANCE AND MODERN ESSAYS: PRESENTED TO VIVIAN DE SOLA PINTO IN CELEBRATION OF HIS SEVENTIETH BIRTHDAY, ed by G. R. Hibbard (Lond: Routledge & Kegan Paul, 1966), pp. 189-97.

Satire, for DHL, is the coupling of antipathy and sympathy, of recoil and flow. It is best sustained in "The Man Who Loved Islands," in which "tragic implications release a sympathetic flow."

2788 Draper, R[onald] P. "A Short Guide to D. H. Lawrence Studies," CRITICAL SURVEY, II (Summer 1966), 222-26.

[A brief, interpretive and evaluative survey of major primary and secondary DHL materials.]

2789 Earl, G. A. "Correspondence," CAMBRIDGE QUARTERLY, I (Summer 1966), 273-75.

[Letter to the Editor in reply to J. C. F. Littlewood, "D. H. Lawrence's Early

Tales," CAMBRIDGE QUARTERLY, I (Spring 1966), 107-24, disputing Littlewood's statement that in the back-washing scene in "Daughters of the Vicar" DHL has made "his characters live and respond from their real selves, in wholeness."] The back-washing scene in "Daughters of the Vicar" is "forced and unconvincing." There are better passages in this work than those selected by Littlewood to demonstrate its virtues.

2790 Eccles, David McA., 1st Viscount. HALF-WAY TO FAITH (Lond: Bles; Phila: Westminster P, 1966), pp. 62-64, 112.

In his Introduction to Dostoevsky's THE GRAND INQUISITOR, "D. H. Lawrence ... considers that as between reality and illusion the Grand Inquisitor was right to attribute the illusion to Christ and the reality to the Church." Picking up "an interesting point made by the Grand Inquisitor," DHL "rides off on his hobby horse and asserts that if men prefer ... 'vivid life' to the accumulation of property they will be real men and happy in the fulfilment of their physical and spiritual nature."

2791 Efron, Arthur. "Lady Chatterley's Lecher," PAUNCH, No. 26 (April 1966), 14-15.

[Reply to Eliseo Vivas, D. H. LAWRENCE: THE FAILURE AND THE TRIUMPH OF ART (1960).] Vivas's chapter on *Lady Chatterley's Lover* is "one of the strangest critical performances in print." He misunderstands DHL's sexual ethic and states that it is of virtually no interest.

2792 Egashira, Teruo. "*Koisuru Onnatachi* no Shudai" (The Theme of *Women in Love*), HUMAN STUDIES (Kanagawa University), No. 32 (Feb 1966), 33-63.

[In Japanese.]

2793 Englander, Ann. "D. H. Lawrence: Technique as Evasion," DISSERTATION ABSTRACTS, XXVII (1967), 2528A. Unpublished dissertation, Northwestern University, 1966.

2794 Fedder, Norman J. THE INFLUENCE OF D. H. LAWRENCE ON TENNESSEE WILLIAMS (The Hague: Mouton, 1966).

Both DHL and Williams suffered childhood poverty and illness, had parents who were hopelessly incompatible, and grew to Oedipal maturity in sordid industrial environments. In their work, both were antimaterialists who sought a meaningful balance between intellectuality and sensuality. But whereas Williams is compassionate toward fragmented people in his work, DHL is contemptuous toward them in his. Whereas Williams encourages perverted sexuality and promiscuity, DHL found both intolerable and destructive; there is a clear distinction between *Blutbrüderschaft* and homosexuality, which DHL saw as a "hopeless sin." Both artists were fascinated by the awakening or destruction of the virginal figure: in treatment of this theme, DHL's *Sons and Lovers* and "The Princess" parallel Williams's "The Important Thing" and THE NIGHT OF THE IGUANA. In I RISE IN FLAME, CRIED THE PHOENIX, Williams concentrates on DHL's tangential obsessions and uses Huxley's edition of DHL's letters as primary source, but the play is such that Frieda's Preface refutes the work it introduces. Various superficial plot and thematic parallels suggest Williams's kinship and indebtedness to DHL: the collections of one-act plays, AMERICAN BLUES and 27 WAGONS FULL OF COTTON, contain incidental echoes of Laurencian themes such as condemnation of decaying values and of industrialism as the real enemy, and one short play, "The Purification," is set in Taos. BATTLE OF ANGELS, rewritten as ORPHEUS DESCENDING, a retelling of the Easter story, includes a marauding fox as in *The Fox*, a wearer of a snakeskin jacket recalling the symbolic reptile in "Snake," a Christ-figure identified with phallic consciousness as in *The Man Who Died,* and an invalid husband whose wife is awakened by a lower-class lover "who has been connected in the past to a neurotically possessive woman" as in *Lady Chatterley's Lover,* though Williams's morbid tone and his working out of the action preclude complete parallel with that novel. The family situation in THE GLASS MENAGERIE corresponds to that in *Sons and Lovers.* The sympathy and morbidity in A STREETCAR NAMED DESIRE recall "The Princess." The flesh versus spirit conflict in SUMMER AND SMOKE and THE ROSE TATTOO are essentially Laurencian. The dark vision of society in CAMINO REAL resembles DHL's in *St. Mawr.* In SWEET BIRD OF YOUTH, a spokesman for tenderness as preferable to rape sounds Laurencian. YOU TOUCHED ME! is an adaptation by Williams and Donald Windham of DHL's story of the same title, though it draws also on *The Fox.* But for all their similarities, DHL and Williams are ultimately different: DHL wrote essentially of wholeness and what should be, whereas Williams concentrates on abnormal human psychology and what is. The Laurencian correspondences are noticeably diminished in Williams's later works.

2795 Foster, Joseph. "First Winter," SOUTH DAKOTA REVIEW, IV (Summer 1966), 29-34; rptd in D. H. LAWRENCE IN TAOS, by Joseph Foster (Albuquerque: University of New Mexico P, 1972), 47-56.

In a log cabin 8,500 feet up a mountain, DHL and Frieda spent the winter of 1922-1923 with two Danish artists, Knud Merrild and Kai Götzsche. They had concerts in the cold winter evenings and arguments about art. The Danes were ordinary men, and DHL could get along with them. He said of his time in Taos, " 'for *greatest* of beauty I have never experienced anything like New Mexico.' "

2796 Fricker, Robert. "David Herbert Lawrence," DER MODERNE ENGLISCHE ROMAN (The Modern English Novel) [1st ed, 1958 (unseen)] ; 2nd ed (Göttingen, 1966), pp. 123-38.

Criticism of modern life and the attempt to close the gap between nature and man are the main themes of DHL's novels. At his best in those novels in which his prophecy does not dominate the tale (*Sons and Lovers, The Rainbow, Women in Love*), Lawrence employs a technique characterized by the open end, variety in perspectives, direct presentation, and a loose structure. In *Sons and Lovers* he shows the artistic and psychological development of the main character. In *The Rainbow* he describes the self-finding process of the individual without offering solutions. He searches for an ideal interpersonal relationship in *Women in Love,* and in *The Plumed Serpent* he uses Aztec rituals to add cosmic dimensions to human love relations. *Lady Chatterley's Lover* focuses on phallic tenderness, making the psychological analysis only a minor matter. [In German.]

2797 Friedman, Alan. "D. H. Lawrence: 'The Wave Which Cannot Halt,'" THE TURN OF THE NOVEL (Lond and NY: Oxford UP, 1966), pp. 130-78; excerpt rvd and rptd as "Suspended Form: Lawrence's Theory of Fiction in *Women in Love*," in TWENTIETH CENTURY INTERPRETATIONS OF "WOMEN IN LOVE": A COLLECTION OF CRITICAL ESSAYS, ed by Stephen J. Miko (Englewood Cliffs, NJ: Prentice-Hall, 1969), pp. 40-49.

Some DHL critics regard the conclusion to *The Rainbow* as unsatisfactorily tentative, but the novel shows clearly that whatever is perfected has been a failure since it has not led into the unknown. The rhythmic inconclusiveness of the novel leaves Ursula at the end unfulfilled but waiting with rich potentiality. This rhythm begins with the early Brangwen men, who feel in the passing seasons "'the wave which cannot halt.'" Numerous crucial passages from *The Rainbow* and *Women in Love* demonstrate DHL's planned thrusts toward a necessary tentativeness of the sort typical of the open form novel. This tentativeness is not accounted for artistically in *Sons and Lovers*. DHL's most startling innovation is his use of the stream of unconsciousness, a phenomenon that represents the most original quality in DHL, though it is manifested in conventional syntax, which he can use because he is presenting feelings themselves as metaphors for something in the dark, beyond feeling.

2798 Gomme, Andor. ATTITUDES TO CRITICISM, with a Preface by Harry T. Moore (Carbondale and Edwardsville: Southern Illinois UP, 1966), pp. 6-7, 127, 131-32, 136-37, 153n.

In his essay "John Galsworthy," DHL emphasizes the importance of emotion rather than reason in literary criticism. The religious element in F. R. Leavis's criticism, as exemplified in his treatment of the "transcendent" quality of certain passages in *The Rainbow,* is related to "the experience of his study of Lawrence," who had called himself "'a passionately religious man.'"

2799 Gordon, David J. D. H. LAWRENCE AS A LITERARY CRITIC (New Haven and Lond: Yale UP [Yale Studies in English Vol. 161], 1966).

DHL's criticism, as represented by *Studies in Classic American Literature, Phoenix,* and scattered remarks in his letters, nonfiction, fiction, and verse, is a major part of his achievement. Though his "primary interests" are in nineteenth- and twentieth-century American, English, Russian, and Italian literature, the novel, and "the relation of art to morality," all his criticism goes beyond formalistic explication and analysis. He developed a "flexible, freewheeling form of [the] critical essay" to explore the relation of art "to the civilization of which it is a vital expression." Believing that "'art-speech is the only truth,'" DHL tried to "reveal deeper and truer implications of a work than the artist himself may have been conscious of." With "'life'" or "'true emotion'" as his standard of value, DHL "read literature mainly as a diagnosis of our psychic illness," often taking for granted "the necessary truth of art," while being enraged by the "falsehood" he detected even in works he admired. Though not "logically consistent," even on its own premises, DHL's criticism, once understood, is "fundamentally coherent." Basically, DHL sought "the Romantic idea of a new center of consciousness" which could transcend "the dualism of mind and body and be the basis for a new idea of community." In DHL's aesthetic, his "theoretical antagonism to traditional form" in the novel, his preference for symbolism over allegory, and his objection to the "subjectification of the outer world" in Romantic poetry, all stem from his "root belief" that " 'life' " is the primary value, a "dynamic conflict of energies" that cannot be permanently conceptualized or formalized. His "lifelong quarrel with the tragic" as artistic mode, as seen in his criticism of Tolstoi and Hardy, results from his "conception of man's nature as radically innocent, of his history as a fall from a recoverable glory, and of his destiny as infinite human possibility." In his treatment of myth and history, DHL's "Romantic view" of a "historical Fall" is less "coherent" than Yeats's and less "plausible" than Eliot's but qualified by a skepticism that made him "unwilling to imagine an ideality beyond" the possible or to maintain "his dream of a perfect art and a perfect society as his personal hope for wholeness and perfection of being came to seem more frail." In history and literature, DHL saw "heroes of death," those who extend human consciousness by destroying dead forms by tragedy or satire, like Dostoevsky, Poe, Hawthorne and Melville, or Hemingway and Huxley, and "heroes of rebirth." DHL's changing views on Whitman illustrate this process and reveal "the limits of ideological criticism." DHL is perhaps the "last Romantic, the last of those radical individualists who set themselves against an entire culture and still stood for something meaningful."

2800 Gordon, David J. "Lawrence as Playwright," NATION (NY), CCII (6 June 1966), 686-87.

Of the eight plays and two fragments collected in *The Complete Plays of D. H. Lawrence*, *The Widowing of Mrs. Holroyd* and *David* "can hold their own in the literature of modern drama." "Both the language and the theme of the Biblical play *David* . . . are in Lawrence's prophetic strain, but with enough modulation of mood, diction, scene and event to make it genuinely dramatic." *Touch and Go* "might be more successful if it were truly a social drama" rather than trying to show that both masters and men should "rise above" the " 'petty' issue" of money and "fight about 'vital beliefs.' " [Touches briefly on several other plays.]

2801 Gordon, David J. "Two Anti-Puritan Puritans: Bernard Shaw and D. H. Lawrence," YALE REVIEW, LVI (Autumn 1966), 76-90.

The anti-Puritans Bernard Shaw and DHL were "as opposed to libertinism and materialism as they were to purity and idealism." Both sought to resolve the conflict between flesh and spirit and felt that strength of will could overcome any evil. Each replaced Victorianism with a "new center . . . of values" based on vital energy.

2802 Gregor, Ian. "What Kind of Fiction Did Hardy Write?" ESSAYS IN CRITICISM, XVI (July 1966), 290-308, espec pp. 293-95.

Both Thomas Hardy and DHL write fiction in which the author's "presence" is important, not as a filter through which the novel is presented, as in Fielding and George Eliot, but as "participant, undergoing the experience of the book with the characters." "The sense of necessary law engraved on one's being . . . dominates the vision of both writers." Although Lettie, Miriam, and Ursula were created "in the shadow of Sue Bridehead," "Lawrence could never accept the tragic conclusion, so apparent in Hardy."

2803 Halperin, Irving. "Unity in *St. Mawr*," SOUTH DAKOTA REVIEW, IV (Summer 1966), 58-60.

St. Mawr, though criticized for lack of unity, is coherently structured around Lou Carrington's journey from Bloomsbury to Las Chivas, a journey of two movements: "first, a strong horizontal one evolving out of Lou's flight from London; and second, a sharply rising movement emergent upon Lou's ascent to Las Chivas."

2804 Harrison, John R. "D. H. Lawrence," THE REACTIONARIES: YEATS, LEWIS, POUND, ELIOT, LAWRENCE: A STUDY OF THE ANTI-DEMOCRATIC INTELLIGENTSIA (Lond: Gollancz, 1966; NY: Schocken Books, 1967), pp. 163-89.

DHL, the most doctrinaire of the writers considered, thought himself prophet, savior, and artist in residence in a superficial society in which industrialism, materialism, and faith in scientific discovery were destroying the sense of wonder so basic to imaginative creativity. Although there is an unattractive vein of self-pity in DHL's works, his basic criticism of the deadening effects of mechanization, materialism, and sexual repression--all inherited from the nineteenth century--is valid. But his remedies are vague or unsatisfactory, the "most obvious objection" to them being that in "the kind of society that Lawrence would like to establish . . . anarchy is always just around the corner." Similarly, while DHL is able to depict failed relationships with sensitivity and vigor, "there are few, if any, convincing portraits" of successful personal relationships. DHL's thwarted quests for a satisfactory society, his consistent equation of democracy (mob rule and mongrelism) with rule by Jewish financiers, and his increasing emphasis on blood sacrifice to appease the dark gods are basic to his works after *Kangaroo*. DHL sought to restore freedom and spontaneity to literature and life, recognized natural superiority as preferable to elected authority, and thought that both could proceed from his love ethic (man-woman, man-man relationships) and could change the world. DHL's emphasis on innate, natural superiority and his contempt for those who would destroy the strong reveal his affinities for and tendencies toward fascism.

2805 Harvey, R. W. "On Lawrence's 'Bavarian Gentians,'" WASCANA REVIEW, I (1966), 74-86.

Free verse, for DHL, never implied lack of art or of work. An examination of the development of "Bavarian Gentians" from its early form as "Glory of Darkness" shows DHL finding out the laws, correcting his tone, structure, and images to achieve "direct utterance."

2806 Häusermann, H. W. "D. H. Lawrence als Dramatiker" (D. H. Lawrence as Playwright), NEUE ZÜRCHER ZEITUNG (1 Jan 1966).

The themes of DHL's ten plays, written between 1912 and 1926, are closely related to the major ideas of his fiction. His plays show that the author attempts to deviate from the realistic tradition of Shavian drama. [In German.]

2807 Heilbut, Anthony Otto. "The Prose of D. H. Lawrence." Unpublished dissertation, Harvard University, 1966. [Listed in Lawrence F. McNamee, DISSERTATIONS IN ENGLISH AND

AMERICAN LITERATURE (NY and Lond: Bowker, 1969), p. 247.]

2808 Hendrick, George. "Jesus and the Osiris-Isis Myth: Lawrence's *The Man Who Died* and Williams's THE NIGHT OF THE IGUANA," ANGLIA (Tübingen), LXXXIV, Nos. 3-4 (1966), 398-406.

Tennessee Williams's THE NIGHT OF THE IGUANA is a deliberate and striking adaptation of DHL's *The Man Who Died*, which it parallels in plot, character, and theme. Both Shannon, the defrocked minister, and the Man Who Died, risen without a mission, suggest Osiris. In the play, Maxine and Hannah are Isis figures, and Judith Fellows plots Shannon's destruction as Judas plotted Jesus'. Other parallels include the giving of the keys (of the kingdom and of the bus), a mock crucifixion, and an act of grace (the releasing of the iguana and of the gamecock as symbols of the phallic reality in the Osiris myth). The central theme of the play, as of the novel, is how to live beyond despair and still live.

2809 Heywood, C[hristopher]. "D. H. Lawrence's *The Lost Girl* and Its Antecedents by George Moore and Arnold Bennett," ENGLISH STUDIES (Amsterdam), XLVII (1966), 131-34.

Most of the many textual resemblances between *The Lost Girl* and Arnold Bennett's ANNA OF THE FIVE TOWNS are superficial because DHL felt that Bennett had not provided "a great kick against misery." The resemblances of DHL's novel to George Moore's A MUMMER'S WIFE are more substantial in that DHL's purpose was to restore fuller and more explicit treatment of the heroine's conflict. [Numerous parallels between *The Lost Girl* and ANNA OF THE FIVE TOWNS and between *The Lost Girl* and A MUMMER'S WIFE are cited.]

2810 Hirashima, Junko. "D. H. Lawrence: *The Rainbow* no Buntai" (D. H. Lawrence: The Style of *The Rainbow*), BAIKA JOSHIDAIGAKU BUNGAKUBU KIYÔ (Baika Joshidaigaku), No. 3 (Dec 1966), 103-38.

[In Japanese.]

2811 Hobsbaum, Philip. "D. H. Lawrence," TIMES LITERARY SUPPLEMENT (Lond), 10 Nov 1966, p. 1023.

[Letter to the Editor in reply to Martin Secker, "D. H. Lawrence," TIMES LITERARY SUPPLEMENT (Lond), 3 Nov 1966, p. 1012. Asking on what information Secker bases his opinion that Clement Shorter is the informer who initiated proceedings against *The Rainbow*, the author says that "all the available facts point to the National Purity League, in the person of its solicitor, Herbert Muskett as the complainant" (evidence cited). See also reply by John Worthen, "D. H. Lawrence," TIMES LITERARY SUPPLEMENT (Lond), 10 Nov 1966, p. 1023; and response by Martin Secker, "D. H. Lawrence," TIMES LITERARY SUPPLEMENT (Lond), 17 Nov 1966, p. 1052.]

2812 Holton, Milne. "Book Reviews," MODERN LANGUAGE

JOURNAL, L (April 1966), 232-33.
The Symbolic Meaning: The Uncollected Versions of "Studies in Classic American Literature," ed by Armin Arnold, collects DHL's early versions of thirteen essays on American literature. "It seems perfectly clear that the essays in their original state are superior as criticism to those published in 1923."

2813 Hudspeth, Robert N. "Duality as Theme and Technique in D. H. Lawrence's 'The Border Line,' " STUDIES IN SHORT FICTION, IV (1966), 51-56.

In "The Border Line," DHL uses duality both "as an aesthetic principle and as a philosophic belief." Katherine Farquhar's two husbands--Alan, masculine in attitude, and Philip, passively meek and "feminine"--represent "possible alternatives" in her "quest for fulfillment." The structure of the story follows Katherine's flight from Philip to Alan," from "illusion to reality," a journey that is "a metaphor for her psychic transformation." The central image, the border line, indicates "the penalty that comes" to those like Philip who cannot "maintain the correct human duality" and "blur the distinctions between masculine and feminine roles."

2814 Irie, Takanori. "Lawrence to Rilke--Shi no Mondai o Megutte" (Lawrence and Rilke--On the Problem of Death), METROPOLITAN (Tôkyô Metropolitan University), XI (1966), 12-23.
[In Japanese.]

2815 Ishikawa, Masafumi. "D. H. Lawrence Kenkyû Shojosaku *Shirokujaku* ni Tsuite" (A Study of D. H. Lawrence, His First Novel: *The White Peacock*), KYÛSHÛ SANGYÔ DAIGAKU KYÔYÔBU KIYÔ (Kyûshû Sangyô University), III (Dec 1966), 69-82.
[In Japanese.]

2816 Itô, Hidekazu. "D. H. Lawrence to Kodoku" (Solitude in D. H. Lawrence), STUDIES IN LANGUAGE AND LITERATURE (Science University of Tôkyô), No. 1 (Dec 1966), 67-88.
[In Japanese.]

2817 Iwata, Noboru. "*St. Mawr* Sairon (II)" (On *St. Mawr* Again [II]), BULLETIN OF THE FACULTY OF LITERATURE (Aichi Prefectural University), No. 17 (Dec 1966), 39-58.
[In Japanese.]

2818 Kai, Sadanobu. "Kyôbô na Junreikô no Ato o Otte--Cornwall" (After the Savage Pilgrimage--Cornwall), STUDIES IN FOREIGN LITERATURES (Ritsumeikan University), No. 12 (May 1966), 1-11.
[In Japanese.]

2819 Kamimura, Tatsuhiko. " 'Kokkyôsen' to D. H. Lawrence" ('The Border Line' and D. H. Lawrence), ENGLISH LITERATURE

REVIEW (Kyôto Women's University), No. 10 (Feb 1966), 11-27. [In Japanese.]

2820 Kaplan, Harold J. "The Naturalist Theology of D. H. Lawrence," THE PASSIVE VOICE: AN APPROACH TO MODERN FICTION (Athens, OH: Ohio UP, 1966), pp. 159-85.

In DHL's fiction, character is not reality but a mask that substitutes for nature and therefore denies a valid life. The hero triumphs when his under-life breaks through the mask and mingles in the vital stream of being, penetrates the solipsistic barrier, and releases human awareness from subjectivity, achieving an "anthropomorphic communication with nature." Only a few of DHL's characters overcome the threat of solipsism, for the price is a struggle too complicated for most people since it involves the theological principles of a private, naturalist myth. The interior force in DHL's characters is so magnified in focus that the active personality as such dissolves into a natural immanence, making it difficult to conceive of them properly as characters. In DHL, the mimetic sensibility pursues immediacy to the point of vanishing into nature, suggesting an ultimate passivity or abstraction in his work. [Contains detailed analysis of "The Prussian Officer."]

2821 Kay, Wallace G. "The Cortege of Dionysus: Lawrence and Giono," SOUTHERN QUARTERLY, IV (Jan 1966), 159-71.

DHL and Jean Giono share the use of both stylistic and biographical characteristics in their development of the Dionysian myth. [Works discussed include DHL's *The Rainbow, Women in Love, The Fox, St. Mawr, The Plumed Serpent,* and *The Man Who Died,* and Giono's LE CHANT DU MONDE, QUE MA JOIE DEMEUSE, and REGAIN.] [See also Wallace G. Kay, "Dionysus, D. H. Lawrence, and Jean Giono: Further Consideration," SOUTHERN QUARTERLY, VI (April 1968), 394-414.]

2822 Kitchin, Laurence. "Colliers," LISTENER AND BBC TELEVISION REVIEW, LXXV (28 April 1966), 618-19.

DHL, who came out of the mining country, achieved in *Sons and Lovers* a novel that has become the most authoritative record of a now nearly extinct breed of men--the colliers--providing data not only on the everyday life of a colliery community but also on the miners themselves, as personified in Walter Morel. With *Lady Chatterley's Lover* the intimacy of the earlier novel has been replaced by the detached view of Mellors on dehumanization. [Literary discussion in a social context.]

2823 Kurono, Yutaka. "*The Rainbow* ni Okeru Byôshahô (D. H. Lawrence no Gengo ni Taisuru Shisei)" (Descriptions in *The Rainbow*: D. H. Lawrence's Attitude toward the Efficacy of Words), SPES (Okayama University), No. 1 (July 1966), 19-20.

[In Japanese.]

2824 "Language and Literature," CHOICE, III (Oct 1966), 644.

The White Peacock, as reissued by Southern Illinois UP (1966), "restores the original passages" bowdlerized in the corrupt text of the Heinemann edition.

2825 Le Breton, Georges. "D. H. Lawrence et l'architecture du roman" (D. H. Lawrence and the Architecture of the Novel), PREUVES, No. 189 (Nov 1966), 70-73.

[This article begins with commentary on Keith Sagar, THE ART OF D. H. LAWRENCE (1966). After quoting from DHL's letters some of his conceptions of the novel, the author wonders that the writers of the "new novel," particularly Nathalie Sarraute and Alain Robbe-Grillet, never mention DHL's name. DHL's structural use of symbols and myths is discussed, with *The Plumed Serpent* cited as illustration.] [In French.]

2826 Lee, Brian. "America, My America," RENAISSANCE AND MODERN ESSAYS: PRESENTED TO VIVIAN DE SOLA PINTO IN CELEBRATION OF HIS SEVENTIETH BIRTHDAY, ed by G. R. Hibbard (Lond: Routledge & Kegan Paul, 1966), pp. 181-88.

DHL interprets the history of America through his own law on the duality of passions and thinks that American colonists sought not only religious freedom but also its opposite, religious oppression. Seen through this filter, the history of America as presented in *Studies in Classic American Literature* is distorted. Differences between the first and second versions of these essays are differences of tone; DHL, in the revised version, evaluates American writers in terms of the principle of realism, comparing the myth to the reality.

2827 Levin, Harry. "The Unbanning of the Books," ATLANTIC MONTHLY, CCXVII (Feb 1966), 77-81; rptd in expanded form in REFRACTIONS: ESSAYS IN COMPARATIVE LITERATURE, by Harry Levin (NY: Oxford UP, 1966), pp. 296-307.

[A discussion of the "unbanning" of James Joyce's ULYSSES, DHL's *Lady Chatterley's Lover*, and Henry Miller's TROPIC OF CANCER after their respective censorship trials.] Although he "was less the dispassionate artist than James Joyce," "Lawrence was a passionate moralist, who preached his unorthodox message with evangelical fervor, and therein lay the strength that could be rallied to his support when *Lady Chatterley's Lover* went on trial at the Old Bailey" in Regina v. Penguin Books, Ltd., "the test case under the new Obscene Publications Act of 1959." "Joyce and Lawrence, each in his unique way, could realize their talents only through expatriation." "The battles for Joyce (inclusion of sex as part of the all-round picture), Lawrence (emphasis on sex as a means of salvation), and Miller (obsession with sex as a nihilistic gesture) have opened the floodgates" to the publication of such works as Vladimir Nabokov's LOLITA and William Burroughs's NAKED LUNCH.

2828 Lid, R. W. (ed). THE SHORT STORY: CLASSIC AND CONTEMPORARY (Phila, NY, and Toronto: J. B. Lippincott, 1966), pp. 185-86.

[Brief headnote.] "The main subject of D. H. Lawrence's fiction is the nature of love, what it can do, what thwarts it, what makes it possible." Although "the realism of the opening pages of 'The Horse Dealer's Daughter' [which is reprinted in the anthology, pp. 186-204] may seem at first in sharp contrast to the events with which the story ends," these too are, in a sense, realistic. "There is nothing symbolic about one person willing another to love."

2829 Liddy, James. "The Figure of Christ in D. H. Lawrence and Edwin Muir," UNIVERSITY REVIEW (Dublin), III (1966), 26-33.

The four Gospels, great archetypal myths of the European consciousness, can be traced in its literary traditions. As that civilization breaks up, the symbols of its canon change also, as seen in the works of DHL and Edwin Muir. DHL, a "deeply religious" revolutionary who struggled with Christian teaching, used the figure of Christ as his focus (*The Man Who Died*) and resurrection through physical love as his vision. Muir, a less gifted writer, made the Incarnation his focal symbol and expressed a reverence, however melancholy, for the organic world. DHL and Muir, by using traditional Christian images rather than the esoteric cycles and symbols of Joyce, Yeats, and Pound, avoid those writers' social isolation and become forerunners of a public, humanistic art which would make creativity once again a concern of the Church.

2830 "Literature," BOOKLIST AND SUBSCRIPTION BOOKS BULLETIN: A GUIDE TO CURRENT BOOKS, LXII (15 April 1966), 799.

The Complete Plays of D. H. Lawrence collects ten plays, which are "more lyrical and passionate in tone and execution than dramatic, reflecting attitudes and preoccupations largely familiar through Lawrence's novels." Except for the date of each play publication and production history is not given.

2831 Littlewood, J. C. F. "Correspondence," CAMBRIDGE QUARTERLY, I (Autumn 1966), 380-82.

[Letter to the Editor in rejoinder to G. A. Earl, "Correspondence," CAMBRIDGE QUARTERLY, I (Summer 1966), 273-75, referring him to Littlewood's earlier discussion of the backwashing scene in "Daughters of the Vicar" as an example of the analysis on which his favorable critical judgment of the tale was based, and reiterating his opinion that "Odour of Chrysanthemums" is a "successful and deeply felt" creation. [See also the article to which G. A. Earl had replied, J. C. F. Littlewood, "D. H. Lawrence's Early Tales," CAMBRIDGE QUARTERLY, I (Spring 1966) 107-24.]

2832 Littlewood, J. C. F. "D. H. Lawrence's Early Tales," CAMBRIDGE QUARTERLY, I (Spring 1966), 107-24.

In pointing out "that Lawrence's power as an artist first decisively appeared ... in his shorter fiction," F. R. Leavis attributed the stories in *The Prussian Officer and Other Stories* to the DHL of the first three novels. On the contrary, they belong to the DHL of *The Rainbow,* since DHL revised all of them for the collection after he had completed the first part of that novel in midsummer 1914. [See also reply by G. A. Earl, "Correspondence," CAMBRIDGE QUARTERLY, I (Summer 1966), 273-75; and rejoinder by J. C. F. Littlewood, "Correspondence," CAMBRIDGE QUARTERLY, I (Autumn 1966), 380-82.]

2833 Mackenzie, Compton. MY LIFE AND TIMES, OCTAVE FIVE: 1915-1923 (Lond: Chatto & Windus, 1966), pp. 164-73, 176-79, 183-85, 189, 190-93, 235.

[In 1919, Mackenzie and DHL had "jolly times" singing popular and old songs, but Frieda "was for ever encouraging her Lorenzo . . . to pull people to pieces," probably an effect of their unhappy wartime experiences. "Yet that silly spying accusation . . . might not have happened if Lawrence had refrained from painting the roof of their cottage with bright stripes of colour." Mackenzie loaned DHL his typewriter, "of which only the red half of the ribbon was still usable," to type the MS of *Fantasia of the Unconscious*. This memoir contains letters from Frieda and DHL in response to Mackenzie's gift of his SYLVIA SCARLET, a letter from DHL about Mackenzie's idea for his mother's Nottingham Repertory Theatre's producing DHL's *The Widowing of Mrs. Holroyd* and *Touch and Go,* three letters from DHL on his travels in Italy and his writing, and two postcards from Raratonga as DHL was preparing for his American journey. See also an earlier version of this memoir, Compton Mackenzie, "Memories of D. H. Lawrence," CERTAIN ASPECTS OF MORAL COURAGE (Garden City, NY: Doubleday, 1962), pp. 104-19, as well as additional reminiscences and comments in other volumes of his ten-volume autobiography, espec MY LIFE AND TIMES, OCTAVE SIX: 1923-1930 (Lond: Chatto & Windus, 1967), pp. 84-85, 131-32, 170; MY LIFE AND TIMES, OCTAVE SEVEN: 1931-1938 (Lond: Chatto & Windus, 1968), pp. 35-36, 282; MY LIFE AND TIMES, OCTAVE EIGHT: 1939-1946 (Lond: Chatto & Windus, 1969), p. 265.]

2834 Major, Mabel. "On a September Sunday--'38," DESCANT, X (Summer 1966), 13-16.

Frieda L served two visitors to the DHL ranch squash blossom omelet, showed them the manuscripts of the three versions of *Lady Chatterley's Lover,* and told them of Mabel Dodge Luhan's persuading her husband, Tony, to steal DHL's ashes--after which Frieda had the urn cemented in the mausoleum, to which she kept the key.

2835 Marnat, Marcel. DAVID HERBERT LAWRENCE (Paris: Éditions Universitaires [Classiques du XXème siècle], 1966).

In spite of a few essays and articles, DHL is largely unknown in France. Drieu La Rochelle, the only writer who knew DHL thoroughly, has read his works with love and commented on the novelist in a lengthy and penetrating preface *L'Homme qui était mort* (*The Man Who Died*) (1933) that is totally ignored. This comprehensive, generous, and well-documented study is the only significant and useful one written in France before World War II. [DHL's life is surveyed in the context of important contemporary political, artistic, and literary events throughout the world.] DHL always thought that sexuality was the intimate drama of every conscience. When he describes the marriages and personal conflicts of three generations in *The Rainbow,* he offers an analysis of the problems of each couple in relation to their society. In spite of the personal achievement of the characters, this novel has an underlying pessimistic tone: DHL has discovered that society is as corrupt as the individual. In *Women in Love,* the essential themes of DHL's future works confusedly appear: distrust of intellectualism and distrust of love, hence the necessity of going beyond the love of woman. *Kangaroo* and *The Plumed Serpent* constitute a diptych that is opposed to *Women in Love*; now the novelist wants to build. *Kangaroo,* the most moving of DHL's books, is largely unread. In *The Plumed Serpent,* love and politics, social, individual, and magical reality blend into the great aspiration of ritual. We shall be able to read this novel when the western world no longer exists, for with this book, DHL tears away the mask and affirms the end of the western world. In 1966, we have the feeling that DHL describes not only the position of Europe since World War II but also the fifty years left for our survival as Europeans. In *Lady Chatterley's Lover,* we find the same antihumanistic trend as in *The Plumed Serpent.* Constance and Mellors embody the individual's achievement, but the novel is paradoxically pessimistic in tone. [The conclusion briefly analyzes the interpretation of DHL today.] [In French.]

2836 Mittleman, Leslie B. "Lawrence's 'Snake' Not 'Sweet Georgian Brown,' " ENGLISH LITERATURE IN TRANSITION, IX (1966), 45-46.

The speaker of "Snake" is horrified by witnessing a symbolic sexual act and, like the Ancient Mariner, must expiate a guilt that he does not understand for a crime against a life force. "Snake" is a symbolist, not a sentimental Georgian, work.

2837 Mizener, Arthur. "D. H. Lawrence," in A HANDBOOK OF ANALYSES, QUESTIONS, AND A DISCUSSION OF TECHNIQUE FOR USE WITH "MODERN SHORT STORIES: THE USES OF IMAGINATION," rvd ed (NY: Norton, 1966), 93-106.

"Odour of Chrysanthemums" embodies a recurrent theme in DHL's fiction: the integrity of the individual. The death of Elizabeth's husband awakens her to the unsatisfactoriness of her marital relationship, in which her demands that her husband be something that he was not alienated her from him. Thus, "Lawrence, in his romantic idealism, thinks it is necessary for a man and a woman to be husband and wife if they are to fulfill their unique, individual selves and truly live their lives." In "The Shadow in the Rose Garden," DHL likewise depicts an alienated married couple, separated in this case by "instinctive and habitual feelings" of class consciousness which have created incompatible expectations. The struggle between a man and a woman to maintain integrity of the self is similarly depicted in "The White Stocking," in which the issue emerges on a subconscious level in a marital spat. Because Elsie and Teddy have "been roused to hurt anger by the injury to elements...beyond the reach of reason," they are forced to "act on feelings that work at a level beneath their conscious, rational minds." DHL's story is "overwhelmingly convincing because it is true, not to what reason tells us people ought logically to feel, but to what...we know people actually do feel." [See also Arthur Mizener (ed). "Part Three: Introduction," MODERN SHORT STORIES: THE USES OF IMAGINATION, rvd ed (NY: Norton, 1967), pp. 427-31, espec pp. 430-31.]

2838 Moore, Harry T. "Preface," *The White Peacock* by D. H. Lawrence (Carbondale and Edwardsville: Southern Illinois UP, 1966), pp. v-viii.

DHL wrote *The White Peacock*, his first novel, while teaching in the Midlands and in Croydon. He brought an advance copy to his dying mother in December 1910; his father was incredulous at the publisher's advance of fifty pounds, as if his son had been a swindler. "The language of the book has . . . little of the intensity" or "distinctive cadences" of DHL's mature prose style. The novel is also less realistic than DHL's later books. Ignoring industrialism, DHL focuses here on an idealized Midlands landscape and even improves the living standards of several characters taken from life. Some of the characters in *The White Peacock* prefigure those of later novels. Leslie Tempest, the young squire Lettie marries, prefigures, in different ways, both Gerald Crich of *Women in Love* and Clifford Chatterley of *Lady Chatterley's Lover*; all three of these country squires "live in the same country house, given a different name" in each novel. Similarly, Annable, the gamekeeper, foreshadows Mellors of *Lady Chatterley's Lover*. But *The White Peacock* should be read not only for these elements but also for its own sake.

2839 Moore, Harry T., and Warren Roberts. D. H. LAWRENCE AND HIS WORLD (NY: Viking P; Lond: Thames & Hudson, 1966).
[A 124-page biography, shorter and sketchier than Harry T. Moore's THE INTELLIGENT HEART (1954) and illustrated, on all but a few pages, with numerous black-and-white photographs. The emphasis in both text and captions is on relating the facts and experiences of DHL's life to his fiction. Contains three pages of bibliographical notes, three pages of chronology, and six pages of notes on the pictures.]

2840 Moravia, Alberto. "Il mito del Messico" (The Myth of Mexico), CORRIERE DELLA SERA (Milan), 20 Nov 1966, p. 3.
DHL, in reaction against western civlization, idealized the Mexican myth. Today, travelling through Mexico, we can easily realize that this myth has disappeared. What DHL called "blood religion" was in the Aztec reality a religion of fear which was exorcised by the sacrifice of human lives. In any case, DHL's ideas on this myth were not so far-fetched because they were acted out long afterwards in German extermination camps. [In Italian.]

2841 Muir, Edwin. "Some Letters of Edwin Muir," ENCOUNTER, XXVI (Jan 1966), 3-10, espec p. 4.
[In a letter to Stephen Hudson (pseud of Sydney Schiff) of 1 Jan 1925, Muir acknowledges that despite DHL's faults of "formlessness, haste, lack of objectivity," his "extraordinary power of vision" comes through in "passages of splendid divination." Although these passages "stick out like isolated peaks," thus blemishing the artistic effect of the whole, "Lawrence's genius is most essentially seen in them."]

2842 Nakamura, Yoshio. "*Lady Chatterley's Lover* ni Tsuite" (On *Lady Chatterley's Lover*), LITERARY SYMPOSIUM (Aichi University), No. 31 (Jan 1966), 237-57.
[In Japanese.]

D. H. LAWRENCE

2843 Nakano, Kimiko. "*Lady Chatterley's Lover* ni Okeru Connie" (Connie in *Lady Chatterley's Lover*), KÔNAN WOMEN'S COLLEGE STUDIES IN ENGLISH LITERATURE, No. 3 (Dec 1966), 54-71. [In Japanese.]

2844 Nardi, Piero. "Introduzione" (Introduction), *Romanzi brevi e frammenti di romanzo* (*The Complete Short Novels and Fragments of Novel*) by D. H. Lawrence (Milan: A. Mondadori, 1966), pp. xv-xxi. The short novels of DHL have major significance precisely because they are short novels and not short stories. They are characterized by the same deep psychological analysis and breadth of themes to be found in the novels. As elsewhere, the autobiographical element prevails, and the writings become confused and less vivid as DHL accentuates the ideological aspect of his message. *The Fox, The Captain's Doll,* and *The Ladybird* are above all psychoanalytic studies; *St. Mawr, The Princess,* and *The Virgin and the Gipsy* primarily reveal DHL's attitude as a prophet; and *The Man Who Died* is the most perfect fictional expression of DHL's "vitalist" belief. [In Italian.]

2845 Newby, Frank Shelton. "Dialectical Form in *The Rainbow* and *Women in Love*," DISSERTATION ABSTRACTS, XXVII (1966), 1062A. Unpublished dissertation, University of California (Berkeley), 1966.

2846 Nin, Anais. "Novelist on Stage," NEW YORK TIMES BOOK REVIEW, 10 April 1966, pp. 4, 33. The eight plays and two fragments collected in *The Complete Plays of D. H. Lawrence* will illluminate DHL's "attempt to crack the surface of naturalism in his novels," but "the dramatic form, with its severe limitations on lyric expression, would not seem suited to Lawrence's aims." "He makes no attempt to break with conventions of the theater, as he did with those of the novel." [Analysis of a scene from *The Widowing of Mrs. Holroyd* and brief discussion of other plays support the author's view.]

2847 Nosaka, Tôsaku. "D. H. Lawrence Dainiki no Okeru Buntai no Ichimen" (Some Features of D. H. Lawrence's Style in His Second Phase), KENKYÛ RONBUN-SHÛ (Miyagi Women's College), No. 27 (Jan 1966), 22-31. [In Japanese.]

2848 Ôhashi, Yasuichirô. "Shijin Lawrence to Shi (Jô)" (D. H. Lawrence: Poet and Death, The First Part), MEMOIRS OF HUMANISTIC AND SOCIAL SCIENCES (Kyôto Technical University), No. 14 (March 1966), 35-60. [In Japanese.]

2849 Okada, Taiji. "D. H. Lawrence to Sensô" (D. H. Lawrence and the War), REVIEW OF KÔBE UNIVERSITY OF MERCANTILE MARINE, PART I: STUDIES IN HUMANITIES AND SOCIAL

SCIENCE, No. 14 (March 1966), 110-32. [In Japanese.]

2850 "Out of the Closet," TIME, LXXXVII (1 April 1966), 104.
The Complete Plays of D. H. Lawrence collects ten "skeletons" in DHL's "literary closet." "As plays, they are quite unplayable." "Essentially, the plays are like sketchbooks--useful for Lawrence in preparation for his other work."

2851 Panichas, George A. "Book Reviews," MODERN LANGUAGE JOURNAL, L (Feb 1966), 123-24.
DHL's poetry does not deserve the neglect of the past but places him among the great twentieth-century poets. Tracing DHL's development as a poet in *The Complete Poems of D. H. Lawrence*, ed by Vivian de Sola Pinto and F. Warren Roberts (1964), shows that he surmounted his unevenness to achieve a control commensurate with his material. [*Paintings of D. H. Lawrence*, ed by Mervyn Levy (1964), is also reviewed.]

2852 Panichas, George A. "E. M. Forster and D. H. Lawrence: Their Views on Education," RENAISSANCE AND MODERN ESSAYS: PRESENTED TO VIVIAN DE SOLA PINTO IN CELEBRATION OF HIS SEVENTIETH BIRTHDAY, ed by G. R. Hibbard, with the assistance of George A. Panichas and Allan Rodway (Lond: Routledge & Kegan Paul; NY: Barnes & Noble, 1966), pp. 199-213; rptd in THE REVERENT DISCIPLINE: ESSAYS IN LITERARY CRITICISM AND CULTURE, by George A. Panichas (Knoxville: University of Tennessee P, 1974), pp. 157-69.
Poetic insights rather than scientific statements give expression to both E. M. Forster's and DHL's views on education. Forster's educational aims are corrective, whereas DHL's are curative. DHL would destroy first and then rebuild. After an unhappy time in public school, Forster attended Cambridge, which represented for him a "recovery of values," whereas Nottingham University College led to DHL's "loss of reverence" for higher education. DHL's reaction developed in the midst of working-class life in the Midlands, whereas Forster's were shaped by the middle class, by a civilized intelligence and humane liberalism and, therefore, by a softness that accepts human limitations. DHL's criticisms of Forster are also criticisms of the Cambridge ethos, a tradition which he felt to be stagnant, superficial, poisonous, and decayed. Whereas Forster would compromise and search for a balance, DHL, for whom the mind and mental consciousness were not goals but instruments, would break the systems down, set up new goals, and begin again. Both Forster and DHL were distressed by the increasing mechanization of the educational process.

2853 PAUNCH, No. 26,"D. H. Lawrence Number" (April 1966), Guest Editor: E. W. Dawson.
Contents, abstracted separately under 1966: Kingsley Widmer, "Notes on the Literary Institutionalization of D. H. Lawrence: An Anti-Review of the Current State of Lawrence Studies," pp. 5-13; Arthur Efron, "Lady Chatterley's Lecher?" pp. 14-15; Wayne Burns, "*Lady Chatterley's Lover*: A Pilgrim's Progress for Our

Time," pp. 16-33; Sandra Barry, "Singularity of Two; the Plurality of One," pp. 34-39; John Doheny, "The Novel is the Bright Book of Life: D. H. Lawrence and a Revised Version of Polymorphous Perversity," pp. 40-59; E. W. Dawson, "Lawrence's Pollyanalytic Esthetic for the Novel," pp. 60-68.

2854 Perkins, Moreland. "Emotion and Feeling," PHILOSOPHICAL REVIEW, LXXV (April 1966), 139-60, espec pp. 155-57.

Lydia Lensky's reaction to Tom Brangwen's proposal of marriage in *The Rainbow* is an example of the novelists' "power to convey to us the emotions felt by their 'characters' " by means of describing "their fictional persons' bodily feeling."

2855 Poirier, Richard. A WORLD ELSEWHERE: THE PLACE OF STYLE IN AMERICAN LITERATURE (NY: Oxford UP, 1966; Lond: Chatto & Windus, 1967), pp. 33, 37-38, 40-49, 50, 72, 78, 115, 124, 144, 154, 236.

In *St. Mawr*, a "gathering of motifs" of "classic American literature," "Lawrence demonstrates the difficulty, in environments conventionalized by social and literary formulations, of trying to find a voice, a personal style appropriate to . . . the 'onward pushing spirit.' " Paralleling "the geographical movement" of its "obvious historical and literary precedents: from old to new worlds," *St. Mawr* incorporates two opposing attitudes characteristic of American literature: "the one imitative, often satiric, often critical, but essentially submissive, in being corrective . . . ; the other creative, daring, often ridiculous in the effort to express a creative ideal of alternative environment where the self can unite its powers with presumably harmonious natural forces." In the interpolated story of the New England woman, "though she fails . . . she represents for Lawrence the positive virtue of effort, of struggle for its own sake." "*St. Mawr* is an astonishing feat in varieties and modulations of style precisely because Lawrence is so anxious to show how nearly impossible it is to be freed of those organizations of language, literary and social, within which human consciousness has chosen to define itself." [Brief discussion of *Studies in Classic American Literature* as "the crucial study of American literature."]

2856 Price, Martin. "E. M. F. and D. H. L.," YALE REVIEW, LV (Summer 1966), 597-601.

Both E. M. Forster and DHL portray the " 'struggle of the individual towards the dark, secret place where he may find reality,' " "that descent into being which overwhelms all measure and demolishes the defensive structures of selfhood," and both depict a society which avoids the struggle by substituting institutional tradition for reality. But whereas Forster's search "does not preclude a skeptical irony," DHL "loathes irony," which is Gudrun's final position in *Women in Love*. [Review of THE CAVE AND THE MOUNTAIN: A STUDY OF E. M. FORSTER, by Wilfred Stone (1966), and THE FORKED FLAME: A STUDY OF D. H. LAWRENCE, by H. M. Daleski (1965).]

2857 Prisco, Michele. "Fantasmi litterari sulla Costa Azzurra" (Literary Ghosts on the French Riviera), COSMORAMA (Rome), VII (Compagnia Italiana Turismo, 1966), 45-48.

DHL's message is based on his aspiration to an imaginary Eden, free of social restrictions. He travelled all his life in search of this paradise. He lived in Italy and described it in a completely unconventional way. [In Italian.]

2858 Pritchett, V[ictor] S. "Lawrence's Laughter," NEW STATESMAN, LXXII (1 July 1966), 18-19.

[Review article on *The Complete Plays of D. H. Lawrence* (1965); Anthony West, D. H. LAWRENCE (1950; 2nd ed, 1966), and Keith Sagar, THE ART OF D. H. LAWRENCE (1966).] DHL may have been attracted to writing plays by hearing that there was money in it, but his "thin, gossipy side" undercuts much of the force in his plays. *The Widowing of Mrs. Holroyd* is marred by the strategy of repetition, used effectively in DHL's fiction, and *Touch and Go* allegorically simplifies the conflict between upper and lower classes, vulgarizing the play into a shallow tract. Some of the plays, like *The Daughter-in-Law* and *The Merry-Go-Round,* reveal a talent for low comedy and farce, but without a "feeling for the artificial," DHL lacked Shaw's ability to carry off larger impudences.

2859 Pritchett, V[ictor] S. "Wells Marches On," NEW STATESMAN (23 Sept 1966), 433-34.

H. G. Wells's prophetic influence, dominant until the end of World War I, was replaced in the twenties by another short-term prophet--DHL. It is the fate of such people to be overtaken by the world, as Kipling and Shaw also were.

2860 Pryce-Jones, D. "Last Glowing Inspiration: Countryside That Inspired," REPORTER, XXXIV (10 Feb 1966), 49-50.

Taos today is "sentimentality at every turn, the gush of a past now meaningless and an equally meaningless present." DHL called the Southwest a show and a playground. The DHL "Shrine" itself has an air about it that makes it seem "as if a thunderstorm charged with electricity were permanently unable to break over this place."

2861 Raina, M. L. "A Forster Parallel in Lawrence's *St. Mawr,*" NOTES AND QUERIES, XIII (March 1966), 96-97.

DHL's reaction to A PASSAGE TO INDIA probably went into his "rendering of the Devil's Chair episode" in *St. Mawr,* as a comparison of its similarities to "Mrs. Moore's experience at the Marabar Caves" suggests.

2862 Reddick, Bryan. "*Sons and Lovers*: The Omniscient Narrator," THOTH, VII (Spring 1966), 68-75.

In *Sons and Lovers,* emotions are ambiguous, even paradoxical. Given this complex notion of human nature, it is appropriate that DHL should try to re-create the emotions of his characters rather than to analyze them logically. The narrator, however, often comments from a broader knowledge than one limited to the story and characters. He tells us, for instance, that Paul believed firmly in his work, that he loved to sleep with his mother, and that Mrs. Morel had a curious, receptive mind. This narrative technique contradicts DHL's conception of the human psyche by implying that emotions can be defined unambiguously and that the narrator knows not only the story materials but also life as a whole. In subsequent novels, such as *Aaron's Rod* and *Lady Chatterley's Lover,* DHL turns to a modern alternative to the omniscient narrator: a "dramatized" narrator, like the ones in Hardy's novels, who participates in the narrative as a man frankly and candidly telling the story.

2863 Remsbury, J[ohn] A. "D. H. Lawrence: Critic of Life." Unpublished dissertation, University of Exeter, 1966. [Listed in Lawrence F. McNamee, DISSERTATIONS IN ENGLISH AND AMERICAN LITERATURE, SUPP I (NY & Lond: Bowker, 1969), p. 247.]

2864 Rieff, Philip. "The Therapeutic as Mythmaker: Lawrence's True Christian Philosophy," THE TRIUMPH OF THE THERAPEUTIC: USES OF FAITH AFTER FREUD (NY: Harper & Row; Lond: Chatto & Windus, 1966; rptd, NY: Harper & Row, Harper Torchbooks, 1968), pp. 189-231; additional references, pp. 2, 8-9, 10-11, 77, 110, 111, 146-47, 178-79, 182, 258.

DHL sets forth in *Psychoanalysis and the Unconscious* and *Fantasia of the Unconscious* the "second faith" that he intended to succeed what he saw as the fallacious philosophies of Christianity and rational science. In the tradition of religious mysticism, DHL aimed at integrating the inner and outer man by advocating the freer expression of man's basically erotic character, which DHL called the "old religious faculty." In his two doctrinal works, DHL proclaimed his trust in man's irrational faculty and his advocacy of innocence of mind, which he believed would allow man to achieve harmony with the universe. Both Freud and DHL turned to the unconscious in their search for an end to the "division between inner and outer life": Freud, believing that the "rational analytic mode" would provide a therapeutic release from inwardness, proposed a science of the irrational that would contain the unconscious; DHL, believing that the "erotic mode" would provide the therapeutic release, advocated a transformation of the unconscious into a religious emotion that is specifically irrational and erotic. Misled by early vulgarizations of psychoanalysis and failing to see the difference between Freud's therapeutic rationalism and its eighteenth-century counterpart, DHL accused Freud of rationalizing man's erotic life and thereby serving as a "new apologist of the old culture." Yet the persistent inward thrust toward the unconscious self to achieve "externality" is the foundation of both DHL's art and Freud's psychoanalysis. [An earlier version of this essay appeared as "A Modern Mythmaker," MYTH AND MYTHMAKING, ed by Henry A. Murray (NY: George Braziller, 1960), pp. 240-75.]

2865 Rogers, Katherine M. THE TROUBLESOME HELPMATE: A HISTORY OF MISOGYNY IN LITERATURE (Seattle: University of Washington P, 1966) pp. 237-47, 249, 254*n*, 256, 257, 263, 268, 269-70, 275.

DHL, although he did not read Freud, was aware of his theories. DHL held reactionary views concerning women--that they are (or should be) passive and that the female is an exclusively sexual being--although his views often are "somewhat disguised by mystical terminology." DHL attempted to tear down the

Victorian idealization of women, but he replaced it with misogyny. He particularly resented and feared the self-sufficient pride of motherhood--a fact that can be accounted for by his feelings toward his own mother. Hence, DHL "found his revenge" by making his most virile characters "abstain from fatherhood, thus depriving the female of what she most wants." Despite his theory of male superiority, however, DHL "found himself irresistibly dependent on women." Therefore, he developed an ethic, which pervades his fiction, wherein an ideal relationship involved the renunciation of will by a woman.

2866 Rohrberger, Mary. HAWTHORNE AND THE MODERN SHORT STORY: A STUDY IN GENRE (The Hague and Paris: Mouton, 1966), pp. 9, 51-53, 58, 74-80, 106, 133, 141.

Although DHL wrote no "clear statement of his philosophy of art," he "saw as basic an understanding of relationships" and eschewed "the idea of truth as an absolute" in favor of the "true symbol" which defies explanation and "cannot be stated discursively." "The Rocking-Horse Winner" is an ironic variant of the fairy tale plot, which on the surface "concerns a youth who is destroyed through his frantic efforts to insure his family's fortune." The story ends, unlike the fairy tale, with the hero's death, the inevitable consequence of the child's having to "live at the mercy of demands which are impossible to meet." The meaning is focused in the rocking horse, the "dominant symbol which encompasses other subsidiary symbols."

2867 Ross, Michael Lawrence. "Nature and Fate in the Early Novels of D. H. Lawrence." Unpublished dissertation, Harvard University, 1966. [Listed in Lawrence F. McNamee, DISSERTATIONS IN ENGLISH AND AMERICAN LITERATURE (NY and Lond: Bowker, 1969), p. 247.]

2868 Rudrum, Alan. "Stage Sons, Stage Lovers," LISTENER AND BBC TELEVISION REVIEW, LXXV (10 Feb 1966), 214-15.

Four of the eight plays collected in *The Complete Plays of D. H. Lawrence* "were written in 1912, the year when Lawrence finished *Sons and Lovers* and began his life with Frieda." [Parallels between the bread burning scene in *A Collier's Friday Night* and *Sons and Lovers* and between the tragedies of *The Widowing of Mrs. Holroyd* and "Odour of Chrysanthemums" are discussed briefly.] *The Daughter-in-Law* is "beautifully worked out in dramatic terms," but DHL was too close to his subject in *The Fight for Barbara* for "artistic success." *David* is "wordy and of ineffable import, written in that slackened biblical rhythm Lawrence employed when his sense of the numinous overcame his sense of humour."

2869 Sagar, Keith M. THE ART OF D. H. LAWRENCE (Cambridge: Cambridge UP, 1966; rptd 1975); excerpt from Chap. II, pp. 28-33, rptd as "The Bases of the Normal," in D. H. LAWRENCE: "SONS AND LOVERS," A CASEBOOK, ed by Gāmini Salgādo (Lond: Macmillan, 1969; Nashville: Aurora Publishers, 1970), pp. 208-15; excerpt from Chap. II, pp. 21-35, rptd with additions as "*Sons and Lovers*," in TWENTIETH CENTURY INTERPRETATIONS OF

D. H. LAWRENCE

"SONS AND LOVERS": A COLLECTION OF CRITICAL ESSAYS, ed by Judith Farr (Englewood Cliffs, NJ: Prentice-Hall, 1970), pp. 42-50; excerpt from Chap. III, pp. 55-68, rptd as "The Third Generation," in TWENTIETH CENTURY INTERPRETATIONS OF "THE RAINBOW": A COLLECTION OF CRITICAL ESSAYS, ed by Mark Kinkead-Weekes (Englewood Cliffs, NJ: Prentice-Hall, 1971), pp. 58-72; excerpt from Chap. VIII, pp. 159-68, rptd as "The Lost Trail: *The Plumed Serpent*," in D. H. LAWRENCE: A COLLECTION OF CRITICISM, ed by Leo Hamalian (NY: McGraw-Hill, 1973), pp. 87-96.

DHL's vision in four phases of his career is correlated with the appropriate form of his art. Regarding *Sons and Lovers* autobiographically is to see it as a case history, not as a novel. Mrs. Morel, rather than dividing Paul psychically through possessiveness, is a norm by which other women are seen as inadequate. Experiencing deeper forces of nature with Clara saves Paul from merging into death. Writing *Sons and Lovers* freed DHL from his mother and "the preoccupation with autobiographical material." In *The Rainbow*, each generation's quest for larger life differs from the others', but all pursue an unattainable rainbow. Whereas in the first two generations, the struggle between the sexes occurs in marriage, Ursula's with Skrebensky, an incomplete human being, occurs before marriage. The evolutionary purpose in the novel moves toward fulfillment in the unknown future. In *Women in Love*, Birkin's problem is individual survival through creativity in an age of societal disintegration. While Gerald and Gudrun's conflict is death oriented, Birkin and Ursula's conflict changes both beneficially. The resolution moves toward a search for a context for their new relationship. DHL was demoralized badly in the post-*Women in Love* period, and the result, in *The Lost Girl, Aaron's Rod,* and *Kangaroo,* was a misanthropy not conducive to good fiction. Cicio's animal-like mindlessness in *The Lost Girl* carries over into *The Captain's Doll* and *The Fox.* Poems in *Birds, Beasts and Flowers,* such as "Snake" and "Fish," register the inaccessible otherness of nonhuman life, though the snake is analogous to the speaker's deeper self. After *The Rainbow* DHL embarks on a search, both internally and externally, for the "dark gods." The female protagonist of "The Woman Who Rode Away" goes too far by accepting literal sacrifice in the Indians' quest for racial resurrection. Style in *St. Mawr* ranges from a casual, sardonic quality in treating Rico to a grave dignity to accommodate the symbolic meanings in St. Mawr, who confronts the characters with whether they are alive. On the ranch Lou attempts both to be alive and to increase her consciousness. The critical censure of *The Plumed Serpent* indicates critics' failure in imaginative participation. DHL's testing manner in developing Kate's mythic quest for rejuvenation transcends preaching, but her absolute submission in marriage to Cipriano abandons DHL's earlier heroines' painful progress toward self-hood. The phallus in *Lady Chatterley's Lover* has many connotations of the earlier rainbow symbol, particularly the relation between people and creativity. The two forms of consciousness, mental and phallic, are represented in Clifford and Mellors and in the Tevershall and Wragby wood settings. The novel fails, in Mellors's Anglo-Saxon love words, to unite a civilized sensibility with a deeper sensitivity to natural man. Resurrection, following the critical illness reflected in "The Flying Fish," becomes a central theme in DHL's last works. In *Etruscan Places,* DHL discovers in the Etruscans the wisdom of fulfilled life and acceptance of death. In *The Man Who Died,* death as part of the creative unknown is thematically associated with the contrast between the Greater Day of the Priestess and the Man and the Lesser Day of materialism. If earlier DHL explored what is dead or dying in civilizations, his poems in *Last Poems* issue from a profound and clarified vision of life and death.

2870 Salgādo, Gāmini. D. H. LAWRENCE: "SONS AND LOVERS" (Lond: Edward Arnold [Studies in English Literature 28], 1966).
[Designed for use in study of the novel by students in Sixth Forms and universities, this study of *Sons and Lovers* provides a chapter-by-chapter analysis and guide to the novel, with emphasis on the basics of the narrative line, characterization and inter-relationships of the characters, and setting, and touches on the ambiguity of the ending. The "Conclusion" places *Sons and Lovers* in the context of early modern industrial society, and "Further Reading" lists selected biographical and critical secondary materials.]

2871 Secker, Martin. "D. H. Lawrence," TIMES LITERARY SUPPLEMENT (Lond), 3 Nov 1966, p. 1012.
[Letter to the Editor noting that Warren Roberts's A BIBLIOGRAPHY OF D. H. LAWRENCE (1963) omitted references to Secker's reissues of *The Rainbow* in Feb 1926 and May 1927 in crown octavo, "bound in exactly the same style as the author's other novels" and consisting "of unbound sheets imported from Thomas Seltzer" and published without alterations under Secker's own cancelled title page. Secker also identifies Clement Shorter, literary editor of THE SPHERE, as the " 'common informer' " who initiated the obscenity proceedings against *The Rainbow* in 1915. See also replies by Philip Hobsbaum and John Worthen, in "D. H. Lawrence," TIMES LITERARY SUPPLEMENT (Lond), 10 Nov 1966, p. 1023; and response by Martin Secker, in "D. H. Lawrence," TIMES LITERARY SUPPLEMENT (Lond), 17 Nov 1966, p. 1052.]

2872 Secker, Martin. "D. H. Lawrence," TIMES LITERARY SUPPLEMENT (Lond), 17 Nov 1966, p. 1052.
[Letter to the Editor in response to Philip Hobsbaum and John Worthen, "D. H. Lawrence," TIMES LITERARY SUPPLEMENT (Lond), 10 Nov 1966, p. 1023.] Although the sheets imported from Thomas Seltzer and used by Martin Secker in his reissue of *The Rainbow* in 1926 and 1927 omitted passages from the 1915 Methuen first edition, the 1926 Secker edition "marked its first reappearance in this country since its suppression." Clement Shorter's name was commonly accepted at the time as the initiator of the proceedings against *The Rainbow,* although in the absence of conclusive evidence, "the identity of the informer must stay a mystery." [See also Martin Secker, "D. H. Lawrence," TIMES LITERARY SUPPLEMENT (Lond), 3 Nov 1966, p. 1012.]

2873 Sepčić, Višnja. "Notes on the Structure of *Women in Love,*" STUDIA ROMANICA ET ANGLICA ZAGRABIENSIA, Nos. 21-22 (1966), 289-304.
In *Women in Love,* DHL adopts a dramatic method in vividly rendered scenes

which depict the clash of characters and convey meaning simultaneously on several levels. Rather than to give traditionally realistic descriptions, DHL's purpose was "to recreate the inner profile of persons, things and events" in a "visionary novel" which captures the "inner rhythms . . . of the contemporary world as they are reflected on the psychical level." Although these scenes all belong to the same category of "the discovery of the irrational in human behaviour," they are all, through DHL's technical skill, executed differently. Some scenes, such as the Arab mare scene, are like "a hallucinatory vision where things, persons and phenomena . . . are brought into a sharp focus so that their inner meaning becomes crystal-clear while time seems to be suspended." Others, such as Gudrun's dance before the bullocks, are similar to hypnosis. Still others, such as Birkin's lying down among flowers and sprinkling himself with fir needles after his near death blow from Hermione, "have a quality of a symbolistic ritual." DHL's variety of techniques is exemplified in the differences between "Moony" and "Rabbit." "Moony" is marked by "discontinuity of narration" and compression and intensification of language to illuminate "the deepest emotional and irrational layers of Birkin's personality" and to suggest "a complex meaning." "Rabbit" is characterized by a "constant interplay between . . . the realistic and the symbolic, the superficial and the deep," the rational and the irrational. [The author makes a detailed analysis of both scenes with, in the case of the former, a consideration of the criticism of the scene by Leavis, Hough, Vivas, Bertocci, Bodkin, and others.]

2874 Simms, Theodore Franklin. "Primitivistic Motifs in the Poetry of D. H. Lawrence," DISSERTATION ABSTRACTS, XXIX (1968), 274A. Unpublished dissertation, New York University, 1966.

2875 Sklare, Arnold B., and William E. Buckler (eds). "D. H. Lawrence," STORIES FROM SIX AUTHORS, 2nd series (NY: McGraw-Hill, 1966), pp. 220-21.
[This anthology includes a biographical headnote, followed by "The Lovely Lady," pp. 221-37; "Odour of Chrysanthemums," pp. 237-55; "England, My England," pp. 256-83; "A Modern Lover," pp. 284-304; "The State of Funk," pp. 304-10; and "Questions for Discussion and Writing" and "Suggestions for Further Reading," pp. 310-13. The headnote stresses DHL's birth "into the poverty, brutality, and drink of an English coal-mining town," "his determined, intelligent mother," his "conflict with the authorities over alleged obscenity," and "his elopement with another man's wife" but says "Lawrence was a moralist, not an immoralist." His "short stories happily embody the best of him."]

2876 "Speech, Theater and Dance," CHOICE, III (Sept 1966), 537. The interest of *The Complete Plays of D. H. Lawrence* lies in the fact that "concepts first developed in a play achieve complete form in a novel or short story."

2877 Spilka, Mark, Kingsley Widmer, and Arthur Efron. [Untitled Exchange of Letters], PAUNCH, No. 27 (Oct 1966), 83-96.
[Mark Spilka's letter to Arthur Efron in reply to Kingsley Widmer, "Notes on the Literary Institutionalization of D. H. Lawrence: An Anti-Review of the Current State of Lawrence Studies," PAUNCH, No. 26 (April 1966), 5-13; "A Sentimental

Reply to Mark Spilka by Kingsley Widmer"; Spilka's rejoinder to Widmer; Arthur Efron's reply to Spilka; Spilka's rejoinder to Efron; and Efron's further reply to Spilka.] **Mark Spilka:** Widmer has become a "reverse sentimentalist," a less than honest "bully of perversity." **Kingsley Widmer:** Spilka, who "has no comprehension of radical critiques of liberal-moral ideology," ignores the "essential point" that "Lawrence's sensibility and views were of a deeply significant revolutionary extremity." Ladies attack DHL because "he demanded a sexually (and generally) passive role for women, reaching obsession in his attacks on 'clitoral orgasms.'" The "pervasive fatuousness and fraudulence of the academic world" should be approached with DHL's "characteristic anger ... for the 'dead-alive.'" **Mark Spilka:** DHL was capable of self-criticism, in *Women in Love* describing Birkin's misanthropy as " 'almost ... an illness' " and Birkin himself as a prig assuming a Salvator Mundi pose. Widmer's view is not new; "it is even *respectable* nowadays to value Lawrence as a radical critic of society" [critics cited]. "But Lawrence is more than a nihilistic social critic; he is also a prophet of individual regeneration." **Arthur Efron:** Spilka's "unbending loyalty to institutional living" makes him unlikely "to give a very wholehearted yes" to DHL's "utter rejection of our whole modern and 'insentient' civilization in *Lady Chatterley's Lover*." **Mark Spilka:** Institutions "of *some* kind" are necessary "in a complex industrial culture." "Can you take seriously, for very long, the kind of society [DHL] presents in *The Plumed Serpent* as an alternative to this one?" **Arthur Efron:** Melville's and DHL's failure "to create in imagination a viable alternative model for institutional organization does not detract at all from the great clarification" that BILLY BUDD and *Lady Chatterley's Lover* give. Readers should "take another look at both Lawrence in the academy and at the academy itself."

2878 Spolton, L. "D. H. Lawrence--Student and Teacher," BRITISH JOURNAL OF EDUCATIONAL STUDIES, XIV (Nov 1966), 18-35. The picture of DHL "as scholarship boy, pupil teacher, college student and eventual elementary school teacher is often overlooked." [DHL's experience in each of these categories is reviewed from standard biographical sources.] Sources of DHL's "informal education" included, through his father, the English "Folk Culture"; through his mother, "the great English Puritan tradition"; and through the Chambers family, wide reading and rich discussions of books. DHL's experience as an uncertified teacher in Eastwood are the basis for Ursula Brangwen's teaching experience in *The Rainbow,* which follows the common "progression from high ideals at the outset through a period of relative deflation to an approach incorporating some satisfactory and satisfying routines." DHL's poem "Discipline" shows his view that "the teacher who is interested, but not emotionally involved, ... can usually help the most." After DHL's two-year course at University College, Nottingham, during which he became "increasingly disillusioned," he went to teach at the Davidson Road School, Croydon. The headmaster, P. F. Smith, rated him highly and later wrote a long reminiscence of him. DHL's schoolmaster poems show the same kind of "alteration between pleasure and distaste" that Ursula experiences. DHL did some of his best teaching in biology; his writing reveals, and both his sister Ada and Jessie Chambers confirm, his knowledge of botany. DHL's educational writings include the textbook *Movements in European History* and the extended essay *Education of the People,* which contrasts "the idealistic and materialistic outlooks," suggests why idealism has failed, and stresses "the importance of the non-mental and affective centres."

2879 Stafford, William, and Frederick Candelaria. THE VOICES OF PROSE (NY: McGraw-Hill, 1966), pp. 176 and 378.

DHL's "independence, his headlong perceptivity and appreciation of vivid writers like Melville, and his constant linking of experience to the emotional concerns of modern man are displayed" in "Herman Melville's MOBY DICK" [which is reprinted in the anthology, pp. 176-88]. "Painted Tombs of Tarquinia," from *Etruscan Places* [which is reprinted in the anthology, pp. 378-80], "an evocation of life from the Etruscan tombs," illustrates the closeness of "life and belief" in DHL.

2880 Stoll, John Edward. "The Search for Integration in the Novels of D. H. Lawrence," DISSERTATION ABSTRACTS, XXVII (1967), 2547A. Unpublished dissertation, Wayne State University, 1966. Rvd and pub as THE NOVELS OF D. H. LAWRENCE: A SEARCH FOR INTEGRATION (Columbia: University of Missouri P, 1971).

2881 Stone, Wilfred. THE CAVE AND THE MOUNTAIN: A STUDY OF E. M. FORSTER (Stanford: Stanford UP; Lond: Oxford UP, 1966), pp. 15, 106n, 114, 116, 118, 121, 155, 165n, 172, 199n, 216-17, 227n, 254, 280, 298, 331n, 345, 352, 378-87, 410.

Forster, like DHL, "is primarily interested in the novel's capacity to explore 'the *passional* secret places of life.' " [Brief references to Laurentian themes of vital life in opposition to living by will in such works as *The Lost Girl, Women in Love, St. Mawr, Etruscan Places,* and *The Man Who Died,* in comparison to similar themes in Forster.] "D. H. Lawrence, a man with no Bloomsbury credentials whatever, gets Forster's highest and most discerning praise." [Forster's comments in his letter, "D. H. Lawrence," NATION AND THE ATHENAEUM, XLVI (29 March 1930), 888, are quoted, together with the discussion it provoked with T. S. Eliot and Clive Bell.] DHL and Forster are alike in several important ways: For both, "the universe echoes with intimations of spiritual realities"; both dealt with the Oedipal problem, DHL in *Sons and Lovers* and Forster in THE LONGEST JOURNEY; though superficially different, they are "in essential agreement" on "the matter of sex"; and finally, they "are alike in loathing what the new world has done to the old."

2882 Stroupe, John S. "D. H. Lawrence's Portrait of Ben Franklin in *The Rainbow,*" IOWA ENGLISH YEARBOOK, II (Fall 1966), 64-68.

DHL's portraits of Benjamin Franklin in *Studies in Classic American Literature* and of Tom Brangwen in *The Rainbow* "have much in common." DHL's Franklin equates "getting on in this world with virtue, and not prospering in it, vice," allows "that the soul is immortal" but reduces it "to practical and mean proportions," and believes that it is "the will of God that civilized white man should prosper," even at the expense of other races like the American natives. "Tom Brangwen is a materialist, a prudent, acquisitive, practical, worldly man of action who attaches himself to the creeping industrialism which is eating up Lawrence's countryside." The acquisitive materialism of both turns people into instruments. In his alternative view of man's instinctual being, the deepest self of the creative unconscious, DHL "sets forth a concept of the mind highly analogous" to that of C. G. Jung.

2883 Suehiro, Yoshitaka. "D. H. Lawrence no Shi ni Okeru Ai to Kodoku ni Tsuite no Kenkyu" (A Study of the Love and Solitude in the Poems of D. H. Lawrence), JOURNAL OF THE SECOND COLLEGE OF ENGINEERING, NIHON UNIVERSITY, Series B, VII (March 1966), 25-35.

[In Japanese.]

2884 Tanner, Tony. "Into the Fire," SPECTATOR, CCVI (7 Jan 1966), 16.

[Review of *The Complete Plays of D. H. Lawrence*.] DHL, by his own account, enjoyed writing his plays, but no one, reading them, "will regret that Lawrence made the novel his major medium." However, three plays, *A Collier's Friday Night, The Widowing of Mrs. Holroyd,* and *The Daughter-in-Law*--"all about mining families--reveal that uncontrived directness in the portrayal of settings and situations which is part of the strength of the best novels." *David* "is a fascinating, impossible piece of writing," marked by the author's changing attitudes toward the figure of David.

2885 Temple, Ruth Z., and Martin Tucker (eds). "D. H. Lawrence," A LIBRARY OF LITERARY CRITICISM (MODERN BRITISH LITERATURE) (NY: Frederick Ungar, 1966), II, 144-64.

Selected excerpts, often brief and with ellipses, from criticism of DHL, 1926 to 1962. Contents, abstracted under year of first publication: Edwin Muir, pp. 144-46, from TRANSITION: ESSAYS ON CONTEMPORARY LITERATURE (1926), pp. 49-63; Desmond MacCarthy, pp. 146-48, from CRITICISM (1932), pp. 248-54; Aldous Huxley, pp. 148-50, from "Introduction," *The Letters of D. H. Lawrence* (1932), pp. xi-xv; John Middleton Murry, pp. 150-52, from REMINISCENCES OF D. H. LAWRENCE (1933), pp. 102-4, 108-9; Norman Douglas, pp. 152-54, from LOOKING BACK (1933), pp, 282-83, 286-87; F. R. Leavis, p. 155, from THE COMMON PURSUIT (1952), p. 284; Stephen Spender, pp. 155-57, from THE CREATIVE ELEMENT (1953), pp. 93, 105-7; A. Alvarez, pp. 157-58, from "D. H. Lawrence: The Single State of Man," THE SHAPING SPIRIT: STUDIES IN MODERN ENGLISH AND AMERICAN POETS (1958), as rptd in A D. H. LAWRENCE MISCELLANY, ed by Harry T. Moore (1959), pp. 342, 349, 351; Richard Aldington, p. 158, from "Foreword," D. H. LAWRENCE: A COMPOSITE BIOGRAPHY, ed by Edward Nehls, Vol. III: 1925-1930 (1959), rptd as "The COMPOSITE BIOGRAPHY as Biography," in A D. H. LAWRENCE MISCELLANY, ed by Harry T. Moore (1959), p. 153; Eliseo Vivas, pp. 158-59, from D. H. LAWRENCE: THE FAILURE AND THE TRIUMPH OF ART (1960), pp. 16-17; review of *Lady Chatterley's Lover,* p. 160, from "A Man in His Senses," TIMES LITERARY SUPPLEMENT (Lond), 4 Nov 1960, p. 708; Raymond Williams, pp. 162-64, from "Letters from Lawrence," MANCHESTER GUARDIAN, 29 March 1962, p. 11.

2886 Thomas, Dylan. SELECTED LETTERS OF DYLAN THOMAS, ed by Constantine Fitzgibbon (Lond: J. M. Dent & Sons, 1966), p. 195.

[In a letter to Henry Treece (16 May 1938), Thomas briefly acknowledges his debt in his early poems to various earlier poets, including "Lawrence (animal poems and the verse extracts from the *Plumed Serpent*)."]

2887 Uchiki, Jôtarô. *"Tentô Mushi* ni Tsuite" (On *The Ladybird*), REPORT OF THE CHIBA INSTITUTE OF TECHNOLOGY (HUMANE STUDIES), No. 8 (Dec 1966), 83-109.

[In Japanese.]

2888 Upadhyaya, L. M. "The Non-Fiction Prose Writings of D. H. Lawrence." Unpublished dissertation, Allahabad University (India). (D. Phil.), 1966.

2889 Wajc-Tenenbaum, Rachel. "Aldous Huxley and D. H. Lawrence," REVUE DES LANGUES VIVANTES, XXXII, No. 6 (1966), 598-610.

The friendship of Aldous Huxley and DHL represented "the attraction force of two diametrically opposed temperaments, instinct and intellect." The two men early discussed DHL's dream of a "community 'based on integrity of character,' " individual fulfillment, and the "completeness" of the group. While DHL's Rananim did not materialize, Huxley joined "a group of chosen highbrows" in California in 1937 and may have presented a version of Rananim in ISLAND (1962). Huxley hints at DHL's creed of the " 'complete man' " in ANTIC HAY (1923) but reflects his own discomfort with sex in the "libertines, satyrs and perverts which people . . . his works." Kingham in "Two or Three Graces" (1926) is a "mischievous image of Lawrence." In POINT COUNTER POINT (1928), he idealizes DHL as Mark Rampion, "a paragon of sanity and balance, to whom a small group of atrophied and tormented personalities are foils." In the treatment of Frieda as Mary Rampion, Huxley stresses the difficulty that "two people with completely different social backgrounds had in working their way through the early years of conjugal life." but otherwise he "actually burked the thorny aspect of Lawrence's marriage." When he wrote BRAVE NEW WORLD (1932), Huxley intended, in presenting the choice between "insanity" (the modern scientific Utopia) and "lunacy" (the Indian village life), to pillory both industrial civilization and the primitivism that DHL advocated. This novel and BEYOND THE MEXIQUE BAY (1934) were "the last symptons of Huxley's interest in Lawrence's theories."

2890 West, Herbert Faulkner. "A Few Random Thoughts on Modern First Editions," AMERICAN BOOK COLLECTOR, XVI (April 1966), 8-10.

DHL is still popular with collectors and librarians, partly as a result of the work of Warren Roberts in publishing a bibliography of DHL editions (1963).

2891 Wickham, Anna. "The Spirit of the Lawrence Women: A

Posthumous Memoir," TEXAS QUARTERLY, IX (Autumn 1966), 31-50.

[Written by a poet who knew the Lawrences in 1915 and whose upbringing was similar to DHL's, this meandering series of reflections on DHL's attack on motherhood distinguishes sharply between DHL the man, who "dealt honestly with me," and DHL the author, who "writes so portentously from the page." To explain this split in DHL and his denigration of motherhood, Wickham suggests the "class war": the "social ambitions" of the Lawrence women helped to drive him out of his class, but neither teaching nor marriage to Frieda afforded him a secure "victory over the superior people." DHL came to associate "all women" with the Lawrence women, and children with his failure to "own" Frieda, who remained attached to her children. Wickham discusses both *The White Peacock* and *Sons and Lovers* in terms of the "class war," with a sharp eye for the difference between the males like Walter Morel and Annable and the women, especially "the mother who would have set him to the teaching, a condition in which he becomes a spiritual eunuch."]

2892 Widmer, Kingsley. "Notes on the Literary Institutionalization of D. H. Lawrence: An Anti-Review of the Current State of Lawrence Studies," PAUNCH, No. 26 (April 1966), 5-13.

The volume of recent academic criticism and scholarship on DHL has reached such proportions that no reasonable summary is possible. Most academic studies falsify DHL by adapting him to "established orders and repressive sensibilities," and most suffer from insularity derived from "*Bureaucratic Jobbing, Academic Busywork, Doctoral Hacking* and *Critical Con-Jobs*"; recent critical and scholarly works fall into one of the above categories. [The DHL studies touched on briefly in this contentious survey include most of the major critical and scholarly books in English in the DHL revival from the late 1940s to the middle 1960s. See also Mark Spilka, Kingsley Widmer, and Arthur Efron, (Untitled Exchange of Letters), PAUNCH, No. 27 (Oct 1966), 83-96, for Spilka's reply to Kingsley Widmer, Widmer's reply to Spilka, Spilka's rejoinder to Widmer, Arthur Efron's reply to Spilka, Spilka's rejoinder to Efron, and Efron's further reply to Spilka.]

2893 Worthen, John. "D. H. Lawrence," TIMES LITERARY SUPPLEMENT (Lond), 10 Nov 1966, p. 1023.

[Letter to the Editor in reply to Martin Secker, "D. H. Lawrence," TIMES LITERARY SUPPLEMENT (Lond), 3 Nov 1966, p. 1012.] Since the 1916 B. W. Huebsch text of *The Rainbow* was the source of the Thomas Seltzer edition of 1924, which in turn became the source of Martin Secker's reissues of 1926 and 1927, the Secker edition "perpetuated" alterations made in the Huebsch edition, including "considerable omissions in the chapters 'Shame' and 'The Bitterness of Ecstasy' and smaller cuts elsewhere." [See also reply to Secker by Philip Hobsbaum, "D. H. Lawrence," TIMES LITERARY SUPPLEMENT (Lond), 10 Nov 1966, p. 1023; and response by Martin Secker, "D. H. Lawrence," TIMES LITERARY SUPPLEMENT (Lond), 17 Nov 1966, p. 1052.]

2894 "Writing the Play," TIMES LITERARY SUPPLEMENT (Lond), 17 Nov 1966, p. 1041.

The Complete Plays of D. H. Lawrence "will hardly increase his reputation." Although his prose fiction reveals "his splendid ear for dialogue and the keenness and accuracy of his observations," DHL's plays are "casual and discursive" in dialogue and "too much a 'slice of life' to have the . . . emotional concentration that the stage needs." [*The Widowing of Mrs. Holroyd, A Collier's Friday Night, Touch and Go, The Daughter-in-Law, The Fight for Barbara,* and *David* are discussed in light of this thesis.] *The Daughter-in-Law* is the best of the plays, and *David*, because it is the most ambitious, fails the worst. Although *David* has a "malicious wit" in parts, "its ponderous solemnity is altogether defeating."

2895 Yamaguchi, Keizabrô. "D. H. Lawrence Kenkyû ni Okeru Jidenteki Yôso (I)" (D. H. Lawrence: Biographical Elements in His Literature [I]), REVIEW OF ARTS AND SCIENCES (Shibaura Institute of Technology), No. 3 (Feb 1966), 54-60.
[In Japanese.]

2896 Yamaguchi, Keizabrô. "D. H. Lawrence Nijû no Higeki" (D. H. Lawrence: Double Tragedy), STUDIES IN ENGLISH LITERATURE (Hôsei University), No. 9 (Feb 1966), 51-62.
[On DHL's handling of tragedy in "Odour of Chrysanthemums" and *The Widowing of Mrs. Holroyd.*] [In Japanese.]

2897 Yamaji, Katsuyuki. "Lawrence Bungaku ni Okeru Shizen" (Nature in D. H. Lawrence's Literature), VOLCANO (Kagoshima University), No. 2 (March 1966), 20-27.
[In Japanese.]

2898 Yamasaki, Susumu. "*Women in Love* ni Nagareru San Shicho (I)" (Three Central Thoughts in *Women in Love* [I]), REPORTS OF HIMEJI INSTITUTE OF TECHNOLOGY, No. 16B (Oct 1966), 10-22.
[In Japanese.]

2899 Yudhishtar. "The Depiction of Conflict in the Novels of D. H. Lawrence." Unpublished dissertation, University of Leeds, 1966.
[Listed in Lawrence F. McNamee, DISSERTATIONS IN ENGLISH AND AMERICAN LITERATURE (NY and Lond: Bowker, 1969), p. 47]. Rvd and pub as CONFLICT IN THE NOVELS OF D. H. LAWRENCE (Edinburgh: Oliver and Boyd; NY: Barnes & Noble, 1969).

2900 Zampa, Giorgio. "I soggiorni di Lawrence" (Lawrence Abroad), LA STAMPA (Turin), 17 March 1966, p. 3.
The Italian experience is a central aspect of DHL's human, creative, and ideological interests. DHL is interested in both ancient and modern Italy as a sunny and fertile country which he contrasts with black and sterile England. [In Italian.]

1967

2901 Agg, Howard. A CYPRESS IN SICILY: A PERSONAL ADVENTURE. Illustrated by Robert Micklewright (Edinburgh: William Blackwood & Sons, 1967), pp. 4, 34-41, 48, 114, 142, 203, 235, 236-38.
[In this travel book, the author recounts how, on his second journey to Taormina, he visited, and later rented, the Villa Fontana Vecchia, where DHL and Frieda "had stayed for the best part of three years" (1920-1922). The book recounts Agg's stay in the villa, with passing references to DHL's earlier stay there, his travel writings about Taormina, and pilgrimages to the villa by Laurentian enthusiasts and scholars.]

2902 Andrews, W. T. " 'Silence' in D. H. Lawrence," NOTES AND QUERIES, ns XIV (July 1967), 252-53.
The "silences" in DHL's novels strengthen the suggestion that he is a "formal and mannered" novelist. "Announced pauses and silences . . . form an integral part of the rhetorical and dramatic structure of Laurentian fiction."

2903 Antonini, Giacomo. "Prima rappresentazione a Londra di una commedia di D. H. Lawrence" (First Performance in London of one of D. H. Lawrence's Plays), IL GAZZETTINO (Venice), 19 Feb 1967, p. 5.
The performance of *The Daughter-in-Law* by the Traverse Theatre of Edinburgh is an important event. Even though DHL was not a great playwright, his treatment of themes like sexual freedom and class struggle has influenced a number of modern dramatists. [In Italian.]

2904 Aoyama, Seiko. " 'Kiku no Ka' ni Okeru Lawrence Bungaku no Hôga" (D. H. Lawrence's Genius in "Odour of Chrysanthemums"), ESSAYS (Tôkyô University), No. 21 (May 1967), 59-72.
[In Japanese.]

2905 Armytage, W. H. G. "Superman and the System," RIVERSIDE QUARTERLY, III (Aug 1967), 44-51.
DHL was an English Germanist who was thought by one editor to have "absorbed" Nietzsche, Marx, and Wagner and who foresaw a "new education" and a "new relation of man."

2906 Baim, Joseph. "Structure in the Short Stories of D. H. Lawrence," DISSERTATION ABSTRACTS, XXVIII (1968), 4162A. Unpublished dissertation, Syracuse University, 1967.

2907 Baker, Ernest A., and James Packman. "Lawrence, David Herbert [1885-1930]," A GUIDE TO THE BEST FICTION: ENGLISH

AND AMERICAN, INCLUDING TRANSLATIONS FROM FOREIGN LANGUAGES, new and enlgd ed (NY: Barnes & Noble, 1967), pp. 290-92.
[Bibliography of DHL's fiction books, listed by date, with short annotation, including commentary, on each.]

2908 Baker, William E. SYNTAX IN ENGLISH POETRY, 1870-1930 (Berkeley: University of California P, 1967), pp. 33, 65-66, 119-20, 133, 137-38.

DHL achieves "fidelity to the pattern of sensation and tentative response, at the expense of grammatical orthodoxy." His use of the catalogue, fragments, and swiftly superimposed images sometimes enables the reader to perceive one thing as another: "The metaphor becomes a mode of perception." [Discusses "Fish," "Tortoise Shout," and "Turkey Cock."]

2909 Beagle, Peter S. "D. H. Lawrence in Taos," HOLIDAY, XLII (Sept 1967), 45, 86-90.

[In conversations in Taos, Joseph Foster sees DHL as the prophet who changed Foster's life; David Garnett thinks DHL's rages, by providing massive doses of adrenalin, prolonged his life; Dorothy Brett thinks DHL's rages were justified because Frieda was a bully; Rachel and Bill Hawk think Brett had a crush on DHL; and John Evans (Mabel Dodge Luhan's son) remembers DHL as a "loathesome man."]

2910 Bentley, Joseph. "Huxley's Ambivalent Responses to the Ideas of D. H. Lawrence," TWENTIETH CENTURY LITERATURE, XIII (Oct 1967), 139-53.

Huxley's fiction and essays show his "preoccupation with the ironic tensions between flesh and spirit," and his satiric technique depends upon this "dualistic consciousness"--the "scientific or scatological imagery" of "vile flesh." This "simple, formulistic technique" seemingly precludes the "passional blood-consciousness" of DHL. Probably the main reason for DHL's hatred of POINT COUNTER POINT, despite Huxley's advocating Lawrentian ideas in it, was his sensing in the portrait of himself as Rampion "elements which subtly but effectively negated his image of himself." Although Huxley's satiric technique reduces "anti-Lawrentian characters . . . to sub-humanity," it also "tends to make the Lawrentian concept absurd and untenable" by rendering "the body devoid of its alleged 'numinous' significance." [Discusses Huxley's satire of DHL's ideas in THOSE BARREN LEAVES and ANTIC HAY.]

2911 Bickerton, Derek. "The Language of *Women in Love*," REVIEW OF ENGLISH LITERATURE, VIII (April 1967), 55-67.

The language of *Women in Love* exhibits vagueness, repetition, and inflation, all of which make most of the novel seem obscure and intangible. Although F. R. Leavis considers DHL a great master of language, the prevailing high opinion of his prose style after *Sons and Lovers* "needs stringent revision."

2912 Bleich, David. "The Determination of Literary Value," LITERA

TURE AND PSYCHOLOGY, XVII (1967), 19-30.
In PRACTICAL CRITICISM, I. A. Richards fails to consider how misreadings of a poem are psychologically connected with the poem that evokes them. Analysis of readers' responses to DHL's "Piano" demonstrates that their "emotional substitutions" for the poetic content are "defenses which appear . . . violently when the reader consciously or unconsciously perceives the poem's failure to provide its own defenses against the [threatening] content it offers." A "bad" poem, thus, requires reader-supplied defenses; a "good" poem does not. Responses to "Piano" either show lack of control or deplore it in the poem, reinforcing the idea that "form" defends against feeling.

2913 Boklund, Gunnar. "Time Must Have a Stop: Apocalyptic Thought and Expression in the Twentieth Century," DENVER QUARTERLY, II (Summer 1967), 69-98, espec 96.
[The author briefly expresses his impatience with the "monolithic solutions" of such "apocalyptic prophets" as DHL and Robinson Jeffers.]

2914 Brett, Dorothy. "Autobiography: My Long and Beautiful Journey," SOUTH DAKOTA REVIEW, V (Summer 1967), 11-71.
[Brett says that the bond between DHL and her was not "love" or "being in love." It was, rather, that DHL, "a light himself," saw a light in her: "Instinctively, intuitively I was close to him."]

2915 Brophy, Brigid, Michael Levey, and Charles Osborne. "D. H. Lawrence: *Lady Chatterley's Lover*," FIFTY WORKS OF ENGLISH AND AMERICAN LITERATURE WE COULD DO WITHOUT (Lond: Rapp & Carroll, 1967; NY: Stein & Day, 1968), pp. 133-34.
The fact that *Lady Chatterley's Lover* is not banned while John Cleland's FANNY HILL is reveals the "cumulative absurdities" of "British thought and actions about books." DHL's novel lacks literary merit, being merely "a straightforward novelette, which fabricates a wish-fulfilment love affair between a very commonplace novelettish hero . . . and an equally commonplace titled novelettish heroine."

2916 Bryden, Ronald. "Strindberg in the Midlands," OBSERVER (Lond), 19 March 1967, p. 25.
Although it has taken, astonishingly, fifty-five years to reach the stage, *The Daughter-in-Law* shows that if DHL was not "an English Chekhov," he could "have become our Strindberg." Within the framework of "a dialect comedy about an overpowering parent and a strong-minded young wife," it explores the same "emotional territory" and mining cottage setting as *Sons and Lovers*. The quarrel scene "is powerful, compulsive drama," and the ending happy, but not frivolous. "Lawrence feared, correctly, that his contemporaries would find his plays too naturalistic and slow, but he was right and they were wrong." [Review of the Royal Court Theatre production, directed by Peter Gill.]

2917 Carroll, LaVon B. "Syzygy: A Study of the Light-Dark Imagery in Five of the Novels of D. H. Lawrence," PROCEEDINGS OF THE UTAH ACADEMY OF SCIENCES, ARTS, AND LETTERS,

XLIV, No. 1 (1967), 139-49.

"Syzygy" best describes the ontology which DHL inherited from English Puritanism. DHL's "major accomplishment" is his "reworking of the unwieldy, ancient, and universal symbols of duality" in a modern British context. Light-dark imagery is associated with the male-female duality, especially in *The Rainbow* and *Women in Love,* where a "constant shifting and . . . intermingling of the light and dark" embodies a functional ambiguity: "light is not always good, and dark is not always bad. There are many confusing manifestations of both."

2918 Cole, William. "Introduction," *D. H. Lawrence: Poems Selected for Young People* (NY: Viking P, 1967), pp. 9-14.

DHL's genius in other genres blinds readers to the quality of his poetry. Genius must have its own voice: many rhyming poems are wonderful, but the "real voice" is only in the free verse. [Concludes with biographical sketch.]

2919 Cowan, James C. "D. H. Lawrence's 'The Princess' as Ironic Romance," STUDIES IN SHORT FICTION, IV (Spring 1967), 245-51; rptd in Chap. V: "The Quest for Symbol and Myth," in D. H. LAWRENCE'S AMERICAN JOURNEY: A STUDY IN LITERATURE AND MYTH, by James C. Cowan (Cleveland and Lond: P of Case Western Reserve University, 1970), pp. 64-70.

In "The Princess," myth links the basic story with ancient modes of action and belief. DHL employs two "structural and thematic motifs": "the fairy tale of the Sleeping Beauty" and the " 'separation-initiation-return' pattern of romance, . . . the monomyth." But DHL "inverts the pattern of quest as the aging princess rejects her would-be prince only to 'return' to an even deeper slumber than before. The result is a brilliantly realized ironic romance." [A detailed analysis of mythic elements in characterization and plot, drawing on Freud, Joseph Campbell, and others.]

2920 Cowan, James C. "Lawrence's Romantic Values: *Studies in Classic American Literature,*" BALL STATE UNIVERSITY FORUM, VIII (Winter 1967), 30-35; rptd in Chap. II: "Lawrence's Romantic Values," in D. H. LAWRENCE'S AMERICAN JOURNEY: A STUDY IN LITERATURE AND MYTH, by James C. Cowan (Cleveland and Lond: P of Case Western Reserve University, 1970), pp. 24-33.

On the evidence of *Studies in Classic American Literature,* in which DHL espouses the critical values of dynamic organicism and rejects those of static mechanism, his critical theory may be defined as romantic, in Morse Peckham's sense of the term. In essays on Cooper and Poe, respectively, DHL set forth a theory for European emigration to America--to slough the old world consciousness and to grow a new consciousness--and applied it to American literature, which he saw as dual in that it involved both disintegration of the old consciousness and formation of a new one. DHL advocated growth and rejected regression to primitivism. Unsympathetic with perfectionist schemes, which were mechanistic in their exertion of conscious will, DHL advocated the unconscious, creative imagination: one's communion with the pristine unconscious is at the heart of one's relation to others and to oneself, for only by this means is a correction of the imbalance between blood and brain, being and knowing, possible.

2921 Coxhead, Gabrielle. "Schemata and Spontaneity: An Approach to Critical Activity, and to the Critical Writings of D. H. Lawrence." Unpublished dissertation, University of Leicester, 1967. [Listed in Lawrence F. McNamee, DISSERTATIONS IN ENGLISH AND AMERICAN LITERATURE, SUPP I: 1964-1968 (NY and Lond: Bowker, 1969), p. 247.]

2922 Craig, David. "Fiction and the Rising Industrial Classes," ESSAYS IN CRITICISM, XVII (Jan 1967), 64-74.

The novel must work by characterizing individuals, but to depict the conditions of, and solutions for, industrial laborers requires "a sense of what we are collectively." The novel has, accordingly, suffered in characterization, as in George Eliot's sentimental rendering of Felix Holt or DHL's treatment of character in "The Industrial Magnate" chapter of *Women in Love,* in both of which practical morality is sacrificed to moral idealism.

2923 Čura, Ileana. "Lawrence's Conception of Art, Morality and the Novel," ZBORNIK FILOZOFSKOG FAKULTETA (Priština), Vol. A, No. 4 (1967), 401-13; enlgd and rptd as Chap. VIII, in D. H. LAWRENCE AS CRITIC, by Ileana Čura-Sazdanić (Delhi: Munshiram Manoharlal, 1969), pp. 171-201; pub in Serbo-Croatian as "Lorensova koncepcija umetnosti, morala i romana," trans from the English by Milivoje Ilić, STREMLJENJA, No. 2 (1976), 247-64.

DHL, believing that "art should be concrete and true to life" as well as "fundamentally moral," saw "the artist's main concern as the working out of the moral problem and the lively representation of reality." DHL's criticism of art in this context leads to his views of Cézanne, whom he admired for struggling free of "ready-made ... 'mental concepts' "; Thomas Mann, whom he considered unwholesome; Shakespeare, whose " 'living rhythm' " he valued; and Dostoievsky, Hardy, and Tolstoy, all of whom, he thought, punished characters for transgressing the " 'human morality, the mechanical system,' " while representing the " 'greater morality' " merely in the background. [Brief discussion of DHL's critical theories of the novel and of *Sons and Lovers, Women in Love,* and *Lady Chatterley's Lover.*]

2924 Dalton, Jack P. "A Note on D. H. Lawrence," PAPERS OF THE BIBLIOGRAPHIC SOCIETY OF AMERICA, LXI (Third Quarter, 1967), 269.

[Reply to F. P. Jarvis, "A Textual Comparison of the First British and American Editions of D. H. Lawrence's *Kangaroo,*" PAPERS OF THE BIBLIOGRAPHICAL SOCIETY OF AMERICA, LIX (Fourth Quarter, 1965), 400-24.] "Pecker" is defined as slang for *spirits, courage,* and *resolution.* Thus, the change to "life" in the American edition is not so startling as Jarvis thinks.

2925 Dawson, Helen. "Running Off with Lawrence," OBSERVER (Lond), 13 Aug 1967, p. 15.

"Suddenly after 27 years [sic]," DHL's "plays are deemed stage-worthy." *The Fight for Barbara* is an overtly autobiographical work," sometimes coy in its sexual euphemisms, but "workably, if naively, constructed." [The author miscounts the thirty-seven years since DHL's death. Review of the Mermaid Theatre production, directed by Robin Midgley, illustrated with a photograph from the production.]

2926 Draper, R[onald] P. "The Sense of Reality in the Work of D. H. Lawrence," REVUE DES LANGUES VIVANTES (Brussels), XXXIII (1967), 461-70.

DHL is concerned with the relationship between the human and the non-human. Reality to him was that which partook of organic process. This is vividly demonstrated in *The Rainbow* when he describes Ursula's observing a living organism under her microscope. One consequence of DHL's having had such a sense of reality was a radical change in his treatment of character. Although in some passages the writing is strained and the meaning obscure, *The Rainbow* is a great novel of human relations given full and satisfying context of unconscious as well as conscious reality. [Commentary on *The Rainbow, Sons and Lovers, Lady Chatterley's Lover*, and some of DHL's shorter fiction.]

2927 Durham, John. "D. H. Lawrence: Outline for a Psychology of Being." Unpublished dissertation, Occidental College, 1967. [Listed in Lawrence F. McNamee, DISSERTATIONS IN ENGLISH AND AMERICAN LITERATURE (NY and Lond: Bowker, 1969), p. 247.]

2928 Erlich, Richard D. "Catastrophism and Coition: Universal and Individual Development in *Women in Love*," TEXAS STUDIES IN LITERATURE AND LANGUAGE, IX (Spring 1967), 117-28.

Following Heraclitus's idea that all creation is in a continual process of destruction and rebirth, DHL works out the first stage of that rebirth in the sexual union of Birkin and Ursula.

2929 Fifield, William. "Joyce's Brother, Lawrence's Wife, Wolfe's Mother, Twain's Daughter," TEXAS QUARTERLY, X (Spring 1967), 69-87.

[This impressionistic essay, in an effort to "recapture the moment when [DHL] wrote his books. . .as a means of getting within the creative process and better understanding it," lingers over a visit to Taos with Frieda and Angelo Ravagli around 1940 and other places where DHL stayed and wrote.] DHL, perhaps starting "as Hardy" in *Sons and Lovers* but later adding some "fantasia" of sexuality and youthful lyricism of his own, grew increasingly sick and petulant. But *The Rainbow,* with Frieda as Ursula "on a dune. . .awaiting her lover," was "written out of love," as *Lady Chatterley's Lover* was revised "out of despair, doggedly."

2930 Fisher, Alan. "A Day Away from Kiowa," SOUTHWESTERN ART (Austin, TX), I, No. 4 (1967), 18-37.

[Discusses DHL and Frieda at Kiowa Ranch, Frieda's return there, and the Lawrences' relationship with Gladys Fisher, sculptor of the fox figure which once adorned the niche above DHL's tomb. Illustrated with a photograph of the fox sculpture.]

>**2931** Friederich, Werner P. "D. H. Lawrence, Esther Landolt, Filippo Sacchi and Nevil Shute," AUSTRALIA IN WESTERN IMAGINATIVE PROSE WRITINGS 1600-1960: AN ANTHOLOGY AND A HISTORY OF LITERATURE (Chapel Hill: University of North Carolina P, 1967), pp. 226-35.

As a writer about Australia, DHL has three shortcomings: he was just barely acquainted with the continent, having visited there only briefly; his novel about Australia, *Kangaroo*, is concerned more with DHL's inner turmoil than with issues of national concern; and his vision of marriage as a "master-serf relationship" is an obtrusive element in his novel. Additionally, DHL has unsuccessfully and inappropriately transplanted a European ideological struggle, between Marxism and fascism, to Australia.

>**2932** Friedland, Ronald Lloyd. "The Craft of D. H. Lawrence's Short Stories: A Study of Five Early Tales," DISSERTATION ABSTRACTS, XXVIII (1967), 1075A. Unpublished dissertation, Columbia University, 1967.

>**2933** Fu, Shaw-shien. "Imagery as Related to Theme in D. H. Lawrence's Poetry," DISSERTATION ABSTRACTS, XXXVII (1967), 1075A. Unpublished dissertation, University of Wisconsin, 1967.

>**2934** Fujii, Kazumi. "1910-Nendai no D. H. Lawrence" (D. H. Lawrence in 1910s), IPPAN KENKYÛ HOKOKU (Seikei University), IV, No. 5 (Dec 1967), 59-74.

[In Japanese.]

>**2935** Galinsky, Hans. "William Carlos Williams. Eine vergleichende Studie zur Aufnahme seines Werkes in Deutschland, England und Italien (1912-1965). Teil II: England und Italien" (William Carlos Williams: A Comparative Study on the Reception of His Work in Germany, England, and Italy [1912-1965]; Part II: England and Italy), JAHRBUCH FÜR AMERIKA-STUDIEN, No. 12 (1967), 167-205.

DHL is one of the first critics to make William Carlos Williams known in England. As DHL's *Studies in Classic American Literature* and his review of Williams's IN THE AMERICAN GRAIN show, their attitudes toward America are similar: both writers share a feeling for the spirit of the land, the urge to clarify the tensions between the American and European cultures, and the ability to summarize in mythical terms. [In German.]

>**2936** Garrett, Peter K. "Scene and Symbol: Changing Mode in the English Novel from George Eliot to Joyce." DISSERTATION ABSTRACTS, XXVII (1967), 4251A. Unpublished dissertation, Yale

University, 1967; rvd and pub as SCENE AND SYMBOL FROM GEORGE ELIOT TO JAMES JOYCE: STUDIES IN CHANGING FICTIONAL MODE (New Haven: Yale UP, 1969).
[One chapter devoted to DHL.]

2937 Gaya Nuño, Antonia. "El lider fascista en la novela inglesa de nuestro tiempo" (The Fascist Leader in the English Novel of Our Time), CUADERNOS HISPANOAMERICANOS, No. 72 (1967), 632-40.
[The growth of the modern political novel is considered in terms of its origins in Huxley's POINT COUNTER POINT, which suggested the possibility of a totalitarian England, and DHL's *Kangaroo*, which considered the possibility of Australian fascism.] [In Spanish.]

2938 Green, Martin. YEATS'S BLESSINGS ON VON HUGEL: ESSAYS ON LITERATURE AND RELIGION (Lond: Longmans, Green, 1967), pp. 26, 44-45, 51-52, 58-59, 61, 62, 94-95, 101, 151, 195, 212-13, 226, 227, 228, 229, 236-38, 241.
To DHL the difference between art and life was that in art one could give free play to the interesting forces in people and eliminate the dull, everyday realities. In *Sons and Lovers,* Paul sometimes rejects a sexual relationship with Miriam because she offers it against her own more spontaneous impulses. Clara, untroubled by her own sexuality, has an equally distorted sense of her instinctive self. In *Women in Love,* Gerald Crich and Birkin are described in opposite terms: Gerald, a perfect human animal, is on his way to death, whereas Birkin, described as pale, thin, shadowy, is always on the road to health and life.

2939 Gross, Theodore, and Norman Kelvin. "D. H. Lawrence," AN INTRODUCTION TO LITERATURE: FICTION, ed by Theodore Gross and Norman Kelvin (NY: Random House, 1967), pp. 205-10.
[This anthology includes *Love Among the Haystacks,* pp. 211-44, and this introduction. Following a brief biography of DHL, the authors indicate DHL's "numerous and interrelated" themes: blood consciousness, sex as a "mystical experience," "class consciousness," "intense hatred of industrialism" and concomitant fascination with primitive cultures. They also touch on DHL's response to his intellectual milieu: his "dream of leadership" in a time of European fascism, and his concern with sex in a time of Freudian influence. The structure of *Love Among the Haystacks,* built around two couples, is typical of much of DHL's fiction. "Ultimately, Lawrence stands outside his time."]

2940 Hamalian, Leo, and Frederick R. Karl (eds.). THE SHAPE OF FICTION: BRITISH AND AMERICAN SHORT STORIES (NY: McGraw-Hill, 1967), pp. 369-70, 531.
[Brief discussion of theme and seven questions for study of "The Horse Dealer's Daughter," which is reprinted in the anthology, pp. 354-69. A brief biographical note on DHL is included, p. 531.]

2941 Handley, Graham. BRODIE'S NOTES ON D. H. LAWRENCE'S "SONS AND LOVERS" (Lond: James Brodie, 1967; rptd, Lond and Sydney: Pan Books, 1976).

[Contains brief biography of DHL, description of his career as a writer, and summary of critical appraisals of his works; discussion of sources and themes of *Sons and Lovers,* its plot, structure, background, characters, and style; and summary of the plot and questions for discussion.] DHL depended less than most writers on reading as a creative inspiration. Instead, he placed confidence in "blood and flesh as distinct from the intellect," thereby bringing to his novels "a new, vivid awareness of the primary things in life." DHL's main concerns are the subconcious, the instinct, and the sexual impulse; however, his treatment of these issues in *Sons and Lovers* differs from that in later works in that it is poetic rather than didactic. DHL's struggles to assert his individuality in the real world are reflected in his novel. The action is based upon autobiographical sources, and the main characters correspond clearly with members of DHL's family and close friends. DHL's strongly individualized style is consciously manipulated in relation to mood; it is characterized by purposeful repetition, vivid imagery, and irony.

2942 Hanson, Christopher. "SONS AND LOVERS" (D. H. LAWRENCE) (Oxford: Blackwell, 1967).

[Introductory critical notes to *Sons and Lovers,* discussing the "aims and structure," "setting," and "characters and relationships."]

2943 Hartogs, Renatus, with Hans Fantel. "Intercourse with Lady Chatterley," FOUR LETTER WORD GAMES: THE PSYCHOLOGY OF OBSCENITY (NY: M. Evans & Delacorte P, 1967), pp. 268-78.

DHL's use of four-letter words in *Lady Chatterley's Lover* illustrates the function of obscene language from a psychological and cultural point of view.

2944 Henry, G. B. McK. "Carrying On: *Lady Chatterley's Lover,*" CRITICAL REVIEW (Melbourne), X (1967), 46-62; rptd in CRITICS ON D. H. LAWRENCE, ed by W. T. Andrews (Lond: George Allen & Unwin; Coral Gables, FL: University of Miami P, 1971), pp. 89-104.

Lady Chatterley's Lover has been misunderstood as "obsessive" in sexuality. But DHL's letters claim the serious purpose of exploring the "passional, secret places of life." DHL became so expert at sheering away layers of "social being" that his characters appear generalized and "representative in the English class structure." DHL's view is that life in the "waste land" is a "meaningless flux," where the individual is an insignificant and chance victim to social "tradition" and fate, and life is reduced to material and mechanical elements: "function" with "no discernible end." Resignation to nothingness, for Connie, leads to a new awareness of the omnipresent beauty of nature and the realization that life continues "beyond and outside herself." The novel "maintains a fine poise between faith and despair."

2945 Hobson, Harold. "At the Drop of a Straw Hat," SUNDAY TIMES (Lond), 13 Aug 1967, p. 21.

Recent productions of DHL's "unfamiliar stage work" suggest that he was a "considerable dramatist," but *The Fight for Barbara* is a disappointment, especially in the dialogue, which does not seem to be "beyond the erotic resources of a child of fifteen." [Review of the Mermaid Theatre production, directed by Robin Midgley.]

2946 Hodin, J. P. [*Paintings of D. H. Lawrence,* ed by Mervyn Levy], ART JOURNAL, XXVI (Spring 1967), 332.
[Brief notice.] "Lawrence [as a painter] was a discovery in the eyes of a wider interested public."

2947 Hogins, J. Burl, and Robert E. Yarber. READING, WRITING, AND RHETORIC (Chicago: Science Research Associates, 1967), p. 490.
[Brief biographical headnote to "Market Day," from *Mornings in Mexico,* which is reprinted in the anthology, pp. 490-93.] "The tempo and tone of the writing match the leisurely pace of the Indians as they plod to the marketplace."

2948 Honig, Edwin. "Lawrence: 'The Ship of Death,'" MASTER POEMS OF THE ENGLISH LANGUAGE, ed by Oscar Williams (NY: Washington Square P, 1967), pp. 954-57.
"The Ship of Death" concerns the passage from one state to another and employs Egyptian and Greek mythology and traditional Biblical imagery to present not an afterlife but the process of the will actively succumbing to death.

2949 "I Cannot Love a Friend Whose Love Is Words," PAUNCH, No. 29 (May 1967), 10-13.
[Using *The Fox* as a point of departure, the anonymous writer discusses her relationship with a man she met in a bar.]

2950 Ishihara, Fumio. "Lawrence Bungaku no Jigen (V)" (The Dimensions of Lawrencean Literature [V]), BULLETIN OF THE FACULTY OF FOREIGN LANGUAGES (Kitakyûshû University), No. 14 (Sept 1967), 1-23.
[Comparison of DHL to Edgar Allan Poe in terms of the open form and closed form in literature.] [In Japanese.]

2951 Jacobson, Dan. "D. H. Lawrence and Modern Society," JOURNAL OF CONTEMPORARY HISTORY, II (April 1967), 81-92; rptd in D. H. LAWRENCE: A COLLECTION OF CRITICISM, ed by Leo Hamalian (NY: McGraw-Hill, Books, 1973), pp. 133-43.
Any discussion of DHL's social and political thought is bound to center on his "intense and unremitting" hatred of modern society. His "theory of human nature and society" is more "consistently argued out from book to book and essay to essay than has generally been allowed." DHL hated modern man's allegiance to the machine and to the production and consumption of material goods, and argued that men should instead be faithful to "non-human forces outside themselves and greater than themselves." He was in a "line" of writers such as Coleridge, Carlyle, Ruskin, Arnold, and Morris who protested against industrialism, though they would have been dismayed by DHL's negative judg-

ment of "modern benevolence," "social justice," "physical comfort," and "the individual 'personality.' " DHL opposed the "automatically ideal humanity" to which "the liberal, the capitalist, the communist, and the Christian" are equally committed. In *Women in Love,* it is Gerald Crich who embodies this "destructive nihilism of the modern world, with its surface kindliness and productiveness and its inner 'malignity.' " But DHL cannot account for his own motives in hating the "gospel of love." In *Kangaroo,* in order to give DHL's alter ego Somers a motive that DHL finds "emotionally convincing," Somers is made to repudiate the Diggers' leader because Kangaroo "has suddenly and absurdly begun to preach the gospel of love." *The Plumed Serpent,* which represents DHL's "most frenzied rejection of the gospel of love in its social, sexual, and religious forms," is his "worst novel," the product of a "bullying, obsessed will" revealed not only in "cruel or vindictive episodes" but also in "vatic assertions that a totally new and better world is imminent." But such flaws are less important than DHL's perception that modern men are "estranged from their own instinctual disposition" and that this estrangement is likely to intensify "as civilizations increase in technological complexity." The best of his work presents to us, with "extraordinary imaginative intensity, those human needs and aspirations which all our progress should ultimately be intended to serve."

2952 Kamimura, Tatsuhiko. "Sei no Heisoku--'Shima o Aishita Otoko' Kara" (The Blockaded Sex--from "The Man Who Loved Islands"), ENGLISH LITERATURE REVIEW (Kyôto Women's University), No. 11 (Nov 1967), 44-61.
[In Japanese.]

2953 Katsumata, Kikuo. "Shôsetsu *Niji* ni Okeru Ursula no Seichô" (Ursula's Growth in *The Rainbow*), KYÛSHÛ SANGYÔ DAIGAKU KYÔYOBÛ KIYÔ (Kyûshû Sangyô University), III, No. 2 (March 1967), 43-57.
[In Japanese.]

2954 Klein, Marcus, and Robert Pack (eds). SHORT STORIES: CLASSIC, MODERN, CONTEMPORARY (Bost: Little, Brown, 1967), p. 357.
[Prefatory biographical note to "The Blue Moccasins," which is reprinted in the anthology, pp. 358-74, mentioning DHL's upbringing as a frail child in a coal mining community, his "attachment to his mother" and his inability to "commit himself to another woman until he eloped with Frieda von Richthofen," their world wide travels, his censorship problems, his phoenix tombstone.]

2955 Knight, G. Wilson. POETS OF ACTION (Lond: Methuen, 1967), pp. 11, 29-31, 171, 177-78, 180, 214, 262.
[Several earlier English literary figures are briefly compared to DHL.] Puritans such as Spenser and Milton, like DHL, oppose "not a physical instinct but an insidious mind-perversion." Milton, in PARADISE LOST, like DHL, "attacks primarily a lustful or unduly mentalized development of sexual energy." Swift's attack in A TALE OF A TUB, on "all over-intellectualization and a will-o'-the-

wisp science" may be related to DHL's attacks on similar targets. Byron's verse drama MARINO FALIERO includes a "strikingly Lawrentian" "prophetic denunciation" of " 'Prurient yet passionless, cold studied lewdness.' "

2956 Kramer, Vicki Weisberg. "D. H. Lawrence: *The Rainbow* and *Women in Love.*" Unpublished dissertation, Harvard University, 1967. [Listed in Lawrence F. McNamee, DISSERTATIONS IN ENGLISH AND AMERICAN LITERATURE (NY & Lond: Bowker, 1969), p. 247.]

2957 Kumar, Raj. THE MODERN NOVEL (Ludhiana, India: Lyall Book Depot, 1967), pp. 84, 96-104.

[A brief account of the English censorship trial of *Lady Chatterley's Lover* (Regina v. Penguin Books, Ltd., 1960) with a discussion of the Obscene Publications Act of 1959 under which proceedings were taken.] The British Parliament is given "kudos" for the "world-wide publicity" the book received as a result of the Act. In India, where "the crude Hicklin test still applies," *Lady Chatterley's Lover* is still banned.

2958 Kurono, Yutaka. "*The Lost Girl* Shiron--Shudai to Gihô Oyobi Hyôka ni Tsuite" (An Essay on *The Lost Girl*--Theme, Technique and Evaluation), OKAYAMA UNIVERSITY: FACULTY OF LETTERS, No. 26 (March 1967), 27-44.

[In Japanese.]

2959 Kuwayama, Taisuke. "D. H. Lawrence no THE FORSYTE SAGA no Hihyô" (D. H. Lawrence's Critical Essay on THE FORSYTE SAGA), STUDIES IN CULTURAL SCIENCE (Nihon University), No. 8 (March 1967), 56-60.

[On DHL's essay "John Galsworthy."] [In Japanese.]

2960 Langman, F. H. "*Women in Love*," ESSAYS IN CRITICISM, XVII (April 1967), 183-206.

Criticism that finds a structural flaw in *Women in Love* in DHL's failure to "solve the problems of civilization that he analyzes" is based on three assumptions: that DHL's intentions can be known apart from the novel and used as a norm for it; that the novel's structure adheres in a simple contrast of Gerald and Gudrun with Ursula and Birkin; that the novel can be judged by whether it offers a viable, practical solution for the problems of civilization. But DHL's intentions outside the novel are beside the point. The differences between the two pairs of lovers is not a simple contrast between a destructive and a creative ending but between a "closed" and an "open" ending. Ursula and Birkin do not find a "solution"; rather, they "trust life" and keep their options open. Gudrun and Gerald select only a limited number of options and when these run out, their relationship ends. DHL's approach is thus "more exploratory than prescriptive." The weakness in the novel is that it has so much structure that believable characterization is sometimes sacrificed to plot needs.

2961 Lee, R[obin] H. "A True Relatedness: Lawrence's View of Morality," ENGLISH STUDIES IN AFRICA, X (Sept 1967), 178-85.

[The final chapter of *The Rainbow* is examined in the light of statements in "Morality and the Novel" and *A Propos of "Lady Chatterley's Lover."*] DHL's conception of morality demands a reconciliation, achieved only in marriage, between the continuously changing individual and the rhythms of the "circumambient universe."

2962 Lerner, Laurence. THE TRUTHTELLERS: JANE AUSTEN, GEORGE ELIOT, D. H. LAWRENCE (Lond: Chatto & Windus; NY: Schocken Books, 1967), pp. 66-71, 78-83, 172-235, 289-91; excerpt from Part I, Chap. IX: "Lawrence's 'Carbon,'" pp. 78-82, rptd in TWENTIETH CENTURY INTERPRETATIONS OF "THE RAINBOW": A COLLECTION OF CRITICAL ESSAYS, by Mark Kinkead-Weekes (Englewood Cliffs, NJ: Prentice-Hall, 1971), pp. 91-95.

DHL believed life impulses from the unconscious, or "carbon" self, to be sacred, though impersonal, because "carbon" is universal. DHL's subject, as he proclaimed (letter to Edward Garnett, 5 June 1914), is carbon, not the "old, stable ego." DHL writes better about the unconscious in his art than in his theoretical works. His descriptions of carbon make even his realistic passages more truthful than the writing of the realists. [Analysis of Chap. XIII of *The Rainbow* illustrates the point.] Artistic failure and success in DHL are related to the "quick and the diseased" in his idea of man. Hence, the fascism (in *Aaron's Rod, Kangaroo, The Plumed Serpent*) and other manifestations of brutality (e.g., in *Lady Chatterley's Lover*) caused by DHL's intolerance toward intellectuals. The blood-mind dialectic in DHL's work is sometimes confusing when he shifts his terminology (as in the *Study of Thomas Hardy* or *St. Mawr*). Verbal inconsistencies of another kind, relating to Birkin and Ursula, mar *Women in Love*.

2963 Levin, Gerald. THE SHORT STORY: AN INDUCTIVE APPROACH (NY: Harcourt, Brace & World, 1967), pp. 296-98.

[Fourteen questions for study on "The Blind Man," which is reprinted in the anthology, pp. 281-96.]

2964 Levin, Gerald. "The Symbolism of Lawrence's *The Fox*," COLLEGE LANGUAGE ASSOCIATION JOURNAL, XI (1967), 135-41.

In *The Fox*, "March in her own way resembles the fox as much as Henry does --perhaps more so. Indeed, it may be said that the fox symbolizes the life force or Eros of each principal."

2965 Lewis, C[live] S[taples]. STUDIES IN WORDS, 2nd ed (Cambridge: Cambridge UP, 1967), pp. 293 and passim.

[Chap. X, "Life," which comments on DHL, does not appear in the 1st ed (1960).] [Sect. VI]: DHL defines "life" as the emotions as opposed to the intellect, and at times, equates non-human existence with "life." According to DHL, we must "live life"; that is, we must pursue the lifestyle that DHL values.

[Sect. VIII] : DHL's use of the word "life" illustrates the modern tendency to convert the term into a Platonic idea. For DHL, sexual desires are transfused from a supra-personal source. All other life exists "to exalt that entity."

2966 McIntosh, Angus. "A Four-Letter Word in *Lady Chatterley's Lover*," PATTERNS OF LANGUAGE: PAPERS IN GENERAL, DESCRIPTIVE AND APPLIED LINGUISTICS, by Angus McIntosh and M. A. K. Halliday (Bloomington: Indiana UP, 1967), pp. 151-64.

The importance of grammatical analysis in translation in general is well illustrated by close scrutiny of DHL's 293 usages of the verb *to know* in *Lady Chatterley's Lover*. All but forty of these can be translated into French with a form of the verb *savoir*, the others with a form of *connaître*. A computer can be instructed to examine the linguistic environments of these usages of *know* so as to make a satisfactory classification of them into the two categories. Such a dichotomy reveals "the extent to which grammatical as distinct from collocational (lexical) criteria are adequate for the solution of problems" in translation.

2967 Mackenzie, Compton. MY LIFE AND TIMES, OCTAVE SIX: 1923-1930 (Lond: Chatto & Windus, 1967), pp. 84-85, 131-32, 170.

[In 1926 Faith Compton Mackenzie, dining alone with DHL in Capri, poured out " 'the secrets of my heart.' " DHL later used these confidences in a story ("The Man Who Loved Islands," unidentified here), which he could not otherwise have written. In 1928, after "The Man Who Loved Islands" appeared, Mackenzie, despite DHL's protest that " 'it's not meant to be Monty,' " threatened an injunction if the story were included in his forthcoming collection, knowing that if Mackenzie's background were used for a Lawrentian caricature the figure would be taken for a portrait.] [See also Faith Compton Mackenzie, MORE THAN I SHOULD (Lond: Collins, 1940), pp. 32-35; as well as an earlier memoir, Compton Mackenzie, "Memories of D. H. Lawrence," CERTAIN ASPECTS OF MORAL COURAGE (Garden City, NY: Doubleday, 1962), pp. 104-119; and other reminiscences and comments throughout the ten-volume autobiography, especially MY LIFE AND TIMES, OCTAVE FIVE: 1915-1923 (Lond: Chatto & Windus, 1966), pp. 164-73, 176-79, 183-85, 189, 190-93, 235; MY LIFE AND TIMES, OCTAVE SEVEN: 1931-1938 (Lond: Chatto & Windus, 1968), pp. 35-36, 282; MY LIFE AND TIMES, OCTAVE EIGHT: 1939-1946 (Lond: Chatto & Windus, 1969), p. 265.]

2968 Manchester, John. "Thoughts on Brett: 1967," SOUTH DAKOTA REVIEW, V (Summer 1967), 3-9.

[Biographical sketch of Dorothy Brett, mentioning her relation to DHL and Frieda, her following DHL to Taos, her memoir LAWRENCE AND BRETT: A FRIENDSHIP (1933) and her painting of DHL, her response to the Indians, and her visits from students and such figures as Aldous Huxley and Georgia O'Keeffe.]

2969 Marcus, Frank. "The Dominant Sex," PLAYS AND PLAYERS, XIV (May 1967), 19.

Although much of the "archaic Midlands dialect" in *The Daughter-in-Law* is "incomprehensible," "the household tasks. . .have an absolute verisimilitude." DHL "knew he was offering emotional truth: he could have learned to express it in dramatic terms." [Review of the Royal Court Theatre production, directed by Peter Gill.]

2970 Marks, W. S., III. "The Psychology of Regression in D. H. Lawrence's 'The Blind Man,'" LITERATURE AND PSYCHOLOGY, XVII (Winter 1967), 177-92.

DHL's "world-weariness and homesickness" and his "sexual nausea and disappointed longing for some kind of homosexual refuge from Frieda" are integrated in "The Blind Man." The story, which corresponds in "mood, character, and action" to a dream related in a letter to Lady Cynthia Asquith (June 1918), "may be understood as a regression fantasy of classic outline held under a strictly conscious and even erudite control." Both internal and external evidence suggest that C. G. Jung's PSYCHOLOGY OF THE UNCONSCIOUS provided "suggestions toward the typology" of DHL's characters "and a rationale for psycho-drama which runs beneath the narrative surface." [Literary analysis is employed to reveal a Jungian archetypal pattern in the story.]

2971 Marnat, Marcel. [Introduction], "L'Esprit de Conquète" (The Spirit of Conquest), LE MONDE, 19 July 1967.

[The author gives a brief summary of DHL's work and writes that the essay presented here (written by DHL in 1924 and previously unpublished) belongs to a series of texts which constitute a transition between *Kangaroo* and *The Plumed Serpent*.] [In French.]

2972 Matsudaira, Yôko. "Lawrence ni Kansuru Ichi Kenkyû (1)" (A Study of Lawrence [1]), SONODA WOMEN'S COLLEGE STUDIES, No. 2 (Nov 1967), 1-27.

[In Japanese.]

2973 Maud, Ralph. "Introduction," THE NOTEBOOKS OF DYLAN THOMAS (NY: New Directions, 1967), pp. 9-42, espec. pp. 12, 13, 16, 17, 26.

Dylan Thomas cited DHL as among the influences on his "'very first and forever unpublishable juvenilia.'" In *The Man Who Died* and "The Risen Lord," DHL perhaps believed Thoreau's concept that Christ was wrong to starve his physical body.

2974 Miko, Stephen Jon. "D. H. Lawrence: His Development as a Novelist," DISSERTATION ABSTRACTS, XXVIII (1967), 236A. Unpublished dissertation, Yale University, 1967: rvd and pub as TOWARD "WOMEN IN LOVE": THE EMERGENCE OF A LAWRENTIAN AESTHETIC (New Haven and Lond: Yale UP, 1971).

2975 Mizener, Arthur (ed.). "Part Three: Introduction," MODERN SHORT STORIES: THE USES OF IMAGINATION, rvd ed

(NY: W. W. Norton, 1967), pp. 427-31, espec pp. 430-31.
DHL's "stories are like an organism with a translucent skin." The surface is intact, yet reveals his "almost infallible sense of how the buried life of the deep feelings moves." [Introduces "Odour of Chrysanthemums" and "The Shadow in the Rose Garden," which are reprinted in the anthology.]

2976 Nardi, Piero. "Introduzione" (Introduction), *Le tre Lady Chatterley (The Three Lady Chatterleys)* (Milan: A. Mondadori, 1967), pp. xv-xxxviii.

The First Lady Chatterley recalls the spontaneity of DHL's early novels and, in the end, leaves the characters uncertain of their futures. In the second version, DHL accentuates the contrast between the cynical rationality of modern society and the gamekeeper's vitality. *Lady Chatterley's Lover,* the third version of the novel, reveals how DHL uses symbolism consciously and explicitly in order to underline his message. [In Italian.]

2977 Nardi, Piero. "Lawrence drammaturgo" (Lawrence as a Playwright), IL RESTO DEL CARLINO (Bologna), 7 April 1967, p. 3.

The performance of *The Daughter-in-Law* brought DHL as a playwright to the attention of English audiences for the first time. Above all autobiographical, DHL's plays develop several themes of his novels. His most theoretically conceived play is *The Merry-Go-Round,* almost a Shavian farce or a comedy in the tradition of Goldoni. Its central theme is the struggle between male and female on a background of sexual and economic interests. [In Italian.]

2978 Nin, Anais. THE DIARY OF ANAIS NIN, 1934-1939, ed and with a Preface by Gunther Stuhlmann (NY: Swallow P and Harcourt, Brace & World, 1967), pp. vi, 15, 27, 28, 31, 32, 45, 51, 54, 146, 202, 228, 229, 240, 289.

[Passing references to her earlier work, D. H. LAWRENCE: AN UNPROFESSIONAL STUDY (1932) and references to DHL's ideas throughout suggest the continuing influence of those ideas on the author. "I went back to intuitions and instinct when I turned to D. H. Lawrence, and then to Henry (Miller), who represents the non-rational."]

2979 Nosaka, Tôsaku. "D. H. Lawrence: 'Taiyo'" (D. H. Lawrence: "Sun"), KENKYÛ RONBUN-SHÛ (Miyagi Women's College), No. 27 (Jan. 1967), pp. 42-60.

[In Japanese.]

2980 Ôhashi, Yasuichirô. "D. H. Lawrence no Shakespeare-Kan" (D. H. Lawrence's View of Shakespeare), SEKAIBUNGAKU (Tôkyô Toritsu University), No. 29 (Oct 1967), 23-33.

[In Japanese.]

2981 Ôhashi, Yasuichirô. "Shijin Lawrence to Shi (Chû)" (D. H. Lawrence: Poet and Death, The Second Part), MEMOIRS OF HU-

MANISTIC AND SOCIAL SCIENCES (Kyôto Technical University), No. 15 (Jan 1967), 115-44.
[In Japanese.]

2982 Okada, Taiji. "D. H. Lawrence Kuroi Me no Hirameki" (D. H. Lawrence: A Spark of Black Eyes), REVIEW OF KÔBE UNIVERSITY OF MERCANTILE MARINE: PART I : STUDIES IN HUMANITIES AND SOCIAL SCIENCE, No. 15 (March 1967), 166-90.
[In Japanese.]

2983 Okumura, Tohru. "Lawrence Shosetsu no Hitotsu no Imi *Musuko to Koibito* kara *Koisuru Onnatachi* Made" (A Meaning of Lawrence's Novels--from *Sons and Lovers* to *Women in Love*), REVIEW OF ENGLISH LITERATURE (Kyôto University), No. 21 (Aug 1967), 103-17.
[In Japanese.]

2984 Okunishi, Akira. "*Niji* no Ketsumatsu to Symbol to Shite no Niji" (The Conclusion of *The Rainbow* and the Rainbow as a Symbol), ATTIC REVIEW (Kyôto Kôgeiseni University), No. 5 (Feb 1967), 24-33.
[In Japanese.]

2985 Oppel, Horst. "D. H. Lawrence: 'Snake,' " DIE MODERNE ENGLISCHE LYRIK: INTERPRETATIONEN (The Modern English Lyric: Interpretations), ed by Horst Oppel (Berlin: E. Schmidt, 1967), pp. 117-36.
There are similarities in theme and word choice between DHL's poem "Snake" and both the story "Sun" and the essay "The Reality of Peace." The structure of the poem, with its rhythmic effects and iterative phrases, is adapted to the theme, the opposition between man and animal. "Snake" is not a romantic nature poem and does not reveal an anthropomorphic point of view since DHL attempts to see the otherness of the animal. [In German.]

2986 "Original Play by Lawrence Revived," TIMES (Lond), 28 Jan 1967, p. 13.
"Written in 1912, just before *Sons and Lovers*," *The Daughter-in-Law* "shows the same preoccupations as the novel." [Brief plot summary.] "The exposition in Act I is rather long drawn out, and there are some embarrassing bits of sexual philosophy in Act IV. . . .But the central quarrel scene between man and wife in Act II cuts like a knife: a painful, wonderfully penetrating encounter which shows Lawrence at his strongest." [Review of the Traverse Theatre, Edinburgh, production, directed by Gordon McDougall. The second deck of the headline to this review calls the play *The Mother-in-Law*.]

2987 Pinto, Vivian de Sola. "The Burning Bush: D. H. Lawrence as a Religious Poet," MANSIONS OF THE SPIRIT, ed by George A.

Panichas (NY: Hawthorne, 1967), pp. 213-35.

DHL, the first poet after the Romantics "powerfully gifted with the religious vision," sought a God vitally present in the flesh as well as the spirit. *The Rainbow* is a meta-history of the inner life of the Brangwens in a setting penetrated by religious vision. DHL, with Ursula, searches "for a bush where God does burn," but, in *Women in Love*, records the failure of the search. *Aaron's Rod, Kangaroo,* and *The Plumed Serpent* are failed experiments to conceive of power. *Birds, Beasts and Flowers* however, shows a religious apprehension of the creative power of nature and its divine "otherness." Marriage, death, and resurrection are the "burning bush" in three theophanies written in DHL's last years. The vision of *Etruscan Places* might be called DHL's "Paradise Regained," and its purest expression is in *Pansies* and *Last Poems*. DHL's work is religious in that we can see in it the striving for the moment "when art will once again tell Man what his God is, and what he himself is."

2988 Potts, Abbie Findlay. "Pipings of Pan: D. H. Lawrence," THE ELEGIAC MODE (Ithaca, NY: Cornell UP, 1967), pp. 395-432.

DHL's laments and love elegies are in the classical, Virgilian tradition. "Discipline" is a sylvan poem in which DHL invades the classroom with vegetal and animal life. The early poems, lacking Apollonian polish and Dionysian measure, have Panic liveliness. DHL's sense of *kinaesthesia* underlies "Love on the Farm" and others. His reference to his verse flying and lapsing can be related to the elegiac distich or the English septenarius. *Amores, Birds, Beasts and Flowers*, and *Look! We Have Come Through!* owe their composition to the Mediterranean Pan influence. Except for "Evangelistic Beasts," the poems in *Birds, Beasts and Flowers* are idylls rather than elegies. In *Look! We Have Come Through!* DHL is the shepherd and Frieda his "Teutonic Cynthia or Lucy." DHL's Biblical preoccupations, however, haunt the Arcadian in him and are only reconciled in *Last Poems,* where the pipes of Pan "yield to the harp of David" in the creation of elegiac Psalms. The characters in the novels are really elegiac tools in whom investigation and rebuttal move toward *anagnorisis*. More energetic than Yeats, and more imaginative than Hardy, DHL is their elegiac successor. DHL is the prime English elegist of the twentieth century.

2989 Remsbury, John. "'Real Thinking': Lawrence and Cézanne," CAMBRIDGE QUARTERLY, II (Spring 1967), 117-47.

The successor to Dr. Johnson, Wordsworth, and Arnold as a critic, DHL arrived at his insights on the basis of "a serious philosophical questioning about human existence." His basic idea was "the mind's slow confrontation...with the fact of the real existence of the body." His climatic achievement as a critic was the "Introduction to These Paintings," which is "a piece of essential European history" dealing with the effects of the fear of syphilis on the English imagination; "a work of art-criticism, appraising the achievement of Cézanne; and...a philosophical excursion into the problems of seeing and knowing."

2990 Rolph, C. H. [pseud of C. R. Hewitt]. "The Literary Censorship in England," KENYON REVIEW, XXIX (June 1967), 401-22; rptd in WILSON LIBRARY BULLETIN, XLII (May 1968), 912-25.

The "climacteric" year in the history of literary censorship came in 1960 with the acquittal of the publisher in Regina v. Penguin Books, Ltd., on the charge of obscenity for publishing *Lady Chatterley's Lover*. The trial marked the first time that "the evidence of experts as to the literary, scientific, or other merits" of a work was considered admissible evidence under the provisions of the Obscene Publications Act of 1959.

2991 Roy, Chitra. "D. H. Lawrence and E. M. Forster: A Study in Values," INDIAN JOURNAL OF ENGLISH STUDIES, VIII (March 1967), 46-58.

DHL's and E. M. Forster's "unshakable faith in life...places them in the direct humanistic tradition of the English novel," though their geniuses are dissimilar in nature. "Far from being primitivists, the novelists are unequivocally committed to the cause of civilization," unlike the "Wasteland" writers limiting "their distaste to the diseases exhibited" and never extending it to civilization itself. DHL's earlier novels are set in England, but after his difficulties during the war years, he turned to other worlds as a means of exploring "wider and larger regions of consciousness." "*The Lost Girl* and *Aaron's Rod* study the effects of a foreign country and culture upon insular ideas and personalities." *Aaron's Rod, Kangaroo,* and *The Plumed Serpent* study "the nature of political action and leadership" and illuminate "the relation between society and politics." DHL returns in *Lady Chatterley's Lover* "to the problem of industrialized civilization in England, and Mellors, the gamekeeper, sums up his total attitude to culture." In *The Man Who Died,* DHL returns to Christianity, while rejecting "the official interpretation of religion," thus reasserting "his faith in life, his belief in humanism, and in the English and Christian way of life." [Forster's novels are similarly surveyed.]

2992 Rukeyser, Muriel. "A Gate to a Meadow," NEW YORK TIMES BOOK REVIEW, 7 May 1967, Sect. 7, Pt. 2, pp. 6, 40, espec p. 40.

"Fertile in many forms," the poems in *D. H. Lawrence: Poems Selected for Young People,* ed. William Cole, "awake answering resonance in the young, in 'any age,' a view of Lawrence in his streaming and raging fascination and love, frank and instinctual."

2993 Sagar, Keith. "'The Best I Have Known': D. H. Lawrence's 'A Modern Lover' and 'The Shades of Spring,'" STUDIES IN SHORT FICTION, IV (Winter 1967), 143-51.

Toward the end of *The White Peacock,* Cyril, the young, intellectual narrator, having deserted his sweetheart, a farmer's daughter, returns unexpectedly to find himself supplanted by a non-intellectual, an episode DHL was "later to use, twice, as the basis of a short story." In "A Modern Lover," the young man is again named Cyril, but put in the third person to allow DHL to focus ironically on his "play-acting" and "priggishness." In the third version, "The Soiled Rose," responsibility for having kept the relationship on "a spiritual plane" is assigned to the lover, Syson, rather than to Hilda, who is finding a "new womanliness" with Pilbeam, a gamekeeper, whose "thin" characterization weakens the story. In his revision, retitled "The Shades of Spring," DHL creates a free woman able to stand apart and invests the gamekeeper "with special strength." The four versions show DHL's deepening understanding of life and consequently of the possibilities of his art.

2994 Sale, Roger. "Who is Frieda Lawrence?" SEWANEE REVIEW, LXXV (April-June 1967), 355-58.

In FRIEDA LAWRENCE: THE MEMOIRS AND CORRESPONDENCE, ed by E. W. Tedlock, Jr. (1961, 1964), the memoir adds "almost nothing to our knowledge of her life," but the correspondence, especially with John Middleton Murry after World War II, is more interesting. The "really great" DHL is "only fitfully in view," but the "glimpses" of the years 1912-1916 suggest how he could have written fiction in that period. From his marriage to Frieda came those books by DHL which make "greatness out of being lost and being human."

2995 Sellers, W. E. "New Light on Auden's THE ORATORS," PMLA, LXXXII (Oct 1967), 455-64.

In diagnosing the modern human condition in THE ORATORS, Auden supports his own ideas with those of DHL because in 1932 DHL was for Auden the "visionary who could lead man out of the wasteland by restoring to him his long-lost psychic balance." In the third section of the first book of THE ORATORS, Auden describes a new society identical to what DHL envisaged in *Fantasia of the Unconscious* and *The Plumed Serpent*, a society in which self-fulfillment and happiness are achieved for all under the direction of a few wise leaders.

2996 Sepčič, Višnja. "Iracionalna motivacija u Lawrenceovu romanu *Zaljubjene zene*" (Irrational Motivation in Lawrence's Novel *Women in Love*), FORUM, Nos. 3-4 (1967), 508-22.

[In Serbo-Croatian.]

2997 Sepčič, Višnja. "A Link Between D. H. Lawrence's *The Trespasser* and *The Rainbow*," STUDIA ROMANICA ET ANGLICA ZAGRABIENSIA, No. 24 (Dec 1967), 113-26.

Although generally dismissed as uncharacteristic of DHL in its "affected anthropomorphism" and "*fin-de-siècle* aestheticism," *The Trespasser* anticipates "the narrative devices Lawrence was to use later," especially in "the technique of symbolic stylization of the action," by which DHL associates character and landscape in a new relationship. [A detailed analysis of "the scene between Ursula and Skrebensky...in the moonlit stackyard on the occasion of Fred Brangwen's wedding supper" demonstrates how the technique functions in the mature fiction of *The Rainbow*. Then a close examination of the scene in which "Siegmund and Helena," lying "on the slope of the hill by the sea," "watch the night sky, meditate on life and their personal destinies," demonstrates DHL's "first clumsy attempt at developing this particular stylistic device" in *The Trespasser*.] The "symbolic stylization of the psychical relationship between the characters" in *The Trespasser* leads to DHL's development in *The Rainbow* of "a new stylistic convention by means of a highly individual application of the techniques of poetry on to narrative prose."

2998 Soldati, Mario. "Lawrence scrittore pigro nelle lettere agli amici" (Lawrence as a Lazy Writer in His Letters to Friends), IL GIORNO (Milan), 25 Oct 1967, p. 3.

DHL's letters are lively and interesting. In some of them, however, the same ideas and judgments are repeated; this feature is probably the evidence of a lazy attitude in DHL as a letter writer. [In Italian.]

2999 Spilka, Mark. "Lawrence's Quarrel with Tenderness," CRITICAL QUARTERLY, IX (Winter 1967), 363-77.

Mellors's courage in *Lady Chatterley's Lover* in affirming tenderness "as part of his masculine strength" and his ability "to accept connection, or dependence on another," are the measure of DHL's success in freeing himself "from maternal dominance," accepting "his masculine heritage," and asserting "his masculine selfhood." But Mellors's limiting his tenderness to Connie, not allowing it to radiate outward "to enrich relations with the world," is the result of DHL's inability to see, finally, that tenderness "is the true maternal heritage by which... we claim the deepest love and release the highest feelings."

3000 Suehiro, Yoshitaka. "D. H. Lawrence no Shokan ni Tsuite no Kenkyû" (A Study of the Letters of D. H. Lawrence), JOURNAL OF THE SECOND COLLEGE OF ENGINEERING, NIHON UNIVERSITY, Series B, VIII, (March 1967), 25-33.

[In Japanese.]

3001 Tao, Sadako. "*Musuko to Koibito* no Nakano Lawrence" (Lawrence in His *Sons and Lovers*), ENGLISH AND AMERICAN STUDIES (Wayô Women's University), No. 5 (Nov 1967), 73-83.

[In Japanese.]

3002 Taylor, John Russell. "First Nights," PLAYS AND PLAYERS, XV (Oct 1967), 40.

The Fight for Barbara, although "not by any standard a very good play," is presented, in the Mermaid production directed by Robin Midgley, as the second half of a double bill, in which it is preceded, with "appealing irony," by a reader's theater program called *Men and Women*, drawn from the writings of DHL, Frieda, and Ernest Weekley, which parallel the play. Thus, "Lawrence's ideas about sex and the sexes are neatly juxtaposed with his own actions in life."

3003 Tetsumura, Haruo. "*The Man Who Died* ni Tsuite (Shûkyô-teki de Arukoto to Sono Hyôgen)" (A Study on *The Man Who Died*: Religiousness as Lawrence's Quintessence), HIROSHIMA STUDIES IN ENGLISH LANGUAGE AND LITERATURE (Hiroshima University), XIV, No. 2 (Dec 1967), 53-65.

[In Japanese.]

3004 Thorn, Fritz. "Politik in kleinen Dosen" (Politics in Small Portions), SUDDEUTSCHE ZEITUNG, 4 April 1967.

DHL's *The Daughter-in-Law* is a social problem play which illustrates the life of a miner's family. Its language and style are realistic, though not in the sense of Galsworthy or Ibsen. The social situation is shown through the states of mind of the characters. [In German.]

3005 Trilling, Lionel (ed). THE EXPERIENCE OF LITERATURE: A READER WITH COMMENTARIES (NY: Holt, Rinehart, & Winston, 1967), pp. 663-74; commentary rptd as " 'Tickets, Please': D. H. Lawrence, 1885-1930," in PREFACES TO THE EXPERIENCE OF LITERATURE, by Lionel Trilling (NY: Holt, Rinehart & Winston [Uniform Edition of Trilling's Works], 1979), pp. 123-27.

[Preface to "Tickets, Please," which is reprinted in the anthology.] DHL is one of the writers who, given women's new status after World War I, wished to resolve the relationship between men and women. While the women in the story are hostile to the male sexual advantage, they are nonplussed by their own actions when they imbalance the situation. DHL directs humor and tenderness toward these women, whose conduct seemingly "unsexes" them but actually underlines their intense sexuality.

3006 Turner, G. R. "Princess on a Rocking-Horse," STUDIES IN SHORT FICTION, V (Fall 1967), 72.

DHL's "The Rocking Horse Winner" was based on real-life "characters in search of an author": Dorothy Brett's sister, Lady Sylvia Brooke (the mother); Brett's brother-in-law, Sir Charles Brooke, White Rajah of Sarawak (the father); and her niece, Leonora Brooke, "the neurotic child who pooled her bets on horse races with a family servant" and "spent hours on end in her bedroom, alone with. . . a rocking horse." Uncle Oscar of the story was Brett herself, the only family member to know about her niece's betting.

3007 Tynan, Kenneth. "Lady Chatterley's Trial (The Old Bailey, 20 October-2 November 1960)," TYNAN RIGHT AND LEFT: PLAYS, FILMS, PEOPLE, PLACES AND EVENTS (Lond: Longmans; NY: Atheneum, 1967), pp. 237, 343, 406-12.

Despite "the waves of pro-Lawrence partisanship. . .from the public gallery," the verdict in the 1960 *Lady Chatterley's Lover* trial (Regina v. Penguin Books) was by no means as certain as it seems in retrospect. Mr. Justice Byrne showed no favor toward the defense, and the expert witnesses delivered "lectures on the nature of literature, clouding the air with semantic evasions." Over the trial hung the fallacy that characters' "immoral behaviour" makes a book "immoral" and thus, by definition, "obscene." Mr. Gerald Gardiner, the defense counsel, restated "the novel's twin themes--the danger that industrialisation would destroy human relationships, and the consequent need to affirm the supremacy of instinct over intellect." "The crucial incident" of the trial was an exchange in which Richard Hoggart called the novel " 'puritanical' " and Mr. Mervyn Griffith-Jones, the counsel for the prosecution, who "exhaled class consciousness" and "disdain," read aloud several "impressive passages," which Hoggart declared were indeed puritanical.

3008 Uchiki, Jôtarô. "*Shinda Otoko* ni Tsuite" (On *The Man Who Died*), SYLVAN (Tôhoku University), No. 12 (Dec 1967), 15-24.

[In Japanese.]

3009 Uehata, Yoshikazu. "D. H. Lawrence no 'Barazono no Kage' ni Okeru Shûkyô Teki Yôso" (Religious Elements in D. H. Lawrence's "The Shadow in the Rose Garden"), BUNGAKU-KAI RONSHÛ (Kônan University), No. 33 (March 1967), pp. 67-83. [In Japanese.]

3010 Waldron, Philip. "Book Reviews," AUMLA: JOURNAL OF THE AUSTRALASIAN UNIVERSITIES LANGUAGE AND LITERATURE ASSOCIATION, No. 27 (May 1967), 122-24.

The Complete Plays of D. H. Lawrence, which includes eight plays and two fragments, is "a slipshod and careless production." *The Daughter-in-Law*, which has affinities with *Sons and Lovers*, is DHL's best play and "one of the best plays by any modern English dramatist." *The Widowing of Mrs. Holroyd* is a less effective and less economical treatment of "Odour of Chrysanthemums." *Touch and Go* reflects DHL's later concerns in *Women in Love*. *David*, "an overwritten and tactless play," "gracelessly sets forth" ideas about which DHL "cared deeply."

3011 Wardle, Irving. "Forgotten Play Shows Power of Genius," TIMES (Lond), 10 August 1967, p. 5.

The Fight for Barbara, "an autobiographical transcript of Lawrence's first months in Italy with the abducted Frieda," "is a dramatization of the opening question, 'Shall we bring it off?' " Although DHL "suppresses all reference to Frieda's three children, and passes off her deserted husband and her parents as a blockish chorus of social conformity," "the play is essentially a duet for the lovers; and on these terms autobiography blazes up into art." [Review of the Mermaid Theatre production, directed by Robin Midgley.]

3012 Wardle, Irving. "Lawrence Play with a Strindberg Touch," TIMES (Lond), 17 March 1967, p. 12.

In *The Daughter-in-Law,* one of a group of "closely naturalistic" plays written in 1912, DHL draws on his parents to show "a mother-dominated young collier going through mental hell" with a wife who has "superior manners and a small inheritance--two factors which destroy the husband's self-respect." "Not even Strindberg has a greater power to convey the feelings of the devitalized male." Although the device by which the couple are unbelievably reunited at the end is mechanical, "what is real is the sense of incurable tension: a bond that holds the characters permanently together." [Review of the Royal Court Theatre production, directed by Peter Gill.]

3013 Wasson, Richard. "Comedy and History in *The Rainbow*," MODERN FICTION STUDIES, XIII (Winter 1967-1968), 465-77.

The central metaphor of *The Rainbow* is marriage, the traditional comic image for fulfillment in personal, social, and sexual terms. In comedy erotic fulfillment is usually blocked by reactive external social forces, but in *The Rainbow* the struggle is to overcome one's personal past, one's infantile, Oedipal images. Tom Brangwen passes into adult sexuality only when he ceases wanting to make Anna a lady, a vicarious sexual wish, and turns to Lydia, who reveals to him how "passionately lovely to himself" he can be. Tom cannot, however, hold back the forces of history. When Anna goes forth into a world where chaos has increased, she marries Will Brangwen, a man who, having lost contact with nature's rhythms, lives primarily by art, and who, lacking any independent, adult self, turns in his weakness to Ursula. His attitude toward her is basically incestuous and death oriented; her resulting feelings of inferiority lead to the problem of sexual dominance in her relationship with Anton Skrebensky. Although freeing herself from her past will be difficult in a civilization which, after the flood at Marsh Farm, has reached a dead end, Ursula assimilates her infantile images, as symbolized in the menacing horses, and works through to a new vision of self--the rainbow.

3014 Waugh, Alec. MY BROTHER EVELYN AND OTHER PROFILES (Lond: Cassell,1967); pub in America as MY BROTHER EVELYN AND OTHER PORTRAITS (NY: Farrar, Straus & Giroux, 1968), pp. 46, 115, 116, 259, 260, 262.
[The author "never met Lawrence," but comments briefly on DHL and Michael Arlen (pseud of Dikran Kouyoumdjian), whom DHL caricatured as Michaelis in *Lady Chatterley's Lover.*]

3015 Weatherby, H. L. "Old-Fashioned Gods: Eliot on Lawrence and Hardy," SEWANEE REVIEW, LXXV (April-June 1967), 301-16.
While both "conceive of a Life Force," Hardy does not share DHL's confidence in it. [The point is discussed with reference to DHL's comments on UNDER THE GREENWOOD TREE, Arabella, and Sue Bridehead.] The " 'emotional paroxysms' " of Hardy's characters are "cured" by their "incorporation into a traditional and rational order," whereas from DHL's viewpoint, "rationality or consciousness" "isolates man" from the "universal flux of the Life Force."

3016 Weintraub, Stanley. BEARDSLEY: A BIOGRAPHY (NY: George Braziller, 1967), pp. 246-47.
DHL planted in *The White Peacock* "a sensitive youth's discovery" of Beardsley's "Atalanta" and the tail-piece to "Salome." [Quotes opening passage from Chap. III.]

3017 Wolpers, Theodor. "Formen mythisierenden Erzählens in der modernen Prosa: Joseph Conrad im Vergleich mit Joyce, Lawrence und Faulkner" (Myth-Making in Modern Prose Narrative: Joseph Conrad Compared with Joyce, Lawrence, and Faulkner), LEBENDE ANTIKE: SYMPOSIUM FÜR RUDOLF SÜHNEL, ed by Horst Meller and Hans-Joachim Zimmermann (Berlin: E. Schmidt, 1967), pp. 397-422.
Myth, for Conrad a symbol of a mysterious reality, enables DHL to analyze the needs of civilized man. Like Conrad he chooses exotic landscapes in *The Plumed Serpent* and "The Woman Who Rode Away." Yet the wilderness does not embody danger but the source of man's rebirth. [In German.]

3018 Yamaguchi, Keizabrô. "D. H. Lawrence Kenkyû ni Okeru Jidenteki Yôso (II)" (D. H. Lawrence: Biographical Elements in His Literature [II]), REVIEW OF ARTS AND SCIENCES (Shibaura

Institute of Technology), No. 4 (Feb 1967), 114-20.
[In Japanese.]

3019 Yamaguchi, Keizabrô. "D. H. Lawrence no Shûkyôteki Tsuikyû (*David* ni Tsuite)" (D. H. Lawrence's Religious Quest--The Biblical Play *David*), BULLETIN OF THE FACULTY OF LIBERAL ARTS (Hôsei University), No. 11 (April 1967), 93-114.
[In Japanese.]

3020 Yamasaki, Susumu. "*Women in Love* ni Nagareru San Shicho (II)" (Three Central Thoughts in *Women in Love* [II]), REPORT OF HIMEJI INSTITUTE OF TECHNOLOGY, No. 17B (Oct 1967), 12-29.
[In Japanese.]

3021 Yasukawa, Akira. "D. H. Lawrence no *David*" (On D. H. Lawrence's *David*), ESSAYS AND STUDIES (Kansai University), XIV, No. 3 (Jan 1967), 1-16.
[In Japanese.]

3022 Yokota, Chuzô. "D. H. Lawrence no *Musuko to Koibito* ni Tsuite" (On D. H. Lawrence's *Sons and Lovers*), BULLETIN OF COLLEGE OF GENERAL EDUCATION (Tôhoku University), VI (March 1967), 75-93.
[In Japanese.]

3023 Zytaruk, George J. (ed.). "Letters to Koteliansky," by D. H. Lawrence, MALAHAT REVIEW, I (Jan 1967), 17-40.
[Editor's Note, pp. 17-18.] The letters from DHL to S. S. Koteliansky, published here for the first time, are authentic documents which enable us to appreciate DHL's capacity for friendship and which enlarge the stature of Koteliansky by revealing his part in DHL's career. [Texts of twenty letters from the years 1914-1919 are published in full. See also George J. Zytaruk (ed.), *The Quest for Rananim: D. H. Lawrence's Letters to S. S. Koteliansky, 1914 to 1930* (1970), which reprints these letters.]

3024 Zytaruk, George J. "The Phallic Vision: D. H. Lawrence and V. V. Rozanov," COMPARATIVE LITERATURE STUDIES, IV, No. 3 (1967), 283-97; rptd as Chap. V in his D. H. LAWRENCE'S RESPONSE TO RUSSIAN LITERATURE (The Hague and Paris: Mouton, 1971), p. 145-68.
DHL's reading, in April 1927, of S. S. Koteliansky's translation of V. V. Rozanov's SOLITARIA enabled him suddenly to grasp the essence of that phallic vision of life "which came to dominate his later writing." He proceeded immediately then to embody this vision in *The Man Who Died* and the second and third versions of *Lady Chatterley's Lover*.

1968

3025 Adelman, Gary. "The Painted Tombs of Tarquinia," D. H. LAWRENCE REVIEW, I (Spring 1968), 75-76.
[Poem on revisiting the Etruscan tombs of Tarquinia, attempting to recreate DHL's experience of them and sometimes quoting DHL's descriptions.]

3026 Adler, Renata. "The Apes, the Fox, and Charlie Bubbles," NEW YORK TIMES, 25 Feb 1968, Sect. 2, pp. 1, 4.
The film version of *The Fox* "makes everything repressed in the book overt and explicit on the screen."

3027 Alexander, Edward. "Thomas Carlyle and D. H. Lawrence: A Parallel," UNIVERSITY OF TORONTO QUARTERLY, XXXVII (April 1968), 248-67.
Carlyle and DHL have many parallel attitudes, chiefly in their common hatred of the mechanization in modern society. Carlyle's balm was work; DHL's sex. Both sought no social reforms and, instead, desired an apocalyptic rebirth, as symbolized in the phoenix. Analytical science, which brought about an unnatural self-consciousness, was the enemy of the dark powers of the unconscious. Democracy and equality bred an enervating striving that sickened and weakened the social order. DHL and Carlyle seek a dictator who can re-establish a principle of aristocracy. This view is reflected in an insistence on an ordained sexual role for women, a reverence for the saving possibilities of work, a religious belief in the harmony of nature over culture. John Stuart Mill and Bertrand Russell stand as contemporary counterparts to Carlyle and DHL respectively.

3028 Amette, Jacques-Pierre. "Lettres Étrangères" (Foreign Letters), LA NOUVELLE REVUE FRANÇAISE, XVI (Aug 1968,) 155-56.
"The Princess" and "The Horse-Dealer's Daughter," centered in the reality of sexual passion, are brutal and powerful short stories that reveal DHL's use of dense metaphors and his yearning after myths. Their theme is the conflict between the social and the natural being. [In French.]

3029 Andersch, Alfred. "Auf der Suche nach dem englischen Roman" (In Search for the English Novel), FRANKFURTER ALLGEMEINE ZEITUNG (Bilder und Zeiten), 21 Sept 1968.
DHL, one of the greatest modern English novelists, is nothing more than the author of a romantic novel (*Lady Chatterley's Lover*) to many German intellectuals. [In German.]

3030 Armytage, W. H. G. "The Novel as the Hole in the Wall: D. H. Lawrence's *Rainbow*," YESTERDAY'S TOMORROWS: A HISTORICAL SURVEY OF FUTURE SOCIETIES (Toronto: Uni-

versity of Toronto P; Lond: Routledge & Kegan Paul, 1968), pp. 106-8; additional references, pp. 215, 244n.
DHL believed that " 'faith and belief and the Temple must be broken'. . . 'And behold, out of the ruins leaps the whole sky.' " Although he "never wrote about the future, his prophetic quality" in *The Rainbow* is paramount, and *Fantasia of the Unconscious* gives "a blue-print for an age to be."

3031 Arnold, Armin. "Genius with a Dictionary: Reevaluating D. H. Lawrence's Translations," COMPARATIVE LITERATURE STUDIES, V (Dec 1968), 389-401.
DHL's translations of the works of Giovanni Verga remain the best available in English, Giovanni Cecchetti's animadversions to the contrary notwithstanding. [See also Giovanni Cecchetti, "Verga and D. H. Lawrence's Translations," COMPARATIVE LITERATURE, IX (Fall 1957), 333-44.]

3032 Ashley, Leonard R. N., and Stuart L. Astor (eds). BRITISH SHORT STORIES: CLASSICS AND CRITICISM (Englewood Cliffs, N. J.: Prentice-Hall, 1968), pp. 148, 163-65.
[This anthology includes "The Rocking-Horse Winner," pp. 149-63, and a brief introductory note, suggesting that Paul's luck is motivated by his "deepest vitality and joy in life," de-emphasizing the importance of sex in the story. Short extracts from other reviews and criticisms are included at the end of the story.]

3033 Asquith, Lady Cynthia. DIARIES, 1915-1918, ed by E. M. Horsley, with a foreword by L. P. Hartley (Lond: Hutchinson, 1968; NY: Knopf, 1969), pp. xi, 16, 18, 19-20, 21, 30, 37, 38, 45-46, 56, 57, 58, 68, 70, 79, 80, 85, 86, 89, 92, 93-95, 96, 97-98, 101, 103, 111, 112, 133, 206, 213, 216, 233-34, 244, 257, 293-94, 295, 296, 299, 355, 356, 357, 359, 361, 362, 364, 365, 367, 369, 372, 376, 382, 415, 416, 417, 418, 419, 421, 423, 424, 431, 433, 480.
[Lady Cynthia records frequent letters and visits from DHL and her thoughts and conversations with others about him at various times in their long friendship. Among the topics she discusses are the following: DHL's "extraordinarily real and living" talk and his "gift of intimacy" and "perceptiveness" (11 May 1915); their discussions of the war, and DHL's "*idee fixe* that 'destruction' is the end, and not the means to an end, in the minds of soldiers" (21 June 1915); his "horror of the absolute deadness of the lives of miners in the new kind of highly organized mines" (20 July 1915); the suppression of *The Rainbow* (10 Nov 1915 and after); DHL's "word-picture" of Lady Cynthia in "The Thimble" (15 Nov 1915); DHL's delightful sense of humor, experienced in person but absent from his books (23 April 1917); his denunciation of Lloyd George "and such-like *canaille*" (29 April 1917); the Lawrences' expulsion from Cornwall (16 Oct 1917); her discussions with DHL on "the disintegration of family life and general collapsing of the moral sense resulting from the war" (4 Dec 1917); the impression that several people have that Lady Cynthia and DHL are in love (18 Feb 1916, 19 Dec 1917); her discussion with others of a "subscription" toward "the possible publication of Lawrence's novel *Goats and Compasses*" (28 Feb 1918); her reading *Women in Love* in manuscript--a "nightmarish,"

"fantastic," and "morbid" work (24 March 1918).

3034 Asselineau, Roger. "Comptes Rendus" (Reviews), ÉTUDES ANGLAISES, XXI (Oct-Dec 1968), 438-39.
The Symbolic Meaning: The Uncollected Versions of "Studies in Classic American Literature," ed by Armin Arnold (1962), collects the first versions of essays written during World War I at the time of DHL's persecution by British authorities for his pacifism and of the suppression of *The Rainbow,* but before his departure for the United States. Free of excessive didacticism and very reasonable in development, these texts were transformed completely when DHL rewrote them in the U. S. in 1922-1923 in the tormented and passionate definitive version, which omitted "The Two Principles," originally written as an introduction to the chapters on Dana and Melville. [In French.]

3035 Baim, Joseph. "The Second Coming of Pan: A Note on D. H. Lawrence's 'The Last Laugh,'" STUDIES IN SHORT FICTION, VI (Fall 1968), 98-100.
"The Last Laugh" can be read most accurately "if one recognizes that each character is symbolic of a different response to the essential nature and spirit of life," embodied in the figure of Pan. A characteristic DHL comment on "the tension between the mind and the body," the story "builds on an ironic reversal of Christ's 'Second Coming,' in which Pan, not Jesus, has the 'last laugh.'" [The symbolism is spelled out in some detail.]

3036 Bauerle, Richard F. "Eberhart's 'Throwing the Apple,'" EXPLICATOR, XXVII (Nov 1968), Item 21.
Although based on DHL's painting *Throwing Back the Apple,* Richard Eberhart's poem "Throwing the Apple" is more than a word picture of it, as is indicated by Eberhart's title, which emphasizes Adam's initiative rather than his mere ability to react.

3037 Baumbach, Jonathan, and Arthur Edelstein (eds). MODERNS AND CONTEMPORARIES: NINE MASTERS OF THE SHORT STORY (NY: Random House, 1968), pp. 187-89.
[Brief commentary on DHL's works introducing the stories "The Prussian Officer," "Tickets, Please," and "The White Stocking," which are reprinted in the anthology, pp. 190-246.] DHL's best stories "capture the pulse of an experience." Although not conventionally so, DHL is a religious writer, for whom the sexual experience is a religious one. For him, there is nothing deader than "mental consciousness" when it outweighs "blood consciousness."

3038 Bayley, John. "A Second Phoenix," SPECTATOR, CCXX (2 Feb 1968), 137-38.
Phoenix II: Uncollected, Unpublished, and Other Prose Works by D. H. Lawrence, ed by Warren Roberts and Harry T. Moore, brings together a number of pieces previously unpublished or now unobtainable. [The author comments briefly on *A Propos of "Lady Chatterley's Lover,"* "Prologue to *Women in Love,"* and *Mr. Noon,* and discusses "Introduction to MEMOIRS OF THE

FOREIGN LEGION" ("the most impressive and remarkable single item in *Phoenix II*") with reference to Norman Douglas's D. H. LAWRENCE AND MAURICE MAGNUS: A PLEA FOR BETTER MANNERS (1924).]

3039 Beachcroft, T[homas] O[wen] THE MODEST ART: A SURVEY OF THE SHORT STORY IN ENGLISH (Lond: Oxford UP, 1968), pp. 48, 117, 120, 161-64, 174, 177, 195, 204-9, 210, 211.

A writer of power and brilliance, DHL is at his best within the limits of the short story form which forces shape and brevity on him. Some early stories, such as "Strike-Pay" and "Odour of Chrysanthemums," are like "miniatures" from the world of *Sons and Lovers*. "The Prussian Officer" must be experienced rather than judged because story and character are swallowed up by a nightmare of self-revelation. DHL is unsurpassed in projecting his own range of human emotions, of the interchanges of feelings, "vibrations in the air" which pass between people. His later stories are cooler, more quietly presented. They range from social satires like "Two Blue Birds" to *The Man Who Died*, in which DHL's "teaching" is brought to its clearest point. DHL is a genius at depicting close personal relations in depth, and often animals and the natural world serve as metaphors for the kind of depths he explores.

3040 Beards, Richard D., assisted by G. B. Crump. "D. H. Lawrence: Ten Years of Criticism, 1959-1968, a Checklist," D. H. LAWRENCE REVIEW, I (Fall 1968), 245-85.

[A checklist of secondary criticism and scholarship which brings up to date the earlier DHL bibliography by Maurice Beebe and Anthony Tommasi, "Criticism of D. H. Lawrence: A Selected Checklist with an Index to Studies of Separate Works," MODERN FICTION STUDIES, V (Spring 1959), 83-98. Entries dated before 1959 are included if they were not listed in the MFS checklist. This bibliography, which covers the period from spring 1959 to summer 1968, is organized into five sections: General, Poetry, Individual Works of Fiction, Non-Fiction Prose, and Drama, with individual works discussed in the items in the General section indexed in the last four sections. With the publication of Richard D. Beards with the assistance of Barbara Willens, "D. H. Lawrence: Criticism: September, 1968--December, 1969: A Checklist," THE D. H. LAWRENCE REVIEW, III (Spring 1970), 70-79, DHLR began its series of annual checklists of secondary criticism and scholarship on DHL.]

3041 Bell, Quentin. BLOOMSBURY (NY: Basic Books, 1968), pp. 11n, 12n, 70-78.

DHL's relationship with Bloomsbury was tenuous, brief, painful, and fraught with dislike for most people connected with it. His deepest aversions were to Duncan Grant, John Maynard Keynes, and Francis Birrell, who made him "dream of beetles." DHL's antipathy was based, perhaps, not on opposing intellectual principles but on his fear of homosexuality in himself after sensing it in others.

3042 Benstock, Bernard. "The Present Recaptured: D. H. Lawrence and Others," SOUTHERN REVIEW, ns IV (Summer 1968), 802-16, espec. 805-9.

A "psychologically false note" in *The White Peacock* (reissued in 1968) is DHL's reduction of the father to "a pathetic nonentity," then killing him off "with a minimum of attention," thus dismissing "with ease a figure who will spring back to life in *Sons and Lovers,* where the maturer artist...would have to come to grips with him." [Also reviews D. H. LAWRENCE AND HIS WORLD, by Harry T. Moore and Warren Roberts; THE FORKED FLAME: A STUDY OF D. H. LAWRENCE, by H. M. Daleski; D. H. LAWRENCE AS A LITERARY CRITIC, by David J. Gordon; and THE ART OF D. H. LAWRENCE, by Keith M. Sagar.]

3043 Blöcker, Günter. "Schwebezustand" (Balance), FRANKFURTER ALLGEMEINE ZEITUNG, 23 Oct 1968.

DHL is more of an artist than a prophet in his short fiction. He did not succeed in resolving the tension between artistic and didactic aims in his novels. [In German.]

3044 Boulton, James T. "Preface" and "Introduction," *Lawrence In Love: Letters to Louie Burrows,* ed by James T. Boulton (Nottingham: University of Nottingham, 1968), pp. vii-xxviii.

Made available in 1966, these 165 letters "treble the number of letters by Lawrence for the period 1906-1910; they double the number for his 'sick year' 1911." Amid unfavorable circumstances, "Louie seemed to offer security, integrity, and the hope of sexual fulfillment," but their relationship failed because DHL sought "an ideal relationship which would provide mutual fulfillment while not denying the individual, the fundamental unity of the two people involved." [Many notes.]

3045 Bowering, Peter. ALDOUS HUXLEY: A STUDY OF THE MAJOR NOVELS (Lond: Athlone P, University of London, 1968; NY: Oxford UP, 1969), pp. 25-26, 28, 55, 66, 77, 78, 81, 91, 93-94, 96, 124, 131, 132, 133-36, 214, 215, 226, 228, 230, 234.

In Huxley's ANTIC HAY, Lypiatt, with his "philosophy of life worship," sometimes seems a burlesque of DHL but often speaks with the voice of the author. In POINT COUNTER POINT and the volume of essays DO WHAT YOU WILL, both published in 1928, Huxley's anti-clericalism and his "growing distrust of intellectualism" are "the result of Lawrence's influence"; in the novel, "The counter theme expresses the Laurentian idea that 'Life is only bearable when the mind and body are in harmony, and there is a natural balance between them.'" Another "measure of Lawrence's influence" is "that the search for spiritual truth...is undertaken in this novel by the perverted Spandrel." In EYELESS IN GAZA, Anthony, sleepless, reads DHL's *The Man Who Died.* Anthony's ultimate rejection of "the concept of the self as a 'succession of unconditioned, uncommitted states'...marked Huxley's final break with Rampion's or Lawrence's doctrine of 'life-worship.'" DHL was filled with despair by the cold, ironic detachment of Huxley's satire in POINT COUNTER POINT, but the sentimentality of Huxley's treatment of the early courtship of DHL and Frieda might have caused him "considerable embarrassment."

3046 Bredsdorff, Elias. "D. H. Lawrence," FREMMEDE DIGTERE I DET 20. ARHUNDREDE (Foreign Writers of the 20th Century), Vol. II, ed by Sven Møller Kristensen (Copenhagen: Gads Forlag, 1968), pp. 19-41.

DHL's revolt was primarily a revolt against reason, and he hated those who intellectualized the sexual instinct. Because man and woman are basically very different, he rejected the struggle for sexual equality. His attitude to women resembles Milton's: women can attain fulfillment only through man. He hated modern industrial society so intensely that he constantly envisioned its downfall; for this reason, there is a streak of anarchy or nihilism in his work. Related to this element are two escape motifs in his work: his desire for withdrawal from European civilization and an almost erotic submersion in nature. *The Man Who Died* is central to DHL's view of life: the "man" is not only Christ but DHL himself rejecting his self-chosen Messianic mission; but he is also mankind which must die before it can truly live. [Biographical account interwoven with critical sketches.] [In Danish.]

3047 Brugière, Bernard. "A Propos de *Women In Love:* Un inedit déconcertant" (A Propos of *Women In Love:* A Disconcerting Unpublished Work), LES LANGUES MODERNES, LXII (March-April 1968), 64.

The previously unpublished prologue to *Women In Love,* which constitutes the first chapter, illuminates the character of Birkin, especially his friendship with Hermione Roddice and his homosexual tendencies which remain latent or sublimated in the novel. [In French.]

3048 Brugière, Bernard. "Lecture critique d'un passage de *Women in Love*" (Critical Reading of a Passage of *Women in Love*), LES LANGUES MODERNES, LXII (March-April 1968), 197-203.

[A commentary on the "Moony" chapter of *Women in Love.*] [In French.]

3049 Bryden, Ronald. "Lawrence Triptych," OBSERVER (Lond), 17 March 1968, p. 31.

Presented in triptych, DHL's "three plays of childhood, marriage and death in a Nottinghamshire village" form "one panorama of English working-class life." "Even separately they have a truth and purity which makes the theatre's normal currency of charm, humour and spectacle seem vulgar." *The Widowing of Mrs. Holroyd,* the last of the trilogy, shows DHL to be "a master of concentration, ...distilling from a naturalism homely as potatoes a fiery, white and ice-cold emotion." [Review of the "Season of Plays" by DHL at the Royal Court Theatre, directed by Peter Gill. See also Ronald Bryden, "Mesmerising Lawrence," OBSERVER (Lond), 3 March 1968, p. 31.]

3050 Bryden, Ronald. "Mesmerising Lawrence," OBSERVER (Lond), 3 March 1968, p. 31.

A Collier's Friday Night is "as exciting an archaeological find as the long ship of Sutton Hoo." With "no clear shape, little sense of an ending," the play is "simply a slice out of the life of a family," in which "nothing happens...that could not happen any Friday evening," but in which "the formality of the ritual lends a monumental quality" to "the body of their lives." "But as in the novels Lawrence conveys that...tiny conflicts are the tips of icebergs drifting infinitely slowly to collision." [Review of the first play in the "Season of Plays" by DHL at the Royal Court Theatre, directed by Peter Gill. See also Ronald Bryden, "Lawrence Triptych," OBSERVER (Lond), 17 March 1968, p. 31.]

   3051 Cassola, Carlo. "Lawrence a Volterra" (Lawrence at Volterra), CORRIERE DELLA SERA (Milan), 2 Oct 1968, p. 3.

The writer of *Sons and Lovers* is a great artist. The same cannot be said of the DHL who wrote *Etruscan Places*. Here DHL is too lengthy and not very objective because he deals with only those aspects and things that confirm his personal interpretation of the Etruscan people. [In Italian.]

   3052 Choudhury, A. F. "The Enemy Territory, A Study of Joseph Conrad, E. M. Forster, and D. H. Lawrence in Relation to Their Portrayal of Evil." Unpublished dissertation, University of Leicester, 1968. [Listed in Lawrence F. McNamee, DISSERTATIONS IN ENGLISH AND AMERICAN LITERATURE, SUPP I (NY and Lond: Bowker, 1969), p. 252.]

   3053 Clark, Ronald W. THE HUXLEYS (NY and Toronto: McGraw-Hill, 1968), pp. 185, 197, 221, 224, 225, 228-31, 275, 350, 351, 353, 354.

Although DHL had not objected to Aldous Huxley's treatment of him as Kingham in "Two or Three Graces" (1926), he rejected his portrait as Rampion in POINT COUNTER POINT (1928) and wrote to Lady Ottoline Morrell: " 'No, I don't like his books: even if I admire a sort of repulsion and repudiation.' " Huxley, however, was greatly influenced by DHL, whom he felt to be " 'superior in kind, not in degree.' " His wife, Maria, conscripted to type the second half of *Lady Chatterley's Lover*, shocked DHL by using a word from the novel. Forty letters from DHL to Huxley were among the valuables lost in the burning of Huxley's house in California in 1961.

   3054 Clor, Harry M. "The Law and the Obscene," DENVER QUARTERLY, III (Summer 1968), 5-24; rptd as "Introduction: The Law and the Obscene," in OBSCENITY AND PUBLIC MORALITY: CENSORSHIP IN A LIBERAL SOCIETY, by Harry M. Clor (Chicago: University of Chicago P, 1969), pp. 3-13; additional references to DHL, pp. 55, 65, 215, 216, 218, 221, 238.

On the basis of the legal criteria of judging a work of literature or film obscene if "its *dominant* tendency" is to arouse lust or sexual response to violence, cruelty or brutality or its lurid portrayal of human torture, death, or the dead body, the presentation of sex is obscene in Cleland's FANNY HILL but not in DHL's *Lady Chatterley's Lover*. [The book reviews Judge Frederick vanPelt

Bryan's decision for the plaintiff in Grove Press v. Christenberry (1959), DHL's definition of pornography as " 'the attempt to insult sex, to do dirt on it,' " the treatment of DHL and others in Eberhard and Phyllis Kronhausen, PORNOGRAPHY AND THE LAW (1959), and the comparison of passages from *Lady Chatterley's Lover* and FANNY HILL.]

    3055 "Collecting Lawrence," TIMES LITERARY SUPPLEMENT (Lond), 7 March 1968, p. 222.

Phoenix II: Uncollected, Unpublished and Other Prose Works by D. H. Lawrence, ed by Warren Roberts and Harry T. Moore, reprints *Reflections on the Death of a Porcupine and Other Essays, Assorted Articles, A Propos of "Lady Chatterley's Lover," Mr. Noon,* "Prologue to *Women in Love,*" and other pieces. In the Introduction to MEMOIRS OF THE FOREIGN LEGION, by Maurice Magnus, a character portrait "done entirely without forcing or affectation or rancour," DHL penetrates beneath the surface "to reveal the curious integrity behind the fraudulent exterior." DHL's moral vision of Magnus's shocking suicide is seen in his courageous insistence "that Magnus chose his own way and must pay the price."

    3056 Collier, Peter. "The Man Who Died," RAMPARTS, VI (Jan 1968), 12-14.

DHL and his legend have become an established part of the Taos, N. M., community. Dorothy Brett's strongest memory of him is "that he was so charming." Two Taos galleries have seven DHL paintings, priced from $2,000 to $15,000. [Includes a full-page color photograph of Dorothy Brett by Baron Wolman, p. 12.]

    3057 Cowan, S. E. "Lawrence's 'The Rocking-Horse Winner,' " EXPLICATOR, XXVII (1968), Item 9.

Hester's gold hair suggests wealth, her green dress luck. She is fickle, Lady Luck, an emblem of *Mala Fortuna*.

    3058 Crump, G. B. "*The Fox* on Film," D. H. LAWRENCE REVIEW, I (Fall 1968), 238-44.

[Review essay on the film version of *The Fox*; directed by Mark Rydell; written for the screen by Lewis John Carlino and Howard Koch.] The subtitle supplied in advertisements of *The Fox*, ". . .symbol of the male," indicates the problem film makers have in translating DHL's symbols and ideas from words into camera images. In addition to certain minor variations from DHL's story, a major and much criticized difference is the filming of three overt sex scenes--one autoerotic, one lesbian, and one heterosexual. These scenes are necessary, however, because film cannot rely, as DHL does in the novella, on authorial exposition of psychological conflict; film must translate such conflict into dramatic action. Although the characterizations of Paul (Henry in the story) and March are simplified for greater clarity, Banford's character is expanded. Seen through the camera's eye instead of DHL's, the movie Banford "must stand alone. . .on equal footing with the other two" in order to be believable, "even at the risk of sentimentality--the regrettable result in this case."

    3059 Dawson, Eugene W. "Love Among the Mannikins: *The Captain's Doll*," D. H. LAWRENCE REVIEW, I (Summer 1968), 137-48.

"Much of Lawrence's best fiction" responds "to a critical reading which incorporates the psychology" of Dr. Trigant Burrow, the American psychoanalyst. Some fiction, such as *The Captain's Doll*, "suggests the possibility of direct influence of Burrow on Lawrence." In his review of Burrow's THE SOCIAL BASIS OF CONSCIOUSNESS: A STUDY IN ORGANIC PSYCHOLOGY, DHL was "sympathetic with Burrow's views on egoism, personality, self versus self-image and 'social image,' and the bearing" of these ideas on love and sexuality. In *The Captain's Doll*, "it is apparent that the 'mannikin' selves are the characteristic alienated, and alienating, 'social' natures which. . .we *project* to others and respond to effectively in them." "The doll image (re. Burrow's self-image) *is* the major theme," signifying, in Leavis's term, the " 'Laurentian challenge to 'personality,' " by asserting the importance of the body element in the love affair between Hannele and Hepburn. "Hannele's creation of the mannikin, and the attitude toward her lover implied in this doll-making, suggests the artificiality . . .of the relationship." Hannele's " 'I'-persona" (DHL's " 'ego. . .that doll-like entity' ") "has projected personalistic, affect-laden love--as symbolized by the life-*like* doll--and. . .Hepburn has passively encouraged her to do so." By the end of the story, Hepburn rejects the doll, and the "odious" still-life painting of it, recognizing both as artificial projections of the true organismic self.

3060 Dawson, Helen. "Green Room," PLAYS AND PLAYERS, XV (May 1968), 57.

The three plays in the "Lawrence season" at the Royal Court Theatre, London--*A Collier's Friday Night, The Daughter-in-Law*, and *The Widowing of Mrs. Holroyd*--"aren't just interesting artist's doodlings, but the work of a considerable playwright." Director Peter Gill put them together "not because they form a trilogy" but because they are linked by a common Eastwood setting.

3061 Deb, Praley Kumar. "An Approach to D. H. Lawrence as Novelist," BULLETIN OF THE DEPARTMENT OF ENGLISH (Calcutta University), ns IV, No. 1 (1968-1969), 39-56.

Criticism on DHL has often focused on extraneous data that "detract us" from being objective about the artistic significance of his work. First, some have seen him as a social reformer, but his social values are mostly derivative. Second, biographical criticism "reveals the man and not the artist." Third, ethical criticism surrounds DHL with "esoteric mysticism," but his religion is "only the religion of sex" that "flows through the whole process of human consciousness independent of any well-defined religious or mystical association." Finally, concerning DHL's "artistic values," many critics "remain almost blind to the radical change which he has brought about in the form and technique of the English novel." The "apparent formlessness" of DHL's novels is "a new mode of capturing the multi-layered and multi-dimensional experiences of human life." In the past, writers such as Fielding, Bennett, and Galsworthy have felt their themes "from the outside" and have observed a strict adherence to the rules of an ideal construction, but DHL writes "from within--from inside the people and scenes he creates." DHL's "open form" novels enable the reader to experience "the unrealized potentialities" of DHL's richly fertile ideas.

3062 Delavenay, Émile. "Le phênix et ses cendres (D. H. Lawrence)" (The Phoenix and Its Ashes [D. H. Lawrence]), ÉTUDES ANGLAISES, XXI (Oct-Dec 1968), 373-80.
[A review of *Phoenix II: Uncollected, Unpublished, and Other Prose Works by D. H. Lawrence,* ed by Warren Roberts and Harry T. Moore (1968).] For the first time, "The Prologue to *Women in Love*" becomes widely accessible, and its publication raises anew the problem of the content of the novel and its real ethical and aesthetic values. Other items in *Phoenix II,* such as "Return to Bestwood," enable the reader to concentrate on the social significance of DHL. [In French.]

3063 De Rougemont, Denis. JOURNAL D'UNE ÉPOQUE: 1926-1946 (Journal of an Epoch: 1926-1946) (Paris: Gallimard, 1968), pp. 209-12, 233-34.
By sacrificing reason to life, DHL and other anti-intellectuals suppress the concern for truth that gives birth to ideas. *Kangaroo* is the only Lawrentian document we know concerning the relationship of an intellectual with the community; this relationship has made him aware of his own situation. [In French.]

3064 D. H. LAWRENCE REVIEW, ed by James C. Cowan, I, No. 1 (Spring 1968).
Contents, abstracted under 1968: "Preface," pp. v-vi [not abstracted]; Langdon Elsbree, "D. H. Lawrence, HOMO LUDENS, and the Dance," pp. 1-30; William H. New, "Character as Symbol: Annie's Role in *Sons and Lovers,*" pp. 31-43; George J. Zytaruk (ed), "The Last Days of D. H. Lawrence: Hitherto Unpublished Letters of Dr. Andrew Morland," pp. 44-50; William A. Fahey, "Lawrence's San Gaudenzio Revisited," pp. 51-59; William Latta, "Lawrence's Debt to Rudolph, Baron Von Hube," pp. 60-62; Marilyn Gaddis Rose, "If Proust Had Been British," pp. 63-72 [not abstracted]; Ben D. Kimpel and T. C. Duncan Eaves, "*The Fight for Barbara* on Stage," pp. 72-74; Gary Adelman, "The Painted Tombs of Tarquinia," pp. 75-76; "Laurentiana," pp. 77-80 [not abstracted]; "Research in Progress," pp. 81-82 [not abstracted], "Notes on Contributors," pp. 83-84, and "Advisory Board," p. 85 [not abstracted].

3065 D. H. LAWRENCE REVIEW, ed by James C. Cowan, I, No. 2 (Summer 1968).
Contents, abstracted under 1968: Evelyn J. Hinz, "D. H. Lawrence's Clothes Metaphor," pp. 87-113; Sarah Youngblood, "Substance and Shadow: The Self in Lawrence's Poetry," pp. 114-28; T. A. Smailes, "The Mythical Bases of *Women in Love,*" pp. 129-36, rvd and rptd from "A Note on Some Mythical Elements in Lawrence's *Women in Love,*" STANDPUNTE, No. 75 (Feb 1968), 213-14; Eugene W. Dawson, "Love among the Mannikins: *The Captain's Doll,*" pp. 137-48; Bernard Benstock, "Personalities and Politics: A View of the Literary Right," pp. 149-69 [not abstracted]; "Laurentiana," pp. 170-73 [not abstracted]; "Research in Progress," p. 174 [not abstracted]; "Notes on Contributors," p. 175, and "Editorial Staff," p. 176 [not abstracted].

3066 D. H. LAWRENCE REVIEW, ed by James C. Cowan, I, No. 3 (Fall 1968) ["Bibliographical Number"].
Contents, abstracted under 1968: Keith Sagar, "The Genesis of *The Rainbow* and

Women in Love," pp. 179-200; T. A. Smailes, *"More Pansies* and *Last Poems:* Variant Readings Derived from MS Roberts E 192," pp. 201-13; Vivian de Sola Pinto and Warren Roberts, "A Note on Editing *The Complete Poems,"* pp. 213-14; David E. Gerard (compiler), "Glossary of Eastwood Dialect Words Used by D. H. Lawrence in His Poems, Plays and Fiction," pp. 215-37; G. B. Crump, *"The Fox* on Film," pp. 238-44; Richard D. Beards, with the assistance of G. B. Crump, "D. H. Lawrence: Ten Years of Criticism, 1959-1968, A Checklist," pp. 245-85; "Laurentiana," pp. 286-88 [not abstracted except for two letters to the editor]; "Research in Progress," p. 289 [not abstracted]; "Notes on Contributors," p. 290, and "Index to Volume One," p. 291 [not abstracted].

3067 Draper, R[onald] P. "Form and Tone in the Poetry of D. H. Lawrence," ENGLISH STUDIES, II (Dec 1968), 498-508.

DHL's early poems do not, for the most part, find their appropriate form. The young man and the demon are very evidently in conflict. "End of Another Home Holiday" is the only early poem which succeeds. The dialect poems, however, allow the poet to escape "literary" phrasing. Most of the best poems are in *Birds, Beasts and Flowers* and *Last Poems*, where the sense of process is realized in the language and rhythms. The mythological poems rediscover antiquity in its Bacchic and gay insouciance. "Bavarian Gentians" and "The Ship of Death" combine the mythic patterns of *Last Poems* with the complex repetitive and aural technique of *Birds, Beasts and Flowers.*

3068 Dudek, Louis. "Poetry as a Way of Life," ENGLISH QUARTERLY, I (June 1968), 7-19.

DHL is a poet who stands in the romantic tradition of Whitman--the tradition of poetry as a liberating element, a "life gospel."

3069 Edwards, John D. "Remarques sur la sensibilité Lawrencienne" (Remarks on the Lawrencean Sensibility), LES LANGUES MODERNES, LXII (March-April 1968), 186-89.

DHL cannot be taxed with being immoral. His sensibility is a sort of cathartic hymn played on the whole gamut of the senses. He is interested in human feelings and sex in so far as they are religious manifestations of man in the universe. [In French.]

3070 Edwards, Lucy I. (compiler). D. H. LAWRENCE: A FINDING LIST: HOLDINGS IN THE CITY, COUNTY AND UNIVERSITY LIBRARIES OF NOTTINGHAM. Preface by David Gerard. (Nottingham: Nottinghamshire County Council, 1968).

[A directory of primary and secondary materials on DHL, including unpublished material and adaptations. Illustrated. This edition is superseded by Sheila M. Cooke (compiler). D. H. LAWRENCE: A FINDING LIST: A CATALOGUE OF PRINTED MATERIAL IN THE COUNTY AND UNIVERSITY LIBRARIES OF NOTTINGHAM, 2nd ed (Nottingham: Nottinghamshire County Council, 1980).]

3071 Elsbree, Langdon. "D. H. Lawrence, HOMO LUDENS, and the Dance," D. H. LAWRENCE REVIEW, I (Spring 1968), 1-30. Johan Huizinga's conclusions in HOMO LUDENS: A STUDY OF THE PLAY-ELEMENT IN CULTURE parallel one of DHL's main tenets and illuminate his use of the dance: " 'Real civilization cannot exist in the absence of a certain play-element, for civilization presupposes limitation and mastery of the self.' " Although his use of the dance changes, DHL's association of the dance with vital playfulness and integrity remain constant. In *The White Peacock*, art, leisure, and the dance are "weapons of class distinction" as well as expressions of vitality. In *Sons and Lovers*, the dance, though not a major symbol, is essential in characterizing Walter Morel and Gertrude; dance also recurs as a leitmotif in the children's dancing and ring games, and in William's dancing, " 'in spite of his mother,' " toward London, Lily, and death. In *The Rainbow* and *Women in Love*, dance is a major symbol; it presents a complex religious vision and becomes what Angelo Bertocci calls a " 'magnetic field of incident, image, and rhythm.' " In these two novels, the dance is "symbolic of destruction or recreation," representing "the degree to which given men and women consent to meet" in a third "principle of being." In *The Rainbow*, "the dance is associated with the circle, the flood, and the moon, each having its cluster of symbolic associations and all relating to the themes of sexual fulfillment and sterility." "In *Women in Love*, Lawrence uses the dance more as a diagnosis of the causes of individual confusion and failure than as a prescription for psychic unity." These dances are distinguished from those in *The Rainbow* by an "insistent topicality" and a "forcing of meaning in the rhetoric." A "preoccupation with the present" and a compulsion to translate "religious vision into 'practical' action" mar the dances in *The Lost Girl, The Boy in the Bush,* and *The Plumed Serpent.* In *Lady Chatterley's Lover*, DHL returns to his fundamental theme of helping " 'to make an *adjustment in consciousness* to the basic physical realities,' " the dance representing man's effort to actualize and participate in the cosmic forces of birth, growth, and death. When DHL's dancers achieve this "sacred play, they achieve order and unity"; when they fail, "sex remains...a matter of will and competition."

3072 Exner, Julian. "Der Theaterrevolutionär D. H. Lawrence. Londoner Entdeckung nach über fünfzig Jahren" (The Revolutionary of the Theatre, D. H. Lawrence. A London Rediscovery after More than Fifty Years), BADISCHE ZEITUNG, 3 April 1968.

DHL's plays are not dramatic either in the modern or the traditional sense. *A Collier's Friday Night* has hardly any structure, but is good for its illustration of conflicts within everyday life. If DHL's plays had been understood by his contemporaries, he might have turned out another Strindberg. His plays do not live by action but by their portrayal of the characters' intense feelings and their unquestioned acceptance of their social milieu. The absence of any indictment, condescension, and pity on the part of the author accounts for DHL's impartiality and realism. [In German.]

3073 Fahey, William A. "Lawrence's San Gaudenzio Revisited," D. H. LAWRENCE REVIEW, I (Spring 1968), 51-59.

The second section of *Twilight in Italy* is divided into two parts. The four short chapters of the second part concern the mountain country behind the Lago di Garda, in particular the San Gaudenzio farm where DHL stayed briefly in early April 1913. "Beginning with a brilliant florilegium that serves as a...prelude to this portion of the book," the San Gaudenzio chapters are shorter than the rest and each focuses on one object: the Fiori family, the dance, Il Duro, and John. As a result, "these figures and activities," presented economically but with intensity, suggest a meaning beyond themselves. Taking up all the foreground, yet not developed at sufficient length to involve us in their individual destinies, the characters here depicted are evidently designed to be allegorical or symbolic in a way that those in the earlier chapters only approximate."

3074 Fairchild, Hoxie Neale. RELIGIOUS TRENDS IN ENGLISH POETRY, Vol. VI: 1920-1965, VALLEY OF DRY BONES (NY and Lond: Columbia UP, 1968), pp. 22, 35, 100, 117-118, 129, 182-83, 193, 200-1, 218, 219-20, 221-22, 225, 226-27, 227-28, 254, 263, 271, 277, 279-81, 288, 290, 292-93, 299, 313-14, 355, 364, 366-70, 387-88, 394, 441, 435.

"D. H. Lawrence was no Communist, but sometimes he sounds like one when he rages at the interdependence of capitalism and the machine civilization which he loathes so intensely." DHL scorned "'foul equality'": "Compared to him Eliot is a sentimental liberal." In "Snake" DHL pictures "A reciprocal union between man and nature; a sundering of that union, with man as the guilty party; hence 'something to expiate.'" [Brief comments on DHL's "solar mysticism" in *The Plumed Serpent* and in his short poems; on his comparison of crucifixion and sex in "Tortoise Shout"; on his "deeply serious" attitude toward Christianity in the poem "The Risen Lord"; and on his "final testimony as the disappointed archapostle of sex."] "Lawrence has too deep a sense of mystery to say 'I am God'; but he does claim, in substance, to be a numinous manifestation of the life force." [See also Hoxie Neale Fairchild, RELIGIOUS TRENDS IN ENGLISH POETRY, Vol. V: 1880-1920: GODS OF A CHANGING POETRY (NY and Lond: Columbia UP, 1962), pp. 261, 276-84, 323.]

3075 Fernandez, Diane. "D. H. Lawrence et le regard froid" (D. H. Lawrence and the Cold Eye), PREUVES, CCVIII (June-July 1968), 81-82. [In French.]

In "The Princess," the father inculcates in his daughter a need for solitude, which results in her frigidity in the disastrous relationship with Romero, the dark guide of a New Mexican ranch. [Extended discussion of the story in this context.] In "The Horse-Dealer's Daughter," in contrast, Mabel is saved from drowning by Dr. Ferguson, for whom she immediately conceives a wild passion. The story turns on unconscious motivation.

3076 Fernandez, Diane. "D. H. Lawrence, la femme et la mort" (D. H. Lawrence, Woman and Death), LES LETTRES NOUVELLES, May-June 1968, pp. 150-56.

In "The Princess" and "The Horse-Dealer's Daughter," as well as in other works by DHL, death is identified either with voluptuous unconstraint close to suicide or with the degradation of the other, described sadistically. In the background stands a parental image that one rejoins if it is dead or that one runs away from if it is living. DHL's hankering after absolute love hides, in fact, an attraction to death in so far as death obliterates the torments of sex. "The Princess" and "The Horse-Dealer's Daughter" are concerned not with eroticism but with impotence, rancor, and man's yearning after his lost integrity. Their main theme is not passion but escape. [In French.]

3077 Fiderer, Gerald. "D. H. Lawrence's *The Man Who Died:* The Phallic Christ," AMERICAN IMAGO, XXV (1968), 91-96.

The major dialectical opposition revealed in a symbolic pattern in *The Man Who Died* is the sun-sea imagery. By means of several references to the sun as a penetrating force and to the sea as the receiver and transformer of this force, Christ is shown to be the Christ-Osiris.

3078 Ford, George H. "Book Reviews," CRITICISM, X (Fall 1968), 352-55.

Phoenix II: Uncollected, Unpublished, and Other Prose Works by D. H. Lawrence, ed by Warren Roberts and Harry T. Moore, reprints two entire collections, *Reflections on the Death of a Porcupine and Other Essays* and *Assorted Articles;* two uncollected short stories, "The Mortal Coil" and "The Thimble"; and such pieces as "Prologue to *Women in Love*" and "Art and the Individual." The latter essay, a talk given by DHL as a young schoolteacher, "which can serve as a useful lead-in to all his writings," shows him to be, from the beginning, committed "to the principle of what he calls 'sympathy.'"

3079 *"The Fox,"* AMERICA, CXVIII (2 March 1968), 298, 300.

The situation in DHL's *The Fox* is credible in terms of "the social and economic structure and the status of women" in his day, but changes in these conditions in the contemporary world indicate the basic problem in trying to update the novella in the film version.

3080 Fraser, G. S. LAWRENCE DURRELL: A CRITICAL STUDY (NY: Dutton, 1968), pp. 10, 15-20, 44, 82, 102, 120, 129, 140, 150, 152.

Lawrence Durrell shares with DHL a distaste for the drabness and pettiness of twentieth-century England. Both writers deplore a failure of happy, direct, and spontaneous interrelationships. . .the deadening and sterilizing effect of social self-conceit, and of self protective self-enclosure"; both felt that such were the effects of a class system that promotes "malice that is bred by a pervading pretentiousness based on a pervading sense of insecurity."

3081 French, Philip. "A Major Miner Dramatist," NEW STATESMAN, ns LXXV (22 March 1968), 390.

Although it is unlikely that DHL's plays will be regarded as highly as his fiction, Peter Gill's direction of *A Collier's Friday Night, The Daughter-in-Law,* and *The Widowing of Mrs. Holroyd* at the Royal Court Theatre in London (March and April, 1968) establishes DHL as a major playwright of the naturalist tradition. This trilogy comprises DHL's best work in drama, with each play closely related to his fiction without being overshadowed by it and the three related to each other by theme and Eastwood setting.

3082 Fulmer, Bryan O. "The Significance of the Death of the Fox in D. H. Lawrence's *The Fox*," STUDIES IN SHORT FICTION, V (Spring 1968), 275-82.

The "popular reading" of *The Fox* sees Henry dominating March at the end, but "the symbolic death of the fox" is an earlier "reverberation" suggesting greater ambiguity. In killing the fox, "an unconscious sex totem and probably a depository for [March's] soul," Henry is substituting himself; but dead, the fox can no longer externalize her soul and "submerge her strong will." She ceases to speak of Henry as a fox and enters into a "battle of wills": she determines "never to relax her conscious will," he is still "the confident, willful hunter"--a battle that is to continue.

3083 Furbank, P. N. "Further Phoenix," LISTENER, LXXIX (1 Feb 1968), 145.

[Review of *Phoenix II: Uncollected, Unpublished, and Other Prose Works by D. H. Lawrence,* ed by Warren Roberts and Harry T. Moore (1968).] In the "oscillation between involvement and withdrawal" which is the pattern of some of DHL's finest fictions, the "withdrawal seems more necessary to him than the involvement." For example, the hero of *Kangaroo* never really gets in the least "involved" in Australian politics. And readers rarely feel "personally involved" with DHL's characters. The "involvement-fearing side" of DHL comes out vividly in his prose portrait of Maurice Magnus in the "Introduction" to MEMOIRS OF THE FOREIGN LEGION by Maurice Magnus; DHL's "masterly study" of Magnus--" one of the finest things" in this collection--is "genial but not warmhearted." In the unfinished *Mr. Noon,* however, "Everything is genial; and his rib-tickling facetious tone as narrator, though a finely calculated dramatic invention, is at the same time a voice quite natural to him." *Mr. Noon,* "The Thimble," "The Mortal Coil," and the essays "Him with his Tail in his Mouth," and "The Novel" are "masterpieces and abundantly justify this well-edited new collection."

3084 Gadda Conti, Giuseppe. "Una lettera inedita di D. H. Lawrence" (D. H. Lawrence: An Unpublished Letter), ENGLISH MISCELLANY (Rome), XIX (1968), 335-38.

Carlo Linati was the first Italian critic to write about DHL, with whom he exchanged some letters. One of DHL's letters to Linati is particularly interesting because it contains a defense of his art. Linati is important not only as a literary critic but also because he contributed to making Italian readers aware of many interesting foreign writers. [In Italian.]

3085 Garcia, Reloy. "Adam in Nottingham: Literary Archetypes in the Novels of D. H. Lawrence," DISSERTATION ABSTRACTS INTERNATIONAL, XXX (1969), 720A. Unpublished dissertation, Kent State University, 1968.

3086 Gass, William H. "From Some Ashes No Bird Rises," NEW YORK REVIEW OF BOOKS, XI (1 Aug 1968), 3-4; rptd in FICTION AND THE FIGURES OF LIFE, by William H. Gass (NY: Knopf, 1970), pp. 212-21.

[Review of *Phoenix: The Posthumous Papers of D. H. Lawrence*, ed by Edward D. McDonald (rptd 1968) and *Phoenix II: Uncollected, Unpublished, and Other Prose Works by D. H. Lawrence*, ed by Harry T. Moore and Warren Roberts (1968).] When DHL "allowed things, landscapes, people, to enter *him*," he wrote "perfect miracles of living form and sensuous language." Most of the time, however, he "composed elaborate and desperate daydreams...recreating himself, rewriting his forlorn history." Driven to write about sex, he could not write well about it. For him, "sex was suicidal" and so he turned "to an abstract, incantational shorthand" which renders nothing clearly or precisely.

3087 Gelli, Piero. "Introduzione" (Introduction), *Figli e amanti (Sons and Lovers)* (Milan: Garzanti, 1968), pp. 7-13.

DHL in his youth was very much affected by his parents' conflict-ridden relationship. Only in maturity was he able to overcome this trauma, when he tried to arrive at a compromise between instinctive, natural, and at times violent, life, will, and rationality. DHL was not particularly concerned with the formal aspects of his writings, but wanted only to communicate his ideas: the search for a more significant relationship among men, the condemnation of industrialism, eroticism as a means of liberation. *Sons and Lovers* is an autobiographical novel which is developed on two main levels: a basic level which follows the tradition of naturalism and realism, and a psychological level which tries to grasp the deepest motivations of human behavior. [In Italian.]

3088 Gerard, D[avid] E. (compiler). "Glossary of Eastwood Dialect Words Used by D. H. Lawrence in His Poems, Plays and Fiction," D. H. LAWRENCE REVIEW, I (Fall 1968), 215-37; slightly rvd and rptd as "A Glossary of Nottinghamshire Dialect and Mining Terms," in A D. H. LAWRENCE HANDBOOK, ed by Keith Sagar (Manchester: Manchester UP; NY: Barnes & Noble, 1982), pp. 166-76.

[Glossary including dialect words, colliery terms, and "ordinary English words distorted by accent" from the Eastwood area, with quoted examples of their use in DHL's works supplied by the editor of the D. H. LAWRENCE REVIEW.]

3089 Gilbert, Sandra Mortola. "Acts of Attention: The Major Poems of D. H. Lawrence," DISSERTATION ABSTRACTS INTERNATIONAL, XXX (1969), 721A. Unpublished dissertation, Columbia University, 1968: rvd and pub as ACTS OF ATTENTION: THE POEMS OF D. H. LAWRENCE (Ithaca and Lond: Cornell UP, 1972).

3090 Gilman, Richard. "What's Left of Lawrence," NEW REPUBLIC, CLVIII (23 March 1968), 31-36.

Nothing in *Phoenix II: Uncollected, Unpublished, and Other Prose Works by D. H. Lawrence*, ed by Harry T. Moore and Warren Roberts, equals the best piece in *Phoenix: The Posthumous Papers of D. H. Lawrence*, ed by Edward D.

McDonald. DHL the prophet, fully represented in *Phoenix II,* is particularly irrelevant now that the artist must be concerned with man in society and not just with the quality of personal life.

3091 Gindin, James. "Society and Compassion in the Novels of D. H. Lawrence," CENTENNIAL REVIEW, XII (Fall 1968), 355-74; rptd in HARVEST OF A QUIET EYE: THE NOVEL OF COMPASSION, by James Gindin (Bloomington: Indiana UP, 1971), pp. 205-21.

In the novels of DHL "in which the action takes place before World War I," compassion is unnecessary because "escape from society, industrial or otherwise, the ability to remain unshaped and undefined by one's immediate environment" is still possible, though never complete or permanent. "In the novels set in the postwar world, escape is impossible." These novels, with the exception of *Lady Chatterley's Lover,* "are full of compassion for the searching human being."

3092 Gray, Simon. "Lawrence the Dramatist," NEW SOCIETY, XI (21 March 1968), 423-24; rptd in D. H. LAWRENCE: A CRITICAL ANTHOLOGY, ed by H. Coombes (Harmondsworth, Middlesex, England: Penguin Books, 1973), pp. 453-57.

At the climax of *The Widowing of Mrs. Holroyd,* when the mourning widow speaks to the pathetic and vulnerable body of her husband, DHL seems to be "rediscovering the sources of the great choric threnodies in Greek tragedy." The scene "establishes the profound relationships" between the casual rituals of the mining family and the concluding ritual of preparing the body for burial. In *A Collier's Friday Night,* "the collier's frequent exclusion from the stage is not ...a dramatic representation of his exclusion from the household, but a mark of Lawrence's inability to control [such themes] within the form of the conventional play." Similarly, *The Daughter-in-Law,* though filled with "the uniquely Laurentian insight into the feelings that keep men and women alien to each other in marriage," brings the problems to a climax and resolves them with "un-Laurentian simplicity." [Review of "D. H. Lawrence: A Season of Plays" (*The Widowing of Mrs. Holroyd, A Collier's Friday Night,* and *The Daughter-in-Law*), produced at the Royal Court Theatre, London, directed by Peter Gill, February-March 1968.]

3093 Green, Martin. "D. H. Lawrence, Phoenix," MONTH, CCXXV (May 1968), 307-9.

[Review of *Phoenix II: Uncollected, Unpublished, and Other Prose Works by D. H. Lawrence,* ed by Warren Roberts and Harry T. Moore (1968).] DHL survives as a novelist rather than as a thinker, though his vitality as a novelist derives from his being a thinker.

3094 Hanson, Barry. "Rehearsal Logbook," PLAYS AND PLAYERS, XV (April 1968).

[Detailed log (August 1965 to February 1968) of director Peter Gill's preparations and rehearsals of the Royal Court Theatre productions of *A Collier's Fri-*

day Night, The Daughter-in-Law, and *The Widowing of Mrs. Holroyd,* presented in the DHL "Season of Plays," February-March 1968. Pre-World War I social and mining conditions are researched, period photographs of mining life are discovered in the National Coal Board archives, the original Eastwood houses on which DHL's settings are closely modelled are sought out, and properties are accumulated for authenticity of detail. Rehearsals, begun in the parish hall of a church, are later moved to a rehearsal room and eventually to a theater. Various exercises in mime, silent acting, and other dramatic exercises are used. Two actresses' problems with washing the body of Holroyd are gradually overcome and resolved into a finished ritual. Gill's direction emerges as a work of "total commitment": "What he teaches about acting is physical, practical and immediate."]

3095 Harris, Wendell V. "Molly's 'Yes': The Transvaluation of Sex in Modern Fiction," TEXAS STUDIES IN LITERATURE AND LANGUAGE, X (1968), 107-18.

[In a discussion of sex as a life affirmative theme in modern fiction, DHL is considered among several other writers.]

3096 Hartung, Philip T. "Bubbly But Sad," COMMONWEAL, LXXXVII (1 March 1968), 656.

The Fox, in the "oddball, . . . at times offensively so," film version directed by Mark Rydell, is fancied up "with some sex scenes that even Lawrence didn't include. So now the story is more sick than Lawrence made his subtle writing," although as in the original the hero wins by a contrivance.

3097 Henestrosa, Mario Alejandro. DAVID HERBERT LAWRENCE Y MEXICO (David Herbert Lawrence and Mexico) (Mexico: Subsecretaria de Educacion Publica [Cuadernos de Lectura Popular 137], 1968).

Although DHL's experiences in New Mexico were quite intense, he could not write his projected American novel there. Evidently, New Mexico lacked that touch of passion, violence, mystery, and permanent sadness which would convulse his spirit the first time he confronted Mexico. DHL's arrival in Mexico was almost unnoticed except for two brief inclusions in the UNIVERSAL and EXCELSIOR newspapers. The latter misspelled his name, and this small insult may have had something to do with his aversion to Mexico City. While in Mexico City he visited the ruins of Teotihuacan, where the house of Quetzalcoatl is enclosed by the serpent. It is conceivable that during that visit he began to give shape to *The Plumed Serpent,* since a strong parallel can be seen between Kate's initial impressions and those of DHL. In the second chapter, "Tea-Party in Tlacolula," Mrs. Norris is based on the well-known anthropologist Zelia Nuttall, whom DHL met. Characters' comments in this section point up the decadence of Mexico City in order to make evident Kate's desire to find redemption in the countryside. Kate's trip to Chapala is similar to DHL's own trip: all the physical and spiritual details are well captured, though reality is somewhat distorted by the necessities of plot. On the whole, DHL captured Mexico's true essence better than any other foreign writer. Full of violent contrasts, the Mexico that

DHL observed had emerged from a revolution and had changed its exterior trappings quite often. While DHL disliked these externals of the country's constant mutability, what was intrinsic and permanent captivated him. The plot of *The Plumed Serpent* demanded an initial nonconformity with the environment, almost a revulsion against any pre-established values. The protagonist had to be hostile to the city and its people to establish the contrast that would make evident her slow immersion into the true essence of the country and her--and by extension, DHL's--eventual conquest by it. This explanation may not justify the harshness with which DHL criticizes certain aspects of Mexico; he wrote what he believed to be true and did so with honesty and courage. His sensibility grasped certain aspects of the country that were being forgotten by Mexicans. Mexico has always appreciated what is beautiful, and this is the reason its national critics have always been so benevolent with DHL, despite his going too far in his desire to penetrate the almost impenetrable. [In Spanish.]

3098 Hinz, Evelyn J. "D. H. Lawrence's Clothes Metaphor," D. H. LAWRENCE REVIEW, I (Summer 1968), 87-113.
[This study concentrates on the presence and significance of the clothes metaphor in *Sons and Lovers, Women in Love,* and *Lady Chatterley's Lover.*] In accepting the "view of civilized man as the...*clothed* man, and regarding many aspects of civilization as *insane*," DHL uses a clothes metaphor to delineate "varying types and degrees of modern *malaise*." "While the significance and function of a sartorial reference is...conditioned by its...context," some characteristic usages can be established: the Edenic, the psychological, and the Carlylean. For DHL, "the Fall means the birth of self-consciousness"; its implications are psycho-moral rather than...religious." DHL uses clothes to suggest psycho-moral attitudes of his characters, as an index to their psychic integrity, and to reveal "the symbolic roles played by the actors in his drama of the sick psyche." The clothes metaphor also functions to emphasize the discrepancy between personality and individuality; since "personality...is associated with costume,...none of the *vital* characters are 'smart dressers.'" "Clothes are the terms of an old base world.'" Like Carlyle, DHL also "describes religion, social institutions, and conventions in terms of garments which society and its members wear, outgrow, and cast off." The clothes metaphor emphasizes "the externality of social forms"; clothing, textile, and tailoring images suggest the restricting nature of marriage, education, class, and convention. In *Sons and Lovers,* for example, the collar illustrates "the way in which a single clothing image is given both a technical and thematic function." In addition, the awareness that DHL's "use of clothes is metaphoric" makes "his 'stripping' scenes less sensational and more meaningful." DHL "is not a sex-obsessed, atavistic primitivist but a highly responsible and skillful artist who exhorts: 'Let there be no accommodation at this issue.'"

3099 Hobson, Harold. "Oratoria on the Terraces," SUNDAY TIMES (Lond), 17 March 1968, p. 49.
DHL's "trilogy of Nottinghamshire miner plays" "has proved that naturalism, when it is the expression of integrity and high tragic vision, is extremely powerful." The early part of *The Widowing of Mrs. Holroyd* is "almost unbearably painful" in its truthful "rendering of the unhappiness of a family," and "the

long final scene..., in which the dead miner is ceremonially laid out and washed by his alienated wife and his mother is a union of naturalism and ritual." [Review of the third play in the DHL "Season of Plays" in the Royal Court Theatre productions, directed by Peter Gill.]

3100 Hoggart, Richard. "The Voices of Lawrence," NEW STATESMAN, ns LXXV (24 May 1968), 796-97.
[Review of *Phoenix II: Uncollected, Unpublished, and Other Prose Works by D. H. Lawrence,* ed by Warren Roberts and Harry T. Moore (1968).] In "Introduction to MEMOIRS OF THE FOREIGN LEGION," DHL achieves a superbly authentic voice in the sense of making all accessible tones embody his particular way of seeing the world. When his writing is not assured, it acquires the voice of the "nagging shrill...working class," reflecting the presence of his mother. He is most effective when his prophetic note is controlled by a "particular, exact and powerful demand on his emotional integrity."

3101 Holland, Norman N. THE DYNAMICS OF LITERARY RESPONSE (NY: Oxford UP, 1968), pp. 37, 44, 255-58, 260.
DHL's "The Rocking-Horse Winner" is a story about a desperate hunger for love for which there is no satisfaction. It is a story about not being fed, "*not* (except by dying) achieving union with a mother." Although the story carries elements of myth, it "does not give us the kind of resonance, the sense of an antediluvian self prior to our historical individuality, that knowing myths in other works so often does."

3102 Hollander, Robert B., and S. E. Lind (eds). THE ART OF THE STORY (NY: American Book Co., 1968).
[This anthology includes "The Blind Man," pp. 299-319, the editors' commentary on the story, biographical information on DHL, and study questions at the end of the story.] The ironic mode together with the verbal irony in the title ("Who is *really* blind?") leads the reader to understand, through a seemingly objective approach, DHL's point of view.

3103 Holroyd, Michael. LYTTON STRACHEY: A CRITICAL BIOGRAPHY, Vol. I: THE UNKNOWN YEARS (1880-1910) (Lond: William Heinemann; NY: Holt, Rinehart and Winston, 1968), pp. 126-27, 157, 262n, 321n.
[Brief discussions of DHL's dismissal of Bertrand Russell as "all 'Disembodied Mind,'" his statement that the Cambridge set (Duncan Grant, Keynes, Birrell) made him "'dream of beetles,'" his caricature of Grant as Duncan Forbes in *Lady Chatterley's Lover,* his view that James Elroy Flecker's poem THE GOLDEN JOURNEY TO SAMARKAND "'only took place on paper,'" and the "Bloomsburies'" contempt for DHL as at the head of "the less well educated."]

3104 Holroyd, Michael. "Sex, Censorship, and D. H. Lawrence," LYTTON STRACHEY: A CRITICAL BIOGRAPHY, Vol. II: THE YEARS OF ACHIEVEMENT (1910-1932) (Lond: William Heinemann; NY: Holt, Rinehart and Winston, 1968), pp. 158-64; additional references to DHL, pp. 5, 6, 136, 136n, 187, 189, 221n, 330, 528, 562n, 642-43.

[Brief discussions of DHL's friendship with Lady Ottoline Morrell and Mark Gertler, whom he caricatured in *Women in Love* as Hermoine Roddice and Loerke; his favorable response to Duncan Grant in 1915; his " 'black fury,' " at the talk of the "Bloomsburies"; his view of David Garnett's LADY INTO FOX as " 'mere playboy stuff,' " i.e., "more Bloomsbury verbiage, empty and meaningless"; his opinion that Gertler's *The Merry-Go-Round* is " 'the best *modern* picture I have seen' "; his caricature of Dora Carrington as Ethel Cane in "None of That"; and Lytton Strachey's and DHL's aversion for each other. Despite this antipathy, Strachey felt compelled to support DHL's cause in 1915 when *The Rainbow* was suppressed, but declared DHL's pictures in the suppressed exhibition at the Warren Gallery in 1929 to be " 'all wretched things' " with neither composition nor point " '--not even that of indecency.' "]

3105 Howard, Daniel F. A MANUAL TO ACCOMPANY "THE MODERN TRADITION: AN ANTHOLOGY OF STORIES" (Bost: Little, Brown, 1968), pp. 10-12.

Although "The Prussian Officer" "seems to invite pathological interpretation" in which "the murder is an erotic act," concentration on the style shows this interpretation to be "over-simple" by revealing linguistic equivalents of the dramatic action. The content of "Two Blue Birds" "presents marriage as atrophied through over-refinement, while the style subversively exposes our "self-flattering tendency to accept an attractive character at face value." "One meaning of the allegory [in "The Man Who Loved Islands"] involves Lawrence's own stance as a writer" and "the paradox. . .that the writer--like the islander--can realize this world only through art, a restricting 'minute world of pure perfection, made by man himself.' " [Includes questions and suggestions for writing on each story.]

3106 Howard, Daniel F. THE MODERN TRADITION: AN ANTHOLOGY OF SHORT STORIES (Bost: Little, Brown, 1968), pp. 268-70, 535-36.

["Introductory Notes" and "Biographical Sketch" to accompany "The Prussian Officer," "Two Blue Birds," and "The Man Who Loved Islands," which are reprinted in the anthology, pp. 271-332.] Concerned with "the human tendency to create satisfying illusions," DHL differs from writers like Henry James in recognizing "one world which lies beneath the surface, demanding to be acknowledged before any kind of unique life is possible." "Associated with the characters' tendency to overlay their essential selves with the routines of society is their tendency to allow intellect to usurp the role of instinct."

3107 Howarth, Herbert. "D. H. Lawrence, From Island to Glacier," UNIVERSITY OF TORONTO QUARTERLY, XXXVII (April 1968), 215-29.

DHL's *The Trespasser* follows Flaubert in its theme of a reckless, sentimental escape to solve the problems of a fruitless male-female relationship. The "question of bovarism" is stimulated by its urgent presence in English society: personal dissatisfactions resulting from strivings brought on since the Education Acts. Despite Hueffer's criticism of its early form, *The Trespasser*, using home and island symbolically, contrasts dream and reality. With Wagnerian parallels, DHL shows the sufferings of both Helena and Siegmund. The motifs of sun and navigator elucidate the theme of male strength vs. female needs, later to be similarly explored in *The Captain's Doll*, written after DHL rejected Flaubert's meticulousness for a more vital flow in his style.

3108 Howarth, Herbert. "Impersonal Aphrodite," MOSAIC, I, No. 2 (1968), 74-86.

Lawrence Durrell's preference for the impersonal, deific archetype to individual psychology was influenced by DHL's rejection of the individual for the element of which he is a manifestation. Even in the traditional *The Trespasser*, DHL is moving toward impersonal and, in a sense, collective psychic forces which function beneath the surface. Words like "protoplasm," "plasm," "nucleus," and "nucleolating" point to DHL's quest for the sensation of primal life. [Examples are cited from *Sons and Lovers, The Rainbow, Women in Love, The Ladybird,* and *Lady Chatterley's Lover*.] In *Women in Love*, Birkin learns through the concept of Aphrodite to risk abandonment of the ego and submission to impersonal, corruptive forces of "death" in hope of rebirth. In later novels, DHL found other gods, such as Isis in Search, through whom to project the impersonal life. [Contains brief discussion of the use of archetypes by such writers as Moore, Yeats, Conrad, and Ford in contrast to the way DHL used them.]

3109 Hsia, Adrian. D. H. LAWRENCE: DIE CHARAKTERE IN DER HANDLUNG UND SPANNUNG SEINER KURZGESCHICHTEN (D. H. Lawrence: The Characters of His Short Stories in Action and Tension) (Bonn: H. Bouvier [Abhandlungen zur Kunst-, Musik- und Literaturwissenschaft, Vol. 56], 1968).

The differences among DHL's short stories can be viewed chronologically: his early short stories are characterized by autobiographical influences, his stories of the middle period use "good" characters to illustrate his concept of life, and his later stories are dominated by "bad" characters or satirical elements. Since character is the center of the short stories, this study examines the role of the narrator, the direct and indirect portrayal of the heroes, and the relation between action and personae. DHL achieves psychological depth best in the role of the detached omniscient narrator. The dualism of the physical and the spiritual in his philosophy comes to the fore in stereotyped characters whom DHL occasionally caricatures for ironic purposes, particularly in his satiric short stories. DHL defies the character who is one-sided, either physically or spiritually, and demands a balance, which he only occasionally portrays in his short stories (e. g., in "You Touched Me"). The study of character groupings explains this dualistic concept, which is apparent in the opposition of the sexes or of characters embodying either "mind" or "blood knowledge." Hence, action and tension are subordinated to character and serve chiefly as the author's commentary. Tension emerges from the interactions of often contrasting individuals and is increased by the use of several structural devices, such as unexpected revelations, repetitions, changes of scene, or even supernatural elements (e. g., in "The Border Line"). The situations often, though not always, have several culmination points which coincide with the development of DHL's idea of life. DHL's short stories are more suited than his novels to his impressionistic technique of capturing "moments of crucial experience." [In German.]

3110 Huttar, Charles A. (ed). LITERATURE AND RELIGION: VIEWS ON D. H. LAWRENCE (Holland, MI: Hope College [Papers Collected for MLA Seminar 15], 1968).
[Multilithed, spiral-bound book, with papers paginated individually.] Contents, abstracted under 1968: Charles A. Huttar, "Introduction" [not abstracted]; Mother Adelyn O'Connell, R.S.C.J., "The Concept of Person in D. H. Lawrence's *The Rainbow*," pp. 1-17; Nancy M. Tischler, "The Rainbow and the Arch," pp. 1-22; James G. Murray, " 'Screaming in Pentecost,' " pp. 1-10; Hubertien H. Williams, "Lawrence's Concept of Being," pp. 1-17; E. C. Vanderlip, "The Morality of D. H. Lawrence," pp. 1-8; Johan H. Stohl, "Man and Society: Lawrence's Subversive Vision," pp. 1-8.

3111 Itô, Hidekazu. "Death-Drift karano Dasshutsu (Lawrence no Shoki no Shôsetsu ni Tsuite)" (An Escape from Death-drift: On Lawrence's Early Novels), STUDIES IN LANGUAGE AND LITERATURE (Science University of Tôkyô), No. 2 (March 1968), 20-50.
[In Japanese.]

3112 Iwata, Noboru. "*The White Peacock* ni Tsuite" (On *The White Peacock*), BULLETIN OF THE FACULTY OF LITERATURE (Aichi Prefectural University), No. 19 (Dec 1968), 1-16.
The White Peacock is considered with regard to the following points: the symbolism of "Nethermere," "the white peacock," and so on; the first-person narrative form; and the significance of the main characters. The conclusion is that *The White Peacock* is a charge against the Victorian matriarchy through the use of archetypal symbols. [In Japanese.]

3113 Jeffers, Robinson. THE SELECTED LETTERS OF ROBINSON JEFFERS, 1897-1962, ed by Ann N. Ridgeway, with "Foreword" by Mark Van Doren, photographs by Leigh Wiener (Baltimore: Johns Hopkins UP, 1968), pp. 194, 208, 218, 230, 246.
[Jeffers places DHL among the important figures in the English novel and among the "memorable names...who broke down some set of conventions or 'ideals.' " In July 1934 he visited "Loud, charming, cordial Frieda" and "Angelino" at the DHL ranch near Taos.]

3114 Johnson, Dale Springer. "The Development of the Non-Formalistic Modern English Novel and Its Relation to D. H. Lawrence's *Sons and Lovers*," DISSERTATION ABSTRACTS INTERNATIONAL, XXX (1969), 726A. Unpublished dissertation, University of Michigan, 1968.

3115 Kael, Pauline. "Making Lawrence More Lawrentian," NEW YORKER, LXIII (10 Feb 1968), 100-5; rptd in FILM 68/69: AN ANTHOLOGY BY THE NATIONAL SOCIETY OF FILM CRITICS, ed by Hollis Alpert and Andrew Sarris (NY: Simon & Schuster, 1969), pp. 194-99; rptd in GOING STEADY, by Pauline Kael (Boston: Little, Brown, 1970), pp. 29-35; rptd (NY: Bantam Books, 1971), pp. 35-43.

A comparison of Mark Rydell's film version of *The Fox* with the original shows that DHL's novel "is still too subtle to be made into a movie" for a mass audience without updating it with "the sexual platitudes" which in movies pass for "Freudian modernism."

    3116 Kai, Sadanobu. "Kyôbô na Junreikô no Ato o Otte--Sicilia" (After the Savage Pilgrimage--Sicily), STUDIES IN FOREIGN LITERATURES (Ritsumeikan University), No. 15 (Jan 1968), 63-79.

[In Japanese.]

    3117 Kamei, Shunsuke. "Whitman to Lawrence" (Whitman and Lawrence), EIGO SEINEN, No. 114 (1968), 430-32.

[In Japanese.]

    3118 Kanzaki, Daigorô. "D. H. Lawrence no Kirisuto-Kyo-Kan ni Tsuite" (On D. H. Lawrence's View of Christianity), CRITICAL ESSAYS ON ENGLISH LITERATURE (Kyôto Industrial University), No. 1 (Jan 1968), 51-65.

[In Japanese.]

    3119 Kauffmann, Stanley. "Three for the Road," NEW REPUBLIC, CLVIII (9 March 1968), 24.

Although "the outlines of the story have been preserved," the film version of *The Fox* fails "because the screenwriters, Lewis John Carlino and Howard Koch, have adapted the novella less for the screen than for screen vogues. Lawrence was concerned with the forces implied in action; the film is much more interested in explicit actions."

    3120 Kay, Wallace G. "Dionysus, D. H. Lawrence, and Jean Giono: Further Considerations," SOUTHERN QUARTERLY, VI (April 1968), 394-414.

["Further Considerations" of the subject of an earlier article by Wallace G. Kay, "The Cortege of Dionysus: Lawrence and Giono," SOUTHERN QUARTERLY, IV (Jan 1966), 159-71.] While DHL and Giono are both concerned with the Dionysian aspect of man's life and the necessity for union with nature, their approaches differ in that DHL draws characters who have lost the "blood awareness" and seek to get it back, whereas Giono's characters have never lost it. [Cites DHL's "Pan in America," "City Life," *The Rainbow*, and *Fantasia of the Unconscious*, and Giono's LE CHANT DU MONDE.]

    3121 Keith, W. J. "D. H. Lawrence's *The White Peacock*: An Essay in Criticism," UNIVERSITY OF TORONTO QUARTERLY, XXXVII (April 1968), 230-47.

It is an oversimplification to say that *The White Peacock* is influenced by Hardy and embodies in embryonic form subsequent Laurentian themes and characters. A study of DHL's writing habits and attitudes towards his emerging fiction, as seen in his letters and autobiographical prose, shows his clear scheme as it struggles through problems of structure. The first person narration, from the point of view of the youthful Cyril, grows more complex as he adopts a cynical behavior as a defensive posture against the struggles in the last part of the novel. Many detailed observations, frequently seen as excessive, are relevant as a unifying focus for the earlier chapters. The "centrality of tone" carries the novel through to artistic fulfillment, despite admitted limitations.

3122 Kermode, Frank. "Lawrence and the Apocalyptic Types," CRITICAL QUARTERLY, X ["Word in the Desert": Tenth Anniversary Number] (Spring-Summer 1968), 14-33; rptd as "D. H. Lawrence and the Apocalyptic Types," in CONTINUITIES, by Frank Kermode (Lond: Routledge & Kegan Paul; NY: Random House, 1968), pp. 122-51; and rptd as "Lawrence and the Apocalyptic Types," in D. H. LAWRENCE: "THE RAINBOW" AND "WOMEN IN LOVE": A CASEBOOK, ed by Colin Clarke (Lond: Macmillan, 1969; Nashville: Aurora Publishers, 1970), pp. 203-218.

Women in Love, like George Eliot's MIDDLEMARCH, is "a novel explanatory of crisis, and it achieves its explanations by means which may be called historical and typological." "Obsessed with apocalypse from early youth," DHL was specifically a Joachite, identifying his age as the moment of transition from the epoch of Love, which had followed the epoch of Law, into the last age, that of the Holy Spirit, a synthesis of Law (Woman) and Love (Man). "Ritual descent into hell followed by rebirth--that is the character of Lawrence's transitional period," a movement he "can signify only by sex." *Women in Love* is DHL's attempt to create a fictional art appropriate to the age.

3123 Kimpel, Ben D., and T. C. Duncan Eaves. "*The Fight for Barbara* on Stage," D. H. LAWRENCE REVIEW, I (Spring 1968), 72-74.

The 1967 Mermaid Theatre (London) production of *The Fight for Barbara*, preceded by "Men and Women," an anthology from the writings of DHL and others, deliberately emphasizes "the autobiographical aspects of the play," "the similarity of its situation to that of Lawrence and Frieda Weekley in their first months together." DHL's "main weakness is apparent whenever the two lovers do not occupy the center of the stage. As often in his novels, the subsidiary characters are pallid, even wooden." But Barbara, like many of DHL's successful women characters, is not merely DHL "in skirts" but an objectified character, able to furnish "vital dramatic conflict."

3124 Kinkead-Weekes, Mark. "The Marble and the Statue: The Exploratory Imagination of D. H. Lawrence," IMAGINED WORLDS: ESSAYS ON SOME ENGLISH NOVELS AND NOVELISTS IN HONOUR OF JOHN BUTT, ed by Maynard Mack and Ian Gregor (Lond: Methuen, 1968), pp. 371-418; excerpts, pp. 371-93, 407-10, 412-18, rptd as "The Marble and the Statue," in TWENTIETH CENTURY INTERPRETATIONS OF "THE RAINBOW": A COLLECTION OF CRITICAL ESSAYS, ed by Mark Kinkead-Weekes (Englewood Cliffs, N. J.: Prentice-Hall, 1971), pp. 96-120.

The Rainbow and *Women in Love* are the culmination of five separate novels and two long essays. These two novels, DHL's greatest works, originate in what began as *The Insurrection of Miss Houghton* and what ultimately became *The Lost Girl*. Their evolution can be traced through the various drafts of *The Sisters* and *The Wedding Ring*. In his *Study of Thomas Hardy*, DHL works out a "theology of marriage" which leads to the exploration of human relationships in *The Rainbow*. Similarly, "The Crown" links *The Rainbow* with *Women in Love*. Surviving fragments enable us to see that the first *Sisters* was probably an "Ur-version" of *Women in Love,* while the second *Sisters* was probably an "Ur-*Rainbow*." *The Wedding Ring* brought the second *Sisters* close to *The Rainbow*, though it also went on into what is now *Women in Love*. The Hardy *Study* is particularly valuable in that it shows how the imaginative exploration of *The Rainbow* grows out of the *Study*. The evolution of the episode in Lincoln Cathedral demonstrates that quite vividly. [Frequent quotations from fragments and early drafts of the works in question provide illustrative examples.]

3125 Kitazawa, Shigehisa. "Lawrence Bungaku no Hassei" (The Early Works and Life of Lawrence), DOKKYO STUDIES IN ENGLISH (Dokkyo University), No. 2 (June 1968), 92-124; rvd and rptd as Chap. I: "Refracted Love," in D. H. LAWRENCE: HIS LITERATURE AND HIS LIFE, by Shigehisa Kitazawa (Tokyo: Bokusui-Shobo, 1973).

[The first article in a four-part series, based on an extensive study of the life and works of DHL, which seeks to reveal the "real substance" of his literature and its significance in our age. See also Shigehisa Kitazawa, "Lawrence: Ai no Tansaku" (Lawrence in Love), DOKKYO STUDIES IN ENGLISH, No. 3 (June 1969), 17-51; "Lawrence: Ai o Koeru Mono" (Lawrence Beyond Love), DOKKYO STUDIES IN ENGLISH, No. 5 (March 1971), 1-50; and "Lawrence: Ai to Kodoku" (Lawrence: Love and Solitude), DOKKYO STUDIES IN ENGLISH, No. 6 (May 1972), 123-72.] [In Japanese.]

3126 Klein, Robert C. "I, Thou, and You in Three Lawrencian Relationships," PAUNCH, No. 31 (1968), 52-70.

The concept "I," the ego, the self, expresses man's conceit. "Thou" is an alien form of being such as money or God which people feel is greater than themselves. Through love, man enters a new world that pivots not upon himself but on "You," his beloved. Each of these concepts is useful in examining the relationships of Paul and Miriam (*Sons and Lovers*), Will and Anna (*The Rainbow*), and Connie and Mellors (*Lady Chatterley's Lover*).

3127 Kleinbard, David J. "The Invisible Man Made Visible: Representation of the Unconscious in the Writings of D. H. Lawrence," DISSERTATION ABSTRACTS INTERNATIONAL, XXX (1969), 727A-728A. Unpublished dissertation, Yale University, 1968.

3128 Knight, Arthur. "Growing Pains," SATURDAY REVIEW (NY), LI (10 Feb 1968), 40, 55.

"The scenes of nudity, autoeroticism, and lesbianism" that producer Raymond Stoss has introduced into the film version of *The Fox*, directed by Mark Rydell, may be, as the producer thinks, in " 'good taste' " but also cut the film off from the "lucrative family market."

3129 Kobayashi, Toshiro. "Lawrence and Etruria," ESSAYS AND STUDIES IN ENGLISH LANGUAGE AND LITERATURE (Sendai, Japan), Nos. 53-54 (1968), 59-78.

3130 Koga, Masakazu. "Lawrence no Motometa Mono--Shi to Yami no Sekai" (About Lawrence's Death and Darkness), CRITICAL ESSAYS ON ENGLISH LITERATURE (Kyôto Industrial University), No. 1 (Jan 1968), 66-79.

[In Japanese.]

3131 Kretzmer, Herbert. [*A Collier's Friday Night*], DAILY EXPRESS (Lond), 1 March 1968.

Although DHL had "little notion" of dramatic structure, *A Collier's Friday Night* is packed with such minute detail, such accurate observation, that one is gradually sucked into the small, slow, humdrum world of the collier." [Review of the Royal Court Theatre production, directed by Peter Gill. See also review by Herbert Kretzmer, ("D. H. Lawrence: A Season of Plays"), DAILY EXPRESS (Lond), 15 March 1968.]

3132 Kretzmer, Herbert. ["D. H. Lawrence: A Season of Plays"], DAILY EXPRESS (Lond), 15 March 1968.

The Widowing of Mrs. Holroyd almost hypnotically pulled the audience "into an appreciation of the minute by minute details of the world of the collier." [Review of the three productions (*A Collier's Friday Night, The Daughter-in-Law,* and *The Widowing of Mrs. Holroyd*) in the DHL "Season of Plays" at the Royal Court Theatre, directed by Peter Gill. See also review by Herbert Kretzmer, (*A Collier's Friday Night*), DAILY EXPRESS (Lond), 1 March 1968.]

3133 Krupat, Arnold. "The Artist as Revolutionary," CATHOLIC WORLD, CCVIII (Nov 1968), 89-90.

[Review of *Phoenix II: Uncollected, Unpublished, and Other Prose Works by D. H. Lawrence,* ed by Warren Roberts and Harry T. Moore.] "The call to revolution" in DHL's work is confusing because he "never understood that political revolution was not separate from or antithetical to sexual revolution but, rather, the natural consequence of it." "Lawrence can be breathtakingly clear-sighted and appallingly blind at one and the same time." "Behind some of Lawrence's celebrations of life--and implied by them--there is often a 'racist' attitude." [Verbal examples are cited and discussed.] "Serious as these charges are against Lawrence the thinker, they are not fatal to the work of Lawrence the artist," who, "unlike the political revolutionary, . . . does not have to enunciate a practical program."

3134 Kuwayama, Taisuke. "D. H. Lawrence no 'John Galsworthy'" (D. H. Lawrence's "John Galsworthy"), STUDIES IN CULTURAL SCIENCE (Nihon University), No. 9 (March, 1968), 40-44.

[In Japanese.]

3135 Lambert, J. W. "Plays in Performance," DRAMA, LXXXIX (Summer 1968), 19-30.

[Review of *A Collier's Friday Night, The Daughter-in-Law,* and *The Widowing of Mrs. Holroyd,* in the Royal Court Theatre productions, directed by Peter Gill.] DHL's three colliery plays are different, yet much the same. They are alike in that they contain "the intangible elixer of truth"; they are different in that the first is merely a sketch for material which is given substance in the other two plays of the trilogy. *The Daughter-in-Law* is the best play, although the extraordinary concluding scene of *The Widowing of Mrs. Holroyd* unifies life and ritual by dignifying a response to grief that has "nothing to do with loss, only with charity."

3136 Latta, William. "Lawrence's Debt to Rudolph, Baron Von Hube," D. H. LAWRENCE REVIEW, I (Spring 1968), 60-62.

The 1901 book GRISELEIA IN SNOTINGHSCIRE and its author, Rudolph, Baron Von Hube, Vicar of Greasley, became DHL's sources for Rudolph, Baron Skrebensky, Vicar of Briswell, and his "History of the Parish of Briswell," in Chap. VII of *The Rainbow*. Von Hube's book also probably fired DHL's imagination for his story "A Fragment of Stained Glass." [See also quoted responses in "Laurentiana," D. H. LAWRENCE REVIEW, I (Fall 1968), 287-88.

3137 "Laurentiana," D. H. LAWRENCE REVIEW, I (Fall 1968), 287-88.

[Two letters to the Editor are quoted in response to William Latta, "Lawrence's Debt to Rudolph, Baron Von Hube," D. H. LAWRENCE REVIEW, I (Spring 1968), 60-62.] **George H. Ford**: "A reading of 'Love Among the Haystacks' would enable one to locate von Hube's parsonage more precisely." **Keith Sagar**: DHL also made use of Baron von Hube in an early poem, "The Death of the Baron," and in the play *The Merry-Go-Round*. [Harry T. Moore's suggestion that "the Baron is caricatured as Baron Rudolph von Ruge" in *The Merry-Go-Round* is cited.]

3138 Lester, John A., Jr. JOURNEY THROUGH DESPAIR, 1880-1914: TRANSFORMATIONS IN BRITISH LITERARY CULTURE (Princeton: Princeton UP, 1968), pp. xiv, 13, 74, 75, 89, 90, 100, 117, 163, 168, 171-72.

[Brief, passing references to DHL's " 'belief in the blood, the flesh, as being wiser than the intellect,' " with supporting evidence from his letters to Ernest Collings (17 Jan 1913) and Willard Johnson (autumn 1922); to DHL's use of sexual love to reveal "most dramatically...the underlying harmony" in the cosmos, with the example of Paul and Clara in *Sons and Lovers;* and to the inability to distinguish between "revelations of a higher reality" and simply moments of intensity with the example of Will Brangwen in the cathedral in *The Rainbow*.]

3139 Lewis, Peter. [*A Collier's Friday Night*], DAILY MAIL (Lond), 1 March 1968.

Although *A Collier's Friday Night* presents a "detailed picture" of DHL's Eastwood home, "nothing really happens but the slow passing of time." [Review of the Royal Court Theatre production, directed by Peter Gill.]

3140 McCabe, Thomas Harper. "Rhythm in D. H. Lawrence's Short Stories," DISSERTATION ABSTRACTS, XXIX (1968), 609A. Unpublished dissertation, University of Wisconsin, 1968.

3141 Mackenzie, Compton. MY LIFE AND TIMES, OCTAVE SEVEN: 1931-1938 (Lond: Chatto & Windus, 1968), pp. 35-36, 282.

[Rpts his review of *The Man Who Died* for the DAILY MAIL: "A great deal of nonsense has been written about D. H. Lawrence since his death, and now...

we have a great deal of nonsense written by D. H. Lawrence about Our Lord."]
[See also an earlier memoir, Compton Mackenzie, "Memories of D. H. Lawrence," CERTAIN ASPECTS OF MORAL COURAGE (Garden City, NY: Doubleday, 1962, pp. 104-19; as well as other reminiscences and comments throughout the ten-volume autobiography, especially MY LIFE AND TIMES, OCTAVE FIVE: 1915-1923 (Lond: Chatto & Windus, 1966), pp. 164-73, 176 - 79, 183-85, 189, 190-93, 235; MY LIFE AND TIMES, OCTAVE SIX: 1923-1930 (Lond: Chatto & Windus, 1967), pp. 84-85, 131-32, 170; MY LIFE AND TIMES, OCTAVE EIGHT: 1939-1946 (Lond: Chatto & Windus, 1969), p. 265.]

3142 Madonna, Michèle. "Le primitivisme dans *Women in Love*" (Primitivism in *Women in Love*), LES LANGUES MODERNES, LXII (March-April 1968), 190-96.

The fact that modern civilization cannot or need not go back to a primitive past but can still be, through its structure and systems, in sympathy with primitive civilizations shows that primitivism unquestionably means more than a step backwards or the simple wish to escape the modern world by returning to a rudimentary way of life. [DHL's attitude towards primitivism is examined in an analysis of *Women in Love,* in which primitivism can be found on three different levels: "the non-human," "the human," and "the unknown." Every theme in the novel is part of a dialectic which is the very structure of the whole. After an examination of the various processes leading the characters from primitivism to immorality, the author concludes that DHL is not a theoretician using the novel as a means to illustrate his philosophy but an artist whose method is essentially intuitive.] [In French.]

3143 Marks, W. S., III. "D. H. Lawrence and His Rabbit Adolph: Three Symbolic Permutations," CRITICISM, X, No. 3 (1968), 200-16.

By tracing the "gradual crystallization of a rabbit episode" from the chapter "Acquaintances" in *Paul Morel* through the sketch "Adolph" and the chapter "Rabbit" in *Women in Love,* one can show that DHL's "specific ability to manage" such an animal interlude so that it yields "a rich vein of poetic and psychologic insight" is "the product of a thorough assimilation of what post-Romantic predecessors had already done as well as a lively interest in the psychoanalytical theories of his contemporaries." "A distinctive product of his author's daemon at work, Adolph re-emerges through the vortices of memory and imagination transfigured from a biographical character into a completed literary symbol of archetypal proportions."

3144 Marland, Michael. "Introduction," *The Widowing of Mrs. Holroyd* and *The Daughter-in-Law,* by D. H. Lawrence (Lond: Heinemann Educational, 1968), pp. xi-xxxvi.

[Finding "nothing in print on Lawrence as a playwright," the author offers background information on the two plays, examining in particular the source of *The Widowing of Mrs. Holroyd* in "Odour of Chrysanthemums" and supplying a glossary of Nottinghamshire dialect words and mining terms used in the plays.]

3145 Marnat, Marcel. "L'envers d'un conte de fées" (The Other Side of a Fairy Tale), LA QUINZAINE LITTÉRAIRE, No. 47 (15-31 March 1968), 3-4.

[Review of *"La Princesse" et "La Fille du Marchand de chevaux"* ("The Princess" and "The Horse-Dealer's Daughter"), trans by Pierre Leyris (Paris: Mercure de France, 1968); *La Dame exquise* ("The Lovely Lady"), trans by Jeanne Fournier-Pargoire (Paris: Calmann-Levy, 1935; rptd 1967); and five other stories.] In Taos in 1924-1925, DHL, in spite of the first attacks of tuberculosis, was working on *Mornings in Mexico, St. Mawr*, "The Woman Who Rode Away," and *The Plumed Serpent*. "The Princess" includes some of DHL's most lyrical descriptions, but the character of Romero seems somewhat schematized. "The Lovely Lady" is among DHL's most fascinating works--dense, concise, mature, and very "modern." The protagonist of "The Man Who Loved Islands" is so carefully and fully dehumanized that he can be mistaken for the elements themselves. [Brief comments on the other stories considered. Illustrated with a black and white photograph of Knud Merrild's portrait of DHL and a photo of the adolescent DHL.] [In French.]

3146 Marnat, Marcel. [*"La Princesse" et "La Fille du marchand de chevaux"* ("The Princess" and "The Horse-Dealer's Daughter"), trans by Pierre Leyris], LE MONDE, 13 April 1968.

"The Horse-Dealer's Daughter" was published only three years before "The Princess," but it belongs with the works written in DHL's "first manner." This short story marks a transition. *St. Mawr*, which belongs to the same period as "The Princess," would have been a better choice for translation and presentation with it here. Sex and religion are for DHL two means of communication and contact for man. [In French.]

3147 Martin, Richard. "Abgeschiedenheit und Auferstehung: Die Entfaltung eines Motivs in D. H. Lawrences letzten Kurzgeschichten" (Seclusion and Resurrection: The Development of a Theme in D. H. Lawrence's Last Short Stories), POETICA (Munich), Hefte 2 (1968), pp. 70-78.

"The Man Who Was Through with the World," "The Man Who Loved Islands," and *The Man Who Died* are variations on the theme of man's retreat from the civilized world to solitude. The first two stories illustrate man's fruitless efforts at achieving completeness by renouncing human society. *The Man Who Died* outlines man's "resurrection" to a new consciousness of human love which should preserve a person's "individual integrity." [In German.]

3148 Martz, Louis L. "Portrait of Miriam: A Study in the Design of *Sons and Lovers*," IMAGINED WORLDS: ESSAYS ON SOME ENGLISH NOVELS AND NOVELISTS IN HONOUR OF JOHN BUTT, ed by Maynard Mack and Ian Gregor (Lond: Methuen, 1968), 343-69.

The problem of narrative objectivity in DHL's autobiographical novel, *Sons and Lovers*, can be solved if we recognize that the book has the essential structure of a triptych, with a major scene of suffering in the center (Chapters 7-11) and two smaller scenes on either side, focusing our attention on the center of the drama. The mode of the opening section resembles Victorian realism with an omniscient narrator who presents the milieu and family with objectivity. However, in the second section, the story of Miriam and Paul, the narrative method changes. Now we cannot trust the analytical commentary of the narrator, who seems an extension of Paul's consciousness, echoing and magnifying Paul's confusions of feeling and judgment. These confusions are not artistic failures but the results of a deliberate over-painting of the action by Paul's stream of consciousness. Although we cannot tell where the truth lies from the stream of consciousness alone, we can tell it from the action, which often belies Paul's one-sided, cruel comments to and about Miriam.

3149 Matsudaira, Yôko. "Lawrence Kenkyû (2)" (A Study of Lawrence [2]), SONODA WOMEN'S COLLEGE STUDIES, No. 3 (Dec 1968), 87-106.
[Treats DHL as a "researcher and thinker" rather than as a novelist, and discusses DHL's search not only for an aesthetic truth but also for "a truth that would solve all human problems including his own."] [In Japanese.]

3150 Mellen, Joan. "Morality in the Novel: A Study of Five English Novelists: Henry Fielding, Jane Austen, George Eliot, Joseph Conrad, and D. H. Lawrence," DISSERTATION ABSTRACTS, XXIX (1968), 1543A. Unpublished dissertation, City University of New York, 1968.

3151 Mendel, Sydney. "Shakespeare and D. H. Lawrence: Two Portraits of the Hero," WASCANA REVIEW, III, No. 2 (1968), 49-60.
DHL's development from *Sons and Lovers* to *Lady Chatterley's Lover* is similar to Shakespeare's development from HAMLET to ANTONY AND CLEOPATRA. Both Hamlet and Paul Morel are rebellious sons who talk more than they act and know they talk too much. Their respective fathers, unlike the sons, inhabit the real world, not the world of the thinker or artist. For both young men, hatred of the father "contains a strong element of sexual jealousy." Both ANTONY AND CLEOPATRA and *Lady Chatterley's Lover* establish the superiority of heart values over head values. Antony and Mellors, both middle-aged, earthy men, are presented as "images of quintessential manhood," as opposed to the colder, more intellectual Caesar and Clifford Chatterley.

3152 Michener, Richard L. "Apocalyptic Mexico: *The Plumed Serpent* and THE POWER AND THE GLORY," UNIVERSITY REVIEW (Kansas City), XXXIV (June 1968), 313-16.
The Plumed Serpent and THE POWER AND THE GLORY illustrate a similar use of symbolic journeys in religious fiction. In each novel the principal character seeks to cast off the deadened state, brought on by materialism, by submitting to a power beyond the individual and his petty social concerns. Graham Greene and DHL differ, however, in their basis for religious conviction, Greene espousing an ultimate, transcendent divine purpose, and DHL finding divinity within, as well as beyond, man.

3153 Mills, Ralph J., Jr. "Three Poets in Fine Editions," POETRY, CXII (May 1968), 127-30.

[Review of *D. H. Lawrence: Poems Selected for Young People*, ed by William Cole, drawings by Ellen Raskin (1967); THE WORKS OF ANNE BRADSTREET, and THE POEMS OF STEPHEN CRANE: A CRITICAL EDITION.] "D. H. Lawrence's poetry has achieved...something like the reputation it deserves." This selection of his poems, "grouped under the headings of *Animals; Man, Woman, Child; Celebrations and Condemnations;* and *Love*," is a fine introduction to DHL's poetry "for anyone."

3154 M[orgenstern], J[oseph]. "Sandy's Week," NEWSWEEK, LXXI (19 Feb 1968), 92.

"*The Fox*, D. H. Lawrence's murky novella about a man's destruction of a tacit lesbian love, has been partly modernized and wholly exteriorized" in the screen adaptation by Lewis John Carlino and Howard Koch, directed by Mark Rydell, but the "clanking plot is still old hat in modern dress."

3155 Mori, Haruhide. "Articles on D. H. Lawrence: A Bibliography, 1916-1965," KÔBE MISCELLANY (Kôbe University), No. 5 (March 1968), 105-41.

[A checklist.]

3156 Morrison, Claudia C. "D. H. Lawrence and American Literature," FREUD AND THE CRITIC: THE EARLY USE OF DEPTH PSYCHOLOGY IN LITERARY CRITICISM (Chapel Hill: University of North Carolina P, 1968), pp. 203-25; additional references to DHL, pp. ix, 40-42, 137-39, 148, 150, 156, 159n, 229.

DHL's criticism in *Studies in Classic American Literature* "represents a highly idiosyncratic application of the principles of depth psychology to literature." DHL, who "disliked Freudian psychology" as "mechanistic," wrote *Psychoanalysis and the Unconscious* and *Fantasia of the Unconscious* to set forth his own "essentially religious" system in which the unconscious, equated with the "Holy Ghost," is "the area of man's deepest being." Fundamentally dualistic, with "two centres of opposition, the sympathetic and the voluntary, the cerebral and the sensual, mental knowing and 'blood-consciousness,'" DHL's "physiological schematization of the individual becomes increasingly more complex, expanding finally into an eight-fold division." The critic's function, DHL believed, "was primarily to judge, not to analyze and classify." The critic himself could be evaluated on the basis of his emotional aliveness, intellectual capability, and moral honesty. Since "duplicity was a characteristic of all art,...the critic's function...was always to translate the art-communication into prose communication." "Equating the art work and the dream," DHL said, the reader must "disregard what the American artist said" and discover "the ultimate statement of a fictional work" in "its unconscious meaning." [Detailed discussion of DHL's essays on individual American authors.] Despite its "factual errors and radically unconventional readings of American authors," *Studies in Classic American Literature*, which states DHL's belief in the moral function of art to change "the blood," is a "significant critical achievement."

3157 Morse, Stearns. "The Phoenix and the Desert Places," MASSACHUSETTS REVIEW, IX (1968), 773-84.
DHL and Robert Frost are alike in family, community, cultural background, personal experiences such as their early love affairs, degree of formal education, and educational interests. They are alike also in that the poetry of both is unique and marked by a "kinesthetic and tactile quality: neither writes like anyone else."

3158 Moynahan, Julian (ed). D. H. LAWRENCE, "SONS AND LOVERS": TEXT, BACKGROUND, AND CRITICISM (NY: Viking Critical Library Edition], 1968).
Contents, abstracted under year of first publication: Julian Moynahan, "Editor's Preface," pp. vii-x [not abstracted]; "A Lawrence Chronology," pp. xi-xiii [not abstracted]. **I: "Sons and Lovers": The Text** [not abstracted]; **II: "Sons and Lovers": Contexts of Response: Early Reviews:** [Untitled anonymous review], pp. 423-24, from "Fiction," ATHENAEUM, No. 4469 (21 June 1913), 668; "*Sons and Lovers*," pp. 425-27, from SATURDAY REVIEW (Lond), CXV (21 June 1913), 780-81; [Louise Maunsell Field], "Mother Love, pp. 428-31, from "Mother Love: Mr. Lawrence's Remarkable Study of Family Life," NEW YORK TIMES, 21 Sept 1913, Sect. 6, p. 479. **Starting from the Village:** DHL, "Nottingham and the Mining Countryside," pp. 432-41 [not abstracted]; Ada Lawrence Clarke, "[A Reminiscence]," pp. 442-45, from EARLY LIFE OF D. H. LAWRENCE TOGETHER WITH HITHERTO UNPUBLISHED LETTERS AND ARTICLES, by Ada Lawrence and G. Stuart Gelder (Lond: Martin Secker, 1932), pp. 8-11; William Edward Hopkin, "[A Personal Memoir]," pp. 446-51, from D. H. LAWRENCE: A COMPOSITE BIOGRAPHY, ed by Edward Nehls, Vol. I: 1885-1919 (Madison: University of Wisconsin P, 1957), pp. 21-25; Norman Shrapnel, "[A View from the Pit]," p. 452, from "Eastwood Turns the Immortal Memory to Account," MANCHESTER GUARDIAN, 18 March 1955, p. 7. **Poems of a Son and Lover:** DHL, Excerpt from "Foreword to *Collected Poems*," pp. 453-54 [not abstracted]; DHL, Excerpts from two letters to Rachel Annand Taylor, pp. 455-56 [not abstracted]; May Chambers Holbrook, "['Mother is Dead']," pp. 457-60, from [Untitled Memoir], in Chap. VI: "The Chambers Papers," D. H. LAWRENCE: A COMPOSITE BIOGRAPHY, ed by Edward Nehls, Vol. III: 1925-1930 (Madison: University of Wisconsin P, 1959), pp. 618-20; DHL, "Poems: 1910-1912": "End of Another Home Holiday," pp. 461-63; "Endless Anxiety," p. 463; "The End," p. 464; "The Bride," pp. 464-65; "The Virgin Mother," pp. 465-66; "Sorrow," p. 466; "Dolour of Autumn," p. 467; "The Inheritance," pp. 468-69; "Silence," p. 469; "Brooding Grief," p. 470; "Last Words to Miriam," pp. 470-71; "Submergence," pp. 471-72; "The Shadow of Death," pp. 472-73; "Spirits Summoned West," pp. 474-77 [not abstracted]; **Two Women:** Jessie Chambers, "[The Clarification that Time Brings]," pp. 478-85, from D. H. LAWRENCE: A PERSONAL RECORD, by "E. T." (1935), 2nd ed rvd (Lond: Frank Cass; NY: Barnes & Noble, 1965), pp. 190-92, 193, 197-98, 201-2, 203-4, 214-15, 216, 219-20, 222-23; Frieda Lawrence Ravagli, "[As I Look Back]," pp. 486-90, from "NOT I BUT THE WIND. . ." (NY: Viking P, 1934), pp. 3-6, 55-57. **Lawrence and Psychoanalysis:** DHL, letter to Edward Garnett (14 Nov 1912), pp. 491-92 [not abstracted]; Simon O. Lesser, "[Two Modes of Insight]," pp. 493-97, from FICTION AND THE UNCONSCIOUS (Boston:

Beacon P, 1957), pp. 173-78; Sigmund Freud, "The Most Prevalent Form of Degradation in Erotic Life," pp. 498-510, from THE COLLECTED PAPERS OF SIGMUND FREUD, Chap. XII, Vol. IV, ed by Ernest Jones (NY: Basic Books, 1959), 203-216 [not abstracted]; J[ohn] Middleton Murry, "[Genius and a Syndrome]," pp. 511-17, from LOVE, FREEDOM AND SOCIETY (Lond: Jonathan Cape, 1957), pp. 59-65; Philip Rieff, "Two Honest Men," pp. 518-26, from LISTENER, LXIII (5 May 1960), 794-96. **Lawrence and Literary Criticism**: Dorothy Van Ghent, "On *Sons and Lovers*," pp. 527-46, from THE ENGLISH NOVEL: FORM AND FUNCTION (NY: Holt, Rinehart and Winston, 1953), pp. 245-61; Mark Spilka, "How to Pick Flowers," pp. 547-59, from THE LOVE ETHIC OF D. H. LAWRENCE (Bloomington: Indiana UP, 1955), pp. 39-59; Julian Moynahan, "*Sons and Lovers*: The Search for Form," pp. 560-76, from THE DEED OF LIFE: THE NOVELS AND TALES OF D. H. LAWRENCE (Princeton: Princeton UP, 1963), pp. 13-31; G[eorge] H. Ford, "The 'S' Curve: Persephone to Pluto," pp. 577-96, from DOUBLE MEASURE: A STUDY OF THE NOVELS AND STORIES OF D. H. LAWRENCE (NY: Holt, Rinehart and Winston, 1965), pp. 28-47; Alfred Kazin, "Sons, Lovers and Mothers," pp. 597-610, from Introduction to *Sons and Lovers* (NY: Randon House [Modern Library Edition], 1962); also pub as "Sons, Lovers, and Mothers," PARTISAN REVIEW, XXIX (Summer 1962), 373-85; **Topics for Discussion and Papers**, pp. 611-18 [not abstracted]; **Bibliography**, pp. 619-22 [not abstracted].

3159 Muggeridge, Malcolm. "The Dreaming Woman," LISTENER, LXXX (25 July 1968), 104-7; excerpt rptd as "An Interview with Helen Corke," by Malcolm Muggeridge, in D. H. LAWRENCE: INTERVIEWS AND RECOLLECTIONS, ed by Norman Page, Vol. I (Lond: Macmillan P; Totowa, NJ: Barnes & Noble, 1981), pp. 79-86.
[An interview with Helen Corke. Main topics discussed include her relationship with DHL, the background materials for *The Trespasser* and DHL's characterization of Siegmund, her relationship with Jessie Chambers and her knowledge of the DHL-Chambers relationship, her knowledge of DHL's relationship with his mother, and her evaluation of DHL's sexuality ("he was near what I would call the middle of the spectrum relating to sex, with the extreme masculine at one end, the extreme feminine at the other end").]

3160 Munro, John M. "D. H. Lawrence," ENGLISH POETRY IN TRANSITION: 1880-1920 (NY: Pegasus, 1968), p. 259.
While DHL owes much to the Imagists, his experiments in free verse are his great contribution. [Selected poems follow.]

3161 Murray, James G. " 'Screaming in Pentecost,' " LITERATURE AND RELIGION: VIEWS ON D. H. LAWRENCE, ed by Charles A. Huttar (Holland, MI: Hope College [Papers Collected for MLA Seminar 15], 1968), pp. 1-10.
[Analyzing DHL's use of religious language and concepts in his poetry, especially in the *Tortoises* sequence, the author finds a "Christian dimension" in DHL's use of Christian metaphors and his concern for the essential nature of religion. He concludes that "if Lawrence never did come to 'our' [i.e., Christian] point of

view, in several important ways [e.g., DHL's faith in life and hope, in expressing whatever love one has, in working for human dignity and freedom] we have come to his."] [Multilithed, spiral-bound book, with papers paginated individually.]

3162 Nardi, Piero. "Dal racconto al film. *La volpe* di Lawrence" (From Short Story to Film: Lawrence's *The Fox*), IL RESTO DEL CARLINO (Bologna), 8 Nov 1968, p. 3.

In DHL's story *The Fox* the Lesbian problem is not the main theme of the story, as it would appear from the film version. Furthermore, many subtle aspects of DHL's tale cannot be rendered by the film medium. [Includes comment on the film version, *The Fox*, a Raymond Stross production, directed by Mark Rydell, with Sandy Dennis, Keir Dullea, and Anne Heywood (1968).] [In Italian.]

3163 "New Movies," TIME, XCI (16 Feb 1968), 91-92.

DHL, "a paladin of explicit sex in a world still impressed by censors, . . .might be surprised to see how his novella *The Fox* had to be fixed up for 1968 movie audiences. Sex had to be put in rather than taken out." Director Mark Rydell heats the movie up "with three gratuitous physical set-tos," one heterosexual, one lesbian, one autoerotic. "But the creaky, mechanical ending (for which Lawrence deserves the blame) is a culpable cop-out."

3164 New, William H. "Character as Symbol: Annie's Role in *Sons and Lovers*," D. H. LAWRENCE REVIEW, I (Spring 1968), 31-43.

Whether the ambiguous ending of *Sons and Lovers* is negative or positive remains a matter of critical disagreement. "But no ending exists in isolation; it depends for its meaning on the way in which earlier scenes have prepared for it." A key scene in *Sons and Lovers* is the mercy killing of Gertrude Morel. "Paul does not act alone at that moment; his sister Annie is there, too, aiding. . .him." "Through a consideration of Annie's role, we can come to a clearer understanding of what Paul's actions mean." Throughout the book, Annie "is linked consistently with childhood," thus becoming "the link between the central character and one of the central themes," that of growing from childhood to maturity.

3165 Nightingale, Benedict. "On the Coal Face," PLAYS AND PLAYERS, XV (May 1968), 18-21, 51.

DHL's eight plays "deserve attention" for their intelligent exploration of "personal relationships" without imposing "any preconceived meaning." Written in "straightforward and resilient" language that authentically asserts the miners' voices, the three plays directed by Peter Gill in the Royal Court Theatre production--*A Collier's Friday Night, The Daughter-in-Law,* and *The Widowing of Mrs. Holroyd*--are "tremendously alive." In all three, the "older women tend to be formidable," the younger women intelligent, and the men often inarticulately angry." [The discussion of individual plays and performances is illustrated with seven photographs from the productions.]

3166 Nin, Anaïs. THE NOVEL OF THE FUTURE (NY: Macmillan, 1968; rptd NY: Collier Books, 1970), pp. 3, 12, 20, 57, 75, 78, 99, 113, 116, 117, 118, 123, 134, 143, 145, 168.

"Modern students in the fifties could not understand the symbolism of D. H. Lawrence." DHL "spoke of our need for the symbol by which to express truths which are unbearable or unacceptable." An exception among male writers, he "had an intuition of women's feelings." In his repetition of key words such as "livingness" and "flow," DHL sought to depict "heightened moments of living." "If novels had seemed to die it was because they dealt, as D. H. Lawrence said, with dead symbols, dead matter expressed in dead language." DHL was the most important influence on the author "because he sought a language for instinct, emotion, and intuition, the most inarticulate part of ourselves." He accurately stated "that our biggest problem in fiction was how to *transport the living essence of a character into the novel without its dying in the process.*" To accomplish this, "we must have first. . .the passionate experience, then the analysis." [See also Anaïs Nin, D. H. LAWRENCE: AN UNPROFESSIONAL STUDY (1932), the writing of which she discusses in the present study.]

      3167 Noguchi, Yoshika. "Miriam ni Tsuite" (On Miriam), ENGLISH STUDIES (Nihon University), No. 18 (March 1968), 53-61.
[On Miriam in *Sons and Lovers.*] [In Japanese.]

      3168 "Notes on D. H. Lawrence and One Reader," PAUNCH, No. 33 (Dec 1968), 10-21.
[A discussion relating DHL and his works to the anonymous male reader's own life experience through his personal responses to several works: *Fantasia of the Unconscious:* DHL's dualism, "the clue" to his "metaphysic," "is complex, and sometimes contradictory"; *Sons and Lovers* (on Clara): "Paul could just as easily have locked the outhouse door and beat off; it could have saved him much money in train-fares and much pain in getting beat up by an irate husband"; *Women in Love* (on male friendship): "It is absurd to think of homosexuality in this context. Critics who try to make DH out as a repressed faggot are stupid." *The Rainbow,* "England, My England," and "The Blind Man" are also discussed.]

      3169 O'Connell, Adelyn, R.S.C.J. "The Concept of Person in D. H. Lawrence's *The Rainbow,*" LITERATURE AND RELIGION: VIEWS ON D. H. LAWRENCE, ed by Charles A. Huttar (Holland, MI: Hope College [Papers Collected for MLA Seminar 15], 1968), pp. 1-7; rvd and rptd with author's name listed as Adelyn Dougherty, in CHRISTIANITY AND LITERATURE, XXI, No. 4 (1972), 15-22.
[Comparing DHL's concept of self with that expressed by post-Lawrentian Christian writers such as Father Robert Johann in WISDOM IN DEPTH and Teilhard de Chardin in THE DIVINE MILIEU, this paper analyzes the cyclic search for self-realization and self-fulfillment in perfect union with another in *The Rainbow.*] [Multilithed, spiral-bound book, with papers paginated individually.]

      3170 Okada, Taiji. "D. H. Lawrence: Chatterley Fujin no Ai no Kaishin" (D. H. Lawrence: Lady Chatterley's Conversion of Love), REVIEW OF KÔBE UNIVERSITY OF MERCANTILE MARINE: PART I, STUDIES IN HUMANITIES AND SOCIAL SCIENCE, No. 16 (March 1968), 1-22.
[In Japanese.]

3171 Palmer, Paul R. "D. H. Lawrence and the 'Q. B.' in Sardinia," COLUMBIA LIBRARY COLUMNS, XVIII (Nov 1968), 3-9.

In *Sea and Sardinia*, "as well as in his other travel books, the author develops themes which reveal as much about himself as an exile and world explorer, as they do about the countries and people which are the actual subjects." ["Q.B." stands for "Queen Bee," DHL's nickname for Frieda in *Sea and Sardinia*.]

3172 Panter-Downes, Mollie. "Letter from London," NEW YORKER, XLIV (11 May 1968), 101-2.

[Review of *A Collier's Friday Night, The Daughter-in-Law,* and *The Widowing of Mrs. Holroyd,* as produced at the Royal Court Theatre (1968).] In a generally unsatisfactory London theatre season, the three plays by DHL seem very real. Each of the three recalls the landscape of *Sons and Lovers* and presents themes familiar to DHL readers. The plays are simple and direct; they have a nobility heightened by the Shakespearean-sounding phrases and the "thee's" and "thou's" of Derbyshire dialect.

3173 Pearson, Alice Canby. "*The Fox*," FILMS IN REVIEW, XIX (March 1968), 177-78.

[Review of the film *The Fox*, directed by Mark Rydell from the screenplay by Lewis John Carlino and Howard Koch.] "The film is a more forthright treatment of lesbianism than are Lawrence's symbolisms and beatings about the bush."

3174 Pierle, Robert C. "D. H. Lawrence's *Studies in Classic American Literature:* An Evaluation," SOUTHERN QUARTERLY (Hattiesburg, MS), VI (April 1968), 333-40.

For what it shows of the workings of DHL's critical mind, *Studies in Classic American Literature* is valuable, despite inaccuracy in details and DHL's attempt to interpret everything according to his personal idea of human psychology.

3175 Pinto, Vivian de Sola, and Warren Roberts. "A Note on Editing *The Complete Poems*," D. H. LAWRENCE REVIEW, I (Fall 1968), 213-14.

[A reply to T. A. Smailes, "*More Pansies* and *Last Poems:* Variant Readings Derived from MS Roberts E 192," THE D. H. LAWRENCE REVIEW, I (Fall 1968), 201-13, commenting on the practical editorial problems in editing DHL manuscripts and the difficulties involved in choosing from several versions of the same poem.]

3176 "Poetry for Pleasure," TIMES LITERARY SUPPLEMENT (Lond), 3 Oct 1968, p. 1109.

D. H. Lawrence: Poems Selected for Young People, ed by William Cole, will be exciting for readers over eleven, but "for children who write as well as read, Lawrence's rough effrontery and his seemingly casual non-style make him a highly dangerous model."

3177 Poole, R[oger] H[enry]. LAWRENCE AND EDUCATION (Nottingham: University of Nottingham, Institute of Education

[Education Papers, No. 8], 1968); rvd, enlgd, and rptd in *D. H. Lawrence: A Selection,* ed by R. H. Poole and P. J. Shepherd (Lond: Heinemann Educational Books, 1970), pp. 25-37.

DHL's essays on education, Education of the People and Democracy," force us to rethink "first principles." He "contests so cherished a belief as equality," "attacks the formula of the ideal," "views the state as a glorified public convenience," and insists on natural spontaneity. For DHL, education is concerned with "identity," not with "superficial requirements"; its problem is "the fate of the individual in the mass society." But individual identity is often lost to ideal systems in education, such as examinations, which enforce standardization. DHL's advocacy of "a hierarchical caste system which accumulates its way upwards toward the 'supreme utterer' " shows his sympathy with fascism and "the cult of the leader." In the "closed rather than...open society" which DHL envisions, teachers and inspectors have great power, and the caste system operates on the basis of natural ability. [The educational program which DHL proposes is summarized.] DHL demanded "that parents should not sentimentalize their children" but that "the child's personality should be respected." DHL's dilemma was that "education was learning to escape from the 'tyranny of the upper centres'...so as to live spontaneously, yet this process...had to be learned."

3178 Pritchett, V[ictor] S. "The Anti-Soporific Art," NEW STATESMAN, ns LXXVI (6 Dec 1968), 793-94.

Such stories as "The Prussian Officer," *The Fox,* "The Rocking-Horse Winner," and "The Man Who Loved Islands" assert intensely and superbly what is often diffuse and questionable in DHL's novels.

3179 Rahv, Philip. "On Leavis and Lawrence," NEW YORK REVIEW OF BOOKS, XI (26 Sept 1968), 62-68; rptd in LITERATURE AND THE SIXTH SENSE, by Philip Rahv (NY: Houghton Mifflin, 1969), pp. 289-306.

[Review of F. R. Leavis, ANNA KARENINA AND OTHER ESSAYS (1967).] Although occasionally perceptive in his general remarks, DHL "is nearly always wrong-headed, absurdly doctrinaire" in the specifics of his literary criticism. Nor is DHL, as Leavis maintains, a great novelist. In the interest of his message he is "all too prone to disregard the modifications, reservations, and strategic reversals imposed by the discipline of novelistic art."

3180 Rajiva, Stanley F. "The Empathetic Vision," LITERARY HALF-YEARLY, IX, No. 2 (1968), 49-70.

A critical examination of the best poems in *Birds, Beasts and Flowers* shows how the sensitivity and compassion of DHL's approach to the natural world make for the rightness of his poetic vision and of the poetic forms he chose to express that vision.

3181 Randall, Richard S. CENSORSHIP OF THE MOVIES: THE SOCIAL AND POLITICAL CONTROL OF A MASS MEDIUM (Madison, Milwaukee, and Lond: University of Wisconsin P, 1968;

rptd 1970), pp. 33, 52-53, 58, 62, 67, 69, 116, 137, 219, 228.
After the New York Board of Regents refused to license the film version of *Lady Chatterley's Lover* on grounds that it "was immoral in presenting adultery 'as a desirable, acceptable, and proper pattern of behavior,'" the New York Court of Appeals sustained the censorship order, which required deletion of a scene in the cabin showing Mellors and Connie lying on a cot in a state of undress and a scene in which, after unzipping her dress, he comments that she has nothing on under it. In contrast, the United States Supreme Court decision, in Kingsley International Pictures v. Board of Regents (1959), "held that a licensing standard of 'sexual immorality,' having been construed to ban a film depicting adultery as a desirable way of life, was in effect a bar to the discussion of ideas," a freedom protected by the First Amendment to the U.S. Constitution.

3182 Rawlinson, D. H. "Extracts from Novels: A Comparison of Passages from Thackeray and Lawrence" and "Aphorisms by Franklin and Lawrence," THE PRACTICE OF CRITICISM (Cambridge: Cambridge UP, 1968), pp. 121-27, 134-40.

As an exercise in "practical criticism," parallel passages from Thackeray's VANITY FAIR and DHL's "The White Stocking" are compared. "Both passages describe a clash between a wronged husband and an unfaithful wife"; both involve tension and violence; "and, in each, the wife has been attracted to the lover by the cheap glamour of an affair with a rich man." "This comparison," however, "asks us to consider a representative difference between the great novelist [DHL] and the lesser novelist [Thackeray]...,the difference between the genuinely dramatic and the falsely dramatic in a novel." In another exercise, parallel passages from Franklin and DHL, quoted from DHL's "Benjamin Franklin" in *Studies in Classic American Literature,* show "that, even in these brief, terse moral directives...prose quality is as much a part of the meaning as it is in ...continuous passages." Whereas Franklin is "safe, sound and respectable" and conveys his thought in "the stale, insipid dullness of conventional moralising," DHL is "less obvious..., and his nostrums have to be understood as a whole if they are to be understood individually,.. because his thought is more penetrating and profound" and conveyed metaphorically.

3183 Read, Herbert. "D. H. Lawrence," THE CULT OF SINCERITY (Lond: Faber & Faber, 1968), pp. 160-77.

DHL was "'an irregular genius,'" deficient in "the faculty of reasoning" that is "requisite for a symmetrical genius." But "whatever other powers Lawrence may have lacked, he had the capacity to rouse enthusiasm and inspire the minds of his contemporaries." As *Psychoanalysis and the Unconscious* and *Fantasia of the Unconscious* show, "Lawrence was first and foremost...a quasi-philosopher," with the "'polly-analytics'" deriving as inferences from his books. "Instead of deploring" his "'vituperation,'" we should be glad he was "moved enough, angry enough, to rip the veil from our sham civilization." The fact that DHL's "ideas are not to be reconciled with any existing social tendency" does not invalidate them, although his contempt for modern "democracy" earned him the opprobrious, and erroneous, charge of fascism. "The writer nearest to Lawrence is Whitman." Although DHL's paintings have survived only because of his literary genius, they remind us that he did not confine himself to writing. "Not immortal, not masterpieces, not 'great,' " DHL's paintings "are visual evidence of the struggle of a great spirit to liberate himself from" fear and return to the garden from which man had been banished.

3184 Rembar, Charles. THE END OF OBSCENITY: THE TRIALS OF "LADY CHATTERLEY," "TROPIC OF CANCER," AND "FANNY HILL" (NY: Random House, 1968; Lond: Andre Deutsch, 1969), pp. 59-160.

["*Lady Chatterley:* The Trial," pp. 59-113; "*Lady Chatterley;* The Federal Courts," pp. 114-51; "*Lady Chatterley:* Postscript," pp. 152-60.] After *Lady Chatterley's Lover* was banned from the mails, a trial took place within the Post Office Department (Washington, D. C.) on 14 May 1959 before a "Judicial Officer," Charles D. Ablard, acting as judge, with Rembar representing Grove Press, the publisher, and Saul J. Mindel and J. Carroll Schueler appearing for the Post Office. Witnesses for Grove Press included Barney Rosset, president of the company, and Malcolm Cowley and Alfred Kazin, literary critics [extracts of testimony given]. Ablard's "order" refused to decide the issue but referred it to Postmaster General Arthur Summerfield, who later ruled that "community standards" precluded the book's being "transmitted in the mails." On 10 June 1959, Grove Press and Reader's Subscription Service sued New York Postmaster Robert Christenberry in U. S. District Court, asking "that the book be declared not obscene and that Christenberry be directed to forward the mail." Four months after Judge Frederick vanPelt Bryan, who presided, ruled in favor of the plaintiffs, the court of appeals upheld the opinion. ["Postscript" discusses the subsequent British trial (Regina v. Penguin Books, Ltd., 1960), in which the issue of morality "thoroughly obscured" "the question of freedom."]

3185 Roberts, Warren, and Harry T. Moore. "Introduction," *Phoenix II: Uncollected, Unpublished, and Other Prose Works by D. H. Lawrence* (NY: Viking P, 1968), pp. ix-xv.

The first *Phoenix* "made little impression": Clifton Fadiman, e.g., wondered "why had readers in the 1920s taken Lawrence seriously." Within a few years, DHL was "almost entirely forgotten." But shortly after World War II, "he had a marvellous resurrection. Readers began to see that he had written more trenchantly than most about the causes of modern evils." They "also came to appreciate Lawrence's expressional powers, his vitally charged language." [Comments introduce the selections included in the anthology.]

3186 Rogers, W. G. "Charity-boy of Literature," LADIES BOUNTIFUL (Lond: Victor Gollancz, 1968), pp. 79-135.

Paradoxically, DHL put women on a pedestal but wanted them to worship him. "Women rallied repeatedly to his rescue, sometimes with minor contributions, sometimes with lifesaving munificence." Whether their relationships were brief or enduring, "he made frank use of them." From Jessie Chambers, " a gift one would not have expected him to accept consisted literally of some passages from her letters embodied in his fiction." Although Harriet Monroe's assistance as an editor was "routine," Amy Lowell was prudently benevolent in gifts of money and a typewriter. Hilda Doolittle sheltered the Lawrences in her London flat when they were expelled from Cornwall. Viola Meynell lent them her cottage in Greatham, Sussex. DHL repaid the Meynells with the "slander" of "England, My England," with its "merciless caricature" of Percy Lucas, Wilfrid Meynell's son-in-law, as Egbert. Like a rebellious child, DHL "took an almost venomous pleasure in biting again and again the hands that fed him." Lady Ottoline Morrell, who championed DHL, is pilloried as Hermione, "the only unreservedly malignant characterization" in *Women In Love*. [Detailed discussion of the DHL-Ottoline Morrell relationship.] Mabel Dodge Luhan, after reading *Sea and Sardinia*, brought DHL to Taos. [Long discussion of Mabel Dodge Luhan's life, her patronage of the arts, her marriages.] Mabel, Frieda, and Dorothy Brett fought over DHL, and he joined in the "scrap." "Lawrence may have paid more in palaver, frayed nerves, and strained emotions for the help [he received from women] than it was worth."

3187 Rossman, Charles Raymond. "Organic Wholeness of Being in Selected Novels of D. H. Lawrence," DISSERTATION ABSTRACTS, XXIX (1969), 315A. Unpublished dissertation, University of Southern California, 1968.

3188 Roston, Murray. BIBLICAL DRAMA IN ENGLAND FROM THE MIDDLE AGES TO THE PRESENT DAY (Lond: Faber & Faber, 1968), pp. 240, 264, 275-79.

Both Yeats and DHL sought to recover the magic of the Scriptures destroyed by the age of reason by returning to a more primitivist reading of them. But whereas Yeats soon turned from Christianity to the occult, DHL, imbued from childhood with a sense of the "wild mystery" of Christianity, fought for a revitalized Christianity that would recognize the creative and pro-creative forces in nature. In *The Man Who Died* he blends the Christian with the pagan cycle of death and resurrection in an attempt to "reimplant religion with the physical world." DHL's purpose in *David* is also to reveal the passion within religion. The prose of the play echoes biblical prose, but it is not pastiche. Saul's sin against God is interpreted by DHL as a turning away from the "Hidden Sun," the life force of nature. The young David symbolizes a reabsorption into the divine forces of nature, a submission.

3189 Roy, Kamal. "*Sons and Lovers* or The Sin Against the Holy Ghost," MODERN REVIEW (Calcutta), CXXIII, No. 4 (April 1968), 264-69, and No. 5 (May 1968), 341-50.

[**Part I**]: DHL differs from his contemporaries most in seeing love not "as an absolute ideal or as an end in itself" but "as a means to self-fulfillment." Claiming "the priority of life over love," DHL saw lovers as two rivers whose courses often cross but never stand still. Through coition man acquires fresh energy, which is then expressed in creative action. Only in "a complex network of relationships with our lady-love, friends, the natural world and ultimately with God or the Infinite" do "we consummate our 'Holy Ghost,' " the principle of individuality that unifies mind, psyche, and soul, in a "oneness of being."
[**Part II**]: In *Sons and Lovers,* "Gertrude and Walter Morel dramatize the typi-

cal Lawrentian dialectic" between "intellect, and intuition and instinct." Paul becomes involved with Miriam, who resembles his mother in her "fixed principles" and her "intellectual, hence mechanical approach to life." While Paul also contributes to the "impasse" in their affair, the self-knowledge that he acquires makes his redemption possible by revealing to him the disparity between his vision and his actual life. Although Gertrude tries to hold on to him, she recognizes, in a moment of self-revelation, that by doing so, "she is actually ruining him and arresting" his full development. Paul contributes much to the "restoration" of Clara, who "is the direct antithesis of Miriam," but his "refusal to wallow in passion as she demands prompts her to go back to Dawes." Left only with "the spiritual love of his dead mother," Paul recognizes that "to cling to her is to embrace death," and that, as a worshipper of life, he cannot do. His "conversion to the Lawrentian metaphysic" complete, Paul recognizes "the paramount importance of instinct in life and of the fundamental human loneliness." "Finally his 'Holy Ghost' emerges triumphant."

3190 Russell, Bertrand. THE AUTOBIOGRAPHY OF BERTRAND RUSSELL, Vol. II : 1914-1944 (Lond: George Allen & Unwin; Bost: Atlantic Monthly P, Little, Brown, 1968), pp. 10-16, 58, 59-65, 127; excerpt also pub as "Autobiography: 1914-1918," HARPER'S MAGAZINE, CCXXXVI (Jan 1968), 31-39.

[Russell's "brief and hectic" friendship with DHL began with a wish to reform human relations, but their views about the reform needed were diametrically opposed. While Russell was a pacifist, DHL was ambivalent about the War: since his wife was German, he could not be wholly patriotic; on the other hand, his "hatred of mankind" made him think "both sides must be right." DHL found the Cambridge intellectuals to whom Russell introduced him "dead, dead, dead." He and Russell considered undertaking a joint venture in writing and lectures, but their irreconcilable differences soon emerged: "I was a firm believer in democracy, whereas he had developed the whole philosophy of Fascism before the politicians had thought of it." Russell rejected DHL's "mystical philosophy of 'blood' " as "frankly rubbish." DHL's letter (14 Sept 1915) denouncing Russell's pacifism as hypocrisy, cloaking the " 'lust to jab and strike,' " had such a "devastating effect" on Russell that he "contemplated suicide." DHL was "his wife's mouthpiece": "Somehow she had imbibed prematurely the ideas afterwards developed by Mussolini and Hitler." When DHL "realized that other people existed he hated them.... In sex alone he was compelled to admit that he was not the only human being in the universe." [See also *D. H. Lawrence's Letters to Bertrand Russell*, ed and with an Introduction by Harry T. Moore (1948).]

3191 Ruthven, K. K. "The Savage God: Conrad and Lawrence," CRITICAL QUARTERLY, X (Spring-Summer 1968), 39-54.

Though they belong to a "later, theoretical, retrospective phase," *The Rainbow* and *Women in Love*, like Conrad's HEART OF DARKNESS, exemplify "savage primitivism," "a particularly intense" nineteenth-century form of primitivism which focused on primitive Africans, "merged with current anarchism, and culminated in a desire to destroy European civilization." "What is peculiar to Lawrence's treatment of this theme is the way it merges with the ancient belief in resurrection.... the destruction of the old is necessary for the emergence of the new."

3192 Sagar, Keith. "The Genesis of *The Rainbow* and *Women in Love*," D. H. LAWRENCE REVIEW, I (Fall 1968), 179-99.

DHL had finished *Paul Morel* by December 1912 and was planning a new novel, *Scargill Street*, a life of Robert Burns. By January 1913, however, he was at work on a " 'most fascinating' " novel, *The Insurrection of Miss Houghton* (eventually published as *The Lost Girl*). By mid-March, he " 'put it aside to do a pot-boiler,' " beginning *The Sisters*, the initial sketch of which he finished in June 1913. He revised this version, completing 340 pages by 25 November; on 30 December 1913 he wrote to Garnett that he would call the novel "The Wedding Ring." The third version was begun in February 1914 and finished by mid-May; its title was *The Rainbow*. DHL wrote the *Study of Thomas Hardy* that autumn, and announced to Pinker in October another revision of *The Rainbow*. Three hundred pages were done by 5 January 1915, when DHL decided to " 'split the book into two volumes.' " *The Rainbow* was finished by the end of February; the volume held back was to become *Women in Love*. After "a series of disappointments, frustrations, humiliations" throughout 1915, DHL began work on " 'the second half of *The Rainbow*' " in April 1916; he finished "four-fifths of 'the fourth and final draft' " in July. The bulk of this manuscript is new material. Unlike the "organic structure of *The Rainbow*," the structure of *Women in Love* seems "arbitrary." "Nor are the novel's positive symbols--star equilibrium and singleness of being--rooted in its life," but "derive entirely from Birkin's preaching, which in turn derives from *The Crown*." The other titles DHL considered-- "Noah's Ark," "Day of Wrath," "The Latter Days"--"indicate the centrality in Lawrence's 1916 vision of the theme of the end of the world which makes the spirit of *Women in Love* so radically different from the buoyancy of the early months of 1915 when *The Rainbow* was bended and set firm."

3193 Sandoval, Patricia Ann Rice. "D. H. Lawrence: A Study of His Poetic Theories," DISSERTATION ABSTRACTS, XXIX (1968), 912A. Unpublished dissertation, University of Michigan, 1968.

3194 Sândulescu, C. G. "Lawrence Dramaturg" (Lawrence the Playwright), CONTEMPORANUL, IV (4 Oct 1968), 4.

DHL's plays have finally found public recognition owing chiefly to performances by the Mermaid and Royal Court Theatres, London. His plays are strongly autobiographical, especially *The Fight for Barbara*, in which he dramatizes his experiences with Frieda von Richthofen after she had deserted Ernest Weekley. Strength of dialogue is shown in *The Daughter-in-Law*, a play about human relationships within a miner's family, dealing with the tensions of everyday life. DHL's philosophy of life is deeply influenced by his childhood experience of the contrast between nature and industry. [In Romanian.]

3195 Sawamura, Kan. "Lawrence no Mother-Complex" (Lawrence and the Mother Complex), JIN-BUN RONSHÛ (Waseda University), No. 5 (Feb 1968), 91-100.

[In Japanese.]

3196 Schneider, Daniel J. "Techniques of Cognition in Modern Fiction," JOURNAL OF AESTHETICS AND ART CRITICISM, XXVI (Spring 1968), 317-28, espec pp. 318, 324-25, 327-28.

In *The Rainbow*, one of many attempts in the modern novel to determine form without aesthetic considerations, DHL attempts to record the actuality of human experience by divorcing scene from the determinants of plot, and characters from "the aesthetic requirements to behave sympathetically or unsympathetically." DHL isolates two psychic impulses in perpetual, unresolved conflict: "the sympathetic impulse to unite with others in pure fusion, and the 'volitional' impulse to hold oneself intact, independent, free of relationship with others." His experiment with concentrating on isolated motive forces strongly suggests that "the determinants of artistic structure may lie, not in the artist's imagination or in the aesthetic requirements of the work but in the actualities of life itself."

3197 Schneiderman, Leo. "Notes on D. H. Lawrence's *Studies in Classic American Literature*," CONNECTICUT REVIEW, I (April 1968), 57-71.

"Unbalanced, extreme, and filled with private symbolism," the final versions of *Studies in Classic American Literature* provide "us with a psychological portrait of [DHL], without disguise, and without the pseudo-objectivity of the original drafts."

3198 Schorer, Mark. LAWRENCE IN THE WAR YEARS ([Stanford, CA]: Stanford University, 1968).

During the First World War, DHL called on Lady Ottoline Morrell to help form a colony of about twenty "decent" people to be called Rananim; but everything failed--friendships with Bertrand Russell and John Middleton Murry collapsed, *The Rainbow* was suppressed, DHL was ordered out of Cornwall as a spy, and his marriage seemed threatened. [Includes "a check list of his correspondence in the Charlotte Ashley Felton Memorial Library of the Stanford University Libraries on the occasion of an exhibition in the Albert M. Bender Room, 30 October 1968."]

3199 Schorer, Mark. "The Life of D. H. Lawrence," D. H. LAWRENCE (NY: Dell, 1968), pp. [3]-[106].

[This biography constitutes Part I of the book. Part II consists of "Selections from the Works of D. H. Lawrence."] Seeing himself as a prophet, DHL seriously believed he could change the world by encouraging "the flowering of a whole new human consciousness"--one based upon a rejection of modern life and an affirmation of primitive mysticism. His "first great novel," *Sons and Lovers*, is historically important because it was the first work of fiction "to impress readers with the availability of modern psychological theory as a means of understanding relationships." In this autobiographical novel in which DHL explores the consequences of the Oedipal complex, the central character desires "the extinction of personality,...what we could call 'social character,' the ego, and a yearning for the dissolution of the individuality in the vast forms of nature, the not-me, in the primitive condition of life." His second major work, *The Rainbow*, is a novel of "psychic symbolism." Based upon a central symbol of "integration of body and spirit in a renewed individual consciousness," *The Rainbow* "develops through a complex orchestration of dualities seeking resolution, or balance." The years following the publication of *The Rainbow* were filled with bitter rage, caused by efforts to suppress DHL's work, alienation from England during the First World War, and the dissolution of friendships; also, there was the matter of DHL's frustrated efforts to establish a deep relationship with another man. With *Women in Love*, his greatest novel, DHL undertook a revolutionary mode of characterization in which characters become more than merely social beings; they are presented as "naked psyches." The theme of this novel "has been dramatized in terms of the struggle between...'Will' (...a death impulse...) and 'Being' (that integration of the total self in which is life)." In the years following the publication of *Women in Love*, the Lawrences moved frequently, and the long-standing desire to establish a utopian community remained elusive. DHL was tormented by a "frustrated 'societal impulse,' and in the four novels following *Women in Love* he began to seek out ways of bringing his people into vital social relationships." As DHL's restlessness intensified, the role of setting became increasingly important in his novels; also his interest in politics is reflected in *Aaron's Rod, Kangaroo,* and *The Plumed Serpent*, novels written in the early to mid 1920s. Frustrated in his attempts to discover a utopian society among various primitive cultures, DHL turned his attention in later works to grim prophecy. In *Lady Chatterley's Lover*, DHL delivered his final assessment of English society. *Apocalypse*, his final work, is "a plea for the necessity of spontaneity in human activity."

3200 Schorer, Mark. THE WORLD WE IMAGINE: SELECTED ESSAYS (NY: Farrar, Straus, Giroux, 1968).
Contents on DHL, abstracted under year of first publication: "Technique as Discovery," pp. 2-23, from HUDSON REVIEW, I (Spring 1948), 67-87; "*Women in Love* and Death," pp. 107-21, from HUDSON REVIEW, VI (Spring 1953), 34-47; "On *Lady Chatterley's Lover*," pp. 122-46, from EVERGREEN REVIEW, I (1957), 149-78; "Poste Restante: Lawrence as Traveler," pp. 147-61, from "Introduction," POSTE RESTANTE: A LAWRENCE TRAVEL CALENDAR, by Harry T. Moore (Berkeley and Los Angeles: University of California P, 1956), pp. 1-18; "Two Houses, Two Ways: The Florentine Villas of Lewis and Lawrence," pp. 195-218, from NEW WORLD WRITING, No. 4 (NY: New American Library of World Literature, 1953), pp. 136-54.

3201 Seymour-Smith, Martin. "Such a Rotter," SPECTATOR, CCXXI (27 Dec 1968), 914.
Lawrence in Love: Letters to Louie Burrows, ed by James T. Boulton, makes known, in 165 letters and postcards published for the first time, DHL's relationship with the young lady to whom he was engaged for fifteen months from late 1910 to early 1912. The letters reveal DHL's typical attitude toward Louie as a "mixture of sarcasm and puzzled affection." "They help to fill out that 'biography of the emotional and inner life,' " illuminate DHL's novels such as *The Rainbow*, in which Louie appears as Ursula, and reveal DHL as "an intensely gifted young man not yet embittered by disease and sexual incapacity."

3202 Sheed, Wilfrid. [*The Fox*], ESQUIRE, LXIX (Feb 1968), 20.

[Review of the film version of *The Fox*, with only tangential reference to the story.] "Verily a dog, this baby, full of arty camera work and soul music that have nothing to do with the matter on hand."

3203 Shepherd, P. J. "Introductory Commentary," *The Rainbow*, by D. H. Lawrence (Lond: Wm Heinemann, 1968), pp. ix-xxxvi.

[Introductory notes discussing characters and themes in *The Rainbow*, which is viewed as a transitional work in DHL's canon and his major achievement in the novel.]

3204 Shimizu, Kohya. "D. H. Lawrence no Center Symbolism" (D. H. Lawrence's Center Symbolism), ESSAYS (Tohoku University), No. 10 (Dec 1968), 35-52.

[The symbols of tree, dance, and lake in *The Plumed Serpent* are examined with regard to "center symbolism," which provides an important clue to the understanding of DHL's symbolism.] [In Japanese.]

3205 Shorter, Eric. [*A Collier's Friday Night*], DAILY TELEGRAPH (Lond), 1 March 1968.

The "photographic realism" on which both the author and the director rely makes the two hours of *A Collier's Friday Night* "pass very slowly." [Review of the Royal Court Theatre production, directed by Peter Gill. See also review by Eric Shorter, ("D. H. Lawrence: A Season of Plays"), DAILY TELEGRAPH (Lond), 15 March 1968.]

3206 Shorter, Eric. ["D. H. Lawrence: A Season of Plays"], DAILY TELEGRAPH (Lond), 15 March 1968.

"Social realism as a means of poignant dramatic expression" marks DHL's "posthumous success" as a playwright. [Review of the three productions (*A Collier's Friday Night, The Daughter-in-Law,* and *The Widowing of Mrs. Holroyd*) in the DHL "Season of Plays" at the Royal Court Theatre, directed by Peter Gill. See also review by Eric Shorter, (*A Collier's Friday Night*), DAILY TELEGRAPH (Lond), 1 March 1968.]

3207 Smailes, T[homas] A. "*More Pansies* and *Last Poems*: Variant Readings Derived from MS Roberts E192," D. H. LAWRENCE REVIEW, I (Fall 1968), 201-213; rptd as Appendix 3: "*More Pansies* and *Last Poems*: Corrigenda Derived from MS Roberts E192," in SOME COMMENTS ON THE VERSE OF D. H. LAWRENCE by T. A. Smailes (Port Elizabeth, South Africa: University of Port Elizabeth, 1970), pp. 93-97.

[A list of variant readings and corrigenda to the indicated section of *The Complete Poems of D. H. Lawrence*, ed by Vivian de Sola Pinto and F. Warren Roberts (1964). Includes photographic facsimiles (not reproduced in Appendix 3 of the book) of three pages of MS Roberts E192, "the only original source of *More Pansies* and *Last Poems*." See also reply by Vivian de Sola Pinto and

Warren Roberts, "A Note on Editing *The Complete Poems*," D. H. LAWRENCE REVIEW, I (Fall 1968), 213-14; and T[homas] A. Smailes, "Lawrence's Verse: More Editorial Lapses," NOTES AND QUERIES, ns XVII (Dec 1970), 465-66.]

3208 Smailes, T[homas] A. "A Note on Some Mythical Elements in Lawrence's *Women in Love*," STANDPUNTE, No. 75 (Feb 1968), 55-58; rvd and rptd as "The Mythical Bases of *Women in Love*," D. H. LAWRENCE REVIEW, I (Summer 1968), 129-36.

Understanding the significance of mythic allusions associated with Gerald and Gudrun in *Women in Love*, since their meaning is consistent with the prevailing optimism of DHL's other work, prevents overemphasis on the "pessimistic nature of Gudrun's victory" in the conflict. Mythic allusions to Gerald Crich fall into two complementary groups, which present him respectively as Hermes and as Germanic hero. As Hermes, the herald of death who summons souls to the underworld, Gerald "has singled out Gudrun for death," although her "eventual escape is implicit" in allusions to the related myth of Proserpine. As Germanic hero, Gerald is also "equated with Loki," with Fenrir the wolf, and with soldier heroes such as Sigurd, all of whom perish with the industrial magnate in "a winter Twilight of the Gods."

3209 Smith, Bob L. "D. H. Lawrence's *St. Mawr*: Transposition of Myth," ARIZONA QUARTERLY, XXIV (Autumn 1968), 197-208.

St. Mawr continues DHL's quest for a myth to give meaning and order to modern, mechanized society. The novel restates the familiar Lawrentian theme: that the consequences of his "cardboard, let's be happy world" are overrefinement and the destruction of man as man. St. Mawr, as totem, embodies what is left of the Pan spirit in England, and Lewis astride the stallion is the last remnant of the centaur myth: recognizing this and the necessity of preserving the "last male thing" in the universe, Lou and Mrs. Witt transpose the horse and what he embodies to America. The horse is revitalized as horse, the centaur exists only figuratively, and the Spirit of Pan is rediscovered in the natural objects of the land itself. None of these changes would have been possible in DHL's dead England. By transposing the myths to America, DHL metaphorically prevented their extinction, "unrefined" them, and suggested that they might regain something of their original stature.

3210 Sobchack, Thomas J. "Social Criticism in the Novels of D. H. Lawrence," DISSERTATION ABSTRACTS, XXIX (1968), 1235A. Unpublished dissertation, City University of New York, 1968.

3211 Sommers, Joseph. AFTER THE STORY: LANDMARKS OF THE MODERN MEXICAN NOVEL (Albuquerque: University of New Mexico P, 1968), pp. 128-32.

DHL's use of pre-Hispanic myth in his romanticized vision of Mexico (*The Plumed Serpent*) influenced Carlos Fuentes (WHERE THE AIR IS CLEAR). However, whereas DHL envisioned primitivism as a refuge from modern society,

Fuentes saw the Indian past as "a vital current in the contemporary Mexican psyche." DHL approached his subject from the standpoint of a European outsider and was influenced by a "more simplistic pre-World War II thought," projecting an answer to the moral dilemma which he had posed. Fuentes, on the other hand, writes during a more disillusioned period and therefore leaves the dilemma unresolved, "affirming only the imperative nature of the search" for an answer. Fuentes has been influenced by DHL, then, only in the sense that "he has incorporated similar thematic material, even a similar theme, into WHERE THE AIR IS CLEAR."

3212 Spano, Joseph. "A Study of Ursula (of *The Rainbow*) and H. M. Daleski's Commentary," PAUNCH, No. 33 (Dec 1968), 21-33.

H. M. Daleski, failing to note that Ursula's character is weakened by her persistent, personal pride, does not include in his quotation from *The Rainbow* a paragraph which, if included, would alter his interpretation of the character. [See also H. M. Daleski, THE FORKED FLAME: A STUDY OF D. H. LAWRENCE (1965), pp. 107-25.]

3213 Spurling, Hilary. "Old Folks at Home," SPECTATOR, CCXX (22 March 1968), 378-79.

The performances at the Royal Court Theatre of *A Collier's Friday Night, The Daughter-in-Law,* and *The Widowing of Mrs. Holroyd*, directed by Peter Gill, reveal that DHL had the ability to shape a scene and to write amusing dialogue. They also reveal, however, that DHL's sense of humor is limited, that his treatment of characters can be patronizing and embarrassing, and that his plays are not remarkable.

3214 Stilwell, Robert L. "The Multiplying of Entities: D. H. Lawrence and Five Other Poets," SEWANEE REVIEW, LXXVI (Summer 1968), 520-35.

The Complete Poems of D. H. Lawrence, ed by Vivian de Sola Pinto and F. Warren Roberts, will be of value only to DHL's devoted advocates. DHL "was among the most prolifically uneven English poets since Wordsworth and Shelley." Much of his output is unrecognizable as poetry, and this edition documents his work from "his careless worst to his careless best."

3215 Stohl, Johan H. "Man and Society: Lawrence's Subversive Vision," LITERATURE AND RELIGION: VIEWS ON D. H. LAWRENCE, ed by Charles A. Huttar (Holland, MI: Hope College [Papers Collected for MLA Seminar 15], 1968), pp. 1-8.

[Placing DHL's concept of love outside the Christian love ethic, the author insists on DHL's unorthodox world view, in which "spontaneous human interaction" is in conflict with repressive "conditioning we receive during childhood." "The central conflict in his vision of human existence is not between society and the individual, but between two modes of being in the world": "the way of compulsion" vs. "the way of pure spontaneity." Brief discussions of the essays "Education of the People" and "Love" and of *The Man Who Died* provide supporting evidence.] [Multilithed, spiral-bound book, with papers paginated individually.]

3216 Stoll, John E. D. H. LAWRENCE'S "SONS AND LOVERS": SELF-ENCOUNTER AND THE UNKNOWN SELF (Muncie, IN: Ball State University [Ball State Monograph No. 11; Publications in English, No. 7], 1968); rvd and incorporated as "Self-Encounter and the Unknown Self: *Sons and Lovers*," in THE NOVELS OF D. H. LAWRENCE: A SEARCH FOR INTEGRATION, by John E. Stoll (Columbia: University of Missouri P, 1971), pp. 62-105.

For DHL, the conscious and unconscious are irreconcilable aspects of mind. Attempts to integrate them lead to the destruction by consciousness of the unconscious well-springs of the psyche. The triumph of the socially conditioned conscious mind, DHL believed, often leads to incest or homosexuality. The struggle between conscious and unconscious led to a deep split in DHL's own personality, which in turn is manifested in the imagery and characters of his fiction, most notably *Sons and Lovers*. In *Sons and Lovers*, the light versus dark imagery reflects the struggle between consciousness and the Freudian unconscious, as does the crippling Oedipal bond between Paul Morel and his mother that leaves him unable to love Miriam because she is a surrogate for his mother and that renders his love for Clara effeminate and submissive because he has identified himself so deeply with his mother's consciousness.

3217 Sturm, Ralph D. "Lawrence: Critic of Christianity," CATHOLIC WORLD, CCVIII (Nov 1968), 75-79.

DHL rejected Christianity--at least what he knew as Christianity--reluctantly and then engaged in "a sincere search for meaning in an attitude of Post-Christianity." He is most convincing, however, when he makes his insistence on fully human, physical love "a completion of Christianity--as he does in *The Man Who Died*." Thus the evidence seems to indicate that DHL rejected, not the Christ of the Gospels, but the modern perversions of the simple Christian message.

3218 Suwabe, Hitoshi. "Ego and the Cosmos," STUDIES IN HUMANITIES (Ibaraki University), No. 2 (Dec 1968), 41-60.

[Treats DHL's last years. DHL's disgust at the modern world with its self-obsessed and fragmentary individuals and his assertion of sex to be the combiner of their egos are traced and examined in such works as *Aaron's Rod, Lady Chatterley's Lover,* and *The Man Who Died*. DHL's egocentric "Macrocosm" and hatred of the "masses," clearly and violently expressed in his posthumous *Apocalypse*, are seen critically as a self-contradictory conclusion to his own life-long doctrines.]

3219 Thody, P[hilip] M. W. FOUR CASES OF LITERARY CENSORSHIP: AN INAUGURAL LECTURE (Cambridge: Leeds UP, 1968), pp. 4-5, 7-13.

[Lecture delivered at the University of Leeds, pub as a monograph of 26 pages. The author draws comparisons among the French censorship cases involving Gustave Flaubert's MADAME BOVARY and Charles Baudelaire's LES FLEURS DU MAL, the British proceedings against *Lady Chatterley's Lover* (Regina v. Penguin Books, Ltd., 1960), and the French banning of Jean Genet's play THE BALCO-

NY.] The meaning of the jury's acquittal of *Lady Chatterley's Lover* is ambiguous, meaning either that the book is "not obscene" or that it "is immoral" but " 'nevertheless so good as literature that it ought to be published.' " It might have been argued that in putting "forward an alternative to the Christian view of marriage" that "laid more stress upon the needs of the body, DHL "was in no way 'depraving or corrupting' previously innocent readers, and that he was even offering a necessary reform." But the tactics of the defense to justify the book "by reference to its supposedly Christian content" prevented "two fundamental points" from being made: that we must allow even opinions we disagree with to be published openly; and that even if we think them likely to "deprave" readers, we must allow publication of books of high literary value.

3220 Thompson, Leslie M. "A Lawrence-Huxley Parallel: *Women in Love* and POINT COUNTER POINT," NOTES AND QUERIES, XV (Feb 1968), 58-59.

Huxley's borrowing of Rupert Birkin's remark about murderers and murderees reveals his "indebtedness to Lawrence," but his giving the remark to Spandrell rather than to Rampion "underscores [his] customary ironic use of borrowed material."

3221 Thwaite, Anthony. "Versions," NEW STATESMAN, ns LXXVI (1 Nov 1968), 600.

D. H. Lawrence: Poems Selected for Young People, ed by William Cole, includes widely anthologized pieces from *Birds, Beasts and Flowers,* as well as many from *Pansies* and *Nettles.* However central to DHL, those from "the peevish/satirical grouping" are not good poems but rancorous and boring.

3222 Tiedje, Egon. "D. H. Lawrence: 'Bavarian Gentians,' " DIE ENGLISCHE LYRIK: VON DER RENAISSANCE BIS ZUR GEGENWART (The English Lyric: From the Renaissance to the Present), ed by Karl Hein Goller (Dusseldorf, 1968), Vol. II, pp. 321-35.

[Line-by-line discussion of "Bavarian Gentians," its rhythm, its mythical allusions, and the difficulties arising from the existence of four versions (the first two entitled "Glory of Darkness").] The central theme of death reflects DHL's feeling of an approaching end. The connection of the Hades motive with the myth of Persephone suggests that the author reinterprets death as the fulfillment of life and the merging of the body with the cosmic powers. [In German.]

3223 Timko, Michael, and Clinton F. Oliver (eds). THIRTY-EIGHT SHORT STORIES: AN INTRODUCTORY ANTHOLOGY (NY: Knopf, 1968).

[This anthology includes "The Horse-Dealer's Daughter," pp. 335-53, and biographical information on DHL, focusing on his unhappy childhood, emphasizing the importance of his mother, his education, his marriage, his anti-war sentiments, and his problems with the censors.]

3224 Tischler, Nancy M. "The Rainbow and the Arch," LITERA-

TURE AND RELIGION: VIEWS ON D. H. LAWRENCE, ed by Charles A. Huttar (Holland, MI: Hope College [Papers Collected for MLA Seminar 15] , 1968), pp. 1-22.
[*The Rainbow* is discussed with emphasis on DHL's "use of mystical language for sexuality and the translation of Christian symbolism into his own terms." The rainbow, in contrast to various "false arches," is "a central symbol in Lawrence's mystique of sex." Analysis of "The Cathedral" chapter, Ursula's final vision of the rainbow, and the novel's thematic relation to such works as *Women in Love* and *David* provide supporting evidence. DHL's religious faith and hope have much in common with the Christian mystic's.] [Multilithed, spiral-bound book, with papers paginated individually.]

3225 Travis, Leigh. "D. H. Lawrence: The Blood-Conscious Artist," AMERICAN IMAGO, XXV (1968), 163-90.
DHL's works as a whole are permutations of the mind-consciousness vs. blood-consciousness dualism modeled on his parents in *Sons and Lovers*. Analysis of four stories, "The Woman Who Rode Away," "The Princess," "The Daughters of the Vicar," and *The Man Who Died*, each written at a different point in DHL's career, reveals the informing ghosts of Mr. and Mrs. Morel. The conflict between these two provides a scheme, the essence of which is a Lawrentian *rite de passage*, through which the later mind-conscious female seeks a blood-conscious experience. [The six basic stages of the *rite de passage* are discussed as they are revealed in the four stories.] DHL's dualistic approach to reality "has the hard lines of inflexible doctrine" because DHL did not explore the complexities of his basic subject; hence, the "mechanically patterned" quality of too much of his work.

3226 Uchiki, Jôtarô. *"Tsubasa Aru Hebi* ni Tsuite" (On *The Plumed Serpent*), REPORT OF RIKKYÔ UNIVERSITY (HUMANE STUDIES), No. 23 (May 1968), 1-47.
[In Japanese.]

3227 Uehata, Yoshikazu. "*St. Mawr* no Hyôka o Megutte" (On Some Appreciations of *St. Mawr*), BUNGAKU-KAI RONSHÛ (Kô-nan University), No. 36 (March 1968), 125-48.
[In Japanese.]

3228 Vanderlip, E. C. "The Morality of D. H. Lawrence," LITERATURE AND RELIGION: VIEWS ON D. H. LAWRENCE, ed by Charles A. Huttar (Holland, MI: Hope College [Papers Collected for MLA Seminar 15] , 1968), pp. 1-8.
[Measuring DHL's philosophy against a Christian world view, the author finds a "full response" to DHL difficult because of DHL's "affirmation of primitivism." "A Christian critique. . .could maintain a view which is disinterested in the sense that it has no desire to elevate ethics above aesthetics. But it should maintain the right to demur at the level of the absolutizing of anything over God." DHL reaches that level when he "absolutizes sex," thus failing both in his stated moral aim and in his artistic objective. Brief references to *The Plumed Serpent* and discussion of "Tickets, Please" provide supporting evidence.] [Multilithed, spi-

ral-bound book, with papers paginated individually.]

3229 Van Tine, James Gaylord. "Major Polarities in the Shorter Fiction of D. H. Lawrence," DISSERTATION ABSTRACTS, XXIX (1969), 3160A. Unpublished dissertation, Claremont Graduate School, 1968.

3230 Walcutt, Charles Child, and J. Edwin Whitesell (eds.). THE EXPLICATOR CYCLOPEDIA, Vol. III: PROSE (Chicago: Quadrangle Books, 1968), pp. 120-24.
[Reprints four items from EXPLICATOR on works by DHL.] Contents on DHL, abstracted under year of first publication: Richard B. Vowles, " 'The Blind Man,' " pp. 120-21, from EXPLICATOR, XI (Dec 1952), Item 14; Carol Haseley, *The Rainbow*," pp. 121-22, from EXPLICATOR, XIX (June 1961), Item 70; R. E. Wiehe, " 'Tickets, Please,' " pp. 122-23, from EXPLICATOR, XX (Oct 1961), Item 12; William A. Fahey, "*The White Peacock*," pp. 123-24, from EXPLICATOR, XVII (Dec 1958), Item 17.

3231 Wall, James M. "Voyeuristic," CHRISTIAN CENTURY, LXXXV (20 March 1968), 360-61.
The film version of *The Fox* [directed by Mark Rydell], "fails miserably to catch Lawrence's vision. Lawrence was concerned with the mysterious depths into which the venturesome March plunges in the hope of finding happiness, only to be dashed against the shoals of the unattainable, The fox symbolizes this otherness. But...the symbolism vanishes and the film becomes a commercially oriented analysis of a frustrated lesbian love affair," leaving us "with very little Lawrence."

3232 Wardle, Irving. "Pay Day for Young Lawrence," TIMES (Lond), 1 March 1968, p. 12.
"Like most of Lawrence's early writing *A Collier's Friday Night* represents a struggle to come to terms with his upbringing." Although "it is an autobiographical record of his Eastwood home with no incidents beyond those of the average payday," the play should not be dismissed as artless. DHL "was fully capable of distancing himself from the subject so as to present an unsentimental study of the mechanics of domestic love." [Review of the Royal Court Theatre production, directed by Peter Gill, as the opening play of the DHL season.]

3233 Waters, Frank. "Quetzalcoatl Versus D. H. Lawrence's *Plumed Serpent*," WESTERN AMERICAN LITERATURE, III (1968), 103-13.
DHL, concerned with the tragic split between the conscious and the unconscious, urges us, in such works as *St. Mawr* and "The Woman Who Rode Away," to go against modern mechanization of life and return to the dark realm of instinctive wisdom. *The Plumed Serpent*, which traces the rise of a revolutionary Quetzalcoatl religion of blood consciousness, whose leaders, Ramón and Cipriano, plan to rid Mexico of Catholicism and Americanism, became DHL's vehicle for one of the most horrible prophecies ever written. The prophecy came true in 1933 with

Adolf Hitler as a German Don Ramón, for whose plans *The Plumed Serpent* could have served better than MEIN KAMPF. The fictional Quetzalcoatl movement and Nazism share similar goals and methods, but DHL knew nothing of the actual ritual premises of Indian ceremonialism. [The author surveys the Quetzalcoatl myth among the Toltecs and Aztecs.] What DHL restores to Mexico in *The Plumed Serpent*, his Bible of racial divisiveness, is an Aztec barbarization of the religion of Quetzalcoatl.

3234 West, Ray B., Jr. "The Use of Point of View and Authority in 'The Blind Man,'" READING THE SHORT STORY (NY: Crowell, 1968), pp. 105-17; also pub in THE ART OF WRITING FICTION, by Ray B. West, Jr. (NY: Crowell, 1968), pp. 223-36.

DHL as narrator of "The Blind Man" has limited omniscience. Isabel Pervin, as the character in conflict, reflects the principal events. Maurice and Bertie are fixed characters and opposites. Occasionally DHL makes short, interpretive comments while employing a shifting point of view--from Isabel to Maurice to Bertie and back to Isabel--usually gracefully but sometimes awkwardly. Though the conflict is not resolved since the two men do not successfully come together, Maurice's blindness is shown to be a lesser evil than Bertie's inability to touch anyone.

3235 Westbrook, Max. "The Poetical Spirit: Sacrality and the American West," WESTERN AMERICAN LITERATURE, III (Fall 1968), 193-205.

DHL in *Apocalypse* forcefully elaborates three tenets central to American sacrality (i.e., the belief in God as energy): (1) Man's basic self is collective, and it is as such that he is prone to shape or betray his primordial energies; (2) Though all men may be equal by political or ethical criteria, they are not so ontologically, and to say they are is to cut oneself off from the undemocratic, primordial reality; (3) The non-biblical, non-idealized gods of the universe are not representatives of reality; they *are* reality.

3236 Whitaker, Thomas R. WILLIAM CARLOS WILLIAMS (NY: Twayne Publishers [Twayne United States Authors 143], 1968), pp. 58, 77-78, 82-84, 86, 92, 94, 97, 122, 124-25, 168.

DHL in "America, Listen to Your Own" called for reintegrating the demon of savage America which the Puritans and Spaniards had rejected. For both DHL and William Carlos Williams in the 1920s, puritanism was a "murderous force ...that causes souls to perish." Williams's "Elegy for D. H. Lawrence" uses Lawrentian images to establish a parallel between DHL and the snake, which is "no netherworld god but a glassy image of the self," and shows DHL subtly contradicting "his own vision by desperate efforts to force change." In Williams's "A Sort of a Song," which harks back to DHL's "Song of a Man Who Has Come Through," the snake becomes "an emblem of the reconciling poetic attention itself."

3237 White, T. H., and David Garnett. THE WHITE / GARNETT LETTERS, ed by David Garnett (NY: Viking P, 1968), pp. 13, 30-31, 111, 254, 306.

[The correspondence of T. H. White and David Garnett. Brief, passing references to DHL.]

3238 Willey, Frederick. "The Novel and the Natural Man: Reality in Fiction Since Cervantes," MICHIGAN QUARTERLY REVIEW, VII (Summer 1968), 104-18.

DHL describes the novel as the "Book of Life." Unlike Dreiser, he sought to liberate and idealize "blood consciousness," a naturalistic endowment. Actually, glorification of sex is not original with DHL, who is anticipated by Fielding in this.

3239 Williams, Hubertien H. "D. H. Lawrence: The Making of a Poet," DISSERTATION ABSTRACTS, XXIX (1969), 4028A. Unpublished dissertation, Bowling Green State University, 1968.

3240 Williams, Hubertien H. "Lawrence's Concept of Being," LITERATURE AND RELIGION: VIEWS ON D. H. LAWRENCE, ed by Charles A. Huttar (Holland, MI: Hope College [Papers Collected for MLA Seminar 15], 1968), pp. 1-17.

DHL's characters, Ursula excepted, can be divided into three groups--those dominated by spirituality, those dominated by sensuality, and those dominated by intellectuality. DHL's concept of being demanded a harmonious reconciliation of spirit, flesh, and intellect. [Discussion of poems in *Birds, Beasts and Flowers, Pansies,* and *Last Poems* and references to theoretical ideas in other works by DHL provide supporting evidence.] [Multilithed, spiral-bound book, with papers paginated individually.]

3241 Williams, Raymond. DRAMA FROM IBSEN TO BRECHT (Lond: Chatto & Windus, 1968; NY: Oxford UP, 1969; rptd Harmondsworth, Middlesex: Penguin Books, 1973), pp. 21, 75, 257-60, 320, 336, 337.

Not finding the expected audience for the plays he wrote between 1909 and 1914, DHL left the drama, though in the twenties *The Widowing of Mrs. Holroyd* was produced, he revised *The Married Man* (1926), and he wrote *Touch and Go* (1920) and *David* (1926). The problem was that his "plays of working class life" were "outside the modes of the contemporary theatre." "He was interested in a kind of play which, without theatrical devices, embodied a rhythm of contemporary life." The plays "overlap with the novels and stories": *A Collier's Friday Night* with *Sons and Lovers, Touch and Go* with *Women in Love, The Daughter-in-Law,* written in "a dialect which is not just a variant of printed English, but the shape and sound of a particular way of living," with the early stories of mining life. [A detailed comparison of *The Widowing of Mrs. Holroyd* and its source, "Odour of Chrysanthemums," shows that the play lacks the advantages of mobility within the larger setting and the varied narrative voice and expression of inward feelings available to DHL in the story.] DHL admired Chekhov and Synge, though he rejected the latter's "rounded off" artistic perfection. In both DHL and Strindberg there is a " 'fusion of the class-war and the sex-war.' "

3242 Young, Archibald M. "Rhythm and Meaning in Poetry: D. H. Lawrence's 'Snake,'" ENGLISH, XVII (Summer 1968), 41-47.

"Poetry of the present," controlled by "an immediate dramatic presence, rather than a formally remote condition," imitates "a sensitive mind responding to ambiguous demands as it undergoes a process of changing experience." The constantly changing rhythmic patterns of "Snake" establish variations in mood and are therefore justified in terms of emotional as opposed to formal unity.

3243 Young, B. A. [*A Collier's Friday Night*], FINANCIAL TIMES (Lond), 2 March 1968.

A plotless but not a shapeless play, *A Collier's Friday Night* is "continually absorbing. The dialogue is wonderfully recorded, and the emotions are truly felt and transmitted." [Review of the Royal Court Theatre production, directed by Peter Gill. See also review by B. A. Young, ("D. H. Lawrence: A Season of Plays"), FINANCIAL TIMES (Lond), 19 March 1968.]

3244 Young, B. A. ["D. H. Lawrence: A Season of Plays"], FINANCIAL TIMES (Lond), 19 March 1968.

DHL's "plays are still life studies in which the reactions of a group of people are examined in relation to a strong central situation." [Review of the three productions (*A Collier's Friday Night, The Daughter-in-Law,* and *The Widowing of Mrs. Holroyd*) in the DHL "Season of Plays" at the Royal Court Theatre, directed by Peter Gill. See also review by B. A. Young, (*A Collier's Friday Night*), FINANCIAL TIMES (Lond), 2 March 1968.]

3245 Youngblood, Sarah. "Substance and Shadow: The Self in Lawrence's Poetry," D. H. LAWRENCE REVIEW, I (Summer 1968), 114-28.

Neither the poems of *Look! We Have Come Through!* nor others are as "ingenuously autobiographical" as DHL's 1928 preface to his *Collected Poems* implies. DHL intends, as earlier prefaces show, to embody the personal as well as the archetypal and universal, and his poetry shows the patterns of balance and imbalance between the two. "The Wild Common" is a fitting introduction to the poems because it details the interplay between the "I" of the ego and undifferentiated life. DHL's unevenness results from an often partial vision which disjoins the personal from its roots in the impersonal, as is shown in the failure of "The Virgin Mother" and the success of "Troth with the Dead." *Look! We Have Come Through!* should be read as the expression of a phase of development of the self, and *Birds, Beasts and Flowers* as the record of a confrontation with "the world of non-human but animate creatures," noting the greater objectivity the "out there" allows. The power of *Last Poems* proceeds from the organic development of the theme of selfhood throughout.

3246 Zytaruk, George J. "Book Reviews," DALHOUSIE REVIEW, XLVIII (Fall 1968), 410-12.

Many of the essays collected in *Phoenix II: Uncollected, Unpublished, and Other Prose Works by D. H. Lawrence,* ed by Warren Roberts and Harry T. Moore, were already available, and the editors' account of DHL's collaboration with

S. S. Koteliansky in translating Russian writers is insupportable where Dostoevsky is concerned and inadequately documented for I. A. Bunin. "The real value of *Phoenix II* is in such pieces as 'Mr. Noon,' " two interesting autobiographical pieces, and the long out of print "Introduction to MEMOIRS OF THE FOREIGN LEGION, by Maurice Magnus."

3247 Zytaruk, George J. (ed). "The Last Days of D. H. Lawrence: Hitherto Unpublished Letters of Dr. Andrew Morland." D. H. LAWRENCE REVIEW, I (Spring 1968), 44-50.

Dr. Andrew Morland visited DHL "in Bandol during the latter part of January 1930." The four previously unpublished letters were "written between 2 February 1930 and 9 March 1930"; "three of these are addressed to S. S. Koteliansky and one to Mark Gertler." The letters "record Dr. Morland's diagnosis of Lawrence's condition in those crucial days just a month and a half before his death"; they "also point to Koteliansky's and Gertler's concern for Lawrence's welfare and reveal how instrumental these two were in arranging the visit." [Texts of the four letters are published in full.]

1969

3248 Adams, Elsie B. "A 'Lawrentian' Novel by Bernard Shaw," D. H. LAWRENCE REVIEW, II (Fall 1969), 245-53.

George Bernard Shaw's youthful novel, CASHEL BYRON'S PROFESSION (1885-1886), anticipates in its characters and incidents DHL's *Lady Chatterley's Lover*, although the similarities do not necessarily indicate direct influence. Shaw's novel is about the love of a prize-fighter, Cashel Byron, for an aristocratic lady, Lydia Carew. While "far from a defense of 'the phallic reality,' " as *Lady Chatterley's Lover* is, Shaw's novel nevertheless concerns a lady who "finds in the life of the body an escape from the sterile life of the mind." Both novels share the same basic plot, similar settings, essentially the same central characters and, on occasion, even the same scenes. However, "Shaw's and Lawrence's views on sexuality are hardly compatible," and one is finally more "impressed by the differences between the two novels" and the two writers: taking the same materials, one "writes a satire on aristocratic propriety and human frailty, and the other writes a poetic defense of sensual love."

3249 Allendorf, Otmar. "Die Bedeutung Thomas Hardys fur des Frühwerk von D. H. Lawrence" (Thomas Hardy's Influence on the Early Work of D. H. Lawrence). Published dissertation, Philipps-Universität Marburg/Lahn, 1969. [Listed in Lawrence F. McNamee, DISSERTATIONS IN ENGLISH AND AMERICAN LITERATURE, SUPP. II: 1969-1973 (NY and Lond: Bowker, 1974), p. 355.] Pub as DIE BEDEUTUNG THOMAS HARDYS FÜR DES FRÜHWERK VON D. H. LAWRENCE (Universität Marburg/Lahn, 1969).

Numerous references to Thomas Hardy in DHL's letters, fiction, and criticism suggest Hardy's direct influence on DHL. DHL's pre-1914 poetry and fiction have both themes and techniques in common with Hardy; and the *Study of Thomas Hardy*, written in 1914, comes to terms with Hardy in an evaluation that marked a turning point, after which Hardy's influence ceased to be important for DHL. The relation between the poems of DHL and Hardy must be inferred from their context in Georgian England and from the poems themselves. Identifying himself with other Georgian poets, DHL wrote nature lyrics and valued sincerity, simplicity, and fidelity to life. Like Hardy, DHL wrote ballad-like poems and used dialect, dramatic situations, and women speakers. "Snap-Dragon," the best of DHL's early poems, differs from other Georgian poetry and contains elements developed in his later work. Of Hardy's novels, JUDE THE OBSCURE impressed DHL most; the Sue Bridehead character reverberates among DHL's early women characters such as Lettie, Helena, Miriam, and Hermione. In narrative technique and structure, *Sons and Lovers* parallels JUDE: the young protagonist of each is torn between a spiritual and a sensual woman, and both novels are structured on contrasts (dark-light, body-spirit, village-town). DHL's method of presenting landscape in *The White Peacock* is indebted to THE RETURN OF THE NATIVE and TESS OF THE D'URBERVILLES. DHL's early characterization owes something to Hardy, with whom he shared an interest in psychology, especially female psychology. The *Study of Thomas Hardy*, which marked an important stage in DHL's development as a thinker, criticizes Hardy's negative attitude toward sexuality. In the process, DHL, by implication, criticizes his own earlier position: whereas he had formerly criticized such vital characters as Walter Morel, he now praises such vital Hardy characters as Arabella Donn and Alec d'Urberville and devalues the spiritual principle he had presented favorably in Gertrude Morel. In the *Study* DHL employed, for the first time, the critical method he later called "saving the tale from the artist." DHL's critique has been influential of subsequent Hardy criticism, and parts of it are now generally accepted. [In German.]

3250 Altenberg, Bengt. "A Checklist of D. H. Lawrence Scholarship in Scandinavia, 1934-1968," D. H. LAWRENCE REVIEW, II (Fall 1969), 275-77.

DHL's work was one of the influences in a primitivist literary movement which "became a strong force in Swedish literature" in the 1930s. "Scholarly interest in his work," however, "has never been widespread in Scandinavia." [The checklist includes four books and sixteen articles, with titles listed both in original Scandinavian languages and in English translation.]

3251 Amette, Jacques-Pierre. "Lectures" (Readings), LA NOUVELLE REVUE FRANÇAISE, ns XVII (July 1969), 158.

Each story in *England, My England and Other Stories* [trans into French by Léo Dilé as *Île, mon Île et autre nouvelles* (1968)] is like an image, and the whole represents a slow motion picture. With DHL, the sky is alive, trees are moving, and the unconscious makes its appearance. The novelist should have reaped other rewards than the scandal of *Lady Chatterley's Lover*. [In French.]

3252 Andrews, W. T. "Laurentian Indifference," NOTES AND

QUERIES, ns XVI (July 1969), 260-61.
In *The Rainbow* and more obviously in *Women in Love* the flow of passion tends to conceal "the want of any real exchange of human sympathies." DHL's "indifferent" or detached characters represent an egotism "almost entirely self-bound and rigorously anti-social," which cannot be reconciled "with his frequently avowed aim of restoring and releasing the flow of sympathy between man and woman." Laurentian indifference tends "towards an unnatural limiting rather than a freeing of vital human emotions."

3253 Arnold, Armin. "D. H. Lawrence als Lehrer und Philosoph" (D. H. Lawrence as Teacher and Philosopher), NEUE ZÜRCHER ZEITUNG, 28 Sept 1969.

Two recent books, *Lawrence in Love: Letters to Louie Burrows*, ed by James T. Boulton (Nottingham: University of Nottingham, 1969), and Émile Delavenay, D. H. LAWRENCE: L'HOMME ET LA GENÈSE DE SON OEUVRE: LES ANNÉES DE FORMATION: 1885-1919 (Paris: Librairie C. Klincksieck, 1969), fill biographical gaps in DHL's early life and provide some keys to his intellectual development. [In German.]

3254 Arnold, Armin (ed). "Three Unknown Letters from Frieda Lawrence to Bertrand Russell," D. H. LAWRENCE REVIEW, II (Summer 1969), 157-61.

[The three letters, written in 1916, 1935, and 1948, are part of the Bertrand Russell Collection at McMaster University in Hamilton, Ontario. Texts of the three letters are printed in full.]

3255 Balbert, Peter Henry. "D. H. Lawrence and the Psychology of Rhythm: The Meaning of Form in *The Rainbow*," DISSERTATION ABSTRACTS INTERNATIONAL, XXX (1970), 3934A. Unpublished dissertation, Cornell University, 1969; rvd and pub as D. H. LAWRENCE AND THE PSYCHOLOGY OF RHYTHM: THE MEANING OF FORM IN "THE RAINBOW" (The Hague: Mouton, 1974).

3256 Baldeshwiler, Eileen. "The Lyric Short Story: The Sketch of a History," STUDIES IN SHORT FICTION, VI (Summer 1969), 443-53.

[DHL mentioned briefly on p. 449.] The structure of "The Blind Man" is "guided by the shape of feeling." "The Christening" shows "a group in the throes of intense and contradictory feeling" and derives its structure from the "ebb and flow of emotion."

3257 Bareiss, Dieter. "Die Vierpersonenkonstellation im Roman: Strukturuntersuchungen zur Personenführung. Dargestellt an N. Hawthornes THE BLITHEDALE ROMANCE, G. Eliots DANIEL DERONDA, H. James' THE GOLDEN BOWL und D. H. Lawrences *Women in Love*" (The Novel with Four Principal Characters: Studies on Character-Grouping in N. Hawthorne's THE BLITHEDALE

ROMANCE, G. Eliot's DANIEL DERONDA, H. James's THE GOLDEN BOWL, and D. H. Lawrence's *Women in Love*). Published dissertation, Erlangen-Nurnberg, 1969. [Listed in Lawrence F. McNamee, DISSERTATIONS IN ENGLISH AND AMERICAN LITERATURE, SUPP. II: 1969-1973 (NY and Lond: Bowker, 1974), p. 440.] Pub as DIE VIERPERSONENKONSTELLATION IM ROMAN: STRUKTURUNTERSUCHUNGEN ZUR PERSONENFÜHRUNG. DARGESTELLT AN N. HAWTHORNES "THE BLITHEDALE ROMANCE," G. ELIOTS "DANIEL DERONDA," H. JAMES' "THE GOLDEN BOWL" UND D. H. LAWRENCES "WOMEN IN LOVE" (Bern: Lang [Europäische Hochschulschriften, Reihe Angelsächsische Sprachen und Literatur, 1], 1969).

Although neglected by most literary theoreticians, the study of character-grouping serves to illuminate significant interrelations between structure and theme in any novel. T. S. Eliot, in his comments on Hawthorne and James, and DHL, early in his career, recognized the importance of character-grouping. DHL declared, " 'The usual plan is to take two couples and develop their interrelationships' "--a structural principle which he found in George Eliot. This study involves a comparative analysis of the character-grouping of the four principal characters in four novels (THE BLITHEDALE ROMANCE, DANIEL DERONDA, THE GOLDEN BOWL, and *Women in Love*) by English and American authors. The plots of the four novels are similar in reducing the quartet of characters to a tercet at the end. But the four novels are dissimilar in that the two English novels have simple personal relationships among characters conditioned by their environment against complex backgrounds with large panoramic effects, whereas the two American novels have complex personal relationships among characters whose behavior is psychologically rather than socially determined against meager backgrounds. Thus, there is a clear relationship between an author's handling of character-grouping and his handling of milieu. [In German.]

3258 Baron, Carl E. "Two Hitherto Unknown Pieces by D. H. Lawrence," ENCOUNTER, XXXIII (Aug 1969), 3-5.

[Offers a correction to Armin Arnold, "D. H. Lawrence's First Critical Essays: Two Anonymous Reviews Identified," PUBLICATIONS OF THE MODERN LANGUAGE ASSOCIATION, LXXIX (March 1964), 185-88, which had identified DHL's first critical essays as reviews of H. G. Fiedler's OXFORD BOOK OF GERMAN VERSE and Jethro Bithell's THE MINNESINGERS. Baron cites evidence to suggest that DHL anonymously reviewed CONTEMPORARY GERMAN POETRY, edited by Jethro Bithell, for ENGLISH REVIEW, Nov 1911, and wrote a "backpage" article, "With the Guns," for the MANCHESTER GUARDIAN (1914). The two articles are reprinted in full. See also Armin Arnold, D. H. LAWRENCE AND GERMAN LITERATURE WITH TWO HITHERTO UNKNOWN ESSAYS BY D. H. LAWRENCE (1963).]

3259 Barrière, Francoise. "*Women in Love* ou le roman de l'antagonisme" (*Women in Love* or the Novel of Antagonism), LES LANGUES MODERNES, LXIII (May-June 1969), 293-303.

DHL's universe is manichean; conflict is at its core. For DHL conflict represents a dynamic element and can be reduced to two opposing forces that are confronted in man as well as in society and the cosmos. One of these forces leads to dissolution, the other to cohesion. This double movement can be observed in the plot, the characters, and the play of metaphors in *Women in Love*; it gives the novel its unity despite its apparent complexity. In man the two antagonistic principles are "mind-consciousness" and "blood-consciousness"; when one prevails over the other, the result is imbalance, bringing about disintegration and death, a process clearly illustrated in the characters of *Women in Love*. [In French.]

3260 Barry, J. "Oswald Spengler and D. H. Lawrence," ENGLISH STUDIES IN AFRICA, XII (Sept 1969), 151-61.

Both Spengler in THE DECLINE OF THE WEST and DHL in *The Rainbow* and *Women in Love* regard the imposition of knowledge upon creativity as a disaster. Both agree that what befalls is determined by character and not by an external fate. Thus, Gerald's death is implicit in his character as revealed in his actions, for he (and to a lesser extent Hermione and Loerke) fulfills all the requirements of the Spenglerian soul in Faustian decline. This reductive process is manifested as a will to mastery that can end only in death. Birkin, on the other hand, moves from mental bondage to instinctive life, the *katharsis* that Spengler describes as seeing "the tortured mythical soul breathe again."

3261 Beards, Richard D. "D. H. Lawrence and the *Study of Thomas Hardy*, His Victorian Predecessor," D. H. LAWRENCE REVIEW, II (Fall 1969), 210-29.

The fact that the largest portion of DHL's *Study of Thomas Hardy* is about DHL's own ideas indicates that he found in the earlier novelist's work the same concerns he was fictionalizing in his own. In addition to the Hardy study and DHL's letters, there are other points of contact: (1) "Hardy's influence on Lawrence's first novel," *The White Peacock*; (2) "evidence throughout Lawrence's novels that he learned from Hardy" various "technical skills"; (3) their three "shared thematic and sympathetic concerns." First, both novelists offer characters who are revealed and defined by means of the strength and validity of their connection to the natural environment. Second, both "are centrally concerned with the establishment of permanent and meaningful sexual relationships." Third, both have a natural sympathy for a certain kind of hero, called the "aristocrat" in DHL's Hardy study--the man or woman who is above the common, isolated by choice, aware of the "otherness" in each individual, capable of emotional spontaneity and sexual fulfillment. DHL condemns Hardy's "ambivalent attitude toward his" aristocrats, seeing the suffering and death of the individualist as " 'the root of Hardy's pessimism' " and the result of Hardy's bourgeois vindictiveness.' " In his own novels, DHL "is solidly behind his aristocrats," but cannot avoid putting them "into similar predicaments."

3262 Beckham, Richard Hamilton, Sr. "The Ritual of Love: A Study of Symbolic Technique in D. H. Lawrence's Shorter Fiction," DISSERTATION ABSTRACTS INTERNATIONAL, XXXI (1970), 1259A. Unpublished dissertation, Kent State University, 1969.

3263 Beker, Miroslav. " 'The Crown,' 'The Reality of Peace,' and *Women in Love*," D. H. LAWRENCE REVIEW, II (Fall 1969), 254-64.

DHL's essays "The Crown" and "The Reality of Peace" are pertinent to an interpretation of *Women in Love*. In "The Crown," the conflict between the Lion and the Unicorn reveals the polarity between " 'Destruction and Creation [as] the two relative absolutes between the opposing infinites.' " In the prison of the self-conscious ego, growth is impossible and nothing is left "but the process of corruption." But when ego melts away, then " 'the spirit of destruction is divine' " because it " 'opens the soul' " to change. The image of pernicious corruption in "The Crown," the aristocratic carrion birds, resembles Hermione Roddice. Images of divine destruction, such as the swan, mud, ooze, water, water lily, lotus, and snake, however, are attached to Birkin and Gudrun. Birkin's acceptance of corruption as an antithetical counterpart of creation and growth and Ursula's unashamed recognition of " 'dark shameful things' " reflect DHL's plea, in "The Reality of Peace," for recognition of the forces of corruption and dissolution as belonging to life. Our self-conscious civilization, DHL thought, "wants to triumph over death and over the concept of man as part of nature." Gerald Crich thus becomes "a symbol of modern civilization," the "persistent self...who is destroyed and who lapses into 'utter stone darkness.' " Birkin's ideals, on the other hand, include a deliberate acceptance of destruction and corruption.

3264 Bhat, Vishnu. "D. H. Lawrence's Sexual Ideal," LITERARY HALF-YEARLY, X (Jan 1969), 68-73.

DHL's sexual ideal was high: to make the sexual relation valid and precious instead of shameful.

3265 Billington, Michael. "With Lawrence in Derbyshire," ILLUSTRATED LONDON NEWS, CCLV (22 Nov 1969), 24.

The film version of *Women in Love*, directed by Ken Russell, is poorest at its most literal and best in its recreation of the period.

3266 Bloom, Edward A., and Lillian D. Bloom. THE VARIETY OF FICTION: A CRITICAL ANTHOLOGY (NY: Odyssey P, 1969), 374-77.

[This anthology includes "The Rocking-Horse Winner," pp. 359-74, and a "Commentary," which states the theme as "the corrupting, the killing effects of money and other gross forms of materialism upon a so-called civilized modernity" and which, in explanation of DHL's theme, quotes extracts from his letters to Charles Wilson (28 Dec 1928), Lady Cynthia Asquith (16 Aug 1915), and Willard Johnson (9 Jan 1924).]

3267 Boulton, James T. "D. H. Lawrence's 'Odour of Chrysanthemums': An Early Version," RENAISSANCE AND MODERN STUDIES, XIII (1969), 5-11.

Twenty-seven pages of printer's proofs of "Odour of Chrysanthemums" from the papers of Mrs. Louisa Heath (Louie Burrows), now in the possession of the University of Nottingham, "enable us to form a clear view of three stages in the composition of one of the best of Lawrence's early stories": (1) the proof sheet version, (2) the proof sheet version with added manuscript revisions, and (3) the published version in the ENGLISH REVIEW, June 1911. [There follows an account of revisions made in the stages of composition.]

3268 Burwell, Rose Marie. "Recent Books on Modern Fiction: British," MODERN FICTION STUDIES, XV (Winter 1969-1970), 577-79.

Incomparable in terms of the biographical information it gives about DHL, *Lawrence in Love: Letters to Louie Burrows,* ed by James T. Boulton, gives little information about Louie Burrows except for the editor's introduction. DHL's commitment to the engagement was less than Louie's. Within a few "months of the proposal Lawrence's letters become briefer, more perfunctory." The importance of these letters is their relevance to the composition of *Sons and Lovers.* After his recovery from his serious illness of 1911, DHL broke the engagement in February 1912--only to form a permanent attachment with Frieda Weekley within six weeks.

3269 Burwell, Rose Marie Read. "A Chronological Catalogue of D. H. Lawrence's Reading from Early Childhood," DISSERTATION ABSTRACTS INTERNATIONAL, XXX (1970), 3937A. Unpublished dissertation, University of Iowa, 1969; rvd and pub as "A Catalogue of D. H. Lawrence's Reading from Early Childhood," THE D. H. LAWRENCE REVIEW, III (Fall 1970), iii-vi, 193-324.

3270 Butler, Gerald Joseph. "*The Rainbow* and D. H. Lawrence's Repudiation of Sex Tragedy," DISSERTATION ABSTRACTS INTERNATIONAL, XXXI (1970), 752A. Unpublished dissertation, University of Washington, 1969.

3271 Carter, John. "*The Rainbow* Prosecution," TIMES LITERARY SUPPLEMENT (Lond), 27 Feb 1969, p. 216.

[Contains three previously unpublished and heretofore unknown letters concerning *The Rainbow* prosecution in 1915. The letters, from DHL, Methuen & Co., and J. B. Pinker and addressed to G. Herbert Thring, Secretary of the Society of Authors, were intended to provide information that would support the Society's legal intervention in DHL's behalf. In a statement of 7 Dec 1915, printed here with the letters, the Society decided against such action.]

3272 Cavitch, David. D. H. LAWRENCE AND THE NEW WORLD (NY: Oxford UP, 1969); excerpt from Chap. III, pp. 61-76, rptd in D. H. LAWRENCE: A COLLECTION OF CRITICISM, ed by Leo Hamalian (NY: McGraw-Hill, 1973), pp. 54-64.

DHL was an unequivocal Romantic who regarded art as expressive of the personality of the artist. More than that, DHL believed that art could be restorative, that it could help integrate the personality by recovering the submerged passionate and sensual self and fusing it with consciousness. His first effort, through art, to emerge into a psychically liberated, sensual mode of selfhood was through the composition of *Sons and Lovers*. That largely autobiographical novel depicts a young man's partially successful effort to free himself from bondage to his mother, and simultaneously to liberate his own guilt-free, masculine sexuality. Paul Morel, at book's end, has learned to associate his own sexuality with the benign forces of nature, but unknown to himself, he has also completely internalized the ideal values of his mother. Paul is left with a severe confusion of sexual roles, which was also DHL's own, and with the choice either of finding a man to identify himself with or seeking a man's love effeminately. Birkin in *Women in Love* openly faces and seeks to satisfy the femininity and bisexual longings that he shares with his creator, both within the novel as published and, in particular, in the "Prologue" that DHL later suppressed, probably to disguise his own homosexuality. In that novel, Birkin is DHL's spokesman, Gudrun is the persona for the homoerotic desires which DHL included in the "Prologue," but which shamed him, and Gerald is the object of those desires. Following *Women in Love*, DHL suppressed his craving for male love, and he depicts his masculine characters as similarly suppressing their homoerotic yearnings. In his later work, DHL came to experience America as a place where his contained homosexual sensuality might be liberated. Thus, the landscapes, particularly the mountains, and the figures, such as powerfully sensual horses, in the American works often symbolize the desired masculine love-object. But DHL could never free himself from his self-suppression, nor could he liberate his fictional recreations of himself. The final works, including *Lady Chatterley's Lover*, thus come from a man who has forfeited the quest for sensual and emotional wholeness, and who instead indulges escapist idylls which disguise his own homosexual urges with a portrayal of simplistic male-female relationships.

3273 Cecil, Robert. LIFE IN EDWARDIAN ENGLAND (Lond: B. T. Batsford; NY: G. P. Putnam's Sons ["English Life Series"], 1969), p. 160.

The suppression of *The Rainbow* showed the reassertion of "the old prudery" by a reading public that preferred to have the sexual theme "wrapped in a tissue of unreality" as in H. de Vere Stacpole's THE BLUE LAGOON (1908).

3274 Christie, Ian Leslie. "*Women in Love*," SIGHT AND SOUND, XXXIX (Winter 1969-70), 49-50.

The film version of *Women in Love*, directed by Ken Russell, emerges "not so much as an 'adaptation' of Lawrence's monumental novel, but as a kind of critical re-creation," "one strand" of which "is to find a number of occasions for broad humour."

3275 Cipolla, Elizabeth. "The *Last Poems* of D. H. Lawrence," D. H. LAWRENCE REVIEW, II (Summer 1969), 103-19.

Many poems in *Last Poems* owe their genesis to the Mediterranean Sea, especially as it was historically important to the Etruscans. "Maximus" and "The Man of Tyre" refer to Maximus of Tyre in Gilbert Murray's FIVE STAGES OF GREEK RELIGION. The paradoxical combination of light and darkness in "Bavarian Gentians" and the marriage of Persephone and Pluto are "the soul's consummation in the darkness of death." The darkness suggests Satan's fall and directly leads into "Lucifer" and on to the "falling" in "The Hands of God," "Abysmal Immortality," and "Only Man." "The Ship of Death" sequence "forms a counterpart to *Look! We Have Come Through!*" The segments from MS B not printed in *Last Poems* explain DHL's symbolism in the ship and its victualing. "Shadows" is a testament of DHL's faith in the merging in the greater unconscious and of the merging of the darkness of the soul with the limitless darkness of death. "Phoenix" is anticlimactic, but perhaps appropriate as a closing.

3276 Clarke, Colin (ed). D. H. LAWRENCE: "THE RAINBOW" AND "WOMEN IN LOVE": A CASEBOOK (Lond: Macmillan, 1969; Nashville: Aurora Publishers, 1970).
Contents, abstracted under year of first publication: "Acknowledgements," p. 7, and A. E. Dyson, "General Editor's Preface," pp. 9-10 [not abstracted]; Colin Clarke, "Introduction," pp. 11-22; **Part One: The Author on the Novels**: DHL, "Letters to Edward Garnett and Others (1913-20)," pp. 25-31, excerpts from four letters to Garnett and one letter each to J. B. Pinker, Waldo Frank, and Martin Secker, rptd from *The Collected Letters of D. H. Lawrence,* ed by Harry T. Moore (1962) [not abstracted]; **Part Two: Documents Relating to "Women in Love"**: George H. Ford, "Introductory Note to D. H. Lawrence's Prologue to *Women in Love,*" pp. 35-42, rptd from TEXAS QUARTERLY, VI (Spring 1963), 92-97; DHL, "Prologue to *Women in Love,*" pp. 43-62, rptd from TEXAS QUARTERLY, VI (Spring 1963), 98-111 [not abstracted]; DHL, "Foreword to *Women in Love*" (1920), pp. 63-64 [not abstracted]; **Part Three: Critical Studies**: John Middleton Murry, "A Review of *Women in Love,*" pp. 67-72, rptd from "The Nostalgia of Mr. D. H. Lawrence," NATION AND THE ATHENAEUM, XXIX (13 Aug 1921), 713-14; John Middleton Murry, "*The Rainbow,*" pp. 73-77, rptd from SON OF WOMAN: THE STORY OF D. H. LAWRENCE (Lond: Jonathan Cape, 1931), pp. 87-92; John Middleton Murry, "The Fundamental Equivocation of *Women in Love,*" pp. 77-90, rptd from SON OF WOMAN: THE STORY OF D. H. LAWRENCE (Lond: Jonathan Cape, 1931), pp. 123-37; Mary Freeman, "Lawrence and Futurism," pp. 91-103, rptd from D. H. LAWRENCE: A BASIC STUDY OF HIS IDEAS (Gainesville: University of Florida P, 1955), pp. 70-81; Roger Sale, "The Narrative Technique of *The Rainbow,*" pp. 104-16, rptd from MODERN FICTION STUDIES, V (Spring 1959), 29-38; S. L. Goldberg, "*The Rainbow:* Fiddle-Bow and Sand," pp. 117-34, rptd from ESSAYS IN CRITICISM, XI (Oct 1961), 418-24; G. Wilson Knight, " 'Through. . .Degradation to a New Health'-- A Comment on *Women in Love,*" pp. 135-41, excerpt rptd from "Lawrence, Joyce and Powys," ESSAYS IN CRITICISM, XI (Oct 1961), 403-17; Julian Moynahan, "Ritual Scenes in *The Rainbow,*" pp. 142-50, rptd from THE DEED OF LIFE: THE NOVELS AND TALES OF D. H. LAWRENCE (Princeton: Princeton UP, 1963), pp. 63-72; H. M. Daleski, "*Women in Love:* 'Firm Singleness and Melting Union,' " pp. 151-66, rptd from THE FORKED FLAME: A STUDY OF D. H. LAWRENCE (Evanston: Northwestern UP, 1965), pp. 174-87; George H. Ford, "*Women in Love:* The Degeneration of Western Man," pp. 167-87, rptd from DOUBLE MEASURE: A STUDY OF THE NOVELS AND STORIES OF D. H. LAWRENCE (NY: Holt, Rinehart, 1965), pp. 189-207; Ronald Gray, "*Women in Love* and the German Tradition in Literature," pp. 188-202, rptd from THE GERMAN TRADITION IN LITERATURE, 1871-1945 (Cambridge: Cambridge

UP, 1965), pp. 340-54; Frank Kermode, "Lawrence and the Apocalyptic Types," pp. 203-18, rptd from CRITICAL QUARTERLY, X (Spring-Summer 1968), 14-33; Colin Clarke, " 'Living Disintegration': A Scene from *Women in Love* Reinterpreted," pp. 219-34, excerpts rptd from RIVER OF DISSOLUTION: D. H. LAWRENCE AND ENGLISH ROMANTICISM (Lond: Routledge & Kegan Paul; NY: Barnes & Noble, 1969), pp. 88-110; "Select Bibliography," pp. 235-36 [not abstracted]; "Notes on Contributors," pp. 237-38 [not abstracted].

3277 Clarke, Colin. "Introduction," D. H. LAWRENCE: "THE RAINBOW" AND "WOMEN IN LOVE": A CASEBOOK, ed by Colin Clarke (Lond: Macmillan, 1969; Nashville: Aurora Publishers, 1970), pp. [11]-22.

Significant commentary on *The Rainbow* and *Women in Love* begins with John Middleton Murry's SON OF WOMAN (1931); earlier studies now have little to offer the student of DHL. Horrified by the corruption which pervades *Women in Love,* Murry failed to recognize Birkin's efforts "to become whole through *incorporating* corruption." Despite his distortions, however, Murry managed to call attention to what remains the crucial theme in DHL's fiction. DHL's reputation declined during the 1930s and 1940s for a variety of reasons. During this period, F. R. Leavis "waged war against misconceptions that retarded a recognition of Lawrence's distinction and stature." Recognizing *The Rainbow* and *Women in Love* as DHL's masterpieces, Leavis demonstrated, in D. H. LAWRENCE: NOVELIST (1955), how each novel "mediates a moral-religious vision of experience, communicated through a fully realized imaginative rendering of life." The shortcoming of Leavis's criticism is his failure to come to terms with the demonic side of DHL and his "deeply ambivalent treatment of the theme of corruption." The first of these qualities has been recognized by Mary Freeman, G. Wilson Knight, and Kingsley Widmer. Although the second of these qualities has received some attention in recent studies by Mark Kinkead-Weekes and K. K. Ruthven, who examines the theme of corruption, "what is wanting is the complementary emphasis: a due recognition that in the world of *Women in Love*... the processes of dissolution and renewal can never, in fact, be dissociated...that there is after all only the one process, the ambivalent process of reduction."

3278 Clarke, Colin. " 'Living Disintegration': A Scene from *Women in Love* Reinterpreted," D. H. LAWRENCE: "THE RAINBOW" AND "WOMEN IN LOVE": A CASEBOOK, ed by Colin Clarke (Lond: Macmillan, 1969; Nashville: Aurora Publishers, 1970), pp. [219]-34; rvd and absorbed in Chap. III: "*Women in Love*: Individuality and Belonging," in RIVER OF DISSOLUTION: D. H. LAWRENCE AND ENGLISH ROMANTICISM, by Colin Clarke (Lond: Routledge & Kegan Paul; NY: Barnes & Noble, 1969), pp. 88-110.

Critics have generally regarded the forces of dissolution and disintegration which DHL presents in *Women in Love* as "life-destructive." However, closer examination reveals that these forces are frequently positive or "positive-negative." They are negative when they are revealed in characters like Gerald and Hermione, whose "false integrity" binds them to a separateness based on an exultant sense of their own advantages which cuts them off from human bonds. An example of "life-enhancing" dissolution, on the other hand, can be recognized in Ursula, whose dissolution puts her "in contact with the rhythms of living and dying." Some of the best moments in the novel, like the chapter "Moony," are those in which "tribute is paid at one and the same time" to dissolution and its opposing force. In effect, two Romantic ideals, the paradisal and the demonic, confront each other in *Women in Love,* and neither is affirmed at the expense of the other.

3279 Clarke, Colin. RIVER OF DISSOLUTION: D. H. LAWRENCE AND ENGLISH ROMANTICISM (Lond: Routledge & Kegan Paul; NY: Barnes & Noble, 1969); excerpt from Part II, Chap. I, pp. 45-68, rptd as "Reductive Energy in *The Rainbow,*" in D. H. LAWRENCE: A COLLECTION OF CRITICISM, ed by Leo Hamalian (NY: McGraw-Hill, 1973), pp. 33-53.

DHL criticism virtually began with John Middleton Murry's SON OF WOMAN, because Murry correctly perceived that DHL in *Women in Love* discovered a positive virtue in degradation. Leavis, George Ford, and Mark Spilka, for instance, illustrate the "single-mindedness" of "moralistic" critics who gloss over DHL's moral ambivalence to posit in his work clear-cut and absolute distinctions between "corruption" and "non-corruption," or destruction and creation. But such a bifurcation is simply a distortion of DHL's work, and will lead readers of the major fiction hopelessly astray. A reader might gain a proper sense of DHL's ambiguous attitude toward corruption by placing DHL in the "Romantic tradition." DHL inherited from the English Romantic poets a tradition of concepts and imagery which expresses a deeply ambiguous, paradoxical attitude toward corruption, reduction, disintegration, and dissolution. Like the Romantics, DHL is endlessly concerned with the process "of dying into being, the lapsing of consciousness which is yet the discovery of a deeper consciousness." This lapsing often takes the form, in the novels, of images of falling or dissolving, and no matter how pejorative or negative the image might seem, it is apt to call to mind, as well, its possible positive meanings.

These ambiguities are to be seen in *The Rainbow*, one of the most elaborately vitalistic of DHL's novels, in the images of positive reductiveness manifested by Will Brangwen and Skrebensky, as well as by Ursula. But *Women in Love* even more clearly illustrates how DHL depicts beauty as a product of the reductive process. *Women in Love* reveals DHL as fascinated by what he attacks, and virtually all the major characters demonstrate the notion that creativity is nourished by degradation. This moral paradox represents DHL's deepest insight into moral reality. Yet it is an insight that DHL abandons in later works, like *The Plumed Serpent* and *Lady Chatterley's Lover,* where moral complexity gives way to a simplistic bifurcation of creativity versus degradation, much like the vision that Leavis, Ford, and Spilka attribute to the earlier novels.

3280 Colmer, John. "HOWARDS END Revisited," LITERARY HALF-YEARLY, X (July 1969), 9-22.

Forster's HOWARDS END and *Lady Chatterley's Lover* both seek to establish, though by very different methods, a connection between the emotional health of the individual and the health of society.

3281 Comerford, Anthony. "*Women in Love,*" TIMES LITERARY SUPPLEMENT (Lond), 11 Dec 1969, p. 1426.

[Letter to the editor.] On the evidence of a passage near the end of *Women in Love* ("Ursula could but think of the Kaiser's: 'Ich habe es nicht gewollt' "), the chronological setting of the story must be post-war Europe and not pre-war England as commonly assumed. If the Kaiser's remark could not have been known in England until 1918, then DHL either did not complete *Women in Love* in 1916, as is commonly believed, or must have at least tinkered with it later. [See also reply by George Ford in letter to the editor, *"Women in Love,"* TIMES LITERARY SUPPLEMENT (Lond), 12 Feb 1970, p. 169.]

3282 Consolo, Dominick P. (ed.). D. H. LAWRENCE: "THE ROCKING-HORSE WINNER" (Columbus, OH: Merrill [The Merrill Literary Casebook Series], 1969).
Contents, abstracted under year of first publication: Dominick P. Consolo, "Introduction," pp. 1-5; "Chronology of Significant Dates," pp. 6-8 [not abstracted]; D. H. Lawrence, "The Rocking-Horse Winner," pp. 9-22 [not abstracted]; Harry T. Moore, "Some Notes on 'The Rocking-Horse Winner,' " pp. 23-25, from THE LIFE AND WORKS OF D. H. LAWRENCE (NY: Twayne, 1951), pp. 277-79; W. D. Snodgrass, "A Rocking-Horse: The Symbol, the Pattern, the Way to Live," pp. 26-36, from HUDSON REVIEW, XI, No. 2 (Summer 1958), 191-200; Carolyn Gordon and Allen Tate, "Commentary on 'The Rocking-Horse Winner,' " pp. 37-40, from THE HOUSE OF FICTION, 2nd ed. (NY: Scribner's, 1960), pp. 227-30; Robert Gorham Davis, "Observations on 'The Rocking-Horse Winner,' " pp. 41-42, from INSTRUCTOR'S MANUAL FOR TEN MODERN MASTERS: AN ANTHOLOGY OF THE SHORT STORY, 2nd ed. (NY: Harcourt, Brace, 1959), pp. 49-50; Kingsley Widmer, "The Triumph of the Middleclass Matriarch," pp. 43-46, rptd from THE ART OF PERVERSITY: D. H. LAWRENCE'S SHORTER FICTIONS (Seattle: University of Washington P, 1962), pp. 92-95; Roy Lamson, Hallett Smith, Hugh Maclean, Wallace W. Douglas, "A Critical Analysis," pp. 47-51, from THE CRITICAL READER, rvd ed. (NY: Norton, 1949), pp. 542-47; W. R. Martin, "Fancy or Imagination: 'The Rocking-Horse Winner,' " pp. 52-54, rptd from COLLEGE ENGLISH, XXIV (Oct 1962), 64-65; William D. Burroughs, "No Defense for 'The Rocking-Horse Winner,' " pp. 55-56, rptd from COLLEGE ENGLISH, XXIV (Jan 1963), 323; Robert G. Lawrence, "Further Notes on D. H. Lawrence's Rocking-Horse, p. 57, rptd from COLLEGE ENGLISH, XXIV (Jan 1963), 324; Frank O'Connor [pseud of Michael O'Donovan], "Poe and 'The Rocking-Horse Winner,' " pp. 58-59, rptd from THE LONELY VOICE: A STUDY OF THE SHORT STORY (Cleveland & NY: World, 1962, rptd 1965), pp. 153-55; James Hepburn, "Disarming and Uncanny Visions: Freud's 'The Uncanny' with Regard to Form and Content in Stories by Sherwood Anderson and D. H. Lawrence," LITERATURE AND PSYCHOLOGY, IX (Winter 1959), 9-12; E. W. Tedlock, Jr., "Values and 'The Rocking-Horse Winner,' " pp. 69-70, rptd from D. H. LAWRENCE: ARTIST AND REBEL (Albuquerque: University of New Mexico P, 1963), pp. 209-10; W. S. Marks III, "The Psychology of the Uncanny in Lawrence's 'The Rocking-Horse Winner,' " pp. 71-83, rptd from MODERN FICTION STUDIES, XI (Winter 1965-1966), 381-92; Frank Amon, "D. H. Lawrence and the Short Story," pp. 84-94, from THE ACHIEVEMENT OF D. H. LAWRENCE, ed by Frederick J. Hoffman and Harry T. Moore (Norman: University of Oklahoma P, 1953), 222-34; Frederick W. Turner III, "Prancing to a Purpose: Myths, Horses, and True Selfhood in Lawrence's 'The Rocking-Horse Winner,' " pp. 95-106 (1969, 1st pub).

3283 Consolo, Dominick P. "Introduction," D. H. LAWRENCE: "THE ROCKING-HORSE WINNER," ed by Dominick P. Consolo (Columbus, OH: Merrill, 1969), pp. 1-5.

The polarity in DHL's life, culminating in his relationship with Frieda, is a dynamic principle in his art. In "The Rocking-Horse Winner," failure of womanliness is expressed in Hester. The simplicity of the style reinforces the hardness in her which destroys her son, and her final illumination comes too late.

3284 Cowan, James C. "D. H. Lawrence's Quarrel with Christianity," LITERATURE AND THEOLOGY, ed by Thomas F. Staley and Lester F. Zimmerman (Tulsa: University of Tulsa [Department of English Monograph Series, No. 7], 1969), pp. 32-43; rptd in D. H. LAWRENCE'S AMERICAN JOURNEY: A STUDY IN LITERATURE AND MYTH, by James C. Cowan (Cleveland and Lond: P of Case Western Reserve University, 1970), pp. 34-44.

DHL's heroes, from Paul Morel to the risen "man who died," seek to reconcile a "duality of religious motive." The Church does not help in co-ordinating flesh and spirit but, as in the cathedral chapter of *The Rainbow*, only confirms their opposition. In *Twilight in Italy*, DHL redefines the Christian Trinity in a Hegelian synthesis in which God the Father (flesh) and Christ the Son (spirit) are reconciled in the Holy Ghost, an idea derived from the doctrine of Joachim of Flora, whose work DHL discusses in *Movements in European History*. In his later works, DHL's syncretic polytheism affirms the open manifestation of the unknown god variously in different cultures, and "The Risen Lord" and *The Man Who Died* reject the halfness of conventional Christianity.

3285 Čura-Sazdanić, Ileana. D. H. LAWRENCE AS CRITIC (Delhi: Munshiram Mancharial, 1969).

DHL's "truly moral value" lies more in "his social, than literary criticism." 'Arnold's conviction that...literature is 'a criticism of life' " is echoed in DHL's affirmation that " 'Nothing is important but life.' " Arnold sees "the intrinsic value" of culture as "its potentiality as a counter-weight to machinery"; Carlyle condemns the fact that "Philosophy, Science, Art, Literature, all depend on machinery." DHL, in "Nottingham and the Mining Countryside," "condemns the ugliness and squalor of the new industrial society," and, in *Women in Love*, "he underlines the disastrous effect of the machine on the individual." Both Arnold and DHL made claims for "the wholeness of human life," and F. R. Leavis and the contributors to SCRUTINY continued in "Arnoldian succession" from their work. Among DHL's contemporaries, E. M. Forster and Aldous Huxley responded "intelligently and spontaneously" to his achievement, while T. S. Eliot and Wyndham Lewis launched "two heavy attacks on Lawrence." [Criticism of DHL by Forster, Huxley, and Leavis is examined in detail.] "Lawrence's explicit condemnation of industrialism as an attitude of mind continues the line of Carlyle and the nineteenth century tradition. But his social values...are strikingly personal." DHL demonstrates "the increasing 'bondage' of industrialism" in *The White Peacock, Sons and Lovers,* and *Women in Love*, and records his sardonic view of "the ugliness of industrial surroundings" in *The Rainbow* and *Lady Chatterley's Lover*. DHL's conception of art, morality, and the novel "proceeds from the conviction that a work of art should be concrete and true to life."

3286 Cushman, Keith. "Literature," LIBRARY JOURNAL, XCIV (1 April 1969), 1499-1500.
Lawrence in Love: Letters to Louie Burrows, ed by James T. Boulton, clarifies DHL's "relationship with Louie, an elusive subject in the past," and "doubles the number of letters published from the years 1906 to 1912."

3287 Cushman, Keith Maxwell. "D. H. Lawrence at Work: The Making of *The Prussian Officer and Other Stories*," DISSERTATION ABSTRACTS, XXI (1970), 1267A. Unpublished dissertation, Princeton University, 1969; rvd and pub as D. H. LAWRENCE AT WORK: THE EMERGENCE OF THE "PRUSSIAN OFFICER" STORIES (Charlottesville: UP of Virginia, 1978).

3288 Daniel, John. "D. H. Lawrence--His Reputation Today," LONDON REVIEW, VI (Winter 1969/1970), 25-33.
DHL's novels do not involve today's students as complete works of art. He wrote about women only to the degree that his female characters sought oblivion in the hypothetical male as he himself sought some greater social absorption for the miner's son dislocated from his own class. His nostalgia for the security of the working-class world is also a nostalgia for the fixed roles in the family and in marriage. In *A Propos of "Lady Chatterley's Lover"* his longing for the firm world of the past leads him to advocate a kind of feudalism. He was in many ways the last real Victorian. [Also mentions "The Fox," "The Woman Who Rode Away," and "Odour of Chrysanthemums."]

3289 [Davis, Peter]. "D. H. Lawrence in Taos," LISTENER, LXXXII (11 Sept 1969), 336-39.
[Narrative account of DHL's life in Taos, New Mexico, Sept 1922-Sept 1925, interspersed with direct comments from reminiscences by Dorothy Brett, Frank Waters, Warren Roberts, Joseph Foster, Willard ("Spud") Johnson, and William Hawk, as broadcast on BBC 2. These reminiscences were also the basis for Peter Davis's documentary film, D. H. LAWRENCE IN TAOS (1969). (Illustrated with black and white photographs of the "Lawrence Shrine," Mabel and Tony Luhan, and Dorothy Brett, Frieda Lawrence, and Mabel Luhan.)]

3290 Delany, Paul (ed). "D. H. Lawrence: Twelve Letters," D. H. LAWRENCE REVIEW, II (Fall 1969), 195-209.
[These letters in the Columbia University Library range in date from July 1918 to January 1929 and are addressed to Nancy Henry, Marie M. Meloney, Thomas Seltzer, A. D. Hawk, Richard Aldington, Dorothy Yorke, Jonathan Cape, and Lady Ottoline Morrell.]

3291 Delavenay, Émile. "D. H. Lawrence entre six femmes et entre deux cultures" (D. H. Lawrence among Six Women and between Two Cultures), ÉTUDES ANGLAISES, XXII (April-June 1969), 152-58.
Lawrence in Love: Letters to Louie Burrows, ed by James T. Boulton (1969),

an important addition to Lawrentian documentation from 1908 to 1912, gives some precise details about DHL's apprenticeship as a writer and throws more light on his relationships with Louie Burrows and Jessie Chambers. It also provides the reader with commentaries on the poems "Snap-Dragon" and "The Hands of the Betrothed." [In French.]

>3292 Delavenay, Émile. "D. H. Lawrence: L'Homme et la genèse de son oeuvre. Les Années de formation (1885-1919)" (D. H. Lawrence: The Man and the Genesis of His Work, the Formative Years: 1885-1919). Published dissertation, Thèse d'État, Sorbonne University, 1969. Pub as D. H. LAWRENCE: L'HOMME ET LA GENÈSE DE SON OEUVRE. LES ANNÉES DE FORMATION (1885-1919) (Paris: C. Klincksieck, 1969); pub in English as D. H. LAWRENCE: THE MAN AND HIS WORK, THE FORMATIVE YEARS: 1885-1919, trans by Katharine M. Delavenay (Lond: Wm. Heinemann; Carbondale: Southern Illinois UP, 1972).

[In this "genetic" analysis, DHL's work is considered in chronological order until the end of 1919 and viewed as a confession which reveals more about DHL than his biographies do. The study falls into three sections: Part I: "Child of the Midlands" evokes the period of DHL's childhood, his years at Nottingham University College, and his love experiences at the time he was writing his earliest works. A discussion of *The White Peacock* and *The Trespasser* is followed by an analysis of the short stories of the 1910-1912 period, showing how DHL was to use some of the same material in *Sons and Lovers*. The analysis of this novel leads to conclusions not only about DHL's literary vocation and the paths he was to follow as a writer but also about the most deeply-seated traits of his character. Part II: "The Exile" traces the evolution of the man and the artist during the years 1912-1919. The author approaches DHL's major works of the period through a study of the conflicts and contradictions which reveal the deep disturbance of his psyche during the time in which they were taking shape. A study of DHL's personal experience illuminates the birth of new ideas in his mind around 1913 and his conviction that he had found the panacea for the evils of mankind as well as the emergence of the Lawrentian hero and of a feminine type which owes much both morally and physically to Frieda. The difficulty that DHL had in adapting himself to society on the national scale and his consequent temptations to create his own micro-society are directly related to the profound psychological shock he experienced as a result of the war. The author's analysis of the doctrine revealed in the *Study of Thomas Hardy*, "The Crown," and *Twilight in Italy* shows that DHL cannot receive ethics as separated from aesthetics, that his "vision of the world is such that he isolates the hero even more than he had in 1914." The originality of *The Rainbow* lies not only in its being a chronicle of three generations but also in the fact that it is DHL's "first attempt at total artistic creation," "at giving a new interpretation of the entire experience of the novelist." A study of the positive and negative aspects of *Women in Love* shows that "the writer's attempt at synthesis is only partially successful because the main ideas governing his work do not form a coherent whole and the oppositions and contrasts are not always entirely clear and conclusive." The novel marks a turning point and the end of what may be regarded as the work of the young DHL. In a final chapter, the author discusses the underlying significance of DHL's work as a whole through 1919, commenting on DHL's creative vision, his Messianism and his aesthetic conception of the "poetry of the present." A third section, "Documents" (included only in the French edition, in which it is published as a separate volume) includes four appendices: "Two Unedited Documents on Lawrence's Youth"; "D. H. Lawrence's Program of Studies"; "The DAILY TELEGRAPH Report of the *Rainbow* Police Court Case"; "Letters and Documents of Jessie Chambers Wood" (abstracted separately under 1969); Bibliography, "Original Texts of Citations in Translation," and Index.] [This work of "genetic" criticism has evoked, in addition to the usual reviews (not abstracted), several critiques of the "genetic" approach to DHL. See especially "The Lawrence Industry," TIMES LITERARY SUPPLEMENT (Lond), 18 Dec 1970, pp. 1496-98; a reply by Émile Delavenay in a Letter to the Editor with a rejoinder by the reviewer, "D. H. Lawrence," TIMES LITERARY SUPPLEMENT (Lond), 15 Jan 1971, p. 69; and William Walsh, "D. H. Lawrence and the Genetic Approach," ÉTUDES ANGLAISES, XXVI (July-Sept 1973), 327-30.] [In French.]

3293 "D. H. Lawrence," FRANKFURTER ALLGEMEINE ZEITUNG, 30 June 1969.

The reaction of French critics to the reissue of DHL's works by two well-known French publishers, Stock and Calmann-Levy, abolishes the notion of the writer as a sexual fanatic and a fascist. [In German.]

3294 "D. H. Lawrence and Louie Burrows," TIMES LITERARY SUPPLEMENT (Lond), 1 May 1969, p. 465.

Lawrence in Love: Letters to Louie Burrows, ed by James T. Boulton (1968), adds to our knowledge of DHL's early life, but Louie herself "remains as veiled, and the relationship as mysterious, as ever." DHL frequently comes off as the type of emotional bully his whole work protests against, and in the end, the reader's sympathies are all with Louie.

3295 D. H. LAWRENCE REVIEW, ed by James C. Cowan, II, No. 1 (Spring 1969) ["John Middleton Murry Number"].

Contents, abstracted under 1969: Dorothy Brett, "John Middleton Murry" (pencil drawing), p. iv [not abstracted]; James C. Cowan, "Preface," v-vi [not abstracted]; F. A. Lea, "Murry and Marriage," pp. 1-21 [not abstracted]; John Middleton Murry, "A Letter from Murry on Marriage" (holographic facsimile with copy), pp. 22-23 [not abstracted]; Richard Rees, "Politics of a Mystic," pp. 24-31; James R. Bennett, "THE PROBLEM OF STYLE," pp. 32-46 [not abstracted]; C. G. Thayer, "Murry's SHAKESPEARE," pp. 47-59 [not abstracted]; Philip Mahone Griffith, "Middleton Murry on Swift: 'The *nec plus ultra* of Objectivity'?" pp. 60-67; Richard Harter Fogle, "Beauty and Truth: John Middleton Murry on Keats," pp. 68-75 [not abstracted]; Ernest G. Griffin, "The Circular and the Linear: The Middleton Murry-D. H. Lawrence Affair," pp. 76-92; Christian Moe, "Playwright Lawrence Takes the Stage in London," pp. 93-97; "Laurentiana," pp. 98-100 [not abstracted]; "Research in Progress,"

p. 101 [not abstracted]; "Notes on Contributors," p. 102 [not abstracted].

3296 D. H. LAWRENCE REVIEW, ed by James C. Cowan, II, No. 2 (Summer 1969).
Contents, abstracted except as noted under 1969: Elizabeth Cipolla, "The *Last Poems* of D. H. Lawrence," pp. 103-19; George J. Zytaruk, "D. H. Lawrence's Reading of Russian Literature," pp. 120-37; John C. Alexander, "D. H. Lawrence and Teilhard de Chardin: A Study in Agreements," pp. 138-56, rvd and rptd from "Teilhard de Chardin and D. H. Lawrence: A Study in Agreements," ORMOND PAPERS, I (1966), 5-13; Armin Arnold (ed), "Three Unknown Letters from Frieda Lawrence to Bertrand Russell," pp. 157-61; George Hendrick, " '10' and the Phoenix," pp. 162-67 [not abstracted]; Elsie B. Adams, "Lawrence Among the Christians: MLA, 1968," pp. 168-71 [not abstracted]; Sadanobu Kai, Yasuichirô Ôhashi, Taiji Okada, and Toru Okumura, "A Checklist of D. H. Lawrence Articles in Japan, 1951-1968," pp. 172-91; "Laurentiana," p. 192 [not abstracted]; "Notes on Contributors," p. 193 [not abstracted].

3297 D. H. LAWRENCE REVIEW, ed by James C. Cowan, II, No. 3 (Fall 1969).
Contents, abstracted under 1969: Paul Delany (ed.), "D. H. Lawrence: Twelve Letters," pp. 195-209; Richard D. Beards, "D. H. Lawrence and the *Study of Thomas Hardy*, His Victorian Predecessor," pp. 210-29; S. Ronald Weiner, "The Rhetoric of Travel: The Example of *Sea and Sardinia*," pp. 230-44; Elsie B. Adams, "A 'Lawrentian' Novel by Bernard Shaw," pp. 245-53; Miroslav Beker, " 'The Crown,' 'The Reality of Peace,' and *Women in Love*," pp. 254-64; Suzanne Henig, "D. H. Lawrence and Virginia Woolf," pp. 265-71; William F. Hall, "The Image of the Wolf in Chapter XXX of D. H. Lawrence's *Women in Love*," pp. 272-74; Bengt Altenberg, "A Checklist of D. H. Lawrence Scholarship in Scandinavia, 1934-1968," pp. 275-77; "Laurentiana," pp. 278-80 [not abstracted]; "Notes on Contributors," p. 281, and "Index to Volume Two," p. 282 [not abstracted].

3298 D. H. LAWRENCE'S "WOMEN IN LOVE" (NY: United Artists, [1969]).
["United Artists Pressbook," a manual of advertisements and promotional copy for the film version of DHL's novel, written for the screen and produced by Larry Kramer, directed by Ken Russell, with Alan Bates, Oliver Reed, Glenda Jackson, and Jennie Linden.] " 'Women in Love' could only have been filmed today, now that the screen has attained a new and adult freedom."

3299 Donnerstag, Jürgen. "Die Stilentwicklung im Werke von D. H. Lawrence" (Stylistic Development in the Work of D. H. Lawrence). Published dissertation, University of Köln, 1969. [Listed in Lawrence F. McNamee, DISSERTATIONS IN ENGLISH AND AMERICAN LITERATURE, SUPP II: 1969-1973 (NY & Lond: Bowker, 1974). Pub as DIE STILENTWICKLUNG IM WERKE VON D. H. LAWRENCE (1969).
Some critics have wrongly accused DHL of being a careless stylist. His development as a writer shows that his style takes on its peculiar Lawrentian shape ac-

cording to the development of his philosophy. "Rhyming Poems" in *The Collected Poems of D. H. Lawrence* (1928) and *The White Peacock* are representative of DHL's earliest stage, in which he is indebted to Thomas Hardy and the Pre-Raphaelites to a large extent, though subsequent typical features have already turned up; e.g., symbolic imagery, irregular syntax, kinaesthetic elements, departure from traditional meter, and a lyrical quality in his descriptive prose. In a second phase of development, exemplified by *Look! We Have Come Through!* and *The Rainbow*, DHL breaks completely away from the conventional and occasionally sentimental cliches he uses in his earlier works. Free verse, abstract language, and the choice of key images, no longer purely ornamental, point to the importance of instinct and spontaneity in DHL's world. DHL's third period of stylistic development, as seen in *Birds, Beasts and Flowers*, is marked by ambiguous symbols and fragmented sentences, which appeal to the reader's sensual, not intellectual, understanding. In *The Plumed Serpent* DHL takes up again realistic techniques, as in *Sons and Lovers* and *Lady Chatterley's Lover*, and draws on mythological images. Here the difference between prose and lyrics becomes less distinct, thus expressing the author's concern with sense-consciousness. [In German.]

3300 "Drama," TIMES LITERARY SUPPLEMENT (Lond), 6 March 1969, p. 253.

The Widowing of Mrs. Holroyd and *The Daughter-in-Law*, with an introduction by Michael Marland, "deserve a wide audience," "though Lawrence's feeling for place is so intimate a part of the plays that it may be risky to attempt them with those who have no direct acquaintance with the dialect and accent." *The Daughter-in-Law*, DHL's best play, is "a fine and moving piece of work."

3301 "Drama," TIMES LITERARY SUPPLEMENT (Lond), 20 Nov 1969, p. 1345.

The Widowing of Mrs. Holroyd, A Collier's Friday Night, and *The Daughter-in-Law*, collected in *Three Plays by D. H. Lawrence*, with an introduction by Raymond Williams, are all related to DHL's early fiction. While the first two suffer by this comparison, *The Daughter-in-Law* is "an extremely fine, moving play" which does what writers of the last fifteen years have been trying to do.

3302 Draper, R[onald] P. D. H. LAWRENCE (NY: Humanities P [Profiles in Literature Series], 1969).

[Brief, lucid account of DHL's biography and the history of his literary reputation is followed, under the headings "Style," "Characterization," "Themes," and "Symbolism," by a series of extracts from DHL's fiction and non-fiction prose, with the author's analytic commentaries. Critical judgments are standard: DHL was released from his tie to his mother by Frieda; his works are closely related to his life; *The Rainbow* and *Women in Love* represent his finest achievement; the three leadership novels are of questionable value. Favorable judgments of DHL are balanced by quotations of negative criticism by T. S. Eliot and Katherine Anne Porter. Includes "Select Bibliography" and "Suggested Sequence of Reading" for those unfamiliar with DHL's work.]

3303 Enroth, Clyde. "Introduction," JOYCE AND LAWRENCE, ed by Clyde Enroth (NY: Holt, 1969), pp. 1-7.
[In this Introduction to an anthology of their work, the editor contrasts Joyce and DHL in terms of their "Apollonian" and "Dionysian" qualities.]

3304 Fernandez, Diane. "A Visionary," LA QUINZAINE LITTÉRAIRE, 1-15 Jan 1969, pp. 10-11.
[Review of selected DHL essays translated by Thérèse Aubray and collected in *Homme d'abord*, ed by Marcel Marnat (Paris: Union Generale d'Editions, 1969).] DHL is not the champion of wild erotism but a visionary like Blake. The major idea of the essays is that we must not mistake conscience for knowledge. *Psychoanalysis and the Unconscious* makes clear why DHL does not admit Freud's discoveries. [In French.]

3305 "First stab at the blood lust," MANCHESTER GUARDIAN, 30 July 1969, p. 6.
[Promotional feature story on director Christopher Miles and his making of the film *The Virgin and the Gypsy*.] "More than the fevered rationalisation of Lawrence's own social misdemeanour in whisking Prussian Frieda away from stuffy old von Richthofen" (*sic*), the story "is a restatement of his beliefs about the generally claustrophobic condition of society, about the life force, about freedom, about sexuality, and...a girl realising her womanhood." [Compare with D. H. LAWRENCE'S "THE VIRGIN AND THE GYPSY" (NY: Chevron Pictures, (1970).]

3306 Ford, George H. "Lawrence in Love," NEW YORK TIMES BOOK REVIEW, 9 March 1969, p. 8.
Lawrence in Love: Letters to Louie Burrows, ed by James T. Boulton, "fills in...a gap in our knowledge" about his relations with the girl to whom he was engaged before he met Frieda Weekley and who served as the main prototype for Ursula Brangwen in *The Rainbow*. Although an obscure figure, Louie and her family "were of crucial importance" in providing DHL "with a mine of insights into personal and family relationships that he would draw on" in *The Rainbow* and *Women in Love*.

3307 Frankes, James R., and Isadore Traschen (eds). SHORT FICTION: A CRITICAL COLLECTION, 2nd ed (Englewood Cliffs, NJ: Prentice-Hall, 1969).
[This anthology includes "The Blind Man" (pp. 149-67), commentary on the story, and questions following the commentary.] Darkness and touch, the two main symbols of "The Blind Man," are linked, respectively, with blood-consciousness and blood-contact. Isabel resolves her conflict when Bertie collapses under Maurice's touch. She realizes that Bertie, a symbol of civilization, can never "touch" her. Only Maurice, to whom darkness is compatible, can break through Isabel's fears of intimacy.

3308 Friedman, Alan. "Suspended Form: Lawrence's Theory of Fiction in *Women in Love*," TWENTIETH CENTURY INTERPRE-

TATIONS OF "WOMEN IN LOVE": A COLLECTION OF CRITICAL ESSAYS, ed by Stephen J. Miko (Englewood Cliffs, NJ: Prentice-Hall, 1969), pp. 40-49; contains rvd material from THE TURN OF THE NOVEL, by Alan Friedman (NY and Lond: Oxford UP, 1966).

DHL's revolutionary theory of fiction and of experience is revealed by the absence of a definitive conclusion in *Women in Love*. Although the ending of the novel has been attacked because the major characters fail to reach any permanent stability, the "final impulse toward expansion...cannot be considered an aberration"; rather, it is a case of DHL's having asserted "the dignity of maintaining through the course of life an unresolved, suspended experience." DHL's views apply to art as well as to experience, for he "has actually embedded an essay on the theory of fiction within the text of his novel." Without losing its artistic integrity, the dialogue in *Women in Love* encompasses "calculated theoretical and formal statements" about the ends of fiction.

3309 Gamache, Lawrence B. "Brangwen Men in *The Rainbow*: A Study of the Function of Two Male Characters." Unpublished dissertation, University of Ottawa, 1969. [Listed in CANADIAN THESES, 1969/70 (Ottawa: National Library of Canada, 1972), p. 133

3310 Garrett, Peter K. "D. H. Lawrence: The Revelation of the Unconscious," SCENE AND SYMBOL FROM GEORGE ELIOT TO JAMES JOYCE: STUDIES IN CHANGING FICTIONAL MODE (New Haven: Yale UP, 1969), pp. 181-213.

DHL differs from Conrad, James, and other modern novelists who experimented with point of view in that he does not depend on his characters' consciousness to describe a realm of experience which lies below the conscious mind; that is, he does not rely on his characters' conscious perception to indicate a meaning which it cannot grasp. DHL, therefore, depends on omniscient narration more frequently than most twentieth-century writers; his narrators typically have access to both conscious and unconscious thought and thus can expound on both analytically. But more important to DHL's attempts to explore unconscious thought are his powerful symbolic scenes in which unconscious states are examined by means of dramatic presentation. In such scenes, DHL avoids using symbols abstractly (meaning does not lie *beyond* the symbol), preferring to explicate an unconscious state through the concrete emotional intensity of a scene (meaning is "created by Lawrence's emphasis"). Correlary techniques employed frequently in DHL's fiction include incantatory language and patterns of imagery.

3311 "General," in "Briefly Noted," NEW YORKER, XLV (10 May 1969), 167.

Lawrence in Love: Letters to Louie Burrows, ed by James T. Boulton, DHL's letters to the young school teacher to whom he became engaged in 1910, when his mother was dying, and whom he "jilted" in early 1912, shows that "Lawrence was stubborn, self-centered, and, while generous with advice, stingy with disinterested concern."

3312 Gerber, Philip L., and Robert J. Gemmett (eds). "The Dream of Logic: A Conversation with Ihab Hassan," UNIVERSITY OF WINDSOR REVIEW, V (Fall 1969), 27-37.

[A conversation among Ihab Hassan, Gregory FitzGerald, and William Heyen, poet. Concerning DHL as a critic: in *Studies in Classic American Literature*, DHL is an impressionistic critic who does not operate in a closed, overly systematic way --an admirable quality since Hassan thinks that most criticism has tended too much towards the systematic "dream of logic."]

3313 Glicksberg, Charles I. THE IRONIC VISION IN MODERN LITERATURE (The Hague: Martinus Nijhoff, 1969), pp. 22, 77-78, 174-75, 180, 243, 244.

In "The Risen Lord" and *The Man Who Died*, DHL makes the "iconoclastic interpretation" that in "the Resurrection, Christ risen in the flesh," having "outlived his false mission," "brings out the true meaning and mystery of the Passion" by turning to "life itself" and "the beauty of the sensuous world." Though he was unaware of "the dead end of metaphysical irony to which his speculations brought him," DHL was the forerunner of "those writers who, though knowing that God is dead, continued to concern themselves with the religious quest." DHL recognized that Dostoevski's " 'moral hostility to the devil is mixed with secret worship of the devil.' " But unlike writers who came after him, DHL had an optimism which prevented his considering that life might be finally meaningless.

3314 Goldberg, Michael. "Lawrence's 'The Rocking-Horse Winner': A Dickensian Fable?" MODERN FICTION STUDIES, XV (Winter 1969-70), 525-36.

Between DOMBEY AND SON and "The Rocking-Horse Winner" there are significant resemblances in subject matter, theme, language, and characters: both stories deal with the death of a child named Paul, whose parents live by the "cash nexus" in an emotionally sterile environment; both boys die of a spiritual disease caused by this environment; both have a wizard-like quality which enables them to penetrate the mysteries of the adult world. To show Dickens's influence on the story is to emphasize a matter of greater importance than the Freudian theme: the death of natural instincts in a world obsessed with money and status. [See also addendum by Michael K. Goldberg, "Dickens and Lawrence: More on Rocking Horses," MODERN FICTION STUDIES, XVII (Winter 1971-1972), 574-75.]

3315 Gomme, Andor. "Criticism and the Reading Public," THE MODERN AGE, ed by Boris Ford (Baltimore: Penguin Books [The Pelican Guide to English Literature, Vol. VII], 1969), pp. 367-74.

For DHL the "living novel" is continually changing as life changes and "will be true to [the living moment] only if it presents life whole and openly: so its morality is never a fixed counter, but always draws its validity from the conditions of the time and place."

3316 Gordon, David J. "*Women in Love* and the Lawrencean

Aesthetic," in TWENTIETH CENTURY INTERPRETATIONS OF "WOMEN IN LOVE": A COLLECTION OF CRITICAL ESSAYS, ed by Stephen J. Miko (Englewood Cliffs, NJ: Prentice-Hall, 1969), pp. 50-60.

DHL's heightened rhetoric in *Women in Love* leads the reader to apprehend some meaning beyond the superficial human interest of the traditional novel--"something more allegorical, ideational, abstract." The form and style of the novel depend upon "a tension of opposites: between the 'poetic' interests in states and the 'novelistic' interest in characters." DHL departs from traditional novelistic technique by adding a symbolic overtone to the "psycho-metaphysical encounters" which serve also to advance the plot. DHL's basic thematic aim in *Women in Love* is an attack on egoism, which he regards as the chief impediment to spontaneity. The term *egoism,* as DHL thinks of it, "signifies a combination of defensive conceit *and* a sense of unworthiness," and the struggle against egoism is dramatized in the two heterosexual relationships depicted in the novel. DHL's novel is flawed, however, by a contrary strain of fatalism. Thus, "despite his great courage and intelligence, Lawrence himself could not eliminate from his novel evidence of unconscious fears."

3317 Green, Martin. "Shorter Reviews," KENYON REVIEW, XXXI, No. 3 (1969), [411]-15.

Lawrence in Love: Letters to Louie Burrows, ed by James T. Boulton (1968), covers the six years (1906-1912) during which "the crucial choices were made that determined the shape he would give to his experience, to his personality, to his talent," choices reflected in the progress of DHL's relationship with Louie Burrows. DHL's naive interest in non-literary concerns appeals to a "British" sensibility, which approves of unselfconscious writers.

3318 Grey, Elizabeth. BEHIND THE SCENES IN THE THEATRE (Lond: J. M. Dent, 1969), pp. 39-40.

Some stage directions in *The Daughter-in-Law* were not clear to Peter Gill, director of the Royal Court Theatre production (1968), until he went to Eastwood and saw the house DHL had lived in and described in the play.

3319 Griffin, Ernest G. "The Circular and the Linear: The Middleton Murry-D. H. Lawrence Affair," D. H. LAWRENCE REVIEW, II (Spring 1969), 76-92.

The terms "circular" and "linear" suggest that although Murry and DHL met and felt a common destiny, "Murry soon began a circuitous course separating at an ever greater distance from the tangential course of Lawrence." Both were "literary men" who dreamed of "a new human society" and sought a "new kind of love-communion to effect the change." While both "felt the inadequacy of purely rational approaches to knowledge," "it is paradoxically in their mutual emphasis on mystical experience that they ... divide." For Murry, such an experience was not ... meta-physical but immediate," not a return to unity but a going beyond to profounder " 'mystic knowledge in disintegration and dissolution.' " DHL fictionalized the relationship with Murry in *Women in Love* (completed 1916), in four stories written in 1924 ("Smile," "The Border Line," "Jimmy and the Desperate Woman," and "The Last Laugh"), and most sympathetically in his play *David* (published 1926). Murry deals with the relationship in SON OF WOMAN: THE STORY OF D. H. LAWRENCE (1931), WILLIAM BLAKE (1933), ADAM AND EVE: AN ESSAY TOWARDS A NEW AND BETTER SOCIETY (1944), and LOVE, FREEDOM AND SOCIETY (1957). Murry attempts "to incorporate the life and art of Lawrence...in the Christian humanist tradition--no easy task," if the views of Birkin and David represent those of DHL himself. [See also Ernest G. Griffin's treatment of the same material in "The Meaning of Lawrence," JOHN MIDDLETON MURRY (1969), pp. 121-40.]

3320 Griffin, Ernest G. "The Meaning of Lawrence," JOHN MIDDLETON MURRY (NY: Twayne [TEAS 72], 1969), pp. 121-41.
DHL thought that Murry would be the "topographer" of his "pioneering work," mapping out the structure of his meanings. Although Murry never became the desired disciple, he "never ceased to worry" about "what had *happened* in his relationship" with DHL. Murry believed that DHL "determined to escape his true destiny of spiritual awareness by transforming it into love of woman--of which he was not capable." *Fantasia of the Unconscious* and *Aaron's Rod*, for Murry DHL's greatest works, reveal the essential DHL, " 'the great life-adventurer of modern times.' " In subsequent evaluations, Murry includes a comparison of DHL and Blake in WILLIAM BLAKE and of DHL and Albert Schweitzer in LOVE, FREEDOM AND SOCIETY, which Murry believed his most important essay on DHL. [Elements of this essay appear in a somewhat different form in Griffin's "The Circular and the Linear: The Middleton Murry-D. H. Lawrence Affair," D. H. LAWRENCE REVIEW, II (Spring 1969), 76-93.]

3321 Griffith, Philip Mahone. "Middleton Murry on Swift: 'The *nec plus ultra* of objectivity'?" D. H. LAWRENCE REVIEW, II (Spring 1969), "John Middleton Murry Number," 60-67.
DHL referred to Swift's CASSINUS AND PETER in *Lady Chatterley's Lover* and again in *A Propos of "Lady Chatterley's Lover."* Murry follows DHL in denying "that the body is more gross than the mind" and in accusing Swift of combining " 'his horror at the fact of human evacuation with a peculiar physical loathing of women.' " The responses of both "are symptomatic...of their own inability to reconcile flesh and spirit and of that peculiar atmosphere of lower or lower-middle class prudery that...pervades the work of both men."

3322 Hall, William F. "The Image of the Wolf in Chapter XXX of D. H. Lawrence's *Women in Love*," D. H. LAWRENCE REVIEW, II (Fall 1969), 272-74.
The "Lawrentian wolf" in *Women in Love* represents "destructive gluttony as the creature of Nordic myth"; it is also related to the abstractions of "power, force, and will," and to "the disruption of a natural order." In this regard, the wolf image in Chapter XXX may also have been prompted by "the famous 'degree' speech of Ulysses in Shakespeare's TROILUS AND CRESSIDA."

3323 Henig, Suzanne. "D. H. Lawrence and Virginia Woolf," D. H. LAWRENCE REVIEW, II (Fall 1969), 265-71.

Virginia Woolf's 1923 essay, "How It Strikes a Contemporary," is the basis for the notion that she was unsympathetic to DHL's writings. The root of Woolf's difficulty in coming to terms with DHL's work lay in "his candid treatment of sex" and, later, in her feminist views. By 1931, however, in "Notes on D. H. Lawrence," published posthumously in THE MOMENT AND OTHER ESSAYS (1947), Woolf was able to render an objective assessment of DHL's work. Although she could never read him without a sense of "'frustration'" she recognized "her affinity to Lawrence" and came to "appreciate his attempts to liberate literature from the lingering Victorianism of the past."

3324 Holloway, John. "The Literary Scene," THE MODERN AGE, ed by Boris Ford (Baltimore: Penguin Books [The Pelican Guide to English Literature, Vol. VII], 1969), pp. 81-86.

"D. H. Lawrence was the most impassioned and persistent" writer of the twentieth century in diagnosing "the psychic dangers besetting his society." In his later work he searches for "a new source of vitality," a necessity in society's transformation from rural to industrial, urban life. Within the psyche DHL finds a source of "integrity and unity" which strengthens the style of both his prose and his poetry. It is through his struggle to overcome his own weaknesses that DHL becomes "a master in fiction."

3325 Howard-Hill, T. H. "Lawrence, David Herbert, 1885-1930," BIBLIOGRAPHY OF BRITISH LITERARY BIBLIOGRAPHIES (Oxford: Clarendon P, 1969), pp. 390-91.

[Bibliography of bibliographies, Items 4011-4022.]

3326 Hudspeth, Robert N. "Lawrence's 'Odour of Chrysanthemums': Isolation and Paradox," STUDIES IN SHORT FICTION, VI (Fall 1969), 630-36.

DHL's preference for "Odour of Chrysanthemums" is justified by the "aesthetic control and imaginative subtlety" with which DHL fused "image, scene, and atmosphere into a finely controlled work." In the first part of the story, these elements collaborate to create "the static reality of blight and futility that dominate Elizabeth's life"; in the second part, they stress Elizabeth's deepened understanding "of what isolation is"--the "paradoxical human necessity to surrender yet remain inviolate."

3327 Humma, John B. "From Transcendental to Descendental: The Romantic Thought of Blake, Nietzsche, Lawrence," DISSERTATION ABSTRACTS INTERNATIONAL, XXX (1970), 4454A. Unpublished dissertation, Southern Illinois University, 1969.

3328 Huxley, Aldous. LETTERS OF ALDOUS HUXLEY, ed by Grover Smith (Lond: Chatto & Windus; NY & Evanston, IL: Harper & Row, 1969), pp. 85-86, 88, 88n, 95, 187, 248, 275, 275n, 288, 294, 295, 300, 304, 305, 313-14, 315, 327, 328, 330-33, 334, 335-37, 335n, 338-40, 339n, 340n, 342, 343, 346-47, 346n, 349n, 350, 352-53, 355, 357-58, 362, 364, 365, 409, 421-22, 422n, 432, 455-

59, 502, 544n, 559, 620, 665-66, 666n, 683, 715, 715n, 813, 830-31, 832-33, 834-36, 875n, 876-77, 876n, 878-79, 884n, 885, 888, 889, 904, 929-30, 929n; see also letters to Frieda Lawrence Ravagli, pp. 334-35, 455-59, 500-1, 502-4, 733-34.

[Huxley's letters reflect a continuing relationship with DHL, whom he met briefly in 1915, with whom he had a warm friendship from 1926 until DHL's death in 1930, and whose ideas continued to interest Huxley. Huxley comments ironically (Nov 1915) that it is "serious books" like *The Rainbow* that have censorship problems rather than popular novels. He repeats an erroneous story (23 June 1920) that DHL, "the slightly insane novelist," had lost his artistic talent along with his complexes as a result of psychoanalysis. Later he reports (2 Nov 1926 and 23 Jan 1928) on his growing friendship with DHL, comments (13 July 1929 and 2 Aug 1929) on DHL's advancing tuberculosis, writes Julian Huxley (3 March 1930) news of DHL's death, and begins making plans (8 March 1930) for his edition of DHL's letters. Huxley denies (July 1930) having "'done' Lawrence" in TWO OR THREE GRACES, comments (19 July 1931) on *Lady Chatterley's Lover*, and denounces J. M. Murry's SON OF WOMAN as "vindictive" (8 Sept 1931 and 25 Sept 1931). He also discusses (14 Aug 1940 and 7 Oct 1940) Melchior Lengyel's projected dramatic version of *Lady Chatterley's Lover*, and comments (21 Nov 1957, 25 Nov 1957, and 4 Dec 1957) on his own novel and play THE GENIUS AND THE GODDESS. To Matthew Huxley (24 Jan 1960 and 4 Dec 1960) he writes concerning the proposed sale of DHL manuscripts to the University of Texas.]

3329 Jones, Brian. "Poets' Letters," LONDON MAGAZINE, ns IX (June 1969), 87-90.

Lawrence in Love: Letters to Louie Burrows, ed by James T. Boulton, reflecting "a sensibility at the height of its powers," has "the organic shape of one of his best novels." "Repeatedly, in these letters, [DHL] curbs his passion for fear of upsetting Louisa," who represents for him, at most, "a healthy ordinariness," and most of his comments about "their relationship indicate clearly the distance between them." [Also reviews LETTERS FROM EDWARD THOMAS TO GORDON BOTTOMLEY, ed by R. George Thomas.]

3330 Joshi, Krishna Nand. "The Lawrencean Dilemma: A Study in Lawrence-Brewster Correspondence," THE WEST LOOKS AT INDIA: STUDIES IN THE IMPACT OF INDIAN THOUGHT ON SHELLEY, EMERSON, THOREAU, WHITMAN, RUSKIN, TENNYSON, D. H. LAWRENCE AND JAMES JOYCE (Bareilly, India: Prakash Book Depot, 1969), pp. 93-109.

DHL's fascination with the East is reflected in his correspondence with Earl Brewster, which reveals the novelist's ambivalence, "his longing for the East blended with a preference for the West," his attraction to some tenets of Buddhism and aversion to others, his interest in Hinduism and the symbols of Tantric mysticism but his hatred for life in the East as he had seen it in Ceylon when he visited the Brewsters in 1922.

3331 Junkins, Donald. "D. H. Lawrence's 'The Horse Dealer's

Daughter,'" STUDIES IN SHORT FICTION, VI (Winter 1969), 210-13.

As "a journey toward the center of Mabel's being," "The Horse Dealer's Daughter" "couches the unreality of the fantastic journey in the framework of a contemporary myth," to dramatize "in modern terms the ancient psychological truths." Mabel "the isolate," to survive, must "die out of her old existence" and awaken "to the flesh," to the "universal rhythms of life itself." [The article delineates a variety of mythic themes and "mythological motifs"--e.g., three brothers, the drudging daughter, the hero risking death--some of them readily apparent.]

3332 Juta, Jan. "Portrait in Shadow: D. H. Lawrence," COLUMBIA LIBRARY COLUMNS, XVIII (May 1969), 3-16.

[Reminiscence by Juta, whose portrait of DHL (1920) hangs in the National Portrait Gallery, London. During the course of their friendship, Juta realized that the basic aspect of DHL that he must "try to portray" was "the Lawrence with a vision in his eyes of a world of beauty, where in awful majesty the truth would reign."]

3333 Kai, Sadanobu. "Kyôbô na Junrei no Ato o Otte--New Mexico" (After the Savage Pilgrimage--New Mexico), STUDIES IN FOREIGN LITERATURES (Ritsumeikan University), No. 18 (June 1969), 1-17.

[Discusses the influence of New Mexico and the American landscape on DHL. Visiting the Kiowa Ranch, Lobo, New Mexico, in 1963, the writer was "shocked" at the sight of the vast desert between the San Juan Mountains and the Sangre de Cristo Mountains: "What a terrible Rananim!"] [In Japanese.]

3334 Kai, Sadanobu, Yasuichirô Ôhashi, Taiji Okada, and Tôru Okumura. "A Checklist of D. H. Lawrence Articles in Japan, 1951-1968," D. H. LAWRENCE REVIEW, II (Summer 1969), 172-91.

[This checklist of articles on DHL published in Japan from February 1951 to May 1968 is divided into five sections: General, Poetry, Individual Works of Fiction, Non-Fiction Prose, and Drama. Each entry gives the author's name, the title in Japanese, a descriptive title in English, and publication information. See also a supplement, Sadanobu Kai, Yasuichirô Ôhashi, Taiji Okada, and Tohru Okumura, "A Checklist of D. H. Lawrence Articles in Japan, 1968-1975," D. H. LAWRENCE REVIEW, X (Summer 1977), 193-208.]

3335 Kaul, Dwarka N. "D. H. Lawrence and the Revolt against Naturalism." Unpublished dissertation, Bristol University, 1969. [Listed in Lawrence F. McNamee, DISSERTATIONS IN ENGLISH AND AMERICAN LITERATURE, SUPP. II: 1969-1973 (NY & Lond: Bowker, 1974), p. 366.]

3336 Kawabata, Takashi. "D. H. Lawrence Ron (*The Trespasser* no Romansu ni Tsuite)" (On D. H. Lawrence: A Love Affair in *The Trespasser*), RESEARCH BULLETIN OF OBIHIRO UNIVER-

SITY, III, No. 4 (Jan 1969), 30-56.

The Trespasser is important in examining DHL's early idea of love. Siegmund tries to love Helena through "blood consciousness," but Helena loves him through "day-consciousness." She cannot love him as a man but only as what she thinks him in her mind. DHL seemed to believe that love through "blood consciousness" could give us the will to live. [In Japanese.]

3337 Kim, Dong-son. D. H. LAWRENCE'S MALE LEADERSHIP IDEAS IN "AARON'S ROD," "KANGAROO," AND "THE PLUMED SERPENT" (Seoul, Korea: Hankuk University of Foreign Studies ["In Commemoration of the 15th Anniversary of the Founding"], 1969).

[This 153-page monograph examines the three leadership novels in the context of DHL's Utopian search for Rananim and his theories, explored also in the two psychological essays, *Psychoanalysis and the Unconscious* and *Fantasia of the Unconscious*, of the union of man and man.] *Aaron's Rod* expresses DHL's desire for both his wife and his friends to submit to him. "Out of sexual failure Lawrence developed the theory of balance," which included not only marriage in which "he came to insist on the woman's utter submission to man" but also the " 'additional marriage' " of *Blutbrüderschaft* with a man. *Kangaroo*, a travel book written in careless form, is closer to reality, with Australian characters based on DHL's shipboard acquaintances. [Detailed discussion of Richard Lovat Somers's involvement in Australian political activities, his relationships with Jack Callcott, Ben Cooley, and Willie Struthers, and his ultimate skepticism about Cooley's love ideal.] DHL's and Frieda's "marital battle" in Mexico, culminating in Frieda's return to England, is reflected in the poem "Bibbles" and in *The Plumed Serpent*, in DHL's ruthlessly denying Kate Leslie her " 'satisfaction' " in sex and insisting on her final submission to Cipriano's male power. DHL's ultimate rejection of the return to the savage state and of "the reciprocity of power" is evident in *St. Mawr*, "The Woman Who Rode Away," the essay "Herman Melville's MOBY DICK," and letters to Rolf Gardiner and Witter Bynner.

3338 Kim, Dong-son. A STUDY OF D. H. LAWRENCE: "LADY CHATTERLEY'S LOVER" AND "THE MAN WHO DIED" (Seoul, Korea: Hankuk University of Foreign Studies, 1969).

The work of DHL's last period presents the theme of salvation through " 'phallic tenderness,' " *Lady Chatterley's Lover*, DHL's "desperate attempt to destroy the mechanism of the industrial world and to defy the puritanism that emphasizes mind and intellect" at the expense of blood and flesh, "was written less for delight in a passionate love. . .than as a kind of sermon on sex." *The Man Who Died*, through a reversal of the Christian story of the Resurrection, expresses DHL's "relief at coming alive out of the very maw of death" and embodies "his long-cherished desire for the miraculous life." [In Korean.]

3339 Kinkead-Weekes, Mark. "Eros and Metaphor: Sexual Relationship in the Fiction of D. H. Lawrence," TWENTIETH CENTURY STUDIES, I (Nov 1969), 3-19; rptd in LAWRENCE AND WOMEN, ed by Anne Smith (Lond: Vision P; NY: Barnes & Noble, 1978), pp. 101-21.

In descriptions of sexual relationship, DHL explores the polar extremes of, on the one hand, the intensive, private bodily experience of sexuality and, on the other, the extensive, relational, public experience that such sexuality makes possible. Sex is seen as a mode of inconclusiveness, seeking to relate the whole self to the whole other, and both to the rhythms of the natural universe. At the same time, sex is an opposite process, not only joining-up but also singling out into "each thing in itself." Similarly, DHL's mixed mode of narration is both a reaching out from the authorial self into others and the natural world, and an analysis in which the author struggles to clarify himself. Eros is metaphor both within the novels and as a description of the relationship between author and fictive process, as in the Foreword to *Women in Love* where DHL likens the acts of writing and sex. DHL's development, from *Sons and Lovers* through *Lady Chatterley's Lover*, shows the difficulty of maintaining an equilibrium between Eros as an intensive experience and Eros as a metaphor of extensive, inclusive relationship.

3340 Kissane, Leedice M. "D. H. Lawrence, Ruth Suckow, and 'Modern Marriage,'" RENDEZVOUS (Idaho State University), IV (1969), 39-45.

Ruth Suckow lived in New Mexico for part of 1929, and it was probably during this period that she and her husband read the work of DHL. This experience led Suckow to write, "Modern Figures of Destiny: D. H. and Frieda Lawrence," in which she views DHL's novels from *The Rainbow* to *Lady Chatterley's Lover* as evangelical anti-feminist statements. In her novel THE FOLKS (1934) Suckow shows "unmistakable signs" of a "Lawrentian conviction" about marriage. [See Ruth Suckow, "Modern Figures of Destiny: D. H. Lawrence and Frieda Lawrence," D. H. LAWRENCE REVIEW, III (Spring 1970), 1-30.]

3341 Kitazawa, Shigehisa. "Lawrence: Ai no Tansaku" (Lawrence in Love), DOKKYO STUDIES IN ENGLISH (Dokkyo University), No. 3 (June 1969), 17-51; rvd and rptd as Chap. II: "A Search for Love," in D. H. LAWRENCE: HIS LITERATURE AND HIS LIFE, by Shigehisa Kitazawa (Tokyo: Bokusui-Shobo, 1973).

[The second article in a four-part series, based on an extensive study of the life and works of DHL, which seeks to reveal the "real substance" of his literature and its significance in our age. See also Shigehisa Kitazawa, "Lawrence Bungaku no Hassei" (The Early Works and Life of Lawrence), DOKKYO STUDIES IN ENGLISH, No. 2 (June 1968), 92-124; "Lawrence: Ai o Koeru Mono" (Lawrence Beyond Love), DOKKYO STUDIES IN ENGLISH, No. 5 (March 1971), 1-50; and "Lawrence: Ai to Kodoku" (Lawrence: Love and Solitude), DOKKYO STUDIES IN ENGLISH, No. 6 (May 1972), 123-72.] [In Japanese.]

3342 Klingopulos, G. D. "The Literary Scene," FROM DICKENS TO HARDY, ed by Boris Ford (Baltimore: Penguin Books [The Pelican Guide to English Literature, Vol. VI], 1969), pp. 59-116, espec pp. 61, 69, 87, 90, 92-93, 99, 108, 110.

Modern writers like Conrad, Yeats, Forster, Eliot, and DHL carry "a stage further the great debates about human resistance initiated by the Romantic poets." When one looks for modern works that transcend Walter Pater's "hesitations," one can be sure only of DHL, whose novels "actually show how 'matter' and 'spirit', 'nature' and 'morality' 'play inextricably into each other,' with the overwhelming effect of redeeming life."

3343 Klingopulos, G. D. "Notes on the Victorian Scene," FROM DICKENS TO HARDY, ed by Boris Ford (Baltimore: Penguin Books [The Pelican Guide to English Literature, Vol. VI], 1969), pp. 11-66, espec pp. 13, 14, 22, 44, 49.

Although DHL oversimplified in blaming "a particular class of people" for the uncontrollable processes "which overwhelmed the older patterns of life in the late eighteenth and nineteenth centuries," his values lie outside the usual economic concepts of most social historians.

3344 Koga, Masakazu. "D. H. Lawrence ni Mirareru Nigensei ni Tsuite" (On the Duality in D. H. Lawrence), SANDAI REVIEW OF ENGLISH STUDIES (Kyôto Sangyô University), No. 1 (March 1969), 47-62.

DHL's literary works are complicated because of the duality of the experience of his early life. This unique aspect is examined concretely in the works of his early and middle periods. [In Japanese.]

3345 Koljevič, Svetozar. "Engleski romansijeri o realizmu romana" (English Novelists on Realism in the Novel), KNJIŽEVNA SMOTRA, No. 2 (1969-1970), 25-32.

[DHL is one of the novelists considered.] [In Serbo-Croatian.]

3346 Kuramochi, Saburô. "Shôsetsu wa ika ni Owaru ka? D. H Lawrence no Shôsetsu to 'Kaishin' " (How to End a Novel? D. H. Lawrence's Novels and "Conversion"), EIGO SEINEN, No. 115 (1969), 224-26.

[In Japanese.]

3347 "Language and Literature," CHOICE, VI (Dec 1969), 1396.

While parts of *Phoenix: The Posthumous Papers of D. H. Lawrence*, ed by Edward D. McDonald (reissued 1968) have been reprinted in other collections, "over one-half of it is still relatively unknown except to specialists." *Phoenix II: Uncollected, Unpublished, and Other Prose Works by D. H. Lawrence*, ed by Warren Roberts and Harry T. Moore, "is a valuable contribution to the making of the permanent Lawrence canon."

3348 Lass, Abraham H., and Norma L. Tasman (eds). THE SECRET SHARER AND OTHER GREAT STORIES (NY: New American Library, Mentor Book Edition, 1969), pp. 62-63.

[Brief critical and biographical headnote to "The Rocking-Horse Winner," which is reprinted in the anthology, pp. 63-78.] On the obvious level "a simple story about what people live for and by," "on a deeper, more fundamental level, 'The Rocking-Horse Winner' is an angry, bitter parable for our times, a scathing attack on the way our materialistic society corrupts and ultimately dehumanizes the individual." [Biographical note mentions DHL's Eastwood background, his "discovery" by Ford Madox Ford, his gifts as a prose stylist, his "uncanny insight into men and women" in his major novels, and his "possessive, domineering" mother.]

3349 Leavis, F[rank] R[aymond]. ENGLISH LITERATURE IN OUR TIME AND THE UNIVERSITY (Lond: Chatto & Windus, 1969), pp. 34n, 51, 69, 107, 129-30, 135, 139, 148-49, 150, 153, 154-57, 161-67, 170, 179, 180; excerpt, pp. 154-57, rptd in D. H. LAWRENCE: A CRITICAL ANTHOLOGY, ed by H. Coombes (Harmondsworth, Middlesex, England: Penguin Books, 1973), pp. 457-60.

DHL's "moral perception is a manifestation of his genius, being the fineness of his sense of life--his sense of the difference between what makes *for* life and what makes against it." Both DHL and T. S. Eliot "were distinguished as critics," and both were profoundly engaged by HAMLET. But DHL saw " 'classiosity' " as " 'bunkum' ": "His distinctive contribution to criticism...was a new sense of the kind of thing significance might be." DHL's comments on HAMLET in "The Theatre," in *Twilight in Italy*, may be compared with Eliot's essay on HAMLET.

3350 "Literature," BOOKLIST AND SUBSCRIPTION BOOKS BULLETIN: A GUIDE TO CURRENT BOOKS, LXV (1 July 1969), 1203.

Lawrence in Love: Letters to Louie Burrows, ed with an introduction and notes by James T. Boulton, contains 165 letters and cards which "shed light on a youthful Lawrence and on a little-known early friendship and 15-month engagement."

3351 Littlewood, J. C. F. "Son and Lover," CAMBRIDGE QUARTERLY, IV (Winter 1969-1970), 323-61; excerpt rptd as "The Best of *Sons and Lovers* and a Deeper Truth," in D. H. LAWRENCE: A CRITICAL ANTHOLOGY, ed by H. Coombes (Harmondsworth, Middlesex, England: Penguin Books, 1973), pp. 460-76.

Because DHL was not free to allow the story to come "through him, with an effect of steady disinterested truth," *Sons and Lovers* is unsatisfactory as a novel and uncharacteristic of DHL's best work. In omitting from the novel a picture of the harmony and joy of his early friendship with Jessie Chambers, DHL betrayed not only the truth of his relationship with her but also the larger human truth involved in his mother's life and in his relationship with her.

3352 Mackenzie, Compton. MY LIFE AND TIMES, OCTAVE EIGHT: 1939-1946 (Lond: Chatto & Windus, 1969), p. 265.

[In H. G. Wells's last talk with the author, he said: "That fellow Lawrence. I think that book of his, what was it called? *Sons and Lovers*? I thought that that was quite good, but why did he go to Arabia?" Not wanting to suggest that Wells was confused, Mackenzie replied: "No, I've never been able to understand why Lawrence did that. He is the last man I can imagine leading Bedouins."] [See also an earlier memoir, Compton Mackenzie, "Memories of D. H. Lawrence," CER-

TAIN ASPECTS OF MORAL COURAGE (Garden City, NY: Doubleday, 1962), pp. 104-19, as well as other reminiscences and comments throughout the ten-volume autobiography, especially MY LIFE AND TIMES, OCTAVE FIVE: 1915-1923 (Lond: Chatto & Windus, 1966), pp. 164-73, 176-79, 183-85, 189, 190-93, 235; MY LIFE AND TIMES, OCTAVE SIX: 1923-1930 (Lond: Chatto & Windus, 1967), pp. 84-85, 131-32, 170; MY LIFE AND TIMES, OCTAVE SEVEN: 1931-1938 (Lond: Chatto & Windus, 1968), pp. 35-36, 282.]

3353 Mallett, Richard. "At the Cinema," PUNCH, CCLVII (19 Nov 1969), 842-43.
The film version of *Women in Love* disappoints expectations. [Caricature of the four principals nude.]

3354 Mason, H. A. "Lawrence in Love," CAMBRIDGE QUARTERLY, IV (Spring 1969), 181-200.
[Review-essay on *Lawrence in Love: Letters to Louie Burrows,* ed by James T. Boulton, (1968).] DHL's life is exemplary in revealing "a common human nature" which gives "definition to our intermittent existences." Because his life sometimes looms larger than his art, we need to dream our way through the recorded facts into the truth about his relationship with his mother, his father, Louie Burrows, and Jessie Chambers. Contrary to Boulton's conclusions, it was probably Jessie Chambers rather than Louie Burrows who was DHL's sensual love.

3355 Meckier, Jerome. "Huxley's Lawrencian Interlude: The 'Latin Compromise' That Failed," ALDOUS HUXLEY: SATIRE AND STRUCTURE (Lond: Chatto & Windus, 1969), pp. 78-123; additional references to DHL, pp. 1-2, 5-6, 10, 25, 29, 31-34, 36-38, 48-51, 54, 72, 77, 151, 153-54, 156-57, 160, 172, 187.
"Beginning with Kingham in 'Two or Three Graces' (1926), and extending through Rampion of POINT COUNTER POINT (1928), Miles Fanning of 'After the Fireworks' (1929), and the Savage of BRAVE NEW WORLD (1932), Huxley presents--...at times satirically--four protagonists who partially resemble D. H. Lawrence." Huxley and DHL employed the roman à clef to satirize some of the same individuals, such as Philip Heseltine and Lady Ottoline Morrell. Whereas DHL "presents himself" as correcting "the mentalization of one's instincts or feelings," Huxley came to feel that DHL tended "towards another form of imbalance: the emotionalization of the mind." DHL's portrait of Huxley as Hammond in *Lady Chatterley's Lover* and Huxley's portrait of DHL as the over-emotional Kingham in "Two or Three Graces" reflect these criticisms. DHL's philosophy of "blood," expressed as early as 1912, reappears in *The Rainbow*; it is one side of a balance in *Women in Love* and of an imbalance in *The Plumed Serpent*, in which characters "deliberately try to live by the blood philosophy." Mark Rampion, Huxley's portrait of DHL in POINT COUNTER POINT, is often the satiric norm against which other characters are measured, but also often satirized as a man who misses no opportunity to theorize. Another DHL portrait, the aging Miles Fanning in "After the Fireworks," is comically pursued by Pamela Tarn, whose overtures he evades with "sparkling conversation" before finally succumbing to her in a

broadly farcical affair. BRAVE NEW WORLD, "an extended critique of *The Plumed Serpent* and of Lawrence's post-1920 thought, juxtaposes the direction the industrial West appears to be taking with the path Lawrence, who may be loosely identified with the Savage, would prefer it to follow." Huxley makes additional references to DHL in BEYOND THE MEXIQUE BAY and EYELESS IN GAZA. The Huxley-DHL relationship reveals the 1920s "as an era of personal satire" in the novel. Although Huxley gradually discarded "even the aspects of Lawrence he once approved of," DHL "was the biggest challenge Huxley ever faced."

3356 Merivale, Patricia. PAN THE GOAT-GOD: HIS MYTH IN MODERN TIMES (Cambridge: Harvard UP, 1969), pp. 91, 99, 103, 114, 117, 123, 124, 129, 130, 135, 144, 145, 147, 149, 153, 158, 159, 170, 178, 184, 192, 194-219, 222, 226, 227, 228, 263n, 272n, 280n.

Few British writers before DHL took the Dionysian power of the Pan myth seriously. He not only creates many Pan-like fictional figures (especially in *The Plumed Serpent* and *St. Mawr*) but also is himself compared to Pan. His essay "Pan in America" delineates both the beauty and the terror of the goat-god within man, a force which later approaches divinity in his continuing Pan-Christ dialectic. The Pan figure, however, is not synonymous with the Laurentian "Dark Hero," representing only one of his manifestations. [Incorporates Patricia Merivale, "D. H. Lawrence and the Modern Pan Myth," TEXAS STUDIES IN LITERATURE AND LANGUAGE, VI (Autumn 1964), 297-305 with many additional references in a wider discussion of the issues in modern literature.]

3357 Miko, Stephen J. "Introduction," TWENTIETH CENTURY INTERPRETATIONS OF "WOMEN IN LOVE": A COLLECTION OF CRITICAL ESSAYS, ed by Stephen J. Miko (Englewood Cliffs, NJ: Prentice Hall, 1969), pp. 1-19.

The completion and publication of *Women in Love* represents an important turning point in DHL's career, since it signals the resolution of the author's preoccupation, dating back to adolescence, with his virility and his relationships with women. DHL's character was significantly shaped by his attachment to his mother, and although he claimed that with the writing of *Sons and Lovers* he had "shed his sickness," DHL's sensitivity and self-consciousness, products of a traumatic childhood, continued to lead him to make unreasonable demands on family, friends and society in general. DHL was deeply troubled by the effects of World War I, especially a kind of materialism which "substitutes quantities for qualities, . . . reduces the sacred to the secular, unlimited possibility to possibilities of arrangement and manipulation." This was DHL's primary concern in *Women in Love*, revealed most tellingly through the dialectical presentation of relationships between characters. There are basically two kinds of characters in the novel: "the intellectual, who abstracts and thereby falsifies and inhibits natural impulse" (Hermione), and "the sensualist, who channels his energies by deliberate exclusion of humanistic concern, and therefore becomes both narcissistic and destructive" (Loerke). Because the novel "places its central values in the search for 'fulfillment,' both extremes--violence and sensuality on one hand, abstraction and intellectuality on the other--become identical in misdirecting natural vitality."

3358 Miko, Stephen J. (ed.). TWENTIETH CENTURY INTERPRE-
TATIONS OF "WOMEN IN LOVE": A COLLECTION OF CRITICAL
ESSAYS (Englewood Cliffs, NJ: Prentice-Hall, 1969).
Contents, abstracted under year of first publication: Stephen J. Miko, "Introduction," pp. 1-19 (1969); **Part One: "Interpretations"**: George H. Ford, "Dies Irae," pp. 20-39, from his DOUBLE MEASURE: A STUDY OF THE NOVELS AND STORIES OF D. H. LAWRENCE (NY: Holt, Rinehart, and Winston, 1965), pp. 184-207; Alan Friedman, "Suspended Form: Lawrence's Theory of Fiction in *Women in Love*," pp. 40-49, rvd espec for this anthology and including material from his THE TURN OF THE NOVEL (NY: Oxford UP, 1966); David J. Gordon, "*Women in Love* and the Lawrencean Aesthetic," pp. 50-60 (written espec for this anthology, 1969); Julian Moynahan, "The Discovery of Form," pp. 61-72, from THE DEED OF LIFE: THE NOVELS AND TALES OF D. H. LAWRENCE (Princeton: Princeton UP, 1963), pp. 72-89; Mark Spilka, "No Man's Land," pp. 73-84, from THE LOVE ETHIC OF D. H. LAWRENCE (Bloomington, IN: Indiana UP, 1955), pp. 148-73, abridged; Eliseo Vivas, "The Substance of *Women in Love*," pp. 85-96, from D. H. LAWRENCE: THE FAILURE AND THE TRIUMPH OF ART (Evanston, IL: Northwestern UP, 1960), pp. 237-54, abridged; **Part Two: "View Points"**: Robert B. Heilman, pp. 97-103, from "Nomad, Monads, and the Mystique of the Soma," SEWANEE REVIEW, LXVIII (Oct-Dec 1960), 650-56; Edwin Honig, pp. 103-105, from DARK CONCEIT: THE MAKING OF ALLEGORY (Evanston, IL: Northwestern UP, 1959), pp. 165-68; Leone Vivante, pp. 105-110, from A PHILOSOPHY OF POTENTIALITY (Lond: Routledge & Kegan Paul, 1955), pp. 90-93; Daniel A. Weiss, pp. 111-13, from OEDIPUS IN NOTTINGHAM: D. H. LAWRENCE (Seattle: University of Washington P, 1962), pp. 100-101, 102-104; "Chronology of Important Dates," pp. 115-16 [not abstracted]; "Notes on the Editor and Contributors" [not abstracted].

3359 Miles, Kathleen M. THE HELLISH MEANING: THE DEMONIC MOTIF IN THE WORKS OF D. H. LAWRENCE (Carbondale, IL: Southern Illinois University Monographs, 1969).
DHL's fiction from *Women in Love* to *Lady Chatterley's Lover* reveals his intense search for a method to achieve a balance between "blood consciousness" and the willful and emotionless cerebral consciousness. In these works, DHL draws on traditional demonic imagery to depict three categories of "mechanized monsters": "Fatal Man," the aristocratic, coldly efficient, passionless creatures like Jim Bricknell, Gerald Crich, and Rico Carrington; "Demon Lover," a class embodying the extreme of "blood consciousness," men who use their minds to exploit their emotions, such as Uncle Tom Brangwen, Loerke, and Cipriano; and "Destructive Women," a single class of "female fiends" who combine aspects of the two other categories, including both exclusively cerebral women and those who know and exploit sensation, such as Hermione, Gudrun, Carlota, and Bertha Coutts.

3360 Miller, James E., Jr., and Bernice Slote. THE DIMENSIONS OF THE SHORT STORY: A CRITICAL ANTHOLOGY (NY and

Toronto: Dodd, Mead, 1969), p. 561.
[Brief biographical note mentioning DHL's parentage (a "coal-miner father and a literate, ambitious mother"), his early fiction, his elopement with Frieda, their world wide travels, his censorship problems. "Two Blue Birds" is reprinted in the anthology, pp. 363-76.]

3361 Mitra, A. K. "Revisions in Lawrence's 'Wedding Morn,' " NOTES AND QUERIES, ns XVI (July 1969), 260.
The editors of *The Complete Poems of D. H. Lawrence* (1964) are incorrect in asserting that the version of "Wedding Morn" appearing in *The Collected Poems of D. H. Lawrence* (1928) is unchanged from its earlier publication in *Love Poems and Others* (1913). There are punctuation changes and linguistic variations, and two lines are added.

3362 Moe, Christian. "Playwright Lawrence Takes the Stage in London," D. H. LAWRENCE REVIEW, II (Spring 1969), 93-97.
Both *The Daughter-in-Law* and *The Widowing of Mrs. Holroyd* have "dramatic movement" marked by "exciting emotional confrontations, and stageworthy dialogue." Although DHL seems "indifferent to conventional dramatic structure," the plays "are absorbing theatrical pieces" with "compelling characterizations of women." However, DHL's tendency to focus on his female characters makes his male characters seem less fully developed. The result does not disturb the effect of *The Daughter-in-Law,* "the better of the two plays," but in *The Widowing of Mrs. Holroyd,* DHL's "failure to let Holroyd demonstrate the cause of the marriage's deterioration" is a dramatic flaw. The effect of both productions "depends heavily on their adherence to environmental details." Although this dependence at first "seems to be old-fashioned naturalism," it soon becomes "theatrically compelling." [Review of the Royal Court Theatre productions, directed by Peter Gill, 7 and 14 March 1968.]

3363 Moody, H. L. B. "African Sculpture Symbols in a Novel by D. H. Lawrence," IBADAN, No. 26 (Feb 1969), 73-77.
The West African statuettes in *Women in Love* embody a "human dignity" unrealized by Gerald Crich, who "represents the rational mind." Gerald finds the sculpture " '*barbaric*,' " not " '*high* art,' " but Birkin recognizes that " 'there are centuries and centuries of development in a straight line behind that carving; it is an awful pitch of culture.' " DHL's use of the words "mindless" and "sensual" suggests that the carving, "existing in the dimensions of space," is not to be interpreted by intellectual analysis but apprehended by the senses, "as an artefact expressing in all finality something which cannot otherwise be articulated." In "Moony" Birkin experiences "a passing mood of revulsion" for the African figures but later wonders " 'how far these West Africans had gone beyond the phallic cult.' " The passage ends with DHL's distinction between the two opposites, "the burning death abstraction of the Sahara" and the frozen abstraction of "the Arctic north."

3364 Nardi, Piero. "Louie, Miss Incontentabile" (Louie, Miss Dissatisfaction), CORRIERE DELLA SERA (Milan), 16 Feb 1969, p. 3.

Lawrence in Love: Letters to Louie Burrows, ed and with "Introduction" and notes by James T. Boulton (1968), shows how important this woman was in the sentimental, intellectual, and professional aspects of DHL's life. [In Italian.]

3365 Nin, Anais. THE DIARY OF ANAIS NIN, 1939-1944, ed and with a Preface by Gunther Stuhlmann (NY: Harcourt, Brace, 1969), pp. ix, 12, 15, 17, 31, 39, 100-1, 107, 110, 122, 160, 174, 196, 214, 233, 256, 259, 271.

[Laurentian ideas frequently come to mind as the author meets and relates to others: She meets Caresse Crosby--all "flowing" and Laurentian "livingness." She meets Mabel Dodge Luhan--"all WILL as she had revealed herself in her book on Lawrence." She meets Kenneth Patchen and finds in his manuscript "some process of destruction the opposite of Lawrence's phoenix rising from the ashes." She sees in two young girls and their lovers a deceptive buoyancy, like DHL's description, "All rosy and healthy on the outside, but all ashes inside." "D. H. Lawrence began to give instinct a language, he tried to escape the clinical." The author wonders "how D. H. Lawrence knew so much about how woman felt in sexual intercourse. How well he described two kinds of orgasms," one passive and miraculous, the other anxious and striving. She continues to study her "three gods of the deep"--Dostoevsky, DHL, and Proust--and feels that Carson McCullers's REFLECTIONS IN A GOLDEN EYE owes much to DHL.]

3366 Nishimura, Kôji. "Nigenron no Yukue" (Outcome of Dualism), EIGO SEINEN, No. 115 (1969), 624-26.
[On DHL's dualism.] [In Japanese.]

3367 Nott, Kathleen. "Lawrence by Himself," A SOUL IN THE QUAD (Lond: Routledge & Kegan Paul, 1969), pp. 297-319.
More fully integrated than *Women in Love*, *The Rainbow*, with its "fusion of idea, belief and concept, with perception," reveals a "moral real" from within: "we can accept Lawrence's moral vision because we stand in the middle of it and see it--because the moral real is welded within the language" in "a true vision of human beings and human relations." In *Women in Love*, on the contrary, DHL interferes "with the order of creation if it suits his prophetic purpose," as in his use of rabbit and moon images "to convey motivelessness and moral impotence on the part of . . . his characters." [Detailed discussion of the "rabbit" scene.] As in *Lady Chatterley's Lover*, DHL advocates "a form of sexual intercourse between man and woman which is commonly practiced by homosexuals," so in *Women in Love*, he hints at "nameless 'perversions' and 'obscenities,' " "*psychological perversities*, [which] are fitted into the prophetic schema of a man-woman relationship which" DHL attempts "to generalize by illegitimate means" as "the 'great overlord' and bully of his material." While DHL preached spontaneity and "inveighed against 'sex in the head,' " "in the later books it is hard to locate it anywhere else." Believing himself "a committed Prophet," DHL "stirs the wonder whether any propaganda anywhere might not be a misuse of language."

3368 Nott, Kathleen. "Lawrence by Leavis," A SOUL IN THE QUAD (Lond: Routledge & Kegan Paul, 1969), pp. 283-96.

[An expansion of ideas expressed by the author in "Whose Culture?" LISTENER AND BBC TELEVISION REVIEW, LXVII (12 April 1962), 631-32, and (19 April 1962), 677-78.] DHL, especially in his later work, is outside "The Great Tradition" as formulated by F. R. Leavis as a moral and aesthetic tradition in the English novel. Although according to Leavis, DHL exemplified the "quality of reverence," he "increasingly disliked and despised the human." With "'aristocratic' exclusiveness and contempt for the underprivileged (and...sycophancy toward the rich)," "the later Lawrence repudiated the workers." Even in his earlier, sympathetic writings, the workers are presented not as "prisoners of the mine and a mine-exploiting society, but as prisoners of their women." DHL probably "disliked his own origins, and visited this on the unprivileged workers as a class."

3369 Ober, William B., M. D. "Lady Chatterley's *What?*" ACADEMY OF MEDICINE OF NEW JERSEY BULLETIN, XV (March 1969), 41-65; rptd in BOSWELL'S CLAP AND OTHER ESSAYS: MEDICAL ANALYSES OF LITERARY MEN'S AFFLICTIONS, by William B. Ober, M. D. (Carbondale and Edwardsville: Southern Illinois UP; Lond and Amsterdam: Feffer & Simons, 1979), pp. 89-117.

[The author focuses on the role that the combination of DHL's "progressive pulmonary tuberculosis and psychosexual conflicts played in shaping the failure" which *Lady Chatterley's Lover* is. Asserting that "one cannot come to grips with Lawrence's solution" to the "sexual problem" in that novel "without taking into account his [DHL's] own psychological development," he traces DHL's "Oedipal" attachment to his mother, his difficult "adjustment to adult heterosexuality" with Jessie Chambers and other young women, and his union with Frieda, noting that DHL's running off with his professor's wife (a woman older than he and the mother of three children) was in effect an attempt to "resolve his Oedipus complex by embracing it."] There is evidence that DHL's apparent impotence during the last five years of his life probably resulted from his advanced pulmonary tuberculosis. *Lady Chatterley's Lover,* in which he compensated for "his loss of potentia" by displacing it onto Clifford while presenting Mellors as always the "potent, sexually agile male," was thus "written not only in a mood of anger against the world, but one of impotence and frustration" as well. DHL repressed his own homosexual tendencies, but they appeared in his art; e.g., in the latent homosexual relationship between Mellors and the colonel he had served under in India and in the "advocacy of buggery" in the deliberately "planted" hints that Mellors and Connie engage in "*coitus per anum.*" The "failure of *Lady Chatterley's Lover* as a work of art" results from DHL's violation of his own "sexual creed" of forthrightness in his concealment of anal intercourse in "covert and oblique" descriptions. Finally, Mellors, who is presented as "the complete sexual man," was DHL's "image of himself, not as he was but as he would have liked to be." [See also reply in review by Paul Fussell, THE BOY SCOUT HANDBOOK AND OTHER OBSERVATIONS (NY and Oxford: Oxford UP, 1982), pp. 85-88, espec. pp. 86-87, refuting Ober's psychoanalytic approach to DHL and others.]

3370 Ogawa, Yoshio. "Lawrence Zakko" (Notes on Lawrence), BULLETIN OF ST. MARGARET'S (St. Margaret's Junior College), No. 1 (Dec 1969), 88-101.

[After a brief sketch of DHL's life and works, the meaning of his being called an autobiographical novelist is considered.] DHL's major works are so closely related in structure that they form one great cycle of his main current of thought, in which conflicts between man and woman and between man and man are gradually brought into harmony through sex and finally settled in the realm of the dark gods. Sex in DHL is a symbol of vitality, most brilliantly shown in *Lady Chatterley's Lover*. Paradoxically, DHL is so purely puritanical as to be regarded as against puritanism. [In Japanese.]

3371 Ort, Daniel. "Lawrence's *Women in Love*," EXPLICATOR, XXVII (Jan 1969), Item 38.

DHL did not think impotence and sterility synonymous. The bullocks before which Gudrun dances in *Women in Love* are sterile. She dominates them as she later does Gerald, who is obviously not impotent, though his relationship with Gudrun is sterile.

3372 Parkinson, Thomas. "Reflections on Allen Ginsberg as Poet," CONCERNING POETRY, II (Spring 1969), 21-24.

Ginsberg's quarrel, like that of Blake, Whitman, and DHL, is with the misuse of cerebral power that impairs "their sympathy with their bodies and with others."

3373 Peckham, Morse. ART AND PORNOGRAPHY: AN EXPERIMENT IN EXPLANATION (NY and Lond: Basic Books, 1969), pp. 19-22, 25, 26, 32, 36, 192, 241.

In *Pornography and Obscenity*, DHL "gives a typical anti-intellectual argument against pornography, which, as he says, he would be happy to censor.... It is an argument based upon the purported psychological effect of pornography.... Thus 'obscene' sexual stimulation emanating from such a writer as Boccaccio is good because it redirects the individual from mob self-consciousness to true individuality, while 'pornographic' sexual stimulation confirms the individual in mob self-consciousness," of which DHL believes "masturbation is the *cause*." Since DHL was "a post-Nietzschean romantic, interested in the transvaluation of all values," "some of the forms" of release from self-consciousness are "a little unattractive." [The author briefly compares the theories on pornography and censorship set forth by DHL, Margaret Mead, Steven Marcus, and Judge John M. Woolsey, all four of whom define pornography as, in effect, "the presentation of sexual material such that the response to it is of negative value."]

3374 Piccolo, Anthony. "Strategies of Crisis in the Shorter Fiction of D. H. Lawrence," DISSERTATION ABSTRACTS INTERNATIONAL, XXXI (1970), 1286A. Unpublished dissertation, New York University, 1969.

3375 Pinto, Vivian de Sola. "Blake and Lawrence," in WILLIAM BLAKE: ESSAYS FOR S. FOSTER DAMON, ed by Alvin H. Rosenfeld (Providence, RI: Brown UP, 1969), pp. 84-106.

[DHL's comments on Blake and the affinities between the two writers are examined.] Although DHL criticized Blake as a mental " 'Knower,' " he admires Blake's "intuitional awareness" and his imaginative treatment of the body. Both Blake and DHL derived from a religious tradition of Puritan dissenters, and both fought a life of mechanical toil. Both were taken up by the "artistic intelligentsia," against whom both reacted violently. Both have "a profound 'sensuous understanding,' a deep, instinctive religious apprehension of the wonder of creative vitality." Both are "deeply conscious of the tragic split in human consciousness caused by excessive development of the analytic intellect at the expense of the imaginative and sensual life," and both "stress the dehumanization of society caused by abstract thought and mechanical organization." As prophetic artists, "both needed the framework of a myth in symbolism and a literary form." Blake was "naturally a visionary," whereas DHL's "genius was that of a keen-eyed observer of life," but "Lawrence's fiction can be read as a cycle of religious vision" closely resembling "the cycle of Blake's poetry." Both present the fundamental theme of "unity in diversity or the tension between opposites." Blake's archetypal symbolism "provides a valuable guide to the inner meanings" of DHL's fiction. As THE MARRIAGE OF HEAVEN AND HELL is "Blake's most Lawrentian work," so *Women in Love* is DHL's "most Blakean." [Detailed comparison of the two works.] A major theme of DHL's later writings, in Blakean terms, is "Enitharmon striving toward the condition of Jerusalem." Both Blake and DHL for a time flirted with political solutions, but both "at the end of their careers were preoccupied with the character of Jesus." "The final testament of both writers is that a solution is only to be found in the individual soul."

3376 Pinto, Vivian de Sola. "Reviews," MODERN LANGUAGE REVIEW, LXIV (Jan 1969), 159-60.

Phoenix II: Uncollected, Unpublished, and Other Prose Works by D. H. Lawrence, ed by Warren Roberts and Harry T. Moore, shows that DHL, like Blake and Coleridge, often expressed himself more revealingly in " 'occasional' and fragmentary pieces than in...more carefully constructed works." The existence of the collection "could be justified alone by the reprinting of...three major works": the Introduction to MEMOIRS OF THE FOREIGN LEGION by Maurice Magnus, "The Crown," and *A Propos of "Lady Chatterley's Lover."*

3377 Pinto, Vivian de Sola. "Swinburne and D. H. Lawrence," TIMES LITERARY SUPPLEMENT (Lond), 20 Feb 1969, p. 185.

[Letter to the Editor, citing a passage in a letter by DHL to Barbara Low (11 Sept 1916) in which DHL generously calls Swinburne "a great revealer."]

3378 Pirenet, Colette. "La structure symbolique de *Women in Love*" (The Symbolic Structure of *Women in Love*), ÉTUDES ANGLAISES, XXII (April-June 1969), 138-51.

In the general symbolic design of *Women in Love*, most of the important symbols become elements of structural unity. The relationship between the two couples creates a sort of counterpoint in parallel, juxtaposed, or contrasted chapters. These relationships are characterized by defiance, in the case of Gudrun and Gerald, and by quarrel, in the case of Birkin and Ursula, who find harmony after experiencing conflict. The "Rabbit" and "Moony" chapters are the climaxes in the cycle of conflicts between the two sets of lovers. Not all the chapters have the same density; they belong to different "genres." Chapters of social comedy are to be found between periods of crisis. The chapter "The Industrial Magnate" constitutes a pause in the story, the other chapters being arranged symmetrically, and this structure partly accounts for the deep meaning of the novel. *Women in Love* is a diptych in which the chapters where symbols prevail throw light on the chapters devoted to the description of real life. [Preceded by a brief introduction by Émile Delavenay, pp. 137-38.] [In French.]

3379 Praz, Mario. "Cosi parlò Lawrence" (Thus Spoke Lawrence), VIDEO (Turin), Aug 1969, pp. 43-48.

In his colliery plays DHL showed a particular ability in the construction of naturalistic dialogue. This mimetic capacity is also apparent in *David*, where DHL imitates biblical language superbly. The colliery plays are all autobiographical and belong to the tradition of bourgeois realism in the theater. On the whole, the recurrent elements of DHL's plays are the contrast between two points of view represented by two characters, the criticism of the social system, the man-woman relationship, and the conception of love as the essence of life. [In Italian.]

3380 Press, John. A MAP OF MODERN ENGLISH VERSE (Lond and NY: Oxford UP, 1969), 93-97.

DHL's main contribution to modern verse was his skill in embodying the rhythms of his sensual perceptions. Although fully capable of writing in normal modes, he frequently chooses not to. *Look! We Have Come Through!* is a bold attempt but fails, while *Birds, Beasts and Flowers* is "a triumphant ordering of themes." Although *Pansies* and *Nettles* are mostly poor, *Last Poems* refutes Blackmur and insures DHL's status as a great poet.

3381 Pritchard, William H. "Lawrence and Lewis," AGENDA, VII, No. 3--VIII, No. 1 (Autumn/Winter 1969-1970) "Wyndham Lewis Special Issue," pp. 140-47; rptd as "Wyndham Lewis and Lawrence," IOWA REVIEW, II (Spring 1971), 91-96.

DHL and Wyndham Lewis, despite their uncomplimentary views of each other, had much "in common as critics and novelists." Early recognized by Pound, both were willing to appear "detestable" in order to convey their message. Both are "notable for their ironic humor" especially as critics--and "a violence of thought," in imagining themselves, through their protagonists, as "lonely heroes" who "come up hard against women who won't quite yield to their heroic male versions of themselves." Both DHL's *Kangaroo* and Lewis's SELF CONDEMNED are books of exile which "look back on England with a mixture of loathing and nostalgia." DHL, the "partisan of the body," fills *Kangaroo* and *Women in Love* with "argument, hesitations, qualifications, but always talk and more talk." Lewis, the "wordy satirist," sounds like DHL in his attempt, in SELF CONDEMNED, to articulate emotional states. "Invaluable critics of literature and society," DHL and Lewis are "the two more significant English novelists of our century."

3382 Pritchett, V[ictor] S. "Busy and Candid," NEW STATESMAN, LXXVII (24 Jan 1969), 120.

"D. H. Lawrence eventually became a letter writer of a far higher order" than is evident in *Lawrence in Love: Letters to Louie Burrows*, ed by James T. Boulton, "but this was long after his youthful correspondence with Louie Burrows, a schoolteacher to whom he was once engaged." [Also reviews LETTERS OF ARNOLD BENNETT, ed by James Hepburn, Vol. II: 1889-1915.]

3383 Pritchett, V[ictor] S. "The History of Mr Wells," NEW STATESMAN, ns LXXVIII (14 Nov 1969), 698-99.

H. G. Wells was representative of the emerging lower middle class in Edwardian England. The sense of moral values is strong in the early Wells, but he lost it to a materialistic progress. DHL escaped the full vulgarity of the Edwardian daydream of the lower middle class. The social historian will get much from Wells, but from DHL he will gain a more nourishing view of what had gone wrong.

3384 Reddick, Bryan Dewitt. "Tone in Dramatic Narrative," DISSERTATION ABSTRACTS INTERNATIONAL, XXXI (1970), 2397A. Unpublished dissertation, University of California at Davis, 1969.

[Includes discussion of DHL.]

3385 Rees, Richard. "Politics of a Mystic," D. H. LAWRENCE REVIEW, II (Spring 1969), 24-31.

Frieda Lawrence was contemptuous of John Middleton Murry's " 'pity' for the underprivileged," but in 1932 "she consented to give a talk to my local branch of the Independent Labour Party" on " 'My Life with Lawrence,' " which "the Marxist dialecticians in the audience refrained from heckling."

3386 Rhode, Eric. "Chumship," LISTENER, LXXXII (20 Nov 1969), 713.

Larry Kramer's script for the film version of *Women in Love* "follows the original story to the letter," but misunderstanding DHL's intentions, "misses the spirit." The film provides evidence for the novel's implication that DHL's "response to the war was to espouse German values--*Wille zur Macht,* mystical conjunctions, Romantic symbolism."

3387 Rolph, C. H. [pseud of C.R. Hewitt]. BOOKS IN THE DOCK (Lond: Andre Deutsch, 1969), pp. 12, 13, 16, 19, 42, 52, 59, 64, 69, 70, 81, 82-83, 108.

[Brief discussions of DHL's British censorship cases: the 1960 censorship trial of *Lady Chatterley's Lover* (Regina v. Penguin Books); the 1915 police seizure and burning of *The Rainbow*; the 1929 seizure by postal authorities, with the support of Sir William Joynson-Hicks, 1st Viscount Brentford, the Home Secretary, of the manuscript of *Pansies*; and the July 1929 police raid on the exhibition of DHL's paintings at the Warren Galleries.]

3388 Roth, Russell. "The Inception of a Saga: Frederick Manfred's BUCKSKIN MAN," SOUTH DAKOTA REVIEW, VII (Winter 1969-1970), 87-99.

Manfred's Buckskin Man tales show the influence of DHL's *Studies in Classic American Literature* (particularly his interpretation of James Fenimore Cooper's Leatherstocking Tales), William Carlos Williams's IN THE AMERICAN GRAIN, and William Faulkner's novels.

3389 Rothkopf, Carol Zemen. "SONS AND LOVERS": A CRITICAL COMMENTARY (NY: American R. D. M., 1969).
[Study guide for *Sons and Lovers*.]

3390 Salgādo, Gāmini. D. H. LAWRENCE, "SEA AND SARDINIA," "THE RAINBOW": NOTES ON LITERATURE NO. 100 (Lond: The British Council, 1969).
[Study guide.]

3391 Salgādo, Gāmini. "Introduction," D. H. LAWRENCE: "SONS AND LOVERS," A CASEBOOK, ed by Gāmini Salgādo (Lond: Macmillan, 1969; Nashville: Aurora Publishers, 1970), pp. 11-17.

Sons and Lovers could have been DHL's first novel, since here he deals with what he must "get out of his system." The Morels and the Leiverses are drawn from life, even though DHL is unfair to Jessie Chambers as Miriam in the novel. Oedipal possibilities are also relevant, even though Freudian criticism often ignores the "palpable surface" of a novel and uses non-literary criteria as a basis for judgment. The novel is also remarkable for introducing new geographic and social areas to fiction, and as a *Bildungsroman*.

3392 Salgādo, Gāmini (ed.). D. H. LAWRENCE: "SONS AND LOVERS," A CASEBOOK (Lond: Macmillan, 1969; Nashville: Aurora Publishers, 1970).

Contents, abstracted under year of first publication: "Acknowledgements," p. 7; A. E. Dyson, "General Editor's Preface," pp. 9-10 [not abstracted]; Gāmini Salgādo, "Introduction," pp. 11-17. **Part I: "Extracts from Letters"**: "From Lawrence's Letters" (1910-1916) [one letter to Sydney S. Pawling, one to Rachel Annand Taylor, six to Edward Garnett, three to A. W. McLeod, and one to Barbara Low], pp. 21-27, from *The Collected Letters of D. H. Lawrence*, 2 vols., ed by Harry T. Moore (Lond: William Heinemann, NY: Viking P, 1962) [not abstracted]; "From Frieda Lawrence's Letters" [two letters to Edward Garnett and two to Harry T. Moore], pp. 28-29, from FRIEDA LAWRENCE: THE MEMOIRS AND CORRESPONDENCE, ed by E. W. Tedlock, Jr. (Lond: William Heinemann, 1961; NY: Knopf, 1964); DHL, "Original Foreword to *Sons and Lovers* (1913)" [Letter to Edward Garnett], pp. 30-37, from *The Letters of D. H. Lawrence*, ed by Aldous Huxley (Lond: William Heinemann; NY: Viking P, 1932), pp. 97-104 [not abstracted]. **Part II: "Early Comment and Original Reviews"**: Comment by "E. T." [pseud of Jessie Chambers], pp. 41-49, excerpts from D. H. LAWRENCE: A PERSONAL RECORD (Lond: Jonathan Cape, 1935),

pp. 190-213; DHL, "Last Words to Miriam" (1913), pp. 52-54 [not abstracted]; Reviews: pp. 55-56, from "Fiction," ATHENAEUM, No. 4,469 (21 June 1913), 668; pp. 56-58, from "*Sons and Lovers*," SATURDAY REVIEW (Lond), CXV (21 June 1913), 780-81; pp. 58-60, from P[erceval] G[ibbon], "A Novel of Quality," BOOKMAN (Lond), XLIV (Aug 1913), 213; pp. 60-61, from "Current Fiction," NATION (NY), XCVII (11 Dec 1913), 564; pp. 61-66, from Alfred [Booth] Kuttner, "*Sons and Lovers*," NEW REPUBLIC, II (10 April 1915), 255-57.
Part III: "Recent Criticism": Alfred Booth Kuttner, A Freudian Appreciation (1916), pp. 69-94, from "*Sons and Lovers*: A Freudian Appreciation," PSYCHOANALYTIC REVIEW, III (July 1916), 295-317; J[ohn] Middleton Murry, "Son and Lover" (1931), pp. 95-105, from Chap. I: "Son and Lover," in SON OF WOMAN: THE STORY OF D. H. LAWRENCE (Lond: Jonathan Cape, 1931), pp. 23-38; Mark Schorer, "Technique as Discovery" (1948), pp. 106-111, from HUDSON REVIEW, I (Spring 1948), 67-87; Dorothy Van Ghent, "On *Sons and Lovers*" (1953), pp. 112-29, from THE ENGLISH NOVEL: FORM AND FUNCTION (NY: Holt, Rinehart, 1953), pp. 245-61; Seymour Betsky, "Rhythm and Theme: D. H. Lawrence's *Sons and Lovers*" (1953), pp. 130-43; from THE ACHIEVEMENT OF D. H. LAWRENCE, ed by Frederick J. Hoffman and Harry T. Moore (Norman: University of Oklahoma P, 1953), pp. 131-43; Frank O'Connor [pseud of Michael O'Donovan], "*Sons and Lovers*" (1955), pp. 144-51, from THE MIRROR IN THE ROADWAY: A STUDY OF THE MODERN NOVEL (N. p.: A. D. Peters, 1955; NY: Knopf, 1956), pp. 270-79; Graham Hough, "Adolescent Love" (1956), pp. 152-59, from THE DARK SUN: A STUDY OF D. H. LAWRENCE (Lond: Gerald Duckworth, 1956; NY: Macmillan, 1957), pp. 47-54; Simon Lesser, "Form and Anxiety" (1957), pp. 160-63, from FICTION AND THE UNCONSCIOUS (Lond: Peter Owen; Bost: Beacon P, 1957), pp. 175-78; David Daiches, "Lawrence and the Form of the Novel" (1960), pp. 164-70, from "D. H. Lawrence," in THE NOVEL AND THE MODERN WORLD, rvd ed (Chicago: University of Chicago P, 1960), pp. 139-47; Eliseo Vivas, "The Triumph of Art" (1960), pp. 171-76, from Chap. VII: "*Sons and Lovers*," in D. H. LAWRENCE: THE FAILURE AND THE TRIUMPH OF ART (Evanston, IL: Northwestern UP, 1960; Lond: Allen & Unwin, 1961), pp. 180-85; Maurice Beebe, "The Artist Theme" (1964), pp. 177-90, from "Lawrence's Sacred Fount: The Artist Theme of *Sons and Lovers*," TEXAS STUDIES IN LITERATURE AND LANGUAGE, IV (Winter 1963), 539-52, rptd in IVORY TOWERS AND SACRED FOUNTS: THE ARTIST AS HERO IN FICTION FROM GOETHE TO JOYCE, by Maurice Beebe (NY: New York UP, 1964), pp. 101-13; H. M. Daleski, "The Release: The First Period," pp. 191-207, from THE FORKED FLAME: A STUDY OF D. H. LAWRENCE (Evanston: Northwestern UP, 1965), pp. 49-63; Keith Sagar, "The Bases of the Normal," pp. 208-215, from THE ART OF D. H. LAWRENCE (Cambridge: Cambridge UP, 1966), pp. 28-33; Laurence Lerner, "Blood and Mind: The Father in *Sons and Lovers*," pp. 216-20, from THE TRUTHTELLERS: JANE AUSTEN, GEORGE ELIOT, D. H. LAWRENCE (Lond: Chatto & Windus; NY: Schocken, 1967), pp. 210-14.

3393 Secor, Robert. "Language and Movement in 'Fanny and Annie,'" STUDIES IN SHORT FICTION, VI (Summer 1969), 395-400.
Following the practices of David Lodge, Wayne Booth, and others, if we stick as

"close as possible" to DHL's language in "Fanny and Annie," we can see clearly "Fanny's movement toward release from (and not submission to) her sensation of doom": Fanny's sense of doom, as evoked by DHL's rhetoric, is that of returning to a "fixed and predictable world of the past," of which Harry's sexuality is a part; when, however, Annie's mother interrupts the ceremony, "the unusual has happened" and the language changes. Fanny can now re-enter a relationship with Harry "with a sense of renewed life instead of deadly familiarity," and the story ends with "the unqualified language of independence, choice, and release." [A number of passages analyzed.]

3394 Sepčić, Višnja. "The Category of Landscape in D. H. Lawrence's *Kangaroo*," STUDIA ROMANICA ET ANGLICA ZAGRABIENSIA, Nos. 27-28 (1969), 129-52.

In *Kangaroo*, "the political plot is inadequate" because it has no correlation with the wider social ambience of Australia. DHL characterizes the continent in his travel sketches as a vast, sparsely inhabited space, not yet subjugated by man, and the Australians themselves as casual, coarse, good-humored, and democratic. Kangaroo's " 'philosophy' is in fact an incongruous mixture" of DHL's views on spontaneity and instinct and "the relics of the Christian ethics" he wishes to discard. Although of questionable value "as a novel of ideas or as a political novel," *Kangaroo* has values to be found in the portrayal of Richard Lovat Somers, whose "tormented split in consciousness is projected upon the Australian tropics." Similarly, "he occasionally identifies himself with various forms of non-human life," especially fish--"cold, self-sufficient, rapacious"--as an embodiment of the "anti-norm" he proposes. [Detailed analysis of quoted passages describing Somers's response to fish and the seacoast, the Australian bush, and the moonrise over the sea.] DHL's use of landscape to bring about "the fusion of the subjective and the objective" represents "a distinct contribution to the twentieth century novelistic technique." Flawed structurally by its lack of progression, *Kangaroo* "consists of a sequence of moves and countermoves that follow the basic oscillation of Somers's mind" and "ends indecisively, leaving all the old problems unsolved" and the future uncertain.

3395 Shimizu, Kohya. "*Women in Love* ni Okeru Necrophilous Characters ni Tsuite" (On "Necrophilous Characters" in *Women in Love*), BULLETIN OF STUDIES IN HUMANITY (Kagawa University), No. 27 (Dec 1969), 35-56.

The theme of evil in *Women in Love* may be one of the most puzzling points which tend to mislead the readers of this novel. Erich Fromm's terminology, "necrophilous character vs. biophilous character," is used to elucidate the theme. [In Japanese.]

3396 Slade, Tony. D. H. LAWRENCE (Lond: Evans, [Literature in Perspective], 1969; NY: Arco [Literary Critiques], 1970).

[This "balanced introduction" to DHL gives an account of his life and background, his parentage, education and marriage, his censorship problems, his views of sex, his critical theories of morality and the novel, his technical innovations. The author devotes separate chapters to the early novels, *The Rainbow* and *Women in Love*, the later novels, the short novels and stories, and the poetry. Critical judgments are standard: the various kinds of "crippling" love in *Sons and Lovers*; the "central affirmation" of marriage in *The Rainbow* and *Women in Love*; the perceptive characterization of Gerald and Gudrun in *Women in Love*; the "patchy" quality of the leadership novels; the "important social theme" of *Lady Chatterley's Lover*; the thematic treatment of "personal relationships" in the short fiction; the "lack of control" in DHL's poetry; the symbolic treatment of the natural world in *Birds, Beasts and Flowers*. DHL's work suggests "the reconstitution of reason upon a new basis" and "a concept of humanity of greater profundity than we have known before."]

3397 Smailes, T[homas] A. "D. H. Lawrence: Poet," STANDPUNTE, No. 85 (Oct 1969), 24-36.

DHL was a poet who was forced to write prose for a living. A comparison of his verse with that of Hopkins, Yeats, and Eliot is all the evidence needed to prove him the peer of these men. [The major part of this essay is devoted to comparison of DHL's poems with poems on related themes by the other three poets.]

3398 Smailes, T[homas] A. "D. H. Lawrence's *Birds, Beasts and Flowers*," STANDPUNTE, No. 84 (Aug 1969), 26-40; rptd as Chap. IV: "*Birds, Beasts and Flowers*" in SOME COMMENTS ON THE VERSE OF D. H. LAWRENCE, by T[homas] A. Smailes (Port Elizabeth: University of Port Elizabeth, South Africa [General Series A11], 1970), pp. 36-51.

In *Birds, Beasts and Flowers* DHL displays a masterly use of a perfected free-verse style in which image, symbol, and allusion blend with natural speech rhythms to form highly complex poetry. Although DHL's verse is of uneven quality, it is always stimulating. [Includes close analyses of selected poems.]

3399 Smailes, Thomas Allen. "The Verse of D. H. Lawrence," Unpublished dissertation, University of Port Elizabeth (Port Elizabeth, South Africa), 1969. [Listed in GESAMENTLIKE KATALOGUS VAN PROEFSKRIFTE EN VERHANDELINGE VAN DIE SUID-AFRIKAANSE UNIVERSEITE (Union Catalogue of Theses and Dissertations of South African Universities), Supp. No. 11 (1969) (Potchefstroom: Potchefstroom University for C. H. E., 1971), p. 48.] Rvd and pub as SOME COMMENTS ON THE VERSE OF D. H. LAWRENCE (Port Elizabeth, South Africa: University of Port Elizabeth [General Series A11], 1970).

3400 Smith, Elton. "Redemptive Snobbishness in Nietzsche, Lawrence, and Eliot," NEWSLETTER OF THE CONFERENCE ON CHRISTIANITY AND LITERATURE, XVIII (Spring 1969), 30-35.

Nietzsche, DHL, and T. S. Eliot are spiritual aristocrats who, echoing the suggestion that the Bible makes decided human distinctions, see a kind of hierarchy of redemptive possibilities.

3401 Sobchack, Thomas. "*The Fox*: The Film and the Novel," WESTERN HUMANITIES REVIEW, XXIII (Winter 1969), 73-78. Although much of the dialogue is taken from DHL, Mark Rydell's film version of *The Fox* lacks the density of DHL's prose and the "graphic complexity" of the narrative point of view. Hence, the film misses "the essential quality of the novel": DHL's "evocation of the ambiguous and enigmatic nature of the relationships between men and women." [Detailed analysis of how and why the film fails.]

3402 Squires, Michael George. "The Pastoral Novel: Studies in George Eliot, Thomas Hardy, and D. H. Lawrence," DISSERTATION ABSTRACTS INTERNATIONAL, XXXI (1970), 370A. Unpublished dissertation, University of Maryland, 1969: rvd and pub as THE PASTORAL NOVEL: STUDIES IN GEORGE ELIOT, THOMAS HARDY, AND D. H. LAWRENCE (Charlottesville: UP of Virginia, 1974).

3403 Stein, Walter. CRITICISM AS DIALOGUE (Cambridge: Cambridge UP, 1969), pp. 11, 13, 18-19, 22, 44, 55, 61, 73-83, 207-8, 218-20, 222, 246.
"Lawrence's turning away from full tragic exposure springs from an active, central refusal--directly related to the direction of his achieved growth." Although "his early work indicates a sensibility potentially fully open to the tragic," his work from the end of *Sons and Lovers* on contains "episodes of loss or defeat, characters that destroy or are destroyed, the vision of a destructive civilization." *The Rainbow* "offers some profound, direct challenges to Christian perspectives" as DHL perceives them. "The Industrial Magnate" chapter of *Women in Love* "poses...searching questions about the relations between natural human values and charity, and between Christian ideals of service and a destructive social activism." "It is obviously impossible for a Christian to read Lawrence...without... radically reconsidering not only the whole theology of sex but also the place of sacrifice in human relations, and the place of natural fulfilment in the life of grace." DHL's "hostility to a conventional rationalism" is seen in his presentation of "Ursula's experience over the microscope" as "a sort of Transfiguration." But the "natural self" that DHL advocates "is only capable of love and human compassion so far as the other person...can consummate this sacred egoism." Skrebensky and Clifford Chatterley fail as natural conductors of " 'infinity.' " DHL simultaneously affirms " 'oneness with the infinite' " and denies "the transcendence of the 'Eternal,' " affirms " 'baptism to another life' " and denies "both its sacrificial source and infinite *otherness*." [Discusses Raymond Williams's treatment of DHL and Tolstoy in MODERN TRAGEDY (1966).] [Christian criticism.]

3404 Stewart, James Ecclestone. "The Evolution and Source of Some Themes of Spontaneity in D. H. Lawrence's Writing until 1914." Unpublished dissertation, Cambridge University, 1969. [Listed in TITLES OF DISSERTATIONS AT CAMBRIDGE UNIVERSITY, 1968-1969 (Cambridge: Cambridge University Press, 1970), p. 13; and in Lawrence F. McNamee, DISSERTATIONS IN ENGLISH AND

AMERICAN LITERATURE, SUPPLEMENT II: 1969-1973 (Lond and NY: R. R. Bowker, 1974), p. 366.]

3405 Stock, Noel. "Fragmentation and Uncertainty," POETRY AUSTRALIA, XXXI (Dec 1969), 41-44.
Artists have betrayed their art by wallowing in uncertainty and "indulging in the anarchies attendant upon self-pity." Modern romanticists like DHL are "sad heirs" to a depleted tradition which did not look beyond the Waste Land because they did not realize how far it extended.

3406 Thomas, Donald. A LONG TIME BURNING: THE HISTORY OF LITERARY CENSORSHIP IN ENGLAND (Lond: Routledge & Kegan Paul; NY: Praeger, 1969), pp. 4, 209, 292, 302-3, 308, 312-13, 314n.
[Details in brief the censorship problems of *Lady Chatterley's Lover, Sons and Lovers, The Rainbow,* and *Women in Love*, and mentions in passing *Pornography and Obscenity.*]

3407 Trail, George Y. "Prolegomena to the Poetry of D. H. Lawrence," DISSERTATION ABSTRACTS INTERNATIONAL, XXX (1970), 3479A. Unpublished dissertation, University of Missouri at Columbia, 1969.

3408 Traschen, Isadore. "The Form of the Literature of Crisis," SOUTH ATLANTIC QUARTERLY, LXVIII (Winter 1969), 16-26.
The archetype of death and rebirth gives shape to the literature of the modern period. DHL (with Yeats, Gide, Mann, Joyce, Miller, Camus, Faulkner, Hemingway, Grass, etc.) depicts death, or the crisis in values, yet creates images of renewal by setting "the life of the blood, sex and silence against mentalism, abstraction, and chatter."

3409 Truchler, Leo. "Zur Spätlyrik von D. H. Lawrence" (On D. H. Lawrence's Late Poems), DIE NEUEREN SPRACHEN (Frankfurt), ns XVIII (1969), 600-606.
In his late poems, DHL translates the artistic program of his "Poetry of the Present" into man's self-fulfillment through union with the universe. His most successful attempt to connect the celebration of the now with a cosmic consciousness is "The Ship of Death," where the speaker's abstention from epigrammatic and didactic intrusions shows a perfect convergence of meaning and form. [In German.]

3410 Turner, Frederick W., III. "Prancing in to a Purpose: Myths, Horses, and the True Selfhood in Lawrence's 'The Rocking-Horse Winner,'" D. H. LAWRENCE: "THE ROCKING-HORSE WINNER," ed by Dominick P. Consolo (Columbus, OH: Merrill [The Merrill Literary Casebook Series], 1969), pp. 95-106.
"The Rocking-Horse Winner" belongs to the final period in which DHL attempted "to slough off the old skin of self and become a new Adam, unsponsored and

free." The myth of Bellerophon and Pegasus is central: the mythic hero is in exile from "the warm homeland of natural parental affection," and with the aid of his magic horse he accomplishes a series of victories. Unlike Bellerophon's, however, Paul's last ride is a triumph, for his motive is not pride but complete unselfishness, and in his death he escapes from the egocentricity of his relatives into a "cosmic consciousness."

3411 Weiner, S. Ronald. "The Rhetoric of Travel: The Example of *Sea and Sardinia*," D. H. LAWRENCE REVIEW, II (Fall 1969), 230-44.

Critics like Wayne Booth and Kenneth Burke generally agree that a work of art is a selection from reality which "implicitly tries to persuade us that reality is one thing rather than another, which...aims at our emotional acceptance of a condition we may in some sense call true." "That travel literature is as amenable to such selectivity as fiction or poetry seems obvious." "To the extent that a travel book seeks to persuade us that a given impression of a locale is a true one, we may speak of its general rhetorical intention." DHL's travel books, however, "go one step further": they "seek positively to change the reader." DHL "clearly conceived of his artistic role as prophetic and homiletic"; he is concerned with the "vital recognition of wonder and mystery within and without the self," as necessary condition to "the achievement of...individuality," and he feels deeply "about the special role of locale in human self discovery and individuation." "The travel books may be understood as an extension of the use of place encountered in the fiction, and that use is centrally homiletic"; they are "rhetorically molded fables of the modern sensibility in search of unspoiled being." This essay demonstrates "some of the strategies of form, image, and style he employs in attempting to fulfill his rhetorical aim."

3412 Williams, Raymond. "Introduction," *Three Plays by D. H. Lawrence: A Collier's Friday Night, The Daughter-in-Law, The Widowing of Mrs. Holroyd* (Harmondsworth, Middlesex, England: Penguin Books, 1969), pp. 7-14.

DHL's three colliery plays--*A Collier's Friday Night, The Daughter-in-Law,* and *The Widowing of Mrs. Holroyd*--were written in 1909, at the time of his early success in publishing his poetry and fiction. "Rejecting the only body of serious new drama in England," that of Shaw and Galsworthy, DHL identified his "relevant predecessors"--Synge, for his "drama based on the experience and the talk of ordinary people," and Chekhov, for his "relevant dramatic form--dismissed by some theorists...as formless." DHL chose "a particular kind of naturalism" in which "the dramatic reality is created by a scrupulous fidelity to the way people talk...: not probable dialogue, in stage terms, but the dramatic action coming out of these rhythms which are the shapes of particular lives and of a common life." DHL at an "early stage of his work, met and identified a major problem of modern dramatic form: the contradiction between the detail and closeness of fiction...and the habits of theatre, and of most traditional drama, in which posture, rhetoric, formality and presentation...had been the ordinary means." "In his later plays, he moved to a brittle stagey talk,...or to stage discussion of a presented kind,...or, finally,...to the traditional, reminiscent, scriptural rhythms of *David*." Unable to find his audience in the theater of his day, DHL was doing in his earliest plays what the dramatists of the past ten or fifteen years have been doing.

3413 "*Women in Love*," FILMS AND FILMING, XVI (Dec 1969), 10-11.
[A photo layout of six stills from the film version of *Women in Love*, including one shot each of Ursula and Birkin, Gudrun and Gerald, Ursula and Gudrun, and Birkin nude in the woods, and two shots of Gerald and Birkin in the nude wrestling scene. On p. 7, preceding, is a full page advertisement for the film.]

3414 Wood, Jessie Chambers. "Letters and Documents of Jessie Chambers Wood," Appendice IV in D. H. LAWRENCE: L'HOMME ET LA GENÈSE DE SON OEUVRE, LES ANNÉES DE FORMATION: 1885-1919: DOCUMENTS (D. H. Lawrence: The Man and the Genesis of His Work, The Formative Years: 1885-1919: Documents), by Émile Delavenay (Paris: Librairie C. Klincksieck, 1969), pp. 664-710; Sect. 3: "Letters from Mrs. Jessie Chambers Wood to Émile Delavenay, 1933 to 1935," pp. 667-98, contains twenty-three letters rptd in George J. Zytaruk (ed), "The Collected Letters of Jessie Chambers," D. H. LAWRENCE REVIEW, XII (Spring-Summer 1979), 59-107, 110-12, 116-17, 126-27, 128-30, with additional letters to Delavenay, pp. 131-33, 155-59.
[This appendix includes the following documents: (1) "Questions submitted by E. Delavenay to Jessie Chambers," (2) "Extracts from Jessie Chambers's replies," (3) "Letters from Mrs. Jessie Chambers Wood to Emile Delavenay, 1933 to 1935," (4) "Extracts from Jessie Chambers's original draft of D. H. LAWRENCE: A PERSONAL RECORD (Ms. 1)." The letters contain a wealth of factual information about DHL's early life and the genesis of *Sons and Lovers*. They also reveal the development of Jessie Chambers's memoir and provide major evidence for Delavenay's study.]

3415 Wood, Paul Alonzo Christopher. "The Primitive Element in the Fiction of D. H. Lawrence," DISSERTATION ABSTRACTS INTERNATIONAL, XXXI (1970), 1298A. Unpublished dissertation, New York University, 1969.

3416 Yamaguchi, Tetsuo. "*Shinda Otoko* ni Tsuite" (On *The Man Who Died*), SHIKOKU CHRISTIAN COLLEGE TREATISES, No. 15 (March 1969), 23-35.
In *The Man Who Died* DHL treats Christ's resurrection as the transfiguration not out of the flesh but into the flesh and gives high praise to "the great atonement" by tenderness in sexual love. But his idea of sexual love is so romantic that it fails to give a sense of truth to this story. [See also a reconsideration of these views in Tetsuo Yamaguchi, "*Shinda Otoko* Saikô" (Reconsideration of *The Man Who Died*), SHIKOKU CHRISTIAN COLLEGE TREATISES, No. 29 (March 1974), 156-67.] [In Japanese.]

3417 Yoshii, Mitsuo. "D. H. Lawrence no Sekai" (The World of D. H. Lawrence), ENGLISH LITERATURE (Waseda University), No. 35 (Nov 1969), 32-43.

DHL penetrated into the cul-de-sac of the progress of modern science and technology and of humanism since the Renaissance. Putting the matter of life and death into his main theme, he tried to solve the problem of modern civilization through pursuit of the relation between man and man, man and universe. [DHL's standpoint is compared to those of T. E. Hulme, Paul Valery, and Walt Whitman.] [In Japanese.]

3418 Yoshimura, Hirokazu. "*The Rainbow* no Characters ni Tsuite--Tom Brangwen to 'Darkness' "(On the Characters in *The Rainbow*--Tom Brangwen and "Darkness"), STUDIES IN FOREIGN LITERATURES (Ritsumeikan University), No. 18 (June 1969), 70-88.

[The first of three articles on the characters in *The Rainbow;* this one discusses the process of Tom Brangwen's realization of the full meaning of "darkness." See also Hirokazu Yoshimura, "*The Rainbow* no Characters ni Tsuite--Will Brangwen: 'A Sick Foetus' "(On the Characters in *The Rainbow*--Will Brangwen: "A Sick Foetus"), STUDIES IN FOREIGN LITERATURES (Ritsumeikan University), No. 21 (Jan 1971), 19-40, and "*The Rainbow* no Characters ni Tsuite--Heishi: Anton Skrebensky" (On the Characters in *The Rainbow*--Anton Skrebensky: A Soldier), STUDIES IN FOREIGN LITERATURES (Ritsumeikan University), No. 23 (Dec 1971), 100-21.] [In Japanese.]

3419 Yudhishtar. CONFLICT IN THE NOVELS OF D. H. LAWRENCE (Edinburgh: Oliver & Boyd [Biography and Criticism, 12]; NY: Barnes & Noble, 1969); excerpt from Chap. VI, "The Changing Scene," pp. 210-30, rptd as "The Changing Scene: *Aaron's Rod*," in D. H. LAWRENCE: A COLLECTION OF CRITICISM, ed by Leo Hamalian (NY: McGraw-Hill [Contemporary Studies in Literature], 1973), pp. 65-80.

DHL, the most important English writer of the twentieth century, is among the greatest novelists. Unfortunately, critical response to DHL for the past half-century, despite its volume and variety, has failed to grasp the essence of either the man or the artist, but has often belabored the obvious or proved downright misleading. Aesthetic criticism, based on too narrow a conception of art, has not responded sympathetically to DHL's vision on the basis of his own artistic intentions but on the basis of preconceived aesthetic standards and thus has failed to recognize that, with rare exceptions, DHL fully realized his purposes. The urgency of DHL's message justified his disregard for the formal completeness of such writers as Joyce and Proust, with their intensely self-conscious art. [The author surveys DHL's "worldview," points up the inadequacies of critical approaches to DHL from the vantage point of symbolism, psychoanalytic theory, or social realism, and proposes instead to isolate DHL's sensitive awareness and treatment of the element of "conflict" in the "series of relationships between man and his circumambient universe" in his novels. Taking DHL's novels chronologically, he views them as revelations of the conflict inherent in various relationships and as representing stages in DHL's development and as exploratory steps in his "spiritual odyssey." Taking his point of departure from selected critical opinions of each novel, he proceeds by descriptive paraphrase and occasional analytic commentary on each.] "It is not as...static, 'immortal' works of art, but as...living, moving 'bright book[s] of life' which are going to help us to live, as nothing else can that Lawrence's novels can have the supreme importance they have for us." [Appendix discusses, and takes issue with, the interpretation by John Sparrow and others of "the night of sensual passion" in *Lady Chatterley's Lover* as "*penetratio per anum.*"]

3420 Zaslove, Jerald. "Counterfeit and the Use of Literature," WEST COAST REVIEW, III (Winter 1969), 5-19.

Art, for certain writers, including DHL, neither imitates reality nor gives a deeper vision of it but instead is a conflict with and unmasking of repressive forces. Conflict is more basic to their art than either ambiguity or coherence. Both Connie Chatterley and Anna Karenina try to create their own language to express the deep reality within them and to escape the sort of counterfeit which in *Women in Love* kills Gerald. *Lady Chatterley's Lover* embodies all of DHL's ideas on the counterfeit, and personal fulfillment is fundamentally opposed to the entire culture. DHL does what literature should do: lead us to think the unthinkable and reveal our "bogus mastery" of life.

3421 Zeraffa, Michel. PERSONNE ET PERSONNAGE: LE ROMANESQUE DES ANNÉES 1920 AUX ANNÉES 1950 (Person and Personage: The Novel of the Years 1920 to 1950) (Paris: Éditions Klinksieck, 1969), pp. 227-34; additional references pp. 54-56, 77, 83, 91, 143, 236, 247, 310, 413.

DHL uses the language of psychoanalysis to discuss the relationship between the individual person and the social person, but he saw the danger in psychoanalysis of isolating from the We a Me considered as an intrinsic entity. DHL was critical of Proust and Joyce, and DHL's character was the antithesis of Joyce's Dedalus in his view of the Other. DHL is sympathetic to comparative psychology and history, but this psychology is very different from that of modern writers such as Virginia Woolf in that the All, for DHL, is not a reassembling of the interior but immediate experience. DHL also accused Flaubert and Thomas Mann of maintaining an aesthetic distance from life as from leprosy. In DHL's fiction man is part of a continuum progressive and progressing through desire, in which the dynamism involves not only a diversity of mental aspects but also multiple aspects of social life. [In French.]

3422 Zytaruk, George J. "Book Reviews," DALHOUSIE REVIEW, XLIX (Summer 1969), 267-68.

Lawrence in Love: Letters to Louie Burrows, ed by James T. Boulton, is "singularly undistinguished" as a group of love letters--DHL's manner of expressing love is too trite. But the letters are "invaluable" for the presentation of "the painful birth of artistic genius," for "the portrait of the struggling artist," and for "the wealth of new material" they afford for scholars.

3423 Zytaruk, George J. "D. H. Lawrence's Reading of Russian

Literature," D. H. LAWRENCE REVIEW, II (Summer 1969), 120-37; rvd and rptd as Chap. I in D. H. LAWRENCE'S RESPONSE TO RUSSIAN LITERATURE, by George J. Zytaruk (The Hague: Mouton, 1971), pp. 13-37.

The purpose of this essay is to determine "the extent of Lawrence's reading of Russian literature" in order to establish a basis for analyzing his response to Russian writers. Evidence indicates that from 1909 on DHL read extensively in Tolstoy and Dostoevsky, examining not only their major works but also their letters and journals, as translated by S. S. Koteliansky, and biographies and criticism of them. Significantly, DHL's "most concentrated period of reading Dostoevsky" was 1914-1916, when he was formulating his own " 'philosophy.' " Later he re-read Dostoevsky for his introduction to Koteliansky's translation of THE GRAND INQUISITOR (1930). While his only direct reference to Turgenev is to A SPORTSMAN'S SKETCHES, Jessie Chambers also mentions DHL's fondness for FATHERS AND SONS and RUBIN. DHL was familiar with the works of Anton Chekhov, Maxim Gorky, I. A. Bunin, and Alexander Kuprin, again largely through translations by Koteliansky. His letters and essays also contain references to Andreyev, Artzybashev, and Gogol. While DHL was aware of the Russian thinker Dimitry Merezhkovsky, he was more familiar with three other Russian philosophers, Vladimir Solovyov, Leo Shestov, and V. V. Rozanov, the last of whom "made the greatest impression" on him. DHL's refusal "to acknowledge the Russian writers as the greatest writers of all time does not...mean that he was not influenced by them." The extent of his reading of the Russians "points to his deep involvement in their work." An examination of DHL's response to Russian literature could, therefore, "serve as an index to his own critical ideas and of his development as an artist."

1970

3424 Allendorf, Otmar. "The Origins of Lawrence's 'Study of Thomas Hardy,'" NOTES AND QUERIES, ns XVII (Dec 1970), 466-67.

It seems likely that Bertram Christian, editor of the "Writers of the Day" series published by Messrs. Nisbet & Co., commissioned DHL to write a book on Thomas Hardy for the series but later rejected it.

3425 Alpers, Anthony. "D. H. Lawrence Letters," QUEEN'S QUARTERLY, LXXVII (Summer 1970), 297.

The Quest for Rananim: D. H. Lawrence's Letters to S. S. Koteliansky, 1914 to 1930, ed by George J. Zytaruk, shows that Koteliansky, to whom DHL wrote more letters than "exist to any other of his friends," evoked "the *good* side of Lawrence." [Praises the "nearly impeccable" editing.]

3426 Alpert, Hollis. "Up the Rebels," SATURDAY REVIEW (NY), LIII (25 July 1970), 37.

The film version of *The Virgin and the Gypsy,* directed by Christopher Miles, captures the theme of DHL's original novel with informed grace and restraint.

3427 Alter, Robert. "Eliot, Lawrence, and the Jews," COMMENTARY, L (Oct 1970), 81-86; rptd as "Eliot, Lawrence and the Jews: Two Versions of Europe" in DEFENSES OF THE IMAGINATION: JEWISH WRITERS AND MODERN HISTORICAL CRISIS, by Robert Alter (Phila: Jewish Publication Society of America, 1978), pp. 137-51.

John Harrison's THE REACTIONARIES (1967) misrepresents *Kangaroo* and DHL's attitude towards Jews. *Kangaroo* is essentially a religious novel and the Jews "are the ultimate adversary. . .because the Jews are the source of European values which. . .alienate man from his natural world." Love as compassion is essentially a Jewish message, and God the Father, for DHL, is a Jew. For Eliot, by contrast, the Jew is "the archetypal outsider, a European who is not a Christian."

3428 Andrews, Nigel. "*The Virgin and the Gypsy*," SIGHT AND SOUND, XXXIX (Autumn 1970), 220-21.

In the film version of *The Virgin and the Gypsy,* "the antagonism between civilised and elemental values is caught in the juxtaposition of the. . .two opening shots — churchyard and waterfall — and highlighted throughout by incidental images." DHL "overstated his case" in a book too "schematic and axe-grinding" to be visualized in "'realistic' terms," but director Christopher Miles's use of realistic details and counterpoint between images, characters, and camera movements serves the theme well.

3429 Arlen, Michael J. EXILES (NY: Farrar, Straus & Giroux, 1970), pp. 66, 71, 202, 218.

[In this memoir of his parents, the author says that his father, Michael Arlen (pseud of Dikran Kouyoumdjian), as a young writer, brought his stories to DHL for criticism. DHL took a "genuine interest" in the senior Arlen, but later put him into *Lady Chatterley's Lover* as Michaelis.]

3430 Armstrong, Marion. "Spirited Creatures," CHRISTIAN CENTURY, Continuing NEW CHRISTIAN, LXXXVII (16 Sept 1970), 1099.

The film of *Women in Love,* written for the screen and produced by Larry Kramer, directed by Ken Russell, "is alive with the thrusting and conflicting ideologies which form the book's main interest." But DHL saw Hermione "more deeply," "and therefore gave to the scene where she whams Birkin over the head with a paperweight a sinister death-centered import not apparent in the film." [Superficial.]

3431 Atkins, John. "Lawrence's Social Landscape," BOOKS AND BOOKMEN, XV (July 1970), 24-26.

"The social landscape of Lawrence's midlands is a vision of industrial purgatory, but behind it and even alongside of it there is a purer, sweeter landscape which we might still be wise enough to save."

3432 Barber, David S. "Can a Radical Interpretation of *Women in Love* Be Adequate?" D. H. LAWRENCE REVIEW, III (Summer 1970), 168-74.
[Reply to Mary Louise Briscoe and Martha Vicinus, "Lawrence among the Radicals: MMLA, 1969: An Exchange," D. H. LAWRENCE REVIEW, III (Spring 1970), 63-69.] Although Vicinus's "radical aesthetic" in effect rejects *Women in Love,* her "reaction to the novel shows how forcefully it dramatizes the problems that modern industrial society has created" and "forces her to seek a better" solution than DHL's. It is DHL's dramatization of the search for "alternatives to modern society,...not any particular solution, that matters."

3433 Barbier, Françoise-Marie, and Simone Rozenberg. "Lawrence/Freud," in RÉFLEXIONS ET DIRECTIVES POUR L ÉTUDE DE D. H. LAWRENCE: "WOMEN IN LOVE" (Thoughts and Directives for the Study of D. H. Lawrence: *Women in Love*), by Anne-Marie Fraisse (Paris: Minard [Carnets des Lettres Modernes], 1970), pp. 106-18.
[In an examination of correspondences between Freudian theory and *Women in Love,* the authors discuss Birkin's homosexual tendencies in "Gladiatorial" and elsewhere in relation to mother fixation, the displacement of Gerald's violent desire for possession in "Rabbit," the reception of *Sons and Lovers* in the London psychoanalytic milieu of 1914, DHL's rejection in *Psychoanalysis and the Unconscious* and *Fantasia of the Unconscious* of the Freudian theories of the unconscious, dream analysis, and the incest motive, and DHL's affinities with Jung.]
[In French.]

3434 Baron, C[arl] E. "More Is Less," SPECTATOR, CCIV (18 April 1970), 524-25.
[Letter to the Editor in reply to Ann Wordsworth, "More Is Less," SPECTATOR, CCIV (21 March 1970), 384.] Several items in *The Quest for Rananim: D. H. Lawrence's Letters to S. S. Koteliansky, 1914 to 1930,* ed by George J. Zytaruk, invite reflection: "what it meant to Lawrence that Koteliansky was Jewish; why the SIGNATURE venture...was conducted...with so little thought given to building up a readership; whether 'Rananim' should simply be dismissed as an absurd utopian scheme...or whether it gives rise to thoughts about Lawrence's marriage and closest relationships." Of interest too is DHL's reference to Dr. David Eder, a Freudian analyst, who may have been the source of DHL's information about syphilis in "Introduction to These Paintings."

3435 Beards, Richard D., with the assistance of Barbara Willens. "D. H. Lawrence: Criticism; September, 1968–December, 1969; A Checklist," D. H. LAWRENCE REVIEW, III (Spring 1970), 70-79.
[A bibliography of the year's works in DHL criticism and scholarship, divided into five sections: General, Poetry, Individual Works of Fiction, Non-Fiction Prose, and Drama.]

3436 Bell, Michael. "The Shift from a Romantic to a Primitive View of Life in D. H. Lawrence, with Particular Reference to Differences in the Language of *The Rainbow, Women in Love,* and *The Plumed Serpent.*" Unpublished dissertation, University of London, 1970. [Listed in Lawrence F. McNamee, DISSERTATIONS IN ENGLISH AND AMERICAN LITERATURE, SUPP II (NY and Lond: Bowker, 1974), p. 369.]

3437 Bergonzi, Bernard. THE SITUATION OF THE NOVEL (Lond: Macmillan; Pittsburgh: University of Pittsburgh P [Critical Essays on Modern Literature Series], 1970; rptd 1972), pp. 11, 15, 22, 36, 42, 99, 140, 149, 164.

DHL described the novel as "'the one bright book of life'" and saw "the form in a non-generic and ahistorical way." The Radcliffe-Tolson relationship in David Storey's RADCLIFFE alludes to that of Birkin and Crich in *Women in Love.* The opening chapters of C. P. Snow's TIME OF HOPE, "describing the boy's ambiguous relations with his possessive and ambitious mother," recalls the DHL of *Sons and Lovers.*

3438 Biles, Jack I. "An Interview in London with Angus Wilson," STUDIES IN THE NOVEL, II (Spring 1970), 76-87.

DHL treats sex as a ritual which isolates people from society and which precludes liking and warmth. The result is the dehumanization of sex.

3439 Blanchard, Margaret. "Men in Charge : A Review of *Women in Love,*" WOMEN: A JOURNAL OF LIBERATION (Baltimore, MD), (Fall 1970), pp. 31-32.

Director Ken Russell's film of *Women in Love* blurs the novel's focus: "the relationship between power and love." DHL's "cosmic sexual drama" obscures social issues of classism and sexism. The most convincing relationship is that between Birkin and Gerald Crich. Non-exclusive marriage relationships are not extended to women and are impossible in a capitalist society.

3440 Blevins, Winifred. "Lawrence's *Women in Love:* Word to Image," LOS ANGELES HERALD EXAMINER, 12 April 1970, Sect. G, p. 4.

[Review of the film version of *Women in Love* discussing the problems of translating DHL's conceptions in the novel into cinematic terms.]

3441 Bloom, Harold. "First and Last Romantics," STUDIES IN ROMANTICISM, IX (Fall 1970), 225-32.

DHL, a "Last Romantic," claimed as his "First Romantic" influence the Etruscans, when actually his "First Romantic" influences were Whitman and Hardy.

3442 Bogan, Louise. "D. H. Lawrence," A POET'S ALPHABET: REFLECTIONS ON THE LITERARY ART AND VOCATION, ed by Robert Phelps and Ruth Limmer (NY: McGraw-Hill, 1970), pp. 276-82.

[Reviews of *Birds, Beasts and Flowers* (1923) and *Selected Poems,* ed by Kenneth Rexroth (1948).] *Look! We Have Come Through!* constituted a break in DHL's dark, intense poetry. He henceforth cried for merging while maintaining spiritual isolation. *Birds, Beasts and Flowers, Twilight in Italy,* and *Studies in Classic American Literature* show an emphasis on isolation and escape from humanity. *Birds, Beasts and Flowers* advances the idea that love is not important to the integrated individual, but DHL is sometimes slightly hysterical about his thesis. The genius will remain under the invective and didacticism perhaps necessary because DHL is "at every point refused."

3443 Briscoe, Mary Louise, and Martha Vicinus. "Lawrence among the Radicals: MMLA, 1969: An Exchange," D. H. LAWRENCE REVIEW, III (Spring 1970), 63-69.

[Exchange on the New University Conference workshop in "Radical Approaches to Literature: D. H. Lawrence's *Women in Love*," led by Martha Vicinus and Dave Schiller and held at the Midwest Modern Language Association meeting in St. Louis on 25 Oct 1969.] **Briscoe:** The NUC critics, attempting to break away from the methods of New Criticism and "to get at larger questions, especially social values," emphasized, in their discussion of *Women in Love,* "such things as the male-female polarity, male supremacy, the dehumanizing effects of industrialism, the strained language, and the illusory quality of the novel's 'solution' to the problems it deals with"; but there is "nothing radical" in such criticism.
Vicinus: Avoiding formal discussions to consider topics relevant to teachers, the NUC used *Women in Love* "as a case study for defining both how a radical would approach literature and how he would work toward a definition of a radical aesthetic theory." Recognizing "the novel's greatness, particularly in its diagnosis of society," but rejecting its solutions, "I find myself forced to break the integrity of the novel by accepting only a part of it." While DHL's treatment of the working class is superficial, "his analysis of the Criches as forces participating in a life-destroying form of industrialization is undeniably powerful." The solution offered in "the relationship of Birkin and Ursula" is contradictory and elitist. Their new life depends on their giving up the old and "linking their futures with each other alone," but "neither could be 'free' without the surplus wealth of the very society they despise and reject." [See also David S. Barber, "Can a Radical Interpretation of *Women in Love* Be Adequate?" D. H. LAWRENCE REVIEW, III (Summer 1970), 168-74.]

3444 Buckley, Jerome H. "Autobiography in the English *Bildungsroman,*" THE INTERPRETATION OF NARRATIVE: THEORY AND PRACTICE, ed by Morton W. Bloomfield (Cambridge: Harvard UP [Harvard English Studies, 1]; Lond: Oxford UP, 1970), pp. 93-104.

Sons and Lovers, in the tradition of the English *Bildungsroman* which includes THE PRELUDE, THE MILL ON THE FLOSS, and DAVID COPPERFIELD, illustrates the possible strength and potential weakness of the genre. The strength lies in the objective control of autobiographical material in the first two-thirds of the novel, and the weakness in the loosening of that control in the final third, which allows DHL to justify Paul's actions rather than to explore the possibilities of his character. The end of the novel, with its affirmation, does not follow logically the preceding development of Paul's character but is imposed from outside, from DHL's experience and perspective.

3445 Burgess, Anthony. THE NOVEL NOW (NY: Pegasus, 1970; Lond: Faber & Faber, 1971) pp. 19, 29-30, 33, 65, 148, 154, 209.
Compared with the exquisite Ronald Firbank and the great experimentalists, DHL seems lumpish, traditional, even pedestrian, but his brief career is a glory of various creation. His passionate affirmation of the life of the body and the emotions gives distinction to work which is stylistically often slipshod, formless, and repetitive. The wonder of novels like *Sons and Lovers, The Rainbow, Women in Love,* and *The Plumed Serpent* lies not only in their passion but also in their power to evoke the feel, smell, and color of living things, and in the way DHL's rhythms drive home the doctrine of man's kinship with the natural world. Although at times we may disparage, parody, and sneer about "deep dark bitter belly-tension," inevitably we go back to DHL, one of the great fresheners and renewers.

3446 Burke, Herbert. "One Man's Lawrence," MYSTERIOUS EAST, Dec 1970, pp. 16-19.
The Quest for Rananim: D. H. Lawrence's Letters to S. S. Koteliansky, 1914 to 1930, ed by George J. Zytaruk (1970), is "impressive" and "authoritative." Recent important films have stimulated general interest in DHL as prophet and revolutionary questioner of the world as it is. These letters contribute to our understanding of DHL's struggles to transform the world and of his quest for an ideal community.

3447 Burns, Robert. "The Novel as a Metaphysical Statement: Lawrence's *The Rainbow,*" SOUTHERN REVIEW (Adelaide), IV (1970), 139-60.
The Rainbow, often seen as a religious work by a seer or visionary, is actually a "metaphysical statement" offering a thorough conceptualization of experience in an intellectually fashioned narrative which insists that "fullness of being is more likely to come from answering to the inclinations of the blood than to the demands of the intellect." DHL rigorously demonstrates the interdependence of man and nature, and man, woman, and children. Beyond ordinary reality, DHL asserts the Infinite of which his characters hope to become aware, but he has no sense of the creative role that mind can play in freeing man from the schemes of nature.

3448 Burwell, Rose Marie. "A Catalogue of D. H. Lawrence's Reading from Early Childhood," D. H. LAWRENCE REVIEW, III (Fall 1970), iii-vi, 193-324; rptd with "Addenda" as "A Checklist of Lawrence's Reading," in A D. H. LAWRENCE HANDBOOK, ed by Keith Sagar (Manchester: Manchester UP; NY: Barnes & Noble, 1982), pp. 59-125.
[A revised and re-edited version of the author's "A Chronological Catalogue of D. H. Lawrence's Reading from Early Childhood," DISSERTATION ABSTRACTS INTERNATIONAL, XXX (1970), 3937A. Unpublished dissertation, University of Iowa, 1969. The entire issue of the D. H. LAWRENCE REVIEW (Fall 1970) is devoted to the catalogue.] The catalogue, which lists DHL's reading by year from 1901 through 1930, organizes evidence for its entries from correspondence, memoirs, biographies, and the non-fictional prose. It includes "every book, play,

poem, essay, and manuscript" which such evidence establishes that DHL read. Re-reading is catalogued, as are periodicals and newspapers, and reviews. "The annotation of each entry is intended. . .to indicate the extent of Lawrence's acquaintance with that item, not to establish his reaction to it." The catalogue includes indexes of authors, newspapers and periodicals, subjects, and authors by national origin. [See also Rose Marie Burwell, "A Catalogue of D. H. Lawrence's Reading from Early Childhood: Addenda," D. H. LAWRENCE REVIEW, VI (Spring 1973), 86-99.]

> **3449** Canby, Vincent. "Lawrence's Philosophy in Subordinate Role," NEW YORK TIMES, 26 March 1970, p. 58; somewhat expanded in NEW YORK TIMES, 29 March 1970, Sect. 2, p. 1; rptd in THE NEW YORK TIMES FILM REVIEWS: A ONE-VOLUME SELECTION, 1913-1970, ed by George Amberg (N.p.: Arno P, 1971), pp. 468-69.

In the novel *Women in Love*, the four central figures "are not so much characters as points of view that are constantly shifting. In the film, they remain fixed as they enact various Laurentian parables about the war between the sexes that can sometimes end in death." Although it necessarily simplifies the novel's ideas, the film is "faithful to Lawrence" in capturing the sensuous "physical contact between people and between people and nature" and in the treatment of "the relationship between the two men." "The movie, like the novel, seems to be propagandizing for a kind of bisexuality that looks terribly confused."

> **3450** Canby, Vincent. "Screen: 'Virgin and the Gypsy' Opens," NEW YORK TIMES, 1 July 1970, p. 50.

Although written near the end of his life as a spin-off from *Lady Chatterley's Lover*, *The Virgin and the Gypsy* "can be read as seminal Lawrence." For the film version, director Christopher Miles and screen writer Alan Plater "have used the novella almost as if it were a scenario, and. . .they have gotten most of it on film, with the exception of some ironies that separate the novella from more ordinary women's fiction."

> **3451** Carballo, Emmanuel. "Prólogo" (Prologue), *D. H. Lawrence: viva y muera México* (D. H. Lawrence: Live and Die in Mexico) (México City: Editorial Diógenes, S. A. [Antologías Temáticas 3], 1970), pp. 9-17.

[A prologue to an anthology of work by DHL, much of it relating to Mexico.] DHL found in his mother the necessary stimulus to put into practice his conceptions about life. He considered love to be the basic and most important function of humans. Frieda later replaced his mother and showed DHL that the basic relationship between a man and a woman consists in battling. Sometimes DHL identifies himself with Mellors and sometimes with Clifford. In other words, at times he wanted to be, like his father, a rude, efficient, and simple man, and at times he wanted to feel like the victim of a mechanized and inhuman society. Once DHL decides to distance himself from his family in order to love Frieda, he finds that he has two choices: he can either let himself be considered a respectable man or let himself be considered a restless man. He opts for the second choice. Mexico, like Australia, Taos, and Italy, was for DHL a pretext for evasion and search. He travelled through Mexico to try to find here a lost paradise. He did not understand the political, social, or economic reality of the country. DHL's Mexico is, at the same time, a falsified Mexico, and a Mexico which deserves a better treatment. At times we are as he painted us, and at times we are better than he believed us to be. [In Spanish.]

3452 Carroll, Kathleen. *"Women in Love* Is Stunning Film," NEW YORK DAILY NEWS, 26 March 1970, p. 79.
[Favorable review of the film version of *Women in Love*.]

3453 Chapman, R. T. "Lawrence, Lewis, and the Comedy of Literary Reputations," STUDIES IN THE TWENTIETH CENTURY, No. 6 (Fall 1970), 85-95.
Authors who run afoul of the literary establishment, as DHL did with his portrayal of sexual activity in *The Rainbow, Women in Love,* and *Lady Chatterley's Lover*, and as Wyndham Lewis did with his criticism of the social and political mores, must depend on a "lobby" of critics to restore them to favor. As DHL was resurrected by his lobbyist, F. R. Leavis, in the fifties, so will Lewis be by his lobby in the seventies.

3454 Chapple, J. A. V. DOCUMENTARY AND IMAGINATIVE LITERATURE, 1880-1920 (Lond: Blandford P, 1970), pp. 72-79, 80, 81-82, 83, 92n, 107, 156n, 213, 233.
The inferno of the colliery village which DHL envisions in Chap. XII of *The Rainbow* has spread to a general " 'corruption triumphant and unopposed' " in the final paragraphs of the novel, which are presented in a style that transcends "workaday prose" in "a high intensity of imagery and rhythmic utterance." DHL, "turning away from the simple pattern of a story told largely for its own sake," produced a myth which, "with its triple movement of degeneration, crisis and rebirth, tends to control the course of his novels in an extraordinary way." Reflecting the decline of rural values in the modern world, "a way of seeing the course of history became the essential form of" *The Rainbow*. In "England, My England," the rural setting takes us back to "the mythological world" with "roots stretching far back into the past; in this case to a very remote and even pre-human past." Although there is much "direct statement of values" in this story, "what proof or demonstration there is resides in the creative substance of passages" descriptive of nature.

3455 Chauhan, Pradyumna S. "D. H. Lawrence and the Making of an American Myth," DISSERTATION ABSTRACTS INTERNATIONAL, XXXI (1971), 6048A. Unpublished dissertation, Duke University, 1970.

3456 Clark, L. D. "The Apocalypse of Lorenzo," D. H. LAWRENCE REVIEW, III (Summer 1970), 141-60.
This essay undertakes an examination in some detail of biblical and literary apocalyptic tradition and of "the two periods of Lawrence's life when his apocalyptic inclinations manifested themselves most strongly": the years of World War I, and the period from his reading of Frederick Carter's DRAGON OF THE

APOCALYPSE in 1923, while writing *The Plumed Serpent*, until his death. Rejecting allegory, DHL saw symbols as perceptions in the blood contributing to deeper perceptions about the relationship between the human and the divine. "In his quest for closer correspondences than those afforded by the Christian tradition, he brought to his last book...a life-long study of paganism and occultism," including a recent reading of J. M. Pryse's THE APOCALYPSE UNSEALED. The way in which DHL used the Book of Revelation can be seen in his handling of various images, such as the Four Horsemen, the twin figure, the Magna Mater, and the figure of Christ. During World War I, DHL wrote six prophetic essays, collectively entitled "The Crown," and pleaded for " 'a new religious era.' "

3457 Cohen, Judith Dana. "The Violation or Fulfillment of Individuality in Marriage as Seen in Selected Works of D. H. Lawrence," DISSERTATION ABSTRACTS INTERNATIONAL, XXXI (1971), 5392A. Unpublished dissertation, University of Pennsylvania, 1970.

3458 Cohen, Richard. "*Virgin and the Gypsy, The*," MONTHLY FILM BULLETIN (British Film Institute, Lond), XXXVII (Aug 1970), 161-62.
"Lawrence did his delicate and finely balanced tale an unwitting disservice in calling it *The Virgin and the Gypsy*--thus implying strong contrasts and an explicit moral," "polarities" which are emphasized in director Christopher Miles's film version. [Synopsis of the plot of the film.]

3459 Coleman, John. "Writing It Again," NEW STATESMAN, LXXVIII (14 Nov 1970), 704.
While Leavis is right in suggesting that adapting DHL's work for film is an " 'obscene undertaking,' " the film version of *Women in Love* has both splendors and flaws.

3460 Connell, Charles. "D. H. Lawrence, 1885-1930," WORLD FAMOUS REBELS (Lond: Hamlyn Publishing, 1970), pp. 219-30.
[Brief, popular account of DHL's life.]

3461 Cooke, Regina. "His Ashes Rest with His Heart; Near Taos," TAOS ARTS 1970, A Special Report in TAOS NEWS (Taos, NM), 3 Sept 1970, p. 3.
DHL's ashes were sealed in the crypt in the "shrine" at Kiowa Ranch near Taos in a ceremony on 15 Sept 1935.

3462 Cowan, James C. D. H. LAWRENCE'S AMERICAN JOURNEY: A STUDY IN LITERATURE AND MYTH (Cleveland & Lond: P of Case Western Reserve University, 1970).
DHL's "pilgrimage" to the American continent, where he remained, with one interruption, for three years, 1922-1925, "follows the pattern of the quest hero of romance," described by Joseph Campbell as " '*separation--initiation--return*,' " a "paradigm which becomes the dominant structural and thematic image in his fiction of the period." DHL found "the symbols and myths whereby...western

civilization might be revived" in commitment to "the romantic values...of dynamic organicism rather than static mechanism." In *Movements in European History,* DHL proposes "to show the 'Spirit,' the impersonal force of the past," which moves in successive waves by a "twofold motive" of peace and "martial triumph." In *Psychoanalysis and the Unconscious* and *Fantasia of the Unconscious,* DHL divides the human body vertically between "the ventral sympathetic region and the dorsal voluntary region" and horizontally between "the lower sensual plane" and "the upper spiritual plane," with the "four psychic or dynamic centers" of his "personality theory" differentiated in function as the positive, incorporative solar plexus is polarized by the negative, delimiting lumbar ganglion as modes of identifying the self, and the positive, adoring cardiac plexus is polarized by the negative, analytical thoracic ganglion as modes of relating to the other. *Studies in Classic American Literature* reflects DHL's romantic "values of change and growth, imperfection and diversity, the creative imagination and the unconscious mind." DHL's redefinition of the Christian Trinity in *Twilight in Italy,* in which the Holy Ghost reconciles the opposites of God the Father (flesh) and Christ the Son (spirit), informs his exploration of possible means of "religious regeneration." In four anti-Murry stories, J. M. Murry is either "mercilessly ridiculed" ("Smile," "Jimmy and the Desperate Woman") or "killed off" ("The Border Line," "The Last Laugh"). In "The Princess," DHL ironically "inverts the pattern of quest" in the Sleeping Beauty fairy tale as Dolly "rejects her would-be prince only to 'return' to an even deeper slumber than before." In "The Woman Who Rode Away," the woman is made both to represent and to reject the crucified god of Christianity in her role as "traditional *pharmakos* of fertility rites." The dual purpose of *St. Mawr* results in its "dual methods, social satire and myth," with Rico Carrington as the chief target in DHL's attack on affectation, Mrs. Witt as the instrument of attack, and the stallion St. Mawr embodying the "mythic potential" "that could revive the waste-land society." *The Plumed Serpent,* structured on thematic and mythic dualities presented through color imagery, "the counters of violence and nakedness," and rituals which recall the inversions of the Black Mass, is characterized by a "failure in coherence between the realistic and metaphorical modes." In the fragmentary story "The Flying Fish," Gethin Day, recovering from a sickness near to death, sets out on the "return" voyage to his ancestral home Daybrook "in search of his own selfhood," on a ship accompanied by schools of porpoises and flying fish, the figures respectively for the "instinctive energy of the creative unconscious" and the transitory flight of "individual life into...consciousness." As *The Man Who Died* shows, the reconciliation of flesh and spirit "in a new, syncretic religious order is the basis" for DHL's ultimate faith that in the reborn man the kingdom of the Holy Ghost is at hand." [This work of myth criticism has evoked, in addition to the usual reviews (not abstracted), several critiques of this mythic approach as applied to DHL. See especially John B. Vickery, "D. H. Lawrence: Critics and Archetypes," PSYCHOLOGICAL PERSPECTIVES, II (Spring 1971), 70-77, espec pp. 71-73; and Charles Rossman, "Myth and Misunderstanding D. H. Lawrence," BUCKNELL REVIEW, XXII (Fall 1976), "Twentieth-Century Poetry, Fiction, Theory," 81-101.]

3463 Crist, Judith. "*Love* Is a Many-Splendored Thing," NEW

YORK, III (30 March 1970), 9.

The film version of *Women in Love*, brilliantly written by Larry Kramer and directed by Ken Russell, is a beautiful, unexploitative visual expression of the themes of passion and doom in the novel.

3464 Crump, G. B. "Doctoral Dissertations on D. H. Lawrence, 1931-1969: A Bibliography," D. H. LAWRENCE REVIEW, III (Spring 1970), 80-86.

[A listing of dissertations on DHL drawn from various printed sources and from responses to queries. See also Gerald M. Garmon, "Doctoral Dissertations on D. H. Lawrence: Bibliographical Addenda," D. H. LAWRENCE REVIEW, V (Summer 1972), 170-73; Dennis Jackson, "Doctoral Dissertations on D. H. Lawrence: Bibliographical Addenda," D. H. LAWRENCE REVIEW, VIII (Summer 1975), 236-41; Fleda Brown Jackson, "Doctoral Dissertations and Masters Theses on D. H. Lawrence: Bibliographical Addenda," D. H. LAWRENCE REVIEW, X (Fall 1977), 299-308.]

3465 DeMaio, Don. "*Women in Love*," DISTANT DRUMMER (Philadelphia), No. 82 (23 April 1970), p. 9.

The film version of *Women in Love* captures the essential quality of DHL's novel.

3466 "D. H. Lawrence," TAOS NEWS (Taos, NM), 21 May 1970.

Contents, abstracted under 1970: Kathy Gosliner, " 'And what about the ranch, the little ranch in New Mexico. The time is different there...,' " p. 1; "Lawrence in New Mexico: There is the pristine; something unbroken...," p. 2; Mabel M. Kuykendall, "Lawrence the Poet: His Webs Were Spun from His Own Vitals," p. 3; "Lawrence the Painter: 'Everything that can possibly be painted has been painted...visual arts are at a dead end,' " pp. 4-5; John Manchester, "Meanwhile Back at the Ranch," p. 6. [Special feature section.]

3467 "D. H. Lawrence: Man of the Century," SAN FRANCISCO CHRONICLE, 1 Aug 1970, p. 14.

People who knew DHL in Taos claim he would have hated the festival planned for Sept 30-Oct 4, 1970, but scholars are enthusiastic. [See also related story, "Exciting, Glorious Man," SAN FRANCISCO CHRONICLE, 1 Aug 1970, p. 14.]

3468 D. H. LAWRENCE REVIEW, ed by James C. Cowan, III, No. 1 (Spring 1970).

Contents, abstracted under 1970: Ruth Suckow, "Modern Figures of Destiny: D. H. Lawrence and Frieda Lawrence," with "Introduction," by Ferner Nuhn, pp. 1-31; Charles Rossman, "The Gospel According to D. H. Lawrence: Religion in *Sons and Lovers*," pp. 31-41; T. A. Smailes (ed), "D. H. Lawrence: Seven Hitherto Unpublished Poems," pp. 42-46; Robert E. Gajdusek, "A Reading of 'A Poem of Friendship,' A Chapter in Lawrence's *The White Peacock*," pp. 47-62; Mary Louise Briscoe and Martha Vicinus, "Lawrence Among the Radicals: MMLA, 1969: An Exchange," pp. 63-69; Richard D. Beards, with the assistance of Barbara Willens, "D. H. Lawrence: Criticism: September, 1968-December, 1969: A Checklist," pp. 70-79; G. B. Crump, "Doctoral Dissertations on D. H.

Lawrence, 1931-1968: A Bibliography," pp. 80-86; "Laurentiana," pp. 87-91 [not abstracted] ; "Notes on Contributors," p. 92 [not abstracted].

3469 D. H. LAWRENCE REVIEW, ed by James C. Cowan, III, No. 2 (Summer 1970).

Contents, abstracted under 1970: Reloy Garcia, "The Quest for Paradise in the Novels of D. H. Lawrence," pp. 93-114; Evelyn J. Hinz, "Juno and *The White Peacock*: Lawrence's English Epic," pp. 115-35; E. San Juan, "Theme versus Imitation: D. H. Lawrence's 'The Rocking-Horse Winner,' " pp. 136-40; L. D. Clark, "The Apocalypse of Lorenzo," pp. 141-60; Keith Sagar, " 'Little Living Myths': A Note on Lawrence's *Tortoises*," pp. 161-67; David S. Barber, "Can a Radical Interpretation of *Women in Love* Be Adequate?," pp. 168-74; Charles Rossman, "Lawrence on the Critics' Couch: Pervert or Prophet?," pp. 175-85 [not abstracted] ; "Laurentiana," pp. 186-90 [not abstracted] ; "Research in Progress," p. 191 [not abstracted] ; "Notes on Contributors," p. 192 [not abstracted].

3470 D. H. LAWRENCE REVIEW, ed by James C. Cowan, III, No. 3 (Fall 1970).

Contents, abstracted under 1970: Rose Marie Burwell, "A Catalogue of D. H. Lawrence's Reading from Early Childhood," pp. iii-vi, 193-324; "Laurentiana," pp. 325-29 [not abstracted] ; "Index to Volume III," p. 330 [not abstracted].

3471 D. H. LAWRENCE'S "THE VIRGIN AND THE GYPSY" (NY: Chevron Pictures, [1970]).

["Exhibitors Showmanship Manual," or press book, of advertisements and promotional copy for the film version of DHL's novel, produced by Kenneth Harper, directed by Christopher Miles, with Joanna Shimkus, Franco Nero, and Honor Blackman.] DHL's "last and most penetrating manuscript, 'The Virgin and the Gypsy' was discovered and published after his death in 1930. It created a furor, some critics maintaining the work was an erotic masterpiece, others that it should be kept out of the hands of decent people." The novel "proved to be his final statement of vindication for Frieda's having walked out on the stuffy von Richthofen, her husband [sic] before Lawrence."

3472 Draper, R[onald] P. (ed.). D. H. LAWRENCE: THE CRITICAL HERITAGE (Lond: Routledge & Kegan Paul, 1970; rptd with corrections, 1979; NY: Barnes & Noble, 1970).

Original reviews and short commentaries are organized under various titles by DHL preceded by bibliographical headnotes. Contents, abstracted under year of first publication: "General Editor's Preface," p. v; "Acknowledgements," pp. xii-xiv; "Note on the Text," p. xv; "Abbreviations," p. xvi [prefatory matter not abstracted] ; [R. P. Draper], "Introduction," pp. 1-29 (1970); Henry Yoxall, [Comment on Four Poems], pp. 31-32, from "Books and Pictures," SCHOOLMASTER, LXXVI (25 Dec 1909), 1242; [*The White Peacock*], p. 33, from "List of New Books and Reprints," TIMES LITERARY SUPPLEMENT (Lond), 21 Jan 1911, pp. 34-35; Allan Monkhouse, [*The White Peacock*], pp. 34-35, from "A Promising Novel," MANCHESTER GUARDIAN, 8 Feb 1911, p. 5; [*The*

White Peacock], pp. 36-37, from "An Interesting Novel," MORNING POST (Lond), 9 Feb 1911, p. 2; Violet Hunt, [*The White Peacock*], pp. 38-39, from "A First Novel of Power," DAILY CHRONICLE (Lond), 10 Feb 1911, p. 6; [*The White Peacock*], pp. 40-41, from DAILY NEWS (Lond), 14 Feb 1911, p. 3; Henry Savage, [*The White Peacock*], pp. 42-43, from "Fiction," ACADEMY, LXXX (18 March 1911), 328; [*The Trespasser*], pp. 44-45, from "Two Realists: Russian and English," ATHENAEUM, No. 4, 414 (1 June 1912), 613-14; Basil de Selincourt, [*The Trespasser*], pp. 46-47, from "New Novels," MANCHESTER GUARDIAN, 5 June 1912, p. 5; [*The Trespasser*], pp. 48-49, from "An Interesting Novel," MORNING POST (Lond), 17 June 1912, p. 2; [*The Trespasser*], p. 50, from "The Woman Who Kills," NEW YORK TIMES BOOK REVIEW, 17 Nov 1912, Sect. 6, p. 677; Edward Thomas, [*Love Poems and Others*], pp. 51-52, from "More Georgian Poetry," BOOKMAN (Lond), XLIV (April 1913), 47; Ezra Pound, [*Love Poems and Others*], pp. 53-54, from "In Metre," NEW FREEWOMAN, I (1 Sept 1913), 113; [*Love Poems and Others*], pp. 55-57, from "Three Poets," NATION (Lond), XVI (14 Nov 1914), 220-21; [*Sons and Lovers*], pp. 58-59, from STANDARD (Lond), 30 May 1913, p. 5; [*Sons and Lovers*], pp. 60-61, from "New Novels," SATURDAY WESTMINSTER GAZETTE, XLI (14 June 1913), 17; Harold Massingham, [*Sons and Lovers*], pp. 62-64, from "A Novel of Note," DAILY CHRONICLE (Lond), 17 June 1913, p. 3; [*Sons and Lovers*], pp. 65-66, from "*Sons and Lovers*," SATURDAY REVIEW (Lond), CXV (21 June 1913), 780-81; Lascelles Abercrombie, [*Sons and Lovers*], pp. 67-68, from "The Poet as Novelist," MANCHESTER GUARDIAN, 2 July 1913, p. 7; [*Sons and Lovers*], pp. 69-72, from NATION (Lond), XIII (12 July 1913), 577-78; Louise Maunsell Field, [*Sons and Lovers*], pp. 73-75, from "Mother Love: Mr. Lawrence's Remarkable Story of Family Life," NEW YORK TIMES BOOK REVIEW, 21 Sept 1913, Sect. 6, p. 479; Alfred Kuttner, [*Sons and Lovers*], pp. 76-80, from "*Sons and Lovers*," NEW REPUBLIC, II (10 April 1915), 255-57; [*The Prussian Officer*], pp. 81-83, from "Novels," OUTLOOK (Lond), XXXIV (19 Dec 1914), 795-96; [Extracts from Lawrence's letters concerning *The Rainbow*, including extracts from six letters to Edward Garnett, three to J. B. Pinker, and one to Waldo Frank], pp. 84-88 [not abstracted]; [*The Rainbow*], pp. 89-90, from STANDARD (Lond), 1 Oct 1915, p. 3; Robert Lynd, [*The Rainbow*], pp. 91-92, from "The Downfall," DAILY NEWS (Lond), 5 Oct 1915, p. 6; James Douglas, [*The Rainbow*], pp. 93-95, from "Books and Bookmen," STAR (Lond), 22 Oct 1915, p. 4; Clement Shorter, [*The Rainbow*], pp. 96-97, from "A Literary Letter," SPHERE, LXIII (23 Oct 1915), 104; H. M. Swanwick, [*The Rainbow*], pp. 98-99, from "Mr. Lawrence's Novel," MANCHESTER GUARDIAN, 28 Oct 1915, p. 5; Catherine Carswell, [*The Rainbow*], pp. 100-1, from GLASGOW HERALD, 4 Nov 1915, p. 4; [News Article on Prosecution of *The Rainbow*], pp. 102-3, from "*The Rainbow*. Destruction of a Novel Ordered," TIMES (Lond), 15 Nov 1915, p. 3; J. C. Squire, [Discussion of the suppression of *The Rainbow*], pp. 104-7, from Solomon Eagle [pseud of J. C. Squire],"Books in General," NEW STATESMAN, VI (20 Nov 1915), 161; John Galsworthy, [Letter to J. B. Pinker], pp. 108-9, From THE LIFE AND LETTERS OF JOHN B. GALSWORTHY, ed by H. V. Marrot (NY: Charles Scribner's Sons, 1935), p. 433; Francis Bickley, [*Amores*], pp. 110-12, from "D. H. Lawrence," BOOKMAN (Lond), LI (Oct 1916), 26-27; Edward Garnett, "Art and the Moralists:

Mr. D. H. Lawrence's Work," pp. 113-20, from DIAL, LXI (16 Nov 1916), 377-81; John Gould Fletcher, [*Look! We Have Come Through!*], pp. 121-24, from "A Modern Evangelist," POETRY: A MAGAZINE OF VERSE, XII (Aug 1918), 269-74; Conrad Aiken, [*Look! We Have Come Through!*], pp. 125-31, from "The Melodic Line," DIAL, LXVII (9 Aug 1919), 97-100; Louis Untermeyer, [New Poems], pp. 132-35, from "D. H. Lawrence," NEW REPUBLIC, XXIII (11 Aug 1920), 314-15; Douglas Goldring, extract from "The Later Work of D. H. Lawrence," pp. 136-40, from REPUTATIONS: ESSAYS IN CRITICISM (Lond: Chapman & Hall, 1920), pp. 67-78; Virginia Woolf (unsigned), [*The Lost Girl*], pp. 141-43, from "Postscript or Prelude?" TIMES LITERARY SUPPLEMENT (Lond), 2 Dec 1920, p. 795; Katherine Mansfield, [*The Lost Girl*, Dec 1920], pp. 144-45, from THE SCRAPBOOK OF KATHERINE MANSFIELD, ed by John Middleton Murry (Lond: Constable, 1939), pp. 156-57; Edward Garnett, [*The Lost Girl*], pp. 146-47, from MANCHESTER GUARDIAN, 10 Dec 1920, p. 5; [John Middleton] M[urry], [*The Lost Girl*], pp. 148-50, from "The Decay of Mr. D. H. Lawrence," ATHENAEUM, 17 Dec 1920, p. 836; Francis Hackett, [*The Lost Girl*], pp. 151-54, from "The Surplus Woman," NEW REPUBLIC, XXVI (16 March 1921), 77-78; Abel Chevalley, [On Lawrence], pp. 155-56, from LE ROMAN ANGLAIS DE NOTRE TEMPS (Oxford: Oxford UP, 1921), pp. 229-32, pub as THE MODERN ENGLISH NOVEL, trans by Ben Ray Redman (NY: Knopf, 1925), pp. 236-38; John Macy, [*Women in Love* and *The Lost Girl*], pp. 157-60, from "The Art of D. H. Lawrence," NEW YORK EVENING POST LITERARY REVIEW, 19 March 1921, pp. 3-4; Evelyn Scott, [*Women in Love* and *The Lost Girl*], pp. 161-64, from "A Philosopher of the Erotic," DIAL, LXX (April 1921), 460; [*Women in Love*], pp. 165-67, from SATURDAY WESTMINSTER GAZETTE, LVIII (2 July 1921), 14-15; J[ohn] M[iddleton] Murry, [*Women in Love*], pp. 168-72, from "The Nostalgia of Mr. D. H. Lawrence," NATION AND THE ATHENAEUM, XXIX (13 Aug 1921), 713-14; Francis Hackett, [*Sea and Sardinia*], pp. 173-76, from "A Week in D. H. Lawrence," NEW REPUBLIC, XXIX (11 Jan 1922), 184; J[ohn] M[iddleton] Murry, [*Aaron's Rod*], pp. 177-80, from "Two Remarkable Novels," NATION AND THE ATHENAEUM, XXXI (12 Aug 1922), 655-56; Edward Shanks, [*Aaron's Rod*], pp. 181-83, from "Fiction," LONDON MERCURY, VI (Oct 1922), 655-57; J[ohn] M[iddleton] Murry, [*Fantasia of the Unconscious*], pp. 184-87, from ALGEMEEN HANDELSBLAD, 31 March 1923, *Derde blad*, p. 9; [*England, My England*], pp. 188-90, from "England, My England," NEW YORK TIMES BOOK REVIEW, 19 Nov 1922, Sect. 3, pp. 13-14; [*The Ladybird* (volume)], pp. 193-94, 191-92, from "Three Stories," TIMES LITERARY SUPPLEMENT (Lond), 22 March 1923, p. 195; Charles Marriott, [*The Ladybird* (volume)], pp. 193-94, from "Life," MANCHESTER GUARDIAN, 6 April 1923, p. 7; [*The Ladybird* (volume)], pp. 195-96, from "*The Ladybird*," SPECTATOR, CXXX, (14 April 1923), 630-31; Edward Shanks, "Mr. D. H. Lawrence: Some Characteristics," pp. 197-207, from LONDON MERCURY, VIII (May 1923), 64-75; Stuart P. Sherman [*Studies in Classic American Literature*], pp. 208-13, from "America is Rediscovered," NEW YORK EVENING POST LITERARY REVIEW, 20 Oct 1923, pp. 143-44; [*Kangaroo*], pp. 214-16, from "A Novel with a Difference," TIMES LITERARY SUPPLEMENT (Lond), 20 Sept 1923, p. 617; Alyse Gregory, [*Kangaroo, Psychoanalysis and the Unconscious, Fantasia of the Unconscious,* and *Studies in Classic American Literature*], pp. 217-23, from "Artist Turns Prophet," DIAL, LXXVI (Jan 1924), 66-72; [*Birds, Beasts and Flowers* and *Love Poems and Others* (reissue)], pp. 224-27, from "Mr. Lawrence's Verse," TIMES LITERARY SUPPLEMENT (Lond), 13 Dec 1923, p. 864; Edwin Muir, [*Birds, Beasts and Flowers*], pp. 228-31, from "Poetry in Becoming," FREEMAN, VIII (2 Jan 1924), 404-5; L. P. Hartley, [*The Boy in the Bush*], pp. 232-34, from "Fiction," SPECTATOR, CXXXIII (13 Sept 1924), 364, 366; John Franklin, [*The Boy in the Bush*], pp. 235-39, from "New Novels," NEW STATESMAN, XXIII (27 Sept 1924), 706; Lloyd Morris, [*The Boy in the Bush*], pp. 240-42, from "Mr. Lawrence and the Frontiers of Civilization," NEW YORK TIMES BOOK REVIEW, 26 Oct 1924, Sect. 3, pp. 9, 17; Edwin Muir, "D. H. Lawrence," pp. 243-49, from NATION (NY), CXX (11 Feb 1925), 148-50, also pub as "Contemporary Writers (II-D. H. Lawrence)," NATION AND THE ATHENAEUM, XXXVII (4 July 1925), 423-27; Stuart P. Sherman, [Review of *St. Mawr*], pp. 250-57, from "Lawrence Cultivates His Beard," NEW YORK HERALD TRIBUNE BOOKS, 14 June 1925, Sect. 5, p. 1; Edward Sackville West, [*Reflections on the Death of a Porcupine and Other Essays* and *David: A Play*], pp. 258-62, from "A Modern Isaiah," NEW STATESMAN, XXVII (10 July 1926), 360-61; Charles Marriott, [*The Plumed Serpent*], pp. 263-64, from "The Quest," MANCHESTER GUARDIAN, 29 Jan 1926, p. 9; L. P. Hartley, [*The Plumed Serpent*], 265-67, from SATURDAY REVIEW (Lond), CXLI (30 Jan 1926), 129-30; Katherine Anne Porter, [*The Plumed Serpent*], pp. 268-71, from "Quetzalcoatl," NEW YORK HERALD TRIBUNE BOOKS, 7 March 1926, Sect. 6, pp. 1, 2; Richard Aldington, "D. H. Lawrence as Poet," pp. 272-74, from SATURDAY REVIEW OF LITERATURE, II (1 May 1926), 749-50; T. S. Eliot, [extract from "The Contemporary Novel" (original English text of "Le Roman Anglais Contemporain")], pp. 275-77, pub in French in LA NOUVELLE REVUE FRANÇAISE, XXVIII (1 May 1927), 669-75; [*Lady Chatterley's Lover*], pp. 278-80, from "Famous Novelist's Shameful Book: A Landmark in Evil," JOHN BULL, XLIV (20 Oct 1928), 11; J[ohn] M[iddleton] Murry, [Review of *Lady Chatterley's Lover*], pp. 281-84, from "The Doctrine of D. H. Lawrence," NEW ADELPHI, II (June-Aug 1929), 367-70; [*Lady Chatterley's Lover*, Authorized Expurgated Edition], pp. 285-86, from "*Lady Chatterley's Lover*," TIMES LITERARY SUPPLEMENT (Lond), 25 Feb 1932, p. 130; V. S. Pritchett, [*Lady Chatterley's Lover*, Authorized Expurgated Edition], pp. 287-88, from "*Lady Chatterley's Lover*," FORTNIGHTLY REVIEW, CXXXI (1 April 1932), 536-37; Henry Hazlitt, [*Lady Chatterley's Lover*, Authorized Expurgated Edition], from "Bowdlerized Lawrence," NATION (NY), CXXXV (7 Sept 1932), 214-15; André Malraux, "Preface" to *L'Amant de Lady Chatterley*, trans by Charles K. Colhoun, pp. 293-97, originally pub as "D. H. Lawrence et l'erotisme. A propos de *l'Amant de Lady Chatterley*" (D. H. Lawrence and Eroticism: A Propos of *Lady Chatterley's Lover*), LA NOUVELLE REVUE FRANÇAISE, XXXVIII (Jan-June 1932), 136-40, and first pub in English translation in CRITERION, XII (Jan 1933), 215-19; W[illiam] B[utler] Yeats, [Comments on *Lady Chatterley's Lover*, 22 and 25 May 1933], p. 298, from THE LETTERS OF W. B. YEATS, ed by Allan Wade (Lond: Rupert Hart-Davis, 1954), p. 810; J. C. Squire, [*The Collected Poems of D. H. Lawrence*], pp. 299-302, from OBSERVER, 7 Oct 1928, p. 6; T. W. Earp, [*The Paintings of D. H. Lawrence*], pp. 306-308, from "Mr. Lawrence on Painting," NEW STATESMAN, XXXIII (17 Aug 1929), 578; [*Pansies*], pp. 309-11, from "Mr. Lawrence's Pansies," TIMES LITERARY SUPPLEMENT (Lond), 4 July 1929, p. 532; Mark Van Doren, [*Pansies*], pp. 312-13 from "For Thoughts," NEW YORK HERALD TRIBUNE BOOKS, 15 Dec 1929, p. 15; [*Pornography and Obscenity*], pp. 314-17, from "Pornography and the Censorship," NEW STATESMAN, XXXIV (23 Nov 1929), 219-20; E. M. Forster, [*Pornography and Obscenity*], pp. 318-21, from "Mr. D. H. Lawrence and Lord Brentford," NATION AND THE ATHENAEUM, XLVI (11 Jan 1930), 508-509; [Obituary], pp. 322-23, from "Mr. D. H. Lawrence: A Writer of Genius," TIMES (Lond), 4 March 1930, p. 11; [Obituary], pp. 324-26, from "Mr. D. H. Lawrence: Novelist and Poet," MANCHESTER GUARDIAN, 4 March 1930, p. 12; [Obituary], pp. 327-29, from "Death of Mr. D. H. Lawrence," GLASGOW HERALD, 4 March 1930, p. 5; J. C. Squire, [Obituary: "the 'precious residuum'"], pp. 330-34, from "D. H. Lawrence," OBSERVER (Lond), 9 March 1930, p. 6; Paul Rosenfeld, [An assessment of Lawrence's work], pp. 335-39, from "D. H. Lawrence," NEW REPUBLIC, LXII (26 March 1930), 155-56; Arnold Bennett, [Obituary: "a tribute of admiration"] pp. 340-42, from "D. H. Lawrence's Delusion," EVENING STANDARD (Lond), 10 April 1930, p. 9; E. M. Forster, [On Lawrence's art and ideas], pp. 343-47, from "D. H. Lawrence," LISTENER, III (30 April 1930), 753-54; Alan Reynolds Thompson, [On Lawrence], pp. 348-58, from "D. H. Lawrence: Apostle of the Dark God," BOOKMAN (NY), LXXIII (July 1931), 492-99; T. S. Eliot, ["The victim and the sacrificial knife"], pp. 359-64, from "Son of Woman," CRITERION, X (July 1931), 768-74; "Bibliography" [not abstracted].

3473 Draper, R[onald] P. "Introduction," D. H. LAWRENCE: THE CRITICAL HERITAGE, ed by R[onald] P. Draper (Lond: Routledge & Kegan Paul; NY: Barnes & Noble, 1970), pp. 1-29.
DHL was a controversial writer who attracted a great amount of commentary during his life. Even the favorable early reviewers of *The White Peacock* were uneasy about his methods and material, but DHL took pains with, and was prepared to defend, the structure of his work from *The White Peacock* on. Some critics, such as Pound and Edward Thomas, saw him as an ally "in the cause of a new kind of expression that should be modern in subject matter and independent of the jaded poetic diction." With the publication of *The Prussian Officer and Other Stories, The Widowing of Mrs. Holroyd,* and *The Rainbow,* critics began to find his work strange and unnatural. Two collections of short fiction, *England, My England and Other Stories* and *The Ladybird,* received some of the most complimentary reviews published in DHL's lifetime, but his theoretical works were "damned." The reviews of *Studies in Classic American Literature* reveal "not only the critical reaction to *Studies,* but the very state of Lawrence's reputation at this time," i.e., that he was "queer," "singular," too subjective, too eccentric. [Draper goes on to highlight and sum up the import of the reviews included in this volume and ends with a discussion of DHL's reputation in other countries and his later critical reputation. He cites F. R. Leavis as becoming DHL's "best advocate and critic."]

3474 Durr, R. A. POETIC VISION AND THE PSYCHEDELIC EX-

PERIENCE (Syracuse, NY: Syracuse UP, 1970), pp. 103-5, 137-38, 160-61, 168-69, 189-91, 225-27, 236-39, 246-49.

Psychedelic experience yields much the same content as the great mystic poets have reported. DHL, "one of the great prophets of the new beginning in our time," maintained that ego dominance is categorically evil and urged entry into the "not me." DHL's entire work "centers upon the distinction between one's true self (the 'Holy Ghost') and the spurious ideas of oneself which constitute the ego."

3475 Eagleton, Terry. EXILES AND ÉMIGRÉS: STUDIES IN MODERN LITERATURE (NY: Schocken Books; Lond: Chatto & Windus, 1970), pp. 9, 14, 18, 139, 191-213, 223.

DHL applied to modern England working-class values assimilated as a child. In *Sons and Lovers* the basis of Morel's human dislocation is the obtrusion into the home of a physically and financially harsh world of work. Paul follows his mother's drive toward a broader, more conscious world, but because of her love, he can neither escape nor re-enter the working class. The insight with which DHL handles working-class family life reveals his own surmounting of barriers that made Paul's movement beyond it tentative and uncertain. Ursula's transcendence in *The Rainbow* represents DHL's judgment in the conflict between individual creative potential and a dehumanizing society. Though Ursula retains a living connection with the society of her youth, she moves toward a fuller society accessible to a more conscious individual. The taut relation between an expanding consciousness and a working environment becomes in *Women in Love* an impassable gap. Lacking the immediacy of *The Rainbow, Women in Love,* in its rarefied relationships and disembodied talk, is too far removed from the society it depicts. Similarly *Lady Chatterley's Lover* fails because DHL is out of touch with the palpable realities of his own society. DHL's refusal to find cheap ways out of the impasse of modern society depicted in his revolutionary analysis of it affected the quality of his art but helped him to realize a deeper understanding of that society than most other writers.

3476 Eichrodt, John M. "Doctrine and Dogma in *Sons and Lovers*," CONNECTICUT REVIEW, IV (Oct 1970), 18-32.

DHL's central concern in *Sons and Lovers* is not the sexual disorientation of "Edwardian lads with dominating mothers" but the religious dislocation caused by the clash "between the old religions and modern thought." The novel is a religious parable, "although Lawrence used...sexual or amatory situation and terminology to make effective his essentially religious concerns."

3477 "Exciting, Glorious Man," SAN FRANCISCO CHRONICLE, 1 Aug 1970, p. 14.

[Interview with Dorothy Brett in which she says that DHL, "an exciting, wonderful person," would have hated the idea of the Taos "festival" in his honor, planned for 30 Sept-4 Oct 1970. See also related story, "D. H. Lawrence: Man of the Century," SAN FRANCISCO CHRONICLE, 1 Aug 1970, p. 14.]

3478 Fabrizio, Ray, Edith Karas, and Ruth Menmuir. INSTRUC-

TOR'S MANUAL FOR "THE RHETORIC OF NO" (NY: Holt, Rinehart & Winston, 1970); 2nd ed., (1974), pp. 20-21, 30.
"Sex Versus Loveliness" "may seem tame" in its discussion of sex in comparison to contemporary explicit descriptions, but DHL's "concept of sex as necessary for beauty, and therefore joy, is an engaging one," which "can be more thoroughly understood by reading his novels." In the "Benjamin Franklin" essay, "as in most of his critical studies, Lawrence's own spirit of rebellion colored his view of his subject." ["Suggestions for Writing" are given for both essays.]

3479 Fabrizio, Ray, Edith Karas, and Ruth Menmuir. THE RHETORIC OF NO (NY: Holt, Rinehart & Winston, 1970), 2nd ed. (1974), pp. 267, 272, 371, 380.
[Introducing "Sex Versus Loveliness" and "Benjamin Franklin," which are reprinted in the anthology, pp. 267-71 and 371-79, respectively, brief headnotes mention criticism of DHL's "nonconformist" nature, for "his unconventional private life as well as for his frank treatment of love and sex in his novels." Both essays are followed by questions "For Discussion."]

3480 Farber, Stephen. *"Women in Love,"* HUDSON REVIEW, XXIII (Summer 1970), 321-26.
"What makes *Women in Love* great is exactly what makes it untranslatable," even into film. The film version, directed by Ken Russell, produced and written for the screen by Larry Kramer, is faithful to the complexity of the novel, but it "would be bewildering to anyone who did not know the book." Only someone who shared DHL's peculiar, sensual mysticism could give immediacy to the film, but Russell and Kramer admire from a distance. The question remains, "What is the purpose of the film?"

3481 Farmer, David. "The Bibliographical Potential of a 20th Century Literary Agent's Archive: The Pinker Papers," LIBRARY CHRONICLE OF THE UNIVERSITY OF TEXAS AT AUSTIN, ns No. 2 (Nov 1970), 27-35.
[Brief mention of DHL with reference to his agent, J. B. Pinker.] The Pinker archive at the University of Texas at Austin contains over 4,000 items of J. B. Pinker's correspondence with DHL, John Galsworthy, H. G. Wells, Arnold Bennett, Aldous Huxley, Robert Graves, George Moore, and others.

3482 Farmer, David Robb. "A Descriptive and Analytical Catalogue of the D. H. Lawrence Collection at the University of Texas at Austin," DISSERTATION ABSTRACTS INTERNATIONAL, XXXI (1971), 6053A. Unpublished dissertation, University of Texas at Austin, 1970.

3483 Farmer, David. "An Unpublished Version of D. H. Lawrence's Introduction to *Pansies,*" REVIEW OF ENGLISH STUDIES, XXI (May 1970), 181-84.
[A brief publication history of *Pansies* together with the entire early version of the introduction for the unexpurgated version taken from the holograph notebook for *Pansies.*]

3484 Farr, Judith. "Introduction," TWENTIETH CENTURY INTERPRETATIONS OF "SONS AND LOVERS": A COLLECTION OF CRITICAL ESSAYS, ed by Judith Farr (Englewood Cliffs, NJ: Prentice-Hall, 1970), pp. 1-23.
[Includes a brief sketch of DHL's life and the biographical material in *Sons and Lovers*, a summary of contemporary and subsequent critical responses to it, a brief discussion of basic themes, including a comparison between Paul and Byron's Childe Harold, comments on the relevance of industrialism and the role of women to the novel, and a discussion of language and mythic associations.]

3485 Farr, Judith (ed). TWENTIETH CENTURY INTERPRETATIONS OF "SONS AND LOVERS": A COLLECTION OF CRITICAL ESSAYS (Englewood Cliffs, NJ: Prentice-Hall, Inc., 1970).
Criticism and reviews are organized under two categories, "Interpretations" and "View Points," followed by an appendix, chronology, and notes. Contents, abstracted under year of first publication: Judith Farr, "Introduction," pp. 1-23; **Part I: Interpretations:** Virginia Woolf, "Notes on D. H. Lawrence," pp. 24-47, from THE MOMENT AND OTHER ESSAYS (Lond: Hogarth P, 1947), pp. 79-82, (NY: Harcourt, Brace, 1948), pp. 93-98; Daniel A. Weiss, "The Mother in the Mind," pp. 28-41, from OEDIPUS IN NOTTINGHAM: D. H. LAWRENCE (Seattle: University of Washington P, 1962), pp. 39-68; Keith Sagar, "*Sons and Lovers*," pp. 42-50, from THE ART OF D. H. LAWRENCE (Cambridge: Cambridge UP, 1966), pp. 21-35; Mark Spilka, "Counterfeit Loves," pp. 51-63, from THE LOVE ETHIC OF D. H. LAWRENCE (Bloomington: Indiana UP, 1955; Lond: Dennis Dobson, 1965), pp. 60-89; George H. Ford, "The 'S' Curve: Persephone to Pluto," pp. 64-73, from DOUBLE MEASURE: A STUDY OF THE NOVELS AND STORIES OF D. H. LAWRENCE (NY: Holt, Rinehart, 1965), pp. 28-44; Alfred Kazin, "Sons, Lovers, and Mothers," pp. 74-84, from "Introduction" to *Sons and Lovers* (NY: Random House, 1962), pp. vii-xix; **Part II: View Points:** DHL [Selections from letters, including four to Louie Burrows, six to Edward Garnett, among them the "Foreword to *Sons and Lovers*," three to A. W. McLeod, and one each to Helen Corke and Barbara Low], pp. 85-94 [not abstracted]; Frieda Lawrence, [Extracts from four letters to Edward Garnett], pp. 94-95, from FRIEDA LAWRENCE: THE MEMOIRS AND CORRESPONDENCE, ed by E. W. Tedlock, Jr. (Lond: William Heinemann, 1961; NY: Knopf, 1964), pp. 185, 196, 202; Edward Garnett [On *Sons and Lovers*], p. 95, from FRIDAY NIGHTS (NY: Knopf, 1922), pp. 154-55; Wyndham Lewis, [DHL's basic principles], pp. 95-96, from PALEFACE: THE PHILOSOPHY OF THE "MELTING POT" (Lond: Chatto & Windus, 1929), pp. 280-81; Ernest Selliere, [Walter Morel], p. 96, from DAVID-HERBERT LAWRENCE ET LES RÉCENTES IDÉOLOGIES ALLEMANDES (Paris: Boivin et Cie, 1936), pp. 176-78 (editor's trans); Karl Menninger, [Mother fixation in *Sons and Lovers*], p. 97, from LOVE AGAINST HATE (NY: Harcourt, Brace, 1942), p. 57; Mark Schorer, [DHL's personal involvement in *Sons and Lovers*], pp. 97-99, from "Technique as Discovery," HUDSON REVIEW, I (Spring 1948), 75-78; Father William Tiverton [pseud of Martin Jarrett-Kerr], [The conclusion of *Sons and Lovers*], pp. 99-101, from D. H. LAWRENCE AND HUMAN EXISTENCE (Lond: Rockliff, 1951; rptd: Lond: SCM P, 1961), pp. 47-49; Frank O'Connor [pseud

of Michael O'Donovan], [The relevance of DHL's background], pp. 101-5, from THE MIRROR IN THE ROADWAY (NY: Knopf, 1956), pp. 270-78; Kingsley Widmer, [The conclusion of *Sons and Lovers*], p. 105, from THE ART OF PERVERSITY: D. H. LAWRENCE'S SHORTER FICTIONS (Seattle: University of Washington P, 1962), pp. 225-26; Appendix: Selections from the May Chambers Holbrook Papers," pp. 106-15, from D. H. LAWRENCE: A COMPOSITE BIOGRAPHY, Vol. III, ed by Edward Nehls (Madison: University of Wisconsin P, 1959), pp. 554, 557-58, 558-59, 567-68, 570, 573-74, 578, 583-84, 593-96, 618-19, 620; **Chronology of Important Dates**, pp. 116-17 [not abstracted]; **Notes on the Editor and Contributors**, pp. 118-19 [not abstracted].

3486 Findlater, Richard. COMIC CUTS: A BEDSIDE SAMPLER OF CENSORSHIP IN ACTION. With drawings by William Rushton (Lond: Andre Deutsch, 1970), pp. 7, 15, 37-38, 63, 94-109.
[Quotes various passages from DHL's works which censors found offensive: a passage cut from the first edition of *The White Peacock* and the inoffensive paragraph which DHL was required to write to replace it; several passages in *The Rainbow* which resulted in its suppression; fourteen poems cut from the first edition of *Pansies* after the MS was seized in the mail. Also quotes Lord Chamberlain's instructions that there be no bed onstage and that Connie and Mellors be properly clothed in a 1961 stage version of *Lady Chatterley's Lover*.]

3487 Ford, George. "*Women in Love*," TIMES LITERARY SUPPLEMENT (Lond), 12 Feb 1970, p. 169.
[Letter to the editor in reply to Anthony Comerford's letter to the editor, "*Women in Love*," TIMES LITERARY SUPPLEMENT (Lond), 11 Dec 1969, p. 1426.] DHL's incorporation of a quotation from the Kaiser fixes neither the chronological setting nor the composition dates of *Women in Love*.

3488 Foster, Joseph. "What was it like...to know Lawrence?" TAOS ARTS 1970, A Special Report in TAOS NEWS (Taos, NM), 3 Sept 1970, pp. 4-5.
A man of integrity, contemplation, and profound wisdom, DHL illumined life for others, penetrating their depths but destroying mediocrity. [Brief reminiscence of DHL in Taos.]

3489 "400 attend D. H. Lawrence festival," TAOS NEWS (Taos, NM), 8 Oct 1970, pp. 1, 2.
At the DHL festival in Taos (30 Sept-4 Oct 1970), DHL's pictures and other Laurentiana were exhibited and panel discussions were presented by old friends, poets, novelists, and scholars. [See also related stories, "Scholars honor D. H. Lawrence here," TAOS NEWS (Taos, NM), 1 Oct 1970, pp. 1-2; and "Reception Honors D. H. Lawrence Festival Panelists as Exhibition Opens," TAOS NEWS (Taos, NM), 8 Oct 1970, pp. 8-9.]

3490 Fraisse, Anne-Marie. RÉFLEXIONS ET DIRECTIVES POUR L'ÉTUDE DE D. H. LAWRENCE: "WOMEN IN LOVE" (Thoughts and Directives for the Study of D. H. Lawrence: *Women in Love*)

(Paris: Minard [Carnets des Lettres Modernes], 1970).
[Intended for the use of students, this guide through the various problems confronting the reader of *Women in Love* deals with two main subjects: the universe of the novel and the characters presented, and symbolic representation in the novel. Also includes Françoise-Marie Barbier and Simone Rozenberg, "Lawrence/Freud," pp. 106-18 (abstracted separately).] [In French.]

3491 Francis, Miller, Jr. "*Women in Love*," GREAT SPECKLED BIRD (Atlanta), 25 May 1970, p. 21.

Relating "crucially to change in our world," "the film of *Women in Love* appears to have avoided the mistakes D. H. Lawrence made when he was trying to come to grips with the Sexism and Male Supremacy of Western culture." [Brief discussion of the film with regard to its relevance to contemporary social issues.]

3492 Fraser, Grace Lovat. IN THE DAYS OF MY YOUTH (Lond: Cassell, 1970), pp. 133-52.

[Memoir of the friendship between DHL and the author, then Grace Crawford, in 1909-1911, when DHL was teaching in Croydon and moving into the literary world of London. Coming to tea at the author's home with Ezra Pound, DHL "projected a feeling of cool detachment rather than of shyness." "He had something which Ezra lacked: a sense of humour." The three discussed modern poetry, especially Francis Thompson, and Italian poetry. "The friendship between [DHL] and Ezra always seemed to me an odd and uneasy one for they were so wildly dissimilar." Eleven of DHL's letters to her are quoted in full, as is a poem, "Song," sent in a Christmas card. DHL read and commented on Gerhart Hauptmann's ELGA, Aleister Crowley's verse, AMBERGRIS, and other works. He also wrote to her about his parents, brothers, and sisters, and sent her the manuscript of *A Collier's Friday Night* to read.]

3493 Friedman, Alan. "The Other Lawrence," PARTISAN REVIEW, XXXVII (Spring 1970), 239-53.

Despite previously held critical views, DHL, on subsequent readings, rises above technical shortcomings many perceive when forcing a traditional assessment. DHL adds to the expected subject matter of the English novel (morals, manners, money, marriages) the new subject of mysticism. Together with Henry James and James Joyce, DHL probes the deeper aspects of the self, enlarging reality in fiction. It was DHL who searched in symbolic action and language for the generic form to yield the sources of energy that were later expressed in the stream of consciousness technique. Drawing parallels between DHL and Freud is misleading, for DHL perceived the psyche in his characters as an extra-human dimension that he presents through the physical. Trying to illuminate this dark complication through words became DHL's challenge. Unlike Joyce, he does not distort conventional verbalization but exaggerates emotional signals through physical sensation. If the reader can realize that the locale of the scenes frequently shifts to the under-conscious, he will see that DHL's artistry transcends previous expectations of the novel. The deliberate harshness of many contemporary novelists is an attempt, influenced by DHL, at a nakedness that confronts the reader with revelation.

3494 Fu, Shaw-shien. "Death in Lawrence's *Last Poems*: A Study of Theme in Relation to Imagery," TAMKANG REVIEW (Taiwan), I (April 1970), 79-91.

DHL's central image in "The Ship of Death" begets the theme of the poem and the surrounding images. The apples refer to the "sorb-apples" of *Birds, Beasts and Flowers,* and thus to decay and "hellish experience." "Phoenix" emphasizes DHL's belief in rebirth. "Bavarian Gentians" continues the theme of "Medlars and Sorb-Apples" but emphasizes the "intoxication of darkness" and, like "The Ship of Death," is an expansion on a single image. While many DHL poems use imagery for "decoration or illumination," in *Last Poems,* his best volume, imagery creates his themes.

3495 Fujiwara, Masuko. "D. H. Lawrence to T. Hardy (I)" (D. H. Lawrence and T. Hardy [I]), KATAHIRA (Chuba Katahira), No. 7 (June 1970), 193-220.

[In this first of two articles, the writer observes that Hardy and DHL seem to have some kinship in their literary sensibilities and taste, traces Hardy's influence on DHL during the period of his literary apprenticeship, and reviews critics' estimates of DHL's early writings in connection with Hardy. See also Masuko Fujiwara, "Egdon to Nethermere" (Egdon and Nethermere), D. H. LAWRENCE STUDIES (The D. H. Lawrence Studies Circle, Kyoto), No. 1 (April 1973), 145-91.] [In Japanese.]

3496 Gajdusek, Robert E. "A Reading of 'A Poem of Friendship,' a Chapter in Lawrence's *The White Peacock*," D. H. LAWRENCE REVIEW, III (Spring 1970), 47-62.

DHL's first novel, *The White Peacock,* "studies the dynamics of creativity. . .and challenges the Christian vision with pagan alternatives"; it establishes "mechanics of creativity for the artist that are. . .indistinguishable from those of his Nature gods." "A Poem of Friendship" is "a great creation myth"; the chapter confronts the question of "how to effect conception where the order of nature has been violated and the maternal principle is lacking." In answer, it affirms "cyclical nature," in which new life emerges from death and in which the synthesis of heaven and earth, of spirit and flesh, is fundamental. Thus, "George moves from his role as a man to the assumption of his role as fertility God presiding over this necessary synthesis"; he is "both Christ and Nature God, setting in motion the cyclical action that his life and death illustrate." As Charon, he is the "symbol of the mediator between the actual and the ideal," the "prototypical artist," as well as the dying and resurrecting god. Cyril, the artist figure whose powers are inadequate, "needs synthesis with George before creativity is truly possible for him." In his mythic union with George, Cyril "participates in nature's cycles;. . .as George's lover-child in the drying episode, he submits and bows to serve the will of the God-father-lover."

3497 Garcia, Reloy, and James Karabatsos (eds). A CONCORDANCE TO THE POETRY OF D. H. LAWRENCE (Lincoln: University of Nebraska P, 1970).

[This computer-generated concordance, keyed to *The Complete Poems of D. H.*

Lawrence, ed by Vivian de Sola Pinto and F. Warren Roberts (NY: Viking P, 1964), is divided into three parts: a word index, nine appendices classifying predominant interests in DHL's poetry, and a page-line index.]

3498 Garcia, Reloy. "The Quest for Paradise in the Novels of D. H. Lawrence," D. H. LAWRENCE REVIEW, III (Summer 1970), 93-114.

The "conflict between the woods and the city," the "central organizing metaphors" in DHL's novels, encompasses a second conflict between the regionalist and the prophet whose chief concern lay not in nature but in the city. Thus, the "one constant" in DHL's search for "sanctuary" in the modern world is "the search itself." There are four stages in DHL's "quest for paradise." The first four novels present "the Midlands as paradise and the encroaching industrial world" as hell. But with the ending of *The Rainbow,* DHL breaks the tie to the Midlands and emerges as "the prophet, whose central concern is man rather than nature." This second stage, also including *Women in Love, The Lost Girl,* and *Aaron's Rod,* "is typified by repeated displacements to the Continent." In the third stage, *Kangaroo* and *The Plumed Serpent* are "versions of the entrance into paradise motif." In the fourth stage, "the quest is internalized" in *Lady Chatterley's Lover.* After *The Rainbow,* DHL is "less concerned with space, natural harmony, and objectivity, than with time and confinement, personal conflict, and the working out of a purely subjective vision of the world." In *Kangaroo* and *The Plumed Serpent,* the single setting constitutes both heaven and hell, a paradise having "the *same* objective as the industrial hell" of earlier novels—"to break the hero's organic chain of being." The "burden of rebirth" is therefore placed on the protagonists, driving their visions inward. In *Lady Chatterley's Lover,* "the heaven-hell struggle is not the conflict itself" but the manner in which the characters transcend it. In this "story of personal regeneration amid social and natural decay," the Lawrentian protagonists transcend "environments and conflicts," and posit "permanent values only in the relations of select and vital human beings."

3499 Gatti, Hilary. "D. H. Lawrence and the Idea of Education," ENGLISH MISCELLANY (Rome), XXI (1970), 209-31.

In an age of educational reform and optimism, DHL was pessimistic about the state of public education in England. In his most extended statement on the subject, the essay "Education of the People," he castigates the falsity of a reformed educational system which sheltered children for a few years, in the atmosphere of pure ideals, from the realities of a materialistic society, only to eject those children into such a society at a certain arbitrary moment. For DHL the greatest mistake of modern education was the excessive attention given to the deepest layers of childish consciousness. These layers, the child's flame of life, should be left alone, and the young person's uniqueness should be nurtured by the teaching of true separateness rather than the illusory kind of togetherness that DHL always despised in modern society. DHL did not, however, conceive of the child as a spiritual innocent, but believed that the child's greatest merit was its capacity to grow into adulthood. DHL's main preoccupation with education was defining what it is possible to teach. His example of how he thought actual teaching should be done is in the "Classroom" chapter of *Women in Love*. In "Education of the People," he outlines a scheme for education which takes its guiding force from a kind of pre-Raphaelite anti-industrialism.

3500 Geduld, Harry M. "Lawrence, Sex, and Celluloid," HUMANIST, XXX (March-April 1970), 31.

The "cold bath" of rereading *Women in Love* provides "the shock of discovering from a novel published in 1921 the shortcomings of the cinema's treatment of sex nearly 50 years later" in the film version. DHL, who recognized "animalism" "as the suppressed 'element' in most modern...'rationalizations' of sex," would have understood "much screen sex" as "pornography...providing mental masturbation through narcissistic fantasies." "The film version of *Women in Love* conveys comparatively little of Lawrence's sexual credo," but "if it encourages humanists to go on and sample the novel," it will have "justified itself."

3501 Gerard, Lillian N. "Of Lawrence and Love," FILM LIBRARY QUARTERLY, III (Fall 1970), 6-12.

Despite the thematic complexities of *Women in Love,* film director Ken Russell has translated DHL's characters into cinematic realities, visualizing them in all their "naked philosophical ambivalence."

3502 Gerard, Lillian N. "*The Virgin and the Gypsy* and D. H. LAWRENCE IN TAOS, " FILM LIBRARY QUARTERLY, IV (Winter 1970-1971), 36-42.

In many ways DHL's book is superior to the film of *The Virgin and the Gypsy,* directed by Christopher Miles from the screenplay by Alan Plater, for several false notes are struck and the ending seems abrupt. The characters, however, are impeccable. D. H. LAWRENCE IN TAOS, a forty-minute documentary film made for BBC by Peter Davis, centers on the three women who cared for DHL--Frieda Lawrence, Mabel Dodge Luhan, and Dorothy Brett. Despite its home movie qualities, the film is of interest to those who are fascinated by DHL.

3503 Gibbs, Jean. "Dorothy Livesay and the Transcendentalist Tradition," HUMANITIES ASSOCIATION BULLETIN (Canada), XXI (Spring 1970), 24-39.

The tension between Laurentian sexual explicitness and narcissism and Thoreauvian asexual oneness with nature produces the unifying principle underlying Dorothy Livesay's poetry.

3504 Gibson, Jeremy. "*Women in Love*," OCTOPUS (Ottawa), III (19 June 1970), 15.

The film version of *Women in Love*, though sometimes "gimmicky," captures DHL's ideas but is lacking in characterization and passion.

3505 Gilliatt, Penelope. "This England, This Past," NEW YORKER, XLVI (4 July 1970), 71; rptd in FILM 70/71: AN ANTHOLOGY BY THE NATIONAL SOCIETY OF FILM CRITICS, ed by David Denby (NY: Simon & Schuster, 1971), pp. 217-20.

Director Christopher Miles's film *The Virgin and the Gypsy*, adapted by Alan Plater from DHL's novella, opens with Sunday rituals of church and dinner that allegorically embody "bourgeois England between the wars." Granny (Fay Compton) is a "less gross figure than the prognathous monster in the book." Yvette (Joanna Shimkus) is a Sleeping Beauty, and the Gypsy (Franco Nero) a melodramatic yet commanding presence. The film is highly intelligent in its truthfulness to DHL's strength and its sure grasp on his love of England and his hatred of her rituals.

3506 Glicksberg, Charles I. MODERN LITERARY PERSPECTIVISM (Dallas: Southern Methodist UP, 1970), pp. 21, 27, 42-43, 46-48, 118-24, 130-48, 191.

DHL opposed vehemently the intellectualization of life and art in the twentieth century. Because he felt they were hostile to poetic and religious vision, DHL rejected Freudian psychology and scientific materialism. He held that "instead of being dominated by the cult of rational efficiency and scientific coordination, man must rely on his intuitions"; in so doing, DHL was not "refuting the theories of science" but rather "asserting the autonomy of the creative imagination." Hence DHL's interest in myth, "archetypal symbols that are precognitive," and his " 'belief in the blood, the flesh, as being wiser than the intellect.' " DHL saw in myth an avenue whereby modern man could overcome the kind of overdeveloped consciousness which destroys spontaneity. However, DHL suffered from a "conflict between untrammeled individuality and the need to be part of some transcendent social purpose," for he strove on the one hand to protect "the sacredness of his individuality," while on the other hand "he detested modern man because he personalized everything in the universe."

3507 Goldknopf, David. "Realism in the Novel," YALE REVIEW, LX (Autumn 1970), 69-84.

Examples from *Women in Love* reflect both the visionary and realistic tendencies of the often misinterpreted DHL. As "idiosyncratic" a writer as DHL seems, he "was able to respect the fundamental process of realism: the process that begins with the acceptance, in its full, brute embrace, of an existential and communal world."

3508 Goode, John. "D. H. Lawrence," in THE TWENTIETH CENTURY, ed by Bernard Bergonzi (Lond: Barrie & Jenkins, Sphere Books, 1970), pp. 106-52.

DHL deplored "the kind of didacticism...which tries to impose a moral order on experience," but saw his fiction as a vehicle for social change in that it "tries above all to *depose* order and discover instead the meaning for the individual in the flux of life itself." DHL therefore seeks no answers which transcend historical change. In the first period of his career (up to 1912), DHL's work is characterized by "a pervasive and complex rhythm...between a powerful need for human relationship and an intense dynamic of self-realization." During these years, DHL perceived his role as that of an affirmer in the aftermath of "the total negation of bourgeois morality by Flaubert and Hardy." DHL's second period (1913-1919) brought "the definitive declaration of war" between him and the middle-class public. The two great novels of this period, *The Rainbow* and *Women in Love*, are concerned with "the modes of consciousness. . .realized in the sexual realtionships which exist within" "a dying society." In his final phase (1919-1930), DHL continued his battle with the world "whose institutions and culture drove him into exile." His writing during this period is disappointing because he was unable to find a satisfactory progression for his basic theme: affirmation of life independent of social institutions. The "key text" of this period is *Aaron's Rod*, in which self-sufficiency is shown to be inadequate by itself since "the emancipated self needs to discover real contact and real community." It is not until DHL returns, in *Lady Chatterley's Lover*, to "his most central concern, the changing consciousness of those who inhabit an industrial society, that we get a real sense of what he was trying to make articulate."

3509 Gosliner, Kathy. "And what about the ranch, the little ranch in New Mexico. The time is different there," TAOS NEWS, 21 May 1970, "D. H. Lawrence" section, p. 1.
[Journalistic feature giving an account of DHL's and Frieda's coming, at the invitation of Mabel Dodge Luhan, to Taos, which became for DHL "a spiritual home"; their move to Del Monte ranch to escape Mabel and to gain the solitude DHL needed for writing; DHL's wish to establish Rananim, which led to Dorothy Brett's accompanying the Lawrences back after their visit to England; the deterioration of DHL's health in Mexico, their return to the ranch for a time before their departure for Europe in 1925; and the cremation of DHL's body and interment on the ranch in 1935. (The date of DHL's death is given erroneously as 2 March 1935.) Illustrated with a drawing of DHL.]

3510 Hamilton, Jack, and Dan McCoy. "*Women in Love*," LOOK MAGAZINE, XXXIV (24 Feb 1970), 32-37.
The film of *Women in Love* by director Ken Russell and producer-screenplay writer Larry Kramer, destined to become a motion picture classic, distills DHL's favorite theme: "lust vs. love on the sexual battleground, and the need for freedom to love more than one person, to satisfy all one's needs, without guilt or mental breakdown." [Illustrated with color stills from the film.]

3511 Heuzenroeder, John. "D. H. Lawrence's Australia," AUSTRALIAN LITERARY STUDIES, IV (Oct 1970), 319-33.
Hurriedly written and printed from the first draft, *Kangaroo* is unintegrated thematically. Richard Lovat and Harriet Somers's views of Australia and its people fluctuate with little apparent reason, though Harriet's common sense rescues the novel from the excesses of "mystico-political speculation." DHL saw Australia as a possible center for world-wide spiritual regeneration, a possibility probably precluded by Australian carelessness and recklessness. Like Kingsley and Trollope, DHL felt Australia needed the European "hierarchical social structure to maintain power" and order.

3512 Hinz, Evelyn J. "Juno and *The White Peacock*: Lawrence's English Epic," D. H. LAWRENCE REVIEW, III (Summer 1970), 115-35.

A detailed study of the literary dimensions of *The White Peacock* reveals that, externally, the novel has three major parts, with each part divided into nine chapters. "Supporting the tri-partite external structure...are three types of geographic and temporal dimensions--the mythological, the historical, and the personal or topical," each operating continuously "as well as being the focal concern in one of the three parts." DHL's use of the triple pattern thus gives the work its unique form and expresses its central themes; it reflects a movement from the general to the specific, from the past to the present, and from the natural world to the interior world of personal problems. The persistence of the literary allusions suggests that they are "intended to support the tri-partite structure rather than to pad the story." With Lettie as Juno, *The White Peacock* is DHL's "British epic, with England as Troy." "In theme and tone," the novel "is both national and elegiac,...yet mythic and hopeful." The "mythological allusions establish the heroic lineaments of the characters, historical allusions nationalize them, while the contemporary quotations expose the chinks in their armour."

3513 Hirth, Mary. "Cyril Connolly Exampled: An Exhibit on 'The Modern Movement,'" LIBRARY CHRONICLE OF THE UNIVERSITY OF TEXAS AT AUSTIN, ns, No. 1 (March 1970), 39-47.

DHL was selected for exhibit because of the extensive holdings in manuscripts, proof copies, inscribed first editions, and related material. Of most interest are the items relating to *Lady Chatterley's Lover*, especially the three complete manuscript versions, accompanied by one of the extremely rare blue paper copies. Other materials relate to *Sons and Lovers* and to *Sea and Sardinia*.

3514 Hochman, Baruch [Baruj Hojman]. ANOTHER EGO: THE CHANGING VIEW OF SELF AND SOCIETY IN THE WORK OF D. H. LAWRENCE (Columbia: University of South Carolina P, 1970).

There is a pervasive tension between self and society in the works of DHL. Throughout his life, he sought ways to allay such tension, even to conceive of "another ego" which would be different from the conventional "social and moral ego of character" and which could exist in harmony both with the natural world and with civilization. DHL felt that the West was destructive and deathly, yet he held a hopeful countervision of salvation. That hopeful vision evolves through stages, beginning with an emphasis in the early works on radical individualism and ending with communalism. In the first phase of DHL's work, through *Women in Love*, characters like Birkin and Ursula struggle to separate themselves from their morally and socially conventional backgrounds in a quest for autonomous and spontaneous selves which transcend the dualisms of flesh and spirit, impulse and duty. The "natural self," discovered through sexual love, stands at odds with society. Yet the antagonism between self and society is not necessary or inherent: it is only *conventional* society that is the enemy of the natural self. In the second phase of his work, DHL explores the possible social orders which might nourish, rather than repress, the spontaneous, autonomous being. In works like *Aaron's Rod, Kangaroo,* and *The Plumed Serpent*, DHL is searching for a continuity among the impulsive, passionate life of the body, the life of the human community, and the vital energies of nature and the cosmos. In this phase, DHL no longer regards deep sexual love as the only medium to being but is now concerned with fulfillment of societal (political) needs as well as erotic ones. Late works like *Apocalypse* represent DHL's effort to lead consciousness and selfhood out of the pattern of history and back to the potent, living cosmos as the matrix for individual being.

3515 Horwath, William Frank. "The Ache of Modernism: Thomas Hardy, Time and the Modern Novel," DISSERTATION ABSTRACTS INTERNATIONAL, XXXI (1970), 4164A. Unpublished dissertation, University of Michigan, 1970.
[Includes discussion of DHL.]

3516 Huxley, Julian. MEMORIES (Lond: George Allen & Unwin; NY: Harper & Row, 1970), p. 160.
[Taking the spacious chalet Les Arolles at Diablerets for the winter of 1927, Julian Huxley was visited there by Aldous and Maria Huxley, soon joined by DHL and Frieda. Maria typed the MS of *Lady Chatterley's Lover*. DHL's outbursts of "impotent rage" whenever they talked about "scientific matters" were especially directed at Julian. Discussions of "the possibility of mankind's genetic improvement" particularly infuriated DHL, "who believed that more power exercised by 'the dark loins of man', greater freedom for our instincts and intuitions, would solve the world's troubles."]

3517 Hyde, G. M. "D. H. Lawrence as Translator," DELOS, IV No. 4 (1970), 146-74.
Although DHL's attitude toward Russian literature was always ambivalent, he found in Leo Shestov an echo of his own conviction that "immortality is in the vividness of life, not in the loss of life." His own ideas were considerably influenced in the process of translating Shestov's *All Things Are Possible*. DHL's translations from the Italian "bulk larger," of course. He was attracted to Giovanni Verga's "peasant realism" and especially to that writer's "art speech," which was "rooted in dialect." DHL's exclusive use of this idiom in his translation of Verga's *Cavalleria Rusticana* makes this collection of stories "more satisfying"than the earlier *Little Novels of Sicily*. There is "not a hint of translatorese," and it seems "marvelously faithful." Unlike Giovanni Cecchetti's translation of the same stories, DHL's has a "feeling for the rhythms of Verga's masterly dialogue." [See also G. M. Hyde, D. H. LAWRENCE AND THE ART OF TRANSLATION (Lond and Basingstoke, England: Macmillan P; Totowa, NJ: Barnes & Noble, 1981).]

3518 Ishibashi, Magoichiro. "Lawrence no Shi 'Hebi' no Hyôgen Style ni Tsuite" (On the Style of "Snake"), JOURNAL OF OSAKA INDUSTRIAL UNIVERSITY, No. 31 (Dec 1970), 1-9.
Because of its originality and vitality, DHL's "Snake" is a masterpiece among twentieth century poems. Its style is influenced by Whitman rather than by the Imagists. [The characteristics of DHL's versification are analyzed.] [In Japanese.]

3519 Iwata, Noboru. "Lawrence no Shôsetsu o Ronjiru tame no Oboegaki" (Preliminary Notes about Lawrence's Fiction), MULBERRY (Aichi Prefectural University), No. 20 (March 1970), 125-39.

This article evaluates the mythopoeic logic--which is not always latent but is subtle and sometimes opposite to the narrative logic--in DHL's fiction. This evaluation is based on the attempt to "save the tale from the artist who created it," as DHL himself advised. [In Japanese.]

3520 Jacobson, Denise. "*Women in Love*," WILLAMETTE BRIDGE (Portland, OR), III (29 May 1970), 22.

The situations in the sometimes eloquent film version of *Women in Love* are difficult to relate to contemporary experience.

3521 James, Stuart B. "Western American Space and the Human Imagination," WESTERN HUMANITIES REVIEW, XXIV (Spring 1970), 147-55.

The setting of *St. Mawr* is a savage country where the supports of civilization and tradition dissipate and are burned away.

3522 Joffe, Phil. "*Women in Love*: The Minor Characters," BOLT (Durban, South Africa), I, No. 3 (1970), 3-8, 45-46.

The minor characters of *Women in Love* are foils to the major quartet, illustrating that, though this civilization will decay, individuals may choose to avoid annihilation. Minette, Halliday, and Loerke, all damned, point up the major opposing symbols of decay: purely sensual understanding (African) and icy, abstract knowledge (Nordic). Sado-masochistic, sensuous, but devoid of emotion, Minette combines both the Nordic and African ways. Halliday's nihilistic world reflects "prephallic primitivism" from both Africa and the abstract Futurists. Loerke is the complete negation of life: intelligent, talented, yet sub-human in his reductive sensuality. Like Birkin he rejects society and its notions of love but, with his cynical view of women, perverts any alternative and goes beyond Gerald in his worship of the mechanical. Only the individual may live in unison with woman; "civilization must die."

3523 Johnsen, William A. "Toward a Redefinition of the Modern: Joyce, Yeats, Eliot, Lawrence." Unpublished dissertation, University of Illinois, 1970. [Listed in Lawrence F. McNamee, DISSERTATIONS IN ENGLISH AND AMERICAN LITERATURE, SUPP. II: 1969-1973 (NY & Lond: Bowker, 1974), p. 253.]

3524 Johnston, Walter Eugene. "Character and Rhetoric in Prose Fiction," DISSERTATION ABSTRACTS INTERNATIONAL, XXXI (1970), 6614A. Unpublished dissertation, Cornell University, 1970. [Includes discussion of Conrad, DHL, and Faulkner.]

3525 Joost, Nicholas, and Alvin Sullivan. D. H. LAWRENCE AND "THE DIAL" (Carbondale and Edwardsville: Southern Illinois UP: Lond and Amsterdam: Feffer & Simons, 1970).

Next to Ford's ENGLISH REVIEW, Thayer's and Watson's THE DIAL first published the greatest number of DHL's works and helped most to establish his audience in America. DHL liked the "coterie atmosphere of the little magazines." Thanks to Pound's and Aldington's help, and the compatibility of interests between himself and Thayer, DHL's fiction, essays, criticism, and poetry were published in THE DIAL. Mabel Dodge Luhan discovered DHL through THE DIAL, and Marianne Moore, editor of the periodical in its last years, admired and published his work. Among the works by DHL appearing first in THE DIAL were "The Fox," "The Woman Who Rode Away," "The Man Who Loved Islands," sections of *Sea and Sardinia*, "Adolf," "Rex," "Pomegranate," "Snake," "Apostolic Beasts," and ten poems from *Pansies*. Frequent reviews of and advertisements for DHL's work were also carried in THE DIAL. [First four chapters, dealing with DHL's coming to THE DIAL and his subsequent dealings with Thayer, Mabel Dodge Luhan, and Marianne Moore, are the most substantial parts of the book.]

3526 Kael, Pauline. "Lust for 'Art,'" NEW YORKER, XLVI (28 March 1970), 97-101; rptd in DEEPER INTO MOVIES, by Pauline Kael (Bost: Little, Brown, Atlantic Monthly Press Book, 1973), pp. 138-42.

Written for the screen and produced by Larry Kramer and directed by Ken Russell, the film of *Women in Love*, "a Gothic sex fantasy on themes" from DHL's novel, is photographed in a style which seems deceptively to be a film equivalent of DHL's purple passages without DHL's "reaching for clarity." Russell's failure to do justice to the novel is particularly unfortunate if it leads the reader who has not read the original to refrain from reading it. Although often faithful to selected portions of DHL's text, particularly the dialogue, the movie fails to supply clues to the motives behind the text, motives always supplied by DHL. Russell's style is overwrought and purposeless and depicts a romantic universe quite at odds with the themes and characters of DHL's novel.

3527 Kai, Sadanobu. "Kyôbô na Junrei no Ato o Otte--Kokyô Eastwood" (After the Savage Pilgrimage--Eastwood), STUDIES IN FOREIGN LITERATURES (Ritsumeikan University), No. 19 (March 1970), 1-20.

DHL once wrote to one of his disciples: " 'Go to Walker St--and stand in front of the third house--and look.... I know that view better than any in the world. That's the country of my heart.'" Visiting Eastwood in 1963, the writer followed that advice faithfully and detected the fact that all of DHL's residences abroad had been taken up on the model of that Walker Street house of his youth. That frank confession of DHL's (" 'When you have run a long way from HOME & MOTHER, then you realize that the earth is round, and if you keep on running you'll be back on the same old door-step. Like a fatality.... A mother: a gorgon. A home: a torture box' ") should be made a key to the secret of "the savage pilgrimage." [In Japanese.]

3528 Kain, R[ichard] M. "*Lady Chatterley's Lover*," TIMES LITERARY SUPPLEMENT (Lond), 8 Jan 1970, 34.

[Letter to the Editor, describing a variant copy of a pirated ed of *Lady Chatterley's Lover* not cited in Warren Roberts, A BIBLIOGRAPHY OF D. H. LAWRENCE (1963).]

3529 Kanfer, Stefan. "Fast Company," TIME, XCVI (13 July 1970), 72.

"To D. H. Lawrence, life was a series of primal contests.... Reason lay on one side, passion on the other, and woe betide the maiden who chose the wrong path." "No story--and no film--better reveals Lawrence's moral absolutism than *The Virgin and the Gypsy*." [Review of the film version, directed by Christopher Miles.]

3530 Kauffmann, Stanley. "*The Virgin and the Gypsy*," NEW REPUBLIC, CLXIII (1 Aug 1970), 24; rptd in FILM 70/71: AN ANTHOLOGY BY THE NATIONAL SOCIETY OF FILM CRITICS, ed by David Denby (NY: Simon & Schuster, 1971), pp. 220-21.

The film version of "*The Virgin and the Gypsy* is fairly faithful to the D. H. Lawrence original and is therefore fairly silly." Made from a posthumous, unrevised novella that "foolishly simplifies" some of DHL's characteristic themes, the film, "directed by Christopher Miles, is a color-me-passionate primer, full of italicized symbols." "In the film Mrs. Fawcett is not Jewish, which omits not only Lawrence's persistent anti-Semitism...but his fascination with her as the outsider."

3531 Kauffmann, Stanley. "*Women in Love*," NEW REPUBLIC, CLXII (18 April 1970), 20.

While some of the "cinematic elements" of director Ken Russell's film version of *Women in Love* are "remarkable," the "least successful" element is Larry Kramer's screenplay, which "sniffs out the 'action' " and minimizes discussion. "The crucial chapter in the book, the conversation [in "Mino"] when Ursula goes alone to Birkin's house for tea, is reduced to a snippet." DHL's inquiry into "the opportunities and burdens of new freedom...depends on its *form*, as a novel," for its vitality.

3532 Kettle, Arnold. "D. H. Lawrence--Some New Letters," MOSAIC, IV, No. 1 (1970), 123-26.

The two hundred new letters printed for the first time in *The Quest for Rananim: D. H. Lawrence's Letters to S. S. Koteliansky, 1914 to 1930,* ed by George J. Zytaruk, add nothing substantial to our understanding of DHL, although he wrote them during the time he was writing some of his most important works. No letters from Koteliansky are included. The collection gives unjustified emphasis to DHL's interest in Rananim.

3533 Kistel, Paul Daniel. "Nature in the Poetry of D. H. Lawrence," DISSERTATION ABSTRACTS INTERNATIONAL, XXXI (1971), 4169A. Unpublished dissertation, University of California at Los Angeles, 1970.

3534 Knight, Arthur. "Liberated Classics," SATURDAY REVIEW

(NY), LIII (21 March 1970), 50-52.
Screenwriter and producer Larry Kramer and director Ken Russell deserve high commendation for translating *Women in Love* into film lovingly, sensitively, and knowingly. The cast is uniformly excellent, and the film succeeds in capturing fully "the sensual immediacy of Lawrence's prose style."

3535 Koga, Masakazu. "Ishmael no Higeki to Syokuzai--'England, My England' o Megutte" (Ishmael's Tragedy and Redemption in "England, My England"), SANDAI REVIEW OF ENGLISH STUDIES (Kyôto Sangyô University), No. 2 (March 1970), 41-54.
In the "Death" of Egbert in "England, My England," we can see the redemption as in the sacrifice of Christianity. [This parallel is considered minutely, referring to other stories from the Bible.] [In Japanese.]

3536 Krishnamurthi, M[atighatta] G[undappa]. D. H. LAWRENCE: TALE AS A MEDIUM (Mysore, India: Rao & Raghavan, 1970).
In approaching the works of DHL, it is more fruitful to experience the work of art than to focus on patterns, motifs, and dichotomies. For this reason, the stories discussed here are quoted extensively and grouped according to theme. Stories dealing with the theme of the danger of reliance upon ideas or the Ideal are "The Princess" and "None of That." Stories concerned with achieving pure relationships with ourselves, others, and the Universe are "England, My England," "Things," and "The Man Who Loved Islands." Love stories which emphasize the "warm flow of common sympathy" between people and the delicacy of sexual relationships are "You Touched Me," *The Fox*, and "The Horse-Dealer's Daughter." Other stories concern the deeper needs and morality of man and present the idea that desire is holy: *The Virgin and the Gipsy* and "The Blue Moccasins." The theme of marriage is explored in "Sun," "The Woman Who Rode Away," "Two Blue Birds," "The Blind Man." Stories concerning mother-child relationships are "The Lovely Lady," "Mother and Daughter," and "The White Stocking."

3537 Kuhn, Helen Weldon. "*Women in Love*," FILMS IN REVIEW, XXI, (April 1970), 241-42.
None of the "literary allusiveness" of *Women in Love*, which "is practically unreadable today save as a literary curiosity," is conveyed in the "cinematization, nor are the psycho-socio maunderings that accompanied Lawrence's tubercular preoccupation with sex." Although Larry Kramer's script and Ken Russell's direction only compound the confusion of the novel, the film "cryptically sets forth Lawrence's notion" that men require close associations with other men in addition to women.

3538 Kuramochi, Saburô. "The Background Description in the Novels of D. H. Lawrence," BULLETIN (Kyôritsu Women's University), No. 16 (May 1970), 1-46.
[Emphasizes the important part the locale (such as forests, lakes, and the sea) plays in DHL's novels and discusses the correlation between those scenes and the thematic development of the novels.]

3539 Kuykendall, Mabel M. "Lawrence the Poet: His Webs Were Spun from His Own Vitals," TAOS NEWS, 21 May 1970, "D. H. Lawrence" section, p. 3.

[Journalistic feature, surveying DHL's published volumes of poetry, culminating in *The Complete Poems of D. H. Lawrence*, edited by Vivian de Sola Pinto and F. Warren Roberts (1964).] Although overshadowed by his prose fiction, DHL's poems, especially those on his parents, on his relationship with Frieda, and on birds, animals, and flowers, are often fine. Many of the poems in *Pansies,* however, are "nonsense."

3540 Kuykendall, Mabel M. "A wealth of literature had its beginning here...," TAOS ARTS 1970, A Special Report in TAOS NEWS (Taos, NM), 3 Sept 1970, pp. 25, 27.

Writers intimately identified with Taos include Dorothy Brett, John Collier, Judson Crews, Marion Estergreen, Max Evans, Blanche C. Grant, Joseph Foster, Spud Johnson, D. H. and Frieda Lawrence, Mabel Dodge Luhan, Frank Waters, and Victor White. [Bibliography included.]

3541 Lainoff, Seymour. "The Wartime Setting of Lawrence's 'Tickets, Please,'" STUDIES IN SHORT FICTION, VII (Fall 1970), 649-51.

Central to "Tickets, Please" is "its essential character as a tale of wartime, acted out on the civilian home front during World War I." The story "contrasts the surface camaraderie and sense of release and adventure promoted during war with the real lawlessness and bleakness underlying these manifestations."

3542 Langbaum, Robert. THE MODERN SPIRIT: ESSAYS ON THE CONTINUITY OF NINETEENTH AND TWENTIETH CENTURY LITERATURE (NY: Oxford UP, 1970), pp. 114-18.

Although DHL's rank as a poet "is still unsettled," he "sets the style for the new nature poetry." "Fish" and the conclusion of "Snake," if too didactic, recognize Ruskin's pathetic fallacy as an operative factor in cognition.

3543 "Language and Literature," CHOICE, VII (June 1970), 544.

Lawrence in Love: Letters to Louie Burrows, ed by James T. Boulton, is of special interest to students of DHL. "Louie is...the prototype of Ursula in *The Rainbow.*"

3544 Laurent, C. "E. M. Forster et D. H. Lawrence" (E. M. Forster and D. H. Lawrence), LES LANGUES MODERNES, LXIV (July-Aug 1970), 281-88.

DHL and Forster were contrasting contemporaries: DHL was a prophet, but he lacked the humor and irony of Forster. Despite their dissimilar social origin and education, their novelistic technique and their inspiration share some common features: both denounce the values of the middle class, particularly those which maim the individual. Preoccupation with sex is at the core of Forster's works-- some critics to the contrary notwithstanding--though less obviously so than in DHL's works. Nature is important to both writers. Despite their differences, DHL and Forster both fought the same hypocrisy with weapons which were less different than they first appeared. [Includes a comparison of HOWARDS END and *Sons and Lovers* as works of moral realism.] [In French.]

3545 "Lawrence and His Publisher," TIMES LITERARY SUPPLEMENT (Lond), 13 Nov 1970, p. 1319.
[Review of *Letters from D. H. Lawrence to Martin Secker, 1911-1930*, ed by M[artin] S[ecker] (1970) and LETTERS FROM A PUBLISHER: MARTIN SECKER TO D. H. LAWRENCE & OTHERS, 1911-1929 (1970).] Although the accord between DHL and Martin Secker was never perfect, theirs was plainly a genuine alliance. DHL reproved Secker for sending a few copies of *The Lost Girl* to American customers, when Thomas Seltzer was planning to bring the book out in New York. He rejected an offer to sell *The Rainbow* to Secker outright for £200. Secker balked at *Lady Chatterley's Lover* in 1928 and omitted a dozen "pansies," despite DHL's injunction not "to make just a bourgeois little book of the *Pansies*." Not a scholarly edition, the volume of DHL letters has few notes and several errors in transcription, though it is beautifully produced. Secker's letters to DHL include his "refusal to tamper with the text of *Women in Love* 'in order to bring it down to the Mudie-Boots level.'"

3546 "Lawrence at the Ranch," TAOS NEWS (Taos, NM), 21 May 1970, Sect. B, p. 5.
DHL at the ranch never rested but worked constantly at writing, milking, riding, chopping wood. [Includes "Lawrence: A Chronology," and "The Unwritten Book," on the abortive collaboration between Mabel Dodge Luhan and DHL.]

3547 "The Lawrence Industry," TIMES LITERARY SUPPLEMENT (Lond), 18 Dec 1970, pp. 1496-98.
D. H. Lawrence: A Selection, ed by R. H. Poole and P. J. Shepherd (1970), "serves no rational purpose," but *The Quest for Rananim: D. H. Lawrence's Letters to S. S. Koteliansky, 1914 to 1930*, ed by George J. Zytaruk (1970), the product of "the steadiest and most uncomplicated" friendship of DHL's life, is "a minor but interesting addition" to his published works. [This review-article, which also considers Émile Delavenay, D. H. LAWRENCE: L'HOMME ET LA GENÈSE DE SON OEUVRE. LES ANNÉES DES FORMATION (1885-1919) (1969), Ileana Čura-Sazdanič, D. H. LAWRENCE AS CRITIC (1969), David Cavitch, D. H. LAWRENCE AND THE NEW WORLD (1969), and James C. Cowan, D. H. LAWRENCE'S AMERICAN JOURNEY: A STUDY IN LITERATURE AND MYTH (1970), suggests that DHL scholarship has become an academic industry. Contains critical commentary on DHL, some of it in rebuttal of views expressed in books under review.]

3548 "Lawrence in New Mexico: There is the pristine; something unbroken...," TAOS NEWS, 21 May 1970, "D. H. Lawrence" section, p. 2.
[Journalistic feature.] DHL hated America's emphasis on power and money, but in New Mexico "he felt apart from the industrialization...which dissipated man's energy and destroyed his initiative." DHL was happiest in the solitude of Kiowa Ranch, and one of his greatest experiences was attending the St. Geronimo dances at Taos Pueblo.

3549 "Lawrence Program Taking Form," TAOS NEWS, 21 May 1970, p. 1.

[News item announcing details of plans for the D. H. Lawrence Festival in Taos (30 Sept-4 Oct 1970).]

3550 "Lawrence the Painter: 'Everything that can possibly be painted has been painted...visual arts are at a dead end,'" TAOS NEWS, 21 May 1970, "D. H. Lawrence" section, pp. 4-5.

[Journalistic feature.] Although he had been painting occasionally since childhood, "it is quite apparent from Lawrence's later paintings that he never studied human anatomy." Bored by pictures, he was critical of the work of Knud Merrild and Dorothy Brett and displeased by the Futurists' glorification of machinery, but he had some affinities with the Dadaists and especially admired Cézanne. The vibrancy of DHL's best paintings transcends his flaws of technique and composition. [Illustrated with black and white photographic reproductions of *Fauns and Nymphs, Close-Up (Kiss),* and *Red Willow Trees.*]

3551 Lerman, Leo. "Love," MADEMOISELLE, LXXI (May 1970), 120.

Ken Russell's film version of *Women in Love* successfully transfers the ideas and characters of the novel to the screen.

3552 Levin, Bernard. "Wives and Servants," THE PENDULUM YEARS: BRITAIN AND THE SIXTIES (Lond: Jonathan Cape, 1970); pub in America as RUN IT DOWN THE FLAGPOLE: BRITAIN IN THE SIXTIES (NY: Athenaeum, 1971), pp. 282-308, espec pp. 282-94, 298, 299, 300-301.

[In this account of the 1960 English censorship trial of *Lady Chatterley's Lover* (Regina v. Penguin Books Ltd.), the author discusses T. S. Eliot's rejection of the request that he be a witness for the prosecution; the prosecutor, Mr. Mervyn Griffith-Jones's cross-examination of Graham Hough; the "literary anthropomorphism" of the law in such a trial; the defense attorney, Mr. Gerald Gardiner's summing up; and the subsequent publication in Britain without prosecution of such books as Philip Roth's PORTNOY'S COMPLAINT and William Burroughs's THE NAKED LUNCH as a result of DHL's "hedge-breaking work's having been "the subject of the 'test case' in 1960."]

3553 McDonald, Edward D. "Foreword," *The Centaur Letters,* by D. H. Lawrence (Austin: Humanities Research Center, University of Texas, 1970), pp. 7-10.

These DHL letters relate to the publication by the Centaur Book Shop, Philadelphia, of Edward D. McDonald's A BIBLIOGRAPHY OF THE WRITINGS OF D. H. LAWRENCE (1925) and DHL's *Reflections on the Death of a Porcupine and Other Essays* (1925). Genuinely interested in both books, DHL cooperated fully with Harold T. Mason and was, if bewildered at first, immensely helpful in supplying information. His letters reflect his delight with both books and his lack of disappointment when *Porcupine* moved slowly in sales. When he left America, he "fully intended to return to New Mexico, but it was not to be." The next four years until his death were productive but emotionally taxing; there was "no healing" his outrage over such tribulations as the attacks on *Lady Chatterley's Lover.*

3554 Maes-Jelinek, Hena. CRITICISM OF SOCIETY IN THE ENGLISH NOVEL BETWEEN THE WARS (Paris: Société d'Éditions "Les Belles Lettres," 1970), pp. 11-110.

There is much social criticism in DHL, but a study of society is not his primary object. He is interested instead in those deeper trends in civilization which thwart the instinctive life of the individual. His basic theme is the impersonal life urge pervading the universe. Contemporary society, failing to balance mind and instinct, male and female, violates the morality of life itself. In *The White Peacock*, the decline of agriculture and the increasing dominance of women destroy the integration of personal relationships and natural beauty. In *Sons and Lovers*, though Mrs. Morel is more complete than Miriam and Clara, whose respective spiritual and physical love are both inadequate, Paul's consciousness is split by the influence of women and Puritanism in religion. In *The Rainbow*, as communal life collapses, women consciously turn to the outside world for individual freedom. Tom and Lydia achieve harmony; but Anna, more involved with the outside world, triumphs over Will; and Ursula's desire for a fuller life takes her into a dehumanizing world and destroys her lover. Emerging reborn from this experience in *Women in Love*, Ursula must engage in a contest with Birkin which he must win for them to achieve a harmonious balance. Here the consequences of the change recorded in *The Rainbow* are obvious: social life is meaningless, the dominance of the mind destroys the body's instinctiveness, and will triumphs. Gerald, a creature of will who recognizes social disintegration, attempts to order society mechanically but can only destroy. Birkin and Ursula face life responsibly and achieve a qualified success, outside society. *Aaron's Rod* attempts to re-establish the social context by accepting the "power-image," but fails to create a situation in which Lilly's leadership could function. DHL rejects democracy because it standardizes men, but *Kangaroo* shows that the quest for something to replace it must be religious, not political. In *The Plumed Serpent*, a creed does irradiate the lives of Ramón and Cipriano, but the European Kate resists commitment and finally accepts it only with misgivings. After this novel, DHL loses interest in power. *Lady Chatterley's Lover* asserts that only through tenderness between men and women can the mechanical deadness of industrial society be escaped. "Phallic marriage" transforms Connie more than any other DHL heroine, and real life does survive.

3555 Majolo, Renato. "David H. Lawrence," ALTO ADIGE (Bolzano), 2 Dec 1970, p. 3.

[Review of *Il pavone bianco, Il trasgressore, Figli e amanti (The White Peacock, The Trespasser, Sons and Lovers)*, with an "Introduction" by Piero Nardi (1970).] The Foreword to *Sons and Lovers* points out for the first time DHL's ambition as a philosopher. But he was a really great artist only when he avoided theoretical attitudes. This is the reason that his best novels are his early ones, *The White Peacock, The Trespasser,* and *Sons and Lovers.* [In Italian.]

3556 Manchester, John. "The Brett Story," NEW MEXICO CULTURAL NEWS, Supplement to ENCANTO MAGAZINE (Albuquerque, NM), III (Sept 1970), 2-5.

In March 1924, Dorothy Brett arrived in Taos, where she was one of the "unholy triumvirate" (with Frieda and Mabel Dodge Luhan) jealously vying for DHL's attention. After his death, Brett remained in Taos, where she became a well-known painter of American Indian ceremonials. [Illustrated with nine photographs of DHL, Brett and Frieda, paintings by Brett, and Nicholai Fechin's *Portrait of Brett*. See also John Manchester, "A Day on the Ranch, 1924: Kiowa Ranch, Taos," ENCANTO MAGAZINE AND NEW MEXICO CULTURAL NEWS (Albuquerque, NM), III, "D. H. Lawrence Commemorative Issue" (Sept 1970), 2-4.]

3557 Manchester, John. "Meanwhile Back at the Ranch," TAOS NEWS, 21 May 1970, "D. H. Lawrence" section, p. 6; rptd as "A Day on the Ranch, 1924: Kiowa Ranch, Taos," ENCANTO MAGAZINE AND NEW MEXICO CULTURAL NEWS, "D. H. Lawrence Commemorative Issue," September 1970, pp. 2-3.
[Recreates the activities of DHL, Dorothy Brett, Trinidad, and Mabel and Tony Luhan on a typical day at Kiowa Ranch in 1924. Illustrated with ten photographs of DHL, Brett, Brett's cabin, Brett, Manchester, and Trinidad, and three of Brett's paintings. See also John Manchester, "The Brett Story," NEW MEXICO CULTURAL NEWS, Supplement to ENCANTO MAGAZINE (Albuquerque, NM), III (Sept 1970), 2-5.]

3558 Marković, Vida E. THE CHANGING FACE: DISINTEGRATION OF PERSONALITY IN THE TWENTIETH-CENTURY BRITISH NOVEL, 1900-1950 (Carbondale & Edwardsville: Southern Illinois UP, 1970), pp. 19-37, 137, 138, 142, 157n, 160n, 163n.
DHL's exploration of the unconscious area below the surface of personality or ego in his characters set him apart from most artists of his time. In his view woman was closer to nature than man. By submitting to and moving with the rhythm of the unconscious, DHL believed, the conscious being becomes free. *The Rainbow*, one of the first "psychoanalytical novels," explores the growth of a child's mind, following Ursula Brangwen from babyhood to young-womanhood to develop the theme of "woman becoming individual, self-responsible, taking her own initiative."

3559 Marshall, Tom. THE PSYCHIC MARINER: A READING OF THE POEMS OF D. H. LAWRENCE (NY: Viking P; Lond: Wm Heinemann, 1970).
[Begins with a survey of criticism and reviews of DHL's poetry.] DHL's early poetry shows him formulating the myth of the voyage and other ideas he developed more fully later; coming to grips with problems concerning guilt, his mother, Jessie Chambers, and Helen Corke; and gradually achieving greater objective clarity in treating experience. Beginning with *Look! We Have Come Through!*, the influence of Whitman is evident as DHL moves closer to his organic free verse forms and the patience and discipline they require, though he lacked Whitman's persona and his large "tidal movements." In *Bay*, DHL develops his idea that war, the death agony of the old order, "might also be the birth pangs of the new." *Birds, Beasts and Flowers*, like all great poetry, transcends influence and fuses objective and subjective modes. The sense of "otherness" which allows DHL his

unique achievement in this volume emerges in "The Song of a Man Who Has Come Through" and "New Heaven and Earth." The poems from *The Plumed Serpent* "constitute a vivid mythic expression of the psychic revolution Lawrence desired." In *Pansies* and *More Pansies*, DHL proclaims his "cyclic theory of ever-renewed creative change" and probably sees himself as a chief prophet of the new era. *Last Poems*, written in the last months of DHL's life, contains his finest poems, radiantly embodying the themes of "the potential splendor of man, the body of God inherent in all struggling life, the supreme beauty of the physical world; the mechanical. . .ego as the only source of evil; and the acceptance of death as the last and deepest consummation of the marriage with the cosmos." "The Ship of Death" shows that DHL's "whole ambition. . .has been to act as a guide of souls." The best poets of today, particularly Robert Lowell and Ted Hughes, have benefited from the Laurentian "discipline of truth to feeling." Like Yeats, Pound, and Eliot, DHL was sensitive to the disintegration of our time, but unlike them he did not wish to institute a new orthodoxy. "Other poets have achieved a more uniform level of quality, but no other poet in our time has seen so far or so much."

3560 Mather, Rodney. "Patrick White and Lawrence: A Contrast," CRITICAL REVIEW (Melbourne), No. 13 (1970), 34-50.

DHL and Patrick White differ strikingly in novelistic approach. DHL, in expansive language and "plastic" narrative, traces the "instinctual life-flicker" of individuals, dwelling on semi-conscious states of transcendence. White, in comparatively "brittle" prose, jumps from object to object, dramatizing individuals not particularly in touch with nature. Confronting reality as an unrevealed mystery, DHL wonderingly acknowledges the enigma, while White bundles together the incomprehensible details. White witnesses experience from a detached point of view that maintains narrative distance; DHL is involved so directly in experience that he is sometimes unable to see beyond it.

3561 Melchiori, Barbara. " 'Objects in the Powerful Light of Emotion,' " ARIEL (Calgary, Canada), I (Jan 1970), 21-30.

While the flower imagery was very deliberately and consciously employed in *Sons and Lovers*, often quite effectively but in an artistic display that the reader feels called upon to pause and admire, the shoe imagery makes a less overt demand and, being altogether better integrated, continues, instead of interrupting, the narrative. Yet the shoes, no less than the flowers, are "objects seen in the powerful light of emotion" and contribute to what DHL rightly defined as the visual character of this novel. DHL was probably not indebted to Freud and psychoanalysis for his symbolism, relying instead on his own observation and on the literary models of HAMLET and OEDIPUS, which simply helped DHL to give structure to the material.

3562 Meyers, Jeffrey. " 'The Voice of Water': Lawrence's *The Virgin and the Gipsy*," ENGLISH MISCELLANY (Rome), XXI (1970), 199-207.

The Virgin and the Gipsy explores various modes of love. The unseen Cynthia, Yvette's mother, is the touchstone of life, opposed to the Rectory household dominated by the parasitic Granny. This sterile family seeks to consume the lives of Yvette and Lucille, the sisters who have returned from school. The Gipsy is in the tradition of DHL's earthy, passionate men, and Yvette, though ambivalent, eventually falls under his power. Into this complex situation come the Eastwoods, whose vital relationship stands between Yvette's alternatives of conventional marriage to Leo and wild nomadic life with the Gipsy, who tells her to be braver in her body and to "listen for the voice of water." These prophecies are fulfilled in the climactic flood scene, which, like the floods in *Sons and Lovers* and *The Rainbow*, suggests powerful destruction and regeneration through sexuality. The sexual consummation comes after the Gipsy has rescued Yvette, as DHL's description of the warming and regenerative embrace makes clear. Yvette is transfigured by her new passsionate awareness.

> **3563** Millett, Kate. "D. H. Lawrence," SEXUAL POLITICS (Garden City, NY: Doubleday, 1970; Lond: Rupert Hart-Davis, 1971), pp. 237-93.

Lady Chatterley's Lover elevates male genitals to the status of godhead and marks, within the total canon of DHL's work, the ascendancy of male supremacy into a mystical religion, as well as the satisfaction of DHL's private, sadistic demand that women be intimidated and subordinated. Such attitudes are foreshadowed in DHL's earliest works. *Sons and Lovers*, for example, depicts Paul Morel as a young man who sexually abuses, then nonchalantly abandons, Miriam and Clara. *The Rainbow* reveals DHL at a stage of sympathy for women, but even then Ursula is feared as a rival to men and is fanally portrayed as a monster who destroys men. *Women in Love, Aaron's Rod,* and *The Plumed Serpent,* along with shorter works like *The Fox* and "The Woman Who Rode Away," chart the progression of DHL's increasing hatred and fear of women, and his desire to master them sexually. Frequently, the sexual abuse of women in these works results from the suppressed homosexuality of the male characters, as well as perhaps of their creator, DHL. [This influential work of feminist criticism has not only spawned numbers of other feminist responses to DHL but has also evoked several critiques of Millett's critical methods and opinions. See especially Norman Mailer, "The Prisoner of Sex," HARPER'S MAGAZINE, CCXLII (March 1971), 41-46, 48, 50, 52-60, 68-72, 77-92, espec. pp. 70-72, 77-79; also pub as THE PRISONER OF SEX (Bost: Little, Brown, 1971), pp. 126-60 and passim; Peter Brookesmith, "The Future of the Individual: Ursula Brangwen and Kate Millett's SEXUAL POLITICS," HUMAN WORLD, No. 10 (Feb 1973), 42-65; John Hoyles, "D. H. Lawrence and the Counter-Revolution: An Essay in Socialist Aesthetics," D. H. LAWRENCE REVIEW, VI (Summer 1973), 173-200, espec. pp. 184-95; Janice Harris, "D. H. Lawrence and Kate Millett," MASSACHUSETTS REVIEW, XV (Summer 1974), 522-29; Bjorn Tysdahl, "Kvinnesak og skjonnlitteratur. D. H. Lawrence: *The Rainbow*" (Feminism in Fiction: D. H. Lawrence, *The Rainbow*), EDDA (Oslo), LXXV, No. 1 (1975), 29-36; and Lydia Blanchard, "Love and Power: A Reconsideration of Sexual Politics in Lawrence," MODERN FICTION STUDIES, XXI (Autumn 1975), 431-43.]

> **3564** Millett, Robert. "Greater Expectations: D. H. Lawrence's *The Trespasser*," in TWENTY-SEVEN TO ONE: A POTPOURRI

OF HUMANISTIC MATERIAL PRESENTED TO DR. DONALD GALE STILLMAN, ed by Bradford D. Broughton (Ogdensburg, NY: Ryan P, 1970), pp. 125-32.

The Trespasser, DHL's most neglected novel, foreshadows some of his later developments. Helena is a modern, self-sufficient woman who cannot give herself and rejects Siegmund because he does not match her ideal vision of him. She has no real contact with him or with the natural world, and the idealized nature of her love dooms the relationship.

3565 Moorer, Clarence Alan, Jr. "The Poetry of D. H. Lawrence," DISSERTATION ABSTRACTS INTERNATIONAL, XXXI (1971), 6065A. Unpublished dissertation, University of Virginia, 1970.

3566 Morelle, Paul. "De l'obscénité en littérature" (Of Obscenity in Literature), LE MONDE, 3 Jan 1970, p. 1.

[Review of *Eros et les chiens* (Eros and the Dogs), essays by D. H. Lawrence, trans by Therese Lauriol, selected and presented by Marcel Marnat (Paris: Christian Bourgois, 1969); includes "Prologue to *Women in Love,*" "Hymns in a Man's Life," "Art and Morality," "The Good Man," "The Novel and the Feelings," "Surgery for the Novel–or a Bomb," "Morality and the Novel," "Why the Novel Matters," *Pornography and Obscenity*, "Making Love to Music," "Making Pictures," "Introduction to These Paintings," "We Need One Another."] From his very first works, DHL was taxed with obscenity. In order to defend himself, he wrote the essays collected here. These texts can be compared with the writings of Wilhelm Reich, THE FUNCTION OF THE ORGASM in particular. DHL and Reich originally shared Freud's views. Later DHL chose a different way because he believed that psychoanalysis ran the risk of reducing sexuality to a mere hygienic necessity. Nature must be respected, as DHL says in "Morality and the Novel," in which he is very close to Celine and Zola ("La Littérature obscène" [1880]). [In French.]

3567 M[orgenstern], J[oseph]. "Body and Soul," NEWSWEEK, LXXV (6 April 1970), 97.

Larry Kramer's screenplay for the film version of *Women in Love* "can't cope with the complexities of Lawrence's great and sometimes obscure exploration of love and marriage. Lawrence tried to arrive at a unified ideal of love–body and spirit, thought and feeling all coming together in 'one single, pure activity'–and tried to reveal impediments to such love–repression, inhibition, jealousy, petty domesticity, the antihuman onslaughts of industrialism."

3568 "Movies," PLAYBOY, XVII (April 1970), 38.

"Male and female nudity are shown with complete frankness–but without a hint of exploitation in the course of *Women in Love,*" directed by Ken Russell, written and produced by Larry Kramer. In the film, "created with keen intelligence, integrity and meticulous period flavor, Lawrence's ideas about life and love retain remarkable potency."

3569 Murphy, Richard Michael. "The Structures of Authorial Control in the Travel Books of D. H. Lawrence," DISSERTATION ABSTRACTS INTERNATIONAL, XXXII (1972), 3960A. Unpublished dissertation, University of Texas at Austin, 1970.

3570 Nahal, Chaman. D. H. LAWRENCE: AN EASTERN VIEW (South Brunswick: Thomas Yoseloff; NY: A. S. Barnes, 1970; Delhi: Atma Ram, 1971).

Although DHL was attracted by India, his knowledge of Hindu scriptures, deriving from secondary sources, was small. Affinities between DHL's thought and the approach to life in the Vedas include the total joy in experience, the integral relation of the physical to the spiritual life, and the realization of the self. *The White Peacock* embodies the Hindu outlook that the "sum of the pleasures of existence far exceeds the sum of the pain of existence." Sex to DHL represents the innate life force, the flow of feeling between individuals culminating in the sacramental form of married love validated not by ritual but by the depth of desire. DHL never believed that women were inferior to men but that the two sexes were different. Love in his earlier novels is more conventional than in *The Rainbow* and *Women in Love,* in which some characters have the same love-transcending instinctual urge found in THE MAHABHARATA. DHL's sensitivity to the autonomy and otherness of woman would have been impossible without Frieda. The man-to-man relationship in *Women in Love* is not homosexuality but the fulfillment of purpose a man craves after successful sexual relationship with a woman. The relationship of Birkin and Ursula is based not on love, passion, or phallicism but, as in Vedantic philosophy, on the Beyond. DHL accepts the role of mind in human life but says in *Psychoanalysis and the Unconscious* and *Fantasia of the Unconscious* that it has its limits. To DHL, God is what *is.* DHL is the artist of the Self in a time of mass society, and right and wrong in his work are grounded not on moral criteria but on the sense of Self. In *The Man Who Died,* DHL rejects Christianity's claim to exclusive truth. The novella is impressive in encompassing DHL's central attributes: delight in creation, love and marriage, and self-realization, which together comprise what DHL calls the fourth dimension, in which the individual is involved in the Infinite. In the final section of *Last Poems,* DHL addresses himself to physical death. As in Vedantic philosophy, engaging the unknown meant not only physical death but also in the capacity to die to the past so as fully to experience the new in the hereafter. DHL's wonder for life in all its unity, variety, and capacity for renewal is not mere curiosity but sensitivity to the *isness* of living.

3571 Nardi, Piero. "Due rivoluzionari individualisti" (Two Individualistic Revolutionaries), CORRIERE DELLA SERA (Milan), 12 March 1970, p. 3.

Although DHL's program for a new society was riddled with contradictions, he really tried, nevertheless, to put it into effect. Many of his friends, Bertrand Russell in particular, were too individualistic to participate in DHL's ideal community. [In Italian.]

3572 Nardi, Piero. "Introduzione" (Introduction), *Il pavone bianco,*

Il Trasgressore, Figli e amanti (The White Peacock, The Trespasser, Sons and Lovers) (Milan: A. Mondadori, 1970), pp. 15-49.

The White Peacock contains some of the major themes which DHL was to develop in his later novels, such as the attack on modern mechanization. Many characters reflect real people and prefigure future characters. *The Trespasser* represents the relationship between DHL and Helen Corke. The non-liberation of Siegmund reflects DHL's defeat because of Helen's refractoriness. *Sons and Lovers* is the glorification of DHL's mother and her victory over "Miriam," but the real victim of the novel is Paul, whose final hopelessness is not to be ascribed to his mother's death but to the conflict between the spiritual fulfillment he finds in his relationship with Miriam and the sexual fulfillment he reaches with Clara. The solution to this fundamental contradiction is brought to DHL by Frieda and his discovery of Freudianism. [In Italian.]

3573 Nardi, Piero. "Introduzione" (Introduction), *La ragazza perduta—La verga di Aronne (The Lost Girl—Aaron's Rod)* (Milan: A. Mondadori, 1970), pp. xv-xxxi.

The Lost Girl, written in the same period as *Women in Love,* is an analysis of the DHL-Frieda and man-woman relationship. *The Lost Girl* is centered on the contradiction between a woman's aspiration to independence and her need of a man to fulfill her primordial sexual desires. In *Aaron's Rod* the fundamental problem is the relationship between men and the submission of a man to another man who possesses leadership qualities. This novel is above all ideological and is often weighted down with digressions, while the best passages reflect DHL's travel experiences. [In Italian.]

3574 Negriolli, Claude. "La Symbolique de D. H. Lawrence" (The Symbolism of D. H. Lawrence). Published dissertation, Académie de Rennes, 1970. [Listed in CATALOGUE DES THÈSES DE DOCTORAT SOUTENUE DEVANT LES UNIVERSITÉS FRANÇAIS, 1971 (Paris: Cercle de la Librairie, 1973), p. 797.] Pub as LA SYMBOLIQUE DE D. H. LAWRENCE (Paris: Presses Universitaires de France, 1970).

[Employing a structuralist method, the author analyzes and classifies DHL's symbolism in terms of the opposition between reason and instinct and the symbols for the integration of these contraries. He examines in three chapters "the elements": light and dark, moon and sun, water and earth, air and fire, north and south, Arctic and African, mountain and valley, city and country. He devotes one chapter each to "human existence": the head and the loins, the nordic races and the southern races, the intellectual and the sensual, the colors white, gray, yellow, and clear blue and the colors black, red, brown, green, and dark blue; to "beasts": unicorn and lion, lamb and tiger, bird and serpent; and to "flowers": the rose and the vine, trees, and fruits. The study culminates in a chapter on DHL's system of symbolism, with a synoptic table classifying his symbols for reason, instinct, and the integration of these opposites in the terms discussed in the foregoing chapters. An appendix, "The Symbolic Structure of 'The Blind Man,' " tabulates symbols associated with the opposing characters, Bertram Reid and Maurice Pervin, and the symbols for the integration of these contraries.] [In French.]

3575 Niethammer, Carolyn. "D. H. Lawrence: Precursor of Today's Spiritual Youth," TUCSON DAILY CITIZEN (Tucson, AZ), 17 Oct 1970, pp. 4-5.

In the view of critics attending the D. H. Lawrence Festival in Taos, NM, 30 Sept-4 Oct 1970, DHL sought "spiritual regeneration" in a return to blood knowledge in the New World, but found Americans materialistic consumers in whom "the God-image had collapsed." [Illustrated with four photographs by Charles Linck of the DHL ranch and tomb.]

3576 Nishimura, Kôji. "Rananim no Yume" (Dream of Rananim), EIGO SEINEN, No. 116 (1970), 637-38.
[In Japanese.]

3577 NOTES FOR AN EXHIBIT AT THE LAWRENCE RANCH, THE D. H. LAWRENCE FESTIVAL, TAOS, NEW MEXICO, 30 SEPTEMBER-4 OCTOBER 1970 (Austin: Humanities Research Center, University of Texas, 1970).

[(Pamphlet.) Annotated checklist of seventeen items from the D. H. Lawrence collection at the Humanities Research Center exhibited at the D. H. Lawrence Festival.]

3578 Ogar, Richard. "*Women in Love* Love," BERKELEY BARB (Berkeley, CA), 1-7 May 1970, p. 17.

Although it "introduces the Male Organ to America" in the nude wrestling scene, the film version of *Women in Love* is not titillating. "Where the film succeeds is in capturing the mood--the FEEL...--of Lawrence's novel," recreating certain scenes with "startling...authenticity."

3579 Oster, Art. " 'I Want to Drown in Flesh...,' " KALEIDOSCOPE (Milwaukee), III (26 June 1970), 10.

While it contains flashes of greatness if not perfection, the film version of *Women in Love* only compounds DHL's tendency to become mired in symbolism.

3580 Panichas, George A. "The End of the Lamplight," MODERN AGE (Chicago), XIV (1970), 65-74.

Although Lady Cynthia Asquith is often thought of as having been treated unjustly by DHL in his fiction, her memoirs reveal that she thought him an extraordinary person and that he held both her and her husband in high esteem, partially because they understood the implications of the war better than other members of the upper classes did. Although DHL usually makes invidious comparisons between upper and lower classes, at the expense of the upper classes, his writing in the war years shows a realization that only a few intellectuals, mostly members of the upper classes, understood his prophetic utterances.

3581 Patmore, Derek. D. H. LAWRENCE AND THE DOMINANT MALE (Lond: Covent Garden P, 1970).

[Pamphlet.] The fact that DHL's most ambitious play, *David*, has never been adapted for the contemporary theater is regrettable. The play presents echoes of DHL's "secret longing for male companionship, and of his frustrated love and friendship for. . .John Middleton Murry." Also, it builds upon a theme, the dominant male, which is pervasive throughout DHL's work. Although film versions of DHL's novels reveal that he had "a vivid sense of drama in his writing," his lack of expertise in technical matters dissuaded him from persevering as a playwright.

3582 Phillips, Gene D. "An Interview with Ken Russell," FILM COMMENT, VI (Fall 1970), 10-17, espec. p. 12.

[Ken Russell, director of the film version of *Women in Love*, discusses the nude wrestling scene as the symbolic embodiment not of homosexuality but of the need for an "intimate relationship" between the two men "that is different from, but which nevertheless complements the heterosexual relationship that each has in marriage." See also Russell's account of the conception and filming of this scene in a chapter on the making of the film in AN APPALLING TALENT: KEN RUSSELL, by John Baxter (Lond: Michael Joseph, 1973), pp. 167-82.

3583 Purdy, Strother B. "On the Psychology of Erotic Literature," LITERATURE AND PSYCHOLOGY, XX, No. 1 (1970), 23-29, espec. 27-28.

Lady Chatterley's Lover pushes "the psychological novel a great distance closer to sexual awareness" but is programmatic and marred by an underlying strain of misogyny.

3584 "Quartet of Soloists," TIME, XCV (13 April 1970), 103, 106-7.

DHL encouraged " 'belief in the blood,' " but "his books are models of calculation. . . . Although Lawrence celebrated the phallus and sang the masculine principle, his every work is marked by an almost feminine hysteria that nags as it argues." "The adapters of *Women in Love* can hardly be blamed for the instability of their film. . .Neither the book nor the film has a conventional plot" but moves "from segment to segment." "In the book," the dialogue of the four principal characters "has the semblance of argument. In the film the quartet is composed of soloists who listen only to themselves." In the book, the nude wrestling scene dramatizes DHL's "wish for a return to the presexual child-state. In the film's formal, choreographic version," it "seems little more than another cinematic plea for homosexuality." Although "the beauty and energy of the novel flow between the lines," the film "oscillates" between opposites, "without once adopting a coherent point of view."

3585 Ragussis, Michael. "The Double Perspective: A Study of D. H. Lawrence's Novels," DISSERTATION ABSTRACTS INTERNATIONAL, XXXII (1971), 451A. Unpublished dissertation, Johns Hopkins University, 1970.

3586 Raina, M. L. "The Wheel and the Centre: An Approach to *The Rainbow*," LITERARY CRITERION (Mysore, India), IX (Summer 1970), 41-55.

The Rainbow is a successful expression of DHL's mythic consciousness, which derives from a religious response to experience.

    3587 Raya, Gino. "Tre donne interno a Lawrence" (Three Women around Lawrence), NUOVA ANTOLOGIA (Rome), Aug 1970, pp. 573-76.

Frieda Lawrence, Mabel Dodge Luhan, and Dorothy Brett each wrote a book of memoirs on her relationship with DHL. In Taos, while DHL was trying to achieve a natural way of life, the three women were unable to free themselves of their intellectual attitudes. They were rivals in the worship of DHL's genius, but they were united by their jealousy of outsiders. [In Italian.]

    3588 "Reception Honors D. H. Lawrence Festival Panelists as Exhibition Opens," TAOS NEWS (Taos, NM), 8 Oct 1970, pp. 8-9.

Three hundred persons, including panelists of the DHL Festival, attended an exhibition of "Lawrenciana: A Visual Show" at the Stables Gallery in Taos. [Includes list of pictorial art relating to DHL, five photographs of panelists and guests. See also related stories, "400 attend D. H. Lawrence festival," TAOS NEWS (Taos, NM), 8 Oct 1970, pp. 1, 2; and "Scholars honor D. H. Lawrence here," TAOS NEWS (Taos, NM), 1 Oct 1970, pp. 1-2.]

    3589 Reed, Rex. "Rex Reed at the Movies," HOLIDAY, XLVII (June 1970), 21; rptd in BIG SCREEN, LITTLE SCREEN, by Rex Reed (NY: Macmillan, 1971), pp. 282-83.

The film version of *Women in Love*, written for the screen and produced by Larry Kramer and directed by Ken Russell, "is bold and erotic and filled with D. H. Lawrence's passionate search for sexual fulfillment and love expressed as aesthetic masochism, but there is little humanity in it and a great deal of hysteria." "There are few clues to what kind of people these characters are, and instead of developing Lawrence's theme (greed for self-importance in love versus sexual freedom) Ken Russell throws the movie to clashing effects and bravura technical effects."

    3590 Rice, Susan. "Clichés," MEDIA AND METHODS, VI (May 1970), 12, 14.

[The author admits that she has not read *Women in Love*; however, she finds the film "breathtaking," though the "talk" is "mannered and unrevealing."]

    3591 Rich. "*Women in Love*," VARIETY, CCLVII (19 Nov 1969), 14.

"Lawrence's pungent thoughts about love and marriage, and the attitudes of the two sexes toward them, are not highly original but are shrewdly put over" in the "episodic, but challenging" film version of *Women in Love*, which "captures the flavor" of the original without becoming a "period piece."

    3592 Richardson, John Adkins, and John I. Ades. "D. H. Lawrence on Cézanne: A Study in the Psychology of Critical Intuition," JOURNAL OF AESTHETICS AND ART CRITICISM, XXVIII

(Summer 1970), 441-53.

DHL's understanding of modern painting, particularly Cézanne's, is remarkable. Without "the tools of modern scholarship," DHL went intuitively to the heart of the matter, focussing on Cézanne's artistic struggle, the conflicts and search for resolution. Parallels between the lives and works of DHL and Cézanne suggest that profound critical insight may spring from such intuited relationships. They also suggest "a far deeper alliance between an artist and his critic than is generally recognized."

3593 Ripp, Judith. "*Women in Love*," PARENTS' MAGAZINE, XLV (March 1970), 27.

The film version of *Women in Love* is "thought-provoking" and tasteful.

3594 Roberts, F[rancis] Warren. "D. H. Lawrence, The Second 'Poetic Me': Some New Material," RENAISSANCE AND MODERN STUDIES, XIV (1970), 5-25.

[Description of a holograph notebook in the possession of W. H. Clarke, the son of DHL's sister Ada, presumably that mentioned by Jessie Chambers in D. H. LAWRENCE: A PERSONAL RECORD and a companion to the French notebook discussed by Vivian de Sola Pinto in RENAISSANCE AND MODERN STUDIES, I (1957), 5-34. A selection of twelve unpublished poems from the notebook accompanies the description, followed by an appendix cataloguing the sixty-four published poems with identification of the volume in which each was published. See also F(rancis) Warren Roberts, "D. H. Lawrence, The Second 'Poetic Me': Corrigenda," RENAISSANCE AND MODERN STUDIES, XV (1971), 103-6.]

3595 Robson, W. W. MODERN ENGLISH LITERATURE (Lond and NY: Oxford UP, 1970), pp. xiii, 4, 7, 11, 23, 36, 42-43, 59, 62, 67, 74-75, 82-92, 94, 98, 104-7, 125, 134, 136, 138, 143-44, 147, 156.

The turbulence in DHL's singular personality clouded his literary reputation. Though didacticism often intrudes, his ethical concerns are of value to his artistry and stem from his understanding of the working- and middle-class culture from which he later felt uprooted. Unlike Joyce and many other twentieth-century writers, DHL is widely read by ordinary people. [A literary/bibliographical summary follows.]

3596 Rossman, Charles. "The Gospel According to D. H. Lawrence: Religion in *Sons and Lovers*," D. H. LAWRENCE REVIEW, III (Spring 1970), 31-41.

Two "related groups of images. . .have fundamental importance for. . .the technique and the themes of *Sons and Lovers*": "religious allusions and images, and images of food and eating." These images underscore the religious dimensions of the novel and "the concepts of communion portrayed in it." In the "Foreword to *Sons and Lovers*," written as a letter to Edward Garnett (Jan 1913), DHL argues for the priority of the Flesh; "he declares that Christianity's emphasis on the Word is a blasphemy of the Flesh," in an explicit and intentional "reversal of the Gospel According to St. John!" Paul's struggle to escape his sterile attachment to his mother, to break free from soul-communion with Miriam, and to satisfy his sexual instincts in his union with Clara Dawes thus becomes a "religious quest" to reaffirm the sanctity of the body. The recurrence of religious images and scenes emphasizes this theme, and the numerous "images of food and eating" extend "the theme of the quest for vitalizing physical communion." Through this "poetic structure of allusion, image, and symbol," *Sons and Lovers* depicts a world of "alienated men who have lost contact with their. . .inner selves, with their fellow men, and with organic nature."

  3597 Rotman, Mel. "*Women in Love*," CHEVRON (Waterloo, Ontario), XI (13 Nov 1970), 9.

Treating several kinds of love, the film version of *Women in Love* depicts women as a "potent and deadly force."

  3598 Runyan, Elizabeth. "Escape from the Self: An Interpretation of E. M. Forster, D. H. Lawrence, Virginia Woolf," DISSERTATION ABSTRACTS INTERNATIONAL, XXXI (1971), 5423A. Unpublished dissertation, Kent State University, 1970.

  3599 Sagar, Keith. " 'Little Living Myths': A Note on Lawrence's *Tortoise*," D. H. LAWRENCE REVIEW, III (Summer 1970), 161-67.

DHL's *Tortoises* sequence is one long poem in six sections. In "Baby Tortoises" the tortoise "both represents and embodies" the first evolutionary steps out of non-life toward the "affirmation of selfhood": "The biochemical origins of life, the highest pitch of evolution--the human life-adventure, both are contained in this 'Ulyssean atom,' " the signs of which are carried on the "Tortoise Shell." Why the plan of the shell is cruciform is explored in "Tortoise Family Connections" as Ulysses-Adam becomes Osiris-Christ, torn to become resurrected. In "Tortoise Shout" the "tortoise scream, in extremis," "is 'consummatum est' which means both 'it is finished' and 'it is accomplished.' " Only through the violation of the self in sex and death can man find wholeness, which involves contact with the creative process, with God. "Coition and death have both the same purpose. They are the necessary condition of birth and rebirth."

  3600 Samuels, Marilyn Schauer. "Water, Ships, and the Sea: Unifying Symbols in Lawrence's *Kangaroo*," UNIVERSITY REVIEW (Kansas City), XXXVII (Oct 1970), 46-57.

Descriptions of water, ships, and the sea provide a "symbolic language" that links the relationships of Somers's life, both inner and exterior: his longing for a river of harmonious friendship with others, his sense of alienation by symbolic oceans which separate, the puzzling complexities of different depths of water. Even the long "Nightmare" chapter can be seen as part of the unified water language. Although not one of DHL's great novels, *Kangaroo* is a sensitive work of fiction. [Contains a detailed schema and many examples.]

  3601 San Juan, E[piphanio], Jr. "Theme versus Imitation:

D. H. Lawrence's 'The Rocking-Horse Winner'," D. H. LAWRENCE REVIEW, III (Summer 1970), 136-40; rptd in FROM FICTION TO FILM: D. H. LAWRENCE'S "THE ROCKING-HORSE WINNER," ed by Gerald R. Barrett and Thomas L. Erskine (Encino, CA, and Belmont, CA: Dickenson Publishing, 1974), pp. 70-74.

A persistent error in most formal analyses of fiction is "the easy reduction of the narrative to an allegorical statement of ideas presumed to underlie the work." An example of this mistaken criticism is W. D. Snodgrass's interpretation of "The Rocking-Horse Winner," in which "the rocking-horse is taken to symbolize a massive cluster of ideas ranging from sex to the occult." Rather, what DHL intends in the story "is to imitate an action which, in conceptual terms, may be expressed as the dialectical interplay of fantasy. . .and the worldly. . . , and its ironic effects on Paul's relation with his mother." The power of this imitation resides specifically in the construction of the plot, in the way the elements converge to present the change in Paul's fortune. Any other "inferred implications or significances may be properly defined as constituents of formal parts used to characterize the protagonist, his mother, or the setting. They function as devices to arouse and satisfy a sequence of emotional responses which defines the power of the narrative."

3602 Sayre, Joel. "Whiskers and Criticism," WASHINGTON POST BOOK WORLD, 29 March 1970, p. 8.

[Personal reminiscence. An amusing account of how a young admirer was disillusioned by the eccentricities of DHL's personality.]

3603 Schickel, Richard. "A Past Master in the Hands of a Future One," LIFE, LXVIII (6 March 1970), 14.

Regarded by many critics as DHL's "masterpiece," *Women in Love* is a work of delicate yet radical probings which suggests that the sexual relationship," impinged upon by the forces of "modern culture, industrialism, Christianity," "cannot contain or sustain a fully developed and genuinely healthy emotional life." DHL is "a young man's writer, a man for the season when one first falls in love with ideas and the idea of having ideas." The film version of *Women in Love*, directed with "technical virtuosity" by Ken Russell but unable "to avoid the tedious philosophical wrangles about the larger issues," "is a failure at least in part because of its faithfulness" to the novel.

3604 Schlesinger, Arthur, Jr. *"The Virgin and the Gypsy.* 'tact,' " VOGUE, CLVI (July 1970), 40.

Although DHL died before he could put his "charming novella" into final form, Alan Plater's screenplay for the film version of *The Virgin and the Gypsy*, directed by Christopher Miles, "expands the original with tact and intelligence."

3605 Schlesinger, Arthur, Jr. "*Women in Love*: Fascinating Try," VOGUE, CLV (1 March 1970), 114.

The film version of *Women in Love*, as an adaptation of the novel, is "incomprehensible."

3606 "Scholars Honor D. H. Lawrence Here," TAOS NEWS (Taos NM), 1 Oct 1970, pp. 1-2.
Traditional San Geronimo Day (30 Sept) Indian ceremonies marked the beginning of a five-day DHL festival in Taos "featuring films, paintings and drawings, radio tapes and panel discussions." [Schedule of planned activities included. See also related stories, "400 attend D. H. Lawrence festival," TAOS NEWS (Taos, NM), 8 Oct 1970, pp. 1, 2; and "Reception Honors D. H. Lawrence Festival Panelists as Exhibition Opens," TAOS NEWS (Taos, NM), 8 Oct 1970, pp. 8-9.]

3607 Secker, Martin. LETTERS FROM A PUBLISHER: MARTIN SECKER TO D. H. LAWRENCE AND OTHERS, 1911-1929 (Lond: Enitharmon P, 1970).
[Includes Foreword, pp. i-iv, and forty-four letters by Martin Secker from copies in office letter books.] After their meeting in 1914, Secker and DHL had both friendly and business relations in the publication of DHL's books until his death. [See also Secker's edition of *Letters from D. H. Lawrence to Martin Secker, 1911-1930* (Bridgefort Ivers, Bucks.: Privately published, 1970).]

3608 S[ecker], M[artin]. "Note," *Letters from D. H. Lawrence to Martin Secker, 1911-1930* (Bridgefort Ivers, Bucks.: Privately published, 1970), [p. 7].
[One early letter, the first that DHL wrote to Secker (12 June 1911) survives; the rest of the 196 letters span 13 Sept 1918, when their "acquaintance became a publishing association," until 9 Jan 1930. Following the texts of the letters are additional notes, pp. 129-33.] [See also Martin Secker, LETTERS FROM A PUBLISHER: MARTIN SECKER TO D. H. LAWRENCE AND OTHERS, 1911-1929 (Lond: Enitharmon P, 1970).]

3609 Sepčič, Višnja. "Struktura romana D. H. Lawrencea" (The Structure of D. H. Lawrence's Novels), FILOLOGIJA, 1970, pp. 183-86.
[In Serbo-Croatian.]

3610 Silvestri, Giuseppe. "Tre romanzi di Lawrence" (Three Novels of Lawrence), MESSAGGERO VENETO (Udine), 10 Dec 1970, p. 3.
[Review of *Il pavone bianco, Il trasgressore, Figli e amanti (The White Peacock, The Trespasser, Sons and Lovers)*, with an "Introduction" by Piero Nardi (1970).] DHL's work is very extensive and reflects different and sometimes contradictory aspects of his character. Against intellectualism and mechanization, DHL proposes a primitive way of life and a new religion centered in sexual experience. DHL is one of the most important modern writers, and his artistic qualities are especially apparent in his ability to structure his characters and situations and to describe nature. His first three novels are above all autobiographical. [In Italian.]

3611 Simon, John. "Lawrence in Print and on Film," NEW LEADER, LIII (13 April 1970), 26-28.
Women in Love is "faintly repulsive" in its repetitive language, its contradictory

ideas, and its "obsessiveness." [The author surveys comments by other writers and critics on DHL and this novel.] "The film version of *Women in Love*--produced and written by Larry Kramer...and directed by Ken Russell...--is for all its superficial fidelity to the novel a profound betrayal of it." For example, the nude wrestling scene has a "homosexual coloration" that DHL would have "abhorred," and Loerke is vulgarized as a proto-fascist homosexual who "makes real Nazi sculptures." Other complex Lawrentian symbols are either omitted or reduced to the obvious, and "the artistic-cultural-historic philosophizing" is "consistently decimated."

3612 Singh, Vishnudat. "Lawrence's Use of 'Pecker,'" PAPERS OF THE BIBLIOGRAPHICAL SOCIETY OF AMERICA, LXIV, No. 3 (1970), 355.

A letter to Edward D. McDonald and a line from "Walk to Huayapa" indicate DHL's knowledge of both the British and American meanings of "pecker."

3613 Singh, Vishnudat. "*Women in Love*: A Textual Note," NOTES AND QUERIES, ns XVII (Dec 1970), 466.

By changing Hasan from an Oriental to an Arab, DHL avoided the anomaly of having a Hindu with an Arabic name as well as the possibility of a charge of libel by the Indian Suhrawardy.

3614 Sirkin, Elliott. "*Women in Love*," HARRY (Baltimore), I (1 June 1970), 16-17 [not seen in this form]; enlgd and rptd in FILM QUARTERLY, XXIV (Fall 1970), 43-47.

Larry Kramer, who wrote the screenplay, and Ken Russell, who directed the film of *Women in Love*, "are obviously conscious of all the big themes in the D. H. Lawrence novel": "Mental sex is deplored, the end of the world is speculated over, the purity of a thoroughly balanced love-partnership is longed for, and there's a constant, if very murky, current of wills clashing and desire emerging." The adaptation, however, is "self-defeating": "It doesn't condense the novel, it castrates it." This serious but misguided film is "too slight to infringe on the novel's territory and do any severe damage to its reputation." [Detailed discussion.]

3615 Sitesh, Aruna. "D. H. Lawrence as Literary Critic." Unpublished dissertation, University of Allahabad, 1970. [Listed in D. H. LAWRENCE REVIEW, V (Summer 1972), 173.] Rvd and pub as D. H. LAWRENCE: THE CRUSADER AS CRITIC (Delhi, Bombay, Calcutta, and Madras: Macmillan Co. of India, 1975).

3616 Sitwell, Edith. SELECTED LETTERS, ed by John Lehmann and Derek Parker (Lond: Macmillan, 1970), p. 200.

[In a letter to Goffrey Singleton (11 July 1955), the author says, "I now admire Lawrence *very* much, but not *technically*." This brief but telling statement contrasts with the view of DHL presented in TAKEN CARE OF: THE AUTOBIOGRAPHY OF EDITH SITWELL (1965).]

3617 Smailes, T[homas] A. (ed). "D. H. Lawrence: Seven Hitherto Unpublished Poems," D. H. LAWRENCE REVIEW, III (Spring 1970), 42-46; the poems are rptd as Appendix I: "Verse Not Included in *The Complete Poems*," in SOME COMMENTS ON THE VERSE OF D. H. LAWRENCE, by T[homas] A. Smailes (Port Elizabeth, South Africa: University of Port Elizabeth, 1970), pp. 73-75.

[Briefly introduces and publishes for the first time six poems crossed out in the manuscript of *Last Poems*, MS E192 ("Amphibian," "Salt-Licks," "Widdershins," "War," "The Maleficent Triangle," "Beauty and Truth"), and one from MS E132 ("Fire").]

3618 Smailes, T[homas] A. "Lawrence's Verse: More Editorial Lapses," NOTES AND QUERIES, ns XVII (Dec 1970), 465-66.

[Lists editorial errors in *The Complete Poems of D. H. Lawrence*, ed by Vivian de Sola Pinto and F. Warren Roberts (Lond: Heinemann; NY: Viking P, 1964), emphasizing a refutation of their editorial note on "The Man of Tyre."] The third stanza of "The Man of Tyre" is based on DHL's own experience rather than on Stephen Dedalus's vision of the bathing girl in James Joyce's A PORTRAIT OF THE ARTIST AS A YOUNG MAN. [See also T. A. Smailes, "*More Pansies* and *Last Poems*: Variant Readings Derived from MS Roberts E192," D. H. LAWRENCE REVIEW, I (Fall 1968), 201-213, and Vivian de Sola Pinto and Warren Roberts, "A Note on Editing *The Complete Poems*," D. H. LAWRENCE REVIEW, I (Fall 1968), 213-14.]

3619 Smailes, T[homas] A. "The Evolution of a Lawrence Poem," STANDPUNTE, LXXXIX (June 1970), 40-42.

A comparison of two unpublished variants of "Embankment at Night, Before the War: Charity" with the final version shows that DHL developed technical skill and maturity of outlook between 1909 and 1918. [The two unpublished versions appear in full, taken from MS E317, as numbered in Warren Roberts, A BIBLIOGRAPHY OF D. H. LAWRENCE (1963).]

3620 Smailes, T[homas] A. SOME COMMENTS ON THE VERSE OF D. H. LAWRENCE (Port Elizabeth, South Africa: University of Port Elizabeth Publications Series [General Series A11], 1970).

DHL's juvenile verse (1904-1908) blends fresh observations with forced rhymes and mechanical metrics. "Love on the Farm" and "Snap-Dragon," however, with compelling symbols taken from everyday objects, give indication of the intense individual style to come. The Croydon period verse (1908-1912) ranges from early autobiographical work which lacks universal appeal to skilled free verse expressing complex emotional states. DHL's adaptation of myth emerges as a distinctive quality. The *Look! We Have Come Through!* poems (1912-1918) show that DHL's conjugal "blessedness" and his poetic maturity were attained together. Poems of perfect honesty record DHL's struggle with Frieda and with his own psychological problems. Examination of the evolution of "Piano" and "Charity" from *New Poems* shows that as DHL's verse became less formed it became more significant, with style and content blended in a new maturity. *Birds, Beasts and Flowers* displays a "perfected free verse style in which image, symbol, and allusion blend with natural speech rhythms." *Pansies* and *Last Poems* (1928-1930) show DHL confronting death. Examination of the several drafts of "Bavarian Gentians" shows Aldington's choice for inclusion in *Last Poems* to be DHL's second best version. Confronting death in "The Ship of Death," DHL is "quiet and apprehensive enough to make faith and courage meaningful." [Appendix I includes eight poems from holograph MSS not included in *The Complete Poems of D. H. Lawrence*, ed by Vivian de Sola Pinto and F. Warren Roberts (Lond: Heinemann; NY: Viking P, 1964). Appendix II prints fifteen pages of "some unpublished variants derived from MS E317." Appendix III, "*More Pansies* and *Last Poems:* Corrigenda Derived from MS Roberts E192," offers textual emendations to the versions printed in *Complete Poems*. Appendix IV contains a "chronological re-appraisal" of MS E192 to show that, contrary to Richard Aldington's assumption, in editing *Last Poems*, work in Notebook A and Notebook B proceeded simultaneously, and that the notebooks were, with some exceptions, composed in sequence and show "in the face of imminent death, a steady progress from the relatively trivial to the sublime."]

3621 Spears, Monroe K. DIONYSUS AND THE CITY: MODERNISM IN TWENTIETH CENTURY POETRY (Lond & NY: Oxford UP, 1970), pp. 52, 56, 101-4, 128-30, 148-49.

DHL is perhaps the most Dionysian of the great writers of the century and *Women in Love* "the most richly and transparently psychological novel ever written" as well as a striking example of apocalyptic primitivism. DHL is a lesser artist than James Joyce because the Apollonian is over-balanced by the Dionysian. Historical discontinuity is a basic postulate with DHL, leading to his obsession with time-consciousness and determination to capture a sense of immediacy in his poetry. He rejects aesthetic discontinuity, refusing to separate art from life. DHL was the only "official imagist" of significant talent. DHL does not aim to preserve the present but to experience it more fully. The radicalism of his position and his disinterest in the poem as "art object" link him with many modern painters.

3622 Speirs, James Gordon. "The Background of the Political Philosophy of Conrad and Lawrence," DISSERTATION ABSTRACTS INTERNATIONAL, XXXII (1972), 7007A. Unpublished dissertation, University of Toronto, 1970.

3623 Spender, Stephen. "Form and Pressure in Poetry," TIMES LITERARY SUPPLEMENT (Lond), 23 Oct 1970, pp. 1226-28.

[Brief comment on DHL's use of free verse. Essay taken from "the text of the Inaugural Lecture delivered at University College London, last night."]

3624 Squires, Michael. "Lawrence's *The White Peacock*: A Mutation of Pastoral," TEXAS STUDIES IN LITERATURE AND LANGUAGE, XII (Summer 1970), 263-84; rptd as "Fit for Old Theocritus," in THE PASTORAL NOVEL: STUDIES IN GEORGE ELIOT, THOMAS HARDY, AND D. H. LAWRENCE (Charlottesville: UP of Virginia, 1974), pp. 174-95.

Often dismissed for its lack of "formal perfection," *The White Peacock*, with the "many impulses at work" in its "mixture of lyrical, elegiac, and harshly realistic elements," is linked with the early "pastoral" novels of George Eliot and Thomas Hardy through its "matrix of four attitudes toward rural life, four different expressions of the pastoral impulse: a tinge of antipastoral reflected in the occasional harsh passages about rural life; a modified or realistic pastoral, close to Hardy's, that is reflected in the often idyllic portrait of life at Strelley Mill farm; a portrait of the Beardsall family...who live in a remote rural setting and who enjoy not regular agricultural labor, but the fruits of culture, the beauty of nature, and freedom from any necessary work; and, last, a burlesque of a traditional pastoral picnic, artificial and self-consciously humorous, which depicts cultured urbanites affecting dialect and pretending to be Theocritean rustics." [Each of these four elements is discussed in detail with reference to particulars of the novel.]

3625 Stewart, Bruce. "Where There's Muck There's Polytheism," MONTH, ns I (Feb 1970), 117-19.

DHL, "the last incarnation of Pan" in Britain, has been up to now a "dodgy... proposition" on screen. [The author surveys the three most recent film versions of DHL's works.] *Women in Love*, DHL's "best book," becomes "the best Lawrence film so far," seen with DHL's eyes, in a "faithful and insistent dialectic" that is "pure paganism."

3626 Stoll, John E. "Common Womb Imagery in Joyce and Lawrence," BALL STATE UNIVERSITY FORUM, XI (Spring 1970), 10-24.

Both Joyce and DHL reflect the duality, alienation, and loneliness of their age, but their polar opposition represents the difference between the Catholic and Protestant consciousness secularized. While Joyce's art is "artificial" in the best sense, DHL's emphasizes self-fulfillment at the expense of most social values. The only point at which they are not irreconcilable is in the common womb imagery permeating their work. In each case, the imagery is intrinsic to the characters' search for identity and influences the author's view of human nature. Joyce's achievement is the greater in that he uses each character's plight--suggested often by womb imagery--with ironic detachment and full control, while DHL's use is characterized by misdirection and evasion. Joyce's use of womb imagery throws new light on his thematic concerns, while DHL's tends to obscure his thematic concerns. The fact that womb imagery provides a common denominator between these two authors strongly suggests that sex is a dominant theme in modern literature.

3627 Stoll, John E. "Psychological Dissociation in the Victorian Novel," LITERATURE AND PSYCHOLOGY, XX, No. 2 (1970), 63-73.

"Lawrence did not *have* to discover psychological dissociation (aesthetically, the 'gap' between the author's 'intention' and his achievement: 'Never trust the artist. Trust the tale.') in the American novel." He could just as well have discovered the same thing in the English novel. DHL is "that last and greatest Victorian," who identifies the unconscious as male and consciousness as female.

3628 Stroupe, John H. "Ruskin, Lawrence, and Gothic Naturalism," BALL STATE UNIVERSITY FORUM, XI (Spring 1970), 3-9.

Although critics have recognized similarities in DHL's and John Ruskin's attitudes toward "industrialism and a striving for mechanical perfection" as "essentially dehumanizing," Ruskin's influence on DHL is more pervasive in *Women in Love* than has been previously noted. The major characters in the novel exemplify Ruskin's differentiation of northern from southern European architecture by seeing them as reflections of systems involving *servile ornament* (Greek, Assyrian, Egyptian), *constitutional ornament* (Gothic), and *revolutionary ornament* (modern). Gerald Crich's dilemma and his eventual spiritual vacuum may be explained by the fact that he attempts mechanical perfection at the expense of humanity--his own and that of his miners.

3629 Suckow, Ruth. "Modern Figures of Destiny: D. H. Lawrence and Frieda Lawrence," D. H. LAWRENCE REVIEW, III (Spring 1970), 3-30.

DHL suffers from over-simplified psychoanalytic criticism, in which the "mother complex" has only a negative side, and from the idea that his experience was unique. But he was a product of the Victorian period which, with its insistence on motherhood as the essence of the female being, created a generation of "sons of women." But through his mother and then his wife he saw, as most of his contemporaries were unable to do, the "otherness" of woman's identity. Although this vision made him fear the loss of his maleness, and although he often returned to the Victorian idea of male domination, it was DHL's modern destiny to make himself a man through contact with a woman instead of by defeat of her. He is "the first symbolic figure of this particular passage in human destiny." The poems in *Look! We Have Come Through!* record the struggle in terms of immediate experience; the prose works make up one great book of modern love. *Sons and Lovers* is primarily an elegy for the "virgin mother." Throughout most of his fiction, DHL's themes are primarily two: "the subduing of woman" and "the mating of the virgin and the gypsy." *The Rainbow* is "the great Hymeneal of modern literature" until its ending, in which "personality" obstructs "artistic impersonality." In *Women in Love* the evangelist overtakes the artist. In *Kangaroo*, DHL begins to see the absurdity of his exhortations on "the proper place of woman" but turns to "the solidarity of 'mates.'" In *Aaron's Rod, The Plumed Serpent*, and especially "The Woman Who Rode Away," DHL resorts to every trick to subdue his women characters but achieves "his imaginary victory" only at the sacrifice of "his artistic integrity." In *Lady Chatterley's Lover*, "the most dishonest novel that Lawrence ever wrote," Connie is his first "totally uninteresting woman" and Mellors his "worst caricature of himself." In his last novel, *The Man Who Died*, DHL finally achieves a balanced vision of a union of man and woman as equals, the priest and priestess of love. [The article is preceded by Ferner Nuhn, "Introduction," D. H. LAWRENCE REVIEW, III (Spring 1970), 1-2, and a photograph of Ruth Suckow, facing p. 1.]

3630 Sw[eeney], L[ouise]. "Lawrence's 'Women' Novel as a Film," CHRISTIAN SCIENCE MONITOR, 13 April 1970, p. 4.

Reflecting "the strengths and flaws of the original," the film version of *Women in Love* is "so erotic in some scenes that it sensationalizes even as it illustrates Lawrence's beliefs: his rejection of lust for something 'beyond sex,' a true love between women and men, a brotherhood between men."

3631 Tarratt, Margaret. "An Obscene Undertaking," FILMS AND FILMING, XVII (Nov 1970), 26-30.
The film industry has cashed in on DHL's popular and misleading reputation as an erotic writer, rather than confronting the complex and acute psychological insights of his works. [Comments briefly on five film versions of DHL's works: *The Rocking-Horse Winner* (1949), *L'Amant de Lady Chatterley* (1955), *Sons and Lovers* (1960), *The Fox* (1968), and *Women in Love* (1969). Illustrated with black and white stills from the films.]

3632 Taylor, Kim. "A Phoenix Out of the Ark," PRIVATE LIBRARY (Middlesex), 2nd series, III (Autumn 1970), 110-20.
[Brief memoir of the author's Ark Press and her association with Warren Roberts and the DHL collection at the University of Texas at Austin.]

3633 Tetsumura, Haruo. "*Sons and Lovers* Kenkyû (1)" (A Study of *Sons and Lovers* [1]), BULLETIN OF FACULTY OF EDUCATION (Nagasaki University), No. 19 (March 1970), 27-35.
[Scrutinizes *Sons and Lovers* through DHL's letters to show how he tries to connect his self-exploration with his self-realization, on a personal plane, and how he discovers the functional writing that could produce a successful novel, on an artistic plane.] [In Japanese.]

3634 Thatcher, David S. NIETZSCHE IN ENGLAND, 1890-1914: THE GROWTH OF A REPUTATION (Toronto: University of Toronto P, 1970), pp. 6, 7, 10, 11, 14, 99, 207, 262, 268, 272n, 274.
In the early twentieth century Nietzsche's works were widely available in translation and his impact was obvious. DHL was one of the few Englishmen to appreciate Nietzsche's true stature. [No extended study of DHL and Nietzsche is included, but peripheral references to DHL illustrate Nietzsche's English reputation during a generation in which he was the subject of fierce controversy.]

3635 Travis, Clayton Leigh. "A Wall of Fire, A Wall of Ice: Growth as an Aesthetic Criterion in the Fiction of D. H. Lawrence," DISSERTATION ABSTRACTS INTERNATIONAL, XXXI (1971), 4137A. Unpublished dissertation, University of Michigan, 1970.

3636 Tucker, Betty Jean. "An Archetypal Imagery Study of the Fall of the Family in the Nineteenth-Century English Novel," DISSERTATION ABSTRACTS INTERNATIONAL, XXXI (1970), 5430A. Unpublished dissertation, University of Alabama, 1970.
[Includes discussion of DHL.]

3637 Tucker, Martin. "Lawrence's Women," COMMONWEAL, XCII (15 May 1970), 223.

Desiring "that man allow all sides of his nature to act and interact," DHL "called for freedom of spirit" that could lead men "to their unique qualities of fulfillment," but "believed some submissions could be more fulfilling and 'freeing' than nominal independence." "Granting the difficulties of turning Lawrence's mystical novel into a concrete film, [director Ken] Russell's version of *Women in Love*" is "a lightweight but stunning tribute to one of the forces for freedom in contemporary culture."

3638 Tunander, Britt. "D. H. Lawrence: *Söner och älskande*" (D. H. Lawrence: *Sons and Lovers*), DAGENS NYHETER (Stockholm), 2 May 1970, p. 5.

[Review of new Swedish translation.] *Sons and Lovers* is, to a great extent, a family novel, full of concrete details and everyday atmosphere. Its density and richness are reminiscent of the Russian nineteenth-century novel, especially as the psychological development is revealed by similar means. [In Swedish.]

3639 Wada, Shizuo. "D. H. Lawrence Oboegaki (IV)--*Seishin-Bunseki to Muishiki* to *Muishiki no Gensô* ni Tsuite" (Notes on D. H. Lawrence [IV] --*Psychoanalysis and the Unconscious* and *Fantasia of the Unconscious*), BULLETIN OF KYÛSHÛ SANGYÔ UNIVERSITY, VI, No. 2 (March 1970), 1-62.

[First of a two-part essay on *Psychoanalysis and the Unconscious* and *Fantasia of the Unconscious*.] When we study a novelist, it is usual to abstract his literary theory from his novels. DHL wrote many essays which stated his thinking about literature; among them, *Psychoanalysis and the Unconscious* and *Fantasia of the Unconscious* are significant because they show his inner thinking more directly than do his novels. [See also Shizuo Wada, "D. H. Lawrence Oboegaki (IV)--*Seishin-Bunseki to Muishiki* to *Muishiki no Gensô* ni Tsuite" (Notes on D. H. Lawrence [IV] --*Psychoanalysis and the Unconscious* and *Fantasia of the Unconscious*), BULLETIN OF KYÛSHÛ SANGYÔ UNIVERSITY, VII, No. 1 (Dec 1970), 7-46.] [In Japanese.]

3640 Wada, Shizuo. "D. H. Lawrence Oboegaki (IV)--*Seishin-Bunseki to Muishiki* to *Muishiki no Gensô* ni Tsuite" (Notes on D. H. Lawrence [IV] --*Psychoanalysis and the Unconscious* and *Fantasia of the Unconscious*), BULLETIN OF KYÛSHÛ SANGYÔ UNIVERSITY, VII, No. 1 (Dec 1970), 7-46.

[Second of a two-part essay on *Psychoanalysis and the Unconscious* and *Fantasia of the Unconscious*. See also Shizuo Wada, "D. H. Lawrence Oboegaki (IV)-- *Seishin-Bunseki to Muishiki* to *Muishiki no Gensô* ni Tsuite" (Notes on D. H. Lawrence [IV] --*Psychoanalysis and the Unconscious* and *Fantasia of the Unconscious*), BULLETIN OF KYÛSHÛ SANGYÔ UNIVERSITY, VI, No. 2 (March 1970), 1-62.] [In Japanese.]

3641 Walsh, Moira. "*Women in Love*," AMERICA, CXXII (23 April 1970), 456.

The fact that DHL was more a polemicist than an artist makes it hard to distinguish between the inadequacies of his vision and the inadequacies of the film adaptation of *Women in Love*. However, director Ken Russell visually supports DHL's "thesis that male-female relationships are frustrating and unsatisfactory at best, and only bearable for a man when supplemented by a close male comradeship."

3642 Weightman, John. "Trifling with the Dead," ENCOUNTER, XXXIV (Jan 1970), 50-53.

The film version of *Women in Love* muddles DHL's meaning, altering some "features of the novel" and compounding its ambiguities. "The subject-matter of the novel" deals with "social or class relationships on the one hand, and personal and sexual relationships on the other." But the implausible relationships between an art-mistress and the lord of the manor and between a school-inspector and the lady of the manor show the unrealistic treatment of class-relationships in the book. The heart of the novel is in the personal relationships, which explore both "Birkin's homosexual attraction to Crich" and the contrast between Hermione as his "Dark Lady" and Ursula as his "Fair Lady." "Possibly the reason why Birkin and Gudrun...find Ursula and Crich unsatisfactory is that the latter are sexually 'normal,' and do not understand...the desire to take sex into the second, and truly mystic, phase." [Detailed comparison of the novel and the film cites the film's "poetic" treatment of the "naked wrestling scene," its "boring" treatment of conventional heterosexual copulation, and its "impertinent liberty" in the use of commercial ragtime music, which DHL regarded as decadent.]

3643 Whitehorn, Ethel. "*Women in Love*," in "Motion Picture Previews," PTA MAGAZINE, LXIV (May 1970), 39.

"The film [of *Women in Love*] communicates Lawrence's powerful feeling for nature, his rejection of a middle-class life style, and his exploration into the nature of man and woman on equal terms. A constant eroticism flowing throughout, consonant with the author's search for sexual freedom, reaches a high point in a nude wrestling scene between the two men." [Brief notice.]

3644 Wilding, Michael. "Between Scylla and Charybdis: *Kangaroo* and the Form of the Political Novel," AUSTRALIAN LITERARY STUDIES, IV (Oct 1970), 334-48.

DHL's letters indicate that the deviation of *Kangaroo* from the form of earlier works was "conscious and deliberate," comparable to the Joycean structural innovations in ULYSSES. DHL's "Scylla and Charybdis" is to steer between the two extremes of romantic adventure in plot and "bourgeois realism" in details. He comes to suspect the "single subsuming image" and "coherent pattern" as distortions of truth. Debates and conversations are presented directly "like pasted in newspaper cuttings." Redundancies and carelessness make the experiment unsuccessful, and *Kangaroo* stands as a casebook of the problems of the political novel.

3645 Wilding, Michael. "'A New Show': The Politics of *Kangaroo*," SOUTHERLY, XXX, No. 1 (1970), 20-40; rptd as "Kangaroo: 'a new show,'" in POLITICAL FICTIONS, by Michael Wilding (Lond: Routledge & Kegan Paul, 1980), pp. 150-91.

In *Kangaroo* there is a tension between the impulse to involvement and rejection of politics. Ultimately DHL rejects both the "money-bond" of capitalists and the "love-bond" of socialists in favor of "faith in his dark gods." The "new show" is the end of traditional and conventional politics and the openness to new possibilities. DHL's impulse toward individuality is expressed in the "recurrent Lawrentian flight" from all social involvement. *Kangaroo* gives a running commentary on the "impulse towards political action," but in a larger context it is inadequate and idiosyncratic.

3646 Williams, Raymond. THE ENGLISH NOVEL FROM DICKENS TO LAWRENCE (NY: Oxford UP, 1970), pp. 169-84.

Like George Eliot and Thomas Hardy, DHL writes about a class new to literature, and in his early stories the sense of community comes alive through a "miracle of language." Feeling with his characters, he alters the educated language of the novelist to the informal and colloquial. This sense of community, of the reality of other people apart from our observation of them, constitutes the essence of *The Rainbow,* where the pressure of change compels a struggle for a new, radical reality, one that requires a new language that is individual rather than communal. In *Women in Love* the novel itself is radically simplified to a new form, powerful but rigid, in order to concentrate on isolated relationships. The inconclusiveness of the ending is DHL's acknowledgement of the sense of loss of community. In *Lady Chatterley's Lover* he attempts to regain it, and goes back to ordinary language.

3647 Wordsworth, Ann. "More Is Less," SPECTATOR, CCIV (21 March 1970), 384.

DHL's plans for Rananim began on a walking tour through the Lake District with Koteliansky before the war, but "the important letters about Rananim are to Bertrand Russell and Lady Ottoline Morrell and other literary friends; Lawrence only mentions the scheme to Kot." The lengthy correspondence collected in *The Quest for Rananim: D. H. Lawrence's Letters to S. S. Koteliansky, 1914 to 1930,* ed by George J. Zytaruk, contains "far too much day-to-day directive, not enough literary discussion, and too little gossip" to be usefully revealing. With few exceptions, "the lived experience" is lacking. "Perhaps the whole problem of publishing complete collections, trivia, post cards, and all, is due for a reconsideration." [See also reply in a Letter to the Editor by C. E. Baron, "More Is Less," SPECTATOR, CCIV (18 April 1970), 524-25.]

3648 Yamaguchi, Tetsuo. "D. H. Lawrence no Bungaku Hihyô" (D. H. Lawrence's Literary Criticism), SHIKOKU CHRISTIAN COLLEGE TREATISES, No. 18 (March 1970), 83-95.

The characteristics of DHL's literary criticism are examined through a discussion of his essay "Herman Melville's MOBY DICK" in *Studies in Classic American Literature.* DHL's criticism is not logical, but it has emotional power to attract readers because he vividly shows his direct feelings toward a work he tries to criticize. [In Japanese.]

3649 Yoshii, Mitsuo. "D. H. Lawrence no Môhitotsu no Jiga--

'Shima o Aishita Otoko' o Chûshin ni" (The Other Ego of D. H. Lawrence--On "The Man Who Loved Islands"), LITERARY MAN, XIII, No. 3 (March 1970), 46-55.

In DHL there was always a wish for keeping pure aloneness in parallel with a wish for living connection with others. In "The Man Who Loved Islands," DHL rejected false human relations in the mass and experimented with the possibility of the ultimate isolation of the protagonist, in whom he projected himself. This isolation is a necessary experience for a next step toward his rebirth. [In Japanese.]

3650 Yoshii, Mitsuo. "D. H. Lawrence Oboegaki—Sakuchû-Jinbutsu no Tokuchô" (The Features of the Characters in D. H. Lawrence's Novels), SHURA, No. 2 (Dec 1970), 63-74.

DHL was a writer who projected himself in his characters. In his early days he loved his mother, but later he was inclined to deny the cultural values which his mother represented and to esteem the simple nature which his father represented. [The chief features of the main characters in all of DHL's longer novels are analyzed in an effort to define the point of this transition.] [In Japanese.]

3651 Yoshii, Mitsuo. "Hôkai to Kyôki no Sôzô—*Tsubasa Aru Hebi* Ron" (A Creation in Collapse and Insanity of Self—On *The Plumed Serpent*), SHURA, No. 1 (June 1970), 47-63.

DHL's concern with politics reached its peak as the " 'leader-cum-follower' " conception in *The Plumed Serpent*. [DHL's ideas on politics are discussed with reference to his ideas on the relation between the individual and the mass, between the individual self and conjugal love, democracy, Christian love of neighbors, and love for one's fellow men.] [In Japanese.]

3652 Z., P. D. "Woman in Love," NEWSWEEK, LXXVI (13 July 1970), 92.

[Review of the film *The Virgin and the Gypsy*, directed by Christopher Miles, written for the screen by Alan Plater.] "Why Lawrence now? His passionate proclamations in favor of feeling, his insistence on the superiority of spontaneous reactions, his rapturous evocation of sexual liberation for women—all these were pitched to a rigidly inhibited turn-of-the-century society. The same can't be said for our world." Hence, Miles "decided to answer this question by treating 'The Virgin and the Gypsy' as a period piece."

3653 Zytaruk, George J. "Introduction," *The Quest for Rananim: D. H. Lawrence's Letters to S. S. Koteliansky, 1914 to 1930*, ed by George J. Zytaruk (Montreal and Lond: McGill-Queen's UP, 1970), pp. xi-xxxvi.

[Traces the production of other collections of DHL's letters and discusses S. S. Koteliansky's background and his relationship with DHL. Of these 343 letters, 104 appear in *The Collected Letters of D. H. Lawrence,* 2 vols., ed by Harry T. Moore (NY: Viking P; Lond: Heinemann, 1962). Many notes.] This collection of letters to one individual permits one to "assess Lawrence's capacity for sustaining human relationships." DHL's motives for helping Koteliansky with his translations were entirely altruistic. In the letters Koteliansky "soon takes on the character of a Lawrencean alter-ego." The insight into DHL given here "cannot be derived from other sources."

1971

3654 Abbas, Ali Abdalla. "The River and the Marsh: The Interdependence between the Public and Private Aspects of Life in the Novels of D. H. Lawrence, with Special Reference to *The Rainbow, Women in Love, Kangaroo,* and *Lady Chatterley's Lover*." Unpublished dissertation, Sussex University, 1971. [Listed in Lawrence F. McNamee, DISSERTATIONS IN ENGLISH AND AMERICAN LITERATURE, SUPP II (NY & Lond: Bowker, 1974), p. 367.]

3655 Abrams, M. H. "Four Versions of the Circuitous Return: Marx, Nietzsche, Eliot, Lawrence," NATURAL SUPERNATURALISM: TRADITION AND REVOLUTION IN ROMANTIC LITERATURE (NY and Lond: W. W. Norton, 1971; rptd Norton Library, 1973), pp. 313-24, espec. pp. 323-24; additional references to DHL, pp. 38, 373.
Apocalypse illustrates DHL's adherence to the Romantic conception of "the circuitous return." The book presents DHL's Romantic vision that man and the universe were once one but became separated, a condition which can be reversed only if man gets back in tune with nature.

3656 Alberto, Giovanni. "Un ricordo da Spotorno" (A Remembrance from Spotorno), LA FIERA LETTERARIA (Rome), 20 June 1971, p. 11.
Mrs. Serafina Astengo Ravagli tells about the period when DHL and Frieda lived in Villa Bernarda, Mrs. Astengo's villa in Spotorno. [In Italian.]

3657 Al-Dabbagh, Abdullah M. "The Social and Political Ideas of D. H. Lawrence." Unpublished dissertation, Cambridge University, 1971. [Listed in Lawrence F. McNamee, DISSERTATIONS IN ENGLISH AND AMERICAN LITERATURE, SUPP II: 1969-1973 (NY & Lond: Bowker, 1974), p. 367.]

3658 Alldritt, Keith. THE VISUAL IMAGINATION OF D. H. LAWRENCE (Evanston, IL: Northwestern UP; Lond: Arnold, 1971). [This study of the visual element as a distinctive feature of DHL's prose fiction is founded on two premises: first, that works of art can reflect individual states of consciousness, social orders, or historical periods; second, that DHL's literary technique "was powerfully affected by his very considerable experience of painting." Focusing on the novels written between 1910 and 1920, the book traces DHL's visual style from the initial influences of nineteenth-century art to those of modernism.] From *The White Peacock* to *Women in Love,* DHL's "main category of perception and the main subject of his novels is process," and "the evolving consciousness of main characters is rendered" largely through art images. In *The White Peacock,* George Saxton fails to evolve because he abandons new perceptions gained through observing art. Paul Morel, on the other hand, accomplishes the necessary evolution in *Sons and Lovers* which depicts Paul's relationships with three women as stages in his development as an artist. While landscape description is a dominant visual mode in *The White Peacock,* in *Sons and Lovers* DHL adds interior scenes and more fully visualized characters. In *The Rainbow,* Will Brangwen is characterized by his changing taste in art, as DHL presents a study of the Victorian consciousness through an analysis of the late-nineteenth century artist. Although Will never reaches a "balanced consciousness," Ursula achieves a resolution to the conflict between seen and visionary reality. The epic vision of *The Rainbow* is distinguished by its "great numinous tableaux, each expressing "a quintessential moment in the history of the Brangwens." In these iconographic passages, DHL, drawing on his knowledge of art rather than on literary tradition, adds to the faithful representation of seen actuality the principles of artistic design and balance, in rhythmic alterations of stability and movement, light and darkness. Although DHL was generally unsympathetic to modernist artists like Duncan Grant, Roger Fry, and Clive Bell, whose work and theories he knew, the influence of modernism accounts for the technical innovations of *Women in Love,* in which an elliptical narrative presents a structure of contrast and tension rather than of process and sequence and in which antithesis and counterforce are rendered through the complex relationships of the four main characters as a means of expressing contemporary experience. In *Women in Love,* works of art reveal character (Gudrun, Loerke) or serve as a focus for major crises (the West African statuette, Loerke's mechanistic sculpture). The conventional appearances of the seen world are called into doubt as the discontinuous structure of the novel presents a series of scenes which provide the background of dying forms. Since these dying forms "deny phenomena their actuality," Birkin struggles to escape from outworn and static perceptions and to see life new and revitalized. The attempt to render experience without resort to conventional images creates a verbal complexity not always convincing, but because of its thematic richness, *Women in Love* rises above its flaws. In DHL's later work, however, the continuing modernist influence "signifies the loss of the particular cultural synthesis that his greatest novels record."

3659 Allendorf, Otmar. "Criticism of D. H. Lawrence in German, 1923-1970: A Bibliography," D. H. LAWRENCE REVIEW, IV (Summer 1971), 210-20.
[A checklist of German-language secondary materials on DHL published in Austria, Germany, and Switzerland, including books, sections of books, doctoral theses, articles, and reviews, and giving for each both its German title and its English translation. Since most of the material is general in nature, the checklist is not subdivided into sections.]

3660 Amette, Jacques-Pierre. "D. H. Lawrence (L'adaptation des oeuvres cinématographiques)" (D. H. Lawrence: The Cinematographic Adaptation of the Works), LA NOUVELLE REVUE FRANÇAISE, XIX (Feb 1971), 108-9.

Thanks to the movies, DHL is re-edited. This is the end of his purgatory because the cinema makes the public at large familiar with the novelist's themes. Ken Russell's adaptation of *Women in Love* is more successful than Christopher Miles's adaptation of *The Virgin and the Gypsy*. On the whole, the power of the cinema is profitable to DHL's works as far as sensuality is concerned, but his works become poorer where reflection, narration, action, and rhythm are concerned. The cinema schematizes literature. [In French.]

3661 Andrews, W. T. (ed). CRITICS ON D. H. LAWRENCE (Lond: George Allen & Unwin; Coral Gables, FL: University of Miami P [Readings in Literary Criticism 9], 1971).

Reviews and articles are organized under three periods of approximately two decades each to show the chronological development of DHL criticism in English. Contents, abstracted under year of first publication: W. T. Andrews, "Introduction," pp. ix-xi. **Critics on D. H. Lawrence: 1911-1930:** D. H. Lawrence, [Excerpt], p. 13, from "Autobiographical Sketch" [not abstracted]; "D. H. Lawrence as a Woman Novelist," p. 14, from "New Novels," ATHENAEUM, No. 4348 (10 Feb 1911), 217; [*The White Peacock*], pp. 14-15, from "Novels," SATURDAY REVIEW (Lond), CXI (13 May 1911), 589-90; P[erceval] G[ibbon], "*Sons and Lovers*--'A Novel of Quality,' " pp. 15-16, from BOOKMAN (Lond), XLIV (Aug 1913), 213; Ford Madox Hueffer, [Comment on *The Trespasser*], p. 16, quoted in Richard Aldington, PORTRAIT OF A GENIUS, BUT... (Lond: Wm Heinemann, 1950); Ezra Pound, [Letter to Harriet Monroe, 23 Sept 1913], pp. 16-17, from Letter 23 in THE LETTERS OF EZRA POUND, 1907-1941, ed by D. D. Paige (NY: Harcourt, Brace, 1950); [*The Rainbow*], p. 17, from ATHENAEUM, No. 4594 (13 Nov 1915); G. W. de Tunzelmann, [Letter to the Editor on the suppression of *The Rainbow*], pp. 17-18, from "*The Rainbow*," ATHENAEUM, No. 4595 (20 Nov 1915), 369; [John Middleton] M[urry], "The Decay of Mr. D. H. Lawrence," pp. 18-20, from ATHENAEUM, 17 Dec 1920, p. 836; J. Middleton Murry, "The Nostalgia of Mr. D. H. Lawrence," pp. 20-24, from NATION AND THE ATHENAEUM, XXIX (13 Aug 1921), 713-14; J. Middleton Murry, [*Aaron's Rod*], pp. 24-27, from "Two Remarkable Novels," NATION AND THE ATHENAEUM, XXI (12 Aug 1922), 655-56; J. Middleton Murry, [*Fantasia of the Unconscious*], p. 27, from "Relevancy," NATION AND THE ATHENAEUM, XXXIII (31 March 1923), 984-85; J. D. Beresford, [*Kangaroo*], pp. 27-28, from "Some Autumn Novels," NATION AND THE ATHENAEUM, XXXIV (8 Dec 1923); E. B. C. Jones, [*England, My England and Other Stories*], p. 28, from "Recent Fiction," NATION AND THE ATHENAEUM, XXXV (23 Feb 1924), 738; Conrad Aiken [*Studies in Classic American Literature*], pp. 28-31, from "Mr. Lawrence: Sensationalist," NATION AND THE ATHENAEUM, XXXV (12 July 1924), 482; Edwin Muir, [*The Plumed Serpent*], pp. 31-32, from "Fiction," NATION AND THE ATHENAEUM, XXXVIII (20 Feb 1926), 719; Barrington Gates, [*Pansies*], pp. 32-33, from "Poetry," NATION AND THE ATHENAEUM, XLV (27 July 1929), 572; Richard Church, [*Pansies*], pp. 33-34, from "Three Established Poets," SPECTATOR, CXLIII (3 Aug 1929), 164-65. **Critics on D. H. Lawrence: 1930-1950:** Catherine Carswell, "Introductory Note," p. 35, from THE SAVAGE PILGRIMAGE: A NARRATIVE OF D. H. LAWRENCE, rvd ed (Lond: Chatto & Windus, 1932); V[ita] Sackville-West, [*The*

Virgin and the Gipsy], p. 36, from SPECTATOR, CXLIV (28 June 1930), 1055-56; James Joyce, [Letters to Harriet Shaw Weaver, 27 Sept 1930 and 17 Dec 1931], pp. 36-37, from LETTERS OF JAMES JOYCE, ed by Stuart Gilbert (Lond: Faber & Faber, 1957); Virginia Woolf, "Notes on D. H. Lawrence," pp. 37-40, from THE MOMENT AND OTHER ESSAYS (Lond: Hogarth P, 1947), pp. 79-82 (NY: Harcourt, Brace, 1948), pp. 93-98; Lord David Cecil, [*The Letters of D. H. Lawrence*, ed by Aldous Huxley], pp. 40-41, from "D. H. Lawrence in His Letters," SPECTATOR, CXLIX (18 Nov 1932), 695-96; Aldous Huxley, [Excerpt], pp. 41-43, from "Introduction," *The Letters of D. H. Lawrence*, ed by Aldous Huxley (Lond: Wm Heinemann; NY: Viking P, 1932), pp. x-xiii; Theodore Spencer, "Is Lawrence Neglected?" pp. 43-44, from SATURDAY REVIEW OF LITERATURE, XV (31 Oct 1936), 13; David Garnett, [*Phoenix: Posthumous Papers of D. H. Lawrence*, ed by Edward D. McDonald], pp. 44-47, from "Books in General," NEW STATESMAN AND NATION, XII (21 Nov 1936), 812; W. H. Auden, "Some Notes on D. H. Lawrence," pp. 47-51, from NATION (NY), CLXIV (26 April 1947), 482-84. **Critics on D. H. Lawrence Since 1950**: Roger Dataller, "Elements of D. H. Lawrence's Prose Style," pp. 52-57, from ESSAYS IN CRITICISM, III (Oct 1953), 413-24; T. B. Tomlinson, "Lawrence and Modern Life: *Sons and Lovers, Women in Love*," pp. 58-66, from CRITICAL REVIEW (Melbourne), No. 8 (1965), 3-18; Edward Engelberg, "Escape from the Circles of Experience: D. H. Lawrence's *The Rainbow* as a Modern *Bildungsroman*," pp. 67-80, from PUBLICATIONS OF THE MODERN LANGUAGE ASSOCIATION OF AMERICA, LXXVIII (March 1963), 103-13; F. H. Langman, "*Women in Love*," pp. 81-86, from ESSAYS IN CRITICISM, XVII (April 1967), 183-93; Curtis Atkinson, "Was There Fact in D. H. Lawrence's *Kangaroo*?" pp. 87-88, from MEANJIN QUARTERLY, XXIX (Sept 1965), 358-59; G. B. McK. Henry, "Carrying On: *Lady Chatterley's Lover*," pp. 89-104, from CRITICAL REVIEW (Melbourne), No. 10 (1967), 46-62; H. M. Daleski, "The Tiger and the Lamb: The Duality of Lawrence," pp. 105-8, from THE FORKED FLAME: A STUDY OF D. H. LAWRENCE (Evanston: Northwestern UP, 1965), pp. 20-31; Eugene Goodheart, "*The Man Who Died*," pp. 109-16, from THE UTOPIAN VISION OF D. H. LAWRENCE (Chicago: University of Chicago P, 1963), pp. 149-59; George A. Panichas, "Voyage of Oblivion," pp. 117-23, from ADVENTURE IN CONSCIOUSNESS: THE MEANING OF D. H. LAWRENCE'S RELIGIOUS QUEST (The Hague: Mouton, 1964), pp. 180-92; "Select Bibliography," pp. 125-26 [not abstracted].

3662 Armstrong, Marion. "Cold Hands Warmed," CHRISTIAN CENTURY, Continuing NEW CHRISTIAN, LXXXVIII (3 Feb 1971), 168-69.

[Review of the film *The Virgin and the Gypsy*, directed by Christopher Miles, written for the screen by Alan Plater.] "The great cinematic advantage of *The Virgin and the Gipsy* over *Women in Love* is its narrative directness and simplicity." [Superficial.]

3663 Baim, Joseph. "Past and Present in D. H. Lawrence's 'A Fragment of Stained Glass,'" STUDIES IN SHORT FICTION, VIII (Spring 1971), 323-26.

Often dismissed, "A Fragment of Stained Glass" "warrants attention" because its "theme becomes a major organizing motif" in DHL's fiction and because "its structure and narration are. . .well-wrought and effectively disposed." The story "builds on the tension" between the fifteenth century, "when men were fully attuned to passional experience," and "modern, industrialized England," when the capacity for "meaningful connection" with the universe is declining. The theme is "the need for a rebirth of the will to resist de-humanization."

3664 Baldwin, Alice. "The Structure of the Coatl Symbol in *The Plumed Serpent*," STYLE, V (Spring 1971), 138-50.

Linguistically, the vision of *The Plumed Serpent* is based upon two symbols, the bird "quetzal" and the snake "coatl" of ancient Indian religions. The snake symbolism is carefully structured, the bird symbolism is not, and this leads to DHL's failure in establishing tension between the two after he has indicated that it exists.

3665 Barber, David S. "Community in *Women in Love*," NOVEL: A FORUM ON FICTION, V (Fall 1971), 32-41.

Birkin and Ursula in *Women in Love* choose to be officially married as an expression of a need for a social bond beyond marriage. As Birkin works toward communion with culture, he gradually realizes that the transcendent moment may involve using another person. Neither "star equilibrium," exclusively a timeless moment, nor "proud singleness," which moves toward isolation, is adequate. Birkin abandons theorizing to accept the truth of Ursula's faith in tender, non-transcendent love, which is a form of unity in duality and the model for society's relation to itself. Birkin's quest is ultimately for communion and community. The isolation of "proud singleness" produces Loerke, an embodiment of social hatred.

3666 Baron, C[arl] E. "Lawrence's Influence on Eliot," CAMBRIDGE QUARTERLY, V (Spring 1971), 235-48.

T. S. Eliot's response to DHL, though largely negative, was not entirely so, as Eliot's comment in an unpublished letter on DHL's statement on " 'stark directness' " in poetry shows. DHL "placed" Eliot in Sir Clifford Chatterley's discussion of ordered emotion in literature in *Lady Chatterley's Lover*. According to Martin Jarrett-Kerr, other unpublished letters show that Eliot "modified his view of Lawrence." Possibly DHL touched on matters that Eliot found painful and difficult, yet "felt he had to handle." This idea seems plausible in light of a comparison of a passage in "The Crown" with a passage in LITTLE GIDDING which employs the same metaphor of the Dove for the Holy Ghost and echoes other verbal phrases and imagery. References to Eliot in THE AUTOBIOGRAPHY OF BERTRAND RUSSELL, 1914-1944 (1968), provide additional evidence of Laurentian sources, in *Women in Love* and "The Crown," for Eliot's ideas on knowledge in FOUR QUARTETS. And a passage in THE DRY SALVAGES parallels a passage on "the science of augury" in *Etruscan Places*. The cumulative effect of the evidence suggests that DHL and Eliot are, "in essentials, much closer to each other than Pound and Joyce were to each other," and that "Eliot, in his poetry, paid as radical and sincere a tribute to the power of Lawrence's writing as he possibly could." [Cited passages from DHL and Eliot are quoted and discussed fully.]

3667 Beards, Richard D. "The Checklist of D. H. Lawrence Criticism and Scholarship, 1970," D. H. LAWRENCE REVIEW, IV (Spring 1971), 90-102.

[This annual checklist brings up to date the two earlier ones by Richard D. Beards published in D. H. LAWRENCE REVIEW in the fall 1968 and spring 1970 issues. The checklist is sub-divided into five parts: General, Poetry, Individual Works of Fiction, Non-Fiction Prose, and Drama.]

3668 Beebe, Maurice. "Joyce and the Meanings of Modernism," LITTERS FROM ALOFT: PAPERS DELIVERED AT THE SECOND CANADIAN JAMES JOYCE SEMINAR (Tulsa, OK: University of Tulsa Monograph Series No. 13, 1971), pp. 15-25.

On the basis of four criteria--"modernism is formalistic"; "modernism is characterized by an attitude of detachment and ambivalence that we may put under the general heading of irony"; "modernist literature makes use of myth not as a discipline of belief but as a means of ordering art"; and "modernist art is reflexive in that it turns back upon itself"--DHL is judged not to be a modernist.

3669 Beer, John. "D. H. Lawrence," TIMES LITERARY SUPPLEMENT (Lond), 24 Sept 1971, p. 1148.

[Letters to the Editor in reply to Keith Sagar, "D. H. Lawrence," TIMES LITERARY SUPPLEMENT (Lond), 10 Sept 1971, p. 1086.] DHL's "Red Wolf" trots toward the sunrise, thus toward the east. DHL's revision was to remove a complication, not to change a mistake. Sagar should let DHL's revision stand. [See also comment by M. B. Mencher, "D. H. Lawrence," TIMES LITERARY SUPPLEMENT, 17 Sept 1971, pp. 1119, and reply to Mencher by Harry T. Moore, "D. H. Lawrence," TIMES LITERARY SUPPLEMENT (Lond), 1 Oct 1971, p. 1177.]

3670 Bellamy, William. THE NOVELS OF WELLS, BENNETT, AND GALSWORTHY, 1890-1910 (NY: Barnes & Noble, 1971), pp. 1, 2, 9, 16, 41, 43, 47, 113, 214, 217, 229, 232.

In evaluating a modernism which dates from 1880 to the present, it is time to re-evaluate the 1920s criticism by Virginia Woolf and D. H. Lawrence, who thought modernism began about 1910. DHL attacked Galsworthy in "John Galsworthy" in SCRUTINIES BY VARIOUS WRITERS (1928).

3671 Bellow, Saul. "Culture Now: Some Animadversions, Some Laughs," MODERN OCCASIONS, I (Winter 1971), 162-78, espec. 169, 172.

DHL's view that Melville's MOBY-DICK represents the doom of white civilization is the "supreme source" of similar views expressed by contemporary black writers such as Cecil M. Brown and Leroi Jones and echoed by the white liberal literary community. [An extract from DHL's essay on MOBY-DICK supports the point.]

3672 Bhalla, Brij Mohan. "The Mutual Flame: The Quest for Self-Hood in Relation to Form in the Later Novels of D. H. Lawrence," DISSERTATION ABSTRACTS INTERNATIONAL, XXXII (1971), 3292A. Unpublished dissertation, University of Wisconsin, 1971.

3673 Birnbaum, Milton. ALDOUS HUXLEY'S QUEST FOR VALUES (Knoxville: University of Tennessee P, 1971), pp. vii, 4, 6, 11, 17, 23, 24, 25, 55, 57, 58, 61, 69, 95, 109, 119, 126, 127, 133, 139, 150, 153, 156, 163, 176, 177, 181, 182, 188n, 199n, 201n.

POINT COUNTER POINT "describes the problem of the disintegrated personality of our times, a personality not living in accordance with the philosophy of the instinctive life which Huxley, under the influence of D. H. Lawrence, was then advocating." Mark Rampion, "Huxley's first ideal character [,] is a fusion of Greek culture" and the Lawrentian ideal: "the person who lived instinctively, spontaneously, realistically, intuitively, fully." In DO WHAT YOU WILL, Huxley "endorses Lawrence's prescription of. . .a 'natural love' that is free from the artificial restraints of the Platonic, Christian, and romantic notions," yet "he cannot get so passionately involved about love as did Lawrence." As DHL denounced "science and the mechanization it has brought into our lives," Rampion speaks of " 'Jesus's and Newton's and Henry Ford's disease.' All three diseases could be eliminated, both Lawrence and Huxley felt, by the rejection of science, technology, and traditional Christianity." Huxley, however, criticized DHL because he never " 'looked through a microscope.' "

3674 Boulton, James T. "Introduction to the New Edition," *Movements in European History,* by D. H. Lawrence (Oxford: Oxford UP, 1971), pp. vii-xxiv.

Count Dionys Psanek's concern in *The Ladybird* with " 'Obedience, submission, faith, belief, responsibility, power' " became DHL's subject in *Movements in European History*, published in 1921 under the pseudonym "Lawrence H. Davison" as a text for " 'junior forms in grammar, or upper forms in primary schools.' " Minor editorial censorship was made by the publisher, and DHL had to excise praise of Luther and criticism of the Pope in the 1925 edition for the Irish Roman Catholic schools market, though the textbook was never commercially successful. Although DHL attempts " 'not. . .a formal, connected textbook, but a series of vivid sketches of movements and people,' " his framework was conventional. DHL found "two 'great passions' " at work in history: " 'the passion of pride and power and conquest, and the passion of peace and production.' " A supreme leader in both is needed, he believed, but neither Italian Fascism nor Soviet Communism, relying "on bullying and brutality," could produce one.

3675 Bradbury, Malcolm. THE SOCIAL CONTEXT OF MODERN ENGLISH LITERATURE (NY: Schocken, 1971), pp. 32, 51, 79, 86-87, 145n.

Although the city in the work of Forster and DHL is seen as culturally discontinuous and polarized against the agrarian world, their response is neither provincial nor nostalgic but an imaginative engagement with the city as a metaphor of a ruined or misused England. In *Kangaroo*, DHL described 1915 as the end of the old world. Though hoping for "a phoenix rebirth, he...created a familiar imaginative pattern for the century--that of an historical process caught between two moments of turn with both purgative and disastrous meanings."

3676 Brayfield, Peg. "Lawrence's 'Male and Female Principles' and the Symbolism of 'The Fox,'" MOSAIC, IV, No. 3 (1971), 41-65.

The major symbolic pattern of "The Fox" makes aesthetic and psychological sense if one recognizes that the central conflict in both March's character and the plot derives from DHL's *Study of Thomas Hardy*, wherein he equates the Female Principle with the body and the Male Principle with the mind. March's conflict is between the two principles, which she sees symbolized in the fox and which Henry sees in March as well as the fox. He therefore kills the fox, for he wants March to live by the Female Principle alone and realizes unconsciously that the fox represents him to March only in a partial and unsatisfactory way.

3677 Burns, Robert. "The Novel as a Metaphysical Statement: Lawrence's *The Rainbow*," SOUTHERN REVIEW (Adelaide, South Australia), IV (1971), 139-60.

"*The Rainbow* is essentially a metaphysical statement" which concerns "the terms or conditions within which human life occurs" and which aims to comprehend through an "engagement with experience" of a "conceptional" rather than a religious sort. The opposing tendencies of the Brangwen men, a life of involvement, subjectivity, and "sensual satiety at the expense of conceptual awareness," and of "the woman," a way "of dissociation, of a deliberate seeking an exercise of the will away from the material and the accidental towards the expansiveness and the (logical) certainties of abstract thought and of the linguistic address of experience," "define the two poles of possibility between which each individual of the succeeding generations" lives. "Fullness of being will be enjoyed by that individual whose life is...a lived reconciliation of these two tendencies," but in the case of a "necessary choice," it "is more likely to come from answering to the inclinations of the blood than to the demands of the intellect." [Detailed discussion of the individual characters of each generation of Brangwens: Tom and Lydia, Will and Anna, and Ursula.] DHL rigorously "traces out the effect of whole upon part, part upon whole, and part upon part." In the close narrative texture, religious, "quasi-evangelical" passages "read as a mere embroidering, an arbitrary addition," "to conceal, or to inflate, the familiar here-and-now nature of the general plan" because DHL's metaphysical "plan of the nature of existence...is really not a very illuminating one."

3678 Carrington, [Dora]. CARRINGTON: LETTERS AND EXTRACTS FROM HER DIARIES, ed and with an Introduction by David Garnett, with a Biographical Note by Noel Carrington (NY: Holt, Rinehart, 1971), pp. 24, 84, 90, 283-84.

[Carrington, who did not like the Lawrences, mentions them in several letters: she refers, in Dec 1915, to DHL's plan to go to Florida; in Nov 1917, to his expulsion from Cornwall; in Nov 1917, to "his German wife in all her grossness"; and on 4 March 1924, to seeing the Lawrences at a party at Dorothy Brett's house the day before the three "set off in an ocean liner for Mexico": "Lawrence was very rude to me of course...Apparently he came back this winter expecting to be greeted as the new Messiah."]

3679 Chavis, Geraldine Giebel. "Ursula Brangwen: Toward Self and Selflessness," THOTH, XII (Fall 1971), 18-28.

Ursula Brangwen in *The Rainbow* and *Women in Love* finds her "meaningful identity" by two routes: through self and selflessness. Her character development, "based on her subliminal responses to life's pains and joys," follows "a cyclical pattern in which hope and disillusionment alternate." These unconscious responses are those of an idealist who must constantly face reality and transcend disillusionment: her adored father's thwarting of her strong will, leading to a "solidification of self"; her desire in college for both an "almost mystical knowledge of life" and "the opportunity for independence and equality"; her "passionate quest for selfhood" as only "her vision"; the "nadir" of her experience in her encounter with the male power of the horses; and finally her epiphany of the rainbow, encompassing Ursula's fear of death and love of life, her "attempt to define a utopian state of existence on earth and to clarify her 'religion' of self and selflessness," and which remains her hope for a "fulfilling union with a being outside herself," a hope realized in *Women in Love*. In her "spiritual and physical communion" with Birkin, Ursula is able to "purge herself of the destructive egotistical will," while still retaining the "dignity of her selfhood." Through her submission to "selfless, spiritual union with Birkin," she is able at last to relate "the highest self-fulfillment to the loftiest selflessness."

3680 Chung, Chong-Wha. "The Leadership Novels of D. H. Lawrence." Unpublished dissertation, Manchester University, 1971. [Listed in Geoffrey M. Paterson and Joan E. Hardy (eds), INDEX TO THESES, XXI (1970-71), (Lond: Aslib, 1973), p. 21.]

3681 Clancy, Jack. "The Film and the Book: D. H. Lawrence and Joseph Heller on the Screen," MEANJIN QUARTERLY, XXX (March 1971), 96-101.

Although literary and cinematic techniques are similar, the ways of "seeing" in a novel and in a film are different because the film must be visual and concrete while a novel is abstract and conceptual. Therefore, it is a mistake to attempt literalness in transforming a novel into a movie as Ken Russell did in *Women in Love*. Christopher Miles's film *The Virgin and the Gypsy* comes off much better because the simpler story could be filmed as a character unfolding in a real situation.

3682 Clark, L. D. "The D. H. Lawrence Festival: Kiowa Ranch, New Mexico, September 30-October 4, 1970," D. H. LAWRENCE REVIEW, IV (Spring 1971), 44-60.

[An informal report on the people, both professional and non-professional, ideas, reminiscences, exchanges, and debates at the D. H. Lawrence Festival at Taos. Illustrated with twenty-seven photographs by LaVerne Harrell Clark and Judith R. Cowan.]

3683 Clupper, Beatrice Blong. "The Male as Principle in D. H. Lawrence's Fiction," DISSERTATION ABSTRACTS INTERNATIONAL, XXXII (1972), 5778A. Unpublished dissertation, University of Illinois at Urbana-Champaign, 1971.

3684 Coleman, Arthur. EASTWOOD THROUGH BYGONE AGES: A BRIEF HISTORY OF THE PARISH OF EASTWOOD (Eastwood: Eastwood Historical Society, 1971), pp. 107-13.
[Brief biographical account of DHL, his birthplace, parentage, and education, and his fictional use of Eastwood. Some Eastwood residents think that DHL's father was "unjustly villified" in Sons and Lovers and dispute the accuracy of "the domestic disturbances" depicted in the novel. "It was not until thirty years after [DHL's] death...that Eastwood began to afford him the recognition so richly deserved as a novelist," but now "a new generation" can appreciate his work. Illustrated with a photograph of DHL's birthplace on Victoria Street. The book also contains accounts of DHL's friend W. E. Hopkin, the colliery, and many places that were used as settings in DHL's Midlands fiction.]

3685 Corke, Helen. "D. H. Lawrence: The Early Stage," D. H. LAWRENCE REVIEW, IV (Summer 1971), 111-21.
[This memoir is the substance of a paper presented to the D. H. Lawrence Festival in Taos, New Mexico, on 1 October 1970. It discusses briefly DHL's boyhood and youth, concentrating on the period of his teaching at the Davidson Road School in Croydon, his first meeting with the author, and his writing of *The Trespasser*.]

3686 Cowell, Catherine R. "The Lawrentian Philosophy of Communication: An Analysis of Selected Essays of D. H. Lawrence," DISSERTATION ABSTRACTS INTERNATIONAL, XXXII (1972), 6582A. Unpublished dissertation, University of Denver, 1971.

3687 Crump, G. B. "Gopher Prairie or Papplewick?: *The Virgin and the Gipsy* as Film," D. H. LAWRENCE REVIEW, IV (Summer 1971), 142-53.
[Review essay of *The Virgin and the Gypsy,* produced by Kenneth Harper, directed by Christopher Miles, written for the screen by Alan Plater (1970).] As one of DHL's lesser achievements, *The Virgin and the Gipsy* seems an unlikely source for a film adaptation, but no doubt the "clash of value systems, implied in the...title and dramatized in the final cataclysm" attracted director Miles and screenwriter Plater to the story. "In trying to discover appropriate visual and dramatic cues for the tense inner conflict of Lawrence's novella, Miles and Plater have too often settled for the facile and obvious rather than the difficult and subtle. As a result, they end by distorting the effect of the original until in some ways it is almost unrecognizable." Distortions in characterization and misinterpretations of DHL's ideas about class conflicts show "that it is not always possible to duplicate the effects of one medium in another."

3688 Crump, G. B. "*Women in Love*: Novel and Film," D. H. LAWRENCE REVIEW, IV (Spring 1971), 28-41.

[Review essay of *Women in Love,* written for the screen and produced by Larry Kramer, directed by Ken Russell (1970).] One would expect the "realistic" level of DHL's work "to be well served by an objective medium like film." For all the plausibility of its acting and precise detail in its mounting, however, *Women in Love* as film is not totally satisfying as a realistic work. Although Pauline Kael blames Russell's direction for this failure, it is "primarily created by Lawrence's fidelity in the novel to a more profound vision of personality than can be accommodated by strict verisimilitude." [Analysis of acting, screenplay, and direction in relation to the novel.] The movie "frequently seems to be a pretentious melodrama full of gratuitous emotion, murky symbolism, and deliberate obfuscation in the treatment of motives." These failures are also flaws in the novel; DHL's "rejection of 'the old stable ego--of the character' does not relieve him of his responsibility to make his people consistent and plausible." The great value of the film version, however, lies in its confirmation of "the skill with which Lawrence registered the buried rhythms of society and character" and in its dramatization of the "larger rhythms of peace and violence." "Because of the interior quality of its action, the movie, like the book, is best regarded as a poem constructed around a richly-textured pattern of symbols and images." The "abiding interest" of the "film is that it suggests something of the novel's totality of vision."

3689 Cushman, Keith. "D. H. Lawrence at Work: The Making of 'Odour of Chrysanthemums,' " JOURNAL OF MODERN LITERATURE, II (Winter 1971-1972), 367-92; rvd and rptd as Chap. III: " 'Odour of Chrysanthemums,' " in D. H. LAWRENCE AT WORK: THE EMERGENCE OF THE "PRUSSIAN OFFICER" STORIES, by Keith Cushman (Charlottesville: UP of Virginia, 1978), pp. 47-76.

If we trace DHL's working of the material for "Odour of Chrysanthemums," we can trace his artistic apprenticeship. His heavily symbolic use of flower images was doubtless in hopes of an early magazine offer; he was rewarded by sale of the story to the ENGLISH REVIEW in 1909. Ford Madox Ford recalls discovering DHL's genius upon reading the first paragraph. The biographical background only begins with DHL's uncle's death in an accident in a mine; the many other family connections in the story ultimately reflect on DHL's marriage to Frieda and his concept of separateness. In its three versions, two of which are published, "Odour of Chrysanthemums" contains situations also treated in *The White Peacock, The Rainbow,* and *The Widowing of Mrs. Holroyd.* [Includes a detailed comparison of the texts of "Odour of Chrysanthemums" and similar passages from the other three works cited.]

3690 Cushman, Keith. "The Making of 'The Prussian Officer': A Correction," D. H. LAWRENCE REVIEW, IV (Fall 1971), 263-73; absorbed in Chap. V: " 'The Prussian Officer' and 'The Thorn in the Flesh,' " in D. H. LAWRENCE AT WORK: THE EMERGENCE OF THE "PRUSSIAN OFFICER" STORIES, by Keith Cushman (Charlottesville: UP of Virginia, 1978), pp. 167-73.

[Takes issue with the opinion of Roger Dataller, "Mr. Lawrence and Mrs. Woolf," ESSAYS IN CRITICISM, VIII (Jan 1958), 48-59, that by considering the printed magazine and collected versions of DHL's stories we can follow his revisions; the manuscript versions must also be considered.] DHL did not add 1,500 words to "Honour and Arms," the magazine version of "The Prussian Officer"; they "can be found in the holograph that antedates both magazine and book texts." "Throughout his career, Lawrence had to face the problem of writing to the length that magazine editors wanted to publish." "Magazine publication was a source of ready cash. . . . Austin Harrison bought 'Honour and Arms' for the ENGLISH REVIEW but wanted a shorter text." DHL agreed, knowing that "the full text would be published in his first collection of tales at the end of the year." Although DHL did extensively recast "The Thorn in the Flesh," "the most significant knowledge that emerges from a careful scrutiny of the different versions of 'The Prussian Officer' is the fact that Lawrence allowed the 'best short story' he had ever done to be cut for magazine publication." [See also exchange of letters by Brian H. Finney and Keith Cushman, in "Laurentiana," D. H. LAWRENCE REVIEW, V (Fall 1972), 331-32.]

3691 Delavenay, Émile. "Comptes Rendus" (Reviews), ÉTUDES ANGLAISES, XXIV (April-June 1971), 206-7.
The Quest for Rananim: D. H. Lawrence's Letters to S. S. Koteliansky, 1914 to 1930, ed by George J. Zytaruk, a collection of 326 letters in Koteliansky's bequest to the British Museum, is an important contribution to scholarship for what these letters reveal not only of DHL's relations with "Kot" (with one significant gap in the correspondence between March 1924 and December 1925) but also of his relations with his editors and agents, with John Middleton Murry and Katherine Mansfield, with Richard Aldington and Hilda Doolittle, and with the psychoanalysts Dr. Barbara Low and Dr. David Eder, whose notes for those years would be of great importance. [In French.]

3692 Delavenay, Émile. "David Herbert Lawrence et la crise de conscience américaine" (David Herbert Lawrence and the Crisis of American Conscience), LE MONDE, 8 Jan 1971, p. 13.
[A comment on The D. H. Lawrence Festival at Taos, New Mexico, 30 Sept-4 Oct 1970. The symposium reflected in its diversity of participants and conflicting points of view the current crisis in the American conscience.] [In French.]

3693 Delavenay, Émile. "D. H. Lawrence," TIMES LITERARY SUPPLEMENT (Lond), 15 Jan 1971, p. 69.
[Letter to the Editor in reply to "The Lawrence Industry," TIMES LITERARY SUPPLEMENT (Lond), 18 Dec 1970, pp. 1496-98, with a rejoinder by the anonymous reviewer. Refutes the reviewer's "disregard for context" and preference for "the Lawrence legend to some uncomfortable facts," and maintains the correctness of Delavenay's "chronological approach" to DHL. The reviewer responds to four specifics of Delavenay's letter.]

3694 Delavenay, Émile. "D. H. Lawrence," TIMES LITERARY SUPPLEMENT (Lond), 10 Sept 1971, p. 1086.
[Letter to the Editor in reply to a letter by Malcolm Pittock, "D. H. Lawrence," TIMES LITERARY SUPPLEMENT (Lond), 20 Aug 1971, p. 999.] Pittock's facts are correct, but "the question of the King's Scholarship Examination of

December, 1904, is rather more involved." DHL was "one of eleven successful men classed in the First Division, Group I, among whom THE TEACHER divided its prize of £60 since 'there has been no classification in order of merit available.'" [See also reply to Pittock by Harry T. Moore, "D. H. Lawrence," TIMES LITERARY SUPPLEMENT (Lond), 10 Sept 1971, p. 1086.]

  3695 Delavenay, Émile. D. H. LAWRENCE AND EDWARD CARPENTER: A STUDY IN EDWARDIAN TRANSITION (Lond: William Heinemann; NY: Taplinger, 1971).

[Originally a "Thèse Complémentaire" presented at the Sorbonne, Paris, 1969.] Internal evidence in DHL's novels points to extensive influence by Edward Carpenter, evident, among other places, in the similarity of ideas presented in Carpenter's LOVE'S COMING OF AGE and in DHL's manuscript of *The Sisters* and the novel *Women in Love*. For example, Rupert Birkin's obsession with homosexuality is explained by a comparison with Gerald Crich in Carpenterian terms. Crich illustrates Carpenter's "man the ungrown" who is limited in his ability to accept different kinds of love, while Birkin is the prototype of the man of the future whose character is a combination of both male and female qualities, which Carpenter ascribes to the man of homogenic nature, or "urning." Carpenter provided DHL with a "mental attitude" which manifests itself in the novels, but the influence was not acknowledged by DHL because Carpenter was not prestigious, because DHL may have been ashamed to admit such extensive borrowing, or because DHL was afraid of suffering guilt by association in defending homosexuality.

  3696 Delavenay, Émile. "D. H. Lawrence et Sacher-Masoch: Contribution à l'étude d'une sensibilité moderne" (D. H. Lawrence and Sacher-Masoch: Contribution to the Study of a Modern Sensibility), LE ROMANTISME ANGLO-AMÉRICAIN: MÉLANGES OFFERTS À LOUIS BONNEROT (Paris: Didier, 1971), pp. 345-70; also pub in English as "D. H. Lawrence and Sacher-Masoch," trans by Katharine M. Delavenay, D. H. LAWRENCE REVIEW, VI (Summer 1973), 119-48.

[Detailed discussion of Gilles Deleuze's psychological study, in SACHER-MASOCH: AN INTERPRETATION, of the tortures of the "suprasensual" hero as "'so many moments of ascension towards the ideal'" and of the typical masochian character as "'a victim in search of a tyrant.'"] DHL's masochism can be viewed as "a fundamental psychological attitude linked with those 'behaviour patterns of bondage and humiliation' which are known to have been" operative in his relationship with his mother and later with Frieda. Certain of his images re-echo obsessively from one work to another, suggesting a process of gradual discovery of the significance of persistent impressions from childhood and youth. Such exploration is remarkable for its sincerity and respect for raw psychological data, but it is also remarkable for a certain reticence, a block which from 1919 on led DHL at times to reject the systematic interpretations of psychoanalysis. In any case, cruelty "is a keynote in the ambivalent, complex interplay of identifications between the novelist and his characters." A survey of the more prominent examples of this relationship in the novels, the short fiction, and the poetry reveals that we are faced with an invariant feature of DHL's literary creation of characters which springs not from a preconceived, abstract view of the universe but from the very nature of his phantasms and day-dreams. "The Soiled Rose," written in 1911 during DHL's convalescence from pneumonia, not only contains a typical erotic scene involving a cloak of wild animal skins but also "offers further evident suggestions of masochism in its widest sense: . . .fetishism, castration complex, dependence on woman--mother and mistress--fear of and attraction toward the virile hero and rival, exclusion of the father, contrast between debilitating civilization and mother nature, rites of the hunt, agriculture and rebirth: all find their place in this story." Although significantly revised and published in *The Prussian Officer and Other Stories* under the more innocuous title "The Shades of Spring," the story, in its original version, contains revealing passages which "rule out all possibility of any influence of Freud through Frieda" but which show the story to be, in DHL's own admission, " 'like sick man's work.' " [In addition to "The Soiled Rose," the article comments briefly on *The White Peacock, Sons and Lovers, Love Poems and Others* ("Cruelty and Love," "Cherry Robbers," "Snap-Dragon," "Virgin Youth"), *Women in Love*, and *Lady Chatterley's Lover*, and draws comparisons with the psychological ideas of Krafft-Ebing and Deleuze and the literary themes and imagery of Baudelaire's LES FLEURS DU MAL and Sacher-Masoch's VENUS IN FURS.] [In French.]

3697 D. H. LAWRENCE REVIEW, ed by James C. Cowan, IV, No. 1 (Spring 1971).

Contents, abstracted under 1971: James C. Cowan, "Preface," pp. v-vi [not abstracted]; Leslie M. Thompson, "D. H. Lawrence and Judas," pp. 1-19; George J. Zytaruk, " 'The Undying Man': D. H. Lawrence's Yiddish Story," pp. 20-27; G. B. Crump, "*Women in Love*: Novel and Film," pp. 28-41; Keith Sagar, "Four Paintings by D. H. Lawrence," pp. 42-43; L. D. Clark, "The D. H. Lawrence Festival: Kiowa Ranch, New Mexico, September 30-October 4, 1970," with photographs by LaVerne H. Clark and Judith R. Cowan, pp. 44-60; Harry T. Moore, "Some New Volumes of Lawrence's Letters," pp. 61-73; James R. Bennett, "The Novel, Truth, and Community," pp. 74-89 [not abstracted]; Richard D. Beards, "The Checklist of D. H. Lawrence Criticism and Scholarship, 1970," pp. 90-102; "Laurentiana," pp. 103-8 [not abstracted]; "Contributors," pp. 109-10 [not abstracted.]

3698 D. H. LAWRENCE REVIEW, ed by James C. Cowan, IV, No. 2 (Summer 1971).

Contents, abstracted under 1971: Helen Corke, "D. H. Lawrence: The Early Stage," pp. 111-21; Evelyn J. Hinz, "*The Trespasser*: Lawrence's Wagnerian Tragedy and Divine Comedy," pp. 122-41; G. B. Crump, "Gopher Prairie or Papplewick?: *The Virgin and the Gipsy* as Film," pp. 142-53; Keith Sagar, "D. H. Lawrence: Dramatist," with photographs by Douglas H. Jeffery, pp. 154-82; Giles Mitchell, "Feeling and Will in the Modern Novel," pp. 183-96 [not abstracted]; Langdon Elsbree, "The Writer as Professional," pp. 197-211 [not abstracted]; Otmar Allendorf, "Criticism of D. H. Lawrence in German; 1923-1970, A Bibliography," pp. 210-20; "Laurentiana," pp. 221-24; "Research in Progress," p. 225 [not abstracted]; "Contributors," p. 226 [not abstracted].

3699 D. H. LAWRENCE REVIEW, ed by James C. Cowan, IV, No. 3 (Fall 1971).
Contents, abstracted under 1971: Egon Tiedje, "D. H. Lawrence's Early Poetry: The Composition-Dates of the Drafts in MS E 317," pp. 227-52; John Worthen, "D. H. Lawrence and Louie Burrows," pp. 253-62; Keith Cushman, "The Making of 'The Prussian Officer': A Correction," pp. 263-73; Ordelle G. Hill and Potter Woodbery, "Ursula Brangwen of *The Rainbow:* Christian Saint or Pagan Goddess?" pp. 274-79; George J. Zytaruk, "What Happened to D. H. Lawrence's *Goats and Compasses?*" pp. 280-86; Jeanie Wagner, "A Botanical Note on *Aaron's Rod*," pp. 287-90; Donald Gutierrez, "Circles and Arcs: The Rhythm of Circularity and Centrifugality in D. H. Lawrence's *Last Poems*," pp. 291-300; Ben D. Kimpel, "One Lawrence from Two Viewpoints," pp. 301-13 [not abstracted]; Margarida Losa and John Remsbury, "D. H. Lawrence: A Secondary Bibliography for Portugal," pp. 314-17; "Laurentiana," pp. 318-21 [not abstracted]; "Contributors," pp. 322-23, and "Index to Volume Four," pp. 324-25 [not abstracted].

3700 Dorner, Marjorie Leone. "The *Blutbrüderschaft* Theme in the Fiction of D. H. Lawrence," DISSERTATION ABSTRACTS, XXXII (1972), 4607A. Unpublished dissertation, Purdue University, 1971.

3701 Eastman, Donald Roger. "The Concept of Character in the Major Novels of D. H. Lawrence," DISSERTATION ABSTRACTS INTERNATIONAL, XXXIII (1973), 7500A. Unpublished dissertation, University of Florida, 1971.

3702 Ekner, Reidar. "Blommornas språk eller säg det med blommor" (The Language of Flowers or Say It with Flowers), GÖTEBORGS HANDELS-OCH SJÖFARTSTIDNING (Gothenburgh), 9 July 1971, p. 3.
Sons and Lovers can be relished at many levels. The natural scenery, especially the flowers, plays an important symbolic role in the novel, marking the progression of events and the changing human relationships. [Review of new Swedish translation.] [In Swedish.]

3703 Fairbanks, N. David. "Strength through Joy in the Novels of D. H. Lawrence," LITERATURE AND IDEOLOGY, No. 8 (1971), pp. 67-78.
DHL and his heroes and heroines suffer the oppression of the petty bourgeoisie in a decayed and parasitic society, yet DHL, in his function as fascist writer, offers an analysis of their problems which stresses the spiritual over the material and so does not call for the overthrow of existing exploitative conditions.

3704 Ferrier, Carole. "The Earlier Poetry of D. H. Lawrence: A Variorum Text, Comprising All Extant Incunabula and Published Poems Up to and Including the Year 1919," Vols. I and II, DISSERTATION ABSTRACTS INTERNATIONAL, XXXV (1975), 6709A. Unpublished dissertation, University of Auckland, 1971.

3705 Flatley, Guy. "Must Glenda Always Be So Neurotic?," NEW YORK TIMES, 7 Feb 1971, Sect. 2, pp. 13, 16.

[Interview with Glenda Jackson, "the screen's champion castrator" and winner of the New York Film Critics award for her role in Ken Russell's film version of *Women in Love* as Gudrun Brangwen, whom she describes as " 'Like so many of Lawrence's women, . . . a fabrication, a woman created to fit in with his philosophy,' " yet possessing a " 'fascinating . . . *mysterious* element.' "] The male relationship in the story is not homosexual but an illustration of DHL's " 'theory about the bond of two men being greater than the love between a man and a woman,' " since the latter " 'eventually *has* to be sexual.' "

3706 Ford, George, Frank Kermode, Colin Clarke, and Mark Spilka. "Critical Exchange: On 'Lawrence Up-Tight': Four Tail-Pieces," NOVEL: A FORUM ON FICTION, V (Fall 1971), 54-70.

[Three responses to Mark Spilka, "Lawrence Up-Tight, or the Anal Phase Once Over," NOVEL, IV (Spring 1971), 252-67, with Spilka's rejoinder.] **Ford**: Spilka is correct in saying that the drive in *Women in Love* is through sick experiences toward healthy ones. **Kermode**: DHL's dissolution metaphysic shows that "Excurse" involves not anal penetration but the lumbar ganglia as the origin of DHL's apartness, though the anal act can be a way of dissolution whose purpose is to burn out shame, as in Ursula's feeling of freedom after Birkin buggers her. **Clarke**: Spilka's metaphor of the digestive process is tautological. DHL was not capable of sustained use of the language of paradox. **Spilka**: Birkin's shame is dispelled verbally by Ursula. Kermode's remarks on the lumbar ganglia mystique are distorted and out of context. Clarke misquotes the original article on the subject of metaphor and paradox.

3707 Fricker, Robert. "David Herbert Lawrence," in ENGLISCHE DICHTER DER MODERNE (English Writer of the Modern Period), ed by Dieter Riesner and Rudolf Suehnel (Berlin: Erich Schmidt, 1971), pp. 338-50.

In Germany DHL has often been suspected of siding with National Socialist ideas, of favoring the decline of Western civilization, and of justifying violence. As DHL's shorter fiction shows, he is more the advocate of human regeneration than the apostle of a cultural breakdown. In his short stories, which do not differ thematically from his novels, he attacks materialism and the Puritan-bourgeois way of life. His object, man's return to nature, never lapses into a romantic or pastoral attitude, but resembles Hardy's solution in THE RETURN OF THE NATIVE, though he does not share Hardy's pessimistic outlook. DHL's message is most convincing when it is free of mythological undertones and based on individual experience. [In German.]

3708 Frye, Northrop. THE CRITICAL PATH (Bloomington: Indiana UP, 1971), pp. 90-91.

Much of DHL's work belongs to the pastoral tradition, emphasizing a closeness between man and nature often betrayed by civilized life. In *The Plumed Serpent* and elsewhere, the psychologically primitive almost lapses into the historically primitive, but DHL's regressive myth is separable from his social vision. DHL opposes to technology the mythopoeic imagination, yet, like other modern writers, he cannot become the focus of a myth of freedom because such poets have a tendency to be converted to dogmatic creeds.

3709 Geracimos, Ann. "In D. H. Lawrence Country They Still Hold a Grudge," NEW YORK TIMES, 6 June 1971, Sect. 10, pp. 35, 48-49.
[A tour through Nottingham and environs, citing passages descriptive of landscape from fiction and correspondence of DHL.] Resentment lingers on account of DHL's use of neighbors as models for his fictional characters.

3710 Gill, Stephen. "The Composite World: Two Versions of *Lady Chatterley's Lover*," ESSAYS IN CRITICISM, XXI (Oct 1971), 347-64.
There are three objections to *Lady Chatterley's Lover:* Mellors's unlikable character, Mellors's unrealistic hope that his example will renew society, and the novel's structure, which is flawed by being not naturalistic enough to be realistic yet too naturalistic to be a moral fable. These three objections cannot be raised against the first version of the book.

3711 Glicksberg, Charles I. THE SEXUAL REVOLUTION IN MODERN AMERICAN LITERATURE (The Hague: Martinus Nijhoff, 1971), pp. 29, 123, 131-32, 135, 137, 139, 147, 155, 237, 238.
DHL never made the error of thinking sex as important or the same thing as a creative life purpose. While *The Rainbow* was censored for sexual indecency, other novels of the time less overtly concerned with perversion were allowed publication. For serious and gifted novelists, such as Proust, Hardy, Faulkner, and DHL, sex involved not only the senses but the imagination as well.

3712 Goldberg, Michael K. "Dickens and Lawrence: More on Rocking Horses," MODERN FICTION STUDIES, XVII (Winter 1971-1972), 574-75.
[An addendum to Michael Goldberg, "Lawrence's 'The Rocking-Horse Winner': A Dickensian Fable?" MODERN FICTION STUDIES, XV (Winter 1969-1970), 525-36, identifying two Dickensian references to rocking-horses mentioned by George Ford but not cited in the earlier Goldberg article on the subject.]

3713 Green, Martin. "Cottage Realism," MONTH, 2nd ns, IV (Sept 1971), 85-88.
DHL has a pious feeling toward rural domestic values such as well-buttered bread, birth, babies, and flowers, a tradition of self-rooting in the past and in the country shared by Raymond Williams, Richard Hoggart, and Tolstoy. This sensibility avoids the formation of an artistic elitism, affirming instead, by its conservatism, the traditional roles of man, woman, and family. The general reader finds in the writings of these men values which correspond to his good memories of childhood and to his orthodox ambitions within society, though such traditional British beliefs are now imaginatively sterile.

3714 Green, Martin. "Old Flames at the Ranch," LONDON MAGA-

ZINE, ns, X (March 1971), 69-83; rptd in D. H. LAWRENCE: A CRITICAL ANTHOLOGY, ed by H. Coombes (Harmondsworth, Middlesex, England: Penguin Books, 1973), pp. 477-84.
[Commentary on the D. H. Lawrence Festival, Taos, NM, 30 Sept-4 Oct 1970, when scholars, creative writers, and older people who had known DHL participated in a series of panel discussions at the Lawrence ranch near Taos. The greater part of the article, which is often satirical in tone, concerns people and events rather than the content of the discussions, with particular emphasis on E. W. Tedlock, Jr., Helen Corke, Sean Hignett, Robert Bly, and Émile Delavenay.]

3715 Gurko, Jane. "The Flesh Made Word: A Study of Narrative and Stylistic Techniques in Five Novels by D. H. Lawrence." Unpublished dissertation, University of California at Berkeley, 1971. [Listed in Lawrence F. McNamee, DISSERTATIONS IN ENGLISH AND AMERICAN LITERATURE, SUPP II (NY and Lond: Bowker, 1974), p. 368.]

3716 Gutierrez, Donald. "Circles and Arcs: The Rhythm of Circularity and Centrifugality in D. H. Lawrence's *Last Poems*," D. H. LAWRENCE REVIEW, IV (Fall 1971), 291-300; rptd in LAPSING OUT: EMBODIMENTS OF DEATH AND REBIRTH IN THE LAST WRITINGS OF D. H. LAWRENCE, by Donald Gutierrez (Rutherford, Madison, Teaneck, NJ: Fairleigh Dickinson UP, 1980), pp. 118-28.
In spite of DHL's tendentiousness, exhortation, talkyness, fragmentariness, and eschatological solemnity in *Last Poems*, many of the poems cohere in a design of selflessness (centrifugality) and selfishness (circularity), or between mechanistic self-centeredness and "an identification or integration with the living forces of the universe." Circularity is most often shown in a negative light, while centrifugality is praised. Death becomes a movement "away from ourselves, a centrifugal descent." [Individual poems are discussed in the context of this thesis.]

3717 Hand, Nancy Walker. "The Anatomy of a Genre: The Modern Novelette in English," DISSERTATION ABSTRACTS INTERNATIONAL, XXXII (1972), 5228A. Unpublished dissertation, Kent State University, 1971.
[Includes discussion of Conrad, Faulkner, Henry James, DHL, O'Hara, Porter, Stein, Steinbeck, Wharton.]

3718 Hartung, Rudolf. "Vorkämpfer einer 'Sex'-Revolution. D. H. Lawrence über Pornographie und Obszönität" (Pioneer of a "Sex" Revolution: D. H. Lawrence on Pornography and Obscenity), SÜDDEUTSCHE ZEITUNG, 13 Oct 1971.
[Review article on *Pornographie und Obszönität und andere Essays über Liebe, Sex und Emanzipation (Pornography and Obscenity and Other Essays on Love, Sex, and Emancipation)*, trans by Elisabeth Schnack (Zurich, 1971).] Like Freud, DHL has contributed much to modern sexual emancipation, although he would not like to be identified with the modern sex mania and the scientific treatment of sex. His attitude toward sex (which for him is an inadequate word) is very

serious and not to be confused with dissolute life. Sex represents man's intuitive forces, which are threatened by civilization. [In German.]

3719 Hays, Peter L. THE LIMPING HERO: GROTESQUES IN LITERATURE (NY: New York UP, 1971), pp. 7-8, 35-38, 39, 41, 47, 55, 59, 77-79, 80, 82, 84, 133, 206.

DHL's fiction contains fertility figures and sterility figures to communicate DHL's belief that "all people who, whether in pursuit of wealth, or God, or knowledge denied their physical beings...thereby denied part of their lives." In *The Man Who Died,* DHL records the escape of Christ "from ascetic denial to a richer, fuller life that includes sexual experience." DHL depicts a rebirth which does not serve as a symbol for other men, but which instead allows one man to live more fully. DHL's sterility figure is Clifford Chatterley, whose disability symbolizes "both the decayed power of the nobility...and the unhealthiness that Lawrence felt was inherent in a mechanized state that transfigured the land and turned men into grimy, unfeeling servants of industrialism."

3720 Hill, Ordelle G., and Potter Woodbery. "Ursula Brangwen of *The Rainbow:* Christian Saint or Pagan Goddess?" D. H. LAWRENCE REVIEW, IV (Fall 1971), 274-79.

Although Ursula's "namesake of Christian legend has significance...at the stage ...where she herself recognizes it," "a sounder explanation of Ursula's name and character at the conclusion of the novel can be found in the pagan roots of the ...legend" in Horsel, "the Swabian goddess of the moon," who was also "associated with horses." DHL's Ursula descends from both the Christian saint and the pagan goddess, but it is "the pagan portion of her spiritual inheritance [which] sustains her at the close of *The Rainbow,*" "defining the basis of her self-realization and her hope for the future in the values of the pre-Christian past."

3721 Hilton, Enid. "Correspondence Section," PHOENIX (Haydenville, MA), III (Spring-Summer 1971), 191-96.

[Letter to the Editor, commenting on the D. H. Lawrence Festival in Taos (30 Sept-4 Oct 1970), her memories of DHL at Mountain Cottage and Villa Mirenda, her smuggling copies of the first edition of *Lady Chatterley's Lover* to subscribers in England, the suppressed exhibition of DHL's pictures at the Warren Gallery, and her brief recollections of Alice Dax.]

3722 Hinz, Evelyn J. "*The Trespasser:* Lawrence's Wagnerian Tragedy and Divine Comedy," D. H. LAWRENCE REVIEW, IV (Summer 1971), 122-41.

The Trespasser has a tripartite structure in which time is the basic feature: "the work is cyclic--from the present to the past to the present." In details, each section (a frame story, a second frame, and the central narrative itself) evidences a chronological movement. The archetypal paradox that history repeats itself yet represents continual change is the "thematic version of the dual time perspective that provides the structure" of the novel. Each of the three main characters "embodies the paradox dramatized in the frame story"; each "is required to represent an ethos and at the same time to act as a product of the cultural conflict." The tragedy thus "consists in the Germanic Siegmund's movement from Helena--the natural mythos--to Beatrice--the Christian; however, the tragedy itself takes place within the Christian-Beatrice framework." The novel is thus concerned "with two tragedies--the cultural or historical--and the domestic; and the latter is a consequence of the former." Archetypally, Siegmund must choose not between two women but between two cultures--Beatrice and self-renunciation or Helena and self-preservation. In choosing the Christian, he becomes unheroic and hangs himself. "Helena's ability to recover" and take a new lover, in keeping with the archetypal concept of time, shows that "nature and myth eternally repeat themselves."

3723 Hinz, Evelyn J. "A Word about Influences--and Unprofessional Studies," THE MIRROR AND THE GARDEN: REALISM AND REALITY IN THE WRITINGS OF ANAIS NIN (Columbus: Ohio State University Libraries, 1971), pp. 15-32.
[Discussion of Anais Nin and DHL in terms of influence and affinities on the basis of her first book, D. H. LAWRENCE: AN UNPROFESSIONAL STUDY (1932).] Nin uses DHL to explain her own theory of the superiority of personal, anti-rational perception of "reality" to the limitations of objective, scientific "realism." DHL, discovering the world to be a projection of himself, achieves ultimate objectivity by surrendering his own personality and consciously embodying his projection in a work of art. Nin's method is like DHL's in *Studies in Classic American Literature,* where he used the writers he discussed to expound his own ideas.

3724 Hooker, Jeremy. "To Open the Mind," PLANET, Nos. 5/6 (Summer 1971), pp. 59-63.
Charles Olson's "projective" or "open" verse offers, rather than the "arrested moment," natural speech in the act of movement. Olson has close affinities to DHL in his search for the man beneath the social being and his attempt to rediscover himself as primal man in nature. Ultimately their poems are acts in affirmation of life rather than discursive talking about it.

3725 Hoyt, William R., III. "Re: 'D. H. Lawrence's Appraisal of Jesus.' (A Response to William E. Phipps)," CHRISTIAN CENTURY, continuing NEW CHRISTIAN, LXXXVIII (14 July 1971), 861-62.
[Letter to the Editor in reply to William E. Phipps, "D. H. Lawrence's Appraisal of Jesus," CHRISTIAN CENTURY, LXXXVIII (28 April 1971), 521-24.] Though DHL's works can erase "the Gnostic ghost" in Jesus, to ascribe a full Christian interpretation to them is theologically unsound. As literary critics have pointed out, DHL uses Christian images for his own metaphorical purposes. His God is immanent but not transcendent. His sexual desires are described but not cured. Decrying altruism, he cannot understand any basis for self-giving. DHL's message may liberate some elders in our society, but its youth need a broader concept, as do those confused in a period of change. [See also further reply to both Phipps and Hoyt by James B. Sipple, "D. H. Lawrence and 'Man's Ontological Solitude,' " CHRISTIAN CENTURY, LXXXVIII (17 Nov 1971), 1365-66.]

3726 Hyde, Virginia Mae. "The Artist Priest and the Cosmic Landscape: D. H. Lawrence's Debt to Medieval and Renaissance Graphic

Arts," DISSERTATION ABSTRACTS INTERNATIONAL, XXXII (1972), 5792A. Unpublished dissertation, University of Wisconsin, 1971.

3727 Inniss, Kenneth. D. H. LAWRENCE'S BESTIARY: A STUDY OF HIS USE OF ANIMAL TROPE AND SYMBOL (The Hague and Paris: Mouton, 1971; NY: Humanities P, 1972).

DHL was an unusual novelist in that his novels are concerned less with social relationships than with states of being and the relationship between individuals and the natural world of bird, beast, and flower. All of DHL's works--novels, poems, travel books, and other expository prose--emerge from a poetic worldview which posits a traditional dichotomy between wilderness and civilization, but reverses traditional evaluation by embracing the wilderness as a "numinous dark" where God has not yet died and where DHL might "find his salvation." This dark wilderness is a source of value, a place of potentiality, impulse, sensations, and physicality, in contrast to the constraints of the rationally ordered city. In his works, "blood" metaphorically conveys this darkness, wilderness, and beasts. Moreover, the dark wilderness of the animal kingdom is not merely the realm of the "other," but also an objective correlative for a state of consciousness. Different animals are emblematic of different states; for example, the tiger and the lion represent the sensual energy of the human "animal self," whereas the dove and the unicorn stand for the passivity of the "spiritual self." Similarly, numerous beasts represent, in DHL's poems and novels, aspects and qualities of being. Analysis of the beast imagery in DHL's poetry from 1917 onward reveals that the earliest poetry contains little insistent doctrine or rhetoric, but instead celebrates the wonder of nature. The later poetry, however, becomes increasingly doctrinal, depicting DHL's quarrel with Christianity and his concern for emergent, sensual selfhood. Analysis of animal imagery in the fiction and non-fiction prose reveals a similar pattern, from purely passionate experience in the early works, to a powerfully dramatic engagement with questions of being and ethics in the works of the middle period, to an increasingly desperate and embittered quest to get life "straight from the source,"amidst a destructive social and political order in the final works. Toward the end of his career, DHL sought with religious fervor, first, to sketch a redeemed world of animism (chiefly in *The Plumed Serpent)*, and then to create animal-like humans appropriate to his mature vision. These late characters, like Mellors and the man who died, are no longer tiger-like, but are more like worldly wise, wounded deer, who survive through the use of intelligence and through evasion of battle with the evils of society. But if the tiger has been defeated, the passive unicorn has not won. These last characters maintain the flame of mystery found only in the dark wilderness.

3728 Ito, Takehisa. "Lawrence no Chichioyatachi--*Sons and Lovers* no Ichimen" (Fathers of Lawrence: An Aspect of *Sons and Lovers)*, RESEARCH REPORTS OF KURUME TECHNICAL COLLEGE, No. 15 (March 1971), 35-43.

[This essay deals exclusively with two fathers related to the novelist: his collier father, John Arthur Lawrence, and Walter Morel, the father of the Morels in *Sons and Lovers*. It hopes to do justice to those unmindfully ill-treated male parents by paying them due attention and restoring them to their proper significance. It also attempts to consider what a father really meant to the son of the two fathers.] [In Japanese.]

3729 Ito, Toyoji. "Lawrence to Huxley" (Lawrence and Huxley), STUDY OF CULTURAL SCIENCE (Niigata University), No. 40 (March 1971), 29-87.

[This paper first seeks to reveal the "image" of DHL through discussion of certain biographies and of his own works. Then it treats DHL's influence on Aldous Huxley and Huxley's description of some characters in DHL's image.] [In Japanese.]

3730 Janik, Del Ivan. "D. H. Lawrence: The Poetry of Intuition," DISSERTATION ABSTRACTS INTERNATIONAL, XXXII (1971), 3309A. Unpublished dissertation, Northwestern University, 1971.

3731 Kai, Sadanobu. "Kyôbô na Junrei no Ato o Otte--Garuda-Kohan nite" (After the Savage Pilgrimage--Lago di Garda), STUDIES IN FOREIGN LITERATURES (Ritsumeikan University), No. 23 (Dec 1971), 122-37.

On the Lago di Garda, DHL and Frieda spent their own private honeymoon in 1912-1913. Visiting Gargnano, on the Lago di Garda, and rereading *Twilight in Italy,* the writer could not help regarding the Lago di Garda as an enlarged replica of the Moorgreen Reservoir at the bottom of DHL's "beloved home valley" near Eastwood. [In Japanese.]

3732 Ketters, David. "New Worlds for Old: The Apocalyptic Imagination, Science Fiction and American Literature," MOSAIC, V (Fall 1971), 37-57.

"Apocalypse" is redefined as a critical term including both negative and positive or "visionary" values. In DHL's *Apocalypse,* "apocalypse" means bitter wish-fulfillment and thirst for power among the underprivileged.

3733 Kinkead-Weekes, Mark. "Introduction," TWENTIETH CENTURY INTERPRETATIONS OF "THE RAINBOW": A COLLECTION OF CRITICAL ESSAYS, ed by Mark Kinkead-Weekes (Englewood Cliffs, NJ: Prentice-Hall, 1971), pp. 1-10.

The Rainbow represents a turning point in DHL's career as a novelist. His marriage and departure from England in 1912 having allowed him to put to rest the turmoil with which he had dealt in *Sons and Lovers,* DHL was prepared to recast autobiographical materials so as to achieve a universal point of view, "to plot the inner history of a changing England over three generations." After the publication of the novel, as casualties in the First World War mounted, the faith of *The Rainbow* was supplanted in DHL's mind by "a grimmer apocalyptic vision of a world dominated by urges of death and destruction." Thus, within the context of DHL's canon, *The Rainbow* is "both a beginning and an end." His art as a novelist declined thereafter; hence, "*The Rainbow* stands revealed as the foundation of his greatest work." It is also the last of DHL's works "written with a successful novelist's confidence that there exists a public capable of responding to his powers." The opening of the novel, with its universal, pastoral setting, sets up "a rich tension between social history and universal vision." There is a shift, however, in the first chapter to a particularized environment with characters "who take over from the archetypal Men and Women of the opening" and face the "challenge to *marry* their oppositions, for, like Blake, Lawrence believed that human progress springs from contraries, and that conflict is creative." Thus, the structure of the novel entails "a progressive series, in which the human potential becomes richer from generation to generation, but the challenge of the marriage of opposites becomes more and more difficult." *The Rainbow* is founded upon a new approach to character, for DHL has completed the shift from a nineteenth-century concern with behavior to a twentieth-century concern with consciousness.

3734 Kinkead-Weekes, Mark (ed). TWENTIETH CENTURY INTERPRETATIONS OF "THE RAINBOW": A COLLECTION OF CRITICAL ESSAYS (Englewood Cliffs, NJ: Prentice-Hall, 1971).
Contents, abstracted under year of first publication: Mark Kinkead-Weekes, "Introduction," pp. 1-10 (1971); **Part One: "A Perspective":** Marvin Mudrick, "The Originality of *The Rainbow*," pp. 11-32, from SPECTRUM, III (Winter 1959), 3-28; **Part Two: "Interpretations":** H. M. Daleski, "The First and Second Generation," pp. 33-57, excerpted from Chap. III: "Two in One: The Second Period," in THE FORKED FLAME: A STUDY OF D. H. LAWRENCE (Lond: Faber & Faber; Evanston: Northwestern UP, 1965), pp. 79-106; Keith Sagar, "The Third Generation," pp. 58-72, excerpted from Chap. III: "The Perfect Medium, 1913-1914," in THE ART OF D. H. LAWRENCE (Cambridge: Cambridge UP, 1966), pp. 55-68; **Part Three: "View Points":** George H. Ford, "The Rainbow and the Bible," pp. 73-82, excerpted from Chap. VI: "*The Rainbow* as Bible," in DOUBLE MEASURE: A STUDY OF THE NOVELS AND STORIES OF D. H. LAWRENCE (NY: Holt, Rinehart, 1965), pp. 126-37; William Walsh, "The Childhood of Ursula," pp. 82-91, excerpted from "The Writer and the Child" in THE USE OF IMAGINATION (Lond: Chatto & Windus, 1959), pp. 163-74; Laurence Lerner, "Lawrence's 'Carbon,'" pp. 91-95, from THE TRUTHTELLERS (Lond: Chatto & Windus; NY: Schocken, 1967), pp. 78-82; **Part Four: "The Making of 'The Rainbow'":** Mark Kinkead-Weekes, "The Marble and the Statue," pp. 96-120, from IMAGINED WORLDS: ESSAYS ON SOME ENGLISH NOVELS AND NOVELISTS IN HONOUR OF JOHN BUTT, ed by Ian Gregor and Maynard Mack (Lond: Methuen, 1968), pp. 371-93, 407-10, 412-18; **Chronology of Important Dates,** pp. 121-22 [not abstracted]; **Notes on the Editor and Contributors,** p. 123 [not abstracted].

3735 Kitazawa, Shigehisa. "Lawrence: Ai o Koeru Mono" (Lawrence Beyond Love), DOKKYO STUDIES IN ENGLISH (Dokkyo University), No. 5 (March 1971), 1-50; rvd and rptd as Chap. III: "Beyond Love," in D. H. LAWRENCE: HIS LITERATURE AND HIS LIFE, by Shigehisa Kitazawa (Tokyo: Bokusui-shobo Co., 1973).
[The third article in a four-part series, based on an extensive study of the life and works of DHL, which seeks to reveal the "real substance" of his literature and its significance in our age. See also Shigehisa Kitazawa, "Lawrence Bungaku no Hassei" (The Early Works and Life of Lawrence), DOKKYO STUDIES IN ENGLISH, No. 2 (June 1968), 92-124; "Lawrence: Ai no Tansaku" (Lawrence

in Love), DOKKYO STUDIES IN ENGLISH, No. 3 (June 1969), 17-51; and "Lawrence: Ai to Kodoku" (Lawrence: Love and Solitude), DOKKYO STUDIES IN ENGLISH, No. 6 (May 1972), 123-72.] [In Japanese.]

3736 Kleinbard, David J. "Laing, Lawrence, and the Maternal Cannibal," PSYCHOANALYTIC REVIEW, LVIII (Spring 1971), 5-13.

R. D. Laing's concepts of ontological insecurity and the oral self apply to DHL. Paul Morel in *Sons and Lovers* suffers from ontological insecurity, has fantasies of implosion, and engages in "protective self-division," feeling that others relate only to his shell or false self. Paul also depersonalizes both Miriam and Clara because he fears them. The roots of the problem are in his relationship with his mother, upon whom his sense of his own being depends entirely.

3737 Knoll, Robert F. "*Women in Love*," FILM HERITAGE, VI (Summer 1971), 1-6.

Although the film version of *Women in Love*, produced and written for the screen by Larry Kramer and directed by Ken Russell (1969), is a serious attempt to render DHL's novel into a reasonable cinematic facsimile, it is only partially successful because it spends more time exploring the novel's weaknesses than exploiting its richness.

3738 Konishi, Eirin. "Kodoku no Jissô: D. H. Lawrence Joron" (A Stranger's Reality: An Introductory Essay on D. H. Lawrence), MEMOIRS OF THE FACULTY OF GENERAL EDUCATION (Ehime University), No. 3 (Feb 1971), 1-25.

[DHL as a man is examined chiefly through his letters and poems.] [In Japanese.]

3739 Krieger, Robert Neal. "D. H. Lawrence's Eclectic Symbolism: The Erotic Design of *Look! We Have Come Through*," DISSERTATION ABSTRACTS INTERNATIONAL, XXXII (1971), 1516A.

Unpublished dissertation, University of Washington, 1971.

3740 La Belle, Jenijoy. "Theodore Roethke and Tradition: 'The Pure Serenity of Memory in One Man,' " NORTHWEST REVIEW, XI (Summer 1971), 1-18.

Roethke's "The Meadow Mouse" results from his admiration of DHL's *Birds, Beasts and Flowers,* and he borrows DHL's rhythm and language.

3741 Lacy, Gerald Morris. "An Analytical Calendar of the Letters of D. H. Lawrence," DISSERTATION ABSTRACTS INTERNATIONAL, XXXII (1972), 5795A. Unpublished dissertation, University of Texas at Austin, 1971.

3742 "Language and Literature," CHOICE, VIII (April 1971), 226.

The Quest for Rananim: D. H. Lawrence's Letters to S. S. Koteliansky, 1914 to 1930, ed by George J. Zytaruk, is unified by "Lawrence's obsessive quest for an ideal male relationship."

3743 Lee, Robin Herbert. "Morality and Tradition in the English Novel, as Seen in the Relationship Between George Eliot and D. H. Lawrence." Unpublished dissertation, University of Witwatersrand (Johannesburg, South Africa), 1971. [Listed in GESAMENTLIKE KATALOGUS VAN PROEFSKRIFTE EN VERHANDELINGE VAN DIE SUID-AFRIKAANSE UNIVERSEITE (Union Catalogue of Theses and Dissertations of South African Universities), Supp. No. 13 (1971) (Potchefstroom: Potchefstroom University for C. H. E., 1972), p. 52.

3744 Littlewood, J. C. F. "Lawrence Old and New," ESSAYS IN CRITICISM, XXI (April 1971), 195-204.

Few of the items on DHL before 1930 in the representative selection in D. H. LAWRENCE: THE CRITICAL HERITAGE, edited by R. P. Draper (1970), have "permanent critical value." "The period 1930-36...must be the key focus" if the "undertaking" was to be "truly historical," since it was in those years that much of DHL's work was published and some of his "most influential contemporaries," such as Aldous Huxley and F. R. Leavis, gave "their considered accounts of his work as a whole." [Also reviews David Cavitch, D. H. LAWRENCE AND THE NEW WORLD (1969).]

3745 Locke, Raymond Friday. "Anais Nin and the Paintings of D. H. Lawrence" collected with "A D. H. Lawrence Postscript" by Anais Nin, MANKIND: THE MAGAZINE OF POPULAR HISTORY, III (August 1971), 18-21.

Anais Nin saw DHL's paintings with "fleshy figures" and trees reminiscent of "Gauguin's nature worship" except that they are sunless, grey-toned, English figures. [Illustrated with color reproductions of DHL's paintings. Knud Merrild's portrait of DHL is erroneously identified as a self-portrait by DHL.]

3746 Lodge, David. THE NOVELIST AT THE CROSSROADS AND OTHER ESSAYS ON FICTION AND CRITICISM (Ithaca, NY: Cornell UP, 1971), pp. 7, 46-48, 49-50, 155, 178, 205, 237, 248, 255, 277, 279-81, 291.

Consideration of the open endings of DHL's novels raises the question "of how you distinguish between a good inconclusive novel and a bad one." Samuel Beckett's PING, with its "bleakly metaphysical rendering of the consciousness of the dying Christ," recalls *The Man Who Died*. Norman O. Brown's use of "the resurrection of the body" as a concluding slogan in LIFE AGAINST DEATH, was not original but traceable to DHL, Nietzsche, and Freud. A modernist "holding utterly different views of 'life' from Virginia Woolf, and of myth from T. S. Eliot, but making considerable play with both terms, was D. H. Lawrence." An "affective" critic, DHL made a "heterodox assimilation of psychological theories of all kinds," which, through *Studies in Classic American Literature*, influenced American criticism.

3747 Losa, Margarida, and John Remsbury. "D. H. Lawrence: A

Secondary Bibliography for Portugal," D. H. LAWRENCE REVIEW, IV (Fall 1971), 314-17.
[This bibliography lists DHL studies only for Continental Portugal. The checklist is divided into three sections: Translations, Graduate Theses, and Criticism in Learned Journals.]

3748 McLeod, Karen. "Reviews," REVIEW OF ENGLISH STUDIES, ns XXII (Aug 1971), 378-80.
The Quest for Rananim: D. H. Lawrence's Letters to S. S. Koteliansky, 1914 to 1930, ed by George J. Zytaruk, contains 346 letters, 126 of them previously published and the remaining 220 "concerned chiefly with domestic and business affairs." "The letters are interesting for what they reveal of Lawrence as a friend, and for their clear charting of his indecisive moods." [Also reviews D. H. LAWRENCE AND THE NEW WORLD, by David Cavitch.]

3749 Mailer, Norman. "The Prisoner of Sex," HARPER'S MAGAZINE, CCXLII (March 1971), 41-46, 48, 50, 52-60, 68-72, 77-92; espec pp. 70-72, 77-79; also pub as THE PRISONER OF SEX (Bost: Little Brown, 1971), pp. 126-60 and passim; rptd (NY: New American Library [Signet Books], 1971), pp. 99-116 and passim.
[The author uses his response to writings of the Women's Liberation movement, especially Kate Millett's SEXUAL POLITICS (1970), focusing on the sections on Mailer, Henry Miller, and DHL, as a means of stating his own attitude toward women.] DHL understood women "as they have never been understood before." DHL is "perhaps a great writer, certainly flawed, and abominably pedestrian in his language" and "unendurably didactic" at times. There are in all his books "unmistakable tendencies toward the absolute domination of women by men." But DHL "was not trying to sell dictatorial theorems, he was also trying to destroy them." He moved from "the adoration of his mother in *Sons and Lovers* and. . .of the womb in *The Rainbow* to worship of the phallus and male will" in the religion of *The Plumed Serpent*. He flirted with homosexuality in *Women in Love* and *Aaron's Rod* and expressed the "outright lust" for women's murder in "The Woman Who Rode Away." "Having purged his blood of murder," he could "now go on to write *Lady Chatterley*." DHL's "emotional odyssey" took him back, in "the five last years of his dying," to the worship of woman's beauty, "even her procreative beauty," and he was able at last to leave off his quest for power in the male world and to return to what he had started with, "to his first knowledge that the physical love of men and women" is our "salvation."

3750 Mannin, Ethel. YOUNG IN THE TWENTIES: A CHAPTER OF AUTOBIOGRAPHY (Lond: Hutchinson, 1971), pp. 33, 53, 55, 56, 95-97, 107, 127-28, 143.
In the twenties, "the voices we listened to urged us away from the pre-war taboos and inhibitions; they were the voices of Freud, D. H. Lawrence, Aldous Huxley, Dr. Marie Stopes, Bertrand Russell." The banning of THE WELL OF LONELINESS and the publication of *Lady Chatterley's Lover*, both in 1928, were "the two great literary excitements" of the decade. *Lady Chatterley's Lover*, though "sincerely admired" at the time, was "novelettish, and the sexual antics rather

silly, and all the ranting about sex and the good life intolerable." DHL's disguising the Armenian Michael Arlen as the Irish Michaelis in the novel is "absurd" and does not work. The "police seizure" of *Pansies* and of DHL's paintings was "puerile." "It is difficult to see where Lawrence could have gone" next--though *Apocalypse*, "anti-Christian and anti-democracy, all his latent Fascism breaking through," gives some indication.

3751 Martin, Graham. D. H. LAWRENCE'S "THE RAINBOW" (Bletchley, Bucks., England: Open UP [Humanities: A Foundation Course: Industrialisation and Culture, Units 35-36], 1971).

[Notes and guide to study of DHL's *The Rainbow*, concentrating on two main issues: "the novel's method and structure" and "Lawrence's criticism of industrial society," with discussion divided into six parts: (1) Characterization, (2) (2) Symbolism, (3) Social History, (4) Marriage, (5) Religion, (6) Industrialization.] (1) DHL's " 'belief...in the blood, the flesh, as being wiser than the intellect' " underlies his attempt in *The Rainbow* to reveal, instead of " 'the old stable *ego*-- of the character' " the "carbon" element of " 'another *ego*, according to whose action the individual is unrecognisable, and passes through, as it were, allotropic states.' " DHL's method of characterization reflects his ideas about personality, "gives the reader direct access to levels of experience beyond the normal consciousness of the characters," and reveals his judgment of his characters. (2) In *The Rainbow*, there is "much variation in the complexity and density of symbolic meaning." The "recurrence" of scenes (e.g., the harvest/courting rituals of Will and Anna, then later of Anton Skrebensky and Ursula) allows for "sensitive discriminations, and connections between them." (3) "The structure of the novel reflects a general social movement, which industrialisation brought about, from a rural and agricultural pattern of life to a pattern based on towns and factories." (4) *The Rainbow* may be called "a novel about three marriages, two that succeed and one that fails, because marriage is the relationship that the novel explores in depth." Writing the novel during his first years with Frieda, DHL saw "a vital connection between marriage and his art." [The attitude toward marriage in *The Rainbow* is extensively compared to that in the Anglican BOOK OF COMMON PRAYER.] (5) "The Brangwens want from religion 'the sense of the eternal and the immortal, not a list of rules for everyday conduct.' " DHL thought that Christianity was centered more in the Crucifixion than in the Resurrection. "To him, the Church year celebrates not the mysteries of the Christian faith, but 'the cycle of *creation*,'...which controls the life of nature." [In terms of these principles, the author discusses DHL's concept of eternity and time, analyzes the Cathedral chapter in detail, and discusses Ursula's attitude toward Christianity.] (6) DHL attacks "the results of industrialisation" in "Ursula's visit to the new colliery town of Wiggiston" and in her experience in education, both as college student and as teacher. In Ursula's criticism of the " 'great machine,' " DHL carries on the tradition of the Victorian Social Critics, especially Morris. DHL shows that "the quality of personal experience illustrates the 'mechanical' influence of industrialisation," an influence which Ursula fights but to which Skrebensky succumbs. [The conclusion suggests further questions not explored in this work: DHL's attitude toward such questions as education and

and the suffragette movement, the success or failure of the final chapters, the novel's extension of "our awareness of ourselves, and of other people."]

3752 Matsubayashi, Yoshinori. "Shokubutsu yori Mita Lawrence no Sakufû--*The White Peacock* to *Sons and Lovers* o Chûshin ni" (Lawrence's Flower-Presentation Technique in *The White Peacock* and *Sons and Lovers*), MEMOIRS OF SUZAKA COLLEGE OF TECHNOLOGY, No. 4 (Feb 1971), 81-90.

[Traces the progress DHL made in flower-presentation technique by comparing the function of plants found in *The White Peacock* in terms of their kind and frequency with that in *Sons and Lovers*.] [In Japanese.]

3753 Mencher, M. B. "D. H. Lawrence," TIMES LITERARY SUPPLEMENT (Lond), 17 Sept 1971, p. 1119.

[Letter to the Editor, commenting on Keith Sagar, "D. H. Lawrence," TIMES LITERARY SUPPLEMENT (Lond), 10 Sept 1971, p. 1086, and Malcolm Pittock, "D. H. Lawrence," TIMES LITERARY SUPPLEMENT (Lond), 20 Aug 1971, p. 999.] What does it matter if DHL came first in a public examination, or if he made a geographical mistake in "Red Wolf"? [See also reply to Sagar by John Beer, "D. H. Lawrence," TIMES LITERARY SUPPLEMENT (Lond), 24 Sept 1971, p. 1148; and reply to Mencher by Harry T. Moore, "D. H. Lawrence," TIMES LITERARY SUPPLEMENT (Lond), 1 Oct 1971, p. 1177.]

3754 Menon, K. P. K. "The Impact of Symbolism on Story and Character in D. H. Lawrence's *The Rainbow*," LITERARY STUDIES: HOMAGE TO DR. A. SIVARAMASUBRAMONIA AIYER (Trivandrum, India: St. Joseph's P, 1971), pp. 23-33.

The symbolism of *The Rainbow* is a colossal failure since it has made the characters and incidents utterly irrational, even absurd.

3755 Mickelson, Anne Zadorozna. "Vital Life versus Sterile Denial: A Study of Family and Sexual Relationships in the Works of Thomas Hardy and D. H. Lawrence," DISSERTATION ABSTRACTS INTERNATIONAL, XXXII (1972), 5191A. Unpublished dissertation, Rutgers University, 1971.

3756 Miko, Stephen J. TOWARD "WOMEN IN LOVE": THE EMERGENCE OF A LAWRENTIAN AESTHETIC (New Haven: Yale UP [Yale Studies in English, Vol. 177], 1971).

DHL's first two novels are pervasively concerned with nature. The failures of George and Cyril in *The White Peacock* entail their frustrated yearnings to discover in nature an order or purpose that they lack in their culturally shaped beings, whereas *The Trespasser* depicts a fundamental conflict between the values of nature and the values of civilization. By moving closer to personal experience, depicted with vivid realism, DHL began to solve, in *Sons and Lovers,* the problems in narrative tone and values of the first two novels. What appear to be DHL's wavering and shifting loyalties and judgments in this novel emerge not from the confused moral judgments that some critics have assumed but from DHL's uniquely dialectical narrative perspective, whereby he can momentarily sympathize with, and render the truth of, the point of view and experience of each and all characters. *The Rainbow* makes it clear that the problems that DHL faced in his earlier books--such as defining the nature of male-female relationship and exploring the relationship of nature (the body) to civilization (consciousness, morality)-- are in essence an individual's quest for self-fulfillment, involving several paradoxes. For instance, DHL's characters continue to be recognizable, individual ego-identities, yet strive for transcendence of the ego; and self-realization is often achieved through self-abnegation. For the first time, in *The Rainbow,* DHL depicts man, woman, and nature in relations which do not imply an opposition between the moral and the vital. Many of the ideas dramatized in *The Rainbow* and shared by *Women in Love* are discussed overtly in several of DHL's prose tracts written during the period, especially the *Study of Thomas Hardy* and "The Crown." *The Rainbow* is an optimistic book written in the face of civilization's apparent bent toward self-destruction. In contrast, *Women in Love* confronts the cultural destructiveness--the flux of corruption--directly, in the effort to gain an understanding of death in order that life might move beyond it. *Women in Love,* more than any of DHL's books, succeeds in the struggle for conscious definition, both aesthetically and intellectually, by confronting in clear perspective a greater range of problems than ever before. Although *Women in Love* is the record of DHL's and his characters' struggle into consciousness, it is also paradoxically about the relationship of human beings to the unknown. The most deathly of the characters have frozen their potential for development through forms of relationship which deny the unknown in themselves and in the other. Birkin and Ursula break out of the pattern of domination and submission, which marks all other relationships in the novel, through a mutual submission to the unknown. To depict the characters in *Women in Love,* their extremes of reduction, their relationships to one another and to the unknown, DHL necessarily moved beyond the technical mode of realism toward symbolic scenes and sometimes merely symbolic characters.

3757 Mizener, Arthur. THE SADDEST STORY: A BIOGRAPHY OF FORD MADOX FORD (NY: World, 1971), pp. xx, xxi, 38, 65, 150, 168-73, 219, 221, 235, 264, 281, 282, 417, 435.
Ford's editorial ability is shown by his acceptance of "Odour of Chrysanthemums" after reading only the first paragraph. Ford discovered DHL's talent, cultivated his friendship, and, over a one-and-a-half-year period, published thirteen of his poems and a story in ENGLISH REVIEW. During the winter of 1909-1910, Ford became preoccupied by the magazine and by Violet Hunt, and DHL felt slighted, but in December 1911, DHL saw the two together and described them as happy. In 1913, Ford "used *Sons and Lovers* to show that only the natural life of the lower classes retained any of the quality of feudal existence," which Ford thought " 'the most satisfactory form' " for society. In 1915, Ford "had an unhappy encounter with the Lawrences" in which Frieda spoke disparagingly of the " 'Dirty Belgians!' " and of the uniform he was wearing, charges which she later indignantly denied. By 1935, Ford was out of sympathy with DHL and found him " 'difficult to re-read.' "

3758 Mizuhara, Sho. "D. H. Lawrence no 'The Princess' no Kenkyu" (A Study of D. H. Lawrence's "The Princess"), MEMOIRS OF MEJIRO GAKUEN WOMEN'S JUNIOR COLLEGE, No. 7 (March 1971), 71-84.

In "The Princess," the illusions which the heroine's father inculcates in her form her strange character. Her costumes and manner are based on illusion, but the Lawrencean control of tone does not permit us to feel it in the same way that we feel her father's fantasies. Many of the details seem double-edged. Although this story seems to end in the author's irony and negation of the heroine's sterility, the last five lines suggest the "fulfillment." [In Japanese.]

3759 Moore, Harry T. "D. H. Lawrence," TIMES LITERARY SUPPLEMENT (Lond), 10 Sept 1971, p. 1086.

[Letter to the Editor in reply to Malcolm Pittock, "D. H. Lawrence," letter to the editor, TIMES LITERARY SUPPLEMENT (Lond), 20 Aug 1971, p. 999. See also reply by Emile Delavenay, TIMES LITERARY SUPPLEMENT (Lond), 10 Sept 1971, p. 1086.]

3760 Moore, Harry T. "D. H. Lawrence," TIMES LITERARY SUPPLEMENT (Lond), 1 Oct 1971, p. 1177.

[Letter to the Editor in reply to M. B. Mencher, "D. H. Lawrence," TIMES LITERARY SUPPLEMENT (Lond), 17 Sept 1971, p. 1119.] Mencher aligns himself with the outmoded New Critics. "Red Wolf" is not a minor poem. [See also Keith Sagar, "D. H. Lawrence," letter to the editor, TIMES LITERARY SUPPLEMENT (Lond), 10 Sept 1971, p. 1086, and reply by John Beer, "D. H. Lawrence," TIMES LITERARY SUPPLEMENT (Lond), 24 Sept 1971, p. 1148.]

3761 Moore, Harry T. "Preface," in *The Boy in the Bush,* by D. H. Lawrence and M. L. Skinner (rptd: Carbondale & Edwardsville: Southern Illinois UP; Lond & Amsterdam: Feffer & Simons, 1971), pp. vii-xxviii.

The Boy in the Bush originated in DHL's collaboration with Mollie Skinner, a nurse whom he met in Western Australia in 1922. When she sent him her MS, then called "The House of Ellis," in 1923, he offered to " 're-cast it, and make a book out of it.' " Although he told her he "wrote the whole book over again, from start to finish," it is difficult to tell, since the MS of "The House of Ellis" is lost, exactly how much it was altered. Although Miss Skinner claimed to have seen nothing further of the book until it was published, DHL's letter to Martin Secker (4 April 1924) requesting some "little changes to please her" makes this statement doubtful. The typescript sent to Secker is probably the one now at Columbia University. But "the most interesting document relating to *The Boy in the Bush*...is the copy of it which M. L. Skinner marked up for Edward Garnett" in 1924 and which is now at the University of Texas Humanities Research Center. [Analyses of several passages she marked as DHL revisions follow.] Among the passages attributed to DHL is the section from p. 341 to the end of the novel. Rose Anne Lee, in an unpublished University of Texas dissertation, concludes, on the basis of her statistical analysis of the Texas copy and the Columbia typescript, that " 'the majority of the credit must go to Miss Skinner' "--238 out of 369 pages. Nevertheless, "the writing throughout is distinctly Lawrencean, and the book should rank as a Lawrence novel, though Mollie Skinner's extremely important contribution should be noted." Early reviews of the novel were mixed, and subsequent books on DHL have largely ignored it. On "one level an adventure story, with various excursions into romance," *The Boy in the Bush* also delineates "the changes that time makes in communities and their members." The novel offers a great deal: "the change in a man, his experiences in love, a fight to the death, and ultimate good fortune. And Lawrence adds, among other ingredients, Jack Grant's Utopian vision."

3762 Moore, Harry T. "Some New Volumes of Lawrence's Letters," D. H. LAWRENCE REVIEW, IV (Spring 1971), 61-71.

[Review essay of *Lawrence in Love: Letters to Louie Burrows,* ed by James T. Boulton (1968); *The Quest for Rananim: D. H. Lawrence's Letters to S. S. Koteliansky, 1914 to 1930,* ed by George J. Zytaruk (1970); *Letters from D. H. Lawrence to Martin Secker, 1911-1930,* ed by Martin Secker (1970); and LETTERS FROM A PUBLISHER: MARTIN SECKER TO D. H. LAWRENCE AND OTHERS (1970).] These volumes of letters show DHL "to be, as always, an absorbing correspondent." The letters to Louie Burrows allow us "to trace the formation of Lawrence as we could never quite do before; his letters to Koteliansky help us to follow his later development" and illuminate this important literary association. Professors Boulton and Zytaruk have written informative and useful introductions to their respective collections. The letters to Martin Secker give "the fullest presentation of Lawrence's business side," while the publisher's letters to DHL "bring out Secker's magnanimity in dealing with a somewhat difficult author." As Zytaruk notes in his introduction, it is now " 'imperative to have every authentic document made available for examination.' " The time has certainly come for "a university press" to bring out a full edition of all of DHL's correspondence. [In 1979 Cambridge UP began publication of a seven-volume edition of *The Letters of D. H. Lawrence,* under the general editorship of James T. Boulton.]

3763 M[oore], L[eslie] [pseud of Ida Baker]. KATHERINE MANSFIELD: THE MEMORIES OF L. M. (Lond: Michael Joseph, 1971), pp. 79, 80, 83, 84, 91, 92, 93, 94, 97, 133, 207n.

[Passing references to DHL's and Frieda's "close yet difficult relationship" with John Middleton Murry and Katherine Mansfield, DHL's contributions to RHYTHM, THE BLUE REVIEW, and SIGNATURE, the Lawrences' quarrels, and the Murrys' "turning away from Lawrence's constant preoccupation with sex."]

3764 Moore, T. Inglis. SOCIAL PATTERNS IN AUSTRALIAN LITERATURE (Berkeley & Los Angeles: University of California P, 1971), pp. 66, 67, 84, 99, 100, 123, 224, 305, 311.

[Brief discussion of DHL's description of the Australian bush and "the influence of the bush on the people" in *Kangaroo* and *The Boy in the Bush.*] DHL had a sense of the freedom in Australia from "the old English inequalities," but his criticism that the Colonies " 'make for *outwardness'* " has an "acid truth." In his treatment of "mateship," however, DHL's introduction of "a physical attraction as operating between Somers and Kangaroo or Jack Callcott" is "a false note, an English concept quite alien to the Australian ethos."

3765 Mortland, Donald E. "The Conclusion of *Sons and Lovers:* A Reconsideration," STUDIES IN THE NOVEL, III (Fall 1971), 305-15.
A survey of criticism on the question of Paul Morel's future at the conclusion of *Sons and Lovers* reveals that some critics believe that Paul will not survive, some see the ambiguity as an artistic failure, and some, like Moynahan, see Paul as pulled between psychological and vital matrices. However, the parallels between Paul and Morel show that Paul, because of his overdeveloped consciousness, cannot integrate the vital into his being and, therefore, merges with it in death. The psychological and the vital both thus triumph in Paul's "drift toward death."

3766 Nahal, Chaman. THE NARRATIVE PATTERN IN ERNEST HEMINGWAY'S FICTION (Rutherford, Madison, & Teaneck, NJ: Fairleigh Dickinson UP, 1971), pp. 17, 31, 41-42, 144-45, 191, 195.
DHL comes closer than other modern writers, such as Woolf, Eliot, and Joyce, to Bergson's *durée*. DHL's " 'mindlessness' is symbolic of the dark forces functioning in the universe and in man. . . . But even in his case, it is a 'discussion' of mindlessness rather than a creative presentation of it." Both DHL and Hemingway intuitively accept "the mystic 'other,'. . .that other force, which runs parallel to and delimits the life of man." But whereas "Lawrence accepted the religious basis of life and proceeded to build his stories on" it, Hemingway, though basically a "religious artist" too, remained a doubting skeptic.

3767 Nardi, Piero. "Carteggi Lawrence" (Lawrence's Correspondence), LA FIERA LETTERARIA (Rome), 20 June 1971, pp. 9-11.
[Review of *Letters from D. H. Lawrence to Martin Secker, 1911-1930* (1970) and *The Quest for Rananim: D. H. Lawrence's Letters to S. S. Koteliansky, 1914 to 1930,* ed by George J. Zytaruk (1970).] DHL's correspondence with his publisher, Martin Secker, and his friend, S. S. Koteliansky, offers new insights into his life and the events leading to the publication of his works, as well as into his ideological attitude to modern society. [In Italian.]

3768 Nin, Anais. THE DIARY OF ANAIS NIN, 1944-1947, ed and with a Preface by Gunther Stuhlmann (NY: Harcourt, Brace, 1971), pp. vii, 35, 58, 61, 66, 85, 86, 115, 142, 205, 206, 222.
[This period is marked by the author's gradual disengagement from DHL. "D. H. Lawrence wrote against merging. But it is this merging I love and seek." Visiting Frieda Lawrence in New Mexico in summer 1947, the author finds, instead of the "tall, imposing woman" of DHL's descriptions, "a tiny old lady, all smiles and liveliness." DHL's paintings there are filled with "fleshy figures," but unlike Gauguin's they are English, "not sun tanned," in gray tones "as if long covered by winter." But Miss Nin, "as reluctant to go into the past of my literary loves as of my human ones," does not stay at the mountain cottage where DHL first lived. Despite its artist's colony, she decides not to visit Lake Chapala, where DHL had lived in Mexico, but goes instead to Acapulco.]

3769 Ocampo, Victoria. "El hombre que murió (D. H. Lawrence)"

(The Man Who Died--D. H. Lawrence), SUR, CCCXXIX (1971), 33-56. Like Kierkegaard, DHL believes that anguish is closely related to the spirit. While DHL is eternally prey to anguish, he rebels, at the same time, against the spirit from which it emanates. This seems to be his life drama. DHL wants us to follow the dark and deep wells of our instincts, which will not eventually betray us. Our submission to this flux of restlessness and obscure attractions or repulsions is a first principle for DHL. As a result, he feels cruelly lacerated by contradictions. The truth is destroyed within him constantly, and for it to be found again it becomes necessary to seek it everywhere, even in lies. Man, as DHL sees him, is a thought adventurer. Consequently, the novel becomes for him the means to articulate his thought adventures. DHL's thirst for travel is the expression of a peculiar mental state which leads him to believe that Europe has lost its flavor. To find what he is seeking, DHL goes first to Australia and then to America. His Australian novel, *Kangaroo,* is of particular interest to us South Americans because it reveals an insight relevant not only to Australia but also to our own continent. Men like Jack Callcott, who with their conscious virility become aggressive against those who do not learn to accommodate themselves to their masculinity, form a part as well of the South American scene. Jack's wife reveals another aspect of the Australian character that is close to ours: the desire to seek surety in life. Do not we in Latin America still have the feeling of being adolescents in search of a firm pathway whenever we are close to Europeans? *Kangaroo* is one of DHL's most suggestive novels, and it moves us because of its cry of anguish that the world is waiting either for a new wave of generosity or a great wave of death. [In Spanish.]

3770 Ohkawa, Hiroshi. "D. H. Lawrence no Jûjika--*Musuko to Koibito* Ron" (On D. H. Lawrence's *Sons and Lovers),* JOURNAL OF THE FACULTY OF FOREIGN LANGUAGES (Komazawa University), No. 7 (March 1971), 45-60.
[On DHL's venture into his own consciousness and his death as a social being in *Sons and Lovers.*] [In Japanese.]

3771 Orrell, Herbert M. "D. H. Lawrence: Poet of Death and Resurrection," CRESSET, XXXIV (March 1971), 10-13.
DHL's poetic form is modeled on Whitman's free verse and wedded with mythological imagery which attempts to capture the thought and feeling of pre-Socratic man. [Donne's "Holy Sonnet X" ("Death, be not proud") and DHL's "The Ship of Death" are compared, showing that DHL presents a convincing experience of death and resurrection.]

3772 Osborne, Marianne M. "The Hero and the Heroine in the British *Bildungsroman:* DAVID COPPERFIELD and A PORTRAIT OF THE ARTIST AS A YOUNG MAN, JANE EYRE and *The Rainbow."* Unpublished dissertation, Tulane University, 1971. [Listed in Lawrence F. McNamee, DISSERTATIONS IN ENGLISH AND AMERICAN LITERATURE, SUPP II (NY and Lond: Bowker, 1974), p. 341.]

3773 Ostendorff, Bernhard. DER MYTHOS IN DER NEUEN WELT.

EINE UNTERSUCHUNG ZUM AMERIKANISCHEN MYTH CRITICISM (The Myth in the New World: A Study on American Myth Criticism), (Frankfurt, 1971), pp. 89-106.

For DHL, the aim of art is to represent life and to destroy the discrepancy between mind and blood. He discovers the gulf between intellect and life in American literature *(Studies in Classic American Literature)*, i.e., in the tensions between the aesthetic and intellectual intentions of Poe, Hawthorne, and Melville, in whose works allegorical traits embody the quest for knowledge. DHL unmasks such American ideals as the American Dream, democracy, and liberty. [In German.]

3774 Perosa, Sergio. "La regione e l'istinto" (Reason and Instinct), CORRIERE DELLA SERA (Milan), 10 Jan 1971, p. 13.

[Review of *Il pavone bianco, Il trasgressore, Figli e amanti (The White Peacock, The Trespasser, Sons and Lovers)*, with an "Introduction" by Piero Nardi (1970).] To understand DHL's first novels there is no need to look for hints of his later ideology. *The White Peacock, The Trespasser,* and *Sons and Lovers* are based on the contrast between intellectual and instinctive characters, a reflection of the main dichotomy of DHL's existence. These novels can be appreciated for their freshness and spontaneity, even though their language and structure are often ingenuous and weak. [In Italian.]

3775 Petrič, Vladimir. "Seksualno jevandeje po D. H. Lorensu" (The Sexual Gospel of D. H. Lawrence), SAVREMENIK: MESEČNI KNJIŽEVNI CASOPIS, No. 7 (1971), 74-81.

[In Serbo-Croatian.]

3776 Phillips, Gene D., S. J. "Sexual Ideas in the Films of D. H. Lawrence," SEXUAL BEHAVIOR, I (June 1971), 10-16.

DHL's theme of the woman of status who must choose between her secure life and involvement with "an 'outsider' of lower social rank" is treated in all the films from DHL's fiction. Sexual insights in DHL's novels come as the culmination of gradual development, but film convention speeds up the process unrealistically and makes overt what was implicit in the fiction. [Illustrated with stills from the films made from DHL's fiction.]

3777 Phipps, William E. "D. H. Lawrence's Appraisal of Jesus," CHRISTIAN CENTURY, continuing NEW CHRISTIAN, LXXXVIII (28 April 1971), 521-24.

Several recent theological assessments prove the growing Christian appreciation of DHL. His portrait of Jesus in *The Man Who Died (The Escaped Cock)* presents a teacher and healer who finds his vice was the "greed of giving," in which altruism replaced sexuality. If modern man is to have a spiritual resurrection, he should follow the new life of DHL's Jesus, who liberates himself in mystical, sexual union. DHL's fiction follows a controversy in the Church over the sensual temperament of the historical Jesus, whose marriage parables suggest that he was married young, in the Hebrew tradition. The roots of *agape* in the Hebrew *aheb* show a joining of physical and spiritual love which can be seen in DHL's desire for a balanced life. DHL's overreaction to a repressed culture, however, resulted in a dualism which seemed to stress the flesh. His repudiation of Christianity, his emphasis on blood as death rather than blood as life, his view of sexual intimacy as transcendent are "significant contributions." [See also replies by William R. Hoyt III, "Re: 'D. H. Lawrence's Appraisal of Jesus.' (A Response to William E. Phipps)," CHRISTIAN CENTURY, LXXXVIII (14 July 1971), 861-62; and James B. Sipple, "D. H. Lawrence and 'Man's Ontological Solitude,' " CHRISTIAN CENTURY, LXXXVIII (17 Nov 1971), 1365-66.]

3778 Pinto, Vivian de Sola. "D. H. Lawrence," in THE POLITICS OF TWENTIETH CENTURY NOVELISTS, ed by George Andrew Panichas (NY: Hawthorne Books, 1971), pp. 30-50.

DHL has been denounced as reactionary and proto-Fascist, but Frieda's testimony denies this. He was actually a "religious genius" who was incomprehensible to the rationalist liberals who denounced and over-simplified him. His vision is achieved out of deep psychological traumas which he transcends. DHL as preacher and as manic is sometimes mistaken about politics; DHL as either prophetic poet or down-to-earth Midlander is not. *Sons and Lovers*, *The Rainbow*, and *Women in Love* are concerned with the destruction of individual sexuality by mechanized society; the only proto-Fascist there is Gerald, who is destroyed by his own ideal. In the crisis of his estrangement from England during the war and his rejection of Christianity, DHL sometimes sounds as if he desired a possibly dictatorial great man, but even then the other sides of his character are not obliterated. Aaron Sisson in *Aaron's Rod* remains unconvinced of the possibility of what Lilly preaches, and Lovat Somers in *Kangaroo* rejects both Fascism and Bolshevism. Don Ramón's revolution in *The Plumed Serpent* is opposed by the fascists, and even when it succeeds, DHL remains aware of the dangers of military tyranny. In his final phase, DHL rejects the idea of the hero and the possibility of significant political action. The "pictorial thinking" of his works after *The Plumed Serpent* depicts the individual regeneration which is essential before anything can be done politically and places him with prophetic poets like Blake, not with reactionaries like Pound.

3779 Pittock, Malcolm. "D. H. Lawrence," TIMES LITERARY SUPPLEMENT (Lond), 20 Aug 1971, p. 999.

[Letters to the Editor.] In the King's Scholarship examination in 1904, DHL placed in the First Division of the First Class, a distinction shared by fifty-five students that year; he was not "first in England and Wales" as reported by Harry T. Moore and Edward Nehls. In the 1908 Teacher's Certificate examination, DHL received distinctions in four subjects: math, history and geography, French, and botany; he did not receive distinction in education as reported by Jessie Chambers. [See also replies by Emile Delavenay and Harry T. Moore, "D. H. Lawrence," TIMES LITERARY SUPPLEMENT (Lond), 10 Sept 1971, p. 1086.]

3780 Powell, Lawrence Clark. "Southwest Classics Reread: *The Plumed Serpent*, by D. H. Lawrence," WESTWAYS, LXIII (Nov 1971), 18-20, 46-49; rptd as "D. H. Lawrence: *The Plumed Serpent*," SOUTHWEST CLASSICS: THE CREATIVE LITERATURE OF THE ARID LANDS, ESSAYS ON THE BOOKS AND THEIR WRITERS

(Los Angeles: Ward Ritchie P, 1974; rptd 1975), pp. 81-91.
DHL's three-year sojourn in the Southwest made an "immediate, strong and creative" impact on his work. "The Princess" places a sophisticated lady, modelled on Dorothy Brett, and a primitive man in a symbolic New Mexican setting. "The Woman Who Rode Away" takes revenge on Mabel Dodge Luhan by "offering her up" as a sacrificial victim. The two stories are "at the zenith of his Southwest writing." *The Plumed Serpent*, regarded as a failure by some because DHL did not himself embrace the primitive religion, achieves greatness in its mythopoeic vision of Mexico through the revolutionary revival of the religion of the Toltecs. [Includes photograph of DHL on horseback, p. 80.]

3781 Prasad, Suman P. "The Tragic Vision in the Novels of Thomas Hardy and D. H. Lawrence." Unpublished dissertation, University of Leicester, 1971. [Listed in Lawrence F. McNamee, DISSERTATIONS IN ENGLISH AND AMERICAN LITERATURE, SUPP II (NY & Lond: Bowker, 1974), p. 357]; rvd and pub as THOMAS HARDY AND D. H. LAWRENCE: A STUDY OF THE TRAGIC VISION IN THEIR NOVELS (New Delhi: Arnold-Heinemann, 1976).

3782 Pritchard, R. E. D. H. LAWRENCE: BODY OF DARKNESS (Lond: Hutchinson University Library, 1971).
This survey of DHL's writings proceeds from a Freudian analysis of his psychological make-up as it is expressed in recurrent images in his fiction, a practice justified by DHL's rejection of any distinction between "the life" and "the work," both of which were events in the great "thought-adventure" or "savage pilgrimage." DHL's imagery of the "living body of darkness," the buried self, and the "dark sun" refers to the unconscious, primary being beneath and suppressed by self-conscious existence, which he tried to liberate in himself through his fictions. It may be defined as the "non-human" life in the dark security of the womb that is akin to death, of which ordinary living is the negation; the primary, preconscious forces in nature, of which the sexual forces are the most obvious, but which also include the even more suppressed and therefore more fundamental anal-excretory complex–the "primal loam" and excremental flow that, though unliving, fertilizes new life and asserts the essential validity of the organic body; the reality of the material and physical; the anal core of the individual self-sufficient being; and subsuming all these, "the ground of all being," that which, while not itself individual or living, is yet the primary reality, the source and essence of the living phenomenal world that serves to manifest it. It may be interpreted as the unconscious or as the immanent God in man. [The analysis of specific works freely associates the principal characters or personae in stories and poems (e.g., Siegmund, Paul Morel, Rupert Birkin) with DHL himself. Includes analyses according to these principles of DHL's major works, with individual studies of *The Rainbow, Women in Love, England, My England,* and treatments of *The Lost Girl, Aaron's Rod, Kangaroo, The Plumed Serpent, Lady Chatterley's Lover, The Man Who Died, Last Poems,* and other works in cumulative discussions.]

3783 Pritchett, V[ictor] S. "The Upholstered Prison," NEW STATESMAN, ns LXXXII (8 Oct 1971), 479-80.

E. M. Forster's MAURICE, written ten years earlier, is the male version of DHL's *Lady Chatterley's Lover,* revealing the same concern with class-consciousness and societal paralysis. Fortunately, the sexual pedagogy which gives DHL's novel an oppressive sense of Cause is absent.

> **3784** Radmehr, Manouchehr. "Formen und Funktionen der Raumdarstellung in den Short Stories von D. H. Lawrence" (Forms and Functions of the Depiction of Space in the Short Stories of D. H. Lawrence). Unpublished dissertation, Gottingen University (Germany), 1971. [Listed in Lawrence F. McNamee, DISSERTATIONS IN ENGLISH AND AMERICAN LITERATURE, SUPP II (NY & Lond: Bowker, 1974), p. 368.] [In German.]

> **3785** Raskin, Jonah. THE MYTHOLOGY OF IMPERIALISM: RUDYARD KIPLING, JOSEPH CONRAD, E. M. FORSTER, D. H. LAWRENCE, AND JOYCE CARY (NY: Random House, 1971), pp. 5-6, 12, 17, 18, 19, 36, 96, 97-98, 196-97, 198-99, 200-205, 252-56, 272, 291, 293.

Unlike his contemporaries, DHL did not hesitate to destroy; tearing down decadent institutions, he sought a new social order and urged his readers "to make a revolution for life." DHL's "sense of chaos" was a healthy antidote to T. S. Eliot's concern for tradition. Because he perceived the "power of wealth and the machine over man," DHL had a far greater awareness of evil than traditional English novelists like George Eliot. DHL's plots dwell on conflict rather than serenity; he is "ready to lose everything, throw it all away if it is rotten, and start anew." In short, DHL stands apart from the imperialistic mainstream of English literature because he recognized "that art does not rest on money, that aesthetic young ladies and practical businessmen are not the basis for the England of the future." [Includes a comparison of *Women in Love* to George Eliot's MIDDLEMARCH and Conrad's NOSTROMO.]

> **3786** Remsbury, Ann, and John Remsbury. "D. H. Lawrence and Art," REVISTA DA FACULDADE DE LETRAS (University of Lisbon), Série III, No. 12 (1971), 101-29; rptd as "Lawrence and Art," in D. H. LAWRENCE: A CRITICAL STUDY OF THE MAJOR NOVELS AND OTHER WRITINGS, ed by A[ndor] H. Gomme (Hassocks, Sussex, England: Harvester P; NY: Barnes & Noble, 1978), pp. 190-218.

Although interesting to the critic or the student of art, DHL's paintings are flawed by a "stiltedness" which is owing to his preoccupation with depicting the human body. Although his idealized paintings fail adequately to render DHL's conception of "the real existence of the body," the prose "Introduction to These Paintings" provided DHL with an appropriate medium in which to convey his theories about art. Rejecting the extremes of an idealized, non-representational style on the one hand and literal photographic observation on the other hand, DHL's focus as an art critic was the perceptual process in the mind of the painter. Believing that "imagination is continuous with perception," DHL viewed the great painter as a seer--a belief appropriately in keeping with his whole apology for art and literature. The parallel, in literature, to what DHL believed Cézanne had accomplished in painting, was a prose fiction of "bare facts...facts without authorial comment and, particularly, without the sense of straining after an effect."

3787 Roberts, F[rancis] Warren. "D. H. Lawrence, The Second 'Poetic Me': Corrigenda," RENAISSANCE AND MODERN STUDIES, XV (1971), 103-6.

[Corrects over 100 errors in his earlier article, "D. H. Lawrence, The Second 'Poetic Me': Some New Material," RENAISSANCE AND MODERN STUDIES, XIV (1970), 5-25.]

3788 Ross, Michael L. "The Mythology of Friendship: D. H. Lawrence, Bertrand Russell, and 'The Blind Man,' " in ENGLISH LITERATURE AND BRITISH PHILOSOPHY, ed by S. P. Rosenbaum (Chicago: University of Chicago P, 1971), pp. 285-315.

Although their friendship began well, Bertrand Russell's pragmatic approach to social reform infuriated DHL, who saw it as evading the "universal spiritual catharsis" that was needed. In denouncing Russell, DHL is attempting to change him and recover a sense of solidarity with him. "The Blind Man" is a product of this unresolved conflict: Bertie Reid resembles Russell as DHL saw him, and Maurice Pervin's situation corresponds to DHL's own feelings of entrapment and isolation brought about by the war. Blindness also suggests the ultimate reality of blood-consciousness and thus is a source of power as well as of agony to Pervin. It enables him to destroy Reid's shell, as DHL was unable to do with Russell, and to triumph over him. Ironically, however, the destruction of the shell means the destruction of Reid himself, and the victory is hollow. Neither DHL nor Pervin manages to liberate the friend he desires, but the artistry of the story transforms DHL's personal resentment into myth.

3789 Rudrum, Alan. "Philosophical Implications in Lawrence's *Women in Love*," DALHOUSIE REVIEW, LI (Summer 1971), 240-50.

DHL's remarks on morality and the novel are important for his view that only the novelist "can help us rescue ourselves from our automatisms." The "Gerald-plot and the Birkin-plot" represent DHL's two opposed beliefs: Birkin represents "the claims of Erigenia's Holy Spirit in the world," Gerald the acceptance of life as a "finite, regular, orderly mechanism." Because Gerald's philosophy predominates in the world, "it takes a will of a different kind not to acquiesce to it." *Women in Love* is thus "a criticism of a fiction: the fiction by which Gerald organizes his world."

3790 Sagar, Keith. "D. H. Lawrence," TIMES LITERARY SUPPLEMENT (Lond), 10 Sept 1971, p. 1086.

[Letter to the Editor.] Since DHL changed one of the "easts" in "Red Wolf" for the English edition of *Birds, Beasts and Flowers*, would it not be justifiable, in editing a selection of his poems, to change the other two also? [See also reply by John Beer, TIMES LITERARY SUPPLEMENT (Lond), 24 Sept 1971, p. 1148; comment by M. B. Mencher, TIMES LITERARY SUPPLEMENT (Lond), 17 Sept

1971, p. 1119; and reply to Mencher by Harry T. Moore, TIMES LITERARY SUPPLEMENT (Lond), 1 Oct 1971, p. 1177.]

3791 Sagar, Keith. "D. H. Lawrence: Dramatist," D. H. LAWRENCE REVIEW, IV (Summer 1971), 154-82.
Of the eleven plays which DHL wrote, only three were published (*The Widowing of Mrs. Holroyd* [1914], *Touch and Go* [1920], and *David* [1926]) and only two were produced (*The Widowing of Mrs. Holroyd* [1920, 1926], and *David* [1927]) during DHL's lifetime. He saw none of these productions, which were received with little critical interest and mixed reviews. It was not until the 1960s, with Peter Gill's "sensitive and painstaking productions" at the Royal Court Theatre, London, of *A Collier's Friday Night, The Widowing of Mrs. Holroyd*, and *The Daughter-in-Law*, that DHL was revealed to be a major twentieth-century English dramatist. *A Collier's Friday Night* is a naturalistic play unlike others of the period; "never before had working-class family life been presented with such immediacy and authenticity." The greatest strength of the play, "and Lawrence's greatest strength as a dramatist," lies in "the quality of the dialogue, and of the silences." Dealing with the same situation, but with the thematic focus shifted to the husband and wife, *The Widowing of Mrs. Holroyd* and *The Daughter-in-Law* have the same strengths of the earlier play. The power of the tragic ending of *The Widowing of Mrs. Holroyd* is "one of the great moments in modern drama." Of the other plays, *The Merry-Go-Round, The Married Man, The Fight for Barbara*, and *Touch and Go* fail to achieve authenticity as drama for various reasons; *Noah's Flood* and *Altitude* are fragments. *David*, DHL's most difficult play, explores the father's role and themes of brotherhood and leadership. [Illustrated with the program cover and seven photographs by Douglas H. Jeffery of the Royal Court Theatre's season of three DHL plays in 1968.]

3792 Sagar, Keith. "Four Paintings by D. H. Lawrence," D. H. LAWRENCE REVIEW, IV (Spring 1971), 42-43; two of the poems, "Boccaccio Story" and "Resurrection," rptd in THE REEF AND OTHER POEMS, by Keith Sagar, with Introduction by Ted Hughes (Ilkley, West Yorkshire: Poem Pamphlets, 1980), p. [9].
[Four short poems describing four of DHL's paintings in imagery drawn from the paintings: "Boccaccio Story," "Red Willow Trees," "Resurrection," and "Summer Dawn."]

3793 Sagar, Keith. "Introduction," *The Mortal Coil and Other Stories*, by D. H. Lawrence, ed by Keith Sagar (Harmondsworth, Middlesex, England: Penguin Books, 1971, rptd 1972), pp. 7-9.
While the first two sketches, "Adolf" and "Rex," are "reminiscences of childhood written in middle life," the remaining fourteen stories collected here "were all written in Lawrence's twenties." "A Prelude," submitted in Jessie Chambers's name to the NOTTINGHAMSHIRE GUARDIAN contest for the best Christmas story, won the prize of three pounds and was published in December 1907. The frustration of DHL's relationships with Jessie, Louie Burrows, and Helen Corke, which he was unable to bring "to a satisfactory sexual footing," is reflected in "The Old Adam" and "The Witch a la Mode." The "strike situation" of 1912

is the background for "The Miner at Home" and "Her Turn." After his elopement to the Tyrolese Alps with Frieda Weekley in the spring of 1912, DHL wrote "A Chapel among the Mountains" and "A Hay Hut among the Mountains," continuing with the same characters in "Once." "The Thimble," based on an incident involving the Herbert Asquiths, is "in some ways preferable to 'The Ladybird' which apparently grew out of it." "The Mortal Coil," which DHL called " 'one of my purest creations,' " was never included in any collections published in his lifetime.

3794 Sagar, Keith. "Introduction," *The Princess and Other Stories,* by D. H. Lawrence, ed by Keith Sagar (Harmondsworth, Middlesex, England: Penguin Books, 1971; rptd 1972, 1974, 1976, 1978), pp. 7-12.

The twelve stories collected here "all date from the last eight years of Lawrence's life." "The Wilful Woman" is the unfinished "train" episode from DHL's aborted collaboration with Mabel Dodge Luhan in a book based on her experience. "The Princess" adapts a theme suggested by Catherine Carswell of a baby girl's upbringing by savages in isolation as a goddess. "The Overtone" derives from DHL's discovery in New Mexico of a name for his "dark god": Pan. DHL's notes [reproduced here] indicate how he planned to end his fragmentary story "The Flying Fish," which grows out of his experience of near-fatal illness in Mexico in 1925. "Sun," collected in *The Woman Who Rode Away* (1928) in the expurgated version, was published by the Black Sun Press (1926) in unexpurgated form [reprinted here for the first time]. "The Man Who Was Through with the World," another story which DHL began and abandoned in 1927, reveals "much more sympathy for Henry the Hermit than he had for Cathcart in *The Man Who Loved Islands.*" In "A Dream of Life," "mistakenly called 'Autobiographical Sketch' in *Phoenix,*" DHL awakens after a thousand years' sleep near Eastwood "to find himself near a handsome town among gentle people who combine" the best qualities of Etruscan civilization and Midlands mining communities. "The Undying Man," another fragment, was based on a Yiddish folk tale sent to him by S. S. Koteliansky, whose translation of the original shows how the story ends [conclusion reproduced here]. "The Blue Moccasins," "Things," and "Mother and Daughter," written in late 1928, "are typical of the satirical and often cruel stories of this period."

3795 Sanders, Scott R. "Studies in the Language of D. H. Lawrence." Unpublished dissertation, Cambridge University, 1971. [Listed in Lawrence F. McNamee, DISSERTATIONS IN ENGLISH AND AMERICAN LITERATURE, SUPP II (NY & Lond: Bowker, 1974), p. 367.]

3796 Scholes, Robert (ed). SOME MODERN WRITERS: ESSAYS AND FICTION BY CONRAD, DINESAN, LAWRENCE, ORWELL, FAULKNER, AND ELLISON (NY: Oxford UP, 1971), pp. 73-74.

[Biographical sketch, mentioning DHL's ambivalent feelings for his parents, his physical illnesses, his life with Frieda, his problems with censorship, and his informal style, and introducing selections by DHL: "Three Essays on Art and Literature" ("Surgery for the Novel--or a Bomb," "Art and Morality," and "Why the Novel Matters"), "Reflections on the Death of a Porcupine," and "The Woman Who Rode Away," which are reprinted in the anthology, pp. 175-242.]

3797 Sencourt, Robert. T. S. ELIOT: A MEMOIR, ed by Donald Adamson (Lond: Garnstone P, 1971), pp. 173-75; (NY: Dodd, Mead, 1971), pp. 87, 93, 226-27.

T. S. Eliot at first thought DHL "the most interesting of the rising novelists" because of his explorations of the unconscious and his "frankness in dealing with sexual relations." But he did not sympathize with the imagists' view that DHL was "superhuman." Eliot planned, "if necessary," to appear for the defense in the 1960 British censorship trial of *Lady Chatterley's Lover* (Regina v. Penguin Books Ltd.). Although he found much in DHL "distasteful if not deplorable, he still preferred unveiled nakedness to the drapery of prudery."

3798 Sharma, Radhe Shyam. "The Symbol as Archetype: A Study of Symbolic Mode in D. H. Lawrence's *Women in Love*," OSMANIA JOURNAL OF ENGLISH STUDIES (Hyderabad, India), VIII, No. 2 (1971), 31-53.

"The tendency to dissolve the literary symbol in the primary mode of the 'symbolic form' or in the undifferentiated 'archetype' " raises "the aesthetic problems implied in their application as valid tools of literary criticism." [Discussion of various neo-Kantian theories of symbol and "symbolic form" and of Jungian and other theories of archetype.] DHL's "symbolic mode...is archetypal in the Jungian sense" of "a dialectic through which man apperceives and integrates his rational, sub-rational and transpersonal experience into new modalities of experience, . . . a process whereby individual consciousness is dissolved into a new creative synthesis." In *Women in Love,* Gudrun, in her dance before the cattle, seeks not to be creatively polarized with them but "negatively polarised to the power of the super-self," a destructive polarity which she then initiates with Gerald Crich. "The archetypal quest for balance in the novel fails, because the characters fail to relate it to concrete living contexts and seek it in individual terms." The nude wrestling scene between Birkin and Gerald symbolizes not homosexuality but "the futility of reconciling power without love with intellect without power." "The tragedy in *Women in Love* is...a tragedy of false polarities, which produce only disintegration and dissolution." DHL's aesthetic theory "accepts the totality of the structure of art as well as its contextuality in relation to the whole."

3799 Shimizu, Kohya. "Lawrence to Marinetti" (Lawrence and Marinetti), BULLETIN OF STUDIES IN HUMANITY (Kagawa University), No. 31 (Sept 1971), 95-122.

[Discusses DHL's sharp interest in Italian Futurism and its leader Marinetti, and portrays DHL as both an aesthetic futurist and a moral anti-futurist.] [In Japanese.]

3800 Shimizu, Kohya. "*The Rainbow* Saikô" (*The Rainbow* Reconsidered), BULLETIN OF STUDIES IN HUMANITY (Kagawa University), No. 30 (March 1971), 1-29.

Although some critics say that there is no development among the couples of the three generations in *The Rainbow,* the writer cannot agree with this view. The "dissolution theme" in this novel marks a considerable transition in DHL's work. [In Japanese.]

    3801 Sipple, James B. "D. H. Lawrence and 'Man's Ontological Solitude,'" CHRISTIAN CENTURY, continuing NEW CHRISTIAN, LXXXVIII (17 Nov 1971), 1365-66.

[Letter to the Editor in reply to William E. Phipps, "D. H. Lawrence's Appraisal of Jesus," CHRISTIAN CENTURY, LXXXVIII (28 April 1971), 521-24; and William R. Hoyt III, "Re: 'D. H. Lawrence's Appraisal of Jesus.' (A Response to William E. Phipps)," CHRISTIAN CENTURY, LXXXVIII (14 July 1971), 861-62.] Within the central focus of his fiction on "'man's ontological solitude,'" DHL is an experimentalist, exploring various possible solutions to the problem. Missing "the wide range of experimental models" that he employs, some critics also "miss the decisive development toward Christianity which is the major thrust of Lawrence's career; namely, the bringing together of nature and history within the theological circle." In his early works the solution to the "ontological tragedy" is found in what DHL calls "darkness." In the later works "the struggle is to turn the darkness to day, to bring nature and history into effective connection," a quest devalued by "a theological stance that presupposes a radical split between nature and history (and between nature and grace)." Both Phipps and Hoyt mistakenly literalize *The Man Who Died,* which is rather a mythic embodiment of the theological quest.

    3802 Smith, Frank Glover. D. H. LAWRENCE: "THE RAINBOW" (Lond: Edward Arnold, 1971).

DHL opens *The Rainbow* in a manner reminiscent of the traditional English novel, which traces the history of a family and a setting, but soon reverses the conventional "downward motion, of narrowing and enclosing" and moves in "a forward, upward motion, a movement of enlargement and release." The stylistic rhythms and metaphors in DHL's description of setting in the first chapter set the theme and tone of his narrative by revealing man's "blood-tie with the cosmos." DHL's characters illustrate a reversal of sexual roles: "the Brangwen women, striving for knowledge and for differentiation, turn from the way of blood-intimacy," while the men are adolescent in nature, "remarkable for their verve, wit, and insight." This reversal of roles leads to DHL's "morality of relationship," a major concern in the novel, which begins with the courtship and marriage of Tom and Lydia, and continues in a narrative spiral with Anna Lensky's maturation and marriage to Will Brangwen. Believing that "selfhood is attained in the fulfilment of a passional relationship" and denying the "'stable ego,'" DHL developed his theory of dynamic polarity and explored a level of consciousness which defies moral absolutes. The "morality of relationship" is further examined in the attitudes of parents and children. Tom Brangwen's unhealthy relationship with his step-daughter, Anna, based upon mutual dependence, is contrasted with Lydia's relationship with her growing sons, "forcing them into independence." The precocious consciousness aroused in Ursula by the troubled relationship with her father, Will Brangwen, however, also has the effect of "widening the circle of life," of provoking an early desire for self-discovery. Consequently, the adolescent Ursula is prepared to strive for the "achievement of new selfhood by a relation that includes the extrapersonal, the connection with the cosmos witnessed in the sacrament of sexual passion." Although this ideal is not realized in Ursula's early relationships, with Anton Skrebensky and Winifred Inger, she is prepared, by the end of the novel, for the kind of relationship which is idealized in *Women in Love*.

3803 Spears, Logan. TOLSTOY AND CHEKHOV (Lond: Cambridge UP, 1971), pp. 227-37.

DHL hated Tolstoy and argued that Tolstoy's Christianity would not work, but ANNA KARENINA made a deep impression on him and influenced *The Rainbow*. Neither Levin nor Tom Brangwen grasps abstract thought, and for both marriage is the central fact, changing them into towers of strength. Tom is destroyed by "industrial waters," while Ursula continues, whereas in Tolstoy, it is the woman who is destroyed by machinery and Levin who survives. Skrebensky is weak like Vronsky; both are made by and for the state. But whereas Ursula knows what is wrong with the life her lover wants for them, Anna Karenina does not. DHL deliberately misinterprets Tolstoy, judging on didactic intent rather than artistic fact. Both authors see life as a quest for illumination, and both feel successful only in real marriage.

3804 Speirs, John. POETRY TOWARDS NOVEL (Lond: Faber & Faber, 1971), pp. 326-33.

Although Thomas Hardy records a vanishing rural England, George Eliot's great successor is DHL, not Hardy. *The Rainbow* conveys the falling away of the older world while *Women in Love* presents the new world already in existence. Unlike Eliot, however, and in affinity with Blake and Wordsworth, DHL recognizes that human relationships cannot be dissociated from the non-human universe around them. DHL sees the unconscious as the roots of conscious life, not as the dustbin of suppressed impulses. The great nineteenth- and twentieth-century novelists are carriers of the poetic tradition of earlier periods.

3805 Spilka, Mark. "Lawrence Up-Tight, or the Anal Phase Once Over," NOVEL: A FORUM ON FICTION, IV (Spring 1971), 252-67.

Colin Clarke, like G. Wilson Knight and Frank Kermode, sees the supremely creative sex act in *Women in Love* as an anal act which may lead to wholeness in heterosexual love. The unpublished "Prologue" to the novel, however, shows that Birkin must "work through" both his " 'living desire' " for Gerald Crich and his "deathly attachment" to Hermione before he can establish a relationship of creative sexual love with Ursula. [Review essay on Colin Clarke, RIVER OF DISSOLUTION: D. H. LAWRENCE AND ENGLISH ROMANTICISM (1969). See also George Ford, Frank Kermode, Colin Clarke, and Mark Spilka, "Critical Exchange: On 'Lawrence Up-Tight': Four Tail-Pieces," NOVEL, V (Fall 1971), 54-70.]

3806 Stoll, John E. THE NOVELS OF D. H. LAWRENCE: A SEARCH FOR INTEGRATION (Columbia: University of Missouri P, 1971).

DHL's use of imagery, especially light and dark and womb imagery, is directly related to his theory of consciousness, which manifests both his "self-division and his attempt to overcome duality through art." In DHL's theory, consciousness, imposed from without by the mother as "culture carrier," is internalized as reason, cutting the child off from his vital self. For the child to become aware of this, both psychic and social upheaval are needed. Reconciling consciousness with the unconscious leads only to loss of male identity; instead the former must be rejected as the psyche takes on its own identity. But since DHL never shows how social consciousness can be destroyed without also destroying the individual, there is an imbalance between ends and means. Two opposed aims, to explore the known self and to show the emergence of the vital self, characterize DHL's work. In *The White Peacock*, DHL fails to link the incestuous tie between Cyril and Lettie with the problem of manhood. The white peacock is associated with death and defilement and the woman as destroyer. Lettie's consciousness is divorced from passion and makes her cruel to the man she dominates, but DHL identifies himself too closely with Cyril to confront the issue objectively. *The Trespasser* treats the incest theme more directly. In Siegmund and Helena, DHL rejects both the passive male and the victimizing female. DHL's claim that neurosis affects only the consciousness limits *Sons and Lovers*. Freudian implications about incest remain, despite DHL's intentions; although he attempts to present Miriam as devouring and Mrs. Morel as vital, their similarity is established in light imagery. In *The Rainbow*, DHL attempts to extend the problem of consciousness to society as a whole but does not show that the Brangwens' problems are rooted in their common humanity. In *Women in Love*, the quest is subordinated to examination of the social ills that make it necessary. *Aaron's Rod, Kangaroo,* and *The Plumed Serpent* extend the vital self into a social and political program in which personal male leadership replaces mechanized society, but the characters are unconvincing, and the connection between their dissolving and reborn selves is assumed, not shown. In *Lady Chatterley's Lover* DHL uses mental consciousness only as a frame of reference and concentrates on the phallic. In evading the conscious self rather than uprooting it, DHL ultimately subverts his own thesis.

3807 Strickland, Geoffrey. "The First *Lady Chatterley's Lover*," ENCOUNTER, XXXVI (Jan 1971), 44-52, rptd in D. H. LAWRENCE: A CRITICAL STUDY OF THE MAJOR NOVELS AND OTHER WRITINGS, ed by A[ndor] H. Gomme (Sussex, England: Harvester P; NY: Barnes & Noble, 1978), pp. 159-74.

The first version of *Lady Chatterley's Lover* is superior to the third in that, although DHL wanted to contrast the primitive and the sophisticated, he failed to do so since he made Parkin-Mellors a relatively educated man suitable for Connie to marry. Parkin stresses the differences between himself as an individual and Connie as a member of a higher class. The third version, in which Connie and Mellors are going to live as genteel farmers, offers no way to react to the English industrial failure. The frank language is not realistic, and the novel is immoral in presenting love as the supreme value, contrary to DHL's teachings elsewhere.

3808 Sullivan, Alvin. "Days of THE FHOENIX," JOURNAL OF MODERN LITERATURE, II (Sept 1971), 137-43.

[Detailed literary history of the little magazine THE PHOENIX (1938-1940, publication resumed 1970). The editor, James P. Cooney, took a worshipful attitude toward DHL's philosophy while appearing to ignore his inconsistencies. Reprinting many of DHL's letters despairing at World War I, Cooney opposed World War II and anticipated the "coming of the new epoch" that would save the world from both Fascism and Marxism.]

 3809 Suzuki, Shunzi. "*Niji* to *Koisuru Onnatachi*--Shin naru Sei. Rakuen e no Michi" (A Study of *The Rainbow* and *Women in Love*: Rebirth to Real Life), NAGOYA REVIEW OF ENGLISH STUDIES (Nagoya University), No. 11 (Dec 1971), 38-54.

The Rainbow and *Women in Love* were originally intended to be a single book, *The Sisters*, but *The Sisters* was, in effect, divided into the two books, which are very different in tone. DHL says repeatedly in his letters that these two novels, though different, are " 'sequels' " or " 'an organic, artistic whole' "; but many critics, such as F. R. Leavis and George H. Ford, do not agree with him and make convincing cases to the contrary. However, it is necessary to read them as " 'an organic, artistic whole,' " if we are to grasp the organic theme of the two novels. This " 'organic, artistic whole' " can be demonstrated through the study of the " 'double rhythm of creating and destroying ' " which DHL comments on in the "Edgar Allan Poe" essay in *Studies in Classic American Literature*. This thematic " 'double rhythm' " flows through *The Rainbow* and *Women in Love*, making two contrasting curves of descent and ascent, so that it symbolically suggests that the central theme is "rebirth to real life." [In Japanese.]

 3810 Swingewood, Alan. "Problems of Method," in THE SOCIOLOGY OF LITERATURE, by Diana Laurenson and Alan Swingewood (Lond: MacGibbon & Kee, 1971), pp. 83-86, 152-53.

Although DHL dealt frankly and explicitly with sexual relations in his fiction, his anti-democratic sentiments led him to write novels which "are rarely. . .social in the sense that milieu is concretely realized." In his three most important novels, in fact, DHL "writes almost to the exclusion of extrapersonalized themes." He believed that men and women are inherently different and therefore rejected the notion that conventional sex roles are the product of socialization. DHL's "message" is that since "women are by nature different from men they will strive towards intellectual equality at the risk of losing their essential being, their femininity." Thus, DHL "succeeds only in isolating the erotic element in love and rarely grasps the social determinations of human emotions." Instead, DHL believes that human relationships are the products of non-social factors, of "the dark brooding of the blood."

 3811 Tabuchi, Hiroyuki. "D. H. Lawrence no *Seishin-Bunseki to Muishiki* Oyobi *Muishiki no Gensôkyoku* Kanken (1)" (On D. H. Lawrence's *Psychoanalysis and the Unconscious* and *Fantasia of the Unconscious* [1]), KEIZAI SHŪSHI (Nihon University), XLI (Nov 1971), 43-53.

[First of two articles on *Psychoanalysis and the Unconscious* and *Fantasia of the Unconscious*.] The two psychoanalytic essays provide a secure foundation for understanding DHL's philosophy of the "unconscious," which can be traced back to his belief that the development of mental conceptions has devastated our love, sex, and education, making the dynamic relation between us quiescent. The contradictory wording, the lack of clarity in argument, and the confusing and tedious explanation for which these essays have often been criticized seem to have their raison d'etre: full effectiveness in asserting DHL's quasi-scientific terms in these essays should be regarded as nothing more than symbols expressing his intuitive cognition of life. [Includes discussion of the "Laurentian unconscious and its function," "parent and child," and "love and education." See also Hiroyuki Tabuchi, "D. H. Lawrence no *Seishin-Bunseki to Muishiki* Oyobi *Muishiki no Gensôkyoku* Kanken (2)" (On D. H. Lawrence's *Psychoanalysis and the Unconscious* and *Fantasia of the Unconscious* [2]), KEIZAI SHUSHI (Nihon University), XLII (Nov 1972), 56-68.] [In Japanese.]

3812 Tetsumura, Haruo. "*Sons and Lovers* Kenkyû (2)" (A Study of *Sons and Lovers* [2]), BULLETIN OF FACULTY OF EDUCATION (Nagasaki University), No. 20 (March 1971), 11-22.
Mark Spilka's criticism that *Sons and Lovers* "is only outwardly conventional" raises two questions: what is "outwardly" and what is "conventional"? The "conventional" may be considered the traditional strict treatment of time, consistent point of view, and other characteristics of nineteenth-century novels which may be called naturalistic. "Outwardly" can be considered DHL's personality as a man and as a novelist. [In Japanese.]

3813 Thompson, Leslie M. "D. H. Lawrence and Judas," D. H. LAWRENCE REVIEW, IV (Spring 1971), 1-19.
DHL's reaction to the Judas figure is complex and contradictory. He "exults in Judas's betrayal of Christ as a. . .necessary assertion of freedom," comparable to DHL's own militant individualism. Yet "Judas became to Lawrence a haunting symbol of betrayal, and the fear generated by this vision increased in direct relation to Lawrence's growing seriousness about his 'mission' to save society." His idea of "Judas as a liberator" derives from his belief that Christianity's "teaching of meekness and humility had drained life of its vitality and joy." In *Apocalypse*, he attributes Judas's betrayal to a lack in Jesus rather than to a weakness in Judas. In *The Man Who Died*, the "Christ figure realizes his shortcomings and confesses that it is Judas, not he, who has been wronged." But DHL's increasing "fear of betrayal coincides directly with his developing view of himself as a Christ figure." The "paradoxical views of Judas as both betrayer and liberator underscore a basic contradiction in Lawrence's philosophy. He claimed the right to total freedom. . .for himself," but refused to grant such freedom to his disciples. Parallel "conflicts between individualism, annihilation of self, and fear of betrayal recur repeatedly in Lawrence's fiction."

3814 Tiedje, Egon. "D. H. Lawrence's Early Poetry: The Composition-Dates of the Drafts in MS E317," D. H. LAWRENCE REVIEW, IV (Fall 1971), 227-52.
[A detailed description of MS E317 extends and corrects the description given by Vivian de Sola Pinto in his "D. H. Lawrence: Letter-Writer and Craftsman in Verse," RENAISSANCE AND MODERN STUDIES, I (1957), 5-34. Tiedje's

article is followed by "Appendix: Chronological Chart of MS E317."] [See also a reply by Carole Ferrier and the response by Egon Tiedje in "D. H. Lawrence's Pre-1920 Poetry: The Textual Approach: An Exchange," D. H. LAWRENCE REVIEW, V (Summer 1972), 149-57.]

3815 Tomatsu, Ryoichi. "Chichioya ni Taisuru D. H. Lawrence no Kanjô--Ishiki to Muishiki" (The Feeling of D. H. Lawrence Towards His Father--Conscious and Unconscious), REVIEW (Sapporo College of Commerce), No. 7 (Dec 1971), 21-30.

It is generally known that when DHL was composing *Sons and Lovers*, he bore hatred toward his father and that later he felt sympathy toward him. If the novel is read with care, however, DHL's sympathy and identification with his father are evident in it, even if these feelings were unconscious when DHL was composing it. [In Japanese.]

3816 Toyokuni, Takashi. "*Women in Love*--A Study of the Man-Woman Relationship," ENGLISH LITERATURE IN HOKKAIDO (Muroran Institute of Technology), No. 16 (June 1971), 31-47.

[Analyzes *Women in Love* from the viewpoint of the man-woman relationship in an effort to illuminate DHL's view of this relationship.]

3817 Toyokuni, Tokashi. "*Women in Love*--A Study of Three Relationships," MEMOIRS OF THE MURORAN INSTITUTE OF TECHNOLOGY, VII, No. 2 (Sept 1971), 285-322.

[Analyzes *Women in Love* from the viewpoint of three relationships--the man-woman relationship, the man-man relationship, and the man-cosmos relationship.]

3818 Tripathy, Biyot Kesh. "*Lady Chatterley's Lover:* A Trembling Balance," BULLETIN OF THE DEPARTMENT OF ENGLISH (Calcutta University), ns VII, No. 2 (1971-1972), 75-89; rptd in THE MAJOR NOVELS OF D. H. LAWRENCE: AN APPROACH TO HIS ART AND IDEAS, by Biyot K. Tripathy (Bhubaneswar, India: Pothi Publications, 1973), pp. 105-21.

Lady Chatterley's Lover has two related themes: the story of personal aspirations, and the social background as the reality in which the lovers seek to realize these aspirations. The careful division of sympathy between Connie and Clifford gives the novel a technical objectivity in which opposites maintain a constant balance.

3819 Veitch, Douglas W. "The Fictional Landscape of Mexico: D. H. Lawrence, Graham Greene and Malcolm Lowry." Unpublished dissertation, University of Montreal, 1971. [Listed in Lawrence F. McNamee, DISSERTATIONS IN ENGLISH AND AMERICAN LITERATURE, SUPP. II: 1969-1973 (NY & Lond: Bowker, 1974), pp. 367-68.] Rvd and pub as LAWRENCE, GREENE AND LOWRY: THE FICTIONAL LANDSCAPE OF MEXICO (Waterloo, Ontario, Canada: Wilfrid Laurier UP, 1978).

3820 Vickery, John B. "D. H. Lawrence: Critics and Archetypes," PSYCHOLOGICAL PERSPECTIVES, II (Spring 1971), 70-77.

[Review essay on James C. Cowan, D. H. LAWRENCE'S AMERICAN JOURNEY (1970); Sven Armen, ARCHETYPES OF THE FAMILY IN LITERATURE; and DHL's *The Rainbow*.] More than "creative artist" or "critic," DHL was "a living, experiencing, suffering human being in touch with all facets of his nature." His idea that dynamic polarity underlies creativity "adumbrates certain Jungian conceptions." Aware of the dangers of both "immersion in the unconscious" and "exclusive reliance on the conscious mind," DHL sought, in "The Flying Fish," to synthesize these opposing modes of psychic experience. *The Rainbow*, an extension of the Victorian omnibus novel in form, purges love of "its illusions and deceptions" and treats it as "authentic, genuine experience which contributes to creative growth."

3821 Wada, Shizuo. "D. H. Lawrence Oboegaki (V)--*Kitsune* ni Kansuru Ichibunseki" (Notes on D. H. Lawrence [V] : An Analysis of *The Fox*), BULLETIN OF KYÛSHÛ SANGYÔ UNIVERSITY, VII, No. 2 (Feb 1971), 1-28.

DHL's theory of the unconscious is a key to understanding his short novel *The Fox*, which may be analyzed according to the heroine's unconscious. [See also Shizuo Wada, "D. H. Lawrence Oboegaki (IV)--*Seishin-Bunseki to Muishiki* to *Muishiki no Genso* ni Tsuite" (Notes on D. H. Lawrence [IV] : *Fantasia of the Unconscious* and *Psychoanalysis and the Unconscious*), BULLETIN OF KYÛSHÛ SANGYÔ UNIVERSITY, VI, No. 2 (March 1970), 1-62, and "D. H. Lawrence Oboegaki (IV)--*Seishin-Bunseki to Muishiki* to *Muishiki no Genso* ni Tsuite" (Notes on D. H. Lawrence [IV] : *Fantasia of the Unconscious* and *Psychoanalysis and the Unconscious*), BULLETIN OF KYÛSHÛ SANGYÔ UNIVERSITY, VII, No. 1 (Dec 1970), 7-46.] [In Japanese.]

3822 Wagner, Jeanie. "A Botanical Note on *Aaron's Rod*," D. H. LAWRENCE REVIEW, IV (Fall 1971), 287-90.

For DHL "the botanist" there would have been a "significance in the term 'Aaron's rod' which was distinct from Biblical or pagan symbolism." The yellow mullein, "a heavily stalked plant," is commonly known by that name and traditionally has "potent medicinal value" and serves "as a fly trap for destructive insects." DHL satirizes "the attitudes of Aaron's admirers. . .by picturing them all drawn like insects by the sweetness of the flute." [Illustrated with a photograph of the plant growing on the DHL ranch in New Mexico.]

3823 Wallenstein, Barry. "D. H. Lawrence," VISIONS AND REVISIONS: AN APPROACH TO POETRY (NY: Crowell, 1971), pp. 246-48.

Although many of DHL's poems are marred by his essential moralism, some transcend petty values. [Reprints early and late versions of "Renascence," "Violets," "Piano," "Man's Image," and "Bavarian Gentians."]

3824 Wallmann, Jürgen P. "Mysterien vom Sex. D. H. Lawrences Essays über Liebe, Emanzipation und ähnliches" (Mysteries of Sex: D. H. Lawrence's Essays on Love, Emancipation, and the Like), BADISCHE ZEITUNG, 13 Dec 1971.

[Review of *Pornographie und Obszönität und andere Essays über Liebe, Sex und*

Emancipation (Pornography and Obscenity and Other Essays on Love, Sex, and Emancipation), trans by Elisabeth Schnack (Zurich, 1971).] DHL's reputation as a pornographic writer is nonsensical. He is more than just a frivolous iconoclast of Victorian sex taboos. The purpose of his essays is to show sex as a mystery of life and as a source of man's naturalness. [In German.]

3825 Weaver, Mike. WILLIAM CARLOS WILLIAMS: THE AMERICAN BACKGROUND (Cambridge: Cambridge UP, 1971), pp. 149-51.

Reflections on the Death of a Porcupine was influenced by DHL's reading of Madame Blavatsky's THE SECRET DOCTRINE and Frazer's THE GOLDEN BOUGH, "but from Lawrence the myth was readily available to Williams as an immediate talisman, to be worked out in full in the last book of PATERSON." Williams sympathized with DHL's idea of " 'the spark which springs from out of the balance' " between man and the living universe and with DHL's "attack on religion and philosophy," which is akin to Williams's attack on academics for putting a padlock on knowledge.

3826 Woodings, R. B. "Reviews," STUDIA NEOPHILOLOGICA (Stockholm), XLIII, No. 2 (1971), 596-98.

Although potentially of great value, the 346 letters collected in *The Quest for Rananim: D. H. Lawrence's Letters to S. S. Koteliansky, 1914 to 1930,* ed by George J. Zytaruk, show that "Lawrence revealed little of what was really in his mind to this friend." Harry T. Moore had already published "most of the immediately relevant material" in *The Collected Letters of D. H. Lawrence* (1962). [Attacks the book as an example of "industrial" scholarship, Zytaruk's introduction as "unjustified," and his editorial annotations as "spurious."]

3827 Worrell, J. "*Sea and Sardinia,*" OBSERVER (Lond), [Weekly Colour Supplement], 3 Jan 1971, pp. 22-27.

Sea and Sardinia is a remarkable, blunt, "maddening, bad-tempered and wholly fascinating book," filled with "sharp observations" and "many passages of lyrical beauty." DHL expresses his hatred of socialism, his admiration for the Sardinian male's maleness, comments on the "execrable food" and the little railway train, but "tells little of the country" itself. [The author retraces "the Lawrence trail" by railway and bus through the mountains and into the villages of Sorgono, Cagliari, Tonara, Gavoi, Nuoro, and Terranova (now called Olbia), commenting on what has changed and what has not since DHL's tour in 1921. Illustrated with two photographs of contemporary Sardinia and accompanied by tourist information on expenses for a holiday in Sardinia.]

3828 Worthen, John. "D. H. Lawrence and Louie Burrows," D. H. LAWRENCE REVIEW, IV (Fall 1971), 253-62.

Lawrence in Love: Letters to Louie Burrows, ed by James T. Boulton (1968), is not "the 'major collection of Lawrence manuscripts'. . .claimed by the wrapper." "There is, in fact, virtually nothing we can call 'Lawrence in Love' here." The importance of the letters lies in what "they barely contain," the unseen drama of a split in background, need, and fundamental ambition. They reveal a DHL who feared and resisted the division between man and artist which the relationship forced on him and who, after the disastrous year of 1911, ended the association.

3829 Yokota, Chūzō. "D. H. Lawrence no 'The Prussian Officer' ni Tsuite" (On D. H. Lawrence's "The Prussian Officer"), BULLETIN OF COLLEGE OF GENERAL EDUCATION (Tôhoku University), XII (Feb 1971), 66-89.

If we consider "The Prussian Officer" in the light of DHL's other works, it is quite evident that it is concerned not only with various other aspects of human beings but with sadism and homosexuality as well. [In Japanese.]

3830 Yoshii, Mitsuo. "Lawrence *Niji* Ronkô (I)--Buntai to Kôsei o Chûshin to Shite" (On Lawrence's *The Rainbow* [I] --Some Characteristics of Style and Structure), WASEDA REVIEW, No. 10 (July 1971), 1-13.

[First of three articles on *The Rainbow*.] In *The Rainbow* DHL devised a new metaphorical style suitable for describing the inner, unconscious self in the characters. The main characters want spiritual adventures outside and beyond themselves. It is their centrifugal movement toward the unknown world that determines the structure of the novel. [Style and structure are discussed with reference to the generation of Tom and Lydia Brangwen.] [See also Mitsuo Yoshii, "Lawrence *Niji* Ronkô (II)--Buntai to Kôsei o Chûshin to Shite" (On Lawrence's *The Rainbow* [II] --Some Characteristics of Style and Structure), WASEDA REVIEW, No. 11 (Sept 1972), 46-56, and "Lawrence *Niji* Ronkô (III)--Buntai to Kôsei o Chûshin to Shite" (On Lawrence's *The Rainbow* [III] --Some Characteristics of Style and Structure), WASEDA REVIEW, No. 12 (Sept 1973), 97-109.] [In Japanese.]

3831 Yoshimura, Hirokazu. "*The Rainbow* no Characters ni Tsuite-- Heishi: Anton Skrebensky" (On the Characters in *The Rainbow*-- Anton Skrebensky: A Soldier), STUDIES IN FOREIGN LITERATURES (Ritsumeikan University), No. 23 (Dec 1971), 100-121.

[Third of three articles on the characters in *The Rainbow*.] [Discusses Anton Skrebensky's futility and limitations as a soldier, and mentions briefly his relation to other male characters in *The Rainbow*.] [See also Hirokazu Yoshimura, "*The Rainbow* no Characters ni Tsuite--Tom Brangwen to 'Darkness' " (On the Characters in *The Rainbow*--Tom Brangwen and "Darkness"), STUDIES IN FOREIGN LITERATURES (Ritsumeikan University), No. 18 (June 1969), 70-88, and "*The Rainbow* no Characters ni Tsuite--Will Brangwen: 'A Sick Foetus' " (On the Characters in *The Rainbow*--Will Brangwen: "A Sick Foetus"), STUDIES IN FOREIGN LITERATURES (Ritsumeikan University), No. 21 (Jan 1971), 19-40.] [In Japanese.]

3832 Yoshimura, Hirokazu. "*The Rainbow* no Characters ni Tsuite-- Will Brangwen: 'A Sick Foetus' " (On the Characters in *The Rainbow*--Will Brangwen: "A Sick Foetus"), STUDIES IN FOREIGN LITERATURES (Ritsumeikan University), No. 21 (Jan 1971), 19-40.

[Second of three articles on the characters in *The Rainbow*.] Will Brangwen is fundamentally "a sick foetus," for he is a man who is bound to his selfishness and who cannot break the shell of self which covers all of his life. [See also Hirokazu Yoshimura, "*The Rainbow* no Characters ni Tsuite--Tom Brangwen to 'Darkness' " (On the Characters in *The Rainbow*--Tom Brangwen and "Darkness"), STUDIES

IN FOREIGN LITERATURES (Ritsumeikan University), No. 18 (June 1969), 70-88, and "*The Rainbow* no Characters ni Tsuite--Heishi: Anton Skrebensky" (On the Characters in *The Rainbow*--Anton Skrebensky: A Soldier), STUDIES IN FOREIGN LITERATURES (Ritsumeikan University), No. 23 (Dec 1971), 100-121.] [In Japanese.]

3833 Zytaruk, George J. "D. H. Lawrence's Hand in the Translation of Maxim Gorki's REMINISCENCES OF LEONID ANDREYEV," YALE UNIVERSITY LIBRARY GAZETTE, XLVI (July 1971), 29-34. [Contains facsimile of first page of the original typescript of S. S. Koteliansky's translation of Maxim Gorki's REMINISCENCES OF LEONID ANDREYEV, with DHL's manuscript revisions.] Examination of the recently discovered typescript indicates that DHL carefully considered his changes, sometimes even crossing out his own revisions. The portion most thoroughly reworked by DHL is the opening page. DHL's stylistic changes in word choice or word order show that he was concerned with precision of diction, disliked the pretentious phrase, and preferred the straightforward Anglo-Saxon vocabulary.

3834 Zytaruk, George J. D. H. LAWRENCE'S RESPONSE TO RUSSIAN LITERATURE (The Hague and Paris: Mouton, 1971). Although DHL's study of Russian never proceeded very far, he read much Russian literature and at one point thought Tolstoy, Turgenev, and Dostoyevsky the greatest of novelists. Through S. S. Koteliansky, Russian short stories, criticism, biography, and philosophy as well as novels were available to him. DHL also collaborated with Koteliansky in translating several Russian works, turning the latter's rough versions into polished English. DHL's responses to Tolstoy and Dostoyevsky were ambivalent. Judging Tolstoy's novels by their emotional effects on himself, DHL tends to misread characters, making no distinction between their amiability as people and their effectiveness as fictional characters. In *The Rainbow,* however, he turns this personal response to good account, creating in Ursula a successful Anna Karenina who has the strength to leave an inadequate lover and continue her search for personal fulfillment. Despite his criticism of Tolstoy for creating such a character as Vronsky, DHL creates a similar one in Anton Skrebensky, realizing as a novelist that not all characters can be "quick." DHL did not share the enthusiasm many of his contemporaries felt for Dostoyevsky. It seemed to him that Dostoyevsky had rejected his own sensual being and thus, in his novels, presented sensuality as repulsive. The emphasis on the spiritual makes his characters self-important and will-dominated. DHL's artistic response to Dostoyevsky is revealed by the resemblance between Svdrigailov and Loerke, and in *The Man Who Died,* where DHL's returned Christ, instead of being silent like Dostoyevsky's in THE GRAND INQUISITOR, explicitly rejects his former role and, hence, Christianity. Comparatively little critical attention has been paid to DHL's reactions to V. V. Rozanov, although DHL saw him as the only Russian with a positive, sensuous view of life. While he objected to Rozanov's typically Russian introspection, DHL found in SOLITARIA the phallic vision later embodied in *The Man Who Died* and *Lady Chatterley's Lover.*

3835 Zytaruk, George J. " 'The Undying Man': D. H. Lawrence's

Yiddish Story," D. H. LAWRENCE REVIEW, IV (Spring 1971), 20-27.
One aspect of DHL's literary collaboration with others is his work in editing S. S. Koteliansky's translations of various Russian writers. An unfinished story titled "The Undying Man," first published in *Phoenix: The Posthumous Papers of D. H. Lawrence* (1936), enables us to see DHL's use of "someone else's material" in his own creative work. The story is DHL's version of "Maimonides and Aristotle," one of two Yiddish stories which Koteliansky's mother set down for him and which he translated and sent to DHL in 1926 or 1927. [The original story, as translated by Koteliansky, is printed here from Koteliansky's manuscript.] "Taking little more than the core of the original story. . ., Lawrence reveals a rare inventiveness of detail and an ability to endow his narrative with profound implications."

3836 Zytaruk, George J. "What Happened to D. H. Lawrence's *Goats and Compasses*?" D. H. LAWRENCE REVIEW, IV (Fall 1971), 280-86.
Available evidence suggests that *Goats and Compasses,* announced by Philip Heseltine as " 'Mr. Lawrence's philosophical work' " to be published privately by "The Rainbow Books and Music," was actually the provisional title for the second part of the manuscript of *The Sisters,* which was eventually to become *Women in Love.* "This version of the novel probably did not" exceed "the sixty-five pages represented by the surviving manuscript of an early version of the first two chapters." [See also reply by Charles L. Ross and rejoinder by George J. Zytaruk in "*Goats and Compasses* and/or *Women in Love:* An Exchange," D. H. LAWRENCE REVIEW, VI (Spring 1973), 33-46, and further comment by Keith Sagar, "*Goats and Compasses* and *Women in Love* Again," D. H. LAWRENCE REVIEW, VI (Fall 1973), 303-8.]

1972

3837 Al-Fishawy, W. M. "A Descriptive Bibliography of the Works of John Middleton Murry, with a Critical Study of His Life and Thought and an Assessment of His Views on D. H. Lawrence." Unpublished dissertation, University of Birmingham, 1972. [Listed in Lawrence F. McNamee, DISSERTATIONS IN ENGLISH AND AMERICAN LITERATURE (NY and Lond: Bowker, 1974), p. 264.]

3838 Alinei, Tamara. "Imagery and Meaning in D. H. Lawrence's *The Rainbow,*" YEARBOOK OF ENGLISH STUDIES, II (1972), 205-211.
The personages in *The Rainbow* are not characters in the usual sense. Their characteristics develop only by means of recurrent imagery. Human qualities are described in terms of natural processes and objects. Significant relationships are expressed in terms of roots and plants; the avoidance of relationship is presented in wind images. Flowers also symbolize desirable relationships and vitality. As-

sociation of wind imagery with Tom Brangwen suggests his divided attitude, for he desires both to achieve and to avoid relationship with Lydia.

3839 Allison, Christopher FitzSimons. GUILT, ANGER, AND GOD: THE PATTERNS OF OUR DISCONTENTS (NY: Seabury P, 1972), pp. 24-25, 26, 27, 32, 38, 72, 138.

DHL advocated a return to nature and trusted in "blood consciousness" as a source of wholeness. Hence, he "welcomed the imminent end of Western culture," scorned Freudian teachings as a new version of Christian moralism which would intellectualize the erotic and destroy creative spontaneity, and dismissed Marxist preoccupation with the practical at the cost of the spiritual.

3840 Allott, Miriam. "Reviews," NOTES AND QUERIES, ns XIX (Feb 1972), 69-70.

Lawrence in Love: Letters to Louie Burrows, ed by James T. Boulton, collects 165 letters written between 1906 and 1912 to the girl to whom he was engaged for fifteen months. The material, unexamined in her lifetime, is wholly new in revealing who Louie Burrows was and the part she played in DHL's emotional life. DHL was somewhat perfunctory in the letters and deliberately withheld much of himself, such as the details of his composition of *The White Peacock*, which he freely discussed in his letters to Blanche Jennings in 1908-1910.

3841 Arnold, Armin. D. H. LAWRENCE (Berlin: Colloquium Verlag, 1972).

[In this short introduction, the author surveys DHL's life and work under the headings "Son and Lover," "Two Romantic Years," "War," "The Way Out of England!," "Into the World," and "The Last Years." The details of DHL's life are covered--his Eastwood working-class and Congregationalist background, his winning the "King's Scholarship," his education at University College Nottingham, his friendship with Jessie Chambers, his teaching in Croydon and friendship with Helen Corke, his engagement to Louie Burrows, the death of his mother, his elopement with Frieda, their experiences in Cornwall during the war years, DHL's plans for Rananim, their leaving England to travel on the Continent and eventually in Ceylon, Australia, New Mexico, and Mexico, their return to Europe during the last five years of DHL's life. The author draws on published memoirs and biographies and relates DHL's life to the works he was writing in each period.] [In German.]

3842 Asahi, Chiseki. "*Koisuru Onnatachi* ni Okeru Ichikôsatsu" (A View of the Darkness and Light Duality in *Women in Love*), EDGEWOOD REVIEW (Sonada Women's Junior College), No. 1 (Feb 1972), 1-44.

In *Women in Love*, more than in his other novels, DHL uses imagery of "darkness" and "light" to express a profound symbolism. This dualistic symbolism is explored in terms of both the inner world (the events, thoughts, and actions of human beings) and the outer world (the natural and social environments). In the outer world, this duality is to be found both in nature, in the contrast between the pit and the world outside it, black and white, and root and stalk, and in society, in the contrast between social and antisocial attitudes, the individual and the mass, and nature and knowledge. [In Japanese.]

3843 Baim, Joseph. "D. H. Lawrence's Social Vision," IN HONOR OF AUSTIN WRIGHT, ed by Joseph Baim, Ann L. Hayes, and Robert J. Gangwere (Pittsburgh: Carnegie-Mellon University [Carnegie Series in English No. 12], 1972), pp. 1-9.

Although DHL is regarded as a major writer, his social vision is usually dismissed. Bertrand Russell's charges of Fascism are repeated, but DHL was actually suspicious of all institutions and political systems and knew that even the utopia envisioned in *The Plumed Serpent* could not exist in reality. Attributing modern misery to men's accepting the repression of human values which followed upon industrialism, DHL believed that only with the sexual emotion do men now recognize that they are deluding themselves with false feelings. Real sexuality requires harmony of body and mind and a revaluation of traditional attitudes about sex. Sex is the most profound way of relating to something outside the self; without real, total marriage, no social system can be meaningful. By fictional example DHL hoped to move at least some individuals toward this goal.

3844 Ballin, Michael. "D. H. Lawrence and William Blake: A Comparative and Critical Study," DISSERTATION ABSTRACTS INTERNATIONAL, XXXIV (1974), 5154A. Unpublished dissertation, University of Toronto, 1972.

3845 Barber, Janet, IHM. "Mexican *Machismo* in Novels by Lawrence, Sender, Fuentes," DISSERTATION ABSTRACTS INTERNATIONAL, XXXIII (1972-1973), 3630A. Unpublished doctoral dissertation, University of Southern California, 1972. [Author listed incorrectly as Janet B. Ihm in Lawrence F. McNamee, DISSERTATIONS IN ENGLISH AND AMERICAN LITERATURE, SUPP. II (NY and Lond: Bowker, 1974), p. 369.]

[Considers *The Plumed Serpent*.]

3846 Baron, Carl Edward. "Aspects of the Life and Thought of D. H. Lawrence, 1912-1916." Unpublished dissertation, Cambridge University, 1972. [Listed in Lawrence F. McNamee, DISSERTATIONS IN ENGLISH AND AMERICAN LITERATURE, SUPP II (NY and Lond: Bowker, 1974), p. 368.]

3847 Baron, C[arl] E. "D. H. Lawrence's Early Paintings," in YOUNG BERT: AN EXHIBITION OF THE EARLY YEARS OF D. H. LAWRENCE, compiled by Lucy I. Edwards, David Phillips, Arnold Rattenbury, and Jo Barnes (Nottingham: Castle Museum, Nottingham Castle, 1972), pp. 32-40.

To bring to light early artistic influences on DHL challenges our easy assumptions about his modernism, "places him, at least for the first twenty-five years of his life, firmly within nineteenth-century provincial English life," and makes intelligible "the remarkable expansion of his consciousness from 1912 onwards." DHL's "early artistic experience" developed first in such activities as drawing, copying pictures, painting firescreens and little boxes, looking at prints and visiting Nottingham museum exhibitions; then in exploring London galleries and teaching art. Greiffenhagen's *An Idyll* particularly obsessed him. Between 1912 and 1919, he continued to copy pictures of the Italian masters and to work into his novels references to these painters and to the Futurists, West African art, Mexican art, and others. His understanding of the art world enabled him to write "an outstandingly attractive essay on Cézanne." [See also C. E. Baron, "The Nottingham Festival D. H. Lawrence Exhibition, 1972," D. H. LAWRENCE REVIEW, VII (Spring 1974), 19-57, which reproduces fifty items of art, photography, and memorabilia from the exhibition.]

3848 Beatty, C. J. P. "Konrad Lorenz and D. H. Lawrence," NOTES AND QUERIES, ns XIX (Feb 1972), 54.

Lorenz's description in KING SOLOMON'S RING of wolves fighting for the leadership of the pack suggests that DHL, as evidenced by his description of the fight between Paul Morel and Baxter Dawes in *Sons and Lovers,* understood the close relationship between men and animals at the instinctual level. DHL's awareness was perhaps furthered by Thomas Hardy's description in THE MAYOR OF CASTERBRIDGE of the fight between Henchard and Farfrae.

3849 Bedient, Calvin. ARCHITECTS OF THE SELF: GEORGE ELIOT, D. H. LAWRENCE, AND E. M. FORSTER (Berkeley, Los Angeles, and Lond: University of California P, 1972), pp. 1-4, 21-25, 27-30, 98-195, 267-69.

"The great importance of George Eliot, Lawrence, and Forster" is to be grasped within the "post-Christian struggle to devise a significant idea of the self." Both DHL and Forster, in their emphasis on the holiness of the body, may be understood as in part reacting to Victorianism, including the self-abnegation advocated by Eliot and the destruction of any of her characters who pit themselves against society. Whereas in Eliot wholeness, understood in the societal sense, was achieved by accepting traditional mores, in DHL harmony with the world begins with a turning "downward" to the blood, the "streams of the flesh, there to find regeneration in the 'inconceivable.'" DHL, though a poetic genius, is difficult and "eccentric" because of his "erotic mysticism." *Sons and Lovers* reveals "the genesis of an aesthetic metaphysical vision" of the self as "single," "integral," and "vital." In *The Rainbow,* "the vital self develops organically--learning separation as well as union, becoming intellectual as well as sensuous--" to emerge as a "soul." In this novel, DHL's acknowledgment of "'the great impersonal'" becomes a "continuous radiance." What is implicit in *The Rainbow* becomes "hard-edged" and "intensified, given an apocalyptic heat," in *Women in Love,* in which the vital self comes to "the modern industrial world...bearing a sword." In *The Plumed Serpent,* in a cosmology consisting of "two adjacent worlds, one temporal, the other eternal," "Being is a world apart" and "the vital self ceases to be the 'goal' of life." DHL's attempt politically "to adjust his metaphysic of a universal spontaneity to his hatred of the 'democratic mob'" leads, in *Aaron's Rod* and *Kangaroo,* to the expression of his undisguised "personal interest in the exercise of power." In *Lady Chatterley's Lover,* a "peaceful" and "idyllic...book by a dying vitalist," "morbidity" has given way to "a profound and life-affirming tenderness." DHL's achievement was to restore "a sense of wonder to the body of the world ...including...the human body," "as an inhabitant of a universe of desire," in which the vital self is rooted.

3850 Beer, John. "Ford's Impressions of the Lawrences," TIMES LITERARY SUPPLEMENT (Lond), 5 May 1972, p. 520.

Ford Madox Ford's description in RETURN TO YESTERDAY of a visit to the DHL home lacks factual precision but remains an accurate impression of the advanced intellectual and cultural climate among the more progressive young adults of Nottingham during the period. [See also reply by Malcolm Elwin, "Ford and Lawrence," TIMES LITERARY SUPPLEMENT (Lond), 19 May 1972, p. 576.]

3851 Bell, Michael. PRIMITIVISM (Lond: Methuen [The Critical Idiom 20], 1972), pp. 12-22, 28-42, 44-46, 48-52, 55, 59-61, 65, 67, 70-72, 77-79, 81-82.

"Primitive modes of feeling pervade a work like *The Rainbow* even though it has few overtly primitivist motifs and is anything but atavistic in its overall values." DHL forces words "to extend their area of meaning yet without obvious wrenching from their 'normal' sense." DHL conveys "the radically different sense of time in a world of primitive subjectivity" "as an aspect of the movement of feeling, of the cyclic and rhythmic processes of life." The primitivist "sense of the emotional life as a movement of elemental and impersonal forces lends" to "commonplace" events a "ritualistic feel." [Examples include the dressing ritual in *The Rainbow* and the laying out of the dead in *The Widowing of Mrs. Holroyd.*] In "The Ship of Death," "perhaps his most impressive and beautiful achievement in the primitivist spirit," "Lawrence has left an especially moving testament to his own natural piety in the matter of death." "The primitivist endeavour in *The Plumed Serpent*" fails because "the cosmic piety of Ramón and his followers" has an "imposed or factitious quality about it." "The sense of cosmic rhythm that informs *The Rainbow* is stuck as an empty idea on Kate's experiences in Mexico." [Compares DHL's use of the primitivist mode with that of Conrad, T. S. Eliot, Joyce, Yeats, and William Golding, with support from Frazer and Jung.]

3852 Bell, Quentin. VIRGINIA WOOLF: A BIOGRAPHY, Vol. II: MRS. WOOLF, 1912-1941 (Lond: Hogarth P, 1972); rptd together with Vol. I, but with separate pagination (NY: Harcourt, Brace, 1972), pp. 50, 65, 105, 151, 162, 185.

Virginia Woolf thought both DHL and E. M. Forster brilliant but "marching in the wrong direction"; her friend Ethel Smyth said that Mrs. Woolf was "jealous of literary excellence; (couldn't see the point of D. H. Lawrence until he was dead)." Still, "her natural allies were (not without some reservations)" Forster, DHL, Eliot, Joyce, and Strachey.

3853 Bennett, Michael. A VISITORS GUIDE TO EASTWOOD AND THE COUNTRYSIDE OF D. H. LAWRENCE (Nottingham: Nottinghamshire County Council, Leisure Services Libraries Division, 1972), 3rd ed: (1975).

[This guide book includes a map of Eastwood streets and a guide to four tours of the Lawrence family houses, the town, the "Lawrence Country" north of Eastwood, and the village of Cossall. Brief notes on the Hopkin collection of DHL material in Nottinghamshire County Library, travel information, and a selected bibliography are included. Illustrated with map and drawings by Michael Kirk.]

3854 Bertelsen, Evelyn Jeannette. "The Poetry of D. H. Lawrence: A Study of Technique and Development." Unpublished dissertation, University of London, 1972. [Listed in Lawrence F. McNamee, DISSERTATIONS IN ENGLISH AND AMERICAN LITERATURE, SUPP II (NY and Lond: Bowker, 1974), p. 368.]

3855 Black, Michael. "That Which Is Perfectly Ourselves; I: Phèdre and the Knowledge of the Self," HUMAN WORLD, No. 6 (Feb 1972), 3-16, espec pp. 9, 11; rptd in THE LITERATURE OF FIDELITY, by Michael Black (Lond: Chatto & Windus; NY: Barnes & Noble, 1975).
"Lawrence's plea through Birkin in *Women in Love* that two people committed to each other in love should leave the ego behind 'so that that which is perfectly ourselves may take place within us'" is contrasted with Racine's view that we do not "*know* what is perfectly ourselves" and with what DHL regarded as Flaubert's withdrawal from life. [A passage from *Women in Love* (Chap. II: "Shortlands") is quoted to show that the question involves more than "the emotional life." See also Michael Black, "That Which Is Perfectly Ourselves; IV: Connie Chatterley," HUMAN WORLD, No. 8 (Aug 1972), 45-54.]

3856 Black, Michael. "That Which Is Perfectly Ourselves; IV: Connie Chatterley," HUMAN WORLD, No. 8 (Aug 1972), 45-54; rptd in THE LITERATURE OF FIDELITY, by Michael Black (Lond: Chatto & Windus; NY: Barnes & Noble, 1975), pp. 184-98.
Whereas "Karenin's full complexity" is conveyed in Tolstoy's ANNA KARENINA, Clifford Chatterley in *Lady Chatterley's Lover* is "a type Lawrence detested anyway": "the moral issue in the book is first simplified and then grossly rigged." Similarly, Vronsky is simple and narrow but has the capacity to grow with his love; Mellors, though deeper and more complicated, "has almost no moral weight" because he does not admit allegiances. "Two of the limitations of *Lady Chatterley's Lover* are echoed in the rest of Lawrence": "this blankness about children and family life," and the fact that "the couple must have a place and function in the world." After "the complete human cycle" of *Sons and Lovers* and the first two generations of *The Rainbow*, the question of the effect of "industrialization on family and emotional life" arises in inchoate form near the end of *The Rainbow* but is dodged in *Women in Love*. After *The Rainbow*, DHL never again showed how "the conflicts of one generation threaten to deform the next by making strange demands on it," but "the rest of his work is a meditation on how" to avoid that situation. DHL calls into question "the egoism for two;...living for the other;...the conventional passion, with the merging of identities;...a life of mutual accommodation where the other person is 'known'." "For Lawrence that was literally death," and "his Lawrence figures in the novels have a commitment

to escaping that condition." DHL's "figures of speech, with the inevitable ambiguity of metaphor, are more satisfying than his concepts, and turn his 'thought' into a tragic vision." [See also Michael Black, "That Which Is Perfectly Ourselves; I: Phèdre and the Knowledge of the Self," HUMAN WORLD, No. 6 (Feb 1972), 3-16, espec pp. 9, 11.]

3857 Bordinat, Philip. "The Poetic Image in D. H. Lawrence's *The Captain's Doll*," WEST VIRGINIA UNIVERSITY BULLETIN: PHILOLOGICAL PAPERS, XIX (July 1972), 45-49.

In *The Captain's Doll*, DHL brings poetry and prose together, especially in "the poetic image." The images in the story are "congruent," "in balance," and dictated by thematic context. The story contains three "contexts": the "glacial, the animal, and the human." Since the context involves the conflict between "the power idea of marriage" and the "equality idea," the animal images reflect the "intensity of the battle" and the "elemental pain" that both of the married partners feel. The glacier is a symbol of the "natural power" that Alexander exerts over Hannele, and when he finally conquers it, Hannele's "submission gives added symbolic significance" to his conquest.

3858 Boulton, James T. "Foreword," YOUNG BERT: AN EXHIBITION OF THE EARLY YEARS OF D. H. LAWRENCE (Nottingham: Castle Museum, Nottingham Castle, 1972), pp. 5-6.

While "the Nottingham-Eastwood region did not...exclusively mould Lawrence," his essay "Nottingham and the Mining Countryside" "has been used in this exhibition almost as a handbook for his early years" and his "genius was permanently rooted in the region."

3859 Bradbrook, Muriel C. LITERATURE IN ACTION (Lond: Chatto & Windus, 1972), pp. 133-35.

Kangaroo is as much about DHL as about Australia. He responds to the violence and beauty in both the landscape and the people and to the easygoing camaraderie of the Australians.

3860 Brashear, Lucy M. "Lawrence's Companion Poems: 'Snake' and *Tortoises*," D. H. LAWRENCE REVIEW, V (Spring 1972), 54-62.

In both "Snake" and *Tortoises*, which DHL came to think of as a unit, a speaker "discerns both mortal and divine characteristics" in an observed reptile. The specifics of the later tortoise poems show that the rejection of the snake is the speaker's symbolic "protest of his own subservience to sexuality" and his fear of loss of self in coitus. The final recognition is that tortoise, man, and snake are all driven by the necessity of existence itself.

3861 Bridson, D. G. THE FILIBUSTER: A STUDY OF THE POLITICAL IDEAS OF WYNDHAM LEWIS (Lond: Cassell, 1972), pp. 65, 76-79, 81, 83, 84, 90, 91, 93, 114, 115.

"When he finds writers of the calibre of D. H. Lawrence and Sherwood Anderson indulging in" Rousseauist "sentimentality" about the primitive as "Noble

Savage," Lewis "moves up his artillery." *Mornings in Mexico* was "the occasion for Lewis's heavy sarcasm." DHL thought the Indian and the white " 'way of consciousness different from and fatal to' " each other, but that he "himself had a knack for instinctively 'understanding' " "the way of consciousness" of the Indian, the bat, the tortoise, and Bibbles. Lewis in PALEFACE links DHL's "noble savagery with the pessimism of Spengler." He also accuses DHL of " 'a glorification of the Feminine principle.' " DHL and his disciples were "at fault in their insistence upon the 'unassimilable seed in the matrix' of race."

3862 Brotherston, J. G. "Revolution and the Ancient Literature of Mexico, For D. H. Lawrence and Antonin Artaud," TWENTIETH CENTURY LITERATURE, XVIII (July 1972), 181-89.

DHL and Artaud reject "Marxism as a European idolatry...the blighting product of a continent whose traditions and philosophy" man must escape "in order to save himself." For both, "true revolution was impossible without the discovery of 'living culture' and Mexico was one of the last places...to find it." Though most "of the 'ancient Mexican' part of *The Plumed Serpent* may be wholly Lawrence's invention," "the main weight of the imaginative effort to recreate the Indian world" rests on particular texts and "the function of the written word is predominant." Artaud rejected DHL's "reliance on an educated, lettered hero as a leader of the masses and super-prophet of the new religion." "With wavering confidence," DHL "asserted the status of his redeeming avatars through literature itself: Artaud remained unprotected to the end, disdaining all reaction." [Some analysis of *The Plumed Serpent*.]

3863 Buckley, B. R. "Lawrence's Novels: Themes and Precedents." Unpublished dissertation, Warwick University, 1972. [Listed in Geoffrey M. Paterson and Joan E. Hardy (eds), INDEX TO THESES, XXIII (1971-72) (Lond: Aslib, 1974), p. 23.]

3864 Bullock, Alice. "D. H. Lawrence Sat Here," NEW MEXICAN (Santa Fe, NM), 21 May 1972, pp. 7-8.

[The history of the DHL ranch near San Christobal, which includes its being sold by the original homesteaders to a family who raised goats on it, figures in *St. Mawr*. Illustrated with photographs.]

3865 Burgess, Anthony. "Introduction," *D. H. Lawrence and Italy: Twilight in Italy, Sea and Sardinia, Etruscan Places*, ed by Anthony Burgess (NY: Viking P, 1972), pp. vii-xiii.

DHL's three Italian travel books are not Baedekers but indispensable guides to the vast country called "Lawrence." *Twilight in Italy*, a misnomer for a book brimming with DHL's sense of beginning a new life in Southeastern Europe with "the aristocratic Frieda von Richthofen" as his lover, consists of seven studies concerning life around Lake Garda. *Sea and Sardinia*, coming after DHL's dark years in the War and bitter alienation from England, was written in six weeks after visiting the island for one week. DHL's last travel book, *Etruscan Places*, more influential on non-specialists than Etruscological scholarship, concerns the evidence DHL found in the tombs of Etruria for his phallic metaphysic. DHL's dark gods--his concern with love and loins and instinct--dramatize an area of life perilous to deny. They inhabit his three books on Italy awesomely.

3866 Burns, Wayne. THE PANZAIC PRINCIPLE (Vancouver, BC: Pendejo P, 1972).
[Pamphlet of 84 pages, incorporating "The Panzaic Principle," PAUNCH, No. 22 (Jan 1965), 1-31, with "The Panzaic Principle Part II."] DHL's "belligerent and eloquent" statement "of the conflict between the real and the ideal" in a passage on Cézanne's apples [quoted in full] in "Introduction to These Paintings" shows that he was right in saying that Christian humanist civilization glorifies " 'the spirit, the mental consciousness.' " The idea that Sancho Panza's belly "has given the lie to Dulcinea and in fact all of Don Quixote's ideals--much as Lady Chatterley's guts give the lie to Clifford and his ideals" is the foundation of "the Panzaic principle": "In Lawrence's as in all other novels, . . .the guts are always right; it is an axiom or principle of the novel that they are always right, that the senses of even a fool can give the lie to even the most profound abstractions of the noblest thinker." This principle is denied by the "normative perspectivism" of critics such as Ian Watt and Dorothy Van Ghent and the view of Falstaff presented by Robert B. Heilman and Cleanth Brooks, but supported by the critical ideas of Ortega y Gasset and DHL. [Part II] : "The Panzaic is not synonymous with the sexual, or the Dionysian, or the Rabelasian, or the Lawrentian. . . . By their very nature Panzaic characters cannot be so elevated--and still remain Panzaic." Mellors is not a Panzaic but a heroic character, DHL's idealized self-image. "Murder, suicide, and rape" neither express our animal impulses nor, when exploited for sensationalism or titillation, as in the grossly oversimplified movie version of *The Fox,* function Panzaically.

3867 Chambers, Jonathan David. "Memories of D. H. Lawrence," RENAISSANCE AND MODERN STUDIES, XVI (1972), 5-17.
[The author recalls the years (roughly 1902-1908) when DHL regularly visited the Chambers family at the Haggs. The Lawrence and Chambers children went to Eastwood schools and played together, and the families often met at the Congregational Chapel. Chambers rehearses the "deep division" in the Lawrence household and its profound effect on "Bert."] By 1902, DHL was a steady member of the Chambers "family circle," in which he became the "leader of our festivities," teaching others songs and dances, introducing chess and cards, leading charades and directing little dramas, and in summer, helping during haymaking. DHL always "had flocks of girls around him," but in what was "still a puritan society," no lovemaking was involved. Jessie Chambers, DHL's equal "in emotional depth" if not in intellect, was "an ideal companion" for him, sharing his extensive reading and helping him to "realize his genius." But because of "the bitter, unsleeping jealousy and the possessiveness of his mother," their love was "not to be." DHL also feared "being absorbed by her. . .and was defeated by her ingrained puritanism." In 1907, at twenty-two, DHL launched an "open rebellion" against Chapel religion and Chapel morality. In 1908, he left for Croydon and "never came to the Haggs again." Jessie's frustration over his subsequent portrayal of their relationship in *Sons and Lovers* precipitated the end of their "idyllic friendship."

3868 Chapman, Robert T. " 'Parties...Parties...Parties': Some Images of the 'Gay Twenties,' " ENGLISH, XXI (Autumn 1972), 93-97.

Since Plato the social gathering has been used in literature as a context for drawing characters together and for discussion of ideas, and the convention continues in the twentieth-century "conversation novel" of Norman Douglas, Wyndham Lewis, and Aldous Huxley. *Women in Love* uses the life-styles of the frequenters of Garsington and the Cafe Royal to symbolize a pervasive decadence. In the party at Breadalby, an attack upon Lady Ottoline Morrell, all acquiesce in a "sickness unto death" in which spontaneous life is strangled by the intellect and the will to destruction.

3869 Choudbury, Sheila Lahiri. "D. H. Lawrence: The Two Versions--*Studies in Classic American Literature* and *The Symbolic Meaning*," ESSAYS AND STUDIES (Jacavpur University, India), II (1972), 76-83.

Impressed by his reading of MOBY-DICK in 1916, DHL began his essays on American literature. The composition coincided with DHL's desire to leave England for the new territory of America. In 1923 in America, he rewrote the essays for publication by Thomas Seltzer as *Studies in Classic American Literature*, dramatically changing them by omitting much of the "philosophy" and making them more critical in approach. He also altered his prose style drastically from the conventional, almost pedagogical style of the earlier essays to the style R. P. Blackmur calls "hysterical" for the *Studies*. This change can be ascribed to the impact of American "yellow journalism," which had gained in popularity since the nineteenth century. In their reviews, Henry Seidel Canby had no hesitation in recognizing an "American style in Mr. Lawrence," and Stuart P. Sherman, by calling him a "genuine American," links DHL to H. L. Mencken and his SMART SET. This "hysterical" style is perhaps traceable to DHL's disillusionment with the American literary scene in the nineteen-twenties.

3870 Christian, Roy. "Lawrence's Country Revisited: The Erewash Valley," COUNTRY LIFE (Lond), CLII (6 July 1972), 19-21.

DHL described his native Erewash Valley as " 'an extremely beautiful countryside,' " but a modern visitor is unlikely to find it so. Today "industry is gradually reverting to the position it held in Lawrence's father's time when life in the valley 'was a curious cross between industrialism and the old agricultural England.' " [Short travel sketch, illustrated with seven black and white photographs by Frank Rodgers of DHL's birthplace in Eastwood; Woolaton Hall, on the Eastern Edge of the Valley; Moorgreen Reservoir, High Park Woods; Cromford Canal, Ironville; Ruined Furnaces, Ironville; Saxon Cross in the Churchyard at Stapleford; and Remains of Beauville Priory.]

3871 Coombes, H[enry]. "B. B. C.," in "Correspondence and Comments," HUMAN WORLD, No. 9 (Nov 1972), 62-65.

[After brief discussions of opposing examples of communism (the captioned pictures of Castro, Mao, and Tito in RADIO TIMES) and fascism (an anti-communist parable in Dennis Wheatley's THE FORBIDDEN TERRITORY), the author comments that "apparent opposites have a way of becoming the same thing in the end." As an alternative, he recommends the final chapter of DHL's *Apocalypse* for "a beauty, a wholesomeness, a moral idealism of the kind we neglect at our peril in a world more and more littered with junk and poison, the issue of greed, pride of the wrong sort, stupidity, self-deceptions."]

3872 Corke, Helen. "Laurentiana," D. H. LAWRENCE REVIEW, V (Summer 1972), 174-75.
[Letter to the Editor, commenting that critics like Anais Nin ignore DHL's origins and reviewing briefly his "chest weakness" from boyhood, his violating "the moral dictates of our native community," his "pitiful dream of Rananim."]

3873 Cowan, James C. "Lawrence's Phoenix: An Introduction," D. H. LAWRENCE REVIEW, V (Fall 1972), 187-99.
[Introduction to the special "Phoenix Number" of the D. H. LAWRENCE REVIEW.] DHL first presented the phoenix image in terms of "theoretical pattern" in "The Crown" and in Will Brangwen's butter mold in *The Rainbow*. In the concluding chapter of *Aaron's Rod*, the image becomes "a 'self-form,' resembling Jung's archetype," while in *Kangaroo*, it is used wittily by Harriet Somers to deflate Lovat's "pretensions to male superiority." The decline of the power and values embodied in the phoenix image in the modern world is suggested in "St. John," a poem in *Birds, Beasts and Flowers*, and in the name which Mrs. Witt gives to Geronimo Trujillo in *St. Mawr*. "The pattern of both plot and imagery" in *Lady Chatterley's Lover*, the first edition of which had a phoenix design on the cover, "suggests the personal and metaphysical implications" of the ancient fable. In "Give us Gods," in *Pansies*, the phoenix hangs " 'over the gold egg of all things.' " In the final poem, "Phoenix," in *Last Poems*, DHL relates the phoenix to his assent to death and faith in rebirth. [Illustrated with photographs of two representations of the phoenix in the ranch house yard at the Lawrence Kiowa Ranch near Taos, New Mexico.]

3874 Cushman, Keith. " 'A Bastard Begot': The Origins of D. H. Lawrence's 'The Christening,' " MODERN PHILOLOGY, LXX (Nov 1972), 146-48; rvd and enlgd as Appendix B: "The Origins of 'The Christening,' " in D. H. LAWRENCE AT WORK: THE EMERGENCE OF THE "PRUSSIAN OFFICER" STORIES, by Keith Cushman (Charlottesville: UP of Virginia, 1978), pp. 216-23.
"The Christening" (1912) is a significant but underrated story because DHL jeers at conventional morality without lapsing into sentimentality or other kinds of intrusiveness as he does in the *Laetitia* fragment and in *The White Peacock* itself, begun in 1906. The difference is shown in DHL's change of attitude toward an early friend of his, George Neville, who had fathered two illegitimate children.

3875 Cushman, Keith. "Fiction," LIBRARY JOURNAL, XCVII (1 Nov 1972), 3616.
John Thomas and Lady Jane is "20,000 words longer than *Lady Chatterley's Lover*" but "mercifully...less polemical." "It is especially exhilarating to come

upon some scenes that were later cut," such as the "superb" scene of "Connie's visit to her lover's lodgings in Sheffield near the end of the novel."

> **3876** Cushman, Keith. "Lawrence's Use of Hardy in 'The Shades of Spring,' " STUDIES IN SHORT FICTION, IX (Fall 1972), 402-4; rvd and absorbed in Chap. V, " 'The Shades of Spring,' " in D. H. LAWRENCE AT WORK: THE EMERGENCE OF THE "PRUSSIAN OFFICER" STORIES, by Keith Cushman (Charlottesville: UP of Virginia, 1978), pp. 116-47.

"The Shades of Spring" is DHL's "best and most interesting attempt in the early short fiction to resolve...autobiographical materials" concerning his "relationship with Jessie Chambers." Despite the personal nature of the story, DHL adapted an episode from Thomas Hardy's UNDER THE GREENWOOD TREE to provide an ending for his tale.

> **3877** Davie, Donald. "A Doggy Demos: Hardy and Lawrence," THOMAS HARDY AND BRITISH POETRY (NY: Oxford UP, 1972; Lond: Routledge & Kegan Paul, 1973), pp. 130-51.

Although DHL ignored Hardy's declaration that free verse "would come to nothing in England," he still owes to Hardy his confessional mode. As Hardy succeeds only when his poems are in "repose," so with DHL as he moves to his mature style of the early 1920s. Like Hardy, DHL took risks, as the virulently anti-democratic "Bibbles" shows. "Poetry of the Present" is adroitly tactful but unconvincing. Either there is room for Shakespeare or all is fluid with no room for the impediment of fixity. DHL asks us to destroy all images, but it is neither surprising nor disgraceful that we have not. Prophetic poetry is necessarily inferior because it is above judiciousness. Society can sometimes afford the prophet, but it cannot dispense with the poet. [The essay incorporates much of Donald Davie's "Sincerity and Poetry," MICHIGAN QUARTERLY REVIEW, V (Winter 1966), 3-8.]

> **3878** de Filippis, Simonetta. "Sociologia e ideologia della classe operaia in *Touch and Go* di D. H. Lawrence" (Sociology and Ideology of the Working Class in D. H. Lawrence's *Touch and Go*), ANNALI ISTITUTO UNIVERSITARIO ORIENTALE, NAPOLI, SEZIONE GERMANICA, XV, No. 3 (1972), 185-206.

DHL was one of the first English dramatists to deal with the problems of the working class. The main theme in *Touch and Go* is in fact the class struggle. From this play and its preface, DHL's ideological position comes out very clearly and he appears very individualistic and conservative. Some of his interpretations of working-class attitudes, which can be found also in the essay "Nottingham and the Mining Countryside" and in some of his poems, can be criticized because DHL assumes the position of the artist who does not belong to any class. Furthermore, at that time, DHL was in search of an alternative to the values of industrial society. [In Italian.]

> **3879** Delavenay, Émile. "Comptes Rendus" (Reviews), ÉTUDES ANGLAISES, XXV (Oct-Dec 1972), 576.

[Review of *La Princesse, suivi de La Fille du Marchand de Chevaux* ("The Princess" followed by "The Horse Dealer's Daughter"), trans by Pierre Leyris.] These two stories are as dissimilar in their subject, their atmosphere, and their style as it is possible for two works by DHL to be. The style of "The Princess" in the original is spare and simple even in the picturesque but well-balanced descriptions of the landscape of New Mexico. The translation, in contrast, is less than easy in its rendering of dialogue and the language of the day. [Examples given.] [In French.]

3880 Dennis, Nigel. "Angry Visitor: The Landscape and D. H. Lawrence," AN ESSAY ON MALTA (Lond: John Murray, 1972), pp. 28-42, espec pp. 36-41.

Approaching Malta from the sea in 1920, DHL rhapsodically describes its landscape at sunrise in his "Introduction" to MEMOIRS OF THE FOREIGN LEGION, by Maurice Magnus. But touring " 'that dreadful island' " by car, he soon sees it with complete accuracy " 'as stark as a corpse, no trees, no bushes even: a fearful landscape.' " [The author's own descriptions of the Maltese landscape are interspersed with references to and brief quotations from DHL's descriptions of Malta and Taormina.]

3881 D. H. LAWRENCE REVIEW, ed by James C. Cowan, V, No. 1 (Spring 1972).

Contents, abstracted under 1972: Shalom Rachman, "Art and Value in D. H. Lawrence's *Women in Love*," pp. 1-25; Evelyn J. Hinz, "*Sons and Lovers*: The Archetypal Dimensions of Lawrence's Oedipal Tragedy," pp. 26-53; Lucy M. Brashear, "Lawrence's Companion Poems: 'Snake' and *Tortoises*," pp. 54-62; Marguerite Bartelle McDonald, "An Evening with the Lawrences," pp. 63-66; George Y. Trail, "Toward a Lawrencian Poetic," pp. 67-81 [not abstracted]; Alice Heath, "The Checklist of D. H. Lawrence Criticism and Scholarship, 1971," pp. 82-92; "Laurentiana," pp. 93-95 [not abstracted]; "Contributors," p. 96 [not abstracted].

3882 D. H. LAWRENCE REVIEW, ed by James C. Cowan, V, No. 2 (Summer 1972).

Contents, abstracted under 1972: Michael Kirkham, "D. H. Lawrence's *Last Poems*," pp. 97-120; David Farmer, "D. H. Lawrence's 'The Turning Back': The Text and Its Genesis in Correspondence," pp. 121-31; Larry V. LeDoux, "Christ and Isis: The Function of the Dying and Reviving God in *The Man Who Died*," pp. 132-48; Carole Ferrier and Egon Tiedje, "D. H. Lawrence's Pre-1920 Poetry: The Textual Approach: An Exchange," pp. 149-57; Keith Cushman, "Putting Lawrence in His Place: Recent Studies in Modern Literature and Culture," pp. 158-69 [not abstracted]; Gerald M. Garmon, "Doctoral Dissertations on D. H. Lawrence: Bibliographical Addenda," pp. 170-73; "Laurentiana," pp. 174-82 [only Letter to the Editor from Helen Corke is abstracted]; "Contributors," p. 183 [not abstracted].

3883 D. H. LAWRENCE REVIEW, ed by James C. Cowan, V, No. 3 (Fall 1972) ["Phoenix Number"].

Contents, abstracted under 1972: Barbara Meier James, "Phoenix" (Frontispiece, painting), p. iii [not abstracted]; James C. Cowan, "Lawrence's Phoenix: An Introduction," pp. 187-99; Jessie Poesch, "The Phoenix Portrayed" [illustrated with 20-page section of art reproductions in black and white and color], pp. 200-237 [not abstracted]; Douglas J. McMillan, "The Phoenix in the Western World from Herodotus to Shakespeare," pp. 238-67 [not abstracted]; Lyna Lee Montgomery, "The Phoenix: Its Use as a Literary Device in English from the Seventeenth Century to the Twentieth Century," pp. 268-323; "Laurentiana," pp. 324-32 [only a brief comment on the publication of *John Thomas and Lady Jane* is abstracted]; "Contributors," p. 333, and "Index to Volume Five," p. 334 [not abstracted].

3884 Doheny, John Rodney."The Novel Is the Book of Life: Illustration of Argument or Insight into Experience," DISSERTATION ABSTRACTS INTERNATIONAL, XXXIII (1972), 2369A. Unpublished dissertation, University of Washington, 1972.

3885 Donoghue, Denis. "The Four 'Lady Chatterleys,'" LISTENER, LXXXVIII (14 Sept 1972), 342-43.

The differences among the three versions of *Lady Chatterley's Lover* "are matters of great literary interest." *The First Lady Chatterley* "is a plain, unwrapped story." Sir Clifford Chatterley's conversation with Connie about the dark and light horses in Plato's PHAEDRUS occurs in the first two versions but not in the third. The first version is "free of anal intercourse," but the "secret places are investigated" in the second and third versions. One can imagine "a possible fourth version" in which Clifford is not paralyzed and starts off even with Mellors, and Connie "is forced to turn upon herself the scrutiny which she turns...upon others" in the third version.

3886 Donoghue, Denis. "Prometheus in Straits," TIMES LITERARY SUPPLEMENT (Lond), 10 Nov 1972, pp. 1371-73; rptd in THIEVES OF FIRE, by Denis Donoghue (Lond & NY: Oxford UP, 1974), pp. 111-39.

[The last of the 1972 T. S. Eliot Memorial Lectures, delivered 2 Nov 1972 at the University of Kent at Canterbury, pub in slightly shortened form in TIMES LITERARY SUPPLEMENT but in complete form in THIEVES OF FIRE.]
DHL's fiction is Promethean "in the sense that its demands are endless, his art is most deeply engaged when the action is propelled by desire, and the desire goes beyond anything that can be named." The essentially Lawrentian feeling "is a profound spiritual restlessness, a Promethean urge to transfigure life by driving it beyond itself." Accepting the Promethean idea that the harmony of man and nature was disrupted by the theft of knowledge, DHL alternately "hates consciousness for the division it has caused between body and spirit" and "celebrates it for the intensity [and] anguish, which it makes possible." While his novels represent "attempts to drive beyond consciousness to a new unity," DHL does not want to return to a prelapsarian condition but rather to write about the modern world "as if it had now to be transfigured." His major novels have one theme: "the possibility of redeeming human relationships, so that they can par-

ticipate in the great natural adventure of creation and imagination." *Fantasia of the Unconscious* is the "handbook for this enterprise." The later fiction displays DHL's determination "to clear the decks, rid the world of its broken faith, and start again; by a cleansing violence, as in *Lady Chatterley's Lover*, or by a retreat to the desert, as in *St. Mawr*." In *The Rainbow*, DHL posits two kinds of will, which correspond to two kinds of energy. When his heroes and heroines quarrel about love, "they are really quarrelling about will, its nature, force and direction." T. S. Eliot's charges against DHL stem from Eliot's belief in an absolute moral law, an idea rejected by DHL, who saw the fundamental moral issue as "the relation between one person and another, as an extension of the relation between a person and himself."

3887 Duffy, Martha. "Then and Now," TIME, C (18 Sept 1972), 98.

"Because *Lady Chatterley's* shortcomings are so well known, it is possible to enjoy the unexpected virtues of this version [*John Thomas and Lady Jane*]." The character of the gamekeeper, who is called Parkin here, is a "substantial improvement" over Mellors, but "the florid, much laughed at language is still there." While the second version of the novel will not replace the third as the "accepted version of Lady Chatterley's story, it is at least nothing for Lawrence lovers to be ashamed of."

3888 Edwards, Lucy I., David Phillips, Arnold Rattenbury, and Jo Barnes (comps.). YOUNG BERT: AN EXHIBITION OF THE EARLY YEARS OF D. H. LAWRENCE (Nottingham: Castle Museum, Nottingham Castle, 1972).

[Catalogue to the exhibition at the Castle Museum, Nottingham Castle, Nottingham, 8 July to 29 Aug 1972, prepared by the Nottingham Festival Committee: James T. Boulton, chairman; Lucy I. Edwards, Local History Department of Nottingham's Central Library; David Phillips, Keeper of Art at the Castle Museum; and Arnold Rattenbury, poet and exhibition designer. The exhibition of 293 items of art, photography, and memorabilia is divided into nine parts as follows: (1) **Eastwood**: Items 1-69, mostly photographs of village, country, and mining life; (2) **Nottingham**: Items 70-91, contemporary photographs of the city in DHL's time, a catalogue and other items associated with J. H. Haywood's (Jordan's in *Sons and Lovers*), and photographs of Mrs. Lydia Lawrence and Jessie Chambers; (3) **The Pagans**: Items 92-115, photographs, autograph albums, posters, and postcards associated with the Pagans, a group of young teachers and teacher-trainees around DHL--including Jessie Chambers, Louie Burrows, George H. Neville, and others--and their activities; (4) **Imitation**: Items 116-69, paintings by the young DHL; (5) **Croydon**: Items 170-202, photographs, banners and sashes of the Women's Suffrage Movement, paintings, and DHL MSS written in Croydon; (6) **Europe**: Items 203-15, photographs of Frieda Weekley and her family, a map of DHL and Frieda's journeys in Europe, paintings DHL did there, postcards, and DHL's *Rainbow* drawing; (7) **Reputation**: Items 216-26, the phoenix symbol and photographs of ten literary figures with their appraisals of DHL's reputation; (8) **The War**: Items 227-75, photographs of DHL at the outbreak and the end of the Great War, war posters, and the complete Home Office file on *The Rainbow;* (9) **Creation**: Items 276-93, photographs of DHL during the war, DHL's wartime letters to Mr. and Mrs. Willie Hopkin, paintings by Duncan Grant and Mark Gertler, decorations by DHL, the Ajanta frescoes, postcards, and DHL's headstone in Vence. The catalogue also contains James T. Boulton, "Foreword," pp. 5-6, and C. E. Baron, "D. H. Lawrence's Early Paintings," pp. 32-40 (abstracted separately). See also C. E. Baron, "The Nottingham Festival D. H. Lawrence Exhibition, 1972," D. H. LAWRENCE REVIEW, VII (Spring 1974), 19-57, which reproduces fifty items from the exhibition.]

3889 Elsbree, Langdon. "The Purest and Most Perfect Form of Play: Some Novelists and the Dance," CRITICISM, XIV (Fall 1972), 361-72.
In DHL, as in Jane Austen, George Eliot, and Thomas Hardy, the dance "signifies the kinds of love and marriage a community permits," and it "objectifies a character's inner life." The "closer to us the novelist and setting are in time, the more likely the dance represents the failure of community and the isolation of characters." In DHL, "the dance becomes a means of apprehending and diagnosing a deeper self...whose integrity and vitality" are threatened by industrialism and materialism and "by a desperate ethic of sheer sensation." In *The Rainbow* and *Women in Love*, the dance scenes become what Huizinga calls sacred play--"the ritual effort to participate in the cosmic forces of birth, growth, and death." DHL often shows us "characters who strive to attain sacred play but cannot because sex for them is a matter of sensation, will, and domination." [See also Langdon Elsbree, "D. H. Lawrence, HOMO LUDENS, and the Dance," D. H. LAWRENCE REVIEW, I (Spring 1968), 1-30.]

3890 Elwin, Malcolm. "Ford and Lawrence," TIMES LITERARY SUPPLEMENT (Lond), 19 May 1972, p. 576.
[Letter to the Editor in reply to John Beer, "Ford's Impressions of the Lawrences," TIMES LITERARY SUPPLEMENT (Lond), 5 May 1972, p. 520.] Douglas Goldring's warning that "Ford's reminiscences are 'quasi-fictional' " is borne out by Beer's article. If Ford had ever visited Nottingham and met DHL's friends, "would not the event have been mentioned by Jessie Chambers"? [Examines statements in Ford's RETURN TO YESTERDAY about his visiting the Lawrences and shows their inconsistency with known facts about DHL's whereabouts and statements in DHL's letters.]

3891 Emmett, V. J., Jr. "Structural Irony in D. H. Lawrence's 'The Rocking-Horse Winner,' " CONNECTICUT REVIEW, V (April 1972), 5-10.
The parallels between "The Rocking-Horse Winner" and the fairy tale form are systematically imperfect, producing "an ironic distortion that subverts the traditional values of the fairy tale." DHL's main strategy is to use the manner and some of the elements of the fairy tale but to bend the form away from the romantic comedy ending and "into something more nearly resembling tragedy."

3892 Fadiman, Regina. "The Poet as Choreographer: Lawrence's 'The Blind Man,' " JOURNAL OF NARRATIVE TECHNIQUE, II (Jan 1972), 60-67.

The structure of "The Blind Man" may be seen in terms of a classical ballet, choreographed for three dancers. Isabel, the wife, is placed in the center of the stage with the two men on opposite sides of her, objectifying her inner conflict. Pervin, her blind husband, has been forced by blindness to discover the world of touch, the means by which DHL's characters achieve creative, phallic consciousness, but his darkness is terrifying to Isabel. Bertie Reid represents the intellectual who has lost his sense of touch. Their conflict is basic to modern civilization, where coordination between hand and eye are lost. Isabel moves toward first one, then the other, and finally floats off with her husband, "carried aloft into his fuller world of being."

3893 Farmer, David. "D. H. Lawrence's 'The Turning Back': The Text and Its Genesis in Correspondence," D. H. LAWRENCE REVIEW, V (Summer 1972), 121-31.

The Letters of D. H. Lawrence, edited by Aldous Huxley (1932), prints a fragment of a poem, section "iii," as complete. *The Complete Poems of D. H. Lawrence,* edited by Vivian de Sola Pinto and Warren Roberts (1964), prints the fragment as "We Have Gone Too Far." "The Turning Back," published here for the first time complete in three parts from a holograph draft, dated 1 November 1915, in a pocket notebook now at the University of Texas at Austin, is integral with ideas DHL expressed in his 1915 correspondence concerning the war.

3894 Farmer, David. "Textual Alterations in 'NOT I, BUT THE WIND...,'" NOTES AND QUERIES, ns XIX (Sept 1972), 336.

In all editions of Frieda Lawrence's "NOT I, BUT THE WIND..." except the first one, privately printed in Santa Fe in July 1934, there are silent changes and omissions in DHL's letter to Frieda dated 7 July 1929.

3895 Ferrier, Carole. "D. H. Lawrence: An Ibsen Reference," NOTES AND QUERIES, ns XIX (Sept 1972), 335-36.

The title of DHL's poem "Nils Lykke" is a reference to a character in Ibsen's LADY INGER OF OSTRAT, a young knight with a look in his eyes that women can never forget.

3896 Ferrier, Carole, and Egon Tiedje. "D. H. Lawrence's Pre-1920 Poetry: The Textual Approach: An Exchange," D. H. LAWRENCE REVIEW, V (Summer 1972), 149-57.

[Carole Ferrier's reply to Egon Tiedje, "D. H. Lawrence's Early Poetry: The Composition Dates of the Drafts," D. H. LAWRENCE REVIEW, IV (Fall 1971), 227-52, and Tiedje's rejoinder to her.] **Ferrier:** Tiedje has not consulted all available manuscripts of DHL's early poetry and "he has not taken into account the contemporary manuscripts." MS E317 records fair copies, the dating of which on the basis of biographical evidence is unsound and misleading. The chronology of the poems is less important than the developments of each poem. **Tiedje:** In working with texts, "the most we can hope for is probability and plausibility, not absolute certainty." Biography cannot be transcended until it is established. While it is agreed that "more attention should be given to the analysis of versions," this approach is complementary to, rather than exclusive of, other approaches.

Contemporary manuscripts are not offered by Miss Ferrier. Finally, " 'stylistic evidence' easily becomes a self-fulfilling prophecy," and "the usefulness of 'published drafts' is limited."

3897 "A Few Novels," NEW REPUBLIC, CLXVII (16 Sept 1972), 32-33.

"All three versions [of *Lady Chatterley's Lover*] are as much about class as about sex--about the rape of the countryside by mining as well as about the seduction of a gentlewoman frustrated by marriage to a war-impotent mineowner." "The final chapters" of *John Thomas and Lady Jane* "not only rank among Lawrence's best writing, but close the novel more effectively than do the other texts."

3898 Finney, Brian. "Additional Bibliographical Information on Some D. H. Lawrence Stories," NOTES AND QUERIES, ns XIX (Sept 1972), 337.

"The Christening" was first published in THE SMART SET (Feb 1914). [Finney also lists early, but not first, periodical appearances, none of them recorded in previous bibliographies, of "A Sick Collier," "A Fragment of Stained Glass," "Strike-Pay," "Her Turn," and "The Witch à la Mode."]

3899 Finney, Brian H. "The Hitherto Unknown Publication of Some D. H. Lawrence Short Stories," NOTES AND QUERIES, ns XIX (Feb 1972), 55-56.

The first published versions of five of DHL's stories in periodicals are identified: "The Fox" in HUTCHINSON'S STORY MAGAZINE (Nov 1920), "The Blue Moccasins" in EVE: THE LADY'S PICTORIAL (22 Nov 1928), "Smile" in NEW MASSES (June 1926), "The Rocking-Horse Winner" in HARPER'S BAZAAR (July 1926). A DHL letter indicates that "In Love" appeared in HUTCHINSON'S (Jan 1928), though this publication cannot yet be confirmed.

3900 Finney, Brian H., and Keith Cushman. "Laurentiana," D. H. LAWRENCE REVIEW, V (Fall 1972), 331-32.

[Exchange of letters: Brian H. Finney's reply to Keith Cushman, "The Making of 'The Prussian Officer': A Correction," D. H. LAWRENCE REVIEW, IV (Fall 1971), 263-73, and Cushman's rejoinder to him.] **Finney**: DHL's unpublished letter to J. B. Pinker (15 Sept 1914) provides evidence that DHL objected to magazine condensation of "Honour and Arms" (the first published version of "The Prussian Officer") in ENGLISH REVIEW. **Cushman**: While "Mr. Finney's new evidence speaks for itself," DHL "later in his career...did not mind if a magazine condensed a tale or novella so long as book publication restored the cuts."

3901 Fisher, Jack. "Three Paintings of Sex: The Films of Ken Russell," FILM JOURNAL, II, No. 1 (1972), 34-43.

[A discussion of three films directed by Ken Russell, with frequent references to DHL and *Women in Love*.] Whereas DHL's forte was "his ability to turn emotion into action, and by the action to discover some of the outlines of the emotion,

Russell turns emotion into moving paintings." [Illustrated with scenes from the film version of *Women in Love*.]

3902 Foster, Joseph. D. H. LAWRENCE IN TAOS (Albuquerque: University of New Mexico P, 1972).
[First person memoir.] DHL, a spiritual nomad, had reached the limit of his endurance in Europe, and his willingness to come to Taos coincided with Mabel Dodge Luhan's wish to have him come. Attracted to the Taos Indians, DHL said he wanted to " 'transfer all my life to America' "; both intrigued and annoyed by the Indians, he wrote no major book about them. Mabel Luhan felt that DHL was the only person who could bring Taos and the Indians alive in his writing and wanted to write a book with him (a plan Frieda disapproved of totally); Mrs. Luhan's real intention, however, was to dominate DHL and to have him formulate her experience of the Southwest. After DHL and Frieda left Luhan's ranch for her mountain cabin (Del Monte Ranch), Luhan and DHL became enemies. DHL was preoccupied with his exile from Europe; America represented dead space and liberty to him. When he arrived in Mexico, DHL first loved the essentialness and the sense of wonder in the Mexicans. But he also felt fear there because of the disordered social conditions and because he saw the tenor and beauty of the country's past in its present and feared the totality of man's past suffering, violence, and crime. Back on the ranch near Taos (Lobo, later renamed Kiowa Ranch), DHL recovered from the severe illness he had contracted in Mexico. His relationship with Mabel Dodge Luhan was over. Although Frieda and DHL often appeared at odds, they were really as one. [See also refutation of much of this memoir in a review by Mark Schorer, "A Book So Bad It Was Impossible to Put Down," NEW YORK TIMES BOOK REVIEW, 16 Jan 1972.]

3903 Fotheringham, Richard. "Expatriate Publishing: P. R. Stephensen and the Mandrake Press," MEANJIN, XXXI (June 1972), 183-88.
P. R. Stephensen (1901-1965), the Australian man of letters, joined with Edward Goldston in Feb 1929 to form the Mandrake Press for the purpose of publishing a volume of reproductions of DHL's paintings to appear simultaneously with the exhibition of these paintings at the Warren Gallery on 14 June 1929. When the police raided the exhibition and removed thirteen paintings, they took four copies of the Mandrake Press volume, which were burned after the trial. The remaining copies sold out instantly to the profit of DHL, Goldston, and Stephensen. Stephensen later lent his name as printer to an unexpurgated edition of *Pansies* in June 1929, and Mandrake Press printed DHL's "My Skirmish with Jolly Roger" in June 1930.

3904 Fox, Carol Lorraine Tyler. "The Artistic and Critical Significance of D. H. Lawrence's *Studies in Classic American Literature*," DISSERTATION ABSTRACTS INTERNATIONAL, XXXIII (1973), 5172A-73A. Unpublished dissertation, Case Western Reserve University, 1972.

3905 Fraser, G. S. "The English Novel," in THE TWENTIETH-CENTURY MIND: HISTORY, IDEAS, AND LITERATURE IN

D. H. LAWRENCE

BRITAIN, ed by C. B. Cox and A. E. Dyson, Vol. II: 1918-1945 (Lond, Oxford, & NY: Oxford UP, 1972), pp. 373-416.

"Joyce and Lawrence are the two giants of our period" (post-1918). *The Lost Girl,* in which DHL exploits a "conventional vein of lower-middle-class comedy," "is mainly interesting for the Italian passages at the end." *Aaron's Rod* and *Kangaroo* were "rapidly improvised...'anti-novels,'" expressing DHL's concern for "masculine independence" from society and women, yet the necessity of "male-to-male relationship." "The political melodrama, which composes the outer plot or framework of *Kangaroo,* is at once a projection and exorcism" of DHL's vindictiveness about his treatment during the war and his "relived anger and fear." [Detailed discussion.] Although "the ideologue" rather than "the artist" is in "command" of *The Plumed Serpent,* "the one great success in this romance about the revival of an ancient and cruel central American religion is the character of the heroine, Kate." In *Lady Chatterley's Lover,* DHL returns to the careful workmanship and Nottingham-Derbyshire coalfield setting of *Women in Love.* Connie, the "least vital" of DHL's heroines, has "a pathetic, hurt, touching quality." Sir Clifford "symbolizes a class system" which no longer rules by "virile dominance [as] in feudal times, but which today works only from the head." [Detailed discussion of male "fears of castration, impotence, inadequacy" in the novel, and their relevance to the reassertion of male dominance in the anal intercourse scene.] "The best way to take Lawrence's novels from *Aaron's Rod* to *Lady Chatterley's Lover* is as Kierkegaardian 'stages on life's way': records of the dialectic of a great soul's exploration of the open road."

3906 Friedman, Alan. "The Novel," in THE TWENTIETH-CENTURY MIND: HISTORY, IDEAS, AND LITERATURE IN BRITAIN, ed by C. B. Cox and A. E. Dyson, Vol. I: 1900-1918 (Lond, Oxford, & NY: Oxford UP, 1972), pp. 414-46, espec pp. 415, 424, 432, 435-40.

"The single greatest master of the novel in this period seems unquestionably to have been D. H. Lawrence.... Possessed...of conviction in himself, faith in the novel, and genius, he directed his attention less to the novels and manners of his time...than to something at once more elemental and more tenuous, the inward conditions of human existence." As a philosophical, political, apocalyptic, and psychological novelist, "Lawrence was driven to experiment with the texture and form of fiction." *Sons and Lovers* is "more than a psychological portrait,...an autobiographical confrontation," or a "story of trapped sexual passion." Its psychological context is established finally not by authorial exposition but "by non-rational vision and by physical details." *The Rainbow* and *Women in Love,* although not identical twins, "form parts of a single experiment" in "direct literary rendering of his characters' unconscious," but rather than "pulverizing *verbal* consciousness" as Joyce did, DHL distorts "emotional awareness" to take us "into another region of the unconscious." The structure of *Women in Love* "is built less on the plotting of action than on the plotting of symbols." One important interest in DHL's fiction is "the excitement of his restless theorizing," beneath which "lay his intuitive psychological theory whose implications were religious," his belief in "'blood-consciousness'" and his resistance to "the tyranny of consciousness."

3907 Furbank, P. N. "How Lawrence Wrote Out the Preaching and the Pathos," TIMES (Lond), 31 Aug 1972, p. 7.

The First Lady Chatterley is not "a revolutionary polemic or manifesto" like its successors but a beautiful, simple, pastoral tale which emphasizes social and political class issues rather than "full-length descriptions of sexual orgasms." *John Thomas and Lady Jane*, the least effective of the three, is "too noisily preachy." The evolution of DHL's conception of the novel is clarified by reading the two earlier versions, which reveal that in the scene in which Mellors and Connie decorate their body hair with flowers Mellors is celebrating sexual liberation and that in the scene in which Clifford runs his wheelchair over the bluebells DHL is rejecting pathos. [Also reviews Émile Delavenay, D. H. LAWRENCE: THE MAN AND HIS WORK: THE FORMATIVE YEARS, 1885-1919 (1969).]

3908 Gant, Roland. "Publisher's Note," *The First Lady Chatterley*, by D. H. Lawrence (Lond: Wm Heinemann, 1972), pp. v-vii.

This ed of *The First Lady Chatterley* follows DHL's original undivided narrative, unlike the 1944 Dial Press ed, which divided the book into 24 chapters. All three drafts of this novel are now available to readers, presenting a unique opportunity to examine the creative methods of one of the greatest novelists of the twentieth century. *The First Lady Chatterley* is, perhaps, the best of the three versions.

3909 Gant, Roland. "Publisher's Note," *John Thomas and Lady Jane*, by D. H. Lawrence (Lond: Wm Heinemann, 1972), pp. v-vii; rvd and enlgd as "Editor's Introduction," *John Thomas and Lady Jane*, by D. H. Lawrence (NY: Viking P, 1972), pp. v-ix.

The second draft of *Lady Chatterley's Lover* is published here for the first time in English. Only the third version ends with " 'John Thomas says good-night to Lady Jane, a little droopingly, but with a hopeful heart.' " Yet the use of *John Thomas and Lady Jane* as a title for the second version is justified, not merely to avoid confusion with *The First Lady Chatterley* and *Lady Chatterley's Lover* but also because of DHL's wish to call his book that. [Includes a brief history of the publication of the novel in three different versions.] [American version discusses the differences between *John Thomas and Lady Jane* and *Lady Chatterley's Lover*, noting that in the former, which contains about twenty thousand more words than the latter, Connie is a more womanly woman, Clifford a more convincing crippled man, and Oliver Parkin, the gamekeeper, more tender, compassionate, and understanding than Mellors. The scene of the tea party in Bill Tewson's house, omitted in the final version, is DHL at his best, and the ending is entirely different from that of *Lady Chatterley's Lover*.]

3910 Garcia, Reloy, and James Karabatsos (eds). A CONCORDANCE TO THE SHORT FICTION OF D. H. LAWRENCE (Lincoln: University of Nebraska P, 1972).

[This computer-generated concordance is divided into two parts consisting of word indices to the short stories and to the short novels of DHL. Words are listed by page and line number and are not shown in context. The texts used are *The Complete Short Stories of D. H. Lawrence*, 3 vols. (NY: Viking P, Compass Book ed, 1961), *Four Short Novels of D. H. Lawrence* (NY: Viking P,

Compass Book ed, 1965), *St. Mawr* and *The Man Who Died* (NY: Knopf, Vintage Book ed, 1953), and *The Virgin and the Gipsy* in *The Short Novels of D. H. Lawrence,* Vol. 2 (Lond: Wm Heinemann, 1956). A list of errata for the texts used is included.]

3911 Garcia, Reloy. STEINBECK AND D. H. LAWRENCE: FICTIVE VOICES AND THE ETHICAL IMPERATIVE (Muncie, IN: Ball State UP [Steinbeck Monograph Series, No. 2], 1972).

Working independently from different cultures and temperaments, John Steinbeck and DHL developed similar concepts of art and the function of the artist. Both conceived of art as a moral force, and "both championed the troubled spirit in the dark night of the Western soul." While both saw themselves as moral activists, both voiced moral anguish and were compelled to withdraw into nature, primitivism, history, or the world of myth and symbol. These conflicts between the public and private selves, between public commitment and private withdrawal, shape their work and govern their aesthetic distance.

3912 Garmon, Gerald M. "Doctoral Dissertations on D. H. Lawrence: Bibliographical Addenda," D. H. LAWRENCE REVIEW, V (Summer 1972), 170-73.

[Addenda to G. B. Crump, "Doctoral Dissertations on D. H. Lawrence, 1931-1969: A Bibliography," D. H. LAWRENCE REVIEW, III (Spring 1970), 80-86. See also Dennis Jackson, "Doctoral Dissertations on D. H. Lawrence: Bibliographical Addenda," D. H. LAWRENCE REVIEW, VIII (Summer 1975), 236-41, and Fleda Brown Jackson, "Doctoral Dissertations and Masters Theses on D. H. Lawrence: Bibliographical Addenda," D. H. LAWRENCE REVIEW, X (Fall 1977), 299-308.]

3913 Gilbert, Sandra M. ACTS OF ATTENTION: THE POEMS OF D. H. LAWRENCE (Ithaca, NY: Cornell UP, 1972).

DHL defines poetry as "a new effort of attention [which] 'discovers' a new world within the known world." As opposed to the integrated vision of the novel, poetry is a passive receiving of "bits" of visionary illumination. The early poems show the struggle between DHL's "demon" and the "young man" trying to find himself in his *fin de siècle* forebears. Imagism had a more decided effect on DHL than did the Georgians. The dialect poems treat complex subjects more appropriate to novels. Poems of "searing honesty" like "Cherry Robbers," "Snap-Dragon," and "Love on the Farm" allow DHL to integrate the "young man," the "demon," and the novelist into a productive artistic self. The "mother" poems, psychologically amazing in their depth of perception, often show a new ease with disciplined form. The new integrated style of *Look! We Have Come Through!* begins in 1912 when DHL meets Frieda and becomes a poet of the body with an organic style. "Bei Hennef" marks the bridge between "Rhyming" and "Unrhyming" poems, as the crutch of rhyme is cast away and rhythms begin to be "determined by the stress of feeling." DHL's commitment to the objective "other" in *Look! We Have Come Through!* allows the greater objectivity of the visionary anti-romantic poetry of *Birds, Beasts and Flowers*, which successively view animals and plants (1) as pure "otherness," (2) as the "otherness" of the primitive world and the future, (3) as the "otherness" of the "living cosmos," and (4) as the "otherness" within ourselves, move through the recognition of the necessity of death prior to the fulfillment of rebirth. DHL turns, in *The Plumed Serpent*, to a "yearning myth," depicting man as he should be in poems indebted to Methodist hymns, the English Bible, and, in their incantatory quality, to Indian and Aztec religious songs. *Pansies* is best understood by comparison to cartoons or, in its deliberate fragmentation, to Pound's CANTOS or Ginsberg's "Kaddish." The *Nettles* poems derive their style from the journalistic prose of *Assorted Articles. Last Poems*, preoccupied with the divine and the problem of evil, is religious, incantatory, meditative, and worshipful. "Bavarian Gentians" uses repetition as incantation to introduce the realms of death to which DHL totally commits himself.

3914 Gill, Richard. HAPPY RURAL SEAT: THE ENGLISH COUNTRY HOUSE AND THE LITERARY IMAGINATION (New Haven: Yale UP, 1972), pp. 147-55 and passim.

DHL uses the manorial seat, Wragby Hall, as more than a setting for *Lady Chatterley's Lover*. In depicting "the moral collapse of the stately home and its traditions," DHL reveals "the failure of a class through the inadequacy of one of its male members." DHL's model for Wragby Hall was Lamb Close, a mansion in Eastwood, where he grew up. Although DHL had a measure of esteem for the English class system of the past--for the ability of squires to be "at one with the people"--he felt that the individualism of the cultured classes in the present had destroyed what he admired. Thus, the "lifeless, shut-in atmosphere" of Wragby Hall emphasizes DHL's view of what had happened to England's aristocracy. Connie escapes the stifling effects of class prejudice by joining Mellors in a farm cottage. DHL's attitudes, however, are ambivalent; while depicting the death of an aristocratic order, he is also "objecting to the failure of its best representatives to resist the industrial, mechanical forces he found ugly and dehumanizing." Wragby Hall, therefore, is indicted more for what it fails to be than for what it is, and DHL's indictment "implies a kind of lament for lost opportunities."

3915 Gill, Stephen. "Reviews," NOTES AND QUERIES, ns XIX (Sept 1972), 354-55.

"Of the 226 previously unpublished letters" in *The Quest for Rananim: D. H. Lawrence's Letters to S. S. Koteliansky, 1914 to 1930*, ed by George J. Zytaruk, "only a small handful are of any real interest." "Koteliansky's solidity was a pivotal point around which Lawrence could whirl," but the relationship is not of sufficient interest for outsiders to "justify this expensive and elaborate volume." "Dating is the only problem posed by the letters in the British Museum." [See also reply by George J. Zytaruk and rejoinder by Stephen Gill, in "Replies," NOTES AND QUERIES, ns XX (April 1973), 143-44.]

3916 Goldknopf, David. THE LIFE OF THE NOVEL (Chicago: University of Chicago P, 1972), pp. 57, 68, 119, 121, 178, 188-91, 193, 197, 203, 209-12, 213.

DHL's visionary philosophy rested on a concretely realistic base which accurately presents the contemporary scene. Exemplifying both the visionary and the realistic in DHL is Hermione's attempt to kill Birkin in *Women in Love*. The authority of her act is not her prior motives but the realistic handling of the sudden violence through compression of fact, sentiment, and idea. Even the following scene in which Birkin wades naked through long grass has circumstantial justification. Rather than being a Fascist, DHL, who knew the ravaging of spirit by twentieth-century technology and its societal instrumentation, was actually England's most democratic novelist since Defoe. Relying on the original unit of the novel, the autonomous ego, DHL projected his characters, even in short fiction, through their self-defining intensity of being, counterpoising the appeal of this world with love and religion, which are thus experienced as deeply as the social forces.

3917 Gouirand, Jacqueline. "Tradition et Innovation: D. H. Lawrence, romancier de l'inexprimé" (Tradition and Innovation: D. H. Lawrence, Novelist of the Unsaid), ACTES DU CONGRÈS DE NANCY, DE LA S.A.E.S. (Paris: Didier, 1972), pp. 219-41.

DHL's art, born of experience, expresses his vision that is both anchored in reality and projected into a spiritual universe. In the early works the natural setting invites the reader to enter a familiar world; in the later, more symbolic works the meaning of life becomes more and more interiorized. Although traditional elements are found in *The White Peacock* and *Sons and Lovers*, family chronicles in which the scenes of everyday life and the dialogue reflect reality, *Sons and Lovers*, in some respects, breaks away from the influence of the naturalists. The turning point in DHL's development as a writer came in 1913-1914, in his innovations in character and structure. In his analysis of a succession of moods in presenting his characters' psychology, the novelist reflects the turmoil of contemporary society. In *The Rainbow* and *Women in Love*, DHL crystallizes into prose the gushing of the unconscious into areas of consciousness. In order to understand DHL's new conception of character, we must distinguish two categories of "dark mental processes": the human and the non-human element of the "unknown" "otherness," expressed by the "darkness." Releasing his characters from a moral background, DHL concentrates on " 'the way our sympathy flows and recoils.' " The originality of DHL's innovation reveals that he is the novelist of "the unuttered." [In French.]

3918 Gould, Eric H. "The Presence of America in the Works of D. H. Lawrence." Unpublished dissertation, King's College, University of London, 1972. [Listed in Lawrence F. McNamee, DISSERTATIONS IN ENGLISH AND AMERICAN LITERATURE, SUPP II (NY and Lond: Bowker, 1974), p. 368.]

3919 Guerrini, Tito. "Da Lawrence a Ken Russell" (From Lawrence to Ken Russell), LA FIERA LETTERARIA (Rome), 16 Jan 1972, p. 28.

[Review of the film version of *Women in Love,* written for the screen and produced by Larry Kramer, directed by Ken Russell.] *Women in Love* can be related to *Sons and Lovers* by its setting and the psychology of its characters, while it also contains certain themes which recur in *Lady Chatterley's Lover.*

It is the novel in which DHL tries to reach the highest expression of his philosophy of sex. Ken Russell catches this point in his film version of the novel, and this is the main reason that *Women in Love* can be considered his best film and a work of art. [In Italian.]

>3920 Gurko, Leo. "D. H. Lawrence's Greatest Collection of Short Stories--What Holds It Together," MODERN FICTION STUDIES, XVII (Summer 1972), 173-82.

In addition to themes, such as those involving the Sleeping Beauty and the Pluto-Persephone myth, a major structural motif of the three stories in the *Ladybird* volume *(The Ladybird, The Captain's Doll, The Fox)* is a movement in which the chief males in each story cease to be mere emblems, or "reductions," and become fully male. This liberation process, in each story, expands symbolically to become a resurrection involving a necessary death. All of DHL's major fiction from this time on contains the death-resurrection pattern, often to the artistic or moral detriment of the story, as in *The Plumed Serpent,* with its Aztec-like ritual murders.

>3921 Gutierrez, Donald. "Lawrence's *The Virgin and the Gipsy* as Ironic Comedy," ENGLISH QUARTERLY (Waterloo, Ont.), V (Winter 1972-1973), 61-69; rptd as Chap. III, in LAPSING OUT: EMBODIMENTS OF DEATH AND REBIRTH IN THE LAST WRITINGS OF D. H. LAWRENCE, by Donald Gutierrez (Rutherford, Madison, Teaneck, NJ: Fairleigh Dickinson UP; Lond and Toronto: Associate University Presses, 1980), pp. 55-67.

Northrop Frye's definition of Menandrine comic irony as locating the enemy of society within the society in a seat of power supports a view of *The Virgin and the Gipsy* as sophisticated comedy achieved through ironic contrasts of the narrative with romance elements and literary analogues, though the conventional comedic formation of a new society around the hero and heroine is violated. The deepest irony is the subsistential, rather than erotic, embrace that the life-renewing gipsy gives the virgin to prevent her freezing to death after a flood that has drowned Granny, the main obstruction to the young people's self-realization. The chief analogues are Guy de Maupassant's novella YVETTE, concerning a French virgin whose coming-of-age is the realization that her mother runs a brothel and still takes lovers, and Tennyson's "The Lady of Shalott," concerning a young woman, doomed by magic to non-fulfillment sexually, who becomes a victim of the sentimental Victorian attachment to virginity and denial of the female drive to full womanhood.

>3922 Haegert, John. "D. H. Lawrence and the Idea of the Erotic." Unpublished dissertation, University of Chicago, 1972. [Listed in Lawrence F. McNamee, DISSERTATIONS IN ENGLISH AND AMERICAN LITERATURE, SUPP II (NY & Lond: Bowker, 1974), p. 368.]

>3923 Harper, Howard M., Jr. "*Fantasia* and the Psychodynamics of *Women in Love,*" in THE CLASSIC BRITISH NOVEL, ed by Howard

Harper, Jr., and Charles Edge (Athens: University of Georgia P, 1972), pp. 202-19.

"*Women in Love* represents the most complex stage in the development" of DHL's great myth of regeneration from a corrupt civilization. The expression of his prophetic vision, as the "unique story" presents "the movement of four major characters through 'allotropic states' of being in their search...for wholeness," required the invented language of *Fantasia of the Unconscious,* which represents DHL's "most explicit attempt to 'explain' human nature." Although not valid scientifically, the theory set forth, "seen symbolically, as a complex metaphor for the expression of psychological insight,...is profound." [The theory of psychic anatomy expounded in *Fantasia* is explained briefly in terms of the polarity between the two centers of the lower, sensual plane and the two centers of the upper, spiritual plane, as a basis for a detailed analysis of *Women in Love,* which is placed in the context of "the search for wholeness" in the novels that precede and follow it.]

3924 Heath, Alice C. "The Checklist of D. H. Lawrence Criticism and Scholarship, 1971," D. H. LAWRENCE REVIEW, V (Spring 1972), 82-92.

[The annual bibliography of works about DHL is divided into five sections: General, Poetry, Individual Works of Fiction, Non-Fiction Prose, and Drama.]

3925 Hinz, Evelyn J. "The Beginning and the End: D. H. Lawrence's *Psychoanalysis* and *Fantasia,*" DALHOUSIE REVIEW, LII (Summer 1972), 251-65.

DHL first denigrates Freudian psychoanalysis as unscientific in methodology, then introduces his own system, based on "the recognition of a precognitive mode of perception," as "more scientific." Inconsistencies arise, not from any purpose to "affirm the irrational" but from DHL's attempts to demonstrate "the rationality of his insights." *Psychoanalysis and the Unconscious* answers the challenge of science "on its own ground"; *Fantasia of the Unconscious* demonstrates that the artist "should feel stimulated by the discoveries of science." *Psychoanalysis* argues for the "empirical validity of intuition and ancient wisdom." *Fantasia* argues for the "independent authority of intuition; subjective, mythological truths are justified...because they verify each other." *Fantasia* is "an archetypal work" whose basic structure is "cyclic, and thus affirmative of the pagan and cosmic perspective."

3926 Hinz, Evelyn J. "Rider Haggard's SHE: An Archetypal 'History of Adventure,'" STUDIES IN THE NOVEL, IV (Fall 1972), 416-31.

DHL was not in error in associating "a heart of darkness" with Rider Haggard's SHE. The book, in spite of its popularity, is one that would have appealed to DHL because of its mythological, archetypal study of the idea that progress equals decline.

3927 Hinz, Evelyn J. "*Sons and Lovers:* The Archetypal Dimensions of Lawrence's Oedipal Tragedy," D. H. LAWRENCE REVIEW, V (Spring 1972), 26-53.

This essay is concerned "with the artistic consequences of the interaction of the topical and the universal in *Sons and Lovers,* with the way in which Lawrence gives a domestic plot 'classical' proportions by employing the archetypal rationale: 'history repeats itself.' " The original "Foreword" to the novel demonstrates that DHL "was familiar with the usurpation-matriarchy implications of the original Oedipus legend,...that he viewed Christianity as the historical example of the Son usurping from the Father,...that he saw excessive formalism and individualism as later recurrences of the Word usurping the Flesh, and...that he recognized that human relations are...an index to...and a consequence of cultural situations." [Myth criticism exploring the archetypal nature of *Sons and Lovers* in terms of both incidents and imagery.]

3928 Horney, Larry J. "The Emerging Woman of the Twentieth Century: A Study of the Women in D. H. Lawrence's Novels *The Rainbow* and *Women in Love*," DISSERTATION ABSTRACTS INTERNATIONAL, XXXIII (1972), 275A. Unpublished dissertation, Ball State University, 1972.

3929 Howe, Florence. "Feminism and Literature," in IMAGES OF WOMEN IN FICTION: FEMINIST PERSPECTIVES, ed by Susan Koppelman Cornillon (Bowling Green,OH: Bowling Green U Popular P, 1972), pp. 253-77, espec pp. 264-66.

DHL "helped to liberate parts of the western world from a Christian-Puritan ethic that regarded sexuality as unclean." However, he "honestly and convincingly portrays sexual man," not woman. In theory, his "star-equilibrium" is "very appealing," but it never functions "on levels beyond the personal; women are wives and men are writers, thinkers, coal miners, farmers, or other workers of the world." A woman, according to DHL, "needs a man, needs marriage and a monogamous heterosexual relationship to be complete."

3930 "Humanities," CHOICE, IX (July-Aug 1972), 632.

Movements in European History "provides adequate evidence" that DHL, though a "major novelist," was "not a great historian." However, it "provides insights into Lawrence's political and social views."

3931 Ishibashi, Magoichiro. "Lawrence no 'Nôjô no Koi' Kenkyû" (A Study of Lawrence's "Love on the Farm"), JOURNAL OF OSAKA INDUSTRIAL UNIVERSITY, No. 35 (Oct 1972), 1-11.

The versification of "Love on the Farm," one of DHL's elementary love poems, is a mixture of intelligence and intuition. His thoughts about nature in the poem obviously come from his great love for animals and plants. [In Japanese.]

3932 Ito, Toyoji. "*Niji* ni Tsuite" (On *The Rainbow*), STUDY OF CULTURAL SCIENCE (Niigata University), No. 42 (Jan 1972), 1-47.

[This paper treats of impersonal elements, images of new birth, and conflict between man and woman in *The Rainbow*. Particular examples discussed include Tom's and Lydia's experience during the proposal and acceptance, Will's experience in Lincoln Cathedral, and the conflict between Ursula and Skrebensky.] [In Japanese.]

3933 Ivker, Barry. "Schopenhauer and D. H. Lawrence," XAVIER UNIVERSITY STUDIES, XI, No. 2 (1972), 22-36.

Although it cannot be proved that DHL read Schopenhauer's THE WORLD AS WILL AND REPRESENTATION, he did read some of Schopenhauer's essays in translation, and his work from the period of *The Rainbow* and *Psychoanalysis and the Unconscious* shows definite influence by Schopenhauer.

3934 Kalnins, Mara. "A Study of Style: The Development of D. H. Lawrence's Style in *The Prussian Officer* Tales." Unpublished dissertation, Edinburgh University, 1972. [Listed in Lawrence F. McNamee, DISSERTATIONS IN ENGLISH AND AMERICAN LITERATURE, SUPP II (NY and Lond: Bowker, 1974), p. 368; and Geoffrey M. Patterson and Joan E. Hardy (eds), INDEX TO THESES, XXV, Pt. 1 (Lond: Aslib, 1976), p. 6, Item 241.

3935 Kamimura, Tatsuhiko. "D. H. Lawrence: Opening to the Wordless World--Toward *The Plumed Serpent* (1)," ENGLISH LITERATURE REVIEW (Kyoto Women's University), No. 16 (Nov 1972), 20-33.

The world-view of the four corners area of the Amerindians to whom DHL was exposed during his stay in America powerfully influenced him: their whole conception of time is central to *The Plumed Serpent*. DHL's mission seems to have been to stress a return to the center of the universe, to see the facts beyond the mundane life, first of all, then to allow the "unfathomable life-mystery" gradually and naturally to reveal itself in *The Plumed Serpent*. [See also Tatsuhiko Kamimura, "D. H. Lawrence: Opening to the Wordless World--Toward *The Plumed Serpent* (2)," ENGLISH LITERATURE REVIEW (Kyoto Women's University), No. 17 (Dec 1973), 25-34.]

3936 Kaneko, Masanobu. "D. H. Lawrence to Morality" (D. H. Lawrence and Morality), MEMOIRS OF THE FACULTY OF GENERAL EDUCATION (Kumamoto University), No. 7 (Feb 1972), 23-41.

Surveying the life and thought of DHL, who considers that " 'Nothing is important but life,' " one finds at the root of his metaphysic an image of "All moves." The image in itself is not new, but his way of thinking is his own, belonging neither to "realism" nor to the "idealism" of the past. DHL's view of "morality" is shown in such statements as " 'Man must be moral, at the very root moral' " and " 'The essential function of art is moral,' " and in his conclusion, " 'Morality is that delicate, for ever trembling *balance* between me and my circumambient universe.' " The fine things in DHL come in unexpectedly between trifle and trifle. [In Japanese.]

3937 Kay, Wallace G. "Lawrence and *The Rainbow*: Apollo and Dionysus in Conflict," SOUTHERN QUARTERLY, X (April 1972), 209-22.

The Rainbow is an account of the struggle between the Dionysian "blood impulse" of the earlier Brangwen men with the Apollonian instincts of the women who want the "spoken world" of ratiocination for their children. Neither can exist without the other and the rainbow at the end of the novel holds the hope and promise of fusion of the two.

3938 Kay, Wallace G. "*Women in Love* and *The Man Who Died*: Resolving Apollo and Dionysus," SOUTHERN QUARTERLY, X (July 1972), 325-39.

The movement in *Women in Love* and *The Man Who Died* works toward Dionysian wholeness of being in the characters who survive. This involves fusion with the Apollonian as it comes from the sexual union of man and woman, but without rejection of the spiritual realization the man may have already achieved.

3939 Kennedy, Richard. A BOY AT THE HOGARTH PRESS, illustrated by Richard Kennedy, with an "Introduction" by Bevis Hillier (Lond: Whittington P; rptd Lond: Heinemann Educational Books, 1972), pp. ix, 34-35.

In a discussion of DHL, Virginia Woolf "talked about working class writers being under a disadvantage, like women, as writers." DHL's paintings in the banned exhibition "were done pretty crudely. It looked as if he had taken off his clothes and then sat down and painted himself: working in the nude at the nude." However, "the Woolfs are taking his part over the prosecution."

3940 Kirkham, Michael. "D. H. Lawrence's *Last Poems*," D. H. LAWRENCE REVIEW, V (Summer 1972), 97-120.

DHL's *Last Poems* is best read "as a single work forming a loosely connected sequence of thought," the purpose of which is to "steady him in the face of death." Although much of the thought is inherited from previous work, "the challenge of the fact of death to a doctrine centered on physical existence" produced a new doctrine, metaphorically referring to the moon, by which death is transcended by the spirit alone. "Invocation to the Moon," "Prayer," and "The Man of Tyre" show the moon imagery in its function as imaginative memory which allows DHL to maintain his faithfulness to the physical and sexual and simultaneously to depart the physical body. A close examination of "The Man of Tyre," "For the Heroes Are Dipped in Scarlet," "The Greeks Are Coming," and "Lord's Prayer" shows DHL in sure command of rhythm and tone, exemplifying the organic relationship of his technique to his theme. [See also Michael Kirkham's correction of a printing error in this article in "Laurentiana," D. H. LAWRENCE REVIEW, V (Fall 1972), 332.]

3941 Kitazawa, Shigehisa. "Lawrence: Ai to Kodoku" (Lawrence: Love and Solitude), DOKKYO STUDIES IN ENGLISH (Dokkyo University), No. 6 (May 1972), 123-72; rvd and rptd as Chap. IV: "Love and Solitude," in D. H. LAWRENCE: HIS LITERATURE AND HIS LIFE, by Shigehisa Kitazawa (Tokyo: Bokusui-Shobo, 1973).

[The fourth article in a four-part series, based on an extensive study of the life and works of DHL, which seeks to reveal the "real substance" of his literature and its significance in our age. See also Shigehisa Kitazawa, "Lawrence Bungaku no Hassei" (The Early Works and Life of Lawrence), DOKKYO STUDIES IN

ENGLISH, No. 2 (June 1968), 92-124; "Lawrence: Ai no Tansaku" (Lawrence in Love), DOKKYO STUDIES IN ENGLISH, No. 3 (June 1969), 17-51; and "Lawrence: Ai o Koeru Mono" (Lawrence Beyond Love), DOKKYO STUDIES IN ENGLISH, No. 5 (March 1971), 1-50.] [In Japanese.]

3942 Konishi, Eirin. "Futatsu no Ikikata: D. H. Lawrence no *Koisuru Onnatachi* ni Tsuite" (Two Ways of Living: A Study of *Women in Love*), MEMOIRS OF THE FACULTY OF GENERAL EDUCATION (Ehime University), No. 4 (March 1972), 47-83.
[Through an analysis of Birkin and Gerald in *Women in Love*, the characteristics of DHL's thought are examined.] [In Japanese.]

3943 Kuramochi, Saburô. "*Sons and Lovers*: The Search for Freedom--An Un-Freudian Appreciation," BULLETIN (Kyôritsu Women's University), XIX (March 1972), 1-50.
Sons and Lovers is generally interpreted from the Freudian point of view. This essay, however, attempts to throw another light upon the novel and point out the son's psychic struggle with his dominant mother.

3944 Lachman, Roy Ernest. "The Open Form in Fiction," DISSERTATION ABSTRACTS INTERNATIONAL, XXXIII (1973), 5129A. Unpublished dissertation, University of Michigan, 1972.
[*The Rainbow* and *Kangaroo* are considered as examples of the "open form" in the novel.]

3945 "Laurentiana," D. H. LAWRENCE REVIEW, V (Fall 1972), 324-25.
[Brief notice of the publication in English of *John Thomas and Lady Jane*, the second version of *Lady Chatterley's Lover*, noting that Parkin, as the gamekeeper is called here, is "more aggressive" than Mellors and the ending "starkly unsentimental."]

3946 LeDoux, Larry V. "Christ and Isis: The Function of the Dying and Reviving God in *The Man Who Died*," D. H. LAWRENCE REVIEW, V (Summer 1972), 132-48.
Part I of *The Man Who Died*, first published as "The Escaped Cock," "focuses on Christ rising, healing, becoming increasingly aware of the urge of life" around him and within himself. Only in Part II "is Christ able to achieve an integration of mind and body, to accept the touch of physical vitality." Here "Christ is identified with the dying-reviving gods of near-Eastern mythology," demonstrating not only "the grounding of the gospel in the ancient archetype but also" the creation of "a new myth capable of revitalizing Christianity." The Isis-Osiris myth thus unifies both parts and embodies "the two major themes--the physical renewal of man and woman and the symbolic renewal of. . .sterile Christianity." Frazer's treatment of the dying-reviving god archetype in THE GOLDEN BOUGH illuminates DHL's novella and reveals the carefully worked out parallels between the story and the myth. The significance of Christ and the priestess lies in their humanity. It is "no ordinary man" who "revitalizes" her womb, however, but

"the prophet" of a new religion. DHL has "shown Christ learning how to love--vitally, with his body." "Lawrence's Christ bases himself and his church, and the society which it implies, on the rock of phallic marriage, . . . the most ancient and vital representation of Dionysian fecundity."

3947 Lee, Robin. "The 'Strange Reality of Otherness': D. H. Lawrence's Social Attitudes," STANDPUNTE, XXV (Aug 1972), 3-10.
DHL recognized the unconscious "quick self" as the *fons et origo* of human existence, and *Sons and Lovers* is a record of its protection from the possessive aspirations of others. *Fantasia of the Unconscious* stresses that this "spontaneous living soul" is in a constant state of flux and underlies all relationships. This doctrine of the spontaneous being lies at the core of the DHL novel, a genre he used to "*restore* into life" the sympathetic flow between man and woman that had once existed in Etruscan civilization but was repugnant to the people who banned DHL's books. His contemporaries believed in the sovereignty of the will and in the mechanistic forces of the industrial revolution. DHL's novels are a wholesome type of Sleeping Beauty myth, a utopian vision of "man alive" in a living rather than a mechanized community.

3948 Lucas, Robert [pseud of Robert Ehrenzweig]. FRIEDA VON RICHTHOFEN. IHR LEBEN MIT D. H. LAWRENCE (Frieda von Richthofen: Her Life with D. H. Lawrence) (Munich: Kindler, 1972); pub in English as FRIEDA LAWRENCE: THE STORY OF FRIEDA VON RICHTHOFEN AND D. H. LAWRENCE, trans by Geoffrey Skelton (NY: Viking P; Lond: Secker & Warburg; and N.p.: Macmillan of Canada, 1973).
[Briefly sketches the descent of the von Richthofen family and discusses in detail Frieda's youth in Metz, her education, her first love affairs, the unhappy relations of her parents, her marriage to Professor Ernest Weekley, and several additional affairs, one of them with the German psychiatrist Dr. Otto Gross, whose unconventional ideas on love impressed her.] After she eloped with DHL to escape unsatisfactory circumstances, their relations were happy, despite frequent disputes over DHL's demands for supremacy and Frieda's lifelong desire to keep contact with her children. The Lawrences' marriage, their negative experiences in England during the First World War, DHL's plans for a utopian colony called Rananim, their frequent stays in Germany and Italy, and their journeys to Ceylon, Australia, and Mexico left an impression on DHL's literary work. Relations between the two gradually worsened in the middle and late 1920s because of DHL's growing irritability, his sickness, and his later impotence. This explains Frieda's brief affair with John Middleton Murry and her later love of Angelo Ravagli, with whom she lived after DHL's death. The rivalries among Mabel Dodge Luhan, Dorothy Brett, and Frieda continued even after DHL's death and calmed down only after the dedication of the DHL commemorative chapel near Taos. DHL portrayed many of his acquaintances in his fiction and appeared in fictional guise in some novels by others. [DHL's works are discussed insofar as they reflect the development of his marriage to Frieda. It is argued that her influence on him was so profound that most of his work is "a continuous dialogue with Frieda, sometimes loving, sometimes full of hate."]

3949 Macaulay, Peter S. "Reviews," ENGLISH STUDIES (Amsterdam), LIII (Oct 1972), 473-75.

During his difficult time in the war years, DHL relied on the friendship of S. S. Koteliansky. *The Quest for Rananim: D. H. Lawrence's Letters to S. S. Koteliansky, 1914 to 1930*, ed by George J. Zytaruk, illuminates that relationship, including DHL's part in polishing Kot's translation of Leo Shestov's ALL THINGS ARE POSSIBLE, I. A. Bunin's "The Gentleman from San Francisco," and other Russian works. [Also reviews David Cavitch, D. H. LAWRENCE AND THE NEW WORLD (1969).]

3950 McCabe, Thomas H. "Rhythm as Form in Lawrence: 'The Horse Dealer's Daughter,'" PMLA: PUBLICATIONS OF THE MODERN LANGUAGE ASSOCIATION, LXXXVII (Jan 1972), 64-68.

DHL's use of rhythm, basic to his conception of the meaning of life, significantly shapes his fictional art, especially in the short stories. This rhythm takes two forms: (1) repetition of scenes, phrases, etc., and (2) such unique Laurentian devices as attraction-and-revulsion of characters and images expanded incrementally and progressively toward a psychic resolution. DHL disliked mechanical rhythm in which everything fits. "The Horse Dealer's Daughter" has DHL's unique rhythmic form, moving from death to life. When Dr. Fergusson rescues Mabel, using his warmth of life against the death represented by the pond and Mabel's will, he brings her back into the rhythm of life and a new relationship in which neither dominates but each has the courage to be true to himself.

3951 McDonald, Marguerite Bartelle. "An Evening with the Lawrences," D. H. LAWRENCE REVIEW, V (Spring 1972), 63-66.

[A memoir about the author's first meeting with DHL and Frieda in New York in September, 1925. Her husband, Edward D. McDonald, had recently published the first bibliography of DHL's writings. The reminiscence is notable for its picture of DHL as a charming, witty, and thoughtful dinner companion.]

3952 Marković, Vida E. "Ursula Brangwen," in PODELJENA LICNOST (Belgrade, 1972), pp. 74-94.

[In Serbo-Croatian, trans from the original English text.]

3953 Meinke, Norman Dale. "D. H. Lawrence: Vitalism and the Universal Indefinite," DISSERTATION ABSTRACTS INTERNATIONAL, XXXIII (1973), 6922A. Unpublished dissertation, University of Oregon, 1972.

3954 Mibu, Ikuo. "*Shirokujaku* no Kôsatsu--Lettie o Chûshin ni" (Lettie in *The White Peacock*), STUDIES IN ENGLISH LITERATURE, No. 5 (Feb 1972), 195-210.

Lettie in *The White Peacock* could not find a man who could satisfy her strong sense of vanity. She is a "white peacock." [In Japanese.]

3955 Montgomery, Lyna Lee. "The Phoenix: Its Use as a Literary Device in English from the Seventeenth Century to the Twentieth

Century," D. H. LAWRENCE REVIEW, V (Fall 1972), 268-323, espec pp. 320-21.
[Brief discussion of Tennessee Williams's use of the "phoenix symbol" as "the single whole metaphor for the little one-act play about the death of Lawrence, I RISE IN FLAME, CRIED THE PHOENIX," and of several Lawrentian themes developed there.]

3956 Moore, Harry T. "D. H. Lawrence to Henry Savage: Two Further Letters," YALE UNIVERSITY LIBRARY GAZETTE, XLVI (April 1972), 262-67.
Two undated letters from DHL to Henry Savage (31 October 1913 and 15 November 1913?) extend the argument of his letter to Ernest Collings (17 January 1913) on his belief in "the blood, the flesh, as being wiser than the intellect." DHL maintains that " 'spirit and flesh should be finely balanced,' but...that they are not in juxtaposition." [The text of the two letters, first published here, is reprinted in *The Letters of D. H. Lawrence*, Vol. II, ed by George J. Zytaruk and James T. Boulton (Cambridge: Cambridge UP, 1981), pp. 94-96 and 100-2. See also Harry T. Moore, "D. H. Lawrence to Henry Savage: An Introductory Note," YALE UNIVERSITY LIBRARY GAZETTE, XXIV (July 1959), 24-33.]

3957 Moore, Harry T. "*John Thomas and Lady Jane*," NEW YORK TIMES BOOK REVIEW, 27 Aug 1972, p. 7.
John Thomas and Lady Jane gives fresh views on *Lady Chatterley's Lover* and new perspectives on DHL's entire work. It is, furthermore, superior to *Lady Chatterley's Lover* in that the narrator presents the story more intensely and more satisfactorily; the characters are more convincing and more vital; the love scenes are more candid, vivid, and tender; and Sir Clifford Chatterley is more credible and sympathetic than the caricature in the third version of the novel.

3958 Mori, Haruhide. "Ushinawareta Bunmyaku--Lawrence ni Okeru Kigekisei" (A Lost Trend--Lawrence's Comic Spirit), KÔBE MISCELLANY (Kôbe University), No. 6 (1972), 119-33.
[In Japanese.]

3959 Moynahan, Julian. "Pastoralism as Culture and Counter-Culture in English Fiction, 1800-1928," NOVEL: A FORUM ON FICTION, VI (Fall 1972), 33-34.
Aware of the death of feeling in the divorce between culture and agriculture, DHL preserved the English tradition of "deep pastoral," as in Emily Brontë's WUTHERING HEIGHTS, as opposed to "mere pastoral," by transforming it. He keeps elements of maiden worship and nature, but turns against culture, hoping for its regeneration through passional relationships.

3960 Moynahan, Julian. "Will the Real Lady Chatterley...," WASHINGTON POST BOOK WORLD, 27 Aug 1972, pp. 1, 15.
From the outset of work on the subject of his three versions of *Lady Chatterley's Lover*, DHL recognized "that a lot of class difference vanishes when people take their clothes off, and that the Anglo-Saxon four-letter words for bodily parts and

functions form a vocabulary that is neither 'low' nor 'high' but essentially classless." *The First Lady Chatterley*, in its bullying and bitterness, is untrue to "the realities of the British class system." *Lady Chatterley's Lover* will "always be preferred for its beautiful rituals of lovemaking, for its magical descriptions of the woodland realm, for its supremely satisfying rendering of the slow awakening of a wholesome passion." *John Thomas and Lady Jane*, which ends realistically with another gamekeeper's interrupting the couple's lovemaking, is "the most touching, believable and contemporary version." [Illustrated with photograph of DHL.]

3961 Mueller, William R. "D. H. Lawrence: The Paradisal Quest," CELEBRATION OF LIFE: STUDIES IN MODERN FICTION (NY: Sheed & Ward, 1972), pp. 145, 146, 148-68, 188, 273-74.

DHL's characters, most often seen in conjunction with other characters, depend less on solitary introspection than characters in Joyce or Sartre. The major characters in *Sons and Lovers, The Rainbow, Women in Love,* and *Lady Chatterley's Lover* all seek a relationship which is "mutually fulfilling" and which enables them, as a couple, "to glimpse paradise." The intensity and complexity of the male-female relationships in DHL is greater than that of characters in Mann, Conrad, and Sartre. For DHL, the male-female bond is the "ground basis for the paradisal quest which informs the whole of his own life and that of his fiction as well." In *The Rainbow*, Tom Brangwen always believes that Lydia alone "can bring him to human completion." The material success of Gerald Crich or Sir Clifford Chatterley is brutal and incomplete because they have not really known women. DHL believed that women also were capable of "brutal, violent power": in their effort to extend their horizons, Gertrude Morel, Anna Brangwen, and Gudrun Brangwen master their men. There needs to be a balance, in DHL's mythology, between sun and moon, between the power which unifies and merges and that which makes each separate being distinct and integral. DHL writes vividly and poignantly of the essential aloneness of the individual, but he always searches for those rare moments of conjunction with another--the lost paradise.

3962 Nardi, Piero. "Un amore di Lawrence" (A Woman Who Attracted Lawrence), LA FIERA LETTERARIA (Rome), 13 Feb 1972, pp. 15-17.

In 1913 DHL met the Asquiths for the first time, and his personality struck them. Lady Cynthia Asquith was then very young and beautiful, and DHL showed a particular interest in her, even though he was waiting for Frieda's divorce. His admiration for Lady Cynthia is apparent in some of his writings and perhaps also in some paintings. [In Italian.]

3963 Nardi, Piero. "Introduzione" (Introduction), *Il purosangue (St. Mawr)* (Milan: A. Mondadori, 1972), pp. 21-27.

St. Mawr is a protest against western civilization. The main character of this novel is a stallion, representing real life, in contrast with an English gentleman who is a symbol of European decadence. [In Italian.]

3964 Oates, Joyce Carol. "Candid Revelations: On *The Complete Poems of D. H. Lawrence*," AMERICAN POETRY REVIEW, I (Nov-Dec 1972), 11-13; rptd as "The Candid Revelation: Lawrence's Aesthetics," in THE HOSTILE SUN: THE POETRY OF D. H. LAWRENCE, by Joyce Carol Oates (Los Angeles: Black Sparrow P, 1973), pp. 9-22.

Judgment becomes irrelevant because reading DHL's poems becomes a mystical experience of life celebration. He seeks to transcend the private self to create a more than human equilibrium. The poems in *Birds, Beasts and Flowers* are remarkable because they take their subjects seriously. DHL's "real technique" is in questions, not answers, in presenting the process of thinking, not formal structures.

3965 Oates, Joyce Carol. "The Hostile Sun: The Poetry of D. H. Lawrence," MASSACHUSETTS REVIEW, XIII (Autumn 1972), 639-56; slightly rvd and rptd as "New Heaven and Earth: Lawrence's Transformations," in THE HOSTILE SUN: THE POETRY OF D. H. LAWRENCE, by Joyce Carol Oates (Los Angeles: Black Sparrow P, 1973), pp. 23-57; and rptd as "The Hostile Sun: The Poetry of D. H. Lawrence," in NEW HEAVEN, NEW EARTH: THE VISIONARY EXPERIENCE IN LITERATURE, by Joyce Carol Oates (NY: Vanguard, 1974), pp. 37-81.

DHL's main battle is between the self and its "Other," symbolized by the sun. In *Look! We Have Come Through!* DHL's marriage "must be considered epiphenomenal in relationship to the deeper, less personal emotions he attempts to comprehend." "New Heaven and Earth" shows the discovery of the "other," as "Humiliation" protests against it. The treatment of the "otherness" of animals in *Birds, Beasts and Flowers* is unique in poetry. "The He-Goat" shows the necessity of a contrary force to the ego, paralleling Freud's theories in CIVILIZATION AND ITS DISCONTENTS, but recognizing the "absolute need for sublimation of basic instincts." DHL worships the sun because it is hostile; he is not a Romantic because he does not seek oneness with nature. DHL's writing, fine when he worships the "Other," is forced when he tries to usurp its position.

3966 Ogawa, Yoshio. "Sei no Shôka (*Shinda Otoko* o Chûshin ni)" (The Sublimation of 'Sex'--Chiefly Concerning *The Man Who Died*), BULLETIN OF ST. MARGARET'S (St. Margaret's Junior College), No. 4 (Dec 1972), 83-118.

[Examines the significance of sex as an approach to DHL's works. Part I explains the revival in *The Man Who Died* of the risen man's sexual instinct; the illicit union of the slaves is the prelude to the greater life of the flesh. Part II examines DHL's expression of sexuality in *The Rainbow* and *Lady Chatterley's Lover* as the inner history of woman's sexuality: a development from sensuality to emotion, from emotion to idea, through eight different experiences--the development, that is, from foreignness to response, from response to affection. Finally, in *The Man Who Died*, the carnal communion is the sublimation of the secular union of the flesh.] [In Japanese.]

3967 Ohkawa, Hiroshi. "Ishiki Tankyûsha D. H. Lawrence--Shojosaku *Shirokujaku* Ron" (D. H. Lawrence: Adventurer into Consciousness--On *The White Peacock*), JOURNAL OF THE FACULTY OF FOREIGN LANGUAGES (Komazawa University), No. 8 (March 1972), 52-65.
[On DHL's originality in his first novel, *The White Peacock*, and its connection with his later works.] [In Japanese.]

3968 Ohkawa, Hiroshi. "Bunmei to Kyôki--D. H. Lawrence no *Shojo to Jipushi* Ron" (Our Mad Civilization--On D. H. Lawrence's *The Virgin and the Gipsy*), JOURNAL OF THE FACULTY OF FOREIGN LANGUAGES (Komazawa University), No. 8 (March 1972), 114-43.
[With references to *The Virgin and the Gipsy*, the writer discusses the difficulty of being resurrected and the way of escaping from the pressures of the elderly.] [In Japanese.]

3969 Ohkawa, Hiroshi. "Rogosu to Nikutai no Bunri--D. H. Lawrence no *Shinda Otoko* Ron" (The Separation of the Logos from the Body--On D. H. Lawrence's *The Man Who Died*), JOURNAL OF FOREIGN LITERATURE (Komazawa University), No. 8 (Nov 1972), 37-52.
[On the dual meanings of death and the resurrection of the body in *The Man Who Died*.] [In Japanese.]

3970 Olivier, T. "The Culture Chasm: Bantu Education and the Use of English," THEORIA, XXXIX (Oct 1972), 49-60.
[Comments are reproduced from essays by English 1 students on DHL's poem "Piano" to demonstrate how very little English language and Western Culture the isolationist Bantu Education Department has taught the African to whom it grants university entrance.] [Compare I. A. Richards's account of Cambridge undergraduates' responses to "Piano" in "Poem 8," PRACTICAL CRITICISM (Lond: K. Paul, Trench, Tribner; NY: Harcourt Brace & World, 1929), pp. 99-112.]

3971 Orr, Christopher James. "D. H. Lawrence: The Evolution of His Political Thought 1914-1930," DISSERTATION ABSTRACTS INTERNATIONAL, XXXIII (1973), 6926A-27A. Unpublished dissertation, Pennsylvania State University, 1972.

3972 Osman, Arthur. "The Town Lawrence Forsook," TIMES (Lond), 16 Nov 1972, p. 1.
[News feature.] The Nottinghamshire County Council's "proposal to rehabilitate the Erewash valley...as a tourist attraction associated with Lawrence" has been met with "a noticeable lack of warmth" from some quarters in Eastwood, where DHL is "still regarded as 'that mucky man.'" The "anti-Lawrence faction" was led by Alderman Charles Limb, who thought Willy Hopkin more significant and "a marvelous chap." DHL's childhood home is being restored by the Association

of Young Writers, and the County Council is considering establishment of "a Lawrence centre." [Illustrated with photos of DHL and Hopkin.]

3973 Paik, Nack-Chung. "A Study of *The Rainbow* and *Women in Love* as Expressions of D. H. Lawrence's Thinking on Modern Civilization." Unpublished dissertation, Harvard University, 1972. [Listed in AMERICAN DOCTORAL DISSERTATIONS 1972-73 (Ann Arbor, MI: University Microfilm International, 1975), p. 315.]

3974 Plant, Raymond. "Social Thought," in THE TWENTIETH-CENTURY MIND: HISTORY, IDEAS, AND LITERATURE IN BRITAIN, ed by C. B. Cox and A. E. Dyson, Vol. II: 1918-1945 (Lond, Oxford, & NY: Oxford UP, 1972), pp. 68-105, espec pp. 70, 88, 97-98.
The twentieth-century "critique of industrialism found its most influential expression in [R. H.] Tawney's ACQUISITIVE SOCIETY, and in some novels and essays of D. H. Lawrence." Gerald Crich's purely functional approach to the management of industry in *Women in Love* is comparable to the replacement of " 'the conception of purpose by that of mechanism' " in the latter seventeenth century as discussed by Tawney.

3975 "Poetry," TIMES LITERARY SUPPLEMENT (Lond), 25 Aug 1972, p. 1006.
D. H. Lawrence: Selected Poems, ed by Keith Sagar, fills the need for "a good comprehensive selection of Lawrence's poetry," though every reader will notice some noteworthy omissions.

3976 "Poetry," TIMES LITERARY SUPPLEMENT (Lond), 1 Dec 1972, p. 1469.
The third edition of *The Complete Poems of D. H. Lawrence,* ed by Vivian de Sola Pinto and Warren Roberts, now the sole charge of Roberts, "has gone to more authoritative manuscripts or early published texts for some of the last group of poems" and includes twelve representative poems from the "Clarke Notebook," which was formerly owned by Ada Lawrence Clarke. Comparison of early variants with later drafts of DHL's poems shows that his revised versions were usually improvements.

3977 Pratt, Annis. "Women and Nature in Modern Fiction," CONTEMPORARY LITERATURE, XIII (Autumn 1972), 481-83.
Sons and Lovers, a *Künstlerroman* like May Sinclair's MARY OLIVIER, A LIFE and James Joyce's A PORTRAIT OF THE ARTIST AS A YOUNG MAN, is the narrative of a young artist emerging from an "intensely Oedipal" family situation. "Paul finds Miriam's naturism," her love and handling of flowers, "as distasteful as her earlier mysticism," reflecting DHL's disapproval of a "female phenomenon." Her "appreciation of nature, a force emanating from the center of her own psyche, is devalued" because it does not derive from submissiveness. Similarly, "Clara is not a 'she' but an 'it' to Paul," who reduces her to a "vaguely representative bubble." After literally murdering his mother, Paul heads "towards the city in quest of an identity which has had as its preliminary phase a trial-by-woman."

3978 Pugh, Bridget. THE COUNTRY OF MY HEART: A LOCAL GUIDE TO D. H. LAWRENCE (Nottingham: Nottinghamshire Local History Council, 1972).

[A description of the "Lawrence country" of Eastwood, Nottingham, and the surrounding countryside, including brief synopses of the novels, plays, and several stories which have Eastwood, Nottingham, Derbyshire, and the surrounding rural areas as major settings. DHL's descriptions of local people and places and how they sometimes differ from the actual people and places are discussed, as well as DHL's suppression of personal feeling in order to depict factual details. Illustrated with several photographs, drawings, and maps, and four tours that can be made in the area, and photographs from plays and stills from films made from DHL's works.]

3979 Rachman, Shalom. "Art and Value in D. H. Lawrence's *Women in Love*," D. H. LAWRENCE REVIEW, V (Spring 1972), 1-25.

The power in DHL's writings does not "emanate from wholeness of being and inner strength, but rather from. . .an intense struggle to devise illusory theories for the. . .justification of self and the denigration of social reality." DHL's supreme value, the " 'spontaneous-creative fulness of being,' " does not mean "self-fulfillment" but "a cultivation of a mystical state, . . .an evasion of responsibility to one's fellow men and to society." "*Women in Love* is an achievement of verbal consciousness" and "a concrete demonstration of a personal vision and belief," but its picture of contemporary society is inaccurate: the presentation of industry, for example, ignores both the pressing problems and the possibilities which confront industry. Gerald Crich is not a tragic figure but "a mistake of nature" who arouses our wonder but not pity or terror. In Birkin, DHL provides a definition and an example of selfishness that can hardly be surpassed. "*Women in Love* is undoubtedly a work of art," but "we would do well to pay close attention to the values embodied in the book before making any exaggerated claims for them."

3980 Rickards, Maurice. WHERE THEY LIVED IN LONDON (Lond: David & Charles; NY: Taplinger, 1972), pp. 82-83.

DHL stayed in the ground floor flat at Byron Villas, Vale of Health, London NW3, in the fall of 1915 at the time of the suppression of *The Rainbow*. [Photographs of an external view of the villas, Jan Juta's portrait of DHL, a First World War poster.]

3981 Rossi, Patrizio. "Lawrence's Two Foxes: A Comparison of the Texts," ESSAYS IN CRITICISM, XXII (July 1972), 265-78.

DHL seems to have regarded the first version of *The Fox* as little more than a fairy tale of the sleeping princess. It contains no violence, not even the killing of the fox, and ends with the three principals in a state of truce. The additions, which occur mainly in the last parts of the published version, do not take into account some important matters contained in the first version; hence there are inconsistencies in the story as a whole.

3982 Rowland, Paul Gabriel. "The Precarious Prophets, Thomas Carlyle and D. H. Lawrence." Unpublished dissertation, University of Sussex, 1972. [Listed in Lawrence F. McNamee, DISSERTATIONS IN ENGLISH AND AMERICAN LITERATURE, SUPP II (NY and Lond: Bowker, 1974), p. 522.]

3983 Ruthven, K. K. "On the So-Called Fascism of Some Modernist Writers," SOUTHERN REVIEW (Adelaide), V (Sept 1972), 225-30.

The term "fascism" meant something different during the period *l'entre deux guerres* than it did after World War II and than it does now. Writers such as Yeats, DHL, Pound, Eliot, and Wyndham Lewis have been called fascists, and people are as shocked and titillated by this as they used to be by evidence of sexual deviancy. It is important to see "the distortions which result when a literary critic assumes that his key-term is in no way problematic."

3984 Sagar, Keith. "Introduction," *D. H. Lawrence: Selected Poems,* ed by Keith Sagar (Harmondsworth, Middlesex, England: Penguin Books, 1972), pp. 11-17.

DHL's poems need to be read in selection. These 150 out of nearly 1,000 poems are those on which DHL's claim to greatness rests, and DHL is a great poet in every sense, including the technical. Early versions rather than the versions in *The Collected Poems of D. H. Lawrence* (1928) are used here because it is more important to have what DHL wrote than what he thought he should have written. DHL comes to maturity as man and poet in *Look! We Have Come Through!,* the discipline of which is spiritual, emotional, and linguistic. *Birds, Beasts and Flowers* presents DHL's "almost occult" penetration into other beings, dramatic confrontations between the human and the non-human potently evoking spirit of place. In *Last Poems* DHL is no longer flippant, exasperated, or spiteful, as he often was in *Pansies,* and the clarity and splendor of these poems testify to DHL's depth of vision.

3985 Sasaki, Manabu. "D. H. Lawrence no Ai ni Tsuite" (On the Laurentian Conception of Love), BULLETIN OF REITAKU UNIVERSITY, XIII (March 1972), 20-71.

It is DHL's firm belief that the ideal of Christianity is impossible because it makes demands greater than the nature of man can bear. If you love your neighbor as yourself, then you run the risk of being absorbed by him. In the end, Christ's way of loving people is all resistance and no love--which, in the opinion of the author of *Apocalypse,* is the history of democracy. The risen man in *The Man Who Died* says, " 'but my mission is over, and my teaching is finished, and death has saved me from my own salvation.' " [In Japanese.]

3986 Schorer, Mark. "A Book So Bad It Was Impossible to Put Down," NEW YORK TIMES BOOK REVIEW, 16 Jan 1972.

[This review of Joseph Foster, D. H. LAWRENCE IN TAOS (1972), refutes Foster's claim to intimate knowledge of DHL; briefly recounts the known facts of the Lawrences' stay in America; shows that many of Foster's "reminiscences" are "fictionalized" from memoirs by others and the "reported dialogues...paraphrases or almost direct quotations from Lawrence's own fiction" (examples in DHL's work cited by page number); and refutes Foster's description of the manuscript of *Sons and Lovers.*]

3987 Schulman, Norma Miriam. "D. H. Lawrence's *Birds, Beasts and Flowers:* Five Kinds of Poetry," DISSERTATION ABSTRACTS INTERNATIONAL, XXXIV (1973), 789A. Unpublished dissertation, Tufts University, 1972.

3988 Sepčić, Višnja. "Realism Versus Symbolism: The Double Patterning of *Sons and Lovers,*" STUDIA ROMANICA ET ANGLICA ZAGRABIENSIA, Nos. 33-36 (1972-1973), 185-208; also pub in Serbo-Croatian as "No raskršću realizma i simbolizma" (At the Crossroads of Realism and Symbolism), UMJETNOST RIJEČI, No. 1 (1975), 29-52 [not seen in this form].

Sons and Lovers, a "double-faced novel...with one face turned...towards the traditional realistic novel with its vivid description of characters and milieus, and with the other face...towards the modern psychological novel which probes the deeper layers of personality," "follows the characteristic turn of twentieth-century literature from the external to the internal, from large social panoramas to the particularities of the inner life of an individual." The scene in which William's coffin is brought home (Chap. VI) illustrates DHL's mastery of realistic scenic representation, and the scene between Walter and Gertrude after Morel cuts little William's hair (Chap. I) illustrates DHL's method of presenting "the emotional and erotic life of his characters." [Both scenes are quoted and examined in detail.] "The swing scene between Paul and Miriam" and "the wild-rose bush episode" (Chap. VII), which "fuses in an indissoluble union the two levels of meaning, literal and metaphorical," "are on the main line of development" leading to the great novels of DHL's next phase. [The two scenes are quoted and examined in detail.] Employing both the "creative imagination" and "the insights gained by painful personal experience," DHL "released the tragical potential of his complex theme" "to suggest the universal in a highly specific local milieu and subtly to define, in its modern disguise, an archetypal human experience."

3989 Shakir, Evelyn Catherine. "'New Blossoms of Me'--The Poetry of D. H. Lawrence," DISSERTATION ABSTRACTS INTERNATIONAL, XXXIII (1972), 1742A. Unpublished dissertation, Boston University, 1972.

3990 Sharma, Radhe S. "D. H. Lawrence's *The Rainbow:* A Note on the Contextuality of the Symbol," OSMANIA JOURNAL OF ENGLISH STUDIES (Hyderabad, India), IX, No. 1 (1972), 21-25.

Because the changing hues of the rainbow symbolize the changing layers of human consciousness, it is organically linked with the thematic and symbolic structure of the novel.

3991 Shields, E. F. "Broken Vision in Lawrence's *The Fox,*" STUDIES IN SHORT FICTION, IX (Fall 1972), 353-63.

The revised ending of *The Fox,* though close to being right, is distracting and misleading. This is caused by a split in the persona of the narrator: the persona of the first part is DHL the artist; that of the second part is DHL the thinker. Two years after the first version, DHL tried and failed to recapture his artistic vision.

    3992 Shimizu, Kohya. "*Lady Chatterley's Lover* Shiron--Koritsu to Kizuna no Gyakusetsu o Megutte" (On *Lady Chatterley's Lover*--Concerning the Paradox between Isolation and Bond), BULLETIN OF STUDIES IN HUMANITY (Kagawa University), No. 32 (March 1972), 47-73.

The ambiguity between isolation and bond in DHL's last phase may be seen in a comparison among three characters, Connie, Clifford, and Mellors, in *Lady Chatterley's Lover*. [In Japanese.]

    3993 Silet, Charles L. P. "A Checklist of THE SEVEN ARTS," SERIF, IX (Summer 1972), 15-21.

THE SEVEN ARTS, which lasted one year (twelve issues), from November 1916 through October 1917, included two works of fiction by DHL: "The Mortal Coil" in the ninth issue, pp. 280-305, and "The Thimble" in the fifth, pp. 435-48.

    3994 Skinner, M[ary] L[ouise]. THE FIFTH SPARROW (Sydney, Australia: Sydney UP, 1972; Lond: Angus & Robertson, 1973), pp. 109-33.

[Autobiography.] DHL was "a man of great spiritual integrity who had not discarded the long long thoughts of boyhood--nor a boy's wilfulness and explosive fits of temper and defiance of authority." The hero of *The Boy in the Bush* [drawn in the likeness of Mollie Skinner's brother] is only a slight exaggeration of his real-life counterpart. The identity of DHL's collaborator on *The Boy in the Bush* was a matter of confusion and controversy among contemporary critics.

    3995 Skurnick, Blanche Jacqueline. "D. H. Lawrence: A Study of His Shorter Fiction," DISSERTATION ABSTRACTS INTERNATIONAL, XXXIII (1972), 330A. Unpublished dissertation, Columbia University, 1972.

    3996 Smith, Grover. FORD MADOX FORD (NY and Lond: Columbia UP [Columbia Essays on Modern Writers, No. 63], 1972), pp. 3, 18, 42-43.

DHL possibly influenced Ford's poetry. "The two have in common an intense, subjective relation between poet and poem, *in* the poem, and also an 'imagistic' technique allied to Ford's prose impressionism."

    3997 "*Sons and Lovers*," PAUNCH, No. 35 (1972), pp. 26-31.

[After reading *Sons and Lovers*, the anonymous writer recognized his own Oedipal relationships with his parents.]

    3998 Squires, Michael. "Pastoral Patterns and Pastoral Variants in *Lady Chatterley's Lover*," ELH, XXXIX (March 1972), 129-46; rvd and rptd as Chap. IX: "*Lady Chatterley's Lover:* 'Pure Seclusion,'" in THE PASTORAL NOVEL: STUDIES IN GEORGE ELIOT,

THOMAS HARDY, AND D. H. LAWRENCE, by Michael Squires (Charlottesville: UP of Virginia, 1974), pp. 196-212.

Critical focus on *Lady Chatterley's Lover* should be shifted from the ethical, social, and sexual issues to an examination of the novel as a modern adaptation of the pastoral tradition. DHL's continuation of pastoral conventions can be recognized, first, in the plot, which involves a journey from a sophisticated, corrupt, urban world to an idealized world of rural innocence, and second, in the blending into the structure of three variant traditions--the pastoral of innocence, the pastoral of solitude, and the pastoral of happiness. The pastoral of innocence can be seen in Connie's escape into a world characterized by "simplicity, natural beauty, and rejection of money and power"; the pastoral of solitude in the retreat of Mellors, who wishes to escape industrialized society and domineering women; and the pastoral of happiness in the definition of happiness as the consummation of erotic desire. DHL departs from the traditional pastoral pattern of "retreat--reorientation--return" by having his lovers permanently retreat to an unindustrialized Canada at the end of the novel rather than using the perspective achieved through pastoral retreat to deal more effectively with the real world. This deviation from tradition is a weakness which mars the universality of the novel.

3999 Stein, Marian L. "Affirmations and Negations: Lawrence's 'Whitman' and Whitman's Open Road," **WALT WHITMAN REVIEW,** XVIII (1972), 63-67.

DHL attacks Whitman for his failure to divorce "sympathy" from Jesus' "love" and Paul's "charity." However, DHL takes partial statements for the whole. A question in "To a Common Prostitute," which neither Whitman nor DHL resolves, is whether the act can be separated from the person. Whitman, because he is writing poetry, need not define his assumptions and terms; but DHL needs to in his analytical essay. Perhaps the best answer is Whitman's admission of self-contradiction in "Song of Myself."

4000 Stohl, Johan H. "D. H. Lawrence and the Religious Imagination: A Study of Sex, Rhetoric, and Ritual in the Major Novels." Unpublished dissertation, University of Chicago, 1972. [Listed in AMERICAN DOCTORAL DISSERTATIONS 1971-72 (Ann Arbor, MI: University Microfilm International, 1974), p. 332.]

4001 Swigg, Richard. LAWRENCE, HARDY, AND AMERICAN LITERATURE (Lond and NY: Oxford UP, 1972).

[Through the focus of Thomas Hardy's art and ideas, Part I examines DHL's view of "Tragedy and the Unconscious," as expressed in *The White Peacock, The Trespasser, Sons and Lovers, The Rainbow, Women in Love,* and the *Study of Thomas Hardy.* Part II, "Four Americans and the Adversities of Morality," examines the philosophic "adaptations" of Poe, Hawthorne, Melville, and Cooper. Part III, "Lawrence and the American Fiction," relates *Studies in Classic American Literature* (both the first and final versions), *The Rainbow,* and *Women in Love* to American literature.] In the preface to *Touch and Go,* DHL observes that tragedy is a " 'working out of some passional problem within the soul of man,' "a working out in which there must be a " 'supreme *struggle.*' " In this view, tragedy is "a forward movement undertaken by the soul at a high level of self-responsibility." Without this "struggle into consciousness," there is simply "passive fatalism." In his early novels, DHL is unable to work free of blind necessity, but in *The Rainbow* and *Women in Love,* he creates "a new kind of moral art" which refuses to settle for absolutes or "inherited forms of fatalism." Through his reading of Hardy, Poe, Hawthorne, Melville, and Cooper, DHL was able to sharpen his sense of tragic dilemma, of what he calls the "passional problem." There are two stages in DHL's reading of Hardy and the Americans--an early stage and a "re-reading and re-assessment." The later reading was tempered by his own struggle with artistic creation and search for meaning. In DHL's writing from *The White Peacock* to *Women in Love* and in his essays on American literature, his "struggle with his own and others' writing is at its most illuminating." DHL was influenced especially by Hardy's technique of admitting tragedy through a "middle distance" in his works, of standing "behind an intervening filter or 'philosophy' partly sheltered from the...contingency." Poe, Hawthorne, Melville, and Cooper each attempted to come to terms with the vast, white waste of American moral ambiguity, and consciously to create meaning and morality from that waste, hence to create the possibility for tragedy. [Extensive discussion.] DHL in *Studies in Classic American Literature* finds that he also must shed the "discriminating European sensibility" to make an "imaginative transfer to America." DHL, in *Women in Love,* is "nearer than ever before to the specially American quality of disorder"; against this false freedom in disorder, DHL posits the freedom of finding "something you really *positively want to be.*" In his essay on Cooper, DHL sees true myth as concerned not with disintegration but with the "'onward adventure of the integral soul'" toward an organic reality.

4002 Tabuchi, Hiroyuki. "D. H. Lawrence no *Seishin-Bunseki to Muishiki* Oyobi *Muishiki no Gensôkyoku* Kanken (2)" (On D. H. Lawrence's *Psychoanalysis and the Unconscious* and *Fantasia of the Unconscious* [2]), KEIZAI SHŪSHI (Nihon University), XLII (Nov 1972), 56-68.

[Second of two articles on *Psychoanalysis and the Unconscious* and *Fantasia of the Unconscious.*] It is quite clear that in his two essays on the unconscious, DHL praises the vital blood-sexual relationship between man and woman and the dynamic interchanges of life inspired by it. He seems, however, to hesitate in admiring sex in the mere monistic conception because "sex" belongs to the night-self, which it is desirable to balance with the day-self. After all, what DHL seeks in these two essays is "dualism," "harmony," or "unison," which should be the one and only way to perfect active spontaneity. [Discusses the relation between man and woman, and between men and men, and the quest for harmony between passion and intellect.] [See also Hiroyuki Tabuchi, "D. H. Lawrence no *Seishin-Bunseki to Muishiki* Oyobi *Muishiki no Gensôkyoku* Kanken (1)" (On D. H. Lawrence's *Psychoanalysis and the Unconscious* and *Fantasia of the Unconscious* [1]), KEIZAI SHUSHI (Nihon University), XLI (Nov 1971), 43-53.] [In Japanese.]

4003 Tenenbaum, Elizabeth B. "Concepts of the Self in the Modern Novel." Unpublished dissertation, Stanford University, 1972. [Listed in Lawrence F. McNamee, DISSERTATIONS IN ENGLISH AND AMERICAN LITERATURE, SUPP II (NY and Lond: Bowker, 1974), p. 363] ; rvd and pub as THE PROBLEMATIC SELF: APPROACHES TO IDENTITY IN STENDHAL, D. H. LAWRENCE, AND MAL-RAUX (Cambridge, MA, and Lond: Harvard UP, 1977).

4004 Terry, Chris J. "F. W. Nietzsche and D. H. Lawrence: A Comparative Study." Unpublished dissertation, Kent University at Canterbury, 1972. [Listed in Geoffrey M. Paterson and Joan E. Hardy (eds), INDEX TO THESES, XXIII (1972-73) (Lond: Aslib, 1975).]

4005 Thulin, Richard Lee. "Men and Women in the Writings of David Herbert Lawrence and of Certain Contemporary Theologians: A Dialogue in Theology and Literature," DISSERTATION ABSTRACTS INTERNATIONAL, XXXIII (1972), 2487A. Unpublished dissertation, Boston University School of Theology, 1972.

4006 Toyokuni, Takashi. "D. H. Lawrence's *The Fox*--The Triumph of the Man's World," MEMOIRS OF THE MURORAN INSTITUTE OF TECHNOLOGY, VII, No. 3 (Sept 1972), 351-62.
[Analyzes the world of *The Fox,* elucidating the conflict between the two worlds--the world of man and that of woman--and the triumph of the man's world.]

4007 Toyokuni, Takashi. "D. H. Lawrence's *The Ladybird*--A Modern Myth," ENGLISH LITERATURE IN HOKKAIDO (Muroran Institute of Technology), No. 17 (June 1972), 40-53.
[Analyzes *The Ladybird* from the standpoint of the Nietzschean view of myth--the conflict and harmony in the two worlds of Dionysus and Apollo--and evaluates the novel.]

4008 Tudor, Kathleen Richardson. "The Androgynous Mind in W. B. Yeats, D. H. Lawrence, Virginia Woolf and Dorothy Richardson," DISSERTATION ABSTRACTS INTERNATIONAL, XXXV (1974), 1126A-27A. Unpublished dissertation, University of Toronto, 1972.

4009 Turroni, Giuseppe. *"Donne in Amore"* (*Women in Love*), FILMCRITICA (Rome), XXIII (March 1972), 153.
The film version of *Women in Love* owes something to the false gothic of Ronald Firbank as well as to the master, DHL. [In Italian.]

4010 Ulmer, Gregory Leland. "D. H. Lawrence and the Rousseau Tradition," DISSERTATION ABSTRACTS INTERNATIONAL, XXXIII (1973), 4436A-37A. Unpublished dissertation, Brown University, 1972.

4011 Vaccarelli, Mary Motta. "Nostalgia for Sicily: The Fictional Modes of Giovanni Verga and D. H. Lawrence," DISSERTATION

ABSTRACTS INTERNATIONAL, XXXII (1972), 7013A. Unpublished dissertation, Catholic University of America, 1972.

4012 Van Tassel, Daniel E. "The Search for Manhood in D. H. Lawrence's *Sons and Lovers*," COSTERUS, No. 3 (1972), 197-210.

The ambiguity of love in the title of *Sons and Lovers* suggests the dilemma Paul faces in his search for manhood. His inordinate intimacy with his mother makes it difficult to harmonize mother love with his growing need for adult love. Frustrated love leads to unconscious cruelty towards Clara and especially Miriam. The novel can be analyzed as a series of triangles with Paul at an angle, tugged in two unsatisfactory directions.

4013 Vickery, John B. "*The Plumed Serpent* and the Reviving God," JOURNAL OF MODERN LITERATURE, II (Nov 1972), 505-32; rvd and rptd in Chap. IV: "Myth and Character: The Dialectic of Scapegoat and Reviving God," in MYTHS AND TEXTS: STRATEGIES OF INCORPORATION AND DISPLACEMENT, by John B. Vickery (Baton Rouge and Lond: Louisiana State UP, 1983), pp. 102-31.

We see the influence of Frazer's THE GOLDEN BOUGH on DHL's *The Plumed Serpent* in the mimetic pattern of relationships between the human and the mythic, especially the resurrection of the god from a waste land world. DHL's satiric mode, as seen in the bullfight scene, draws the mythic into the human action, following Kate's initial rejection of her quest for enlightenment. Death, the victim, and purification are all revealed through ritual; as Kate observes these, she seeks the appropriate way. [This thesis is explored through detailed analysis of *The Plumed Serpent*.]

4014 Von Broembsen, Francesca Ferraris. "Moses Off the Mountain: Readings in Paul Valery and D. H. Lawrence." Unpublished dissertation, Harvard University, 1972. [Listed in AMERICAN DOCTORAL DISSERTATIONS 1971-72 (Ann Arbor, MI: University Microfilm International, 1974), p. 231.]

4015 Von Eckardt, Wolf. "Visiting Frieda: The Woman in D. H. Lawrence's Life," WASHINGTON POST BOOK WORLD, 27 Aug 1972, pp. 2, 8.

[An account of the author's visit in summer 1941 to Frieda Lawrence and Angelo Ravagli at Kiowa Ranch near Taos. The author is related to Frieda through her sister, Else Jaffe.]

4016 Wagner, Geoffrey. ANOTHER AMERICA: IN SEARCH OF CANYONS (Lond: Allen & Unwin, 1972), pp. 76, 105, 111, 133, 174-76, 189-91.

[Brief, passing references to DHL on the American Indian, DHL and Emily Dickinson on the snake (with poetic treatments of the subject by both reprinted in Appendix C), and a visit to DHL's Kiowa Ranch near Taos and the "Shrine" containing his ashes.]

4017 Walker, Grady Joe. "The Influence of the Bible on D. H. Lawrence as Seen in His Novels," DISSERTATION ABSTRACTS INTERNATIONAL, XXXII (1972), 5810A. Unpublished dissertation, University of Tulsa, 1972.

4018 Wasserman, Jerry. "*St. Mawr* and the Search for Community," MOSAIC, V, No. 2 (1972), 113-23.

"*St. Mawr* discloses a world in which the community and all its codes have lost all their potency." Rejecting the "sexual alternative" proposed in earlier and affirmed in later works by DHL, "and, in fact, all significant human relationship," Lou Witt "finds a substitute for the communal life she lacks in a mystical, quasi-sexual union with the 'wild spirit' of the New Mexico landscape." While *Sons and Lovers* presented an integrated community, the "process of community disintegration" can be traced from *The Rainbow* and *Women in Love* to its culmination in *St. Mawr,* in which all of the major characters suffer the psychic trauma of the Great War and the deracinated condition of displaced colonials in England. With the two grooms disqualified as sexual partners, for different reasons, Lou turns to a "solitary life" for which there is "much authority" in DHL's writings, but the likelihood that her projected life at the ranch will lead to more sterility is suggested by DHL's own responses to New Mexico. "The hopes Lawrence had for a successful communal or sexual life for modern man reach their nadir in *St. Mawr,*" a fact which points up the difficulty of the process whereby he arrived at his hopeful vision of "phallic marriage" in *The Man Who Died*.

4019 Watanabe, Junko. "Orufeusu no Fukkatsu--D. H. Lawrence Oboegaki" (Orpheus Resurrected--A Note on D. H. Lawrence), COLLECTED ESSAYS (Kyôritsu Women's Junior College), No. 15 (March 1972), 41-61.

DHL, a great thought-adventurer in human consciousness, advocated vitalism and the love ethic, but he showed, at the same time, a profound concern with the dark, deep world of death, which reflects his unique mysticism of the earth, of the dark god, of the "blood-consciousness," ideas quite central to his whole body of thought. As revealed in such short fictions as *The Man Who Died,* "The Last Laugh," and *The Ladybird,* these ideas are closely connected with the doctrines of Orphism, with its emphasis on death and rebirth, the mystery of dark night, and the world of Hades. In this tradition DHL can be regarded as Orpheus resurrected in modern times, trying to unite fragmented man with the great Life of the Universe by searching for the world of stillness and fulfillment in the multiplicity of life in our time. [In Japanese.]

4020 Wayland, James Ward. "D. H. Lawrence: A Study of His Prose Style," DISSERTATION ABSTRACTS INTERNATIONAL, XXXIII (1973), 3680A. Unpublished dissertation, University of California, Los Angeles, 1972.

4021 "Wholeness Through Conflict," TIMES LITERARY SUPPLEMENT (Lond), 10 March 1972, p. 280.

"However rich a forcing ground it may be for doctoral theses, *Women in Love* is a lesser, and less satisfying, work" than *The Rainbow*. Some of DHL's judgments in *Movements in European History* "now sound odd, though his brand of hero-worship has more persuasiveness today than it could have had fifty years ago." [Review of Stephen J. Miko, TOWARD "WOMEN IN LOVE": THE EMERGENCE OF A LAWRENTIAN AESTHETIC (1971); DHL, *Movements in European History* (new ed, 1971); and Joseph Foster, D. H. LAWRENCE IN TAOS (1972).]

4022 Willison, I. R. (ed). "David Herbert Lawrence," THE NEW CAMBRIDGE BIBLIOGRAPHY OF ENGLISH LITERATURE, Vol. IV: 1900-1950 (Cambridge: Cambridge UP, 1972), 481-503.
[Bibliography arranged in the following categories: bibliographies, collections and selections, primary works with translations and letters listed separately, secondary materials subdivided into books and chapters in books, and articles in periodicals.]

4023 Wise, James N. "Emerson's 'Experience' and *Sons and Lovers*," COSTERUS, VI (1972), 179-221.
Ralph Waldo Emerson's essay "Experience," which contains the statement that for contact with reality " 'we would even pay the costly price of sons and lovers,' " sets forth ideas "which are inherent in the lives" of the characters in *Sons and Lovers*, particularly Paul Morel, although no claim is made for direct influence. These ideas may be summarized "in terms of seven central concerns": (1) "the Reality of death which encapsulates the tension between" lethargy and creative potential; (2) "the Illusions of existence which make up our daily lives"; (3) "man's Temperament which is the inner core of mood and impulse"; (4) recognition that existence is "on the Surface and is transitory" clarifies "the significance of spontaneity"; (5) "Surprise encompasses the impact" of "excess, sensation, potentiality, and vigor"; (6) these represent "the Subjectiveness of our reality"; (7) the context of reality is "the utter Successiveness of human existence." "Belief in one's self, and a clear understanding of the difference between acting and knowing may enable man to 'realize his world' " and transform " 'genius into practical power.' " [The detailed examination of these ideas, as expressed in thematic motifs in *Sons and Lovers*, is presented in seven corresponding sections, which follow the development of Emerson's argument in "Experience."]

4024 Woodcock, George. DAWN AND THE DARKEST HOUR: A STUDY OF ALDOUS HUXLEY (NY: Viking P, 1972), pp. 131-33 and passim.
The Huxley of the thirties was shaped by earlier conflicts, especially those of the period of DHL's influence, when Huxley questioned whether intellectual abstraction could lead us to a dangerous lack of awareness of reality. The intensity of the relationship with DHL was not always reciprocated. Although DHL encouraged him to write the essays in DO WHAT YOU WILL and filled a psychological need of Huxley's transitional phase, he was often a harsh critic of Huxley's works. After DHL's death, Huxley, while editing DHL's letters, experienced a conversion to mysticism that is presented in EYELESS IN GAZA; later, in Mexico, he was able to shake off DHL's hold. Huxley denied that the character Kingham in

TWO OR THREE GRACES was patterned after DHL, though parallels are evident. Overall, DHL's influence on Huxley's writing was equal to that of Dostoevsky but less than that of Proust, Malraux, and Gide.

4025 Woodeson, John. MARK GERTLER: BIOGRAPHY OF A PAINTER, 1891-1939 (Lond: Sidgwick & Jackson, 1972; Toronto and Buffalo: University of Toronto P, 1973), pp. 109, 159, 160-61, 177-78, 186, 207, 223, 226-27, 235, 238, 240, 256, 260-61, 272, 278-79, 326-27, 354-55.

Mark Gertler met DHL by September 1914. After DHL moved to Cornwall, he sent "a steady flow of letters" to Gertler about his plans for starting an overseas colony to make a "new life" and offering advice on such matters as Gertler's pessimism and his love affair with Dora Carrington. Both were pacifists who shared a dislike of "officious patriotism." DHL praised Gertler's painting *The Merry-Go-Round* as " 'terrible and dreadful,' " the product of 3,000 years of Jewish consciousness, " 'the best *modern* picture I have seen' "; but he warned Gertler against burning his "flame" out too fast. DHL thought Gilbert Cannan's MENDEL, a fictional treatment of Gertler, a merely journalistic " 'statement without creation.' " In time Gertler found DHL disturbing and, by 1925, no longer wanted to see him.

4026 Yamasaki, Susumu. "Atarashii Kyôkantai no Tankyu--*The Plumed Serpent* no Ichikôsatsu" (The Quest for a New Human Relationship--A Study of *The Plumed Serpent*), REPORTS OF HIMEJI INSTITUTE OF TECHNOLOGY, No. 22B (Oct 1972), 33-50.

Men are generally not associated with each other except by the so-called "cash-nexus." In *The Plumed Serpent*, DHL rejects the false human relationship motivated by the "cash-nexus," and suggests a new human relationship ultimately comparable to "orientalism," especially Zen Buddhism or Dhyāna. [In Japanese.]

4027 Yoshii, Mitsuo. "Lawrence *Niji* Ronkô (II)--Buntai to Kôsei o Chûshin to Shite" (On Lawrence's *The Rainbow* [II] --Some Characteristics of Style and Structure), WASEDA REVIEW, No. 11 (Sept 1972), 46-56.

[Second of three articles on *The Rainbow*.] [Style and structure are discussed with reference to the generation of Will and Anna Brangwen.] [See also Mitsuo Yoshii, "Lawrence *Niji* Ronkô (I)--Buntai to Kôsei o Chûshin to Shite" (On Lawrence's *The Rainbow* [I] --Some Characteristics of Style and Structure), WASEDA REVIEW, No. 10 (July 1971), 1-13, and "Lawrence *Niji* Ronkô (III)-- Buntai to Kôsei o Chûshin to Shite" (On Lawrence's *The Rainbow* [III] --Some Characteristics of Style and Structure), WASEDA REVIEW, No. 12 (Sept 1973), 97-109.] [In Japanese.]

4028 Yoshitake, Yoshinori. "D. H. Lawrence no Whitman Ron" ("Whitman" by D. H. Lawrence), SYLVAN (Tôhoku University), No. 16 (March 1972), 1-14.

This study examines, first, DHL's general viewpoints, then his view of Walt Whitman in the "Whitman" essay in *Studies in Classic American Literature*. DHL objects to the abstract ideas of "Man," "Love," "People," etc., seen in Whitman's poetry. DHL has sympathy with Whitman, but thinks that Whitman made some mistakes. [In Japanese.]

1973

4029 Adam, Ian. "Lawrence's Anti-Symbol: The Ending of *The Rainbow*," JOURNAL OF NARRATIVE TECHNIQUE, III (May 1973), 77-84.

The horses at the end of *The Rainbow* are neither hallucinated nor real nor symbolic. They provide a means for DHL to develop Ursula's character in her connection of the conscious with the unconscious. Ursula must come into contact with powers underlying the natural world. The horses are simultaneously part of both her real world and her psyche. They are the real thing, the inconceivable part of the unconscious that DHL describes in *Psychoanalysis and the Unconscious* as being knowable only by direct experience.

4030 Appel, George Fowler. "Modern Masters and Archaic Motifs of the Animal Poem," DISSERTATION ABSTRACTS INTERNATIONAL, XXXIV (1973), 717A. Unpublished dissertation, University of Minnesota, 1973.

[Chap. III compares and contrasts the "objective" animal poetry of DHL and Marianne Moore.]

4031 Bair, Hebe [later Hebe Riddick Mace]. "Lawrence as Poet," D. H. LAWRENCE REVIEW, VI (Fall 1973), 313-25.

D. H. Lawrence: Selected Poems, ed and with an introduction by Keith Sagar (1972) provides a useful selection, although it contains some poems of questionable merit and omits a few that deserve attention. *The Complete Poems of D. H. Lawrence*, ed by Vivian de Sola Pinto and Warren Roberts (issued in paperback, 1971) corrects numerous errors contained in the 1964 hardcover edition. Corrections made on the publisher's master sheets indicate a rough total of 414 revisions, both mechanical and substantive, involving 243 poems. Although the substantive revisions are of more interest to the general reader, the 96 corrections in punctuation, especially in the placement of commas, are significant to the prosodist, since DHL uses the comma to control the free verse line by establishing units of stress patterns within its boundaries. [Also reviews ACTS OF ATTENTION: THE POEMS OF D. H. LAWRENCE, by Sandra M. Gilbert (1973).]

4032 Baldanza, Frank. "*Sons and Lovers*: Novel to Film as a Record of Cultural Growth," LITERATURE/FILM QUARTERLY, I (Jan 1973), 64-70.

While some of the departures from DHL's text made by Jack Cardiff, director of Jerry Wald's production of *Sons and Lovers,* are felicitous, notably the explorations of the oedipal dimensions of the novel, others, such as the foreshortenings used to tighten the plot, do aesthetic violence to the "looseness and random impulsiveness that is at the heart of Lawrence."

    4033 Barr, William. "The Metaphor of Apocalypse in the Novels of D. H. Lawrence," Vols. I and II, DISSERTATION ABSTRACTS INTERNATIONAL, XXXIV (1974), 6623A. Unpublished dissertation, University of Michigan, 1973.

    4034 Beards, Richard D. "The Checklist of D. H. Lawrence Criticism and Scholarship, 1972," D. H. LAWRENCE REVIEW, VI (Spring 1973), 100-108.
[The annual checklist is divided into five sections: General, Poetry, Individual Works of Fiction, Non-Fiction Prose, and Drama. DHL's poetry has "come under increased scrutiny in 1972," and criticism of film adaptations of DHL's work continues.]

    4035 Beauchamp, Gorman. "Lawrence's 'The Rocking-Horse Winner,'" EXPLICATOR, XLI (Jan 1973), Item 32.
In "The Rocking-Horse Winner," love equals luck equals lucre. To give his mother love, Paul must have the lucre which comes of luck, the equivalent of sexual potency, lucre of sperm. His mother's cry is orgasmic.

    4036 Becker, Henry, III. "*The Rocking-Horse Winner*: Film as Parable," LITERATURE/FILM QUARTERLY, I (Jan 1973), 55-63.
The integrity of Anthony Pelissier's film *The Rocking-Horse Winner* derives mainly from its writer-director's fidelity to DHL's story, though the effect is certainly enhanced by the skillful use of specifically cinematic techniques such as montage, angle shots, and juxtaposition of visual images to develop the irony of DHL's theme.

    4037 Bedford, Sybille. ALDOUS HUXLEY: A BIOGRAPHY, Vol. I: 1894-1939; Vol. II: 1939-1963 (Lond: Chatto & Windus, 1973); rptd in one volume ed: (NY: Alfred A. Knopf and Harper & Row, 1974), pp. 60-61, 69-71, 80, 178-80, 183, 186, 188-94, 198-200, 206-7, 209-13, 217, 221-28, 232, 235, 237, 263, 307, 325, 601, 605-6, 612-14, 656, 660-61, 664, 675, 677, 685, 710; on Frieda Lawrence Ravagli, pp. 183-84, 224, 361, 381, 388, 392, 403, 406, 414, 422-24, 441-42, 446, 466, 532, 560, 632, 634n, 735, 740-41.
Aldous Huxley met DHL in 1915, when DHL was full of plans for a Utopian colony in Florida. The two met again in Florence in 1926, when DHL was already very ill. Huxley admired DHL for obeying his creative genius, whereas Huxley, in all humility, did not believe in his own. DHL and Maria Huxley understood each other well, and Maria typed parts of the manuscript of *Lady Chatterley's Lover*. DHL did not always see eye to eye with Aldous and Julian Huxley on science, particularly ideas on physiology and evolution, and sometimes proclaimed unreasonably, "All scientists are liars." Although Huxley found DHL's anti-intellectualism curious in such a well-read man, Huxley thought him extraordinary as a human being and found his perception of the world intense and

exciting. DHL worked like a man possessed, sometimes writing for eighteen hours a day. In a 1957 letter, Huxley says that Frieda, a woman of enormous vitality, completely free of neurosis, helped keep DHL alive for five years beyond the time he might have died. Although DHL and Frieda had a profound love relationship, this did not prevent her having affairs with others. DHL was angry about these affairs but was too dependent on Frieda to leave her.

4038 Beker, Miroslav. "Lawrenceov obračun sa svojim suvremenicima" (Lawrence's Dispute with His Contemporaries), in MODERNA KRITIKA U ENGLISKOV I AMERICI (Zagreb: Liber Mladost, 1973), pp. 225-49.
[In Serbo-Croatian.]

4039 Betsky-Zweig, S. " 'Floutingly in the Fine Black Mud': D. H. Lawrence's 'The Horse Dealer's Daughter,' " DUTCH QUARTERLY REVIEW OF ANGLO-AMERICAN LETTERS, III (1973), 159-64.
"The Horse Dealer's Daughter" fulfills its promise only with the appearance of Jack Fergusson to rescue Mabel Pervin from the pond into which, unable to imagine life, she has walked in an attempt to join her mother in death. "It is the mutual touch (both deep thrusts and graspings and gentle reachings) that give birth to Mabel as a woman and Jack as a man" from the animal state in which each has formerly existed. The rescue scene demonstrates DHL's "firm hold. . . on fictional technique for describing acts of sex, of intercourse." "Triumphantly the story of the pain of the real loss of real virginity," "The Horse Dealer's Daughter" is finally as much the man's story as the woman's. "A new body must come to him, one earned by the broken membrane of his heart, not by the broken membrane of sex."

4040 Billington, Michael. "*The Merry-Go-Round* at the Royal Court," GUARDIAN (Manchester), 8 Nov 1973, p. 12.
The staging of DHL's plays makes clear that "British theatre has been sitting on a goldmine. No other native dramatist in the early part of the century dealt so intelligently with personal relationships" or "painted such a vivid picture of British provincial life." *The Merry-Go-Round,* unlike the trilogy of plays presented in the earlier DHL season, is "a theatrical hybrid": "a comedy laced with pain and passion," but as in those plays, "emotion is expressed through physical ritual as much as through words." [Review of the Royal Court Theatre production, directed by Peter Gill.]

4041 Bishop, David R., S.J. "Form and Content in Lawrence's Poetry," SPIRIT: A MAGAZINE OF POETRY, XL (Spring-Summer 1973), 18-23.
While DHL is a major novelist, he is not a great poet. His early poems are uneven, with forced rhymes and diction. Revision was almost unthinkable to him. His art is too close to experience, leaving "nothing out" and giving us "reality, warts and all." The poems of *Birds, Beasts and Flowers* are excellent in descriptive quality and force, and "The Ship of Death" has wonderful rhythm and fluidity

of movement. DHL's poetry remains, rather than a major force, only "jottings in a very imaginative commonplace book."

4042 Bobbitt, Joan. "Lawrence and Bloomsbury: The Myth of a Relationship," ESSAYS IN LITERATURE (University of Denver), I (Sept 1973), 31-42.

"The Lawrence-Bloomsbury 'relationship' did not fail; it simply failed to materialize." DHL was antipathetic to most of the Bloomsbury figures because of their Platonism, their "faith in the ultimate supremacy of the intellect," their belief in "art for art's sake," and their "lifestyle."

4043 Bonadeo, Barbara Bates. "D. H. Lawrence's View of the Italians," ENGLISH MISCELLANY (Rome), XXIV (1973-1974), 271-97.

Twilight in Italy, Etruscan Places, and *Sea and Sardinia* reveal DHL's feeling that "the cultural disposition of the contemporary Italian has remained...pre-Christian" and "mediaeval." Two distinct but interacting ideas are apparent in his thesis: the arrest of the spiritual and intellectual development of the Italian, and his inherent sensuality. Ancient man (the Etruscan, for example) drew into himself all he could of the " 'vitality' of the universe." Since knowledge and power came to him through the senses, it was "disclosed bodily." DHL called the organization of society in which this divine power was passed down from a superior being to each segment of society the "aristocratic principle." [Discussion of DHL's view of the ORESTIA trilogy and HAMLET.] Man, in his effort to cast off the old-world man, "leaned to the opposite extreme and attempted to deny the flesh in favor of the spirit." The Italians, however, have retained the old self. For them, "Creativity stems not from the mind, but from the blood, through procreation." But in *Sea and Sardinia,* DHL's "strong emotional appeal for Italians," which had been so prevalent in the earlier *Twilight in Italy,* is "conspicuously absent." He sees the people as full of self-pity and overly sympathetic, at the expense of the intellect. Italian women and men can have no real relationship because they approach each other "exclusively on the sexual level" and spiritual intimacy between two people has no place in the Italian culture. Because the Italian people "have made consummation of the self the only infinite," Italian civilization seemed to DHL one that has "fully completed its life cycle and has come to rest, perhaps forever," and one that gives, at last, a "feeling of sterility."

4044 Boulton, James T. (gen. ed.), PROSPECTUS AND NOTES FOR VOLUME EDITORS: "THE LETTERS OF D. H. LAWRENCE" (Cambridge: Cambridge UP, 1973).

[An 18-page pamphlet limited to 350 copies, setting forth "The Case for an Edition" of DHL's letters, "The Plan" for seven volumes under the general editorship of James T. Boulton with six of the individual volumes to be edited or co-edited by others, and the "Editorial Principles" to be employed in preparing a uniform edition. Four DHL letters to Louie Burrows, Ada Lawrence, and Vere H. G. Collins are printed with editorial apparatus and notes by Boulton as examples. See also James T. Boulton, "The Cambridge University Press Edition of Lawrence's Letters, Part 4," in D. H. LAWRENCE: THE MAN WHO LIVED, ed by Robert B. Partlow, Jr., and Harry T. Moore (Carbondale & Edwardsville: Southern

Illinois UP, 1979), pp. 223-28; and the Cambridge Edition of *The Letters of D. H. Lawrence,* of which Vol. I: 1901-1913, ed by James T. Boulton, was published on 10 Sept 1979.]

4045 Bradbury, Malcolm. POSSIBILITIES: ESSAYS ON THE STATE OF THE NOVEL (NY: Oxford UP, 1973), pp. 5, 7, 81, 84, 87, 92, 106, 120, 122, 126-27, 133, 142, 153, 161, 176, 184.
Modernism, regarded as a manipulation of artistic content according to the "logic of metaphor, form, or symbol" rather than as traditional narrative or psychological progress, can be found in the new novel of DHL. *Lady Chatterley's Lover* is dominated by the ordeal of war, which in turn leads to the "bad time" Mellors predicts. The War was for DHL both the end of something and the beginning of something else. In DHL's version of the novel of consciousness, unlike those of Henry James and James Joyce, the function of the novel is to break down the "old stable ego" and present the vitalist and deathly forces evolving in people in an apocalyptic period.

4046 Brandabur, A[gnes] M. "The Ritual Corn Harvest Scene in *The Rainbow*," D. H. LAWRENCE REVIEW, VI (Fall 1973), 284-302.
A reading of Jane Harrison's ANCIENT ART AND RITUAL "helps to clarify the precise character of the rituals" that are important in *The Rainbow* and therefore "provides insight into the mythic quality of the novel." Her discussion of "art coming out of ritual, specifically out of magical ritual dances," "accords with the idea of the truly religious" which DHL "was to articulate in *Apocalypse* and other essays." "In *The Rainbow,* Lawrence has envisioned the yearly cycle of planting, growing, and reaping. . . . The foreshortening of time lends to human generations the same cyclic rhythms as that of the vegetation year." "The individual ritual dances. . .are like those described" in Harrison's study: " 'dromena,' things done to regenerate fructifying power." *The Rainbow* defines "the moment when skepticism changes the attitude with which the community performs the sacred ritual." A detailed analysis of the ritual elements in the courtships of the three generations, focusing on the ritual corn harvest scene involving Will and Anna, supports these conclusions.

4047 Brandeis, R. C. "Male Relationships in the Work of D. H. Lawrence." Unpublished dissertation, University of Leicester, 1973.
[Listed in Lawrence F. McNamee, DISSERTATIONS IN ENGLISH AND AMERICAN LITERATURE, SUPP II (NY & Lond: Bowker, 1974), p. 369.]

4048 Brookesmith, Peter. "The Future of the Individual: Ursula Brangwen and Kate Millett's SEXUAL POLITICS," HUMAN WORLD, No. 10 (Feb 1973), 42-65.
Ursula Brangwen in *The Rainbow* is a positive portrait of a woman seeking her identity in the modern world, not DHL's attack on the new woman. Ursula is a member of probably the first generation to see an opposition between individual and society, particularly in emotional relations with other people and in the manner or sphere in which she earns a living. [In part a reply to Kate Millett, "D. H.

Lawrence," SEXUAL POLITICS (Garden City, NY: Doubleday, 1970; Lond: Rupert Hart-Davis, 1971), pp. 237-93.]

4049 Burwell, Rose Marie. "A Catalogue of D. H. Lawrence's Reading from Early Childhood: Addenda," D. H. LAWRENCE REVIEW, VI (Spring 1973), 86-99.

[Addenda and corrigenda to Rose Marie Burwell, "A Catalogue of D. H. Lawrence's Reading from Early Childhood," D. H. LAWRENCE REVIEW, III (Fall 1970), iii-vi, 193-324, including "six new titles...which reveal or organize new evidence."

4050 Capey, A. C. "Sin, Obedience and Duty: The English Teacher and Moral Values," HUMAN WORLD, No. 10 (1973), 9-17.

In DHL's hostility to the values--especially "duty"--of the vicarage in "Daughters of the Vicar," we can see a sign of the modern estrangement from the church. For all the deep familiarity with religious language shown in *The Rainbow* and the Blakean echoes in *The Virgin and the Gipsy*, DHL's ignorance of the church is a twentieth-century phenomenon.

4051 Carey, John. "D. H. Lawrence's Doctrine," in D. H. LAWRENCE: NOVELIST, POET, PROPHET, ed by Stephen Spender (Lond: Weidenfeld & Nicholson; NY: Harper & Row, 1973), pp. 122-34.

Although DHL might have disclaimed thought, he had "a set of passions and hatreds that he turned into beliefs," which he desired to impose on others. Though he thought education cold and useless, "blood knowledge" was his religion, as between men and women "blood contact" was better than mental communion. Linking sight to thought and touch to blood knowledge, DHL, in "The Blind Man," *The Fox, The Plumed Serpent*, and "The Woman Who Rode Away," shows a preference for the more profound non-visual senses and the instincts. In sex, DHL spoke for "mindlessness" and male dominance, as in *The Ladybird*. His novels are not fully intelligible without reference to his anatomical theory outlined in *Psychoanalysis and the Unconscious* and *Fantasia of the Unconscious*. In terms of society, he prefers a natural aristocracy which he never fully explains but which is akin to the Calvinistic notion of "the elect." While "the Lawrentian aristocrat hates to see people suffering," he blames them "for forcing their ugly woes on his attention." DHL's social ideals, focusing on the destruction of all he hates, are more negative than positive. Though DHL has been called a fascist, many of his ideas are similar to those of Yeats, Carlyle, and Arnold. Despising benevolence and pity, DHL despises Christianity also. To replace the dying Christian God, DHL "propounded a dark cosmology and darkish after-life," as in *The Plumed Serpent*. Though he later disavowed the leadership cult of that novel and spoke for tenderness in *Lady Chatterley's Lover*, it is a tenderness without compassion. Only in his books is DHL's thought alive; it cannot be reduced to a schematic philosophy.

4052 Colquhoun, Keith. "In Love with Lawrence," OBSERVER (Lond), [Weekly Colour Supplement], 9 Sept 1973, pp. 61, 63, 65.

[Feature article based on an interview with Dorothy Brett, centering on her accompanying DHL and Frieda to New Mexico in 1924 and remaining there ever since. Brett discusses the Cafe Royal Dinner (December 1923), life at the ranch in 1924, DHL's approach to women, his life with Frieda (" 'a bossy woman' "), and her own relationship with Frieda in New Mexico after DHL's death. Illustrated with a large photograph by Neil Libbert of Dorothy Brett in her studio home in Taos.]

4053 Coniff, Gerald William. "The Plays of D. H. Lawrence," DISSERTATION ABSTRACTS INTERNATIONAL, XXXIV (1974), 5095A-5096A. Unpublished dissertation, Pennsylvania State University, 1973.

4054 Coombes, H[enry] (ed). D. H. LAWRENCE: A CRITICAL ANTHOLOGY (Harmondsworth, Middlesex, England: Penguin Books, 1973).

Contents, abstracted under year of first publication: **"Preface,"** p. 25 [not abstracted]; **"Table of Dates,"** pp. 27-33 [not abstracted]; H. Coombes, "Introduction," pp. 37-56 (1973). **Part One: "Contemporaneous Criticism"**: [H. Coombes], "Introduction," pp. 57-59 [not abstracted]; Excerpts from 164 of DHL's letters, pp. 61-209 [not abstracted]; and the following, often very brief cuttings, from letters and reviews between 1911 and 1930: [*The White Peacock*], pp. 62-63, from "An Interesting Novel," MORNING POST (Lond), 9 Feb 1911, p. 2; [Four excerpts from Frieda Lawrence's letters], pp. 65-66, 85, 154, 184, from FRIEDA LAWRENCE: THE MEMOIRS AND CORRESPONDENCE, ed by E. W. Tedlock, Jr. (Lond: Heinemann, 1961; NY: Knopf, 1964); [*The Trespasser*], pp. 68-69, from "The Woman Who Kills," NEW YORK TIMES BOOK REVIEW, 17 Nov 1912, Sect. 6, p. 677; [Two excerpts from Ezra Pound's letters], pp. 72, 80, from THE LETTERS OF EZRA POUND, 1907-1941, ed by D. D. Paige (NY: Harcourt, Brace, 1950), pp. 17-22; Edward Thomas, [*Love Poems and Others*], pp. 74-75, from "More Georgian Poetry," BOOKMAN (Lond), XLIV (April 1913), 47; [*Sons and Lovers*], pp. 76-77, from "*Sons and Lovers,*" SATURDAY REVIEW (Lond), CXV (21 June 1913), 780-81; Ezra Pound, [*Love Poems and Others*], pp. 78-79, from "In Metre," NEW FREEWOMAN, I, No. 6 (Sept 1913), 113; Henry James, [Excerpt], p. 86, from "The New Novel," TIMES LITERARY SUPPLEMENT (Lond), 19 March 1914, pp. 1-2; John Galsworthy, [Excerpts from two letters]. pp. 87, 101-2, from LIFE AND LETTERS OF JOHN GALSWORTHY, ed by H. V. Marrot (NY: Scribner's, 1935) [not seen in this form]; A[lan] N. M[onkhouse], [*The Prussian Officer and Other Stories*], pp. 94-95, from MANCHESTER GUARDIAN, 17 Dec 1914 [not abstracted]; Robert Frost, [Excerpt from letter (12 June 1915)], p. 97 [not abstracted]; James Douglas, [*The Rainbow*], pp. 98-101, from "Books and Bookmen," STAR (Lond), 22 Oct 1915, p. 4; Edward Garnett, [Excerpt]. p. 109, from "Art and the Moralists: Mr. D. H. Lawrence's Work," DIAL, LXI (16 Nov 1916), 379-81; Catherine Carswell, [Excerpt], p. 118, from THE SAVAGE PILGRIMAGE: A NARRATIVE OF D. H. LAWRENCE (Lond: Secker & Warburg, 1932), p. 101; John Gould Fletcher, [*Look! We Have Come Through!*], pp. 119-22, from "A Modern Evangelist," POETRY: A MAGAZINE OF VERSE, XII (Aug 1918), 269-74; Douglas Goldring, [Excerpt], pp. 133-34, from "The Later Work of D. H. Lawrence," REPUTATIONS: ESSAYS IN CRITICISM (Lond: Chapman & Hall, 1920), pp. 67-78; Virginia Woolf (anonymously), [*The Lost Girl*], pp. 134-37, from "Postscript or Prelude?" TIMES LITERARY SUPPLEMENT (Lond), 2 Dec 1920, p. 795; J[ohn] M[iddleton] Murry, [*Women in Love*], pp. 138-43, from "The Nostalgia of Mr. D. H. Lawrence," NATION AND THE ATHENAEUM, XXIX (13 Aug 1921), 713-14; W. Charles Pilley, [*Women in Love*], pp. 143-45, from "A Book the Police Should Ban," JOHN BULL, XXX (17 Sept 1921), 4; T. S. Eliot, [Excerpt], p. 147, from "London Letter," DIAL, LXXIII (Sept 1922), 329-31; [*The Ladybird* volume], pp. 148-49, from "Three Stories," TIMES LITERARY SUPPLEMENT (Lond), 22 March 1923, p. 195; T. S. Eliot, [Excerpt], p. 150, from "Contemporary English Prose," VANITY FAIR, July 1923 [not abstracted]; [*Kangaroo*], pp. 150-53, from "A Novel with a Difference," TIMES LITERARY SUPPLEMENT (Lond), 20 Sept 1923, p. 617; Herbert J. Seligmann, [Two excerpts], pp. 154-56, 157-58, from D. H. LAWRENCE: AN AMERICAN INTERPRETATION (NY: Thomas Seltzer, 1924), pp. 1-4, 9-12, 72-74; Paul Rosenfeld, [Excerpt], pp. 166-74, from MEN SEEN: TWENTY-FOUR MODERN AUTHORS (NY: Dial P, 1925), pp. 45-62; Charles Marriot, [*The Plumed Serpent*], pp. 175-76, from "The Quest," MANCHESTER GUARDIAN, 29 Jan 1926, p. 9; C. H. Rickword, [*The Plumed Serpent*], pp. 177-79, from CALENDAR OF MODERN LETTERS, April 1926 [not abstracted]; Edmund Wilson, [*Lady Chatterley's Lover*], pp. 198-201, from "Signs of Life: *Lady Chatterley's Lover*," NEW REPUBLIC, LIX (3 July 1929), 184-85; [*Pornography and Obscenity*], pp. 209-12, in "Pornography and the Censorship," NEW STATESMAN, XXXIV (23 Nov 1929), 219-20; Catherine Carswell, [Excerpt from letter], pp. 212-13, from "D. H. Lawrence," TIME AND TIDE, XI (14 March 1930), 342; Paul Rosenfeld, [Obituary], pp. 214-18, from "D. H. Lawrence," NEW REPUBLIC, LXII (26 March 1930), 155-56; E. M. Forster, [Letter to the Editor], pp. 218-19, from "D. H. Lawrence," NATION AND THE ATHENAEUM, XLVI (29 March 1930), 888; T. S. Eliot, [Letter to the Editor], p. 209, from "D. H. Lawrence," NATION AND THE ATHENAEUM, XLVII (5 April 1930), 11; E. M. Forster, [Letter to the Editor], pp. 219-20, from "D. H. Lawrence," NATION AND THE ATHENAEUM, XLVII (12 April 1930), 45; Clive Bell, [Letter to the Editor], p. 220, from "D. H. Lawrence," NATION AND THE ATHENAEUM, XLVII (19 April 1930), 76-77; E. M. Forster, [Letter to the Editor], pp. 220-21, from "D. H. Lawrence," NATION AND THE ATHENAEUM, XLVII (26 April 1930), 109; Arnold Bennett, [Obituary], pp. 221-23, from "D. H. Lawrence's Delusion," EVENING STANDARD (Lond), 10 April 1930, p. 9. **Part Two: "Campaigning 1930-1950":** "Introduction," pp. 225-26 [not abstracted]; F. R. Leavis, [Excerpt], pp. 227-33, from D. H. LAWRENCE (Cambridge: Gordon Fraser ["Minority Pamphlet No. 6"], 1930), pp. 27-33; J[ohn] M[iddleton] Murry, [Excerpt], pp. 233-41, from SON OF WOMAN: THE STORY OF D. H. LAWRENCE (Lond: Jonathan Cape, 1931), pp. 31-36; T. S. Eliot, "Son of Woman" (review), pp. 241-47, from CRITERION, X (July 1931), 768-74; Catherine Carswell, [Three excerpts], pp. 247-52, from THE SAVAGE PILGRIMAGE: A NARRATIVE OF D. H. LAWRENCE (Lond: Secker & Warburg, 1932), pp. 69-72, 66-67, 138-39; F. R. Leavis, [Excerpt], pp. 252-54, from "Reminiscences of D. H. Lawrence," SCRUTINY, I, No. 2 (Sept 1932), 189-91; Aldous Huxley, [Excerpt], pp. 254-64, from "Introduction," *The Letters of D. H. Lawrence,* ed by Aldous Huxley (Lond: Heinemann; NY: Viking P, 1932), pp. ix-xxxii; Harold Nicolson [*The Letters of D. H. Lawrence,* ed by Aldous Huxley], pp. 264-67, from "D. H. Lawrence," NEW STATESMAN AND NATION, IV (1 Oct 1932), 376; F. R. Leavis, "The Living Lawrence," pp. 267-70, from LISTENER, 5 Oct 1932, pp. iv-vii [not abstracted]; Aldous Huxley, "Lawrence in Etruria," pp. 270-74, from SPECTATOR, CXLIX (4 Nov 1932), 629; F. R. Leavis, "D. H. Lawrence and Professor Irving Babbitt," pp. 274-81, from SCRUTINY, I (Dec 1932), 273-79; F. R. Leavis, [Excerpt], pp. 281-86, from "Restatement for Critics," SCRUTINY, I (March 1933), 315-23; W. B. Yeats, [Excerpts from two letters (22 May 1933 and 25 May 1933)], pp. 286-87, from THE LETTERS OF W. B. YEATS, ed by Allan Wade (Lond: Rupert Hart-Davis, 1954; NY: Macmillan, 1955), pp. 810-11; Jessie Chambers, [Seven excerpts], pp. 287-98, from D. H. LAWRENCE: A PERSONAL RECORD, by "E. T." (Lond: Jonathan Cape, 1935), pp. 103-5, 81-82, 115-19, 190-97, 201-4, 222-23; Frieda Lawrence, [Two excerpts], pp. 299-302, from "NOT I, BUT THE WIND..." (NY: Viking P, 1934; Lond: Heinemann, 1935), pp. 52, 65-69; F. R. Leavis, "The Wild Untutored Phoenix," pp. 302-9, from SCRUTINY, VI (Dec 1937), pp. 352-58; Frieda Lawrence, "A Bit about Lawrence," pp. 309-13, from FRIEDA LAWRENCE: THE MEMOIRS AND CORRESPONDENCE, ed by E. W. Tedlock, Jr. (Lond: Heinemann, 1961; NY: Knopf, 1964), pp. 130-34; F. R. Leavis, [Excerpt], pp. 313-18, from "Thought and Emotional Quality in Poetry," SCRUTINY, XIII (Spring 1945), 55-59; F. R. Leavis, [Excerpt], pp. 318-21, from THE GREAT TRADITION: GEORGE ELIOT, HENRY JAMES, JOSEPH CONRAD (Lond: Chatto & Windus; NY: George W. Stewart, 1948), pp. 23-27; H. Coombes, [Letter to the Editors, with reply by F. R. Leavis], pp. 322-26, from "Comment: D. H. Lawrence Placed," SCRUTINY, XVI (March 1949), 44-47; Frieda Lawrence, [Excerpt from a letter], p. 326, from FRIEDA LAWRENCE: THE MEMOIRS AND CORRESPONDENCE (Lond: Heinemann, 1961; NY: Knopf, 1964), p. 293; F. R. Leavis, "The Novel as Dramatic Poem: *St. Mawr,*" pp. 326-49, from SCRUTINY, XVII (Spring 1950), as rvd and rptd in D. H. LAWRENCE: NOVELIST, by F. R. Leavis (Lond: Chatto & Windus, 1955), pp. 225-45. **Part Three: "Later Criticism 1951-1971":** [H. Coombes], "Introduction," pp. 353-54 [not abstracted]; Bertrand Russell, [BBC Talk], pp. 355-59, from "Portraits from Memory--III," LISTENER, XLVIII (24 July 1952), 135-36; F. R. Leavis, "Lawrence and Art" [Excerpt], pp. 359-80, from D. H. LAWRENCE: NOVELIST (Lond: Chatto & Windus, 1955), pp. 31-50; F. R. Leavis, "Shaw Against Lawrence," pp. 381-84, from SPECTATOR, CXCIV (1 April 1955), pp. 397-99; Phillip Trotter, [Three excerpts], pp. 384-93, from Edward Nehls (ed), D. H. LAWRENCE: A COMPOSITE BIOGRAPHY, Vol. III: 1925-1930 (Madison: University of Wisconsin P, 1959), 190-92, 329-31, 365-67; F. R. Leavis, "Romantic and Heretic?" pp. 393-97, from SPECTATOR, CCII (6 Feb 1959), pp. 196-97; F. R. Leavis, "Lawrence After Thirty Years" (an address given at the University of Nottingham, 17 June 1960), pp. 398-407; D. W. Harding, "Lawrence's Evils," pp. 408-13, from SPECTATOR, CCV (11 Nov 1960), 735-36; F. R. Leavis, "The New Orthodoxy," pp. 413-19, from SPECTATOR, CCVI (17 Feb 1961), 229-30; F. R. Leavis, "Genius as Critic," pp. 419-23, from SPECTATOR, CCVI (24 March 1961), 412-14; Barbara Lucas, "A propos of 'England, My

England,' " pp. 424-30, from TWENTIETH CENTURY, CLXIX (March 1961), 288-93; Andor Gomme (anonymously), [*The Collected Letters of D. H. Lawrence*, ed by Harry T. Moore], pp. 430-35, from "Friends and Enemies," TIMES LITERARY SUPPLEMENT (Lond), 27 April 1962, pp. 273-75; W. H. Auden, "D. H. Lawrence," pp. 435-42, from "Two Bestiaries," THE DYER'S HAND (NY: Random House, 1948), as rptd (Lond: Faber & Faber, 1963), pp. 285-95; D. J. Enright, "A Hate for Wisdom," pp. 442-48, from NEW STATESMAN, ns LXVIII (30 Oct 1964), 653-54; D. W. Harding, "Courting," pp. 448-50, from NEW STATESMAN, ns LXIX (23 April 1965), p. 650; D. W. Harding, "Womenfolk," pp. 450-52, from NEW STATESMAN, ns LXX (24 Sept 1965), 441-42; Simon Gray, "Lawrence the Dramatist," pp. 453-57, from NEW SOCIETY, XI (21 March 1968), 423-24; F. R. Leavis, [Excerpt], pp. 457-60, from ENGLISH LITERATURE IN OUR TIME AND THE UNIVERSITY (Lond: Chatto & Windus, 1969), pp. 154-57; J. C. F. Littlewood, "The Best of *Sons and Lovers* and a Deeper Truth," pp. 460-76, from "Son and Lover," CAMBRIDGE QUARTERLY, IV (Winter 1969-1970), 323-61; Martin Green, "Old Flames at the Ranch," pp. 477-84, from LONDON MAGAZINE, ns X (March 1971), 69-83. "**Select Bibliography**," pp. 485-86 [not abstracted].

4055 Coombes, H[enry]. "Introduction," D. H. LAWRENCE: A CRITICAL ANTHOLOGY, ed by H. Coombes (Harmondsworth, Middlesex, England: Penguin Books, 1973), pp. 37-56.

The history of critical opinion about DHL is a stormy one. T. S. Eliot is central to this history because his seemingly impersonal but nonetheless passionate moral censure made respectable the set of value-assumptions about DHL with which a host of other commentators would condemn him for two decades. John Middleton Murry and Bertrand Russell must bear responsibility for the "hate and destructiveness" slander. F. R. Leavis is, of course, DHL's great champion.

4056 Corbin, Richard Johnstone. "Unity and Meaning in D. H. Lawrence's *Birds, Beasts and Flowers*," DISSERTATION ABSTRACTS INTERNATIONAL, XXXIV (1973-1974), 4250A-51A. Unpublished dissertation, Tulane University, 1973.

4057 Craig, David. "Lawrence and Democracy," THE REAL FOUNDATIONS: LITERATURE AND SOCIAL CHANGE (Lond: Chatto & Windus, 1973; NY: Oxford UP, 1974), pp. 143-67.

As wise and deep as DHL's analysis of human nature is, his pronouncements on social problems are wild and even silly. DHL failed to grasp the facts of labor movements and industrial strife during the late nineteenth and early twentieth centuries and consequently failed to appreciate the new social orders which came out of these movements. A comparison of DHL's version of this social and industrial evolution in "The Industrial Magnate" chapter of *Women in Love* with the existing facts clearly demonstrates DHL's prejudices and his incomprehension of the real social and industrial conditions of his time. This incomprehension and his own sense of alienation result in a negative social doctrine which does not adequately assess the prevailing conditions of modern society and contributes nothing to its betterment. [Craig's essay "Love and Society: MEASURE FOR

MEASURE and Our Own Time," in SHAKESPEARE IN A CHANGING WORLD, ed by Arnold Kettle (Lond: Lawrence & Wishart; NY: International Publishers, 1964), pp. 195-216, is also rptd here as Chap. I: "Shakespeare, Lawrence and Sexual Freedom," pp. 17-38.]

4058 Crump, G. B. "Lawrence and the LITERATURE/FILM QUARTERLY," D. H. LAWRENCE REVIEW, VI (Fall 1973), 326-32.

[Review-essay on the "D. H. Lawrence Number" of LITERATURE/FILM QUARTERLY, I (Jan 1973), focusing on a critique of the problems inherent in criticism treating the relationship between film and literature as applied to DHL.]

4059 Cushman, Keith. "D. H. Lawrence and Nancy Henry: Two Unpublished Letters and a Lost Relationship," D. H. LAWRENCE REVIEW, VI (Spring 1973), 21-32.

Nancy Henry is represented in *The Letters of D. H. Lawrence,* ed by Aldous Huxley (1932), by five letters omitted from *The Collected Letters of D. H. Lawrence,* ed by Harry T. Moore (1962). She does not appear in any of the DHL memoirs and biographies, including Edward Nehls (ed), D. H. LAWRENCE: A COMPOSITE BIOGRAPHY, 3 vols. (1957, 1958, 1959). However, she received "at least eight letters from Lawrence between July 1918 and February 1919," all of them "related to the writing of *Movements in European History,* providing. . . our clearest knowledge of the composition of Lawrence's history textbook." The letters suggest also that the relationship was a personal as well as a professional one. Two previously unpublished early letters in the sequence, including a letter about Mrs. Henry from DHL to J. B. Pinker, his London literary agent, are published here.

4060 Cushman, Keith. AN EXHIBITION OF FIRST EDITIONS AND MANUSCRIPTS FROM THE D. H. LAWRENCE COLLECTION OF JOHN E. BAKER, JR. (Chicago: Joseph Regenstein Library, The University of Chicago, 1973).

[Exhibition catalogue of seven pages, limited to 500 copies. Introduction and checklist of 114 items in the Baker collection exhibited at the Joseph Regenstein Library, The University of Chicago, November and December, 1973. See also Keith Cushman, "A Profile of John E. Baker, Jr. and His Lawrence Collection," D. H. LAWRENCE REVIEW, VII (Spring 1974), 83-88; and A CATALOGUE OF TWENTIETH CENTURY LITERATURE, collected by John E. Baker, Jr. (Desbarats, Ontario, 1977), a 102-page catalogue of the complete Baker collection.]

4061 Cushman, Keith. "The Making of D. H. Lawrence's 'The White Stocking,' " STUDIES IN SHORT FICTION, X (Winter 1973), 51-64; rvd and enlgd as Chap. VI: " 'The White Stocking,' " D. H. LAWRENCE AT WORK: THE EMERGENCE OF THE "PRUSSIAN OFFICER" STORIES (Charlottesville: UP of Virginia, 1978), pp. 148-66.

The first version of "The White Stocking," written about 1907, is lost, but the text, as published in SMART SET in Oct 1914, "is drastically different from that included in *The Prussian Officer* just two months later." A comparison of the two versions shows "how Lawrence added some of his most characteristic concerns to the 'rich and complex sense of ordinary life' with which he began." While "the marriage of Ted and Elsie Whiston is not a facsimile" of DHL's and Frieda's, "the experience of the first two years of this marriage" gave DHL "the insight that allowed him to transform 'The White Stocking' into a first-rate story." [Contains detailed analyses.]

4062 Daniel, John Turner. "The Influence of the English Class Structure on the Work of D. H. Lawrence," DISSERTATION ABSTRACTS INTERNATIONAL, XXXIV (1973-1974), 4252A. Unpublished dissertation, University of Minnesota, 1973.

4063 Davies, J. V. "Introduction," *Lawrence on Hardy and Painting: "Study of Thomas Hardy" and "Introduction to These Paintings,"* ed by J. V. Davies (Lond: Heinemann Educational Books, 1973), pp. 1-9.

DHL's study of Hardy is central to the study of DHL's own work because in it the novelist is discovering what he himself, living in a particularly portentous time of disjunction in European civilization, really believes. The Hardy essay manifests an indwelling attentiveness to fundamental truths about the psyche and the human condition. DHL's preoccupation with the nature of perception lies very near the source of his creative impulse. In the same way that his concern with the nature of experience often expresses itself in visual analogies, his remarkable "Introduction to These Paintings" concerns the re-creation of the realities of human experience.

4064 Davis, Patricia C. "Chicken Queen's Delight: D. H. Lawrence's *The Fox*," MODERN FICTION STUDIES, XIX (Winter 1973-1974), 565-71.

Given Henry's desire for a passively feminine woman, it would seem that he would have chosen Banford instead of the more independent March. But Henry fears femininity, equating it with possessiveness. He prefers March because she is masculine and therefore appeals to the homoerotic drive in him. DHL's own repressed homosexual feelings kept him from recognizing this and led to the morally unsatisfactory aspects of the story, such as the murder of Banford. Henry and March are, for all practical purposes, two male figures.

4065 Delavenay, Émile. "Études Lawrenciennes" (Lawrencian Studies), ÉTUDES ANGLAISES, XXVI (July-Sept 1973), 320-26.

[Review essay.] In *The Complete Poems of D. H. Lawrence*, ed by Vivian de Sola Pinto and F. Warren Roberts (1 vol. paperback ed., 1971), the editors have corrected a number of errors which had slipped into their two-volume edition of 1964 and have augmented their notes, sometimes considerably. *Movements in European History*, reissued in 1971 with an Introduction by James T. Boulton, was originally published in 1921. When DHL demanded the addition of an anti-democratic epilog for the second edition of

1925, Oxford University Press refused to publish it. [Also reviews THE PSYCHIC MARINER: A READING OF THE POEMS OF D. H. LAWRENCE, by Tom Marshall; THE D. H. LAWRENCE REVIEW, IV (Fall 1971) and V (Spring and Summer 1972); D. H. LAWRENCE'S BESTIARY: A STUDY OF HIS USE OF ANIMAL TROPE AND SYMBOL, by Kenneth Inniss; LAWRENCE, HARDY, AND AMERICAN LITERATURE, by Richard Swigg; TOWARD "WOMEN IN LOVE": THE EMERGENCE OF A LAWRENTIAN AESTHETIC, by Stephen J. Miko; D. H. LAWRENCE: "THE RAINBOW," by Frank Glover Smith; D. H. LAWRENCE'S RESPONSE TO RUSSIAN LITERATURE, by George J. Zytaruk; ACTS OF ATTENTION: THE POEMS OF D. H. LAWRENCE, by Sandra M. Gilbert; and LAWRENCE, by Frank Kermode.] [In French.]

4066 Derrick, John Bruce. " 'Widdershins': Reversed Parental Identification and Narrative Point of View in the Work of D. H. Lawrence." Unpublished dissertation, University of California at Berkeley, 1973. [Listed in Lawrence F. McNamee, DISSERTATIONS IN ENGLISH AND AMERICAN LITERATURE, SUPP II (NY and Lond: Bowker, 1974), p. 369.]

4067 de Wofe, Ivor. "A Protest by D. H. Lawrence," in "Sociable Housing," ARCHITECTURAL REVIEW, CLIV (Oct 1973), 222.
[A brief headnote introducing a reprint of excerpts from "Nottingham and the Mining Countryside" notes that DHL wrote the essay at the request of the then editor of ARCHITECTURAL REVIEW.]

4068 D. H. LAWRENCE REVIEW, ed by James C. Cowan, VI, No. 1 (Spring 1973).
Contents, abstracted under 1973: Peter L. Irvine and Anne Kiley, "D. H. Lawrence: Letters to Gordon and Beatrice Campbell," pp. 1-20; Keith Cushman, "D. H. Lawrence and Nancy Henry: Two Unpublished Letters and a Lost Relationship," pp. 21-31; Charles L. Ross and George J. Zytaruk, *"Goats and Compasses* and/or *Women in Love*: An Exchange," pp. 33-46; Charles Rossman, "Four Versions of D. H. Lawrence," pp. 47-70 [not abstracted]; Margaret Bolsterli, "Studies in Context: The Homosexual Ambience of Twentieth Century Literary Culture," pp. 71-85 [not abstracted]; Rose Marie Burwell, "A Catalogue of D. H. Lawrence's Reading from Early Childhood: Addenda," pp. 86-99; Richard D. Beards, "The Checklist of D. H. Lawrence Criticism and Scholarship, 1972," pp. 100-108; "Laurentiana," pp. 109-15 [only a Letter to the Editor by W. J. Keith is abstracted]; "Contributors," pp. 116-17 [not abstracted].

4069 D. H. LAWRENCE REVIEW, ed by James C. Cowan, VI, No. 2 (Summer 1973).
Contents, abstracted except as noted under 1973: Émile Delavenay, "D. H. Lawrence and Sacher-Masoch," pp. 119-48, trans by Katharine M. Delavenay from the original publication in French as "D. H. Lawrence et Sacher-Masoch:

D. H. LAWRENCE

Contribution a l'étude d'une Sensibilité Moderne," in LE ROMANTISME ANGLO-AMERICAIN: MELANGES OFFERTS À LOUIS BONNEROT (Paris: Didier, 1971), pp. 345-70; John Remsbury, *"Women in Love* as a Novel of Change," pp. 149-72; John Hoyles, "D. H. Lawrence and the Counter-Revolution," pp. 173-200; Winston Weathers, "Mythology in Modern Literature," pp. 201-13 [not abstracted]; Richard DiMaggio, "A Note on *Sons and Lovers* and Emerson's 'Experience,'" pp. 214-16; Gerald Garmon, Patsy C. Howard, and Edmund A. Bojarski, "Theses on D. H. Lawrence: 1931-1972: A Bibliography with Addenda of Senior Theses and Works in Progress," pp. 217-30; "Laurentiana," pp. 231-34 [only a Letter to the Editor from Harry T. Moore is abstracted]; "Contributors," p. 235 [not abstracted].

4070 D. H. LAWRENCE REVIEW, ed by James C. Cowan, VI, No. 3 (Fall 1973).

Contents, abstracted under 1973: John Stevens Wade, "D. H. Lawrence in Cornwall: An Interview with Stanley Hocking," pp. 237-83; A. M. Brandabur, "The Ritual Corn Harvest Scene in *The Rainbow*," pp. 284-302; Keith Sagar, *"Goats and Compasses* and *Women in Love* Again," pp. 303-8; Brian H. Finney, "A Profile of Mr. George Lazarus and His Lawrence Collection of Manuscripts and First Editions," pp. 309-12; Hebe Bair, "Lawrence as Poet," pp. 313-25; G. B. Crump, "Lawrence and the LITERATURE/FILM QUARTERLY," pp. 326-32; Carole Ferrier, "D. H. Lawrence's Pre-1920 Poetry: A Descriptive Bibliography of Manuscripts, Typescripts, and Proofs," pp. 333-59; "Laurentiana," pp. 360-63 [not abstracted]; "Research in Progress," pp. 364-65 [not abstracted]; "Contributors," p. 366, and "Index to Volume Six," pp. 367-68 [not abstracted].

4071 D. H. LAWRENCE STUDIES (Kyôto), No. 1, *"Shirokujaku"* (*The White Peacock* Number) (April 1973).

Contents, abstracted under 1973: Sadanobu Kai, Foreword, pp. 1-3 [not abstracted]; Iwao Nishimura, [*Shirokujaku* (*The White Peacock*)], pp. 4-36 [not abstracted]; Masakazu Koga, *"Shirokujaku* ni Okeru Shizen to Ningen" (Nature and Man in *The White Peacock*), pp. 37-52; Hirokazu Yoshimura, *"Shirokujaku* no Jinbutsu o Megutte--Cyril Beardsall o Chûshin ni" (A Study of Cyril Beardsall in *The White Peacock*), pp. 53-73; Yasushi Sugiyama, *"Shirokujaku* ni Okeru Sei no Yakudô to Shi" (Quickening of Life and Death in *The White Peacock*), pp. 75-94; Masako Yoshida, *"Shirokujaku* ni Okeru Ambivalence no Mondai" (An Inquiry into Ambivalence in *The White Peacock*), pp. 95-122; Kaien Kitazaki, "A. Huxley no Shiten kara no *Shirokujaku* Ron" (A Study of *The White Peacock* from A. Huxley's Viewpoint), pp. 123-43; Masuko Fujiwara, "Egdon to Nethermere" (Egdon and Nethermere), pp. 145-91; *The White Peacock* Bibliography [not abstracted]. [In Japanese.]

4072 DiGaetani, John Louis. "Wagnerian Patterns in the Fiction of Joseph Conrad, D. H. Lawrence, Virginia Woolf, and James Joyce," DISSERTATION ABSTRACTS INTERNATIONAL,

XXXIV (1974), 7745A. Unpublished dissertation, University of Wisconsin (Madison), 1973. Rvd and pub as RICHARD WAGNER AND THE MODERN BRITISH NOVEL (Lond: Associated University Presses, 1978).

4073 DiMaggio, Richard. "A Note on *Sons and Lovers* and Emerson's 'Experience,' " D. H. LAWRENCE REVIEW, VI (Summer 1973), 214-16.

The title of *Sons and Lovers* "may have been suggested" to DHL by a passage in Emerson's essay "Experience." The essay "brings into focus an unsentimental view of grief resulting from the death of a loved one."

4074 Donoghue, Denis. " 'Till the Fight is Finished': D. H. Lawrence in His Letters," in D. H. LAWRENCE: NOVELIST, POET, PROPHET, ed by Stephen Spender (Lond: Weidenfeld & Nicolson; NY: Harper & Row, 1973), pp. 197-209.

Like his works of fiction, DHL's letters cannot be taken at face value because they are subject to some of the same forces which are at work in the fiction. The letters must be read with a sense of their belonging to the creative work. While the spitefulness of some of the letters is disturbing, with DHL one must take the rough with the smooth, for this is his authenticity. In friendship as in art, DHL demanded tension, energy, and spontaneity. In his later years, he turned away from people "and looked to the earth itself for the only genuine values." Even in some of his most bitter and hostile letters there is gentleness and tact.

4075 Drabble, Margaret. "Lawrence's Aphrodite," ENCOUNTER, No. 41 (Aug 1973), 77-79.

[Review of Robert Lucas, FRIEDA LAWRENCE, trans by Geoffrey Skelton, commenting briefly on Frieda's "disastrous" sexual relation with Ernest Weekley, the difficulties of life with DHL, and the "cheering" account of her old age.]

4076 Elder, John Clark. "Towards a New Objectivity: Essays on the Body and Nature in Faulkner, Lawrence, and Mann," DISSERTATION ABSTRACTS INTERNATIONAL, XXXIV (1974), 7228A. Unpublished dissertation, Yale University, 1973.

[Focuses on *Sons and Lovers, The Rainbow,* and *Women in Love.*]

4077 Ellmann, Richard. GOLDEN CODGERS: BIOGRAPHICAL SPECULATIONS (NY: Oxford UP, 1973), pp. 114, 117-18, 120, 121, 122, 124, 154.

[Brief discussion of DHL's being "attracted by images of Christ" and willingness "to revise Christianity and its metaphors," his use of the cross as "emblematic of the failure to cohabit properly," his sharing with Joyce the treatment of "the forbidden as well as the commonplace" and with Yeats of "an exaltation of spontaneous ignorance," his use of key words such as "light" and "dark" in *The Rainbow* and *Women in Love.*]

4078 Exner, Julian. "Theater pro und contra 'Women's Lib'. Nuentdeckter D. H. Lawrence und umfunktionierter Shakespeare" (Theater for or against "Women's Lib". A Rediscovered Play by D. H. Lawrence and a Re-interpreted Play by Shakespeare), FRANKFURTER RUNDSCHAU (15 Dec 1973).

Unlike DHL's other plays, *The Merry-Go-Round* has strong comic traits. Its happy ending makes it almost the proletarian counterpart to AS YOU LIKE IT. Despite the comedy form, the play is full of intricate social and erotic tensions. [Review of the performance of DHL's play at the Royal Court Theatre and of Charles Merowitz's production of THE TAMING OF THE SHREW.] [In German.]

4079 Faas, Egbert. "Charles Olson and D. H. Lawrence: Aesthetics of the 'Primitive Abstract,'" BOUNDARY 2, II, Nos. 1-2 (1973-1974), 113-26.

Olson was directly influenced by DHL's criticism of Western civilization: his rejection of Christianity for its "fall into teleological, future-oriented thinking about the beyond"; his rejection of Socratic abstract thought; his search for a "living cosmos" in North American Indians, Mexicans, pre-Socratic cultures, and "the debris of our own civilization." Like DHL, "Olson lacked the 'critical intelligence' and erudition to relate his insights to the mainstream of Western thought of which they remain a product, however much they tend to reverse it."

4080 Fenby, George. "The Organic Self (A Study of Selected English Working-Class Fiction)," DISSERTATION ABSTRACTS INTERNATIONAL, XXXIII (1973), 6352A-53A. Unpublished dissertation, University of Connecticut, 1973.

[Includes discussion of Lawrence, Sillitoe, Storey, Braine, Waterhouse.]

4081 Ferrier, Carole. "D. H. Lawrence's Pre-1920 Poetry: A Descriptive Bibliography of Manuscripts, Typescripts, and Proofs," D. H. LAWRENCE REVIEW, VI (Fall 1973), 333-59.

[Part A gives detailed descriptions, listings, and locations of manuscripts, typescripts, and proofs of DHL's pre-1920 poetry, superseding all previous bibliographies; Part B gives further details of individual manuscripts, typescripts, and proofs described in Part A. Also includes a "Key to Abbreviations and Clue Titles" and a partial list of errors in *The Complete Poems of D. H. Lawrence*, ed by Vivian de Sola Pinto and Warren Roberts (rvd ed., 1971).]

4082 "Fiction," in "Notes on Current Books," VIRGINIA QUARTERLY REVIEW, XLIX (Spring 1973), lvii.

John Thomas and Lady Jane is "much more serious in intent with somewhat less obtrusive sexual encounters" than *Lady Chatterley's Lover*. But the "sociological aspects" of the story are emphasized, with Clifford as the symbol of the impotent upper classes, the virile gamekeeper as "the hope of mankind," and Connie as "the hapless Jane, upon whose body the working class might avenge itself by debasing her."

4083 Filippi, Zivan. "D. H. Lawrence--Mit o ponovnom rodenju" (D. H. Lawrence: The Myth of Rebirth), KNJIŽEVNA SMOTRA, No. 16 (1973), 41-60.
[On the thematic myth of rebirth in *The Plumed Serpent*.] [In Serbo-Croatian.]

4084 Finney, Brian Hubert. "The Artistic Development of D. H. Lawrence as a Writer of Short Stories." Unpublished dissertation, London University, 1973. [Listed in Lawrence F. McNamee, DISSERTATIONS IN ENGLISH AND AMERICAN LITERATURE, SUPP II (NY and Lond: Bowker, 1974), p. 369.]

4085 Finney, Brian H. "A Profile of Mr. George Lazarus and His Lawrence Collection of Manuscripts and First Editions," D. H. LAWRENCE REVIEW, VI (Fall 1973), 309-12.
[A description of the manuscripts, letters, and first editions of DHL's novels, collected over forty years, by George Lazarus.]

4086 Finney, Brian H. "Two Missing Pages from *The Ladybird*," REVIEW OF ENGLISH STUDIES, XXIV (May 1973), 191-92.
It is evident from the holograph of *The Ladybird* that two pages of the MS, falling between pp. 48 and 51, have been omitted in all published texts. The missing material is included here.

4087 Ford, George. "Jessie Chambers' Last Tape on D. H. Lawrence," MOSAIC, VI (Spring 1973), 1-12.
Jessie Chambers wrote fiction in order to achieve a true perspective on DHL, but felt that her fiction failed in this regard. She was more successful in her aim, because of what she writes about DHL the man, in her letters to S. S. Koteliansky, none of which so far has been published. According to Jessie, DHL's personal failures lie in his subjection to his mother and his rejection of Christianity.
[Includes extracts (pp. 8-12), largely restricted to her comments on DHL, from sixteen letters from Jessie Chambers to Koteliansky, written 1936-1938, and one letter written in 1943. See also George J. Zytaruk (ed), "The Collected Letters of Jessie Chambers," D. H. LAWRENCE REVIEW, XII, Nos. 1 and 2 (Spring and Summer 1979), 1-237, espec pp. 134-55, 160-84, 185-87, which includes the full texts of thirty-nine letters from Jessie to Koteliansky and three letters by her husband John R. (Jack) Wood to Koteliansky.]

4088 Fujiwara, Masuko. "Egdon to Nethermere" (Egdon and Nethermere), D. H. LAWRENCE STUDIES (Kyoto), No. 1 (April 1973), 145-91.
[The second of two articles on Hardy and DHL.] Egdon Heath in Hardy's THE RETURN OF THE NATIVE is not only the natural background of the story but also the symbolic embodiment of a supernatural will controlling the movements of the characters in the novel. A similar relation between natural scenes and characters can be seen in DHL's *The White Peacock*. Comparative study of the two works makes clear that, while DHL had learned much from his literary master, his achievement had finally come to be much different from Hardy's. [See

also Masuko Fujiwara, "D. H. Lawrence to T. Hardy (I)" (D. H. Lawrence and T. Hardy [I]), KATAHIRA (Chuba Katahira), No. 7 (June 1970), 193-220.] [In Japanese.]

4089 Garmon, Gerald, Patsy C. Howard, and Edmund A. Bojarski. "Theses on D. H. Lawrence: 1931-1972: A Bibliography with Addenda of Senior Theses and Works in Progress," D. H. LAWRENCE REVIEW, VI (Summer 1972), 217-30.

[This bibliography lists 168 master's and nineteen honor's theses. See also Dennis Jackson, "Theses on D. H. Lawrence: Bibliographical Addenda," D. H. LAWRENCE REVIEW, VIII (Spring 1975), 106-12; Toshitaka Shirai, "A Checklist of Theses on Lawrence in Japan, 1968-1973," D. H. LAWRENCE REVIEW, VIII (Summer 1975), 233-35; and Fleda Brown Jackson, "Doctoral Dissertations and Masters Theses on D. H. Lawrence: Bibliographical Addenda," D. H. LAWRENCE REVIEW, X (Fall 1977), 299-308.]

4090 Garnett, David. "Frieda and Lawrence," in D. H. LAWRENCE: NOVELIST, POET, PROPHET, ed by Stephen Spender (Lond: Weidenfeld & Nicolson; NY: Harper & Row, 1973), pp. 37-41; rvd and rptd as "D. H. Lawrence and Frieda," in GREAT FRIENDS, by David Garnett (Lond: Macmillan, 1979), pp. 74-93.

[Biographical comment about Frieda's first marriage to Ernest Weekley and her meeting with DHL. Includes a memoir of Garnett's meetings with the Lawrences: Frieda seemed like a "lioness"; DHL seemed more alive than most human beings.]

4091 Gerber, Stephen. "Character, Language, and Experience in 'Water Party,' " PAUNCH, Nos. 36-37 (April 1973), 3-29.

In *Women in Love,* DHL's language, rather than giving "a direct literary rendering of his character's unconscious," as Alan Friedman asserts, modulates among conscious, preconscious, and unconscious responses.

4092 Gersh, Gabriel. "In Search of D. H. Lawrence's *Sea and Sardinia,*" QUEEN'S QUARTERLY, LXXX (1973), 581-88.

During the brief visit to Sardinia which DHL imposed on himself and Frieda early in 1921, he showed little interest in the history or totality of Sardinia. Moreover, his account of the trip, in *Sea and Sardinia*, is filled with boring personal squabbles, grievances, strident generalizations, and sexual antagonisms. Yet a second reading of the account pushes these personal details into diminished footnotes. What remains, the essence of the book, is a series of intensely felt, beautiful landscapes and episodes which reveal DHL's marvelous power to be intensely alive to the experience of the moment.

4093 Glicksberg, Charles I. "D. H. Lawrence and the Religion of Sex," THE SEXUAL REVOLUTION IN MODERN ENGLISH LITERATURE (The Hague: Martinus Nijhoff, 1973), pp. 88-117; additional references to DHL pp. xii, xvi, xix, 36, 73, 74, 119, 120, 132, 143, 161, 184, 186.

DHL was "a religious artist, . . .who sought fullness of life, the release of the vital impulses, the affirmation of the whole man." To him, "love...is sacramental in character," but he exalts Eros, not Agape, and presents sexual union as the expression not of sin and suffering but of liberation and ecstasy. In *The White Peacock,* Annable is a "personification of Nature." In his scathing denunciation of Lettie, DHL "begins his diatribes against the destructive woman" who "renounces her intrinsic selfhood" and endeavors to dominate the male in the war of the sexes. The theme is further developed in *The Trespasser* in Siegmund's relationship with Helena, a moody, dreaming woman who rejects the animal in humanity. In *Sons and Lovers,* while examining Paul's sexual conflict, "his refusal to face the truth about his passionately physical desires," DHL moves "toward a coherent, rounded presentation of his love ethic." In *Aaron's Rod,* he takes up "the problem of love and the limitations of marriage," rejecting the Christian view of love, which, he felt, "leads to the immolation of body and soul." In *The Rainbow,* DHL made a revolutionary attack on conventional morality and presented sex as "a serious, normal, central preoccupation of mankind." In *Women in Love,* Birkin chooses instinctive blood knowledge in sensuality with Ursula over Hermione's feminist, mental knowledge. Gerald Crich, the potent, sexually attractive "male conquistador," is "marked for destruction in his relationship with Gudrun," the dominating, intellectual woman. In *Lady Chatterley's Lover,* DHL's "aim was to reinstate the primacy of the phallic consciousness" in "the harmonious integration of mind and body, flesh and spirit." For DHL, "sexuality is a surrogate for religion," and he describes the sexual experience in numinous language.

4094 Green, Eleanor H. "The Works of D. H. Lawrence in Relation to the Ideas of Schopenhauer and Nietzsche." Unpublished dissertation, University of Nottingham, 1973. [Listed in Lawrence F. McNamee, DISSERTATIONS IN ENGLISH AND AMERICAN LITERATURE, SUPP II (NY & Lond: Bowker, 1974), p. 369.]

4095 Greiff, Louis K. "The Rhythm of Perfection: A Study and Reappraisal of D. H. Lawrence's 'Leadership Novels'--*Aaron's Rod, Kangaroo,* and *The Plumed Serpent,*" DISSERTATION ABSTRACTS INTERNATIONAL, XXXIV (1974), 6641A. Unpublished dissertation, Syracuse University, 1973.

4096 Gullason, Thomas A. "Revelation and Evolution: A Neglected Dimension of the Short Story," STUDIES IN SHORT FICTION, X (Fall 1973), 348-56.
[Takes issue with Mark Schorer's assertion that the short story " 'is an art of moral revelation, the novel an art of moral evolution' " and with his analysis of "The Horse Dealer's Daughter."] What "evolves" in "The Horse Dealer's Daughter" "are the characters of Mabel Pervin and Dr. Fergusson, their ambiguous and ambivalent relationship, and the theme." These are "reenforced and heightened by the cyclical, spiraling, and advancing structure of the work; and by a variety of motifs and images that echo and reecho as musical counterpoint." "Revelation alone leaves the experience" in the story "isolated and private," "a brief encounter and sudden change in two people." Evolution gives "the isolated incident a sense of public value...and a universalizing quality."

4097 Gutierrez, Donald. "The Pressures of Love: Kinesthetic Action in an Early Lawrence Poem," CONTEMPORARY POETRY, I (Winter 1973), 6-20.

DHL's early poem "Lightning" uses kinesthetic imagery of strain, tension, or muscular activity to indicate emotional intensity. The poem depicts a girl torn between sexual love and fear, and a youth's frustration and rage at her condition. "Light," effected by lightning, reveals her deep terror of a sexual act, whereas darkness, in a reversal of the usual Laurentian pattern, embodies his ignorance rather than instinctual power. DHL uses similar kinesthetic diction in the cherry-orchard scene in *Sons and Lovers* in which Paul tries to induce Miriam to have sexual relations but finds her involuntarily opposed to the idea. The situation may also be related to DHL's theory in "Introduction to These Paintings" of the paralysis induced in the Renaissance mind by the fear of syphilis.

4098 Hamalian, Leo (ed). D. H. LAWRENCE: A COLLECTION OF CRITICISM (NY: McGraw-Hill [Contemporary Studies in Literature], 1973).

Contents, abstracted under year of first publication: Leo Hamalian, "Introduction," pp. 1-13; DHL, "Autobiographical Sketch," pp. 14-16 [Not the same as his "Autobiographical Sketch" in *Assorted Articles* (1930), 172-82; not abstracted]; Frieda Lawrence, "D. H. Lawrence, the Failure," pp. 17-19, from FRIEDA LAWRENCE: THE MEMOIRS AND CORRESPONDENCE, ed by E. W. Tedlock, Jr. (Lond: Heinemann, 1961; NY: Knopf, 1964), pp. 437-39; Anais Nin, "Lawrence's World," pp. 20-21, from D. H. LAWRENCE: AN UNPROFESSIONAL STUDY (Paris: E. W. Titus, 1932; rptd Lond: Neville Spearmann, 1961), pp. 4-5; Alfred Kazin, "Sons, Lovers, and Mothers," pp. 22-32, from PARTISAN REVIEW, XXIX (Summer 1962), 373-85, and from "Introduction," *Sons and Lovers* by D. H. Lawrence (NY: Random House, Modern Library, 1962), pp. vii-xix; Colin Clarke, "Reductive Energy in *The Rainbow*," pp. 33-53, from RIVER OF DISSOLUTION: D. H. LAWRENCE AND ENGLISH ROMANTICISM (Lond: Routledge & Kegan Paul; NY: Barnes & Noble, 1969), pp. 45-68; David Cavitch, "On *Women in Love*," pp. 54-64, from D. H. LAWRENCE AND THE NEW WORLD (NY: Oxford UP, 1969), pp. 61-76; Yudhishtar, "The Changing Scene: *Aaron's Rod*," pp. 65-80, from CONFLICT IN THE NOVELS OF D. H. LAWRENCE (Edinburgh: Oliver & Boyd; NY: Barnes & Noble, 1969), pp. 210-30; Anthony Beal, "On *Kangaroo*," pp. 81-86, from D. H. LAWRENCE (Edinburgh: Oliver & Boyd, 1961), pp. 69-77; Keith Sagar, "The Lost Trail: *The Plumed Serpent*," pp. 87-96, from THE ART OF D. H. LAWRENCE (Cambridge: Cambridge UP, 1966), pp. 159-68; Graham Hough, "On *Lady Chatterley's Lover*," pp. 97-108, from THE DARK SUN: A STUDY OF D. H. LAWRENCE (Lond: Gerald Duckworth, 1956; NY: Macmillan, 1957), pp. 149-66; Monroe Engel, "The Continuity of Lawrence's Short Novels," pp. 109-17, from HUDSON REVIEW, XI (Summer 1958), 201-9; Kenneth Rexroth, "The Poetry of D. H. Lawrence," pp. 118-32, from "Introduction," *D. H. Lawrence: Selected Poems* (NY: New Directions, 1948; rptd NY: Viking P, Compass Books, 1959), pp. 1-23; Dan Jacobson, "D. H. Lawrence and Modern Society," pp. 133-43, from JOURNAL OF CONTEMPORARY HISTORY, II, No. 2 (April 1967), 81-92; "Bibliography," pp. 145-51 [not abstracted].

4099 Hamalian, Leo. "Introduction," D. H. LAWRENCE: A COLLECTION OF CRITICISM, ed by Leo Hamalian (NY: McGraw-Hill, 1973), pp. 1-13.

"During most of Lawrence's creative career, few critics were tuned into his novels, stories, poetry, plays, criticism, and 'pollyanalytics,'" but major critics of the "'Lawrence revival' of the fifties" read him with the "imaginative response" his work requires. [Briefly traces the high points of DHL's life, then surveys the articles and excerpts rptd in this collection.]

4100 Hardy, Barbara. "Women in D. H. Lawrence's Works," in D. H. LAWRENCE: NOVELIST, POET, PROPHET, ed Stephen Spender (Lond: Weidenfeld & Nicolson; NY: Barnes & Noble, 1973), pp. 90-121.

DHL is hard on women "as he sheds and fails to shed his Oedipal sickness." Both Jessie Chambers and Helen Corke believed it difficult for DHL to accept mind in women. Though he had a continual battle with the female, *Look! We Have Come Through!* and *More Pansies* can be praised for his admission that "men and women are alike" and for his knowledge of sexual feeling. While DHL often seems to stereotype women, he does the same with male characters. "Where he seems most chauvinistic he is probably most personal," as in "The Woman Who Rode Away," which can be revealingly compared to "The Ship of Death." Some of the images of male-female conjunction which DHL uses in *Women in Love* occur also in *Look! We Have Come Through!* Though DHL's eros "makes no claims to generosity" in its discovery of self and other through respect, it does have an affinity with agape. If DHL could not sympathize with the suffragettes, he could sympathize with Ursula's quest for liberation. Even when he uses the women characters as "instruments," he has moments which show the women as human beings.

4101 Harris, Janice Hubbard. "Mode and Development in D. H. Lawrence's Tales," DISSERTATION ABSTRACTS INTERNATIONAL, XXXIV (1974), 5960A. Unpublished dissertation, Brown University, 1973. Extensively rvd and pub as THE SHORT FICTION OF D. H. LAWRENCE (New Brunswick, NJ: Rutgers UP, 1984).

4102 Hashimoto, Makinori. "Hebi to Tsuki to Shochoshugi: D. H. Lawrence no Sozoryoku" (Serpent, Moon, and Symbolism in D. H. Lawrence), OBERON, XV, No. 1 (1973), 96-119.

[In Japanese.]

4103 Haya, Kenichi. "Lawrence o do yomuka" (How to Read Lawrence), EIGO SEINEN, No. 119 (1973), 134-35.

[In Japanese.]

4104 Heath, Alice C. "Characterization and the Concept of the Self in the Novels of D. H. Lawrence," DISSERTATION ABSTRACTS INTERNATIONAL, XXXV (1974), 3743A. Unpublished dissertation, Temple University, 1973.

4105 Hebert, Hugh. "The Whipper-in," GUARDIAN (Manchester), 7 Nov 1973, p. 12.

DHL wrote to Edward Garnett (1 Feb 1913) with regard to his plays, "an audience might be found in England for some of my stuff, if there were a man to whip 'em in. It's the producer that is lacking, not the audience." The "man to whip 'em in" did not turn up until more than fifty years later, in the person of Peter Gill, director of the DHL season of plays in 1968 and of the 1973 Royal Court Theatre production of *The Merry-Go-Round*. [Profile-interview of Peter Gill.]

4106 Heilbrun, Carolyn G. TOWARD A RECOGNITION OF ANDROGYNY (NY: Alfred A. Knopf, 1973); pub in England as TOWARDS ANDROGYNY: ASPECTS OF MALE AND FEMALE IN LITERATURE (Lond: Gollancz, 1973), pp. 101-10 and passim.

While DHL deserves the opprobrium of feminists, who see him as the arch-chauvinist he undoubtedly was, *The Rainbow*, seen as a separate work from *Women in Love*, is prophetic in its exploration of a world in which the lost "feminine" impulse is reborn. It is significant that in this myth of re-creation of the spiritual, rebirth consists of claiming spiritual rather than physical parenthood; hence, the rebirth is through a female who is recognized not by her physical parent but by the spiritual parent whose child she becomes.

4107 Herban, Patricia L. "The Theme of War in the Writings of D. H. Lawrence," DISSERTATION ABSTRACTS INTERNATIONAL, XXXIV (1974), 7757A. Unpublished dissertation, University of Pennsylvania, 1973.

4108 Hinz, Evelyn J. "Lorenzo Mythistoricus: Studies in the Archetypal Imagination of D. H. Lawrence," DISSERTATION ABSTRACTS INTERNATIONAL, XXXIII (1973), 6871A. Unpublished dissertation, University of Massachusetts, 1973.

4109 Hinz, Evelyn J. "Novels and Novelists," QUEEN'S QUARTERLY, LXXX (Spring 1973), 137-38.

Not only does *John Thomas and Lady Jane* "have a finished quality that distinguishes it from the typical draft but also there is such a radical difference in the controlling perspective" of this second version and the third version of *Lady Chatterley's Lover* "that one is tempted to view them as two independent approaches to the same material." *John Thomas and Lady Jane* "fulfills the novelistic requirements of the 'great tradition,'" whereas *Lady Chatterley's Lover* "belongs to that 'divergent strain' of the novel characterized by its mythic quality," a "generic difference" that accounts for their "qualitative difference."

4110 Hoffman, Lois. "A Catalogue of the Frieda Lawrence Manuscripts in German at the University of Texas," LIBRARY CHRONICLE OF THE UNIVERSITY OF TEXAS AT AUSTIN, ns VI (Dec 1973), 87-105.

[Catalogue of 133 German letters which are part of the Frieda Lawrence collection of MSS in the Humanities Research Center of the University of Texas at Austin. Included are 58 letters from Frieda to her mother between 1900 and 1930 with many references to DHL, 16 letters from Dr. Otto Gross to the young Frieda, and miscellaneous letters to and from Frieda and the Richthofens. Illustrated with photographs of Frieda, her sisters Else and Johanna, and their mother.]

4111 Howe, Marguerite Beede. "D. H. Lawrence as Ego Psychologist: Self and Being in the Novels," DISSERTATION ABSTRACTS INTERNATIONAL, XXXVII (1976), 3643A. Unpublished dissertation, Columbia University, 1973. Rvd and pub as THE ART OF THE SELF IN D. H. LAWRENCE (Athens: Ohio UP, 1977).

4112 Hoyles, John. "D. H. Lawrence and the Counter-Revolution: An Essay in Socialist Aesthetics," D. H. LAWRENCE REVIEW, VI (Summer 1973), 173-200.

This essay reviews the assessments of DHL's work by Christopher Caudwell, STUDIES IN A DYING CULTURE (1938), and Kate Millett, SEXUAL POLITICS (1970), as examples of Marxist and feminist criticism, "pointing out. . . limitations and contradictions, . . .and suggesting. . .new bases for" a socialist aesthetic. According to Caudwell, DHL is a "bourgeois artist who. . .exposes the contradictions in bourgeois society" but is unable to solve them. He "regresses to Fascism"; "instead of advancing beyond the limitations of bourgeois culture, he shares that culture's profound neurosis and returns to the primitive." "Caudwell does not recognize. . .that Lawrence develops a concept of collective neurosis which is not. . .applicable to Fascism but to the vacuous bankruptcy of bourgeois social relations." "One of the flaws in Kate Millett's approach to Lawrence is her inability to provide any correlation between sociological and aesthetic judgments." Her criticism of DHL's works amounts to "special pleading" in which analysis is tailored to fit the theory. For DHL, "sexual politics means not the war of the sexes conducted in a transcendental vacuum. . . , and not a metaphysic of male chauvinism to which his art is subdued, but a full and frank investigation through the creative imagination of the relationship between class and sexuality, between the interior life of the individual" and his universe. "The way in which an artist reflects the complexities of his culture irrespective of any ideological positions which can be extrapolated from" his art must be justly examined by the critic.

4113 Hugger, Ann-Grete. "The Dichotomy between Private and Public Sphere: Sex Roles in D. H. Lawrence's Novels," LANGUAGE AND LITERATURE (Copenhagen), II (Nov 1973), 127-36.

In *Women in Love* DHL wanted to demonstrate that woman's wish for equality and participation is false ideology because it leads to destruction of true femininity. The alienating effect of industrialism can be overcome only in personal relationships withdrawn from society. Sexual experience thus comes to play an all-important role, since here man can still be spontaneous and vital. Hence several of DHL's novels end with a socially isolated marriage based on an ancient sex-role pattern. The social isolation is partly the result of a regressive sexual ideology, partly of a corresponding social ideology based on a regressive, "back to nature" critique of capitalist industrial society.

4114 Hulley, Kathleen. "Disintegration as Symbol of Community: A Study of *The Rainbow, Women in Love*, LIGHT IN AUGUST, PRISONER OF GRACE, EXCEPT THE LORD, NOT HONOUR MORE, and HERZOG," DISSERTATION ABSTRACTS INTERNATIONAL, XXXIV (1974), 6643A-44A. Unpublished dissertation, University of California at Davis, 1973.

4115 Huxley, Juliette. "Ottoline," ADAM INTERNATIONAL REVIEW, Nos. 370-75 (1973), pp. 92-93.
[Memoir of Lady Ottoline Morrell at Garsington, recalling the *tableaux vivantes* presented at Christmas 1916 which DHL used in *Women in Love*.]

4116 Ichihashi, Katsue. "Lawrence to Shibetsugo no Frieda" (Frieda Bereaved of Lawrence), HERON (Saitama University), No. 7 (Feb 1973), 33-42.
[An introduction to the activities of Frieda Lawrence during her widowhood, as derived from FRIEDA LAWRENCE: THE MEMOIRS AND CORRESPONDENCE, ed by E. W. Tedlock, Jr. (1961). Among the topics discussed are Frieda's recovery from the shock of DHL's death, the solution to the matter of inheritance, her life at Kiowa Ranch with Angelo Ravagli, her deep love for the children born of her first marriage to Ernest Weekley, and her correspondence with John Middleton Murry revealing their one-time intimacy.] [In Japanese.]

4117 Imaizumi, Haruko. "*Koisuru Onnatachi* ni Okeru Lawrence no Ai no Kannen" (The Idea of Love in Lawrence's *Women in Love*), DOSHISHA LITERATURE (Doshisha University), No. 27 (Nov 1973), 51-66.
[Examining DHL's idea of love in *Women in Love*, the author first clarifies the meaning of Birkin's term "star-equilibrium," then compares this concept with Martin Buber's "I-Thou" relationship. To DHL, everything in the universe is of, from, and by the unknown "dark God."] [In Japanese.]

4118 "The Immorality of Lady Chatterley," TIMES LITERARY SUPPLEMENT (Lond), 27 April 1973, pp. 471-72; rptd as "The Three Lady Chatterleys," ESSAYS AND REVIEWS FROM TLS, XII (Lond: Oxford UP, 1974), pp. 103-14.
The First Lady Chatterley is "the least offensive" of the three versions: "lacking the crudely opposed contrasts of *John Thomas and Lady Jane* and more especially of *Lady Chatterley's Lover*, it is more honest in observation," but "more obscure in purpose." But "the 'symbolic' abstractions which he imposed on his vision of the real world" trapped DHL. The development of his "idea" through three successive versions "brought fully into the open how mechanical is the view it offers of the possibilities of the life we can live now--and how much hatred lies within its assumption of tenderness." [See also replies by Geoffrey

Strickland and by Malcolm Muggeridge (not abstracted), in "Lady Chatterley," TIMES LITERARY SUPPLEMENT (Lond), 11 May 1973, p. 528.]

4119 Irvine, Peter L., and Anne Kiley (eds). "D. H. Lawrence: Letters to Gordon and Beatrice Campbell," D. H. LAWRENCE REVIEW, VI (Spring 1973), 1-20.

"The D. H. Lawrence Collection of the University of Cincinnati Library holds fourteen letters from Lawrence to Gordon Campbell, later Lord Glenavy, and his wife, Beatrice." Five of these letters were published in *The Collected Letters of D. H. Lawrence*, ed by Harry T. Moore (1962); four others were quoted briefly in Moore's THE INTELLIGENT HEART: THE STORY OF D. H. LAWRENCE (1954); and several others are quoted briefly in Lady Glenavy's memoir, TODAY WE WILL ONLY GOSSIP (1964). Nine letters from DHL to the Campbells are published here "in their entirety for the first time." They provide "glimpses into personal relationships within the Lawrence circle during the war years and, more important, into Lawrence's reactions to wartime society." Most of the letters also refer to DHL's plans for a utopian community, Rananim.

4120 Jacobson, Sibyl. "The Paradox of Fulfillment: A Discussion of *Women in Love*," JOURNAL OF NARRATIVE TECHNIQUE, III (Jan 1973), 53-65.

The search for fulfillment is the underlying metaphor of *Women in Love*. The paradoxical nature of the images used as vehicles for psychological characterization allows a double perspective essential to the theme that fulfillment is both necessary and impossible. Patterns of organic imagery, burden imagery, and stellar imagery are especially significant.

4121 James, Clive. "D. H. Lawrence in Transit," in D. H. LAWRENCE: NOVELIST, POET, PROPHET, ed by Stephen Spender (Lond: Weidenfeld & Nicolson; NY: Harper & Row, 1973), pp. 159-69; rptd in FIRST REACTIONS: CRITICAL ESSAYS, by Clive James (NY: Alfred A. Knopf, 1980), pp. 74-86.

DHL's spiritual odyssey across several continents was both a quest for meaning and an attempt to escape from all that he had revolted against. DHL was a dreamer who never found things "important enough," whose intimacy with a place bred "unease," and who thus searched for a significance that this world has never supplied. Though it is often impossible to reconcile the opposing things he says, DHL was never bothered by his contradictions. He could effortlessly reproduce reality, as in *Sea and Sardinia, Twilight in Italy, Kangaroo, The Plumed Serpent*, despite his "now-rampant mysticism." *Etruscan Places* is a gentle book, "the book of a strong man dying." The closest DHL ever came to finding a home was the Kiowa ranch in New Mexico, as can be told by reading *St. Mawr* and "Reflections on the Death of a Porcupine."

4122 Janik, Del Ivan. "Toward 'Thingness': Cézanne's Painting and Lawrence's Poetry," TWENTIETH CENTURY LITERATURE, XIX (April 1973), 119-28.

DHL's "Art and Morality" and "Introduction to These Paintings" reveal "the special intuitive consciousness" he saw in Cézanne's work and can be "read as retrospective descriptions" of DHL's "own poetic development." In writing of Cézanne's struggle to free his art "from the element of chiche," DHL characterized "his own attempt to give human intuition its rightful place in poetry and fiction." Just as Cézanne abandoned the "principles of 'good drawing' " and the " 'kodak-vision,' " DHL concluded that the traditional poetic forms were obstacles to "an intuitive expression of the 'thingness' of things." [Contains brief discussions of "The Hand of the Betrothed," and *Birds, Beasts and Flowers.*]

4123 Kabiljo-Šutić, Simha. "Filozofija vitalizma D. H. Lorensa i O. Hakslija--Uticaj i paralele" (The Philosophy of Vitalism in D. H. Lawrence and A. Huxley: Influence and Parallels), KNJIŽEVNAK KRITIKA, No. 3 (1973), 29-54.
[In Serbo-Croatian.]

4124 Kabiljo-Šutić, Simha. "Književno Prijateljstvo D. H. Lorensa i O. Hakslija" (The Literary Friendship of D. H. Lawrence and A. Huxley), SAVREMENIK: MESEČNI KNJIŽEVNI CASOPIS, XXXVII (1973), 338-52.
[After brief biographical sketches outlining the many striking differences between DHL and Aldous Huxley--their family and social backgrounds, education, personalities and temperaments, creative styles, and literary judgments are all widely divergent--the author traces the evolution of the two artists' close and lasting friendship.] Huxley was for DHL a source of both private and public support and encouragement, voicing respect for DHL as man and artist, even when DHL was in virtually total disrepute. Although DHL had reservations about Huxley's ideas and works, he inspired a significant change in the development of Huxley's ideas and writings. The Laurentian inspiration is seen most clearly in the sympathetic portrait of Rampion in POINT COUNTER POINT. [In South Slovenian.]

4125 Kai, Sadanobu. "Kyôbô na Junrei no Ato o Otte--Villa Mirenda" (After the Savage Pilgrimage--Villa Mirenda), STUDIES IN THE HUMANITIES (Ôsaka Medical College), No. 4 (March 1973), 76-85.
Visiting the Villa Mirenda in 1963, the writer found in the valley behind it that pinewood, which, like the wood in *Lady Chatterley's Lover*, symbolized for DHL his "HOME & MOTHER" forever.] [In Japanese.]

4126 Kamimura, Tatsuhiko. "D. H. Lawrence: Opening to the Wordless World--Toward *The Plumed Serpent* (2)," ENGLISH LITERATURE REVIEW (Kyôto Women's University), No. 17 (Dec 1973), 25-34.
[Examines DHL's inner experiences and elucidates a rich and proud ritual expressed in *The Plumed Serpent.*] Modern man does not have the opportunity or the capacity to work out in satisfactory terms the inner-relation of man and his experiences. *The Plumed Serpent*, by putting this relation in a different context, may save us from the modern predicament through ritual, a version of initiation

for modern man. [See also Tatsuhiko Kamimura, "D. H. Lawrence: Opening to the Wordless World--Toward *The Plumed Serpent* (1)," ENGLISH LITERATURE REVIEW (Kyoto Women's University), No. 16 (Nov 1972), 20-33.]

4127 Kanatani, Nobuo. "*Koisuru Onnatachi* Kenkyû--Lawrence no Gendai Gôrishugi Hihan" (A Study of *Women in Love:* Lawrence's Criticism of Modern Rationalism), JOURNAL OF TSUDA COLLEGE, No. 5 (March 1973), 39-53.

Some of the major characters of *Women in Love*, deeply immersed in modern rationalism, are destined to self-destruction in their strained attempts to conquer matter (mankind as well as nature) by mind. The book is both an analysis of this suicidal tendency of rationalism and a quest for a way out of the present crisis. [In Japanese.]

4128 Kauffmann, Stanley. "Three Cities," NEW REPUBLIC, CLXIX (15 Dec 1973), 22.

The Widowing of Mrs. Holroyd "shows that, as Lawrence was Britain's first significant working-class novelist, so he was also the first significant working-class dramatist." [Review of the production at the Long Wharf Theater, New Haven, CT.]

4129 Kawabata, Takashi. "D. H. Lawrence Ron (*Sons and Lovers* ni Okeru Lawrence no Ningenzô)" (On D. H. Lawrence: His View of Man in *Sons and Lovers*), RESEARCH BULLETIN OF OBIHIRO UNIVERSITY, IV, No. 1 (March 1973), 10-38.

In *Sons and Lovers*, DHL reviewed his own past so honestly and sincerely that he had to deny his mother as well as Jessie Chambers; he could find no hope for the future in a world symbolized by them. DHL believes that the effort to save ourselves from the ugly, suffocating world by the pursuit of happiness results in the "forcing of all human energy into a competition of mere acquisition." As an alternative means of salvation, he advocates that one must follow his conscientious, spontaneous self and also realize in others the reality of their Otherness. [In Japanese.]

4130 Kazin, Alfred. "The Writer as Political Crazy," PLAYBOY, XX (June 1973), 107-8, 136, 206-9; espec pp. 108, 136.

"An amazingly evocative novelist, essayist and poet," DHL "became the most viciously authoritarian of political pseudo philosophers" after the "blow to his shaky masculinity" of being rejected for military service on medical grounds in World War I. Having been taught by his mother "to despise the lower orders," DHL, in *Kangaroo* and *The Plumed Serpent*, expressed "thoroughly brutal," feverishly anti-democratic political views. Few writers in English can convey "the feel of life" as DHL can, but his pronouncements "about women, society, peasants, the Etruscans and their art" were "alternately repulsive and ridiculous." "A strain of personal cruelty" runs through DHL's fantasies of "unlimited domination over others"; but his "belief in blood knowledge," though analogous to Nazi rhetoric about " 'blood and soil,' " has a comic pretentiousness.

D. H. LAWRENCE

4131 Keith, W. J. "Laurentiana," D. H. LAWRENCE REVIEW, VI (Spring 1973), 109-10.
[Letter to the Editor.] DHL specialists "have memoirs and biographical studies galore;...letters;...mountains of critical commentary;...reprints of minor works;...bibliographies"--everything, in fact, except established texts of DHL's works. DHL's publishers should be persuaded "that a new scholarly edition is essential." [See also supporting letter by Harry T. Moore, "Laurentiana," D. H. LAWRENCE REVIEW, VI (Summer 1973), 231-32; and announcement by Michael Black, "Laurentiana," D. H. LAWRENCE REVIEW, VIII (Fall 1975), 375-76.]

4132 Kermode, Frank. LAWRENCE (Lond: Fontana/Collins, 1973); also pub in America as D. H. LAWRENCE (NY: Viking P [Modern Masters Series], 1973).
To define the modernity of DHL we must focus on the novels and certain long stories. For the important critical job is to show how the visionary is contained by the novelist, how DHL created a "metaphysic" *(Study of Thomas Hardy)* as an heuristic instrument without allowing it to dominate his fictions. Beginning with *The Rainbow,* and continuing through the rest of the canon, every work has a doctrinal double which spurred DHL to artistry but which had to be subdued in the act of writing fiction. DHL was an ideologue as well as an artist, and the originality and formal inventiveness of his fiction derives from the racking and transformation of ideas by living narrative. His methods of rewriting reflect his concern to criticize his own dogmatism by submitting texts to continuous, even last-minute rewritings designed to create the illusion of " 'the rhythm of a living thing' " ("German Books: Thomas Mann"). *Women in Love* is the most highly developed product of DHL's dualistic intentions; it proceeds by obscuring doctrines with narrative symbolisms capable in their nature of more general and more doubtful interpretation. At their best DHL's novels have a beneficent instability, containing but criticizing ideology. [Divided into four sections--i. "1913-1917," ii. "1917-1921," iii. "1922-1925," iv. "1925-1930"--with subsections on the novels and major ideological essays of each period.]

4133 Kermode, Frank. "The Novels of D. H. Lawrence," in D. H. LAWRENCE: NOVELIST, POET, PROPHET, ed by Stephen Spender (Lond: Weidenfeld & Nicolson; NY: Harper & Row, 1973), pp. 77-89.
In writing *The White Peacock* DHL was learning his trade. Annable, the most interesting character, was not planned but an "intruder" whom DHL kept. *The Trespasser,* DHL's Wagnerian novel, taken from the story of a true Wagnerian, Helen Corke, depicts the ethereal type of woman "whose culture castrated" her man. This theme led directly to DHL's evolving a non-Freudian theory of "the main source of men's troubles--the mother as mistress" in *Sons and Lovers,* in which DHL's random technique--telling here, showing there--is not employed for the sake of form but to make the novel "quick." *The Lost Girl* is another "study in repression and redemption." In *The Rainbow* and *Women in Love,* constantly subverting "conventional expectations," DHL takes more freedom with form. In the posthumously published Foreword to *Sons and Lovers,* DHL evolved his theory of the polarity of male and female, love and law, flesh and word which he

developed further in the *Study of Thomas Hardy* and "The Crown" into the metaphysic underlying *The Rainbow* and *Women in Love*. In these novels, and to a lesser extent in *Aaron's Rod, Kangaroo,* and *The Plumed Serpent,* the tale saves the artist by the intrusion of critiques of the metaphysic, voiced by such characters as Ursula, Hermione, and Loerke. *The Rainbow* and *Women in Love* are the climax of DHL's career. After writing them he becomes more dogmatic and less receptive to new ideas and impressions. Though *The Plumed Serpent* sometimes triumphs, it is too often hysterical and full of the faults of DHL's "now perpetual exasperation." "Most of Lawrence is in *Lady Chatterley's Lover,*" a book easily criticized or laughed at, but one "founded on a kind of self-recognition" which allows it to stand beside *The Rainbow* and *Women in Love*.

4134 Kitazaki, Kaien. "A. Huxley no Shiten kara no *Shirokujaku* Ron" (A Study of *The White Peacock* from A. Huxley's Viewpoint), D. H. LAWRENCE STUDIES (Kyôto), No. 1 (April 1973), 123-43.
[The purpose of this study is to demonstrate the accuracy of Aldous Huxley's view of DHL as an artist. *The White Peacock* is examined from Huxley's unique perspective as expressed in his "Introduction" to his edition of *The Letters of D. H. Lawrence* (1932).] [In Japanese.]

4135 Kitazawa, Shigehisa. D. H. RORENSU, SONO BUNGAKU TO JINSEI (D. H. Lawrence, His Literature and His Life) (Tôkyô: Bokusui-Shobo, 1973).
[This study attempts to elucidate the "meaning" implied in DHL's writings through a close examination of his major novels, with some references to his short stories, poems, and essays. The final chapter centers on DHL's literary attack on the "materialism" of modern civilization, which has caused men to lose *l'élan vital*. The book concludes with an extensively detailed, 28-page "Chronology of the Life of Lawrence" and a 46-page bibliography of primary and secondary works.] [In Japanese.]

4136 Koga, Masakazu. "*Shirokujaku* ni Okeru Shizen to Ningen" (Nature and Man in *The White Peacock*), D. H. LAWRENCE STUDIES (Kyôto), No. 1 (April 1973), 37-52.
In *The White Peacock,* nature is very beautiful, the characters move toward destruction, and nature and people become more distant from each other. [The meaning of the novel is considered in relation to the background of the times.] [In Japanese.]

4137 Kuczkowski, Richard. "Lawrence's 'Esoteric' Psychology: *Psychoanalysis and the Unconscious* and *Fantasia of the Unconscious,*" DISSERTATION ABSTRACTS INTERNATIONAL, XXXV (1974), 1107A. Unpublished dissertation, Columbia University, 1973.

4138 Kuramochi, Saburô. "*Chatterley-Fujin no Koibito* no Mori" (Forest in *Lady Chatterley's Lover*), EIGO SEINEN, No. 118 (1973), 642-43.
[In Japanese.]

4139 Kuramochi, Saburô. "Mothers in Love--An Aspect of *Women in Love*," BULLETIN (Kyôritsu Women's University), XX (March 1973), 1-23.

The central women characters in *Women in Love* are rather characteristic of domineering "mothers" instead of "loving women." Thus, the idea of "freedom together" is important to the hero in this work.

4140 Lacy, Gerald M. "Commentary," in *The Escaped Cock*, by D. H. Lawrence, ed by Gerald M. Lacy (Los Angeles: Black Sparrow P, 1973), pp. 121-70.

["Commentary" on *The Escaped Cock* is divided into ten sections: "I. Introduction: Lawrence and the Resurrection Theme, II. Chronology: Influences and Works, III. From Story to Novel, IV. Dating the Composition of Part II, V. Publication: The Novel and the Watercolor Decorations, VI. The Final Statement, VII. The Manuscripts, VIII. The Text, IX. Table of Variants, X. Bibliography."] The theme of DHL's last major novel rose directly out of his near fatal illness in Mexico in 1925. In *The Escaped Cock* DHL resolved and "completed" the resurrection theme which was left unresolved in the fragment "The Flying Fish." In this novel he fuses the Christian myth of resurrection with one of the oldest accounts of the same myth, the story of Isis and Osiris. *The Escaped Cock* is not so much a critique of Christianity as a movement beyond it. It is post-Christian, not pre-Christian. DHL was influenced in his working of the resurrection theme by John Middleton Murry, who was writing a book on Christ; by Dorothy Brett, who did a painting of the crucifixion with Pan in the foreground; and especially by his trip to the Etruscan tombs, where he was impressed "by the brilliant sense of life, not death."

4141 Leavis, F[rank] R[aymond]. "Lawrence After Thirty Years," D. H. LAWRENCE: A CRITICAL ANTHOLOGY, ed by H. Coombes (Harmondsworth, Middlesex, England: Penguin Books, 1973), pp. 398-407.

[Address given at the University of Nottingham, 17 June 1960, at the opening of the conference and exhibition, "D. H. Lawrence After Thirty Years, 1930-1960," 17 June-30 July 1960.] [Discusses the limitations of critical assessments of DHL thirty years earlier by T. S. Eliot, E. M. Forster, John Middleton Murry, and Leavis himself.] Asserting DHL's "creative genius" is less paradoxical today than it was thirty years ago when CRITERION printed no obituary of him, though it so honored Robert Bridges and Harold Munro. "The difference in the conception of Art represented by Lawrence and Eliot" reflects a difference in values of profound importance for civilization. Eliot's "profound antipathy" for DHL, as seen in the "critical theorizing of THE SACRED WOOD," represents the "ethos of Flaubert, for whom art is the justifying perfection." DHL's conception of art as "the servant of life" represents the opposing view that sees no "separation between the man who lives and the mind that creates." It does not follow, however, that his art is the "romantic" expression of a "personality." What DHL's many memoirists "found irresistible...was not merely an intense vitality,...and not at all a dominating ego, but a profound and unquestionable disinterestedness, the manifestation of a rare kind of responsibility." DHL's use of the word "moral" with reference to art is "irreplaceable, unmisleading, and justified," for this "formula" repudiated the conception of art by which Eliot distinguished between what is said and the way it is said. But *Women in Love*, like THE WASTE LAND, is "in kind and in achieved actuality," an "organic whole" and "one of the world's major creations." If DHL was "a radical and potent counter-influence to the aesthetic, the esoteric, and the sophisticated" in the age of Eliot, Joyce, Valery, and Clive Bell, he was equally "an enemy of the didactic" in the age of "Marxizing." DHL "stood unequivocally for the integrity of art," which was for him "the inviolability of the human spirit."

4142 Lee, Robert. "D. H. Lawrence and the Australian Ethos," SOUTHERLY, XXXIII (1973), 144-51.

Australian literati view *Kangaroo* with distaste because they think it hastily composed "with insufficient experience of the country." DHL wrote *Kangaroo* at the rate of 3500 words a day, and he spent only three months in Australia. His prime concern is with the nature of love, especially between men. Two concepts of love are worked out on the political level: the "egalitarian...mate-love of socialists" and the non-materialistic social ideal, "love of man for man." Although DHL makes a human and universal rather than a national statement, his complex treatment of Australian political issues and techniques has been given insufficient credit. Unfortunately, he did not recognize that Whitmanesque mate-love "had some validity in preserving and extending a fabric of civilization" over the vast emptiness of the continent.

4143 Lee, Robin. "Irony and Attitude in George Eliot and D. H. Lawrence," ENGLISH STUDIES IN AFRICA, XVI (March 1973), 15-21.

Irony, rooted in an agreement between author and reader on a disparity between actual and ideal, disappears before DHL's generously tragic vision of the discrepancies between human aspiration and achievement. His prophetic outrage at the control of "man alive" by will and by machine makes him write with a combined orientation that sees past and future simultaneously, and makes him envisage a future that is utopian because it is traditional. DHL accepted the Industrial Revolution as irreversible, but with revolutionary zeal he uses his novels to show that the values of the golden age and a sense of community can be preserved.

4144 Lindley, David. "Lawrentian Places, II: Eastwood Revisited," HUMAN WORLD, No. 11 (May 1973), 50-54.

Comparing Eastwood with Siena, DHL called it " 'a bit of a place.' " [The author recounts in detail his revisiting DHL's native town and the less than enthusiastic attitudes toward DHL expressed by two elderly people, a former miner who regarded him as " 'one for the women...Always after it,' " and a seamstress who thought DHL unfair to his father. See also F(rederick) I. Owen, "Lawrentian Places, I: A Chapel and a Hay-Hut among the Mountains: 1971," HUMAN WORLD, No. 11 (May 1973), 39-49.]

4145 LITERATURE/FILM QUARTERLY, ed by Thomas L. Erskine, I (Jan 1973), "D. H. Lawrence Number."

Contents on DHL, abstracted under 1973: Harry T. Moore, "D. H. Lawrence and the Flicks," pp. 3-11; Sam Solecki, "D. H. Lawrence's View of Film," pp. 12-16; Joan Mellen, "Outfoxing Lawrence: Novella into Film," pp. 17-27; Julian Smith, "Vision and Revision: *The Virgin and the Gypsy* as Film," pp. 28-36; James F. Scott, "The Emasculation of *Lady Chatterley's Lover*," pp. 37-45; Ana Laura Zambrano, "*Women in Love*: Counterpoint on Film," pp. 46-54; Henry Becker, III, "*The Rocking-Horse Winner*: Film as Parable," pp. 55-63; Frank Baldanza, "*Sons and Lovers*: Novel to Film as a Record of Cultural Growth," pp. 64-70. [This special number is illustrated with a line drawing of DHL, p. (2); and black and white stills from the film versions of *The Fox*, pp. 20, 25; *L'Amant de Lady Chatterley*, pp. 39, 42; *Women in Love*, pp. 48, 52; *The Rocking-Horse Winner*, pp. 58, 62. See also a critique of literature/film criticism as applied to DHL in a review-essay by G. B. Crump, "Lawrence and the LITERATURE/FILM QUARTERLY," D. H. LAWRENCE REVIEW, VI (Fall 1973), 326-32.]

4146 Lucie-Smith, Edward. "The Poetry of D. H. Lawrence--With a Glance at Shelley," in D. H. LAWRENCE: NOVELIST, POET, PROPHET, ed Stephen Spender (Lond: Weidenfeld & Nicholson; NY: Harper & Row, 1973), pp. 224-33.

DHL is the only English-born modernist poet of importance to survive the First World War. Whereas with T. S. Eliot we are "presented with an elaborately wrought, polished surface," DHL "dramatizes the way in which the mind encounters and apprehends experience." Though most critics place DHL and Shelley at opposite poles, DHL had an instinctive regard for Shelley. Both thought poetry should be natural; both were exiles from England. DHL is a bridge between the great writers of the nineteenth-century Romantic movement and our own epoch. DHL's "naturalness," like that of the Romantics, is "at its deepest level a moral virtue."

4147 Mackenzie, D. Kenneth M. "THE FOX" (Milton Keynes, England: Open UP, 1973).

[Study guide to *The Fox*.]

4148 McLaurin, Allen. VIRGINIA WOOLF: THE ECHOES ENSLAVED (Cambridge: Cambridge UP, 1973), pp. 20, 53, 64, 92, 101-4, 119.

Roger Fry, Virginia Woolf, and DHL have in common "the problem of self-consciousness and autonomy." Birkin's copy of the Chinese goose, which Fry would approve, is set against "the geometrical, industrial art of Loerke, which is full of the sadistic expressionism which Fry saw and abhored in much German art." There are two kinds of repetition in *Women in Love*: "Set against Birkin's idea of rhythmical, flame-like movement is a life dominated by routine and by machinery, by hateful repetition," a principle of "dehumanisation" which "Gerald symbolises." Fry's LAST LECTURES, especially his "dislike of the machine-made" and his "idea that freedom from repetition" comes from the unconscious, are in line with DHL's ideas.

4149 Malafry, Hugh David. "The Word and the Flesh: A Study of the Cosmological Interest of D. H. Lawrence," DISSERTATION ABSTRACTS INTERNATIONAL, XXXIV (1973-1974), 4271A. Unpublished dissertation, University of Denver, 1973.

4150 Mann, Charles W. "D. H. Lawrence: Notes on Reading Hawthorne's THE SCARLET LETTER," NATHANIEL HAWTHORNE JOURNAL (1973), pp. 9-25.

What are presumably DHL's initial notes on THE SCARLET LETTER, preserved in Thomas Stanley Hocking's farm diary of July 1921, reveal the origin of DHL's copious use of quotations, though these sometimes vary from both the Everyman and Centenary Editions, as well as his interest in "the demonic and exotic underpinnings of the puritan tale" and his fascination with Pearl. [DHL's notes are included in facsimile and transcription, pp. 13-25.]

4151 Mansfield, Elizabeth Reed. "Solitary Confinement: A Study of D. H. Lawrence's Early Fiction," DISSERTATION ABSTRACTS INTERNATIONAL, XXXV (1974), 1111A. Unpublished dissertation, Cornell University, 1973.

4152 Mellen, Joan. "Outfoxing Lawrence: Novella into Film," LITERATURE/FILM QUARTERLY, I (Jan 1973), 17-27; rptd in WOMEN AND THEIR SEXUALITY IN THE NEW FILM, by Joan Mellen (NY: Horizon P, 1973), pp. 216-28.

Mark Rydell's film *The Fox* is a caricature of DHL's novella because DHL understood that the psychological "truth" of the story depended on sexuality's remaining under the surface while Rydell makes explicit what should be a matter of nuances of consciousness. It is DHL's point that the unconscious presence of forces rules one's everyday life; Rydell translates this subtle understatement into an assault of explicit visual images.

4153 Meyer, Horst E. "An Addendum to the D. H. Lawrence Canon," PAPERS OF THE BIBLIOGRAPHICAL SOCIETY OF AMERICA, LXVII (Winter 1973), 458-59.

[Attempts to solve the "long-lived bibliographical puzzle" concerning DHL's essay "Germans and English," which appeared for the first time in English in *Phoenix II: Uncollected, Unpublished, and Other Prose Works by D. H. Lawrence*, ed by Warren Roberts and Harry T. Moore (1968). It had earlier appeared in an Italian version, as "Tedeschi e Inglesi" in LA CULTURA (Nov 1934), translated from a German version which had not been previously traced.] The unrecorded German original of "Tedeschi e Inglesi" was published by Anton Kippenberg's Insel Verlag, as "Ein Brief von D. H. Lawrence an das Inselschiff" in the quarterly DAS INSELSCHIFF (Leipzig, 1927), pp. 285-93. The German version of DHL's essay, "be it a translation by an anonymous hand or Lawrence's original, is a rather clumsy performance," with few of the "stylistic felicities" of the text published in *Phoenix II*.

4154 Meyers, Jeffrey. "D. H. Lawrence and Homosexuality," LONDON MAGAZINE, XIII (Oct-Nov 1973), 68-98; also pub in D. H. LAWRENCE: NOVELIST, POET, PROPHET, ed by Stephen Spender (Lond: Weidenfeld & Nicholson; NY: Harper & Row, 1973), pp. 135-46; and rptd in HOMOSEXUALITY AND LITERATURE, 1890-1930, by Jeffrey Meyers (Montreal: McGill-Queen's UP, 1977), pp. 131-61, with additional references to DHL pp. 2, 10-11, 13, 15-18, 32, 60, 90, 100, 112-13, 117, 165, 167-68, 171, 173, 175-79.

DHL believed that his "intrinsic" sexual nature was dual "and that his male and female elements were in conflict." This gave him great insight into the female being, but it "also caused him to see sexual relationships in terms of struggle rather than harmony." He describes mutually destructive conflicts between men and women in his fiction as well as an "alternative" search for fulfilling relationships between men. His conflicting attitudes about male love appear most notably "in four overt homosexual scenes: the swimming idyll in *The White Peacock* (1911), the wrestling match in *Women in Love* (1920), the nursing episode in *Aaron's Rod* (1922), and the initiation ceremony in *The Plumed Serpent* (1926)." Modelled on the biblical friendship of David and Jonathan, these scenes invariably occur after a "frustrating humiliation with a woman." DHL's conflicting feelings about the validity of homosexual experience resulted in an "ambiguity of presentation" in his novels. All his life DHL "felt threatened by dominating and possessive women," one of whom was Frieda. Most critics have failed to admit the sexual implications of the scenes between Birkin and Gerald in *Women in Love* and, later, the anal intercourse scene between Birkin and Ursula, in which DHL equates the anus with the source of life.

4155 Mibu, Ikuo. "Muishiki no Jiga--*Shinda Otoko* o Chûshin ni" (Unconscious Self--A Study of *The Man Who Died*), STUDIES IN CIVIC AND NATURAL SCIENCES (Nihon University), No. 43 (Nov 1973), 23-52.

DHL had the gift which enabled him to know unconsciously the invisible, unknown world. The power which works unconsciously in a man's deeper self is strong, and a man cannot suppress it completely. [Examines *The Man Who Died* in the light of these ideas.] [In Japanese.]

4156 Milley, Frederick George. "The Ritual of Becoming: A Study of the Short Stories of D. H. Lawrence," DISSERTATION ABSTRACTS INTERNATIONAL, XXXV (1974), 466A. Unpublished dissertation, Purdue University, 1973.

4157 Mizuhara, Sho. "D. H. Lawrence no *St. Mawr* ni Okeru Shôchôsei(1)" (Symbolism in D. H. Lawrence's *St. Mawr* [1]), MEMOIRS OF MEJIRO GAKUEN WOMEN'S JUNIOR COLLEGE, No. 9 (March 1973), 63-74.

[First of a two-part article.] In *St. Mawr*, the horse St. Mawr, full of life, urges Lou, who has been leading an insubstantial life, into awakening to real existence. But why did DHL forget about the horse-hero near the end of the book and become absorbed by the ranch? No critic except Alan Wilde has dealt effectively with this difficult problem. The more Lou's understanding grows, the less important St. Mawr's function becomes; by the time Lou is completely awakened to reality, St. Mawr is gone. Symbolically, St. Mawr represents deep impulses of life that are thwarted in the modern world, while Rico, the antithesis of St. Mawr, stands for the modern civilized world. [See also Sho Mizuhara, "D. H. Lawrence no *St. Mawr* ni Okeru Shôchôsei (2)" (Symbolism in D. H. Lawrence's *St. Mawr* [2]), MEMOIRS OF MEJIRO GAKUEN WOMEN'S JUNIOR COLLEGE, No. 10 (Dec 1973), 101-11.] [In Japanese.]

4158 Mizuhara, Sho. "D. H. Lawrence no *St. Mawr* ni Okeru Shôchôsei (2)" (Symbolism in D. H. Lawrence's *St. Mawr* [2]", MEMOIRS OF MEJIRO GAKUEN WOMEN'S JUNIOR COLLEGE, No. 10 (Dec 1973), 101-11.

[Second of a two-part article. Abstracted under Sho Mizuhara, "D. H. Lawrence no *St. Mawr* ni Okeru Shôchôsei (1)" (Symbolism in D. H. Lawrence's *St. Mawr* [1]), MEMOIRS OF MEJIRO GAKUEN WOMEN'S JUNIOR COLLEGE, No. 9 (March 1973), 63-74.] [In Japanese.]

4159 Moore, Harry T. "D. H. Lawrence and the Flicks," LITERATURE/FILM QUARTERLY, I (Jan 1973), 3-11.

[An account of the author's efforts in the 1930s to interest Hollywood filmmakers such as Merian Cooper and Jesse L. Lasky in filming DHL's novels and of his reactions to the six films that have been made from DHL's works: *L'Amant de Lady Chatterley, The Rocking-Horse Winner, Sons and Lovers, The Fox, Women in Love,* and *The Virgin and the Gypsy.*]

4160 Moore, Harry T. "Laurentiana," D. H. LAWRENCE REVIEW, VI (Summer 1973), 231-32.

[Letter to the Editor in support of the letter by W. J. Keith, "Laurentiana," D. H. LAWRENCE REVIEW, VI (Spring 1973), 109-10.] The necessity of establishing "Lawrence editions that are not corrupt" is illustrated by a "textual crux," in the last episode of *Sons and Lovers*, in which Paul's "whimpered" unaccountably became "whispered." The variously corrupted text of *Women in Love* is another case in point. [See also announcement by Michael Black, "Laurentiana," D. H. LAWRENCE REVIEW, VIII (Fall 1975), 375-76.]

4161 Morrill, Claire. A TAOS MOSAIC: PORTRAIT OF A NEW MEXICO VILLAGE (Albuquerque: University of New Mexico P, 1973), pp. 106-28.

DHL was the magnet which drew together the "three women of Taos," Mabel Dodge Luhan, Dorothy Brett, and Frieda Lawrence. Never a part of Taos, DHL lived first on the edge and later twenty miles out at the ranch. He did not develop any close ties with the Pueblo Indians, yet their religion, coupled with the natural landscape of New Mexico, had a profound effect on him. [Contains an account of the DHL Festival at Taos, 30 Sept-4 Oct 1970, and discusses people who were DHL's friends in Taos.]

4162 Nardi, Piero. "Introduzione" (Introduction), *Il serpente piumato (The Plumed Serpent)* (Milan: A. Mondadori, 1973), pp. 18-23.

In DHL's ideology, America symbolizes a negative force, the death of any spontaneous action. *The Plumed Serpent* condemns the American way of life and asserts the rights of nature and instinct through the glorification of archaic North American civilizations. [In Italian.]

4163 Nightingale, Benedict. "The Trouble with Harry," NEW STATESMAN, LXXXVI (16 Nov 1973), 748-49.

Although *The Merry-Go-Round* has much the same setting, it has none of the "intimate sense of the nuances of life (and death) in a mining community" that characterize *The Widowing of Mrs. Holroyd, The Daughter-in-Law,* or *A Collier's Friday Night,* the three plays directed by Peter Gill in the DHL season of 1968. Although three-quarters through the play the conflicts seem to offer enormous dramatic potential, DHL abruptly changes course and concludes the play in a comic vein with several scarcely credible marriage arrangements. [Review of the Royal Court Theatre production, directed by Peter Gill.]

4164 Nudel, Harry. "Conscious Mad: The Nature of Self in D. H. Lawrence," DISSERTATION ABSTRACTS INTERNATIONAL, XXXIV (1974), 5198A. Unpublished dissertation, State University of New York at Buffalo, 1973.

4165 Oates, Joyce Carol. THE HOSTILE SUN: THE POETRY OF D. H. LAWRENCE (Los Angeles: Black Sparrow P, 1973).

[Reprints the author's earlier "Candid Revelations: On *The Complete Poems of D. H. Lawrence,*" AMERICAN POETRY REVIEW, I (Nov-Dec 1972), 11-13, as "The Candid Revelation: Lawrence's Aesthetics," pp. 9-22; and "The Hostile Sun: The Poetry of D. H. Lawrence," MASSACHUSETTS REVIEW, XIII (Autumn 1972), 639-56, as "New Heaven and Earth: Lawrence's Transformations," pp. 23-57.] DHL's poems "are meant to be spontaneous works, spontaneously experienced; they are not meant to give us the sense of grandeur or permanence which other poems attempt, the fallacious sense of immortality that is an extension of the poet's ego. Yet they achieve a kind of immortality precisely in this: that they transcend the temporal, the intellectual."

4166 Ogawa, Yoshio. "*Apocalypse* Oboegaki" (Some Notes on *Apocalypse*), BULLETIN OF ST. MARGARET'S (St. Margaret's Junior College), No. 5 (Feb 1973), 13-27.

This paper explores DHL's religious attitude in *Apocalypse*. In Chapters I-IX, he writes about his religious life from childhood and about the writer of the Revelation. He also gives his criticism of the text in which everything seems to be based on old pagan consciousness. He concludes that Revelation shows the weak side of Christianity by longing for the destruction of all earthly power and the reign of saints in ultimate glory. Against this idea, DHL puts forth Vitalism or the living religion and expresses his religion so brilliantly that he is not a preacher but a writer of religious literature in the true sense. [In Japanese.]

4167 Ohkawa, Hiroshi. "Kûzen no Shin-Minshushugi-Setsu--D. H. Lawrence no Seizetsunaru Ningenkôsei Ron" (On New Democracy of D. H. Lawrence), JOURNAL OF THE FACULTY OF FOREIGN LANGUAGES (Komazawa University), No. 2 (March 1973), 55-68.
[On DHL's proposal of a new democracy in order to keep newly alive with the disclosure of the defects and the ghastly ideas in our democracy.] [In Japanese.]

4168 Okada, Taiji. "D. H. Lawrence no Rananim ni Tsuite (1)" (On D. H. Lawrence's Rananim [1]), BULLETIN OF THE FACULTY OF TEXTILE SCIENCE (Kyôto University of Industrial Arts and Textile Fibers), VII, No. 1 (Feb 1973), 159-70.
[The first of two articles concerning DHL's Rananim. Attempts to clarify DHL's plan for Rananim by discussing the following problems: (1) the original operating factors of the Rananim plan, (2) DHL's close connection with the Russian Jewish emigré, S. S. Koteliansky, (3) the organization of Rananim, (4) its meaning, and (5) DHL's relation to Lady Ottoline Morrell. See also Taiji Okada, "D. H. Lawrence no Rananim ni Tsuite (2)" (On D. H. Lawrence's Rananim [2]), BULLETIN OF THE FACULTY OF TEXTILE SCIENCE (Kyôto University of Industrial Arts and Textile Fibers), VIII, No. 2 (Feb 1974), 331-47.] [In Japanese.]

4169 Okumura, Tohru. "Lawrence no Leadership Novels ni Tsuite--*Aaron no Tsue* kara *Tsubasa Aru Hebi* made" (On Lawrence's Leadership Novels--From *Aaron's Rod* to *The Plumed Serpent*), REVIEW OF ENGLISH LITERATURE (Kyôto University), No. 31 (Dec 1973), 46-62.
In what are called "leadership novels," DHL wants to establish the superiority of man over woman on the grounds that man should pursue more impersonal problems beyond love. But it is apparent that DHL has not succeeded in this attempt. After all, he cannot help denying the superiority of man over woman in order to return to the tender love between man and woman in *Lady Chatterley's Lover.* So it can be said that his insistence on leadership has turned out to be his wish-fulfillment. [In Japanese.]

4170 Okumura, Tohru. "Nikutai no Fukkatsu--*Chatterley-Fujin no Koibito*" (The Resurrection of the Body--*Lady Chatterley's Lover*), REVIEW OF ENGLISH LITERATURE (Kyôto University), No. 30 (March 1973), 51-63.
In his symbolic novel *Lady Chatterley's Lover,* DHL satirically criticizes the lack of tender love between man and woman in the modern industrial world, where money and machines govern human beings. Clifford Chatterley symbolizes the destruction of living human relationships by industrialism. The resurrection of the body is symbolically attained through the tender love between Constance Chatterley and Oliver Mellors. [In Japanese.]

4171 Onodera, Takeshi. "Forster to Lawrence" (Forster and Lawrence), EIGO SEINEN, No. 119 (1973), 454-55.
[In Japanese.]

4172 "On Resisting the Lawrence Course," PAUNCH, Nos. 36-37 (1973), 30-38.
[From the perspective of *Sons and Lovers,* the anonymous writer recalls her own sexual development amid brutal familial relationships.]

4173 Owen, F[rederick] I. "Lawrentian Places, I: A Chapel and a Hay-Hut among the Mountains: 1971," HUMAN WORLD, No. 11 (May 1973), 39-49.
Although in "A Chapel among the Mountains" and "A Hay Hut among the Mountains" DHL, because of his imperfect German and the poor light, missed or mistook some details of the chapel and its ex voto pictures, he compensated with wonderful descriptive powers. [The author recounts in detail his revisiting in 1971 the Isar valley setting of DHL's early travels with Frieda. See also David Lindley, "Lawrentian Places, II: Eastwood Revisited," HUMAN WORLD, No. 11 (May 1973), 50-54.]

4174 Pace, Billy J. "D. H. Lawrence's Use in His Novels of Germanic and Celtic Myth from the Music Dramas of Richard Wagner," DISSERTATION ABSTRACTS INTERNATIONAL, XXXIV (1973-1974), 3423A-24A. Unpublished dissertation, University of Arkansas, 1973.

4175 Paterson, John. "D. H. Lawrence: The One Bright Book of Life," THE NOVEL AS FAITH: THE GOSPEL ACCORDING TO JAMES, HARDY, CONRAD, JOYCE, LAWRENCE, AND VIRGINIA WOOLF (Boston: Gambit, 1973), pp. 143-83; additional references to DHL, pp. x-xi, 208-9, 223, 228, 230, 231, 234, 240, 244, 246, 250, 254, 262, 271, 275, 276, 278, 280, 281, 283, 284, 292.
In the modern period, the novel was, as DHL called it, " 'the one bright book of life.' " "To write it was to keep the faith. To read it was to receive the faith." In DHL, "connection" with others is of central importance. In his work, connection often has a mystical dimension not found in other modern novelists, but it is a mysticism which in no way involves the transcendently supernatural. To DHL, the artist, by discovering the "unknown" in himself, by letting his unconscious nature work for him, creates life--and art--out of himself. DHL hopes that the new feelings emerging from his deepest self can help to create a new society. Thus the novel becomes an imitation of an inner reality and a creation of an outer reality; hence, DHL's rejection of the Flaubertian view of authorial detachment. If the Lawrentian "deity was *in* man and nature, not outside them," then there is no absolute which is independent of temporal and local contingencies. Things "achieved their reality from their relations to each other." The novel is, therefore, DHL says, " 'the highest example of subtle inter-relatedness that man has discovered.' " [Further references to DHL discuss his opinions of Wilde, Emily Brontë, Maupassant, Dostoevsky, Flaubert, Dickens, Balzac, Wells, Bennett, Tolstoy, Aldous Huxley, Scott, Stevenson, Cooper, Zola, Turgenev, Verga, Hardy, Melville, Plato, Conrad, Whitman, Mann, Anatole France, Proust, Dorothy Richardson, George Eliot, Fielding, and the Bible.]

4176 Phillips, Steven R. "The Double Pattern of D. H. Lawrence's

'The Horse Dealer's Daughter,'" STUDIES IN SHORT FICTION, X (Winter 1973), 94-97.

In "The Horse Dealer's Daughter," there are "two presentations of the rebirth pattern," the first Mabel's rescue from the pond, the second back at the farm. This double pattern "divides the story into two equal parts, with the second descent reinforcing the first." DHL seems to say that "such moments of spiritual union are very fragile," and that "the double pattern. . .is not the final pattern of love, for love requires continual affirmation."

4177 Pittock, Malcolm. "Lawrence's 'Art and the Individual,'" ÉTUDES ANGLAISES, XXVI (July-Sept 1973), 312-19.

If the influence of Herbartian ideas on "Art and the Individual" is the most obvious one, the evidence this early paper provides for DHL's having read Tolstoy's WHAT IS ART? is of greater immediate importance. DHL does not make use of all of Tolstoy's distinctions or follow them completely, but he accepts Tolstoy's view that art transmits feelings and not truths.

4178 Pollak, Paulina Salz. "The Letters of D. H. Lawrence to Sallie and Willie Hopkin," JOURNAL OF MODERN LITERATURE, III (Feb 1973), 24-34.

The thirty-seven letters to old Eastwood friends, Sallie and Willie Hopkin, reveal DHL's intimate and warm relationship with them. His reliance on this friendship at important junctions in his life, including his marriage, and his interest in Socialism, influenced by Willie's religious commitment to that cause, are revealed in these moving letters, written between 1910 and 1929, which often chart the rise and fall of his philosophies and his reactions to the reception of his works.

4179 Porter, Peter. "Collaborators," NEW STATESMAN, ns LXXXVI (16 Nov 1973), 741-42.

[Review of *The Boy in the Bush*, rptd (1971), and Mollie Skinner, THE FIFTH SPARROW.] *The Boy in the Bush*, an unjustly neglected but remarkable collaboration of special interest to Australians, is entirely DHL's in tone but Mollie Skinner's in surface details. Thus, her accurate account of the pioneering age becomes in DHL's hands an imposing spiritual quest, indeed "one of the best books to come out of Australia."

4180 Procter, Margaret Ruth. "E. M. Forster and D. H. Lawrence as Novelists of Ideas." Unpublished dissertation, University of Toronto, 1973. [Listed in Lawrence F. McNamee, DISSERTATIONS IN ENGLISH AND AMERICAN LITERATURE, SUPP II (NY & Lond: Bowker, 1974), p. 365.]

4181 Pujals, Esteban. "La Poesía de Yeats, Lawrence y de la Mare" (The Poetry of Yeats, Lawrence, and de la Mare), LA POESÍA INGLESA DEL SIGLO XX (English Poetry of the Twentieth Century) (Barcelona: Editorial Planeta, 1973), pp. 31-37, espec pp. 34-36.

DHL was a somewhat autobiographical poet whose poetry, informed by a religion of the blood and the instincts, reflected concretely the experience and the imagery of the countries in which he travelled. His art is direct and sensual, dramatic and impressionistic, at times ironic, and always puts forth his idea that the natural, physical desires and emotions of man ought to predominate over reason. [In Spanish.]

4182 Ramos Suarez, Jorge. "El Poema 'Snake,' de D. H. Lawrence, y la 'Elegía a un Moscardón Azul,' de Damaso Alonso: Una Influencia Admitida y Dos Sensibilidades Diferentes" (The Poem "Snake," by D. H. Lawrence, and the "Elegía a un Moscardón Azul," by Damaso Alonso: An Admitted Influence and Two Different Sensibilities), CUADERNOS HISPANOAMERICANOS (Madrid), Nos. 280-82 (1973), 274-83.

Damaso Alonso himself noted similarities between his poem "Elegía a un Moscardón Azul" and DHL's "Snake." The themes and motives which underlie DHL's poem are converted in Alonso's "Elegía" into an anguished cry of pain and disconsolation over the inadequacy of communication. The two poems, emerging from two different sensibilities, the one spontaneous, the other contemplative, reveal a common interior structure. Unlike the traditional poet, who speaks through a mask, DHL, the poet of vital expression, speaks directly without a mask. The product of the instantaneous life of the moment, DHL's poetry, in accordance with his theory in "Poetry of the Present," resembles the eternal where all is imperfect, fluid, and ephemeral. The serpent in "Snake" is simple and local but has cosmic dimensions, embodying that part of man's obscure internal motivations which mysteriously govern human conduct. Man is only the conduit through which these themes emerge from our profound being. Alonso, preoccupied with life and death, examines the death of the "moscardón," whose eyes reveal a soul which was like a great fire, elevating the insect to the status of king, as DHL's description of the "Snake" had done. [In Spanish.]

4183 Ravilious, C. P. "Lawrence's 'Chladni Figures,' " NOTES AND QUERIES, ns XX (Sept 1973), 331-32.

In his letter about *The Rainbow* to Edward Garnett (5 June 1914), DHL refers to the lines sand takes when one draws a fiddle-bow across a fine tray delicately sanded. The reference is to a phenomenon in acoustics first demonstrated by the German physicist E. F. F. Chladni, who was investigating vibration in sonorous bodies. The induced patterns in the sand, still known as Chladni's figures, evince a residual indeterminancy and thus stand as a suggestive equivalent to DHL's conception of character.

4184 Rawlings, Carl Donn. "Prophecy in the Novel," DISSERTATION ABSTRACTS INTERNATIONAL, XXXIV (1973-1974), 2575A.
Unpublished dissertation, University of Washington, 1973.
[Includes discussion of Forster, Emily Brontë, Melville, Dostoyevsky, and DHL.]

4185 Remsbury, John. "*Women in Love* as a Novel of Change," D. H. LAWRENCE REVIEW, VI (Summer 1973), 149-72.

The "true drama" of *Women in Love* "lies with Gudrun, Gerald, and Loerke," of whom DHL writes "not as a moralist but as a candid observer of his age. . . .

The novel is organized around a conception of history and social change" rather than around what Leavis calls " 'a concern for moral health.' " Gudrun "is by no means the 'radically corrupt' figure" she is often taken to be. In the novel, scenes "are not fortuitous 'background' merely, but impressions registered through the eyes of different characters, helping to define them." DHL shuffles "his characters in and out of their familiar habitats when he wants to show them up," so that "the movement from place to place forms the structure of the novel." The novel puts forth its "green shoots--Gerald, Breadalby, Birkin, Ursula, Gudrun-- and finally sprouts Loerke," the ultimate "product of a century of change. It is the twentieth century" that is " 'the little obscene monster.' " Birkin is "a superb portrait of today's intellectual, dimly...feeling a dis-ease about" things, while Gerald is DHL's "summary of what counted most in nineteenth-century England." In reacting against him, Gudrun develops the modern critical spirit. Loerke and Gudrun abandon society and, "with their art as a focus of value," they, "no less than Birkin and Ursula, have become 'free' like the nomads, with a rootless cosmopolitan future."

4186 Reuben, Elaine. "Feminist Criticism in the Classroom, or, 'What Do You Mean We, White Man?' " WOMEN'S STUDIES, I (1973), 315-25.

Lady Chatterley's Lover is a good text for exploring the possibilities of radical feminist criticism not only because it is so blatantly chauvinistic but also because people are still prone to appreciate DHL's prescriptions for their sexual and psychological problems without analyzing them.

4187 Roberts, Mark. "D. H. Lawrence and the Failure of Energy," THE TRADITION OF ROMANTIC MORALITY (Lond & Basingstoke: Macmillan, 1973), pp. 322-48; additional references to DHL, pp. 19, 108, 295, 373-74.

To the modern world, DHL's thinking, like that of Locke to the eighteenth century, "has provided a corpus of acceptably coherent doctrine expressing the characteristic assumptions and the orientations of the time." His writing, furthermore, can be viewed as "the culmination of the Romantic moral tradition," which since has become decadent. DHL's attitudes are set forth most fully and succinctly in *Psychoanalysis and the Unconscious* and *Fantasia of the Unconscious*, in which he divided the human body into "poles" or "dynamic centres of consciousness." DHL believed that the center of consciousness called the intellect was not, by itself, a reliable foundation upon which to make choices. Because he held that knowledge derives only from past experience and therefore is "dead," DHL tacitly reversed the Platonic position: Plato's "shadowy realities...become vital things," while Ideas and Forms "are in principle completely knowable" and hence dead. Thus, DHL believed that the intellect put man in a prison, for whenever he is faced with a dilemma, the intellect can only "pace endlessly round and round the same circle of past experience" and cannot know the future. Consequently, DHL felt that what was needed was "the creative spontaneity" which he attributed to "the vital centres of consciousness." Contrary to prevalent interpretations of his work, however, he did not hold that one "vital centre" (specifically, the one governing sexual behavior) was superior to another; he believed that all should function in a kind of balance. Therefore, DHL rejected traditional Christian teaching "not because of its belief in making a harmony of the forces of the soul but because of its excessive belief in reason."

 4188 Rosenberg, Judith Guttenberg. "Elements of Existentialism and Phenomenology in the Works of D. H. Lawrence," DISSERTATION ABSTRACTS INTERNATIONAL, XXXIV (1974), 7779A-80A. Unpublished dissertation, University of Illinois, 1973.

 4189 Ross, Charles L. "From 'The Sisters' to *The Rainbow* and *Women in Love*: A Textual and Critical History, 1913-17." Unpublished dissertation, Oxford University, 1973. [Listed in Geoffrey M. Paterson and Joan E. Hardy (eds), INDEX TO THESES, XXIV (1973-1974) (Lond: Aslib, 1975), p. 6.] Rvd and pub as THE COMPOSITION OF "THE RAINBOW" AND "WOMEN IN LOVE": A HISTORY (Charlottesville: UP of Virginia, 1979).

 4190 Ross, Charles L., and George J. Zytaruk. "*Goats and Compasses* and/or *Women in Love:* An Exchange," D. H. LAWRENCE REVIEW, VI (Spring 1973), 33-46.
[Charles L. Ross's reply to George J. Zytaruk, "What Happened to D. H. Lawrence's *Goats and Compasses?*" D. H. LAWRENCE REVIEW, IV (Fall 1971), 280-85; and Zytaruk's rejoinder to him.] **Ross:** Available evidence, especially that of several unpublished DHL letters, suggests that Lady Cynthia Asquith's confusing reference to *Goats and Compasses* as a "novel" are slips of the memory. Despite Zytaruk's contention that they are the same, the lost "philosophy" and "the first draft of *Women in Love*" were "two different works." **Zytaruk:** DHL had a substantially completed version of *Women in Love* in hand by 22 April 1914. The manuscripts DHL burned before leaving Cornwall were probably his own copy of *Goats and Compasses*, the lost chapters of "The Reality of Peace," and perhaps some poems. It is unlikely that Lady Cynthia Asquith was mistaken about the literary type. Ross's scholarship does not explain how she knew that the work contained a "lampoon" of Lady Ottoline Morrell. [See further discussion by Keith Sagar, "*Goats and Compasses* and *Women in Love* Again," D. H. LAWRENCE REVIEW, VI (Fall 1973), 303-8.]

 4191 Rossi, Patrizio. " 'The Fox' e 'La Lupa': D. H. Lawrence lettore di Verga" ("The Fox" and "La Lupa": D. H. Lawrence, Reader of Verga), ENGLISH MISCELLANY (Rome), No. 24 (1973-1974), 299-320.
DHL's reading and translation of Giovanni Verga's "La Lupa" influenced *The Fox*. [In Italian.]

 4192 Rossi, Patrizio. "Verga e l'Italia nella corrispondenza di D. H. Lawrence" (Verga and Italy in the Correspondence of D. H. Lawrence), ANNALI ISTITUTO UNIVERSITARIO ORIENTALE, NAPOLI, SEZIONE ROMANZA, XV, No. 1 (1973), 25-43.
Italy was very important both in DHL's life and in his artistic career. The reading

of Giovanni Verga's works and the discovery of the places described in them were important events in DHL's life. He admired Verga so much that he translated some of his best works in spite of the negative opinion of the English publishers. All this emerges clearly from many of DHL's letters to his friends. [In Italian.]

4193 Roth, Mary Beth. "Tiresias Their Muse: Studies in Sexual Stereotypes in the English Novel," DISSERTATION ABSTRACTS INTERNATIONAL, XXXIV (1974), 6604A. Unpublished dissertation, Syracuse University, 1973.

"Explores the ambivalent fascination" reflected in "the underlying attitudes in the works of Dickens, Meredith, Hardy, Lawrence, and Joyce toward sensual or sexual women."

4194 Russell, John. "D. H. Lawrence and Painting," in D. H. LAWRENCE: NOVELIST, POET, PROPHET, ed by Stephen Spender (Lond: Weidenfeld & Nicolson; NY: Harper & Row, 1973), pp. 234-43.

DHL's paintings would probably not be "ranked higher than curiosities" were they by anyone besides DHL. What is most important about them is the intensity of DHL's commitment to painting. "Lawrence liked pictures for what he got out of them and not for their status in the hierarchies." DHL uses his oil paintings, painted toward the end of his life, as a means of setting up a direct confrontation with the authorities and with the English art world. The paintings do not merit discussion on the level of lasting art, but in the context of DHL's total work, as a testament to his effort, like Cézanne's, "to describe the world as it really is, and as it had never been described before."

4195 Russell, Ken, in AN APPALLING TALENT: KEN RUSSELL, by John Baxter (Lond: Michael Joseph, 1973), pp. 167-82.

[A first-person account by director Ken Russell of the making of the film version of *Women in Love*. By his account, Russell had a substantial but, at Larry Kramer's insistence, uncredited collaboration with Kramer in writing the final shooting script and was responsible for preserving in the film a number of sequences from the novel not included in Kramer's original version of the screenplay. Also included are accounts of the casting, the parallel between Gudrun's and Isadora Duncan's dancing, the conception and filming of the nude wrestling scene, and the problem of incorporating Lawrencian philosophical dialogue in a film for a general audience.]

4196 Sagar, Keith. "*Goats and Compasses* and *Women in Love* Again," D. H. LAWRENCE REVIEW, VI (Fall 1973), 303-8.

[Further discussion of the arguments advanced in George J. Zytaruk, "What Happened to D. H. Lawrence's *Goats and Compasses*?" D. H. LAWRENCE REVIEW, IV (Fall 1971), 280-86; and Charles L. Ross and George J. Zytaruk, "*Goats and Compasses* and/or *Women in Love*: An Exchange," D. H. LAWRENCE REVIEW, VI (Spring 1973), 33-46.] The ideas suggested by the title *Goats and Compasses* are "central" to "The Reality of Peace," which "either *is Goats and Compasses*" or "the 'new half' which remained to be written on 25 Feb. 1916." Involved in completing *Women in Love* by mid-April 1916, DHL would "lose interest" in *Goats and Compasses,* but "he later salvaged most of it for *At the Gates,* a 140 page book of which only "The Reality of Peace" essays have survived." DHL "continued to propose alternative titles [for *Women in Love*] right up to publication in 1920." One of these titles may well have been *Goats and Compasses,* and that may have been "the last title Lady Cynthia [Asquith]" had heard from DHL "when she made her diary entries in February and March 1918."

4197 Sale, Roger. MODERN HEROISM: ESSAYS ON D. H. LAWRENCE, WILLIAM EMPSON, & J. R. R. TOLKIEN (Berkeley: University of California P, 1973), pp. 1, 2, 11-15, 16-106, 107, 108, 113, 121, 124, 131, 135, 140, 144, 177, 184, 188, 193, 199, 218, 239, 240, 241, 246-48, 250-55.

Modern heroism is exemplified in the writer who rejects the Myth of Lost Unity, defies generally held attitudes about the fragmentation of civilization and the alienation of the individual, and strives to achieve a community, however small. The composition history of *Sons and Lovers* and the events of DHL's life during this period show how his struggles enabled him to render a unified story and to come to terms with himself as an artist while achieving "partial release from the mother love that had so restricted him." His next novel, *The Rainbow,* conveys a sense of history, that "of woman becoming individual over the course of three generations." Since the energies at work in *The Rainbow* emerge in "patterns larger than the individual," DHL's personal problems are seen as "paradigmatic of the culture's," revealing that heroism which results from an individual's "bringing his culture into focus as he clarifies the needs of his own life." With Birkin and Ursula in *Women in Love,* a new relationship is finally realized, but in the last third of the novel "what was creative and hopeful...became paralyzed." DHL had "rendered as fully as anyone had the collapse" of civilization, "and he had found, in the human consciousness pushing itself to the verge of annihilation, a heroic countermotion." But having "gone as far as he could" imaginatively, "he could only repeat himself in the last fourteen years of his life."

4198 Salter, K. W. "Lawrence, Hardy, and 'The Great Tradition,'" ENGLISH, XX, No. 113 (Summer 1973), 60-65.

DHL's insight in the *Study of Thomas Hardy* on the split in Hardy between the "sensuous understanding" of the novels and their undramatic and so unconvincing "metaphysic" is equally applicable to his own work, especially *Women in Love.* Hardy's strength lies in the depiction of fear--fear of the future, of change, of life itself. DHL, in contrast, celebrates the present, welcoming change as a condition of life. For DHL, as for Hardy in TESS OF THE D'URBERVILLES, refusal to change an idea is the great corruption. Mr. Massy's willful treatment of Mary Lindley in "Daughters of the Vicar" and Gerald Crich's of Gudrun Brangwen in *Women in Love* follow and develop Hardy's insight on Angel Clare's idea-ridden rejection of Tess once he finds that she is not pastorally pure.

4199 Sanders, Scott. D. H. LAWRENCE: THE WORLD OF THE MAJOR NOVELS (Lond: Vision P, 1973); also pub as D. H. LAWRENCE: THE WORLD OF THE FIVE MAJOR NOVELS (NY:

Viking P, 1974).

DHL's five major novels--*Sons and Lovers, The Rainbow, Women in Love, The Plumed Serpent,* and *Lady Chatterley's Lover*--are his response to specific historical circumstances such as class division, DHL's alienation from all social groups, increased individual mobility, decay of organized religion, widespread education, growth of cities and industry, rise of the working class, and the First World War. DHL's changes in the novel form reflect general changes in thought about the relation of man to society. DHL responded either directly to the works of such thinkers as Marx, Weber, Durkheim, Frazer, Darwin, and Pavlov, or to the "historical developments which their thought mirrored." His fiction reveals conflicts in his own life, which coincided with vast changes in thought and society. DHL's world view is constructed from a "fundamental opposition between nature and culture," which emerges in his related psychological, social, political, aesthetic, and religious views; the categories of his thought shift continually as he tries to reconcile the "opposite terms of his dialectic." In *The Rainbow* the conflict is between the natural and the social selves, in *Women in Love* between "the African way (nature, body) and the Arctic way (culture, mind)," in *The Plumed Serpent* between the primitive and the modern, and in *Lady Chatterley's Lover* between the truths of science and the truths of fiction and between language and silence. Bolder in exploring the deeper areas of the self than Proust, Mann, Woolf, or Joyce, DHL can best be compared with Picasso and Kandinsky, Freud and Pavlov. "In Lawrence's novels we encounter in heightened form the essential pressures, fears and hopes of our age."

4200 Schermbrucker, William Gerald. "Strange Textures of Vision: A Study of the Significance of Mannered Fictional Techniques in Six Selected Novels of D. H. Lawrence, William Faulkner, and Patrick White, Together with a Theoretical Introduction on 'The Novel of Vision,'" DISSERTATION ABSTRACTS INTERNATIONAL, XXXV (1974), 473A. Unpublished dissertation, University of British Columbia, 1973.

4201 Scott, James F. "The Emasculation of *Lady Chatterley's Lover*," LITERATURE/FILM QUARTERLY, I (Jan 1973), 37-45.
DHL's intentions in *Lady Chatterley's Lover* are thwarted in Marc Allegret's film by staginess, prissiness, prudery, and the effect of being "too French." In addition, the director failed to confront the complexity latent in Connie Chatterley's options, which developed from a milieu of rising feminine consciousness.

4202 Seidl, Frances. "Lawrence's 'The Shadow in the Rose Garden,'" EXPLICATOR, XXXII (Oct 1973), Item 9.
In "The Shadow in the Rose Garden," the young wife's memories of her former lover are tainted when she discovers, in the garden which she used to visit with him, that he is now a lunatic. The taint spreads to her feelings for her husband, and her marriage dies. The garden in which her husband is shown is the Garden of Eden, containing over-ripe, near-decaying fruit, symbolizing both her marriage and the psychic taint.

4203 Seymour-Smith, Martin. FUNK & WAGNALLS GUIDE TO MODERN WORLD LITERATURE (NY: Funk & Wagnalls, 1973), pp. 267-69.

Although DHL's poems and criticism are not wholly successful, the former failing in language and the latter self-indulgent if often brilliant, his short stories and novels justify his reputation. His egotistical personality, his relationship with women, beginning with a complex oedipal struggle with his mother, and his angry rebellion against bourgeois English society are overshadowed by the vitality of his ideas. But DHL's "solar-plexus" theory of sexuality reveals an arrested personal development and lack of liberation, which mar the quality of his love-making scenes. Although F. R. Leavis hails him as the century's greatest writer, this critic's adulation keeps him from pointing out the dangerous aspects of DHL's ideology. DHL's novels are inspired in intent but "ruined" by vituperation. The best of his short stories, however, show his genius "unpoisoned" and present his artistic fulfillment.

4204 Shimizu, Kohya. "D. H. Lawrence ni Okeru Seishoku to Sôzô no Kairi o Megutte" (The Distinction between Creation and Procreation in D. H. Lawrence), STUDIES IN ENGLISH LITERATURE (English Literary Society of Japan, Tokyo), L, No. 1 (Nov 1973), 63-77.

The theme of procreation for DHL is interposed ambiguously, as both a link and a wedge, between creation and sex. DHL's remarks on procreation are contradictory, leading to a discrepancy between creativity and procreativity in his work. Critics have advanced three unconvincing reasons for DHL's attitude of reluctance toward procreation: his Oedipus complex, his sense of ethical responsibility for the child, and his supposed inclination toward sexual perversity. But a fourth, more persuasive reason is the metaphysic of "purposelessness." DHL draws a sharp distinction between true creation and false creation or production in the difference between existence and being, function and flowering, mechanical force and life itself. True creation is not revealed in the motivated purpose of producing the seeds or the children but only in the "excess" and "overflow" of being. ["Rose of All the World," *Lady Chatterley's Lover,* and *Study of Thomas Hardy* are examined briefly in support of this argument.] In the process of the phallic reconsecration of sex, DHL eliminates procreation from his idea of sex and from the core of his category of creation. [In Japanese.]

4205 Shimizu, Kohya. "Loerke as a Futurist--Some Modernistic Aspects in *Women in Love,*" STUDIES IN HUMANITY BY THE COLLEGE OF LIBERAL ARTS (Kanazawa University), No. 11 (March 1973), 47-81.

Although we can discover various reasons for Loerke's mysterious qualities in *Women in Love,* the most important of these may be the modernistic elements of his character as evidenced in his Futurist inclination.

4206 Sillitoe, Alan. "D. H. Lawrence and His District," in D. H. LAWRENCE: NOVELIST, POET, PROPHET, ed by Stephen Spender (Lond: Weidenfeld & Nicolson; NY: Harper & Row, 1973), 42-70;

rptd as "Lawrence and District," in MOUNTAINS AND CAVERNS: SELECTED ESSAYS, by Alan Sillitoe (Lond: W. H. Allen, 1975), pp. 128-44.

Although after his elopement with Frieda DHL never returned to the Midlands except for brief visits, he remained preoccupied for some time with his home district. Setting many of his novels there, if only as a point of departure as in *Aaron's Rod* or *The Lost Girl,* DHL was preoccupied with the ugliness of Nottinghamshire in *The Rainbow* and *Lady Chatterley's Lover.* "Infatuated with strong landscapes, grandiose and dangerous scenery," DHL loved the Eastwood of his childhood but was disturbed by the ugliness of the collieries. He found the class system there suffocating and felt England was like a coffin sinking into the sea.

4207 Sissman, L. E. "The Second Lady Chatterley," NEW YORKER, XLVIII (6 Jan 1973), 73-75.

John Thomas and Lady Jane is "the full-blown novel implicit in the shorter version, . . . not a full-blown tract on the inequities of English sexuality; its characters are too resistant, because too individualized and, literally, peculiar to become the mere bearers of message." DHL, in the knowledge that he was dying and determined to "leave posterity a posthumous message," in *Lady Chatterley's Lover* sacrificed characterization to that message. But in *John Thomas and Lady Jane,* Clifford is rounded, believable, and vulnerable rather than merely "a selfish, monstrous symbol of impotent, imperialist business ethics"; Connie, fragile and alive, is "drawn slowly into the affair with the gamekeeper," who is "decidedly lower-class"; and Mrs. Bolton, subtly divided in loyalty between the miners and Clifford, is "one of the remarkable supporting characters of English fiction." *John Thomas and Lady Jane* is more than the equal of *Lady Chatterley's Lover* in technique, "simply because it is conceived and executed as more of a novel, less of an importunity."

4208 Smart, William. "D. H. Lawrence," EIGHT MODERN ESSAYISTS, 2nd ed (NY: St. Martin's P, 1973), pp. 91-94.

Although DHL's success as a novelist and short story writer often obscures his achievement as a poet and essayist, his essays, on travel, "psychology, religion, and a variety of moral and philosophical issues," though sometimes disturbing, are very fine. [This account is preceded by a brief biography and a full-page photograph of DHL, and followed by four of DHL's essays, "Adolf," "Nottingham and the Mining Countryside," "Pan in America," and "Why the Novel Matters," pp. 95-129.] [DHL was not included in the first edition of this book.]

4209 Smith, Julian. "Vision and Revision: *The Virgin and the Gypsy* as Film," LITERATURE/FILM QUARTERLY, I (Jan 1973), 28-36.

Director Christopher Miles's film version of *The Virgin and the Gypsy* is an intelligent reshaping of the original material which makes an interesting film in its own right and inspires a reconsideration of DHL's novella.

4210 Solecki, Sam. "D. H. Lawrence's View of Film," LITERATURE/FILM QUARTERLY, I (Jan 1973), 12-16.

DHL disapproved of film as an art form because it evokes only a mental response, not a sensual, emotional one, from the audience and because of its obscene treatment of sex.

4211 Solomon, Gerald. "The Banal, and the Poetry of D. H. Lawrence," ESSAYS IN CRITICISM, XXIII (July 1973), 254-67.

The banal in DHL's poetry is sometimes overcome by an instinctive leap into the "outer darkness." This darkness shows his aversion to the sort of self-knowledge manifested in revising. DHL may use the banal in reaction against effete poeticizing, but not as a conscious poetic device. DHL's poetry would have been better had he been able to criticize his own poems.

4212 Spender, Stephen. "D. H. Lawrence, England and the War," in D. H. LAWRENCE: NOVELIST, POET, PROPHET, ed by Stephen Spender (Lond: Weidenfeld & Nicolson; NY: Harper & Row, 1973), pp. 71-76.

By 1922 DHL had lost all tolerance for industrial England. DHL always considered himself English, but the England he loved was pre-1914. For DHL the war killed the old England of *The White Peacock* and of the opening section of *The Rainbow*. To a degree the war also killed part of DHL, "a man who died several deaths," one of which was "the rending out of his body of his vision of an England that was both intensely of the earth and intensely of the spirit." When the war came, he decided he could choose neither England nor Europe, so he chose himself--his genius. From this point on he became an outsider. DHL often contradicted himself, at times feeling a revival of England was possible, but quarreling with Bertrand Russell over the means. *Aaron's Rod* describes these conflicting thoughts and emotions and, of all his books, is "the one most revealing of his psychology." The story "England, My England" also depicts the death of the old England.

4213 Spender, Stephen (ed). D. H. LAWRENCE: NOVELIST, POET, PROPHET (Lond: Weidenfeld & Nicolson; NY: Harper & Row, 1973).

Contents, abstracted under year of first publication: Diana Trilling, "D. H. Lawrence and the Movements of Modern Culture," pp. 1-7 (1973); Barbara Weekley Barr, "Memoir of D. H. Lawrence," pp. 8-36, rptd from Edward Nehls (ed), D. H. LAWRENCE: A COMPOSITE BIOGRAPHY, Vol. I: 1885-1919 (Madison: University of Wisconsin P, 1957), 162-63, 320-21; Vol. II: 1919-1925 (Madison: University of Wisconsin P, 1958), 294-95; Vol. III: 1925-1930 (Madison: University of Wisconsin P, 1959), 7, 8-9, 20-26, 53-54, 57-58, 137-40, 162-63, 188-89, 282-84, 427-28, 434-36, 448-49, 466-67, 485; David Garnett, "Frieda and Lawrence," pp. 37-41 (1973); Alan Sillitoe, "D. H. Lawrence and His District," pp. 42-70 (1973); Stephen Spender, "D. H. Lawrence, England and the War," pp. 71-76 (1973); Frank Kermode, "The Novels of D. H. Lawrence," pp. 77-89 (1973); Barbara Hardy, "Women in D. H. Lawrence's Works," pp. 90-121 (1973); John Carey, "D. H. Lawrence's Doctrine," pp. 122-34 (1973); Jeffrey Meyers, "D. H. Lawrence and Homosexuality," pp. 135-46, rptd from LONDON MAGAZINE, XIII (Oct-Nov 1973), 68-98; Clive James, "D. H. Lawrence in Transit," pp. 159-69 (1973); Tony Tanner, "D. H. Lawrence and America," pp. 170-96 (1973);

Denis Donoghue, " 'Till the Fight Is Finished': D. H. Lawrence in His Letters," pp. 197-209 (1973); A. Alvarez, "Lawrence's Poetry: The Single State of Man," pp. 210-23, rptd from THE SHAPING SPIRIT: STUDIES IN MODERN ENGLISH AND AMERICAN POETS, by A. Alvarez (Lond: Chatto & Windus, 1958); Edward Lucie-Smith, "The Poetry of D. H. Lawrence--With a Glance at Shelley," pp. 224-33 (1973); John Russell, "D. H. Lawrence and Painting," pp. 234-43 (1973). [The volume is illustrated with numerous photographs of DHL and his contemporaries and of people and places important in his life and fiction.]

4214 Spiegel, Alan Harvey. "Fiction and the Camera Eye: A Study of Visual Form in the Modern Novel," DISSERTATION ABSTRACTS INTERNATIONAL, XXXIV (1974), 5205A. Unpublished dissertation, University of Virginia, 1973.
[Includes discussion of DHL.]

4215 Squires, Michael. "Teaching a Story Rhetorically: An Approach to a Short Story by D. H. Lawrence," COLLEGE COMPOSITION AND COMMUNICATION, XXIV (May 1973), 150-56.
DHL's basic rhetorical strategy in "The Man Who Loved Islands" is to employ the deductive form of argument, "opening the story with a premise, then narrowing to the psychological analysis of a single mind." To maintain the proper tension between idea and illustration, however, he modifies within the story his treatment of tone, distance, and point of view, so that he successfully persuades the reader both to accept the syllogistic argument of the story and to sympathize with the character who is the illustration of the idea.

4216 Stern, Eva I. "D. H. Lawrence and Pierre Drieu la Rochelle: A Cry Against Decadence," DISSERTATION ABSTRACTS INTERNATIONAL, XXXIV (1974), 6663A. Unpublished dissertation, Indiana University, 1973.

4217 Stern, J. P. ON REALISM (Lond & Bost: Routledge & Kegan Paul, 1973), pp. 77, 99, 194.
Changing historical situations made it possible for DHL's miners to be more realistic than similar working-class characters in Hardy.

4218 Stewart, Kay Lanette. "The Rhetoric of the Confession: Essays in Theory and Analysis," DISSERTATION ABSTRACTS INTERNATIONAL, XXXIV (1974), 5997A. Unpublished dissertation, University of Oregon, 1973.
[Includes discussion of DHL. *The Rainbow* is an example of "the romance (involved climax-directed)."]

4219 Stoker, Richard Judge. "Fiction: The Search for Friendship," DISSERTATION ABSTRACTS INTERNATIONAL, XXXIV (1973), 792A-93A. Unpublished dissertation, State University of New York at Buffalo, 1973.
[One chapter is devoted to male friendship in *Women in Love*.]

4220 Strickland, Geoffrey. "Lady Chatterley," TIMES LITERARY SUPPLEMENT (Lond), 11 May 1973, p. 528.
[Letter to the Editor in reply to "The Immorality of Lady Chatterley," TIMES LITERARY SUPPLEMENT (Lond), 27 April 1973, pp. 471-72.] In the third version of *Lady Chatterley's Lover,* DHL made manliness acceptable, associated manliness with tenderness, and advocated "an unapologetic gratification of one's own and another's needs." But *The First Lady Chatterley* is a "much finer novel," in which "Clifford and Connie are much more suitable companions. . .and Connie's lover much more alien to her" than in the third version. [Followed by a response from the anonymous author of the original review article admitting "verbal inconsistency" (not abstracted).]

4221 Sugiyama, Yasushi. "*Shirokujaku* ni Okeru Sei no Yakudô to Shi" (Quickening of Life and Death in *The White Peacock*), D. H. LAWRENCE STUDIES (Kyôto), No. 1 (April 1973), 75-94.
The Japanese have a strong belief that there is an undercurrent of vital force everywhere in the cosmos and that the same life force exists in every living creature. This essay attempts to find this life force in *The White Peacock.* [In Japanese.]

4222 Suzuki, Shunzi. "*The White Peacock* Shiron--Cyril ni Shiten o Oita Shudai Kaishaku" (A Study of *The White Peacock:* Interpretation of the Theme from Cyril's Point of View), NAGOYA REVIEW OF ENGLISH STUDIES (Nagoya University), No. 12 (April 1973), 1-11.
The White Peacock is sometimes misunderstood because the significant roles in the action are taken not by Cyril, the narrator, but by Lettie, his sister, and George, his friend. In order to understand the deep-rooted theme, however, we need to study the relation between such central symbols as Nethermere (Cyril's home country) and the white peacock and between Cyril as narrator and the author himself. In the course of the novel, Cyril gradually comes to separate himself from those feminine elements symbolized by Nethermere and the white peacock. This process of separation constitutes the theme and sets the tone of *The White Peacock* and foreshadows the next stage of the conflict in *Sons and Lovers.* [In Japanese.]

4223 Swinden, Patrick. "Growing Pains," UNOFFICIAL SELVES: CHARACTER IN THE NOVEL FROM DICKENS TO THE PRESENT DAY (Lond: Macmillan; NY: Harper & Row, Barnes & Noble Imports, 1973), pp. 158-202, espec pp. 160-81.
In *Sons and Lovers,* "Miriam and Clara are not to be blamed for Paul's failures with them. The tie with the mother prevents him from making any satisfactory tie with another person." But this "long view" of these relationships emerges from a succession of "short views" in individual scenes through which DHL develops his characters. [Discussion.] DHL's letter to Edward Garnett (5 June 1914) reduces character to an impersonal "quiddity," which is "integral to personality but alien to it." Ultimately, DHL "persuades us to approach his characters at three levels": first, as "personalities" in social relationships; then in dissolution

of personality in commitment to the blood or in passage through " 'allotropic states' "as the requisite to "final self discovery"; and finally, in their elemental existence in " 'free proud singleness.' " [Extended discussion of characterization in *The Rainbow* and limited references to *Women in Love* explain DHL's practice in light of this theory.]

    4224 Tanner, Tony. "D. H. Lawrence and America," in D. H. LAWRENCE: NOVELIST, POET, PROPHET, ed by Stephen Spender (Lond: Weidenfeld & Nicolson; NY: Harper & Row, 1973), pp. 170-96.

DHL underwent a mental crisis during his American sojourn of 1922-1925. To his friends he sometimes appeared mad, though some of his conflicts had to do with marital strains and "an inability to resolve his feelings about relationships with men." Perhaps DHL never wrote a travelogue of America because so much of urban America meant nothing to him, and "only the desert" had "a fascination." Finding only an "outside life" in America and nothing inside, DHL thought America exhausted the soul, though in the Southwest there was something "pristine" and unbroken. Mabel Dodge Luhan writes of DHL's ambivalent feelings about the Indians, the mountains, the "mystic life," and essays such as "Certain Americans and an Englishman," "Taos," and "Indians and an Englishman" reveal this ambivalence. The three most important stories DHL wrote in America, *St. Mawr,* "The Woman Who Rode Away," and "The Princess," have as theme a modern white woman coming into contact with the "unsocialized savagery of the American landscape," and "imagine three different conclusions to the experience."

    4225 Thody, Philip. HUXLEY: A BIOGRAPHICAL INTRODUCTION (NY: Scribner's, 1973), pp. 9, 18, 21, 33-36, 38, 40, 43, 44, 46-47, 62, 66, 70, 108, 110, 115, 118, 131.

After a first meeting in 1915, Aldous Huxley and DHL were not to renew their friendship for nearly ten years. During and after 1926, DHL's influence was strong, leading Huxley to a new religious awareness and away from previous intellectual attitudes. Maria Huxley typed the MS of *Lady Chatterley's Lover* in Italy. Huxley's POINT COUNTER POINT (1928) showed DHL's personality and ideas in Rampion, though DHL called the character a "dreadful windbag" and criticized Huxley's obsession with "physical suffering and acts of physical violence" as being out of touch with his essential humanism. After DHL's encouragement to write on "the great perverts," Huxley published DO WHAT YOU WILL (1929). Theirs was a stable relationship until after DHL's death and Huxley's edition of DHL's letters, after which Huxley's worship abated. He later called DHL's ideas the "Doctrine of Cosmic Pointlessness."

    4226 Toyokuni, Takashi. "*The Trespasser* ni Okeru Shinwateki Yôso ni Tsuite--D. H. Lawrence no Shinwa no Sekai" (Mythical Elements in *The Trespasser*--D. H. Lawrence's World of Myth), MEMOIRS OF THE MURORAN INSTITUTE OF TECHNOLOGY, VIII, No. 1 (Oct 1973), 63-86.

The Trespasser is not merely a story of love and death in the world of Wagnerian myth but also a "nature myth" which extols the communion between man and the cosmos. [In Japanese.]

4227 Trease, Geoffrey. D. H. LAWRENCE: THE PHOENIX AND THE FLAME (Lond: Macmillan; NY: Viking P, 1973).
[A biography of DHL reconstructed from Frieda Lawrence, "NOT I, BUT THE WIND..." (1934); E. T. [pseud of Jessie Chambers], D. H. LAWRENCE: A PERSONAL RECORD (1935); Harry T. Moore, THE INTELLIGENT HEART: THE STORY OF D. H. LAWRENCE (1954); Edward Nehls (ed), D. H. LAWRENCE: A COMPOSITE BIOGRAPHY, 3 vols (1957, 1958, 1959); and *Lawrence in Love: Letters to Louie Burrows*, ed by James T. Boulton (1968). Includes illustrations, a chronology of DHL's life and times, and "Some Books for Further Reading." Trease, who grew up in Nottingham and attended the same schools as DHL, was twenty-four years DHL's junior and never met him. He knew the DHL country, however, and talked with some of the people who figured in DHL's life, such as Ernest Weekley, David Chambers, and some of DHL's schoolmasters.]

4228 Trilling, Diana. "Lawrence and the Movements of Modern Culture," NEW YORK TIMES BOOK REVIEW, 4 Nov 1973, Sect. 7, p. 65; rptd in D. H. LAWRENCE: NOVELIST, POET, PROPHET, ed by Stephen Spender (Lond: Weidenfeld & Nicolson; NY: Harper & Row, 1973), pp. 1-7; rptd in WE MUST MARCH, MY DARLINGS, by Diana Trilling (NY & Lond: Harcourt, Brace, Jovanovich, 1977), pp. 295-303.
Among major twentieth-century writers, DHL "is unique for the ambiguous response he receives from his readers." Our evaluation of his books has regularly changed. In the 1930s, his doctrine was seen as "an appeal...for the release of sexuality," and *Lady Chatterley's Lover*, which is little discussed today, was his most famous book; a humorless book, it is puritanical and misogynistic yet idealistic.

4229 Tripathy, Biyot K. THE MAJOR NOVELS OF D. H. LAWRENCE (Bhubaneswar, India: Pothi Publications, 1973).
After a lengthy explication of DHL's major novels, we can make some generalizations about their structure and characterization. Most of the novels on English life and society are given two distinct time schemes: objective, chronological narrative, where life is presented in general, and subjective, character-centered narrative, where life becomes specific. A study of DHL's approach to characterization reveals that he conceives of each individual as a distinct identity, and it would be unjustifiable to consider his characters as types. Finally, an examination of sources other than the novels will help elaborate and clearly define DHL's ideas.

4230 Vickery, John B. THE LITERARY IMPACT OF "THE GOLDEN BOUGH" (Princeton: Princeton UP, 1973), pp. 74, 82, 93, 119, 122, 125, 130, 138, 163, 200-201, 280-93, 294-325, 326.
DHL's interest in myth and anthropology began as early as 1911, and he was reading Frazer by 1915 and Gilbert Murray and Sir Edward B. Tylor soon after. His early poetry reflects his interest in myth, and *Amores* carries specific references to rituals described by Frazer and Jane Harrison. *Birds, Beasts and Flow-*

ers develops vegetative and animal aspects of the dying and reviving god and equates the return of vegetation with the return of the deity. In his last years, DHL, like Yeats, invokes the myths of THE GOLDEN BOUGH as talismans. Like Frazer's primitives, DHL refuses to distinguish between the animate and the inanimate. The basic coordinates of DHL's vision of the reborn man-god are the necessity of death, acceptance of sacrificial communion, and attainment of a new life. The drama of the dying and reviving god is a major *leitmotif* in DHL's fiction. From *The Rainbow* on, DHL intensifies his heroes by referring to them as demons, devils, or ghosts to emphasize sudden eruptions of the psyche in contrast to the inflexibility of society. Among the archetypes which DHL employs are the stranger, the virgin, the sacred prostitute, the witch, the hanged man, and the scapegoat. The power of the underworld is a vital part of DHL's fiction best associated with Harrison's view of the chthonic gods and related phallic worship prior to the cerebral Olympians. DHL's characters repeatedly exhibit the primitive consciousness which stands in contrast to Frazer's rationalistic temper but which was his subject. DHL's landscape is also mythically charged. In general, myth and ritual function in DHL's fiction over a six-part scale: (1) representations of a concealed anthropological dimension of life; (2) a satiric device favorably contrasting mythico-ritualistic ancient life to profane modern life; (3) a combination of these two in concealed totemism; (4) myth as second or double plot; (5) direct mythmaking (as in *The Man Who Died*); and (6) myths of the dead, mostly to be found in the short fiction. There are four main kinds of stories: endurance, criticism, combat, and questing, which, if considered sequentially, are a development similar to the myth of the dying and reviving god.

4231 Vidas, Louise Walczak. "The Single Green Light and the Splendid and Terrible Spectrum: A Study of the Secular Romance Quest in the Novels of Thomas Hardy and D. H. Lawrence," DISSERTATION ABSTRACTS INTERNATIONAL, XXXIV (1973), 1298A-99A. Unpublished dissertation, University of Illinois, 1973.

4232 Wade, John Stevens. "D. H. Lawrence in Cornwall: An Interview with Stanley Hocking," D. H. LAWRENCE REVIEW, VI (Fall 1973), 237-83.
[Conversations between the author and Stanley Hocking who, as a boy of sixteen, knew DHL and Frieda when they lived in Cornwall in 1916. "The Hocking family had been tenants on Tregerthen farm for several hundred years." Illustrated with two photographs of the author and Hocking and of Tregerthen farm.]

4233 Walsh, William. "D. H. Lawrence and the Genetic Approach," ÉTUDES ANGLAISES, XXVI (July-Sept 1973), 327-30.
DHL, in the role of "the Writer as Teacher," endeavored both to recover a "lost element" essential to "a healthy human nature" but "no longer operative in the modern consciousness" and "to define its character and conditions." For him, however, "the didactic purpose was subordinate to the larger purpose,...namely, the tactful and intelligible communication of life, and of the life of feeling and of values as well as of reason." These principles inform his critical writing on the novel, which conceives the novel as "very different from, more complex, more

important than, the novel conventionally understood." "A novelist who took his art so seriously. . .had to be more than a fanatical advocate. . .of the irrational and the immediate." [These comments serve as a long background to a discussion of Émile Delavenay's D. H. LAWRENCE: L'HOMME ET LA GENÈSE DE SON OEUVRE: LES ANNÉES DE FORMATION (1885-1919), which, Walsh thinks, in its "genetic approach," blurs the distinction between "the essential and the less significant work."]

4234 Wardle, Irving. "*The Merry-Go-Round,*" TIMES (Lond), 8 Nov 1973, p. 13.

In *The Merry-Go-Round,* DHL "sets his ruling obsessions in comic perspective," although he "is no less interested here than elsewhere in the full naturalistic apparatus, and in powerfully self-willed characters." "What preserves the comic line is that the characters are. . .on the same big wheel which flings them this way and that before spinning them off into final partnerships." [Review of the Royal Court Theatre production, directed by Peter Gill, illustrated with a four-column wide photograph.]

4235 Watanabe, Junko. "Erosu no Nimensei--D. H. Lawrence no *Women in Love* o Megutte" (The Ambivalence of Eros--A Study of D. H. Lawrence's *Women in Love*), COLLECTED ESSAYS (Kyôritsu Women's Junior College), No. 16 (Jan 1973), 1-19.

This article attempts to clarify the dual aspect of eros, focusing on the love between Birkin and Ursula in *Women in Love.* DHL, strongly opposed to the prevalent view of eros based on a false idea of love, a sentimental, superficial feeling, devoted himself to the restoration of divine eros as a unifying force of life; but what he saw revealed as a result of his exploration was the ambivalence of eros: eros as an affirmative, creative force making possible a new mode of life and eros as a destructive force leading man and woman ultimately to self-negation, death. Despite his bent toward pessimism and nihilism, produced by his relentless insight into human reality, DHL never lost an affirmative view of life, a hope for new life, trusting man's instinct, a view which is most typically indicated by Birkin's struggle against the death-impulse involved in eros. *Women in Love* shows DHL's deepened understanding of man's self-contradiction as revealed in the ambivalence of eros and his belief in the ultimate force of life. [In Japanese.]

4236 Wellard, James. "Sir Richard Burton and D. H. Lawrence," THE SEARCH FOR THE ETRUSCANS (Lond: Thomas Nelson & Sons; Lond: Sphere Books, Cardinal Edition, 1973), pp. 75-91, espec pp. 80, 87-91; additional references, pp. 25-26, 43, 45, 212, 213.

"The Etruscans tended to be regarded as innately decadent until. . .D. H. Lawrence. . .presented them in an entirely new light" for "lovers of spontaneous life forms." Although not a "professional Etruscologist," DHL "prepared himself conscientiously for the task," and his "intuitive approach" "makes us feel that we are not merely spectators but companions on his travels." Despite the low academic opinion of Etruscan art, DHL "remained eloquently anti-museum in his appraisal of the Etruscans," using his senses rather than his intellect in freely interpreting their art, "whether it is their tomb paintings or their bronzes or their burial urns."

4237 Weston, Edward. THE DAYBOOKS OF EDWARD WESTON, Vol. I: MEXICO, ed by Nancy Newhall (Millerton, NY: Aperture, 1973), pp. 101, 102, 103, 120, 159, 168, 181, 191, 198.
[Introduced to Edward Weston by Luis Quintanilla on 2 Nov 1924, DHL promised to sit for the photographer. At the sitting the two were on amiable but superficial terms. Weston found the negatives "not technically up to standard," though DHL was pleased with the printed profile. Includes Weston's negative response to *The Plumed Serpent*.]

4238 Weston, Edward. THE DAYBOOKS OF EDWARD WESTON, Vol. II: CALIFORNIA, ed by Nancy Newhall (Millerton, NY: Aperture, 1973), pp. 247, 249, 264, 271.
[While complaining of the publishers' reshaping of his portraits, Weston admits that he is "not at all proud" of his "poor technical job" on the DHL portrait. For DHL's reaction to the photographs--"I like them very much"--see his letter to Edward Weston of ?18 Dec 1924 in *The Collected Letters of D. H. Lawrence*, ed by Harry T. Moore (NY: Viking P, 1962), II, 824.]

4239 Widmer, Kingsley. "Lawrentian Manias: A Review of Recent Studies of D. H. Lawrence," STUDIES IN THE NOVEL, V (Winter 1973), 547-58.
[Review essay of *John Thomas and Lady Jane:* "the final *Lady Chatterley's Lover* is generally better written, more sexually significant, and makes crucial change in the social theme"; and of five books on DHL.]

4240 Widmer, Kingsley. "The Pertinence of Modern Pastoral: The Three Versions of *Lady Chatterley's Lover*," STUDIES IN THE NOVEL, V (1973), 298-313.
A study of the three versions of *Lady Chatterley's Lover* reveals an ambivalent movement from a proletarian to a pastoral fictional world. The third version, a romance, shows that there can be no resolving agreement between a mechanized social world and the two lovers. The development through the three versions results in the unjustly severe treatment of Clifford. British critics are incorrect in emphasizing the buggery question; what should be emphasized is the removal of Mellors's "proletarian identification." DHL suggests unconvincingly that all society should become pastoral. The final version of the novel is flawed by stridency and misogyny, but in form it is the best of the three.

4241 Wiley, Paul L. "D. (David) H. (Herbert) Lawrence," THE BRITISH NOVEL: CONRAD TO THE PRESENT (Northbrook, IL: AHM Publishing [Goldentree Bibliographies in Language and Literature], 1973), pp. 71-77.
[A selected bibliographical checklist in four parts: Texts, Bibliographies, Critical and Biographical Books, and Critical Essays.]

4242 Wilkin, Andrew. "Introduction" and "Glossary," in *Little Novels of Sicily*, by Giovanni Verga, trans by D. H. Lawrence (Harmondsworth, Middlesex, England: Penguin Books, 1973).

"Guided largely by personal instinct and artistic taste," DHL, in his translation of Verga's *Little Novels of Sicily*, was not hampered greatly by his reliance on the dictionary. Although "his knowledge of Italian was limited," his translations "often capture the tone and atmosphere of the original."

4243 Williams, Raymond. THE COUNTRY AND THE CITY (NY: Oxford UP; Lond: Chatto & Windus, 1973), pp. 170, 171, 194, 196, 198, 213, 251, 252, 264-68, 270-71, 299.

Like Eliot and Hardy, DHL is part of a cultural and educational pattern that is actually more central to English life than Oxbridge, and he shares with them the crisis of mobility. His landscape is a mixture of the old country and the new city, and DHL himself is on a cultural border, with the worlds of both mine and farm on one side and those of education and art on the other. Conflicts resulting from this division are internal and subjective in *Sons and Lovers* and are overwhelmed by the relationship with the mother. Crises in *The Rainbow* affect the way in which history is seen. The male sexual imagery expressing relationship to the land is a central metaphor; women move away from this relationship into consciousness of class and education. The historical narrative at the beginning is a projection of the mother's attitudes described directly in *Sons and Lovers*. Industrialism consistently manifests death in DHL's work. Its eventual opposition is not in the farming community with which *The Rainbow* begins but in primitivism. DHL does not have a conventional idea of old, unspoiled England; his objection is not to towns per se but to our false towns, and he never sees real ones in England, so that even when a vital life is achieved, as in *Lady Chatterley's Lover*, the problem of maintaining it in "a necessary working world" remains.

4244 Williams, Raymond. "Introduction," *D. H. Lawrence on Education*, ed by Joy and Raymond Williams (Harmondsworth, Middlesex, England: Penguin Books, 1973), pp. 7-13.

DHL is one of the first major writers to share in what has become an important pattern for writers: he was born in a working-class family, got his education on scholarships, and went on to teach in an ordinary school. Education for DHL was not a specialized subject but a set of active decisions about how life should be lived. In the light of such a belief, DHL's own views on education, at times contradictory, must be read and understood in the context of his ongoing experience. He does not offer a systematic position on education, but, rather, he gives a flow of observations, feelings, and ideas. [A selection of DHL's writings on education, including "Education of the People" and sections of *The Rainbow* and *Women in Love*.]

4245 Wilson, Raymond J. "Transactional Analysis and Literature," DISSERTATION ABSTRACTS INTERNATIONAL, XXXIV (1974), 7793A. Unpublished dissertation, University of Nebraska, 1973.

[Chapter Seven applies the "script concept of transactional analysis" to *Sons and Lovers*.]

4246 "With the Accent on English," TIMES LITERARY SUPPLEMENT (Lond), 13 April 1973, pp. 404-6.

THE OXFORD BOOK OF TWENTIETH CENTURY ENGLISH VERSE should have included more of DHL's animal poems and allotted him more space "as the only successful practitioner of free verse in these islands until the 1960s."

4247 Woodward, A. G. "The Artist and the Modern World," ENGLISH STUDIES IN AFRICA, XVI (March 1973), 9-14.
Joyce, DHL, and Yeats typify the belief that progress is achieved through the individual rather than through technology and the sense of alienation that has developed between the artist and society. Ursula's encounter with the horses in *The Rainbow* is a world-transforming piece of Romanticism such as we find in Blake.

4248 Yamashita, Kazuichiro. "D. H. Lawrence *Seishin-Bunseki to Muishiki* ni Tsuite (I)" (On *Psychoanalysis and the Unconscious* by D. H. Lawrence [I]), ENGLISH LANGUAGE AND LITERATURE (Chūo University), No. 13 (March 1973), 103-24.
[First of two articles on *Psychoanalysis and the Unconscious*. This study analyzes Chapters I and II of *Psychoanalysis and the Unconscious*, first criticizing DHL's comment on Sigmund Freud, then discussing DHL's vitalism and his opposition to idealism. See also Kazuichiro Yamashita, "D. H. Lawrence *Seishin-Bunseki to Muishiki* ni Tsuite (II)" (On *Psychoanalysis and the Unconscious* by D. H. Lawrence [II]), ESSAYS IN CELEBRATION OF THE NINETIETH ANNIVERSARY OF CHŪO UNIVERSITY (Chūo University, Aug 1975), pp. 167-88.] [In Japanese.]

4249 Yanada, Noriyuki. "D. H. Lawrence no 'Sun' Kenkyû--Sono Shudai to Hôhô" (The Theme and Technique of D. H. Lawrence's "Sun"), JOURNAL OF HOKKAIDO UNIVERSITY OF EDUCATION, XXIII, No. 2 (Feb 1973), 123-37.
"Sun" presents the process in which Juliet, an American woman who has been worn out with civilization, recovers her life by mating with the sun. Full of rich symbols and wonderfully unified images, and closely connected with DHL's own scheme of mythology, this short story reveals the fantastic world of the last stage of his writing career. "Sun" may be called "an unfinished myth" because Juliet cannot yet find the man who will complete her resurrection. [In Japanese.]

4250 Yoshida, Masako. "*Shirokujaku* ni Okeru Ambivalence no Mondai" (An Inquiry into Ambivalence in *The White Peacock*), D. H. LAWRENCE STUDIES (Kyôto), No. 1 (April 1973), 95-122.
[The writer discusses DHL's attitude toward the natural and the civilized sides of human life, as represented respectively by George and Cyril in *The White Peacock*. The tragic ending of the novel, the ruin of George's life, seems to indicate DHL's ambivalent attitude toward these two sides.] [In Japanese.]

4251 Yoshii, Mitsuo. "Jubaku kara no Ridatsu--Lawrence *Musuko to Koibito* Ron" (A Release from Bondage--On Lawrence's *Sons and Lovers*), JOURNAL OF THE COLLEGE OF LIBERAL ARTS (Toyama University), No. 5 (March 1973), 129-49.

In analyzing the conflict in *Sons and Lovers* between Paul's love for his mother and his love for Miriam, we can see latent signs that he will overcome his mother complex, abandon his mother's standards (reason, knowledge, will) and turn toward his father's standards (simplicity, wildness, emotion). [In Japanese.]

4252 Yoshii, Mitsuo. "Lawrence *Niji* Ronkô (III)--Buntai to Kôsei o Chûshin to Shite" (On Lawrence's *The Rainbow* [III] --Some Characteristics of Style and Structure), WASEDA REVIEW, No. 12 (Sept 1973), 97-109.

[Third of three articles on *The Rainbow*.] [Style and structure and the open ending of *The Rainbow* are discussed with reference to the generation of Ursula Brangwen and Anton Skrebensky. See also Mitsuo Yoshii, "Lawrence *Niji* Ronkô (I)--Buntai to Kôsei o Chûshin to Shite" (On Lawrence's *The Rainbow* [I] --Some Characteristics of Style and Structure), WASEDA REVIEW, No. 10 (July 1971), 1-13; and "Lawrence *Niji* Ronkô (II)--Buntai to Kôsei o Chûshin to Shite" (On Lawrence's *The Rainbow* [II] --Some Characteristics of Style and Structure), WASEDA REVIEW, No. 11 (Sept 1972), 46-56.] [In Japanese.]

4253 Yoshimura, Hirokazu. "D. H. Lawrence no Shôsetsu ni Okeru Shizen-Byôsha ni Tsuite--'Tsuki' no Byôsha o Chûshin ni" (On D. H. Lawrence's Descriptions of 'the Moon' in His Novels), STUDIES IN FOREIGN LITERATURES (Ritsumeikan University), No. 26 (March 1973), 79-99.

[Traces each stage in the changes in DHL's descriptions of the moon from *The White Peacock* to *Women in Love*.] [In Japanese.]

4254 Yoshimura, Hirokazu. "*Shirokujaku* no Jinbutsu o Megutte-- Cyril Beardsall o Chûshin ni" (Cyril Beardsall in *The White Peacock*), D. H. LAWRENCE STUDIES (Kyôto), No. 1 (April 1973), 53-73.

In *The White Peacock*, Cyril Beardsall has the roles of both narrator and mouthpiece for the author's personal feelings and ideas. The interrelation between his roles and the descriptions in *The White Peacock* is discussed briefly. [In Japanese.]

4255 Yoshimura, Hirokazu. "*The Trespasser* no Jinbutsu ni Tsuite-- Cecil Byrne to Hampson o Megutte" (Cecil Byrne and Hampson in *The Trespasser*), STUDIES IN FOREIGN LITERATURES (Ritsumeikan University), No. 25 (Dec 1973), 71-88.

We can find elements of DHL's Döppelganger in both Cecil Byrne and Hampson among the characters of *The Trespasser:* Byrne represents the author's personal feelings, while Hampson preaches the author's metaphysical ideas. [In Japanese.]

4256 Zambrano, Ana Laura. "*Women in Love:* Counterpoint on Film," LITERATURE/FILM QUARTERLY, I (Jan 1973), 46-54.

The film version of *Women in Love*, directed by Ken Russell from a screenplay by Larry Kramer, is an interpretation rather than a rendering of the novel. The rich texture of the film is a result of using themes from DHL's other work as well as visual juxtaposition of settings as counterpoint to the philosophic intent of the novel.

4257 Zytaruk, George J. "The Chambers Memoirs of D. H. Lawrence--Which Chambers?" RENAISSANCE AND MODERN STUDIES, XVII (1973), 5-37.

The so-called "Chambers Papers," which Edward Nehls, in D. H. LAWRENCE: A COMPOSITE BIOGRAPHY, Vol. III (1959), attributes to May Chambers Holbrook, may in fact have been written by her sister Jessie. The papers, found in typescript in the house of their brother Bernard in Saskatchewan, were attributed to May by another brother, Professor J. D. Chambers, although her name appears on neither the typescript nor the handwritten manuscript. The "Chambers Papers" are similar to Jessie Chambers's D. H. LAWRENCE: A PERSONAL RECORD by E. T. (1935) in verbal phrasing and literary style, sequence of incidents, and content, but not in narrative point of view. S. S. Koteliansky, who had read the forty manuscript pages of the novel Jessie was writing about her experiences with DHL, told her that she needed more "novelists' tricks" to "transform the material" into a "credible novel." One can conclude that on this advice Jessie adopted the narrative point of view of her sister May and sent her a carbon copy of the typescript. Jessie's inability, as she told Koteliansky, to "invent incidents" for her novel accounts for the close parallel between her earlier memoirs and the "novel." Finally, J. D. Chambers's statement that "May 'knew everybody' " but that " '*she held herself aloof from D. H. Lawrence and his circle*' " makes it impossible to accept her "as the author of the second memoir." [See also reply by John Worthen, "The Chambers Memoirs of D. H. Lawrence: A Reply," RENAISSANCE AND MODERN STUDIES, XIX (1975), 98-107; and rejoinder by George J. Zytaruk, "The Chambers Memoirs of D. H. Lawrence--Which Chambers?: A Reply to Mr. John Worthen," RENAISSANCE AND MODERN STUDIES, XIX (1975), 108-11.]

4258 Zytaruk, George J., and Stephen Gill. "Replies," NOTES AND QUERIES, ns XX (April 1973), 143-44.

[George J. Zytaruk's reply to Stephen Gill's review of *The Quest for Rananim: D. H. Lawrence's Letters to S. S. Koteliansky, 1914 to 1930*, ed by George J. Zytaruk, in "Reviews," NOTES AND QUERIES, ns XIX (Sept 1972), 354-55; and Gill's rejoinder to him. The exchange concerns the dates assigned by Zytaruk to letters number 24, 26, 108, 110, 111, 198.]

1974

4259 Adamowski, T[homas] H. "Character and Consciousness: D. H. Lawrence, Wilhelm Reich, and Jean-Paul Sartre," UNIVERSITY OF TORONTO QUARTERLY, XLIII (Summer 1974), 311-34.

Although DHL's critique of character may have been neglected by scholars because he was not a Freudian or a social scientist, the intellectual complexity of his work is comparable to that of Herbert Marcuse, Norman O. Brown, Paul Goodman, Wilhelm Reich, and other psychoanalytically influenced critics. In DHL's view, the human dilemma derives from the demands of an "ideal self," begotten of an idea, which transforms the individual into "an actor who forgets that he is acting."

Through sexuality, however, the individual can break free of the "character armour" imposed on him by this ideal self. Although DHL and Reich were ideologically incompatible concerning human sexuality, they did share a common belief that "properly achieved sexual relationships reveal a 'natural' self that is prior to the everyday self of character," "the dark self in the mysterious labyrinth of the body," as opposed to the "armour of repression" which is usually defined, incorrectly, as the self. Thus, DHL's fictional characters are in search of experience which will make them complete; those who succeed are willing to surrender their stable, conventional selves in order to "gain an ultimate unity which cannot itself be stable." This unity or equilibrium, enjoyed by lovers on a non-conscious level (the kind of equilibrium sought by Rupert Birkin in *Women in Love*), is remote but possible in DHL's fiction.

4260 Adamowski, T[homas] H. "*The Rainbow* and 'Otherness'," D. H. LAWRENCE REVIEW, VII (Spring 1974), 58-77.

Understanding DHL's idea of "otherness" and its manifestation in *The Rainbow* enables us "to understand the relationships that exist in the novel among the following: the...notion of a core to the self, the sensitivity of the book towards distance and conflict among selves, and the moments during which they seem to come into harmony with each other." DHL is "concerned not with the psychology of character but with the ur-form of human reality that is prior to any psychic container filled with 'traits' and motives," that other " 'center of consciousness' " the "pre-cognitive," "dark" self. A concern with the uniqueness of the self risks seeing the Other as nonessential or adversary. DHL's solution is "a fusion of *desires* (not of individuals themselves) in a 'fourth dimension,' " in which the Other "becomes the symbol of all that we feel lacking in ourselves." Characters in *The Rainbow* try to escape "partial existence by means of flight into the ecstasies offered by religion, art, and knowledge." "In the reciprocal incarnation of sexuality, there is a reciprocal tolerance of otherness, for it is the Other that one needs to complete oneself." In *The Rainbow,* this complex notion of otherness is revealed in the moments of recognition of self and other by the main characters, and in the conflicts and harmonies which occur in their relationships with each other.

4261 Asahi, Chiseki. " 'Jets of Sunlight,' " STUDIES OF SONODA WOMEN'S COLLEGE, No. 9 (Dec 1974), 143-55.

In the phrase "jets of sunlight" in "The Wild Common" there is a significant reflection of the primitive sensibility found in DHL's poems, of his interest in animism and natural piety. DHL uses color elements in his poetry to enhance what is signified by this unique phrase.

4262 Baker, James R. "Lawrence as Prophetic Poet," JOURNAL OF MODERN LITERATURE, III (July 1974), 1219-38.

The very crises DHL predicted have come to pass and reaffirm his role as a prophet, especially as can be seen in his poetry written between 1920 and 1930. Though the experiences DHL foretold were accepted by only a few of his contemporaries, his psychological and social analyses are now accepted by a large number of our writers and theorists. DHL's negative diagnosis of the machine civilization and its cities is balanced in some poems by a faith in the organic beauties and energies of the universe, and a hope that the younger generation will help to heal the spiritual sickness. The most prophetic of the poems, which reach beyond the consciousness of the predictive, foresee a return to the passions and actions inspired by, and integrated with, the cosmic.

4263 Baker, Paul Geoffrey. "A Critical Re-examination of D. H. Lawrence's *Aaron's Rod*," DISSERTATION ABSTRACTS INTERNATIONAL, XXXVI (1975), 1515A. Unpublished dissertation, University of Toronto, 1974; rvd and pub as A REASSESSMENT OF D. H. LAWRENCE'S "AARON'S ROD" (Ann Arbor, MI: UMI Research P [Series No. 31], 1983).

4264 Balbert, Peter. D. H. LAWRENCE AND THE PSYCHOLOGY OF RHYTHM: THE MEANING OF FORM IN "THE RAINBOW" (The Hague & Paris: Mouton [Studies in English Literature, 99], 1974).

[This study focuses on a close reading of *The Rainbow* as a demonstration of the interrelationship of form and meaning in DHL's fictional work with the intent to show the specific connections between DHL's doctrines and the fundamental rhythmic structures of his narratives. The principal argument is that *The Rainbow* represents "a meticulously planned three-stage process," using "the symbol of the womb after conception as a metaphor" for rebirth into "unfettered freedom and organic wholeness." Both the "psychology of this development *and* its metaphorical equivalent" are articulated in DHL's "pollyanalytical" essays; the discussion here, however, considers only those "pollyanalytical" theories pertinent to *The Rainbow*. It is "directed not towards meaning *and* form, but the meaning of form--that is, the psychology of rhythm," and describes how the "rhythmic arrangement of phrases, character gradations, incidents, 'expanding' and 'fixed' symbols, and interweaving themes" make a coherent whole, becoming the form which DHL's "meaning must take." The analysis focuses "on the male as antagonist and the female as protagonist," correcting the lack of emphasis, in previous criticism, on the female as central to the novel. The statement of theory and methodology is followed by a detailed analysis of *The Rainbow* from the "emasculation and incomplete birth" in the relationships of Tom and Lydia and of Will and Anna to "the metaphor delivered" in Ursula, who becomes "the organic Word made flesh."]

4265 Baron, C[arl] E. "The Nottingham Festival D. H. Lawrence Exhibition, 1972," D. H. LAWRENCE REVIEW, VII (Spring 1974), 19-57.

The "1972 Nottingham Festival D. H. Lawrence Exhibition," which assembled DHL's early paintings and representative artifacts of his youth, contributed to an understanding of the worth of his cultural heritage. "The artists Lawrence copied were popular," and sometimes talented, but "the sweet world of the magazines and books from which" he copied was "banal" and "theatrical," though it provided him with "the range of reference he could deploy later" in hundreds of allusions to art scattered throughout his writings. "There is a striking difference between the genteel and respectable early paintings and the resolutely unbuttoned efforts of his later years," possibly reflecting "the struggle with gentility within himself." What is significant "is not so much the inferior art his early environment put before him, as the vocabulary for the passions which he inherited." [Includes photographs of fifty items exhibited at the Nottingham Festival D. H. Lawrence Exhibition, 1972. See also C(arl) E. Baron, "D. H. Lawrence's Early Paintings," in YOUNG BERT: AN EXHIBITION OF THE EARLY YEARS OF D. H. LAWRENCE, compiled by Lucy I. Edwards, David Phillips, Arnold Rattenbury, and Jo Barnes (Nottingham: Castle Museum, Nottingham Castle, 1972), pp. 32-40.]

4266 Barrett, Gerald R., and Thomas L. Erskine (eds). FROM FICTION TO FILM: D. H. LAWRENCE'S "THE ROCKING-HORSE WINNER" (Encino & Belmont, CA: Dickenson Publishing, 1974). Casebook on DHL's "The Rocking-Horse Winner" and the adaptation as a screenplay by Anthony Pelissier, with criticism organized under each. Contents, abstracted under year of first publication: Gerald R. Barrett and Thomas L. Erskine, "Preface," p. vii [not abstracted]; **Introduction**: Gerald R. Barrett, "From Fiction to Film," pp. 2-33; **The Short Story**: DHL, "The Rocking-Horse Winner," pp. 36-49 [not abstracted]; **Criticism of the Short Story**: Wallace W. Douglas, Roy Lamson, Hallett Smith, Hugh N. MacLean, "Critical Analysis of 'The Rocking-Horse Winner,'" pp. 52-57, from THE CRITICAL READER, rvd ed, ed by Roy Lamson, Hallett Smith, Hugh N. MacLean, Wallace W. Douglas (NY: Norton, 1949, 1962), pp. 416-21; W. D. Snodgrass, "A Rocking-Horse: The Symbol, the Pattern, the Way to Live," pp. 58-69, from THE HUDSON REVIEW, XI (Summer 1958), 191-200; E. San Juan, Jr., "Theme Versus Imitation: D. H. Lawrence's 'The Rocking-Horse Winner,'" pp. 70-74, from D. H. LAWRENCE REVIEW, III (Summer 1970), 136-40; **The Film**: "The Rocking-Horse Winner," Adapted for the Screen by Anthony Pelissier, Final Shooting Script (6 April 1949), 76-201 (pub 1974); **Criticism of the Film**: Henry Becker III, "'The Rocking-Horse Winner': Film as Parable," pp. 204-13, from LITERATURE/FILM QUARTERLY, I (Jan 1973), 55-63; Joan Mellen, "'The Rocking-Horse Winner' as Cinema," pp. 214-23 (pub 1974); Julian Smith, "The Social Architecture of 'The Rocking-Horse Winner,'" pp. 224-30 (pub 1974); Gerald R. Barrett and Thomas L. Erskine, "Suggestions for Papers," pp. 232-33; "Annotated Bibliography," pp. 236-38 [not abstracted].

4267 Bayer, Roberta M. "Voyage into Creativity: The Modern Künstlerroman: A Comparative Study of the Development of the Artist in the Works of Hermann Hesse, D. H. Lawrence, James Joyce and Theodore Dreiser," DISSERTATION ABSTRACTS INTERNATIONAL, XXXV (1975), 7245A. Unpublished dissertation, New York University, 1974.

4268 Beards, Richard D. "The Checklist of D. H. Lawrence Criticism and Scholarship, 1973," D. H. LAWRENCE REVIEW, VII (Spring 1974), 89-98.
[The annual checklist is divided into five sections: General, Poetry, Individual Works of Fiction, Non-Fiction Prose, and Drama.]

4269 Beards, Richard D. "*Sons and Lovers* as Bildungsroman," COLLEGE LITERATURE, I (Fall 1974), 204-17.

Paul Morel in *Sons and Lovers* is a Bildungsroman protagonist, "an apprentice to life," who aims to achieve an ideal of ambition, "fulfillment of which will heighten his sense of self." He defines his values "in regard to four critical concerns: vocation, mating, religion, and identity." Additionally, he searches "for the right relationship to the transcendent and non-human in the universe." Because DHL reveals so well "this mystical level of identity," he provides for the Bildungsroman and all fiction "a deeper interpenetration of the human and vital natural world than had been previously envisioned."

4270 Beirne, Raymond M. "Lawrence's Night-Letter on Censorship and Obscenity," D. H. LAWRENCE REVIEW, VII (Fall 1974), 321-22.

[Reprints with comment DHL's telegram on censorship to Thomas Seltzer (9? Feb 1923), in response to New York Supreme Court Justice John Ford's announced intention to seek prosecution of *Women in Love* after finding his daughter reading the novel. DHL's night-letter was originally published in NEW YORK TIMES, 11 Feb 1923, p. 18; rptd under the heading "*Women in Love* Again," PUBLISHER'S WEEKLY, 24 Feb 1923, p. 580; rptd as Letter 58 in *D. H. Lawrence: Letters to Thomas and Adele Seltzer,* ed by Gerald M. Lacy (Santa Barbara: Black Sparrow P, 1976), p. 65.]

4271 Boulton, James T. " 'D. H. Lawrence: Study of a Free Spirit in Literature,' A Note on an Uncollected Article," RENAISSANCE AND MODERN STUDIES, XVIII (1974), 5-6.

[Two-page note which introduces W. H. Roberts, "D. H. Lawrence: Study of a Free Spirit in Literature," which had appeared originally in MILLGATE MONTHLY (May 1928) and which is rptd here, pp. 7-16.] Roberts's 1928 article is noteworthy as one of the earliest "general critical assessments" of DHL in England and as one aimed at working men "interested in ideas." DHL took "issue with Mr. Roberts's comment on the 'verbose obscurity' which, in his view, occasionally mars Lawrence's verse." [A passage is quoted from DHL's 13 May 1928 letter to Roberts.]

4272 Brown, Homer O. " 'The Passionate Struggle into Conscious Being': D. H. Lawrence's *The Rainbow,*" D. H. LAWRENCE REVIEW, VII (Fall 1974), 275-90.

The emphasis in the opening passage of *The Rainbow* is "on the experience of touch, on tactile and kinesthetic imagery; the passage is hardly visualized at all." The reader participates in an experience that is immediate and not fully conscious for the Brangwens but that is presented from the highly conscious point of view of the narrator. The Brangwen men are caught in the flow of blood process, but the women seek liberation through expanded consciousness, "not simply a greater intellectuality." "The true movement for modern man. . .is always outward to a fuller consciousness beyond that of the mind, and this movement"--the " 'passionate struggle into conscious being' "--"is the controlling direction of both the action and the point of view" in the novel. DHL's repetitive style is related to point of view, which must both "adapt itself to the ever-widening consciousness of the characters and stand detached from it." The point of view develops concurrently with the experience of the characters, from a "vastly generalized group experience" to the "gradually accumulating weight and particularity of detail" in the more than last half of the novel "devoted to Ursula and her groping toward selfhood." "Ursula reaches self-definition not only through her widening range of experience but also by constant transcending of each experience, a constant rejection of and separation from what is not herself."

4273 Buckley, Jerome Hamilton. SEASON OF YOUTH: THE BILDUNGSROMAN FROM DICKENS TO GOLDING (Cambridge: Harvard UP, 1974), pp. viii, 13, 17, 19, 21, 79, 97, 105, 115, 123, 143, 178, 204-24, 225, 231-33, 248, 250, 254, 256, 272, 279, 282, 313, 316-20.

DHL's *Sons and Lovers* is perhaps "the most passionately autobiographical of all major English novels"; however, the fictional component of the novel determines method and pattern, and it is clear that DHL was conscious of writing in the tradition of the Bildungsroman. The following conventions of the genre are evident in *Sons and Lovers:* troubled relationships between the hero and members of his family, a provincial setting, a concern for money and economic security, a hero with an aesthetic sensibility, and a plot which entails the education of the hero. DHL's complex and painful relationships with his mother and with Jessie Chambers serve as the autobiographical sources for his novel. In the second half of the book, however, "analysis tends more and more to displace delineated action." This tendency encourages Freudian interpretations of this novel and of other of DHL's works which relate to his feelings for his mother--interpretations which DHL could not understand and bitterly resented. Unlike other novelists in the tradition of the Bildungsroman, DHL "regards his fictional counterpart [Paul Morel] without irony; he condones most of Paul's conduct and presents his moodiness, sentimentality, arrogance, and rage as if they were all necessary concomitants, perhaps even tokens, of the artistic temperament." DHL's message is essentially "the Nietzschean individualism, defiantly amoral, that shocked Jessie Chambers."

4274 Burwell, Rose Marie. "Schopenhauer, Hardy and Lawrence: Toward a New Understanding of *Sons and Lovers,*" WESTERN HUMANITIES REVIEW, XXVIII (Spring 1974), 107-17.

Examination of DHL's "knowledge and acceptance of Schopenhauer's view of human relationships" shows that in *Sons and Lovers* "character motivations recognized as Freudian blended with. . .unrecognized. . .Schopenhauerian" assumptions. DHL's conception of Sue Bridehead's character in his *Study of Thomas Hardy* was embodied in the character of Miriam Leivers. In addition, "both the elder Morels and Baxter and Clara Dawes are perceived. . .as having wrought upon one another a mutual destruction similar to that which destroyed Jude and Sue" in JUDE THE OBSCURE.

4275 Carstarphen, Sally S. "The Divided Sympathetic Bond: A Study of D. H. Lawrence's Drama." Unpublished dissertation, University of North Carolina at Greensboro, 1974. [Listed in D. H.

LAWRENCE REVIEW, VIII (Summer 1975), 237.]

4276 Cavitch, David. "Merging--with Fish and Others," D. H. LAWRENCE REVIEW, VII (Summer 1974), 172-78.
Birds, Beasts, and Flowers shows DHL, in a difficult period of adjustment, attempting to re-establish his connections to the object world so important in its "otherness" to the bases of morality in private and public life. "Fish" shows DHL entertaining, in its early section, a fantasy of narcissistic merging which in the second section is rejected for the "unknown" phallic pike, redirecting his sadistic impulses away from the maternal to a male adversary the destruction of which, with its imagery of masturbation, results in a destruction of the self as well as the other. Chastened, DHL withdraws into a condition of passivity and wonder.

4277 Chabrowe, Leonard, and James Cooney. "U. S. Discoverer of Henry Miller Returns for Today's Unknowns--James Cooney: The Literary Phoenix," NEW YORK SMITH, Summer 1974, pp. 2, 11, 31.
DHL saw the "bankruptcy" of capitalist democracy, the Russian revolution, and Christianity, and sought means of resurrection, symbolized in the phoenix. [Transcript of interview on WBAI-FM, New York, with James Cooney, editor of THE PHOENIX (Woodstock, NY).]

4278 Chaddock, Bruce E. "Authorial Presence in the Novel," DISSERTATION ABSTRACTS INTERNATIONAL, XXXV (1975), 4505A-6A. Unpublished dissertation, Cornell University, 1974.
[Extended discussion of *The Rainbow.*]

4279 Chinol, Elio. "Introduzione" (Introduction), *Il pavone bianco (The White Peacock)* by D. H. Lawrence (Rome: Newton Compton Italiana, 1974), pp. 7-13.
The White Peacock is generally considered one of DHL's minor works even by critics such as F. R. Leavis, who acknowledged the genius of this author. The importance of this novel emerges if it is seen in relation to DHL's later works and as representative of a first phase in which the fundamental themes are already present: the conflict between consciousness and the unconscious, mind and body, civilization and nature. As for the man-woman relationship, it is treated in terms of both conflict and love. Particularly vivid is DHL's sense of nature. [In Italian.]

4280 Chrisman, Reva Wells. "Ursula Brangwen in the University: D. H. Lawrence's Rejection of Authority in *The Rainbow*," KENTUCKY PHILOLOGICAL ASSOCIATION BULLETIN, I (1974), 9-16.
Jessie Chambers's "hunch" that DHL wanted "the University to compensate for his lack of a father is. . .substantiated in Ursula's experience." DHL thought that in the interests of a society based on money and mechanized efficiency, "the University subverts the vital Dionysian energies in the service of Apollonian order." One of the " 'allotropic states' through which the ego passes" in *The Rainbow* is "the masculine sense of authority." Ursula has both "the Brangwen women's capacity for out-reaching" and "the Brangwen men's consciousness of the blood."

Thus, she suspects "the spuriousness of an institution which seeks to transmit wisdom without a knowledge of the blood." She dislikes abstract mathematics but enjoys the education class, "which brings the theory of education to life." Although she looks for a way into life through Skrebensky, she finds her salvation in "rejecting the society which has destroyed Skrebensky's soul." "She must 'await' rather than 'create' the man with whom she will enter the 'unknown.'" There are biographical parallels between Ursula and DHL in their educational and teaching experiences, which thematically signal DHL's break with traditional masculine authority. "Womb imagery is used repeatedly...to represent the gestation of an age, conceived in the artist's mind, but not yet born." Ursula's achievement is to hold in balance the two polarities--inner and outer, dark and light, blood and consciousness. The validity of DHL's prophetic assessment of civilization, however, is ultimately less important than his aesthetic contribution in the novel.

4281 Clarke, Richard. "Autobiography, Doctrine, and Genre Comparison in the Plays of D. H. Lawrence," DISSERTATION ABSTRACTS INTERNATIONAL, XXXV (1974), 1091A. Unpublished dissertation, Florida State University, 1974.

4282 Cline, C. L. "A Visit to Frieda," LIBRARY CHRONICLE OF THE UNIVERSITY OF TEXAS AT AUSTIN, ns No. 7 (Spring 1974), 37-41.
[Account of informal negotiations with Frieda Lawrence by Cline for her DHL collection for the Humanities Research Center, University of Texas at Austin. Due to a lack of immediate funds and Frieda's death several days later, the deal was not completed. However, much of the collection found its way to Austin anyway, in the T. E. Hanley and E. D. McDonald collections.]

4283 "Commentary," TIMES LITERARY SUPPLEMENT (Lond), 11 Jan 1974, p. 33.
[Discussion of plans by the Cambridge UP to undertake "a real endeavour to give us the full corpus of Lawrence's letters in a sound edition," which is important in establishing accurate texts. See also Letter to the Editor by John Carswell, "Lawrence Letters," TIMES LITERARY SUPPLEMENT (Lond), 1 Feb 1974, p. 108 (not abstracted).]

4284 Cooney, Seamus. "The First Edition of Lawrence's Foreword to *Women in Love*," LIBRARY CHRONICLE OF THE UNIVERSITY OF TEXAS AT AUSTIN, ns No. 7 (Spring 1974), 71-79.
There are three extant versions of DHL's Foreword to *Women in Love,* formerly thought to have been first published in 1936 by Gelber, Lilianthal, Inc. as *D. H. Lawrence's Unpublished Foreword to "Women in Love," 1919,* indicating that 1936 was not the first publication date but that two states of an earlier edition were used for advertising at the time of the novel's first publication in 1920. One state of this edition varies at only one point from the 1936 version. [The three versions are reproduced here as well as a table of variant readings for comparison.]

4285 Corke, Helen. "The Writing of *The Trespasser*," D. H. LAWRENCE REVIEW, VII (Fall 1974), 227-39.
[A third-person narrative account of the author's meeting with DHL and the details of their relationship. It focuses on the genesis of *The Saga of Siegmund* and its transformation into *The Trespasser*.]

4286 Cowan, James C. "Laurentiana," D. H. LAWRENCE REVIEW, VII (Summer 1974), 218-19.
The "underlying structure" of *The Widowing of Mrs. Holroyd* is made clear in "repeated ritual actions" that balance the first two acts with the third. While "the play turns on...moral ambivalence and blind pride," Mrs. Holroyd, "alone with the body of her husband,...reaches...tragic perception." [Review of the Long Wharf Theater production in New Haven, CT, broadcast on PBS television (1974).]

4287 Cowan, James C. "Lawrence's Criticism of Melville," MELVILLE SOCIETY EXTRACTS, XIX (1974), 6-9.
In *Studies in Classic American Literature*, DHL sees Melville as a myth-maker, whose work embodies the conflict between mental consciousness and "blood consciousness." Though modern man cannot regress to the savage consciousness of Melville's Polynesians, DHL believed, we can "take a great curve in their direction onwards." In his view, the "marriage" between Ishmael and Queequeg was a possible means of reconciling pagan and Christian consciousness, had Ishmael not been caught up in Ahab's quest. Nevertheless, DHL thinks Melville the finest "poet of the sea" and MOBY-DICK "a great book."

4288 Cushman, Keith. "A Profile of John E. Baker, Jr., and His Lawrence Collection," D. H. LAWRENCE REVIEW, VII (Spring 1974), 83-88.
[A description of the nearly complete assemblage of DHL first editions and the typescripts, autograph manuscripts, and corrected galley sheets of DHL's works in the collection of John E. Baker, Jr. (Illustrated with a photograph of Baker.) See also Keith Cushman, AN EXHIBITION OF FIRST EDITIONS AND MANUSCRIPTS FROM THE D. H. LAWRENCE COLLECTION OF JOHN E. BAKER, JR. (Chicago: Joseph Regenstein Library, The University of Chicago, 1973), an introduction and checklist of 114 items from the collection exhibited at the Joseph Regenstein Library, The University of Chicago, November and December, 1973; and A CATALOGUE OF TWENTIETH CENTURY LITERATURE, collected by John E. Baker, Jr. (Desbarats, Ontario, 1977), a 102-page catalogue of the complete Baker collection.]

4289 Cushman, Keith. "A Profile of John Martin and His Lawrence Collection," D. H. LAWRENCE REVIEW, VII (Summer 1974), 199-205.
[A description of the DHL first editions in mint condition, the paintings, and other DHL materials in the collection held by John Martin.] [The collection was acquired by McFarlin Library of the University of Tulsa, which held a special exhibition on 8 December 1975, as reported in "Laurentiana," D. H. LAWRENCE REVIEW, IX (Spring 1976), 172.]

4290 Czuchlewski, Ellen Dugan. "D. H. Lawrence: The Prophet and His Voice," DISSERTATION ABSTRACTS INTERNATIONAL, XXXV (1974), 1650A-51A. Unpublished dissertation, Fordham University, 1974.
[On DHL's poetry.]

4291 Davies, Russell. "*The Merry-Go-Round,*" PLAYS AND PLAYERS, XXI (Jan 1974), 50-51.
Although "by no means omnicompetent," DHL was a "tactful and relaxed stage-craftsman." The new production of *The Merry-Go-Round,* however, is enhanced by director Peter Gill's excision of "improbable stage-directions and extraneous snooping Poles." "The bizarre truce [DHL] imposes on the play's conflicts" in "the rib-tickling bonhomie of the last five minutes" is in "unacceptable contrast with the preceding couple of hours." "Had Lawrence been true to himself and the course of his play," *The Merry-Go-Round* would have been more durable. [Review of the Royal Court Theatre production, illustrated with four photographs.]

4292 de Filippis, Simonetta. "Minatori e anime superiori: conflitti famigliari e lotta delle classi nei teatro autobiografico di D. H. Lawrence" (Miners and Superior Souls: Family Conflicts and Class Struggle in D. H. Lawrence's Autobiographical Theatre), ANNALI ISTITUTO UNIVERSITARIO ORIENTALE, NAPOLI, SEZIONE GERMANICA-ANGLISTICA, XVII, No. 2 (1974), 7-59.
The analysis of *A Collier's Friday Night, The Daughter-in-Law,* and *The Widowing of Mrs. Holroyd* brings out explicitly the complex significance of the three characters that recur in this trilogy: the father, the mother, and the woman. These, in fact, appear as symbolic figures through which DHL represents his own interior struggle for his identity. This struggle, however, involves a greater conflict: that between two cultures, two classes competing for the mind of the young DHL. The conflict is resolved, in the end, by his claiming the supremacy of the rights of the artist's individuality, by rejecting any class identity, and by recognizing instinct and spontaneity as the only positive values. [In Italian.]

4293 Delavenay, Émile, and W. J. Keith. "Mr. Rolf Gardiner, 'The English Neo-Nazi': An Exchange," D. H. LAWRENCE REVIEW, VII (Fall 1974), 291-94.
[Émile Delavenay's reply to W. J. Keith, "Spirit of Place and *Genius Loci:* D. H. Lawrence and Rolf Gardiner," D. H. LAWRENCE REVIEW, VII (Summer 1974), 127-38, and Keith's rejoinder to him.] **Delavenay**: To refute Keith's inference that Delavenay's designation of Rolf Gardiner as a "pro-Nazi" is inaccurate, the texts of the evidence in question, the news item "D. H. Lawrence in a Black Shirt: Berlin Busy Finding Fascists (From Our Special Correspondent)," OBSERVER (Lond), 4 Feb 1934, and Rolf Gardiner's letter to the editor, "D. H. Lawrence in a Black Shirt," OBSERVER (Lond), 11 Feb 1934, are printed in full. **Keith**: The news item can hardly be taken seriously. "If Gardiner 'regarded Lawrence as the god of the younger generation,'...then he might himself, like Lawrence, have 'looked upon Fascism and Communism alike with a certain disgust.'" Moreover,

"for an anonymous reporter to call Gardiner 'the English neo-Nazi' in 1934 is one thing; for a literary scholar to dismiss him...as 'le pro-Nazi' after the Second World War is another."

4294 De Saint Jean, Robert. JOURNAL D'UN JOURNALISTE (Journal of a Journalist) (Paris: Grasset, 1974), pp. 88, 94, 127, *et passim.*

The success of *Lady Chatterley's Lover* is attributable to the frankness with which this novel shows how far behind woman is in comparison with man, as far as sexual enjoyment is concerned. According to Gabriel Marcel, only two men in his life looked like born poets: DHL and Rilke. [In French.]

4295 D. H. LAWRENCE REVIEW, ed by James C. Cowan, VII, No. 1 (Spring 1974).

Contents, abstracted under 1974: John B. Vickery, "D. H. Lawrence's Poetry: Myth and Matter," pp. 1-18; C. E. Baron, "The Nottingham Festival D. H. Lawrence Exhibition, 1972" [illustrated with 32-page section of art reproductions in black and white], pp. 19-57; T. H. Adamowski, "*The Rainbow* and 'Otherness,'" pp. 58-77; Takashi Toyokuni, "A Modern Man Obsessed by Time: A Note on 'The Man Who Loved Islands,'" pp. 78-82; Keith Cushman, "A Profile of John E. Baker, Jr., and His Lawrence Collection," pp. 83-88; Richard D. Beards, "The Checklist of D. H. Lawrence Scholarship for 1973," pp. 89-98; "Laurentiana," pp. 99-104 [not abstracted]; "Research in Progress," p. 105 [not abstracted]; "Contributors," p. 106 [not abstracted].

4296 D. H. LAWRENCE REVIEW, ed by James C. Cowan, VII, No. 2 (Summer 1974).

Contents, abstracted under 1974: Daniel J. Schneider, "The Symbolism of the Soul: D. H. Lawrence and Some Others," pp. 107-26; W. J. Keith, "Spirit of Place and *Genius Loci*: D. H. Lawrence and Rolf Gardiner," pp. 127-38; Jeffrey Meyers, "*The Rainbow* and Fra Angelico," pp. 139-55; Bryan D. Reddick, "Point of View and Narrative Tone in *Women in Love*: The Portrayal of Interpsychic Space," pp. 156-71; David Cavitch, "Merging--with Fish and Others," pp. 172-78; Del Ivan Janik, "The Two Infinites: D. H. Lawrence's *Twilight in Italy*," pp. 179-98; Keith Cushman, "A Profile of John Martin and His Lawrence Collection," pp. 199-205; Charles L. Ross, "Art and 'Metaphysic' in D. H. Lawrence's Novels," pp. 206-17 [not abstracted]; "Laurentiana," pp. 218-22 [only James C. Cowan, Review of *The Widowing of Mrs. Holroyd*, is abstracted]; "Research in Progress," p. 223 [not abstracted]; "Contributors," pp. 224-25 [not abstracted].

4297 D. H. LAWRENCE REVIEW, ed by James C. Cowan, VII, No. 3 (Fall 1974).

Contents, abstracted under 1974: Helen Corke, "The Writing of *The Trespasser*," pp. 227-39; George J. Zytaruk (ed), "Dorothy Brett's Letters to S. S. Koteliansky," pp. 240-74; Homer O. Brown, "'The Passionate Struggle into Conscious Being': D. H. Lawrence's *The Rainbow*," pp. 275-90; Émile Delavenay and W. J. Keith, "Mr. Rolf Gardiner, 'The English Neo-Nazi': An Exchange," pp. 291-94; Charles Rossman, "Toward D. H. Lawrence and His Visual Bestiary," pp. 295-308 [not abstracted] ; Giles Mitchell, "Lawrence, Others, and the Self," pp. 309-20 [not abstracted] ; Raymond M. Beirne, "Lawrence's Night-Letter on Censorship and Obscenity," pp. 321-22; "Laurentiana," pp. 323-29 [not abstracted] ; "Research in Progress," pp. 330-31 [not abstracted] ; "Contributors," pp. 332-33, and "Index to Volume VII," pp. 334-35 [not abstracted].

4298 D. H. LAWRENCE STUDIES (Kyôto), No. 2, "*Shinnyusha*" (*The Trespasser* Number) (Nov 1974).
Contents, abstracted under 1974: Sadanobu Kai, "Foreword: The Isle of Wight in a Living Myth," pp. 1-3; Hirokazu Yoshimura, "*Shinnyusha* no Wagnerteki Yôso o Megutte" (Wagnerian Elements in *The Trespasser*), pp. 5-28; Kaien Kitazaki, "*The Trespasser* ni Okeru 'Saihô' ni Tsuite" ("The West" in *The Trespasser*), pp. 29-45; Yasushi Sugiyama, "*Shinnyusha* ni Okeru Shi to Sei" (Death and Life in *The Trespasser*), pp. 47-64; Iwao Nishimura, "The Secret of *The Trespasser*--Traced in Siegmund's Tragedy," pp. 65-97; Masuko Fujiwara, "*Shinnyusha* ni Okeru Genjitsu to Yume" (Reality and Dream in *The Trespasser*), pp. 99-116; "Synopses" [in English] , pp. 117-23 [not abstracted] ; *The Trespasser* Bibliography, pp. 125-28 [not abstracted]. [In Japanese.]

4299 Dignon, Hugh Alexander. "Love and Courtship in the Novels of George Eliot, Thomas Hardy, and D. H. Lawrence: A Comparative Study," DISSERTATION ABSTRACTS INTERNATIONAL, XXXV (1975), 4425A-26A. Unpublished dissertation, New York University, 1974.

4300 Ditsky, John M. " 'Dark, Darker than Fire': Thematic Parallels in Lawrence and Faulkner," SOUTHERN HUMANITIES REVIEW, VIII (Fall 1974), 497-505.
DHL and William Faulkner use a similar language to express their parallel visions of the role of Nature in relation to man's character. Though Faulkner never overtly mentions DHL's influence, he read DHL during the Twenties, and recent criticism suggests similarities in their characterization. A relationship in stylistic diction can also be shown, especially by a close analysis of Chapter IV of *The Rainbow*. The use here of nature images to point up the intensity of the drama in a scene is also found in SANCTUARY, AS I LAY DYING, and THE WILD PALMS.

4301 Dobrowolny, Welleda. "D. H. Lawrence and Italy." Unpublished dissertation, University of Trieste, 1974. [Listed in D. H. LAWRENCE REVIEW, X (Fall 1977), 301.]

4302 Doheny, John. "Lady Chatterley and Her Lover," WEST COAST REVIEW, VIII (1974), 51-56.
The publication of *John Thomas and Lady Jane* gives a unique opportunity to watch DHL developing a novel. The first version is merely a draft, but the sharpening of issues and Mellors's preaching in the third version require DHL to sacrifice Parkin's and Connie's vitality as developing characters to allow Mellors to function merely as his spokesman. The three versions represent not a smooth development

into a perfect apologue but a struggle between the instinctive novelist interested in character and human dilemmas and the "impatient philosopher" that DHL became in his last years.

4303 Dooley, D. J. COMPTON MACKENZIE (NY: Twayne [TEAS 173], 1974), pp. 5, 7, 26-27, 56, 57, 92-93, 129, 130, 132.

The friendship between DHL and Compton Mackenzie included at one time plans for a trip to the South Seas which resulted in DHL's using Mackenzie as a model for "The Man Who Loved Islands." Mackenzie's critical response to DHL's writing, especially *Lady Chatterley's Lover,* was outrage at his language and his treatment of sex and God.

4304 Drabble, Margaret. ARNOLD BENNETT (NY: Knopf, 1974), pp. 31, 97, 107, 235, 253, 254, 287, 289, 313, 316, 317, 328, 341.

Arnold Bennett immediately recognized *The Lost Girl* as a work of "genius" and DHL as "far and away the best of the younger school." This was particularly perceptive in view of the fact that *The Lost Girl* was in some ways an ironic and critical comment on THE OLD WIVES' TALE or ANNA OF THE FIVE TOWNS--its heroine, too, is a draper's daughter who escapes the dark, ruined world of the Midlands into a new country. Unlike DHL, Bennett could conceive of salvation without sex. Sophia endures and Anna endures, whereas DHL's Alvina Houghton escapes in the arms of an Italian lover in a subjugation that many women would consider a fate worse than death. "How interesting it is that Bennett...should have made all his true heroines fight till the end, with an inner indestructible core, whereas Lawrence's women find themselves only in submission and destruction."

4305 Eisenstein, Samuel A. BOARDING THE SHIP OF DEATH: D. H. LAWRENCE'S QUESTER HEROES (The Hague: Mouton [De proprietatibus litterarum, series practica, 42], 1974).

DHL's novels deal with the quest of the hero--the process of his growth and development in mass man as he becomes an individual. He never ceases to explore himself and the world for the way to wholeness. The books in which these processes are most apparent are DHL's least successful ones as works of art: *The White Peacock, The Trespasser, The Lost Girl, Aaron's Rod, Kangaroo,* "The Woman Who Rode Away," *The Man Who Died,* and "The Ship of Death." These works most clearly illustrate the snares and pitfalls the potential hero must experience on his way to individuation. A comparison with the hero prototype in religious and mythological literature enables one to understand the otherwise puzzling behavior of many DHL heroes. Similarly, seemingly arbitrary symbols are made clear when compared to those in religious and mythological works. The purpose of the quest is to find oneself; where the struggle leads is a mystery, but DHL's heroes are analogous to Michelangelo's slaves struggling to free themselves from the mass of marble in which they have their origin. DHL felt that the hero was required to undertake a spiritual odyssey: the processes of initiation, rites of passage, death, and rebirth cannot be avoided if the hero is to realize his potential. He must encounter and assimilate the unknown to live in harmony in his higher and lower centers--both physical and spiritual. Heroes begin as undifferentiated lumps and painfully individuate or perish. No hero ever succeeds wholly, but he works to bring himself into being. DHL's stories and novels offer hope to his readers and a message which may help the reader to release his own creative energies.

4306 Feldmann, Hans Eugene. "The Function of Heresy in Modern Literature: Studies in the Major Fiction of Thomas Hardy, E. M. Forster, and D. H. Lawrence," DISSERTATION ABSTRACTS INTERNATIONAL, XXXVI (1975), 1524A. Unpublished dissertation, University of Maryland, 1974.

4307 "Fiction," BOOKLIST, LXX (15 April 1974), 907.
The Escaped Cock, ed with a commentary by Gerald M. Lacy, restores the original title to the "metaphysical novella" published in Britain and the United States as *The Man Who Died* and adds "portions omitted in all previous editions although they are extant in the manuscript. Important letters related to the work" are also included.

4308 Fitz, L. T. " 'The Rocking-Horse Winner' and THE GOLDEN BOUGH," STUDIES IN SHORT FICTION, XI (Spring 1974), 199-200.
[A brief note on three names--Singhalese, Malabar, and Mirza--used in "The Rocking-Horse Winner" for the horses and found in Frazer.] Malabar is mentioned twice in THE GOLDEN BOUGH, once concerning the transfer of the people's sins to a scapegoat, as Paul is a scapegoat for the "sins of his loveless family," and once concerning the King of Calicut in Malabar, who had "godlike power" for twelve years, then had to cut his throat, again showing similarity to Paul.

4309 Fogel, Stanley. " 'And all the little typtopies': Notes on Language Theory in the Contemporary Experimental Novel," MODERN FICTION STUDIES, XX (Autumn 1974), 328-36.
DHL is like the "metafictionists" such as John Barth, Donald Barthelme, and Robert Coover in rejecting the traditional referential use of language by trying to strip away language, urging the reader toward the inarticulate preconscious. [Description of techniques used is included.] DHL "used language in a way that is anathema to William Gass, Vladimir Nabokov, and the whole Joyce-influenced school of present-day novelists."

4310 Foster, John Burt, Jr. "Nietzsche and the Novel of Cultural Crisis: A Study of Image and Idea in D. H. Lawrence and André Malraux," DISSERTATION ABSTRACTS INTERNATIONAL, XXXV (1975), 4516A-17A. Unpublished dissertation, Yale University, 1974.

4311 Freeman, Alma Susan. "The Androgynous Ideal: A Study of Selected Novels by D. H. Lawrence, James Joyce, and Virginia Woolf," DISSERTATION ABSTRACTS INTERNATIONAL, XXXVI (1975), 877A-78A. Unpublished dissertation, Rutgers University, 1974.

4312 Fujiwara, Masuko. "*Shinnyusha* ni Okeru Genjitsu to Yume" (Reality and Dream in *The Trespasser*), D. H. LAWRENCE STUDIES (Kyôto), No. 2 (Nov 1974), 99-116.

[After analyzing contradictory changes of DHL's viewpoint in handling the main characters of *The Trespasser* and in the pursuit of the symbolic function of the moon in relation to the lovers, the writer concludes that there are three ways of interpreting the meaning of "trespass": (1) Siegmund's trespassing the rules of normal social behavior on a realistic level, (2) Siegmund's trespassing Helena's Zauberland on the level of dream, and (3) Siegmund's stepping into death (the central theme of the novel).] [In Japanese.]

4313 Gadda Conti, Giuseppe. "Introduzione" (Introduction), *Il pavone bianco* (*The White Peacock*) (Milan: Rizzoli, 1974), pp. 9-16.

In *The White Peacock* nature is represented in all its beauty and vitality, but it is detached from the other aspects of life and assumes a mythical dimension. This novel is very symbolic and shows DHL's effort to overcome everyday reality. The dialogue of the characters seems artificial because DHL was above all a poet and was unable to adhere strictly to the rules of narrative technique. [In Italian.]

4314 Gallo, Rose. "Mythic Concepts in D. H. Lawrence," DISSERTATION ABSTRACTS INTERNATIONAL, XXXV (1975), 3739A. Unpublished dissertation, Rutgers University, 1974.

4315 Gates, Norman T. THE POETRY OF RICHARD ALDINGTON: A CRITICAL EVALUATION AND AN ANTHOLOGY OF UNCOLLECTED POEMS (University Park & Lond: Pennsylvania State UP, 1974), pp. 9, 10, 12-15, 26, 28, 30-32, 36, 66, 77, 91-92, 106, 108, 119n, 120n, 121, 125-26, 137, 158.

Although influence is difficult to assess, Richard Aldington's poems often echo Lawrencian themes and imagery. Aldington's LIFE QUEST contains a "direct answer" to DHL's "The Ship of Death," and "A Grave" was "probably intended" for DHL. Aldington, who consistently admired and defended DHL's work from the beginning, says in an unpublished letter that "Lawrence and not Eliot followed the authentic line."

4316 Gidley, Mick. "Antipodes: D. H. Lawrence's *St. Mawr*," ARIEL (Calgary, Canada), V (Jan 1974), 25-41.

St. Mawr develops by the tension of various antitheses associated with the horse: "Ancient Mysteries and Modern Knowledge; Animal and Human; and Nature and Society." Lou senses that the order of society is deformed since men in control, like Rico and Dean Vyner, lack the pure animal manliness of men in positions of servitude, such as Lewis, the Welsh groom, who is in touch with the mystery of St. Mawr. To escape this desolation, Lou and Mrs. Witt journey westward away from the unreality of London toward the reality of the wilderness in America. This journey provides syntheses to the various antitheses, and the ranch on the edge of the Rockies becomes sacred to Lou. But since the wilderness fails her ideal in two ways, seeming not only so primeval as to antedate sex itself but also fallen from ideal order as a result of man's degrading influence, it actually increases the distance between nature and society by defeating all notions of a harmonious civilization. The vitality of the horse fades before the spirit of the continent. The poles of the novel turn out to be spurious, and the "constitution of illusion and reality" emerges as the central concern in Lou's question, "What was real?" For Mrs. Witt the reality that impinges most forcefully on her consciousness is death; for Lou it is, first, her awareness of "positive evil" as a pervasive force in the world, then of the wilderness itself as a vision of truth which supersedes it. The "spirit of place" of the ranch gives Lou a final reality that is all-embracing, considering death a manifestation of the primordial life principle. Lou seems called to a mission of the spirit in a way that makes her predestined, capable of being one of the elect.

4317 Gill, Richard. "Invitation to Garsington," VIRGINIA QUARTERLY REVIEW, L (1974), 198-214.

[An account of Garsington Manor, the Tudor manor of Lady Ottoline Morrell and Philip Morrell, M. P., and "the kind of life that Lady Ottoline attempted to create for her guests" in the "golden years" from 1915 to 1926.] Among the visitors to Garsington was DHL, who participated in the amateur theatricals and *tableaux vivants,* once staging OTHELLO with himself playing the Moor. Ottoline introduced DHL to Bertrand Russell; the two jointly planned an attack on the military policy of the government, but the friendship ended in "mutual recriminations." Later DHL's grotesque caricature of Ottoline as Hermione Roddice in *Women in Love* wounded and disillusioned her.

4318 Gouirand, Jacqueline. "Sur trois manuscrits de D. H. Lawrence, *The White Peacock, The Trespasser, The Rainbow:* Contribution à l'étude de la création littéraire" (Concerning Three Manuscripts of D. H. Lawrence, *The White Peacock, The Trespasser, The Rainbow:* Contribution to the Study of Literary Creation). Unpublished dissertation, Thèse Doctorat de Troisième Cycle, University of Nice, 1974. [Listed in D. H. LAWRENCE REVIEW, VIII (Summer 1975), 238; and in CATALOGUE DES THÈSES DE DOCTORAT SOUTENUES DEVANT LES UNIVERSITÉS FRANÇAISES, ns Année 1974 (Paris: Cercle de la Librairie, 1978), p. 1018, Item 12806.]

[Compares MSS of *The White Peacock* and *The Trespasser* with published versions of these novels; classifies and analyzes all known variant MSS, typescripts, and printed texts of *The Rainbow;* and examines DHL's method of literary creation in *The Rainbow.*] [In French.]

4319 Green, Eleanor H. "Blueprints for Utopia: The Political Ideas of Nietzsche and D. H. Lawrence," RENAISSSANCE AND MODERN STUDIES, XVIII (1974), 141-61.

Nietzsche's "anti-democratic and elitist ideas" greatly impressed DHL, as evidenced in the leadership novels, *Aaron's Rod, Kangaroo,* and *The Plumed Serpent.* DHL's "natural aristocrat" is based partly on Nietzsche's conception of the superman. In *Aaron's Rod,* Lilly, the DHL character, is "weak, arrogant," and, if the Nietzschean "higher man," "far from prepossessing." In *Kangaroo,* the fascist Kangaroo assigns "love" the place in the cosmos that DHL and Nietzsche give to power, while the Communist Struthers, who wants rule by the masses, ascribes to no "god-passion" and preaches love without a full heart. Hence, the final response of the DHL character, Somers, is an "abnegation of all political activity." In *The Plumed Serpent,* Mexico is the "snake" that tries to capture and pull down to its level the "bird" Kate, who is "the embodiment of a conscious white culture that, at the same time, has lost its deep roots in the earth." Just as Nietzsche speaks of the "importance of myth in the creation of culture," so Ramón tries to give back to the people a symbolic structure by reviving the Aztec deities. As social and political thinkers, however, Nietzsche and DHL are not to be taken literally. Their contribution is their common emphasis on the "union of the whole individual with nature and the universe, the affirmation of life in all its manifestations and the discovery of a new meaning and direction within life."

4320 Green, Martin. THE VON RICHTHOFEN SISTERS: THE TRIUMPHANT AND THE TRAGIC MODES OF LOVE: ELSE AND FRIEDA VON RICHTHOFEN, OTTO GROSS, MAX WEBER, AND D. H. LAWRENCE, IN THE YEARS 1870-1970 (NY: Basic Books, 1974).
[Biographical study of Else and Frieda von Richthofen, their German intellectual background, and their relationships with Otto Gross, Max Weber, DHL, Edgar Jaffe, and others. The book sees the two sisters' lives, their antithetical voices, their differing modes of love, their rejection of conventional marriages and alliances, Else tragically, Frieda triumphantly, with men who embodied their own deepest commitments, as emblematic of the opposite ways of consciousness available to women in the first half of the twentieth century. Whereas Else sought university study in the social sciences, a career, personal independence, and prominence in rational debate and political reform, Frieda left her husband and children for a life of ideological eroticism and of virtual "co-authorship" of DHL's books: "Lawrence, or Lawrence-and-Frieda, became a genius by accepting her discipline and thus entering the world of Woman, enacting in his own life the principles of the erotic movement." The ideas of Gross, a disciple of Freud, an anti-democratic revolutionary, and Schwabing's culture hero of sexual liberation, are related through Else and Frieda, both of whom had affairs with Gross, to DHL's psychoanalytic, sexual, and religious ideas. The book examines DHL's contacts, indirectly through Gross and directly through Else and Edgar Jaffe, with the *kosmische Runde* (the Cosmic Circle) and the ideas of Alfred Schuler and Ludwig Klages and later with those of the Swiss historian Johann Jakob Bachofen and Alfred Weber. The Jaffes' marriage became the model for that of Mary Lindley and Edward Massy in DHL's "Daughters of the Vicar." The author draws a comparison between DHL and Max Weber and sees F. R. Leavis and Talcott Parsons as their respective heirs.] [See also a point-by-point refutation of what Delavenay calls Green's factual inaccuracies, misquotations, errors, and misleading use of evidence in Émile Delavenay, " 'Making Another Lawrence': Frieda and the Lawrence Legend," D. H. LAWRENCE REVIEW, VIII (Spring 1975), 80-98.]

4321 Grey, Anthony. "Up the Rough Deserted Pasture...the Country of My Heart," IN BRITAIN, XXIX (April 1974), 15-18.
DHL drew more powerfully and openly on his surroundings than any other English

novelist. For this reason it is still possible to visit Eastwood in the Midlands of England and see the actual scenes from which he drew the setting of his books. [Illustrated travel sketch on Eastwood, including local attitudes toward DHL.]

4322 Grigson, Geoffrey. "Leavis against Eliot" and "Lawrence Twice Over," THE CONTRARY VIEW: GLIMPSES OF FUDGE AND GOLD (Lond: Macmillan, 1974), pp. 39-43, 112-18.

[Recounts F. R. Leavis's attack on T. S. Eliot with reference to DHL and accuses Leavis of having a vengeful mind and barbarous taste. Also reprints a 1964 review of D. H. LAWRENCE: A PERSONAL RECORD, 2nd ed, by Jessie Chambers (1965); D. H. LAWRENCE: THE CROYDON YEARS, by Helen Corke (1965); and *The Paintings of D. H. Lawrence,* ed by Mervyn Levy (1964), and suggests that the fact that scholars are swarming to DHL like maggots does not hide the fact that he was a fabricator, a "liar of a kind whose lies prompt him to his weak exclamatory prose."]

4323 Grotte, Margaret Spencer. "The Unsteady Arch: The Place of *The Rainbow* in the Lawrentian Love-Ethic," DISSERTATION ABSTRACTS INTERNATIONAL, XXXV (1975), 6137A. Unpublished dissertation, Cornell University, 1974.

4324 Gunn, Drewey Wayne. AMERICAN AND BRITISH WRITERS IN MEXICO, 1556-1973 (Austin: University of Texas P, 1974), pp. 97, 123, 124, 125, 128-29, 131, 134, 135, 136, 137.

Believing that America held the destiny of the world yet was led destructively by will, DHL saw the Southwest and Mexico, with their Indian cultures, as areas of revitalization. The most significant English-speaking writer who used Mexico as a setting, DHL responded with fear and disgust to the Aztec cruelty he saw at the heart of Mexican culture. *The Plumed Serpent,* flawed by a Fascist sense of a people's destiny, is simple in narrative but characterized by a fantastic vision of early Mexican religion and a complex symbolism, used to convey DHL's ideas on sex, politics, relations between men, and the essence of life and death. *Mornings in Mexico* explores concepts of cosmic creation and destruction. After leaving Mexico, which gave him his most complete contact with the primitive, DHL praised primitivism less.

4325 Hall, R. L. "Expatriate Publishing I," MEANJIN QUARTERLY, XXXIII (June 1974), 170-76.

The reproductions of DHL's paintings were the immediate cause of the breakdown of the Fanfrolico Press. Although P. R. Stephensen, who engineered the publication of the reproductions (*The Paintings of D. H. Lawrence,* 1929), clearly enjoyed flouting bourgeois sensibilities, he did not intend to engage in a crusade against censorship. [See also Jack Lindsay, "Expatriate Publishing II," MEANJIN QUARTERLY, XXXIII (June 1974), 176-79.]

4326 Harris, Janice H. "D. H. Lawrence and Kate Millett," MASSACHUSETTS REVIEW, XV (Summer 1974), 522-29.

Kate Millett in SEXUAL POLITICS (1970) ignores all evidence which opposes her thesis regarding DHL's sexism, failing to note that DHL's heroes typically come into salvation as they take on qualities traditionally associated with the feminine.

4327 Haskell, Molly. FROM REVERENCE TO RAPE: THE TREATMENT OF WOMEN IN THE MOVIES (NY: Holt, Rinehart & Winston; Harmondsworth, Middlesex, England: Penguin Books, 1974), pp. 23, 29, 204, 340-41.

"The emphasis on orgasmic sex is masculine in thrust, finding its apotheosis in the phallic philosophy of D. H. Lawrence." In "opening itself up to sex," in such movies as the film versions of *The Fox, The Virgin and the Gypsy,* and *Women in Love,* "the screen had gone beyond Lawrence; the 'new morality' made it possible to show everything--homosexual and heterosexual copulation--without ever coming to terms with" the audience's repression. Gudrun, as played by Glenda Jackson in *Women in Love,* "is even more abrasive and emasculating than her Lawrentian prototype." "As the poet/prophet of sexual liberation, . . .Lawrence did want sexually demanding women," but feared that, in "their psychological hunger," they would "unman him," as his comments on Hawthorne's women show.

4328 Herrick, Jeffrey Don. "Visionary Sequences: D. H. Lawrence's Major Poetry." Unpublished dissertation, University of Chicago, 1974. [Listed in AMERICAN DOCTORAL DISSERTATIONS 1974-75 (Ann Arbor, MI: University Microfilm International, 1976), p. 289.]

4329 Hesse, Hermann. MY BELIEF: ESSAYS ON LIFE AND ART, ed by Theodore Ziolkowski, trans by Denver Lindley (NY: Farrar, Straus & Giroux, 1974).

[Although Hesse has read only the "castrated" edition of *Lady Chatterley's Lover* trans by Herlitschka, he still finds it one of DHL's most passionate and charming books and admires DHL's defense of love, tenderness, sensuality, nature, and blood against abstract morality. Hesse finds in *St. Mawr* DHL's finest work.]

4330 Hinz, Evelyn J. "D. H. Lawrence and 'Something Called Canada,'" DALHOUSIE REVIEW, LIV (Summer 1974), 240-50.

In *The White Peacock* and *Lady Chatterley's Lover,* Canada "symbolizes the place where liberated beings may go to live their liberated lives." DHL chose Canada because of his acquaintance with Jessie Chambers's brothers, who spoke of emigrating there; his choice persisted because he "never practically pursued his initial belief in the possibilities of the Canadian 'new world.'"

4331 Hope, A. D. "D. H. Lawrence's *Kangaroo*: How It Looks to an Australian," THE AUSTRALIAN EXPERIENCE: CRITICAL ESSAYS ON AUSTRALIAN NOVELS, ed by W. S. Ransom (Canberra: Australian National UP, 1974), pp. 157-73.

Aside from its structural and artistic flaws, DHL's *Kangaroo* is a "comic caricature" of the Australian milieu. The book fails to arise "out of its setting in the way that *Sons and Lovers* can be said to"; instead, it simply uses "certain local references to peg the themes down to some recognisable time and place." Through the character of Somers, with whom he identifies himself, DHL makes the kind of superficial observations about Australia which an inexperienced tourist might make and presents a view of the country which is inaccurate in its depiction of its political climate in the 1920s by imposing upon Australia the Italian fascism with which the author was acquainted.

4332 Humma, John B. "D. H. Lawrence as Friedrich Nietzsche," PHILOLOGICAL QUARTERLY, LIII (Jan 1974), 110-20.

Although DHL disparages Nietzsche's concept of the *Wille zur Macht* (in *Women in Love,* Birkin calls it a "base and petty thing"), DHL insistently advocated it himself. In *Aaron's Rod,* Lilly argues that man must rid himself of the spiritual "love-urge" and embrace the "power-urge." DHL saw Nietzsche's *Wille zur Macht* as essentially an intellectualized love-will. In "Blessed Are the Powerful," he identifies Nietzsche's will-to-power with the Germanic deification of "the egoistic Will of Man." The will DHL praises in *Psychoanalysis and the Unconscious* is the pre-intellectual will of the spontaneous "living unconscious." But this concept of will is precisely what Nietzsche intends to convey, and DHL's failure to comprehend this accounts for his aversion to Nietzsche, who actually anticipated DHL's ideas. Both writers considered consciousness a disease (Nietzsche's THE JOYFUL WISDOM and DHL's *Fantasia of the Unconscious*), both found Socrates guilty of killing the instinctual cosmos with reason (TWILIGHT OF THE IDOLS and *Apocalypse*), both held Christianity to be a religion of death rather than life (THE ANTICHRIST and *Apocalypse*), and both despised bourgeois morality (BEYOND GOOD AND EVIL, THE GENEALOGY OF MORALS, and *A Propos of "Lady Chatterley's Lover"* and "Introduction to These Paintings"). Thus, DHL continues Nietzsche's conceptual world.

4333 Humma, John B. "Melville's BILLY BUDD and Lawrence's 'The Prussian Officer': Old Adam and New," ESSAYS IN LITERATURE (Western Illinois University), I (1974), 83-88.

Character and action in BILLY BUDD and "The Prussian Officer" are analogous. Claggart and the officer symbolize "the fallen Adam" whose disease is his "mental consciousness" and who, envious of the "natural perfection" he has lost, assumes the role of Satan and "attempts to bring the same disintegration" to his former, "mocking" self.

4334 Iida, Takeo. "Shôdô to Ittaisei--*Lady Chatterley's Lover* ni Tsuite (1)" (Impulse and Unity: On *Lady Chatterley's Lover* [1]), KURUME UNIVERSITY JOURNAL, No. 2 (Nov 1974), 159-66.

In *Lady Chatterley's Lover,* Clifford Chatterley symbolizes the man who has superficial desires and no vital impulse. Without deep desires within him, he cannot create any vivid relationships with a woman, Connie, and with the cosmos. This is because he is a slave to an idea of absolute Freedom. He cannot realize that it is an illusion, which disintegrates his own life and destroys the life of nature. [In Japanese.]

4335 Imaizumi, Haruko. "D. H. Lawrence ni Okeru 'Chi' " (The

"Blood" in D. H. Lawrence), ANNUAL STUDY BULLETIN OF HINOMOTO GAKUEN JUNIOR COLLEGE, No. 1 (Dec 1974), 32-41.

According to DHL, blood is life, which is created by the Holy Ghost. In DHL the term *Holy Ghost* is used interchangeably both with *Creator* and with other "Lawrencian terms." DHL's artistic usage is similar to that of the Bible, in which blood is life and Christ's blood, in some verses, almost means the Holy Ghost. [In Japanese.]

4336 Irie, Takanori. KENJA RORENSU (Lawrence the Seer) (Tokyo: Kodansha, 1974).

[This critical biography traces DHL's life and analyzes his major novels, poems, and essays in chronological order, in an effort to illuminate DHL's "world-view." Separate chapters are devoted to discussions of major works by DHL ("The Crown," *The White Peacock, The Rainbow,* and *Apocalypse*), and other chapters focus on DHL's relationship with Frieda, his argument with Bertrand Russell, his travels, his response to the "Spirit of Place," and his ideas on death.] [In Japanese.]

4337 Ishibashi, Magoichiro. "Lawrence no Kaiga to Kaiga-Seishin ni Tsuite" (On the Painting and Its Spirits of Lawrence), JOURNAL OF ÔSAKA INDUSTRIAL UNIVERSITY, No. 39 (April 1974), 1-24.

[The whole spirit of DHL's painting is explored, from the birth of his creative power to his one-man exhibition as a painter. The main points discussed are as follows: (1) DHL's insistence that the intuition and instinct of painters is quite necessary in order to paint the inner side of the object; (2) his intention to vivify his images through his own vision; (3) the close relation between his painting and his literary works.] [In Japanese.]

4338 Janik, Del Ivan. "The Two Infinites: D. H. Lawrence's *Twilight in Italy*," D. H. LAWRENCE REVIEW, VII (Summer 1974), 179-98; rvd and rptd as "The Two Infinites," in THE CURVE OF RETURN: D. H. LAWRENCE'S TRAVEL BOOKS, by Del Ivan Janik (Victoria, BC: University of Victoria [English Literary Studies Monograph Series, No. 22], 1981), pp. 24-42.

Twilight in Italy gives exposition and embodiment to the central conflict on which almost all of DHL's subsequent writings are founded. "In *Twilight in Italy,* this conflict or polarity is expressed in three significant ways: in the pairings of South and North, past and future, and mind and body." The book also reveals another duality: DHL's "vacillation between spontaneity and intellection." "The apparent discontinuity in content and expression and the resulting tension in the texture of the work" are essential to its "form and meaning": "the interplay of descriptive and expository passages makes the book a whole that encompasses the two infinites" manifested in "Italian phallicism and northern rationalism." "The polarity of place. . .is paralleled in *Twilight in Italy* by a polarity of time; a sensual, natural past as against a mentalized, mechanical future." "There is no reconciliation or synthesis" of these polarities "but rather an affirmation of the interplay of opposites." The book, which in its style encompasses both spontaneity and intellection, "only apparently ends in resignation to the triumph of science, the intellect, and the machine"; it "actually brings Lawrence to a crossroads from which he can contemplate the two paths available to man--and, in some sense, accept both."

4339 Jeffers, Thomas Linden. "That Vernal Time: Four English Novels about Growing Up," DISSERTATION ABSTRACTS INTERNATIONAL, XXXVI (1975), 315A-16A. Unpublished dissertation, Yale University, 1974.
[Includes a study of *Sons and Lovers.*]

4340 John, Brian. SUPREME FICTIONS: STUDIES IN THE WORK OF WILLIAM BLAKE, THOMAS CARLYLE, W. B. YEATS AND D. H. LAWRENCE (Montreal & Lond: McGill-Queen's UP, 1974), pp. 24, 42, 64, 73, 76n, 113, 131n, 231-309.
DHL, like Blake and Yeats, was a patriotic writer whose deep concern for his country was qualified by ambivalence. Though vividly aware of evil, DHL was more optimistic about England's fate than Blake or Carlyle. He rejected tragedy and wore the prophet's mask, believing that the novelist could combine art and philosophy to change the world. Like Yeats, Blake, and Carlyle, DHL was a vitalist, opposed to physical and psychical mechanization. His hatred of machines sometimes led to simplistic pronouncements about how to cure social ills. Early critics such as Eliot and Wyndham Lewis argued that DHL was dangerously antiintellectual, but most critics after F. R. Leavis have seen that he favored integration of blood and intellect into a whole self. Though he saw its limitations, DHL's preference for the pagan sense of life and way of knowing led him in his later work to assert the need for a dynamic correspondence between man and the universe. DHL believed that all the universe is created from the self, which is the center or source. *The Plumed Serpent* and *Lady Chatterley's Lover* depict DHL's conflict between the leader/power principle and tenderness. In his last years he came to emphasize the latter. "The Woman Who Rode Away," less ambiguous and more absolute than *The Plumed Serpent,* is, for those reasons, more objectionable. *St. Mawr* is less pompous and determinedly demonic than either of the former. *Lady Chatterley's Lover* is part of DHL's final affirmation of life, "impressive in its sanity, wholesomeness, and maturity of judgment."

4341 Johnston, Walter E. "The Shepherdess in the City," COMPARATIVE LITERATURE, XXIX (Spring 1974), 124-41.
Among twentieth-century experiments with pastoral conventions, "D. H. Lawrence's novels undoubtedly provide the most intricate study of the relationship of 'rustic' and sophisticate, and of natural 'models' for the self-conscious mind; Lawrence is a good example of the Romantic fascination with the primitive as a route to a new faith in the individual. . . . But critics. . .have ignored Lawrence's awareness of the limitations of his musical colliers and gamekeepers and of their experiences of transport."

4342 Jones, Bernard. "The Three Ladies Chatterley," BOOKS AND

BOOKMEN, XIX (March 1974), 46-50.
In *Lady Chatterley's Lover*, as in *The First Lady Chatterley* and *John Thomas and Lady Jane*, DHL failed "to weave his themes--personal relationships and his distrust of industrialism--into a satisfying·artistic whole." His twice rewriting of the novel evidences a coarsening tone and a loosening of unity. The "comparatively pastoral" first version is "sharply conceived and executed." Its "inconclusive" ending is "far more truthful to the natures of the persons. . .than the melodramatic letter of Mellors" which ends *Lady Chatterley's Lover*. *John Thomas and Lady Jane* can be "written off as a wilful pulling out of the original story." There, and more so in the final version, DHL is overcome by his "frantic obsessiveness" with his message, and he becomes "in the end a sentimentalist." His "account of the condition of England" in this version "wrecks the novel." For example, Clifford Chatterley, who "began as a genuinely cultivated person" in the first version, is an unsympathetic "non-person" in the third, where he is made to "stand for" ugly industrialism. In fact, the "most depressing" aspect of DHL's twice rewriting of the story is his progressive "hardening and harshening of the sympathies" with each revision.

4343 Kai, Sadanobu. "Foreword: The Isle of Wight in a Living Myth," D. H. LAWRENCE STUDIES (Kyôto), No. 2 (Nov 1974), 1-3.
In writing *The Trespasser*, DHL went to the Isle of Wight, which became for him both the Isle of the Blessed of Greek mythology and the Isle of Rananim of Lawrencian mythology. [In Japanese.]

4344 Kamitani, Shotaro. "D. H. Lawrence no *Sons and Lovers* ni Tsuite" (On D. H. Lawrence's *Sons and Lovers*), JOURNAL OF YASUDA WOMEN'S UNIVERSITY, No. 4 (March 1974), 1-31.
In *Sons and Lovers*, the notorious ambiguity of DHL's treatment of the "Oedipal love" relationship between Paul and his mother leads us to his acute and direct sense of the relativity of human relationships. Perhaps we need not be too much annoyed with that controversial problem: who is ultimately responsible for the failure and frustration of the several types of human relationship in this work-- Paul, or his mother, or his lovers? DHL himself was not in a position of an ultimate judge, because he is "trying" their love and their process of frustration as he relives his experience, trying every phase of their subtle and complex relationships. It is neither a moral nor a concept of "Oedipal love" that *Sons and Lovers* gives us but the delicately fluid and subtle quality of human experience and the process of awareness and groping pursuit of real human relationships. [In Japanese.]

4345 Kanatani, Nobuo. "Lawrence no Shuyô-Sakuhin ni Okeru Shi no Imi" (Death in the Major Novels of D. H. Lawrence), TSUDA REVIEW (Tsuda College), No. 19 (Nov 1974), 1-17.
In DHL's novels, especially in *Sons and Lovers, The Rainbow,* and *Women in Love,* a man's fear and denial of death is a sign of his final defeat and failure in life. Unless he accepts death as an inevitable phase of the life process, he cannot transcend the Western rationalist civilization in which the legitimacy of the senses is disclaimed and life unfulfilled. [In Japanese.]

4346 Keith, W. J. "Spirit of Place and *Genius Loci:* D. H. Lawrence and Rolf Gardiner," D. H. LAWRENCE REVIEW, VII (Summer 1974), 127-38.

DHL's association with Rolf Gardiner is known through the latter's writings about him and through DHL's correspondence. DHL's initial reaction to the acquaintance was understandably cautious; Gardiner's " 'weird movements' " did suggest "communal heartiness" and "can even be associated with the taint of fascist discipline." Yet DHL "was acute enough to detect something fundamentally genuine and vital in Gardiner's" ideas. DHL's moving letter to Gardiner about Eastwood as " 'the country of my heart' " (3 December 1926) was provoked by Gardiner's report of "his experiences with the Travelling Morrice" and the Yorkshire miners. While DHL's reaction in 1928 to Gardiner's description of the " 'hard work' " on Gore Farm was less enthusiastic, the emphasis in DHL's later work "on man's relation to his natural environment" was influenced by his contact with Gardiner, particularly in his discussion of the natural rhythms of the community in *A Propos of "Lady Chatterley's Lover"* and his concern for the miners in "Nottingham and the Mining Countryside." As a "successful and practical 'complement' " to DHL, Gardiner "was able to translate into the form of an existing and exemplary community a significant segment of Lawrence's prophetic message." [See also reply by Émile Delavenay and rejoinder by W. J. Keith, "Mr. Rolf Gardiner, 'The English Neo-Nazi': An Exchange," D. H. LAWRENCE REVIEW, VII (Fall 1974), 291-94.]

4347 Kennedy, Alan. THE PROTEAN SELF: DRAMATIC ACTION IN CONTEMPORARY FICTION (NY: Columbia UP, 1974), pp. 31n, 64-66, 69n, 70, 119-20, 123.

As a novelist, DHL's "first concern is the integrity and freedom of the individual, admittedly often in open opposition to existing forms of society." Marriage becomes possible only after separateness of being has been achieved. He insists, however, that "since love is a movement towards the centre, there must be another centrifugal force." Although he is "concerned with marriage as much as with individuality," for DHL "the first question is not a social one, it is. . .how to make individuals."

4348 Kim, Dong-son. "An Architect of the Vital Self: A Study of D. H. Lawrence." Unpublished dissertation, Hankuk University of Foreign Studies (Seoul, Korea), 1974. [Listed in Sheila M. Cooke, D. H. LAWRENCE: A FINDING LIST, 2nd ed (Nottingham: Nottinghamshire County Council Leisure Services/Libraries, 1980), p. 40.]

4349 Kitazaki, Kaien. " 'Babariya no Rindô' Oyobi *Shinda Otoko* ni Arawareta D. H. Lawrence no Shisei-Kan" (D. H. Lawrence's Attitude Toward Life and Death in "Bavarian Gentians" and *The Man Who Died*), JOURNAL OF NAGOYA MUNICIPAL WOMEN'S JUNIOR COLLEGE, No. 23 (Feb 1974), 59-71.

In "Bavarian Gentians," the Demeter myth and its concrete image are found in the death and resurrection of a plant as in the thought of Eleusis. This thought of Eleusis is also presented in *The Man Who Died* as the god of the sun in the myth of Osiris, which connects with Isis the Goddess who nourishes life, including "life and death." [In Japanese.]

4350 Kitazaki, Kaien. "*The Trespasser* ni Okeru 'Saihô' ni Tsuite" ("The West" in *The Trespasser*), D. H. LAWRENCE STUDIES (Kyôto), No. 2 (Nov 1974), 29-45.

The sunset image, to which Siegmund consistently turns his eyes in *The Trespasser*, is compared with "the contemplation upon the sunset" as the first expedient step to see the true life or light (Nirvana) taught in "The Pure Land Teaching" in Mahayana Buddhism. From this, it is inferred that DHL's utopian image of Rananim was then in Siegmund's eyes turned toward "the west." [In Japanese.]

4351 Kleinbard, David J. "D. H. Lawrence and Ontological Insecurity," PMLA: PUBLICATIONS OF THE MODERN LANGUAGE ASSOCIATION, LXXXIX (Jan 1974), 154-63.

In *The Rainbow* DHL concentrates on forms of feeling and thought which R. D. Laing, in THE DIVIDED SELF, calls "ontological insecurity." The form it takes in Will Brangwen, whose fantasies imply infantile dependence and a powerful sense of his own unreality, is comparable to Freud's description, in THE PROBLEM OF ANXIETY, of the sources of anxiety. Will's fantasy of drowning is associated with the anxiety of being deprived of a meaningful person (a mother, a lover), a threat that must be warded off by a vigilant self-awareness to maintain a sense of his own reality. Will's dependence on Anna derives from his Oedipal attachment to his mother, as DHL's association of Will with the mother-obsessed Ruskin and Will's craving to return to the symbolic womb of the church bear out. Split between being "master of the house" like his father and the dependence resulting from his involvement with his mother, Will suffers from what Erik H. Erikson calls "role confusion." This identity-confusion also damages his relation with his daughter Ursula, towards whom he behaves as father, sadistic lover, and demanding son. Lacking a "sense of ego identity," Will can never cohere as an integrated human being.

4352 Kuramochi, Saburô. "Gamekeeper no Henbo: *Lady Chatterley's Lover* no Mittsu no Han" (The Transfiguration of the Gamekeeper: The Three Versions of *Lady Chatterley's Lover*), EIGO SEINEN, No. 120 (1974), 214-15.

[In Japanese.]

4353 Lee, Robin H. "Darkness and 'A Heavy Gold Glamour': Lawrence's *Women in Love*," THEORIA, XLII (June 1974), 57-64.

Against a background of social dissolution, DHL asserts the integrity of the individual and explores the possibility of a microcosmic community which could form the basis of a new society. "Coal-Dust" (Chap. 9) demonstrates, by structure and imagery, the relationships and tensions that exist among Gerald, mare, and roadmenders, and between all these and the sisters. Gudrun's fascination with the "glamour" of their surroundings is a spurious nostalgia that, like the squalid "magic" cast over the black fields by the declining sun, invests Gerald and all he represents with the sunset gold of a pinchback romance. Ursula's revulsion is a touchstone which helps the reader reject the false and maintain some sort of faith in the existence of the genuine.

4354 Lindsay, Jack. "Expatriate Publishing II," MEANJIN QUARTERLY, XXXIII (June 1974), 176-79.
[Lindsay, an associate of P. R. Stephensen in the Fanfrolico Press, at first encouraged a showing of DHL's paintings in the belief that they were "of much interest in the whole DHL aesthetic." Lindsay later concluded that the paintings could be reproduced in a profitable book. He did not, however, take up the venture, ultimately, because of his antagonism "to many of DHL's attitudes" and because of his apprehension that publication would provoke police action. Lindsay therefore encouraged Stephensen to form another partnership and to issue the reproductions (*The Paintings of D. H. Lawrence,* 1929) as the first product of the new press (Mandrake Press).] [See also R. L. Hall, "Expatriate Publishing I," MEANJIN QUARTERLY, XXXIII (June 1974), 170-76; and Jack Lindsay, "D. H. Lawrence," FANFROLICO AND AFTER (Lond: Bodley Head, 1962), pp. 149-52.]

4355 McKeown, Marion Smith. "Patterns of Stylistic Change in the Novels of D. H. Lawrence," DISSERTATION ABSTRACTS INTERNATIONAL, XXXV (1975), 6722A-23A. Unpublished dissertation, McGill University, 1974.

4356 Madison, Charles A. "B. W. Huebsch and D. H. Lawrence," IRVING TO IRVING: AUTHOR-PUBLISHER RELATIONS, 1800-1974 (NY & Lond: Bowker, 1974), pp. 191-96.
After his unsatisfactory financial relations with the American publisher Mitchell Kennerley, who paid his royalties with worthless checks, DHL agreed to give *The Rainbow* to B. W. Huebsch, who, to avoid John S. Sumner's censorship, "printed a thousand copies but did not formally publish or promote it." DHL was angry at Huebsch's "minor emendations" and did not appreciate the publisher's circumspect distribution of the novel to interested readers. By a misunderstanding, DHL's agent, J. B. Pinker, held for two years the manuscript of *Women in Love,* which should have gone to Huebsch but which was eventually brought out in a trade edition by Thomas Seltzer, a company on "an infirm financial foundation." DHL's next book, *St. Mawr,* went to Alfred A. Knopf, with whom his relationship came to an end when Knopf decided against publishing *The Collected Poems of D. H. Lawrence.* Huebsch in 1925 joined the partners of the Viking Press, which later took over a number of DHL's earlier books.

4357 Manchester, John. "Introduction," "Lawrence and Brett: A Prologue," and "Epilogue," in LAWRENCE AND BRETT: A FRIENDSHIP, by Dorothy Brett (Santa Fe: Sunstone P, 1974), pp. i-v, vi-xiv, and I-IX.
"Brett was a soul image to Lawrence, a counterpart to his own inner feminine side," whereas Frieda was a projection of the mother-archetype, "either good or devouring." Frieda, Mabel Dodge Luhan, and Brett, in their respective memoirs, all "wanted to justify their own relationship" with DHL. [Surveys Brett's life

before and after DHL, revealing, among the more familiar details of her education, her friendships, and her art, the fact that she had a brief sexual relationship with John Middleton Murry.] Brett appears in *The Boy in the Bush* as Hilda Blessington. Brett was not the "virgin lover" who, in the popular conception, "chased" DHL. Indeed, as several pages excluded from the first edition of her memoir show, DHL twice tried unsuccessfully to make love to Brett in a hotel in Ravello but proved impotent. DHL continued to show concern for Brett in his letters to her. Later, Brett was involved in the plot to steal DHL's ashes.

4358 Matsubayashi, Yoshinori. "D. H. Lawrence Kenkyû--Sono Shi no Hyôka no Kiten ni Tsuite" (On Appraisal Criteria of D. H. Lawrence's Poems), MEMOIRS OF SUZUKA COLLEGE OF TECHNOLOGY, No. 8 (March 1974), 55-65.

The essence of the poems "The Wild Common" and "Baby Tortoise" lies in DHL's enthusiastic faithfulness toward life without any restraint. These works support the idea that poetic forms and other matters related to the category of "rhetoric" have little to do with Lawrentian poetry. And they show the characteristic features (DHL's passion, his warmth, and his ability to see things as they are) which distinguish his poetry. [In Japanese.]

4359 Matsubayashi, Yoshinori. "D. H. Lawrence no Shizen-Byôsha no Shisei ni Tsuite" (On Descriptive Features of D. H. Lawrence's Nature Presentation), MEMOIRS OF SUZUKA COLLEGE OF TECHNOLOGY, No. 9 (Oct 1974), 23-28.

Throughout his novels, essays, and travel books, DHL's description of nature gives us a certain sense of *élan vital*, a product of DHL's "innate and observant" eye for nature and the so-called Western "dual and combative" way of thinking in terms of nature and things natural; for instance, in the positive presentation of the self through the pronoun "I," whose fixedness is quite in contrast with such Japanese first persons as "watashi" and "boku," the usages of which are always dependent on surrounding circumstances. [In Japanese.]

4360 Matsuura, Naomi. "Kotoba no Kochiragawa de--D. H. Lawrence no Shi ni Tsuite" (On This Side of Words--Some Notes towards the Poetry of D. H. Lawrence), ENGLISH LITERATURE REVIEW (Kyôto Women's University), No. 18 (Dec 1974), 65-77.

Aware of the gap between the new sense of reality and old poetic statement, almost all modern poets since Imagism have aimed to create poetry by the destruction of conventional words. But DHL conceived of a "poetry of the immediate present" because his heart beat with "the urgent, insurgent Now," and he believed that words are pure and beautiful in their very nature. Using words according to that philosophy, he was inspired to express transcendental experience in ordinary events--the eternal in the temporal. Thus, as against other modern poets who tried to go beyond the words, DHL stood as "a madman in rapture" on this side of words. [In Japanese.]

4361 Mellen, Joan. " 'The Rocking-Horse Winner' as Cinema," FROM FICTION TO FILM: D. H. LAWRENCE'S "THE ROCKING-

HORSE WINNER," ed by Gerald R. Barrett and Thomas L. Erskine (Belmont & Encino, CA: Dickenson Publishing, 1974), pp. 214-23.

As film, *The Rocking-Horse Winner* (1949), produced by John Mills, written for the screen and directed by Anthony Pelissier, is structured along literary lines as a narrative framed by the arrival and departure of Bassett. Although its confinement largely to the house and grounds accurately reflects its "closed world" themes, the resulting sense of "filmed theatre" is "fatal to the film." By means of parallelism in editing and transitional dissolves, instead of straight cuts, Pelissier emphasizes the simultaneity of events, thus strengthening "the causal connection between Paul's obsession and his mother's extravagance."

4362 Mendel, Sydney. ROADS TO CONSCIOUSNESS (Lond: George Allen & Unwin, 1974), pp. 13, 21, 22, 73, 74-75, 189, 209, 232-51, 263, 265n, 268n, 270n, 275n.

DHL viewed the Fall as a fall into consciousness in which man begins " 'to live from a picture of himself,' " as the Texas cowboys do in *St. Mawr:* " 'inwardly they were self-conscious film heroes.' " DHL "is undoubtedly the major prophet of the gospel of the return to sensation," as his treatment of the theme in "The Blind Man" shows. "Pervin and Bertie Reid represent antithetical principles or modes of being," the lawyer standing "for the head alone, . . .while the blind man" is related to what Edward Carpenter calls " 'the entirety of the bodily organs.' " [Detailed comparison of HAMLET and *Sons and Lovers* in terms of "the hatred of the father" theme and the heroes' treatment of Ophelia and Miriam, and of ANTONY AND CLEOPATRA and *Lady Chatterley's Lover,* in terms of the similar attitudes of Octavius Caesar toward Antony and Clifford toward Mellors and similar themes.]

4363 Metcalf, Neal. THE PURE GAMBLE (Menlo Park, CA: Word Wheel Books, 1974).

[Novel about a DHL disciple, Gabriel Day, who founds a Rananim-like commune on a ranch in Northern California. The ranch "where goats once lived" is called Las Chivas, like the ranch in *St. Mawr,* and the counter-culture established there expresses its values in a number of other Laurentian symbols: a flying fish forged from metal to adorn the roof, horses, whales, a porpoise surging upward in a rainbow design over the image of the cross. Gabriel Day, whose name recalls that of Gethin Day of "The Flying Fish," is as preachy at times as Birkin, but his pronouncements spring from the same urgent need to find a viable alternative lifestyle in the *Dies Irae* atmosphere of the modern world. A humanized, Laurentian Christ-figure, painfully reborn and striving to aid the rebirth of others, he is sacrificed again to the dehumanized god of the machine as a bulldozer, with the dubious legitimacy of "the law" behind it, batters down the hand-built houses of the commune, killing Gabe in the process. On Day's ranch, though the mechanized society wins, the communicants have experienced, however fleetingly and imperfectly, DHL's vision of Rananim.]

4364 Meyers, Jeffrey. "*The Plumed Serpent* and the Mexican Revolution," JOURNAL OF MODERN LITERATURE, IV (Sept 1974), 55-72.

Critics, including William York Tindall, Jascha Kessler, and L. D. Clark, have failed to take Mexican political history into account in analyzing *The Plumed Serpent*. DHL mixes myth and Realpolitik to portray the historical violence and power he associated with the socialism of Villa, Zapata, and Juarez, opposed by the leadership of Cipriano and Ramón, and the rise of Quetzalcoatl in his novel. The work, however, fails to create a meaningful alternative, either mythic or political, to the cruelty of either side, and reveals DHL's lack of a humanistic imagination. [Illustrated throughout by detailed descriptions of relevant Mexican history.]

4365 Meyers, Jeffrey. "*The Rainbow* and Fra Angelico," D. H. LAWRENCE REVIEW, VII (Summer 1974), 139-55; rptd in PAINTING AND THE NOVEL, by Jeffrey Meyers (Manchester: Manchester UP; NY: Barnes & Noble, 1975), pp. 53-64.

The Bible is the literary, and Fra Angelico's *The Last Judgment* the pictorial, source for DHL's "recurrent images of light, gateways, angels, circles, gardens and religious ecstasy" in *The Rainbow*. The iconography of the painting "represents the opposition of salvation and damnation, heaven and hell"; DHL portrays these polarities in the novel "by contrasting illumination and darkness, inclusion and exclusion, consummation and annihilation." Since the novel culminates in Ursula's "heavenly vision of the New Jerusalem," *The Last Judgment* is "both a symbolic center of the narrative" and a source of its biblical imagery, related by the "paradigm" of the opening section to the structure of the novel: "there are three entries into paradise, three transfigurations and three annihilations, one for each Brangwen generation." The two descriptions of the painting "are preceded by the characters' parallel and contrasting responses to religious art" and followed by symbolic dances. Between the two descriptions is the cathedral chapter, which "is thematically related to both." "The architectural metaphor of the rainbow recalls the cathedral, and connects the final judgment of Noah in Genesis with the Last Judgment of Christ in Revelation." Rather than "a logical conclusion to the events of the novel," the rainbow is "a regenerative symbol" that promises Ursula's ultimate " 'transfiguration.' "

4366 Michaels, Jennifer Elizabeth. "The Polarity of North and South: Germany and Italy in the Prose Works of D. H. Lawrence," DISSERTATION ABSTRACTS INTERNATIONAL, XXV (1975), 5417A. Unpublished dissertation, McGill University, 1974; rvd and pub as Jennifer Michaels-Tonks, D. H. LAWRENCE: THE POLARITY OF NORTH AND SOUTH--GERMANY AND ITALY IN HIS PROSE WORKS (Bonn: Bouvier Verlag Herbert Grundmann, 1976).

4367 Miles, Rosalind. THE FICTION OF SEX: THEMES AND FUNCTIONS OF SEX DIFFERENCE IN THE MODERN NOVEL (Lond: Vision P, 1974), pp. 16-21.

DHL is not altogether responsible for the cult of "advanced bullhood," but his work was often a minefield dividing the sexes. Even in his best fiction he never overcame a deep anti-feminism, which can be seen in his attacks upon female possessiveness and, particularly, in the way in which he uses Ursula in *Women in Love* as a mere agent in the growth and career of Birkin. Whatever the effect of DHL's work upon twentieth-century ideas of sexuality, he was the first novelist to achieve an exclusively sexual focus in the presentation of female character.

4368 Miyasaki, Junji. "Shôsetsu no Kôzô to Sono Kaishaku--D. H. Lawrence no Baai" (The Structure of Novels and the Interpretation of D. H. Lawrence), HUMANITIES (Doshisha University), II, No. 3 (July 1974), 41-66.

DHL knows that industrialism has broken down the community in which formerly the relationship between people must have been conserved and developed. DHL's novels provide an experience of such a disintegrated community through the experiences of such protagonists as Connie in *Lady Chatterley's Lover,* Ursula in *Women in Love,* Alfred in "Daughters of the Vicar," and others. It follows that the form reveals the strict correspondence between the structure of the novel and that of the society in which the value of exchange precedes man or in which man is just a machine to produce it. DHL's heroes and heroines should naturally be dynamic and potential, far from being socially impotent. DHL's protagonists always try to get over the dissociated reality and to found a liberated, new, and knowable reality in the structure of feeling. While this structure of feeling is not defined by the author, we can construct it within the structure of the novel through our discernment of tradition. [In Japanese.]

4369 Moore, Harry T. THE PRIEST OF LOVE: A LIFE OF D. H. LAWRENCE (NY: Farrar, Straus & Giroux; Lond: Wm Heinemann, 1974).

[A revised and enlgd version of THE INTELLIGENT HEART: THE STORY OF D. H. LAWRENCE (1954), this biography contains new material based on recently published letters from DHL to Louie Burrows, S. S. Koteliansky, and others, as well as an updated bibliographical essay.]

4370 Mori, Haruhide (ed). A CONVERSATION ON D. H. LAWRENCE (Los Angeles: Friends of the UCLA Library, 1974).

[Transcription of a tape recording of a panel discussion at UCLA Library, 7 March 1952, by Frieda Lawrence, Aldous Huxley, Dorothy G. Mitchell, and Majl Ewing. Huxley links DHL with an English pantheist tradition going back to Thomas Traherne. Intuition evoked a sense of place which came to him from the country itself by a "sixth sense," Frieda says, but his honest expression of feeling sometimes led to a nasty, elemental temper. Huxley comments that DHL rejected "sex in the head" for immediate contact with the cosmos through direct sexual experience that becomes evil only when it is mentalized. Mrs. Mitchell feels that DHL "tends to make women's conflicts. . .too simple."]

4371 Mori, Haruhide. "Shinwa to Genjitsu no Hazama--D. H. Lawrence *Tsubasa Aru Hebi*" (Myth and Reality in D. H. Lawrence's *The Plumed Serpent*), MODERN AGE (Kôbe University), No. 48 (Feb 1974), 1-29.

[In Japanese.]

4372 Mori, Haruhide. "Shisô-Kôzô to Paragraph-Kôzô--Lawrence to Woolf" (Lawrence and Woolf: A Stylistic Approach to Their Thought

Structure and Paragraph Structure), ESSAYS IN HONOUR OF PROFESSOR SHIKO MURAKAMI (1974), pp. 381-93. [In Japanese.]

4373 Mori, Haruhide. "Shiten to Buntai o Megutte" (Point of View and Prose Style), in GENGO TO BUNTAI: HIGASHIDA CHIAKI KYOJU KANREKI KINEN RONBUNSHU (Language and Style: Collected Essays Commemorating the Sixtieth Birthday of Professor Chiaki Higashida), ed by Chiaki Higashida (Osaka: Osaka Kyoiku Tosho, [1974]), pp. 295-305.
[DHL's style is discussed.] [In Japanese.]

4374 Morrell, Ottoline. OTTOLINE AT GARSINGTON: MEMOIRS OF LADY OTTOLINE MORRELL, 1915-1918, ed by Robert Gathorne-Hardy (Lond: Faber and Faber, 1974; NY: Alfred A. Knopf, 1975), pp. 34, 35, 36-40, 41, 55-68, 69-81, 93, 128-29, 139-46, 151, 197, 198, 200-201, 218, 220, 233-34.
[Personal recollections of DHL and Frieda recorded at the time by Lady Ottoline Morrell in her journal or based on letters from DHL and Bertrand Russell, as well as a later evaluation of events and a personal portrait of DHL which she wrote after his death. Ottoline deplores DHL's dependence on Frieda, though she does not try to rescue him from it; comments on his short-lived friendship with Bertrand Russell, to whom she introduced him; expresses her pain at his portrayal of her as Hermione in *Women in Love;* describes their consequent break and eventual partial reconciliation; and gives interesting accounts of other members of DHL's circle, including Dorothy Brett, John Middleton Murry, and Aldous Huxley.]

4375 Mudrick, Marvin. "Lawrence," HUDSON REVIEW, XXVII (Autumn 1974), 424-42.
Although DHL criticized the great Russian authors as cruder than the English writers, both *The Rainbow* and *Women in Love* are "massive studies of marriages," much like ANNA KARENINA. The structure and tone of *Women in Love* are Dostoyevskian and its subject a Tolstoyan concern with "death and dissolution." Although DHL never wrote approvingly of male homosexuality, the excised "Prologue" to *Women in Love* treats at length Birkin's arousal by and love for men; without this "Prologue," the novel is "decapitated." The three leadership novels following *Women in Love* would all be offensive except for their "pathetic weakness." [Review-essay on Harry T. Moore, THE PRIEST OF LOVE: A LIFE OF D. H. LAWRENCE (1974).]

4376 Mulloy, John J. "The Dark God or the Spirit of God," in "The Catholic Tradition" (column), WANDERER (St. Paul, MN), 25 July 1974, p. 5.
DHL, following Nietzsche's purely aesthetic world view, asserts the importance of pagan myth and symbol over traditional Christian morality and mind in man's religious experience. The dangers are that this view omits "considerations of truth in evaluating religion"; that "the spirits of evil" move into the religious vacuum, leaving man prey to spiritualism, diabolism, and "the pseudo-religious worship of blood and soil...found in Nazism"; and that man loses the spiritual

vitality and energy of primitive Christianity, which "motivated the whole man
...with a new life."

    4377 Negriolli, Claude. "L'Univers sémantique de *The Rainbow* de
D. H. Lawrence" (The Semantic Universe of D. H. Lawrence's *The
Rainbow*). Published dissertation, University of Paris VII, 1974.
[Listed in CATALOGUE DES THÈSES DE DOCTORAT SOUTENUES
DEVANT LES UNIVERSITÉS FRANÇAISES, ns Année 1974 (Paris:
Cercle de la Librairie, 1978), p. 1019, Item 12819.] Pub as L'UNI-
VERS SÉMANTIQUE DE "THE RAINBOW" DE D. H. LAWRENCE
(Paris: H. Champion, 1976).
[In French.]

    4378 Nishimura, Iwao. "The Secret of *The Trespasser*--Traced in
Siegmund's Tragedy," D. H. LAWRENCE STUDIES (Kyôto), No. 2
(Nov 1974), pp. 65-97.
[In Japanese.]

    4379 Nishimura, Kôji. "Lawrence Bungaku no Konnichisei" (The
Contemporary Relevance of Lawrence's Works), EIGO SEINEN, No.
120 (1974), 216-17.
[In Japanese.]

    4380 Ogawa, Yoshio. "Shi to Bôkyaku--*Women in Love* kara 'The
Ship of Death' e" (Death and Oblivion--From *Women in Love* to
"The Ship of Death"), BULLETIN OF ST. MARGARET'S (St. Margaret's Junior College), No. 6 (Dec 1974), 145-65.
DHL's extraordinary experience of elopement in 1912 influenced his life and
literature thereafter. It was the liberation from the world of *Sons and Lovers,*
which resulted in his "Unrhyming Poems" and the loose structure of *Women in
Love.* The death theme in this novel and in *Last Poems* is examined, especially
in "The Ship of Death," where "oblivion" refers, with nine different meanings,
to the afterworld. But DHL deals with death without despair and regards death
as the beginning of the journey to new life. DHL can be best understood only
when we grasp him in the rhythm of life and death without exclusive emphasis
on sex. [In Japanese.]

    4381 Ôhashi, Yasuichirô. "Shijin Lawrence to Shi (Ge I)" (D. H.
Lawrence: Poet and Death [The Last Part I]), MEMOIRS OF
HUMANISTIC AND SOCIAL SCIENCES (Kyôto Technical University), No. 22 (Jan 1974), 59-80.
What knowledge of the post-mortem world did DHL have? There are different
kinds of thoughts and beliefs about it all over the world: in general, graves are
the dwellings of the dead, who fly away from them, move about, and at night fly
back to them; the realm of the dead is in the subterranean world; also, it is in the
subaerial world or in the superterrene world; the dead generally live joyless lives
(though, according to ancient Egyptian thought, they live joyful lives); a sea lies
between this world and the other, a sea the dead must cross. Some of DHL's

poems sustain those thoughts and beliefs. [In Japanese.]

4382 Ohkawa, Hiroshi. "D. H. Lawrence no Shôsetsu Ron--Zettai Hitei ni Yoru Ishiki-Tankyû" (On "The Novel" of D. H. Lawrence), JOURNAL OF THE FACULTY OF FOREIGN LANGUAGES (Komazawa University), No. 3 (March 1974), 157-73.

[Discusses DHL's essay "The Novel," in which he makes clear the defects of absolute ideas.] [In Japanese.]

4383 Okada, Taiji. "D. H. Lawrence no Rananim ni Tsuite (2)" (On D. H. Lawrence's Rananim [2]), BULLETIN OF THE FACULTY OF TEXTILE SCIENCE (Kyôto University of Industrial Arts and Textile Fibers), VIII, No. 2 (Feb 1974), 331-47.

[The second of two articles concerning DHL's Rananim.] In 1916, DHL changed a part of his Rananim plan and decided to make his way without any other participants. The reason must be understood in relation to his basic idea of "immortality," which he had been pursuing all his life. [See also Taiji Okada, "D. H. Lawrence no Rananim ni Tsuite (1)" (On D. H. Lawrence's Rananim [1]), BULLETIN OF THE FACULTY OF TEXTILE SCIENCE (Kyoto University of Industrial Arts and Textile Fibers), VII, No. 1 (Feb 1973), 159-70.] [In Japanese.]

4384 Okamura, Naomi. "E. M. Forster no Shôsetsu: Kojin to Shakai no Tanima--D. H. Lawrence to no Hikaku ni Oite" (The Conflict between Society and Individuals in the Novels of E. M. Forster and D. H. Lawrence), RESEARCHER (Tsuda College), No. 8 (Sept 1974), 39-61.

DHL and E. M. Forster, seemingly far apart, have much in common. Especially when the conception of personal relationship through love and sex is analyzed in the novels of the two authors, the development of E. M. Forster from THE LONGEST JOURNEY to MAURICE is quite similar to that of DHL from *Sons and Lovers* to *Lady Chatterley's Lover*. [In Japanese.]

4385 Okunishi, Akira. "Rorensu ni Okeru Kyûshinteki-Shikô to Sono Hyôgen" (Centripetal Thought and Expression in Lawrence), in GENGO TO BUNTAI: HIGASHIDA CHIAKI KYOJU KANREKI KINEN RONBUNSHU (Language and Style: Collected Essays Commemorating the Sixtieth Birthday of Professor Chiaki Higashida), ed by Chiaki Higashida (Osaka: Osaka Kyoiku Tosho, [1974]), pp. 166-84.

DHL's centripetalism can be seen in the circularity of his peculiar style with its " 'continual, slightly modified repetitions.' " His fictions tend to appeal rather to the emotions than to the intellect of the reader. Asking for the reader's participation, the fictions and their episodic chapters lead the reader from the emotional state of mind into the "impersonal," unconscious reality. [In Japanese.]

4386 Pachmuss, Temira. "Dostoevsky, D. H. Lawrence and Carson McCullers: Influences and Confluences," GERMANO-SLAVICA (University of Waterloo), IV (1974), 59-68.

Although DHL professed not to understand Dostoevsky's "poetic universe" and scorned his ideology, DHL's character types, like Raskolnikov, Prince Myshkin, and Stavrogin, "delve into the depths of human experience," questioning the nature and significance of human life, death, love, and will, and constantly seeking transcendence. *The Trespasser* is generally patterned after Dostoevsky's THE GENTLE MAIDEN (1876). They share "circular design," inner monologues, flashbacks, detailed "close-up" technique, colors used as psychological symbols, and dualistic treatment of love as love/hatred. Both DHL and Dostoevsky use religious symbols and myths, as in DHL's references in *The Rainbow* to the "flood," Eve, and the moon, but unlike Dostoevsky, DHL rejected Christian tradition, though Birkin and Gerald in *Women in Love* discuss God, religion, and basic human nature.

4387 Panichas, George A. "Notes on Eliot and Lawrence, 1915-1924," THE REVERENT DISCIPLINE: ESSAYS IN LITERARY CRITICISM AND CULTURE (Knoxville: University of Tennessee P, 1974), pp. 135-56.

DHL and T. S. Eliot, antithetical contemporaries, represent the essential conflict of ideas and ways of living in the twentieth century. Eliot "will never be forgiven" for the orthodoxy of certain of his views or for his defense of the "moral imagination," whereas DHL represents a defiance of whatever is accepted and time-honored. In AFTER STRANGE GODS Eliot charges DHL with "heresy" and says he had a sense of the moment but no sense of history. The visions of both writers were rooted in despair, but DHL's was "a romanticism of despair," and Eliot's a "classicism of despair." To Eliot, DHL's denial and neglect of tradition gives rein to a disastrous individuality. Like DHL, Eliot is "unable to escape personally, biographically, from his work." *Women in Love,* contemporary with THE WASTE LAND, also captures the horror of the years 1915-1924 and presents death as the inescapable condition of a period when "We have no history." DHL's novel is more artistically unified than Eliot's fragmented poem. Despite their differences, DHL and Eliot are our "last great religious visionaries and seekers."

4388 Panichas, George A. THE REVERENT DISCIPLINE: ESSAYS IN LITERARY CRITICISM AND CULTURE (Knoxville: University of Tennessee P, 1974), pp. xii, xvi, 1, 38, 69, 70, 71, 72, 73, 74, 75, 79, 82, 90, 92, 93, 124, 135-56, 157-69, 198, 200, 205-28, 335-50, 379, 387, 391, 392.

[Collection of twenty-two essays on various literary topics from an author writing "as a generalist critic and as a Christian humanist." Includes four essays on DHL, abstracted under year of first publication: "Notes on Eliot and Lawrence, 1915-1924," pp. 135-56 (1974); "E. M. Forster and D. H. Lawrence: Their Views on Education," pp. 157-69, from RENAISSANCE AND MODERN ESSAYS, ed by G. R. Hibbard (Lond: Routledge & Kegan Paul; NY: Barnes & Noble, 1966), pp. 199-213; "F. M. Dostoevsky and D. H. Lawrence: Their Visions of Evil," pp. 205-28, from RENAISSANCE AND MODERN STUDIES, V (1961), 49-75; and "D. H. Lawrence and the Ancient Greeks," pp. 335-50, from ENGLISH MISCELLANY (Rome), XVI (1965), 195-214.]

4389 Panken, Shirley. "Some Psychodynamics in *Sons and Lovers:* A New Look at the Oedipal Theme," PSYCHOANALYTIC REVIEW, LXI (1974-1975), 571-89.

Although the Oedipal theme in *Sons and Lovers* has received ample attention, critics have focused almost exclusively on Mrs. Morel's sons' preoccupation with their mother, overlooking the fact that the entire "family matrix" is involved in the typical Oedipal complex. Specifically, Paul's multi-faceted relationship with his mother bears closer examination. Paul is frustrated "in the resolution of phase-specific tasks--that is, identification with his father, the repression of his Oedipal wishes toward his mother, a commitment to love relationships outside his family--because of...contrapuntal behavioral dynamisms." These include Mrs. Morel's alternating patterns of aloofness and over-solicitousness during Paul's pre-Oedipal stage of development; the "split in Paul's Oedipal feelings" set up by his mother's demonstrated preference for William; Paul's need to be recognized as the dependable child and later to rescue his mother, intensified by "the depreciated images for masculine identification" in the family constellation; Paul's reaction to William's death as "a fulfillment of both sibling and Oedipal rivalries"; his mother's thwarting of Paul's "adolescent need for separation and individuation"; Paul's fear of "emotional death" if he leaves his mother and marries; and his "confusion of personal and sexual definition." Mrs. Morel's exploitation of her sons bears significance not only to DHL's personal trauma, which finally was resolved in a tempestuous relationship with Frieda, but also to what DHL perceived as the plight of the majority of his male contemporaries in England, whose sexual adjustment had been hampered by similar mothering. Thus, the women most admired by men in DHL's culture were those who inhibited male sexuality. In asserting that women diverted love from their husbands to their sons, DHL "challenged Freud's delineation of the Oedipal theme, maintaining it was the mother who set up the incestuous cycle of events."

4390 Pelissier, Anthony. "*The Rocking-Horse Winner,*" in FROM FICTION TO FILM: D. H. LAWRENCE'S "THE ROCKING-HORSE WINNER," ed by Gerald R. Barrett and Thomas L. Erskine (Encino & Belmont, CA: Dickenson Publishing, 1974), pp. 76-201.

[Final shooting script, 6 April 1949, for the Two Cities Films Ltd. production, produced by John Mills, written for the screen and directed by Anthony Pelissier. The script, "the written text that the director and other members of the production staff use to create the film," is unusually detailed in its directions concerning elements of film style: mise-en-scene, camera work, sound, and editing. The editors, Barrett and Erskine, provide extensive annotations on shots, camera placement, camera movement, sound, and lighting; on quotations in the script from DHL's story; and on omissions from the script in the film itself. Illustrated with nineteen black and white stills from the motion picture.]

4391 Pinder, Donna. "The Normalcy of Suffering and Artistic Survival: Literature and Society," PAUNCH, No. 38 (March 1974), 66-78, espec pp. 66, 70-72.

In *Women in Love,* Gerald's and Gudrun's "Falstaffian characteristics are the normalcy of suffering that they live," the repression which emerges in "their contorted debasement of their bodies." Lacking "the ability to search for and express their core of individuality, . . .they begin to protect it in the manner of a fetish, which turns into perversion," torturing "not only themselves but others." Birkin "is both more contradictory in nature and more prone to suffering, but also is trying to get beyond suffering."

4392 Prasad, Madhusudan. "The Autobiographical Element in the Novels of D. H. Lawrence." Unpublished dissertation, University of Allahabad, 1974. [Listed in D. H. LAWRENCE REVIEW, X (Fall 1977), 303.] Rvd and pub as D. H. LAWRENCE: A STUDY OF HIS NOVELS (Bareilly, India: Prakash Book Depot, 1980).

4393 Raddatz, Volker. "Lyrical Elements in D. H. Lawrence's *The Rainbow*," REVUE DES LANGUES VIVANTES, XL, No. 3 (1974), 235-42.

In DHL's concept of the "immediate present," the established dimensions of time and space, representing the world order, are dismissed because they no longer apply to the "deeper stratum" of man's existence with which DHL was concerned. The significance of lyrical components in the fabric of *The Rainbow* can be noticed in the introductory chapter, which presents a panorama of the relationship between nature and man. The lyrical passages in the novel appear most clearly in contrast with the dramatic elements such as the courtship of Tom and Lydia. The time immediately following the wedding of Will and Anna may be regarded as the longest, yet the most coherent, example of lyrical composition in *The Rainbow*.

4394 Reddick, Bryan D. "Point of View and Narrative Tone in *Women in Love*: The Portrayal of Interpsychic Space," D. H. LAWRENCE REVIEW, VII (Summer 1974), 156-71.

Women in Love combines several characteristics of omniscient and dramatic narrative. "The detached narrator is implicit from the beginning"; "as the novel progresses, . . .the narrator comments. . .more openly," but not "until the authority of his observations has been *dramatically* established." "The devices of narrative detachment. . .intensify the ironic complexity of experience" and prevent conventional sympathies and antipathies for the characters. Although "Birkin's values and those implicit in the novel's form are apparently the same," he is also often "criticized by other characters" and by the ironic tone of the narrator, and these attacks are "dramatically supported by Birkin's own behavior." The ironic "detachment with which Birkin's earlier speeches are presented. . .provides dramatic justification for Ursula's charge" at the end that his "desire for a lasting bond with a man is merely. . .'theory' "; but "the dramatic confirmation of Birkin's 'theory' about his relationship with Ursula implies that his 'theory' about Gerald is also valid," underscoring the tragedy of Gerald's death. "The changing relationship. . .between the reader and Birkin dramatizes the ambivalence of all interrelationships within the novel."

4395 Robson, W[illiam] W[allace]. "D. H. Lawrence," ENCYCLOPAEDIA BRITANNICA, 15th ed., Micropedia, X (Chicago: Encyclo-

paedia Britannica, William Benton, Publisher, 1974), pp. 722-25.
[A detailed, authoritative, concise synopsis of DHL's life and work, noting his early recognition by Ford Madox Hueffer, his elopement with Frieda Weekley, his difficulties during the war, his plans for Rananim, his friendships (with Bertrand Russell, Lady Ottoline Morrell, John Middleton Murry, Mabel Dodge Luhan, Dorothy Brett, Aldous Huxley, and others), his personality and genius, his technique and prophetic vision as a novelist, his critical and travel books, and his style. Includes highly selective primary and secondary bibliography.]

4396 Ross, Charles L. "A Problem of Textual Transmission in the Typescripts of *Women in Love*," LIBRARY, 5th series, XXIX (June 1974), 197-205; rvd and absorbed in Chap. V: "The Manuscripts: Three Preliminary Drafts," in THE COMPOSITION OF "THE RAINBOW" AND "WOMEN IN LOVE": A HISTORY, by Charles L. Ross (Charlottesville: UP of Virginia, 1979), pp. 97-114.

DHL prepared duplicate typescripts of the penultimate draft of *Women in Love*, one for publishers and the other for friends. His revisions were so extensive, and his pace so rapid, that he enlisted Frieda's help in transcribing. They worked in a peculiar fashion, so that many pages have transcriptions in *both* hands. Moreover, Frieda mistranscribed or neglected to transcribe a large number of DHL's revisions. Finally, they assembled the typescripts *after* revision, so that each is a mixture of top-copy and carbon-copy. The duplicate sent to DHL's agent, from which the printer's-copy typescript was prepared, is at the University of Toronto; the other is at the Humanities Research Center, the University of Texas. Comparing the Toronto typescript with the printer's-copy, one notes at least twenty-two instances of words or phrases miscopied by Frieda which DHL may have overlooked in revising the printer's-copy and which remain in the published text. The editor of a critical edition should consider reinstating the authorial readings from the typescripts of the penultimate draft.

4397 Rowley, Eugene G. "Individual Instinct and Societal Repression in the Writings of D. H. Lawrence," DISSERTATION ABSTRACTS INTERNATIONAL, XXXV (1974), 3766A. Unpublished dissertation, Tufts University, 1974.

4398 Sasae, Osamu. "*Aaron's Rod* no Futatsu no Jôkei" (Some Remarks on Two Scenes of *Aaron's Rod*), BULLETIN OF FUKUOKA UNIVERSITY OF EDUCATION, No. 24 (1974), 49-56.

DHL's techniques in two passages in *Aaron's Rod* are highly successful in enriching their content. These techniques--e.g., his extensive use of onomatopoeia or symbolic forms--may result from the conflict between his "subjectivistic" disposition and his propagandistic one. [In Japanese.]

4399 Schneider, Daniel J. "The Symbolism of the Soul: D. H. Lawrence and Some Others," D. H. LAWRENCE REVIEW, VII (Summer 1974), 107-26.

DHL's central concern is the relationship between consciousness and the unconscious; his images function to define the nature of the soul, the division within the soul, and the nature of psychic health and psychic disease. The archetypal nature of the symbolism common to DHL, Mann, Hawthorne, Yeats, Hesse, Conrad, Malraux, and Stevens stresses the immensity of the gulf between the two worlds of spirit and flesh. It is reflected topographically in the opposition of "ice-world and sun-world," of sea and sky, and in animal and vegetation imagery which embodies the polarity. Although writers like Stevens have no absolute, DHL searches for the image that unites heaven and earth, night and day, moon and sun; sometimes he discovers this unity in certain individuals, but the rainbow is his most expressive symbol of wholeness. But wholeness is rare, and DHL's stress on the psychic wounds caused by the frustration of unconscious desire leads to an elaborate depiction of a sick world. Illustrations of symbolic illness are numerous in DHL's fiction; "closely associated with the symbolism of disease is that of immobility and imprisonment," of "the reality-unreality pattern" in a "nature-art antithesis," and the elaborate imagery of machines and mechanism.

4400 Schorer, Mark. "D. H. Lawrence: Then, During, Now," ATLANTIC MONTHLY, CCXXXIII (March 1974), 84-88.
[A brief, accurate account of the history of DHL's reputation as a novelist from the time of his death to the present. Contains notes on the publication history of DHL's works when this bears on the growth of his reputation.]

4401 Schwab-Fehlisch, Hans. "*Freitag abend eines Bergmanns.* Ein Stuck von D. H. Lawrence in Bochum" (*A Collier's Friday Night:* A Play by D. H. Lawrence in Bochum), FRANKFURTER ALLGEMEINE ZEITUNG, 19 Feb 1974.
A Collier's Friday Night is a weak play. Its main theme is the yearning for a freer life. The mother, not the collier, is the chief character. [In German.]

4402 Sepčič, Višnja. "Romansijerski eksperiment D. H. Lawrencea" (D. H. Lawrence's Experiment as Novelist), KNJIŽEVNA SMOTRA, No. 17 (1974), 55-65.
[In Serbo-Croatian.]

4403 Sepčič, Višnja. "*The White Peacock* Reconsidered," STUDIA ROMANICA ET ANGLICA ZAGRABIENSIA, No. 38 (Dec 1974), 105-14.
The White Peacock, a "thematic embryo" of DHL's "entire novelistic *oeuvre,*" "announces a number of significant Lawrentian themes" developed in his later work. "The central theme is represented by the author's concentration on the decisive moment in the life of Lettie Beardsall and George Saxton where they ...by an act of deliberate choice [between two life possibilities] determine their own future." The turning point is revealed in two scenes of recognition. For Lettie it is the scene in the wood where she and Leslie Tempest, Cyril and Emily discover in the snowdrops of the dell "the mystery of nature." "The scene represents Lettie's moment of lucid insight into her own personality and destiny," the "life possibilities" which she is throwing away in choosing the intellectual Leslie over the inarticulate George. For George Saxton the moment of insight comes earlier when Cyril tells him of Lettie's engagement to Leslie, and George sits immobile

as if "listening to some far-off future events," aware that "out of inertia and lack of confidence he has allowed his life chance to slip by."

4404 Shibata, Takaharu. RORENSU BUNGAKU NO SEKAI (The Literary World of Lawrence) (Tôkyô: Yashio Shuppan, 1974).
[Part I focuses on "His Character and His Works" and includes separate essays on the psychological complications in *Women in Love,* psychoanalysis and DHL, *The Fox,* DHL and Bertrand Russell, DHL's views on the novel, DHL's love poems, DHL as "A Seeker for Truth in Life," and textual criticism of the three versions of *Lady Chatterley's Lover.* Part II, entitled "Three Critics," includes separate essays on T. S. Eliot, F. R. Leavis, and Eliseo Vivas, and their contrasting "Views" on DHL's literature.] [In Japanese.]

4405 Shimizu, Kohya. "Ambiguity and Isolation in 'The Man Who Loved Islands,' " STUDIES IN HUMANITY BY THE COLLEGE OF LIBERAL ARTS (Kanazawa University), No. 12 (March 1974), 39-60.
The very last phase of DHL's fiction, exemplified by "The Man Who Loved Islands," is neither an abandonment of the communalistic attitude nor a simple affirmation of the individualistic idea, but a perverse integration of both themes.

4406 Sinclair, Stephen G. "Moralists and Mystics: Religion in the Modern British Novel," DISSERTATION ABSTRACTS INTERNATIONAL, XXXV (1975), 7328A. Unpublished dissertation, University of Michigan, 1974.
[Contains a chapter entitled "D. H. Lawrence and the Approach to Mysticism."]

4407 Sklar, Sylvia. "The Relationship between Social Context and Individual Character in the Naturalist Drama, with Special Reference to Chekov, D. H. Lawrence and David Storey." Unpublished dissertation, University of London, 1974. [Listed in Geoffrey M. Paterson and Joan E. Hardy (eds), INDEX TO THESES, XXV, Part I (1976), p. 7.]

4408 Smith, Julian. "The Social Architecture of 'The Rocking-Horse Winner,' " in FROM FICTION TO FILM: D. H. LAWRENCE'S "THE ROCKING-HORSE WINNER," ed by Gerald R. Barrett and Thomas L. Erskine (Encino & Belmont, CA: Dickenson Publishing, 1974), pp. 224-30.
[Critical article on the film of *The Rocking-Horse Winner* (1949), produced by John Mills, written for the screen and directed by Anthony Pelissier.] *The Rocking-Horse Winner,* nearly twenty-five years after it was made, remains an intelligent film adaptation of superior fictional material. The film exhibits a carefully structured spatial and temporal organization; it is "a textbook example of how to tell a story through the environment of its characters." The style of the film, however, is less Laurentian than it is like the Dickens films made in the 1930s and 1940s; in its careful "attention to production values and the full range of characterization," and in its ventures into social commentary it is reminiscent in particular of David Lean's adaptation of GREAT EXPECTATIONS. A marked

contrast is established and maintained throughout the film between Bassett, the possessor of clear-eyed lower-class virtues, and Uncle Oscar, whose similar instincts are confused by his stereotyped ideas of gentlemanly behavior. The role of Bassett, expanded from the character sketched in the original story, thus becomes not only an appropriate vehicle for John Mills but also a direct appeal to the primarily working-class audience in Clement Attlee's Labour government England. The film fails to generate sympathy for Paul; however, its focus on Hester successfully catalogues her initiation into fiscal responsibility--an ironic descent which turns on the ascent of her son's "unfortunate luck." Pelissier and Mills have made "an honest and straightforward film about the sacrifice of innocence."

4409 Solecki, Zdzislaw Zbigniew Sam. "Aspects of Education in the Work of D. H. Lawrence," DISSERTATION ABSTRACTS INTERNATIONAL, XXXVI (1975), 1538A. Unpublished dissertation, University of Toronto, 1974.

4410 Spender, Stephen. LOVE-HATE RELATIONS: A STUDY OF ANGLO-AMERICAN SENSIBILITIES (Lond: Hamish Hamilton, 1974); pub in America as LOVE-HATE RELATIONS: ENGLISH AND AMERICAN SENSIBILITIES (NY: Random House, 1974), pp. 13, 16, 18-20, 115-16, 139, 141, 147, 149, 160, 162, 167-68, 171-72, 173, 181-87, 188-89, 193-94, 196, 204, 226.

In *Studies in Classic American Literature,* "America--or American art--is made to symbolize the decay of old Europe which America has left behind." DHL recognized in Hemingway the American insistence on freedom from connections. He attacked Bennett, Wells, and Galsworthy on essentially the same grounds that Woolf and James did--"that they judged life by social values." World War I killed the England which DHL loved and depicted in descriptions of countryside and farm lands in *The White Peacock* and *The Rainbow.* "England, My England" is DHL's English elegy, with Egbert's death symbolizing the death of old England. The loss of the old England was succeeded in DHL's writings by hatred for the new.

4411 Spilka, Mark. "Lawrence," in THE ENGLISH NOVEL, ed by A. E. Dyson (Lond: Oxford UP [Select Bibliographic Guides], 1974), pp. 334-48.

By 1950 "the world had finally caught up with" DHL and critics began to see his work in "proper context." [Discusses "Texts," "Critical Studies and Commentaries," "Biographies and Letters," "Bibliographies," and "Background Reading," with a bibliography for each. Traces virtually all the critical studies to 1971, emphasizing early work by Tindall, Moore, and Leavis. Discusses the importance of New Criticism for DHL. Observes that there is no major treatment of DHL's affinities with Carlyle, Nietzsche, Blake, or Hardy.]

4412 Squires, Michael. THE PASTORAL NOVEL: STUDIES IN GEORGE ELIOT, THOMAS HARDY, AND D. H. LAWRENCE (Charlottesville: UP of Virginia, 1974), pp. 19-21, 174-212.

[Includes brief comments on *Sons and Lovers, The Rainbow, Women in Love,*

The Lost Girl, The Fox, and *The Plumed Serpent,* and rpts two earlier articles: "Lawrence's *The White Peacock:* A Mutation of Pastoral," TEXAS STUDIES IN LITERATURE AND LANGUAGE, XII (1970), 263-83, rptd as "Fit for Old Theocritus," pp. 174-95; and "Pastoral Patterns and Pastoral Variants in *Lady Chatterley's Lover,*" ENGLISH LITERARY HISTORY, XXXIX (1972), 129-46, rptd as "Pure Seclusion," pp. 196-212.]

4413 Stacy, Paul H. "Lawrence and Movies: A Postscript," LITERATURE/FILM QUARTERLY, II (Winter 1974), 93-95.

Not only does *The Boy in the Bush* have "cinematic force" but it also uses cinematic techniques such as flashbacks and highly visualized descriptions. DHL's poetry is an excellent source for corroborating information on his attitudes toward film.

4414 Sugiyama, Yasushi. "D. H. Lawrence--Sono Yami no Sekai no Tankyû" (D. H. Lawrence--A Search for His "Darkness"), BULLETIN OF N. C. N. A., XV, No. 2 (Oct 1974), 87-103.

The Japanese have had no habit of recognizing nature as an object apart from human beings. This genuine intuition of man's oneness with nature and the universe provides a clue in the search for DHL's "darkness." [This search is pursued in three parts: (1) DHL and Bertrand Russell, (2) DHL and Aldous Huxley, and (3) the world of DHL's darkness--resurrection from "tomb" to "womb."] [In Japanese.]

4415 Sugiyama, Yasushi. "*Shinnyusha* ni Okeru Shi to Sei" (Death and Life in *The Trespasser*), D. H. LAWRENCE STUDIES (Kyôto), No. 2 (1974), 47-64.

DHL wrote from his most palpitant, sensitive self in *The Trespasser*. Although the novel was a revision of the work by Helen Corke, he put his own experience of the death of his mother into it. The concept of the great stream of life which contains both life and death helps to illuminate the theme of *The Trespasser*. [In Japanese.]

4416 Suzuki, Shunzi. "Bannen no Lawrence--Kodoku kara Shinwateki Cosmos e" (The Later Lawrence: Escape from Isolation into Mythical Cosmos), NAGOYA REVIEW OF ENGLISH STUDIES (Nagoya University), No. 13 (July 1974), 35-48.

DHL had a great concern about the relation with others and society; nevertheless, he could not help feeling himself greatly isolated and alienated from society. How to solve the problem of his own sense of isolation must have been a great question to him, from which the question of his relation with the mythical cosmos must inevitably come. Especially in his later days, DHL suffered so much from his illness and from his bitter conflict with his wife that the problem of isolation and its solution through the relation with the mythical cosmos are especially prominent in the late works, such as "The Woman Who Rode Away," "The Man Who Loved Islands," *Lady Chatterley's Lover,* and *The Man Who Died.* The heroes and heroines in these stories are all in the suffering state of isolation and try to find some true relation with others, including the cosmos. Accordingly, DHL's works more and more come to assume mythical backgrounds and methods. [In Japanese.]

4417 Suzuki, Shunzi. "D. H. Lawrence no Cosmos--Sono Shisôshijô no Igi o Motomete" (The Cosmos of D. H. Lawrence: An Approach to Its Meaning in the History of Thought), BULLETIN FOR LANGUAGES AND LITERATURE (Tenri University), No. 90 (March 1974), 66-77.

This paper attempts, first, to clarify a tendency seen commonly in those representative writers who lived in the uneasy pre- and post-First World War period, then to study the meaning of DHL's idea of "cosmos" in his later days. Such writers as Yeats, Joyce, and DHL have a common consciousness of history; i.e., they all seem to long for a return to a pristine universe, to the Great Past where man could experience oneness with the mythical universe. DHL, especially, seems literally to believe in a return to the pristine cosmos through consciousness, so that those who suffer a living death can be restored to a new living relation with cosmos and others. We can find this idea in *Apocalypse* and its realization in *The Man Who Died*. From the viewpoint of the history of thought, the meaning of DHL's "cosmos" can be regarded as the romantic reaction against the static mechanism of the modern world. [In Japanese.]

4418 Taube, Myron. "Fanny and the Lady: The Treatment of Sex in FANNY HILL and *Lady Chatterley's Lover*," LOCK HAVEN REVIEW, No. 15 (1974), 37-40.

Lady Chatterley's Lover "makes a serious statement about life and FANNY HILL is pornography," but there are "certain striking similarities" between the two novels. Both books are "in a sense anti-sexual": in FANNY HILL, the sex act is described with "images of violence" as "a form of combat"; in *Lady Chatterley's Lover*, DHL "spiritualizes the sexual experience." In their treatment of sexual behavior, John Cleland "succeeds" where DHL "fails." Having aimed lower, Cleland was able to create a unity of objective ("titillation") and technique. He succeeds "because he removes his characters from reality": they exist to have sex; they live in a dream world where "orgasms are mutual and frequent"; and "everything holds together because none of it is really believable." In contrast, DHL fails "because he wants his sex to be believed" and at the same time to serve as "a critique of the politico-socio-economic structure." In DHL, sex "rises from the animal to the human to the mythic to the mystical," becomes "a cure for the ills of society," and connects the heroine through the sex act to "some kind of Jungian-Reichian-mythic-unconsciousness." DHL "fails because he tries to make sex do more than it logically can do, either in the structure of society or the structure of the novel."

4419 Taylor, John A. "The Greatness in *Sons and Lovers*," MODERN PHILOLOGY, LXXI (May 1974), 380-87.

The normal course of the hero's early life is the habitual and customary, but *Sons and Lovers* is a history of losses of the world of custom as much as it is of achievements. Such losses as the events surrounding the death of William or the casting off of Morel touch us more than Paul's final dereliction. [Numerous examples show the movement away from the exceptional and beautiful in the early parts of the book to the quotidian of the later parts.] The loss of the customary, which constitutes the early world of Paul and of Ursula in *The Rainbow,* produces the deracinated hero of the leadership novels.

4420 Terry, C[hris] J. "Aspects of D. H. Lawrence's Struggle with Christianity," DALHOUSIE REVIEW, LIV (Spring 1974), 112-29.

DHL's examination of the feminine intelligence is "the main thrust of his struggle with the Bible": his women characters up to the end of *The Rainbow* embody "a disruptive spirit that will liberate rural man from his paradisal confines and usher him into a wider, freer world in which 'knowledge' is approved of rather than forbidden." Because Kate in *The Plumed Serpent* is "too weak to contain Lawrence's fear, disgust, despair, and failure," emotions necessary to the "main thrust" of the novel, the idea of "substitute religion" fails. In *Lady Chatterley's Lover* the "angry Eve-spirit in Lawrence relents in favor of a more saddened and circumspect vision of the world."

4421 Tetsumura, Haruo. " 'Daughters of the Vicar' Kô--Shudai to Hôhô" (The Theme and Its Expression in "Daughters of the Vicar"), HIROSHIMA STUDIES IN ENGLISH LANGUAGE AND LITERATURE (Hiroshima University), XX, No. 1 (April 1974), 15-34.

The consciousness of "class-distinctions," which pursues DHL's imagination to his last novel, finds expression in "Daughters of the Vicar" as a major element, and the theme is, as F. R. Leavis says properly, " 'their defeat--the triumph over them of life.' " It is of searching interest to see DHL's way of expressing the theme in parallel with the theme itself, to take into consideration the period of composition, which falls on the important turning-point in DHL's way of expressing "carbon." DHL wants to see how life forces act upon man beyond his power, and he succeeds in describing the flame of life as it is, without explaining its greatness in words. [In Japanese.]

4422 Teunissen, John J., and Evelyn Hinz. "The Attack on the *Pietà:* An Archetypal Analysis," JOURNAL OF AESTHETICS AND ART CRITICISM, XXXIII (Fall 1974), 43-50.

Feeling that an archetype was manifested in the sculpture, Laszlo Toth, who in 1972 battered Michelangelo's the *Pietà* with a hammer, believed he was attacking the actual divine mother and her dead son. DHL and others prefigured Toth's misinterpretation of the archetype. To DHL the *Pietà* "is a perfect emblem of the spiritual deathliness that our Hellenic and Hebraic ancestors have bequeathed to our Western cultural tradition." DHL saw only the "heavy, broken beauty" of the *Pietà:* in *Women in Love,* Gerald Crich likens the statue to the broken beauty of Halliday, and in *Lady Chatterley's Lover,* Mrs. Bolton, with Clifford Chatterley in her arms, looks like a satirical *Pietà.*

4423 Tibbetts, Robert A. "Addendum to Roberts: Another Piracy of *Lady Chatterley's Lover,*" SERIF, XI (Fall 1974), 58.

[Descriptive bibliographical listing of a piracy of *Lady Chatterley's Lover* that "differs from the eight forgeries and piracies recorded" by Warren Roberts in

Appendix I, B, of A BIBLIOGRAPHY OF D. H. LAWRENCE (1963), and "also from that reported by Richard M. Kain" in TIMES LITERARY SUPPLEMENT (Lond), 8 Jan 1970, p. 34.]

    4424 Toyokuni, Takashi. "A Modern Man Obsessed by Time: A Note on "The Man Who Loved Islands," D. H. LAWRENCE REVIEW, VII (Spring 1974), 78-82.
[Analyzes the treatment of time in "The Man Who Loved Islands" as not only essential to this short story but also closely related to DHL's "self-dissolution" theme.]

    4425 Vickery, John B. "D. H. Lawrence's Poetry: Myth and Matter," D. H. LAWRENCE REVIEW, VII (Spring 1974), 1-18; rvd and rptd as Chap. I: "Myth and Poetics: The Creation of a Cosmos," in MYTHS AND TEXTS: STRATEGIES OF INCORPORATION AND DISPLACEMENT, by John B. Vickery (Baton Rouge & Lond: Louisiana State UP, 1983), pp. 8-26.
DHL's best poetry mediates happily between the mythopoesis of Eliot's THE WASTE LAND and the physicalist givens of Williams's PATERSON in its balanced sense of the realities of matter and the potentialities of myth. The "New World" of DHL's poetry can be defined as a physics in which matter is seen as concrete and animate, moving in a complex pattern of attraction and recoil which can be called love. Myth, for DHL, is the energy force that impels this motion "because ultimately it is the human imagination's direct action on itself." Myth, for him, "is the verbal or narrative form of matter" which possesses, for its basic forms of motion, sex and death, ontological dialectical rituals. "Bavarian Gentians" shows myth merging with mystery, matter with nothingness, and speech with silence, "embracing, but not absorbed into either Eliot's myths or Williams' matter."

    4426 Vitoux, Pierre. "Aldous Huxley and D. H. Lawrence: An Attempt at Intellectual Sympathy," MODERN LANGUAGE REVIEW, LXIX (July 1974), 501-22.
DHL's major influence on Huxley at the time of the composition of POINT COUNTER POINT accounts for that novel's difference from other works in Huxley's canon. Though he looked to DHL for an ideal of wholeness which would fit Jung's character typologies, Huxley did not understand the aspect of intuition in the introvert type such as DHL and therefore makes his Lawrencean character Rampion a "gas-bag," as DHL perceived. [Other Jungian typologies in POINT COUNTER POINT are described.] When DHL ceased to emphasize the ideal of wholeness and turned to the need for connection with the impersonal, Huxley rejected DHL, though in his later mysticism, Huxley seems to be advocating something akin to DHL's impersonal himself.

    4427 Vogelsang, John Daniel. "The Wave of Self in Time to Break: D. H. Lawrence and Virginia Woolf," DISSERTATION ABSTRACTS INTERNATIONAL, XXXV (1974), 1677A. Unpublished dissertation, State University of New York at Buffalo, 1974.

4428 Wada, Shizuo. "D. H. Lawrence Oboegaki (VI)--Jessie Chambers no Tegami" (Notes on D. H. Lawrence [VI] : A Letter by Jessie Chambers), BULLETIN OF KYÛSHÛ SANGYÔ UNIVERSITY, X, No. 2 (Feb 1974), 1-17.

In a letter to Helen Corke (1 June 1933) in the DHL collection of the University of Nottingham Library, Jessie Chambers wrote that she reproached DHL for having become engaged to Louie Burrows. In her memoir, D. H. LAWRENCE: A PERSONAL RECORD by E. T. (1935), a person referred to only as "X" can now be identified as Louie Burrows. It can also be inferred from the letter that DHL's tendency in youth was especially inclined toward women. [The letter in question was published, without identifications of author, recipient, or "X," as " 'E. T.' on D. H. Lawrence: A Letter to a Common Friend," ARENA, I (1950), 61-65; rptd in full as Letter 23: (To Helen Corke), in "The Collected Letters of Jessie Chambers," ed by George J. Zytaruk, D. H. LAWRENCE REVIEW, XII (Spring-Summer 1979), 53-59.] [In Japanese.]

4429 Walker, Cynthia Lucille. "Power and Isolation in the Political Novels of D. H. Lawrence," DISSERTATION ABSTRACTS INTERNATIONAL, XXXV (1975), 7332A. Unpublished dissertation, Purdue University, 1974.

4430 Walker, Ronald G. "The Blood, Border, *Barranca:* The Role of Mexico in the Modern English Novel," DISSERTATION ABSTRACTS INTERNATIONAL, XXXVI (1975), 913A. Unpublished dissertation, University of Maryland, 1974. Rvd and pub as INFERNAL PARADISE: MEXICO AND THE MODERN ENGLISH NOVEL (Los Angeles & Lond: University of California P, 1978).

4431 Widmer, Kingsley. "D. H. Lawrence and Critical Mannerism," JOURNAL OF MODERN LITERATURE, III, No. 4 (1974), 1044-45.

"After half a century of massive Lawrence studies...the impassioned meditations proper to literary criticism often turn synthetic, willful, hyper-sophisticated, narrow yet ornate--in a word, critical mannerism." [Reviews books on DHL by Keith Alldritt, Sandra Gilbert, Stephen J. Miko, and R. E. Pritchard.]

4432 Wilkin, Andrew. "Sulle Traduzioni Lawrenciane delle Novelle di G. Verga" (On the Lawrencian Translations of the Novels of G. Verga), BIOLOGIA CULTURALE, IX (Sept 1974), 122-27.

Although DHL's translations of Giovanni Verga's novels sound good on the whole, their flaws become evident in an examination of the details. [In a side by side comparison, the author considers eleven examples of phrases or sentences from Verga together with their translations by DHL, which he finds to be imperfect.] [In Italian.]

4433 Winegarten, Renee. "Revolutionary Resurrection: D. H. Lawrence," WRITERS AND REVOLUTION: THE FATAL LURE OF

ACTION (NY: New Viewpoints, 1974), pp. 248-60.
DHL believed in the necessity of revolutionary destruction of a moribund world and took himself seriously as a prophet. Rejecting Christianity and disgusted with humanity, he desired a return to "the supposed vital consciousness" of the pagans and shares with Shelley "the nature-image of death as a prerequisite for creation." In DHL this leads to a distasteful indifference to individual life and a lack of sympathy for the doomed. He was contemptuous of democracy and social reformers, and his temporary attractions to both fascism and bolshevism show irresponsibility.

4434 Woodcock, Bruce. "Poetic Fiction: A Study in Representation with Reference to Virginia Woolf and D. H. Lawrence." Unpublished dissertation, University of Leicester, 1974. [Listed in Geoffrey M. Paterson and Joan E. Hardy (eds), INDEX TO THESES, XXVI, Part 2 (1978), p. 7.]

4435 Yamaguchi, Tetsuo. "*Shinda Otoko* Saikô" (Reconsideration of *The Man Who Died*), SHIKOKU CHRISTIAN COLLEGE TREATISES, No. 29 (March 1974), 156-67.
[A reconsideration of views expressed by Tetsuo Yamaguchi in "*Shinda Otoko* ni Tsuite" (On *The Man Who Died*), SHIKOKU CHRISTIAN COLLEGE TREATISES, No. 15 (March 1969), 23-35. When he first discussed *The Man Who Died*, the writer could not accept it because he thought that DHL was lost in the rapture of his impossible and unrealistically idealized view of sexual love. In this paper, he discusses the short novel affirmatively *because* DHL's ideal is so impossible and unrealistic.] DHL is a sad romanticist whose pessimism formed the base for his romanticism. Deep sadness is hidden behind the happy dream presented in *The Man Who Died.* [In Japanese.]

4436 Yamakawa, Kozo. "*Niji* Izen-Igo: Beardsley no *Salome* wo Megutte" (Before and After *The Rainbow:* On Beardsley's *Salome*), EIGO SEINEN, No. 120 (1974), 212-13.
[In Japanese.]

4437 Yamakawa, Kozo. SHISO NO BOKEN: RORENSU NO SHOSETSU (Adventures in Thought: Lawrence's Fiction) (Tôkyô: Kenkyusha, 1974).
[The author traces the transformation and progress of DHL's aesthetic concepts by analyzing, in separate chapters, *Sons and Lovers, The Rainbow, Women in Love, Aaron's Rod, The Plumed Serpent,* and *Lady Chatterley's Lover.* (The final chapter concludes that *Lady Chatterley's Lover* is a "failure.") The author also notes similarities between DHL's aesthetics and those of sculptor Henry Moore, and several photographs of Moore's "primitive" sculptures illustrate the dust jacket of the book and some of its pages.] [In Japanese.]

4438 Yamasaki, Susumu. "Lawrence no Okeru Shikaku to Shokkaku no Mondai--'Ichijiku no Ha' Izen no Kyôi e no Kaiki" (Lawrence's Research for Human Existence Not by Visualization but by Blood-

Contact--Return to the Innocent Stage of Adam and Eve in the Garden of Eden), REPORTS OF HIMEJI INSTITUTE OF TECHNOLOGY, No. 24B (Dec 1974), 103-15.

DHL condemns visual recognition for its falsehood, but he approves of blood-contact because of its truth. He maintains that man can gain his true self by returning to the sinless stage prior to the banishment of Adam and Eve from the Garden. [In Japanese.]

4439 Yanada, Noriyuki. "D. H. Lawrence no Shoki no Tanpen--*Sons and Lovers* no Shûhen" (A Study of D. H. Lawrence's Early Short Stories and *Sons and Lovers*), JOURNAL OF HOKKAIDO UNIVERSITY OF EDUCATION, XXIV, No. 2 (Jan 1974), 129-40.

Most of DHL's early short stories do not have much originality, but they offer tentative interpretations of his youthful experience before he could finally put them in order. These early stories, chiefly "A Modern Lover," "Odour of Chrysanthemums," and "Daughters of the Vicar," also provide clues to the relations of characters in *Sons and Lovers,* in which the stories have been assimilated thematically. [In Japanese.]

4440 Yoshida, Tetsuo. "The Broken Balance and the Negative Victory in *Lady Chatterley's Lover,*" STUDIES IN ENGLISH LITERATURE AND LANGUAGE (Kyûshû University), No. 24 (March 1974), 117-29.

In his essay "Morality and the Novel," DHL observes that " 'Morality in the novel is the trembling instability of the balance. When the novelist puts his thumb in the scale, to pull down the balance to his own predilection, that is immorality.' " In *Lady Chatterley's Lover,* however, DHL himself breaks the balance when he presents Clifford from the perspective of his own view as identified with Connie's. The predilection for the heroine's rebirth prevents the author from analyzing honestly some dubious oscillations of her feelings and leads to the effect that her transformation is passively accomplished.

4441 Yoshimura, Hirokazu. "*Shinnyusha* no Wagnerteki Yôso o Megutte" (Wagnerian Elements in *The Trespasser*), D. H. LAWRENCE STUDIES (Kyôto), No. 2 (Nov 1974), 5-28.

The secrets of DHL's creative world may be explored by examining the Wagnerian elements in *The Trespasser,* for his efforts in groping for his own patterns or forms in the novel are made known to us by his treatment of Wagner's characters and music-dramas. [In Japanese.]

4442 Ziebarth, Janet A. "Sexuality and Social Critique in the Novels of D. H. Lawrence, 1915-1922," DISSERTATION ABSTRACTS INTERNATIONAL, XXXV (1975), 6739A-40A. Unpublished dissertation, Rutgers University, 1974.

4443 Zytaruk, George J. (ed). "Dorothy Brett's Letters to S. S. Koteliansky," D. H. LAWRENCE REVIEW, VII (Fall 1974), 240-74.

"Published here for the first time," Dorothy Brett's letters to S. S. Koteliansky, beginning in August 1921 and continuing sporadically until February 1924, with a last letter from America in 1930, "reveal the manner of woman it was who... gave up the security of her native England and chose as her new home an isolated ranch in New Mexico," the only convert to DHL's Rananim. "The two main themes" in the letters are Brett's "complex feelings for Katherine Mansfield and for Middleton Murry." Murry and Brett had a "temporary liaison" in this period, and "Murry had also been seeing a good deal of Frieda," who, according to him, "proposed...that they become lovers." "An obligation to sustain Murry from complete emotional collapse became" Brett's "burden, about which we would know nothing were it not for these letters to Kot." "When Lawrence returned to England in 1923, he walked straight into this complex tangle of emotional relationships," though "at the infamous Café Royal dinner, [he] was surely unaware of what was going on among his most intimate friends." [Contains twenty-four letters from Brett to Koteliansky, preserved in the Koteliansky papers in the possession of Mrs. Catherine Stoye. Illustrated with four black and white photographs of Brett, Koteliansky, and Koteliansky surrounded by a group of six male friends.]

1975

4444 Adam, Michael [pseud of Kim Taylor]. D. H. LAWRENCE AND THE WAY OF THE DANDELION, with recollections by Frieda Lawrence and woodcuts by Barbara Whitehead (Penzance, Cornwall, England: Ark P, 1975).
[This "tributary essay" includes sections on "Lawrence's Phoenix," "A Matter of Death and Life," "Marriage and the Wheeling Sun," "The Sixth Sense of Wonder," "The Tilt of the Joy of Life," "Flowers and the Silenced Races," "Beyond the Walls of Light," "The Way of the Dandelion," and "A Torch Held Out, to Kindle." Recollections by Frieda Lawrence, originally recorded in 1954 for BBC, were first published as the introduction to *Look! We Have Come Through!* (1958). Besides the twenty woodcuts, illustrations include the portrait of DHL by Jan Juta and a photograph of Frieda.]

4445 Adamowski, T[homas] H. "Being Perfect: Lawrence, Sartre, and *Women in Love*," CRITICAL INQUIRY, II (Winter 1975), 345-68. DHL's perception of himself as a visionary with the means to cure the ills of the "self" forces criticism to look beyond the confines of art itself to the broader context of philosophy for an understanding of his work. For this reason *Women in Love* bears comparison with Sartre's BEING AND NOTHINGNESS since both are explorations of the possibility of achieving perfection for the self.

4446 Aldington, Richard. A PASSIONATE PRODIGALITY: LETTERS TO ALAN BIRD FROM RICHARD ALDINGTON, 1949-1962, ed and with an Introduction by Miriam J. Benkovitz (NY: New York Public Library, Astor, Lenox and Tilden Foundations, 1975), pp. ix, xii, 7-8, 12-13, 16, 30, 37, 39, 49, 52-53, 60, 64, 65n, 71, 90, 103,

121, 123, 124-27, 129n, 131, 136n, 139, 140-42, 150, 154, 161, 162n, 173, 185, 190, 193n, 196n, 208, 228, 229n, 234-37, 241, 242n, 262n, 264, 266n, 267n, 269, 272, 274, 276, 282-84, 287-88, 290.

[Aldington's letters reflect his ongoing interest in DHL, who was his onetime colleague in the Imagist movement; whom he wrote about in various studies, editions, and introductions throughout his life; and whose importance as a writer Aldington continues to defend. Aldington discusses his biographical inclusion of "the Bibbles incident"; DHL's errors in *Studies in Classic American Literature;* DHL's having to write too fast for financial reasons; DHL's fight for "those words" in *Lady Chatterley's Lover,* and the recently won British censorship case involving the novel (Regina v. Penguin Books Ltd., 1960); and the German publication of DHL's work.]

4447 Alinei, Tamara. "Three Times Morel: Recurrent Structure in *Sons and Lovers,*" DUTCH QUARTERLY REVIEW OF ANGLO-AMERICAN LETTERS, V, No. 1 (1975), 39-53.

The structure of *Sons and Lovers* is based on variations of episodes involving Mrs. Morel and one of her sons pitted against the will of Mr. Morel, who is, as a result, morally and symbolically defeated. In subsequent scenes DHL recreates the patterns and meanings of these episodes which express his passionate love for his mother and his strongly ambivalent feelings for his father.

4448 Asahi, Chiseki. "Factors of Romanticism in D. H. Lawrence's Rhyming Poems," STUDIES OF SONODA WOMEN'S COLLEGE, No. 10 (Dec 1975), 77-93.

In his poems, DHL seems to have inherited the primitive sensibility of William Wordsworth, though many outward differences between them cannot be overlooked. [The characteristics of Romanticism in DHL's rhyming poems are studied with reference to Wordsworth's poems.]

4449 Bartel, Roland. "D. H. Lawrence (1885-1930)," in BIBLICAL IMAGES IN LITERATURE, ed by Roland Bartel, with James S. Ackerman and Thayer S. Warshaw (Nashville & NY: Abingdon P, 1975), p. 272.

[Brief headnote to twenty poems by DHL containing biblical allusions, including a number of satirical verses from his last period, reprinted in the book, pp. 272-78, calls attention to his frequent references to the Bible in both his poetry and his fiction.]

4450 Beards, Richard D. "The Checklist of D. H. Lawrence Criticism and Scholarship, 1974," D. H. LAWRENCE REVIEW, VIII (Spring 1975), 99-105.

[The annual checklist is divided into five sections: General, Poetry, Individual Works of Fiction, Non-Fiction Prose, and Drama.]

4451 Bersani, Leo. "Lawrentian Stillness," YALE REVIEW, LXV (Autumn 1975), 38-60; rptd in A FUTURE FOR ASTYANAX:

CHARACTER AND DESIRE IN LITERATURE, by Leo Bersani (Bost: Little, Brown, 1976), pp. 156-85.
Women in Love exemplifies the opposition between agitation and stillness that is characteristic of DHL's writing. The only choice an individual can make in the mind of DHL is a choice between life and death. The experimental nature of his work is evident in the thematic and psychological repetitions of characters whose ultimate goals should be "stillness of being, a state beyond movement and even character." DHL makes an impressive attempt "to use the skepticism inherent to realistic fiction as a means of promoting rather than of deflating projects designed to revolutionize the self."

4452 Black, Michael. "Sexuality in Literature: *Lady Chatterley's Lover*," "Lawrence and 'that which is perfectly ourselves,' " and "Tolstoy and Lawrence: Some Conclusions," in THE LITERATURE OF FIDELITY, by Michael Black (Lond: Chatto & Windus; NY: Barnes & Noble, 1975), pp. 169-83, 184-98, and 199-211.

[*Lady Chatterley's Lover* is examined, in comparison with works by other writers, in the context of love and marriage, the need for self-fulfillment and the need for commitment, the claims of passion and feeling and the claims of society.] *Lady Chatterley's Lover* is a serious work that will always be significant for having taken "the explicit description of sexual acts into English literature." The sensual language of Shakespeare's OTHELLO and the atmosphere of Racine's PHÈDRE are, without explicit details, as "heavily laden with sexuality," and Tolstoy reveals "the same grasp of implicit realities, which are as much emotional as physical," when Karenin exercises his "marital rights" with an unresponsive Anna. "There are whole dimensions left out of Lawrence's novel" that account for the superiority of Tolstoy's; for example, Tolstoy's characterization of Karenin shows a "depth of understanding" lacking in DHL's treatment of Clifford Chatterley. [*Sons and Lovers, The Rainbow,* and *Women in Love* are discussed in terms of the theme "that which is perfectly ourselves," and an extended comparison is drawn between DHL and Tolstoy.]

4453 Blanchard, Lydia. "Love and Power: A Reconsideration of Sexual Politics in Lawrence," MODERN FICTION STUDIES, XXI (Autumn 1975), 431-43.

DHL shows male protagonists destroyed or damaged by female dominance as often as he shows the male maiming the female in the typical power struggle. (Both Kate Millett in SEXUAL POLITICS [1970] and Norman Mailer in THE PRISONER OF SEX [1970] take limited views of the problem.) DHL's hatred of the machine and the intellect poses a special problem for the contemporary female, who feels that she must free herself, by means of intellect, from bondage to the male. The male in DHL is actually crippled by the machine, not by the woman, so that he tries to compensate for his loss of power by dominating the female. DHL's most obviously autobiographical characters, ultimately, want separateness in unity with equality, though some of DHL's non-fiction statements on the matter are chauvinistic. DHL's attempts to resolve the conflict in fictional terms are inconsistent: in the middle period he turns to dominance of woman by man, of man by man, and of mass by dictator; in his last works he turns to experiments with isolation and withdrawal to survive and concerns himself very little with the male-female dominance struggle.

4454 Bobbitt, Joan. "The Aesthetic of Life: Art and the Artist in the Major Novels of D. H. Lawrence," DISSERTATION ABSTRACTS INTERNATIONAL, XXXVI (1975), 2836A-37A. Unpublished dissertation, University of Texas at Austin, 1975.

4455 Boulton, Marjorie. THE ANATOMY OF THE NOVEL (Lond & Bost: Routledge & Kegan Paul, 1975), pp. 8, 12, 21, 65, 71, 76, 81, 94, 126, 127, 130, 136, 137, 150, 158.

DHL's "plots are always...concerned with sincerity and depth in human relationships." In character, "he is a wonderful novelist of love-hate tensions, of struggles for dominance,...but he tells us little about the victories of rational co-operation...." In setting, he is good at handling backgrounds, as in the Australian milieu of *Kangaroo,* which forces Somers to rethink some of his ideas.

4456 Braem, Helmut M. "Lady Chatterley ist nur das Gelbe im Ei. Die Zweitfassung eines beruhmten Romans, zum erstenmal auf deutsch" (Lady Chatterley is merely second-rate. The second version of a famous novel, for the first time in German translation), SÜDDEUTSCHE ZEITUNG, 8 Oct 1975.

John Thomas and Lady Jane, the second version of *Lady Chatterley's Lover,* for the first time available in German translation [trans by Susanna Rademacher (Zürich, 1975)], exposes the weakness of the novel and DHL's weakness as a novelist in general. DHL's language is poor, lacks descriptive strength, and is full of pantheist bathos. His metaphors and imagery are unconvincing and show a remarkable paucity in verbal artistry. All this and the underlying Fascist ideology account for the inferior quality of the novel. [In German.]

4457 Callow, Philip. SON AND LOVER: THE YOUNG LAWRENCE (Lond: Bodley Head, 1975); pub in America as SON AND LOVER: THE YOUNG D. H. LAWRENCE (NY: Stein & Day, 1975).

[A survey of DHL's life from 1885 to 1919, including DHL's Eastwood heritage, family background, and childhood, the character and death of his brother Ernest, DHL's close relationships with his mother and his friendship with Jessie Chambers, his life as a teacher in Croydon, his friendship with Helen Corke and engagement to Louie Burrows, his collapse and recovery in 1911, his elopement with Frieda Weekley and their travels on the Continent, the prosecution of *The Rainbow,* the Lawrences' stay in Cornwall, friendship with John Middleton Murry and Katherine Mansfield, and difficulties with the authorities during the war, the plans for Rananim, and the Lawrences' ultimate departure from England in 1919. Biographical sources for DHL's work of the period are identified. Does not go beyond previous critical biographies.]

4458 Canfield, Ken. "Indian Cultures Appeal More than English Aristocracy," KANSAS CITY STAR, 26 Jan 1975.

[In an interview in Taos, NM, Dorothy Brett briefly recalls her friendship with

DHL. Quotes DHL's poem "Beautiful Old Age."]

4459 Carr, Virginia Spencer. THE LONELY HUNTER: A BIOGRAPHY OF CARSON McCULLERS (Garden City, NY: Doubleday, 1975), pp. 33, 39.
McCullers read *The Rainbow* and *The Prussian Officer and Other Stories,* the title story of which influenced her portrayal of "the homosexually inclined, but impotent Captain Penderton and the primitive, animalistic Private Williams in REFLECTIONS IN A GOLDEN EYE."

4460 Cavallone, Anna Anzi. "Lawrence a Gargnano" (Lawrence in Gargnano), STUDI INGLESI (Rome), II (1975), 401-23.
During the Lawrences' stay in Gargnano (1913), DHL got much of the material for *Twilight in Italy.* [Discusses DHL's relationship with Signor De Paoli, Il Duro, and John; his visit to the puppet theater; his letters from Italy to friends like David Garnett, and his renting rooms from Mrs. Anthony in San Gaudenzio.] [In Italian.]

4461 Cherry, Richard L., Robert J. Conley, and Bernard A. Hirsch. "Rhetorical Analysis," THE ESSAY: STRUCTURE AND PURPOSE (Bost: Houghton, Mifflin, 1975), pp. 254-55.
In "New Mexico" [which is reprinted in the anthology, pp. 249-54], DHL intermingles "three basic approaches" to the rhetorical problem of conveying the revelation that New Mexico represented for him: "he describes New Mexico, he describes the Indians, and he comments on the description, relating it to his notions of religion." [Brief headnote.]

4462 Chesson, Diane Marie. "The Intellectual and Emotional Complex as an Expression of the Consciousness in Joyce, Lawrence, and Woolf," DISSERTATION ABSTRACTS INTERNATIONAL, XXXVI (1976), 6081A. Unpublished dissertation, University of Illinois, 1975.

4463 Clark, Ronald W. THE LIFE OF BERTRAND RUSSELL (Lond: Jonathan Cape and Weidenfeld & Nicolson, 1975), pp. 259-65, 269, 271, 275-76, 290, 292, 310, 549.
When Lady Ottoline Morrell engineered a meeting between DHL and Bertrand Russell, they were immediately drawn to each other. But it was inevitable that the two men, one a believer in *Blutbrüderschaft* with prophetic ideas, the other a calm logician, "would mount their hobby-horses and charge each other full tilt." When Russell took DHL to Cambridge to meet G. E. Moore and John Maynard Keynes, DHL reacted with depression to the obvious homosexuality cloaked in intellectual defenses. Later DHL and Russell planned a series of joint lectures on "The Principles of Social Reconstruction" with such topics as "religion, politics, ...morality, the State, property, marriage, war, taking them to their roots in human nature." But when Russell sent DHL a 22-page draft outline of his plans, DHL wrote his reply across the title page, rejecting it as "social criticism," not "social reconstruction." Russell responded to DHL's schoolmasterly hectoring with self-doubt, and DHL compounded the problem with impractical proposals

for a "'revolution in the state,'" beginning with nationalization of industry, communications media, and the land. In response to an article by Russell, DHL declared that what Russell hated was not falsehood but mankind itself with a "'perverted mental blood-lust.'" For twenty-four hours Russell contemplated suicide before "'the instinct of self-preservation'" asserted itself. DHL felt betrayed as an outsider, indulged as a personality only for a sensation. DHL satirized Russell as Bertie Reid in "The Blind Man" and Sir Joshua Malleson in *Women in Love*. Russell later described him as a megalomaniac, "'one of a long line of people beginning with Heraclitus & ending with Hitler.'"

4464 Colacurcio, Michael J. "The Symbolic and the Symptomatic: D. H. Lawrence in Recent American Criticism," AMERICAN QUARTERLY, XXVII (Oct 1975), 486-501.

During the last ten years a Laurentian school in American literary studies has emerged after decades in which *Studies in Classic American Literature* was overshadowed by more professional, rationalist studies. Richard Poirier in A WORLD ELSEWHERE suggests that American literary style as a mode of verbal freedom corresponds to the specialness that DHL saw in American literature in America's attempt to be absolutely masterless. Quentin Anderson sees DHL as a "symptomatic" critic who reads American classics for what they reveal, or conceal, about deeper cultural illnesses. But since identifying the unconscious with the symbolic as a mode of critical interpretation makes it hard to discuss consciousness and control in relation to literary significance, intentional and symptomatic meanings must be distinguished clearly. Leslie Fiedler's LOVE AND DEATH IN THE AMERICAN NOVEL shows the same tendency to find deeper unwholesome meanings in American literature that he lauds in DHL's *Studies,* and his THE RETURN OF THE VANISHING AMERICAN relies heavily on DHL's epigraph that once the American Indian has been culturally destroyed, the white man will have to face the demon of the continent. Richard Slotkin's REGENERATION THROUGH VIOLENCE suggests that if we accept DHL's thesis that a "spirit of place" has been the dominating factor in shaping the American sensibility, then all rational constructs of national ideology or destiny are excluded, as are the various critical approaches of Parrington, Matthiessen, Fiedelson, and R. W. B. Lewis, a damaging blow to ideological interpretation of American cultural history.

4465 Corke, Helen. IN OUR INFANCY: AN AUTOBIOGRAPHY, Part I: 1882-1919 (Cambridge: Cambridge UP, 1975), pp. viii-x, 137-235.

[The author gives the source and background of *The Trespasser* in a detailed account of her romantic involvement, accompanied by feelings of guilt, with her married violin teacher, "H. B. M." (Herbert Baldwin Macartney, unidentified except by initials), culminating in their brief five-days' affair on the Isle of Wight followed by his suicide, her period of emotional shock in the aftermath, and her ultimate return to life through the friendship of DHL. When Corke showed DHL her retrospective "Freshwater Diary" (printed as an appendix), he asked to use it as the basis for a book, arguing "that the act of expression pre-supposes a reader, and that human experience is the property of humanity." As he wrote the "saga" that was to become *The Trespasser,* she acted as his guide to the characters of

Helena and Siegmund, as he called them. DHL confided in her his ambivalence about Jessie Chambers, with whom Corke later developed a deep friendship. DHL was engaged briefly to Louie Burrows, whose quality of mind he seemed to despise but who would never challenge his mother's claims on him. In *Sons and Lovers,* the author believes, DHL presented his mother's image of Jessie. DHL and Helen went on rambles together, and once he even suggested that they might marry, a clearly impossible match. Includes photographs of the author, "H. B. M.," Jessie Chambers (c. 1908), and DHL (c. 1908).]

4466 Corke, Helen. "Laurentiana," D. H. LAWRENCE REVIEW, VIII (Fall 1975), 378-79.

[Letter to Émile Delavenay, in support of his article, " 'Making Another Lawrence': Frieda and the Lawrence Legend," D. H. LAWRENCE REVIEW, VIII (Spring 1975), 80-98.] "If anyone can claim the distinction of acting as mid-wife to DHL's genius there are only two women who qualify for that honour--his mother and Jessie Chambers." Frieda never "understood the nature of Lawrence's genius" or of "his frequent indisposition."

4467 Cowan, James C. "D. H. Lawrence's Dualism: The Apollonian-Dionysian Polarity and *The Ladybird,*" in FORMS OF MODERN BRITISH FICTION, ed by Alan Warren Friedman (Austin & Lond: University of Texas P, 1975), pp. 73-99.

DHL's dualistic world view, related to the two cultural traditions which Nietzsche calls the Apollonian and the Dionysian, is expressed in symbols which center, as Henry Miller notes, in " '*the resolution of two opposites in the form of a mystery.*' " Culturally, the Apollonian tradition concerns rational, "analytical discriminations in the conscious mind" and "assumes a linear development in a causal sequence" with "objective truth as a reachable end point." The Dionysian tradition, in contrast, concerns intuitive, imaginative syntheses in the creative unconscious and "assumes a cyclic development" with a truth that cannot be defined discursively but only presented in concrete imagery and symbols. In *The Ladybird,* DHL establishes the theoretical opposition between the two traditions in a fictional triangle in which Major Basil Apsley, a modern figure of Apollonian love in decline, and Count Dionys Psanek, an advocate of the resurrection of the Dionysian mystery of power both in the sexual relationship and in political leadership, compete for the soul of Lady Daphne, whose name derives from the Apollo-Daphne myth and who represents the divided modern self. [Parallel passages from *The Ladybird* and Edgar Allan Poe's "The Fall of the House of Usher" are compared stylistically.] Count Dionys, a figure of Laurentian darkness, advocates the creative dissolution discussed in "The Crown" as a means toward regeneration.

4468 Cox, James. "Pollyanalytics and Pedagogy: Teaching Lawrence's Short Fiction," in "On the Teaching of D. H. Lawrence: A Forum," ed by Langdon Elsbree. D. H. LAWRENCE REVIEW, VIII (Spring 1975), 74-77.

[The author suggests in detail how DHL's "pollyanalytic essays"--"Love," "Sex Versus Loveliness," and "The Real Thing"--may be used in teaching the second volume of *The Complete Short Stories of D. H. Lawrence* in a lower division course centered on the relationship between men and women. In an extended example, he shows the applicability of "Sex Versus Loveliness" to "The Horse Dealer's Daughter," with its theme of "the reciprocal kindling of the life-flame in Mabel and Fergusson."]

4469 Crotch, Martha Gordon. MEMORIES OF FRIEDA LAWRENCE (Edinburgh: Tragara P [Edition limited to 175 copies handprinted], 1975).

[The text is "an extract (chapters 62 to 65 complete) from the unpublished memoirs of Mrs. Gordon Crotch, known widely in literary and artistic circles as 'Auntie.'" The author knew Frieda Lawrence in 1930-1931 in Vence, where Frieda and her daughter Barbara Weekley were staying at the Villa Roberman where DHL had died. After Barby returned to her father's home, Frieda stayed with Mrs. Crotch, whom she persuaded to mount an exhibit of DHL's paintings at her house in the Place du Peyra. "A woman of many great qualities. . .with touches of original sin," Frieda gave the impression of "something half tamed" with the gait and "exquisite grace" of a "wild creature" who demanded "life in its pristine state." Frieda and DHL often "loathed each other," and she refused to "coddle" him, even after he had haemorrhaged at the Villa Mirenda, but continued to rouse his determination by the challenge of her "virility." The author recounts a visit to Frieda by Captain Angelo Ravagli's wife and children, just before Frieda and the "Capitano" left for New Mexico together, and gives details of a threat by the owner of the Villa Roberman to attach DHL's pictures to pay for damages to the villa by the three "unruly" children. She also discusses in detail the disagreement between Frieda and the Lawrence family which led to the court ruling in Frieda's favor on the DHL estate. Finally, she recounts the 1934 claim by a town official in Vence that DHL's grave had never been paid for, a charge disputed by Aldous Huxley, an unpleasant controversy which precipitated Frieda's decision to have DHL's remains disinterred, cremated, and returned to Taos. See also "Letters from Frieda Lawrence and Ada Lawrence Clarke to Martha Gordon Crotch," in FRIEDA LAWRENCE AND HER CIRCLE: LETTERS FROM, TO AND ABOUT FRIEDA LAWRENCE, ed by Harry T. Moore and Dale B. Montague (Lond & Basingstoke: Macmillan P; Hamden, CT: Shoe String P, Archon Books, 1981), pp. 42-70.]

4470 Cushman, Keith. "D. H. Lawrence at Work: 'The Shadow in the Rose Garden'," D. H. LAWRENCE REVIEW, VIII (Spring 1975), 31-46.

"The Shadow in the Rose Garden" "achieved its final form only at the culmination of a lengthy evolutionary process." Of the three completely different versions in existence, "the earliest, called 'The Vicar's Garden,' dates from the beginning of Lawrence's career as a short story writer." "'The Vicar's Garden' was rewritten in the summer of 1913 to produce the magazine version of 'The Shadow in the Rose Garden' published in the SMART SET in March 1914. The *Prussian Officer* version emerged in the sweeping recasting of the story in July 1914." The first version depends heavily on DHL's relationship with Jessie Chambers, and on a visible debt to Charlotte Brontë's JANE EYRE, one of DHL's "'favorite English books' " in 1908. "Only as the story developed away from its origin in autobiography...did it begin to achieve an esthetic life of its own." An analysis of the subsequent revisions traces its striking development from the innocuous blandness of its origin to the heightened intensity of its final form. [Includes facsimile of first page of the manuscript of "The Vicar's Garden."]

4471 Cushman, Keith. " 'I am going through a transition stage': *The Prussian Officer* and *The Rainbow*," D. H. LAWRENCE REVIEW, VIII (Summer 1975), 176-97.

The *Prussian Officer* stories and *The Rainbow* should be understood as part of the same great artistic moment. An analysis of the overlapping development of the two books emphasizes the interrelationships between them and indicates that DHL's development as a short story writer is "an integral part of the complicated process in which he became the author of *The Rainbow*." A detailed study of specific aspects of the stories reveals "how fully they reside within the powerful orbit of Lawrence's Brangwen saga." Written shortly before he undertook revisions for *The Prussian Officer and Other Stories*, DHL's "familiar letter to Garnett of June 5, 1914," about " 'the old stable ego--of the character,' " is a central document for any student of DHL's artistic development; some of the complex ideas developed in this letter are embodied not only in *The Rainbow* but also in the final revisions of the stories.

4472 Darroch, Sandra Jobson. OTTOLINE: THE LIFE OF LADY OTTOLINE MORRELL (NY: Coward, McCann & Geohegan, 1975), pp. 15, 147-53, 157, 158-61, 162, 163-65, 166-67, 178, 183, 187-97, 198, 200, 203, 207, 223, 226-27, 231, 239, 240, 241, 242, 251, 253, 257, 267-68, 271-73, 274-75, 277, 278, 280, 282, 287.

In December 1914, Gilbert Cannan brought DHL and Frieda to meet Lady Ottoline Morrell. Through her they later met Duncan Grant, whose work DHL disliked--the first indication that he and Bloomsbury were not to get along. DHL wanted to found a utopian colony, Rananim, to be based not on poverty, humility, and sacrifice, but on riches, pride, and fulfillment. Believing that DHL and Bertrand Russell were similar in their thinking, Ottoline brought them together, with the result that the two men planned a joint venture in lectures and publications. However, when DHL visited Cambridge to meet John Maynard Keynes and others, he was put off by the atmosphere of sodomy, and Russell took an equal dislike to John Middleton Murry, Katherine Mansfield, and S. S. Koteliansky, when DHL introduced him to them. Finally, in September 1915, when DHL wrote to Russell denouncing his pacifism as the hypocritical sublimation into words of the desire " 'to jab and strike, like the soldier with the bayonet,' " Russell, deeply distressed, briefly contemplated suicide. The friendship that had flared between the two men just as quickly burned out. When *The Rainbow* was suppressed, shortly after its publication in 1915, Philip Morrell, M.P., tried to get the ban lifted, and Ottoline wrote to prominent literary figures to collect money for DHL to go to America, though he was later denied clearance to leave the country. In 1915 and 1916, trouble flared between Ottoline and Frieda, who resented being underrated. Stunned by DHL's portrayal of her as Hermione in *Women in Love,* Ottoline wrote furiously to him, every line revealing a wound, and Philip contacted DHL's literary agents and threatened action for libel if the manuscript were published. DHL's attempt at reconciliation in 1918, through Mark Gertler, failed; but in 1927, after twelve years, DHL and Ottoline made up the quarrel. The following year she wrote praising *Lady Chatterley's Lover.* In 1929, she attended the court hearing to decide whether DHL's pictures, seized in the Warren Gallery exhibition, should be destroyed. DHL's last letter to her came in January 1930. After his death, Philip Morrell helped Frieda negotiate a settlement of DHL's estate with his brother and sister. "Ottoline's life, Philip apart, was based on three great friendships--Lawrence, Lytton [Strachey], and Russell."

4473 Davis, Robert Gorham. "Introduction," in *Sons and Lovers,* by D. H. Lawrence (Avon, CT: Printed for the Limited Editions Club, 1975), pp. v-x.

One of the strengths of *Sons and Lovers* is that the "central story needs no interpreting. Nor do the symbols." It is clear from DHL's "letter to his editor David [sic] Garnett" that this was his "own story--or what he thought was his story." [Discussion of the biographical background includes DHL's leading the country in the King's Scholarship examinations, his teaching, and his friendship with Jessie Chambers.] Jessie worked with DHL on two versions of the novel; "the final version, done with furious intensity abroad in the fall of 1912, had come under a radically different influence," namely Frieda Weekley's. Although the first part of the novel is "still close to the social realism of Arnold Bennett and H. G. Wells, the second part...is written with an imaginative sensibility startling to readers of the English novel." "For Lawrence intangible feelings are always fused with the precise tangibility of objects, places, and--above all--action," as when Paul and Clara make love by the river. Later DHL used his novels as vehicles for his message, but *Sons and Lovers* still "bears the stamp" of its origin.

4474 de Filippis, Simonetta. "La fiamma e il volto: studio filologico dell'ideologia del *David* di D. H. Lawrence" (The Flame and the Face: A Philological Study of the Ideology of D. H. Lawrence's *David*), ANNALI ISTITUTO UNIVERSITARIO ORIENTALE, NAPOLI, SEZIONE GERMANICA-ANGLISTICA, XVIII, No. 3 (1975), 7-84.

A direct comparison of DHL's *David* with 1 Samuel 15-20 and a study of DHL's deviation from the biblical text bring to light the ideological implications of the play as well as its general meaning and the author's specific message. In David DHL sees the beginning of a new world-view which replaces the primitive and natural one represented by Saul and the evolution of which will eventually lead to modern Western society. In the final moments of the play DHL expresses the hope of a return to a more meaningful and authentic way of life and religious spirit, as opposed to the prevailing values of industrial civilization. [In Italian.]

4475 Delany, Paul. "Lawrence and E. M. Forster: Two Rainbows," D. H. LAWRENCE REVIEW, VIII (Spring 1975), 54-62.

DHL's sketch representing "Ursula's climactic vision of the rainbow" in the final scene of *The Rainbow* is "indebted to iconographic traditions" which influenced DHL's philosophy at this time and which were epitomized in three paintings: Fra Angelico's *The Last Judgement,* Hans Memling's *Last Judgement,* and Raphael's

Ansidei Madonna. To these should be added another rainbow vision that DHL "was freshly acquainted with": the design by Roger Fry which decorated "the front and rear endpapers" of E. M. Forster's THE CELESTIAL OMNIBUS (1911). In Fry's design, "the bridge between this earth and heaven is a rainbow"; in DHL's drawing, both feet of the bow are set in "the old world: one on the colliery, the other on one of the 'brittle, hard edged new houses.' " The differences between the two "help to define" the opposition between Forster and DHL. "Forster's rainbow points forward in space and time, a symbol of connection and continuity; Lawrence's is a chiliastic sign set athwart the flow of history to mark an epoch of cosmic destruction and rebirth." [Illustrated with black and white reproductions of DHL's sketch for *The Rainbow,* Memling's *Last Judgement,* Raphael's *Ansidei Madonna,* and Fry's design for THE CELESTIAL OMNIBUS.]

4476 Delavenay, Émile. " 'Making Another Lawrence': Frieda and the Lawrence Legend," D. H. LAWRENCE REVIEW, VIII (Spring 1975), 80-98.

"The function of criticism...to inform" is well served by Harry T. Moore's THE PRIEST OF LOVE: A LIFE OF D. H. LAWRENCE (1974), though Moore glosses over DHL's political ideas and his anti-semitism. Contemporary comments, however, completely contradict Martin Green's assertion, in THE VON RICHTHOFEN SISTERS: THE TRIUMPHANT AND THE TRAGIC MODES OF LOVE: ELSE AND FRIEDA VON RICHTHOFEN, OTTO GROSS, MAX WEBER, AND D. H. LAWRENCE IN THE YEARS 1870-1970 (1974), that Frieda was the "maker" of DHL's genius. "Much of what is valuable" in Green's book "is spoilt by a casual approach to facts and disregard for the painful necessities of scholarly presentation." [Some seven pages are devoted to setting the record straight in a point-by-point correction of what the author asserts are factual inaccuracies, misquotations, proofreading errors, and misleading use of evidence in Green's book.] Robert Lucas's FRIEDA LAWRENCE: THE STORY OF FRIEDA VON RICHTHOFEN AND D. H. LAWRENCE (1972, English trans by Geoffrey Skelton 1974) is excellent in "factual presentation" but tedious in its "explanatory digressions." [Review essay. See also reply by Harry T. Moore, in "Laurentiana," D. H. LAWRENCE REVIEW, VIII (Summer 1975), 242-46; and supportive comment by Helen Corke, in "Laurentiana," D. H. LAWRENCE REVIEW, VIII (Fall 1975), 378-79.]

4477 D. H. LAWRENCE REVIEW, ed by James C. Cowan, VIII, No. 1 (Spring 1975).

Contents, abstracted under 1975: Michael L. Ross, "Lawrence's Second 'Sun,' " pp. 1-18; Leslie M. Thompson, "The Christ Who Didn't Die: Analogues to D. H. Lawrence's *The Man Who Died,*" pp. 19-30; Keith Cushman, "D. H. Lawrence at Work: 'The Shadow in the Rose Garden,' " pp. 31-46; Keith Sagar, "The Genesis of 'Bavarian Gentians,' " pp. 47-53; Paul Delany, "Lawrence and E. M. Forster: Two Rainbows," pp. 54-62; Langdon Elsbree (ed), "On the Teaching of D. H. Lawrence: A Forum," pp. 63-79 [includes Joanne Trautmann, "The Body Electric," pp. 65-68; Sanford Pinsker, "Confessions of a Lawrentian Manqué," pp. 68-71; William R. Lowery, "Trivium," pp. 71-74; and James Cox, "Pollyanalytics and Pedagogy: Teaching Lawrence's Short Stories," pp. 74-77, all abstracted separately]; Émile Delavenay, " 'Making Another Lawrence': Frieda and the Lawrence Legend," pp. 80-98; Richard D. Beards, "The Checklist of D. H. Lawrence Criticism and Scholarship, 1974," pp. 99-105; Dennis Jackson, "Theses on D. H. Lawrence: Bibliographical Addenda," pp. 106-12; "Laurentiana," pp. 113-18 [not abstracted]; "Research in Progress," pp. 119-21 [not abstracted]; "Contributors," pp. 122-24 [not abstracted].

4478 D. H. LAWRENCE REVIEW, ed by James C. Cowan, VIII, No. 2 (Summer 1975).
Contents, abstracted under 1975: Michael Squires, "Scenic Construction and Rhetorical Signals in Hardy and Lawrence," pp. 125-46; Chaman Nahal, "The Colour Ambience of Lawrence's Early and Later Poetry," pp. 147-54; Evelyn Shakir, " 'Secret Sin': Lawrence's Early Verse," pp. 155-75; Keith Cushman, " 'I am going through a transition stage': *The Prussian Officer* and *The Rainbow*," pp. 176-97; Charles L. Ross, "The Composition of *Women in Love*: A History, 1913-1919," pp. 198-212; Evelyn J. Hinz, "Lawrence at the MLA, 1974: A Critique," pp. 213-19 [not abstracted]; Kingsley Widmer, "Lawrence as Abnormal Artist," pp. 220-32; Toshitaka Shirai, "A Checklist of Theses on Lawrence in Japan, 1968-1973," pp. 233-35; Dennis Jackson, "Doctoral Dissertations on D. H. Lawrence: Bibliographical Addenda," pp. 236-41; "Laurentiana," pp. 242-50 [only Letter to the Editor from Harry T. Moore is abstracted]; "Research in Progress," p. 251 [not abstracted]; "Contributors," pp. 252-53 [not abstracted].

4479 D. H. LAWRENCE REVIEW, ed by James C. Cowan, VIII, No. 3 ["D. H. Lawrence and Women"] (Fall 1975).
Contents, abstracted under 1975: Charles Rossman, " 'You are the call and I am the answer': D. H. Lawrence and Women," pp. 255-328; Eleanor H. Green, "Schopenhauer and D. H. Lawrence on Sex and Love," pp. 329-45; Virginia Hyde, "Will Brangwen and Paradisal Vision in *The Rainbow* and *Women in Love*," pp. 346-57; Lucia Henning Heldt, "Lawrence on Love: The Courtship and Marriage of Tom Brangwen and Lydia Lensky," pp. 358-70; Brian Finney and Michael L. Ross, "The Two Versions of 'Sun': An Exchange," pp. 371-74; "Laurentiana," pp. 375-80 [only Letter to Émile Delavenay from Helen Corke is abstracted]; "Research in Progress," pp. 381-82 [not abstracted]; "Contributors," p. 383, and "Index to Volume VIII," pp. 384-85 [not abstracted].

4480 D. H. LAWRENCE STUDIES (Kyôto), No. 3, *"Musuko to Koibito"* (*Sons and Lovers* Number) (Sept 1975).
Contents, abstracted under 1975: Sadanobu Kai, "Introducing the *Sons and Lovers* Number," pp. 1-2; Hirokazu Yoshimura, "*Musuko to Koibito* ni Okeru Niku to Kotoba--Sono 'Jogen' o Megutte no Ichikôsatsu" (*Sons and Lovers* and Its Foreword), pp. 3-30; Keiichi Okano, "*Musuko to Koibito* no Higeki--Morel-Fujin ni Mirareru Kikai-Bunmei ni yoru Hakaisei no Shiten yori" (The Tragedy of *Sons and Lovers*--From a Viewpoint of Mrs. Morel's Destructiveness Caused by Machine Civilization), pp. 31-49; Masako Yoshida, "Yami no Sekai e no Tabidachi--Morel-Fujin no Shi ga Imisuru Mono" (A Journey to "Darkness"--What the Death of Mrs. Morel Means), pp. 51-82; Masuko Fujiwara, "*Musuko to Koibito* ni Okeru

Ai no Yukue" (*Sons and Lovers:* How Does Paul's Love Go?), pp. 83-108; Akano Sano, "Paul Morel's Transfiguration in Love," pp. 109-31; Yasushi Sugiyama, "Shinda Musuko to Uchû no Rizumu" (The Son Who Died in the Rhythm of the Universe), pp. 133-56; Haruko Imaizumi, "*Musuko to Koibito* ni Okeru Shûkyôsei" (The "Religions" in *Sons and Lovers*), pp. 157-83; Kaien Kitazaki, "*Musuko to Koibito* ni Okeru Shûkyôteki Sokumen ni Tsuite (Paul no Motomeru 'Kami' no Imi o Megutte)" (Paul's God: A Study of Religious Aspects in *Sons and Lovers*), pp. 185-98; Minoru Nishida, "*Musuko to Koibito* no Okeru Tankyû no Imi to Kôzô" (The Meaning and Structure of Paul's Quest in *Sons and Lovers*), pp. 199-220; "Synopses" [in English], pp. 221-45 [not abstracted]; "*Sons and Lovers* Bibliography," pp. 247-58 [not abstracted]. [In Japanese.]

4481 "D. H. Lawrence's Letters to Catherine Carswell," YALE UNIVERSITY LIBRARY GAZETTE, XLIX, No. 3 (Jan 1975), 253-60.

[Contains the text of seven letters by DHL, with a short introduction and a brief explanation of the circumstances surrounding each letter.] The authenticity of Catherine Carswell's account of DHL in THE SAVAGE PILGRIMAGE: A NARRATIVE OF D. H. LAWRENCE (1932) is enhanced by her quotations from this set of letters, now held by the Yale University Library.

4482 Doré, Joseph, III. "D. H. Lawrence: In Search of the Big 'O,' " DISSERTATION ABSTRACTS INTERNATIONAL, XXXVI (1976), 6699A-6700A. Unpublished dissertation, University of North Carolina at Chapel Hill, 1975.

[On DHL's philosophy in *Psychoanalysis and the Unconscious, Fantasia of the Unconscious, Reflections on the Death of a Porcupine and Other Essays*, "The Two Principles," and *Women in Love*.]

4483 Elsbree, Langdon (ed). "On the Teaching of D. H. Lawrence: A Forum," D. H. LAWRENCE REVIEW, VIII (Spring 1975), 63-79.

[The forum includes introductory comments by Elsbree in which he raises several questions pertinent to the teaching of DHL's work; a sample examination is included in Appendix A, pp. 78-79. Contributions to the forum, abstracted separately under 1975: Joanne Trautmann, "The Body Electric," pp. 65-68; Sanford Pinsker, "Confessions of a Lawrentian Manqué," pp. 68-71; William R. Lowery, "Trivium," pp. 71-74; and James Cox, "Pollyanalytics and Pedagogy: Teaching Lawrence's Short Fiction," pp. 74-77.]

4484 Farrer, Edward Alfred. "The Quest for Being: D. H. Lawrence and Hermann Hesse," DISSERTATION ABSTRACTS INTERNATIONAL, XXXVI (1976), 6671A. Unpublished dissertation, Purdue University, 1975.

4485 Fielding, Michael L. NOTES ON D. H. LAWRENCE'S "SONS AND LOVERS" (Lond: Methuen Educational, 1975).

[Study guide to *Sons and Lovers*.]

4486 Finney, Brian H. "D. H. Lawrence's Progress to Maturity: From Holograph Manuscript to Final Publication of *The Prussian Officer and Other Stories*," STUDIES IN BIBLIOGRAPHY, XXVIII (1975), 321-32.

Two important points emerge from an examination of all the known versions of the twelve stories published in *The Prussian Officer and Other Stories* in 1914. First, every story in the volume was written, rewritten, or revised in 1913 or 1914. The revisions DHL undertook in July 1913 and July 1914 were of a sufficiently drastic nature to warrant dating all the stories in his first collection as the work of 1913-1914. Second, this means that the *Prussian Officer* volume comprises DHL's only fiction between *Sons and Lovers,* a novel in the nineteenth-century tradition, and his next revolutionary, forward-looking book, *The Rainbow*. The enormous gulf separating these two quite different novels is bridged by the short stories. On the basis of an analysis of three of these stories, "The White Stocking," "The Shadow in the Rose Garden," and "Daughters of the Vicar," one may conclude that, in 1913 and 1914, DHL learned to replace a reliance on plotted events by an emphasis on internal feelings, to replace an appeal to sentimentality by a sterner regard for psychological realism, and to replace an intrusive use of autobiographical material by narrative objectivity.

4487 Finney, Brian H. "A Newly Discovered Text of D. H. Lawrence's 'The Lovely Lady,'" YALE UNIVERSITY LIBRARY GAZETTE, XLIX, No. 3 (Jan 1975), 245-52.

The corrected typescript of DHL's short story "The Lovely Lady" in Yale University Library is twice the length of its first published appearance in Lady Cynthia Asquith's THE BLACK CAP: NEW STORIES OF MURDER AND MYSTERY (1927). The shorter, later version is more subtle and less dogmatic than the earlier, longer version.

4488 Finney, Brian, and Michael L. Ross. "The Two Versions of 'Sun': An Exchange," D. H. LAWRENCE REVIEW, VIII (Fall 1975), 371-74.

[Critical exchange including Brian Finney's reply to Michael L. Ross, "Lawrence's Second 'Sun,'" D. H. LAWRENCE REVIEW, VIII (Spring 1975), 1-18; and Ross's rejoinder to Finney.] **Finney**: Evidence supports Keith Sagar's assertion that the 1926 version of "Sun" was expurgated and the 1928 "Black Sun" version unexpurgated. DHL's correspondence indicates that the first version of "Sun" was not only "long" but also "too sexually explicit." "To accept Ross's assumptions one has to see Lawrence as acting in a highly uncharacteristic manner--motivated by greed and deliberately misleading his purchaser with untruths." **Ross**: Finney's evidence is inconclusive and confusing; it says nothing about the internal evidence arising from Ross's comparison of the texts of the two versions of "Sun." DHL would hardly have "exerted himself in 1926 to produce a version not simply shorter and less sexually explicit" but also "far inferior in its diction, structure," and imagery.

4489 Freedman, Richard. THE NOVEL (NY: Newsweek Books, 1975), pp. 13, 119, 121, 122-23, 125, 168-70.

D. H. LAWRENCE

[After a brief biographical sketch, incorrectly identifying Frieda as the "sister of the famous German air ace of World War I," the author comments briefly on DHL's major novels: *Sons and Lovers* is his "great" autobiographical novel. *The Rainbow* and *Women in Love* are "tender in their evocations of love and psychologically acute in their analysis of the conflicting love demands of the sexes." "The older and sicker Lawrence became, however, the more shrill and didactic his tone was to grow, so that such late novels as *The Plumed Serpent* and *Lady Chatterley's Lover* resemble not so much novels as impassioned sermons on the proper relations of the sexes in a modern world devoid of religion, myth, and ritual and given over to a materialistic use of sex." The opening passage of *The Rainbow* is quoted in a section entitled "Great Beginnings."]

4490 Frise, Maria. "M.'s Geheimnis. Unsere Neue Erzählung: 'Der Fremdenlegionär' " (M's Secret. Our New Story: "Introduction to MEMOIRS OF THE FOREIGN LEGION"), FRANKFURTER ALLGEMEINE ZEITUNG, 26 March 1975.

[Introduction to the German translation of DHL's "Introduction to MEMOIRS OF THE FOREIGN LEGION."] DHL's "story" is based on his acquaintance with the American adventurer Maurice Magnus. It is free from the ordinary Laurentian message. Despite his dislike of some of M's traits, DHL tries to do him justice and to probe into the failure and tragic end of M's life. But he does not completely succeed in solving M's secret. [In German.]

4491 Fujiwara, Masuko. "*Musuko to Koibito* ni Okeru Ai no Yukue" (*Sons and Lovers:* How Does Paul's Love Go?), D. H. LAWRENCE STUDIES (Kyôto), No. 3 (Sept 1975), 83-108.

Three women--Paul's mother, Miriam, and Clara--are pictured in *Sons and Lovers* as if they were so selfish and destructive that Paul had to be broken to pieces, but actually, each of them gave him what was essential for his growth as a man. The most greedy and egocentric person in the novel was Paul himself. [In Japanese.]

4492 Fussell, Paul. THE GREAT WAR AND MODERN MEMORY (NY & Lond: Oxford UP, 1975), pp. 23, 76, 90, 174, 220, 233, 244, 276, 314.

DHL's objectification of the "nice sexless Englishman" and his designation of "the adversary in *Kangaroo*" as the "jackals" who stayed at home and "bit us all" so that "blood-poisoning and mortification set in" are like other objectifications of a faceless enemy in the Great War. Unable to describe the war in any but traditional literary language, such writers as Joyce, Eliot, DHL, Pound, and Yeats "were not present at the front to induct them into the new idiom which might have done the job better." It is "entirely English" that DHL, in the scene in *Lady Chatterley's Lover* where the lovers decorate each other's genitals, "should particularize so knowledgeably and precisely" the flowers used. Employing the red flower imagery idiomatic to Great War descriptions of combat, DHL, in "Bombardment," "conceives the town being bombed as 'a flat red lily with a million petals.' "

4493 Ghiselin, Brewster. "D. H. Lawrence and the Peacocks of Atrani," MICHIGAN QUARTERLY REVIEW, XIV (Spring 1975), 119-34.

The peacocks in the church of San Salvatore di Bireto resemble DHL's phoenix, which is a combination of the eagle, the peacock, and the serpent. DHL may have seen the Atrani peacocks in either 1920 or 1926. In DHL's fiction, the serpent is flame, as in *The Man Who Died,* lifting toward the consummation of the phoenix; the serpent curled in a circle, as in *The Plumed Serpent,* is flame sunken into darkness. The serpent, sometimes only implied by the reptilian nature of the peacock aspect of the image, may symbolize the ouroboros, the state of undifferentiation; the eagle aspect of the image may symbolize transcendence realized as action or enactment, as in Will's phoenix in *The Rainbow.*

4494 Gillie, Christopher. "D. H. Lawrence (1885-1930)," MOVEMENTS IN ENGLISH LITERATURE 1900-1940 (Lond & NY: Cambridge UP, 1975), pp. 47-64.

DHL was the first major English novelist of working-class origins. His background accounts for the two distinctive features of his fiction: his disregard for social and stylistic amenities of language and his insistence "that a human being has an identity (an 'ego') beyond the identity that his ordinary social relationships endow him with." DHL believed that it was his mission to show that "social stereotypes had become a tyranny" and that man "was fighting a deadly battle with himself in the dark, not recognizing the enemy as the false idea of himself." The basic aims of DHL's fiction become evident through analysis of *Sons and Lovers, The Fox, The Rainbow,* and *Women in Love.*

4495 Green, Eleanor. "Schopenhauer and D. H. Lawrence on Sex and Love," D. H. LAWRENCE REVIEW, VIII (Fall 1975), 329-45.

In Mrs. Rudolf Dircks's 1897 translation of Schopenhauer's essays, DHL made careful annotations in the chapter entitled "The Metaphysic of Love." This essay discusses the sections of that chapter which DHL marked as particularly relevant, reviews "Schopenhauer's main arguments concerning sex and love," and explores "the use Lawrence made of these ideas in his own work." [Discussion of Schopenhauer's ideas in the chapter.] "The difference in the basic attitudes" of DHL and Schopenhauer is seen in the different "value they place upon life and the will to live." While DHL sometimes accepts Schopenhauer's "withdrawal from the world," "he then also insists on a return to the empirical world and an active participation" in it. With DHL's affirmation of life comes a strong affirmation of the sexual passion. Neither writer thinks that love "brings happiness," and both "condemn sexual promiscuity." But whereas Schopenhauer sees all marriage as an invitation to calamity, DHL upholds marriage as a condition essential to individual fulfillment. Both DHL and Schopenhauer, however, believing that "they had suffered greatly from the role their mothers had played in their lives," "try to discount the importance of maternal love."

4496 Green, Eleanor H. "The *Wille zur Macht* and D. H. Lawrence," MASSACHUSETTS STUDIES IN ENGLISH, V, No. 2 (1975), 25-30.

DHL's condemnation of Nietzsche's *Wille zur Macht* was the result of DHL's misunderstanding of the philosophical idea, which actually resembles his own conception of the "will to power."

4497 Haegert, John W. "Brothers and Lovers: D. H. Lawrence and the Theme of Friendship," SOUTHERN REVIEW (Adelaide, South Australia), VIII (March 1975), 39-50.

Several of DHL's novels have the "special view of friendship" implied in his 1918 statement calling for a return to " 'the old passion of deathless friendship between man and man.' " In *The White Peacock,* "the friendship of George and Cyril. . . stands forth in vivid contrast" to the many "betrayals of one lover by another." In *The Trespasser,* "the deficiencies of erotic partnership are most plainly revealed in a conversation between" Siegmund and Hampson. In *Sons and Lovers,* the fight between Paul Morel and Baxter Dawes is employed "as a means of developing spiritual intimacy between two natural antagonists." Although Gerald refuses Birkin's offer of *Blutbrüderschaft* earlier in *Women in Love,* in the wrestling scene, "Lawrence uses the rhetoric of erotic love to suggest the intensity and profundity of male friendship--a bond no less 'normal' for its physical vitality than the sexual love between man and woman." In *Aaron's Rod,* "the physical intimacy" of Lilly's massaging Aaron's body suggests "a mystical transference of sensual energy." DHL "politicized the role of friendship in *Kangaroo*": Somers repudiates both Cooley's paternalism and Struthers's comradely "merging" without instinctive darkness and individuality. In "Education of the People," DHL still proclaims: " 'Marriage and deathless friendship, both should be inviolable and sacred,' " as complementary "creative passions." [See also reply and further discussion by John Edge, "D. H. Lawrence and the Theme of Comradeship," SOUTHERN REVIEW (Adelaide, South Australia), IX (March 1976), 34-49; and rejoinder by John W. Haegert, "Turning One's Back on Lawrence; Or, The Function of Friendship Once More," SOUTHERN REVIEW (Adelaide, South Australia), XI (March 1978), 72-89.]

4498 Hahn, Emily. LORENZO: D. H. LAWRENCE AND THE WOMEN WHO LOVED HIM (Phila & NY: Lippincott, 1975).

[A popular biography, with chapters organized around the women important in DHL's life: Lydia Lawrence, Jessie Chambers, Helen Corke, Louisa Burrows, Frieda von Richthofen Lawrence, Ivy Low, Lady Ottoline Morrell, Hilda Doolittle, Cecily Lambert and Violet Monk, Mary Cannan, Mabel Dodge Luhan, and Dorothy Brett. The work is designed for those who have no previous knowledge of DHL's life.]

4499 Harmer, J. B. VICTORY IN LIMBO: IMAGISM 1908-1917 (NY: St. Martin's P, 1975), pp. 1, 8, 23, 41, 43, 99-103, 110, 112, 152.

Up to 1915 DHL's poetic affinities were with the Georgians. Ford Madox Hueffer introduced DHL's poems in THE ENGLISH REVIEW in 1909, and DHL was among the contributors to three of Edward Marsh's anthologies of GEORGIAN POETRY. He also contributed to three anthologies of SOME IMAGIST POETS, edited by Amy Lowell 1915 to 1917. DHL "did not regard himself as an imagist," however, and "his relations to the movement were tangential." Ezra Pound admired DHL's Nottinghamshire dialect verse as in "Violets," but DHL's first "recognizably modernist poems," such as "Mosquito," were written in 1920. Although chiefly remembered as a prose writer, DHL produced some animal and nature poems of "remarkable insight and power" in *Birds, Beasts and Flowers*. He "remained unaffected by the newer French poetry," and his later verse frequently employs "the long Whitmanesque line."

4500 Heldt, Lucia Henning. "Lawrence on Love: The Courtship and Marriage of Tom Brangwen and Lydia Lensky," D. H. LAWRENCE REVIEW, VIII (Fall 1975), 358-70.

In *The Rainbow*, "the courtship and marriage of Tom Brangwen and Lydia Lensky [sets] the standard by which all of the other sexual involvements can be judged and [provides]...a rare, fully developed example of exactly what Lawrence has in mind when he speaks of love." DHL presents their marriage as encompassing "both the movement towards unity and the movement towards separateness." "Not until their reconciliation scene" in Chapter III "do the lovers finally approach the mysterious 'other,' " thus dramatizing DHL's "belief that the individual only...exists within a relationship."

4501 Hinz, Evelyn J. "Lawrence at the MLA, 1974: A Commentary," D. H. LAWRENCE REVIEW, VIII (Summer 1975), 213-19.

[Critique of the seminar on DHL presented at the Modern Language Association convention, 27 Dec 1974. The four papers--by Chaman L. Nahal, Evelyn Shakir, Keith Cushman, and Charles L. Ross--are published in the D. H. LAWRENCE REVIEW, VIII (Summer 1975).]

4502 Hyde, Virginia. "Will Brangwen and Paradisal Vision in *The Rainbow* and *Women in Love*," D. H. LAWRENCE REVIEW, VIII (Fall 1975), 346-57.

A comparison of the paradisal motifs surrounding both Will and Ursula in *The Rainbow* and *Women in Love* shows that Ursula's capacity for visionary experience is related to that of her father. Ursula's and Birkin's achievement of "successful union" "is expressed in terms recalling Will's mystical commitments...: his love of church architecture, music, ritual, and Biblical scenes." No degradation in Will can negate this triumphant transmission to Ursula of the quality of vision which has fed her soul and which she, in turn, transmits to Birkin. DHL's language in conveying these visionary experiences indicates, in similarities of diction and imagery, "the intended parallelism among these characters," though Will clings "too exclusively to old forms" while "the Birkins' more open-minded and active response to visionary experience allows a resurgence of faith in life's ineffable dimensions."

4503 Imaizumi, Haruko. "*Musuko to Koibito* ni Okeru Shûkyôsei" (The "Religions" in *Sons and Lovers*), D. H. LAWRENCE STUDIES (Kyôto), No. 3 (Sept 1975), 157-83.

In *Sons and Lovers*, Mrs. Morel's and Paul's religions correspond respectively to the authoritarian religion and the humanistic religion, the two kinds of religion distinguished by Erich Fromm in his theory of religion. By describing Paul's rejection of Mrs. Morel, DHL criticizes and protests against the idolized or authoritarian traditional religion in Europe. [In Japanese.]

4504 Ito, Chikai. "Lawrence ni Okeru 'Otoko' no Keifu (I) (*Sons and Lovers* no Baai)" (The Development of "Manhood" in the Novels of Lawrence [I] : On *Sons and Lovers*), APOSTOLOS (Kyôto University of Education), No. 1 (June 1975), 12-17.

In *Sons and Lovers,* there is an affinity between the Walter-Gertrude and Baxter-Clara relationships. Having tried in vain to reconcile his father with his mother, Paul Morel tries to actualize the reconciliation between Baxter and Clara Dawes in compensation for his former frustrated effort. Although he is unconscious of the meaning of the act, Paul attempts in this way to escape being wholly swallowed up into the mother's world. At the end of the novel, he accepts his father's world. [In Japanese.]

4505 Jackson, Dennis. "Doctoral Dissertations on D. H. Lawrence: Bibliographical Addenda," D. H. LAWRENCE REVIEW, VIII (Summer 1975), 236-41.

[An expansion and continuation of two previous checklists: G. B. Crump, "Doctoral Dissertations on D. H. Lawrence, 1931-1969: A Bibliography," D. H. LAWRENCE REVIEW, III (Spring 1970), 80-86; and Gerald M. Garmon, "Doctoral Dissertations on D. H. Lawrence: Bibliographical Addenda," D. H. LAWRENCE REVIEW, V (Summer 1972), 170-73.]

4506 Jackson, Dennis. "Theses on D. H. Lawrence: Bibliographical Addenda," D. H. LAWRENCE REVIEW, VIII (Spring 1975), 106-12.

[An expansion and continuation of a previous checklist: Gerald Garmon, Patsy C. Howard, and Edmund A. Bojarski, "Theses on D. H. Lawrence: 1931-1972: A Bibliography with Addenda of Senior Theses and Works in Progress," D. H. LAWRENCE REVIEW, VI (Summer 1973), 217-30. See also Toshitaka Shirai, "A Checklist of Theses on Lawrence in Japan, 1968-1973," D. H. LAWRENCE REVIEW, VIII (Summer 1975), 233-35.]

4507 Jacobus, Mary. "Sue the Obscure," ESSAYS IN CRITICISM, XXV (July 1975), 304-28, espec pp. 305-7.

In *Study of Thomas Hardy*, DHL sees Jude in JUDE THE OBSCURE "as divided between the male and female within himself." DHL's influential view of Sue Bridehead's character is that with the female principle atrophied in her, "she embodies the male principle." Since she "is at once self-possessed and self-divided, sexual consummation can only bring desecration to her and negation to Jude," a view that does violence to the complexity of the novel but that "remains surprisingly current."

4508 Janik, Del Ivan. "D. H. Lawrence's 'Future Religion': The Unity of *Last Poems*," TEXAS STUDIES IN LITERATURE AND LANGUAGE, XVI (Winter 1975), 739-54.

The notebook which includes "Bavarian Gentians" and "The Ship of Death," posthumously published as *Last Poems,* is a cohesively organized work expressing

DHL's conviction that life is preparation for death and ultimate rebirth.

4509 Jarrett-Kerr, Martin. "D. H. Lawrence and 'The Spirit of Place,'" in DER ENGLISCHE ESSAY: ANALYSEN (The English Essay: Analyses), ed by Horst Weber (Darmstadt: Wissenschaftliche Buchgesellschaft, 1975), pp. 308-19.

DHL's essays are of three types: literary criticism, "pollyanalytics," and description (nature, travel, activities). [Brief discussion of extracts from each type, including "Fireworks in Florence," the Review of THE WORLD OF WILLIAM CLISSOLD by H. G. Wells, and *Study of Thomas Hardy*.] The first version of "The Spirit of Place" (1918), which establishes American literature as a subject distinct from English literature, contains the substance, though not the phrasing, of DHL's critical dictum, "'Never trust the artist. Trust the tale.'" The tone of the later version (1923) is more chatty, journalistic, and infelicitous in phrasing, and its purpose is more didactic. [Analysis of extracts from the first version demonstrate the organization and figurative language which prepare for DHL's ultimate generalization: "that man can put his prints on his environment, but only because he is already a part of it, and it has already put its distinctive prints on him."]

4510 Jones, David A. "The Third Unrealized Wonder--The Reality of Relation in D. H. Lawrence and Martin Buber," RELIGION AND LIFE, XLIV (Summer 1975), 178-87.

Although neither writer had an influence on the other, DHL and Martin Buber made similar analyses of modern life and offered similar "proposals for restoring meaning to it." Both men recognized and lamented the objectification of experience which accompanied the machine age and believed that life had become "increasingly rationalized" as the significance of the individual diminished. Both writers examined their own experiences in order "to communicate the reality of relationship as the basis for a new kind of knowledge." DHL concerned himself with sexual relationships, hoping to remedy the idealization of erotic experience; he believed that people had "gotten their sex in their heads, whereas...'the root of sanity' is in the genitals." In DHL's view, however, the integrity of the individual must precede successful relationship, since the individual precedes the universe; but it is successful relationship between man and woman which holds the universe together. "The third, unrealized wonder," then, is the dimension of experience which neither derives entirely from the individual nor deprives him of his uniqueness; it is what lies *between* a man and a woman. For Buber, likewise, the "heart of reality" is "betweenness," although it is not perceived exclusively in sexual terms, as it is in the case of DHL.

4511 Jordan, Francis X. "Archetypal Patterns in the Poetry of D. H. Lawrence," DISSERTATION ABSTRACTS INTERNATIONAL, XXXVII (1976), 2197A. Unpublished dissertation, Saint Louis University, 1975.

4512 Kabiljo-Šutić, Simha. "Lorensova poetika" (Lawrence's Poetics), VIDICI, No. 171 (1975), 9.

[DHL's poetic theory.] [In Serbo-Croatian.]

4513 Kai, Sadanobu. "Introducing the *Sons and Lovers* Number," D. H. LAWRENCE STUDIES (Kyôto), No. 3 (Sept 1975), 1-2.

The description in *Sons and Lovers,* Chap. I, of the unborn Paul Morel's melting with his mother reveals that the pattern of DHL's literary work derives from his own blood relationship. [In Japanese.]

4514 Kanzaki, Takashi. "D. H. Lawrence: Sono Kansei ni Tsuite" (D. H. Lawrence: His Sensibility), BULLETIN OF THE FACULTY OF FOREIGN STUDIES (Kitakyûshû University), No. 26 (March 1975), 1-24.

[In Japanese.]

4515 Kegel-Brinkgreve, E. "The Dionysian Tramline," DUTCH QUARTERLY REVIEW OF ANGLO-AMERICAN LETTERS, V, No. 2 (1975), 180-94.

In "Tickets, Please," the female tram conductors, in their attack on John Thomas, led by Annie Stone in a role parallel to that of Agaue, re-enact the frenzied Dionysian religious ritual of the Maenads' rending to pieces of King Pentheus, as dramatized in Euripides' THE BACCHAE. If we are prepared to accept this parallel, "there are many details which can be interpreted as having double meaning, providing links between the two stories." [Detailed examples are given.]

4516 Kester, Joseph. "Sculptural Character in Lawrence's *Women in Love,*" MODERN FICTION STUDIES, XXI (Winter 1975-1976), 543-52.

DHL's theoretical and practical interest in art is reflected in *Women in Love* and other novels. In "Introduction to These Paintings" he finds only in Cézanne a reversal of the trend toward bloodless intellectualizing and a movement toward " 'intuitive apperception' " and physical wholeness. DHL's letter to Edward Garnett (5 June 1914) emphasizes his concern with " 'physiology of matter' " and cites the theories of Marinetti and the Futurists. DHL's " 'another language' " is an attempt to go beyond the temporal art of fiction and the two-dimensional visual art of painting to the three-dimensional art of sculpture. In *The Rainbow* he uses Impressionism in such scenes as Tom Brangwen's return after proposing to Lydia Lensky. But he employs the sculptural analogy in such examples as Tom's committing himself "into her hands" and the descriptions of Lincoln Cathedral. In *Women in Love,* imagery of spatial art defined the characters: Halliday is compared to Christ in a Pietà, Gerald's body in "Gladiatorial" and elsewhere to a beautiful plastic form. While "the essence of the novel is temporality," DHL attempted, by his sculptural conception of characterization in *Women in Love,* the timelessness of non-dimensional space.

4517 King, Nancy. "D. H. Lawrence and German Expressionism." Unpublished dissertation, McGill University, 1975. [Listed in D. H. LAWRENCE REVIEW, VIII (Summer 1975), 239.]

4518 Kinkead-Weekes, Mark. "This Old Maid: Jane Austen Replies to Charlotte Brontë and D. H. Lawrence," NINETEENTH CENTURY FICTION, XXX (Dec 1975), 399-419.

The "passionate individualism" of DHL underlies his "implicit belief that the social is ultimately less real than the private world" and thus accounts for his characterization of Jane Austen as an "old maid" who has set herself apart from vital experience. In DHL's opinion, Austen's lack of imaginative sympathy for her characters causes her to uphold the values of "knowing in apartness" (i.e., rationally and scientifically), as opposed to "knowing in togetherness" (religiously and poetically). Austen's technique can be vindicated partly by the necessity for detachment dictated by the ironic mode in which she has chosen to write; however, beneath the ironic surface there is also "a very humane if deliberately indirect concern with the heart and its deceptions." A contrast between the scene in Sotherton Chapel in MANSFIELD PARK and DHL's cathedral scene in *The Rainbow* reveals Austen's emphasis on the church's "sanction for moral and social value" and DHL's concern with the nature of religious experience and symbols. Austen's further development as a novelist shows that she anticipated DHL's criticism of her fiction.

4519 Kitazaki, Kaien. "*Musuko to Koibito* ni Okeru Shûkyôteki Sokumen ni Tsuite (Paul no Motomeru 'Kami' no Imi o Megutte)" (Paul's God: A Study of Religious Aspects in *Sons and Lovers*), D. H. LAWRENCE STUDIES (Kyôto), No. 3 (Sept 1975), 185-98.

DHL is undeniably a religious writer, but in what respects is he religious? The religious aspects of *Sons and Lovers*, chiefly the meaning of Paul's God, are considered. [In Japanese.]

4520 Koga, Masakazu. "Morel-Ke no Kattô o Megutte" (On the Trouble between the Morels), STUDIES IN FOREIGN LITERATURES (Ritsumeikan University), No. 32 (March 1975), 25-36.

In DHL's biographical novel *Sons and Lovers*, the fatherly principles are opposed to the motherly principles. Paul repels the vulgar characteristics in his mother, but he cannot be wholly on the side of his father. With the death of his mother at the end of the novel, however, Paul begins to make his own way. [In Japanese.]

4521 Koljevič, Svetozar. "Poruke i granice Lorensove umetnosti" (The Messages and Limits of Lawrence's Art), RADOVI A NI U BI H, LVI (1975), Odejeljenje za knjizevnost/umjetnost, Book 2, pp. 75-84. [In Serbo-Croatian.]

4522 Konishi, Nagatomo. D. H. RORENSU SHIJIN TO CHATAREI SAIBAN (D. H. Lawrence: The Poet and the "Chatterley" Trial) (Tôkyô: Umon Shoin, 1975).
[On the censorship trial of *Lady Chatterley's Lover*.] [In Japanese.]

4523 Kunkel, Francis L. "Lawrence's *The Man Who Died:* The Heavenly Cock," PASSION AND THE PASSION: SEX AND RELIGION IN MODERN LITERATURE (Phila: Westminster P, 1975), pp. 37-57, with additional references to DHL pp. 34-35, 96, 119, 135, 164, 169-70, 174, 176, 178, 186-88, 199.

DHL used sex to gain entry to the Godhead; he invoked the mystery of religion through orgasm. A consideration of *The Man Who Died* together with DHL's letters helps us to understand the Lawrentian orchestration of sex and religion.

4524 Kuramochi, Saburô. "D. H. Lawrence to Ottoline Morrell (*Women in Love* no Haikei)" (D. H. Lawrence and Ottoline Morrell-- Figures behind *Women in Love*), BULLETIN OF TÔKYÔ UNIVERSITY OF LIBERAL ARTS AND EDUCATION, XXVI (Jan 1975), 96-110.

A description of Lady Ottoline Morrell's life and a comparison of Lady Ottoline with Hermione in *Women in Love* show that it is not proper to connect her with the fictional character since they are rather different women. [In Japanese.]

4525 Langbaum, Robert. "Lords of Life, Kings in Exile: Identity and Sexuality in D. H. Lawrence," AMERICAN SCHOLAR, XLV (Winter 1975-1976), 807-15; enlgd and rptd as "Identity and Sexuality," in THE MYSTERIES OF IDENTITY: A THEME IN MODERN LITERATURE (NY: Oxford UP, 1977), pp. 251-97.

Believing that the problem of identity is anterior to the problem of sex, DHL constructs a concept of external self that blends the concepts in Wordsworth and Yeats. Self and art are blended in Wordsworth in the sense that Wordsworth regards the external self as primitive and natural. DHL is Yeatsian in realizing that this self has been undermined as a result of Platonism and Christianity. Relatedness between art and culture, in particular, is what DHL, Wordsworth, and Yeats want. This relatedness can be recovered through sexuality only when one unlocks the individual ego and becomes conscious of one's partner's otherness. [Numerous examples are provided of the way relatedness and unrelatedness are symbolized by animals, as in "Tortoise Shout."]

4526 Lea, F[rank] A. "David Herbert Lawrence, 1885-1930," VOICES IN THE WILDERNESS: FROM POETRY TO PROPHECY IN BRITAIN (Lond: Brentham P, 1975), pp. 120-66; additional references, pp. 168-69, 178-81, 182, 183, 184-85, 189.

DHL's ability to "see things as though for the first time" demonstrates a "literary genius" different "from others not just in degree, but in kind." [Discussion of *The Rainbow* for the "aliveness" of its characterizations.] Romantic and Victorian writers, while rejecting *laissez-faire* and the Materialist premise, had "believed it their duty to pursue the general Happiness Here." "It took Lawrence to insist that, if men are not mathematical units, they are neither equal nor even commensurable." "From 1915 onwards, Lawrence never relinquished his war on that 'love and benevolence ideal.'" DHL was not, however, a "modern." He rejected Freudianism because it "derived from the same false conception of human nature as Utilitarianism." [Detailed discussion of the pairings and contrasts in *Women in Love*.] Distrusting "the Delphic 'Know Thyself,'" DHL recognized that "no instinct can manifest itself save in *rapport* with outside objects.'" "Lawrence's 'philosophy'...bears scant resemblance to what normally goes by the name." He thought "naturally in symbols." [Detailed discussion of *Psychoanalysis and the Unconscious* and *Fantasia of the Unconscious*.] In "Education of the People" and *Fantasia of the Unconscious*, DHL opposes "idealism" in education and advocates " 'education according to nature' " with the many learning "practical skills" while only the few go on to " 'schools of mental culture.' " In "Introduction to Pictures," DHL posits the Romantic myth of man's spontaneous, animal consciousness in the past, an epoch resembling the conceptions of Rousseau, Hegel, and Nietzsche. DHL's "Mexican 'detour' " fulfilled "a long-standing dream," engendered by DHL's early reading of Fenimore Cooper. [Discussion of DHL's treatment of Indians in "New Mexico" and a detailed discussion of *The Plumed Serpent*.] As *St. Mawr* and *The Man Who Died* show, "the old epoch has been war upon the 'instinctive, intuitive body,' " a "warfare perpetuated, if not instigated, by Christianity." DHL recognized that "it was not the bourgeois era alone that was perishing; it was the Christian, and with it 'the old England' itself." "From 1926 onwards, . . .we hear less of 'the power mode.' " DHL's "diagnosis was substantially right," but not his prescription. "In *Apocalypse*, Lawrence shows an aptitude worthy of Blake for divining the very different psychological 'principles or characters' projected in the symbolism of *Revelation*." "Both in *The Man Who Died* and repeatedly in the *Last Poems*, he has given us what fewer than half-a-dozen poets since Homer, and none since Nietzsche, have given, a completely new vision of man." [Additional discussion centers on DHL's relationship with John Middleton Murry.]

4527 Lea, F[rank] A. "John Middleton Murry, 1889-1957,"
VOICES IN THE WILDERNESS: FROM POETRY TO PROPHECY
IN BRITAIN (Lond: Brentham P, 1975), pp. 167-90, espec pp. 168-69, 173, 178, 179-80, 181-83, 184-85, 189.

John Middleton Murry's "place in Lawrence hagiography" bears out his view that " 'There are few harder fates for a man of some genius than to be intimately associated with a man of more.' " Discerning the affinity between DHL and Rousseau, he thought that DHL's works could be comprehended only as a whole. DHL commented allegorically on his relationship with Murry in *Women in Love* and *David*. Murry's serialization of *Fantasia of the Unconscious* in the ADELPHI "halved the circulation." Like DHL, Murry saw modern mechanized destruction as the result of organizing society for mass production and ultimately of the bourgeois war on " 'the flesh.' "

4528 Leavis, F[rank] R[aymond]. THE LIVING PRINCIPLE:
"ENGLISH" AS A DISCIPLINE OF THOUGHT (NY: Oxford UP,
1975), pp. 7, 44-45, 49, 54-55, 56, 63, 68, 75-79, 92, 101, 105-6, 238.

A comparison of DHL's "Piano" and Tennyson's "Tears, Idle Tears" shows DHL's poem to be a satisfying whole with a complexity involving something more than "mere emotional flow," while the Tennyson poem is not marked by complexity, offers "emotion for its own sake," and is inferior to the DHL poem. *Phoenix* is "an inexhaustible source of fresh insight, pregnant suggestion, and stimulus to thought," and *Women in Love* should be considered as "a work of heuristic thought."

4529 Leavis, F[rank] R[aymond]. "Thought, Words, and Creativity," SPECTATOR, CCXXXV (19 July 1975), 78-81; absorbed in THOUGHT, WORDS AND CREATIVITY: ART AND THOUGHT IN LAWRENCE, by F. R. Leavis (NY & Lond: Oxford UP, 1976), pp. 15-33.

One need only read *Psychoanalysis and the Unconscious* to realize that T. S. Eliot's evaluation of DHL as "incapable of what is ordinarily called thinking" is incorrect. An examination of the ideas, techniques, and works of the two writers will show DHL a far greater genius than Eliot.

4530 Leland, Richard Wallace. "A Rhetorical Criticism of D. H. Lawrence based upon the Master Tropes of Kenneth Burke," DISSERTATION ABSTRACTS INTERNATIONAL, XXXVI (1975), 3212A. Unpublished dissertation, University of Minnesota, 1975.

4531 Lisk, Thomas David. "Love, Law, and the Nature of Character," DISSERTATION ABSTRACTS INTERNATIONAL, XXXVI (1975), 2198A. Unpublished dissertation, Rice University, 1975.

[Discusses *The Rainbow* and *Women in Love*.]

4532 Lodge, David. "Metaphor and Metonymy in Modern Fiction," CRITICAL QUARTERLY, XVII (Spring 1975), 75-93, espec pp. 86-88.

[Stylistic analysis of the Arab mare scene in *Women in Love*.] DHL employs lexical and syntactical repetitions, earmarks of metonymic style, to create "the kind of effect usually associated with metaphor." His technique is exemplified in the passage from *Women in Love* which immediately follows Gerald's controlling of his panic-stricken Arab mare at the train and describes Gudrun's response to the episode. The metaphorical significance of the passage (Gudrun's contemplation of a kind of sexual domination which both offends and fascinates her) is underscored by DHL's metonymic prose, "forwarded by contiguity, each clause or phrase taking its impetus from an item in the preceding clause or phrase."

4533 Lowery, William R. "Trivium," in "On the Teaching of D. H. Lawrence: A Forum," ed by Langdon Elsbree. D. H. LAWRENCE REVIEW, VIII (Spring 1975), 71-74.

[After parodically reducing DHL to the basic outline of "his social, philosophical, and psychosexual history," the teacher-author learns, from a gnat on the light fixture, that this sort of reductionism is "bullshit" designed to gratify the teacher's selfish "love for power," his "desire to control other minds." Concluding that "Lawrence humbles me every time I read him, because he forces me to see new things," the author suggests some important questions raised by reading DHL.]

4534 MacKenzie, David. "Collection Called One of Finest: Rare D. H. Lawrence Items Acquired by TU," TULSA DAILY WORLD (Tulsa, OK), 23 Nov 1975.

The DHL collection recently acquired by the University of Tulsa from collector John Martin is one of the finest in the world, including first editions, many in mint condition and some signed, over 70 editions of *Lady Chatterley's Lover*, 200 periodical pieces, letters, the painting *Men Bathing*, and screenplays of films from DHL's works.

4535 MacKenzie, David. "Scholars Are 'Lovers' Of Lady Chatterley," TULSA DAILY WORLD (Tulsa, OK), 9 Dec 1975.
[News item.] The DHL collection recently acquired by the University of Tulsa from collector-publisher John Martin is unique for its completeness, depth, and almost new condition. [Quotes Warren Roberts and James C. Cowan on the occasion of the opening of the collection.]

4536 MacKinnon, Kenneth A. "The Relation of D. H. Lawrence's Thought to His Prose Style Up to 1916, Stylistic and Narrative Technique in the Early Novels of D. H. Lawrence." Unpublished dissertation, University of Toronto, 1975. [Listed in D. H. LAWRENCE REVIEW, X (Fall 1977), 302.]

4537 Magarašević, Mirko. "Današnji značaj D. H. Lawrencea" (The Contemporary Significance of D. H. Lawrence), VIDICI, No. 171 (1975), 2.
[In Serbo-Croatian.]

4538 Mahar, Margaret Anne. "The Shape of a History: Eliot, Hardy, and Lawrence," DISSERTATION ABSTRACTS INTERNATIONAL, XXXVI (1975), 3734A. Unpublished dissertation, Yale University, 1975.

4539 Meyers, Jeffrey. PAINTING AND THE NOVEL (Manchester: Manchester UP; NY: Barnes & Noble, 1975), pp. 46-82.
[Three essays on DHL's allusions to paintings in three novels.] DHL used paintings as thematic and structural motifs in his novels. Thus, the attitude of Cyril and George in the homoerotic bathing scene in *The White Peacock* recalls "the limp, passive figure" of the woman "pressed against the powerful male" in Greiffenhagen's *An Idyll;* "the iconography of [Fra Angelico's] *The Last Judgement* represents the opposition of salvation and damnation, heaven and hell," portrayed in *The Rainbow* in contrasting light and darkness; and Mark Gertler's *The Merry-Go-Round* evoked a powerful emotional response in DHL that emerges not only in Loerke's character and mechanistic art but also in various statements of DHL's suggesting an anti-Semitic prejudice.

4540 Mibu, Ikuo. "Ai to Shôtotsu (Anna to Will no Baai)" (Love and Conflict--Anna and Will), STUDIES IN CIVIC AND NATURAL SCIENCES (Nihon University), No. 45 (Nov 1975), 8-18.
In *The Rainbow*, there are repetitions of conflict between Anna and Will, but the repetition makes them become more intimate with each other. [In Japanese.]

4541 Michel-Michot, P[aulette]. "D. H. Lawrence's 'Tickets, Please': The Structural Importance of the Setting," REVUE DES LANGUES VIVANTES, XLI, No. 5 (1975), 464-70.
In "Tickets, Please," "the tramway system, its drivers and passengers, is a vast metaphor for society's rape of the natural countryside turning it into an unnaturally black, industrial area, while prompting in the people a wish for escape and

providing them with false, artificial, mechanised excitement that makes them cling to the tramcar as a refuge of *light* and refuse to enter the cold, natural blackness of the *night,* that darkness which. . .is associated with instinctive life and is the prelude to a regenerative death." DHL's description of the tramway system presents a mock-heroic reversal of values in which "the female is in charge, endowed with male aggressiveness." The ambivalent relationship between Annie and John Thomas dramatizes the battle of the sexes. The collective revenge on John Thomas, which takes place in the girls' waiting room, is paralleled with the " 'darkness and lawlessness of war' " in DHL's "comment on war and violence."

4542 Mizuhara, Sho. "D. H. Lawrence no *The Fox* no Ichikôsatsu (Seishin-Bunseki o Chûshin Toshite)" (A Psychoanalytical Study of D. H. Lawrence's *The Fox*), MEMOIRS OF MEJIRO GAKUEN WOMEN'S JUNIOR COLLEGE, No. 12 (Dec 1975), 97-109.
The thesis of this paper is centered in the theory of Edmund Bergler, M.D., a psychoanalytic psychiatrist, that March in *The Fox* is a masochist. On the assumption that DHL adopted Freudian theories, examples are cited to illustrate March's masochistic characteristics, though she is not solely a masochist because there seems to be some narcissistic identification in the two women's lesbianism. In addition, we should not forget that DHL is not simply putting a case-history into fictional form. [See also Edmund Bergler, M.D., "D. H. Lawrence's *The Fox* and the Psychoanalytic Theory on Lesbianism," JOURNAL OF NERVOUS AND MENTAL DISEASE, CXXVI (May 1958), pp. 488-91.] [In Japanese.]

4543 Moore, Harry T. "Laurentiana," D. H. LAWRENCE REVIEW, VIII (Summer 1975), 242-46.
[Letter to the Editor in reply to Émile Delavenay, " 'Making Another Lawrence': Frieda and the Lawrence Legend," D. H. LAWRENCE REVIEW, VIII (Spring 1975), 80-98, reiterating his views, expressed in THE PRIEST OF LOVE: A LIFE OF D. H. LAWRENCE (1974), that DHL was right to disparage Lloyd George, that DHL's anti-Semitism was "rather mild and secondary," that he was not a Fascist, and that he was "persecuted" and "victimized" during the War.]

4544 Mori, Haruhide. "Cythera e no Shinnyû" (Trespass into Cythera), ESSAYS (Kôbe University), No. 15 (Dec 1975), 11-29.
[In Japanese.]

4545 Mori, Haruhide. "Jôsho to Kâkô--Lawrence, Forster, Woolf, Huxley Ra ni Okeru Ninshiki no Kata ni Tsuite" (Basic Pattern of Thought in Lawrence, Forster, Woolf, and Huxley), MODERN AGE (Kôbe University), No. 50 (July 1975), 51-66.
[In Japanese.]

4546 Mori, Haruhide. "Kujaku no Yukue" (The World of *The White Peacock*), KÔBE MISCELLANY (Kôbe University), No. 7 (Aug 1975), 109-23.
[In Japanese.]

4547 Morris, Tom. "On *Etruscan Places*," PAUNCH, Nos. 40/41 (April 1975), 8-39.

In *Etruscan Places* DHL's German traveling companion, in his response to the tombs of Tarquinia, replaces immediate experience with documented fact, whereas DHL, assuming "that the paintings can reveal to us the substance and quality of Etruscan life," attempts "to describe the Etruscan way of *being* in the world." Unlike "Roman and Gothic architecture," Etruscan houses had "a *natural proportion* in size and substance...which he associates with aliveness and flexibility." Rather than duplicating "the flat, visual and 'real' surface of things," the Etruscan artists extracted qualities from "*within* things that reveal the fully embodied life of the object," a "way of being in touch" that is seen in the flowing body contours of their painting. In asserting themselves against the Etruscans, the Romans moved "against a social-cultural order rooted in the natural world." DHL's historical view equated "the ancient and the new Fascist Romans." Long aware of historical Fascism as opposed to the "fascism" he has been accused of accepting, DHL returned to Italy in 1925, when press censorship and "strict government control" of public organizations characterized Mussolini's "totalitarian" state. DHL's inner-directed Etruscans' "'patience' is opposed to Roman resistance and mastery which result in mental cunning and mechanical force." DHL "ends *Etruscan Places* with two stories" in which "the *work* of art, the making of 'effigies' of the cast-off deadness-in-life, becomes a means towards the truer Etruscan merging of art with fulfilling life."

4548 Mulloy, John J. "D. H. Lawrence and the Worship of the Earth," in "The Catholic Tradition" column, WANDERER (St. Paul, MN), 21 Aug 1975, p. 5.

DHL has been the most influential spokesman for a "vitalistic pantheism" characterized by "the worship of the cosmos as a living being...identified with all other beings in the cosmos." Trying to find religious meaning in a rationalist age and to escape the personal God of Christianity, liberals are often drawn to the "religiosity" of worshiping the "life force." Hence, DHL in *Mornings in Mexico* describes an inability to judge which would paralyze man's reason, in *The Plumed Serpent* advocates a "return to aboriginal paganism," and in *Etruscan Places* denies a transcendent personal God but "makes everything else in the universe personal." The logical inconsistency is that in a universe of pantheistic flow, the critical faculties of a moral critic like DHL would be suspended.

4549 Mulloy, John J. "Nature: God or a Creature of God?" in "The Catholic Tradition" column, WANDERER (St. Paul, MN), 11 Sept 1975, p. 6.

DHL's criticism that Christianity shares with modern science "an intellectualized non-vital conception" of life and nature curiously reverses the usual criticism that Christianity is unscientific. The equation makes Christianity responsible for the devastation of nature wrought by industrialism, but, as Psalm 104 and Hopkins's "God's Grandeur" show, nature in Christian tradition is fresh and individual. DHL's caricature of Christianity derives from his humanistic "wish to avoid any God who is above man, to whom man is accountable."

4550 Mulloy, John J. "Primitivism and the Supernatural," in "The Catholic Tradition" column, WANDERER (St. Paul, MN), 28 Aug 1975, p. 5.

DHL's description in *Etruscan Places* of "the Etruscan drawing...life into himself from a vital source of power really corresponds to that of the magician" in Frazer's THE GOLDEN BOUGH, tapping the source of vital power in order to manipulate it. But what differentiates DHL's inaccurate conception from the actual religion of primitive man is the supernatural character of primitive religion, its breaking "the bounds of natural life and energy" to move between "consciousness of an all-enveloping supernatural power, incomprehensible and mysterious, and of that power as it reveals itself to man in a personal form."

4551 Mulloy, John J. "Sacrificial Practice in Primitive Religion," in "The Catholic Tradition" column, WANDERER (St. Paul, MN), 18 Sept 1975, p. 5.

DHL's superficial version of primitive cosmic vitalism neglects the "need for adoration, for sacrifice and propitiation...for transgression against the holiness" of the numinous Power to which primitive man responded. Cardinal Newman's sermons on primitive sacrifice as well as the specific practices of the American Indians show that DHL's "worship of the life-force owes a great deal to literary inflation and to careful exclusion" of essential religious elements of asceticism and atonement.

4552 Nahal, Chaman. "The Colour Ambience of Lawrence's Early and Later Poetry," D. H. LAWRENCE REVIEW, VIII (Summer 1975), 147-54.

DHL's sensitivity to color amounts, in *Look! We Have Come Through!* and *Last Poems,* to a poetic device for conveying meaning. Using variations on the basic colors of red, green, and black, DHL uses color as epithet, metaphor, or for contrast by juxtaposition. Red and its variations stands for passion, black for extinction, and green for fertility. Often in the early poems the extremes of red and black are combined to suggest a plasticity existing beneath the surface duality of existence. In *Last Poems,* however, green almost completely disappears and the extremes are not allowed to mingle. The emergence of greys in the late poems indicates that DHL has become rigid and dogmatic, doctrinal rather than flexible.

4553 Nakamura, Shiro. "*Chatterley* no Mittsu no Han ni Tsuite" (The Three Versions of *Lady Chatterley's Lover*), MEMOIRS OF ISHIKAWA TECHNICAL COLLEGE, No. 7 (March 1975), 119-29.

It was not until recently that we were able to read the three versions of *Lady Chatterley's Lover* collectively in print. The construction of the story seems to have been better arranged version by version and, as for the characters, such changes are made in Clifford and Mellors as render the behavior of Constance the less unnatural. The bitter class hatred or prejudice in the first version decreases and the mutual confidence between hero and heroine becomes more predominant instead. The philosophy of tenderness ripens gradually, and in the final version this philosophy, together with the renunciation of the ego of man and woman, offers us a unique world. DHL's thought was deepened and his art was refined through the development of the three versions. [In Japanese.]

4554 Nardi, Piero. "Introduzione" (Introduction), *La ragazza perduta (The Lost Girl)* (Milan: A. Mondadori, 1975), pp. 22-26.
The Lost Girl is the study of a woman who tries to affirm her independence but in the end is forced to give it up because of her womanly nature and the primordial need for sex. This novel is a much better example of DHL's art than are *The Plumed Serpent* and *Lady Chatterley's Lover*. [In Italian.]

4555 Nardi, Piero. "Introduzione" (Introduction), *Teatro e prose varie (The Complete Plays and Selected Essays)* by D. H. Lawrence (Milan: A. Mondadori, 1975), pp. xv-lvi.
DHL's colliery plays are mainly autobiographical. *The Married Man* and *The Merry-Go-Round* are essentially farces, but nonetheless reflect DHL's reality. *Touch and Go* is an appeal to humanity against the class struggle and a call to rebuild the world destroyed by war. *David* is DHL's dramatic representation of his blood religion. Furthermore, many of DHL's essays are artistically very important and can be useful in the study of his life and ideology. [In Italian.]

4556 Nathan, John Goldsmith. "The Almost of Satisfaction: A Study of the Major Fiction of D. H. Lawrence," DISSERTATION ABSTRACTS INTERNATIONAL, XXXVI (1975), 2811A-12A. Unpublished dissertation, Wayne State University, 1975.

4557 New, W. H., and H. J. Rosengarten. "David Herbert Lawrence," MODERN STORIES IN ENGLISH (NY: Crowell, 1975), p. 194.
[Biographical headnote to "The Horse Dealer's Daughter," which is reprinted in the anthology, pp. 194-208, mentioning DHL's Nottingham background, censorship problems, and thematic concern with social man versus instinctive man.]

4558 New, W. H., and H. J. Rosengarten. "The Horse Dealer's Daughter," INSTRUCTOR'S MANUAL FOR MODERN STORIES IN ENGLISH (NY: Crowell, 1975), pp. 26-27.
In "The Horse Dealer's Daughter," Mabel Pervin, who has kept aloof from the "coarse sensuality" established in the "connection between the heavy shire horses and the Pervin brothers," moves toward death. She and Dr. Fergusson emerge from their "grisly baptism" in the " 'dead water' " of the pond "changed from their former selves" by a new sexual awareness. "The final section, with its emphasis on the workings of instinct and the mystery of love, conveys Lawrence's mystical views about the nature of sex and the human unconscious."

4559 Nin, Anais. A WOMAN SPEAKS: THE LECTURES, SEMINARS, AND INTERVIEWS OF ANAIS NIN, ed by Evelyn J. Hinz (Chicago: Swallow P, 1975), pp. 36, 62-63, 65, 66, 82, 85, 87, 98, 99, 100, 103, 152, 153-54, 176, 207, 211.
DHL "obtained a great deal of his knowledge of woman by reading the diary of his first love." His ideas about women are "old-fashioned." DHL "was trying to write very often about what women felt. He wrote very much as a woman." He

found it difficult to understand women, but "we do owe him a tremendous debt for his effort to find a language...for feelings, instincts, emotions, and intuitions."

4560 Nishida, Minoru. "*Musuko to Koibito* no Okeru Tankyu no Imi to Kôzô" (The Meaning and Structure of Paul's Quest in *Sons and Lovers*), D. H. LAWRENCE STUDIES (Kyôto), No. 3 (Sept 1975), 199-220.

In George Eliot and Thomas Hardy the eternal world of nature establishes unchangeable "Law" for human beings. In *Sons and Lovers,* however, nature is relative to man's existence. This means that man has lost the outer "Law" which had meant either the home to return to or a firm ground to stand on. Paul, who has keen sensibility, sees clearly his mother's and father's tragedy in the modern world. Paul's quest or groping for new life makes his eye keen, and this keen vision sometimes results in his merciless attitude even toward his parents and lovers. The utterly independent figure of Paul in the modern world, where nobody has a spiritual home or firm ground to support him, is to be seen clearly, especially in his figure in the last scene of the novel. [In Japanese.]

4561 Ogawa, Yoshio. "Watakushi no Lawrence to Butler" (My Lawrence and Butler), BULLETIN OF ST. MARGARET'S (St. Margaret's Junior College), No. 7 (Dec 1975), 45-57.

Each of DHL's works, from *The White Peacock* to "The Ship of Death," is a part of a whole cycle presenting the hero's progress through sex toward death. DHL reveals to us the "oblivion" through which we proceed on board "the Ship of Death" and in which we can meet God and have the chance of rebirth. In Samuel Butler's work, on the other hand, the whole cycle is contained within the novel THE WAY OF ALL FLESH, which reveals not "oblivion" but the dark world of Ernest's heredity. [Also discusses the affinities between DHL and Butler.] [In Japanese.]

4562 Okada, Taiji. "America e Mukau Lawrence" (Lawrence on the Way to America), STUDIES IN HUMANITIES AND SOCIAL SCIENCE (Kôbe University of Mercantile Marine), No. 24 (Oct 1975), 5-37.

This article considers the strange experience, both internally and externally, of DHL, who had left England in November 1919 on a journey that would eventually take him to America. Especially after the War, he had a positive economic connection with American publishers. Then Mrs. Thrasher and Mrs. Mabel Dodge Luhan respectively offered him a way to live in America. But what was it that supported DHL inwardly? It was that "spontaneity," the meaning of which he had made clear in "Education of the People" and which was the first principle of his art. "Spontaneity" was the inner power that motivated DHL to make the journey to America via the East, dreaming his own dream of Rananim. [In Japanese.]

4563 Okada, Taiji. "D. H. Lawrence no Gikyoku *David* ni Tsuite" (On D. H. Lawrence's Drama *David*), STUDIES IN HUMANITIES AND SOCIAL SCIENCE (Kôbe University of Mercantile Marine), No. 23 (Jan 1975), 83-105.

This study attempts to locate DHL's drama *David* as precisely as possible among his works. *David* is a phallic drama rewritten on the basis of DHL's religious experience in recovering from the illness near death in the early months of 1925, though the play has no special and different meaning beyond his other works. [In Japanese.]

4564 Okano, Keiichi. "*Musuko to Koibito* no Higeki--Morel-Fujin ni Mirareru Kikai-Bunmei ni yoru Hakaisei no Shiten yori" (The Tragedy of *Sons and Lovers*--From a Viewpoint of Mrs. Morel's Destructiveness Caused by Machine Civilization), D. H. LAWRENCE STUDIES (Kyôto), No. 3 (Sept 1975), 31-49.

The cause of the tragedy in *Sons and Lovers* is too close a relationship between the sons and their mother. While William succumbs to the destructiveness both of his mother and of machine civilization, Paul " 'would not give in.' " It is Paul's vitality that saves him from falling a victim to the same destructiveness. [In Japanese.]

4565 Orr, Christopher. "D. H. Lawrence and E. M. Forster: From *The White Peacock* to MAURICE," WEST VIRGINIA ASSOCIATION OF COLLEGE ENGLISH TEACHERS BULLETIN, II, No. 2 (1975), 22-28.

The White Peacock, a favorite book with E. M. Forster, influenced the writing of MAURICE, though the influence of MAURICE on the writing of *Lady Chatterley's Lover* is improbable since Forster is not likely in 1915 to have shown DHL the manuscript of MAURICE. DHL's characterization of George Saxton and Annable influenced Forster's conception of Alec Scudder, but Annable more closely resembles Maurice. Both DHL and Forster were influenced by Edward Carpenter.

4566 Perrakis, Phyllis Sternberg. "Creativity in Crisis: D. H. Lawrence and World War I." Unpublished dissertation, University of California at Berkeley, 1975. [Listed in COMPREHENSIVE DISSERTATION INDEX, 1975 SUPP (University Microfilms International), p. 349.]

4567 Petillon, Pierre-Yves. "L'Europe des Amants," CRITIQUE (Paris), XXXI (Dec 1975), 1277-84.

[Review article surveying the time and the interrelationships of the figures in Martin Green's THE VON RICHTHOFEN SISTERS: THE TRIUMPHANT AND THE TRAGIC MODES OF LOVE: ELSE AND FRIEDA VON RICHTHOFEN, OTTO GROSS, MAX WEBER, AND D. H. LAWRENCE, IN THE YEARS 1870-1970 (1974).] [In French.]

4568 Phillips, Steven R. "The Monomyth and Literary Criticism," COLLEGE LITERATURE, II (Winter 1975), 1-16.

An examination of "The Horse Dealer's Daughter" in terms of the monomyth (i.e., of the mythic pattern of separation, initiation, and return as defined by Joseph Campbell in THE HERO WITH A THOUSAND FACES) produces several revisions. Although "the regenerative aspect of the experience of the pond is confirmed," that scene is not the "central episode" but only a preparatory experience to "future spiritual adventure." The "thematic emphasis" shifts from the pond to the farmhouse, so that the meaning of the tale is not in the attempted suicide but in the "sacred marriage."

 4569 Pinsker, Sanford. "Confessions of a Lawrentian Manqué," in "On the Teaching of D. H. Lawrence: A Forum," ed by Langdon Elsbree. D. H. LAWRENCE REVIEW, VIII (Spring 1975), 68-71.
[Although a pro-Joycean, anti-Lawrentian modernist, the author undertook an undergraduate seminar in DHL. While frankly doubting that "a Lawrence seminar is within the emotional range of most undergraduates," he finds value in the "deeper freedom" to be gained in confronting the "variety of angels" which DHL makes one wrestle with, though to see DHL both "steadily and whole" "requires special efforts."]

 4570 Pinto-Muñoz, Ana. " 'Two Marriages' y 'Daughters of the Vicar': dos versiones de un mismo relato de D. H. Lawrence" ("Two Marriages" and "Daughters of the Vicar": Two Versions of the Same Story by D. H. Lawrence). Unpublished dissertation, University of Salamanca, 1975. [Listed in Michael Smith (ed), ANNUAL BIBLIOGRAPHY OF ENGLISH LANGUAGE AND LITERATURE FOR 1975 (Lond: Modern Humanities Research Association, 1978), L, p. 708.]
[In Spanish.]

 4571 Pollnitz, Christopher P. "The Poetry of D. H. Lawrence: Extending Romanticism." Unpublished dissertation, University of Leicester, 1975. [Listed in Geoffrey M. Paterson and Joan E. Hardy (eds), INDEX TO THESES, XXVI, Part 2 (1978), p. 7.]

 4572 Ragussis, Michael. "The False Myth of *St. Mawr:* Lawrence and the Subterfuge of Art," PAPERS ON LANGUAGE AND LITERATURE, XI (Spring 1975), 186-96.
The design of *St. Mawr* is a "complicated pattern of belief and disbelief." The reader suffers the "reversal of feeling" that characters do: he alternately sympathizes with Lou and criticizes her illusions. If the "pattern of lies" in the novel fools the reader, *St. Mawr* fails; "if it first engages our beliefs, and then instigates our criticism," its "formal intentions" succeed. *St. Mawr* "criticizes the morality of easy belief."

 4573 Riesen, David Herman. "Retreat into Wilderness: A Study of the Travel Books of Five Twentieth-Century British Novelists," DISSERTATION ABSTRACTS INTERNATIONAL, XXXVI (1975), 1534A-35A. Unpublished dissertation, University of Wisconsin-Madison, 1975.
[One chapter treats the travel books of Lawrence.]

4574 Rose, Shirley. "Physical Trauma in D. H. Lawrence's Short Fiction," CONTEMPORARY LITERATURE, XVI (Winter 1975), 73-83.

DHL criticism tends to regard "the violence in his work as symptomatic of a perverse and obsessive preoccupation with pain and suffering." This view may be wrong, however: in DHL's short stories "pain is not a means to enlightenment but rather the reverse." DHL condemns physical pain because "it reduces the range of humanness, and is therefore to be strictly avoided." "Sorrow and remorse more likely lead to self-knowledge and so have broader implications than pain itself." Though DHL affirms "the principle that the highest form of courage lies in rejection of suffering," in his stories "none of the characters transcend physical pain. Their capacity for insight disappears in its central focus. If they are to 'know,' they, like the man who died, must first stop hurting. If they do not find release, they remain contained in that narrow single sensation that extinguishes all else." [Stories discussed include "The Woman Who Rode Away," "None of That," and "Odour of Chrysanthemums."]

4575 Ross, Charles L. "The Composition of *Women in Love:* A History, 1913-1919," D. H. LAWRENCE REVIEW, VIII (Summer 1975), 198-212; rvd and enlgd as "The Manuscripts: Three Preliminary Drafts" and "The Final Draft: *Women in Love,*" in THE COMPOSITION OF "THE RAINBOW" AND "WOMEN IN LOVE": A HISTORY, by Charles L. Ross (Charlottesville: UP of Virginia, 1979), pp. 97-114, 115-23; absorbed in "Introduction," *Women in Love,* by D. H. Lawrence (Harmondsworth, Middlesex, England: Penguin Books, 1982), pp. 13-48.

"The history of the composition of *Women in Love* is even more complicated than that of *The Rainbow.* . . . the novel remained in typescript for five years," circulating among various publishers and friends "and undergoing periodic revisions." "To add to this difficulty, the manuscripts and typescripts of the novel are kept in two, widely-separated collections. Most of the materials of 'The Sisters' are owned by the University of Texas," but there is also another "typescript now owned by the University of Toronto." In addition, "a further typescript was prepared from the Toronto typescript. . . . Revised between 1917 and 1919, it was the exemplar for the proof-sheets." "Finally, many of the letters which bear critically on the genesis of the novel have not been published." "Fortunately, the draft materials available for examination are extensive." A detailed analysis of all of these materials reveals "the sequence of composition" and revision of *Women in Love.* [See also two related articles by Charles L. Ross, "A Problem of Textual Transmission in the Typescripts of *Women in Love,*" LIBRARY, 5th series, XXIX (June 1974), 197-205; and "The Revisions of the Second Generation in *The Rainbow,*" REVIEW OF ENGLISH STUDIES, XXVII (Aug 1976), 277-95.]

4576 Ross, Michael L. "Lawrence's Second 'Sun,'" D. H. LAWRENCE REVIEW, VIII (Spring 1975), 1-18.

The form in which DHL's story "Sun" "has generally been known does not represent its author's final wishes." The "revised and expanded text. . .was published in a limited edition. . .by Black Sun Press." A comparison of the two versions demonstrates the superiority of the "Black Sun" version, which it is misleading to call "unexpurgated." Although DHL did use the term, evidence indicates that in 1928 he decided "to rework and expand a tale he had hitherto apparently considered complete." DHL responded to publisher Harry Crosby's request for a manuscript of the 1926 "Sun" by sending him a new version of the story, "altered radically enough to qualify as a saleable item." Many of the changes in the later text represent minor corrections, and relatively few have to do with matters of sexual candor. But the second "Sun" provides "an intriguing parallel" to the long "gestation" of *Lady Chatterley's Lover*. "Both works represent Lawrence's endeavor to achieve a definitive statement of one of his essential themes: the reawakening of woman's vital self." The revised "Sun" preserves the "general plot line" of the original version but includes changes which affect its "essential quality," such as the imagery having "to do with the dominant symbolic force, the sun itself," and "the repositioned and. . .expanded encounter between woman and peasant." The physical juxtaposing of her two suitors forces Juliet to a climactic moment of decision, making her failure of nerve appear all the more discouraging. [See also reply by Brian Finney and rejoinder by Michael L. Ross in "The Two Versions of 'Sun': An Exchange," D. H. LAWRENCE REVIEW, VIII (Fall 1975), 371-74.]

    4577 Rossman, Charles. " 'You are the call and I am the answer': D. H. Lawrence and Women," D. H. LAWRENCE REVIEW, VIII (Fall 1975), 255-328.

Although DHL is the conscious "proponent of *delicately balanced reciprocity* in male-female relationships," some critics, from Simone de Beauvoir to Kate Millett, regard his treatment of the subject "as tainted. . .with his bias of masculine supremacy." This essay examines DHL's work as a whole in order to explore the attitudes towards women dramatized in his writing, the changes these attitudes undergo throughout his career, and the way in which his biographical experience assists us in interpreting them. The essay is organized chronologically in four sections. "The 'idealism' of his mother--the stifling intensity of her love--serves. . .as Lawrence's model for female destructiveness," which is illustrated in "virtually all of the women" in his early novels. *The White Peacock* and *The Trespasser,* however, focus not on destructive women but on weak, self-destructive men, while Paul in *Sons and Lovers* "survives the destructive impact" of his relationships with his mother and with Miriam and Clara. Although *The Rainbow* represents DHL's "period of greatest sympathy for women," affirming woman's "quest for fuller self," *Women in Love* shows DHL's "growing hostility toward women" in the portraits of Gudrun and Hermione, the handling of the Gudrun-Gerald relationship, and the shift from "star equilibrium" to "*Blutbrüderschaft.*" The change in attitude--in redefining women's "proper place"--is seen in DHL's letters and essays, especially *Fantasia of the Unconscious,* and in fiction such as *Aaron's Rod, Kangaroo, The Captain's Doll, The Ladybird,* and *The Fox,* which increasingly asserts a vision of a male-dominated world to which woman must submit, culminating in the ritual sacrifice of a woman in "The Woman Who Rode Away" and "religious totalitarianism,. . .with its subjugation of women," in *The Plumed Serpent.* In his last period, DHL rejects power and primitivism and returns to the sexual union of man and woman as the center of the individual's life. In *Lady*

Chatterley's Lover, both Mellors and Connie "submit" and in their sexual union realize themselves as vital, purposive beings. In *The Man Who Died,* the man "accepts his own guilt," and his union with the priestess of Isis "is the most nearly perfect realization of the reciprocal relationship between man and woman" in DHL's major fiction, as he abandons the "manly mission" and "his hostility toward women" is "outgrown." [See also the author's expansion of the Women in Love section, pp. 273-82, in "D. H. Lawrence, Women, and *Women in Love,*" CAHIERS VICTORIENS & EDOUARDIENS, No. 8 (1979), 93-115.]

4578 Sagar, Keith M. THE ART OF TED HUGHES (Cambridge & NY: Cambridge UP, 1975), pp. 1, 5, 7, 12, 18, 38-45, 63, 66, 77, 78, 90, 123, 141, 153, 164, 165, 166, 196; additional references to DHL in expanded 2nd ed (1978), pp. viii, 168-69, 170, 172, 189, 195, 232-33.

[Frequently citing DHL in epigraphs and passing references, the author draws parallels between Ted Hughes's animal poems in LUPERCAL and DHL's animal poems. He also sees "Ursula's encounter with the horses at the end of *The Rainbow*" as one source of Hughes's story "The Rain Horse." DHL's "Tortoise Shout" is discussed in a detailed note.]

4579 Sagar, Keith. "The Genesis of 'Bavarian Gentians,'" D. H. LAWRENCE REVIEW, VIII (Spring 1975), 47-53.

The holograph notebook of *Last Poems* contains two complete versions of "Bavarian Gentians," written in Sept/Oct 1929 on consecutive pages, the first version extensively revised, the second substantially different and four lines longer. Although the second version is "final and definitive," Richard Aldington, the editor, printed the first version. "Bavarian Gentians," "one of the great poems of the language," is generally known in the wrong version. "Glory of Darkness" does not become "overtly a poem about death" until the second version. In the first version of "Ship of Death," "Persephone's journey to Hades is only an analogy for the journey of the poet's soul," and there is no "idea of the soul as wedding guest." Despite the comparison of gentians to torches in the first version of "Bavarian Gentians," "the implications of the Persephone story" are unrealized until the second version, where the gentians are both phallic and womb-like, both Pluto and Persephone. Hence, "death is a nuptial" in which the soul as wedding guest participates.

4580 Sano, Akano. "Paul Morel's Transfiguration in Love," D. H. LAWRENCE STUDIES (Kyôto), No. 3 (Sept 1975), 109-31.

[In Japanese.]

4581 Scholtes, M. "*St. Mawr:* Between Degeneration and Regeneration," DUTCH QUARTERLY REVIEW OF ANGLO-AMERICAN LETTERS, V, No. 4 (1975), 253-69.

Near the end of his life DHL's vision of society, complicated by extensive reliance on symbol and myth, became bleaker, as *St. Mawr* reflects in discussing "social renewal...almost entirely in terms of a change of 'consciousness' within the individual." The major characters are representative of the three main forces which characterize a period of transition: "the conservative, the critical and the progressive." Rico's "anxiety for the future and his need to provide for it make him voluntarily enter the prison of the establishment he apparently abhors" as an artist. Mrs. Witt, who has none of Rico's crippling fear "but all of his disgust and hatred for the sham world they both move in," is free to assume "the role of critical observer and accuser." Lou Witt, "representative of the regenerative force and of the pioneer into a new world," uses St. Mawr, "an inhabitant of 'an older, heavily potent world,'" as a standard against which to contrast the triviality, sterility, and futility of Rico's world. "Of the different reactions to social change, the escapist or conservative, the cynical, and the idealistic or progressive, the latter was to Lawrence the most important." [Illustrated with portrait of DHL by Kai Gôtzsche.]

4582 Sekiguchi, Masakazu. "Bungaku ni Arawareta Anrakushi" (Euthanasia from Literature), JOURNAL OF RYÛTSÛ KEIZAI UNIVERSITY, XXXII (March 1975), 47-63.
[Examines the meaning of euthanasia in several works of literature, including *Sons and Lovers*. Euthanasia, when circumstances compel it, is presented affirmatively in these works.] [In Japanese.]

4583 Sekiguchi, Masakazu. "*Shirokujaku* Shiron" (On *The White Peacock*), JOURNAL OF RYÛTSÛ KEIZAI UNIVERSITY, XXXII (Feb 1975), 42-61.
[Considers the meaning in *The White Peacock* of the deterioration of George Saxton that holds the book together. Through his relationship with Lettie, which may be compared to that of Adam and Eve, George gradually declines into a condition of physical and spiritual decay.] [In Japanese.]

4584 Shakir, Evelyn. "'Secret Sin': Lawrence's Early Verse," D. H. LAWRENCE REVIEW, VIII (Summer 1975), 155-75.
DHL's cancelled preface to his *Collected Poems* and attitudes expressed in other prose works indicate that his poetry often reveals guilty psychological states and ambivalent feelings toward sexuality and sexual identity, especially as these relate to his parents. DHL's revisions of his earlier work for *The Collected Poems of D. H. Lawrence* (1928) show him, in a period of illness and impotence, "trying to rehabilitate his younger self by transforming him into a more virile figure." His willingness to relinquish fantasies of narcissistic impotence may have allowed the masterful *Last Poems*. Additionally, by accepting human limitations on his power, DHL could free himself from his prevalent early castration fears complexly revealed in the earlier versions of the poems. [Discusses the revisions of "Cruelty and Love" ("Love on the Farm"), "Snap-Dragon," "Piano," "Honeymoon," "Forecast," "Virgin Youth," "Yesternight," "Kisses on the Train," "Last Words to Miriam," and others.]

4585 Shirai, Toshitaka. "A Checklist of Theses on D. H. Lawrence in Japan: 1968-1975," D. H. LAWRENCE REVIEW, VIII (Summer 1975), 233-35.
[Bibliography of master's theses on DHL written in Japan from 1968 to 1975.

The titles in the checklist are given only in English translation.]

4586 Sitesh, Aruna. D. H. LAWRENCE: THE CRUSADER AS CRITIC (Delhi, Bombay, Calcutta, Madras: Macmillan Co. of India, 1975).

DHL's critical judgments are based on his vision of life. The theories on which he based his literary criticism were those on which he established his concept of the "man-woman relationship" as "a first step toward the achievement of man-cosmos relatedness." DHL felt that a successful literary work would supply certain essentials that modern man lacks. It would help him to strike a balance between the intellect and the emotions, to preserve the individual consciousness against the pressures of social consciousness and self-consciousness, and to quicken the relationship between the individual and the living universe. For DHL art is not to be understood in isolation from life, but must deal with the whole man. Emphasis solely upon individual facets of man is anathema to DHL. While no rigid rules can be laid down for assessing a work of art, the artist must be honest with himself both in comprehending the work and in conveying his responses to it. The art form embodies life and depicts the "life flux"; therefore, its structure must fit the particular life it embodies. DHL is not against form as such since it is needed to express creative energy, but he is against traditional, established forms because they represent excessive intellectualization and self-consciousness. Both as artist and as critic, DHL was a moralist whose morality consisted not in a conventional code but in "pure" emotions and relationships and in faithfully depicting and honoring "life."

4587 Sklar, Sylvia. THE PLAYS OF D. H. LAWRENCE (Lond: Vision P; NY: Barnes & Noble, 1975).

DHL's plays are the last of his works to receive scholarly attention. His eight complete plays as well as the fragments, *Altitude* and *Noah's Flood,* deserve to be read and judged in their own right and not just as glosses on the life and work of the novelist and poet. DHL, who saw himself as a writer who wrote in different modes, had a great love for the theater and a talent at charades and all kinds of mimicry. The importance of the dramatic element in all his work is attested to by the stream of dramatizations of DHL's novels and stories. As a young man, DHL greatly admired Ibsen and Chekhov, and later he came to admire Shaw, with mixed feelings. Shaw, seeing a production of *The Widowing of Mrs. Holroyd,* thought the dialogue excellent. This play, *A Collier's Friday Night,* and *The Daughter-in-Law* are DHL's naturalist plays. *The Merry-Go-Round, The Married Man,* and *The Fight for Barbara* are in the tragicomic mode. [Includes an account of the circumstances under which DHL wrote each of these plays, as well as *Touch and Go* and *David,* and gives an analysis of each of them as dramatic literature. A bibliographical note at the end includes editions of and critical work on DHL's plays.]

4588 Small, Michael. "The Tale the Critic Tells: D. H. Lawrence on Nathaniel Hawthorne," PAUNCH, Nos. 40/41 (April 1975), 40-58.

DHL's strictures against asking for "absolutes" and his critical concern that theories should not be applied mechanically to life "should prepare him for understanding Hawthorne," but he still misunderstands the purpose of THE SCARLET LETTER. DHL sees that in mastering passion "Hester becomes cold," that it is hypocrisy rather than adultery that leads to Dimmesdale's decay, and that Hawthorne's moralizing imposes a "meaning that often conflicts with undercurrents in the novel." But in applying to the story "*his* categories" of "mind-consciousness and blood-consciousness," DHL fails to recognize the significance of the forest scene where Hester seeks regeneration without the benefit of " 'human law' or 'higher truth,' " and in imposing his "devil theory on Pearl," he misreads her character. In trusting his own "experience of the tale," "the reader substitutes himself for the teller" and thus risks falsifying the work. Thus, in attempting to rescue the tale from Hawthorne, "Lawrence has. . .partially rewritten the romance."

4589 Smithson, Isaiah. "Structuralism as a Method of Literary Criticism," COLLEGE ENGLISH, XXXVII (Oct 1975), 145-59.
[Essay defining structuralism as a critical method. Includes a detailed structuralist analysis of *The Rainbow*.]

4590 Soliman, Soliman Yousef. "Non-British Setting in Twentieth-Century British Fiction," DISSERTATION ABSTRACTS INTERNATIONAL, XXXVI (1975), 881A-82A. Unpublished dissertation, Indiana University, 1975.
[Includes discussion of DHL's use of foreign settings in his fiction.]

4591 Spilka, Mark. "Lessing and Lawrence: The Battle of the Sexes," CONTEMPORARY LITERATURE, XVI (Spring 1975), 218-40.
Doris Lessing and DHL have in common "the novel's long concern with love and marriage as the accepted resolution for ordinary lives; and their extraordinary heroines--uprooted intellectuals. . .who paint, teach, write, perform--question its acceptability as sharply as they question male sufficiency." While the fiction of both has "an autobiographical intensity," Lessing's and DHL's differences are "considerable": she is more "Joycean than Laurentian in her formal predilections," and while she shares DHL's theme of "the fragmentation of society and of consciousness," she expresses it through "multiple perspectives," whereas DHL could "never give himself up to such fragmentary devices," but always maintains the stance of "the omniscient narrator." While presenting manliness and womanliness as "attractive traits," Lessing and DHL "present them in short supply at a time when the cultural attack against them runs extremely strong." Lessing comes closest to DHL in depicting sexual relations, agreeing with him "on the values of the heterosexual love-act" and "on the difficulties of depicting it." It is "not love or hate which matters but selfhood, as Lessing and Lawrence seem to know, each for his or her own sex chiefly, but also in some sympathetic measure for the other." [Dense, wide-ranging analysis covering a number of works and ideas.]

4592 Springer, Mary Doyle. FORMS OF THE MODERN NOVELLA (Chicago: University of Chicago P, 1975), pp. 25-32, 34, 38, 40, 41, 42, 44, 47, 48, 50, 55, 120, 128, 137, 142-48, 149.

Two of DHL's long stories, "The Woman Who Rode Away" and *The Fox,* serve as examples of two different forms of the modern novella. The former is an "apologue"--a story in which the fictional devices are subordinated to the making of a statement. In this category it joins such stories as Chekhov's "Ward Six," Conrad's "Heart of Darkness," and DHL's own *The Man Who Died* and "The Man Who Loved Islands." *The Fox,* however, more representational than illustrative, is mainly concerned with the development of character through action. Hence it belongs to the category of "serious plots of learning (or failed learning)" along with such stories as Bellow's SEIZE THE DAY, Joyce's "The Dead," and DHL's *The Virgin and the Gipsy.* In "The Woman Who Rode Away," DHL shows great formal skill in causing the reader to surrender normal fictional expectations about the fate of the anonymous woman, by having her "die" figuratively in the first section and by denying the reader access to her at the fatal end of her journey. As a result of the strategy, the reader sees her story as universal rather than personal, a drama of statement rather than character.

4593 Squires, Michael. "Recurrence as a Narrative Technique in *The Rainbow,*" MODERN FICTION STUDIES, XXI (Summer 1975), 230-36.

DHL employs "singular" scenes in *The Rainbow,* scenes which occur only once and which possess unusual power and immediacy, as well as brief "recurrent" scenes, which prepare for the singular scenes. By this means DHL can pace the narrative appropriately and smoothly, for example, by creating the effect of lapsed time without rushing the narrative. [Examples of various techniques typically used in both types of scene are provided.]

4594 Squires, Michael. "Scenic Construction and Rhetorical Signals in Hardy and Lawrence," D. H. LAWRENCE REVIEW, VIII (Summer 1975), 125-46.

Structural analysis shows Hardy and DHL to be "superb scenic craftsmen," who developed a particular kind of fictional scene that captures the stages of conflict and resolution found in courtship and marriage and uses rhetorical signals to mark the stages in the scene's construction. An analysis of the first seven chapters of *The Rainbow* shows that DHL's scenes are "patterned on Hardy's." DHL begins with a "temporal signal," followed by "questions that generate increasing tension" but which, unlike Hardy's, are internal as well as external; the scene then builds to a *"height of tension"* which, like Hardy's revelation, "marks the climax"; a "gesture of conciliation" then signals a bridge between estranged characters, followed by the signal for "closure." In addition DHL uses "process markers"-- "gradually," "suddenly," "at length," and "at last"--which "function as surrogates for. . .external plot" and reveal plot turning inward. Whereas Hardy's "generalizations about the power of external forces" are embodied in his scenic structure, DHL in *The Rainbow* is "less interested in. . .external action, than in internal shifts of feeling." DHL focuses on development and process, Hardy on change. In *The Rainbow,* however, from Chapter VIII on, "the gesture of conciliation fails to be expressed"; the relief from emotional conflict, typical of the first half, disappears. Although "the truncated scenic pattern. . .does not solve the artistic difficulties of the novel's last half," it is "meaningful and intentional." [Includes diagrams of the tensive curve of scenes in *The Rainbow* and JUDE THE OBSCURE.]

4595 Steig, Michael. "Fantasy and Mimesis in Literary Character: Shelley, Hardy, and Lawrence," ENGLISH STUDIES IN CANADA, I (Summer 1975), 160-71, espec pp. 161, 168-71.

George Eliot, Thomas Hardy, and DHL "were all concerned with the troubled emergence of the modern woman." "*Sons and Lovers* can be read as an inversion of JUDE THE OBSCURE." The functions of Sue Bridehead and Miriam are comparable, "but while Jude turns from the heavily physical Arabella to the mentally vivifying Sue, Paul Morel escapes from the increasing desperation of trying to love Miriam physically to the passionate release of his relationship with Clara." DHL's characterization of Miriam, however, rather than being objective, is presented from Paul's point of view.

4596 Steloff, Frances. "In Touch with Genius," JOURNAL OF MODERN LITERATURE, IV, "Gotham Book Mart Issue" (April 1975), 749-882, espec pp. 766, 770, 791, 827, 829, 847, 848, 859.

[Anecdotal first-person memoir, including association of the Gotham Book Mart with various people who had some relation to DHL: the agent J. B. Pinker, a letter to whom by DHL is owned by the Gotham; Christopher Morley, who objected on artistic grounds to a display of DHL's painting *Resurrection;* Anais Nin, who in the early 1940s offered to sell the Gotham copies of her book D. H. LAWRENCE: AN UNPROFESSIONAL STUDY (1932) for one dollar each; Harry T. Moore, who edited *D. H. Lawrence's Letters to Bertrand Russell* (1948), after Frances Steloff had purchased the letters; and Dame Edith Sitwell, who humorously compared DHL's poetry to a Jaeger sweater: "soft, woolly, and hot."]

4597 Stoehr, Taylor. " 'Mentalized Sex' in D. H. Lawrence," NOVEL: A FORUM ON FICTION, VIII (Winter 1975), 101-22.

DHL cannot communicate to us adequately the goal he has in mind--to correct consciousness and therefore destroy pornography--for the goal is experience unmediated by language. DHL hated masturbation and pornography not so much for themselves as for their function in the mental life, a function which is to make one prefer an ideal, a mental construct, to a person. The crisis in culture was not one of sexuality but one of consciousness. [Comparisons of DHL's work with Samuel Richardson's are provided.]

4598 Street, Brian V. THE SAVAGE IN LITERATURE (Lond: Routledge & Kegan Paul, 1975), pp. 10-11, 29, 93, 152, 158-59.

DHL, along with Forster and Conrad, was among the few novelists of the early decades of the twentieth century who treated members of a primitive society with the seriousness and sympathy considered necessary by modern standards for an anthropological understanding. In *The Plumed Serpent* DHL sought to provide interpretations for primitive customs. He gave considerable significance, in his Mexican studies, to the symbolism of colors in Aztec ritual.

4599 Sugiyama, Yasushi. "Shinda Musuko to Uchû no Rizumu"

(The Son Who Died in the Rhythm of the Universe), D. H. LAWRENCE STUDIES (Kyôto), No. 3 (Sept 1975), 133-56.

Paul's sudden redirection--toward life--at the conclusion of *Sons and Lovers* is not credible to some readers. The following four points, however, justify Paul's repudiation of the drift towards death: (1) the rhythm of the universe, (2) the symbol of the clenched fists, (3) the mercy killing of Mrs. Morel, and (4) Paul's rebirth from the Greater Womb. [In Japanese.]

4600 Sullivan, Elizabeth Quay. "1. Lawrence among the Aztecs: Travels, Readings, and Poems. 2. Functions of Disguise in Ben Jonson's Comedies. 3. The Language of the Theater in Hawthorne's Tales and THE SCARLET LETTER." DISSERTATION ABSTRACTS INTERNATIONAL, XXXVI (1976), 6665A. Unpublished dissertation, Rutgers University, 1975.

4601 Sykes, Christopher. EVELYN WAUGH: A BIOGRAPHY (Bost & Toronto: Little, Brown, 1975), p. 433.

Although Evelyn Waugh regarded DHL highly as a writer, he declined the invitation to give evidence for the defense in the 1960 English censorship trial of *Lady Chatterley's Lover* (Regina v. Penguin Books Ltd.) since he thought DHL followed fallacious theories on how to write about sex in fiction. "If he [Waugh] had been asked by the other side he might conceivably have accepted."

4602 Tabuchi, Hiroyuki. "Ai to Koritsu--*Musuko to Koibito* ni Tsuite" (Love and Isolation--On *Sons and Lovers*), KEIZAI SHŪSHI (Nihon University), No. 45 (Nov 1975), 40-58.

In *Sons and Lovers* DHL is aiming at neither an autobiographical sketch of Paul's growth nor a record of his Oedipus complex. The intense contrast arising from the effective arrangement of characters may be primary here, one character being set up in opposition to another. The aspiration to attain "harmony," which later develops into DHL's central message, remains submerged as yet. [In Japanese.]

4603 Teruya, Yoshio. "*The Plumed Serpent* ni Tsuite" (On *The Plumed Serpent*), WASEDA JOURNAL OF GENERAL SCIENCES (Waseda University), No. 12 (Feb 1975), 55-74.

As a political novel *The Plumed Serpent* provides a very interesting theme. The creative opposition between politics and religion produces the "soft bloom of being," which is what Kate has always sought. But the tranquility is destroyed by a sort of altruism expressed in a will to power. [In Japanese.]

4604 Tetsumura, Haryo. " 'Ureshii Yurei no Kageri" (A Study of "Glad Ghosts"), BULLETIN OF FACULTY OF EDUCATION (Nagasaki University), No. 24 (March 1975), 37-44.

In introducing pagan gods, the modal rites of dancing, and the appearance of hyperphysical things and ghosts, DHL had the purpose of incorporating the supernatural into the fabric of the story and of consolidating the short story and the fable. If *The Man Who Died* is properly called a fable, "Glad Ghosts" foreshadows it. [In Japanese.]

4605 Thompson, Leslie M. "The Christ Who Didn't Die: Analogues to D. H. Lawrence's *The Man Who Died*," D. H. LAWRENCE REVIEW, VIII (Spring 1975), 19-30.

DHL's *The Man Who Died* "reflects the cultural milieu of his era, and possibly [his] knowledge of earlier works or comments by Oscar Wilde, William Butler Yeats, Frank Harris, and especially George Moore, all of whom preceded Lawrence in suggesting that Christ did not really die on the cross but returned from the tomb to live out his days on earth." DHL's story "culminates a long period of literary and cultural ferment which by the last quarter of the nineteenth century made unorthodox discussions of Christ if not palatable at least less offensive." "New scientific views,...the ideas of Spinoza, Strauss, Renan," as well as Thomas Henry Huxley's essays and the Oxford Movement contributed to the change in attitude. There is every reason to suppose DHL's familiarity with the work of his predecessors and contemporaries. [Specific analogues are examined in relation to *The Man Who Died*.]

4606 Toyokuni, Takashi. "*Shojo to Jipushi*--Hahaoya no Botsuraku" (*The Virgin and the Gipsy*--The Fall of Mother), ENGLISH LITERATURE IN HOKKAIDO (Muroran Institute of Technology), No. 20 (June 1975), 21-29.

[Considers the meaning of "the flood scene" and the death of Granny, "Mater," in *The Virgin and the Gipsy,* analyzing the inhabitants in the world of anti-life and those in the world of life. [In Japanese.]

4607 Trautmann, Joanne. "The Body Electric," in "On the Teaching of D. H. Lawrence: A Forum," ed by Langdon Elsbree. D. H. LAWRENCE REVIEW, VIII (Spring 1975), 65-68.

[Description of a course in the Humanities Department of the Pennsylvania State University, College of Medicine, called "The Body Electric" and devoted to " 'the artistic, as opposed to the scientific, study of the body.' " Including considerations of William Carlos Williams, John Donne, Robert Graves, Allen Ginsberg, Sylvia Plath, and André Gide, the course devoted its largest segment of time to DHL and Walt Whitman.]

4608 Tysdahl, Bjørn. "Kvinnesak og skjønnlitteratur. D. H. Lawrence: *The Rainbow*" (Feminism in Fiction: D. H. Lawrence, *The Rainbow*), EDDA (Oslo), LXXV, No. 1 (1975), 29-36.

[Detailed discussion and critique of Kate Millett's feminist reading of *The Rainbow* in SEXUAL POLITICS (1970). In particular her view that DHL found Ursula's independent womanhood " 'hard to bear' " is countered by Leavis's suggestion that Ursula's character is the nearest of all the characters to DHL's own. The characterization is discussed in the light of DHL's letter to Edward Garnett (5 June 1914) about the distinction between " 'the old stable ego, of the character' " and " 'another ego.' "] [In Norwegian.]

4609 Unrue, Darlene H. "Lawrence's Vision of Evil: The Power-Spirit in *The Rainbow* and *Women in Love*," DALHOUSIE REVIEW, LV (Winter 1975-1976), 643-54.

DHL perceives evil as an unnatural lust for power--a desire to impose one's will upon another creature. Not only can this "power-spirit" undermine relationships between individuals; it can have an even more pernicious influence upon society at large, where it manifests itself in contemporary religion, in industry, and in warfare. In short, the "power-spirit" can be recognized in any exercise of power which is not directed toward brotherhood. DHL's vision of evil is constant throughout his work, but it is most concentrated in *The Rainbow* and *Women in Love*. In both novels he delineates this vision through pairs of lovers; whether each pair succeeds in establishing "mystic communion" depends upon their willingness to renounce the "power-impulse." [Examines the relationships of Will and Anna and of Ursula and Winifred Inger in *The Rainbow* and those of Birkin and Ursula and Gerald Crich and Gudrun in *Women in Love*.] Analysis of these two novels justifies the conclusion that unfulfilled characters in DHL's fiction are thwarted because of an evil internal to themselves--the lust for power.

4610 von Broembsen, F. "Mythic Identification and Spatial Inscendence: The Cosmic Vision of D. H. Lawrence," WESTERN HUMANITIES REVIEW, XXIX (Spring 1975), 137-54.

DHL's "categories" are non-traditional, defying those who follow the categories of democratic individualism. DHL's "wholesale indictment of western civilization makes any criticism pronounced within its categories if not trivial at least impertinent to Lawrence and pertinent only to the critic's context." In DHL one finds, incomplete and in tension with the "individualistic consciousness of self," a "reaching back to levels of cultural experience antecedent to the discovery of the great dichotomy" between "I" and the world. Place, space, and being are significant categories in DHL's fictional universe. [Discusses *The Plumed Serpent* and *Women in Love*.]

4611 Wallace, Mary Elizabeth. " 'Study of Thomas Hardy': D. H. Lawrence's 'Art-Speech' in the Light of Polanyi's PERSONAL KNOWLEDGE." Unpublished dissertation, University of Kent, 1975. [Listed in D. H. LAWRENCE REVIEW, X (Fall 1977), 304.]

4612 Wallmann, Jürgen P. "Eben nicht nur der Autor der *Lady Chatterley*. Prosawerke von David Herbert Lawrence" (Not Just the Author of *Lady Chatterley*: Prose Works by D. H. Lawrence), BADISCHE ZEITUNG, 28 June 1975.

[Review of *David Herbert Lawrence: Sämtliche Erzählungen und Kurzromans (David Herbert Lawrence: The Complete Tales and Short Novels)* (1975).] DHL is not an exponent of modern pornography. The missionary zeal behind his gospel of erotic Romanticism is often to the detriment of his artistry, particularly in his novels. DHL is at his best in the tales and short novels in which sex becomes a means of widening man's scope of life. [In German.]

4613 West, Alick. "D. H. Lawrence," CRISIS AND CRITICISM, AND SELECTED LITERARY ESSAYS (Norwood, PA: Norwood Editions; Lond: Lawrence & Wishart, 1975), pp. 259-82.

Although there is some reason for Christopher Caudwell's judgment, in STUDIES

IN A DYING CULTURE (1938), that DHL's "revolt against bourgeois relations" reflects his own imprisonment within them, the "highest value" of DHL's work is shown in his "power of wonder that reality is" and his conviction that "our life must be founded in the consciousness of our participation in being." In *The Rainbow* man's "participation in universal being" is achieved first in "relationship with the earth through his work," then "in the sexual love of man and woman." Against this "ground-tone," DHL "shows the working of social change in individual lives," on the one hand, in a "movement away from...inter-relation...with the earth" and toward "individual self-consciousness," and on the other hand, in the frustration of "this desire for a life of self-responsibility." [Detailed discussion of *The Rainbow* supports this thesis.] "The 'carbon' which is his theme is the participation of all individuals in universal being, and the attitude which Lawrence demands toward his characters is that we should recognise that through this participation they are." [Further discussion of the "error" in Caudwell's "general theoretical position."]

4614 Wevill, Sharon Lee Potts. "The Heart Sacrificed to the Sun: Mythos of Reality in D. H. Lawrence's American Fiction," DISSERTATION ABSTRACTS INTERNATIONAL, XXXVII (1976), 345A. Unpublished dissertation, University of Texas at Austin, 1975.

4615 Wicker, Brian. "Lawrence and the Unseen Presences," THE STORY-SHAPED WORLD: FICTION AND METAPHYSICS: SOME VARIATIONS ON A THEME (Lond: Athlone P; Notre Dame, IN: University of Notre Dame P, 1975), pp. 120-33; additional references, pp. 59, 67, 85, 108, 109, 117, 118, 134-36, 137, 142, 143, 149, 151, 156, 157, 195, 196, 202, 205, 206, 208, 209, 210, 212, 216.
For DHL, the modern world was "tragic" but "refused to take itself tragically" because "it had replaced the metaphysical conceptions of man's place in Nature ...by merely illustrative images of Nature." The "attitude to tragic waste" which he attributes to Hardy in *Study of Thomas Hardy* is developed further in "Birkin's moment of cosmic optimism as he is confronted by Gerald's death in *Women in Love*." Nature in *Women in Love,* far from being only a woodland retreat, is intended as " 'the vast incomprehensible pattern of some primal morality.' " This idea is developed most explicitly in *St. Mawr,* in which, in the first half, "the theme of a living and meaningful Nature is embodied in St Mawr himself" and in the second half, in "the Mexican [sic] landscape in which Lou finds herself at the end." The woman in "The Woman Who Rode Away" is the " 'central intelligence" from whose consistent point of view the story is told. "Once that intelligence is extinguished, ...the story freezes into an eternal gesture." *The Man Who Died* shows "what Lawrence makes of a death that is not final": "the cosmic myth of the renovation of man by the sun...made actual in the return to life of the man by the sun's radiance; literally in Part 1...but more profoundly still in the sexual encounter of Part 2." The gamecock, like the horse in *St. Mawr,* "symbolizes 'the greater morality of life itself.' "

4616 Widmer, Kingsley. "Lawrence as Abnormal Novelist," D. H. LAWRENCE REVIEW, VIII (Summer 1975), 220-32.

[Review essay on Scott Sanders, D. H. LAWRENCE: THE WORLD OF THE FIVE MAJOR NOVELS (1973), and John E. Stoll, THE NOVELS OF D. H. LAWRENCE: A SEARCH FOR INTEGRATION (1971). The author includes his list of "the best and 'essential' Lawrence" to show that DHL "should not be understood as primarily a novelist" at all.]

4617 Worthen, John. "The Chambers Memoirs of D. H. Lawrence: A Reply," RENAISSANCE AND MODERN STUDIES, XIX (1975), 98-107.

[This reply to George J. Zytaruk, "The Chambers Memoirs of D. H. Lawrence--Which Chambers?" RENAISSANCE AND MODERN STUDIES, XVII (1973), 5-37, refutes the thesis that Jessie Chambers is the author of the memoir of DHL attributed to May Chambers Holbrook in "The Chambers Papers," D. H. LAWRENCE: A COMPOSITE BIOGRAPHY, ed by Edward Nehls, Vol. III: 1925-1930 (1959), pp. 552-98, 599-608, 609-11, 616-20. See also rejoinder by George J. Zytaruk, "The Chambers Memoirs of D. H. Lawrence--Which Chambers?: A Reply to Mr. John Worthen," RENAISSANCE AND MODERN STUDIES, XIX (1975), 108-11.]

4618 Worthen, John. "Sanity, Madness and *Women in Love*," TRIVIUM, X (May 1975), 125-36.

Early reviewers and subsequent critics have misunderstood DHL's intentions in *Women in Love*. Responses usually characterized as insane are shown to be closer to real experience in the modern era than is generally believed. The dissolution and disintegration of the age are indicated in the title *The Latter Days*, which DHL once considered for the novel.

4619 Yagyu, Naoyuki. "D. H. Rorensu to Kirisutokyō" (D. H. Lawrence and Christianity), in KIRISUTOKYŌ TO BUNGAKU (DAI 3 SHU) (Christianity and Literature, No. 3), ed by Tomoichi Sasbuchi (Tokyo: Kasama Shoin, 1975), pp. 135-54.

[In Japanese.]

4620 Yamashita, Kazuichiro. "D. H. Lawrence *Seishin-Bunseki to Muishiki* ni Tsuite (II)" (On *Psychoanalysis and the Unconscious* by D. H. Lawrence [II]), ESSAYS IN CELEBRATION OF THE NINETIETH ANNIVERSARY OF CHŪO UNIVERSITY (Chūo University, Aug 1975), pp. 167-88.

[Second of two articles on *Psychoanalysis and the Unconscious*.] This study analyzes Chapters III and IV of *Psychoanalysis and the Unconscious*, first criticizing what DHL calls the pristine consciousness, then discussing DHL's treatment of the communion of love between mother and child. [See also Kazuichiro Yamashita, "D. H. Lawrence *Seishin-Bunseki to Muishiki* ni Tsuite (I)" (On *Psychoanalysis and the Unconscious* by D. H. Lawrence [I]), ENGLISH LANGUAGE AND LITERATURE (Chūo University), No. 13 (March 1973), 103-24.] [In Japanese.]

4621 Yoshida, Masako. "Yami no Sekai e no Tabidachi--Morel-Fujin no Shi ga Imisuru Mono" (A Journey to "Darkness"--What the Death of Mrs. Morel Means), D. H. LAWRENCE STUDIES (Kyôto), No. 3 (Sept 1975), 51-82.

The protagonist Paul's psychological and mystical experiences in darkness largely dominate DHL's autobiographical novel, *Sons and Lovers.* The experience DHL gained through his mother's death made him discover the significance of darkness, in other words, "maternal darkness." [In Japanese.]

4622 Yoshii, Mitsuo. "Bunmei no Hôkai-Katei no Naka de--Lawrence *Koisuru Onnatachi* Ron" (In the Dissolution of Civilization--On Lawrence's *Women in Love*), JOURNAL OF THE COLLEGE OF LIBERAL ARTS (Toyama University), No. 7 (March 1975), 65-83.

In *Women in Love* there are two main themes: one is the love mode between man and woman; the other is the author's view of the collapse and dissolution of European civilization which the humanism, science, and technology since the Renaissance have brought about. Through these two themes DHL's ideas as a critic as well as an artist are studied. [In Japanese.]

4623 Yoshii, Mitsuo. "Shisô no Henreki--Lawrence *Aaron no Tsue* Ron" (Pilgrimage in Ideas--On Lawrence's *Aaron's Rod*), WASEDA REVIEW, No. 14 (Sept 1975), 30-47.

DHL's wish to relieve and to lead his fellow men in the world may be seen in *Aaron's Rod* in Lilly's explanation to Aaron of his ideas on the social order and leadership. Lilly's concern with the problems of the accomplishment of an individual self and of the relation between a man and others, a mass and a nation, are examined. [In Japanese.]

4624 Yoshimura, Hirokazu. "*Musuko to Koibito* ni Okeru Niku to Kotoba--Sono 'Jogen' o Megutte no Ichikôsatsu" (*Sons and Lovers* and Its Foreword), D. H. LAWRENCE STUDIES (Kyôto), No. 3 (Sept 1975), 3-30.

This paper first explains DHL's ideas of "Flesh" and "Word" found in the Foreword to *Sons and Lovers,* then considers how these ideas are related to the novel itself. [In Japanese.]

4625 Yoshimura, Hirokazu. "*The Trespasser* no Shizen to Jinbutsu o Megutte--Siegmund no Tankyû to Zasetsu" (A Study of *The Trespasser*--Siegmund's Quest and Collapse), STUDIES IN FOREIGN LITERATURES (Ritsumeikan University), No. 33 (June 1975), 51-79.

This paper deals with four phases of Siegmund, the hero of *The Trespasser:* the first phase is as a bee, the second as an animal, the third as the priest of the sun, and the fourth as an anemone. [In Japanese.]

4626 Youssef, T. I. M. "The Use of Mythology in the Novels of D. H. Lawrence." Unpublished dissertation, University of Glasgow, 1975. [Listed in Geoffrey M. Paterson and Joan E. Hardy (eds), INDEX TO THESES, XXVII, Pt 1 (1979), p. 10.]

4627 Zytaruk, George J. "The Chambers Memoirs of D. H. Lawrence--Which Chambers?: A Reply to Mr. John Worthen," RENAISSANCE AND MODERN STUDIES, XIX (1975), 108-11.
[This rejoinder to John Worthen, "The Chambers Memoirs of D. H. Lawrence: A Reply," RENAISSANCE AND MODERN STUDIES, XIX (1975), 98-107, reasserts Zytaruk's thesis, in "The Chambers Memoirs of D. H. Lawrence--Which Chambers?"RENAISSANCE AND MODERN STUDIES, XVII (1973), 5-37, that Jessie Chambers is the author of the memoir of DHL attributed to May Chambers Holbrook in "The Chambers Papers," D. H. LAWRENCE: A COMPOSITE BIOGRAPHY, ed by Edward Nehls, Vol. III: 1925-1930 (1959), pp. 552-98, 599-608, 609-11, 616-20.] Two kinds of evidence make the hypothesis of Jessie's authorship "plausible" if not "foolproof": (1) "the multiplicity of...[verbal] parallels" between "The Chambers Papers" and D. H. LAWRENCE: A PERSONAL RECORD; and (2) the fact that "what we know from Jessie's correspondence with Koteliansky about the 40-page manuscript [of her 'Novel of Youth']...does fit the characteristics of the memoir attributed to May Chambers."

Index

AUTHORS

Included here are authors of articles and books on Lawrence, editors and compilers of works in which criticism on Lawrence appears. Editors and translators are identified parenthetically: (ed), (trans). Numbers after each name refer to the item(s) in the bibliography where the name occurs.

Abbas, Ali Abdalla: 3654
Abrams, M. H.: 3655
Ackerman, James S. (ed): 4449
Adam, Ian: 4029
Adam, Michael [See Taylor, Kim]
Adamowski, Thomas H.: 4259, 4260, 4445
Adams, Elsie B.: 3248
Adelman, Gary Stephen: 2197, 2361, 3025
Ades, John I.: 3592
Adler, Renata: 3026
Agee, James: 2198
Agg, Howard: 2901
Alberto, Giovanni: 3656
Alcibiade [See Praz, Mario]
Alcorn, John Marshall: 2763
Al-Dabbagh, Abdullah M.: 3657
Aldington, Richard, 2200, 4446
Alexander, Edward: 3027
Alexander, John C.: 2603, 2764
Al-Fishawy, W. M.: 3837
Alinei, Tamara: 3838, 4447
Alldritt, Keith: 3658
Allen, Walter: 2470
Allendorf, Otmar: 3249, 3424, 3659
Allison, Christopher FitzSimons: 3839
Allott, Miriam: 2765, 3840
Alpers, Anthony: 3425
Alpert, Hollis: 3426; (ed): 3115
Altenberg, Bengt: 3250

Alter, Robert: 3427
Altick, Richard D.: 2604
Amado Lévy-Valensi, Eliane: 2201
Amberg, George (ed): 3449
Amette, Jacques-Pierre: 3028, 3251, 3660
Amorós, Andrés: 2766
Andersch, Alfred: 3029
André, Robert: 2202
Andrews, Cicily Isabel Fairfield [pseud West, Rebecca]: 2187
Andrews, Nigel: 3428
Andrews, W. T.: 2767, 2768, 2902, 3252; (ed): 2389, 2394, 2607, 2624, 2744, 2944, 3661
Antonini, Giacomo: 2903
Aoyama, Seiko: 2605, 2904
Appel, George Fowler: 4030
Arlen, Michael J.: 3429
Armstrong, Marion: 3430, 3662
Armytage, W. H. G.: 2062, 2905, 3030
Arnold, Aerol: 2362
Arnold, Armin: 2063, 2064, 2204, 2363, 2364, 2472, 2606, 3031, 3253, 3841; (ed): 2203, 2204, 2296, 3254; (trans): 2364
Asahi, Chiseki: 3842, 4261, 4448
Asakawa, Jun: 2065, 2365, 2366
Ashley, Leonard R. N. (ed): 3032
Asquith, Lady Cynthia: 3033
Asselineau, Roger: 3034

Astor, Stuart L. (ed): 3032
Atkins, John: 3431
Atkinson, Curtis: 2607
Austin, Allan Edward: 2473
Baim, Joseph: 2906, 3035, 3663, 3843; (ed): 3843
Bair, Hebe [later Mace, Hebe Riddick]: 4031
Baker, Ernest A.: 2907
Baker, Ida [pseud Moore, Leslie]: 3763
Baker, James R.: 4262
Baker, Paul Geoffrey: 4263
Baker, William E.: 2908
Balakian, Nona: 2206
Balbert, Peter Henry: 3255, 4264
Baldanza, Frank: 2066, 4032
Baldeshwiler, Eileen: 3256
Baldwin, Alice: 3664
Ballin, Michael: 3844
Bantock, Geoffrey Herman: 2367, 2608
Barbati, Claudio: 2609
Barber, David S.: 3432, 3665
Barber, Janet: 3845
Barbier, Françoise-Marie: 3433
Bareiss, Dieter: 3257
Barfield, Owen: 2610
Barnes, Jo (comp): 3847, 3888
Baron, Carl Edward: 3258, 3434, 3666, 3846, 3847, 4265
Barr, William: 4033
Barrett, Gerald R. (ed): 3601, 4266, 4390, 4408
Barrière, Françoise: 3259
Barry, J.: 3260
Barry, Sandra: 2769
Bartel, Roland: 4449; (ed): 4449
Bartlett, Norman: 2474
Basler, Roy: 2207
Battye, Louis: 2770
Bauerle, Richard F.: 3036
Baumbach, Jonathan (ed): 3037
Baxter, John: 4195
Bayer, Roberta M.: 4267
Bayley, John: 2067, 3038
Beachcroft, Thomas Owen: 3039
Beagle, Peter S.: 2909
Beal, Anthony: 2068
Beards, Richard Douglas: 2611, 3040, 3261, 3435, 3667, 4034, 4268, 4269, 4450
Beatty, C. J. P.: 3848

Beauchamp, Gorman: 4035
Beck, Warren: 2208
Becker, Henry, III: 4036
Beckham, Richard Hamilton, Sr.: 3262
Bedford, Sybille: 2069, 2070, 4037
Bedient, Calvin Bernard: 2475, 2771, 3849
Beebe, Maurice: 2368, 3668
Beer, J. B.: 2209
Beer, John: 3669, 3850
Beirne, Raymond M.: 4270
Beker, Miroslav: 3263, 4038
Bell, Michael: 3436, 3851
Bell, Quentin: 2641, 3041, 3852
Bellamy, William: 3670
Bellow, Saul: 3671
Benkovitz, Miriam J.: 4446
Bennett, Michael: 3853
Benstock, Bernard: 3042
Bentley, Joseph: 2910
Berg, Robert von: 2071
Bergonzi, Bernard: 2210, 2612, 3437; (ed): 3508
Bersani, Leo: 4451
Bertaccini, Renato: 2369
Bertelsen, Evelyn Jeannette: 3854
Betsky-Zweig, S.: 4039
Bhalla, Brij Mohan: 3672
Bhat, Vishnu: 3264
Bickerton, Derek: 2911
Biles, Jack I.: 3438
Billington, Michael: 3265, 4040
Birnbaum, Milton: 3673
Bishop, David R.: 4041
Black, Michael: 3855, 3856, 4452
Blanchard, Lydia: 4453
Blanchard, Margaret: 3439
Bleich, David: 2912
Blevins, Winifred: 3440
Blissett, William: 2772
Blöcker, Gunter: 2370, 3043
Bloom, Edward A.: 3266
Bloom, Harold: 3441
Bloom, Lillian D.: 3266
Bloomfield, Morton W. (ed): 3444
Bo, Carlo: 2212
Bobbitt, Joan: 4042, 4454
Bogan, Louise: 3442
Bogdanovich, Peter: 2213
Bojarski, Edmund A.: 4089
Boklund, Gunnar: 2913
Bompiani, Valentino (ed): 2679
Bonadeo, Barbara Bates: 4043

INDEX OF AUTHORS

Bonner, Marjorie (ed): 2690
Booth, Wayne C.: 2072
Bordinat, Philip: 3857
Boren, James L.: 2613
Boulton, James T.: 3044, 3267, 3674, 3858, 4271; (ed): 3044; (gen. ed.): 4044
Boulton, Marjorie: 4455
Bowering, Peter: 3045
Bradbrook, Frank: 2214
Bradbrook, Muriel C.: 3859
Bradbury, Malcolm: 3675, 4045
Brady, Emily Kuempel: 2215
Braem, Helmut M.: 4456
Bramley, J. A.: 2614
Branda, Eldon S.: 2476
Brandabur, Agnes M.: 4046
Brandeis, R. C.: 4047
Brashear, Lucy M.: 3860
Brayfield, Peg: 3676
Bredsdorff, Elias: 3046
Breit, Harvey (ed): 2690
Brennan, Neil F.: 2615
Brett, Dorothy: 2914, 4357
Bridson, D. G.: 3861
Briscoe, Mary Louise: 3443
Brookesmith, Peter: 4048
Brophy, Brigid: 2371, 2915
Brotherston, J. G.: 3862
Broughton, Bradford D. (ed): 3564
Brown, Homer O.: 4272
Brugière, Bernard: 3047, 3048
Bryden, Ronald: 2916, 3049, 3050
Buckler, William E. (ed): 2875
Buckley, B. R.: 3863
Buckley, Brian: 2616
Buckley, Jerome Hamilton: 3444, 4273
Bugarski, Ranko: 2073
Bullock, Alice: 3864
Burbank, Rex: 2477
Burgess, Anthony: 3445, 3865; (ed): 3865
Burke, Herbert: 3446
Burkill, T. A.: 2247
Burns, Robert: 3447, 3677
Burns, Wayne: 2773, 3866
Burroughs, William D.: 2372
Burwell, Rose Marie: 3268, 3269, 3448, 4049, 4274
Busch, Günther: 2216
Butler, Gerald Joseph: 3270
Callaghan, Morley: 2217

Callow, Philip: 4457
Cameron, Mary Carolyn Davis: 2774
Campbell, Beatrice Elvery [See Glenavy, Lady Beatrice]
Canby, Vincent: 3449, 3450
Candelaria, Frederick: 2879
Canfield, Ken: 4458
Capey, A. C.: 4050
Carballo, Emmanuel: 3451
Carey, John: 4051
Carr, Virginia Spencer: 4459
Carrington, Dora: 3678
Carrington, Noel: 3678; (ed): 2641
Carroll, Kathleen: 3452
Carroll, LaVon B.: 2917
Carstarphen, Sally S.: 4275
Carter, John: 3271
Casey, Paul C.: 2075
Cassola, Carlo: 3051
Cavallone, Anna Anzi: 4460
Cavitch, David Berl: 2775, 2776, 3272, 4276
Cecchi, Emilio: 2478
Cecil, Robert: 3273
Ceserani, Remo: 2218
Chabrowe, Leonard: 4277
Chaddock, Bruce E.: 4278
Chamberlain, Robert L.: 2373
Chambers, J. K. (ed): 2617
Chambers, Jessie [pseud T., E.]: 2617; see also Wood, Jessie Chambers
Chambers, Jonathan David: 2617, 3867
Chambers, Maria Cristina: 2479
Chapman, Robert T.: 3453, 3868
Chapple, J. A. V.: 3454
Charlesworth, Barbara: 2618
Chauhan, Pradyumna S.: 3455
Chavis, Geraldine Giebel: 3679
Cherry, Richard L.: 4461
Chesson, Diane Marie: 4462
Chinol, Elio: 4279
Choudbury, Sheila Lahiri: 3869
Choudhury, A. F.: 3052
Chrisman, Reva Wells: 4280
Christian, Roy: 3870
Christie, Ian Leslie: 3274
Chung, Chong-Wha: 3680
Cipolla, Elizabeth: 3275
Clancy, Jack: 3681
Clark, L. D.: 2220, 2374, 2480, 2619, 3456, 3682

Clark, LaVerne H. (photog): 2220, 3682
Clark, Ronald W.: 3053, 4463
Clarke, Colin: 3277, 3278, 3279, 3706; (ed): 2086, 2107, 2423, 2624, 2639, 2647, 3122, 3276, 3277
Clarke, Richard: 4281
Clements, A. L.: 2221
Cline, C. L.: 4282
Clor, Harry M.: 3054
Clupper, Beatrice Blong: 3683
Coffey, Warren: 2375
Cogan, Lee (ed): 2682
Cohen, John: 2272
Cohen, Judith Dana: 3457
Cohen, Richard: 3458
Cohn, Dorritt: 2777
Colacurcio, Michael J.: 4464
Cole, William: 2918
Coleman, Arthur: 3684
Coleman, John: 3459
Collier, Peter: 3056
Colmer, John: 3280
Colquhoun, Keith: 4052
Comerford, Anthony: 3281
Coniff, Gerald William: 4053
Conley, Robert J.: 4461
Connell, Charles: 3460
Connolly, Cyril: 2222
Consolo, Dominick P.: 3283; (ed): 2291, 2351, 2372, 2407, 2430, 2456, 2694, 3282, 3410
Cooke, Regina: 3461
Coombes, Henry: 2376, 3871, 4054, 4055; (ed): 2114, 2115, 2119, 2248, 2491, 2653, 2654, 3092, 3349, 3351, 3714, 4054, 4055, 4141
Cooney, James: 4277
Cooney, Seamus: 4284
Corbin, Richard Johnstone: 4056
Corke, Helen: 2223, 2620, 2724, 3685, 3872, 4285, 4465, 4466
Cornwell, Ethel F.: 2224
Corsani, Mary: 2621, 2778
Cowan, James Costello: 2481, 2622, 2919, 2920, 3284, 3462, 3873, 4286, 4287, 4467; (ed): 3064, 3065, 3066, 3295, 3296, 3297, 3468, 3469, 3470, 3697, 3698, 3699, 3881, 3882, 3883, 4068, 4069, 4070, 4295, 4296, 4297, 4477, 4478, 4479

Cowan, S. E.: 3057
Cowell, Catherine R.: 3686
Cox, C. B.: 2076, 2377, 2779; (ed): 3905, 3906, 3974
Cox, James: 4468
Coxhead, Gabrielle: 2921
Craig, Alec: 2225
Craig, David: 2226, 2482, 2922, 4057
Crist, Judith: 3463
Cross, Amanda [See Heilbrun, Carolyn G.]
Cross, Gustov: 2484
Crossman, R. H. S.: 2485
Crotch, Martha Gordon: 4469
Crump, G. B.: 3040, 3058, 3464, 3687, 3688, 4058
Cummins, P. D.: 2780
Cunningham, J. S.: 2227
Čura-Sazdanič [also Čura], Ileana: 2623, 2923, 3285
Cushman, Keith: 3286, 3287, 3689, 3690, 3874, 3875, 3876, 3900, 4059, 4060, 4061, 4288, 4289, 4470, 4471
Czuchlewski, Ellen Dugan: 4290
Daiches, David: 2379
Daleski, Herman M.: 2624
Dalton, Jack P.: 2924
Dalton, Robert O.: 2229
Daniel, John: 3288
Daniel, John Turner: 4062
Darroch, Sandra Jobson: 4472
Davie, Donald: 2077, 2078, 2781, 3877
Davies, J. V.: 4063; (ed): 4063
Davies, Russell: 4291
Davis, Edward: 2230, 2486
Davis, Patricia C.: 4064
Davis, Peter: 3289
Davis, Robert Gorham: 4473
Dawson, Eugene W.: 2380, 2782, 3059; (ed): 2853
Dawson, Helen: 2925, 3060
Deb, Praley Kumar: 3061
Decker, Randall E. (ed): 2783
de Filippis, Simonetta: 3878, 4292, 4474
Dehring, Erna: 2079
Dekker, George: 2487
Delany, Paul: 4475; (ed): 3290
Delavenay, Émile: 3062, 3291, 3292, 3414, 3691, 3692, 3693, 3694, 3695, 3696, 3879, 4065, 4293, 4476

INDEX OF AUTHORS

Delavenay, Katharine M. (trans): 3292, 3696
Delbaere-Garant, Jane: 2381
dell'Arco, Mario: 2231
DeMaio, Don: 3465
de Michelis, Eurialo: 2080, 2081
Denby, David (ed): 3505
DeNitto, Dennis: 2784
Dennis, Nigel: 3880
De Rougemont, Denis: 3063
Derrick, John Bruce: 4066
De Saint Jean, Robert: 4294
De Villeneuve-Trans, Roméo: 2625
DeWinter, Oswald: 2232
de Wofe, Ivor: 4067
Díaz de León, Martha: 2626
DiGaetani, John Louis: 4072
Dignon, Hugh Alexander: 4299
DiMaggio, Richard: 4073
Ditsky, John M.: 4300
Dobrowolny, Welleda: 4301
Doheny, John Rodney: 2785, 3884, 4302
Dolch, Martin (ed): 2464
Donald, D. R.: 2489
Donnerstag, Jürgen: 3299
Donoghue, Denis: 2627, 2628, 3885, 3886, 4074
Dooley, D. J.: 4303
Doré, Joseph, III: 4482
Dorner, Marjorie Leone: 3700
Dougherty, Adelyn: 3169
Drabble, Margaret: 4075, 4304
Drain, Richard Leslie: 2236, 2237, 2629
Draper, Ronald P.: 2382, 2490, 2786, 2787, 2788, 2926, 3067, 3302, 3473; (ed): 3472, 3473
Drew, Elizabeth: 2383
Dudek, Louis: 2384, 3068
Duffy, Martha: 3887
Duncan, Iris June Autry: 2630
Dunlap, Dennis: 2244
Durham, John: 2927
Durr, R. A.: 3474
Durrell, Lawrence: 2385
Dutton, Geoffrey: 2386
Dyson, A. E.: 2377, 2631; (ed): 3905, 3906, 3974, 4411
Eagleton, Terry: 3475
Earl, G. A.: 2789
Eastman, Donald Roger: 3701
Eaves, T. C. Duncan: 3123

Eccles, David McA.: 2790
Edelstein, Arthur (ed): 3037
Edge, Charles E. (ed): 2506, 3923
Edwards, John D.: 3069
Edwards, Lucy I. (comp): 3070, 3847, 3888
Efron, Arthur: 2791, 2877
Egashira, Teruo: 2792
Ehrenzweig, Robert [pseud Lucas, Robert]: 3948
Ehrstine, John W.: 2633
Eichrodt, John Morris: 2238, 3476
Eisenstein, Samuel Abraham: 2634, 2635, 4305
Ekner, Reidar: 3702
Elder, John Clark: 4076
Ellmann, Richard: 4077; (ed): 2636
Elsbree, Langdon: 2387, 3071, 3889; (ed): 4468, 4483, 4533, 4569, 4607
Elwin, Malcolm: 3890
Emmett, V. J., Jr.: 3891
Empson, William: 2388
Engelberg, Edward: 2389, 2637
Englander, Ann: 2390, 2793
Enright, Dennis Joseph: 2239, 2491
Enroth, Clyde: 3303
Erlich, Richard D.: 2928
Ernst, Morris L.: 2492
Erskine, Thomas L. (ed): 3601, 4145, 4266, 4390, 4408
Exner, Julian: 3072, 4078
Faas, Egbert: 4079
Fabiani, Enzo: 2240
Fabrizio, Ray: 3478, 3479
Fadiman, Regina: 3892
Fahey, William Arthur: 2493, 3073
Fairbanks, N. David: 3703
Fairchild, Hoxie Neale: 2241, 3074
Fantel, Hans: 2943
Farber, Stephen: 3480
Farmer, David: 3481, 3482, 3483, 3893, 3894
Farr, Judith: 3484; (ed): 2263, 2348, 2351, 2639, 2869, 3484, 3485
Farrer, Edward Alfred: 4484
Fedder, Norman Joseph: 2242, 2794
Feidelson, Charles, Jr. (ed): 2636
Feldmann, Hans Eugene: 4306
Feltes, N. N.: 2391
Fenby, George: 4080
Fernandez, Diane: 3075, 3076, 3304
Ferrier, Carole: 3704, 3895, 3896, 4081

Fiderer, Gerald: 3077
Fiedler, Leslie A.: 2082, 2494
Fielding, Michael L.: 4485
Fifield, William: 2929
Filippi, Zivan: 4083
Findlater, Richard: 3486
Finney, Brian Hubert: 3898, 3899, 3900, 4084, 4085, 4086, 4486, 4487, 4488
Fisher, Alan: 2930
Fisher, Jack: 3901
Fitz, L. T.: 4308
Fitzgerald, Francis Scott: 2392
Fitzgibbon, Constantine (ed): 2886
Flatley, Guy: 3705
Fogel, Stanley: 4309
Foltinek, Herbert: 2496
Ford, Boris (ed): 2153, 3324, 3342, 3343
Ford, Ford Madox [formerly Hueffer, Ford Madox]: 2638
Ford, George H.: 2243, 2393, 2497, 2639, 3078, 3306, 3487, 3706, 4087
Foster, D. W.: 2083
Foster, John Burt, Jr.: 4310
Foster, Joseph: 2795, 3488, 3902
Fotheringham, Richard: 3903
Foulke, Adrienne (trans): 2124
Fox, Carol Lorraine Tyler: 3904
Fraiberg, Selma: 2084
Fraisse, Anne-Marie: 3433, 3490
Francis, Miller, Jr.: 3491
Frankes, James R. (ed): 3307
Fraser, G. S.: 3080, 3905
Fraser, Grace Lovat: 3492
Freedman, Richard: 4489
Freeman, Alma Susan: 4311
Freeman, Donald C. (ed): 2559
French, Philip: 3081
Fricker, Robert: 2796, 3707
Friederich, Werner P.: 2931
Friedland, Ronald Lloyd: 2932
Friedman, Alan Howard: 2498, 2797, 3308, 3493, 3906
Friedman, Alan Warren (ed): 4467
Frierson, William C.: 2640
Frise, Maria: 4490
Frye, Northrop: 3708
Fu, Shaw-shien: 2933, 3494
Fujii, Kazumi: 2934
Fujita, Takashi: 2584

Fujiwara, Masuko: 3495, 4088, 4312, 4491
Fulmer, Bryan O.: 3082
Furbank, P. N.: 3083, 3907
Fussell, Paul: 4492
Gadda Conti, Giuseppe: 3084, 4313
Gajdusek, Robert E.: 3496
Galinsky, Hans: 2935
Gallo, Rose: 4314
Gamache, Lawrence B.: 3309
Gangwere, Robert J. (ed): 3843
Gant, Roland: 3908, 3909
Garcia, Reloy: 3085, 3498, 3911; (ed): 3497, 3910
Gardner, John: 2244
Garmon, Gerald M.: 3912, 4089
Garnett, David: 2245, 3237, 4090; (ed): 3237, 3678
Garrett, Peter K.: 2936, 3310
Gaspar, Leonard (ed): 2253
Gass, William H.: 3086
Gates, Norman T.: 4315
Gathorne-Hardy, Robert (ed): 2421, 4374
Gatti, Hilary: 3499
Gaya Nuño, Antonia: 2937
Gebsattel, Jerome: 2679
Geduld, Harry M.: 3500
Geisler, Rolf (ed): 2679
Gelli, Piero: 3087
Gemmett, Robert J. (ed): 3312
Gentry, Curt: 2246
Geracimos, Ann: 3709
Gerard, David: 3070; (comp): 3088
Gerard, Lillian N.: 3501, 3502
Gerber, Philip L. (ed): 3312
Gerber, Stephen: 4091
Germer, Rudolph: 2247
Gersh, Gabriel: 4092
Gershon, Karen (trans): 2284
Gertler, Mark: 2641
Ghiselin, Brewster: 4493
Gibbs, Jean: 3503
Gibson, Jeremy: 3504
Gidley, Mick: 4316
Gifford, Henry: 2085
Gilbert, Sandra: 2642, 3089, 3913
Gill, Richard: 3914, 4317
Gill, Stephen: 3710, 3915, 4258
Gillès, Daniel: 2499, 2500
Gilliatt, Penelope: 3505
Gillie, Christopher: 2643, 4494

INDEX OF AUTHORS

Gilman, Richard: 3090
Gindin, James: 3091
Glenavy, Lady Beatrice: 2501
Glicksberg, Charles I.: 3313, 3506, 3711, 4093
Gohdes, Clarence: 2502
Goldberg, Michael K.: 3314, 3712
Goldberg, S. L.: 2086
Goldknopf, David: 3507, 3916
Goller, Karl Hein (ed): 3222
Gomme, Andor H.: 2248, 2644, 2645, 2798, 3315; (ed): 3786, 3807
Goode, John: 3508
Goodheart, Eugene: 2087, 2394, 2503
Gordan, John D.: 2646
Gordon, David J.: 2088, 2504, 2799, 2800, 2801, 3316
Gordyshevskaya, M.: 2395
Gosliner, Kathy: 3509
Gottwald, Johannes: 2505
Gouirand, Jacqueline: 3917, 4318
Gould, Eric H.: 3918
Gransden, Karl Watts: 2249
Grant, Douglas: 2396
Gray, Ronald: 2647
Gray, Simon: 3092
Green, Eleanor H.: 4094, 4319, 4495, 4496
Green, Martin: 2089, 2397, 2648, 2938, 3093, 3317, 3713, 3714, 4320
Greenwood, E. B.: 2250
Greet, T. Y. (ed): 2506
Gregor, Ian: 2251, 2649, 2802; (ed): 3124, 3148
Gregory, Horace: 2507
Greiff, Louis K.: 4095
Grey, Anthony: 4321
Grey, Elizabeth: 3318
Gribble, Jennifer: 2252
Griffin, Ernest G.: 3319, 3320
Griffith, Philip Mahone: 3321
Grigson, Geoffrey: 4322
Gross, Theodore: 2939
Grotte, Margaret Spencer: 4323
Grubb, Frederick: 2650
Guerrini, Tito: 3919
Gullason, Thomas A.: 4096; (ed): 2253
Gunn, Drewey Wayne: 4324
Gurko, Jane: 3715

Gurko, Leo: 2254, 2398, 2508, 3920
Gurtoff, Stanley Arthur: 2651
Gutierrez, Donald: 3716, 3921, 4097
Guttmann, Allen: 2509
Haegert, John W.: 3922, 4497
Hagopian, John V. (ed): 2464
Hahn, Emily: 4498
Hall, James B. (ed): 2652
Hall, R. L.: 4325
Hall, Roland: 2255
Hall, William F.: 3322
Halliday, M. A. K.: 2966
Halperin, Irving: 2803
Hamalian, Leo: 4099; (ed): 2263, 2869, 2940, 2951, 3279, 3419, 4098, 4099
Hamilton, Jack: 3510
Hand, Nancy Walker: 3717
Handley, Graham: 2941
Hanson, Barry: 3094
Hanson, Christopher: 2942
Harding, D. W.: 2653, 2654
Hardy, Barbara: 2510, 4100
Hardy, John Edward: 2511, 2512
Harmer, J. B.: 4499
Harper, Howard M., Jr.: 3923; (ed): 3923
Harris, Janice Hubbard: 4101, 4326
Harris, Marguerite (ed): 2513
Harris, Wendell V.: 3095
Harrison, John R.: 2804
Hartley, L. P.: 3033
Hartogs, Renatus: 2943
Hartt, Julian N.: 2399
Hartung, Philip T.: 3096
Hartung, Rudolf: 3718
Harvey, J. R.: 2655
Harvey, R. W.: 2805
Hasegawa, Toshimitsu: 2256
Hashimoto, Hiroshi: 2090
Hashimoto, Makinori: 4102
Haskell, Molly: 4327
Hassall, Christopher: 2257
Haüsermann, H. W.: 2656, 2806
Hawkins, Kenneth B.: 2267
Haya, Kenichi: 4103
Hayes, Ann L. (ed): 3843
Hays, Peter L.: 3719
Heagarty, Mary Alice: 2514
Heath, Alice C.: 3924, 4104
Hebert, Hugh: 4105
Heilbrun, Carolyn G. [pseud Cross, Amanda]: 2091, 2483, 4106

Heilbut, Anthony Otto: 2807
Heldt, Lucia Henning: 4500
Helwig, Werner: 2657
Hendrick, George: 2808
Henestrosa, Mario Alejandro: 3097
Henig, Suzanne: 3323
Henry, G. B. McK.: 2944
Hepburn, James G.: 2658
Heppenstall, Rayner: 2092
Herban, Patricia L.: 4107
Herrick, Jeffrey Don: 4328
Hesse, Hermann: 4329
Heuzenroeder, John: 3511
Hewitt, C. R. [pseud Rolph, C. H.]: 2154, 2990, 3387
Heywood, Christopher: 2809
Hibbard, G. R. (ed): 2826, 2852
Hicks, Granville: 2515
Higashida, Chiaki (ed): 4373, 4385
Hildick, Wallace: 2659
Hill, Ordelle G.: 3720
Hillier, Bevis: 3939
Hilton, Enid: 3721
Hinz, Evelyn J.: 3098, 3512, 3722, 3723, 3925, 3926, 3927, 4108, 4109, 4330, 4422, 4501; (ed): 4559
Hirashima, Junko: 2093, 2400, 2516, 2660, 2810
Hirsch, Bernard A.: 4461
Hirth, Mary: 3513
Hobsbaum, Philip: 2811
Hobson, Harold: 2945, 3099
Hochman, Baruch: 2517, 3514
Hodin, J. P.: 2946
Hoffman, Frederick J.: 2518
Hoffman, Lois: 4110
Hoggart, Richard: 2094, 2095, 2519, 2661, 3100
Hogins, J. Burl: 2947
Hojman, Baruj [See Hochman, Baruch]
Holbrook, David: 2662
Holland, Norman N.: 3101
Hollander, Robert B. (ed): 3102
Holloway, John: 3324
Holroyd, Michael: 3103, 3104
Holtgen, K. J.: 2258
Holton, Milne: 2812
Honig, Edwin: 2948
Hooker, Jeremy: 3724
Hope, A. D.: 4331
Horney, Larry J.: 3928
Horsley, E. M. (ed): 3033
Hortmann, Wilhelm: 2663
Horwath, William Frank: 3515
Hough, Graham: 2259, 2260
Howard-Hill, T. H.: 3325
Howard, Daniel F.: 3105, 3106
Howard, Patsy C.: 4089
Howarth, Herbert: 3107, 3108
Howe, Florence: 3929
Howe, Marguerite Beede: 4111
Hoyles, John: 4112
Hoyt, C. A.: 2520
Hoyt, William R., III: 3725
Hsia, Adrian Rue Chun: 2664, 3109
Hudspeth, Robert N.: 2813, 3326
Hueffer, Ford Madox [See Ford, Ford Madox]
Hugger, Ann-Grete: 4113
Hughes, Ted: 3792
Hulley, Kathleen: 4114
Humma, John B.: 3327, 4332, 4333
Huttar, Charles A. (ed): 3110, 3161, 3169, 3215, 3224, 3228, 3240
Huxley, Aldous: 3328
Huxley, Julian: 3516
Huxley, Juliette: 4115
Hyde, G. M.: 3517
Hyde, Virginia Mae: 3726, 4502
Hyman, Stanley Edgar: 2665
Ichihashi, Katsue: 4116
Idema, James M.: 2096
Iida, Kôsaku: 2401
Iida, Takeo: 4334
Ilić, Milivoje (trans): 2923
Imaizumi, Haruko: 4117, 4335, 4503
Ingamells, John: 2402, 2666
Inniss, Kenneth B.: 2667, 3727
Irie, Takanori: 2668, 2814, 4336
Irvine, Peter L. (ed): 4119
Irwin, W. R.: 2097
Isaacs, Neil D.: 2669
Ishibashi, Magoichiro: 3518, 3931, 4337
Ishihara, Fumio: 2098, 2670, 2950
Ishikawa, Masafumi: 2815
Ito, Chikai: 4504
Itô, Hidekazu: 2816, 3111
Ito, Takehisa: 3728
Ito, Toyoji: 3729, 3932
Ivker, Barry: 3933
Iwata, Noboru: 2099, 2403, 2521, 2671, 2817, 3112, 3519
Jackson, Dennis: 4505, 4506
Jacobson, Dan: 2100, 2951
Jacobson, Denise: 3520

INDEX OF AUTHORS

Jacobson, Sibyl: 4120
Jacobus, Mary: 4507
James, Clive: 4121
James, Stuart B.: 3521
Janik, Del Ivan: 3730, 4122, 4338, 4508
Jarrett-Kerr, Martin: 2101, 2102, 4509
Järv, Harry: 2103
Jarvis, F. P.: 2672
Jeffers, Robinson: 3113
Jeffers, Thomas Linden: 4339
Joffe, Phil: 3522
John, Brian: 4340
Johnsen, William A.: 3523
Johnson, Dale Springer: 3114
Johnson, Spud [See Johnson, Willard]
Johnson, Willard [pseud Johnson, Spud]: 2522, 2523
Johnston, Walter Eugene: 3524, 4341
Jones, Bernard: 4342
Jones, Brian: 3329
Jones, David A.: 4510
Joost, Nicholas: 3525
Jordan, Francis X.: 4511
Jorgensen, Paul A.: 2673
Joshi, Krishna Nand: 3330
Junkins, Donald: 2524, 3331
Juta, Jan: 3332
Kabiljo-Šutić, Simha: 4123, 4124, 4512
Kael, Pauline: 2104, 3115, 3526
Kai, Sadanobu: 2105, 2261, 2818, 3116, 3333, 3334, 3527, 3731, 4125, 4343, 4513
Kain, Richard M.: 3528
Kalnins, Mara: 3934
Kamei, Shunsuke: 3117
Kamimura, Tatsuhiko: 2674, 2819, 2952, 3935, 4126
Kamitani, Shotaro: 4344
Kanatani, Nobuo: 4127, 4345
Kaneko, Masanobu: 3936
Kanfer, Stefan: 3529
Kanzaki, Daigorô: 3118
Kanzaki, Takashi: 4514
Kaplan, Harold J.: 2820
Karabatsos, James (ed): 3497, 3910
Karas, Edith: 3478, 3479
Karl, Frederick R.: 2262; (ed): 2940
Katô, Muneyuki: 2106

Katsumata, Kikuo: 2953
Kauffmann, Stanley: 3119, 3530, 3531, 4128
Kaul, Dwarka N.: 3335
Kawabata, Takashi: 2525, 3336, 4129
Kay, Wallace Grant: 2675, 2821, 3120, 3937, 3938
Kazin, Alfred: 2263, 4130
Kegel-Brinkgreve, E.: 4515
Keith, W. J.: 3121, 4131, 4293, 4346
Keller, Dean H.: 2264
Kelvin, Norman: 2939
Kendle, Burton S.: 2526
Kennedy, Alan: 4347
Kennedy, Richard: 3939; (illus): 3939
Kenner, Hugh (ed): 2676
Kermode, Frank: 2265, 2266, 2677, 3122, 3706, 4132, 4133
Kershaw, Alister (ed): 2418, 2678
Kessler, Jascha: 2527
Kester, Joseph: 4516
Ketters, David: 3732
Kettle, Arnold: 3532; (ed): 2226, 2482
Kiley, Anne (ed): 4119
Kim, Dong-son: 3337, 3338, 4348
Kimpel, Ben D.: 3123
King, Nancy: 4517
King, Willard L.: 2267
Kinkead-Weekes, Mark: 3124, 3339, 3733, 4518; (ed): 2594, 2624, 2639, 2869, 2962, 3124, 3733, 3734
Kirkham, Michael: 3940
Kissane, Leedice M.: 3340
Kistel, Paul Daniel: 3533
Kitazaki, Kaien: 4134, 4349, 4350, 4519
Kitazawa, Shigehisa: 3125, 3341, 3735, 3941, 4135
Kitazawa, Yoshihiro: 2404, 2680
Kitchin, Laurence: 2681, 2822
Klein, Marcus (ed): 2954
Klein, Robert C.: 3126
Kleinbard, David J.: 3127, 3736, 4351
Klingopulos, G. D.: 3342, 3343
Knight, Arthur: 3128, 3534
Knight, G. Wilson: 2107, 2955
Knoll, Robert F.: 3737
Kobayashi, Toshiro: 3129

Koga, Masakazu: 3130, 3344, 3535, 4136, 4520
Koljevič, Svetozar: 2268, 2405, 3345, 4521
Konishi, Eirin: 3738, 3942
Konishi, Nagatomo: 4522
Koppelman, Susan (ed): 3929
Kramer, Vicki Weisberg: 2956
Kretzmer, Herbert: 3131, 3132
Kreuzer, James R. (ed): 2682
Krieger, Robert Neal: 3739
Krishnamurthi, Matighatta Gundappa: 3536
Kristensen, Sven Møller: 3046
Krupat, Arnold: 3133
Kuczdowski, Richard: 4137
Kuhn, Helen Weldon: 3537
Kumar, Raj: 2957
Kunkel, Francis L.: 4523
Kuo, Carol Haseley: 2108
Kuramochi, Saburô: 2109, 2269, 2528, 3346, 3538, 3943, 4138, 4139, 4352, 4524
Kurono, Yutaka: 2823, 2958
Kuwayama, Taisuke: 2959, 3134
Kuykendall, Mabel M.: 3539, 3540
La Belle, Jenijoy: 3740
Lacher, Walter: 2110
Lachman, Roy Ernest: 3944
Lacy, Gerald Morris: 3741, 4140; (ed): 4140
Lainoff, Seymour: 3541
Lambert, J. W.: 3135
Land, Myrick: 2406
Langbaum, Robert: 3542, 4525
Langman, F. H.: 2960
Lanning, George: 2537
Lasch, Christopher: 2684
Laski, Marghanita: 2111
Lass, Abraham H. (ed): 3348
Latta, William Charlton, Jr.: 2685, 2686, 3136
Laurenson, Diana: 3810
Laurent, C.: 3544
Lawrence, Frieda [Mrs. Frieda Lawrence Ravagli]: 2112, 4444
Lawrence, Robert G.: 2407
Lea, Frank A.: 4526, 4527
Leavis, Frank Raymond: 2114, 2115, 2408, 2687, 3349, 4141, 4528, 4529
Le Breton, Georges: 2825
LeDoux, Larry V.: 3946

Lee, Brian: 2826
Lee, Robert: 4142
Lee, Robin Herbert: 2961, 3743, 3947, 4143, 4353
Leland, Richard Wallace: 4530
Lerman, Leo: 3551
Lerner, Laurence: 2409, 2962
Lesser, M. X.: 2271
Lester, John A., Jr.: 3138
Levey, Michael: 2915
Levin, Bernard: 3552
Levin, Gerald: 2963, 2964
Levin, Harry: 2688, 2827
Levin, Richard: 2410
Levy, Mervyn: 2272, 2530; (ed): 2530, 2531, 2533, 2545, 2575
Levy, Raphael: 2532
Lewis, Clive Staples: 2116, 2117, 2965
Lewis, Peter: 3139
Leyris, Pierre (trans): 3146
Lid, R. W. (ed): 2828
Liddy, James: 2829
Limmer, Ruth (ed): 3442
Lind, S. E. (ed): 3102
Lindley, David: 4144
Lindley, Denver (trans): 4329
Lindsay, Jack: 2273, 2533, 4354
Lisk, Thomas David: 4531
Littlewood, J. C. F.: 2831, 2832, 3351, 3744
Lochhead, Marion: 2535
Locke, Raymond Friday: 3745
Lo Curzio, Guglielmo: 2274, 2275, 2411
Lodge, David: 2689, 3746, 4532
Lohf, Kenneth A. (comp): 2276
Longville, Timothy: 2277
Losa, Margarida: 3747
Loth, David: 2118
Lovett, Robert Morss: 2544
Lowe, Victor: 2278
Lowery, William R.: 4533
Lowry, Malcolm: 2690
Lucas, Barbara: 2119
Lucas, Robert [See Ehrenzweig, Robert]
Lucie-Smith, Edward: 4146
Ludwig, Richard M. (ed): 2638
McCabe, Thomas Harper: 3140, 3950
McCann, Charles: 2279
Macaulay, Peter S.: 3949
Macauley, Robie: 2537

INDEX OF AUTHORS

McCoy, Dan: 3510
MacDonald, Dwight: 2120
McDonald, Edward D.: 3553
McDonald, Marguerite Bartelle: 3951
Mace, Hebe Riddick [See Bair, Hebe]
MacInnes, Colin: 2280
McIntosh, Angus: 2966
Mack, Maynard (ed): 3124, 3148
Mackenzie, Compton: 2281, 2282, 2691, 2833, 2967, 3141, 3352
Mackenzie, D. Kenneth M.: 4147
MacKenzie, David: 4534, 4535
McKeown, Marion Smith: 4355
MacKinnon, Kenneth A.: 4536
McLaurin, Allen: 4148
McLeod, Karen: 3748
MacShane, Frank: 2692
McWilliam, G. H.: 2121
Madison, Charles A.: 4356
Madonna, Michèle: 3142
Maes-Jelinek, Hena: 3554
Maetzke, Ernst-Otto: 2412
Magalaner, Marvin: 2122; (ed): 2122
Magaraševič, Mirko: 4537
Mahar, Margaret Anne: 4538
Mahnken, Harry E.: 2693
Mailer, Norman: 3749
Majolo, Renato: 3555
Major, Mabel: 2834
Malafry, Hugh David: 4149
Maldonado Denis, Manuel: 2283
Mallett, Richard: 3353
Manchester, John: 2968, 3556, 3557, 4357
Mandrillo, P.: 2538
Mann, Charles W.: 4150
Mannin, Ethel: 3750
Mansfield, Elizabeth Reed: 4151
Marcus, Frank: 2969
Marcuse, Ludwig: 2284
Markovič, Vida E.: 2413, 3558, 3952
Marks, William Sowell, III: 2539, 2694, 2970, 3143
Marland, Michael: 3144
Marnat, Marcel: 2835, 2971, 3145, 3146
Marshall, Percy: 2285
Marshall, Tom: 3559
Martin, Dexter: 2286, 2287, 2288, 2289, 2290; (ed): 2233, 2234, 2235
Martin, Graham: 3751
Martin, Richard: 3147

Martin, W. R.: 2291, 2695
Martz, Louis L.: 3148
Mason, H. A.: 3354
Massey, Irving: 2696
Masugi, Tadashi: 2123, 2414
Mather, Rodney: 3560
Matsubayashi, Yoshinori: 3752, 4358, 4359
Matsudaira, Yôko: 2972, 3149
Matsuura, Naomi: 4360
Maud, Ralph: 2973
Mauriac, François: 2124
Maxwell, J. C.: 2125
Mayhall, Jane: 2697
Mayhead, Robin: 2698
Meckier, Jerome: 3355
Meinke, Norman Dale: 3953
Melchiori, Barbara: 3561
Mellen, Joan: 3150, 4152, 4361
Meller, Horst (ed): 3017
Mencher, M. B.: 3753
Mendel, Sydney: 3151, 4362
Menmuir, Ruth: 3478, 3479
Menon, K. P. K.: 3754
Merivale, Patricia: 2540, 3356
Metcalf, Neal: 4363
Meyer, Horst E.: 4153
Meyers, Jeffrey: 3562, 4154, 4364, 4365, 4539
Mibu, Ikuo: 2292, 2541, 2542, 3954, 4155, 4540
Michaels-Tonks, Jennifer: 4366
Michaels, Jennifer Elizabeth: 4366
Michel-Michot, Paulette: 2126, 4541
Michener, Richard L.: 3152
Mickelson, Anne Zadorozna: 3755
Miko, Stephen Jon: 2974, 3357, 3756; (ed): 2348, 2423, 2639, 2797, 3308, 3316, 3357, 3358
Miles, Kathleen M.: 3359
Miles, Rosalind: 4367
Miller, Henry: 2385
Miller, James E., Jr.: 3360; (ed): 2543
Miller, Nolan: 2293
Millett, Fred B.: 2544
Millett, Kate: 3563
Millett, Robert: 3564
Millett, Robert Walker: 2699
Milley, Frederick George: 4156
Mills, Ralph J., Jr.: 3153
Mitchell, Peter Tod: 2700
Mitra, A. K.: 3361
Mittleman, Leslie B.: 2836

Miyasaki, Junji: 4368
Mizener, Arthur: 2837, 3757; (ed): 2975
Mizuhara, Sho: 3758, 4157, 4158, 4542
Moe, Christian: 3362
Montale, Eugenio: 2127
Montgomery, Lyna Lee: 3955
Moody, H. L. B.: 3363
Moody, William Vaughn: 2544
Moore, Harry T.: 2128, 2203, 2294, 2295, 2296, 2415, 2416, 2417, 2418, 2545, 2701, 2798, 2838, 2839, 3185, 3759, 3760, 3761, 3762, 3956, 3957, 4159, 4160, 4369, 4543; (ed): 2294
Moore, Leslie [See Baker, Ida]
Moore, T. Inglis: 3764
Moorer, Clarence Alan, Jr.: 3565
Moravia, Alberto: 2840
Morelle, Paul: 3566
Morgenstern, Joseph: 3154, 3567
Mori, Haruhide: 2297, 2298, 2419, 2420, 2546, 2702, 2703, 3155, 3958, 4371, 4372, 4373, 4544, 4545, 4546; (ed): 4370
Morrell, Ottoline: 2421, 4374
Morrill, Claire: 2299, 2704, 4161
Morris, John N.: 2271
Morris, Tom: 4547
Morrison, Claudia C.: 3156
Morse, Donald E.: 2705
Morse, J. Mitchell: 2422
Morse, Stearns: 3157
Mortland, Donald E.: 3765
Moseley, Edwin M.: 2300
Mothersill, Mary: 2129
Moynahan, Julian: 2423, 3959, 3960; (ed): 2263, 2423, 2639, 3158
Mudrick, Marvin: 4375
Mueller, William R.: 3961
Muggeridge, Malcolm: 3159
Muir, Edwin: 2841
Muir, Kenneth: 2130
Muir, P. H.: 2131
Mulloy, John J.: 4376, 4548, 4549, 4550, 4551
Munro, John M.: 3160; (ed): 2506
Murphy, Richard Michael: 3569
Murphy, Terrence J.: 2424
Murray, James F.: 3161
Murray, W.: 2132
Myers, Neil: 2301

Nahal, Chaman Lal: 2133, 3570, 3766, 4552
Nakamura, Shiro: 4553
Nakamura, Yoshio: 2134, 2425, 2547, 2842
Nakano, Kimiko: 2548, 2706, 2707, 2843
Nardi, Piero: 2135, 2302, 2303, 2304, 2305, 2306, 2549, 2550, 2551, 2552, 2708, 2844, 2976, 2977, 3162, 3364, 3571, 3572, 3573, 3767, 3962, 3963, 4162, 4554, 4555
Nathan, John Goldsmith: 4556
Nazareth, Peter: 2307, 2426
Negriolli, Claude: 3574, 4377
New, William H.: 3164, 4557, 4558
Newby, Frank Shelton: 2845
Newhall, Nancy (ed): 4237, 4238
Newman, Paul B.: 2308, 2553
Nicholas, Brian: 2251
Nichols, Ann Eljenholm: 2709
Niethammer, Carolyn: 3575
Nightingale, Benedict: 3165, 4163
Nin, Anais: 2846, 2978, 3166, 3365, 3745, 3768, 4559
Ninomiya, Takamichi: 2427, 2554, 2555, 2710
Nishida, Minoru: 4560
Nishikawa, Masaharu: 2136, 2428
Nishimura, Iwao: 4378
Nishimura, Kôji: 3366, 3576, 4379
Nogara, Gino: 2309, 2556
Noguchi, Yoshika: 3167
Nolte, William H.: 2711
Noon, William T.: 2310
Nordell, Rod: 2311
Nosaka, Tôsaku: 2557, 2847, 2979
Nott, Kathleen: 2312, 3367, 3368
Nudel, Harry: 4164
Oates, Joyce Carol: 3964, 3965, 4165
Ober, William B.: 3369
Ocampo, Victoria: 3769
O'Connell, Adelyn, R.S.C.J.: 3169
O'Connor, Frank [See O'Donovan, Michael]
Oda, Motoi: 2713
O'Donovan, Michael [pseud O'Connor, Frank]: 2430
O'Faolain, Sean (ed): 2137
Ogar, Richard: 3578
Ogawa, Yoshio: 3370, 3966, 4166, 4380, 4561

INDEX OF AUTHORS

Ôhashi, Yasuichirô: 2138, 2313, 2558, 2848, 2980, 2981, 3334, 4381
Ohkawa, Hiroshi: 3770, 3967, 3968, 3969, 4167, 4382
Ohmann, Richard: 2559
Okada, Taiji: 2314, 2560, 2714, 2849, 2982, 3170, 3334, 4168, 4383, 4562, 4563
Okamura, Naomi: 4384
Okano, Keiichi: 4564
Okumura, Osamu: 2139
Okumura, Tôru [also Tohru]: 2140, 2315, 2561, 2715, 2983, 3334, 4169, 4170
Okunishi, Akira: 2984, 4385
Oldsey, Bernard S.: 2316
Oliver, Clinton F. (ed): 3223
Olivier, T.: 3970
Onodera, Takeshi: 4171
Oppel, Horst: 2716, 2985; (ed): 2716, 2985
Orr, Christopher James: 3971, 4565
Orrell, Herbert M.: 3771
Ort, Daniel: 3371
Osborne, Charles: 2915
Osborne, Marianne M.: 3772
Osman, Arthur: 3972
Ostendorff, Berhard: 3773
Oster, Art: 3579
Ôta, Saburô: 2717
Owen, Frederick I.: 4173
Pace, Billy J.: 4174
Pachmuss, Temira: 4386
Pack, Robert (ed): 2954
Packman, James: 2907
Page, Normal (ed): 3159
Paik, Nack-Chung: 3973
Palmer, Paul R.: 3171
Panichas, George Andrew: 2141, 2317, 2318, 2431, 2432, 2563, 2564, 2718, 2851, 2852, 3580, 4387, 4388; (ed): 2987, 3778
Panken, Shirley: 4389
Panter-Downes, Mollie: 3172
Parkinson, Thomas: 3372
Paterson, John: 4175
Patmore, Derek: 3581
Pearsall, Robert Brainard: 2565
Pearson, Alice Canby: 3173
Peckham, Morse: 3373
Peerman, Dean: 2142
Pelissier, Anthony: 4390
Perkins, Moreland: 2854

Perosa, Sergio: 2143, 3774
Perrakis, Phyllis Sternberg: 4566
Peter, John: 2319, 2320, 2433
Peterson, L.: 2566
Petillon, Pierre-Yves: 4567
Petrič, Vladmir: 3775
Pfister, Manfred (ed): 2679
Phelps, Robert (ed): 3442
Phillips, David (comp): 3847, 3888
Phillips, Gene D.: 3582, 3776
Phillips, Steven R.: 4176, 4568
Phipps, William E.: 3777
Piccolo, Anthony: 3374
Pickrel, Paul: 2567
Pieraccini, Leonetta: 2568
Pierle, Robert C.: 3174
Pinder, Donna: 4391
Pinsker, Sanford: 4569
Pinto, Vivian de Sola: 2144, 2145, 2146, 2321, 2434, 2569, 2719, 2987, 3175, 3375, 3376, 3377, 3778; (ed): 2146
Pinto-Muñoz, Ana: 4570
Pirenet, Colette: 3378
Pittock, Malcolm: 2720, 3779, 4177
Plant, Raymond: 3974
Poirier, Richard: 2855
Pollak, Paulina Salz: 4178
Pollnitz, Christopher P.: 4571
Poole, Roger Henry: 3177; (ed): 3177
Porteous, Alexander: 2252, 2322
Porter, Peter: 4179
Potter, Stephen: 2571
Potts, Abbie Findlay: 2988
Powell, Lawrence Clark: 2435, 2572, 3780
Prasad, Madhusudan: 4392
Prasad, Suman P.: 3781
Pratt, Annis: 3977
Praz, Mario [pseud Alcibiade]: 2147, 2199, 2573, 3379
Press, John: 3380
Price, Martin: 2856
Prisco, Michele: 2323, 2574, 2857
Pritchard, R. E.: 3782
Pritchard, William H.: 3381
Pritchett, Victor S.: 2148, 2858, 2859, 3178, 3382, 3383, 3783
Procter, Margaret Ruth: 4180
Pryce-Jones, D.: 2860
Pugh, Bridget: 3978
Pujals, Esteban: 4181
Purdy, Strother B.: 3583

Rachman, Shalom: 3979
Radcliffe, Cyril John, Baron: 2149
Raddatz, Volker: 4393
Radler, Rudolf (ed): 2679
Radmehr, Manouchehr: 3784
Raes, Hugo: 2721
Ragussis, Michael: 3585, 4572
Rahv, Philip: 3179
Raina, M. L.: 2722, 2861, 3586
Rajiva, Stanley F.: 3180
Ramos Suarez, Jorge: 4182
Randall, Richard S.: 3181
Ransom, W. S. (ed): 4331
Raskin, Jonah: 3785
Rattenbury, Arnold (comp): 3847, 3888
Ravagli, Frieda Lawrence [See Lawrence, Frieda]
Ravilious, C. P.: 4183
Rawlings, Carl Donn: 4184
Rawlinson, D. H.: 3182
Raya, Gino: 3587
Raymond, John: 2324
Read, Herbert: 2575, 3183
Reddick, Bryan Dewitt: 2862, 3384, 4394
Reed, Rex: 3589
Rees, Marjorie: 2576
Rees, Richard: 2150, 3385
Rehder, Jessie (ed): 2436
Rembar, Charles: 3184
Remsbury, Ann: 3786
Remsbury, John A.: 2863, 2989, 3747, 3786, 4185
Requardt, Egon: 2151, 2437
Reuben, Elaine: 4186
Rexroth, Kenneth: 2577
Rhode, Eric: 3386
Rice, Susan: 3590
Rich: 3591
Rich, Adrienne: 2723
Richardson, John Adkins: 3592
Rickards, Maurice: 3980
Ricks, Christopher: 2578
Ridgeway, Ann N. (ed): 3113
Rieff, Philip: 2864
Riesen, David Herman: 4573
Riesner, Dieter (ed): 3707
Ripp, Judith: 3593
Robbins, Patricia: 2152
Roberts, Francis Warren: 2438, 2569, 2620, 2724, 2839, 3175, 3185, 3594, 3787; (ed): 2146

Roberts, Mark: 4187
Roberts, Walter: 2328
Robson, William Wallace: 2153, 3595, 4395
Rodway, Allan: 2852
Rogers, Katherine M.: 2865
Rogers, W. G.: 3186
Rohrberger, Mary: 2866
Roland, Christoph: 2725
Rolph, C. H. [See Hewitt, C. R.]
Rose, Shirley: 4574
Rosenbaum, S. P. (ed): 3788
Rosenberg, Judith Guttenberg: 4188
Rosengarten, H. J.: 4557, 4558
Rosenthal, T. G.: 2329
Ross, Charles L.: 4189, 4190, 4396, 4575
Ross, Michael Lawrence: 2867, 3788, 4488, 4576
Ross, Robert H.: 2726
Rossi, Patrizio: 3981, 4191, 4192
Rossman, Charles Raymond: 3187, 3596, 4577
Roston, Murray: 3188
Roth, Mary Beth: 4193
Roth, Russell: 3388
Rothkopf, Carol Zemen: 3389
Rotman, Mel: 3597
Rovit, Earl: 2439
Rowland, Paul Gabriel: 3982
Rowley, Eugene G.: 4397
Rowse, A. L.: 2330
Roy, Chitra: 2991
Roy, Kamal: 3189
Rozenberg, Simone: 3433
Rudrum, Alan: 2868, 3789
Rukeyser, Muriel: 2992
Runyan, Elizabeth: 3598
Russell, Bertrand: 3190
Russell, John: 4194
Russell, Ken: 4195
Ruthven, K. K.: 3191, 3983
Ryals, Clyde de L.: 2331
Ryan, A. P. (ed): 2644
Sagar, Keith M.: 2332, 2333, 2727, 2869, 2993, 3192, 3599, 3790, 3791, 3792, 3793, 3794, 3984, 4196, 4578, 4579; (ed): 3088, 3488, 3793, 3794, 3984
Saibara, Susumu: 2440
St. John-Stevas, Norman: 2155
Sale, Roger: 2728, 2994, 4197

INDEX OF AUTHORS

Salgādo, Gāmini: 2156, 2729, 2870, 3390, 3391; (ed): 2368, 2624, 2869, 3392
Salter, K. W.: 4198
Samuels, Marilyn Schauer: 3600
San Juan, Epiphanio, Jr.: 3601
Sanders, Scott R.: 3795, 4199
Sandoval, Patricia Ann Rice: 3193
Sândalescu, C. G.: 3194
Sano, Akano: 4580
Sargent, Robert: 2157
Sarris, Andrew (ed): 3115
Sasae, Osamu: 4398
Sasaki, Manabu: 3985
Sasbuchi, Tomoichi (ed): 4619
Satin, Joseph: 2579
Saunders, J. W.: 2580
Sawamura, Kan: 3195
Sawyer, Paul W.: 2158
Saxena, H. S.: 2159, 2334, 2441
Sayre, Joel: 3602
Schermbrucker, William Gerald: 4200
Schickel, Richard: 3603
Schlesinger, Arthur, Jr.: 3604, 3605
Schmidt, Johann N.: 2679
Schmidt, Sandra: 2581
Schmoller, Hans: 2335
Schneider, Daniel J.: 3196, 4399
Schneiderman, Leo: 3197
Scholes, Robert: 2582; (ed): 3796
Scholtes, M.: 4581
Schönfeld, Herbert M.: 2160
Schorer, Mark: 2336, 3198, 3199, 3200, 3986, 4400
Schroeter, James: 2161, 2207
Schulman, Norma Miriam: 3987
Schwab-Fehlisch, Hans: 4401
Schwartz, Alan U.: 2492
Scott, James F.: 4201
Secker, Martin: 2871, 2872, 3607, 3608
Secor, Robert: 3393
Seidl, Frances: 4202
Sekiguchi, Masakazu: 4582, 4583
Sellers, W. E.: 2995
Sencourt, Robert: 3797
Sepčič, Višnja: 2730, 2873, 2996, 2997, 3394, 3609, 3988, 4402, 4403
Serraillier, Ian: 2442
Seymour-Smith, Martin: 3201, 4203
Shakir, Evelyn Catherine: 3989, 4584
Sharma, Radhe Shyam: 3798, 3990

Sharpe, Michael C.: 2163
Shaw, Rita Granger: 2731
Sheed, Wilfrid: 2164, 3202
Shepherd, P. J.: 3203; (ed): 3177
Shibata, Takaharu: 4404
Shields, E. F.: 3991
Shimizu, Kazuyoshi: 2583, 2732
Shimizu, Kohya: 3204, 3395, 3799, 3800, 3992, 4204, 4205, 4405
Shimpachirō, Miyata: 2165
Shirai, Toshitaka: 2166, 2337, 2443, 2584, 4585
Shonfield, Andrew: 2167
Shorter, Eric: 3205, 3206
Shruyer, Frederick B.: 2673
Silet, Charles L. P.: 3993
Sillitoe, Alan: 2168, 4206
Silvestri, Giuseppe: 3610
Simms, Theodore Franklin: 2874
Simon, John: 3611
Simpson, Louis: 2585
Sinclair, Stephen G.: 4406
Singh, G. S.: 2733
Singh, T. N.: 2586
Singh, Vishnudat: 3612, 3613
Singleton, Ralph Herbert (ed): 2338
Sinzelle, Claude M.: 2587
Sipple, James B.: 3801
Sirkin, Elliott: 3614
Sissman, L. E.: 4207
Sitesh, Aruna: 3615, 4586
Sitwell, Edith: 2734, 3616
Skelton, Geoffrey (trans): 3948
Skinner, Mary Louise: 3994
Sklar, Robert: 2588
Sklar, Sylvia: 4407, 4587
Sklare, Arnold B. (ed): 2875
Skurnick, Blanche Jacqueline: 3995
Slade, Tony: 3396
Slote, Bernice: 3360; (ed): 2543
Smailes, Thomas A.: 3207, 3208, 3397, 3398, 3399, 3617, 3618, 3619, 3620; (ed): 3617
Small, Michael: 4588
Smart, William: 4208
Smith, Anne (ed): 3339
Smith, Bob L.: 3209
Smith, Elton: 3400
Smith, Frank Glover: 3802
Smith, Grover: 3996
Smith, Julian: 4209, 4408
Smith, L. E. W.: 2444
Smithson, Isaiah: 4589

Sobchack, Thomas J.: 3210, 3401
Soldati, Mario: 2998
Solecki, Zdzislaw Zbigniew Sam: 4210, 4409
Soliman, Soliman Yousef: 4590
Solomon, Gerald: 4211
Sommers, Joseph: 3211
Spano, Joseph: 3212
Sparrow, John: 2169, 2339, 2340, 2445, 2446
Spears, Logan: 3803
Spears, Monroe K.: 3621
Speirs, James Gordon: 3622
Speirs, John: 3804
Spender, Stephen: 2447, 2448, 3623, 4212, 4410; (ed): 4051, 4074, 4090, 4100, 4121, 4133, 4146, 4154, 4206, 4212, 4213, 4224, 4228
Spiegel, Alan Harvey: 4214
Spilka, Mark: 2735, 2877, 2999, 3706, 3805, 4411, 4591; (ed): 2146, 2417, 2449
Spolton, L.: 2878
Springer, Mary Doyle: 4592
Spurling, Hilary: 3213
Squires, Michael George: 3402, 3624, 3998, 4215, 4412, 4593, 4594
Stacy, Paul H.: 4413
Stafford, William: 2879
Staley, Thomas F. (ed): 3284
Stanley, F. R.: 2450
Stavrou, Constantine N.: 2341
Steig, Michael: 4595
Stein, Marian L.: 3999
Stein, Walter: 3403
Steiner, George: 2342, 2451
Steinhoff, Anneliese: 2452
Steloff, Frances: 4596
Stern, Eva I.: 4216
Stern, J. P.: 4217
Steward, James Ecclestone: 3404
Stewart, Bruce: 3625
Stewart, J. I. M.: 2453
Stewart, Kay Lanette: 4218
Stilwell, Robert L.: 3214
Stock, Noel: 3405
Stoehr, Taylor: 4597
Stohl, Johan H.: 3215, 4000
Stoker, Richard Judge: 4219
Stoll, John Edward: 2880, 3216, 3626, 3627, 3806
Stolpe, Herman: 2170

Stone, Wilfred: 2881
Storey, David: 2589
Street, Brian V.: 4598
Strickland, Geoffrey: 2171, 3807, 4220
Strittmatter, Horst: 2679
Stroupe, John S. [also Stroupe, John H.]: 2882, 3628
Stuhlmann, Gunther (ed): 2978, 3365, 3768
Sturn, Ralph D.: 3217
Suckow, Ruth: 3629
Suehiro, Yoshitaka: 2736, 2883, 3000
Suehnel, Rudolf (ed): 3707
Sugiyama, Yasushi: 4221, 4414, 4415, 4599
Sullivan, Alvin: 3525, 3808
Sullivan, Elizabeth Quay: 4600
Sumimoto, Akiko: 2454
Suwabe, Hitoshi: 3218
Suzuki, Shunzi: 3809, 4222, 4416, 4417
Sweeney, Louise: 3630
Swigg, Richard: 4001
Swinden, Patrick: 4223
Swingewood, Alan: 3810
Swinnerton, Frank: 2455
Sykes, Christopher: 4601
T., E. [See Chambers, Jessie]
Tabuchi, Hiroyuki: 3811, 4002, 4602
Talon, Henri: 2737
Tanner, Tony: 2172, 2343, 2884, 4224
Tanselle, G. Thomas: 2590
Tao, Sadako: 3001
Tarratt, Margaret: 3631
Tasman, Norma L. (ed): 3348
Taube, Myron: 4418
Taylor, John A.: 4419
Taylor, John Russell: 3002
Taylor, Kim [pseud Adam, Michael]: 3632, 4444
Tedlock, Ernest W., Jr.: 2456, 2739, 2740; (ed): 2112, 2263, 2348, 2701, 2738, 2739, 2740
Temple, Frédéric-Jacques: 2344; (ed): 2418, 2678
Temple, Ruth Z. (ed): 2352, 2885
Tenenbaum, Elizabeth B.: 4003
Terry, Chris J.: 4004, 4420
Teruya, Yoshio: 4603
Tetsumura, Haruo: 2457, 2458, 2591, 2741, 2742, 3003, 3633, 3812, 4421, 4604

INDEX OF AUTHORS

Teunissen, John J.: 4422
Thatcher, David S.: 3634
Thody, Philip: 2173, 3219, 4225
Thomas, Donald: 3406
Thomas, Dylan: 2886
Thompson, Leslie M.: 3220, 3813, 4605
Thorn, Fritz: 3004
Thulin, Richard Lee: 4005
Thwaite, Anthony: 3221
Tibbetts, Robert A.: 4423
Tiedje, Egon: 3222, 3814, 3896
Tillyard, E. M. W.: 2174
Timko, Michael (ed): 3223
Tischler, Nancy M.: 3224
Titta Rosa, Giovanni: 2743
Tomatsu, Ryoichi: 3815
Tomlinson, T. B.: 2175, 2744
Toraiwa, Masazumi: 2345
Toyokuni, Takashi: 3816, 3817, 4006, 4007, 4226, 4424, 4606
Trail, George Y.: 3407
Traschen, Isadore: 3408; (ed): 3307
Trautmann, Joanne: 4607
Travis, Clayton Leigh: 3225, 3635
Trease, Geoffrey: 4227
Trilling, Diana: 4228
Trilling, Lionel: 3005; (ed): 3005
Tripathy, Biyot Kesh: 3818, 4229
Truchler, Leo: 3409
Tucker, Betty Jean: 3636
Tucker, Martin: 3637; (ed): 2352, 2885
Tudor, Kathleen Richardson: 4008
Tudsbery, M. T.: 2176
Tunander, Britt: 3638
Turnbull, Andrew (ed): 2392
Turnell, Martin: 2177
Turner, Frederick W., III: 3410
Turner, G. R.: 3006
Turroni, Giuseppe: 4009
Tynan, Kenneth: 3007
Tysdahl, Bjørn: 4608
Uchiki, Jôtarô: 2459, 2745, 2746, 2887, 3008, 3226
Uehata, Yoshikazu: 2592, 2747, 3009, 3227
Ulmer, Gregory Leland: 4010
Unrue, Darlene H.: 4609
Unterecker, John (ed): 2619
Upadhyaya, L. M.: 2888
Usui, Yoshitaka: 2460
Vaccarelli, Mary Motta: 4011

Vanderlip, E. C.: 3228
Van Doren, Mark: 3113
Van Tassell, Daniel E.: 4012
Van Tine, James Gaylord: 3229
Veitch, Douglas W.: 3819
Verga, Giovanni: 4242
Vicinus, Martha: 3443
Vickery, John B.: 2461, 2462, 3820, 4013, 4230, 4425
Vidas, Louise Walczak: 4231
Vigorelli, Giancarlo: 2346
Vitoux, Pierre: 4426
Vogelsang, John Daniel: 4427
Volpe, Edmond L.: 2122; (ed): 2122
von Broembsen, Francesca Ferraris: 4014, 4610
Von Eckardt, Wolf: 4015
Wada, Shizuo: 2463, 2593, 2749, 3639, 3640, 3821, 4428
Wade, John Stevens: 4232
Wagner, Geoffrey: 4016
Wagner, Jeanie: 3822
Wajc-Tenenbaum, Rachel: 2889
Walcutt, Charles Child (ed): 2108, 3230
Waldron, Philip: 2178, 2750, 3010
Walker, Cynthia Lucille: 4429
Walker, Grady Joe: 4017
Walker, Ronald G.: 4430
Walker, Warren S.: 2179
Wall, James M.: 3231
Wallace, Mary Elizabeth: 4611
Wallenstein, Barry: 3823
Wallmann, Jürgen P.: 3824, 4612
Walsh, Moira: 3641
Walsh, William: 2594, 4233
Wardle, Irving: 2751, 3011, 3012, 3232, 4234
Warner, Oliver: 2595
Warschausky, Sidney: 2464
Warshaw, Thayer S. (ed): 4449
Wasserman, Jerry: 4018
Wasserstrom, William: 2752
Wasson, Richard: 3013
Watanabe, Junko: 4019, 4235
Waterfield, Lina: 2180
Waters, Frank: 3233
Watson, George: 2347
Waugh, Alec: 3014
Way, Brian: 2596
Wayland, James Ward: 4020
Weales, Gerald: 2181, 2753
Weatherby, H. L.: 3015

Weaver, Mike: 3825
Weaver, Robert: 2182
Weber, Horst (ed): 4508
Weightman, John: 3642
Weiner, S. Ronald: 3411
Weintraub, Stanley: 2465, 2754, 3016
Weisburg, Edzia: 2183
Weiss, Daniel A.: 2348, 2466
Welch, Colin: 2184
Welker, Robert H.: 2185
Wellard, James: 4236
Werner, Alfred: 2186
West, Alick: 4613
West, Herbert Faulkner: 2890
West, Paul: 2755
West, Ray B., Jr.: 3234
West, Rebecca [See Andrews, Cicily Isabel Fairfield]
Westbrook, Max: 3235
Weston, Edward: 4237, 4238
Wevill, Sharon Lee Potts: 4614
Whitaker, Thomas R.: 2188, 3236
White, T. H.: 3237
White, Victor: 2756
White, William: 2349
Whitehead, Barbara (artist): 4444
Whitehorn, Ethel: 3643
Whitesell, J. Edwin (ed): 2108, 3230
Wicker, Brian: 4615
Wickes, George: 2350; (ed): 2385
Wickham, Anna: 2891
Widmer, Eleanor (ed): 2189
Widmer, Kingsley: 2351, 2757, 2877, 2892, 4239, 4240, 4431, 4616; (ed): 2189
Wiehe, R. E.: 2191
Wiener, Leigh (photog): 3113
Wilde, Alan: 2598
Wilding, Michael: 3644, 3645
Wiley, Paul L.: 4241
Wilkin, Andrew: 4242, 4432
Willens, Barbara: 3435
Willey, Frederick: 3238
Williams, Hubertien H.: 3239, 3240
Williams, Joy (ed): 4244
Williams, Oscar (ed): 2948
Williams, Raymond: 2192, 2193, 2352, 2353, 2467, 3241, 3412, 3646, 4243, 4244; (ed): 4244
Williams, William Emrys: 2194
Willingham, John R.: 2354, 2599, 2600, 2601

Willison, I. R. (ed): 4022
Wilson, Colin: 2272, 2355
Wilson, Raymond J.: 4245
Winegarten, Renee: 4433
Winterich, John T.: 2356
Wise, James N.: 4023
Woerner, Gert (ed): 2679
Woerner, Robert Frederick: 2357
Wolf, Harold R.: 2758
Wolpers, Theodor: 3017
Wood, Frederick T.: 2468
Wood, Jessie Chambers: 3414
Wood, Paul Alonzo Christopher: 3415
Woodbery, Potter: 3720
Woodcock, Bruce: 4434
Woodcock, George: 4024
Woodeson, John: 4025
Woodings, R. B.: 3826
Woodward, A. G.: 4247
Wordsworth, Ann: 3647
Worrell, J.: 3827
Worthen, John: 2893, 3828, 4617, 4618
Wright, Raymond: 2195
Yagyu, Naojuki: 4619
Yamada, Noriyuki: 4249
Yamaguchi, Keizabrô: 2358, 2759, 2760, 2895, 2896, 3018, 3019
Yamaguchi, Tetsuo: 3416, 3648, 4435
Yamaji, Katsuyuki: 2196, 2897
Yamakawa, Kozo: 4436, 4437
Yamasaki, Susumu: 2898, 3020, 4026, 4438
Yamashita, Kazuichiro: 4248, 4620
Yanada, Noriyuki: 4249, 4439
Yarber, Robert E.: 2947
Yasukawa, Akira: 3021
Yokota, Chuzô: 3022, 3829
Yoshida, Masako: 4250, 4621
Yoshida, Tetsuo: 4440
Yoshii, Mitsuo: 3417, 3649, 3650, 3651, 3830, 4027, 4251, 4252, 4622, 4623
Yoshimura, Hirokazu: 3418, 3831, 3832, 4253, 4254, 4255, 4441, 4624, 4625
Yoshitake, Yoshinori: 4028
Young, Archibald M.: 3242
Young, B. A.: 3243, 3244
Young, Jessica Hankinson Brett: 2359
Youngblood, Sarah: 3245
Youssef, T. I. M.: 4626
Yudhishtar: 2899, 3419

INDEX OF AUTHORS

Z., P. D.: 3652
Zambrano, Ana Laura: 4256
Zampa, Giorgio: 2360, 2900
Zanger, Jules: 2761
Zaslove, Jerald: 3420
Zeraffa, Michel: 3421
Ziebarth, Janet A.: 4442
Zimmerman, Lester F. (ed): 3284
Zimmermann, Hans-Joachim (ed): 3017
Zinnes, Harriet: 2469
Ziolkowski, Theodore (ed): 4329
Zuckerman, Elliott: 2602
Zytaruk, George John: 2762, 3024, 3246, 3422, 3423, 3653, 3833, 3834, 3835, 3836, 4190, 4257, 4258, 4627; (ed): 3023, 3247, 3414, 3653, 4443

Index

TITLES OF SECONDARY WORKS

Titles of articles in periodicals and chapters in books are in quotation marks; book titles are in upper case; translations of article titles originally appearing in a foreign language are in parentheses, without quotation marks and in lower case; translations of book titles originally appearing in a foreign language are in parentheses and in upper case. Numbers after each title refer to the item in the bibliography where the title appears.

"A Propos de *Women in Love*: Un inedit déconcertant": 3047
"A propos of 'England, My England' ": 2119
(A Propos of *Women in Love*: A Disconcerting Unpublished Work): 3047
"A. Huxley no Shiten kara no *Shirokujaku* Ron": 4134
"*Aaron's Rod* Danshô (Sakuhin to Ningen Lawrence)": 2741
"*Aaron's Rod* no Futatsu no Jôkei": 4398
"Abgeschiedenheit und Auferstehung: Die Entfaltung eines Motivs in D. H. Lawrences letzten Kurzgeschichten": 3147
(About Lawrence's Death and Darkness): 3130
ABOUT LITERATURE: 2519
"The Ache of Modernism: Thomas Hardy, Time and the Modern Novel": 3515
THE ACHIEVEMENT OF E. M. FORSTER: 2209
"Action is Eloquence": 2627
"Acts of Attention: The Major Poems of D. H. Lawrence": 3089
ACTS OF ATTENTION: THE POEMS OF D. H. LAWRENCE: 3089, 3913
"Adam in Nottingham: Literary Archetypes in the Novels of D. H. Lawrence": 3085
"Addendum to Roberts: Another Piracy of *Lady Chatterley's Lover*": 4423
"An Addendum to the D. H. Lawrence Canon": 4153
"Additional Bibliographical Information on Some D. H. Lawrence Stories": 3898
ADVENTURE IN CONSCIOUSNESS: THE MEANING OF D. H. LAWRENCE'S RELIGIOUS QUEST: 2141, 2317, 2318, 2431, 2432, 2563, 2564
(ADVENTURES IN THOUGHT: LAWRENCE'S FICTION): 4437
"Advocate for Eros: Notes on D. H. Lawrence": 2185
"Aesthetic Distance in the Techniques of the Novel": 2514
"The Aesthetic of Life: Art and the Artist in the Major Novels of D. H. Lawrence": 4454
"The Affective Fallacy Revisited": 2735
"Affirmations and Negations: Lawrence's 'Whitman' and Whitman's Open Road": 3999
"African Sculpture Symbols in a Novel by D. H. Lawrence": 3363
"After the Prophet: The Reputation of D. H. Lawrence": 2328
(After the Savage Pilgrimage--Cornwall): 2818
(After the Savage Pilgrimage--Eastwood): 3527

(After the Savage Pilgrimage--Lago di Garda): 3731
(After the Savage Pilgrimage--New Mexico): 3333
(After the Savage Pilgrimage--Sicily): 3116
(After the Savage Pilgrimage--Villa Mirenda): 4125
AFTER THE STORY: LANDMARKS OF THE MODERN MEXICAN NOVEL: 3211
"Afternoons in Italy with D. H. Lawrence": 2479
AFTERNOONS IN ITALY WITH D. H. LAWRENCE: 2479
"Afterthoughts on Regina v. Penguin Books Ltd.": 2339
"Afterword": 2295
AGE OF THE MODERN AND OTHER LITERARY ESSAYS: 2415
"Ai no Shigan *The Rainbow*": 2591
"Ai to Koritsu--*Musuko to Koibito* ni Tsuite": 4602
"Ai to Kunô no Henreki *Miyo Warera Wa Yatte Kita!*": 2140
"Ai to Shôtotsu (Anna to Will no Baai)": 4540
ALDOUS HUXLEY: A BIOGRAPHY: 4037
ALDOUS HUXLEY: A STUDY OF THE MAJOR NOVELS: 3045
"Aldous Huxley and D. H. Lawrence": 2474, 2889
"Aldous Huxley and D. H. Lawrence: An Attempt at Intellectual Sympathy": 4426
ALDOUS HUXLEY: SATIRE AND STRUCTURE: 3355
ALDOUS HUXLEY'S QUEST FOR VALUES: 3673
"The Almost of Satisfaction: A Study of the Major Fiction of D. H. Lawrence": 4556
"Ambiguity and Isolation in 'The Man Who Loved Islands' ": 4405
(The Ambivalence of Eros--A Study of D. H. Lawrence's *Women in Love*): 4235
"America e Mukau Lawrence": 4562
"America, My America": 2826
AMERICAN AND BRITISH WRITERS IN MEXICO, 1556-1973: 4324
"Among the New Books--The Time of Dickens": 2471
"Un amore di Lawrence": 3962
L'AMOUR ET LE DIVIN: 2110
"Anais Nin and the Paintings of D. H. Lawrence": 3745
"Anais Nin's Works Reissued": 2469
"An Analytical Calendar of the Letters of D. H. Lawrence": 3741
"The Anatomy of a Genre: The Modern Novelette in English": 3717
THE ANATOMY OF THE NOVEL: 4455
"Ancora su Lady Chatterley": 2080
" 'And all the little typtopies': Notes on Language Theory in the Contemporary Experimental Novel": 4309
"And what about the ranch, the little ranch in New Mexico. The time is different there": 3509
"The Androgynous Ideal: A Study of Selected Novels by D. H. Lawrence, James Joyce, and Virginia Woolf": 4311
"The Androgynous Mind in W. B. Yeats, D. H. Lawrence, Virginia Woolf and Dorothy Richardson": 4008
"Angry Visitor: The Landscape and D. H. Lawrence": 3880
(The Animal in the Work of D. H. Lawrence): 2079
"ANNA KARENINA": 2687
ANNA KARENINA AND OTHER ESSAYS: 2115, 2408, 2687
"ANNA KARENINA: Thought and Significance in a Great Creative Work": 2687
"Annable no Sôwa": 2136
ANOTHER AMERICA: IN SEARCH OF CANYONS: 4016
" 'Another Ego': The Changing View of Self and Society in the Work of D. H. Lawrence": 2517
ANOTHER EGO: THE CHANGING VIEW OF SELF AND SOCIETY IN THE WORK OF D. H. LAWRENCE: 2517, 3514
"Antipodes: D. H. Lawrence's *St. Mawr*": 4316
"The Anti-Soporific Art": 3178
"The Apes, the Fox, and Charlie Bubbles": 3026
"Aphorisms by Franklin and Lawrence": 3182

INDEX OF TITLES OF SECONDARY WORKS

"*Apocalypse* Oboegaki": 4166
"The Apocalypse of Lorenzo": 3456
"Apocalyptic Mexico: *The Plumed Serpent* and THE POWER AND THE GLORY": 3152
AN APPALLING TALENT: KEN RUSSELL: 4195
"An Approach to D. H. Lawrence as Novelist": 3061
APPROACHES TO THE TWENTIETH-CENTURY NOVEL: 2619
THE APPROPRIATE FORM: AN ESSAY ON THE NOVEL: 2510
"An Archetypal Imagery Study of the Fall of the Family in the Nineteenth-Century English Novel": 3636
"Archetypal Patterns in the Poetry of D. H. Lawrence": 4511
"An Architect of the Vital Self: A Study of D. H. Lawrence": 4348
ARCHITECTS OF THE SELF: GEORGE ELIOT, D. H. LAWRENCE, AND E. M. FORSTER: 2475, 2771, 3849
ARNOLD BENNETT: 4304
ART AND PORNOGRAPHY: AN EXPERIMENT IN EXPLANATION: 3373
"Art and Value in D. H. Lawrence's *Women in Love*": 3979
"Art, Entertainment and Religion": 2384
THE ART OF D. H. LAWRENCE: 2333, 2869
"The Art of Fiction: XXVIII": 2350
THE ART OF PERVERSITY: D. H. LAWRENCE'S SHORTER FICTIONS: 2351
THE ART OF PROSE: 2673
THE ART OF TED HUGHES: 4578
THE ART OF THE SELF IN D. H. LAWRENCE: 4111
THE ART OF THE STORY: 3102
THE ART OF WRITING FICTION: 3234
"Articles on D. H. Lawrence: A Bibliography, 1916-1965": 3155
"The Artist and the Modern World": 4247
"The Artist as Pornographer: The Evaluation of D. H. Lawrence's Genius": 2450
"The Artist as Revolutionary": 3133

"The Artist Priest and the Cosmic Landscape: D. H. Lawrence's Debt to Medieval and Renaissance Graphic Arts": 3726
"The Artist Theme": 2368
"The Artistic and Critical Significance of D. H. Lawrence's *Studies in Classic American Literature*": 3904
"The Artistic Development of D. H. Lawrence as a Writer of Short Stories": 4084
"As a Would-be Messiah, Mr. D. H. Lawrence Endures his Sad Lot Among a Host of Friends": 2406
"Aspects of D. H. Lawrence's Struggle with Christianity": 4420
"Aspects of Education in the Work of D. H. Lawrence": 4409
"Aspects of the Life and Thought of D. H. Lawrence, 1912-1916": 3846
"At the Cinema": 3353
(At the Crossroads of Realism and Symbolism): 3988
"At the Drop of a Stamp": 2205
"At the Drop of a Straw Hat": 2945
"Atarashii Kyôkantai no Tankyu--*The Plumed Serpent* no Ichikôsatsu": 4026
"The Attack on the *Pietà*: An Archetypal Analysis": 4422
ATTITUDES TO CRITICISM: 2798
"Au Nouveau-Mexique sur les pas de D. H. Lawrence": 2344
"Auf der Suche nach dem englischen Roman": 3029
AUSTRALIA IN WESTERN IMAGINATIVE PROSE WRITINGS 1600-1960: AN ANTHOLOGY AND A HISTORY OF LITERATURE: 2931
THE AUSTRALIAN EXPERIENCE: CRITICAL ESSAYS ON AUSTRALIAN NOVELS: 4331
"Authorial Presence in the Novel": 4278
"The Autobiographical Element in the Novels of D. H. Lawrence": 4392
"Autobiography, Doctrine, and Genre Comparison in the Plays of D. H. Lawrence": 4281
"Autobiography in the English *Bildungsroman*": 3444
"Autobiography: My Long and Beautiful

Journey": 2914
THE AUTOBIOGRAPHY OF BERTRAND RUSSELL, Vol. II: 1914-1944: 3190
"The Autoerotic Metaphor in Joyce, Sterne, Lawrence, Stevens, and Whitman": 2669
"B. B. C.": 3871
"B. W. Huebsch and D. H. Lawrence": 4356
" 'Babariya no Rindô' Oyobi *Shinda Otoko* ni Arawareta D. H. Lawrence no Shisei-Kan": 4349
"The Background Description in the Novels of D. H. Lawrence": 3538
"The Background of the Political Philosophy of Conrad and Lawrence": 3622
(Balance): 3043
"The Banal, and the Poetry of D. H. Lawrence": 4211
THE BANNED BOOKS OF ENGLAND AND OTHER COUNTRIES: 2225
"Bannen no Lawrence--Kodoku kara Shinwateki Cosmos e": 4416
"The Bases of the Normal": 2869
(Basic Pattern of Thought in Lawrence, Forster, Woolf, and Huxley): 4545
" 'A Bastard Begot': The Origins of D. H. Lawrence's 'The Christening' ": 3874
" 'Bavarian Gentians' by D. H. Lawrence": 2377
BEARDSLEY: A BIOGRAPHY: 3016
"Die Bedeutung Thomas Hardys für des Frühwerk von D. H. Lawrence": 3249
DIE BEDEUTUNG THOMAS HARDYS FÜR DES FRÜHWERK VON D. H. LAWRENCE: 3249
(Before and After *The Rainbow*: On Beardsley's *Salome*): 4436
"The Beginning and the End: D. H. Lawrence's *Psychoanalysis* and *Fantasia*": 3925
BEHIND THE SCENES IN THE THEATRE: 3318
"Being Perfect: Lawrence, Sartre, and *Women in Love*": 4445
"The Best of *Sons and Lovers* and a Deeper Truth": 3351

"Better History and Better Criticism: The Significance of F. R. Leavis": 2733
"Between Scylla and Charybdis: *Kangaroo* and the Form of the Political Novel": 3644
"Beyond Love": 3735
"Beyond the Pleasure Principle: An Analysis of D. H. Lawrence's 'The Prussian Officer' ": 2361
BIBLICAL DRAMA IN ENGLAND FROM THE MIDDLE AGES TO THE PRESENT DAY: 3188
BIBLICAL IMAGES IN LITERATURE: 4449
"The Biblical Play *David*": 2431
"The Bibliographical Potential of a 20th Century Literary Agent's Archive: The Pinker Papers": 3481
BIBLIOGRAPHY OF BRITISH LITERARY BIBLIOGRAPHIES: 3325
A BIBLIOGRAPHY OF D. H. LAWRENCE: 2438
BIG SCREEN, LITTLE SCREEN: 3589
"Biography": 2211
"*Birds, Beasts and Flowers*": 3398
"Birkin ni Tsuite": 2541
"Black Magic, White Lies": 2184
"Blake and Lawrence": 3375
(The Blockaded Sex--from "The Man Who Loved Islands"): 2952
"Blommornas språk eller säg det med blommor": 3702
"The Blood, Border, *Barranca*: The Role of Mexico in the Modern English Novel": 4430
("The Blood" in D. H. Lawrence): 4335
BLOOMSBURY: 3041
"Blueprints for Utopia: The Political Ideas of Nietzsche and D. H. Lawrence": 4319
"The *Blutbrüderschaft* Theme in the Fiction of D. H. Lawrence": 3700
BOARDING THE SHIP OF DEATH: D. H. LAWRENCE'S QUESTER HEROES: 2634, 2635, 4305
(Body and Illusion: A Note on D. H. Lawrence): 2345
"Body and Soul": 3567
"The Body Electric": 4607
"Book Reviews": 2178, 2812, 2851,

3010, 3078, 3246, 3422
"A Book So Bad It Was Impossible to Put Down": 3986
"A Bookman's Notebook": 2246
"Books": 2637
"Books in English": 2439, 2465
BOOKS IN THE DOCK: 3387
('The Border Line' and D. H. Lawrence): 2819
BOSWELL'S CLAP AND OTHER ESSAYS: MEDICAL ANALYSES OF LITERARY MEN'S AFFLICTIONS: 3369
"A Botanical Note on *Aaron's Rod*": 3822
"The Bottom of the Well": 2319
A BOY AT THE HOGARTH PRESS: 3939
"Brangwen Men in *The Rainbow*: A Study of the Function of Two Male Characters": 3309
"The Breaking Chain: A Study of the Dance in the Novels of Jane Austen, George Eliot, Thomas Hardy, and D. H. Lawrence": 2387
"The Brett Story": 3556
"Brief Mention": 2502
"Briefly Noted": 2748
"British Fathers and Sons, 1773-1913: From Filial Submissiveness to Creativity": 2758
"The British Museum and Solitary Vice": 2371
THE BRITISH MUSEUM IS FALLING DOWN: 2689
THE BRITISH NOVEL: CONRAD TO THE PRESENT: 4241
BRITISH SHORT STORIES: CLASSICS AND CRITICISM: 3032
BRODIE'S NOTES ON D. H. LAWRENCE'S "SONS AND LOVERS": 2941
"The Broken Balance and the Negative Victory in *Lady Chatterley's Lover*": 4440
"Broken Vision in Lawrence's *The Fox*": 3991
"Brothers and Lovers: D. H. Lawrence and the Theme of Friendship": 4497
"Bubbly But Sad": 3096
"Bungaku ni Arawareta Anrakushi": 4582
"Bunmei no Hôkai-Katei no Naka de-- Lawrence *Koisuru Onnatachi* Ron": 4622
"Bunmei to Kyôki--D. H. Lawrence no *Shojo to Jipushi* Ron": 3968
"The Burning Bush: D. H. Lawrence as a Religious Poet": 2987
"Busy and Candid": 3382
"The Call of the South": 2381
"Camus and Lawrence": 2214
"Can a Radical Interpretation of *Women in Love* Be Adequate?": 3432
"Canadian Customs Seize Books": 2074
"The Candid Revelation: Lawrence's Aesthetics": 3964
"Candid Revelations: On *The Complete Poems of D. H. Lawrence*": 3964
"Carlyle and Froude": 2485
CARRINGTON: LETTERS AND EXTRACTS FROM HER DIARIES: 3678
"Carrying On: *Lady Chatterley's Lover*": 2944
"Carteggi Lawrence": 3767
"The Case of *Lady Chatterley's Lover*": 2281
"The Casey Judgement": 2075
CASTLE IN ITALY: AN AUTOBIOGRAPHY: 2180
"A Catalogue of D. H. Lawrence's Reading from Early Childhood": 3269, 3448
"A Catalogue of D. H. Lawrence's Reading from Early Childhood: Addenda": 4049
"A Catalogue of the Frieda Lawrence Manuscripts in German at the University of Texas": 4110
"Catastrophism and Coition: Universal and Individual Development in *Women in Love*": 2928
"The Category of Landscape in D. H. Lawrence's *Kangaroo*": 3394
THE CAVE AND THE MOUNTAIN: A STUDY OF E. M. FORSTER: 2881
(Cecil Byrne and Hampson in *The Trespasser*): 4255
CELEBRATION OF LIFE: STUDIES IN MODERN FICTION: 3961
"The Censor as Aedile": 2169

CENSORS: THE REDE LECTURE: 2149
CENSORSHIP: GOVERNMENT AND OBSCENITY: 2424
CENSORSHIP OF THE MOVIES: THE SOCIAL AND POLITICAL CONTROL OF A MASS MEDIUM: 3181
CENSORSHIP: THE SEARCH FOR THE OBSCENE: 2492
(Centripetal Thought and Expression in Lawrence): 4385
CERTAIN ASPECTS OF MORAL COURAGE: 2281, 2282
"Cézanne in England 1910-1930": 2402, 2666
"The Chambers Memoirs of D. H. Lawrence: A Reply": 4617
"The Chambers Memoirs of D. H. Lawrence--Which Chambers?": 4257
"The Chambers Memoirs of D. H. Lawrence--Which Chambers?: A Reply to Mr. John Worthen": 4627
THE CHANGING FACE: DISINTEGRATION OF PERSONALITY IN THE TWENTIETH-CENTURY BRITISH NOVEL: 3558
"The Changing Scene: *Aaron's Rod*": 3419
"Character and Consciousness: D. H. Lawrence, Wilhelm Reich, and Jean-Paul Sartre": 4259
"Character and Rhetoric in Prose Fiction": 3524
"Character as Symbol: Annie's Role in *Sons and Lovers*": 3164
CHARACTER IN ENGLISH LITERATURE: 2643
"Character, Language, and Experience in 'Water Party' ": 4091
"Characterization and the Concept of the Self in the Novels of D. H. Lawrence": 4104
"Charity-boy of Literature": 3186
"Charles Olson and D. H. Lawrence: Aesthetics of the 'Primitive Abstract' ": 4079
"Chatterley Fujin no Ichiya": 2547
"*Chatterley* no Mittsu no Han ni Tsuite": 4553
"The Chatterley Syndrome": 2770
"*Chatterley*, the Witnesses, and the Law: Black Magic? White Lies?": 2094, 2101, 2187, 2194
"*Chatterley-Fujin no Koibito* no Mori": 4138
"A Checklist of D. H. Lawrence Articles in Japan, 1951-1968": 3334
"The Checklist of D. H. Lawrence Criticism and Scholarship, 1970": 3667
"The Checklist of D. H. Lawrence Criticism and Scholarship, 1971": 3924
"The Checklist of D. H. Lawrence Criticism and Scholarship, 1972": 4034
"The Checklist of D. H. Lawrence Criticism and Scholarship, 1973": 4268
"The Checklist of D. H. Lawrence Criticism and Scholarship, 1974": 4450
"A Checklist of D. H. Lawrence Scholarship in Scandinavia, 1934-1968": 3250
"A Checklist of Lawrence's Reading": 3448
"A Checklist of THE SEVEN ARTS": 3993
"A Checklist of Theses on D. H. Lawrence in Japan: 1968-1975": 4585
"Chichi no Ko Lawrence": 2714
"Chichioya ni Taisuru D. H. Lawrence no Kanjô--Ishiki to Muishiki": 3815
"Chicken Queen's Delight: D. H. Lawrence's *The Fox*": 4064
"Chijô no Shinwa": 2759
"The Childhood of Ursula": 2594
"A Child's Guide to Modern Culture: N Is for New Establishment": 2219
"Christ and Isis: The Function of the Dying and Reviving God in *The Man Who Died*": 3946
"Christ as Artist and Lover: D. H. Lawrence's *Sons and Lovers*": 2300
"Christ Risen": 2564
"The Christ Who Didn't Die: Analogues to D. H. Lawrence's *The Man Who Died*": 4605
(CHRISTIANITY AND LITERATURE, NO. 3): 4619
(CHRONICLES AND SOCIAL NOVELS): 2625
CHRONIQUES ET ROMANS SOCIAUX: 2625
"A Chronological Catalogue of D. H. Lawrence's Reading from Early Childhood": 3269
"Chumship": 3386

INDEX OF TITLES OF SECONDARY WORKS

"The Circle Completes Itself: Notes on the Contemporary Colonial Novel": 2395
"Circles and Arcs: The Rhythm of Circularity and Centrifugality in D. H. Lawrence's *Last Poems*": 3716
"The Circular and the Linear: The Middleton Murry-D. H. Lawrence Affair": 3319
(Class Consciousness of D. H. Lawrence): 2404
THE CLASSIC BRITISH NOVEL: 3923
"Clichés": 3590
"Cold Hands Warmed": 3662
"Collaborators": 4179
"*The Collected Letters of D. H. Lawrence*": 2356
"The Collected Letters of Jessie Chambers": 3414
"Collecting Lawrence": 3055
"Collection Called One of Finest: Rare D. H. Lawrence Items Acquired by TU": 4534
THE COLLECTION OF BOOKS, MANUSCRIPTS, AND AUTOGRAPH LETTERS IN THE LIBRARY OF JEAN AND DONALD STRALEM: 2276
"Colliers": 2822
[*A Collier's Friday Night*]: 3131, 3139, 3205, 3243
(*A Collier's Friday Night*: A Play by D. H. Lawrence in Bochum): 4401
"The Colour Ambience of Lawrence's Early and Later Poetry": 4552
"Comedy and History in *The Rainbow*": 3013
COMIC CUTS: A BEDSIDE SAMPLER OF CENSORSHIP IN ACTION: 3486
"Comment on Leavis": 2415
"Commentary": 4140, 4283
"Commitment and Futility in *The Fox*": 2613
"Commitment and the Straitjacket": 2104
"Common Womb Imagery in Joyce and Lawrence": 3626
"Community in *Women in Love*": 3665
(*The Complete Poems of D. H. Lawrence*): 2127, 2143
"The Composite World: Two Versions of *Lady Chatterley's Lover*": 3710
THE COMPOSITION OF "THE RAINBOW" AND "WOMEN IN LOVE": A HISTORY: 4189, 4396, 4585
"The Composition of *Women in Love*: A History, 1913-1919": 4575
"Comptes Rendus": 3034, 3691, 3879
COMPTON MACKENZIE: 4303
"The Concept of Character in the Major Novels of D. H. Lawrence": 3701
"The Concept of Person in D. H. Lawrence's *The Rainbow*": 3169
"Concepts of the Self in the Modern Novel": 4003
(Concerning Three Manuscripts of D. H. Lawrence, *The White Peacock, The Trespasser, The Rainbow*: Contribution to the Study of Literary Creation): 4318
THE CONCISE ENCYCLOPEDIA OF ENGLISH AND AMERICAN POETS AND POETRY: 2447
"The Conclusion of *Sons and Lovers*: A Reconsideration": 3765
(The Conclusion of *The Rainbow* and the Rainbow as a Symbol): 2984
A CONCORDANCE TO THE POETRY OF D. H. LAWRENCE: 3497
A CONCORDANCE TO THE SHORT FICTION OF D. H. LAWRENCE: 3910
"Confessions of a Lawrentian Manqué": 4569
(The Conflict between Society and Individuals in the Novels of E. M. Forster and D. H. Lawrence): 4384
CONFLICT IN THE NOVELS OF D. H. LAWRENCE: 2899, 3419
(Connie in *Lady Chatterley's Lover*): 2843
"Conscious Mad: The Nature of Self in D. H. Lawrence": 4164
CONSPIRATORS AND POETS: 2491
(The Contemporary English Novel): 2268
THE CONTEMPORARY ENGLISH NOVEL: 2262
(The Contemporary Relevance of Lawrence's Works): 4379

685

(The Contemporary Significance of D. H. Lawrence): 4537
CONTINUITIES: 3122
THE CONTRARY VIEW: GLIMPSES OF FUDGE AND GOLD: 4322
CONTROVERSIAL ESSAYS: 2339, 2340
A CONVERSATION ON D. H. LAWRENCE: 4370
"Correspondence": 2391, 2415, 2789, 2831
"Correspondence Section": 3721
"The Cortege of Dionysus: A Study of the Fiction of D. H. Lawrence and Jean Giono": 2675
"The Cortege of Dionysus: Lawrence and Giono": 2821
"Così parlò Lawrence": 3379
(The Cosmos of D. H. Lawrence: An Approach to Its Meaning in the History of Thought): 4417
"Cottage Realism": 3713
"Counterfeit and the Use of Literature": 3420
THE COUNTRY AND THE CITY: 4243
THE COUNTRY OF MY HEART: A LOCAL GUIDE TO D. H. LAWRENCE: 3978
"Courting": 2653
"The Craft of D. H. Lawrence's Short Stories: A Study of Five Early Tales": 2932
THE CRAZY FABRIC: ESSAYS IN IRONY: 2631
(A Creation in Collapse and Insanity of Self--On *The Plumed Serpent*): 3651
"Creativity in Crisis: D. H. Lawrence and World War I": 4566
CRISIS AND CRITICISM, AND SELECTED LITERARY ESSAYS: 4613
(A Critical Approach to D. H. Lawrence): 2216
CRITICAL ESSAYS: 2153
"Critical Exchange: On 'Lawrence Up-Tight': Four Tail-Pieces": 3706
THE CRITICAL PATH: 3708
(Critical Reading of a Passage of *Women in Love*): 3048
"A Critical Re-examination of D. H. Lawrence's *Aaron's Rod*": 4263

"The Critical Writings of D. H. Lawrence": 2159
CRITICISM AND RESEARCH: 2586
"Criticism and the Reading Public": 3315
CRITICISM AS DIALOGUE: 3403
"Criticism of D. H. Lawrence in German, 1923-1970: A Bibliography": 3659
CRITICISM OF SOCIETY IN THE ENGLISH NOVEL BETWEEN THE WARS: 3554
THE CRITIC'S CREDENTIALS: ESSAYS AND REVIEWS: 2665
CRITICS ON D. H. LAWRENCE: 2389, 2394, 2607, 2624, 2744, 2944, 3661
CRITICS WHO HAVE INFLUENCED TASTE: 2644
" 'The Crown,' 'The Reality of Peace,' and *Women in Love*": 3263
"Culminations: D. H. Lawrence": 2540
THE CULT OF SINCERITY: 3183
THE CULT OF THE EGO: THE SELF IN MODERN LITERATURE: 2503
"The Culture Chasm: Bantu Education and the Use of English": 3970
"Culture Now: Some Animadversions, Some Laughs": 3671
"Current Books": 2228, 2378
"Current Literature 1962": 2468
THE CURVE OF RETURN: D. H. LAWRENCE'S TRAVEL BOOKS: 4338
A CYPRESS IN SICILY: A PERSONAL ADVENTURE: 2901
(Cyril Beardsall in *The White Peacock*): 4254
"Cyril Connolly Exampled: An Exhibit on 'The Modern Movement' ": 3513
"Cythera e no Shinnyû": 4544
"D. (David) H. (Herbert) Lawrence": 4241
"D. H. L. the Second Time Around": 2515
"D. H. L.'s American Digest": 2488
"D. H. Lawrence": 2110, 2122, 2124, 2273, 2335, 2352, 2355, 2362, 2416, 2464, 2544, 2573, 2644, 2659, 2663, 2673, 2755, 2783, 2804, 2811, 2837, 2871, 2872, 2875, 2885, 2893, 2939, 3046,

INDEX OF TITLES OF SECONDARY WORKS

3160, 3183, 3293, 3442, 3466, 3508, 3563, 3669, 3693, 3694, 3753, 3759, 3760, 3779, 3790, 3823, 4208, 4395, 4613
D. H. LAWRENCE: 2068, 2379, 2490, 3199, 3302, 3396, 3841, 4132
"D. H. Lawrence: A Belated Apology": 2126
D. H. LAWRENCE: A COLLECTION OF CRITICAL ESSAYS: 2146, 2417, 2449
D. H. LAWRENCE: A COLLECTION OF CRITICISM: 2263, 2869, 2951, 3272, 3279, 3419, 4098, 4099
D. H. LAWRENCE: A CRITICAL ANTHOLOGY: 2114, 2115, 2119, 2248, 2491, 2653, 2654, 3092, 3349, 3351, 3714, 4054, 4055, 4141
D. H. LAWRENCE: A CRITICAL STUDY OF THE MAJOR NOVELS AND OTHER WRITINGS: 3786, 3807
D. H. LAWRENCE: A FINDING LIST: HOLDINGS IN THE CITY, COUNTY AND UNIVERSITY LIBRARIES OF NOTTINGHAM: 3070
D. H. LAWRENCE: A PERSONAL RECORD: 2617
(D. H. Lawrence–A Search for His "Darkness"): 4414
"D. H. Lawrence: A Season of Plays": 3132, 3206, 3244
"D. H. Lawrence: A Secondary Bibliography for Portugal": 3747
(D. H. Lawrence: A Spark of Black Eyes): 2982
D. H. LAWRENCE: A STUDY OF HIS NOVELS: 4392
"D. H. Lawrence: A Study of His Poetic Theories": 3193
"D. H. Lawrence: A Study of His Prose Style": 4020
"D. H. Lawrence: A Study of His Shorter Fiction": 3995
(D. H. Lawrence: Adventurer into Consciousness–On *The White Peacock*): 3967
"D. H. Lawrence als Dramatiker": 2806
"D. H. Lawrence als Lehrer und Philosoph": 3253
(D. H. Lawrence among Six Women and between Two Cultures): 3291
"D. H. Lawrence: An Eastern Interpretation": 2133
D. H. LAWRENCE: AN EASTERN VIEW: 2133, 3570
"D. H. Lawrence: An Ibsen Reference": 3895
(D. H. Lawrence: An Unpublished Letter): 3084
"D. H. Lawrence and A. N. Whitehead": 2255
"D. H. Lawrence and America": 4224
"D. H. Lawrence and American Literature": 3156
"D. H. Lawrence and Art": 3786
(D. H. Lawrence and Christianity): 4619
(D. H. Lawrence and Class): 2443
"D. H. Lawrence and Critical Mannerism": 4431
"D. H. Lawrence and E. M. Forster: A Study in Values": 2992
"D. H. Lawrence and E. M. Forster: From *The White Peacock* to *MAURICE*": 4565
D. H. LAWRENCE AND EDWARD CARPENTER: A STUDY IN EDWARDIAN TRANSITION: 3695
"D. H. Lawrence and Frieda": 4090
"D. H. Lawrence and German Expressionism": 4517
D. H. LAWRENCE AND GERMAN LITERATURE WITH TWO HITHERTO UNKNOWN ESSAYS BY D. H. LAWRENCE: 2063, 2363, 2364, 2472
"D. H. Lawrence and Hermann Hesse: A Comparative Study of Two Critics on Modern Culture": 2357
"D. H. Lawrence and His District": 4206
"D. H. Lawrence and his Paintings": 2545
"D. H. Lawrence and His Rabbit Adolph: Three Symbolic Permutations": 3143
D. H. LAWRENCE AND HIS WORLD: 2839
"D. H. Lawrence and Homosexuality": 4154
(D. H. Lawrence and India): 2314

(D. H. LAWRENCE AND ITALY): 2621
"D. H. Lawrence and Italy": 4301
"D. H. Lawrence and Judas": 3813
"D. H. Lawrence and Kate Millett": 4326
"D. H. Lawrence and Louie Burrows": 3294, 3828
"D. H. Lawrence and 'Man's Ontological Solitude' ": 3801
"D. H. Lawrence and Modern Society": 2951
(D. H. Lawrence and Morality): 3936
"D. H. Lawrence and Nancy Henry: Two Unpublished Letters and a Lost Relationship": 4059
"D. H. Lawrence and Ontological Insecurity": 4351
(D. H. Lawrence and Ottoline Morrell--Figures behind *Women in Love*): 4524
"D. H. Lawrence and Painting": 4194
"D. H. Lawrence and Pierre Drieu la Rochelle: A Cry against Decadence": 4216
"D. H. Lawrence and Sacher-Masoch": 3696
(D. H. Lawrence and Sacher-Masoch: Contribution to the Study of a Modern Sensibility): 3696
"D. H. Lawrence and Sex": 2307, 2426
(D. H. Lawrence and Society): 2747
"D. H. Lawrence and 'Something Called Canada' ": 4330
D. H. LAWRENCE AND "SONS AND LOVERS": SOURCES AND CRITICISM: 2263, 2348, 2701, 2738, 2739, 2740
(D. H. Lawrence and T. Hardy [I]): 3495
"D. H. Lawrence and Teilhard de Chardin: A Study in Agreements": 2764
"D. H. Lawrence and the Ancient Greeks": 2718
(D. H. Lawrence and the Architecture of the Novel): 2825
"D. H. Lawrence and the Australian Ethos": 4142
(D. H. Lawrence and the Cold Eye): 3075
"D. H. Lawrence and the Counter-Revolution: An Essay in Socialist Aesthetics": 4112
D. H. LAWRENCE AND "THE DIAL": 3525
D. H. LAWRENCE AND THE DOMINANT MALE: 3581
"D. H. Lawrence and the Etruscans": 2257
"D. H. Lawrence and the Failure of Energy": 4187
"D. H. Lawrence and the Flicks": 4159
"D. H. Lawrence and the Genetic Approach": 4233
"D. H. Lawrence and THE GOLDEN BOUGH": 2308
"D. H. Lawrence and the Idea of Education": 3499
"D. H. Lawrence and the Idea of the Erotic": 3922
"D. H. Lawrence and the Impressionistic Technique": 2334
"D. H. Lawrence and the Making of an American Myth": 3455
"D. H. Lawrence and the Modern Pan Myth": 2540
D. H. LAWRENCE AND THE NEW WORLD: 2775, 2776, 3272
"D. H. Lawrence and the New World": 2775
"D. H. Lawrence and the Peacocks of Atrani": 4493
"D. H. Lawrence and the Protestant Crisis": 2238
"D. H. Lawrence and the Psychology of Rhythm: The Meaning of Form in *The Rainbow*": 3255
D. H. LAWRENCE AND THE PSYCHOLOGY OF RHYTHM: THE MEANING OF FORM IN "THE RAINBOW": 3255, 4264
"D. H. Lawrence and the 'Q. B.' in Sardinia": 3171
"D. H. Lawrence and the Religion of Sex": 4093
"D. H. Lawrence and the Religious Imagination: A Study of Sex, Rhetoric, and Ritual in the Major Novels: 4000
"D. H. Lawrence and the Revolt Against Naturalism": 3335
"D. H. Lawrence and the Rousseau Tradition": 4010

INDEX OF TITLES OF SECONDARY WORKS

"D. H. Lawrence and 'The Spirit of Place' ": 4509
"D. H. Lawrence and the *Study of Thomas Hardy,* His Victorian Predecessor": 3261
(D. H. Lawrence and the War): 2849
D. H. LAWRENCE AND THE WAY OF THE DANDELION: 4444
"D. H. Lawrence and the Worship of the Earth": 4548
"D. H. Lawrence and Thomas Mann": 2063
(D. H. Lawrence and Tradition): 2592
"D. H. Lawrence and Trigant Burrow: Pollyanalytics and Phylobiology, An Interpretive Analysis": 2380
"D. H. Lawrence and Virginia Woolf": 3323
"D. H. Lawrence and William Blake: A Comparative and Critical Study": 3844
"D. H. Lawrence and *Women in Love*": 2153
D. H. LAWRENCE, ARTIST AND REBEL: A STUDY OF LAWRENCE'S FICTION: 2456
"D. H. Lawrence as a Critic and Translator of Verga": 2538
D. H. LAWRENCE AS A LITERARY CRITIC: 2088, 2504, 2799
(D. H. Lawrence as a Thinker): 2668
D. H. LAWRENCE AS CRITIC: 2923, 3285
"D. H. Lawrence as Critic": 2623
"D. H. Lawrence as Ego Psychologist: Self and Being in the Novels": 4111
"D. H. Lawrence as Friedrich Nietzsche": 4332
"D. H. Lawrence as Literary Critic": 2088, 3615
(D. H. Lawrence as Playwright): 2806
(D. H. Lawrence as Teacher and Philosopher): 3253
"D. H. Lawrence as Translator": 3517
(D. H. Lawrence as Translator from the Italian): 2778
D. H. LAWRENCE AT WORK: THE EMERGENCE OF THE "PRUSSIAN OFFICER" STORIES: 3287, 3689, 3690, 3874, 3876, 4061
"D. H. Lawrence at Work: The Making of 'Odour of Chrysanthemums' ": 3689

"D. H. Lawrence at Work: The Making of *The Prussian Officer and Other Stories*": 3287
"D. H. Lawrence (Atara Shii Sekai no Kokai)": 2525
"D. H. Lawrence: 'Bavarian Gentians' ": 3222
(D. H. Lawrence: Biographical Elements in His Literature [I]): 2895
(D. H. Lawrence: Biographical Elements in His Literature [II]): 3018
D. H. LAWRENCE: BODY OF DARKNESS: 3782
"D. H. Lawrence: Chatterley Fujin no Ai no Kaishin": 3170
"D. H. Lawrence: Critic of Life": 2863
"D. H. Lawrence: Criticism; September, 1968-December, 1969; a Checklist": 3435
"D. H. Lawrence: Critics and Archetypes": 3820
"D. H. Lawrence Dainiki no Okeru Buntai no Ichimen": 2847
"D. H. Lawrence, D'Annunzio, Wagner": 2772
"D. H. Lawrence: Devout Heretic": 2142
D. H. LAWRENCE: DIE CHARAKTERE IN DER HANDLUNG UND SPANNUNG SEINER KURZGESCHICHTEN: 2664, 3109
(D. H. Lawrence: Double Tragedy): 2896
"D. H. Lawrence: Dramatist": 3791
D. H. LAWRENCE E L'ITALIA: 2621
"D. H. Lawrence, England and the War": 4212
"D. H. Lawrence entre six femmes et entre deux cultures": 3291
"D. H. Lawrence, Esther Landolt, Filippo Sacchi and Nevil Shute": 2931
"D. H. Lawrence et l'architecture du roman": 2825
"D. H. Lawrence et Sacher-Masoch: Contribution à l'étude d'une sensibilité moderne": 3696
(D. H. Lawrence--Existence and Love): 2401
"The D. H. Lawrence Festival: Kiowa Ranch, New Mexico, September 30-October 4, 1970": 3682

"D. H. Lawrence, From Island to Glacier": 3107
A D. H. LAWRENCE HANDBOOK: 3088, 3448
"D. H. Lawrence: His Development as a Novelist": 2974
D. H. LAWRENCE: HIS LITERATURE AND HIS LIFE: 3125, 3341, 3735, 3941
(D. H. LAWRENCE, HIS LITERATURE AND HIS LIFE): 4135
"D. H. Lawrence--His Reputation Today": 3288
(D. H. Lawrence: His Sensibility): 4514
(D. H. Lawrence: His Voyage of Discovery to the New World): 2525
"D. H. Lawrence, HOMO LUDENS, and the Dance": 3071
"D. H. Lawrence in Cornwall: An Interview with Stanley Hocking": 4232
"D. H. Lawrence: In Search of the Big 'O' ": 4482
"D. H. Lawrence in Taos": 2909, 3289
D. H. LAWRENCE IN TAOS: 2795, 3902
"D. H. Lawrence in Transit": 4121
"D. H. Lawrence in viaggio: Frati anarchici, Etruschi e Messicani": 2218
(D. H. Lawrence in 1910s): 2934
D. H. LAWRENCE: INTERVIEWS AND RECOLLECTIONS: 3159
"D. H. Lawrence Kenkyû (II) (Sono Shinpi Shugi o Sasaeru Mono)": 2457
"D. H. Lawrence Kenkyû ni Okeru Jidenteki Yôso (I)": 2895
"D. H. Lawrence Kenkyû ni Okeru Jidenteki Yôso (II)": 3018
"D. H. Lawrence Kenkyû Shojosaku *Shirokujaku* ni Tsuite": 2815
"D. H. Lawrence Kenkyû–Sono Shi no Hyôka no Kiten ni Tsuite": 4358
"D. H. Lawrence Kuroi Me no Hirameki": 2982
"D. H. Lawrence, la femme et la mort": 3076
"D. H. Lawrence (L'adaptation des oeuvres cinématographiques)": 3660
(D. H. Lawrence: Lady Chatterley's Conversion of Love): 3170
"D. H. Lawrence: *Lady Chatterley's Lover*": 2915
"D. H. Lawrence Letters": 3425
"D. H. Lawrence: Letters to Gordon and Beatrice Campbell": 4119
"D. H. Lawrence: L'homme et la genèse de son oeuvre. Les années de formation (1885-1919)": 3292
D. H. LAWRENCE: L'HOMME ET LA GENÈSE DE SON OEUVRE. LES ANNÉES DE FORMATION (1885-1919): 3292
D. H. LAWRENCE: L'HOMME ET LA GENÈSE DE SON OEUVRE, LES ANNÉES DE FORMATION: 1885-1919: DOCUMENTS: 3414
"D. H. Lawrence: Man of the Century": 3467
"D. H. Lawrence--Mit o ponovnom rodenju": 4083
"D. H. Lawrence: Mystical Critic": 2755
"D. H. Lawrence ni Mirareru Nigensei ni Tsuite": 3344
"D. H. Lawrence ni Okeru Ai": 2090
"D. H. Lawrence ni Okeru 'Chi' ": 4335
"D. H. Lawrence ni Okeru Seishoku to Sôzô no Kairi o Megutte": 4204
"D. H. Lawrence ni Okeru Shi no Ishiki": 2428
"D. H. Lawrence ni Okeru Shi to Fukkatsu *Shinda Otoko* no Daimei o Megutte": 2105
"D. H. Lawrence ni Okeru Shi to Fukkatsu--Shocho to Shiteno Fushicho ni Tsuite": 2261
"D. H. Lawrence Nijû no Higeki": 2896
"D. H. Lawrence no Ai ni Tsuite": 3985
"D. H. Lawrence no Ai to Seimei no Rinri": 2736
"D. H. Lawrence no 'Barazono no Kage' ni Okeru Shûkyô Teki Yôso": 3009
"D. H. Lawrence no Bungaku Hihyô": 3648
"D. H. Lawrence no Center Symbolism": 3204
"D. H. Lawrence no Cosmos–Sono

Shisôshijô no Igi o Motomete": 4417
"D. H. Lawrence no *David*": 3021
"D. H. Lawrence no Doku Shin Jidai (I)": 2440
"D. H. Lawrence no Gikyoku *David* ni Tsuite": 4563
"D. H. Lawrence no Hyôgen Keishiki": 2702
"D. H. Lawrence no Ikyôsei": 2358
"D. H. Lawrence no John Galsworthy": 3134
"D. H. Lawrence no Jûjika--*Musuko to Koibito* Ron": 3770
"D. H. Lawrence no Kaikyû Kan": 2443
"D. H. Lawrence no Kaikyûkan (Dai Ikki no Baai)": 2404
"D. H. Lawrence no Kaikyûkan--Dai Sanki no Baai": 2414
"D. H. Lawrence no Kirisuto-Kyo-Kan ni Tsuite": 3118
"D. H. Lawrence no Mashin to Seirei": 2560
"D. H. Lawrence no Mohitotsu no Jiga--'Shima o Aishita Otoko' o Chûshin ni": 3649
"D. H. Lawrence no *Musuko to Koibito* ni Tsuite": 3022
"D. H. Lawrence no Rananim ni Tsuite (1)": 4168
"D. H. Lawrence no Rananim ni Tsuite (2)": 4383
"D. H. Lawrence no *St. Mawr* ni Okeru Shôchôsei (1)": 4157
"D. H. Lawrence no *St. Mawr* ni Okeru Shôchôsei (2)": 4158
"D. H. Lawrence no Saku Hin ni Arawareta Shokubutsu to Sono Gihô ni Tsuite": 2680
"D. H. Lawrence no *Seishin-Bunseki to Muishiki* Oyobi *Muishiki no Gensôkyoku* Kanken (1)": 3811
"D. H. Lawrence no *Seishin-Bunseki to Muishiki* Oyobi *Muishiki no Gensôkyoku* Kanken (2)" 4002
"D. H. Lawrence no Sekai": 2269, 3417
"D. H. Lawrence no Shakespeare-Kan": 2980
"D. H. Lawrence no Shi ni Okeru Ai to Kodoku ni Tsuite no Kenkyu": 2883
"D. H. Lawrence no Shinpishugi (Tsuki no Imisuru Mono)": 2458
"D. H. Lawrence no Shisôteki Igi": 2668
"D. H. Lawrence no Shizen-Byôsha no Shisei ni Tsuite": 4359
"D. H. Lawrence no Shokan ni Tsuite no Kenkyû": 3000
"D. H. Lawrence no Shoki no Tanpen--*Sons and Lovers* no Shûhen": 4439
"D. H. Lawrence no Shôsetsu ni Okeru Shizen-Byôsha ni Tsuite--'Tsuki' no Byôsha o Chûshin ni": 4253
"D. H. Lawrence no Shôsetsu Ron--Zettai Hitei ni Yoru Ishiki-Tankyû": 4382
"D. H. Lawrence no Shûkyôteki Tsuikyû (*David* ni Tsuite)": 3019
"D. H. Lawrence no *Sons and Lovers* ni Tsuite": 4344
"D. H. Lawrence no 'Sun' Kenkyû--Sono Shudai to Hôhô": 4249
"D. H. Lawrence no Tanpen Shôsetsu no Gihô to Stairu": 2760
"D. H. Lawrence no THE FORSYTE SAGA no Hihyô": 2959
"D. H. Lawrence no *The Fox* no Ichikôsatsu (Seishin-Bunseki o Chûshin Toshite)": 4542
"D. H. Lawrence no 'The Princess' no Kenkyu": 3758
"D. H. Lawrence no 'The Prussian Officer' ni Tsuite": 3829
"D. H. Lawrence no Whitman Ron": 4028
"D. H. Lawrence no *Women in Love* ni Tsuite": 2256
"D. H. Lawrence no Working Method": 2337
"D. H. Lawrence: Notes on Reading Hawthorne's THE SCARLET LETTER": 4150
D. H. LAWRENCE: NOVELIST, POET, PROPHET: 4051, 4074, 4090, 4100, 4121, 4133, 4146, 4154, 4206, 4212, 4213, 4224, 4228
"D. H. Lawrence Oboegaki (I)": 2463
"D. H. Lawrence Oboegaki (II) (*Shirokujaku* ni Tsuite)": 2593
"D. H. Lawrence Oboegaki (III) (*Musuko to Koibito* ni Tsuite)": 2749
"D. H. Lawrence Oboegaki (IV)--

Seishin-Bunseki to Muishiki to Muishiki no Gensô ni Tsuite": 3639, 3640

"D. H. Lawrence Oboegaki (V)--*Kitsune* ni Kansuru Ichibunseki": 3821

"D. H. Lawrence Oboegaki (VI)--Jessie Chambers no Tegami": 4428

"D. H. Lawrence Oboegaki--Sakuchû-Jinbutsu no Tokuchô": 3650

"D. H. Lawrence on Cézanne: A Study in the Psychology of Critical Intuition": 3592

"D. H. Lawrence: Opening to the Wordless World--Toward *The Plumed Serpent* (1)": 3935

"D. H. Lawrence: Opening to the Wordless World--Toward *The Plumed Serpent* (2)": 4126

(D. H. Lawrence or Immediate Poetry): 2499

(D. H. LAWRENCE OR THE SCANDALOUS PURITAN): 2500

"D. H. Lawrence ou la Poésie Immédiate": 2499

D. H. LAWRENCE OU LE PURITAIN SCANDALEUX: 2500

"D. H. Lawrence: Outline for a Psychology of Being": 2927

"D. H. Lawrence, Phoenix": 3093

"D. H. Lawrence, Poet": 3397

(D. H. Lawrence: Poet and Death, The First Part): 2848

(D. H. Lawrence: Poet and Death [The Last Part I]): 4381

(D. H. Lawrence: Poet and Death, The Second Part): 2981

"D. H. Lawrence: Poet of Death and Resurrection": 3771

"D. H. Lawrence: Poet without a Mask": 2146

"A D. H. Lawrence Postscript": 3745

"D. H. Lawrence: Precursor of Today's Spiritual Youth": 3575

"D. H. Lawrence, Religious Seeker": 2317

"D. H. Lawrence Ron (*Sons and Lovers* ni Okeru Lawrence no Ningenzô)": 4129

"D. H. Lawrence Ron (*The Trespasser* no Romansu ni Tsuite)": 3336

"D. H. Lawrence, Ruth Suckow, and 'Modern Marriage' ": 3340

"D. H. Lawrence: *St. Mawr*": 2716

"D. H. Lawrence Sat Here": 3864

D. H. LAWRENCE, "SEA AND SARDINIA," "THE RAINBOW": NOTES ON LITERATURE NO. 100: 3390

"D. H. Lawrence *Seishin-Bunseki to Muishiki* ni Tsuite (I)": 4248

"D. H. Lawrence *Seishin-Bunseki to Muishiki* ni Tsuite (II)": 4620

"D. H. Lawrence: Seven Hitherto Unpublished Poems": 3617

"D. H. Lawrence: *Shojo to Jipshi Hihyô*": 2717

"D. H. Lawrence: 'Snake' ": 2985

"D. H. Lawrence: Solipsist oder Prophet einer neuen Gemeinschaft?": 2437

(D. H. Lawrence: Solipsist or Prophet of a New Community?): 2437

"D. H. Lawrence--Some New Letters": 3532

"D. H. Lawrence: *Söner och älskande*": 3638

"D. H. Lawrence: Sono Kansei ni Tsuite": 4514

"D. H. Lawrence--Sono Yami no Sekai no Tankyû": 4414

D. H. LAWRENCE: "SONS AND LOVERS": 2870

(D. H. Lawrence: *Sons and Lovers*): 3638

D. H. LAWRENCE: "SONS AND LOVERS," A CASEBOOK: 2368, 2624, 2869, 3391, 3392

D. H. LAWRENCE: "SONS AND LOVERS": LES ASPECTS SOCIAUX, ÉCONOMIQUES, LA VISION DE L'ARTISTE: 2737

D. H. LAWRENCE, "SONS AND LOVERS": TEXT, BACKGROUND, AND CRITICISM: 2263, 2423, 2639, 3158

(D. H. LAWRENCE: "SONS AND LOVERS": THE SOCIAL AND ECONOMIC ASPECTS AND THE ARTIST'S VISION): 2737

"D. H. Lawrence: *Sons and Lovers, Women in Love*": 2744

"D. H. Lawrence Sonzai to Ai": 2401

"D. H. Lawrence--Student and Teacher": 2878

" 'D. H. Lawrence: Study of a Free Spirit in Literature,' A Note on an Uncollected Article": 4271

(D. H. Lawrence: "Sun"): 2979

INDEX OF TITLES OF SECONDARY WORKS

"D. H. Lawrence: 'Taiyo' ": 2979
D. H. LAWRENCE: TALE AS A MEDIUM: 3536
"D. H. Lawrence: Technique as Evasion": 2793
"D. H. Lawrence: Ten Years of Criticism, 1959-1968, a Checklist": 3040
"D. H. Lawrence: The Blood-Conscious Artist": 3225
(D. H. LAWRENCE: THE CHARACTERS OF HIS SHORT STORIES IN ACTION AND TENSION): 2664, 3109
(D. H. Lawrence: The Cinematographic Adaptation of the Works): 3660
"D. H. Lawrence: The Courage of Human Contact": 2520
(D. H. Lawrence: 'The Creative Genius of Our Time'): 2103
D. H. LAWRENCE: THE CRITICAL HERITAGE: 3472, 3473
D. H. LAWRENCE: THE CROYDON YEARS: 2223, 2620, 2724
D. H. LAWRENCE: THE CRUSADER AS CRITIC: 3615, 4586
"D. H. Lawrence: The Early Stage": 3685
"D. H. Lawrence: The Evolution of a Genius": 2586
"D. H. Lawrence: The Evolution of His Political Thought 1914-1930": 3971
"D. H. Lawrence: The Making of a Poet": 3239
D. H. LAWRENCE: THE MAN AND HIS WORK, THE FORMATIVE YEARS: 1885-1919: 3292
(D. H. Lawrence: The Man and the Genesis of His Work, the Formative Years: 1885-1919): 3292
(D. H. LAWRENCE: THE MAN AND THE GENESIS OF HIS WORK, THE FORMATIVE YEARS: 1885-1919: DOCUMENTS): 3414
"D. H. Lawrence: *The Man Who Died* no Buntai": 2660
(D. H. Lawrence: "The Man Who Loved Islands"): 2516
"D. H. Lawrence: The Man Who Misunderstood Gulliver": 2526
(D. H. Lawrence: The Myth of Rebirth): 4083

"D. H. Lawrence: The One Bright Book of Life": 4175
"D. H. Lawrence: The Paradisal Quest": 3961
D. H. LAWRENCE: THE PHOENIX AND THE FLAME: 4227
"D. H. Lawrence: *The Plumed Serpent*": 2703, 3780
(D. H. LAWRENCE: THE POET AND THE "CHATTERLEY" TRIAL): 4522
"D. H. Lawrence: The Poetry of Intuition": 3730
D. H. LAWRENCE: THE POLARITY OF NORTH AND SOUTH--GERMANY AND ITALY IN HIS PROSE WORKS: 4366
"D. H. Lawrence: The Politics of Irrationality": 2509
"D. H. Lawrence the Preacher": 2139
"D. H. Lawrence: The Prophet and His Voice": 4290
D. H. LAWRENCE: "THE RAINBOW": 3802
"D. H. Lawrence: *The Rainbow* and *Women in Love*": 2956
D. H. LAWRENCE: "THE RAINBOW" AND "WOMEN IN LOVE": A CASEBOOK: 2086, 2107, 2423, 2624, 2639, 2647, 3122, 3276, 3277, 3278
"D. H. Lawrence: *The Rainbow* no Buntai": 2810
"D. H. Lawrence: The Revelation of the Unconscious": 3310
D. H. LAWRENCE: "THE ROCKING-HORSE WINNER": 2291, 2351, 2372, 2407, 2430, 2456, 2694, 3282, 3283, 3410
"D. H. Lawrence, the Russians, and Giovanni Verga": 2606
"D. H. Lawrence, The Second 'Poetic Me': Corrigenda": 3787
"D. H. Lawrence, The Second 'Poetic Me': Some New Material": 3594
(D. H. Lawrence: The Structure of *Women in Love*): 2166
(D. H. Lawrence: The Style of *The Fox*): 2093
(D. H. Lawrence: The Style of *The Man Who Died*): 2660
(D. H. Lawrence: The Style of *The Rainbow*): 2810

(D. H. Lawrence: "The Thorn in the Flesh"): 2400
"D. H. Lawrence: The Triumph of Texture": 2697
"D. H. Lawrence: The Two Versions–*Studies in Classic American Literature* and *The Symbolic Meaning*": 3869
"D. H. Lawrence: 'The Wave Which Cannot Halt' ": 2797
D. H. LAWRENCE: THE WORLD OF THE FIVE MAJOR NOVELS: 4199
D. H. LAWRENCE: THE WORLD OF THE MAJOR NOVELS: 4199
"D. H. Lawrence: Then, During, Now": 4400
(D. H. Lawrence Thirty Years After): 2147
"D. H. Lawrence to Dentô": 2592
"D. H. Lawrence to Henry Savage: Two Further Letters": 3956
"D. H. Lawrence to Indo": 2314
"D. H. Lawrence to Kodoku": 2816
"D. H. Lawrence to Morality": 3936
"D. H. Lawrence to Ottoline Morrell (*Women in Love* no Haikei)": 4524
"D. H. Lawrence to Sensô": 2849
"D. H. Lawrence to Shakai": 2747
"D. H. Lawrence to T. Hardy (I)": 3495
"D. H. Lawrence traduttore dall'italiano": 2778
"D. H. Lawrence trent'anni dopo": 2147
"D. H. Lawrence: *Tutte le poesie*": 2143
"D. H. Lawrence: Twelve Letters": 3290
"D. H. Lawrence–'var tids skapande geni' ": 2103
"D. H. Lawrence: Vitalism and the Universal Indefinite": 3953
(D. H. Lawrence, Woman and Death): 3076
"D. H. Lawrence: *Women in Love* no Kosei": 2166
"D. H. Lawrence, 1885-1930": 2595, 3460
"D. H. Lawrence (1885-1930)": 4449, 4494
"D. H. Lawrence, 1885-1930: *Women in Love*": 2383
"D. H. Lawrence, 1910-1916": 2728
"D. H. Lawrence, 1912-1916": 2728
D. H. LAWRENCE'S AMERICAN JOURNEY: A STUDY IN LITERATURE AND MYTH: 2481, 2622, 2919, 2920, 3284, 3462
"D. H. Lawrence's Appraisal of Jesus": 3777
(D. H. Lawrence's Art of the Novel): 2730
(D. H. Lawrence's Attitude to Love and Religion as Found in *The Rainbow*): 2548
(D. H. Lawrence's Attitude Toward Life and Death in "Bavarian Gentians" and *The Man Who Died*): 4349
"D. H. Lawrence's Australia": 3511
"D. H. Lawrence's Bestiary: A Study of His Use of Animal Trope and Symbol": 2667
D. H. LAWRENCE'S BESTIARY: A STUDY OF HIS USE OF ANIMAL TROPE AND SYMBOL: 2667, 3727
"D. H. Lawrence's Biblical Play *David*": 2431
"D. H. Lawrence's *Birds, Beasts and Flowers*": 3398
"D. H. Lawrence's *Birds, Beasts and Flowers*: Five Kinds of Poetry": 3987
(D. H. Lawrence's Center Symbolism): 3204
"D. H. Lawrence's Clothes Metaphor": 3098
"D. H. Lawrence's Concept of the Risen Lord": 2564
(D. H. Lawrence's Critical Essay on THE FORSYTE SAGA): 2959
(D. H. Lawrence's Demon and Holy Ghost): 2560
"D. H. Lawrence's Doctrine": 4051
"D. H. Lawrence's Dualism: The Apollonian-Dionysian Polarity and *The Ladybird*": 4467
"D. H. Lawrence's Early Paintings": 3847
"D. H. Lawrence's Early Poetry: The Composition-Dates of the Drafts in MS E317": 3814
"D. H. Lawrence's Early Tales": 2832
"D. H. Lawrence's Eclectic Symbolism: The Erotic Design of *Look! We

INDEX OF TITLES OF SECONDARY WORKS

Have Come Through!": 3739
(D. H. Lawrence's Experiment as Novelist): 4402
"D. H. Lawrence's Favourite Jargon": 2767
"D. H. Lawrence's First Critical Essays: Two Anonymous Reviews Identified": 2363, 2472
"D. H. Lawrence's 'Future Religion': The Unity of *Last Poems*": 4508
(D. H. Lawrence's Genius in "Odour of Chrysanthemums"): 2904
"D. H. Lawrence's German Letters": 2364
"D. H. Lawrence's Great Circle: From *Sons and Lovers* to *Lady Chatterley*": 2348, 2466
"D. H. Lawrence's Greatest Collection of Short Stories--What Holds It Together": 3920
"D. H. Lawrence's Hand in the Translation of Maxim Gorki's REMINISCENCES OF LEONID ANDREYEV": 3833
(D. H. Lawrence's John Galsworthy): 3134
"D. H. Lawrence's *Kangaroo*: Fantasy, Fact or Fiction?": 2603
"D. H. Lawrence's *Kangaroo*: How It Looks to an Australian": 4331
"D. H. Lawrence's *Last Poems*": 3940
"D. H. Lawrence's Letters to Catherine Carswell": 4481
D. H. LAWRENCE'S MALE LEADERSHIP IDEAS IN "AARON'S ROD," "KANGAROO," AND "THE PLUMED SERPENT": 3337
(D. H. Lawrence's Mysticism: What the Moon Signifies): 2458
"D. H. Lawrence's Novels as Irritants": 2768
"D. H. Lawrence's 'Odour of Chrysanthemums': An Early Version": 3267
"D. H. Lawrence's Plays: An Annotated Bibliography": 2658
"D. H. Lawrence's Poem 'Masses and Classes'": 2258
"D. H. Lawrence's Poetry: Myth and Matter": 4425
"D. H. Lawrence's Portrait of Ben Franklin in *The Rainbow*": 2882
"D. H. Lawrence's Pre-1920 Poetry: A Descriptive Bibliography of Manuscripts, Typescripts, and Proofs": 4081
"D. H. Lawrence's Pre-1920 Poetry: The Textual Approach: An Exchange": 3896
"D. H. Lawrence's Primitivism": 2527
"D. H. Lawrence's Progress to Maturity: From Holograph Manuscript to Final Publication of *The Prussian Officer and Other Stories*": 4486
"D. H. Lawrence's Quarrel with Christianity": 3284
"D. H. Lawrence's Quarrel with Tragedy": 2504
"D. H. Lawrence's Reading of Russian Literature": 3423
(D. H. Lawrence's Religious Quest--The Biblical Play *David*): 3019
"D. H. Lawrence's Response to Russian Literature": 2762
D. H. LAWRENCE'S RESPONSE TO RUSSIAN LITERATURE: 2762, 3024, 3423, 3834
"D. H. Lawrence's *St. Mawr*: Transposition of Myth": 3209
"D. H. Lawrence's Sexual Ideal": 3264
"D. H. Lawrence's Shorter Fiction: The Question of Chronology": 2473
"D. H. Lawrence's Social Vision": 3843
"D. H. Lawrence's Song of Songs": 2066
D. H. LAWRENCE'S "SONS AND LOVERS" AND "THE RAINBOW," "WOMEN IN LOVE," "THE PLUMED SERPENT": 2642
D. H. LAWRENCE'S "SONS AND LOVERS": SELF-ENCOUNTER AND THE UNKNOWN SELF: 3216
"D. H. Lawrence's Sternest Critic": 2614
"D. H. Lawrence's *Studies in Classic American Literature*: An Evaluation": 3174
"D. H. Lawrence's *The Fox*--The Triumph of the Man's World": 4006
"D. H. Lawrence's 'The Horse Dealer's Daughter'": 3331
"D. H. Lawrence's 'The Horse Dealer's Daughter': An Interpretation": 2331

D. H. LAWRENCE

"D. H. Lawrence's *The Ladybird*--A Modern Myth": 4007

"D. H. Lawrence's *The Lost Girl* and its Antecedents by George Moore and Arnold Bennett": 2809

"D. H. Lawrence's *The Man Who Died*: The Phallic Christ": 3077

"D. H. Lawrence's *The Plumed Serpent*": 2374

(D. H. Lawrence's *The Plumed Serpent*): 2759

"D. H. Lawrence's 'The Princess' as Ironic Romance": 2919

"D. H. Lawrences 'The Rocking-Horse Winner' ": 2566

"D. H. LAWRENCE'S "THE RAINBOW": 3751

"D. H. Lawrence's *The Rainbow*: A Note on the Contextuality of the Symbol": 3990

"D. H. Lawrence's 'The Turning Back': The Text and Its Genesis in Correspondence": 3893

D. H. LAWRENCE'S "THE VIRGIN AND THE GYPSY": 3471

"D. H. Lawrence's *The White Peacock*: An Essay in Criticism": 3121

"D. H. Lawrence's Three Strange Angels": 2761

"D. H. Lawrence's 'Tickets, Please': The Structural Importance of the Setting": 4541

(D. H. Lawrence's Travels: Anarchist Monks, Etruscans and Mexicans): 2218

"D. H. Lawrence's Use in His Novels of Germanic and Celtic Myth from the Music Dramas of Richard Wagner": 4174

"D. H. Lawrence's View of Film": 4210

(D. H. Lawrence's View of Shakespeare): 2980

(D. H. Lawrence's View of Social Class, Especially in His Third Period): 2414

"D. H. Lawrence's View of the Italians": 4043

"D. H. Lawrence's War Letters": 2432

D. H. LAWRENCE'S "WOMEN IN LOVE": 3298

(D. H. Lawrence's Working Method): 2337

D. H. RORENSU SHIJIN TO CHATAREI SAIBAN: 4522

D. H. RORENSU, SONO BUNGAKU TO JINSEI: 4135

"D. H. Rorensu to Kirisutokyō": 4619

"Da Lawrence a Ken Russell": 3919

"Dal racconto al film. *La volpe* di Lawrence": 3162

"Današnji značaj D. H. Lawrencea": 4537

" 'Dark, Darker than Fire': Thematic Parallels in Lawrence and Faulkner": 4300

"The Dark God or the Spirit of God": 4376

DARK NIGHT OF THE BODY: D. H. LAWRENCE'S "THE PLUMED SERPENT": 2374, 2480

DARK PASSAGES: 2618

"Darkness and 'A Heavy Gold Glamour': Lawrence's *Women in Love*": 4353

" 'Daughters of the Vicar' Kô--Shudai to Hôhô": 4421

"David H. Lawrence": 3555

"David Herbert Lawrence": 2796, 3707, 4022, 4557

DAVID HERBERT LAWRENCE: 2835

(David Herbert Lawrence): 2413

(DAVID HERBERT LAWRENCE AND MEXICO): 3097

(David Herbert Lawrence and the Crisis of American Conscience): 3692

"David Herbert Lawrence. Berühmtberüchtigt seine Lady Chatterly--Eine Genie--von düsterer Krankheit gezeichnet": 2725

"David Herbert Lawrence et la crise de conscience américaine": 3692

(David Herbert Lawrence: Notorious for His Lady Chatterley--A Genius--Stricken by an Incurable Disease): 2725

"David Herbert Lawrence: *Sons and Lovers*": 2151

DAVID HERBERT LAWRENCE Y MÉXICO: 3097

"David Herbert Lawrence, 1885-1930": 4526

"David Herbert Lorens": 2413

DAWN AND THE DARKEST HOUR: A STUDY OF ALDOUS HUXLEY: 4024

"A Day Away from Kiowa": 2930
"A Day on the Ranch, 1924: Kiowa Ranch, Taos": 3557
THE DAYBOOKS OF EDWARD WESTON, Vol. I: MEXICO: 4237
THE DAYBOOKS OF EDWARD WESTON, Vol. II: CALIFORNIA: 4238
"Days of THE PHOENIX": 3808
(Death and Life in *The Trespasser*): 4415
(Death and Oblivion--From *Women in Love* to "The Ship of Death"): 4380
(The Death and Resurrection in D. H. Lawrence, II: Phoenix as His Personal Symbol): 2261
(Death and Resurrection in D. H. Lawrence, with Special Reference to *The Man Who Died*): 2105
"Death in Lawrence's *Last Poems*: A Study of Theme in Relation to Imagery": 3494
(Death in the Major Novels of D. H. Lawrence): 4345
"Death-Drift karano Dasshutsu (Lawrence no Shoki no Shōsetsu ni Tsuite)": 3111
THE DEED OF LIFE: THE NOVELS AND TALES OF D. H. LAWRENCE: 2423
DEEPER INTO MOVIES: 3526
"The Defeat of Feminism: D. H. Lawrence's *The Fox* and 'The Woman Who Rode Away'": 2786
"The Defect in Lawrence's Poetry": 2085
DEFENSES OF THE IMAGINATION: JEWISH WRITERS AND MODERN HISTORICAL CRISIS: 3427
"Demons All Along": 2585
"The Depiction of Conflict in the Novels of D. H. Lawrence": 2899
(Descriptions in *The Rainbow*: D. H. Lawrence's Attitude toward the Efficacy of Words): 2823
"A Descriptive and Analytical Catalogue of the D. H. Lawrence Collection at the University of Texas at Austin": 3482
"A Descriptive Bibliography of the Works of John Middleton Murry, with a Critical Study of His Life and Thought and an Assessment of His Views on D. H. Lawrence": 3837
"The Determination of Literary Value": 2912
"Die deutschen Briefe von D. H. Lawrence": 2364
(The Development of "Manhood" in the Novels of Lawrence [I]: On *Sons and Lovers*): 4504
"The Development of the Non-Formalistic Modern English Novel and Its Relation to D. H. Lawrence's *Sons and Lovers*": 3114
"The Dialectic in D. H. Lawrence": 2633
"Dialectical Form in *The Rainbow* and *Women in Love*": 2845
DIARIES, 1915-1918: 3033
THE DIARY OF ANAIS NIN, 1934-1939: 2978
THE DIARY OF ANAIS NIN, 1939-1944: 3365
THE DIARY OF ANAIS NIN, 1944-1947: 3768
"The Dichotomy between Private and Public Sphere: Sex Roles in D. H. Lawrence's Novels": 4113
"Dickens and Lawrence: More on Rocking Horses": 3712
"Dies Irae": 2639
(The Dimensions of Lawrencean Literature, III): 2098
(The Dimensions of Lawrencean Literature [IV]): 2670
(The Dimensions of Lawrencean Literature [V]): 2950
THE DIMENSIONS OF THE SHORT STORY: A CRITICAL ANTHOLOGY: 2543, 3360
"The Dionysian Tramline": 4515
DIONYSUS AND THE CITY: MODERNISM IN TWENTIETH CENTURY POETRY: 3621
"Dionysus, D. H. Lawrence, and Jean Giono: Further Considerations": 3120
"The Discovery of Form": 2423
"Disintegration as Symbol of Community: A Study of *The Rainbow*, *Women in Love*, LIGHT IN AUGUST, PRISONER OF GRACE, EXCEPT THE LORD, NOT HONOUR MORE, and HERZOG": 4114

(The Distinction between Creation and Procreation in D. H. Lawrence): 4204
"The Divided Sympathetic Bond: A Study of D. H. Lawrence's Drama": 4275
DIZIONARIO DELLE OPERE DI TUTTI I TEMPI E DI TUTTE LE LETTERATURE: 2679
"Doctoral Dissertations on D. H. Lawrence: Bibliographical Addenda": 3912, 4505
"Doctoral Dissertations on D. H. Lawrence, 1931-1969: A Bibliography": 3464
"Doctrine and Dogma in *Sons and Lovers*": 3476
DOCUMENTARY AND IMAGINATIVE LITERATURE: 3454
"A Doggy Demos: Hardy and Lawrence": 2781, 3877
"The Dominant Sex": 2969
"Le donne di Lawrence": 2549
"*Donne in Amore*": 4009
"Dorothy Brett's Letters to S. S. Koteliansky": 4443
"Dorothy Livesay and the Transcendentalist Tradition": 3503
"Dostoevsky, D. H. Lawrence and Carson McCullers: Influences and Confluences": 4386
DOUBLE MEASURE: A STUDY OF THE NOVELS AND STORIES OF D. H. LAWRENCE: 2639
"The Double Pattern of D. H. Lawrence's 'The Horse Dealer's Daughter' ": 4176
"The Double Perspective: A Study of D. H. Lawrence's Novels": 3585
"Drama": 3300, 3301
DRAMA FROM IBSEN TO BRECHT: 3241
"The Dream of Logic: A Conversation with Ihab Hassan": 3312
(Dream of Rananim): 3576
"The Dreaming Woman": 3159
"Drei alte Frauen im Hochtal von Taos": 2452
"Die Drzahlformen der Romane von Aldous Huxley und David Herbert Lawrence": 2505
"Duality as Theme and Technique in D. H. Lawrence's 'The Border Line' ": 2813
"Due rivoluzionari individualisti": 3571
"Due romanzi di Lawrence": 2574
THE DYNAMICS OF LITERARY RESPONSE: 3101
"E. M. F. and D. H. L.": 2856
E. M. FORSTER: 2249
(E. M. Forster and D. H. Lawrence): 3544
"E. M. Forster and D. H. Lawrence as Novelists of Ideas": 4180
"E. M. Forster and D. H. Lawrence: Their Views on Education": 2852
"E. M. Forster et D. H. Lawrence": 3544
"E. M. Forster no Shôsetsu: Kojin to Shakai no Tanima--D. H. Lawrence to no Kikaku ni Oite": 4384
"The Earlier Poetry of D. H. Lawrence: A Variorum Text, Comprising All Extant Incunabula and Published Poems Up to and Including the Year 1919": 3704
(The Early Life of D. H. Lawrence--His Life and World [I]): 2440
THE EARLY MEMOIRS (1873-1915) OF LADY OTTOLINE MORRELL: 2421
(The Early Works and Life of Lawrence): 3125
EASTWOOD THROUGH BYGONE AGES: A BRIEF HISTORY OF THE PARISH OF EASTWOOD: 3684
"Eben nicht nur der Autor der *Lady Chatterley*. Prosawerke von David Herbert Lawrence": 4612
"Eberhart's 'Throwing the Apple' ": 3036
"The Economics of Affection": 2632
ECSTASY: A STUDY OF SOME SECULAR AND RELIGIOUS EXPERIENCES: 2111
"Editor's Introduction": 3909
"Editor's Note on the Text": 2569
EDUCATION AND VALUES: ESSAYS IN THE THEORY OF EDUCATION: 2608
EDUCATION IN AN INDUSTRIAL SOCIETY: 2367
"The Education of D. H. Lawrence": 2750

INDEX OF TITLES OF SECONDARY WORKS

(Egdon and Nethermere): 4088
"Egdon to Nethermere": 4088
"Ego and the Cosmos": 3218
EIGHT MODERN ESSAYISTS: 4208
EIGHT MODERN WRITERS: 2453
"Einübung in D. H. Lawrence": 2370
THE ELEGIAC MODE: 2988
"Elements of Existentialism and Phenomenology in the Works of D. H. Lawrence": 4188
"Eliot, Lawrence, and the Jews": 3427
"Eliot, Lawrence and the Jews: Two Versions of Europe": 3427
"The Emasculation of *Lady Chatterley's Lover*": 4201
"The Emerging Woman of the Twentieth Century: A Study of the Women in D. H. Lawrence's Novels *The Rainbow* and *Women in Love*": 3928
"Emerson's 'Experience' and *Sons and Lovers*": 4023
"Emotion and Feeling": 2854
"The Empathetic Vision": 3180
ENCYCLOPAEDIA BRITANNICA: 4395
(End of Literary Illegality): 2073
THE END OF OBSCENITY: THE TRIALS OF "LADY CHATTERLEY," "TROPIC OF CANCER," AND "FANNY HILL": 3184
"The End of the Lamplight": 3580
"An End to Innocence": 2696
"L'en-deçà de la connaissance. Le péché et les voies du salut dans l'ontologie Lawrencienne": 2201
"The Enemy Territory, A Study of Joseph Conrad, E. M. Forster, and D. H. Lawrence in Relation to Their Portrayal of Evil": 3052
ENGLESKI ROMAN XX VEKA: 2413
"Engleski romansijeri o realizmu romana": 3345
ENGLISCHE DICHTER DER MODERNE: 3707
DER ENGLISCHE ESSAY: ANALYSEN: 4509
ENGLISCHE LITERATUR IM 20. JAHRHUNDERT: 2663
DIE ENGLISCHE LYRIK: VON DER RENAISSANCE BIS ZUR GEGENWART: 3222
(ENGLISH AND AMERICAN WRITERS: COMMENTS, NOTES, AND VERSIONS): 2478
(THE ENGLISH ESSAY: ANALYSES): 4508
ENGLISH LITERATURE: A PORTRAIT GALLERY: 2595
ENGLISH LITERATURE AND BRITISH PHILOSOPHY: 3788
ENGLISH LITERATURE IN OUR TIME AND THE UNIVERSITY: 3349
(ENGLISH LITERATURE IN THE TWENTIETH CENTURY): 2663
(THE ENGLISH LYRIC: FROM THE RENAISSANCE TO THE PRESENT): 3222
THE ENGLISH MIDDLE-CLASS NOVEL: 2744
"The English Novel": 3905
THE ENGLISH NOVEL: 4411
THE ENGLISH NOVEL FROM DICKENS TO LAWRENCE: 3646
THE ENGLISH NOVEL IN TRANSITION: 2640
(THE ENGLISH NOVEL OF THE TWENTIETH CENTURY): 2413
(English Novelists on Realism in the Novel): 3345
ENGLISH POETRY IN TRANSITION: 1880-1920: 3160
(ENGLISH POETRY OF THE TWENTIETH CENTURY): 4181
(ENGLISH WRITER OF THE MODERN PERIOD): 3707
"L'envers d'un conte de fées": 3145
"Epilogue": 4357
"Eros and Metaphor: Sexual Relationship in the Fiction of D. H. Lawrence": 3339
"Erosu no Nimensei--D. H. Lawrence no *Women in Love* o Megutte": 4235
THE EROTIC IN LITERATURE: 2118
(An Escape from Death-drift: On Lawrence's Early Novels): 3111
"Escape from the Circles of Experience: D. H. Lawrence's *The Rainbow* as a Modern *Bildungsroman*": 2389
"Escape from the Self: An Interpretation of E. M. Forster, D. H. Lawrence, Virginia Woolf": 3598

D. H. LAWRENCE

"L'Esprit de Conquete": 2971
AN ESSAY ON MALTA: 3880
(An Essay on *The Lost Girl*--Theme, Technique and Evaluation): 2958
THE ESSAY: STRUCTURE AND PURPOSE: 4461
ESSAYS AND REVIEWS FROM TLS: 4118
"Etudes Lawrenciennes": 4065
"L'Europe des Amants": 4567
"Europe of the Lovers": 4567
(Euthanasia from Literature): 4582
(The Evaluation of *St. Mawr*): 2403
EVELYN WAUGH: A BIOGRAPHY: 4601
"An Evening with the Lawrences": 3951
"The Evolution and Source of Some Themes of Spontaneity in D. H. Lawrence's Writing Until 1914": 3404
"The Evolution of a Lawrence Poem": 3619
"Exciting, Glorious Man": 3477
AN EXHIBITION OF FIRST EDITIONS AND MANUSCRIPTS FROM THE D. H. LAWRENCE COLLECTION OF JOHN E. BAKER, JR.: 4060
EXILES: 3429
EXILES AND ÉMIGRÉS: STUDIES IN MODERN LITERATURE: 3475
"An Exit from the Fallen Self": 2776
"Expatriate Publishing I": 4325
"Expatriate Publishing II": 4354
"Expatriate Publishing: P. R. Stephensen and the Mandrake Press": 3903
THE EXPERIENCE OF LITERATURE: A READER WITH COMMENTARIES: 3005
AN EXPERIMENT IN CRITICISM: 2116
"Experts on Trial: A Comment on Mr. Sparrow": 2280
THE EXPLICATOR CYCLOPEDIA, Vol. III: PROSE: 2108, 3230
(Expression of Irritation and Contradiction: Characterization and Imagery in *Women in Love*): 2297
"Extracts from Novels: A Comparison of Passages from Thackeray and Lawrence": 3182
"F. M. Dostoevsky and D. H. Lawrence: Their Visions of Evil": 2141
"F. R. Leavis": 2342
"F. W. Nietzsche and D. H. Lawrence: A Comparative Study": 4004
"Factors of Romanticism in D. H. Lawrence's Rhyming Poems": 4448
(Failure of Art: Ideas and Expression in *Aaron's Rod* and *Kangaroo*): 2419
"The False Myth of *St. Mawr*: Lawrence and the Subterfuge of Art": 4572
THE FAMILIAR FACES: 2245
"Fancy or Imagination? 'The Rocking-Horse Winner' ": 2291
FANFROLICO AND AFTER: 2273
"Fanny and the Lady: The Treatment of Sex in FANNY HILL and *Lady Chatterley's Lover*": 4418
"*Fantasia* and the Psychodynamics of *Women in Love*": 3923
"Fantasmi litterari sulla Costa Azzurra": 2857
"Fantasy and Mimesis in Literary Character: Shelley, Hardy, and Lawrence": 4595
(The Fascist Leader in the English Novel of Our Time): 2937
"Fast Company": 3529
"The Fate of the Self: Self and Society in the Novels of George Eliot, D. H. Lawrence, and E. M. Forster": 2475
(Fathers of Lawrence: An Aspect of *Sons and Lovers*): 3728
(The Features of the Characters in D. H. Lawrence's Novels): 3650
(The Feeling of D. H. Lawrence Towards His Father--Conscious and Unconscious): 3815
"Feminism and Literature": 3929
(Feminism in Fiction: D. H. Lawrence, *The Rainbow*): 4608
"Feminist Criticism in the Classroom, or, 'What Do You Mean We, White Man?' ": 4186
FESTIVAL OF ENGLISH POETRY: 2230
"A Few Novels": 3897
"A Few Random Thoughts on Modern First Editions": 2890
"La fiamma e il volto: studio filologico dell'ideologia del *David* di D. H. Lawrence": 4474
"Fiction": 3875, 4307

INDEX OF TITLES OF SECONDARY WORKS

"Fiction and the Camera Eye: A Study of Visual Form in the Modern Novel": 4214
FICTION AND THE FIGURES OF LIFE: 3086
"Fiction and the Rising Industrial Classes": 2922
THE FICTION OF EXPERIENCE: MODERN SHORT STORIES: 2271
THE FICTION OF SEX: THEMES AND FUNCTIONS OF SEX DIFFERENCE IN THE MODERN NOVEL: 4367
"Fiction: The Search for Friendship": 4219
"The Fictional Landscape of Mexico: D. H. Lawrence, Graham Greene and Malcolm Lowry": 3819
THE FIFTH SPARROW: 3994
FIFTY WORKS OF ENGLISH AND AMERICAN LITERATURE WE COULD DO WITHOUT: 2915
"*The Fight for Barbara* on Stage": 3123
"The Figure of Christ in D. H. Lawrence and Edwin Muir": 2829
FIGURES IN THE FOREGROUND: LITERARY REMINISCENCES: 2455
THE FILIBUSTER: A STUDY OF THE POLITICAL IDEAS OF WYNDHAM LEWIS: 3861
"The Film and the Book: D. H. Lawrence and Joseph Heller on the Screen": 3681
FILM 68/69: AN ANTHOLOGY BY THE NATIONAL SOCIETY OF FILM CRITICS: 3115
FILM 70/71: AN ANTHOLOGY BY THE NATIONAL SOCIETY OF FILM CRITICS: 3505, 3530
"Filozofija vitalizma D. H. Lorensa i O. Hakslija–Uticaj i paralele": 4123
"The Final Draft: *Women in Love*": 4575
THE FINE ART OF LITERARY MAYHEM: A LIVELY ACCOUNT OF FAMOUS WRITERS AND THEIR FEUDS: 2406
"Fine Arts": 2599
"The Fire That Consumes": 2222
"The First and Final Versions of *Lady Chatterley's Lover*": 2489
"First and Last Romantics": 3441
"The First and Second Generations": 2624
"The First Edition of Lawrence's Foreword to *Women in Love*": 4284
THE FIRST HUNDRED YEARS OF WAGNER'S TRISTAN: 2602
"The First *Lady Chatterley's Lover*": 3807
"First Nights": 3002
(First Performance in London of one of D. H. Lawrence's Plays): 2903
FIRST REACTIONS: CRITICAL ESSAYS: 4121
"First stab at the blood lust": 3305
"First Winter": 2795
"Fit for Old Theocritus": 3624
(The Flame and the Face: A Philological Study of the Ideology of D. H. Lawrence's *David*): 4474
"The Flesh Made Word: A Study of Narrative and Stylistic Techniques in Five Novels by D. H. Lawrence": 3715
"The Fleshly Muse": 2495
" 'Floutingly in the Fine Black Mud': D. H. Lawrence's 'The Horse-Dealer's Daughter' ": 4039
(Flowers and Animals in *Sons and Lovers*): 2671
"For D. H. Lawrence": 2157
"Ford and Lawrence": 3890
FORD MADOX FORD: 3996
"Ford's Impressions of the Lawrences": 3850
(Foreign Letters): 2202, 3028
(FOREIGN WRITERS OF THE 20TH CENTURY): 3046
(Forest in *Lady Chatterley's Lover*): 4138
"Foreword": 2530, 3553, 3858
"Foreword: The Isle of Wight in a Living Myth": 4343
"Forgotten Play Shows Power of Genius": 3011
THE FORKED FLAME: A STUDY OF D. H. LAWRENCE: 2624
"Form and Content in Lawrence's Poetry": 4041
"Form and Pressure in Poetry": 3623
"Form and Tone in the Poetry of D. H. Lawrence": 3067

D. H. LAWRENCE

"The Form of the Literature of Crisis": 3408
"Formative Influences on the Work of D. H. Lawrence": 2236
"Formen mythisierenden Erzählens in der modernen Prose: Joseph Conrad im Vergleich mit Joyce, Lawrence und Faulkner": 3017
"Formen und Funktionen der Raumdarstellung in den Short Stories von D. H. Lawrence": 3784
(Forms and Functions of the Depiction of Space in the Short Stories of D. H. Lawrence): 3784
THE FORMS OF FICTION: 2244
FORMS OF MODERN BRITISH FICTION: 4467
FORMS OF THE MODERN NOVELLA: 4592
(Forster and Lawrence): 4171
"A Forster Parallel in Lawrence's *St. Mawr*": 2861
"Forster to Lawrence": 4171
"The Fortress of Aulla and D. H. Lawrence": 2180
FOUR CASES OF LITERARY CENSORSHIP: AN INAUGURAL LECTURE: 3219
"400 attend D. H. Lawrence festival": 3489
"The Four 'Lady Chatterleys' ": 3885
FOUR LETTER WORD GAMES: THE PSYCHOLOGY OF OBSCENITY: 2943
"A Four-Letter Word in *Lady Chatterley's Lover*": 2966
"Four Paintings by D. H. Lawrence": 3792
"Four Versions of the Circuitous Return: Marx, Nietzsche, Eliot, Lawrence": 3655
THE FOURFOLD TRADITION: NOTES ON THE FRENCH AND ENGLISH LITERATURES, WITH SOME ETHNOLOGICAL AND HISTORICAL ASIDES: 2092
"*The Fox*": 3079, 3173
"THE FOX": 4147
[*The Fox*]: 3202
("The Fox" and "La Lupa": D. H. Lawrence, Reader of Verga): 4191
" 'The Fox' e 'La Lupa': D. H. Lawrence lettore di Verga": 4191
"*The Fox* ni Tsuite": 2099
"*The Fox* on Film": 3058
"*The Fox*: The Film and the Novel": 3401
"Fragmentation and Uncertainty": 3405
FRANCIS BRETT YOUNG: A BIOGRAPHY: 2359
" 'Freedom Together' in Lawrence's *Women in Love*": 2695
"*Freitag abend eines Bergmanns*. Ein Stuck von D. H. Lawrence in Bochum": 4401
FREMMEDE DIGTERE I DET 20. ARHUNDREDE: 3046
FREUD AND THE CRITIC: THE EARLY USE OF DEPTH PSYCHOLOGY IN LITERARY CRITICISM: 3156
"Frieda and Lawrence": 4090
"Frieda and the Lawrence Legend": 2756
(Frieda Bereaved of Lawrence): 4116
FRIEDA LAWRENCE: THE MEMOIRS AND CORRESPONDENCE: 2112
FRIEDA LAWRENCE: THE STORY OF FRIEDA VON RICHTHOFEN AND D. H. LAWRENCE: 3948
(FRIEDA VON RICHTHOFEN: HER LIFE WITH D. H. LAWRENCE): 3948
FRIEDA VON RICHTHOFEN. IHR LEBEN MIT D. H. LAWRENCE: 3948
"Friends and Enemies": 2248
FROM DICKENS TO HARDY: 3342, 3343
FROM FICTION TO FILM: D. H. LAWRENCE'S "THE ROCKING-HORSE WINNER": 3601, 4266, 4361, 4390, 4408
(From Lawrence to Ken Russell): 3919
"From Rananim to Thelnetham": 2062
FROM REVERENCE TO RAPE: THE TREATMENT OF WOMEN IN THE MOVIES: 4327
(From Short Story to Film: Lawrence's *The Fox*): 3162
"From Some Ashes No Bird Rises": 3086

INDEX OF TITLES OF SECONDARY WORKS

(From *Sons and Lovers* to *Women in Love*: Toward a More Concrete Sense of Death): 2742
"From the Book-Shelf": 2311
"From 'The Sisters' to *The Rainbow* and *Women in Love*: A Textual and Critical History, 1913-17": 4189
"From Transcendental to Descendental: The Romantic Thought of Blake, Nietzsche, Lawrence": 3327
"The Function of Heresy in Modern Literature: Studies in the Major Fiction of Thomas Hardy, E. M. Forster, and D. H. Lawrence": 4306
FUNK & WAGNALLS GUIDE TO MODERN WORLD LITERATURE: 4203
"Further Notes on D. H. Lawrence's 'Rocking-Horse' ": 2407
"Further Phoenix": 3083
"Further Reminiscences XV": 2131
"Futatsu no 'Hi-Gakkyuteki' Lawrence Ron (Anais Nin to Henry Miller)": 2427
"Futatsu no Ikikata: D. H. Lawrence no *Koisuru Onnatachi* ni Tsuite": 3942
A FUTURE FOR ASTYANAX: CHARACTER AND DESIRE IN LITERATURE: 4451
"The Future of the Individual: Ursula Brangwen and Kate Millett's SEXUAL POLITICS": 4048
"Gamekeeper no Henbo: *Lady Chatterley's Lover* no Mittsu no Han": 4352
THE GARNETT FAMILY: 2091
"Geijutsu no Hôkai--*Aaron's Rod* to *Kangaroo* no Shisô to Hyôgen": 2419
"General": 3311
"Generative Grammars and the Concept of Literary Style": 2559
"The Genesis of 'Bavarian Gentians' ": 4579
"The Genesis of D. H. Lawrence's *The Trespasser*": 2163
"The Genesis of *The Rainbow* and *Women in Love*": 3192
GENGO TO BUNTAI: HIGASHIDA CHIAKI KYOJU KANREKI KINEN RONBUNSHU: 4373, 4385

"Genius as Critic": 2114
"A Genius But . . .": 2578
"Genius with a Dictionary: Reevaluating D. H. Lawrence's Translations: 3031
THE GEOGRAPHICAL BACKGROUND IN THE EARLY WORKS OF D. H. LAWRENCE: 2587
"The Georgian Literary Scene: Secker's World": 2324
THE GEORGIAN REVOLT: RISE AND FALL OF A POETIC IDEAL: 2726
(Gerald Crich in *Women in Love*): 2707
"The German Letters of D. H. Lawrence": 2364
(The German Letters of D. H. Lawrence): 2364
THE GERMAN TRADITION IN LITERATURE: 2647
"Glossary": 4242
"Glossary of Eastwood Dialect Words Used by D. H. Lawrence in His Poems, Plays and Fiction": 3088
"A Glossary of Nottinghamshire Dialect and Mining Terms": 3088
"*Goats and Compasses* and/or *Women in Love*: An Exchange": 4190
"*Goats and Compasses* and *Women in Love* Again": 4196
"God and Man in Twentieth-Century Fiction": 2310
GOING STEADY: 3115
"THE GOLDEN BOUGH: Impact and Archetype": 2461
GOLDEN CODGERS: BIOGRAPHICAL SPECULATIONS: 4077
"Gopher Prairie or Papplewick?: *The Virgin and the Gipsy* as Film": 3687
"The Gospel According to D. H. Lawrence: Religion in *Sons and Lovers*": 3596
"The Great Circle": 2348, 2466
GREAT FRIENDS: 4090
THE GREAT WAR AND MODERN MEMORY: 4492
"The Great War of 1914-1918": 2432
"Great Writers--4: D. H. Lawrence": 2382
"Greater Expectations: D. H. Lawrence's *The Trespasser*": 3564

D. H. LAWRENCE

"The Greatness in *Sons and Lovers*": 4419

(Greek Mythology in D. H. Lawrence's Poetry): 2313

"Green Room": 3060

"Growing Pains": 3128, 4223

A GUIDE TO THE BEST FICTION: ENGLISH AND AMERICAN, INCLUDING TRANSLATIONS FROM FOREIGN LANGUAGES: 2907

GUILT, ANGER, AND GOD: THE PATTERNS OF OUR DISCONTENTS: 3839

"Gûwa (D. H. Lawrence–'The Man Who Loved Islands' no Sekai)": 2516

"The Habitat of *The Plumed Serpent*": 2220

HALF-WAY TO FAITH: 2790

"Hana to Dôbutsu (*Sons and Lovers* no Baai)": 2671

A HANDBOOK OF ANALYSES, QUESTIONS, AND A DISCUSSION OF TECHNIQUE FOR USE WITH "MODERN SHORT STORIES: THE USES OF IMAGINATION": 2837

"Hands Up, America!": 2396

HAPPY RURAL SEAT: THE ENGLISH COUNTRY HOUSE AND THE LITERARY IMAGINATION: 3914

"Hardy to Lawrence: A Study in Naturism": 2763

HARVEST OF A QUIET EYE: THE NOVEL OF COMPASSION: 3091

"A Haste for Wisdom: The Poetry of D. H. Lawrence": 2491

HAUPTWERKE DER ENGLISCHEN LITERATUR DARSTELLUNGEN UND INTERPRETATIONEN: 2679

"The Hawk and the Plover: 'The Polarity of Life' in the 'Jungle Aviary' of D. H. Lawrence's Mind in *Sons and Lovers* and *The Rainbow*": 2096

HAWTHORNE AND THE MODERN SHORT STORY: A STUDY IN GENRE: 2866

"Hawthorne on Don Juan": 2341

"The Heart Sacrificed to the Sun: Mythos of Reality in D. H. Lawrence's American Fiction": 4614

HEAVENS BELOW: UTOPIAN EXPERIMENTS IN ENGLAND, 1560-1960: 2062

"Hebi to Tsuki to Shochoshugi: D. H. Lawrence no Sozoryoku": 4102

THE HELLISH MEANING: THE DEMONIC MOTIF IN THE WORKS OF D. H. LAWRENCE: 3359

"The Hero and the Heroine in the British *Bildungsroman*: DAVID COPPERFIELD and A PORTRAIT OF THE ARTIST AS A YOUNG MAN, JANE EYRE and *The Rainbow*": 3772

HEROES' TWILIGHT: A STUDY OF THE LITERATURE OF THE GREAT WAR: 2612

THE HEYDAY OF SIR WALTER SCOTT: 2077

"Higeki no Keishô (Lawrence no Thomas Hardy Ron)": 2710

"High-Handed Publishers?": 2248

"His Ashes Rest with His Heart; Near Taos": 3461

(HISTORY OF ENGLISH LITERATURE): 2573

A HISTORY OF ENGLISH LITERATURE: 2544

"The History of Mr Wells": 3383

"The Hitherto Unknown Publications of Some D. H. Lawrence Short Stories": 3899

"Hôkai to Kyôki no Sôzô--*Tsubasa Aru Hebi* Ron": 3651

"El hombre que murió (D. H. Lawrence)": 3769

HOMOSEXUALITY AND LITERATURE, 1890-1930: 4154

"The Horse Dealer's Daughter": 4558

"The Hostile Sun: The Poetry of D. H. Lawrence": 3965

THE HOSTILE SUN: THE POETRY OF D. H. LAWRENCE: 3964, 3965, 4165

"How Beastly the Bourgeois Is": 2409

" 'How beastly the bourgeois is': Lawrence's Poetry": 2409

"How Lawrence Wrote Out the Preaching and the Pathos": 3907

(How to End a Novel? D. H. Lawrence's Novels and "Conversion"): 3346

(How to Read Lawrence): 4103

"HOWARDS END Revisited": 3280

INDEX OF TITLES OF SECONDARY WORKS

"Human Subject and Human Substance: Stephen Dedalus of A PORTRAIT OF THE ARTIST and Rupert Birkin of *Women in Love*": 2643
"Humanities": 3930
"A Hungry Woman": 2172
HUXLEY: A BIOGRAPHICAL INTRODUCTION: 4225
THE HUXLEYS: 3053
"Huxley's Ambivalent Responses to the Ideas of D. H. Lawrence": 2910
"Huxley's Lawrencian Interlude: The 'Latin Compromise' That Failed": 3355
" 'I am going through a transition stage': *The Prussian Officer* and *The Rainbow*": 4471
"I Cannot Love a Friend Whose Love is Words": 2949
I LOST IT AT THE MOVIES: 2104
"I soggiorni di Lawrence": 2900
"I, Thou, and You in Three Lawrencian Relationships": 3126
"I viaggi di Lawrence": 2304
" 'I Want to Drown in Flesh...' ": 3579
(The Idea of Love in Lawrence's *Women in Love*): 4117
"Identity and Sexuality": 4525
"The Illusion of *St. Mawr*: Technique and Vision in D. H. Lawrence's Novel": 2598
"The Image of the Wolf in Chapter XXX of D. H. Lawrence's *Women in Love*": 3322
"Imagery and Meaning in D. H. Lawrence's *The Rainbow*": 3838
"Imagery as Related to Theme in D. H. Lawrence's Poetry": 2933
IMAGES OF WOMEN IN FICTION: FEMINIST PERSPECTIVES: 3929
IMAGINED WORLDS: ESSAYS ON SOME ENGLISH NOVELS AND NOVELISTS IN HONOUR OF JOHN BUTT: 3124, 3148
"The Immorality of Lady Chatterley": 4118
"The Impact of D. H. Lawrence on His Contemporaries": 2651
"The Impact of Modernism on Lawrence": 2533
"The Impact of Symbolism on Story and Character in D. H. Lawrence's *The Rainbow*": 3754
"Impersonal Aphrodite": 3108
(Impulse and Unity: On *Lady Chatterley's Lover* [1]): 4334
"In D. H. Lawrence Country They Still Hold a Grudge": 3709
IN HONOR OF AUSTIN WRIGHT: 3843
"In Love with Lawrence": 4052
IN OUR INFANCY: AN AUTOBIOGRAPHY, Part I: 1882-1919: 4465
(In Search for the English Novel): 3029
"In Search of D. H. Lawrence's *Sea and Sardinia*": 4092
(In Search of the Unknown World--*The Rainbow*): 2715
IN THE DAYS OF MY YOUTH: 3492
(In the Dissolution of Civilization--On Lawrence's *Women in Love*): 4622
"In the Footsteps of D. H. Lawrence in Switzerland: Some New Biographical Material": 2064
IN THE LAST ANALYSIS: 2483
"In Touch with Genius": 4596
"In Writing Nothing Fails Like Success": 2148
"Incanto pagano di D. H. Lawrence": 2199
"The Inception of a Saga: Frederick Manfred's BUCKSKIN MAN": 3388
INDEPENDENT ESSAYS: 2169
"Indian Cultures Appeal More than English Aristocracy": 4458
"Indians and Palefaces": 2581
"Individual Instinct and Societal Repression in the Writings of D. H. Lawrence": 4397
INFERNAL PARADISE: MEXICO AND THE MODERN ENGLISH NOVEL: 4430
"The Influence of D. H. Lawrence on Tennessee Williams": 2242
THE INFLUENCE OF D. H. LAWRENCE ON TENNESSEE WILLIAMS: 2242, 2794
"The Influence of the Bible on D. H. Lawrence as Seen in his Novels": 4017
"The Influence of the English Class Structure on the Work of D. H. Lawrence": 4062

"An Informal Bibliography (from June 1960 to April 1962)": 2286
(An Inquiry into Ambivalence in *The White Peacock*): 4250
INSIGHT II: ANALYSES OF MODERN BRITISH LITERATURE: 2464
INSTRUCTOR'S MANUAL FOR MODERN STORIES IN ENGLISH: 4558
INSTRUCTOR'S MANUAL FOR "THE RHETORIC OF NO": 3478
(Intellect and Sex): 2556
"The Intellectual and Emotional Complex as an Expression of the Consciousness in Joyce, Lawrence, and Woolf": 4462
"Intelletto e sesso": 2556
"Intercourse with Lady Chatterley": 2943
THE INTERPRETATION OF NARRATIVE: THEORY AND PRACTICE: 3444
"An Interview in London with Angus Wilson": 3438
"An Interview with Helen Corke": 3159
"An Interview with Ken Russell": 3582
"Into the Fire": 2884
INTRODUCCIÓN A LA NOVELA CONTEMPORÁNEA: 2766
"Introducing the *Sons and Lovers* Number": 4513
"Introduction": 2095, 2204, 2263, 2294, 2442, 2724, 2739, 2918, 2973, 2989, 3044, 3144, 3185, 3277, 3283, 3303, 3357, 3391, 3412, 3473, 3484, 3653, 3733, 3793, 3794, 3865, 3939, 3984, 4055, 4063, 4099, 4242, 4244, 4357, 4473
(Introduction): 2135, 2302, 2303, 2550, 2844, 2976, 3087, 3572, 3573, 3963, 4162, 4279, 4313, 4554, 4555
[Introduction]: 2971
"Introduction: The Law and the Obscene": 3054
(Introduction to D. H. Lawrence): 2370
AN INTRODUCTION TO LITERATURE: FICTION: 2939
(INTRODUCTION TO THE CONTEMPORARY NOVEL): 2766
"Introduction to the New Edition": 3674
"Introduction to the Second Edition": 2617
"Introductory Commentary": 3203
"An Introductory Note to D. H. Lawrence's Prologue to *Women in Love*": 2393
"Introduzione": 2135, 2302, 2303, 2550, 2844, 2976, 3087, 3572, 3573, 3963, 4162, 4279, 4313, 4554, 4555
"The Invisible Man Made Visible: Representation of the Unconscious in the Writings of D. H. Lawrence": 3127
"Invitation to Garsington": 4317
"Iracionalna motivacija u Lawrenceovu romanu *Zaljübjene zene*": 2996
THE IRONIC VISION IN MODERN LITERATURE: 3313
"Irony and Attitude in George Eliot and D. H. Lawrence": 4143
(Irrational Motivation in Lawrence's Novel *Women in Love*): 2996
IRVING TO IRVING: AUTHOR-PUBLISHER RELATIONS, 1800-1974: 4356
"Ishiki Tankyûsha D. H. Lawrence-- Shojosaku *Shirokujaku* Ron": 3967
"Ishikika no Sekai (D. H. Lawrence: *The Fox* no Buntai)": 2093
"Ishmael no Higeki to Syokuzai--'England, My England' o Megutte": 3535
(Ishmael's Tragedy and Redemption in "England, My England"): 3535
IVORY TOWERS AND SACRED FOUNTS: THE ARTIST AS HERO IN FICTION FROM GOETHE TO JOYCE: 2368
"Jessie Chambers' Last Tape on D. H. Lawrence": 4087
"Jesus and the Osiris-Isis Myth: Lawrence's *The Man Who Died* and Williams's THE NIGHT OF THE IGUANA": 2808
" 'Jets of Sunlight' ": 4261
"Jiyû to Sokubaku (D. H. Lawrence: 'The Thorn in the Flesh' no Sekai)": 2400

INDEX OF TITLES OF SECONDARY WORKS

JOHN MIDDLETON MURRY: 3320
"John Middleton Murry, 1889-1957": 4527
"*John Thomas and Lady Jane*": 3957
"Jôsho to Kâkô--Lawrence, Forster, Woolf, Huxley Ra ni Okeru Ninshiki no Kata ni Tsuite": 4545
JOURNAL D'UN JOURNALISTE: 4294
JOURNAL D'UNE ÉPOQUE: 1926-1946: 3063
(JOURNAL OF A JOURNALIST): 4294
(JOURNAL OF AN EPOCH: 1926-1946): 3063
JOURNEY THROUGH DESPAIR, 1880-1914: TRANSFORMATIONS IN BRITISH LITERARY CULTURE: 3138
(A Journey to "Darkness"--What the Death of Mrs. Morel Means): 4621
JOYCE AND LAWRENCE: 3303
"Joyce and the Meanings of Modernism": 3668
"Joyce's Brother, Lawrence's Wife, Wolfe's Mother, Twain's Daughter": 2929
"Jubaku kara no Ridatsu--Lawrence *Musuko to Koibito* Ron": 4251
"Juno and *The White Peacock*: Lawrence's English Epic": 3512
"Kangaroo: 'a new show' ": 3645
"*Kangaroo*: D. H. Lawrence in Transit": 2508
KATHERINE MANSFIELD: THE MEMORIES OF L. M.: 3763
KENJA RORENSU: 4336
" 'Kiku no Ka' ni Okeru Lawrence Bungaku no Hôga": 2904
(KINDLER'S HANDBOOK OF LITERATURE): 2679
KINDLERS LITERATUR LEXIKON: 2679
KIRISUTOKYŌ TO BUNGAKU (DAI 3 SHU): 4619
"Književno Prijateljstvo D. H. Lorensa i O. Hakslija": 4124
"Kodoku no Jissô: D. H. Lawrence Joron": 3738
"*Koisuru Onnatachi* Kenkyû--Lawrence no Gendai Gôrishugi Hihan": 4127
"*Koisuru Onnatachi* ni Okeru Ichikôsatsu": 3842

"*Koisuru Onnatachi* ni Okeru Kôseijô no Tokuchô ni Tsuite": 2745
"*Koisuru Onnatachi* ni Okeru Lawrence no Ai no Kannen": 4117
"*Koisuru Onnatachi* no Shudai": 2792
" 'Kokkyôsen' to D. H. Lawrence": 2819
"Konrad Lorenz and D. H. Lawrence": 3848
"Kotoba no Kochiragawa de--D. H. Lawrence no Shi ni Tsuite": 4360
"Kraj jedne knijiževne i legalnosti": 2073
"Kritische These über D. H. Lawrence": 2216
"Kujaku no Yukue": 4546
"Die Kurzgeschichten von D. H. Lawrence": 2664
"Kûzen no Shin-Minshushugi-Setsu--D. H. Lawrence no Seizetsunaru Ningenkôsei Ron": 4167
"Kvinnesak og skjønnliteratur. D. H. Lawrence: *The Rainbow*": 4608
"Kyôbô na Junrei no Ato o Otte--Garuda-Kohan nite": 3731
"Kyôbô na Junrei no Ato o Otte–Kokyô Eastwood": 3527
"Kyôbô na Junrei no Ato o Otte--New Mexico": 3333
"Kyôbô na Junrei no Ato o Otte–Villa Mirenda": 4125
"Kyôbô na Junreikô no Ato o Otte–Cornwall": 2818
"Kyôbô na Junreikô no Ato o Otte--Sicilia": 3116
LADIES BOUNTIFUL: 3186
"The Lady and Her Horsekeeper: Middleton or Rowley?": 2410
"Lady Chatterley": 2267, 4220
"Lady Chatterley Again": 2320, 2388, 2445
(*Lady Chatterley*: An Evaluated Account of the Much-Debated Novel): 2160
"Lady Chatterley and All That": 2182
"Lady Chatterley and Her Lover": 4302
"*Lady Chatterley*: Eine Darstellung und Würdigung des vielumstrittenen Romans": 2160
"Lady Chatterley for the Last Time I": 2433
"Lady Chatterley for the Last Time II": 2446

"Lady Chatterley in Ottawa": 2270
(Lady Chatterley is merely second-rate. The second version of a famous novel, for the first time in German translation): 4456
"Lady Chatterley ist nur das Gelbe im Ei. Die Zweitfassung eines beruhmten Romans, zum erstenmal auf deutsch": 4456
"*Lady Chatterley* vann processen": 2170
(*Lady Chatterley* Won the Case): 2170
LADY CHATTERLEY'S DAUGHTER: 2152
"Lady Chatterley's Husband": 2227
"Lady Chatterley's Lecher": 2791
"*Lady Chatterley's Lover*": 2176, 3528
"*Lady Chatterley's Lover*: A Correction": 2125
"*Lady Chatterley's Lover*: A PILGRIM'S PROGRESS for Our Time": 2773
"*Lady Chatterley's Lover*: A Pyrrhic Victory": 2173
"*Lady Chatterley's Lover*: A Trembling Balance": 3818
"*Lady Chatterley's Lover* and the Aubade": 2232
(*Lady Chatterley's Lover*--Its Failure and Triumph): 2713
"*Lady Chatterley's Lover* ni Okeru Connie": 2843
"*Lady Chatterley's Lover* ni Tsuite": 2842
"*Lady Chatterley's Lover*: 'Pure Seclusion' ": 3998
"*Lady Chatterley's Lover* Shiron--Koritsu to Kizuna no Gyakusetsu o Megutte": 3992
"*Lady Chatterley's Lover*--Sono Shippai to Shôri": 2713
"*Lady Chatterley's Lover*: The Novel as Ritual": 2295
"Lady Chatterley's Trial (The Old Bailey, 20 October-2 November 1960)": 3007
"Lady Chatterley's *What*?": 3369
"Laing, Lawrence, and the Maternal Cannibal": 3736
"Language and Literature": 2529, 2683, 2824, 3347, 3543, 3742
(LANGUAGE AND LITERATURE: ACTS OF THE EIGHTH CONGRESS OF THE INTERNATIONAL FEDERATION OF THE MODERN LANGUAGES AND LITERATURES): 2128
"Language and Movement in 'Fanny and Annie' ": 3393
(LANGUAGE AND STYLE: COLLECTED ESSAYS COMMEMORATING THE SIXTIETH BIRTHDAY OF PROFESSOR CHIAKI HIGASHIDA): 4373, 4385
(The Language of Flowers or Say It with Flowers): 3702
"The Language of *Women in Love*": 2911
LANGUE ET LITTÉRATURE: ACTES DU VIIIe CONGRÈS DE LA FÉDÉRATION INTERNATIONALE DES LANGUES ET LITTÉRATURES MODERNES: 2128
LAPSING OUT: EMBODIMENTS OF DEATH AND REBIRTH IN THE LAST WRITINGS OF D. H. LAWRENCE: 3716, 3921
"The Last Days of D. H. Lawrence: Hitherto Unpublished Letters of Dr. Andrew Morland": 3247
"Last Glowing Inspiration: Countryside That Inspired": 2860
"The *Last Poems* of D. H. Lawrence": 3275
"The Last Trial of Lady Chatterley": 2069
(The Later Lawrence: Escape from Isolation into Mythical Cosmos): 4416
"Laurentian Indifference": 3252
"Laurentiana": 3137, 3872, 3900, 3945, 4131, 4160, 4286, 4466, 4543
"The Law and Literary Merit": 2192
"The Law and the Obscene": 3054
"Lawrence": 2447, 2453, 4375, 4411
LAWRENCE: 4132
"Lawrence a Gargnano": 4460
"Lawrence a Volterra": 3051
(Lawrence Abroad): 2900
"Lawrence After Thirty Years": 4141
"Lawrence: Ai no Tansaku": 3341
"Lawrence: Ai o Koeru Mono": 3735
"Lawrence: Ai to Kodoku": 3941
"Lawrence amava l'Italia come si ama una bella donne": 2305

INDEX OF TITLES OF SECONDARY WORKS

"1. Lawrence among the Aztecs: Travels, Readings, and Poems. 2. Functions of Disguise in Ben Jonson's Comedies. 3. The Language of the Theater in Hawthorne's Tales and THE SCARLET LETTER": 4600
"Lawrence among the Radicals: MMLA, 1969: An Exchange": 3443
"Lawrence and Art": 3786
"Lawrence and Bloomsbury: The Myth of a Relationship": 4042
LAWRENCE AND BRETT: A FRIENDSHIP: 4357
"Lawrence and Brett: A Prologue": 4357
(Lawrence and Casanova): 2568
"Lawrence and Christ": 2503
"Lawrence and Democracy": 4057
"Lawrence and District": 4206
"Lawrence and E. M. Forster: Two Rainbows": 4475
LAWRENCE AND EDUCATION: 3177
"Lawrence and Etruria": 3129
"Lawrence and Frieda": 2434
(Lawrence and His Critics): 2460
"Lawrence and his Publisher": 3545
(Lawrence and Huxley): 3729
"Lawrence and Lewis": 3381
(Lawrence and Marinetti): 3799
"Lawrence and Marquand": 2349
"Lawrence and Modern Life: *Sons and Lovers, Women in Love*": 2744
"Lawrence and Movies: A Postscript": 4413
"Lawrence and Pascin": 2186
(Lawrence and Rilke–On the Problem of Death): 2814
"Lawrence and 'that which is perfectly ourselves' ": 4452
"Lawrence and the Apocalyptic Types": 3122
(Lawrence and the First World War): 2315
"Lawrence and the LITERATURE/ FILM QUARTERLY": 4058
(Lawrence and the Mother Complex): 3195
"Lawrence and the Movements of Modern Culture": 4228
"Lawrence and *The Rainbow*: Apollo and Dionysus in Conflict": 3937
"Lawrence and the Unseen Presences": 4615
"Lawrence and the War": 2301
"Lawrence and the Wilkinsons": 2332
(Lawrence and Vittorini): 2369
LAWRENCE AND WOMEN: 3339
(Lawrence and Woolf: A Stylistic Approach to Their Thought Structure and Paragraph Structure): 4372
(Lawrence as a Lazy Writer in His Letters to Friends): 2998
"Lawrence as a Painter": 2575
(Lawrence as a Playwright): 2977
"Lawrence as Abnormal Novelist": 4616
"Lawrence as Playwright": 2800
"Lawrence as Poet": 4031
"Lawrence as Prophetic Poet": 4262
"Lawrence at the MLA, 1974: A Commentary": 4501
"Lawrence at the Ranch": 3546
(Lawrence at Volterra): 3051
(Lawrence beyond Love): 3735
"Lawrence Bungaku ni Okeru Shizen": 2897
"Lawrence Bungaku no Hassei": 3125
"Lawrence Bungaku no Jigen (III)": 2098
"Lawrence Bungaku no Jigen (IV)": 2670
"Lawrence Bungaku no Jigen (V)": 2950
"Lawrence Bungaku no Konnichisei": 4379
"Lawrence by Himself": 3367
"Lawrence by Leavis": 2312, 3368
"Lawrence cercava in Italia le tracce di una razza selvaggia": 2360
"Lawrence: Critic of Christianity": 3217
"Lawrence, David Herbert, 1885-1930": 3325
"Lawrence, David Herbert [1885-1930]": 2907
"Lawrence Dramaturg": 3194
"Lawrence drammaturgo": 2977
LAWRENCE DURRELL: A CRITICAL STUDY: 3080
LAWRENCE DURRELL/HENRY MILLER: A PRIVATE CORRESPONDENCE: 2385
"Lawrence e Casanova": 2568
"Lawrence e Vittorini": 2369
"Lawrence etrusco": 2231

D. H. LAWRENCE

"Lawrence/Freud": 3433
LAWRENCE, GREENE AND LOWRY: THE FICTIONAL LANDSCAPE OF MEXICO: 3819, 4425
LAWRENCE, HARDY, AND AMERICAN LITERATURE: 4001
"Lawrence, Hardy, and 'The Great Tradition' ": 4198
"A Lawrence-Huxley Parallel: *Women in Love* and POINT COUNTER POINT": 3220
(Lawrence in Gargnano): 4460
"Lawrence in His Letters": 2265
(Lawrence in His *Sons and Lovers*): 3001
"Lawrence in Italia": 2323, 2346
(Lawrence in Italy): 2323, 2346
"Lawrence in Love": 3306, 3354
(Lawrence in Love): 3341
"Lawrence in New Mexico: There is the pristine; something unbroken ...": 3548
"Lawrence in Old and New Mexico: The Quest and the Art": 2481
"Lawrence in Print and on Film": 3611
LAWRENCE IN THE WAR YEARS: 3198
(Lawrence in Verse): 2081
"Lawrence in versi": 2081
"The Lawrence Industry": 3547
"Lawrence, Joyce and Powys": 2107
"Lawrence Kenkyû (2)": 3149
"Lawrence Letters--The Heart of the Man": 2208
"Lawrence, Lewis, and the Comedy of Literary Reputations": 3453
(Lawrence: Love and Solitude): 3941
(Lawrence Loved Italy as One Loves a Beautiful Woman): 2305
"The Lawrence Mob": 2665
"Lawrence ni Kansuru Ichi Kenkyu (1)": 2972
"Lawrence ni Okeru 'Otoko' no Keifu (I) (*Sons and Lovers* no Baai)": 4504
"Lawrence *Niji* Ronkô (I)--Buntai to Kôsei o Chûshin to Shite": 3830
"Lawrence *Niji* Ronkô (II)--Buntai to Kôsei o Chûshin to Shite": 4027
"Lawrence *Niji* Ronkô (III)--Buntai to Kôsei o Chûshin to Shite": 4252
"Lawrence no Bungaku Hihyô": 2583
"Lawrence no Buntai": 2292
"Lawrence no Chichioyatachi--*Sons and Lovers* no Ichimen": 3728
"Lawrence no Gikyoku no Kansuru Oboegaki: *Mrs. Holroyd, Touch and Go, David*": 2420
"Lawrence no Kaiga to Kaiga-Seishin ni Tsuite": 4337
"Lawrence no Leadership Novels ni Tsuite--*Aaron no Tsue* kara *Tsubasa Aru Hebi* made": 4169
"Lawrence no Mother-Complex": 3195
"Lawrence no Motometa Mono--Shi to Yami no Sekai": 3130
"Lawrence no *Niji* no Kôsei ni Kansuru Ichi Kenkyû": 2459
"Lawrence no 'Nôjô no Koi' Kenkyû": 3931
"Lawrence no Okeru Shikaku to Shokkaku no Mondai--'Ichijiku no Ha' Izen no Kyôi e no Kaiki": 4438
"Lawrence no Rakuen (Risô Shakai 'Rananim' no Kôsatsu)": 2732
"Lawrence no Shi 'Hebi' no Hyôgen Style ni Tsuite": 3518
"Lawrence no Shi ni Arawareta Ganseki to Kôbutsu ni Tsuite": 2138
"Lawrence no Shôsetsu o Ronjiru tame no Oboegaki": 3519
"Lawrence no Shuyô-Sakuhin ni Okeru Shi no Imi": 4345
"Lawrence no Tolstoi Kan (I)": 2554
"Lawrence no Tolstoi Kan (II)": 2555
"Lawrence o do yomuka": 4103
"Lawrence Old and New": 3744
"Lawrence on Love: The Courtship and Marriage of Tom Brangwen and Lydia Lensky": 4500
"Lawrence on Stage": 2751
(Lawrence on the Way to America): 4562
"Lawrence Play Skilfully Adapted to Television": 2113
"Lawrence Play with a Strindberg Touch": 3012
"Lawrence Program Taking Form": 3549
" 'Lawrence Scholarship' and Lawrence": 2408
"Lawrence scoperse l'Australia come un mondo ancora vergine": 2306
"Lawrence scrittore pigro nelle lettere

INDEX OF TITLES OF SECONDARY WORKS

agli amici": 2998
(Lawrence Searched in Italy for the Traces of a Savage Race): 2360
"Lawrence, Sex, and Celluloid": 3500
"Lawrence, Sex and Religion": 2083
"Lawrence Shôsetsu no Hitotsu no Imi *Musuko to Koibito* kara *Koisuru Onnatachi* Made": 2983
(Lawrence: Son of Father): 2714
(Lawrence Student of Etruscan Civilization): 2231
"Lawrence the Dramatist": 3092
"Lawrence the Painter: 'Everything that can possibly be painted has been painted . . . visual arts are at a dead end' ": 3550
(Lawrence the Playwright): 3194
"Lawrence the Poet": 2616, 2719, 2720
"Lawrence the Poet: Achievement and Irrelevance": 2645
"Lawrence the Poet: His Webs Were Spun from His Own Vitals": 3539
(Lawrence the Puritan): 2552
(LAWRENCE THE SEER): 4336
"Lawrence: 'The Ship of Death' ": 2948
"Lawrence to Daiichiji Taisen": 2315
"Lawrence to Hihyôka-Tachi": 2460
"Lawrence to Huxley": 3729
"Lawrence to Marinetti": 3799
"Lawrence to Rilke--Shi no Mondai o Megutte": 2814
"Lawrence to Shibetsugo no Frieda": 4116
"Lawrence Triptych": 3049
"Lawrence Twice Over": 4322
"Lawrence Up-Tight, or the Anal Phase Once Over": 3805
"Lawrence/*Women in Love*: The Contravened Knot": 2619
"Lawrence Zakko": 3370
"Lawrence's Anti-Symbol: The Ending of *The Rainbow*": 4029
"Lawrence's Aphrodite": 4075
"Lawrence's 'Art and the Individual' ": 4177
"Lawrence's 'Chladni Figures' ": 4183
"Lawrence's Companion Poems: 'Snake' and *Tortoises*": 3860
"Lawrence's Concept of Being": 3240
"Lawrence's Conception of Art, Morality and the Novel": 2923

"Lawrence's 'Carbon' ": 2962
(Lawrence's Correspondence): 3767
"Lawrence's Country Revisited: The Erewash Valley": 3870
"Lawrence's Criticism of Melville": 4287
"Lawrence's Debt to Rudolph, Baron Von Hube": 3136
(Lawrence's Discovery of Australia as an Untouched World): 2306
(Lawrence's Dispute with His Contemporaries): 4038
"Lawrence's 'Error' about Hawthorne's Pearl": 2316
"Lawrence's 'Esoteric' Psychology: *Psychoanalysis and the Unconscious* and *Fantasia of the Unconscious*": 4137
(Lawrence's Flower-Presentation Technique in *The White Peacock* and *Sons and Lovers*): 3752
(Lawrence's Idea of Life in *The Virgin and the Gipsy*): 2605
"Lawrence's Imagistic Development in *The Rainbow* and *Women in Love*": 2546
"Lawrence's Influence on Eliot": 3666
"Lawrence's Laughter": 2858
(Lawrence's Love, Real Existence, Alienation, and Bond Themes Seen Mainly Through *Sons and Lovers*): 2106
"Lawrence's 'Male and Female Principles' and the Symbolism of 'The Fox' ": 3676
"Lawrence's Night-Letter on Censorship and Obscenity": 4270
"Lawrence's Non-Human Analogues": 2195
"Lawrence's Novels: Themes and Precedents": 3863
"Lawrence's 'Odour of Chrysanthemums': Isolation and Paradox": 3326
"Lawrence's Other Censor": 2167
"Lawrence's Philosophy in Subordinate Role": 3449
"Lawrence's Phoenix: An Introduction": 3873
(Lawrence's Pilgrimage of Love and Agony--*Look! We Have Come Through!*): 2140
(Lawrence's Poetics): 4512

D. H. LAWRENCE

"Lawrence's Poetry": 2321
(Lawrence's Poetry): 2274
"Lawrence's Pollyanalytic Esthetic for the Novel": 2782
"Lawrence's Quarrel with Tenderness": 2999
"Lawrence's *Rainbow*": 2197
"Lawrence's Republic": 2168
(Lawrence's Research for Human Existence Not by Visualization But by Blood-Contact--Return to the Innocent Stage of Adam and Eve in the Garden of Eden): 4438
(Lawrence's Revolt and His Flight from Civilization): 2212
"Lawrence's Romantic Values": 2920
"Lawrence's Romantic Values: *Studies in Classic American Literature*": 2920
"Lawrence's Sacred Fount: The Artist Theme of *Sons and Lovers*": 2368
"Lawrence's San Gaudenzio Revisited": 3073
"Lawrence's *Sea and Sardinia* Revisited": 2700
(Lawrence's Search for Paradise Lost): 2405
"Lawrence's Second 'Sun' ": 4576
"Lawrence's 'Snake' Not 'Sweet Georgian Brown' ": 2836
"Lawrence's Social Landscape": 3431
"Lawrence's 'Song of a Man Who Has Come Through' ": 2532
(Lawrence's Style): 2292
"Lawrence's *The Man Who Died*: The Heavenly Cock": 4523
"Lawrence's *The Rainbow*": 2108
"Lawrence's 'The Rocking-Horse Winner' ": 3057, 4035
"Lawrence's 'The Rocking-Horse Winner': A Dickensian Fable?": 3314
"Lawrence's 'The Shadow in the Rose Garden' ": 4202
"Lawrence's *The Virgin and the Gipsy* as Ironic Comedy": 3921
"Lawrence's *The White Peacock*: A Mutation of Pastoral": 3624
"Lawrence's 'Tickets, Please' ": 2191
(Lawrence's Travels): 2304, 2411
"Lawrence's Two Foxes: A Comparison of the Texts": 3981
"Lawrence's Use of Hardy in 'The Shades of Spring' ": 3876
"Lawrence's Use of 'Pecker' ": 3612
"Lawrence's Verse: More Editorial Lapses": 3618
"Lawrence's Vicious Art": 2779
(Lawrence's View of Tolstoy [I]): 2554
(Lawrence's View of Tolstoy [II]): 2555
"Lawrence's Views on Character": 2441
"Lawrence's Vision of Evil: The Power-Spirit in *The Rainbow* and *Women in Love*": 4609
"Lawrence's Voices": 2519
"Lawrence's Western Path: *Mornings in Mexico*": 2188
(Lawrence's Wife): 2743
"Lawrence's Women": 3637
(Lawrence's Women): 2549
"Lawrence's *Women in Love*": 3371
"Lawrence's *Women in Love*: Word to Image": 3440
"Lawrence's 'Women' Novel as a Film": 3630
"The Lawrencean Dilemma: A Study in Lawrence-Brewster Correspondence": 3330
"Lawrenceov obračun sa svojim suvreimenicima": 4038
(Lawrencian Studies): 4065
"Lawrentian Manias: A Review of Recent Studies of D. H. Lawrence": 4239
"A 'Lawrentian' Novel by Bernard Shaw": 3248
"The Lawrentian Philosophy of Communication: An Analysis of Selected Essays of D. H. Lawrence": 3686
"Lawrentian Places, I: A Chapel and a Hay-Hut among the Mountains: 1971": 4173
"Lawrentian Places, II: Eastwood Revisited": 4144
"Lawrentian Stillness": 4451
"The Leadership Novels of D. H. Lawrence": 3680
"Leavis Against Eliot": 4322
"Leavis, Lawrence and Porteus [sic] ": 2252
LEBENDE ANTIKE: SYMPOSIUM FÜR RUDOLF SÜHNEL: 3017
"Lecture critique d'un passage de *Women in Love*": 3048

"Lectures": 3251
"Lessing and Lawrence: The Battle of the Sexes": 4591
"Letter from London": 3172
"Una lettera inedita di D. H. Lawrence": 3084
"Letters and Documents of Jessie Chambers Wood": 3414
LETTERS FROM A PUBLISHER: MARTIN SECKER TO D. H. LAWRENCE AND OTHERS, 1911-1929: 3607
"Letters from Lawrence": 2352
LETTERS OF ALDOUS HUXLEY: 3328
"The Letters of D. H. Lawrence": 2222
"The Letters of D. H. Lawrence to Sallie and Willie Hopkin": 4178
THE LETTERS OF F. SCOTT FITZGERALD: 2392
LETTERS OF FORD MADOX FORD: 2638
LETTERS OF JAMES AGEE TO FATHER FLYE: 2198
"Letters to Koteliansky": 3023
(Lettie in The White Peacock): 3954
"Lettres Étrangères": 2202, 3028
(THE LEVELS OF BEING AND KNOWLEDGE AND THEIR RELATIONSHIP TO THE PROBLEM OF EVIL): 2201
"Liberated Classics": 3534
A LIBRARY OF LITERARY CRITICISM (MODERN BRITISH LITERATURE): 2352, 2885
"El lider fascista en la novela inglesa de nuestro tiempo": 2937
THE LIFE AND WORK OF FORD MADOX FORD: 2692
LIFE IN EDWARDIAN ENGLAND: 3273
THE LIFE OF BERTRAND RUSSELL: 4463
"The Life of D. H. Lawrence": 3199
"Life of Letters": 2451
THE LIFE OF THE NOVEL: 3916
"Lilies That Fester: THE LAST OF THE MOHICANS and 'The Woman Who Rode Away' ": 2487
THE LIMPING HERO: GROTESQUES IN LITERATURE: 3719
"The Line of a Life Made Clear": 2336

LINGUISTICS AND LITERARY STYLE: 2559
"A Link Between D. H. Lawrence's *The Trespasser* and *The Rainbow*": 2997
"The Listener's Book Chronicle": 2150, 2259, 2260
"The Literary Censorship in England": 2991
LITERARY CENSORSHIP: PRINCIPLES, CASES, PROBLEMS: 2189
(Literary Criticism of Lawrence): 2583
THE LITERARY CRITICS: A STUDY OF ENGLISH DESCRIPTIVE CRITICISM: 2347
"The Literary Faulkner: His Indebtedness to Conrad, Lawrence, Hemingway, and Other Modern Novelists": 2215
(The Literary Friendship of D. H. Lawrence and A. Huxley): 4124
(Literary Ghosts on the French Riviera): 2857
THE LITERARY IMPACT OF "THE GOLDEN BOUGH": 2461, 4230
THE LITERARY REBEL: 2757
"The Literary Scene": 3324, 3342
LITERARY STUDIES: HOMAGE TO DR. A. SIVARAMASUBROMONIA AIYER: 3754
(THE LITERARY WORLD OF LAWRENCE): 4404
"The Literati of the Four-letter Word": 2082
"Literature": 2354, 2534, 2600, 2830, 3286, 3350
"Literature and History--The Novel": 2175
LITERATURE AND RELIGION: VIEWS ON D. H. LAWRENCE: 3110, 3161, 3169, 3215, 3224, 3228, 3240
LITERATURE AND THE SIXTH SENSE: 3179
LITERATURE AND THEOLOGY: 3284
LITERATURE FOR COMPOSITION: 2682
LITERATURE IN ACTION: 3859
THE LITERATURE OF FIDELITY: 3855, 3856, 4452
LITTERS FROM ALOFT: PAPERS

DELIVERED AT THE SECOND CANADIAN JAMES JOYCE SEMINAR: 3668
" 'Little Living Myths': A Note on Lawrence's *Tortoises*": 3599
"Little Magazines in Australia": 2484
THE LITTLE PACKAGE: PAGES ON LITERATURE AND LANDSCAPE FROM A TRAVELING BOOKMAN'S LIFE: 2572
LIVES AND LETTERS: A HISTORY OF LITERARY BIOGRAPHY IN ENGLAND AND AMERICA: 2604
" 'Living Disintegration': A Scene from *Women in Love* Reinterpreted": 3278
THE LIVING PRINCIPLE: "ENGLISH" AS A DISCIPLINE OF THOUGHT: 4528
"Loerke as a Futurist--Some Modernistic Aspects in *Women in Love*": 4205
"London Letter": 2120
"London 1960: D. H. Lawrence oder purissimus penis (Kaiser Augustus über Horaz)": 2284
(London 1960: D. H. Lawrence or purissimus penis--Emperor Augustus on Horace): 2284
THE LONELY HUNTER: A BIOGRAPHY OF CARSON McCULLERS: 4459
THE LONELY VOICE: A STUDY OF THE SHORT STORY: 2430
(The Long Italian Journey of the Author of *Lady Chatterley*): 2309
A LONG TIME BURNING: THE HISTORY OF LITERARY CENSORSHIP IN ENGLAND: 3406
"The Longest Journey: D. H. Lawrence's *Phoenix*": 2277
"Lords of Life, Kings in Exile: Identity and Sexuality in D. H. Lawrence": 4525
"Lorensova koncepcija umetnosti, morala i romana": 2923
"Lorensova poetika": 4512
"Lorensovo traganje za izgubljenim rajem": 2405
"Lorenzo Mythistoricus: Studies in the Archetypal Imagination of D. H. Lawrence": 4108

LORENZO: D. H. LAWRENCE AND THE WOMEN WHO LOVED HIM: 4498
"*The Lost Girl*: D. H. Lawrence as a 'Dickens of the Midlands' ": 2398
"*The Lost Girl* Oboegaki": 2425
"*The Lost Girl* Shiron--Shudai to Gihô Oyobi Hyôka ni Tsuite": 2958
THE LOST IMAGE OF MAN: 2399
"Lost Paradise": 2536
"The Lost Trail: *The Plumed Serpent*": 2869
(A Lost Trend--Lawrence's Comic Spirit): 3958
(Louie, Miss Dissatisfaction): 3364
"Louie, Miss Incontentabile": 3364
"Love": 3551
"Love Among the Mannikins: *The Captain's Doll*": 3059
(Love and Conflict--Anna and Will): 4540
"Love and Courtship in the Novels of George Eliot, Thomas Hardy, and D. H. Lawrence: A Comparative Study": 4299
(Love and Isolation--On *Sons and Lovers*): 4602
(The Love and Life Ethics of D. H. Lawrence): 2736
"Love and Power: A Reconsideration of Sexual Politics in Lawrence": 4453
"Love and Society: MEASURE FOR MEASURE and Our Own Time": 2226, 2482
"Love and Solitude": 3941
(LOVE AND THE DIVINE): 2110
"Love and Three Generals: A Fable": 2705
(Love Ethic of D. H. Lawrence): 2090
"*Love* Is a Many-Splendored Thing": 3463
"Love, Law, and the Nature of Character": 4531
LOVE-HATE RELATIONS: A STUDY OF ANGLO-AMERICAN SENSIBILITIES: 4410
LOVE-HATE RELATIONS: ENGLISH AND AMERICAN SENSIBILITIES: 4410
"Il lungo viaggio italiano dell'autore di *Lady Chatterley*": 2309
"Lust for 'Art' ": 3526

INDEX OF TITLES OF SECONDARY WORKS

"The Lyric Short Story: The Sketch of a History": 3256
"Lyrical Elements in D. H. Lawrence's *The Rainbow*": 4393
LYTTON STRACHEY: A CRITICAL BIOGRAPHY, Vol. I: THE UNKNOWN YEARS (1880-1910): 3103
LYTTON STRACHEY: A CRITICAL BIOGRAPHY, Vol. II: THE YEARS OF ACHIEVEMENT (1910-1932): 3104
"M.'s Geheimnis. Unsere Neue Erzahlung: 'Der Fremdenlegionar' ": 4490
(M's Secret. Our New Story: "Introduction to MEMOIRS OF THE FOREIGN LEGION"): 4490
"Mabel Dodge Luhan: Sex as Politics": 2684
(MAIN WORKS OF ENGLISH LITERATURE, CONCISE COMMENTARIES AND INTERPRETATIONS): 2679
"A Major Miner Dramatist": 3081
THE MAJOR NOVELS OF D. H. LAWRENCE: 4229
"Major Polarities in the Shorter Fiction of D. H. Lawrence": 3229
" 'Making Another Lawrence': Frieda and the Lawrence Legend": 4476
"Making Lawrence More Lawrentian": 3115
"The Making of D. H. Lawrence's "The White Stocking' ": 4061
"The Making of 'The Prussian Officer': A Correction": 3690
"The Male as Principle in D. H. Lawrence's Fiction": 3683
"Male Relationships in the Work of D. H. Lawrence": 4047
"Man and Society: Lawrence's Subversive Vision": 3215
MAN IN THE MODERN NOVEL: 2512
"The Man Who Died": 3056
"*The Man Who Died*": 2394
(The Man Who Died--D. H. Lawrence): 3769
"*The Man Who Died* ni Tsuite (Shûkyôteki de Arukoto to Sono Hyôgen)": 3003
"The Man Who Lived": 2343
"A Man with Red Hair": 2734
"Manalive": 2102
"Männer mit roten Hosen": 2412
MANSIONS OF THE SPIRIT: 2987
A MANUAL TO ACCOMPANY "THE MODERN TRADITION: AN ANTHOLOGY OF STORIES": 3105
"The Manuscripts: Three Preliminary Drafts": 4396, 4575
A MAP OF MODERN ENGLISH VERSE: 3380
"The Marble and the Statue": 3124
"The Marble and the Statue: The Exploratory Imagination of D. H. Lawrence": 3124
MARK GERTLER: BIOGRAPHY OF A PAINTER, 1891-1939: 4025
"The Marquis on Trial": 2165
MASTER POEMS OF THE ENGLISH LANGUAGE: 2948
(Master Tales): 2657
MASTERS OF THE ENGLISH NOVEL: 2285
MAXIMS & APHORISMS FROM THE LETTERS OF D. H. LAWRENCE: 2513
(The Meaning and Structure of Paul's Quest in *Sons and Lovers*): 4560
"The Meaning of Lawrence": 3320
(A Meaning of Lawrence's Novels--from *Sons and Lovers* to *Women in Love*): 2983
"Meanwhile Back at the Ranch": 3557
"Meisternovellen": 2657
"Melville": 2628
"Melville's BILLY BUDD and Lawrence's 'The Prussian Officer': Old Adam and New": 4333
MEMOIRS OF LADY OTTOLINE MORRELL: A STUDY IN FRIENDSHIP, 1873-1915: 2421
MEMORIES: 3516
"Memories of D. H. Lawrence": 2282, 3867
MEMORIES OF FRIEDA LAWRENCE: 4469
"Men and Women in the Writings of David Herbert Lawrence and of Certain Contemporary Theologians: A Dialogue in Theology and Literature": 4005
"Men in Charge: A Review of *Women in Love*": 3439

(Men in Red Trousers): 2412
" 'Mentalized Sex' in D. H. Lawrence": 4597
"Merging–with Fish and Others": 4276
"*The Merry-Go-Round*": 4234, 4291
"*The Merry-Go-Round* at the Royal Court": 4040
"Mesmerising Lawrence": 3050
(The Messages and Limits of Lawrence's Art): 4521
"Metaphor and Metonymy in Modern Fiction": 4532
"The Metaphor of Apocalypse in the Novels of D. H. Lawrence": 4033
"Mexican *Machismo* in Novels by Lawrence, Sender, Fuentes": 3845
(Mexico as Seen by D. H. Lawrence): 2626
"El México visto por D. H. Lawrence": 2626
"Michinaru Sekai o Motomete–*Niji*": 2715
"Middleton Murry on Swift: 'The *nec plus ultra* of objectivity'?": 3321
"Minatori e anime superiori: conflitti famigliari e lotta delle classi nei teatro autobiografico di D. H. Lawrence": 4292
(Miners and Superior Souls: Family Conflicts and Class Struggle in D. H. Lawrence's Autobiographical Theatre): 4292
"The Miner's Son, Who Was 'No Gentleman' ": 2330
"Miriam ni Tsuite": 3167
THE MIRROR AND THE GARDEN: REALISM AND REALITY IN THE WRITINGS OF ANAIS NIN: 3723
A MIRROR FOR ANGLO-SAXONS: 2089
"A Misreading of Poe's 'Ligeia' ": 2161
"Il mito del Messico": 2840
"Mode and Development in D. H. Lawrence's Tales": 4101
THE MODERN AGE: 2153, 3315, 3324
MODERN ENGLISH LITERATURE: 3595
(THE MODERN ENGLISH LYRIC: INTERPRETATIONS): 2985
(THE MODERN ENGLISH NOVEL): 2796
(THE MODERN ENGLISH NOVEL: INTERPRETATIONS): 2716
"Modern Figures of Destiny: D. H. Lawrence and Frieda Lawrence": 3629
MODERN HEROISM: ESSAYS ON D. H. LAWRENCE, WILLIAM EMPSON, AND J. R. R. TOLKIEN: 2728, 4197
MODERN LITERARY PERSPECTIVISM: 3506
"Modern Literary Primitivism in the Writings of D. H. Lawrence and Other British Novelists": 2784
MODERN LITERATURE AND CHRISTIAN FAITH: 2177
"A Modern Man Obsessed by Time: A Note on 'The Man Who Loved Islands' ": 4424
"Modern Masters and Archaic Motifs of the Animal Poem": 4030
"The Modern Necessity": 2448
THE MODERN NOVEL: 2957
THE MODERN NOVEL IN BRITAIN AND THE UNITED STATES: 2470
MODERN POETRY: STUDIES IN PRACTICAL CRITICISM: 2377
THE MODERN SHORT NOVEL: 2752
MODERN SHORT STORIES: THE USES OF IMAGINATION: 2975
THE MODERN SPIRIT: ESSAYS ON THE CONTINUITY OF NINETEENTH AND TWENTIETH CENTURY LITERATURE: 3542
MODERN STORIES IN ENGLISH: 4557
THE MODERN TALENT: AN ANTHOLOGY OF SHORT STORIES: 2511
THE MODERN TRADITION: AN ANTHOLOGY OF SHORT STORIES: 3106
THE MODERN TRADITION: BACKGROUNDS OF MODERN LITERATURE: 2636
MODERN TRAGEDY: 2467
"Modern Writers: D. H. Lawrence": 2247

INDEX OF TITLES OF SECONDARY WORKS

DIE MODERNE ENGLISCHE LYRIK: INTERPRETATIONEN: 2985
DIE MODERNE ENGLISCHE ROMAN: 2796
DIE MODERNE ENGLISCHE ROMAN: INTERPRETATIONEN: 2716
MODERNS AND CONTEMPORARIES: NINE MASTERS OF THE SHORT STORY: 3037
THE MODEST ART: A SURVEY OF THE SHORT STORY IN ENGLISH: 3039
"La moglie di Lawrence": 2743
"Mollie Skinner and D. H. Lawrence": 2576
"Molly's 'Yes': The Transvaluation of Sex in Modern Fiction": 3095
"The Monomyth and Literary Criticism": 4568
(The Moon in D. H. Lawrence's Poetry): 2558
THE MORAL AND THE STORY: 2251
"Moralists and Mystics: Religion in the Modern British Novel": 4406
"Morality and Tradition in the English Novel, as Seen in the Relationship Between George Eliot and D. H. Lawrence": 3743
"Morality in the Novel: A Study of Five English Novelists: Henry Fielding, Jane Austen, George Eliot, Joseph Conrad, and D. H. Lawrence": 3150
"The Morality of D. H. Lawrence": 3228
"More Books": 2685
"More is Less": 3434, 3647
"*More Pansies* and *Last Poems*: Corrigenda Derived from MS Roberts E192": 3207
"*More Pansies* and *Last Poems*: Variant Readings Derived from MS Roberts E192": 3207
"Morel-Ke no Kattô o Megutte": 4520
THE MORTAL NO: DEATH AND THE MODERN IMAGINATION: 2518
"Moses Off the Mountain: Readings in Paul Valery and D. H. Lawrence": 4014
"The Mother in the Mind": 2348
"Mothers in Love--An Aspect of *Women in Love*": 4139
MOUNTAINS AND CAVERNS: SELECTED ESSAYS: 4206
MOVEMENTS IN ENGLISH LITERATURE 1900-1940: 4494
"Movies": 3568
"Mr. Gifford and D. H. Lawrence": 2144, 2156
"Mr. Rolf Gardiner, 'The English Neo-Nazi': An Exchange": 4293
"Muishiki no Jiga--*Shinda Otoko* o Chûshin ni": 4155
"Mujun to Shôsô no Hyôgen: *Women in Love*, Jinbutsu to Imêji": 2297
"The Multiplying of Entities: D. H. Lawrence and Five Other Poets": 3214
"Must Glenda Always Be So Neurotic?": 3705
"*Musuko to Koibito* ni Okeru Ai no Yukue": 4491
"*Musuko to Koibito* ni Okeru Niku to Kotoba--Sono 'Jogen' o Megutte no Ichikôsatsu": 4624
"*Musuko to Koibito* ni Okeru Shûkyô-sei": 4503
"*Musuko to Koibito* ni Okeru Shûkyô-teki Sokumen ni Tsuite (Paul no Motomeru 'Kami' no Imi o Megutte)": 4519
"*Musuko to Koibito* no Higeki--Morel-Fujin ni Mirareru Kikai-Bunmei ni yoru Hakaisei no Shiten yori": 4564
"*Musuko to Koibito* no Nakano Lawrence": 3001
"*Musuko to Koibito* no Okeru Tankyû no Imi to Kôzô": 4560
"*Musuko to Koibitotachi* o Chûshin to Shite Mita Lawrence no Ai to Jitsuzon to Sogai to Jyûtai": 2106
"The Mutual Flame: The Quest for Self-Hood in Relation to Form in the Later Novels of D. H. Lawrence": 3672
MY BELIEF: ESSAYS ON LIFE AND ART: 4329
MY BROTHER EVELYN AND OTHER PORTRAITS: 3014
MY BROTHER EVELYN AND OTHER PROFILES: 3014

(My Lawrence and Butler): 4561
MY LIFE AND TIMES, OCTAVE FOUR: 1907-1915: 2691
MY LIFE AND TIMES, OCTAVE FIVE: 1915-1923: 2833
MY LIFE AND TIMES, OCTAVE SIX: 1923-1930: 2967
MY LIFE AND TIMES, OCTAVE SEVEN: 1931-1938: 3141
MY LIFE AND TIMES, OCTAVE EIGHT: 1939-1946: 3352
"Mysterien vom Sex. D. H. Lawrences Essays über Liebe, Emanzipation und ähnliches": 3824
THE MYSTERIES OF IDENTITY: A THEME IN MODERN LITERATURE: 4525
(Mysteries of Sex: D. H. Lawrence's Essays on Love, Emancipation, and the Like): 3824
"Myth and Character: The Dialectic of Scapegoat and Reviving God": 4013
"Myth and Poetics: The Creation of a Cosmos": 4426
(Myth and Reality in D. H. Lawrence's *The Plumed Serpent*): 4371
(THE MYTH IN THE NEW WORLD: A STUDY ON AMERICAN MYTH CRITICISM): 3773
(The Myth of Mexico): 2840
(Myth-Making in Modern Prose Narrative: Joseph Conrad Compared with Joyce, Lawrence, and Faulkner): 3017
"Mythic Concepts in D. H. Lawrence": 4314
"Mythic Identification and Spatial Inscendence: The Cosmic Vision of D. H. Lawrence": 4610
"The Mythical Bases of *Women in Love*": 3208
(Mythical Elements in *The Trespasser*--D. H. Lawrence's World of Myth): 4226
"The Mythology of Friendship: D. H. Lawrence, Bertrand Russell, and 'The Blind Man' ": 3788
THE MYTHOLOGY OF IMPERIALISM: RUDYARD KIPLING, JOSEPH CONRAD, E. M. FORSTER, D. H. LAWRENCE, AND JOYCE CARY: 3785

DER MYTHOS IN DER NEUEN WELT. EINE UNTERSUCHUNG ZUM AMERIKANISCHEN MYTH CRITICISM: 3773
MYTHS AND TEXTS: STRATEGIES OF INCORPORATION AND DISPLACEMENT: 4013, 4425
"Narrated Monologue: Definition of a Fictional Style": 2777
THE NARRATIVE PATTERN IN ERNEST HEMINGWAY'S FICTION: 3766
(Narrative Techniques in the Novels of Aldous Huxley and David Herbert Lawrence): 2505
"The Natural Aristocrat in Letters": 2553
NATURAL SUPERNATURALISM: TRADITION AND REVOLUTION IN ROMANTIC LITERATURE: 3655
"The Naturalist Theology of D. H. Lawrence": 2820
"Nature and Fate in the Early Novels of D. H. Lawrence": 2867
(Nature and Man in *The White Peacock*): 4136
"Nature: God or a Creature of God?": 4549
(Nature in D. H. Lawrence's Literature): 2897
"Nature in the Poetry of D. H. Lawrence": 3533
THE NATURE NOVEL FROM HARDY TO LAWRENCE: 2763
NEGLECTED POWERS: ESSAYS ON NINETEENTH AND TWENTIETH CENTURY LITERATURE: 2107
"Never Trust the Editor": 2239
" 'New Blossoms of Me'--The Poetry of D. H. Lawrence": 3989
THE NEW CAMBRIDGE BIBLIOGRAPHY OF ENGLISH LITERATURE: 4022
"A New Collection of D. H. Lawrence Letters": 2246
"New Heaven and Earth: Lawrence's Transformations": 3965
NEW HEAVEN, NEW EARTH: THE VISIONARY EXPERIENCE IN LITERATURE: 3965
"New Light on Auden's THE ORATORS": 2995

INDEX OF TITLES OF SECONDARY WORKS

"New Movies": 3163
"The New Orthodoxy": 2115
THE NEW RADICALISM IN AMERICA (1889-1963): THE INTELLECTUAL AS A SOCIAL TYPE: 2684
" 'A New Show: The Politics of *Kangaroo*": 3645
"New Worlds for Old: The Apocalyptic Imagination, Science Fiction and American Literature": 3732
THE NEW YORK TIMES FILM REVIEWS: A ONE-VOLUME SELECTION: 3449
"A Newly Discovered Text of D. H. Lawrence's 'The Lovely Lady' ": 4487
"Nietzsche and the Novel of Cultural Crisis: A Study of Image and Idea in D. H. Lawrence and André Malraux": 4310
NIETZSCHE IN ENGLAND, 1890-1914: THE GROWTH OF A REPUTATION: 3634
"Nigenron no Yukue": 3366
(A Night Spent by Lady Chatterley): 2547
"*Niji* Izen-Igo: Beardsley no *Salome* wo Megutte": 4436
"*Niji* ni Tsuite": 3932
"*Niji* no Ketsumatsu to Symbol to Shite no Niji": 2984
"*Niji* no Ursula": 2109
"*Niji* to *Koisuru Onnatachi*--Shin naru Sei. Rakuen e no Michi": 3809
"Nikutai no Fukkatsu--*Chatterley-Fujin no Koibito*": 4170
"Nikutai to Sono Kage: D. H. Lawrence Oboegaki": 2345
"1910-Nendai no D. H. Lawrence": 2934
LES NIVEAUX DE L'ÊTRE ET LA CONNAISSANCE DANS LEUR RELATION AU PROBLÈME DU MAL: 2201
"No Defense for 'The Rocking-Horse Winner' ": 2372
"No raskršću realizma i simbolizma": 3988
"Non-British Setting in Twentieth-Century British Fiction": 4590
"The Non-Fiction Prose Writings of D. H. Lawrence": 2888

"The Normalcy of Suffering and Artistic Survival: Literature and Society": 4391
"Nostalgia for Sicily: The Fictional Modes of Giovanni Verga and D. H. Lawrence": 4011
(Not Just the Author of *Lady Chatterley*: Prose Works by D. H. Lawrence): 4612
"Note": 3608
"A Note about Frieda": 2287
"Note by D. M.": 2288
"A Note on D. H. Lawrence": 2924
(A Note on D. H. Lawrence [I]): 2463
(A Note on D. H. Lawrence [II]: A study of *The White Peacock*): 2593
(A Note on D. H. Lawrence [Part III]: On *Sons and Lovers*): 2749
"A Note on Editing *The Complete Poems*": 3175
(A Note on Lawrence [II]): 2065
(A Note on Lawrence [III]): 2365
(A Note on Lawrence [IV]): 2366
"A Note on Some Mythical Elements in Lawrence's *Women in Love*": 3208
"A Note on *Sons and Lovers* and Emerson's 'Experience' ": 4073
THE NOTEBOOKS OF DYLAN THOMAS: 2973
"Notes and Questions on D. H. Lawrence's *Sons and Lovers*": 2422
NOTES FOR AN EXHIBIT AT THE LAWRENCE RANCH, THE D. H. LAWRENCE FESTIVAL, TAOS, NEW MEXICO, 30 SEPTEMBER-4 OCTOBER 1970: 3577
"Notes on Current Books": 2429, 2712, 4082
(Notes on D. H. Lawrence [IV]--*Psychoanalysis and the Unconscious* and *Fantasia of the Unconscious*): 3639, 3640
(Notes on D. H. Lawrence [V]: An Analysis of *The Fox*): 3821
(Notes on D. H. Lawrence [VI]: A Letter by Jessie Chambers): 4428
"Notes on D. H. Lawrence and One Reader": 3168
NOTES ON D. H. LAWRENCE'S "SONS AND LOVERS": 4485

"Notes on D. H. Lawrence's *Studies in Classic American Literature*": 3197
"Notes on Eliot and Lawrence, 1915-1924": 4387
(Notes on *Lady Chatterley's Lover*): 2283
(Notes on Lawrence): 3370
(Notes on Lawrence's Plays: *Mrs. Holroyd, Touch and Go, David*): 2420
"Notes on the Literary Institutionalization of D. H. Lawrence: An Anti-Review of the Current State of Lawrence Studies": 2892
(Notes on *The Lost Girl*): 2425
"Notes on the Structure of *Women in Love*": 2873
"Notes on the Victorian Scene": 3343
"The Nottingham Festival D. H. Lawrence Exhibition, 1972": 4265
"La Nouvelle Vague Anglaise et Strindberg": 2353
"The Novel": 3906
THE NOVEL: 4489
THE NOVEL: A MODERN GUIDE TO FIFTEEN ENGLISH MASTERPIECES: 2383
"The Novel and the Life Standard": 2067
"The Novel and the Natural Man: Reality in Fiction Since Cervantes": 3238
"The Novel as a Metaphysical Statement: Lawrence's *The Rainbow*: 3447, 3677
THE NOVEL AS FAITH: THE GOSPEL ACCORDING TO JAMES, HARDY, CONRAD, JOYCE, LAWRENCE, AND VIRGINIA WOOLF: 4175
"The Novel as Prophecy: *Lady Chatterley's Lover* (1928)": 2251
"The Novel as Puritan Romance: A Comparative Study of Samuel Richardson, The Brontës, Thomas Hardy, and D. H. Lawrence": 2539
"The Novel as the Hole in the Wall: D. H. Lawrence's *Rainbow*": 3030
"The Novel Is the Book of Life: D. H. Lawrence and a Revised Version of Polymorphous Perversity": 2785
"The Novel Is the Book of Life: Illustration of Argument or Insight into Experience": 3884
THE NOVEL NOW: 3445
THE NOVEL OF THE FUTURE: 3166
(The Novel with Four Principal Characters: Studies on Character-Grouping in N. Hawthorne's THE BLITHEDALE ROMANCE, G. Eliot's DANIEL DERONDA, H. James's THE GOLDEN BOWL, and D. H. Lawrence's *Women in Love*): 3257
THE NOVELIST AT THE CROSSROADS AND OTHER ESSAYS ON FICTION AND CRITICISM: 3746
"Novelist on Stage": 2846
"Novels and Novelists": 4109
"Novels in Manuscript: An Exhibition from the Berg Collection, Part II (Conclusion)": 2646
"The Novels of D. H. Lawrence": 4133
THE NOVELS OF D. H. LAWRENCE: A SEARCH FOR INTEGRATION: 2880, 3216, 3806
"The Novels of Patrick White": 2386
"The Novels of Thomas Hardy and D. H. Lawrence: A Comparative Study": 2611
THE NOVELS OF WELLS, BENNETT, AND GALSWORTHY, 1890-1910: 3670
" 'Objects in the Powerful Light of Emotion' ": 3561
"Oboegaki Lawrence (II)": 2065
"Oboegaki Lawrence (III)": 2365
"Oboegaki Lawrence (IV)": 2366
OBSCENE: THE HISTORY OF AN INDIGNATION: 2284
"An Obscene Undertaking": 3631
"De l'obscénité en littérature": 3566
OBSCENITY AND PUBLIC MORALITY: CENSORSHIP IN A LIBERAL SOCIETY: 3054
OBSZÖN: GESCHICHTE EINER ENTRÜSTUNG: 2284
" 'Odour of Chrysanthemums' ": 3689
OEDIPUS IN NOTTINGHAM: D. H. LAWRENCE: 2348, 2466
"Of Lawrence and Love": 3501
(Of Obscenity in Literature): 3566
"Old Flames at the Ranch": 3714
"Old Folks at Home": 3213
"Old-Fashioned Gods: Eliot on

INDEX OF TITLES OF SECONDARY WORKS

Lawrence and Hardy": 3015
"Oliver & Constance / John Thomas & Lady Jane": 2771
"On a September Sunday--'38": 2834
(On *Aaron's Rod* by Lawrence): 2741
(On Appraisal Criteria of D. H. Lawrence's Poems): 4358
(On Birkin): 2541
(On D. H. Lawrence: A Love Affair in *The Trespasser*): 3336
(On D. H. Lawrence: His View of Man in *Sons and Lovers*): 4129
(On D. H. Lawrence: *The Virgin and the Gipsy*): 2717
(On D. H. Lawrence's *David*): 3021
(On D. H. Lawrence's Descriptions of 'the Moon' in His Novels): 4253
(On D. H. Lawrence's Drama *David*): 4563
(On D. H. Lawrence's Late Poems): 3409
(On D. H. Lawrence's *Psychoanalysis and the Unconscious* and *Fantasia of the Unconscious* [1]): 3811
(On D. H. Lawrence's *Psychoanalysis and the Unconscious* and *Fantasia of the Unconscious* [2]): 4002
(On D. H. Lawrence's Rananim [1]): 4168
(On D. H. Lawrence's Rananim [2]): 4383
(On D. H. Lawrence's *Sons and Lovers*): 3022, 3770, 4344
(On D. H. Lawrence's "The Prussian Officer"): 3829
(On D. H. Lawrence's View of Christianity): 3118
(On D. H. Lawrence's *Women in Love*): 2256
(On Descriptive Features of D. H. Lawrence's Nature Presentation): 4359
"On *Etruscan Places*": 4547
(On Lady Chatterley Again): 2080
(On *Lady Chatterley's Lover*): 2842
(On *Lady Chatterley's Lover*--Concerning the Paradox Between Isolation and Bond): 3992
"On Lawrence's 'Bavarian Gentians'": 2805
(On Lawrence's Leadership Novels-- From *Aaron's Rod* to *The Plumed Serpent*): 4169
(On Lawrence's *The Rainbow* [I] -- Some Characteristics of Style and Structure): 3830
(On Lawrence's *The Rainbow* [II] -- Some Characteristics of Style and Structure): 4027
(On Lawrence's *The Rainbow* [III] -- Some Characteristics of Style and Structure): 4252
"On Leavis and Lawrence": 3179
(On Miriam): 3167
ON MORAL COURAGE: 2281, 2282
(On "Necrophilous Characters" in *Women in Love*): 3395
(On New Democracy of D. H. Lawrence): 4167
(On *Psychoanalysis and the Unconscious* by D. H. Lawrence [I]): 4248
(On *Psychoanalysis and the Unconscious* by D. H. Lawrence [II]): 4620
ON REALISM: 4217
(On *Reflections on the Death of a Porcupine*): 2674
"On Resisting the Lawrence Course": 4172
(On *St. Mawr* Again [I]): 2521
(On *St. Mawr* Again [II]): 2817
"On Sincerity: From Wordsworth to Ginsberg": 2781
(On Some Appreciations of *St. Mawr*): 3227
(On *Sons and Lovers*): 2706, 2746
(On the Characteristics in the Composition of *Women in Love*): 2745
(On the Characters in *The Rainbow*-- Anton Skrebensky: A Soldier): 3831
(On the Characters in *The Rainbow*-- Tom Brangwen and "Darkness"): 3418
(On the Characters in *The Rainbow*-- Will Brangwen: "A Sick Foetus"): 3832
"On the Coal Face": 3165
(On the Consciousness of Death in D. H. Lawrence's Works): 2428
(On the Duality in D. H. Lawrence): 3344
(On the Episode of Annable): 2136
(On *The Fox*): 2099
(On *The Ladybird*): 2887
(On the Laurentian Conception of Love): 3985

(On the Lawrencian Translations of the Novels of G. Verga): 4432
(On *The Man Who Died*): 3008, 3416
(On "The Novel" of D. H. Lawrence): 4382
(On the Painting and Its Spirits of Lawrence): 4337
(On *The Plumed Serpent*): 3226, 4603
"On the Psychology of Erotic Literature": 3583
(On *The Rainbow*): 2134, 3932
(On *The Rainbow*: Love as It Is to Be Transcended): 2591
"On the So-Called Fascism of Some Modernist Writers": 3983
(On the Style of "Snake"): 3518
"On the Sun (II)--Three Types of Love in D. H. Lawrence's Literature": 2196
"On the Teaching of D. H. Lawrence: A Forum": 4468, 4483, 4533, 4569, 4607
(On the Trouble between the Morels): 4520
(On *The White Peacock*): 3112, 4583
(On This Side of Knowledge: Sin and the Roads to Salvation in the Lawrentian Ontology): 2201
(On This Side of Words--Some Notes towards the Poetry of D. H. Lawrence): 4360
100 GREAT BOOKS: MASTERPIECES OF ALL TIME: 2780
"One Man's Lawrence": 3446
"The Open Form in Fiction": 3944
"Oratoria on the Terraces": 3099
THE ORDINARY UNIVERSE: SOUNDINGS IN MODERN LITERATURE: 2627
"The Organic Self (A Study of Selected English Working-Class Fiction)": 4080
"Organic Wholeness of Being in Selected Novels of D. H. Lawrence": 3187
"Original Play by Lawrence Revived": 2986
"The Origins of Lawrence's 'Study of Thomas Hardy' ": 3424
"The Origins of 'The Christening' ": 3874

(Orpheus Resurrected--A Note on D. H. Lawrence): 4019
"The Orthodoxy of Enlightenment": 2115
"Orufeusu no Fukkatsu--D. H. Lawrence Oboegaki": 4019
(Ostrich Play: The Evolution of Erotic Literature): 2721
"Oswald Spengler and D. H. Lawrence": 3260
(The Other Ego of D. H. Lawrence--On "The Man Who Loved Islands"): 3649
"The Other Lawrence": 3493
(The Other Side of a Fairy Tale): 3145
"Ottoline": 4115
OTTOLINE AT GARSINGTON: MEMOIRS OF LADY OTTOLINE MORRELL, 1915-1918: 4374
OTTOLINE: THE LIFE OF LADY OTTOLINE MORRELL: 4472
"Our Literary Tocqueville": 2588
(Our Mad Civilization--On D. H. Lawrence's *The Virgin and the Gipsy*): 3968
"Out of the Closet": 2850
(Outcome of Dualism): 3366
"Outfoxing Lawrence: Novella into Film": 4152
(Pagan Enchantment in D. H. Lawrence): 2199
(Paganism in D. H. Lawrence's Literature): 2358
"Pagine di viaggio del romanziere dell'amore": 2240
"The Painted Tombs of Tarquinia": 3025
"The Painter of the Rainbow": 2562
PAINTING AND THE NOVEL: 4365, 4539
"The Paintings of D. H. Lawrence": 2272
"*The Paintings of D. H. Lawrence*": 2655
[*Paintings of D. H. Lawrence*, ed by Mervyn Levy]: 2946
PAN THE GOAT-GOD: HIS MYTH IN MODERN TIMES: 2540, 3356
THE PANZAIC PRINCIPLE: 3866
"The Paradox of Fulfillment: A Discussion of *Women in Love*": 4120

INDEX OF TITLES OF SECONDARY WORKS

"Part Three: Introduction": 2975
" 'Parties . . . Parties . . . Parties': Some Images of the 'Gay Twenties' ": 3868
PASSION AND THE PASSION: SEX AND RELIGION IN MODERN LITERATURE: 4523
A PASSIONATE PRODIGALITY: LETTERS TO ALAN BIRD FROM RICHARD ALDINGTON, 1949-1962: 4446
" 'The Passionate Struggle into Conscious Being': D. H. Lawrence's *The Rainbow*": 4272
THE PASSIVE VOICE: AN APPROACH TO MODERN FICTION: 2820
"Past and Present in D. H. Lawrence's 'A Fragment of Stained Glass' ": 3663
"A Past Master in the Hands of a Future One": 3603
"The Pastoral Novel: Studies in George Eliot, Thomas Hardy, and D. H. Lawrence": 3402
THE PASTORAL NOVEL: STUDIES IN GEORGE ELIOT, THOMAS HARDY, AND D. H. LAWRENCE: 3402, 3624, 3998, 4412
"Pastoral Patterns and Pastoral Variants in *Lady Chatterley's Lover*": 3998
"Pastoralism as Culture and Counter-Culture in English Fiction, 1800-1928": 3959
"Patrick White and Lawrence: A Contrast": 3560
(Pattern in the Style of D. H. Lawrence): 2702
PATTERNS OF EXPOSITION: 2783
PATTERNS OF LANGUAGE: PAPERS IN GENERAL, DESCRIPTIVE AND APPLIED LINGUISTICS: 2966
"Patterns of Stylistic Change in the Novels of D. H. Lawrence": 4355
"Paul Morel's Transfiguration in Love": 4580
"Paul no Higeki–*Musuko to Koibito*": 2561
(Paul's God: A Study of Religious Aspects in *Sons and Lovers*): 4519
"Pay Day for Young Lawrence": 3232
THE PENDULUM YEARS: BRITAIN AND THE SIXTIES: 3552
(PERSON AND PERSONAGE: THE NOVEL OF THE YEARS 1920 TO 1950): 3421
"Personification and De-Personification in D. H. Lawrence's Poetry": 2528
PERSONNE ET PERSONNAGE: LE ROMANESQUE DES ANNÉES 1920 AUX ANNÉES 1950: 3421
"The Pertinence of Modern Pastoral: The Three Versions of *Lady Chatterley's Lover*": 4240
"The Phallic Vision: D. H. Lawrence and V. V. Rozanov": 3024
"Le phénix et ses cendres (D. H. Lawrence)": 3062
"Philosophical Implications in Lawrence's *Women in Love*": 3789
(The Philosophy of Vitalism in D. H. Lawrence and A. Huxley: Influence and Parallels): 4123
(The Phoenix and Its Ashes [D. H. Lawrence]): 3062
"The Phoenix and the Desert Places": 3157
"The Phoenix: Its Use as a Literary Device in English from the Seventeenth Century to the Twentieth Century": 3955
"A Phoenix Out of the Ark": 3632
"Physical Trauma in D. H. Lawrence's Short Fiction": 4574
PIECES OF TIME: PETER BOGDANOVICH ON THE MOVIES: 2213
(Pilgrimage in Ideas--On Lawrence's *Aaron's Rod*): 4623
(Pioneer of a "Sex" Revolution: D. H. Lawrence on Pornography and Obscenity): 3718
"Pipings of Pan: D. H. Lawrence": 2988
"Places, Races and Faces": 2570
(Plants in D. H. Lawrence's Works and His Treatment of Them): 2680
"Plays in Performance": 3135
"The Plays of D. H. Lawrence": 4053
THE PLAYS OF D. H. LAWRENCE: 4587
"The Plays of D. H. Lawrence: Addenda": 2693
"Playwright Lawrence Takes the Stage in London": 3362

D. H. LAWRENCE

"*The Plumed Serpent* and the Eternal Paradox": 2462
"*The Plumed Serpent* and the Mexican Revolution": 4364
"*The Plumed Serpent* and the Reviving God": 4013
"*The Plumed Serpent* ni Tsuite": 4603
"*The Plumed Serpent*: Vision and Language": 2417
"Poe and 'The Rocking-Horse Winner' ": 2430
(The Poem "Snake," by D. H. Lawrence, and the "Elegía a un Moscardón Azul," by Damaso Alonso: An Admitted Influence and Two Different Sensibilities): 4182
"El Poema 'Snake,' de D. H. Lawrence, y la 'Elegía a un Moscardón Azul,' de Damaso Alonso: Una Influencia Admitida y Dos Sensibilidades Diferentes": 4182
"The Poems of D. H. Lawrence": 2145, 2171
"Poe's 'Ligeia' ": 2207
"La Poesía de Yeats, Lawrence y de la Mare": 4181
"Poesia di Lawrence": 2274
LA POESÍA INGLESA DEL SIGLO XX: 4181
"The Poet as Choreographer: Lawrence's 'The Blind Man' ": 3892
"Poet in a Fugitive Cause": 2577
"Poet without a Mask": 2146
"Poetic Fiction: A Study in Representation with Reference to Virginia Woolf and D. H. Lawrence": 4246, 4434
"The Poetic Image in D. H. Lawrence's *The Captain's Doll*": 3857
POETIC VISION AND THE PSYCHEDELIC EXPERIENCE: 3474
"The Poetical Spirit: Sacrality and the American West": 3235
"Poetry": 2601, 3975, 3976
"Poetry as a Way of Life": 3068
"Poetry for Pleasure": 3176
"The Poetry of D. H. Lawrence": 3565
"The Poetry of D. H. Lawrence: A Study of Technique and Development": 3854
"The Poetry of D. H. Lawrence: Extending Romanticism": 4571
"The Poetry of D. H. Lawrence--With a Glance at Shelley": 4146
THE POETRY OF RICHARD ALDINGTON: A CRITICAL EVALUATION AND AN ANTHOLOGY OF UNCOLLECTED POEMS: 4315
(The Poetry of Yeats, Lawrence, and de la Mare): 4181
POETRY TOWARDS NOVEL: 3804
A POET'S ALPHABET: REFLECTIONS ON THE LITERARY ART AND VOCATION: 3442
"Poets' Letters": 3329
POETS OF ACTION: 2955
"Point of View and Narrative Tone in *Women in Love*: The Portrayal of Interpsychic Space": 4394
(Point of View and Prose Style): 4373
"The Polarity of North and South: Germany and Italy in the Prose Works of D. H. Lawrence": 4366
POLITICAL FICTIONS: 3645
(Politics in Small Portions): 3004
"Politics of a Mystic": 3385
THE POLITICS OF TWENTIETH CENTURY NOVELISTS: 3778
"Politik in kleinen Dosen": 3004
"Pollyanalytics and Pedagogy: Teaching Lawrence's Short Fiction": 4468
"Portrait in Shadow: D. H. Lawrence": 3332
"Portrait of D. H. Lawrence, 1909-1910": 2223
"Portrait of Miriam: A Study in the Design of *Sons and Lovers*": 3148
"Portraits of the Artists as Young Men: Fact versus Fiction": 2279
"Poruke i granice Lorensove umetnosti": 4521
POSSIBILITIES: ESSAYS ON THE STATE OF THE NOVEL: 4045
"A Postscript": 2701
"Power and Isolation in the Political Novels of D. H. Lawrence": 4429
THE PRACTICE OF CRITICISM: 3182
(PRACTICE OF MODERN LANGUAGES INSTRUCTION): 2247
"Prancing in to a Purpose: Myths, Horses, and the True Selfhood in Lawrence's 'The Rocking-Horse Winner' ": 3410

PRAXIS DES NEUSPRACHLICHEN UNTERRICHTS: 2247
"The Precarious Prophets, Thomas Carlyle and D. H. Lawrence": 3982
"Preface": 2296, 2838, 3044, 3761
(Preface): 2656
PREFACES TO THE EXPERIENCE OF LITERATURE: 3005
(Preliminary Notes about Lawrence's Fiction): 3519
"The Presence of America in the Works of D. H. Lawrence": 3918
"The Present Recaptured: D. H. Lawrence and Others": 3042
"The Pressures of Love: Kinesthetic Action in an Early Lawrence Poem": 4097
PREVIOUS CONVICTIONS: 2222
THE PRIEST OF LOVE: A LIFE OF D. H. LAWRENCE: 4369
"Prima rappresentazione a Londra di una commedia di D. H. Lawrence": 2903
"The Primitive Element in the Fiction of D. H. Lawrence": 3415
PRIMITIVISM: 3851
"Primitivism and the Supernatural": 4550
(Primitivism in *Women in Love*): 3142
"Le primitivisme dans *Women in Love*": 3142
"Primitivistic Motifs in the Poetry of D. H. Lawrence": 2874
("The Princess" and "The Horse-Dealer's Daughter"): 3146
"Princess on a Rocking Horse": 3006
["*La Princesse*" et "*La fille du marchand de chevaux*"]: 3146
"The Prisoner of Sex": 3749
THE PRISONER OF SEX: 3749
"Private Eye": 2210
(The Problem of Love in Lawrence's Novels): 2551
"A Problem of Textual Transmission in the Typescripts of *Women in Love*": 4396
"Il problema dell'amore nei romanzi de Lawrence": 2551
THE PROBLEMATIC SELF: APPROACHES TO IDENTITY IN STENDHAL, D. H. LAWRENCE, AND MALRAUX: 4003

"Problems of Method": 3810
PROCEEDINGS OF THE NINTH CONGRESS OF THE AUSTRALASIAN UNIVERSITIES' LANGUAGE AND LITERATURE ASSOCIATION: 2538
THE PROFESSION OF ENGLISH LETTERS: 2580
"A Profile of John E. Baker, Jr., and His Lawrence Collection": 4288
"A Profile of John Martin and His Lawrence Collection": 4289
"A Profile of Mr. George Lazarus and His Lawrence Collection of Manuscripts and First Editions": 4085
"Prolegomena to the Poetry of D. H. Lawrence": 3407
"Prológo": 3451
(Prologue): 3451
"Prometheus in Straits": 3886
"Prophecy in the Novel": 4184
"The Prophetic Vogue of the Anti-Heroine": 2206
"The Prose of D. H. Lawrence": 2807
"Prose, Poetry, and Drama": 2468
"The Prose Style of D. H. Lawrence": 2128
PROSPECTUS AND NOTES FOR VOLUME EDITORS: "THE LETTERS OF D. H. LAWRENCE": 4044
THE PROTEAN SELF: DRAMATIC ACTION IN CONTEMPORARY FICTION: 4347
"A Protest by D. H. Lawrence": 4067
[*The Prussian Officer and Other Stories*]: 2609
" 'The Prussian Officer' and 'The Thorn in the Flesh' ": 3690
" 'The Prussian Officer': The Self Divided": 2390
PSEUDONYMS OF CHRIST IN THE MODERN NOVEL: 2300
THE PSYCHIC MARINER: A READING OF THE POEMS OF D. H. LAWRENCE: 3559
(A Psychoanalytical Study of D. H. Lawrence's *The Fox*): 4542
"Psychological Dissociation in the Victorian Novel": 3627
"The Psychology of Regression in D. H. Lawrence's 'The Blind Man' ": 2970

"The Psychology of the Uncanny in Lawrence's 'The Rocking-Horse Winner' ": 2694
"Publisher's Note": 3908, 3909
THE PURE GAMBLE: 4363
"The Purest and Most Perfect Form of Play: Some Novelists and the Dance": 3889
"Il puritano Lawrence": 2552
"Pussum, Minette, and the Africo-Nordic Symbol in Lawrence's *Women in Love*": 2373
"Putevi suvremenog engleskog romana": 2268
"Quartet of Soloists": 3584
(Quest for a New Human Relationship--A Study of *The Plumed Serpent*): 4026
"The Quest for Being: D. H. Lawrence and Hermann Hesse": 4484
THE QUEST FOR LOVE: 2662
"The Quest for Paradise in the Novels of D. H. Lawrence": 3498
"The Quest for Symbol and Myth": 2919
"The Quest for the Self: D. H. Lawrence's *The Rainbow*": 2221
"The Quester Hero: A Study of Creative Evolution in the Fiction of D. H. Lawrence": 2634
"The Question of the Relationships between the Painting and Written Works of D. H. Lawrence": 2699
"A Question of Tone: Some Problems in Autobiographical Writing": 2661
"Quetzalcoatl Versus D. H. Lawrence's *Plumed Serpent*": 3233
(Quickening of Life and Death in *The White Peacock*): 4221
"The Radicalism of *Lady Chatterley's Lover*": 2771
"*The Rainbow* and D. H. Lawrence's Reputation of Sex Tragedy": 3270
"*The Rainbow* and Fra Angelico": 4365
"*The Rainbow* and 'Otherness' ": 4260
"The Rainbow and the Arch": 3224
"*The Rainbow* and the Bible": 2639
"*The Rainbow*: Fiddle-Bow and Sand": 2086
"*The Rainbow* ni Okeru Byôshahô (D. H. Lawrence no Gengo ni Taisuru Shisei)": 2823
"*The Rainbow* ni Okeru D. H. Lawrence no Shisô": 2548
"*The Rainbow* ni Tsuite": 2134
"*The Rainbow* no Characters ni Tsuite--Heishi: Anton Skrebensky": 3831
"*The Rainbow* no Characters ni Tsuite--Tom Brangwen to 'Darkness' ": 3418
"*The Rainbow* no Characters ni Tsuite--Will Brangwen: 'A Sick Foetus' ": 3832
"*The Rainbow* no Kôzô Imeiji no Hassô Oyobi Sakusô to Tenkai": 2298
"*The Rainbow* Prosecution": 3271
(*The Rainbow* Reconsidered): 3800
"*The Rainbow* Saikô": 3800
"Rammel": 2677
"Rananim no Yume": 3576
"Re: 'D. H. Lawrence's Appraisal of Jesus.' (A Response to William E. Phipps)": 3725
THE REACTIONARIES: YEATS, LEWIS, POUND, ELIOT, LAWRENCE: A STUDY OF THE ANTI-DEMOCRATIC INTELLIGENTSIA: 2804
"A Reading of 'A Poem of Friendship,' a Chapter in Lawrence's *The White Peacock*": 3496
READING PROSE FICTION: 2579
READING THE SHORT STORY: 3234
READING, WRITING, AND RHETORIC: 2947
(Readings): 3251
READINGS IN MODERN FICTION: 2486
THE REAL FOUNDATIONS: LITERATURE AND SOCIAL CHANGE: 2226, 2482, 4057
" 'Real Thinking': Lawrence and Cézanne": 2990
"Realism in the Novel": 3507
"Realism Versus Symbolism: The Double Patterning of *Sons and Lovers*": 3988
(Reality and Dream in *The Trespasser*): 4312
THE REALM OF FICTION: SIXTY-ONE SHORT STORIES: 2652
RE-APPRAISALS: SOME COMMON-

INDEX OF TITLES OF SECONDARY WORKS

SENSE READINGS IN AMERICAN LITERATURE: 2397
(Reason and Instinct): 3774
A REASSESSMENT OF D. H. LAWRENCE'S "AARON'S ROD": 4263
"Recent Books on Modern Fiction: British": 3268
"Reception Honors D. H. Lawrence Festival Panelists as Exhibition Opens": 3588
(Reconsideration of *The Man Who Died*): 4435
"Recurrence as a Narrative Technique in *The Rainbow*": 4593
"Redemptive Snobbishness in Nietzsche, Lawrence, and Eliot": 3400
"Reductive Energy in *The Rainbow*": 3279
THE REEF AND OTHER POEMS: 3792
"Reflections of Lawrence": 2723
"Reflections on Allen Ginsberg as Poet": 3372
"Reflections on Professor Wellek's Concept of Realism": 2250
"Reflections on the Final Volume of THE OXFORD HISTORY OF ENGLISH LITERATURE": 2688
RÉFLEXIONS ET DIRECTIVES POUR L'ÉTUDE DE D. H. LAWRENCE: "WOMEN IN LOVE": 3433, 3490
"Refracted Love": 3125
REFRACTIONS: ESSAYS IN COMPARATIVE LITERATURE: 2688, 2827
REGGIE: A PORTRAIT OF REGINALD TURNER: 2754
"Regina v. Penguin": 2325, 2326, 2327
"Regina v. Penguin Books Ltd.: An Undisclosed Element in the Case": 2340
"La regione e l'istinto": 3774
"Rehearsal Logbook": 3094
"The Relation of D. H. Lawrence's Thought to His Prose Style Up to 1916, Stylistic and Narrative Technique in the Early Novels of D. H. Lawrence": 4536
"The Relationship between Social Context and Individual Character in the Naturalist Drama, with Special Reference to Chekov, D. H. Lawrence and David Storey": 4407
(A Release from Bondage--On Lawrence's *Sons and Lovers*): 4251
"The Release: The First Period": 2624
RELIGION IN MODERN ENGLISH DRAMA: 2181
(The "Religions" in *Sons and Lovers*): 4503
(Religious Elements in D. H. Lawrence's "The Shadow in the Rose Garden"): 3009
RELIGIOUS TRENDS IN ENGLISH POETRY, Vol. V: 1880-1920: GODS OF A CHANGING POETRY: 2241
RELIGIOUS TRENDS IN ENGLISH POETRY, Vol. VI: 1920-1965, VALLEY OF DRY BONES: 3074
"The Religious Vision of D. H. Lawrence": 2158
(Remarks on the Lawrencean Sensibility): 3069
"Remarques sur la sensibilité Lawrencienne": 3069
(A Remembrance from Spotorno): 3656
RENAISSANCE AND MODERN ESSAYS: PRESENTED TO VIVIAN DE SOLA PINTO IN CELEBRATION OF HIS SEVENTIETH BIRTHDAY: 2787, 2826, 2852
"Replies": 4258
"A Report on the Final Manuscript": 2740
"The Reputation of D. H. Lawrence: 1912-1960": 2774
(The Resurrection of the Body–*Lady Chatterley's Lover*): 4170
"Retreat into Wilderness: A Study of the Travel Books of Five Twentieth-Century British Novelists": 4573
"Return to Alexandria: Lawrence Durrell and Western Narrative Tradition": 2582
"Revelation and Evolution: A Neglected Dimension of the Short Story": 4096
THE REVERENT DISCIPLINE: ESSAYS IN LITERARY CRITICISM AND CULTURE: 2141, 2718, 2852, 4387, 4388

"Reviews": 2237, 2629, 2765, 3376, 3748, 3826, 3840, 3915, 3949
(Reviews): 3034, 3691, 3879
"Reviews and Comment": 2729
"Revisions in Lawrence's 'Wedding Morn' ": 3361
"Revolution and the Ancient Literature of Mexico, For D. H. Lawrence and Antonin Artaud": 3862
(A Revolutionary of the Theatre, D. H. Lawrence. A London Rediscovery after More than Fifty Years): 3072
"Revolutionary Resurrection: D. H. Lawrence": 4433
"Rex Reed at the Movies": 3589
THE RHETORIC OF FICTION: 2072
THE RHETORIC OF NO: 3479
"The Rhetoric of the Confession: Essays in Theory and Analysis": 4218
"The Rhetoric of Travel: The Example of *Sea and Sardinia*": 3411
"Rhetorical Analysis": 4461
"A Rhetorical Criticism of D. H. Lawrence based upon the Master Tropes of Kenneth Burke": 4530
"Rhythm and Meaning in Poetry: D. H. Lawrence's 'Snake' ": 3242
"Rhythm as Form in Lawrence: 'The Horse Dealer's Daughter' ": 3950
"Rhythm in D. H. Lawrence's Short Stories": 3140
"The Rhythm of Perfection: A Study and Reappraisal of D. H. Lawrence's 'Leadership Novels'--*Aaron's Rod, Kangaroo*, and *The Plumed Serpent*": 4095
RICHARD ALDINGTON: AN INTIMATE PORTRAIT: 2418, 2678
"Richard Aldington in His Last Years": 2418
"Un ricordo da Spotorno": 3656
"Rider Haggard's SHE: An Archetypal 'History of Adventure' ": 3926
"The Ritual Corn Harvest Scene in *The Rainbow*": 4046
"The Ritual of Becoming: A Study of the Short Stories of D. H. Lawrence": 4156
"The Ritual of Love: A Study of Symbolic Technique in D. H. Lawrence's Shorter Fiction": 3262

"Ritual Scenes in *The Rainbow*": 2423
"The River and the Marsh: The Interdependence between the Public and Private Aspects of Life in the Novels of D. H. Lawrence, with Special Reference to *The Rainbow, Women in Love, Kangaroo,* and *Lady Chatterley's Lover*": 3654
RIVER OF DISSOLUTION: D. H. LAWRENCE AND ENGLISH ROMANTICISM: 3278, 3279
"La rivolta di Lawrence e la fuga dalla civiltà": 2212
ROADS TO CONSCIOUSNESS: 4362
"*The Rocking-Horse Winner*": 4390
" 'The Rocking-Horse Winner': A Modern Myth": 2524
" 'The Rocking-Horse Winner' and THE GOLDEN BOUGH": 4308
" 'The Rocking-Horse Winner' as Cinema": 4361
"*The Rocking-Horse Winner*: Film as Parable": 4036
(Rocks and Minerals in D. H. Lawrence's Poetry): 2138
"Rogosu to Nikutai no Bunri--D. H. Lawrence no *Shinda Otoko* Ron": 3969
"Romansijerska tehnika D. H. Lawrencea": 2730
"Romansijerski eksperiment D. H. Lawrencea": 4402
LE ROMANTISME ANGLO-AMÉRICAIN: MÉLANGES OFFERTS À LOUIS BONNEROT: 3696
RORENSU BUNGAKU NO SEKAI: 4404
"Rorensu ni okeru Kyûshinteki-Shikô to Sono Hyôgen": 4385
RUN IT DOWN THE FLAGPOLE: BRITAIN IN THE SIXTIES: 3552
"Running Off with Lawrence": 2925
"Ruskin, Lawrence, and Gothic Naturalism": 3628
"The 'S' Curve: Persephone to Pluto": 2639
"Sacrificial Practice in Primitive Religion": 4551
THE SADDEST STORY: A BIOGRAPHY OF FORD MADOX FORD: 3757

INDEX OF TITLES OF SECONDARY WORKS

"*St. Mawr* and the Search for Community": 4018
"*St. Mawr*: Between Degeneration and Regeneration": 4581
"*St. Mawr* no Hyôka": 2403
"*St. Mawr* no Hyôka o Megutte": 3227
"*St. Mawr* Sairon (I)": 2521
"*St. Mawr* Sairon (II)": 2817
"Sandy's Week": 3154
"Sanity, Madness and *Women in Love*": 4618
"The Santa Fe Gadfly": 2522, 2523
"Satire as a Form of Sympathy: D. H. Lawrence as a Satirist": 2787
"The Savage God: Conrad and Lawrence": 3191
THE SAVAGE IN LITERATURE: 4598
"Scene and Symbol: Changing Mode in the English Novel from George Eliot to Joyce": 2936
SCENE AND SYMBOL FROM GEORGE ELIOT TO JAMES JOYCE: STUDIES IN CHANGING FICTIONAL MODE: 2936, 3310
"Scenic Construction and Rhetorical Signals in Hardy and Lawrence": 4594
"Schemata and Spontaneity: An Approach to Critical Activity, and to the Critical Writings of D. H. Lawrence": 2921
"Scholars Are 'Lovers' Of Lady Chatterley": 4535
"Scholars Honor D. H. Lawrence Here": 3606
"Schopenhauer and D. H. Lawrence": 3933
"Schopenhauer and D. H. Lawrence on Sex and Love": 4495
"Schopenhauer, Hardy and Lawrence: Toward a New Understanding of *Sons and Lovers*": 4274
"Schwebezustand": 3043
SCIENCE AND THE SHABBY CURATE OF POETRY: ESSAYS ABOUT THE TWO CULTURES: 2648
" 'Screaming in Pentecost' ": 3161
"Screen: 'Virgin and the Gypsy' Opens": 3450

SCRITTORI INGLESI E AMERICANI: SAGGI, NOTE E VERSIONI: 2478
"Sculptural Character in Lawrence's *Women in Love*": 4516
"*Sea and Sardinia*": 3827
"The Search for Integration in the Novels of D. H. Lawrence": 2880
"A Search for Love": 3341
"The Search for Manhood in D. H. Lawrence's *Sons and Lovers*": 4012
THE SEARCH FOR THE ETRUSCANS: 4236
"Searcher for Atlantis": 2162
SEASON OF YOUTH: THE BILDUNGSROMAN FROM DICKENS TO GOLDING: 4273
(Seclusion and Resurrection: The Development of a Theme in D. H. Lawrence's Last Short Stories): 3147
"The Second Art of D. H. Lawrence": 2565
"The Second Coming of Pan: A Note on D. H. Lawrence's 'The Last Laugh' ": 3035
"The Second Lady Chatterley": 4207
"A Second Phoenix": 3038
SECOND THOUGHTS: REFLECTIONS ON LITERATURE AND ON LIFE: 2124
"The Secret of *The Trespasser*--Traced in Siegmund's Tragedy": 4378
THE SECRET SHARER AND OTHER GREAT STORIES: 3348
" 'Secret Sin': Lawrence's Early Verse": 4584
"Sei no Heisoku--'Shima o Aishita Otoko' Kara": 2952
"Sei no Shôka (*Shinda Otoko* o Chûshin ni)": 3966
"Seksualno jevandeje po D. H. Lorensu": 3775
SELECTED LETTERS: 2641, 3616
SELECTED LETTERS OF DYLAN THOMAS: 2886
SELECTED LETTERS OF MALCOLM LOWRY: 2690
THE SELECTED LETTERS OF ROBINSON JEFFERS, 1897-1962: 3113
"Self-Encounter and the Unknown Self: *Sons and Lovers*": 3216

D. H. LAWRENCE

(The Semantic Universe of D. H. Lawrence's *The Rainbow*): 4377
"The Sense of Reality in the Work of D. H. Lawrence": 2926
(The Separation of the Logos from the Body--On D. H. Lawrence's *The Man Who Died*): 3969
(Serpent, Moon, and Symbolism in D. H. Lawrence): 4102
"Sex and Language: Obscene Words in D. H. Lawrence and Henry Miller": 2596
"Sex, Censorship, and D. H. Lawrence": 3104
"The Sex Mysticism of D. H. Lawrence": 2224
"The Sex Uproar": 2711
(The Sexual Gospel of D. H. Lawrence): 3775
"Sexual Ideas in the Films of D. H. Lawrence": 3776
SEXUAL POLITICS: 3563
THE SEXUAL REVOLUTION IN MODERN AMERICAN LITERATURE: 3711
THE SEXUAL REVOLUTION IN MODERN ENGLISH LITERATURE: 4093
(Sexual Vitalism): 2766
"Sexuality and Social Critique in the Novels of D. H. Lawrence, 1915-1922": 4442
"Sexuality in Literature: *Lady Chatterley's Lover*": 4452
" 'The Shades of Spring' ": 3876
"Shakespeare and D. H. Lawrence: Two Portraits of the Hero": 3151
SHAKESPEARE IN A CHANGING WORLD: 2226, 2482
"Shakespeare, Lawrence and Sexual Freedom": 2226, 2482
SHAKESPEARE, SPENSER, DONNE: 2266
"The Shape of a History: Eliot, Hardy, and Lawrence": 4538
THE SHAPE OF FICTION: BRITISH AND AMERICAN SHORT STORIES: 2940
"Shelley or Schiller? A Note on D. H. Lawrence at Work": 2243
"The Shepherdess in the City": 4341
SHERWOOD ANDERSON: 2477

"Shi to Bôkyaku--*Women in Love* kara 'The Ship of Death' e": 4380
"The Shift from a Romantic to a Primitive View of Life in D. H. Lawrence, with Particular Reference to Differences in the Language of *The Rainbow, Women in Love,* and *The Plumed Serpent*": 3436
"Shijin Lawrence to Girisha Shinwa": 2313
"Shijin Lawrence to Shi (Chû)": 2981
"Shijin Lawrence to Shi (Ge I)": 4381
"Shijin Lawrence to Shi (Jô)": 2848
"Shijin Lawrence to Tsuki": 2558
"Shinda Musuko to Uchû no Rizumu": 4599
"*Shinda Otoko* ni Tsuite": 3008, 3416
"*Shinda Otoko* Saikô": 4435
"*Shinnyusha* ni Okeru Genjitsu to Yume": 4312
"*Shinnyusha* ni Okeru Shi to Sei": 4415
"*Shinnyusha* no Wagnerteki Yôso o Megutte": 4441
"Shinwa to Genjitsu no Hazama--D. H. Lawrence *Tsubasa Aru Hebi*": 4371
"*Shirokujaku* ni Okeru Ambivalence no Mondai": 4250
"*Shirokujaku* ni Okeru Sei no Yakudô to Shi": 4221
"*Shirokujaku* ni Okeru Shizen to Ningen": 4136
"*Shirokujaku* no Jinbutsu o Megutte-- Cyril Beardsall o Chûshin ni": 4254
"*Shirokujaku* no Kôsatsu--Lettie o Chûshin ni": 3954
"*Shirokujaku* Shiron": 4583
SHISO NO BOKEN: RORENSU NO SHOSETSU: 4437
"Shisô no Henreki--Lawrence *Aaron no Tsue* Ron": 4623
"Shisô-Kôzô to Paragraph-Kôzô--Lawrence to Woolf": 4372
"Shiten to Buntai o Megutte": 4373
"Shôdô to Ittaisel--*Lady Chatterley's Lover* ni Tsuite (1)": 4334
"Shojo to Jipushi--Hahaoya no Botsuraku": 4606
"Shokubutsu yori Mita Lawrence no Sakufû--*The White Peacock* to

INDEX OF TITLES OF SECONDARY WORKS

Sons and Lovers o Chûshin ni": 3752
SHORT FICTION: A CRITICAL COLLECTION: 3307
THE SHORT FICTION OF D. H. LAWRENCE: 4101
"A Short Guide to D. H. Lawrence Studies": 2788
SHORT STORIES: A STUDY IN PLEASURE: 2137
SHORT STORIES: CLASSIC, MODERN, CONTEMPORARY: 2954
(The Short Stories of D. H. Lawrence): 2664
THE SHORT STORY: AN INDUCTIVE APPROACH: 2963
THE SHORT STORY: CLASSIC AND CONTEMPORARY: 2828
"Shorter Reviews": 3317
"Shôsetsu *Niji* ni Okeru Ursula no Seichô": 2953
"Shôsetsu no Kôzô to Sono Kaishaku-- D. H. Lawrence no Baai": 4368
"Shôsetsu wa ika ni Owaru ka? D. H. Lawrence no Shôsetsu to 'Kaishin' ": 3346
"The Significance of the Death of the Fox in D. H. Lawrence's *The Fox*": 3083
" 'Silence' in D. H. Lawrence": 2902
"Sin, Obedience and Duty: The English Teacher and Moral Values": 4050
"Sincerity and Poetry": 2781
"The Single Green Light and the Splendid and Terrible Spectrum: A Study of the Secular Romance Quest in the Novels of Thomas Hardy and D. H. Lawrence": 4231
"Singularity of Two; The Plurality of One": 2769
"Sir Richard Burton and D. H. Lawrence": 4236
THE SITUATION OF THE NOVEL: 3437
"Slabs of Slate": 2589
"Snake": 2444
" 'Snake: A Moment of Consciousness": 2229
"Sobre la lectura de *Lady Chatterley's Lover*": 2283
"Social and Personal Tragedy: Tolstoy and Lawrence": 2467
"The Social and Political Ideas of D. H. Lawrence": 3657
"The Social Architecture of 'The Rocking-Horse Winner' ": 4408
THE SOCIAL CONTEXT OF MODERN ENGLISH LITERATURE: 3675
"Social Criticism in the Novels of D. H. Lawrence": 3210
SOCIAL PATTERNS IN AUSTRALIAN LITERATURE: 3764
"Social Thought": 3974
"Society and Compassion in the Novels of D. H. Lawrence": 3091
"Sociologia e ideologia della classe operaia in *Touch and Go* di D. H. Lawrence": 3878
(Sociology and Ideology of the Working Class in D. H. Lawrence's *Touch and Go*): 3878
THE SOCIOLOGY OF LITERATURE: 3810
"Solipsism and Death in D. H. Lawrence's Late Works": 2776
"Solitary Confinement: A Study of D. H. Lawrence's Early Fiction": 4151
(Solitude in D. H. Lawrence): 2816
SOME COMMENTS ON THE VERSE OF D. H. LAWRENCE: 3207, 3398, 3399, 3617, 3620
(Some Features of D. H. Lawrence's Style in His Second Phase): 2847
"Some Letters of Edwin Muir": 2841
SOME MODERN WRITERS: ESSAYS AND FICTION BY CONRAD, DINESAN, LAWRENCE, ORWELL, FAULKNER, AND ELLISON: 3796
SOME MYTHICAL ELEMENTS IN ENGLISH LITERATURE: 2174
"Some New Volumes of Lawrence's Letters": 3762
(Some Notes on *Apocalypse*): 4166
"Some Psychodynamics in *Sons and Lovers*: A New Look at the Oedipal Theme": 4389
(Some Remarks on Two Scenes of *Aaron's Rod*): 4398
"Son and Lover": 3351
SON AND LOVER: THE YOUNG D. H. LAWRENCE: 4457
SON AND LOVER: THE YOUNG

LAWRENCE: 4457
(The Son Who Died in the Rhythm of the Universe): 4599
"Sons and Lovers": 2869, 3997
"SONS AND LOVERS": A CRITICAL COMMENTARY: 3389
(*Sons and Lovers* and Its Foreword): 4624
"*Sons and Lovers* as Bildungsroman": 4269
"*Sons and Lovers*/D. H. Lawrence": 2780
"SONS AND LOVERS" (D. H. LAWRENCE): 2942
(*Sons and Lovers*: How Does Paul's Love Go?): 4491
"*Sons and Lovers* kara *Women in Love* e (Shi no Gutaitekina Kankaku ni Mukatte)": 2742
"*Sons and Lovers* Kenkyû (1)": 3633
"*Sons and Lovers* Kenkyû (2)": 3812
"*Sons and Lovers* ni Okeru Buntai": 2557
"*Sons and Lovers* ni Tsuite": 2706, 2746
"SONS AND LOVERS": NOTES: 2731
"*Sons and Lovers*: Novel to Film as a Record of Cultural Growth": 4032
"*Sons and Lovers* or The Sin Against the Holy Ghost": 3189
"*Sons and Lovers*: The Archetypal Dimensions of Lawrence's Oedipal Tragedy": 3927
"*Sons and Lovers*: The Artist as Savior": 2512
"*Sons and Lovers*: The Omniscient Narrator": 2862
"*Sons and Lovers*: The Search for Form": 2423
"*Sons and Lovers*: The Search for Freedom--An Un-Freudian Appreciation": 3943
"Sons, Lovers, and Mothers": 2263
A SOUL IN THE QUAD: 2312, 3367, 3368
"Southwest Classics Reread: *The Plumed Serpent*, by D. H. Lawrence": 3780
SOUTHWEST CLASSICS: THE CREATIVE LITERATURE OF THE ARID LANDS, ESSAYS ON THE BOOKS AND THEIR WRITERS: 3779
SOUTHWESTERN BOOK TRAILS: A READER'S GUIDE TO THE HEARTLAND OF NEW MEXICO AND ARIZONA: 2435
SPEAKING TO EACH OTHER: ESSAYS: 2519
"Speech, Theater and Dance": 2876
"Spenser and the Allegorists": 2266
(The Spirit of Conquest): 2971
"Spirit of Place and *Genius Loci*: D. H. Lawrence and Rolf Gardiner": 4346
"The Spirit of the Lawrence Women: A Posthumous Memoir": 2891
"Spirited Creatures": 3430
"Stage Sons, Stage Lovers": 2868
STEINBECK AND D. H. LAWRENCE: FICTIVE VOICES AND THE ETHICAL IMPERATIVE: 3911
STIGMA: THE EXPERIENCE OF DISABILITY: 2770
"Die Stilentwicklung im Werke von D. H. Lawrence": 3299
DIE STILENTWICKLUNG IM WERKE VON D. H. LAWRENCE: 3299
THE "STILL POINT": THEME AND VARIATIONS IN THE WRITINGS OF T. S. ELIOT, COLERIDGE, YEATS, HENRY JAMES, VIRGINIA WOOLF, AND D. H. LAWRENCE: 2224
"The Stockings Are Rough but They Haven't Run": 2494
STORIA DELLA LETTERATURA INGLESE: 2573
STORIES FROM SIX AUTHORS: 2875
THE STORY AT WORK: AN ANTHOLOGY: 2436
THE STORY-SHAPED WORLD: FICTION AND METAPHYSICS: SOME VARIATIONS ON A THEME: 4615
"The Strange Case of Dr Leavis and Mr Lawrence": 2322
"The 'Strange Reality of Otherness': D. H. Lawrence's Social Attitudes": 3947
"Strange Textures of Vision: A Study of the Significance of Mannered

INDEX OF TITLES OF SECONDARY WORKS

Fictional Techniques in Six Selected Novels of D. H. Lawrence, William Faulkner, and Patrick White, Together with a Theoretical Introduction on 'The Novel of Vision' ": 4200

(A Stranger's Reality: An Introductory Essay on D. H. Lawrence): 3738

"Strategies of Crisis in the Shorter Fiction of D. H. Lawrence": 3374

"Strength through Joy in the Novels of D. H. Lawrence": 3703

THE STRENGTH TO DREAM: LITERATURE AND THE IMAGINATION: 2355

"Strindberg and the New Drama in Britain": 2353

"Strindberg in the Midlands": 2916

"Structural Irony in D. H. Lawrence's 'The Rocking-Horse Winner' ": 3891

"Structuralism as a Method of Literary Criticism": 4589

"Structure in the Short Stories of D. H. Lawrence": 2906

(The Structure of D. H. Lawrence's Novels): 3609

(The Structure of Novels and the Interpretation of D. H. Lawrence): 4368

"The Structure of the Coatl Symbol in *The Plumed Serpent*": 3664

(The Structure of *The Rainbow* and a Study of Its Imagery): 2298

"La structure symbolique de *Women in Love*": 3378

"The Structures of Authorial Control in the Travel Books of D. H. Lawrence": 3569

THE STRUGGLE OF THE MODERN: 2448

"Struisvogeltje Spelen: De Evolutie van de Erotische Literatuur": 2721

"Struktura romana D. H. Lawrencea": 3609

STUDIES IN CHANGE: A BOOK OF THE SHORT STORY: 2676

"Studies in the Language of D. H. Lawrence": 3795

STUDIES IN WORDS: 2965

(A Study of D. H. Lawrence, His First Novel: *The White Peacock*): 2815

(A Study of D. H. Lawrence, II: An Aspect of His Mysticism): 2457

A STUDY OF D. H. LAWRENCE: "LADY CHATTERLEY'S LOVER" AND "THE MAN WHO DIED": 3338

(A Study of D. H. Lawrence's Early Short Stories and *Sons and Lovers*): 4439

(A Study of D. H. Lawrence's "The Princess"): 3758

(A Study of "Glad Ghosts"): 4604

(A Study of Lawrence [1]): 2972

(A Study of Lawrence [2]): 3149

(A Study of Lawrence's "Love on the Farm"): 3931

(A Study of *Sons and Lovers* [1]): 3633

(A Study of *Sons and Lovers* [2]): 3812

"A Study of Style: The Development of D. H. Lawrence's Style in *The Prussian Officer* Tales": 3934

(A Study of the Letters of D. H. Lawrence): 3000

(A Study of the Love and Solitude in the Poems of D. H. Lawrence): 2883

"A Study of *The Rainbow* and *Women in Love* as Expressions of D. H. Lawrence's Thinking on Modern Civilization": 3973

(A Study of *The Rainbow* and *Women in Love*: Rebirth to Real Life): 3809

(A Study of the Short Stories of D. H. Lawrence and the Love Theme): 3390

(A Study of *The Trespasser*--Siegmund's Quest and Collapse): 4625

(A Study of *The White Peacock* from A. Huxley's Viewpoint): 4134

(A Study of *The White Peacock*: Interpretation of the Theme from Cyril's Point of View): 4222

" 'Study of Thomas Hardy': D. H. Lawrence's 'Art-Speech' in the Light of Polanyi's PERSONAL KNOWLEDGE": 4611

"A Study of Ursula (of *The Rainbow*) and H. M. Daleski's Commentary": 3212

(A Study of *Women in Love*): 2454

(A Study of *Women in Love*: Law-

rence's Criticism of Modern Rationalism): 4127
(A Study on the Composition of Lawrence's *The Rainbow*): 2459
(A Study on *The Man Who Died*: Religiousness as Lawrence's Quintessence): 3003
(The Style in *Sons and Lovers*): 2557
(Stylistic Development in the Work of D. H. Lawrence): 3299
(The Sublimation of 'Sex'–Chiefly Concerning *The Man Who Died*): 3966
"Substance and Shadow: The Self in Lawrence's Poetry": 3245
"The 'Success' and 'Failure' of D. H. Lawrence": 2293
"Such a Rotter": 3201
"Sue the Obscure": 4507
"Sulle Traduzioni Lawrenciane delle Novelle di G. Verga": 4432
"Superman and the System": 2905
SUPPRESSED BOOKS: A HISTORY OF THE CONCEPTION OF LITERARY OBSCENITY: 2225
SUPREME FICTIONS: STUDIES IN THE WORK OF WILLIAM BLAKE, THOMAS CARLYLE, W. B. YEATS AND D. H. LAWRENCE: 4340
"Sur trois manuscrits de D. H. Lawrence, *The White Peacock, The Trespasser, The Rainbow*: Contribution à l'étude de la création littéraire": 4318
"Surer Than Sure": 2100
"The Survival of Pan": 2097
"Suspended Form: Lawrence's Theory of Fiction in *Women in Love*": 2797, 3308
"Sutures in the Saga of Lorenzo": 2200
"Sweet Georgian Brown": 2615
"Swinburne and D. H. Lawrence": 3377
"The Symbol as Archetype: A Study of Symbolic Mode in D. H. Lawrence's *Women in Love*": 3798
"The Symbolic and the Symptomatic: D. H. Lawrence in Recent American Criticism": 4464
"The Symbolic Structure of *The Plumed Serpent*": 2622
(The Symbolic Structure of *Women in Love*): 3378
"La Symbolique de D. H. Lawrence": 3574
LA SYMBOLIQUE DE D. H. LAWRENCE: 3574
(Symbolism in D. H. Lawrence's *St. Mawr* [1]): 4157
(Symbolism in D. H. Lawrence's *St. Mawr* [2]): 4158
(The Symbolism of D. H. Lawrence): 3574
"The Symbolism of Lawrence's *The Fox*": 2964
"The Symbolism of the Soul: D. H. Lawrence and Some Others": 4399
"Symposium: Pornography and Obscenity. Editorial Comment: The Teaching of Literature": 2076
"Symposium: Pornography and Obscenity. Four-Letter Words": 2117
"Symposium; Pornography and Obscenity. Literature and Morality": 2078
"Symposium: Pornography and Obscenity. The English Censorship Laws": 2155
"Syntax and Style: Ambiguities in Lawrence's *Twilight in Italy*": 2709
SYNTAX IN ENGLISH POETRY, 1870-1930: 2908
"Syzygy: A Study of the Light-Dark Imagery in Five of the Novels of D. H. Lawrence": 2917
T. S. ELIOT: A MEMOIR: 3797
(T. S. Eliot on D. H. Lawrence): 2071
"T. S. Eliot über D. H. Lawrence": 2071
"Taccuino veneziano: la laguna di Lawrence": 2708
TAKEN CARE OF: AN AUTOBIOGRAPHY: 2734
TAKEN CARE OF: THE AUTOBIOGRAPHY OF EDITH SITWELL: 2734
"The Tale the Critic Tells: D. H. Lawrence on Nathaniel Hawthorne": 4588
"Talkies": 2213
"Talkies: A Conversation Piece in Short Takes, Starring the Last Tycoons": 2213

INDEX OF TITLES OF SECONDARY WORKS

"Taos Echoes of D. H. Lawrence": 2299
A TAOS MOSAIC: PORTRAIT OF A NEW MEXICO VILLAGE: 2704, 4161
"Teaching a Story Rhetorically: An Approach to a Short Story by D. H. Lawrence": 4215
(Technique and Style of D. H. Lawrence's Short Stories): 2760
TECHNIQUE IN FICTION: 2537
"Techniques of Cognition in Modern Fiction": 3196
"Techniques of Description: Adjectives, Figures of Speech, Imagery": 2682
"Teilhard de Chardin and D. H. Lawrence: A Study in Agreements": 2764
"Tennessee Williams Borrows a Little Shaw": 2753
"Tentô Mushi ni Tsuite": 2887
"Textual Alterations in 'NOT I, BUT THE WIND . . .' ": 3894
"Textual Changes in *Women in Love*": 2476
"A Textual Comparison of the First British and American Editions of D. H. Lawrence's *Kangaroo*": 2672
"That Vernal Time: Four English Novels about Growing Up": 4339
"That Which Is Perfectly Ourselves; I: Phèdre and the Knowledge of the Self": 3855
"That Which Is Perfectly Ourselves; IV: Connie Chatterley": 3856
" 'The Best I Have Known': D. H. Lawrence's 'A Modern Lover' and 'The Shades of Spring' ": 2993
(Theater for or against "Women's Lib." A Rediscovered Play by D. H. Lawrence and a Re-interpreted Play by Shakespeare): 4078
"Theater pro und contra 'Women's Lib.' Nuentdeckter D. H. Lawrence und umfunktionierter Shakespeare": 4078
"Der Theaterrevolutionär D. H. Lawrence. Londoner Entdeckung nach über funfzig Jahren": 3072
(The Theme and Its Expression in "Daughters of the Vicar"): 4421
(The Theme and Technique of D. H. Lawrence's "Sun"): 4249
"The Theme of Spiritual Death and Rebirth in the Novels of D. H. Lawrence": 2686
"The Theme of the Artist's Isolation in Works by Three Modern British Novelists": 2630
"The Theme of War in the Writings of D. H. Lawrence": 4107
(The Theme of *Women in Love*): 2792
"Theme versus Imitation: D. H. Lawrence's 'The Rocking-Horse Winner' ": 3601
"Then and Now": 3887
"Theodore Roethke and Tradition: 'The Pure Serenity of Memory in One Man' ": 3740
"The Therapeutic as Mythmaker: Lawrence's True Christian Philosophy": 2864
"Theses on D. H. Lawrence: Bibliographical Addenda": 4506
"Theses on D. H. Lawrence: 1931-1972: A Bibliography with Addenda of Senior Theses and Works in Progress": 4089
"They Know They're Monsters: Some Recent Books on Art": 2567
THIEVES OF FIRE: 3886
"The Third Generation": 2869
"The Third Unrealized Wonder--The Reality of Relation in D. H. Lawrence and Martin Buber": 4510
THIRTY-EIGHT SHORT STORIES: AN INTRODUCTORY ANTHOLOGY: 3223
"This England, This Past": 3505
"This Old Maid: Jane Austen Replies to Charlotte Brontë and D. H. Lawrence": 4518
"Thomas Carlyle and D. H. Lawrence: A Parallel": 3027
THOMAS HARDY AND BRITISH POETRY: 2781, 3877
THOMAS HARDY AND D. H. LAWRENCE: A STUDY OF THE TRAGIC VISION IN THEIR NOVELS: 3781
(Thomas Hardy's Influence on the Early Work of D. H. Lawrence): 3249
"The Thomas Seltzer Imprint": 2590
"Thought, Words, and Creativity": 4529

THOUGHT, WORDS, AND CREATIVITY: ART AND THOUGHT IN LAWRENCE: 4529
THOUGHTS AND DIRECTIVES FOR THE STUDY OF D. H. LAWRENCE: "WOMEN IN LOVE"): 3433, 3490
"Thoughts on Brett: 1967": 2968
(Three Central Thoughts in *Women in Love* [I]): 2898
(Three Central Thoughts in *Women in Love* [II]): 3020
"Three Cities": 4128
"Three for the Road": 3119
"The Three Ladies Chatterley": 4342
"The Three Lady Chatterleys": 2130, 4118
(Three Novels by Lawrence): 2275
(Three Novels of Lawrence): 3610
(Three Old Women in Taos): 2452
"Three Paintings of Sex: The Films of Ken Russell": 3901
"Three Poets in Fine Editions": 3153
"Three Separate Ways: Unpublished D. H. Lawrence Letters to Francis Brett Young": 2727
"Three Times Morel: Recurrent Structure in *Sons and Lovers*": 4447
"Three Types of Vitalism in *The Rainbow*": 2289
"Three Unknown Letters from Frieda Lawrence to Bertrand Russell": 3254
(The Three Versions of *Lady Chatterley's Lover*): 4553
(Three Women around Lawrence): 3587
"Three Women of Taos": 2704
"Three Women of Taos: Frieda Lawrence, Mabel Luhan, and Dorothy Brett": 2704
" 'Through . . . degradation to a new health'—A Comment on *Women in Love*": 2107
(Thus Spoke Lawrence): 3379
" 'Tickets, Please': D. H. Lawrence, 1885-1930": 3005
"Das Tier bei D. H. Lawrence": 2079
"The Tiger and the Lamb: The Duality of Lawrence": 2624
" 'Till the Fight is Finished': D. H. Lawrence in His Letters": 4074
"Time Must Have a Stop: Apocalyptic Thought and Expression in the Twentieth Century": 2913
"Tiresias Their Muse: Studies in Sexual Stereotypes in the English Novel": 4193
(To New Mexico in the Steps of D. H. Lawrence): 2344
"To Open the Mind": 3724
TODAY WE WILL ONLY GOSSIP: 2501
TOLSTOY AND CHEKHOV: 3803
"Tolstoy and Lawrence: Some Conclusions": 4452
"Tolstoy, Lawrence, and Tragedy": 2467
"Tone in Dramatic Narrative": 3384
TOWARD A RECOGNITION OF ANDROGYNY: 4106
"Toward a Redefinition of the Modern: Joyce, Yeats, Eliot, Lawrence": 3523
"Toward 'Thingness': Cézanne's Painting and Lawrence's Poetry": 4122
TOWARD "WOMEN IN LOVE": THE EMERGENCE OF A LAWRENTIAN AESTHETIC: 2974, 3756
"Towards a Christian Literary Criticism": 2649
"Towards a New Objectivity: Essays on the Body and Nature in Faulkner, Lawrence, and Mann": 4076
TOWARDS ANDROGYNY: ASPECTS OF MALE AND FEMALE IN LITERATURE: 4106
"Towards the Great Secret": 2571
"The Town Lawrence Forsook": 3972
TRADITION AND DREAM: THE ENGLISH AND AMERICAN NOVEL FROM THE TWENTIES TO OUR TIME: 2470
(Tradition and Innovation: D. H. Lawrence, Novelist of the Unsaid): 3917
"Tradition et Innovation: D. H. Lawrence, romancier de l'inexprimé": 3917
THE TRADITION OF ROMANTIC MORALITY: 4187
(Tragedy Bequeathed: Lawrence on Thomas Hardy): 2710
(The Tragedy of Paul--*Sons and Lovers*): 2561
(The Tragedy of *Sons and Lovers*--

INDEX OF TITLES OF SECONDARY WORKS

From a Viewpoint of Mrs. Morel's Destructiveness Caused by Machine Civilization): 4564
"The Tragic Vision in the Novels of Thomas Hardy and D. H. Lawrence": 3781
"Transactional Analysis and Literature": 4245
"The Transcendental Element": 2204
"The Transcendental Element in American Literature: A Study of Some Unpublished D. H. Lawrence Manuscripts": 2204
(The Transfiguration of the Gamekeeper: The Three Versions of *Lady Chatterley's Lover*): 4352
"The Travail of Erotic Man": 2399
"The Travel Books of D. H. Lawrence: Records of a Spiritual Pilgrimage": 2493
(Travel Books of the Novelist of Love): 2240
"Tre donne interno a Lawrence": 3587
"Tre romanzi di Lawrence": 2275, 3610
(Trespass into Cythera): 4544
"*The Trespasser*: D. H. Lawrence's Neglected Novel": 2254
"*The Trespasser*: Lawrence's Wagnerian Tragedy and Divine Comedy": 3722
"*The Trespasser* ni Okeru 'Saihô' ni Tsuite": 4350
"*The Trespasser* ni Okeru Shinwateki Yôso ni Tsuite--D. H. Lawrence no Shinwa no Sekai": 4226
"*The Trespasser* no Jinbutsu ni Tsuite--Cecil Byrne to Hampson o Megutte": 4255
"*The Trespasser* no Shizen to Jinbutsu o Megutte--Siegmund no Tankyû to Zasetsu": 4625
"The Trial of Lady Chatterley": 2164
THE TRIAL OF LADY CHATTERLEY: REGINA V. PENGUIN BOOKS LIMITED: 2154
"Trifling with the Dead": 3642
"The Triumph and Failure of D. H. Lawrence": 2183
"The Triumph of the Middleclass Matriarch": 2351
THE TRIUMPH OF THE THERAPEUTIC: USES OF FAITH AFTER FREUD: 2864
"Trivium": 4533
"The Trouble with Harry": 4163
THE TROUBLESOME HELPMATE: A HISTORY OF MISOGYNY IN LITERATURE: 2865
"A True Relatedness: Lawrence's View of Morality": 2961
"Truthfulness and Schematism: D. H. Lawrence": 2510
THE TRUTHTELLERS: JANE AUSTEN, GEORGE ELIOT, D. H. LAWRENCE: 2409, 2962
"*Tsubasa Aru Hebi* ni Tsuite": 3226
THE TURN OF THE NOVEL: 2498, 2797
"The Turn of the Novel: Changes in the Pattern of English Fiction Since 1890, Conrad, Forster, and Lawrence": 2498
"Tutte le poesie di D. H. Lawrence": 2127
TWELVE POEMS CONSIDERED: 2444
TWELVE SHORT STORIES: 2122
TWELVE SHORT STORIES, SECOND SERIES: 2122
THE TWENTIETH CENTURY: 3508
TWENTIETH CENTURY INTERPRETATIONS OF "SONS AND LOVERS": A COLLECTION OF CRITICAL ESSAYS: 2263, 2348, 2351, 2639, 2869, 3484, 3485
TWENTIETH CENTURY INTERPRETATIONS OF "THE RAINBOW": A COLLECTION OF CRITICAL ESSAYS: 2594, 2624, 2639, 2869, 2962, 3124, 3733, 3734
TWENTIETH CENTURY INTERPRETATIONS OF "WOMEN IN LOVE": A COLLECTION OF CRITICAL ESSAYS: 2348, 2423, 2639, 2797, 3308, 3316, 3357, 3358
THE TWENTIETH-CENTURY MIND: HISTORY, IDEAS, AND LITERATURE IN BRITAIN: 3905, 3906, 3974
TWENTY-SEVEN TO ONE: A POTPOURRI OF HUMANISTIC MATERIAL PRESENTED TO DR. DONALD GALE STILLMAN: 3564

TWO AND TWENTY: A COLLECTION OF SHORT STORIES: 2338
"Two Anti-Puritan Puritans: Bernard Shaw and D. H. Lawrence": 2801
"Two Hitherto Unknown Pieces by D. H. Lawrence": 3258
(Two Individualistic Revolutionaries): 3571
"The Two Infinites": 4338
"The Two Infinites: D. H. Lawrence's *Twilight in Italy*": 4338
("Two Marriages" and "Daughters of the Vicar": Two Versions of the Same Story by D. H. Lawrence): 4570
" 'Two Marriages' y 'Daughters of the Vicar': dos versiones de un mismo relato de D. H. Lawrence": 4570
"Two Missing Pages from *The Ladybird*": 4086
"Two Modern Incest Heroes": 2084
(Two Novels of Lawrence): 2574
(Two Unprofessional Studies of Lawrence--Anais Nin's and Henry Miller's): 2427
"The Two Versions of 'Sun': An Exchange": 4488
(Two Ways of Living: A Study of *Women in Love*): 3942
TYNAN RIGHT AND LEFT: PLAYS, FILMS, PEOPLE, PLACES AND EVENTS: 3007
"U. S. Discoverer of Henry Miller Returns for Today's Unknowns--James Cooney: The Literary Phoenix": 4277
"Über die Methode des Motivvergleichs--Dargestellt an englishen Literaturwerken": 2496
UNANCESTRAL VOICE: 2610
"The Unbanning of the Books": 2827
"The Uncollected Letters of D. H. Lawrence": 2376
"An Uncollected Poem by Lawrence": 2264
(Unconscious Self--A Study of *The Man Who Died*): 4155
UNDERSTANDING LITERATURE: 2698
UNDERSTANDING WHITEHEAD: 2278
" 'The Undying Man': D. H. Lawrence's Yiddish Story": 3835
"Unity and Meaning in D. H. Lawrence's *Birds, Beasts and Flowers*": 4056
"Unity in *St. Mawr*": 2803
"L'Univers sémantique de *The Rainbow* de D. H. Lawrence": 4377
L'UNIVERS SÉMANTIQUE DE "THE RAINBOW" DE D. H. LAWRENCE: 4377
UNOFFICIAL SELVES: CHARACTER IN THE NOVEL FROM DICKENS TO THE PRESENT DAY: 4223
"An Unpublished Version of D. H. Lawrence's Introduction to *Pansies*": 3483
"The Unsteady Arch: The Place of *The Rainbow* in the Lawrentian Love-Ethic": 4323
"Up the Rebels": 3426
"Up the Rough Deserted Pasture ... the Country of My Heart": 4321
"The Upholstered Prison": 3783
" 'Ureshii Yûrei' no Kageri": 4604
"Ursula Brangwen": 3952
"Ursula Brangwen in the University: D. H. Lawrence's Rejection of Authority in *The Rainbow*": 4280
"Ursula Brangwen of *The Rainbow*: Christian Saint or Pagan Goddess?": 3720
"Ursula Brangwen: Toward Self and Selflessness": 3679
"Ursula in *The Rainbow*": 2594
(Ursula in *The Rainbow*): 2109
(Ursula's Growth in *The Rainbow*): 2953
THE USE OF IMAGINATION: EDUCATIONAL THOUGHT AND THE LITERARY MIND: 2594
"The Use of Mythology in the Novels of D. H. Lawrence": 4626
"The Use of Point of View and Authority in 'The Blind Man' ": 3234
"The Use of the Symbol by English Novelists 1900-1930, with Particular Reference to E. M. Forster, D. H. Lawrence, and Virginia Woolf": 2722
"Ushinawareta Bunmyaku--Lawrence ni Okeru Kigekisei": 3958
"The Utopian Vision of D. H. Lawrence": 2087
THE UTOPIAN VISION OF D. H.

INDEX OF TITLES OF SECONDARY WORKS

LAWRENCE: 2087, 2394
(Utopian World of D. H. Lawrence--A Consideration of "Rananim"): 2732
"Values and 'The Rocking-Horse Winner' ": 2456
"The Variety of D. H. Lawrence": 2193
THE VARIETY OF FICTION: A CRITICAL ANTHOLOGY: 3266
(Venetian Notebook: Lawrence's Lagoon): 2708
"Verga and 'Verismo' ": 2121
"Verse": 2748
"Verse Not Included in *The Complete Poems*": 3617
"The Verse of D. H. Lawrence": 3399
"Versions": 3221
"Il viaggiatore Lawrence": 2411
THE VICTORIAN HOUSEHOLD: 2535
VICTORY IN LIMBO: IMAGISM 1908-1917: 4499
"Die Vierpersonenkonstellation im Roman: Strukturuntersuchungen zur Personenführung. Dargestellt an N. Hawthornes THE BLITHEDALE ROMANCE, G. Eliots DANIEL DERONDA, H. James' THE GOLDEN BOWL und D. H. Lawrences *Women in Love*": 3257
DIE VIERPERSONENKONSTELLATION IM ROMAN: STRUKTURUNTERSUCHUNGEN ZUR PERSONENFÜHRUNG. DARGESTELLT AN N. HAWTHORNES "THE BLITHEDALE ROMANCE," G. ELIOTS "DANIEL DERONDA," H. JAMES' "THE GOLDEN BOWL" UND D. H. LAWRENCES "WOMEN IN LOVE": 3257
(A View of the Darkness and Light Duality in *Women in Love*): 3842
"The Violation or Fulfillment of Individuality in Marriage as Seen in Selected Works of D. H. Lawrence": 3457
"*The Virgin and the Gipsy* ni Tsuite (Lawrence no Tanpen-Shôse-Tsu ni Okeru Seimeishugi no Keifu)": 2605
(*The Virgin and the Gipsy*—The Fall of Mother): 4606
"*The Virgin and the Gypsy*": 3428, 3530
"*The Virgin and the Gypsy* and D. H. LAWRENCE IN TAOS": 3502
"*The Virgin and the Gypsy*. 'tact' ": 3604
"*Virgin and the Gypsy, The*": 3458
VIRGINIA WOOLF: A BIOGRAPHY, VOL. II: MRS. WOOLF, 1912-1941: 3852
VIRGINIA WOOLF: THE ECHOES ENSLAVED: 4148
"Vision and Form in the Works of D. H. Lawrence": 2333
"Vision and Revision: *The Virgin and the Gypsy* as Film": 4209
A VISION OF REALITY: A STUDY OF LIBERALISM IN TWENTIETH-CENTURY VERSE: 2650
"A Visionary": 3304
"Visionary Sequences: D. H. Lawrence's Major Poetry": 4328
VISIONS AND REVISIONS: AN APPROACH TO POETRY: 3823
"A Visit to Frieda": 4282
"Visiting Frieda: The Woman in D. H. Lawrence's Life": 4015
A VISITORS GUIDE TO EASTWOOD AND THE COUNTRYSIDE OF D. H. LAWRENCE: 3853
VISUAL IMAGINATION OF D. H. LAWRENCE: 3658
"Vital Life versus Sterile Denial: A Study of Family and Sexual Relationships in the Works of Thomas Hardy and D. H. Lawrence": 3755
"Vitalismo Sexual": 2766
"Vivas on D. H. Lawrence": 2129
" 'The Voice of Water': Lawrence's *The Virgin and the Gipsy*": 3562
VOICES IN THE WILDERNESS: FROM POETRY TO PROPHECY IN BRITAIN: 4526, 4527
"The Voices of Lawrence": 3100
THE VOICES OF PROSE: 2879
THE VON RICHTHOFEN SISTERS: THE TRIUMPHANT AND THE TRAGIC MODES OF LOVE: ELSE AND FRIEDA VON RICHTHOFEN, OTTO GROSS, MAX WEBER, AND D. H. LAWRENCE, IN THE YEARS 1870-1970: 4320
"Vorkämpfer einter 'Sex'-Revolution.

"D. H. Lawrence über Pornographie und Obszönität": 3718
"Vorwort": 2656
"Voyage into Creativity: The Modern Künstlerroman: A Comparative Study of the Development of the Artist in the Works of Hermann Hesse, D. H. Lawrence, James Joyce and Theodore Dreiser": 4267
"Voyage of Oblivion: The Meaning of D. H. Lawrence's Death Poems": 2318
"Voyeuristic": 3231
"Vs. Diana Trilling's Preface to her Portable Lawrence": 2290
(Wagnerian Elements in *The Trespasser*): 4441
"Wagnerian Patterns in the Fiction of Joseph Conrad, D. H. Lawrence, Virginia Woolf, and James Joyce": 4072
"A Wall of Fire, A Wall of Ice: Growth as an Aesthetic Criterion in the Fiction of D. H. Lawrence": 3635
"The Wartime Setting of Lawrence's 'Tickets, Please'": 3541
"Was There Fact in D. H. Lawrence's *Kangaroo*?": 2607
"Watakushi no Lawrence to Butler": 4561
"Water, Ships, and the Sea: Unifying Symbols in Lawrence's *Kangaroo*": 3600
"The Wave of Self in Time to Break: D. H. Lawrence and Virginia Woolf": 4427
WE MUST MARCH, MY DARLINGS: 4228
"The We's": 2597
"A wealth of literature had its beginning here . . .": 3540
" 'The Wedding' Chapter of D. H. Lawrence's *Women in Love*": 2497
"Wells Marches On": 2859
("The West" in *The Trespasser*): 4350
THE WEST LOOKS AT INDIA: STUDIES IN THE IMPACT OF INDIAN THOUGHT ON SHELLEY, EMERSON, THOREAU, WHITMAN, RUSKIN, TENNYSON, D. H. LAWRENCE AND JAMES JOYCE: 3330
"Western American Space and the Human Imagination": 3521
"What Happened to D. H. Lawrence's *Goats and Compasses*?": 3836
"What Kind of Fiction Did Hardy Write?": 2802
"What was it like . . . to know Lawrence?": 3488
"What's Left of Lawrence": 3090
"The Wheel and the Centre: An Approach to *The Rainbow*": 3586
"Where There's Muck There's Polytheism": 3625
WHERE THEY LIVED IN LONDON: 3980
"The Whipper-in": 4105
"Whiskers and Criticism": 3602
THE WHITE/GARNETT LETTERS: 2337
"*The White Peacock* ni Tsuite": 3112
"*The White Peacock* Reconsidered": 4403
"*The White Peacock* Shiron—Cyril no Shiten o Oita Shudai Kaishaku": 4222
(*The White Peacock*: The Moon and the Peacock): 2123
"*The White Peacock*--Tsuki to Kujaku": 2123
" 'The White Stocking' ": 4061
(Whitman and Lawrence): 3117
("Whitman" by D. H. Lawrence): 4028
"Whitman to Lawrence": 3117
"Who is Frieda Lawrence?": 2994
"Wholeness through Conflict": 4021
"Who's Who in the Lawrence Letters": 2294
"Whose Culture?": 2312
"Why Did the S. A. Censors Ban *Lady Chatterley's Lover*?": 2132
" 'Widdershins': Reversed Parental Identification and Narrative Point of View in the Work of D. H. Lawrence": 4066
[*The Widowing of Mrs. Holroyd*]: 2190
"The Wife's Tale": 2070
"Will Brangwen and Paradisal Vision in *The Rainbow* and *Women in Love*": 4502
"Will the Real Lady Chatterley . . .": 3960

INDEX OF TITLES OF SECONDARY WORKS

"The *Wille zur Macht* and D. H. Lawrence": 4496
WILLIAM BLAKE: ESSAYS FOR S. FOSTER DAMON: 3375
WILLIAM CARLOS WILLIAMS: 3236
(William Carlos Williams: A Comparative Study on the Reception of His Work in Germany, England, and Italy [1912-1965]; Part II: England and Italy): 2935
"William Carlos Williams. Eine vergleichende Studie zur Aufnahme seines Werkes in Deutschland, England und Italien (1912-1965). Teil II: England und Italien": 2935
WILLIAM CARLOS WILLIAMS: THE AMERICAN BACKGROUND: 3825
THE WINE OF ABSURDITY: ESSAYS ON LITERATURE AND CONSOLATION: 2755
"With Lawrence in Derbyshire": 3265
"With the Accent on English": 4246
"Wives and Servants": 3552
"Woman in Love": 3652
A WOMAN SPEAKS: THE LECTURES, SEMINARS, AND INTERVIEWS OF ANAIS NIN: 4559
(A Woman Who Attracted Lawrence): 3962
" 'The Woman Who Rode Away' ": 2635
"Women and Nature in Modern Fiction": 3977
WOMEN AND THEIR SEXUALITY IN THE NEW FILM: 4152
"Women in D. H. Lawrence's Works": 4100
(Women in Early Works): 2542
"*Women in Love*": 2960, 3274, 3281, 3413, 3465, 3480, 3487, 3491, 3504, 3510, 3520, 3531, 3537, 3591, 3593, 3597, 3614, 3641, 3643, 3737
(*Women in Love*): 4009
"*Women in Love*–A Study of the Man-Woman Relationship": 3816
"*Women in Love*–A Study of Three Relationships": 3817
"*Women in Love*: A Textual Note": 3613

"*Women in Love* and the German Tradition in Literature": 2647
"*Women in Love* and the Lawrencean Aesthetic": 3316
"*Women in Love* and *The Man Who Died*: Resolving Apollo and Dionysus": 3938
"*Women in Love* as a Novel of Change": 4185
"*Women in Love*: Counterpoint on Film": 4256
"*Women in Love*: Fascinating Try": 3605
"*Women in Love*: 'Firm Singleness and Melting Union' ": 2624
"*Women in Love*: Individuality and Belonging": 3278
"*Women in Love* Is Stunning Film": 3452
"*Women in Love* Love": 3578
"*Women in Love* ni Nagareru San Shicho (I)": 2898
"*Women in Love* ni Nagareru San Shicho (II)": 3020
"*Women in Love* ni Okeru Gerald Crich": 2707
"*Women in Love* ni Okeru Necrophilous Characters ni Tsuite": 3395
"*Women in Love*: Novel and Film": 3688
(*Women in Love* or the Novel of Antagonism): 3259
"*Women in Love* ou le roman de l'antagonisme": 3259
"*Women in Love* Ron: Shi to Sei": 2454
"*Women in Love*: The Degeneration of Western Man": 2639
"*Women in Love*: The Minor Characters": 3522
"Womenfolk": 2654
"A Word about Influences--and Unprofessional Studies": 3723
"The Word and the Flesh: A Study of the Cosmological Interest of D. H. Lawrence": 4149
WORD FOR WORD: A STUDY OF AUTHORS' ALTERATIONS: 2659
WORD FOR WORD: THE REWRITING OF FICTION: 2659
"Word-List of *The Rainbow*--A Study of D. H. Lawrence's Vocabulary": 2584

D. H. LAWRENCE

"The Works of D. H. Lawrence in Relation to the Ideas of Schopenhauer and Nietzsche": 4094
A WORLD ELSEWHERE: THE PLACE OF STYLE IN AMERICAN LITERATURE: 2855
WORLD FAMOUS REBELS: 3460
(The World of D. H. Lawrence): 2269, 3417
THE WORLD OF SHORT FICTION: AN INTERNATIONAL COLLECTION: 2253
(The World of *The White Peacock*): 4546
THE WORLD WE IMAGINE: SELECTED ESSAYS: 3200
THE WORLDS OF FICTION: STORIES IN CONTEXT: 2506
"Would You Give This Book to a Fifteen-Year Old?": 2217
"The Writer as Painter": 2329
"The Writer as Political Crazy": 4130
"The Writer as Teacher: The Educational Ideas of D. H. Lawrence": 2594
"A Writer in His Letters": 2311
WRITERS AND REVOLUTION: THE FATAL LURE OF ACTION: 4433
WRITERS AT WORK: THE "PARIS REVIEW" INTERVIEWS: 2350
"Writing It Again": 3459
"The Writing of *The Trespasser*": 4285
"Writing the Play": 2894
"Wyndham Lewis and Lawrence": 3381
"Wyndham Lewis: Enemy of the Rose": 2375
"*Yamaarashi no Shi ni Omou* Kara": 2674
"Yame no Sekai e no Tabidachi--Morel-Fujin no Shi ga Imisuru Mono": 4621
YEATS'S BLESSINGS ON VON HUGEL: ESSAYS ON LITERATURE AND RELIGION: 2938
YESTERDAY'S TOMORROWS: A HISTORICAL SURVEY OF FUTURE SOCIETIES: 3030
" 'You are the call and I am the answer': D. H. Lawrence and Women": 4577
YOUNG BERT: AN EXHIBITION OF THE EARLY YEARS OF D. H. LAWRENCE: 3847, 3858, 3888
YOUNG IN THE TWENTIES: A CHAPTER OF AUTOBIOGRAPHY: 3750
"A Young Man Speaking for His Own Generation": 2507
"Zenki Sakuhin no Josei": 2542
"The Zombie's Lair": 2681
"Zur Spätlyrik von D. H. Lawrence": 3409

Index

PERIODICALS AND NEWSPAPERS

Included here are periodicals and newspapers for which entries occur in the bibliography. Numbers after each title refer to the number(s) of the item in the bibliography where the title appears.

ACADEMY OF MEDICINE OF NEW JERSEY BULLETIN: 3369
ADAM INTERNATIONAL REVIEW: 4115
AGENDA: 3381
ALTO ADIGE (Bolzano): 3555
AMERICA: 3079, 3641
AMERICAN BAR ASSOCIATION JOURNAL: 2267
AMERICAN BOOK COLLECTOR: 2890
AMERICAN IMAGO: 3077, 3225
AMERICAN LITERATURE: 2502
AMERICAN POETRY REVIEW: 3964
AMERICAN QUARTERLY: 4464
AMERICAN SCHOLAR: 2185, 4525
ANNALI ISTITUTO UNIVERSITARIO ORIENTALE, NAPOLI, SEZIONE GERMANICA: 3878
ANNALI ISTITUTO UNIVERSITARIO ORIENTALE, NAPOLI, SEZIONE GERMANICA-ANGLISTICA: 4292, 4474
ANNALI ISTITUTO UNIVERSITARIO ORIENTALE, NAPOLI, SEZIONE ROMANZA: 4192
ANNUAL STUDY BULLETIN OF HINOMOTO GAKUEN JUNIOR COLLEGE: 4335
ANTIOCH REVIEW: 2293
AOYAMA JOURNAL OF GENERAL EDUCATION (Aoyama Gakuen University): 2139
APOSTOLOS (Kyôto University of Education): 4504
ARCHITECTURAL REVIEW: 4067
ARIEL: A REVIEW OF INTERNATIONAL ENGLISH LITERATURE: 3561, 4316
ARIZONA QUARTERLY: 3209
ART JOURNAL: 2946
ATLANTIC MONTHLY: 4400
ATTIC REVIEW (Kyôto Kôgeiseni University): 2984
AUSTRALIAN LITERARY STUDIES: 3511, 3644
AUSTRALIAN QUARTERLY: 2474
BADISCHE ZEITUNG: 3072, 3824, 4612
BAIKA JOSHIDAIGAKU BUNGAKUBU KIYÔ (Baika Joshidaigaku): 2516, 2660, 2810
BAIKA TANKIDAIGAKU KENKYUKIYO (Baika Tankidaigaku): 2093, 2400
BALL STATE UNIVERSITY FORUM: 2920, 3626, 3628
BERKELEY BARB (Berkeley, CA): 3578
BIOLOGIA CULTURALE: 4432
BLUE REVIEW: 2063
BOKVANNEN (Stockholm): 2170
BOLD (Durban, South Africa): 3522
BOOK COLLECTOR: 2131, 2658
BOOKLIST: 4307
BOOKLIST AND SUBSCRIPTION BOOKS BULLETIN: A GUIDE

TO CURRENT BOOKS: 2211, 2534, 2830, 3350
BOOK-OF-THE-MONTH CLUB NEWS (NY): 2356
BOOKS ABROAD: 2439, 2465, 2469
BOOKS AND BOOKMEN: 3431, 4342
BOUNDARY 2: 4079
BRIGHAM YOUNG UNIVERSITY STUDIES: 2229
BRITISH JOURNAL OF AESTHETICS: 2402, 2666
BRITISH JOURNAL OF EDUCATIONAL STUDIES: 2878
BULLETIN (Kyôritsu Women's University): 3538, 3943, 4139
BULLETIN FOR LANGUAGES AND LITERATURE (Tenri University): 4417
BULLETIN OF COLLEGE OF GENERAL EDUCATION (Tôhoku University): 3022, 3829
BULLETIN OF FACULTY OF EDUCATION (Nagasaki University): 3633, 3812, 4604
BULLETIN OF FUKUOKA UNIVERSITY OF EDUCATION: 4398
BULLETIN OF KYÛSHÛ SANGYÔ UNIVERSITY: 3639, 3640, 3821, 4428
BULLETIN OF N. C. N. A.: 4414
BULLETIN OF REITAKU UNIVERSITY: 3985
BULLETIN OF ST. MARGARET'S (St. Margaret's Junior College): 3370, 3966, 4166, 4380, 4561
BULLETIN OF STUDIES IN HUMANITY (Kagawa University): 3395, 3799, 3800, 3992
BULLETIN OF THE DEPARTMENT OF ENGLISH (Calcutta University): 3061, 3818
BULLETIN OF THE FACULTY OF FOREIGN LANGUAGES (Kitakyûshû University): 2098, 2670, 2950
BULLETIN OF THE FACULTY OF FOREIGN STUDIES (Kita-kyûshû University): 4514
BULLETIN OF THE FACULTY OF LIBERAL ARTS (Hôsei University): 2759, 3019
BULLETIN OF THE FACULTY OF LITERATURE (Aichi Prefectural University): 2817, 3112
BULLETIN OF THE FACULTY OF TEXTILE SCIENCE (Kyôto University of Industrial Arts and Textile Fibers): 4168, 4383
BULLETIN OF THE NEW YORK PUBLIC LIBRARY: 2646
BULLETIN OF TOKYO UNIVERSITY OF LIBERAL ARTS AND EDUCATION: 4524
BULLETIN OF YAMAGATA UNIVERSITY: 2166, 2584
BUNGAKU-KAI RONSHÛ (Kônan University): 3009, 3227
CAMBRIDGE QUARTERLY: 2789, 2831, 2832, 2989, 3351, 3354, 3666
CANADIAN FORUM: 2075, 2270
CATHOLIC WORLD: 3133, 3217
CEA CRITIC: 2705
CENTENNIAL REVIEW: 3091
CHEVRON (Waterloo, Ontario): 3597
CHICAGO REVIEW: 2129
CHICAGO SUNDAY TRIBUNE MAGAZINE OF BOOKS: 2208
CHOICE: 2529, 2683, 2824, 2876, 3347, 3543, 3742, 3930
CHRISTIAN CENTURY: 2142, 3231
CHRISTIAN CENTURY, Continuing NEW CHRISTIAN: 3430, 3662, 3725, 3777, 3801
CHRISTIAN SCHOLAR: 2564
CHRISTIAN SCIENCE MONITOR: 2311, 2581, 3630
COLLECTED ESSAYS (Kyôritsu Women's Junior College): 2605, 4019, 4235
COLLECTED TREATISES FOR THE 35TH ANNIVERSARY OF KANAGAWA UNIVERSITY: 2401
COLLEGE COMPOSITION AND COMMUNICATION: 2709, 4215
COLLEGE ENGLISH: 2254, 2291, 2372, 2407, 2685, 4589
COLLEGE LANGUAGE ASSOCIATION JOURNAL: 2964
COLLEGE LITERATURE: 4269, 4568
COLUMBIA LIBRARY COLUMNS: 3171, 3332
COMMENTARY: 3427
COMMONWEAL: 3096, 3637
COMPARATIVE LITERATURE:

INDEX OF PERIODICALS AND NEWSPAPERS

2063, 2364, 2777, 4341
COMPARATIVE LITERATURE STUDIES: 2606, 3024, 3031
CONCERNING POETRY: 3372
CONNECTICUT REVIEW: 3197, 3476, 3891
CONTEMPORANUL: 3194
CONTEMPORARY LITERATURE: 3977, 4574, 4591
CONTEMPORARY POETRY: 4097
CORRIERE DELLA SERA (Milan): 2127, 2360, 2840, 3051, 3364, 3571, 3774
COSMORAMA (Rome): 2857
COSTERUS: 4012, 4023
COUNTRY LIFE (Lond): 3870
CRANE REVIEW (Tufts University): 2158
CRESSET: 3771
CRITICAL ESSAYS ON ENGLISH LITERATURE (Kyôto Industrial University): 3118, 3130
CRITICAL INQUIRY: 4445
CRITICAL QUARTERLY: 2076, 2078, 2085, 2117, 2144, 2146. 2155, 2156, 2277, 2321, 2729, 2999, 3122, 3191, 4532
CRITICAL REVIEW (Melbourne): 2175, 2744, 2944, 3560
CRITICAL SURVEY: 2409, 2444, 2788
CRITICISM: 2188, 2301, 2462, 3078, 3143, 3889
CRITICISM AND RESEARCH (Banaras Hindu University): 2586
CRITIQUE (Paris): 4567
CRITIQUE: STUDIES IN MODERN FICTION: 2386
CUADERNOS AMERICANOS: 2626
CUADERNOS HISPANOAMERICANOS (Madrid): 2937, 4182
CULTURAL SCIENCE REPORTS (Kagoshima University): 2196
D. H. LAWRENCE NEWS AND NOTES (California, PA): 2217, 2232, 2233, 2234, 2235, 2248, 2264, 2286, 2287, 2288, 2289, 2290, 2316, 2349
D. H. LAWRENCE REVIEW: 2699, 2730, 2764, 3025, 3040, 3058, 3059, 3064, 3065, 3066, 3071, 3073, 3088, 3098, 3123, 3136, 3137, 3164, 3175, 3192, 3207, 3208, 3245, 3247, 3248, 3250, 3254, 3261, 3263, 3269, 3275, 3290, 3295, 3296, 3297, 3319, 3321, 3322, 3323, 3334, 3362, 3385, 3411, 3414, 3423, 3432, 3435, 3443, 3448, 3456, 3464, 3468, 3469, 3470, 3496, 3498, 3512, 3596, 3599, 3601, 3617, 3629, 3659, 3667, 3682, 3685, 3687, 3688, 3690, 3696, 3697, 3698, 3699, 3716, 3720, 3722, 3747, 3762, 3791, 3792, 3813, 3814, 3822, 3828, 3835, 3836, 3860, 3872, 3873, 3881, 3882, 3883, 3893, 3896, 3900, 3912, 3924, 3927, 3940, 3945, 3946, 3951, 3955, 3979, 4031, 4034, 4046, 4049, 4058, 4059, 4068, 4069, 4070, 4073, 4081, 4085, 4089, 4112, 4119, 4131, 4160, 4185, 4190, 4196, 4232, 4260, 4265, 4268, 4270, 4272, 4276, 4285, 4286, 4288, 4289, 4293, 4295, 4296, 4297, 4338, 4346, 4365, 4394, 4399, 4424, 4425, 4443, 4450, 4466, 4468, 4470, 4471, 4475, 4476, 4477, 4478, 4479, 4483, 4488, 4495, 4500, 4501, 4502, 4505, 4506, 4533, 4543, 4552, 4569, 4575, 4576, 4577, 4579, 4584, 4585, 4594, 4605, 4607, 4616
D. H. LAWRENCE STUDIES (Kyôto): 4071, 4088, 4134, 4136, 4221, 4250, 4254, 4298, 4312, 4343, 4350, 4378, 4415, 4441, 4480, 4491, 4503, 4513, 4519, 4560, 4564, 4580, 4599, 4621, 4624
DAGENS NYHETER (Stockholm): 3638
DAILY EXPRESS (Lond): 3131, 3132
DAILY MAIL (Lond): 3139
DAILY TELEGRAPH (Lond): 3205, 3206
DALHOUSIE REVIEW: 3246, 3422, 3789, 3925, 4330, 4420, 4609
DELO (Belgrade): 2268
DELOS: 3517
DELTA (Cambridge University): 2655
DENVER QUARTERLY: 2913, 3054
DESCANT: 2834
DISTANT DRUMMER (Philadelphia): 3465

DOKKYO STUDIES IN ENGLISH (Dokkyo University): 3125, 3341, 3735, 3941
DOSHISHA LITERATURE (Doshisha University): 4117
DRAMA: 3135
DUTCH QUARTERLY REVIEW OF ANGLO-AMERICAN LETTERS: 4039, 4447, 4515, 4581
EDDA (Oslo): 4608
EDGEWOOD REVIEW (Sonada Women's Junior College): 3842
EIGO SEINEN: 3117, 3346, 3366, 3576, 4103, 4138, 4171, 4352, 4379, 4436
ELH: 3998
ENCANTO MAGAZINE AND NEW MEXICO CULTURAL NEWS: 3557 (See also NEW MEXICO CULTURAL NEWS)
ENCOUNTER: 2094, 2101, 2167, 2184, 2187, 2192, 2194, 2280, 2325, 2326, 2327, 2339, 2340, 2342, 2841, 3258, 3642, 3807, 4075
ENGLISH: 2434, 3242, 3868, 4198
ENGLISH AND AMERICAN STUDIES (Wayô Women's University): 3001
ENGLISH FICTION IN TRANSITION: 2279
ENGLISH LANGUAGE AND ENGLISH AND AMERICAN LITERATURES (Chūo University): 2065, 2366
ENGLISH LANGUAGE AND LITERATURE (Chūo University): 4248
ENGLISH LANGUAGE NOTES: 2526, 2629
ENGLISH LITERATURE (Waseda University): 2136, 2345, 2460, 3417
ENGLISH LITERATURE IN HOKKAIDÔ (Hokkaidô University): 2525, 2713; (Muroran Institute of Technology): 3816, 4007, 4606
ENGLISH LITERATURE IN TRANSITION: 2615, 2836
ENGLISH LITERATURE REVIEW (Kyôto Women's University): 2140, 2315, 2674, 2819, 2952, 3935, 4126, 4360
ENGLISH MISCELLANY (Rome): 2318, 2496, 2718, 2733, 2778, 3084, 3499, 3562, 4043, 4191
ENGLISH QUARTERLY (Waterloo, Ontario): 3068, 3921
ENGLISH RECORD: 2520
ENGLISH STUDIES (Amsterdam): 2237, 2468, 2809, 3067, 3949
ENGLISH STUDIES (Nihon University): 2292, 2541, 2542, 3167
ENGLISH STUDIES IN AFRICA: 2695, 2961, 3260, 4143, 4247
ENGLISH STUDIES IN CANADA: 4595
ESQUIRE: 2069, 2213, 3202
ESSAYS (Kôbe University): 4544
ESSAYS (Tôhoku University): 3204
ESSAYS (Tôkyô University): 2904
ESSAYS AND STUDIES (Jacavpur University, India): 3869
ESSAYS AND STUDIES (Kansai University): 3021
ESSAYS AND STUDIES IN ENGLISH LANGUAGE AND LITERATURE (Sendai, Japan): 3129
ESSAYS BY DIVERS HANDS: 2257, 2661
ESSAYS IN CRITICISM: 2086, 2107, 2163, 2319, 2320, 2376, 2388, 2433, 2445, 2446, 2802, 2922, 2960, 3710, 3744, 3981, 4211, 4507
ESSAYS IN LITERATURE (University of Denver): 4042
ESSAYS IN LITERATURE (Western Illinois University): 4333
ÉTUDES ANGLAISES: 3034, 3062, 3291, 3378, 3691, 3879, 4065, 4177, 4233
EXERCISE EXCHANGE: 2422
EXPLICATOR: 2108, 2191, 2532, 3036, 3057, 3371, 4035, 4202
LA FIERA LETTERARIA (Rome): 2609, 3656, 3767, 3919, 3962
FILM COMMENT: 3582
FILM HERITAGE: 3737
FILM JOURNAL: 3901

INDEX OF PERIODICALS AND NEWSPAPERS

FILM LIBRARY QUARTERLY: 3501, 3502
FILM QUARTERLY: 2104
FILMCRITICA (Rome): 4009
FILMS AND FILMING: 3631
FILMS IN REVIEW: 3173, 3537
FILOLOGIJA: 3609
FINANCIAL TIMES (Lond): 3243, 3244
FOCUS: 2547
FORUM (Houston): 2096
FORUM (South Africa): 2132
FORUM (Zagreb): 2996
FORUM FOR THE MODERN LANGUAGE STUDIES (St. Andrews University): 2688
FRANKFURTER ALLGEMEINE ZEITUNG: 2412, 3043, 3293, 4401, 4490; (Bilder und Zeiten): 3029
FRANKFURTER RUNDSCHAU: 4078
GAKUEN (Shôwa Women's University): 2717
GAZZETTA DEL SUD (Messina): 2274, 2275
IL GAZZETTINO (Venice): 2743, 2903
GENTE (Milan): 2240
GEORGIAN REVIEW: 2341
GERMANO-SLAVICA (University of Waterloo): 4386
IL GIORNALE D'ITALIA (Rome): 2080
IL GIORNO (Milan): 2998
GÖTEBORGS HANDELS-OCH SJÖFARTSTIDNING (Gothenburgh): 3702
GREAT SPECKLED BIRD (Atlanta): 3491
GUARDIAN (Manchester): 4040, 4105
HARPER'S MAGAZINE: 2567, 3190, 3749
HARRY (Baltimore): 3614
HERMATHENA: 2121
HERON (Saitama University): 4116
HIBBERT JOURNAL: 2614
HIROSHIMA STUDIES IN ENGLISH LANGUAGE AND LITERATURE (Hiroshima University): 2458, 2741, 4421
HOLIDAY: 2909, 3589
HORISONT (Vasa, Finland): 2103, 2566
HUDSON REVIEW: 2771, 3480, 4375
HUMAN STUDIES (Kanagawa University): 2792
HUMAN WORLD: 3855, 3856, 3871, 4050, 4144, 4173
HUMANIST: 3500
HUMANITIES (Doshisha University): 4368
HUMANITIES ASSOCIATION BULLETIN (Canada): 3503
IBADAN: 3363
ILLUSTRATED LONDON NEWS: 3265
IN BRITAIN: 4321
INDIAN JOURNAL OF ENGLISH STUDIES: 2159, 2334, 2441, 2991
INOSTRANNAIA LITERATURA (Foreign Literature): 2395
IOWA ENGLISH YEARBOOK: 2882
IOWA REVIEW: 3381
IPPAN KENKYÛ HOKOKU (Seikei University): 2934
JAHRBUCH FÜR AMERIKASTUDIEN: 2935
JAPAN QUARTERLY: 2165
JIN-BUN RONSHÛ (Waseda University): 3195
JOURNAL OF AESTHETICS AND ART CRITICISM: 3196, 3592, 4422
JOURNAL OF CONTEMPORARY HISTORY: 2951
JOURNAL OF FOREIGN LITERATURE (Komazawa University): 3969
JOURNAL OF HOKKAIDO UNIVERSITY OF EDUCATION: 4249, 4439
JOURNAL OF MODERN LITERATURE: 3689, 3808, 4013, 4178, 4262, 4364, 4431, 4596
JOURNAL OF NAGOYA MUNICIPAL WOMEN'S JUNIOR COLLEGE: 4349
JOURNAL OF NARRATIVE TECHNIQUE: 3892, 4029, 4120

JOURNAL OF OSAKA INDUSTRIAL UNIVERSITY: 3518, 3931, 4337
JOURNAL OF RYÛTSÛ KEIZAI UNIVERSITY: 4582, 4583
JOURNAL OF THE AUSTRALASIAN UNIVERSITIES LANGUAGES AND LITERATURE ASSOCIATION: 2178, 2750, 3010
JOURNAL OF THE COLLEGE OF LIBERAL ARTS (Toyama University): 4251, 4622
JOURNAL OF THE FACULTY OF FOREIGN LANGUAGES (Komazawa University): 3770, 3967, 3968, 4167, 4382
JOURNAL OF THE SECOND COLLEGE OF ENGINEERING, NIHON UNIVERSITY: 2736, 2883, 3000
JOURNAL OF TSUDA COLLEGE: 4127
JOURNAL OF YASUDA WOMEN'S UNIVERSITY: 4344
JUBILEE: 2164
KALEIDOSCOPE (Milwaukee): 3579
KANSAI-DAIGAKU BUNGAKU RONSHÛ (Kansai University): 2592
KANSAS CITY STAR: 4458
KANSAS MAGAZINE: 2308
KATAHIRA (Chuba Katahira): 3495
KEIZAI SHÛSHI (Nihon University): 3811, 4002, 4602
KENKYÛ RONBUN-SHÛ (Miyagi Women's College): 2557, 2847, 2979
KENTUCKY PHILOLOGICAL ASSOCIATION BULLETIN: 4280
KENYON REVIEW: 2186, 2451, 2467, 2990, 3317
KNJIŽEVNA SMOTRA: 3345, 4083, 4402
KNJIŽEVNAK DRITIKA: 4123
KÔBE MISCELLANY (Kôbe University): 2427, 2702, 3155, 3958, 4546
KÔNAN WOMEN'S COLLEGE RESEARCHES: 2707
KÔNAN WOMEN'S COLLEGE STUDIES IN ENGLISH LITERATURE: 2548, 2706, 2843
KURUME UNIVERSITY JOURNAL: 4334
KYÛSHÛ AMERICAN LITERATURE (Fukuoka, Japan): 2635
KYÛSHÛ SANGYÔ DAIGAKU KYÔYÔBU KIYÔ (Kyûshû Sangyô University): 2593, 2749, 2815, 2953
KYÛSHÛ SHÔKA DAIGAKU SHÔKEI RONSÔ (Kyûshû Shôka University): 2463
LANGUAGE AND LITERATURE (Copenhagen): 4113
LES LANGUES MODERNES: 3047, 3048, 3069, 3142, 3259, 3544
LETTERATURE MODERNE (Bologna): 2081
LES LETTRES NOUVELLES: 3076
LIBRARY: 4396
LIBRARY CHRONICLE OF THE UNIVERSITY OF TEXAS AT AUSTIN: 3481, 3513, 4110, 4282, 4284
LIBRARY JOURNAL: 2354, 2599, 2600, 2601, 3286, 3875
LIFE: 3603
LISTENER: 3083, 3159, 3289, 3386, 3885
LISTENER AND BBC TELEVISION REVIEW: 2150, 2259, 2260, 2312, 2329, 2519, 2681, 2822, 2868
LITERARY CRITERION (Mysore, India): 3586
LITERARY HALF-YEARLY: 2130, 2227, 2450, 3180, 3264, 3280
LITERARY MAN: 3649
LITERARY SYMPOSIUM (Aichi University): 2099, 2134, 2403, 2425, 2521, 2671, 2732, 2842
LITERATURE AND IDEOLOGY: 3703
LITERATURE AND PSYCHOLOGY: 2331, 2669, 2912, 2970, 3583, 3627
LITERATURE/FILM QUARTERLY: 4032, 4036, 4145, 4152, 4159, 4201, 4209, 4210, 4256, 4413
LOCK HAVEN REVIEW: 4418
LONDON MAGAZINE: 2067, 2371, 3329, 3714, 4154
LONDON REVIEW: 3288
LOOK MAGAZINE: 3510
LOS ANGELES HERALD EXAMINER: 3440
LUGANO REVIEW: 2628
MADEMOISELLE: 3551
MALAHAT REVIEW: 3023

INDEX OF PERIODICALS AND NEWSPAPERS

MANCHESTER GUARDIAN: 3305
MANCHESTER GUARDIAN WEEKLY: 2352
MANKIND: THE MAGAZINE OF POPULAR HISTORY: 3745
MASSACHUSETTS REVIEW: 2728, 2776, 3157, 3965, 4326
MASSACHUSETTS STUDIES IN ENGLISH: 4496
IL MATTINO (Naples): 2323, 2574
MEANJIN QUARTERLY: 2603, 2607, 3681, 3903, 4325, 4354
MEDIA AND METHODS: 3590
MELVILLE SOCIETY EXTRACTS: 4287
MEMOIRS OF HUMANISTIC AND SOCIAL SCIENCES (Kyoto Technical University): 2313, 2558, 2848, 2981, 4381
MEMOIRS OF ISHIKAWA TECHNICAL COLLEGE: 4553
MEMOIRS OF MEJIRO GAKUEN WOMEN'S JUNIOR COLLEGE: 3758, 4157, 4158, 4542
MEMOIRS OF SUZUKA COLLEGE OF TECHNOLOGY: 3752, 4358, 4359
MEMOIRS OF THE FACULTY OF GENERAL EDUCATION (Ehime University): 3738, 3942
MEMOIRS OF THE FACULTY OF GENERAL EDUCATION (Kumamoto University): 3936
MEMOIRS OF THE MURORAN INSTITUTE OF TECHNOLOGY: 3817, 4006, 4226
MENCKENIANA: 2711
MESSAGGERO VENETO (Udine): 3610
METROPOLITAN (Tôkyô Metropolitan University): 2668, 2814
MICHIGAN QUARTERLY REVIEW: 2781, 3238, 4493
MIDWAY: 2204
MODERN AGE (Chicago): 3580
MODERN AGE (Kôbe University): 4371, 4545
MODERN DRAMA: 2431, 2693
MODERN FICTION STUDIES: 2066, 2508, 2694, 3013, 3268, 3314, 3712, 3920, 4064, 4309, 4453, 4516, 4593
MODERN LANGUAGE JOURNAL: 2812, 2851
MODERN LANGUAGE NOTES: 2195
MODERN LANGUAGE REVIEW: 2765, 3376, 4426
MODERN OCCASIONS: 3671
MODERN PHILOLOGY: 2204, 3874, 4419
MODERN REVIEW (Calcutta): 3189
LE MONDE: 2971, 3146, 3566, 3692
IL MONDO (Rome): 2218, 2568
MONTH: 2328, 2649, 3093, 3625, 3713
MONTHLY FILM BULLETIN (British Film Institute, Lond): 3458
MOSAIC: 3108, 3532, 3676, 3732, 4018, 4087
MULBERRY (Aichi Prefectural University): 2454, 3519
NAGOYA REVIEW OF ENGLISH STUDIES (Nagoya University): 3809, 4222, 4416
NATION (NY): 2577, 2800
NEOPHILOLOGUS: 2250
NEUE DEUTSCHE HEFTE: 2452
NEUE ZEITSCHRIFT FÜR ÄRZTLICHE FORTBILDUNG: 2160
NEUE ZÜRCHER ZEITUNG: 2364, 2806, 3253
DIE NEUEREN SPRACHEN (Frankfurt): 2151, 2437, 3409
NEW LEADER: 3611
NEW LEFT REVIEW: 2487, 2596
NEW LETTERS: 2665
NEW MEXICAN (Santa Fe, NM): 3864
NEW MEXICO CULTURAL NEWS, Supplement to ENCANTO MAGAZINE (Albuquerque, NM): 3556
NEW REPUBLIC: 3090, 3530, 3531, 3897, 4128
NEW SOCIETY: 3092
NEW STATESMAN: 2100, 2102, 2239, 2265, 2485, 2491, 2589, 2653, 2654, 2677, 2858, 2859, 3081, 3100, 3178, 3221, 3382, 3383, 3459, 3783, 4163, 4179
NEW YORK: 3463
NEW YORK DAILY NEWS: 3452
NEW YORK HERALD TRIBUNE BOOKS: 2330

NEW YORK REVIEW OF BOOKS: 2578, 3086, 3179
NEW YORK SMITH: 4277
NEW YORK TIMES: 3026, 3449, 3450, 3705, 3709
NEW YORK TIMES BOOK REVIEW: 2148, 2336, 2507, 2846, 2992, 3306, 3957, 3986, 4228
NEW YORKER: 2748, 3115, 3172, 3311, 3505, 3526, 4207
NEWSLETTER OF THE CONFERENCE ON CHRISTIANITY AND LITERATURE: 3400
NEWSWEEK: 2536, 3154, 3567, 3652
NINETEENTH CENTURY FICTION: 2228, 2378, 4518
NORTHWEST REVIEW: 3740
NOTES AND QUERIES: 2125, 2176, 2255, 2258, 2410, 2767, 2768, 2861, 2902, 3220, 3252, 3361, 3424, 3613, 3618, 3840, 3848, 3894, 3895, 3898, 3899, 3915, 4183, 4258
LA NOUVELLE REVUE FRANÇAISE: 2202, 2344, 3028, 3251, 3660
NOVEL: A FORUM ON FICTION: 3665, 3706, 3805, 3959, 4597
NUOVA ANTOLOGIA (Rome): 3587
OBERON: 4102
OBSERVER (Lond): 2751, 2916, 2925, 3049, 3050, 3827, 4052
OCTOPUS (Ottawa): 3504
OKAYAMA UNIVERSITY: FACULTY OF LETTERS: 2958
ORMOND PAPERS (Parkville, Victoria, Australia): 2764
OSAKA LITERARY REVIEW (Ôsaka University): 2298, 2419
OSMANIA JOURNAL OF ENGLISH STUDIES (Hyderabad, India): 3798, 3990
ÔTSUKA REVIEW (Tôkyô University): 2528
PAESE SERA (Rome): 2199
PAPERS OF THE BIBLIOGRAPHICAL SOCIETY OF AMERICA: 2590, 2672, 2924, 3612, 4153
PAPERS ON LANGUAGE AND LITERATURE: 2761, 4572
PARENTS' MAGAZINE: 3593
PARIS REVIEW: 2350
PARTISAN REVIEW: 2084, 2120, 2183, 2263, 2503, 3493
PAUNCH: 2769, 2773, 2782, 2785, 2791, 2853, 2877, 2892, 2949, 3126, 3168, 3212, 3997, 4091, 4172, 4391, 4547, 4588
PERSONA (Rome): 2369
PERSPECTIVE: 2504
PHILOLOGICAL QUARTERLY: 4332
PHILOSOPHICAL REVIEW: 2854
PHOENIX (Haydenville, MA): 3721
PLANET: 3724
PLAYBOY: 2082, 3568, 4130
PLAYS AND PLAYERS: 2969, 3002, 3060, 3094, 3165, 4291
PMLA: PUBLICATIONS OF THE MODERN LANGUAGE ASSOCIATION: 2995, 3950, 4351
POETICA (Munich): 3147
POETRY: 2723, 3153
POETRY AUSTRALIA: 3405
PRELIMINARY ESSAY (Tôhoku University): 2404
PRELUDE (Ôsaka University): 2297, 2420
PREUVES: 2825, 3075
PRIVATE LIBRARY (Middlesex): 3632
PROCEEDINGS OF THE BRITISH ACADEMY: 2266
PROCEEDINGS OF THE UTAH ACADEMY OF SCIENCES, ARTS, AND LETTERS: 2917
LA PROVINCIA (Cremona): 2309, 2556
PSYCHOANALYTIC REVIEW: 2348, 2466, 2758, 3736, 4389
PSYCHOLOGICAL PERSPECTIVES: 3820
PTA MAGAZINE: 3643
PUBLICATIONS OF THE MODERN LANGUAGE ASSOCIATION: 2097, 2161, 2207, 2363, 2373, 2389, 2398, 2472, 2598, 2995, 3950, 4351
PUNCH: 3353
QUADRANT: 2252, 2322
QUEEN'S QUARTERLY: 2384, 2696, 3425, 4092, 4109
LA QUINZAINE LITTÉRAIRE: 3145, 3304
RADOVI A NI U BI H: 4521

RAMPARTS: 2375, 3056
RELIGION AND LIFE: 4510
RENAISSANCE AND MODERN STUDIES: 2141, 3267, 3594, 3787, 3867, 4257, 4271, 4319, 4617, 4627
RENDEZVOUS (Idaho State University): 3340
REPORT OF RIKKYÔ UNIVERSITY (HUMANE STUDIES): 3226
REPORT OF THE CHIBA INSTITUTE OF TECHNOLOGY (HUMANE STUDIES): 2746, 2887
REPORTER: 2588, 2860
REPORTS OF HIMEJI INSTITUTE OF TECHNOLOGY: 2898, 3020, 4026, 4438
RESEARCH BULLETIN OF OBIHIRO UNIVERSITY: 3336, 4129
RESEARCH REPORTS OF KURUME TECHNICAL COLLEGE: 3728
RESEARCH STUDIES (Washington State University): 2633
RESEARCHER (Tsuda College): 4384
IL RESTO DEL CARLINO (Bologna): 2304, 2549, 2552, 2708, 2977, 3162
REVIEW (Sapporo College of Commerce): 3815
REVIEW OF ARTS AND SCIENCES (Shibaura Institute of Technology): 2895, 3018
REVIEW OF ENGLISH LITERATURE: 2332, 2396, 2484, 2911
REVIEW OF ENGLISH LITERATURE (Kyôto University): 2561, 2715, 2983, 4169, 4170
REVIEW OF ENGLISH LITERATURE (Leeds): 2727
REVIEW OF ENGLISH STUDIES: 3483, 3748, 4086
REVIEW OF KÔBE UNIVERSITY OF MERCANTILE MARINE, PART I: STUDIES IN HUMANITIES AND SOCIAL SCIENCE: 2314, 2560, 2714, 2849, 2982, 3170
REVISTA DA FACULDADE DE LETRAS (University of Lisbon): 3786
REVUE DES LANGUES VIVANTES: 2126, 2381, 2889, 2926, 4393, 4541

REVUE GÉNÉRALE BELGE (Brussels): 2499
THE RITSUMEIKAN BUNGAKU (Ritsumeikan University): 2256
RIVERSIDE QUARTERLY: 2905
RONSHÛ (Senshû University): 2109, 2269
SAN FRANCISCO CHRONICLE: 2246, 3467, 3477
SAN FRANCISCO CHRONICLE, THIS WORLD: 2471
SANDAI REVIEW OF ENGLISH STUDIES (Kyôto Sangyô University): 3344, 3535
SANTA FE NEW MEXICAN, PASATIEMPO (Sunday Magazine Section): 2522, 2523
SATURDAY REVIEW: 2200, 2515, 3128, 3426, 3534
SAVREMENIK: MESEČNI KNJIŽEVNI CASOPIS: 3775, 4124
SCIENTIFIC RESEARCHES (Waseda University): 2090
SEKAIBUNGAKU (Tôkyô Toritsu University): 2980
SERIF: 3993, 4423
SEWANEE REVIEW: 2390, 2391, 2408, 2415, 2994, 3015, 3214
SEXUAL BEHAVIOR: 3776
SHAW REVIEW: 2753
SHENANDOAH: 2157
SHIKOKU CHRISTIAN COLLEGE TREATISES: 3416, 3648, 4435
SHIMONOSEKI ECONOMIC REVIEW (Shimonoseki Ichiritsu College): 2457, 2591, 2742
SHIRON (Tôhoku University): 2123, 2337, 2414, 2443, 2583
SHURA: 3650, 3651
LA SICILIA (Catania): 2231, 2411
SIGHT AND SOUND: 3274, 3428
SONODA WOMEN'S COLLEGE STUDIES: 2972, 3149
SOUTH ATLANTIC QUARTERLY: 2565, 3408
SOUTH DAKOTA REVIEW: 2704, 2795, 2803, 2914, 2968, 3388
SOUTHERLY: 3645, 4142
SOUTHERN HUMANITIES REVIEW: 4300
SOUTHERN QUARTERLY: 2821, 3120, 3174, 3937, 3938
SOUTHERN REVIEW (Adelaide):

2735, 3447, 3677, 3983, 4497,
SOUTHERN REVIEW (Baton Rouge): 2755, 3042
SOUTHWEST REVIEW: 2206, 2299, 2756
SOUTHWESTERN ART: 2930
SPECTATOR: 2070, 2114, 2115, 2219, 2343, 2571. 2779, 2884, 3038, 3201, 3213, 3434, 3647, 4529
SPES (Okayama University): 2823
SPIRIT: A MAGAZINE OF POETRY: 4041
LA STAMPA (Turin): 2212, 2900
STANDPUNTE: 3208, 3397, 3398, 3619, 3947
STUDI INGLESE (Rome): 4460
STUDIA NEOPHILOLOGICA (Stockholm): 3826
STUDIA ROMANICA ET ANGLICA ZAGRABIENSIA: 2873, 2997, 3394, 3988, 4403
STUDIES IN BIBLIOGRAPHY: 4486
STUDIES IN CIVIC AND NATURAL SCIENCES (Nihon University): 4155, 4540
STUDIES IN CULTURAL SCIENCE (Nihon University): 2959, 3134
STUDIES IN ENGLISH LANGUAGE AND LITERATURE (Kansai University): 2747
STUDIES IN ENGLISH LITERATURE (English Literary Society of Japan, Tokyo): 3954, 4204
STUDIES IN ENGLISH LITERATURE (Hôsei University): 2358, 2760, 2896
STUDIES IN ENGLISH LITERATURE AND LANGUAGE (Kyûshû University): 4440
STUDIES IN FOREIGN LITERATURES (Ritsumeikan University): 2105, 2138, 2261, 2818, 3116, 3333, 3418, 3527, 3731, 3831, 3832, 4253, 4255, 4520, 4625
STUDIES IN HUMANITIES (Ibaraki University): 3218
STUDIES IN HUMANITIES AND SOCIAL SCIENCE (Kôbe University of Mercantile Marine): 4562, 4563
STUDIES IN HUMANITY BY THE COLLEGE OF LIBERAL ARTS (Kanazawa University): 4205, 4405
STUDIES IN LANGUAGE AND LITERATURE (Science University of Tôkyô): 2816, 3111
STUDIES IN ROMANTICISM: 3441
STUDIES IN SHORT FICTION: 2361, 2524, 2786, 2813, 2919, 2993, 3006, 3035, 3082, 3256, 3326, 3331, 3393, 3541, 3663, 3876, 3991, 4061, 4096, 4176, 4308
STUDIES IN STYLISTICS (Ôsaka Women's University): 2703
STUDIES IN THE HUMANITIES (Ôsaka Medical College): 4125
STUDIES IN THE NOVEL: 3438, 3765, 3926, 4239, 4240
STUDIES IN THE TWENTIETH CENTURY: 3453
STUDIES OF SOCIAL SCIENCE (Kôchi Junior College): 2440
STUDIES OF SONODA WOMEN'S COLLEGE: 4261, 4448
THE STUDIO: 2272
STUDY OF CULTURAL SCIENCE (Niigata University): 3729, 3932
SÜDDEUTSCHE ZEITUNG: 2071, 2370, 2657, 3004, 3718, 4456
SUNDAY HERALD TRIBUNE BOOK WEEK (NY): 2494, 2570, 2585
SUNDAY TIMES (Lond): 2222, 2324, 2945, 3099
SUR: 3769
SYLVAN (Tôhoku University): 2459, 2680, 2745, 3008, 4028
TABLET (Lond): 2210
TAMARACK REVIEW: 2075, 2182
TAMKANG REVIEW (Taiwan): 3494
TAOS ARTS 1970, A Special Report in TAOS NEWS (Taos, NM): 3461, 3488, 3540
TAOS NEWS (Taos, NM): 3466, 3489, 3509, 3539, 3546, 3548, 3549, 3550, 3557, 3588, 3606
TAUROS (Kôbe University): 2554, 2555, 2710
IL TEMPO (Milan): 2147, 2346
IL TEMPO (Rome): 2305, 2306, 2551
TEXAS QUARTERLY: 2220, 2223, 2393, 2418, 2479, 2700, 2891, 2929
TEXAS STUDIES IN LITERATURE

AND LANGUAGE: 2064, 2243, 2368, 2432, 2476, 2497, 2527, 2540, 2928, 3095, 3624, 4508
THEOLOGY: 2083
THEORIA: 2489, 3970, 4353
THOTH: 2221, 2862, 3679
THOUGHT: 2310
THRESHOLD: 2173
TIME: 2205, 2495, 2597, 2850, 3163, 3529, 3584, 3887
TIME AND TIDE: 2168, 2172, 2193, 2382
TIMES (Lond): 2074, 2113, 2632, 2986, 3011, 3012, 3232, 3907, 3972, 4234
TIMES LITERARY SUPPLEMENT (Lond): 2145, 2162, 2169, 2171, 2214, 2248, 2335, 2362, 2416, 2488, 2562, 2616, 2645, 2719, 2720, 2811, 2871, 2872, 2893, 2894, 3055, 3176, 3271, 3281, 3294, 3300, 3301, 3377, 3487, 3528, 3545, 3547, 3623, 3669, 3693, 3694, 3753, 3759, 3760, 3779, 3790, 3850, 3886, 3890, 3975, 3976, 4021, 4118, 4220, 4246, 4283
TORONTO STAR WEEKLY: 2217
LA TORRE: REVISTA GENERAL DE LA UNIVERSIDAD DE PUERTO RICO: 2283
TRANSITION: 2307, 2426
TREATISES IN COMMEMORATION OF THE 15TH ANNIVERSARY OF THE FOUNDATION OF KITA-KYÛSHÛ UNIVERSITY: 2106
TRIJUMF INTELIGENCIJE (Belgrade): 2405
TRIVIUM: 4618
TSUDA REVIEW (Tsuda College): 4345
TUCSON DAILY CITIZEN (Tucson, AZ): 3575
TULANE STUDIES IN ENGLISH: 2622
TULSA DAILY WORLD (Tulsa, OK): 4534, 4535
TV TIMES (Lond): 2190
TWENTIETH CENTURY: 2119
TWENTIETH CENTURY LITERATURE: 3862
TWENTIETH CENTURY STUDIES: 3339

UMJETNOST RIJEČI: 3988
UNIVERSITY OF TORONTO QUARTERLY: 3027, 3107, 3121, 4259
UNIVERSITY OF WINDSOR REVIEW: 3312
UNIVERSITY REVIEW (Dublin): 2829
UNIVERSITY REVIEW (Kansas City): 2553, 2613, 3152, 3600
VARIETY: 3591
IL VERRI (Milan): 2143
VIDEO (Turin): 3379
VIDICI: 4512, 4537
VIRGINIA QUARTERLY REVIEW: 2429, 2461, 2582, 2712, 4082, 4317
VLAAMSE GIDS: 2721
VOGUE: 3604, 3605
VOLCANO (Kagoshima University): 2897
WALT WHITMAN REVIEW: 3999
WANDERER (St. Paul, MN): 4376, 4548, 4549, 4550, 4551
WASCANA REVIEW: 2805, 3151
WASEDA JOURNAL OF GENERAL SCIENCES (Waseda University): 4603
WASEDA REVIEW: 3830, 4027, 4252, 4623
WASHINGTON POST BOOK WORLD: 3602, 3960, 4015
WEST COAST REVIEW: 3420, 4302
WEST VIRGINIA ASSOCIATION OF COLLEGE ENGLISH TEACHERS BULLETIN: 4565
WEST VIRGINIA UNIVERSITY BULLETIN: PHILOLOGICAL PAPERS: 3857
WESTERLY: 2576
WESTERN AMERICAN LITERATURE: 3233, 3235
WESTERN HUMANITIES REVIEW: 2637, 2697, 3401, 3521, 4274, 4610
WESTWAYS: 3780
WILLAMETTE BRIDGE (Portland, OR): 3520
WILSON LIBRARY BULLETIN: 2990
WISCONSIN STUDIES IN CONTEMPORARY LITERATURE: 2509, 2772
WOMEN: A JOURNAL OF LIBERA-

TION (Baltimore, MD): 3439
WOMEN'S STUDIES: 4186
WORD: 2559
WORD IN DER ZEIT (Vienna): 2216
WORLD THEATRE: 2353
XAVIER UNIVERSITY STUDIES: 3933
YALE REVIEW: 2801, 2856, 3507, 4451
YALE UNIVERSITY LIBRARY GAZETTE: 3833, 3956, 4481, 4487
YAMATO BUNKA (Tenri University): 2428
YEARBOOK OF ENGLISH STUDIES: 3838
ZBORNIK FILOZOFSKOG FAKULTETA (Priština): 2923
ŽIVOT: 2073

Index

FOREIGN LANGUAGES

Included here are the languages in which articles and books listed in the bibliography originally appeared. Numbers under each language refer to items in the bibliography where the foreign-language title is given. English-language items are not listed.

Danish: 3046
Dutch: 2721
French: 2110, 2201, 2202, 2344, 2353, 2499, 2500, 2625, 2737, 2825, 2835, 2971, 3028, 3034, 3047, 3048, 3062, 3063, 3075, 3076, 3142, 3145, 3146, 3251, 3259, 3291, 3292, 3304, 3378, 3421, 3433, 3490, 3544, 3566, 3574, 3660, 3691, 3692, 3696, 3879, 3917, 4065, 4294, 4318, 4377, 4567
German: 2071, 2079, 2151, 2160, 2216, 2284, 2364, 2412, 2437, 2452, 2496, 2505, 2656, 2657, 2663, 2664, 2679, 2716, 2725, 2796, 2806, 2935, 2985, 3004, 3017, 3029, 3043, 3072, 3109, 3147, 3222, 3249, 3253, 3257, 3293, 3299, 3409, 3707, 3718, 3773, 3784, 3824, 3841, 4078, 4401, 4456, 4490, 4612
Italian: 2080, 2081, 2127, 2135, 2143, 2147, 2199, 2212, 2218, 2231, 2240, 2274, 2275, 2302, 2303, 2304, 2305, 2306, 2309, 2323, 2346, 2360, 2369, 2411, 2478, 2549, 2550, 2551, 2552, 2556, 2568, 2573, 2574, 2609, 2621, 2708, 2743, 2778, 2840, 2844, 2857, 2900, 2903, 2976, 2977, 2998, 3051, 3084, 3087, 3162, 3364, 3379, 3555, 3571, 3572, 3573, 3587, 3610, 3656, 3767, 3774, 3878, 3919, 3962, 3963, 4009, 4162, 4191, 4192, 4279, 4292, 4313, 4432, 4460, 4474, 4554, 4555
Japanese: 2065, 2090, 2093, 2098, 2099, 2105, 2106, 2109, 2123, 2134, 2136, 2138, 2139, 2140, 2166, 2256, 2261, 2269, 2292, 2297, 2298, 2313, 2314, 2315, 2337, 2345, 2358, 2365, 2366, 2400, 2401, 2403, 2404, 2414, 2419, 2420, 2425, 2427, 2428, 2440, 2443, 2454, 2457, 2458, 2459, 2460, 2463, 2516, 2521, 2525, 2541, 2542, 2547, 2548, 2554, 2555, 2557, 2558, 2560, 2561, 2583, 2591, 2592, 2593, 2605, 2660, 2668, 2670, 2671, 2674, 2680, 2702, 2703, 2706, 2707, 2710, 2713, 2714, 2715, 2717, 2732, 2736, 2741, 2742, 2745, 2746, 2747, 2749, 2759, 2760, 2792, 2810, 2814, 2815, 2816, 2817, 2818, 2819, 2823, 2842, 2843, 2847, 2848, 2849, 2883, 2887, 2895, 2896, 2897, 2898, 2904, 2934, 2950, 2952, 2953, 2958, 2959, 2972, 2979, 2980, 2981, 2982, 2983, 2984, 3000, 3001, 3003, 3008, 3009, 3018, 3019, 3020, 3021, 3022, 3111, 3112, 3116, 3117, 3118,

3125, 3130, 3134, 3149, 3167,
3170, 3195, 3204, 3226, 3227,
3333, 3336, 3341, 3344, 3346,
3366, 3370, 3395, 3416, 3417,
3418, 3495, 3518, 3519, 3527,
3535, 3576, 3633, 3639, 3640,
3648, 3649, 3650, 3651, 3728,
3729, 3731, 3735, 3738, 3752,
3758, 3770, 3799, 3800, 3809,
3811, 3812, 3815, 3821, 3829,
3830, 3831, 3832, 3842, 3931,
3932, 3936, 3941, 3942, 3954,
3958, 3966, 3967, 3968, 3969,
3985, 3992, 4002, 4019, 4026,
4027, 4028, 4071, 4088, 4102,
4103, 4116, 4117, 4125, 4127,
4129, 4134, 4135, 4136, 4138,
4155, 4157, 4158, 4166, 4167,
4168, 4169, 4170, 4171, 4204,
4221, 4222, 4226, 4235, 4248,
4249, 4250, 4251, 4252, 4253,
4254, 4255, 4298, 4312, 4334,
4335, 4336, 4337, 4343, 4344,
4345, 4349, 4350, 4352, 4358,
4359, 4360, 4368, 4371, 4372,
4373, 4378, 4379, 4380, 4381,
4382, 4383, 4384, 4385, 4398,
4404, 4414, 4415, 4416, 4417,
4421, 4428, 4435, 4436, 4437,
4438, 4439, 4441, 4480, 4491,
4503, 4504, 4513, 4514, 4519,
4520, 4522, 4524, 4540, 4542,
4544, 4545, 4546, 4553, 4560,
4561, 4562, 4563, 4564, 4580,
4582, 4583, 4599, 4602, 4603,
4604, 4606, 4619, 4620, 4621,
4622, 4623, 4624, 4625

Korean: 3338
Norwegian: 4608
Romanian: 3194
Russian: 2395
Serbo-Croatian: 2073, 2268, 2405,
   2413, 2730, 2923, 2996, 3345,
   3609, 3775, 3952, 3988, 4038,
   4083, 4123, 4402, 4512, 4521,
   4537, 4570
South Slovenian: 4124
Spanish: 2283, 2626, 2766, 2937,
   3097, 3451, 3769, 4181, 4182,
   4570
Swedish: 2103, 2170, 2566, 3638,
   3702

Index

PRIMARY TITLES

Included here are all titles by Lawrence which occur in titles of articles or books or in the abstracts. Numbers after each title refer to the item in the bibliography where the title appears.

L'Amant de Lady Chatterley, film: 2424, 3181, 3631, 4145, 4201
A Propos of "Lady Chatterley's Lover": 2107, 2126, 2149, 2261, 2283, 2961, 3038, 3055, 3288, 3321, 3376, 4332, 4346
Aaron's Rod: 2068, 2097, 2110, 2394, 2419, 2453, 2456, 2490, 2549, 2621, 2624, 2640, 2662, 2679, 2698, 2141, 2754, 2769, 2862, 2869, 2962, 2987, 2991, 3199, 3218, 3320, 3337, 3419, 3472, 3498, 3508, 3514, 3554, 3563, 3573, 3629, 3661, 3699, 3749, 3778, 3782, 3806, 3822, 3849, 3873, 3905, 4093, 4095, 4098, 4133, 4154, 4169, 4206, 4212, 4263, 4305, 4319, 4332, 4398, 4437, 4497, 4577, 4623
"Abysmal Immortality": 2230, 3275
"Adolf": 3143, 3525, 3793, 4208
"All Soul's Day": 2318
All Things Are Possible, translation: 3517
Altitude: 2693, 3791, 4587
"America, Listen to Your Own": 3236
Amores: 2988, 3472, 4230
"Amphibian": 3617
Apocalypse: 2318, 2610, 2679, 2764, 3199, 3235, 3514, 3655, 3732, 3750, 3813, 3871, 3985, 4046, 4166, 4332, 4336, 4417, 4526

"Apostolic Beasts": 3525
"Art and Morality": 3566, 3796, 4122
"Art and the Individual": 3078, 4177
Assorted Articles: 3055, 3078, 3913, 4098
At the Gates: 4196
"Baby Tortoise": 3599, 4358
"Bavarian Gentians": 2318, 2377, 2776, 2805, 3067, 3275, 3494, 3620, 3823, 3913, 4349, 4425, 4477, 4508, 4579
"Baxter Dawes": 2111
Bay: 3559
"Beautiful Old Age": 4458
"Beauty and Truth": 3617
"Bei Hennef": 2499, 3913
"Benjamin Franklin": 2882, 3479
"Beware the Unhappy Dead": 2318
"Bibbles": 3337, 3877
Birds, Beasts, and Flowers: 2143, 2146, 2377, 2499, 2621, 2708, 2869, 2987, 2988, 3067, 3180, 3221, 3240, 3245, 3299, 3380, 3396, 3398, 3442, 3472, 3494, 3559, 3620, 3740, 3790, 3873, 3913, 3964, 3965, 3984, 3987, 4041, 4056, 4122, 4230, 4276, 4499
"The Bitterness of Ecstasy": 2289, 2893
"Blessed Are the Powerful": 4332
"The Blind Man": 2122, 2449, 2464, 2652, 2963, 2970, 3102, 3168,

3230, 3234, 3256, 3307, 3536,
3574, 3788, 3892, 4051, 4362
4463
"The Blue Moccasins": 2351, 2954,
3536, 3794, 3899
Boccaccio Story, painting: 2562,
3792
"Bombardment": 4492
"The Border Line": 2351, 2678,
2813, 2819, 3109, 3319, 3462
The Boy in the Bush: 2110, 2275,
2302, 2304, 2306, 2369, 2576,
3071, 3472, 3760, 3764, 3994,
4179, 4357
"The Bride": 2720
The Captain's Doll: 2351, 2453,
2482, 2679, 2844, 2869, 3059,
3065, 3107, 3857, 3920, 4577
"The Cathedral": 2111, 3224, 3284
*Cavalleria Rusticana and Other
Stories*, translation: 2121, 2621,
3517
The Centaur Letters: 3553
"Certain Americans and an Englishman": 4224
"A Chapel among the Mountains":
2303, 3793, 4173
"Charity": 3620
"Cherry Robbers": 3696, 3913
"The Christening": 2348, 2442,
2511, 3256, 3874, 3898
"City Life": 3120
"Classroom": 3499
Close-Up (Kiss), painting: 2562
*The Collected Letters of D. H.
Lawrence*: 2200, 2205, 2211,
2222, 2228, 2246, 2248, 2259,
2265, 2293, 2294, 2311, 2330,
2335, 2336, 2343, 2352, 2354,
2356, 2364, 2376, 2378, 2391,
2408, 2429, 2434, 2439, 2451,
2468, 2506, 3276, 3392, 3826,
4054, 4059, 4119, 4238
*The Collected Poems of D. H.
Lawrence*: 2264, 2683, 3158,
3245, 3299, 3361, 3472, 3984,
4356, 4370, 4584
A Collier's Friday Night: 2868,
2884, 2894, 3092, 3241, 3301,
3412, 3492, 4292, 4401, 4587
A Collier's Friday Night, Royal
Court Theatre production:
2632, 3050, 3060, 3072, 3081,
3092, 3093, 3131, 3132, 3135,
3139, 3165, 3172, 3205, 3206,
3213, 3232, 3243, 3244, 3791,
4163
Complete Collection of Travel Books
(Milan): 2135, 2199, 2218,
2240, 2305, 2309, 2323, 2360,
2411
*Complete Plays and Selected Literary
Criticism, Essays* (Milan): 4555
*The Complete Plays of D. H.
Lawrence*: 2751, 2800, 2830,
2846, 2850, 2858, 2868, 2876,
2884, 2894, 3010
*The Complete Poems of D. H.
Lawrence* (London, 1957): 2264
*The Complete Poems of D. H. L
Lawrence*, ed Vivian de Sola Pinto
and F. Warren Roberts: 2146,
2491, 2507, 2519, 2534, 2536,
2569, 2571, 2577, 2585, 2601,
2616, 2629, 2637, 2645, 2665,
2683, 2685, 2719, 2720, 2723,
2729, 2748, 2765, 2851, 3066,
3158, 3175, 3207, 3214, 3361,
3497, 3539, 3617, 3618, 3620,
3893, 3964, 3976, 4031, 4065,
4081, 4165
*The Complete Short Novels and
Fragments of Novel* (Milan): 2844
The Complete Short Stories (Milan):
2303
*The Complete Short Stories of D. H.
Lawrence*: 3910, 4468
"Creative Evolution": 2264, 2288
"The Crown": 3124, 3192, 3263,
3292, 3376, 3456, 3666, 3756,
3873, 4133, 4336
"Cruelty and Love": 3696, 4584
"Cry of the Masses": 2478
"D. H. Lawrence: A Season of
Plays," Royal Court Theatre
productions: 3049, 3050, 3092,
3094, 3099, 3131, 3132, 3135,
3206, 3244, 3791
*D. H. Lawrence and Italy: Twilight in
Italy, Sea and Sardinia, Etruscan
Places*: 3865
D. H. Lawrence on Education: 4244
*D. H. Lawrence: Poems Selected for
Young People*: 2918, 2992, 3153,
3176, 3221
D. H. Lawrence: Selected Poems,

INDEX OF PRIMARY TITLES

ed Keith Sagar: 3975, 3984, 4031
D. H. Lawrence: Selected Tales, ed Ian Serraillier: 2442
D. H. Lawrence: Tutte le Poesie, ed Piero Nardi: 2081, 2127, 2143, 2145, 2171, 2274
D. H. Lawrence's Letters to Bertrand Russell: 3190, 4596
D. H. Lawrence's Unpublished Foreword to "Women in Love": 4284
The Daughter-in-Law: 2858, 2868, 2884, 2894, 2977, 3004, 3010, 3092, 3144, 3194, 3241, 3300, 3301, 3412, 3791, 4292, 4587
The Daughter-in-Law, Royal Court Theatre production: 2916, 2969, 2977, 3012, 3060, 3081, 3092, 3094, 3132, 3135, 3165, 3172, 3194, 3206, 3213, 3244, 3318, 3362, 3791, 4163
The Daughter-in-Law, Traverse Theatre production: 2903, 2986
"Daughters of the Vicar": 2202, 2226, 2348, 2351, 2442, 2453, 2466, 2482, 2789, 2831, 3225, 4050, 4368, 4421, 4439, 4486, 4570
David: 2181, 2420, 2431, 2751, 2800, 2868, 2884, 2894, 3010, 3019, 3021, 3188, 3224, 3241, 3319, 3379, 3412, 3472, 3581, 3791, 4474, 4527, 4555, 4587
David Herbert Lawrence: The Complete Tales and Short Novels: 4612
"The Dead Mother": 2720
"The Death of Pan": 2636
"Death": 2318
"Death and Love": 2619
"Democracy": 2631, 3177
"Difficult Death": 2318
"Discipline": 2878, 2988
"A Dream of Life": 3794
"Edgar Allan Poe": 2161, 2207, 2470, 2506, 3809
"Education of the People": 2367, 2594, 2878, 3177, 3215, 3499, 4244, 4497, 4526, 4562
"Elysium": 2107
"Embankment at Night, Before the War: Charity": 3619
"End of Another Home Holiday": 3067
"The End, the Beginning": 2318

"England, My England": 2119, 2351, 2875, 3168, 3186, 3454, 3535, 3536, 4212, 4410
England, My England and Other Stories: 3251, 3472, 3473, 3661, 3782
"The English Are So Nice": 2230
"Epithalamion": 2499
Eros and the Dogs (Paris): 3566
The Escaped Cock: 3777, 3946, 4140, 4307
Etruscan Places: 2135, 2178, 2231, 2318, 2360, 2621, 2776, 2869, 2879, 2881, 2987, 3051, 3666, 3865, 4043, 4121, 4547, 4548, 4550
"The Evangelistic Beasts": 2708, 2988
"Excurse": 2177, 2619, 2728, 3706
"Fanny and Annie": 3393
Fantasia of the Unconscious: 2110, 2168, 2177, 2282, 2456, 2527, 2608, 2663, 2773, 2833, 2864, 2995, 3030, 3120, 3156, 3168, 3183, 3320, 3337, 3433, 3462, 3472, 3570, 3639, 3640, 3661, 3811, 3821, 3886, 3923, 3925, 3947, 4002, 4051, 4137, 4187, 4332, 4482, 4526, 4527, 4577
The Fight for Barbara: 2693, 2868, 2894, 3002, 3194, 3791, 4587
The Fight for Barbara, Mermaid Theatre production: 2925, 2945, 3011, 3064, 3123, 3194
Fight with an Amazon, painting: 2562
"Fire": 3617
"Fireworks in Florence": 4509
The First Lady Chatterley: 2112, 2489, 2976, 3807, 3885, 3907, 3908, 3909, 3960, 4118, 4220, 4342
"Fish": 2499, 2869, 2908, 3542, 4276
"The Flying Fish": 2869, 3462, 3794, 3820, 4363
"For the Heroes Are Dipped in Scarlet": 2318, 3940
"Forecast": 4584
"Foreword to *Collected Poems*" (1964): 3158, 4370
The Fox: 2093, 2099, 2239, 2244, 2351, 2355, 2394, 2423, 2613, 2679, 2697, 2786, 2794, 2821

2844, 2869, 2949, 2964, 3082,
3162, 3178, 3401, 3525, 3536,
3563, 3676, 3821, 3899, 3920,
3981, 3991, 4006, 4051, 4064,
4147, 4191, 4404, 4412, 4494,
4542, 4577, 4592
The Fox, film: 3026, 3058, 3066,
3079, 3096, 3115, 3128, 3154,
3162, 3173, 3202, 3231, 3401,
3631, 3866, 4145, 4152, 4159,
4327
"A Fragment of Stained Glass":
2303, 2351, 3663, 3898
"German Books: Thomas Mann":
4132
"Germans and English": 4153
"Give Us Gods": 3873
"Glad Ghosts": 2678, 4604
"Gladiatorial": 2453, 3433, 3582,
4154, 4516
"Glory of Darkness": 2805, 3222,
4579
Goats and Compasses: 3033, 3699,
3836, 4068, 4070, 4190, 4196
"The Good Man": 3566
"The Greeks Are Coming!": 2318,
3940
"The Hands of God": 2230, 3275
"The Hands of the Betrothed":
3291, 4122
"Hawthorne's *Blithedale Romance*":
2316
"A Hut among the Mountains":
2303, 3793, 4173
"The He-Goat": 3965
"Her Turn": 3793, 3898
"Herman Melville's *Moby Dick*":
2879, 3337, 3671, 4287
"Herman Melville's *Typee* and
Omoo": 2559, 2487
"Him with His Tail in His Mouth":
3083
"Honeymoon": 4584
"Honour and Arms": 3690
"The Hopi Snake Dance": 2673
"The Horse-Dealer's Daughter":
2137, 2331, 2351, 2828, 2940,
3028, 3075, 3076, 3145, 3146,
3223, 3536, 3879, 3950, 4039,
4096, 4176, 4468, 4557, 4558,
4568
"The Houseless Dead": 2318
"How Beastly the Bourgeois Is":
2409
"Humiliation": 3965
"Hymns in a Man's Life": 3566
I Malavoglia, translation: 2121
"In Love": 3899
"Indians and an Englishman": 4224
"The Industrial Magnate": 3403, 4057
The Insurrection of Miss Houghton:
3124, 3192
"Intimates": 2230
"Introduction to *Memoirs of the
Foreign Legion* by Maurice
Magnus": 2135, 3038, 3055
3246
"Introduction to *Pansies*": 3483
"Introduction to These Paintings":
2273, 2990, 3566, 4097, 4122,
4516
"Invocation to the Moon": 3940
"Italians in Exile": 2064
"Jimmy and the Desperate Woman":
2351, 3319, 3462
"John Galsworthy": 2386, 2644,
2798, 2959, 3134, 3670
John Thomas and Lady Jane: 3875,
3883, 3887, 3897, 3907, 3909,
3945, 3957, 3960, 4082, 4109,
4118, 4207, 4239, 4240, 4302,
4342, 4456
Kangaroo: 2068, 2110, 2261, 2275,
2285, 2301, 2302, 2304, 2306,
2369, 2394, 2419, 2453, 2456,
2484, 2490, 2508, 2509, 2538,
2572, 2603, 2607, 2612, 2624,
2640, 2646, 2648, 2672, 2679,
2754, 2804, 2835, 2869, 2924,
2931, 2937, 2951, 2962, 2971,
2987, 2991, 3063, 3083, 3199,
3337, 3381, 3394, 3427, 3472,
3498, 3514, 3554, 3600, 3629,
3644, 3645, 3654, 3661, 3675,
3764, 3769, 3778, 3782, 3806,
3849, 3859, 3873, 3905, 3944,
4054, 4095, 4098, 4121, 4130,
4133, 4142, 4305, 4319, 4331
4455, 4492, 4497, 4577
Keeping Barbara: 2693
"Kisses on the Train": 4584
"La Lupa," translation: 4191
Lady Chatterley's Lover: 2068, 2072,
2073, 2075, 2083, 2089, 2094,
2095, 2097, 2101, 2107, 2110,
2115, 2118, 2125, 2130, 2132,

INDEX OF PRIMARY TITLES

2152, 2155, 2158, 2160, 2164, 2165, 2167, 2175, 2176, 2184, 2185, 2187, 2189, 2192, 2206, 2217, 2222, 2225, 2227, 2232, 2234, 2235, 2245, 2251, 2255, 2261, 2266, 2278, 2281, 2283, 2284, 2285, 2295, 2307, 2309, 2310, 2311, 2319, 2324, 2339, 2340, 2348, 2355, 2371, 2379, 2384, 2388, 2399, 2410, 2418, 2423, 2424, 2426, 2433, 2445, 2446, 2449, 2453, 2456, 2466, 2470, 2478, 2489, 2490, 2492, 2510, 2520, 2537, 2547, 2568, 2572, 2580, 2596, 2618, 2621, 2624, 2633, 2640, 2662, 2677, 2679, 2681, 2687, 2697, 2705, 2708, 2713, 2718, 2721, 2734, 2766, 2770, 2771, 2773, 2776, 2791, 2794, 2796, 2822, 2827, 2834, 2835, 2838, 2842, 2843, 2853, 2862, 2869, 2877, 2885, 2915, 2923, 2926, 2929, 2943, 2944, 2962, 2966, 2976, 2991, 2999, 3014, 3024, 3029, 3053, 3054, 3071, 3091, 3098, 3103, 3108, 3126, 3151, 3199, 3200, 3218, 3248, 3251, 3272, 3279, 3280, 3285, 3299, 3321, 3328, 3338, 3339, 3340, 3355, 3359, 3367, 3369, 3370, 3396, 3406, 3419, 3420, 3429, 3453, 3472, 3475, 3486, 3498, 3508, 3513, 3516, 3528, 3545, 3553, 3554, 3563, 3583, 3629, 3646, 3654, 3661, 3666, 3696, 3710, 3721, 3749, 3750, 3782, 3783, 3806, 3818, 3834, 3849, 3856, 3873, 3875, 3885, 3886, 3887, 3897, 3905, 3909, 3914, 3919, 3945, 3957, 3960, 3961, 3966, 3992, 3998, 4037, 4045, 4051, 4054, 4082, 4093, 4098, 4109, 4118, 4125, 4138, 4145, 4170, 4186, 4199, 4201, 4204, 4206, 4207, 4220, 4225, 4228, 4239, 4240, 4243, 4294, 4303, 4329, 4330, 4334, 4340, 4342, 4352, 4362, 4368, 4384, 4404, 4412, 4416, 4418, 4420, 4422, 4423, 4437, 4440, 4452, 4456, 4472, 4489, 4492, 4522, 4534, 4553, 4554, 4565, 4576, 4577

Lady Chatterley's Lover, trials: 2069, 2073, 2074, 2075, 2076, 2078, 2080, 2095, 2101, 2115, 2118, 2120, 2126, 2132, 2149, 2154, 2155, 2164, 2165, 2169, 2170, 2173, 2182, 2184, 2189, 2192, 2222, 2225, 2267, 2270, 2280, 2281, 2284, 2295, 2320, 2325, 2326, 2327, 2339, 2340, 2424, 2445, 2446, 2450, 2478, 2492, 2610, 2779, 2827, 2957, 2990, 3007, 3054, 3181, 3184, 3219, 3387, 3406, 3552, 3797, 4446, 4601

"Lady Wife": 2761

The Ladybird: 2097, 2366, 2844, 2887, 3108, 3472, 3473, 3674, 3793, 3920, 4007, 4019, 4054, 4086, 4467, 4577

Laetitia: 3874

"The Last Laugh": 2540, 3035, 3319, 3462, 4019

Last Poems: 2146, 2261, 2318, 2377, 2447, 2637, 2645, 2718, 2776, 2869, 2987, 2988, 3066, 3067, 3175, 3207, 3240, 3245, 3275, 3296, 3380, 3494, 3559, 3570, 3617, 3618, 3620, 3699, 3716, 3782, 3873, 3882, 3913, 3940, 3984, 4380, 4508, 4552, 4579, 4584

"Last Words to Miriam": 4584

The Latter Days: 4618

Lawrence in Love: Letters to Louie Burrows: 3044, 3201, 3253, 3268, 3286, 3291, 3294, 3306, 3311, 3317, 3329, 3350, 3354, 3364, 3382, 3422, 3543, 3762, 3828, 3840, 4227

Lawrence on Hardy and Painting: 4063

Letters from D. H. Lawrence to Martin Secker, 1911-1930: 3545, 3608, 3762

The Letters of D. H. Lawrence, ed. Aldous Huxley: 2198, 2214, 2246, 2265, 2336, 2690, 2885, 3392, 3661, 3893, 4054, 4059, 4134

The Letters of D. H. Lawrence, gen. ed. James T. Boulton: 3762, 3956, 4044

"Life": 2261
"Lightning": 4097
Little Novels of Sicily, translation: 2121, 2778, 3517, 4242
Look! We Have Come Through!: 2140, 2143, 2241, 2723, 2761, 2988, 3245, 3275, 3299, 3380, 3442, 3472, 3559, 3620, 3629, 3739, 3913, 3965, 3984, 4054, 4100, 4444, 4552
"Lord's Prayer": 3940
The Lost Girl: 2068, 2381, 2398, 2406, 2423, 2425, 2453, 2490, 2580, 2621, 2640, 2809, 2869, 2881, 2958, 2991, 3071, 3124, 3192, 3472, 3498, 3545, 3573, 3782, 3905, 4054, 4133, 4206, 4304, 4305, 4412, 4554
Love among the Haystacks: 2178, 2351, 2355, 2939, 3137
Love among the Haystacks and Other Pieces: 2178
"Love on the Farm": 2988, 3620, 3913, 4584
Love Poems and Others: 3361, 3472, 3696, 4054
"Love": 3215, 4468
"The Lovely Lady": 2110, 2151, 2351, 2875, 3145, 3536, 4487
"Making Love to Music": 3566
"Making Pictures": 3566
"The Maleficent Triangle": 3617
"The Man of Tyre": 3275, 3618, 3940
The Man Who Died: 2076, 2105, 2292, 2300, 2318, 2348, 2351, 2394, 2449, 2453, 2503, 2562, 2564, 2619, 2621, 2660, 2678, 2679, 2718, 2776, 2794, 2808, 2821, 2829, 2835, 2844, 2869, 2881, 2973, 2991, 3008, 3024, 3039, 3045, 3046, 3077, 3141, 3147, 3188, 3215, 3217, 3218, 3225, 3284, 3313, 3338, 3416, 3462, 3570, 3629, 3661, 3719, 3746, 3777, 3782, 3801, 3813, 3834, 3882, 3910, 3938, 3946, 3966, 3969, 3985, 4018, 4019, 4155, 4230, 4305, 4307, 4349, 4416, 4417, 4435, 4477, 4493, 4523, 4526, 4577, 4592, 4604, 4605, 4615
"The Man Who Loved Islands": 2110, 2351, 2355, 2442, 2516, 2526, 2639, 2787, 2967, 3105, 3106, 3145, 3147, 3525, 3536, 3649, 3794, 4215, 4295, 4303, 4405, 4416, 4424, 4592
"The Man Who Was Through with the World": 3147, 3794
"Man's Image": 3823
The Mango Tree, painting: 2562
"Manifesto": 2107
"Market Day": 2682
The Married Man: 3241, 3791, 4555, 4587
Mastro-Don Gesualdo, translation: 2121, 2621, 2778
"Maximus": 3275
"Medlars and Sorb-Apples": 3494
Men and Women: 3002, 3123
Men Bathing, painting: 4534
The Merry-Go-Round: 2858, 2977, 3137, 3791, 4078, 4163, 4234, 4555, 4587
The Merry-Go-Round, Royal Court Theatre production: 4040, 4105, 4291
"The Miner at Home": 3793
"Mino": 3531
"A Modern Lover": 2303, 2875, 2993, 4439
"Monkey Nuts": 2442
"Moony": 2619, 2873, 3048, 3363
"Morality and the Novel": 2334, 2506, 2961, 3566, 4440
More Pansies: 2637, 3066, 3175, 3207, 3559, 3618, 3620, 4100
Mornings in Mexico: 2135, 2178, 2188, 2285, 2370, 2412, 2682, 2947, 3145, 3861, 4324, 4548
"The Mortal Coil": 3078, 3083, 3793, 3993
The Mortal Coil and Other Stories: 3793
"Mosquito": 4499
"The Mosquito Knows": 2499
"Mother and Daughter": 2351, 3536, 3794
Movements in European History: 2878, 3284, 3462, 3674, 3930, 4021, 4059, 4065
"Mr. Noon": 3038, 3055, 3083, 3246
"My Skirmish with Jolly Roger": 3903

INDEX OF PRIMARY TITLES

"Nathaniel Hawthorne and *The Scarlet Letter*": 2316, 2341, 4150, 4588
Nettles: 2585, 3221, 3380, 3913
"New Eve and Old Adam": 2351
"New Heaven and Earth": 2107, 3559, 3965
"New Mexico": 2783, 4461, 4526
New Poems: 3620
"The Nightmare": 2301, 2612, 3600
"Nils Lykke": 3895
Noah's Flood: 3791, 4587
"None of That": 2351, 2663, 3536, 4574
"Nottingham and the Mining Countryside": 2506, 3285, 3858, 4067, 4208, 4346
"The Novel": 2782, 3083, 4382
"The Novel and the Feelings": 3566
"Odour of Chrysanthemums": 2098, 2122, 2247, 2303, 2348, 2351, 2423, 2442, 2506, 2627, 2659, 2831, 2837, 2868, 2875, 2896, 2904, 2975, 3010, 3039, 3144, 3241, 3267, 3288, 3326, 3689, 3757, 4439, 4574
"The Old Adam": 2348, 2466, 3793
"Once": 2303, 3793
"Only Man": 3275
"The Overtone": 3794
"Painted Tombs of Tarquinia": 2879, 3025
Paintings of D. H. Lawrence, ed Mervyn Levy: 2495, 2507, 2530, 2531, 2533, 2536, 2545, 2562, 2565, 2567, 2570, 2575, 2577, 2578, 2588, 2589, 2599, 2655, 2712, 2851, 2946, 4322
The Paintings of D. H. Lawrence (Mandrake P): 2118, 3472, 3903, 4325, 4354
"Pan in America": 2097, 2540, 2636, 3120, 4208
Pansies: 2143, 2222, 2499, 2580, 2645, 2723, 2776, 2987, 3221, 3240, 3380, 3387, 3472, 3483, 3486, 3539, 3545, 3559, 3620, 3661, 3750, 3873, 3903, 3913, 3984
Paul Morel: 2701, 3143, 3192
"The People": 2478
"Phoenix": 2261, 3275, 3494, 3873
Phoenix: The Posthumous Papers of D. H. Lawrence: 2102, 2114, 2135, 2162, 2193, 2237, 2277, 2799, 3086, 3090, 3185, 3347, 3661, 3794, 3835, 3873, 4528
Phoenix II: Uncollected, Unpublished, and Other Prose Works by D. H. Lawrence: 3038, 3055, 3062, 3078, 3083, 3086, 3090, 3093, 3100, 3133, 3185, 3246, 3347, 3376
"Piano": 2912, 3620, 3823, 3970, 4528, 4584
The Plumed Serpent: 2062, 2068, 2097, 2110, 2174, 2220, 2275, 2283, 2285, 2290, 2302, 2369, 2374, 2417, 2435, 2437, 2449, 2453, 2456, 2470, 2480, 2490, 2509, 2538, 2540, 2580, 2622, 2624, 2626, 2640, 2642, 2663, 2679, 2703, 2718, 2759, 2777, 2796, 2821, 2825, 2835, 2869, 2877, 2886, 2951, 2962, 2971, 2987, 2991, 2995, 3017, 3071, 3074, 3097, 3145, 3152, 3199, 3204, 3211, 3226, 3228, 3233, 3279, 3299, 3337, 3355, 3356, 3436, 3445, 3456, 3462, 3472, 3498, 3514, 3554, 3559, 3563, 3629, 3651, 3661, 3664, 3708, 3727, 3749, 3778, 3780, 3782, 3806, 3843, 3845, 3849, 3851, 3862, 3905, 3913, 3935, 4013, 4026, 4051, 4054, 4083, 4095, 4098, 4121, 4126, 4130, 4133, 4154, 4162, 4169, 4199, 4237, 4319, 4324, 4340, 4364, 4412, 4420, 4437, 4489, 4493, 4526, 4548, 4554, 4577, 4598, 4603, 4610
"A Poem of Friendship": 3468, 3496, 4154
"Poetry of the Present": 2723, 3409, 3877, 4182
"Pomegranate": 3525
Pornography and Obscenity: 2083, 2327, 2679, 3373, 3406, 3472, 3566, 3718, 3824, 4054
The Portable D. H. Lawrence: 2233, 2290
"Prayer": 3940
"A Prelude," also titled "A Prelude to a Happy Christmas": 2303, 3793

D. H. LAWRENCE

"The Princess": 2351, 2572, 2794, 2844, 2919, 3028, 3075, 3076, 3145, 3146, 3225, 3462, 3536, 3758, 3780, 3794, 3879, 4224

The Princess and Other Stories: 3794

"Prologue to *Women in Love*": 2393, 3038, 3055, 3062, 3078, 3272, 3566, 3805, 4375

"The Prussian Officer": 2303, 2348, 2351, 2355, 2361, 2390, 2466, 2639, 2820, 3037, 3039, 3105, 3106, 3178, 3690, 3699, 3829, 3900, 4333, 4459

The Prussian Officer and Other Stories: 2276, 2348, 2609, 2832, 3287, 3472, 3473, 3696, 3876, 3934, 4054, 4061, 4459, 4470, 4471, 4478, 4486

Psychoanalysis and the Unconscious: 2110, 2252, 2456, 2527, 2636, 2663, 2864, 3156, 3183, 3304, 3337, 3433, 3462, 3472, 3570, 3639, 3640, 3811, 3821, 3925, 3933, 4002, 4029, 4051, 4137 4187, 4248, 4332, 4482, 4526, 4529, 4620

The Quest for Rananim: D. H. Lawrence's Letters to S. S. Koteliansky, 1914 to 1930: 3023, 3425, 3434, 3446, 3532, 3547, 3647, 3653, 3691, 3742, 3748, 3762, 3767, 3826, 3915, 3949, 4258

"Rabbit": 2619, 2873, 3143, 3433

The Rainbow: 2065, 2066, 2068, 2086, 2096, 2107, 2108, 2109, 2110, 2111, 2118, 2134, 2175, 2177, 2193, 2195, 2197, 2221, 2222, 2225, 2235, 2252, 2261, 2276, 2282, 2285, 2289, 2298, 2307, 2322, 2368, 2379, 2382, 2389, 2394, 2421, 2423, 2449, 2453, 2456, 2459, 2470, 2483, 2486, 2490, 2504, 2514, 2537, 2546, 2548, 2550, 2551, 2556, 2572, 2574, 2580, 2584, 2587, 2591, 2594, 2621, 2624, 2633, 2639, 2640, 2642, 2644, 2647, 2659, 2678, 2679, 2697, 2715, 2718, 2728, 2733, 2786, 2796, 2797, 2798, 2810, 2811, 2821, 2823, 2832, 2835, 2845, 2854, 2869, 2871, 2872, 2878, 2882, 2893, 2917, 2926, 2929, 2953, 2956, 2961, 2962, 2984, 2987, 2997, 3013, 3030, 3033, 3034, 3066, 3071, 3104, 3108, 3110, 3120, 3122, 3124, 3126, 3136, 3138, 3168, 3191, 3192, 3196, 3198, 3199, 3203, 3212, 3224, 3230, 3252, 3255, 3260, 3270, 3273, 3276, 3277, 3278, 3279, 3284, 3285, 3292, 3299, 3302, 3306, 3309, 3328, 3340, 3355, 3367, 3390, 3396, 3403, 3406, 3418, 3436, 3445, 3447, 3453, 3454, 3472, 3473. 3475. 3486. 3498. 3508. 3543, 3545, 3554, 3558, 3563, 3570, 3586, 3629, 3646, 3654, 3658, 3661, 3677, 3679, 3689, 3699, 3711, 3720, 3733, 3734, 3749, 3751, 3754, 3756, 3772, 3778, 3782, 3800, 3802, 3803, 3804, 3806, 3809, 3820, 3830, 3831, 3832, 3834, 3838, 3849, 3851, 3856, 3873, 3886, 3888, 3889, 3906, 3917, 3928, 3932, 3933, 3937, 3944, 3961, 3966, 3973, 3980, 3990, 4001, 4018, 4021, 4027, 4029, 4046, 4048, 4050, 4054, 4065, 4070, 4076, 4077, 4093, 4098, 4114, 4132, 4133, 4183, 4189, 4197, 4199, 4206, 4212, 4218, 4223, 4230, 4243, 4244, 4247, 4252, 4264, 4272, 4278, 4280, 4295, 4296, 4297, 4300, 4318, 4323, 4336, 4345, 4351, 4356, 4365, 4375, 4377, 4386, 4393, 4396, 4410, 4412, 4419, 4420, 4436, 4437, 4452, 4457, 4459, 4471, 4472, 4475, 4478, 4479, 4486, 4489, 4493, 4494, 4500, 4502, 4516, 4518, 4526, 4531, 4539, 4540, 4575, 4577, 4578, 4589, 4593, 4594, 4608, 4609, 4613

The Rainbow, prosecution of: 2225, 2580, 3104, 3271, 3292, 3406, 3472, 3661, 4054

"The Real Thing": 2506, 4468

"The Reality of Peace": 2985, 3263, 4190, 4196, (See also *At the Gates* and *Goats and Compasses*)

"Red Geranium and Godly Mignon-

INDEX OF PRIMARY TITLES

ette": 2519
"Red-Herring": 2535
Red Willow Trees, painting: 3792
"Red Wolf": 3669, 3753, 3760, 3790
"Reflections on the Death of a Porcupine": 2674, 3796, 3825, 4121
Reflections on the Death of a Porcupine and Other Essays: 3055, 3078, 3472, 3553, 4482
"Resurrection," essay: 2679
Resurrection, painting: 2562, 3792, 4596
"The Return Journey": 2064
"Rex": 3525, 3793
"Review of H. G. Fiedler's *Oxford Book of German Verse*": 2363, 2472, 3258
"Review of Jethro Bithell's *The Minnesingers*": 2363, 2472, 3258
"Review of *The World of William Clissold* by H. G. Wells": 4509
"The Risen Lord," essay 2973, 3284, 3313
"The Risen Lord," poem: 3074
"The Rocking-Horse Winner": 2084, 2271, 2291, 2338, 2351, 2372, 2407, 2430, 2456, 2464, 2524, 2566, 2669, 2694, 2697, 2866, 3006, 3032, 3057, 3101, 3178, 3282, 3283, 3314, 3348, 3410, 3469, 3601, 3712, 3891, 3899, 4035, 4266, 4308
The Rocking-Horse Winner, film: 3631, 4036, 4145, 4159, 4266, 4361, 4408; script: 4390
"Rose of All the World": 4204
The Saga of Siegmund: 4285
"St. John": 3873
"St. Mark": 2708
St. Mawr: 2097, 2110, 2201, 2226, 2351, 2394, 2403, 2410, 2453, 2482, 2521, 2540, 2598, 2640, 2679, 2716, 2794, 2803, 2817, 2821, 2844, 2855, 2861, 2869, 2881, 2962, 3145, 3146, 3209, 3227, 3233, 3337, 3356, 3462, 3472, 3521, 3864, 3873, 3886, 3910, 3963, 4018, 4054, 4121, 4157, 4224, 4316, 4340, 4356, 4362, 4363, 4526, 4572, 4581, 4615
"Salt-Licks: 3617

Scargill Street: 3192
Sea and Sardinia: 2135, 2360, 2370, 2572, 2621, 2700, 3171, 3186, 3297, 3390, 3411, 3472, 3513, 3525, 3827, 3865, 4053, 4092, 4121
Selected Literary Criticism: 2102
"Sex versus Loveliness": 3478, 4468
"The Shades of Spring": 2303, 2348, 2993, 3696, 3876
"The Shadow in the Rose Garden": 2351, 2579, 2676, 2837, 2975, 3009, 4202, 4470, 4477, 4486
"Shadows": 2318, 3275
"Shame": 2893
"The Ship of Death": 2230, 2318, 2499, 2621, 2948, 3067, 3275, 3409, 3494, 3559, 3620, 3771, 3851, 4041, 4100, 4305, 4315, 4380, 4508, 4561, 4579
The Short Novels of D. H. Lawrence: 3910
"A Sick Collier": 3898
The Sisters: 2091, 2533, 2551, 3124, 3192, 3695, 3809, 3836, 4189, 4575
"Sleep": 2318
"Sleep and Waking": 2318
"Smile": 2128, 3319, 3462, 3899
"Snake": 2229, 2615, 2836, 2869, 2985, 3242, 3518, 3525, 3542, 3860, 3881, 4182
"Snap-Dragon": 2615, 2726, 3249, 3291, 3620, 3696, 3913, 4584
"The Soiled Rose": 2993, 3696
"Song": 3492
"Song of a Man Who Has Come Through": 2761, 3236, 3559
Sons and Lovers: 2068, 2084, 2091, 2096, 2106, 2110, 2111, 2116, 2122, 2151, 2175, 2180, 2201, 2263, 2279, 2285, 2300, 2348, 2353, 2368, 2382, 2422, 2423, 2430, 2449, 2453, 2455, 2456, 2466, 2470, 2490, 2510, 2512, 2514, 2557, 2561, 2580, 2587, 2624, 2633, 2639, 2640, 2642, 2661, 2671, 2678, 2679, 2692, 2701, 2706, 2718, 2724, 2728, 2731, 2737, 2738, 2739, 2740, 2742, 2744, 2746, 2749, 2758, 2780, 2785, 2794, 2796, 2797, 2822, 2862, 2868, 2869,

2870, 2881, 2891, 2911, 2916, 2923, 2926, 2929, 2938, 2941, 2942, 2983, 2986, 3001, 3010, 3022, 3039, 3042, 3051, 3064, 3071, 3087, 3098, 3108, 3114, 3126, 3138, 3148, 3151, 3158, 3164, 3167, 3168, 3172, 3189, 3199, 3216, 3225, 3241, 3249, 3268, 3272, 3285, 3292, 3299, 3339, 3351, 3352, 3357, 3389, 3391, 3392, 3396, 3403, 3406, 3414, 3433, 3437, 3444, 3445, 3468, 3472, 3475, 3476, 3484, 3485, 3513, 3544, 3554, 3555, 3561, 3563, 3572, 3596, 3610, 3629, 3633, 3638, 3658, 3661, 3684, 3696, 3702, 3728, 3733, 3736, 3749, 3752, 3756, 3757, 3770, 3774, 3778, 3806, 3812, 3815, 3848, 3849, 3856, 3867, 3881, 3888, 3906, 3917, 3919, 3927, 3947, 3961, 3977, 3986, 3988, 3997, 4001, 4012, 4018, 4023, 4054, 4069, 4073, 4076, 4093, 4097, 4098, 4129, 4133, 4145, 4160, 4172, 4197, 4199, 4222, 4223, 4243, 4245, 4251, 4269, 4273, 4274, 4331, 4339, 4344, 4345, 4362, 4380, 4384, 4389, 4412, 4419, 4437, 4439, 4447, 4452, 4465, 4473, 4480, 4485, 4486, 4489, 4491, 4494, 4497, 4503, 4504, 4513, 4519, 4520, 4560, 4564, 4577, 4582, 4595, 4599, 4602, 4621, 4624

Sons and Lovers, film: 2104, 2213, 3631, 4032, 4145, 4159

"The Spirit of Place": 4509

"The State of Funk": 2875

"Strike-Pay": 3039, 3898

Studies in Classic American Literature: 2097, 2103, 2161, 2203, 2207, 2260, 2396, 2397, 2478, 2487, 2488, 2559, 2597, 2644, 2679, 2755, 2799, 2855, 2882, 2920, 2935, 3156, 3174, 3182, 3197, 3312, 3388, 3442, 3462, 3472, 3473, 3648, 3661, 3723, 3746, 3773, 3809, 3869, 3904, 4001, 4028, 4287, 4410, 4446, 4464

Study of Thomas Hardy: 2193, 2624, 2962, 3124, 3192, 3249, 3261, 3292, 3297, 3676, 3756, 4001, 4132, 4133, 4198, 4204, 4274, 4507, 4509, 4611, 4615

Summer Dawn, painting: 3792

"Sun": 2351, 2663, 2979, 2985, 3794, 4477, 4479, 4488, 4576

"Surgery for the Novel-- --or a Bomb": 3566, 3796

The Symbolic Meaning: The Uncollected Versions of "Studies in Classic American Literature": 2203, 2204, 2260, 2296, 2465, 2471, 2494, 2502, 2515, 2529, 2581, 2588, 2597, 2600, 2755, 2812, 3034, 3869

"Tabernacle": 2318

"Taos": 4224

"The Test on Miriam": 2653

"The Theatre": 3349

"The Thimble": 3033, 3078, 3083, 3793, 3993

"Things": 2442, 3536, 3794

"The Thorn in the Flesh": 2303, 3690

Three Plays by D. H. Lawrence: 3301, 3412

Throwing Back the Apple, painting: 3036

"Tickets, Please": 2191, 2351, 2442, 3005, 3037, 3228, 3230, 3541, 4515, 4541

"Tortoise Family Connections": 3599

"Tortoise Shell": 3599

"Tortoise Shout": 2908, 3074, 3599, 4525, 4578

Tortoises: 3161, 3469, 3599, 3860, 3881

Touch and Go: 2420, 2751, 2833, 2858, 2894, 3010, 3241, 3791, 3878, 4001, 4555, 4587

The Trespasser: 2068, 2110, 2163, 2223, 2254, 2285, 2453, 2456, 2490, 2580, 2602, 2772, 2997, 3107, 3108, 3159, 3292, 3336, 3472, 3555, 3564, 3572, 3610, 3661, 3685, 3698, 3722, 3756, 3774, 3806, 4001, 4054, 4093, 4133, 4226, 4255, 4285, 4297, 4298, 4305, 4312, 4318, 4343, 4350, 4378, 4386, 4415, 4441, 4465, 4497, 4577, 4625

"The Triumph of the Machine": 2230

INDEX OF PRIMARY TITLES

"Troth with the Dead": 3245
"Turkey Cock": 2908
"The Turning Back": 3882, 3893
Twilight in Italy: 2135, 2218, 2360, 2370, 2621, 2709, 3073, 3284, 3292, 3349, 3442, 3462, 3731, 3865, 4043, 4121, 4296, 4338, 4460
"Two Blue Birds": 2543, 3039, 3105, 3106, 3536
Two Blue Birds and Other Stories: 2656
"Two Marriages": 4570
"The Two Principles": 3034, 4482
"Two Ways of Living and Dying": 2318
"The Undying Man": 3697, 3794, 3835
"The Vicar's Garden": 4470
"Violets": 3823
The Virgin and the Gipsy: 2110, 2202, 2351, 2423, 2482, 2605, 2717, 2844, 3536, 3562, 3661, 3910, 3921, 3968, 4050, 4592, 4606
The Virgin and the Gypsy, film: 3305, 3426, 3428, 3450, 3458, 3471, 3502, 3505, 3529, 3530, 3604, 3652, 3660, 3662, 3681, 3687, 3698, 4145, 4159. 4209, 4327
"The Virgin Mother": 3245
"Virgin Youth": 3696, 4584
"Walk to Huayapa": 3612
"War": 3617
"Water-Party": 2619, 4091
"We Have Gone Too Far": 3893
"We Need One Another": 2506, 3566
"Wedding Morn": 3361
The Wedding Ring: 2389, 3124
"What Have They Done to You-?": 2478
The White Peacock: 2068, 2097, 2110, 2118, 2123, 2136, 2201, 2247, 2285, 2290, 2355, 2421, 2453, 2456, 2470, 2580, 2587, 2593, 2659, 2815, 2824, 2838, 2891, 2993, 3016, 3042, 3071, 3112, 3121, 3230, 3249, 3261, 3285, 3292, 3468, 3469, 3472, 3473, 3486, 3496, 3512, 3554, 3555, 3570, 3572, 3610, 3624, 3658, 3661, 3689, 3696, 3752, 3756, 3774, 3806, 3840, 3874, 3917, 3954, 3967, 4001, 4054, 4071, 4088, 4093, 4133, 4134, 4136, 4154, 4212, 4221, 4222, 4250, 4253, 4254, 4279, 4305, 4313, 4318, 4330, 4336, 4403, 4410, 4497, 4546, 4561, 4565, 4577, 4583
"The White Stocking": 2351, 2837, 3037, 3182, 3536, 4061, 4486
"Whitman": 3999, 4028
"Why the Novel Matters": 2636, 3566, 3796, 4208
"Widdershins": 3617, 4066
The Widowing of Mrs. Holroyd: 2420, 2800, 2833, 2846, 2858, 2868, 2884, 2894, 2896, 3010, 3092, 3099, 3144, 3206, 3241, 3300, 3301, 3412, 3473, 3689, 3791, 3851, 4292, 4587
The Widowing of Mrs Holroyd, Granada TV version: 2113, 2190
The Widowing of Mrs. Holroyd, Long Wharf Theater production: 4128, 4286, 4296
The Widowing of Mrs. Holroyd, Royal Court Theatre Production: 3060, 3081, 3092, 3094, 3132, 3135, 3165, 3172, 3213, 3244, 3249, 3362, 3791, 4163
"The Wild Common": 3245, 4261, 4358
"The Wilful Woman": 3794
"The Witch a la Mode": 2351, 3793, 3898
"The Woman Who Rode Away": 2177, 2351, 2362, 2416, 2453, 2487, 2496, 2635, 2752, 2786, 2869, 3017, 3145, 3225, 3233, 3288, 3337, 3462, 3525, 3536, 3563, 3629, 3749, 3780, 3796, 4051, 4100, 4224, 4305, 4340, 4416, 4574, 4577, 4592, 4615
The Woman Who Rode Away and Other Stories: 3794
Women in Love: 2066, 2068, 2086, 2107, 2110, 2141, 2153, 2166, 2175, 2177, 2183, 2245, 2250, 2255, 2276, 2285, 2297, 2308, 2342, 2353, 2373, 2379, 2382, 2383, 2393, 2406, 2423, 2426, 2449, 2453, 2454, 2456, 2467,

D. H. LAWRENCE

2470, 2476, 2486, 2490, 2497, 2509, 2510, 2514, 2518, 2533, 2537, 2541, 2546, 2549, 2550, 2551, 2553, 2556, 2574, 2580, 2587, 2602, 2619, 2621, 2624, 2633, 2639, 2640, 2642, 2643, 2647, 2648, 2649, 2662, 2679, 2681, 2695, 2707, 2718, 2728, 2733, 2742, 2744, 2745, 2786, 2792, 2796, 2797, 2821, 2835, 2838, 2845, 2856, 2869, 2873, 2877, 2881, 2898, 2911, 2917, 2922, 2923, 2928, 2938, 2951, 2956, 2960, 2962, 2974, 2983, 2987, 2996, 3010, 3020, 3033, 3047, 3048, 3065, 3066, 3071, 3098, 3104, 3108, 3122, 3124, 3142, 3143, 3168, 3186, 3191, 3192, 3199, 3200, 3208, 3220, 3224, 3241, 3252, 3257, 3259, 3260, 3263, 3272, 3276, 3277, 3278, 3279, 3281, 3285, 3292, 3297, 3302, 3306, 3308, 3316, 3319, 3322, 3339, 3355, 3357, 3358, 3359, 3363, 3367, 3371, 3375, 3378, 3381, 3395, 3396, 3403, 3406, 3420, 3432, 3433, 3436, 3437, 3443, 3445, 3449, 3453, 3469, 3472, 3475, 3480, 3490, 3491, 3498, 3499, 3500, 3507, 3514, 3522, 3545, 3554, 3563, 3570, 3573, 3584, 3589, 3603, 3611, 3613, 3621, 3625, 3628, 3629, 3631, 3641, 3646, 3654, 3658, 3661, 3665, 3679, 3688, 3695, 3696, 3697, 3706, 3749, 3756, 3778, 3785, 3789, 3798, 3802, 3804, 3805, 3806, 3809, 3816, 3817, 3836, 3842, 3849, 3856, 3868, 3881, 3889, 3905, 3906, 3916, 3917, 3923, 3928, 3938, 3942, 3961, 3973, 3974, 3979, 4001, 4018, 4021, 4054, 4057, 4065, 4068, 4069, 4070, 4076, 4077, 4091, 4093, 4098, 4100, 4106, 4113, 4114, 4115, 4117, 4120, 4127, 4132, 4133, 4139, 4141, 4148, 4154, 4160, 4185, 4189, 4190, 4196, 4197, 4198, 4199, 4205, 4219, 4223, 4235, 4244, 4253, 4259, 4270, 4284, 4296, 4317, 4327, 4332, 4345, 4353, 4356, 4367, 4368, 4375, 4380, 4386, 4387, 4391, 4394, 4396, 4404, 4412, 4422, 4437, 4445, 4451, 4452, 4463, 4472, 4478, 4479, 4482, 4489, 4494, 4497, 4502, 4516, 4524, 4526, 4527, 4528, 4531, 4532, 4575, 4577, 4609, 4610, 4615, 4618, 4622

Women in Love, film: 3265, 3274, 3298, 3353, 3386, 3413, 3430, 3439, 3440, 3452, 3459, 3463, 3465, 3480, 3487, 3500, 3501, 3504, 3510, 3520, 3526, 3531, 3537, 3551, 3567, 3568, 3578, 3579, 3582, 3584, 3590, 3591, 3593, 3597, 3603, 3605, 3611, 3614, 3625, 3630, 3631, 3637, 3641, 3642, 3643, 3652, 3660, 3681, 3688, 3697, 3705, 3737, 3901, 3919, 4009, 4145, 4159, 4195, 4256

"The Work of Creation": 2288

Yawning, painting: 2562

"Yesternight": 4584

"You Touched Me": 2753, 2794, 3109, 3536